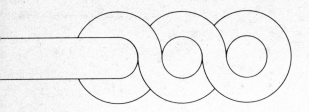

Writing about Literature

*An Anthology
for Reading and Writing*

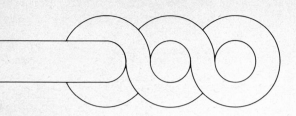

Writing about Literature
An Anthology for Reading and Writing

Lynn Klamkin
Harvard University

Margot Livesey
Tufts University

Holt, Rinehart and Winston
New York   Chicago   San Francisco   Philadelphia
Montreal   Toronto   London   Sydney
Tokyo   Mexico City   Rio de Janeiro   Madrid

Publisher *Susan Katz*
Acquisitions Editor *Charlyce Jones Owen*
Senior Project Editor *Herman Makler*
Production Manager *Robin B. Besofsky*
Art Director *Bob Kopelman*
Text Design *Suzanne Bennett Associates*
Cover Design *Judy Allan/The Designing Woman*

Library of Congress Cataloging-in-Publication Data
Main entry under title:

Writing about literature.

Includes index.
1. English language—Rhetoric. 2. College readers.
3. Criticism—Authorship. 4. Report writing.
5. Literature—Collections. I. Klamkin, Lynn.
II. Livesey, Margot.
PE1479.C7W75 1986   808'.042   85-17747

ISBN 0-03-001508-1

CBS COLLEGE PUBLISHING
Holt, Rinehart and Winston
The Dryden Press
Saunders College Publishing

Acknowledgments of copyright ownership and permission to reproduce works included in this volume begin on page 999.

Preface

In teaching literature we have found that the best way to make sense of a work is to write about it. At the same time, in teaching writing, we have found that one way students learn to write well is by reading good writing. In this book we teach students how to write about literature, and we combine this information with an exciting anthology that includes not only fiction, poetry, and drama but also essays. Essays seem to us no less worthy than the other three genres to be considered as literature, and they often provide a useful model for students' own writing. We hope that this combination makes *Writing about Literature* a book that will enhance students' understanding and appreciation of literature while it improves their writing skills.

Writing about Literature is divided into three parts. The first part teaches students how to read literature and how to write about it. The second part is a thematic anthology. The third part comprises two chapters about more advanced writing topics. At the end of the book there are also biographical information about the authors whose works appear in the anthology and a glossary of literary terms.

In the early chapters we discuss reading and writing in general terms. Chapter 1 shows students how to make their reading more productive by asking questions and by learning what to look for in an essay, story, poem, or play. Chapter 2 explains how to write the first draft of an essay, step by step: how to generate ideas, find a thesis, gather evidence, outline, organize, make transitions, and present a logical conclusion. Chapter 3 uses a question-and-answer format to guide students in revising their drafts. The chapter ends with a sample essay about Tennessee Williams's play *The Glass Menagerie.* We show all the stages of writing this essay, from generating ideas, through a first draft, to the final draft. Chapter 4 covers four kinds of essays students can write: explicatory, analytical, comparative, and argumentative. We explain the differences among these types of essays and show how to organize each type. We emphasize that the division into categories is not rigid and that there is often considerable overlap among them.

Chapters 5–8 focus on writing about essays, fiction, poetry, and drama. We explain the essential features of each genre, using numerous examples from the anthology. The information is presented in easily accessible subsections. It is not necessary, for example, to read all of Chapter 7, "Writing about Poetry," to find the section about imagery, or all of Chapter 8, "Writing about Drama," to locate the section about romantic comedy. Our discussions of the genres are intended to help students to write about literature, and these chapters include a section called Suggestions for Writing, which lists possible approaches to writing about that genre.

The "Writing about . . ." chapters also include examples of works in each genre and sample student essays about those works. In Chapter 5, "Writing about Essays," Maya Angelou's "Graduation" is followed by a sample essay analyzing it. Two short stories, James Joyce's "Araby" and John Cheever's "The Swimmer," appear at the end of Chapter 6, "Writing about Fiction," followed by a sample essay comparing the two. Chapter 7, "Writing about Poetry," ends with Robert Frost's "The Silken Tent" and a student's explication and analysis of that poem.

We break with this format somewhat in Chapter 8, "Writing about Drama," where our example is a three-page play by David Mamet called *The Hat*. This play, like some of the other works in this anthology, has rarely been anthologized. These works are real "finds," to which our students have responded with unusual enthusiasm. The sample essay in Chapter 8 is not about *The Hat* but rather about *Death of a Salesman*, one of the plays in the anthology.

The center of *Writing about Literature* is the thematic anthology. The five themes—Generation to Generation, Struggles, Places, Varieties of Love, and Work and Reward—were chosen because they address all of us. We are defined by our families, our convictions, where we live, our relationships with others, and the work we do. Even when two authors are writing about similar subjects, there is often a dramatic contrast in their attitudes and opinions. This is clear, for example, in two poems, William Butler Yeats's "A Prayer for My Daughter" and Weldon Kees's "For My Daughter": The former shows a father's hopes; the latter ends with despair about the future of all children.

The works in each thematic section are grouped according to genre, in the same order as the "Writing about . . ." chapters: essays, fiction, poetry, and drama. Within each genre we have arranged the works to facilitate comparisons. An essay by Gandhi about civil disobedience follows Thoreau's essay about the same subject. This kind of juxtaposition generates lively classroom discussion.

Some of the works in the anthology are by people who are not known primarily as writers. For example, we include a letter from Mozart to his father, in which many methods of persuasion are at work simultaneously. In "Waitress," which appears in the essay section of Work and Reward, a waitress speaks at once humorously and movingly about her work and her life. Margaret Sanger's essay "The Turbid Ebb and Flow of Misery," in Struggles, shows us what she saw as a nurse working in the Lower East Side of New York City at the turn of the century. These selections help to demonstrate that it is not only professional writers who have something important to say.

Each work in the anthology is followed by questions for writing and discussion. These questions help students look at the work more closely and to find writing topics. We also use the questions to give necessary information about a work and to suggest interesting comparisons between works in the same or different genres. From classroom experience we know that our questions can lead to animated discussions. Besides these questions about individual works, at the end of each section we include thematic questions, which raise more general issues about the section's theme.

The anthology is followed by two more chapters on writing. In Chapter 9 we discuss some ways students can respond to literature other than in formal essays. We give examples of a review, a parody, and a satire and show students how to write their own. We also show students how to use a story, poem, or play as a model for their own writing, and we discuss writing letters and journal entries in a character's voice. This chapter encourages students to become authors or participants in literature.

Chapter 10 is a guide to writing literary research essays. We explain the purpose of research, how to find material, how to make notes, and how to organize a research essay. Following the 1984 *MLA Handbook*, we show how to quote and cite sources. At the end of the chapter we include a research essay on *Billy Budd*. This chapter will help students do research for any course, not just for courses in literature.

Reading and writing are closely connected, and this book makes full use of this connection. Whether or not students intend to pursue careers as writers, teachers, or critics, literature enlarges their knowledge of the world and of their place in it, and the ability to write clearly, persuasively, and concisely is invaluable. But literature is not simply useful; it also adds joy and substance to our lives. The aim of *Writing about Literature* is to help students develop the skills of reading and writing while at the same time enhancing their enjoyment of literature.

Acknowledgments

We are deeply grateful to many people whose suggestions, assistance, and support brought this book to life. Jean Herbert, Jonathan Wilson, and Claudia Yukman, all of Tufts, read parts of the manuscript at critical times and under the pressure of our deadlines. We also would like to thank other Tufts colleagues for their generous help, among them Alan Lebowitz, chairman of the English Department; Linda Bamber, director of Freshman English; and Elizabeth Ammons, Lee Edelman, Frieda Gardner, Marcie Hershman, Marie Howe, Seymour Simckes, Harriet Spiegel, and Michael Ullman.

Our indebtedness extends to our many students, whose insights into literature and whose questions, comments, and writing taught their classmates and us much about the relationship between what students read and the way they write. Those whose contributions were especially important are Sander Eth, Peter Gittleman, Michael Goldberg, Rebecca Harriman, David Hirsch, Bruce Ito, Catherine Payne, Sally Payson, Tamah Solomon, and Jeanne Widen.

Other friends and colleagues made important suggestions about the content of the anthology, or contributed information about their own experience in teaching writing and literature: Sharon Bryant, University of Washington, Seattle; Jay Clayton, University of Wisconsin, Madison; Cynthia E. Cornell, DePauw University; Edward Hirsch, Wayne State University; Harvey Oxenhorn, Harvard University: James Shepard, Williams College; and especially Catherine Tudish, Harvard University Expository Writing Program, Constance C. Cohen, Frances Rosen, Dianne Lamb, and Anne Higgins.

Others who read this book in several stages of development and whose comments were essential to us are John S. Biays, Jr., Broward Community College; Donald C. Barnett, DeAnza College; Flynn Brantley, University of North Carolina, Charlotte; Elizabeth D. Rankin, University of Alabama; Catherine Anne Sherrill, East Tennessee State University; Judith Stanford, Merrimack College; and Kathleen Tickner, Brevard Community College.

We are most grateful to the staff at Holt, Rinehart and Winston who guided us through all of the stages of the book's development. Our editor Charlyce Jones Owen supported the project from its earliest beginnings and guided us toward its completion. We would also like to thank her assistant, Miriam Bravo, for her many contributions. Herman Makler, who oversaw the production, was invaluable. Donna Baum offered her knowledge and encouragement. We would especially like to thank Joan K. Rainer for her guidance and support.

The manuscript for *Writing about Literature: An Anthology for Reading and Writing* was prepared by Judd Holt, whose patience and diligence about our deadlines will not soon be forgotten, and Linda Scola and Sue Edelman. We are grateful to all of them.

There are also several people we wish to single out for specific contributions. It was only through their substantial efforts that the book took shape. Susan Brison, Dartmouth College, made important suggestions about the nonfiction and helped us to develop questions. Louise Kawada made illuminating comments about the poetry and nonfiction and added important insights as she worked on the Instructor's Guide. Two poets, Jane Shore and Tom Sleigh of Tufts and Dartmouth respectively, gave their knowledge selflessly, suggested titles, and helped us to develop questions for the poems. Camille Smith read and commented on the manuscript in its entirety twice; it is impossible to imagine this project ever coming into being without her. Andreas Teuber, Brandeis University, enthusiastically supported the project in its early stages and made valuable suggestions about the ways the works of literature might be grouped. Many of his suggestions are reflected in the nonfiction. David Wallace also saw the manuscript at many critical stages, and his suggestions and support were invaluable and vital to the creation of the book.

Finally, we acknowledge with special feelings of warmth the contribution of Kim Rogal, a fine writer whose love of words touched all who knew him. His encouragement was most directly responsible for bringing our work as teachers of writing and literature to a wider audience of students and teachers.

L.K. / M.L.

Contents

Part II A Thematic Anthology

Generation to Generation

Essays

Struggles

Essays

Fiction

Poetry

Drama

Places

Essays

Fiction

Poetry

Drama

Varieties of Love

Essays

Fiction

Poetry

Drama

Work and Reward

Essays

Fiction

Poetry

Drama

Part III Other Approaches to Writing

9. Other Ways of Reading and Writing   951

10. Writing Literary Research Essays   959

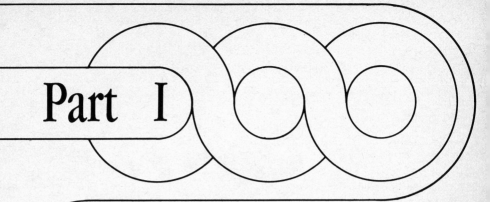

Part I

Writing
about Literature

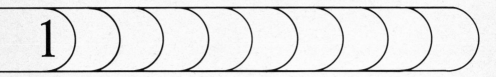

Reading in Depth

I love to lose myself in other men's minds.
CHARLES LAMB

Imagine you are visiting Paris for the first time. First you go to the Eiffel Tower because you know it's there and everyone has told you to see it. You then visit the Rodin museum because Rodin's sculpture has fascinated you since you studied his work in art history class. Next you go walking, not sure where you will end up, intrigued by the new sights, discovering small shops, museums, and churches no one has told you about. This turns out to be the most exciting part of the visit. You have found something on your own, something that was there all along but that you didn't expect to find.

Reading a work of literature for the first time is not unlike visiting a new place. There is an expectation of some sort. We expect to be amused, moved, provoked, or informed. Yet often we discover more than we expect: a new idea, a pleasing use of words, an eloquent argument, a connection with the mind and heart of an author or a character. And on rereading we find even more. Just as every time we return to a city like Paris there is something new and unexpected to see, so too every time we reread a work of literature there is something more to discover.

Finding the deeper meanings in a literary work requires careful reading. Reading literature demands more concentration than, say, skimming a newspaper account of the latest political scandal or checking the baseball standings on the sports page. In much of the reading we do there is no meaning beneath the meaning we see at first glance—nor should there be. With literature we expect more. We want there to be something beneath what we first see, something to make us think or feel or to expand our perception of the world. Often a first reading will give us only a hint of the many meanings to be found in a work.

Asking Questions as You Read

Your reading may be more pleasurable and will certainly be more productive if you have certain questions in mind and read to find the answers. The questions in the following list can apply to any work. In addition, each selection in this book is followed by questions. Looking at these before you reread the selection will help you to focus your reading. It is a good idea to keep paper and pencil beside you so that as you read you can jot down your ideas about the work.

What is this work about? On rereading an essay, story, poem or play, we may find that we have missed an important part of its meaning. In William Carlos Williams' poem "The Horse Show" we know, on first reading, that there is a dialogue between the speaker and his mother. On rereading we start to formulate ideas about why the speaker talks about a horse show at the end of the poem. As we ask ourselves what the words and images add up to, a theme starts to emerge. In stories, poems, and plays the major reason to reread is to discover the deeper meaning or theme.

Nonfiction too may have a theme, but in reading an essay we are usually also trying to discover the author's thesis—the claim the author is making. In his essay "Family Romances" Sigmund Freud maintains that most children need to fantasize that they are adopted. On rereading this essay we come to understand more clearly why Freud makes this claim and how he supports it. We understand his thesis.

Do I like this work? Just as we don't all like the same people or places or foods, we are entitled not to like something we've read. One person may find Elizabeth Barrett Browning's poem "How Do I Love Thee?" moving. Someone else may find it "mushy" or sentimental. Sometimes this dislike will disappear on rereading. Just as we may revise our initial impression of another person as we get better acquainted, reading more deeply may alter our initial reactions to a literary work. We can also reread to try to discover what other people like in the work and to look for ways to justify or explain our dislike. Keep in mind that it is not necessary to like a work to write a good essay about it.

How did the author achieve a particular effect? In Tillie Olsen's story "I Stand Here Ironing" we read about the childhood of a shy, plain girl from a broken home. At the end of the story we learn that she has not become the withdrawn adolescent we might have expected. Instead she has become an extrovert, an entertainer. After the kind of childhood she had, this may seem illogical and surprising. Yet as we reread we notice the clues Olsen has given us that make the outcome plausible.

In rereading an essay, we can ask ourselves how the author has managed to persuade us. We can go back and look at how the argument was constructed and presented. Something about a poem might linger in the mind. Is it a musical effect? Is it something about the particular arrangement of sounds and words? We go back and look. Rereading to see how an effect is achieved in no way diminishes our enjoyment. Rather, it makes us appreciate the skill, the thought, and sometimes the genius of an author.

Is there a particular question I'd like to answer? What does the protagonist *really* think about her husband? Why did the poet include the jarring last line of that poem? Why did the author spend so much time describing the landscape? What is the function in the play of the character who has only two lines? Rereading gives us the luxury of examining a particular aspect of a work. This is particularly important as a step in writing about literature. As you become more experienced as a reader and a writer, you will find that more and more questions present themselves, questions to which there may not be a single right answer but which are in themselves provocative.

Does this work illuminate something in my own life? Literature often mirrors conflicts in our own lives. We see these conflicts condensed, with the author or characters taking the roles of people we might know: the shy daughter, the domineering parent, the disloyal friend, the child who fantasizes. We see some kind of resolution, though not always a happy one, and we can translate the meaning of what happens into our own lives. When rereading, ask yourself if you can identify with the conflict in the work. Does the work give voice to some of your own feelings?

What else can I learn from this work? Through literature we may learn about a place or a way of life that is foreign to our experience. We may travel back through time. Sophocles' play *Antigone,* over two thousand years old, tells us something about life in ancient Greece. Maya Angelou's essay "Graduation" shows us a moment in the life of a young black woman in a small Arkansas town thirty years ago. We feel as if we know what it would have been like to be in her graduating class. Literature can transport us out of our own lives and give us an idea of what it is like to be someone else.

Using Background Information as You Read

Rereading a work may not always give us all the information we need for a full understanding. Literature reflects the historical period in which it was written, the author's personal experiences, and the influence of other writers. Knowing about these aspects of a work can enhance our appreciation of it.

Historical Context

We could not fully understand Jonathan Swift's "A Modest Proposal" if we did not know that when he wrote there was a famine in Ireland. In her diary, Anne Frank frequently mentions an impending Allied attack. In fact D-Day occurred shortly before Anne and her family were captured; this information gives us insight into her diary. Knowing the kinds of restrictions placed on blacks in the South during the time Martin Luther King, Jr., was jailed in Birmingham allows us to appreciate the controlled and reasoned tone of the letter he wrote from jail.

Although investigating the historical context is an important part of gathering information before writing about a work of literature, looking at works solely in this way can make us lose perspective. One of the definitions of a "classic" work of literature is that it is timeless—that its impact does not depend on a reader's familiarity with the time or the circumstances in which it was written. Certainly we do not have to know Elizabethan history to be moved by Shakespeare's love sonnets, and Plato's dialogues can be appreciated by people who have not studied the society of ancient Greece. Learning about the historical background is only one way to deepen your understanding of a work of literature.

Biographical Information

There are literary critics who insist that biographical information about the author should never influence the way we read and interpret literature. They argue that a work must stand on its own merits, that a reader should not need to know anything about the author in order to appreciate the work. Some critics go further, believing that a biographical approach can distort the way we read a work. We believe that biographical information can often enhance our appreciation of a work, and therefore we include brief biographies of the authors of the selections in this anthology. Osip Mandelstam, represented in this book by his "The Stalin Epigram," was a victim of Stalin's regime and probably died on his way to a prison camp. Knowing that the poet was so close to his subject gives us a better understanding of this poem.

In an essay, in contrast to the other genres, the relationship between author and topic is usually made immediately clear. In "A Kiowa Grandmother," N. Scott Momaday tells us in the second sentence that he himself is a member of the Kiowa tribe. We know that he is not writing with the distance of an anthropologist or a reporter. Similarly, Margaret Sanger, in her essay "The Turbid Ebb and Flow of Misery," tells us early on that she is a nurse and that the people about whom she writes are her patients. We could investigate the lives of these authors further, but in these essays some biographical information is already part of the work.

Remember that, like historical context, biographical information should not be your only or primary means of interpretation. Beware of concentrating so closely on the author's life that you neglect more significant aspects of a work: the statement it makes about the larger world, how it reflects your own feelings or conflicts, the author's use of language. Consider that literary scholars have argued for hundreds of years about whether Shakespeare actually wrote all the plays attributed to him. Various scholars have proposed that the plays were written by Sir Walter Raleigh, Ben Jonson, Anne Hathaway, and Queen Elizabeth I, among others. Although these theories are important to many scholars, the plays themselves transcend the question of authorship.

Literary Allusion

A third kind of information that can be useful concerns the links between the work we are reading and other literary works. References to other works, either obvious or subtle, are called *literary allusions.* For example, there are many overt references to Greek tragedies in E. M. Forster's "The Road from Colonus." The title itself is a reference to Sophocles' tragedy *Oedipus at Colonus.* As you will see in Chapter 6, where we discuss Forster's story, recognizing what these references contribute is important to understanding the story as a whole. Forster uses the Greek tragedy to give his story a literary context and a larger meaning; he invites us to compare his hero to Oedipus. Less obviously, John Updike's story "The A & P" refers to the myth of Paris, the Greek shepherd who had to decide which goddess, Hera, Athena, or Aphrodite, was the most beautiful. Forster's allusions are difficult to overlook; Updike's are more obscure. Yet recognizing the literary allusion invites us to make a comparison between Updike's modern characters and the ones in the myth.

Information of any of these types can help you to understand a work, but no kind of outside information is a substitute for reading the text carefully, several times. Whether you are reading a work of literature solely for pleasure or in preparation for writing about it, asking questions as you read, and keeping in mind any relevant background information, will enhance your reading. You will discover more about the work, appreciate the different levels of meaning, and make the work more your own.

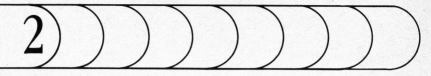

2

Writing a First Draft

The best way to deepen your understanding of a work of literature is to write about it. Writing is a process, made easier if it is organized into steps. In this chapter we describe the various steps of the process, from choosing a thesis, to organizing ideas and making an outline, through writing a draft and revising it. Later, at the end of Chapter 3, we will show all these steps in sequence as we trace one student's writing project from assignment to finished essay.

Before you begin writing you should read the work carefully. It is beneficial to read a shorter work several times. For a longer one, you may have to settle for a couple of thorough readings. Read actively: Ask questions and jot down notes. Sometimes the assignment will shape your reading. For example, you might be asked to analyze Blake's use of irony in "The Chimney Sweeper." As you read the poem, you would focus on the aspects of the poem that are ironic. If the choice of a topic is up to you, you will need to formulate your own questions to ask and answer as you read. Whatever the assignment, there are methods for generating ideas, and for shaping and organizing material, that will help you to write your essay.

Generating Ideas

Good writing topics are not necessarily the result of inspiration. Like the other skills involved in writing an essay, coming up with ideas is something you can learn. Here we will discuss three common techniques. Even if you have been assigned a topic or already have an idea for one, these techniques can help you explore and clarify your ideas. You may want to use all three in conjunction, or you may find one especially helpful.

Freewriting

The premise behind freewriting is that most of us feel inhibited as writers and therefore unconsciously edit out ideas before we can even write them down. In freewriting you force yourself to write and keep writing. Hidden ideas come to light, and you give yourself the chance to decide whether any of them can be useful.

To use freewriting to find a topic, first carefully read the work you intend to write about; then sit down and write whatever comes into your head, even if it has nothing to do with what you have read. Give yourself a set time period, maybe ten or fifteen minutes, and *do not stop writing.* Even if you think you have no ideas, keep writing: Explain that you have no ideas, write the same sentence over and over again, or write down whatever comes to mind on any subject, until something else relevant to your essay assignment occurs to you. Here is an example of freewriting done in preparation for an essay about Frank O'Connor's story "My Oedipus Complex."

> The kid in "My Oedipus Complex" grows up at the end of the story. I wish I could remember if I left my running shoes at the gym or at home. What's an Oedipus complex anyway? The kid likes his mother but it's not like in psych class. In psych class things are really complex. But not complex like the use of complex in the title. Did I ever go through a period in my life when I was especially clinging to my mother? I don't remember it but maybe I did. Maybe my brother was more like that kid.

This reads like a jumble, but it contains the beginnings of some good ideas for topics. Aside from the running shoes, almost all these thoughts could be developed into essays. Here is a list of some topics that emerge:

How does the narrator of the story grow up?

What is the real meaning of the title of the story?

How does the narrator feel about his mother?

Did I express feelings in my own childhood similar to those of the narrator?

Do I know anyone who went through a stage like the one the narrator goes through?

Brainstorming

Brainstorming is similar to freewriting. Immediately after reading the work, write down any and all ideas that come into your head about it. Do not pay attention to the importance or usefulness of each thought as you write it; simply get your thoughts down on paper before you forget them. Here is a brainstorming list for an essay about John Gregory Dunne's essay "Quintana," in which Dunne describes his adopted daughter.

Quintana—very well adjusted

adopted children more wanted than biological children?

nature or nurture?

rights of Quintana v. rights of biological mother

rights of biological mother v. rights of adoptive parents

family?

There are several good topics in this list. For example,

What is a family?

Do adopted children have a right to know their biological parents?

Do the biological parents have a right to privacy?

Which is most important in developing our personalities: our genes or our environment?

Asking Questions

At every stage of writing an essay you are asking yourself questions: Is this the best word? Should I start a new paragraph? Am I being clear? Asking questions can also help you find a topic for your essay. The most basic questions are those used by journalists: who? what? when? where? why? how? Here are some possible answers to these questions about Robert Browning's poem "My Last Duchess."

Who? The Duke

What? Got rid of his first wife—murder? Why doesn't Browning tell us what happened to her?

When? Some time ago, before the poem starts. Now he's looking for a second wife but Browning only tells us at the end of the poem.

Where? In Renaissance Italy, in the Duke's palace.

Why? Because he was jealous, because she did not seem conscious enough of her position as his wife. Maybe she was unfaithful?

How? Suddenly: "then all smiles stopped together."

These answers suggest the following topics:

Why did the Duke behave as he did?

Was his wife guilty of the things he suspects?

Did she deserve what happened to her?

Why does the poet present the story in this way?

What is the effect of being kept in the dark until the end of the poem?

You can ask these basic questions about different subjects in the same work; you can also ask them in a different order to give a different emphasis. For example, if you wanted to focus on the importance of the setting of a story, you could begin with the question "where?"

Besides these all-purpose questions and those listed in Chapter 1, there are also many more specific questions you can ask about a work of literature. What point is the author trying to make? How does the title relate to the rest of the work? What are the intentions of specific characters? Where is the language most striking? Is the work commenting, directly or indirectly, on another work? Does it grow out of a literary tradition? Interviewing yourself about a work of literature, both asking and answering the questions, is an excellent way to find a topic and a central strategy in the whole process of writing. The questions we have provided at the end of each selection in this anthology will help you with this process.

It is worth experimenting with one or all of these techniques for generating ideas: freewriting, brainstorming, asking questions. It is always better to have too many ideas than too few.

Choosing Your Topic

The next step is to review the material you have generated by freewriting, brainstorming, or questioning. Look at your list of possible topics and decide which one to explore further. Choose a topic that interests you. If you aren't interested, your reader probably won't be either. Be aware, however, that the first topic to catch your attention may not be the best.

In addition, your topic must be substantial enough to fit your assignment. There may not be enough material for a good paper about a minor character in a story or about a peripheral idea in an essay. In the essay "On Embryology," Lewis Thomas remarks on the effect of test tube babies on the role of the father. This is an intriguing idea, but it is not one that Thomas goes into; he only mentions it in passing. If you were assigned to write about "On Embryology," this would not be a suitable topic because there is not enough material about it in the text.

On the other hand, beware of topics that are too large. A good topic is one that can be effectively handled in the assigned length of your essay. If you were asked to write a four- to five-page essay on drama, choosing parental influence in *King Lear* would not be a good idea. There is too much to say about the ways Lear and Gloucester influence their children for you to give more than the briefest of overviews. To make this an effective topic, you would have to narrow it to some specific aspect of parental influence. You could compare Gloucester's sons. Why does Edmund, his illegitimate yet favorite son, turn out so much worse than Edgar, the legitimate son? If a topic is too broad for the assignment, your treatment of it will inevitably be superficial.

Determining Your Thesis

Once you have chosen a topic, you need to decide what specific assertion you wish to make about it; that is, you need to choose your thesis. Suppose your topic is the use of symbols in Arthur Miller's play *Death of a Salesman.* What point do you wish to make about the use of those symbols? What do you want to persuade your reader of? What question do you wish to answer? Perhaps you decide to show that the common thread linking the various symbols is how they reveal Willy Loman's nostalgia. This will be the thesis of your essay. You will try to persuade your reader that the symbols are being used in this way. In your finished paper it is not a good idea to write your thesis in the form of a question. However, while you plan what to write, it can be very helpful to think of your thesis as a question that your essay will answer; for example, "How do various symbols reveal Willy Loman's nostalgia?"

One way to determine a thesis is to look for connections among the ideas you have jotted down in your search for a topic. Look again at the example of freewriting about "My Oedipus Complex." Suppose this freewriting is your own. Reading it over carefully, you might choose as a topic the boy's feelings for his mother. You can see that there is a connection between the title of the story, the boy's affection for his mother, and the boy's growing up. You notice that the title is "*My* Oedipus Complex" rather than "*The* Oedipus Complex": In other words, the narrator of the story, who is the boy grown older, describes the feelings of his younger self in this way. So you decide the term *Oedipus complex* is not used seriously. As your thesis, you choose the following: "The narrator's attitude toward the feelings he had for his mother is a playful one." The question you will keep in mind while writing the essay is: "How serious is the narrator in claiming to have had an Oedipus complex?"

Finding Evidence

Once you have determined your thesis, the next step is to look for evidence to support it. At the same time, you should also be looking for any evidence that seems to contradict your thesis. It is a good idea to imagine a reader who disagrees with your thesis and argues against it. Anticipating this reader's arguments and answering them with counterarguments will strengthen your essay and make it more persuasive.

Where you look for evidence in the text of the work depends on your topic and your thesis. Suppose you are writing an essay about Martin Luther King, Jr.'s "Letter from Birmingham Jail," and your topic is racism. Your thesis is that King's letter shows the strength of the opposition the civil rights movement faced. In this case, you would look for evidence in the paragraphs where King explicitly comments on the treatment of blacks in Birmingham at that time. At the same time, you would gather as much information as you could about King's opponents: What kinds of support did they have? Exactly how does King show us their strength?

Your thesis may also involve looking for evidence outside the text. You might, for instance, look not only at "Letter from Birmingham Jail" but also at how newspapers reported the incident at the time. These newspaper articles might furnish supporting evidence of the strength of King's opponents.

When gathering evidence, make careful notes of quotations and ideas that support your thesis. A good method of notetaking is to write each quotation or idea on a separate file card, so that later it will be easy to arrange and rearrange the material. In the top right-hand corner of the card write the subject, for easy reference. At the bottom of the card write the page numbers, so that you can look up the evidence again when you start to write the essay.

> *segregation*
>
> Blacks were not protected by law against segregation in public places.
>
> "Letter," #14

At the end of this chapter we discuss how to use quotations correctly in your essay.

Outlining and Organizing

Once you have gathered your evidence, you are ready to outline your essay. The purpose of an outline is to organize your material in the most effective way to prove your thesis. The term *outline* can be used for anything from an informal list to a detailed summary of what will be done in each paragraph of your essay. As you work on your outline, keep asking yourself what evidence supports each point you want to make, what counterarguments there are, how you can answer them, and how all your ideas or points are connected.

The easiest way to begin to outline is by making a simple list. Suppose you are preparing to write an essay on James Joyce's story "Araby," and your thesis is that the narrator's moods are revealed by the setting of the story. You might make a list like this one:

1. Narrator's home
2. The street

   3. Shopping
   4. Train journey
   5. Bazaar

The next step is to write each item on the list on a separate file card. Using cards makes it easy to organize your outline.

How you organize an essay depends on your subject matter and the points you are trying to make about it. There are two principal methods of organizing the material in an essay: First, you can organize according to the chronology of the work you are discussing—that is, the order in which things appear in the text—or second, you can organize according to the strength of your evidence. When using the second method you may put the strongest evidence first, so that the secondary and supporting material flows naturally from it, or you may arrange the evidence from weakest to strongest to achieve a crescendo effect. The two major organizing methods often overlap; for example, an essay may be structured from the strongest evidence to the weakest, and at the same time, the discussion of each piece of evidence may follow the order of events or ideas in the work you are analyzing.

Depending on your topic, one of these methods will fit your material better than the other. If you are tracing the changes a character goes through or discussing how a situation or an idea develops in the course of a work, it will probably be best to organize your essay by following the chronology of the work. If you are making a general point and supporting it with specific examples, you will have a choice between presenting the examples chronologically and arranging them according to their strength as evidence.

Sometimes the best organization for an essay combines these two methods. For example, the essay as a whole may be structured from the weakest evidence to the strongest, and within that structure the discussion of each piece of evidence may follow the order of events or ideas in the work being analyzed. If you write an essay comparing two works of literature, you will probably use both methods of organization.

Let us look again at the simple outline for "Araby."

   1. Narrator's home
   2. The street
   3. Shopping
   4. Train journey
   5. Bazaar

After you have made an initial list, it is time to bring in the evidence you have gathered. Look at the file cards on which you have written down pieces of evidence, and group them under the headings on the list. When you have arranged them to your satisfaction, you are ready to write a fuller outline. Here is a more formal outline for the essay on "Araby."

   1. Introduction:
      introduce story: "Araby"
      thesis: the setting reveals the narrator's moods
      method for proving thesis: discuss the different settings

2. Narrator's home:
   the blinds
   the broken windows
   the upstairs
3. The street:
   the school
   the houses and gardens
4. Shopping:
   shopping at night narrator feels alone—crowds—darkness/light
5. Train journey:
   the narrator's solitary journey through the dark, past ruined houses, makes him feel superior
6. Bazaar:
   the darkness and light in the building
7. Conclusion

Rereading this outline, you might decide to reverse numbers 2 and 3, to follow the chronology of the story. It seems logical to combine numbers 4 and 5—shopping and the train journey—since they are minor pieces of evidence and you are making roughly the same point about both of them.

The revised and expanded outline might look like this:

1. Introduction:
   introduce story: "Araby"
   thesis: the setting reveals the narrator's moods
   method for proving thesis: discussing the different settings
2. The street:
   the school
   the houses and gardens—general disrepair
3. Narrator's home:
   the blinds
   the broken windows
   the upstairs—"the high cold empty gloomy rooms"
4. Shopping and train journey:
   each takes place at night—in crowds narrator feels solitary—shifts in tone
5. Bazaar:
   darkness and light in the building—darkness disappoints narrator, as does the light, which reveals the seediness of everything
6. Conclusion:
   the settings of this story not only reveal the narrator's moods but also act as a catalyst to transform his feelings

The more fully developed the outline, the easier it is to write the first draft of an essay.

Writing Your Introduction

Be careful how you start your essay. If you look at the essays in this anthology, you will notice that they do not start with phrases like "In this essay I will discuss . . ."; "When I first sat down to write this paper . . ."; "After thinking about the assignment . . ."; "I had a hard time coming up with something to write about. . . ." This kind of opening draws attention to the author rather than allowing the reader to focus on the author's ideas. Such phrases may be helpful as you begin to write, but you should discard them as you develop your essay.

The introduction to your essay should tell the reader what work or works you are writing about. It should also state your thesis clearly and indicate how you plan to prove it.

Here is an introduction to an essay about Keats's poem "On First Looking into Chapman's Homer."

> In Keats's sonnet "On First Looking into Chapman's Homer" the speaker describes his excitement at being able to visit the world of Homer's *Iliad* and *Odyssey* through Chapman's translations. The comparison between reading and traveling runs throughout the poem. It is important to note what aspect of travel is being emphasized. A close look at the poem will show that Keats repeatedly uses words that have to do with seeing and looking. He is drawing attention to the visual and visionary qualities of the experiences.

This paragraph introduces the poem, explains the thesis of the essay—that the poet is comparing reading to traveling in terms of seeing—and indicates that the thesis will be proved by a close look at the poem.

Making Transitions

Transitions are the words or phrases that connect ideas. They show how paragraphs and sentences are related to one another. An essay without transitions seems abrupt, and the reader may not be able to understand the connections between the various parts.

Three kinds of words or phrases are frequently used in transitions: (1) words or phrases that suggest a temporal connection, the order in which things happen, such as *first, then, next, after, while, furthermore, also, in addition, finally;* (2) words or phrases that suggest a causal connection, what caused what, such as *as a result, because;* (3) words or phrases that suggest a contrast, such as *but, yet, although, in spite of, however, nevertheless, whereas, even.*

Here is an excerpt from an essay about Arthur Miller's play *Death of a Salesman.* Notice the use of transitional words and phrases.

> In this sense the house resembles the cars that play such an important part in Willy's life. *Throughout* the play, Miller emphasizes that the convenience machines can bring is bought at a high price. *Although* he is a salesman, and inev-

itably part of the machine age, Willy is often portrayed as a victim of progress. It is no coincidence that the subject his son Biff flunks in high school is math.

> *However,* the house is not seen only in a negative light. It is *also* described as a place in which Willy has invested a considerable amount of himself. He skillfully fixes it up and derives considerable pleasure from doing so. *Even* though more repairs are needed, the work still gives him more satisfaction than his job.

Throughout, although, also, and *even* tell us, the readers, the relationships between various sentences and ideas. The word *however* at the beginning of the second paragraph signals that the information we are about to be given is in contrast to the information we have just been given. Without these words and phrases the sentences would be no more than a list of ideas and examples. Strong transitions are vital for a good essay.

Using Summary

As you write your essay, you will probably need to summarize at least part of the work you are writing about. Even when you can rely on your readers to be familiar with the work, a brief summary may be necessary to remind them of a particular part or to make a point effectively. Look again at the introductory paragraph of the essay about "On First Looking into Chapman's Homer." Although many readers are probably familiar with the sonnet, the author gives a brief, one-sentence summary to remind them of what it is about and as a way to introduce the thesis of the essay.

> In Keats's sonnet "On First Looking into Chapman's Homer" the speaker describes his excitement at being able to visit the world of Homer's *Iliad* and *Odyssey* through Chapman's translations.

There are several important points to keep in mind about summarizing. A summary is always shorter than the original. It should include only main points critical to your thesis, but at the same time it should be as exact as possible. A summary can only be a *part* of a successful essay. It can be a good way to establish a point or to convey useful information to your reader or to step back from an analysis—but it can never stand alone.

Writing Your Conclusion

In the conclusion of your essay you explain what the evidence you have given amounts to and how it proves your thesis. A conclusion should not be simply a restatement of the introduction or a summary of what you have done in the essay; it should offer some fresh perspective on the material you have presented. It is not, however, the place to present a major new piece of information. Different kinds of essays, obviously, require different kinds of conclusions.

A short explication of a poem needs only a brief concluding paragraph. A longer persuasive essay, on the other hand, calls for a longer concluding paragraph, in which you make a final attempt to show your readers why they should agree with you.

In your conclusion, just as in your introduction, you should avoid convenient phrases like "In conclusion . . ."; "To sum up . . ."; "In summary. . . ." These draw attention to the fact that the author has come to the end of the essay. An author who uses such phrases does not trust the reader to see the obvious.

Here is the concluding paragraph of an explication of Robert Frost's sonnet "The Silken Tent."

> So the end of the poem returns us to the beginning; like the tent, the poem is circular. From the last two lines we gain a new and deeper understanding of the metaphor of line one.

The author of this short essay does not need a long concluding paragraph. It is enough to show how the ending of the poem relates to the beginning and to the thesis of the essay.

Here is the conclusion to a five-page research essay about Herman Melville's *Billy Budd*. (The entire essay appears at the end of Chapter 10.)

> Whether or not one sees Vere as an allegory for God, it is clear that the ultimate responsibility does indeed fall to him. He not only welcomes this responsibility, he monopolizes it. Whether or not Vere abuses his power by employing it to justify his own personal biases, it is clear that he takes *too much* responsibility concerning Billy's fate, and for this he *is* to blame.

The thesis of this essay is that Captain Vere is largely responsible for Billy Budd's death. Each sentence in this paragraph is a reformulation of a point that has been proved in the essay. The author is showing how the points combine to prove the thesis.

Quoting Sources

An essential step in writing your first draft is finding appropriate quotations and using them correctly. Each of the sample student essays we provide in this book uses quotations from the work or works being discussed. Quotations can provide evidence in support of your thesis, summarize an idea, or convey the thoughts of other authors about your topic. It is important, however, to be judicious in your use of quotations. You should use them only when they support or enhance your thesis, and they should be as brief as possible. Never quote more than you need, and never include a quotation without commenting on it.

Whatever the source of a quotation, you must attribute it to the person who originally wrote or said it. Not to do so is plagiarism. Stealing an idea is also plagiarism. Even if you restate someone else's idea in your own words, you must give credit to the original author. (For a fuller discussion of how to avoid plagiarism, see Chapter 10.)

Citing Titles

Part of giving credit is, of course, mentioning the title of the work you are quoting. When you mention titles in your essay, be sure to punctuate them correctly. The rules for this are fairly simple:

Titles of short stories, chapters in books, songs, most poems, essays, speeches, and unpublished works all appear in quotation marks.

Titles of books (including collections of plays, essays, fiction, or poetry), plays, periodicals, and long poems such as *Paradise Lost* are underlined or italicized.

Titles of sacred works—the Bible, the Torah, the Koran—have no additional punctuation and are not italicized. The same is true for sections of these works, such as the Old Testament, Genesis, Exodus, and so on. Titles of political documents, such as the Bill of Rights, the Declaration of Independence, and the Magna Carta, are also treated in this way.

Quoting Prose

A short prose quotation—no more than four lines of type—can be typed right in the body of your paragraph. Here is an example from an essay on Tennessee Williams' play *The Glass Menagerie.*

> Laura has been deceiving her mother because she can't bear to disappoint her. "When you're disappointed," she says to Amanda, "you get that awful suffering look on your face, like the picture of Jesus' mother in the museum!" By likening her mother to the Madonna, Laura effectively silences her.

The author of the sample essay divided the quotation with her own words. She could also have written:

> Laura says to Amanda, "When you're disappointed you get that awful suffering look on your face, like the picture of Jesus' mother in the museum!"

Alternatively, the author might have decided to quote only the most important part of the sentence, rather than all of it.

> Laura can't bear to disappoint her mother because, she says, when Amanda is disappointed her expression is "like the picture of Jesus' mother in the museum!"

Note the phrase "she says" in this example, which makes it clear that the quotation is from Laura. Whenever you are quoting a character, be sure that the reader knows which one.

For longer prose quotations you need to use a different format. When typing a long prose quotation, begin the quotation on a new line, indent ten spaces from the left margin, and type the quotation double-spaced. Do not use quotation marks, and do not indent the first line any farther than the ten spaces. If you quote more than one paragraph, indent an additional three spaces for the beginning of the second paragraph. Here is an excerpt from an essay showing the use of a long quotation.

> In Flannery O'Connor's story "Everything that Rises Must Converge" the two main characters, Julian and his mother, react physically to their conflicts. This is not to say that they do not have verbal disagreements, but O'Connor seems to show their anger toward each other through descriptions of their physical behavior.
>
> > They had reached the bus stop. There was no bus in sight and Julian, his hands still jammed into his pockets and his head thrust forward, scowled down the empty street. The frustration of having to wait on the bus as well as ride on it began to creep up his neck like a hot hand. The presence of his mother was borne in upon him as she gave a pained sigh. He looked at her bleakly. She was holding herself very erect under the preposterous hat, wearing it like a banner of her imaginary dignity. There was in him an evil urge to break her spirit. He suddenly unloosened his tie and pulled it off and put it in his pocket.
>
> This passage gives us a very clear visual image of Julian's irritation and his mother's dignity. It is surely no coincidence that his mother is on her way to an exercise class at the Y.

If you are going to include such a long quotation—this is an entire paragraph from the story—be certain that you need it all and that your own work is substantial enough to support its use. In this example, the important part of the quotation for the author's thesis is the part that details the physical reactions of Julian and his mother to their conflicts. There is no need, however, to give every detail of these reactions, and the quotation could be effectively shortened. It would still provide telling evidence if it began with "The presence of his mother. . . ." Remember, when you use a quotation you must add a comment of your own, telling the reader what point you are using it to make.

Quoting Poetry

In quoting poetry there is also a distinction between short and long quotations. A short quotation—not more than three lines of verse—can appear in the body of your text with a slash (/) to mark the line breaks. Here is an example of two lines of poetry quoted in an essay about the sense of mortality in Wordsworth's poems:

> Probably the poet's most famous lines on this subject are from "Ode," which he subtitles "Intimations of Immortality from Recollections of Early Childhood":

"We will grieve not, rather find/Strength in what remains behind." Here again Wordsworth gives us reason to find something beyond the mere pleasures of the present.

When quoting more than three lines from a poem, begin on a new line, indent ten spaces, and do not use quotation marks. Type the quotation double-spaced. Copy the indentation and spacing of the original as accurately as possible. Here is an example from an essay on Keats's sonnet "On First Looking into Chapman's Homer."

> Throughout the poem the speaker emphasizes the visual qualities of his experiences:
>
> Then felt I like some watcher of the skies
>   When a new planet swims into his ken;
> Or like stout Cortez when with eagle eyes
>   He stared at the Pacific—
>
> The common characteristic of the people with whom the speaker compares himself is that they are seeing.

Punctuation for Quotations

As we have indicated, when you use long quotations indenting replaces quotation marks. Shorter quoted material within your text must be placed inside quotation marks.

When you are writing about literature, it often happens that you have a quotation within a quotation. In such a case the main quotation is in double quotation marks, and the quotation within it is in single quotation marks. In the following example, from an essay about O'Connor's "Everything that Rises Must Converge," note the single quotation marks within the double ones.

> According to critic Jane Shore, "Julian's mother is never truly combative with Julian. She retains her own sense of gentility, which sustains her. She says to Julian, 'I most certainly know who I am.'" As the story progresses, however, her sense of identity seems to grow weaker.

There are rules for how to punctuate around quotations. Periods and commas always appear *inside* the quotation marks.

> When Lawrence tells us that "the voices in the house . . . simply trilled and screamed in a sort of ecstasy," he is not necessarily speaking about the supernatural.

> Oscar Cresswell has profited so handsomely from Paul's talents that it seems somewhat hypocritical when he says "he's best gone out of a life where he rides his rocking-horse to find a winner."

Semicolons, colons, and dashes are always placed *outside* the quotation marks. Question marks and exclamation points go inside the quotation marks only if they are part of the quotation, outside if they are part of your own sentence.

> We see how Lear fosters the rivalry among his daughters when he asks Cordelia, "What can you say to draw a third more opulent than your sisters?"

Here it is King Lear who is asking the question, not the author. The question mark inside the quotation marks indicates this. If the question or exclamation is yours rather than the author's you are quoting, place the punctuation outside the quotation marks.

> Can we see a difference when the author says "but his voice was thin, scarcely a thread of sound"?

In this case the quotation is not a question. It is the author who is asking the question, as the punctuation shows.

Sometimes you will want to quote only part of an author's sentence or paragraph. In such a case you may need to use *ellipsis points.* An ellipsis is the omission of one or more words; ellipsis points are the three dots used to mark that omission. Suppose your argument calls for quoting only part of the paragraph from Flannery O'Connor quoted earlier:

> There was no bus in sight and Julian . . . scowled down the empty street. The frustration of having to wait on the bus as well as ride on it began to creep up his neck like a hot hand. . . . He suddenly unloosened his tie and pulled it off and put it in his pocket.

Notice that the first omission, where material has been left out of a sentence, is indicated by three ellipsis points. The second ellipsis occurs after a complete sentence and is marked by a period followed by three ellipsis points. Ellipsis points are necessary in the middle of the quotation but not at the beginning or end. It is not usually necessary to begin or end a quotation with ellipsis points because your reader knows you are not quoting all of the work under discussion.

Though we describe the process of writing as a linear one—a steady progression from generating ideas to writing your conclusion—in actuality writing a first draft often involves using the various steps in different sequences. As you write your first draft you may find yourself outlining for a second or third time. Or you may freewrite to see if your thesis can be made more precise. Try to be flexible in using the techniques. You should not simply follow the steps in this chapter in a mechanical way, but use them in whatever ways are most helpful to the evolution of your first draft.

3

Revision

Revision is an integral part of writing. Frank O'Connor, the author of "My Oedipus Complex," sometimes revised a story as many as fifty times. Most of us do not have the time or the temperament for this kind of repeated reworking of material, but all of us need to revise our material thoroughly at least once. Many writers find the process of revising more enjoyable than that of writing the first draft because in revising they can clarify and focus their ideas.

Questions to Ask as You Revise

By the time you have finished a first draft of your essay, you have already revised a great deal, by selecting, discarding, and reordering material. In this chapter we list questions that will help you turn your first draft into a final, polished essay. If at all possible, you should put your first draft aside, preferably overnight or longer but at least for a couple of hours, before you begin to revise. This will give you some distance from what you have written and help you to look at it more critically.

Does the essay fit the assignment? Reread the instructor's assignment to make sure that you are doing what you were asked. Sometimes you will be given a good deal of choice, but on other occasions your instructor may ask for a very specific type of essay on a specific topic.

   If you find that your essay really doesn't fit the assignment, you should review your essay. Can you make it fit by revising, or should you begin to write again from scratch, salvaging what you can along the way? In either case, you will be faced with considerable rewriting; most instructors will not look kindly on essays that do not carry out the assignment.

Is the first draft too short or too long? If your essay is too short, reexamine your thesis and the evidence you present. It may be that the thesis is not focused or clear enough to be the foundation of a strong essay, or it may be that you have not fully used or explored the evidence in favor of your thesis. This is a good time to go back to the literary work about which you are writing and look for new information or ideas. If your essay includes any unsupported generalizations, look for evidence to support them. Do not be tempted to expand your essay by repeating things you have already said or by including material that is not relevant to your thesis.

If your first draft is too long, it may be that you have chosen a topic that is too broad for the assignment. Check to see if you can give your thesis a narrower focus. Also check to see if you are explaining or summarizing more than you need to or using too many quotations. Then take a careful look at all the points you make in the essay and the evidence you use to support them. Are some of the points unimportant compared to the others? Are there any points you can omit without weakening the essay as whole? Is any of the evidence you present so minor that it can be omitted or just mentioned briefly? If after you answer these questions your essay is still too long, you should consult your instructor to see what he or she would prefer you to do.

Is the point of your essay clear? Be sure your reader will be able to tell early in the essay what point you are making. Does your introduction create expectations that are not fulfilled? Do you keep your thesis in mind throughout? Does your conclusion insist that you have proved something that you haven't? It is a good idea to have a friend read your essay and give you a brief summary of it. Did he or she get out of your paper what you intended? Another way to review your essay is to reread it, make an outline of the finished version, and compare this with your original outline. Did you really do what you set out to do? If your new outline is different, is the difference an improvement?

Is the information presented in a logical order? Do you give the arguments and the evidence in the order that will best make your case? As we said in Chapter 2, the best order is the one that suits your subject matter and your thesis. If the point of your essay is not sufficiently clear, it may be that you are not presenting the material in the best possible order. Look again at your organization.

Do you have strong transitions? Good transitions connect the parts of your essay with one another and show that you are building an argument step by step. Look at your paper again to see if it moves logically from one idea to the next.

Is your writing style clear, consistent, and appropriate? However interesting your thesis, however good your evidence and organization, however strong your transitions, your essay will not succeed if it is poorly written. Try to make your writing as clear, consistent, and appropriate as possible. Reread your first draft sentence by sentence.

Is your writing clear? Too many long sentences or too many long words will confuse your reader. Pay attention to the length of each sentence. Are most of your sentences long with many clauses? Or short and jerky? Try to vary their length. Check for run-on sentences and sentence fragments. At the same time, pay attention to your choice of words. Are you using long words simply to impress your reader? Would a shorter, more common word be clearer?

Is your writing consistent? It is important to choose a level of diction and stick to it. Suppose you were reading a serious discussion of Shakespeare's sonnet "Shall I compare thee to a summer's day?" and the author suddenly switched to much more casual language with a sentence like "It's just like a man to begin by praising his girlfriend and end up by praising himself." This sudden change would be jarring. It would be just as disconcerting to read an essay that skipped back and forth between serious but plain prose and self-consciously "scholarly" sentences.

It is also important to be consistent in your use of tenses. Always discuss a work of literature in the present tense, for example, "King Lear soon comes to realize the mistake he has made in believing Goneril and Regan."

Is your writing style appropriate for your subject? We have already mentioned that you should choose one level of diction and stick to it. The way you should choose that level is by considering your subject matter and your audience. (For a discussion of audience, see the next question.) Your style should do justice to your subject. When writing about an author as serious and formal as Freud it would not be appropriate to write a sentence like "Freud seems to have sex on the brain." On the other hand, an informal style might be entirely appropriate for a review of a new Woody Allen film.

The following suggestions about style come from George Orwell's essay "Politics and the English Language." As you can see, Orwell's advice is to use clear, simple language and to avoid clichés and jargon. His suggestions apply to any essay you may write, whatever its subject.

1. Never use a metaphor, simile or other figure of speech which you are used to seeing in print.
2. Never use a long word where a short one will do.
3. If it is possible to cut a word out, always cut it out.
4. Never use the passive where you can use the active.
5. Never use a foreign phrase, a scientific word or a jargon word if you can think of an everyday English equivalent.
6. Break any of these rules sooner than say anything outright barbarous.

Have you written at the right level for your audience? Unless your instructor asks for an essay written with some other audience in mind, you should assume that your classmates will be your audience. Do they know enough about the work so that you do not need to give elaborate explanations or summaries? Do you try to close the gap between yourself and your audience, taking account of any differences there may be? In his essay "On Embryology" Lewis Thomas writes about the multiplication of cells in the embryo. Although Thomas himself is a doctor and scientist, this essay demands no special knowledge: He assumes his readers will share his awe, whether they are scientists or not.

The fact that your classmates are your audience does not mean that you should write as casually as you would if writing a note to one of your friends. Your essay should address everyone equally, both your friends in the class and the people you know less well. On the other hand, it is inappropriate to be excessively formal; your points will be better understood if you avoid verbal pyrotechnics.

Are you, as the writer of the paper, too visible? Remember not to use self-conscious and convenient phrases such as "when I sat down to write this paper" or "in my opinion." These draw attention to the author of the paper instead of the work of literature.

You as the writer may also be too visible if you let your emotional reactions to your subject show too obviously in your essay. In an essay about Tennessee Williams' *The Glass Menagerie* a student wrote,

> Tom had no excuse for deserting his family that way. It's just unbelievable that he would have been so cruel to them. Tennessee Williams obviously couldn't think of a better way to end his play.

The problem here is self-evident. The writer is reacting too personally to the parts of the play with which he can identify. This does not mean that the author's emotions have no place in an essay about literature; it does mean that an author who shows us his or her emotional reaction to a work must give reasons for that reaction or persuade us to share it.

Have you given your paper an appropriate title? Many students leave their essays untitled. This does them, and their readers, a great disservice. Choosing a title gives you a chance to review your work: Did you accomplish what you set out to do? A title can also help to direct your reader's attention, clarify the point of a paper, convey a deeper meaning, and indicate that you have confidence in the essay. A title is your signature, and you should not be afraid to use one.

How to Type Your Final Draft

Use 8½-by-11-inch paper. Do not use erasable paper, which smudges easily and is hard to write comments on. The entire essay, including quotations, should be double-spaced, with margins of at least an inch on each side. In the top right-hand corner on the first page put your name, the course name or number, and your instructor's name. Type the title of your essay in the center of the first page, about 2 inches from the top. Begin your essay about 2 inches below the title. (If you or your instructor prefers to have a title page, center the necessary information on the title page and begin the text of your essay on a fresh page, about 4 inches from the top.) Number the pages consecutively in the top right-hand corner. It is also a good idea to put your name on each page. Fasten the pages together securely before you hand in your essay.

Always proofread your essay. Because it is easy to overlook mistakes in your own work, we recommend strongly that you ask a friend or friends to read your paper for spelling and punctuation before you type the final draft. You—or a friend—should also proofread the final draft after it is typed. Most instructors will accept a typescript with a few corrections written in neatly in pen or pencil; you should check to see what your instructor expects. Make any necessary corrections as neatly as possible.

Sample Essay

Here we show how one student planned and wrote an essay using the procedures described in Chapter 2 and the questions for revision listed in this chapter. The student's assignment was to write a two- to three-page essay on one of the characters in Tennessee Williams' play *The Glass Menagerie.*

Freewriting

First the student tried freewriting. She sat down, wrote for fifteen minutes, and produced the following material.

> How am I going to get this essay done by tomorrow? I have no idea, besides I want to go and buy some new records. I can't stand spending another evening in the library. This is hopeless, I'm not even writing about the play. *The Glass Menagerie, The Glass Menagerie*—it sounds like a sort of chant. I like the word "menagerie"—it's like a story, sort of old-fashioned. I suppose that's what Laura and Amanda are, old-fashioned. I don't blame Tom for wanting to escape. I mean I wouldn't think of the marines as an escape but I can see why he does—it's the idea of adventure, like the movies. I wonder what happens to Amanda and Laura without him. Somehow I think they are all right.

Some parts of this make sense only to the student, but her freewriting contains some useful material. When she reread it, the idea about Tom's desire for escape seemed promising. She made a note of it as a possible topic and then decided to see what ideas she could come up with by brainstorming.

Brainstorming

The student wrote down everything that came to mind about the play. Her list looked like this:

The Glass Menagerie
Amanda—very dramatic—difficult mother

father abandons family—not really a character

Laura's collection

Jim breaks the unicorn

Is Laura like Tom? or like Amanda?

Why is Laura so weird?

At this point the student ran out of ideas. But looking at this list she noticed that the focus of her interest seemed to have shifted from Tom to Laura. She decided to try asking the journalist's six questions about both Tom and Laura.

Asking Questions

Who?	Tom
What?	Argues with his mother and leaves home
When?	When he was young, during the Depression
Where?	St. Louis
Why?	He wanted to escape, he wanted a different life, his mother and his job were driving him crazy
How?	Suddenly, without really explaining, the only way he could

Reading these answers, the student had the feeling that she was at a dead end. It was true that Tom escaped, but she couldn't see at the moment what else to say about that. She went on to ask the same questions about Laura.

Who?	Laura
What?	Not sure exactly—refused to go along with her mother's schemes?
When?	During the Depression, when she was fairly young; although she's two years older than Tom, so she can't be as young as all that
Where?	St. Louis. In her family's apartment
Why?	Because she's different from other girls. Maybe her father's leaving had something to do with it?
How?	By being passive? By refusing to participate?

The student had trouble answering some of the questions about Laura, but at the same time she realized that she wanted to find out more. Here was something that she wanted to explore in detail. She thought she could raise interesting questions about Laura by looking at one or two scenes and that there would not be too much material for the two- to three-page essay she was assigned.

Determining a Thesis

Now the student had to choose a thesis. What point did she want to make about Laura? What aspect of Laura's character did she want her readers to think about? She reviewed the material she had generated through freewriting, brain-storming, and questioning and wrote down the things she had said about Laura.

>Laura is old-fashioned—keeps a glass collection.
>
>Laura and Amanda are both dependent on Tom.
>
>She's not like other girls.
>
>She doesn't do what Amanda wants.
>
>She's passive.
>
>Is Laura like Amanda? or like Tom?

Looking at these notes, the student decided what her thesis would be:

>Although Laura doesn't argue openly with her mother, nevertheless she opposes her.

The next step was to gather evidence in support of this thesis.

Finding Evidence

The student was writing about Laura, so her evidence came mainly from look-ing at what Laura says and does in the play. She also looked to see what the other characters say about Laura and how they behave toward her. Because she was writing about the relationship between Laura and her mother, she began by rereading the scenes that take place between the two of them.

Using file cards, the student made notes of her evidence. She also noted, in parentheses, any evidence or arguments that might be used by someone arguing *against* her thesis.

---

business school

Laura drops out of typing classes and conceals the fact from Amanda for 6 weeks. (but, it was Amanda's idea for Laura to become a secretary)

Scene II

---

butter

Laura complains about having to ask for credit when sent to buy butter.

Scene IV

gentleman caller

Laura doesn't even ask caller's name. (Why should she, given that it's all Amanda's idea?)

Scene VI

Once she had gathered her evidence, the student was ready to write an outline and organize her material.

Making an Outline

She began by making a simple list:

Business school
Family finances
Butter
Gentleman callers

Passivity

Tom

Amanda's worries

She wrote each item on the list on a separate file card so that she could easily arrange and rearrange the items. Then she grouped the evidence she had gathered under the different headings on the list. She rearranged the material until she found the order that seemed best. Then she wrote a more complete outline.

1. Introduction:
   introduce play
   introduce thesis
   how to prove thesis?
2. Business school:
   Laura refuses to attend and deceives Amanda
3. Family finances:
   Wingfields are poor, see butter incident
4. Gentleman callers:
   Amanda's preoccupation seems silly, but what else will Laura do if she doesn't get married? Scene VI—Laura opposes Amanda
5. Laura's passivity:
   more effective than Tom's arguing; she tends to get her own way
6. Laura loves Tom:
   sympathizes with his frustrations, but doesn't help him
7. Conclusion

Rereading the outline, the student realized that the point about Laura's passivity was part of her thesis and should run throughout the essay. The comment about Tom, although interesting, did not seem strictly relevant. The important point for the student's thesis was not Laura's affection for Tom but the contrast between her behavior and his.

The First Draft

Having reassessed and reorganized her material, the student was ready to begin to write. This is her first draft, with the annotations she later made for revision.

author?

Throughout <u>The Glass Menagerie</u> Amanda

Wingfield struggles with her grown children Tom

and Laura. Tom appears to be the more difficult.

In almost every scene he and Amanda (argue.)   *Example?*
    Don't all
Laura only argues with her mother when she's   *families*
    argue?

Is she really really (desperate.) Her passivity constitutes a very *should state*
"desperate?" real kind of opposition. At two critical moments *thesis more*
    clearly.
in the play, we can see how Laura opposes her

Introduction needed. should describe Amanda's anger and Laura's passivity.

mother. [Laura is the handicapped daughter.)] — *doesn't fit here — cut?*

In Scene II Amanda confronts Laura after discovering that she has not been attending her typing classes at Rubicam's Business College. Laura has been deceiving her mother because she can't bear to disappoint her. "When you're disappointed, you get that awful suffering look on your face, like the picture of Jesus' mother in the museum!" This scene reveals two things → *Amanda's reaction*

about Laura. She does not apologize for wasting the $50 tuition fee for the course, even though it is a considerable sum of money for the Wingfields. Another important point is the care with which Laura deceives Amanda. It is — *New ¶?*

probably true that she cannot bear to disappoint her mother. It is also clear that the deceit prevents Amanda from doing anything about the situation until it is much too late. Laura gets her own way. *How?*

Money is not the main issue here, insert elsewhere!

vague

should emphasize the contrast between Tom and Laura here.

Transition → The finances of the Wingfield household are extremely precarious. When Laura is sent out for butter, Amanda tells her to charge it. Laura says, "Mother, they make such faces when I do that." Clearly, although both Tom and Amanda work, charging things is not a new experience for the Wingfield household.

This should fit in with information in previous ¶.

Is this evidence strong enough? What point does it support?

TRANSITION!

At the beginning of Scene VI Amanda is getting Laura ready to meet the gentleman caller; she tells Laura that the gentleman's name is Jim O'Connor, someone Laura knew in high school. Laura immediately wants to back out but Amanda

Need to summarize better.

forces her to go through with their plans. It is *Is it entirely Laura's fault?* not Laura's fault that nothing comes of her meeting with Jim; he is already engaged to be married; but the reason that Amanda is so anxious and excited is Laura's (fault.) Laura shows *Doesn't work here. Maybe introduce new ¶.* no interest in supporting herself so how will she manage to get a husband?

Is this clear by now? am I assuming too much? Laura's behavior hurts her mother and brother as well as herself. [She causes Amanda *cut?* great anxiety.] While at least Tom does try to help *awkward— sounds jerky.* his mother, however reluctantly, Laura opposes Amanda at every step. Although she appears to be

Probably needs explanation sympathetic to her mother and brother, she is oblivious to the burden she places on their shoulders; she doesn't make the slightest effort to *still like this?* help them. Laura is not only the more difficult of Amanda's children, she is the more dangerous.

Revising the First Draft

After finishing the first draft, the student reread it, asking the questions listed in the first half of this chapter. The essay did fit the assignment. It was rather short, but she found several places where an example or additional evidence or explanation was needed. The point of the essay seemed clear but was not sufficiently well expressed or supported. The information was presented according to the chronology of the play, which seemed the right order, but she saw that some of the information could be more effectively introduced. She noticed she had forgotten to remind her readers of the contrast between Tom and Laura. Also the transitions, the links between the various ideas and pieces of information, were sometimes either weak or nonexistent. The style of writing was awkward in places. Some of the sentences were too short; others, too long and rambling. The student did not feel that she was being too visible: She had avoided using phrases like "in my opinion" and had been careful not to react to her subject too emotionally. She had not yet given her essay a title. As she wrote notes and prepared her final draft, she thought about an appropriate title.

The Final Draft

Passive Resistance

Throughout Tennessee Williams' play The Glass Menagerie Amanda Wingfield struggles with her two grown children, Tom and Laura. On the surface Tom is the more difficult. In almost every scene there are arguments between him and Amanda, ranging from squabbles over table manners to much more serious disputes in which he threatens to leave home. Although Laura rarely argues with Amanda, and never raises her voice to her, she is more successful than Tom in resisting Amanda's plans. Her passive behavior proves more effective than his noisy arguments.

In Scene II we can see the clever way in which Laura uses her quietness to neutralize her mother's anger. Amanda discovers that Laura has not been attending her typing classes at Rubicam's Business College; instead for the last six weeks she has been spending the day walking around or visiting the zoo. When Amanda asks why Laura has been deceiving her, Laura says, "When you're disappointed you get that awful suffering look on your face, like the picture of Jesus' mother in the museum!" It is not a statement to which Amanda, or anyone else, could easily respond. By likening her mother to the Madonna, Laura effectively silences her. This is in sharp contrast to Tom's arguments with Amanda, which never have a resolution but only end because Tom leaves the room.

Intriguing title suggests thesis

Clear introduction to the work and the main characters

Thesis is clearly stated

Introduces evidence, while reminding reader of thesis

Good use of quotation as evidence

Sustains comparision between Tom and Laura

When Amanda attacks Laura after discovering that she has been deceiving her about business college, we cannot help feeling Laura's helplessness. Yet as the scene continues Laura's passive behavior renders her mother momentarily helpless. Laura seems to sense intuitively how vulnerable her mother is to any setback in her plans.

This scene raises other questions about Laura's behavior. She does not apologize for wasting the $50 tuition fee, even though it is a considerable sum of money for the Wingfields. She seems oblivious to the fact that her brother works at a job he hates and that her mother also takes on numerous, unpleasant part-time jobs. Financial worries do not seem to motivate Laura. The only time she seems concerned about the family finances is when she is directly affected by them. When Amanda tells her to charge groceries, she protests because she finds this humiliating.

Good transition—takes the analysis begun in the last paragraph one step further

Laura also seems oblivious to her mother's attempts to find her a husband. When preparations are being made for the gentleman caller, Amanda's frenzied behavior predictably causes Laura to withdraw. This withdrawal makes Amanda even more frantic and determined. When their guest finally arrives she tries wildly to compensate for Laura's shyness. As in the confrontation after Laura drops out of business school, mother and daughter bring out the worst aspects of each other's personality;

Interprets the meaning of the events, rather than simply summarizing

Reference to earlier example helps to show the connection between these two pieces of evidence

they seem destined to force each other into extreme behavior. At this point in the play Amanda's behavior finally drives Tom out of the house, but we know that Laura will continue to live with her mother.

Laura uses her passive behavior to foil any plans Amanda may have for her, even though these plans are based on genuine practical concerns for Laura's future. Throughout the play both Tom and Amanda are manipulated by Laura's apparent helplessness. While they work at jobs they dislike, Laura does nothing to alleviate any of the financial or emotional burdens of the family. Although she is quiet, Laura is stubborn. She is not only the more difficult of Amanda's children, she is the more dangerous.

Conclusion shows how the evidence supports the thesis of the essay and interprets that thesis in a new way

The student has taken an obvious risk by promoting a thesis that presents Laura in an unsympathetic light. However, she succeeds in making a strong case by choosing her arguments carefully and presenting them unemotionally.

4

Explication, Analysis, Comparison, and Argument

In the first three chapters we discussed in general terms what to look for when you read, how to find writing topics, how to write the first draft of your essay, and how to revise. In this chapter we will look at four approaches to writing about literature: explication, analysis, comparison, and argument. Each one has a different purpose, but a single essay may well use more than one. For example, in comparing two poems, you may find that for the comparison to be clear you must first explicate them. Or you may analyze a story and begin by comparing two of the characters. Or you may want to argue against the position taken by the author of an essay and find that you must first do a careful analysis of the text. Knowing the purpose of each of these approaches and how to make use of them will help you give your essays greater clarity and focus.

Explication

To explicate means to explain or make clear. Think about explaining the details of a Chinese dinner to someone unfamiliar with Chinese food: "First we had won-ton soup. That's a clear broth with vegetables and dumplings similar to ravioli. Then we had shrimp chow mein. That's cut-up onion and celery with a sauce containing tiny shrimp." In this case you are explaining terms in detail and presenting them chronologically, following the order of the meal.

When you write an explicatory essay about a work of literature, you make sense of it for yourself and your readers by giving a detailed account of the text. You describe and explain, sentence by sentence—or in the case of a poem, often word by word. Because explication requires looking so closely at the text, it is only practical to explicate a short work or part of a work: a poem, a speech from a play, or a passage from an essay or story. Explication involves studying details. Consequently, it can help you arrive at a deeper understanding of the text. In an essay about a work, however, an explication without interpretation—that is, without a thesis—cannot stand alone. You cannot simply go through the text, line by line, amassing details, without telling your reader what they add up to. Beware of using explication to replace interpretation.

The following example from a student's essay about Keats' sonnet "On First Looking into Chapman's Homer" demonstrates that explication by itself cannot create an adequate essay.

> In the first four lines of the poem Keats describes himself as having seen many different countries. He emphasizes how widely he has traveled both by placing the word "much" at the beginning of the poem and by using four different expressions to refer to all the countries he has seen: "realms of gold," "goodly states," "kingdoms," "western islands." "Realms of gold" sounds very exotic, and we wonder what countries Keats can be talking about. Things become clear in the fourth line. When we read "which bards in fealty to Apollo hold" we realize that Keats has not been traveling at all; he has only been imagining visiting various countries that he has read about.

The author of this explication plods along as if reading the poem for the first time. Although he does pay close attention to the details and the text, he does not treat the poem as a coherent whole. He shows no sense of what the poem is about except on the most obvious level.

Here is the beginning of another essay for the same assignment.

> In Keats's sonnet "On First Looking into Chapman's Homer" the speaker describes his excitement at being able to visit the world of Homer's *Iliad* and *Odyssey* through Chapman's translations. The comparison between reading and traveling runs throughout the poem. It is important to note what aspect of travel is being emphasized. A close look at the poem will show that Keats repeatedly uses words that have to do with seeing and looking. He is drawing attention to the visual and visionary qualities of the experiences.

Unlike the first student, this writer has a thesis, and he pursues it. In the rest of his essay he examines the sonnet line by line, but he always keeps the whole poem in mind and refers to earlier or later parts when appropriate.

Even when you are not writing an explicatory essay, you will often find yourself using explication. Explication of a key passage can be the basis for an analytical essay, for a comparison of two texts, or for an argument.

Analysis

To analyze something means literally to separate it into its components. In a mystery novel, for example, a chemist may analyze a cup of tea and discover that it contains traces of arsenic. Analysis of a literary text involves something more. We do indeed select an element of a work to look at in isolation: symbolism in Yeats's poem "Easter 1916," perhaps, or the use of the supernatural in D. H. Lawrence's story "The Rocking-Horse Winner." But then, unlike the chemist, we must go on to think about how the part contributes to the whole. For example, how does Lawrence's use of the supernatural relate to the main theme of the story? Examining one element in depth helps us to understand the work.

Suppose you are going to write an analysis of John Cheever's short story "The Swimmer." You decide to focus on the use of setting. Ned, the main character, swims through a series of pools. Cheever uses these different swimming pools to suggest Ned's different states of mind. A careful examination of the parts of the story that describe the various pools would not be sufficient to make this a good essay. You need to explain why you decided to write about this particular aspect of the story and how it contributes to the overall theme. The essay might be structured like this.

1. Opening of story and introduction of Ned's journey: why he undertakes it and what it means to him.
2 & 3. Connection between various swimming pools and Ned's thoughts and feelings.
4. Ending of story: Ned realizes that the house he has been swimming toward is no longer his home.
5. Reason for examining this aspect of the story: how the use of swimming pools bears on the main theme.

Of course, this is not the only way to structure such an essay, but it does suggest the importance of connecting the part with the whole. The aim of analyzing a work of literature is to come to an understanding of the whole by thoroughly exploring some part of it.

It should be obvious how analysis differs from explication. The essay on "The Swimmer" deals with only one element of the story. It examines neither the plot nor the voice of the narrator nor the use of language. In fact a thorough explication of even a story as short as "The Swimmer" would require a lengthy essay. You could, however, write an explicatory essay examining the use of swimming pools by restricting yourself to one or two key passages of the story.

Comparison

Works of literature do not exist in a void. Part of the excitement of reading is connecting one work to another, one idea to another, one character or style to another. Probably the most common way in which we make these connections is through comparison. When we look for similarities or differences in two or more works, we are *comparing* those works. Another term for looking at the differences is *contrasting*. In this section we will treat contrast as a form of comparison.

There are many reasons to compare works of literature. First, one work can shed light on another. Robert Hayden's poem "Those Winter Sundays" and Theodore Roethke's poem "My Papa's Waltz" share a subject, the relationship between fathers and sons. By examining the poems together we can appreciate their distinct differences in style and approach. Seeing them side by side, we see each one more clearly. Comparisons can also broaden our approach to works. Initially there may not seem to be much of a basis for comparison in the stories "Araby" and "The Swimmer." The former is set in Catholic Dublin during the early part of the century. The latter is set in upper-middle-class American suburbia. But explaining what these two works have in common allows us to see the broader themes that both authors address, such as the way the characters in both stories use fantasy to escape from the realities of their lives. By focusing on the similarities between the two works, we come to appreciate the universal elements of each. (This essay appears at the end of Chapter 6.)

There are two main categories of comparison: One is comparing two or more works by the same author, such as an early and a late play by Shakespeare; the other is comparing two or more works by different authors.

Of course, there must be some basis for any comparison. In the case of two works by the same author, you can take this for granted. The second case is more complicated. You cannot select works at random and expect to find similarities. The same is true for contrasting. We expect to find differences between works of literature; it is only if there is some connection between them that the differences become worthy of notice.

Sometimes you will have to work surprisingly hard to discover some common element between two works. It might seem promising to compare Andrea Lee's description of Leningrad to Henry James's of Venice since both authors are Americans abroad. Say you decide to write about what they think of the citizens of the countries they are visiting. A careful reading of the two essays, however, reveals that the authors never really describe their attitudes toward the people. The basis for comparison that you had imagined does not exist. Further consideration might reveal some other aspect that you could compare: perhaps the way both authors convey a sense of light and color or how they describe various shopkeepers and vendors.

It is also possible that a common subject may not form the basis for a successful comparison. Both D. H. Lawrence's "The Rocking-Horse Winner" and Frank O'Connor's "My Oedipus Complex" focus on the relationship between a boy and his mother, but this does not necessarily mean that you could compare the two stories in this respect. Being a son is not a very specific concept, and in fact, the two boys are quite different.

To start writing a paper comparing two works of literature, ask yourself the following questions.

1. For essays: Do the authors agree or disagree with each other? What kinds of attitudes do they have about themselves and their readers? What tone do they adopt? Do they offer an argument, or do they rely on description or narration to make their points? If they are writing about the same subject, do they make the same assumptions about it?

2. For fiction: Are the stories about similar characters or similar situations? Are they told from similar points of view? What kinds of language do the two authors use? Do symbols or metaphors play an important part? How does the setting of each story function?

3. For poems: Are the two poems about the same situation or the same emotion? Are the poets using similar forms? How do the sound, the rhythm, and the rhymes contribute to the meaning of each poem? Are there similar figures of speech? Could one poem have influenced the other?

4. For drama: How do two characters respond to similar situations? How are their conflicts resolved? Compare the way in which two plays illuminate the historical period in which they were written.

As in writing any type of essay, you must organize carefully when comparing or contrasting two works. Suppose you have decided to write an essay contrasting Ben Jonson's two sonnets "On My First Son" and "On My First Daughter." Here is one way you might organize the essay.

1. Thesis:
   Although Jonson mourns the death of both his children, he grieves more strongly for his son
2. First difference—attitudes toward child's life and death:
   son
   daughter
3. Second difference—degree of sorrow:
   son
   daughter
4. Third difference—imagery:
   son
   daughter
5. Conclusion

An alternative method of organizing the same material would be to begin in the same way—by introducing the obvious similarities between the two poems—but then to go on and deal first with one poem and then with the other. Such an essay might be organized something like this:

1. Thesis:
   Although Jonson mourns the death of both his children, he grieves more strongly for his son
2. Son:
   attitude toward his life and death
   degree of sorrow
   imagery
3. Daughter:
   attitude toward her life and death
   degree of sorrow
   imagery
4. Conclusion

Both of these methods of organization have advantages. The first method maintains the comparison throughout. The second allows you to look at each work in depth. Be aware, however, that there are also drawbacks to each method. The first can easily deteriorate into little more than a list of similarities and differences unless you scrutinize each of these elements and relate them to a carefully stated thesis. The danger of the second approach is that the essay may separate into two unrelated halves. To avoid such a separation, be sure that in the second half of your essay you refer back to the first half, to remind your reader of key points and to maintain the comparison. You might use phrases like these:

> Jonson does not seem to experience nearly so much regret over the death of his daughter as he does over that of his son. . . . In contrast to his tone in the first sonnet, here Jonson. . . .

So far we have discussed comparisons between two separate works of literature. You can also write an essay comparing two aspects of the same work. For example, you might compare the attitudes of the narrator in "My Oedipus Complex" toward his mother and toward his father. Such an essay would be organized in the same way as a comparison between two different texts.

You can also compare works from different genres. A good example would be the comparison of Sophocles' play *Antigone* with Thoreau's essay "On Civil Disobedience." However, when discussing works from different genres, you should keep in mind the special features of each. It would not be reasonable to write an essay about dialogue in Thoreau and Sophocles because although dialogue is central to drama, it is only occasionally used in essays. Generally, essays comparing works from two different genres will probably focus on the ideas and opinions embodied in the works rather than on the mode of expression.

Argument

If the purpose of your essay is to persuade your reader to accept a particular opinion, you are writing an argument. An argument gives reasons for or against a particular position. In an argument you take the skills of explication, analysis, and comparison one step further. You direct these skills toward a particular opinion. You could explicate John Crowe Ransom's poem "Blue Girls" in order to argue that the speaker is sexist. You could analyze a scene in *Death of a Salesman* to argue that Willy's suicide does not accomplish what he had hoped. You could compare Virginia Woolf's "Professions for Women" with Studs Terkel's "Waitress" and argue that Woolf's position is unrealistic in light of certain economic facts. Although the word *argue* has an emotional connotation, remember that an argument must be carefully built; mere editorializing is not sufficient. An argument will succeed only if you choose your evidence carefully and present it coherently.

Consider writing an essay about the character of Dr. Stockmann in Ibsen's play *An Enemy of the People.* You find Stockmann to be inconsiderate, insensitive, and obstinate. Unless you substantiate this opinion with evidence from the text, your essay will not be taken seriously. Most readers feel alienated by an opinion without facts to support it. To build an argument you must examine specific occasions on which Stockmann antagonizes the other characters in the play and show how he does this. Be sure to consider counterarguments as well. While you maintain that Dr. Stockmann is reprehensible, you could quote his daughter Petra, who believes him to be bold and virtuous. By showing why you disagree with her, you will strengthen your own position.

Here is an outline of an argument about John Gregory Dunne's essay "Quintana." Notice that throughout, the writer of this outline takes into account the *counterarguments*.

1. Thesis: Secrecy in adoption is wrong.
2. Evidence:
   a. Quintana's curiosity about her biological mother seems reasonable. (Counterargument: But so does her biological mother's desire to remain anonymous.)
   b. Quintana's curiosity does not threaten Dunne. (Counterargument: Perhaps it doesn't threaten him now, but he writes about her with so much pride that it is hard to imagine him actually accommodating her biological parents.)
   c. Dunne says that psychological evidence shows that secrecy in adoption is "barbaric." (Counterargument: But what about psychological damage to the biological mother?)
3. Conclusion

There are several ways of organizing your evidence for an argument, and you may have to keep rearranging the evidence to come up with the best structure. Some pieces of evidence will be stronger than others, some more interesting. You could make your most persuasive points early on and then follow them with secondary pieces of evidence to support your thesis. Or you could build your argument from smaller points to larger ones, from weaker evidence to stronger. This is where outlining can be especially helpful. By drawing up several outlines, you can determine by trial and error which organization best serves your essay.

As you organize your arguments about a work of literature, keep the following points in mind:

1. Your argument must come from a commitment to your subject. It is hard to be convincing if your subject is not clear to you or if it seems unimportant to you.

2. Substantiate your position with evidence from the text. An opinion that is not closely connected with the text will seem pointless.

3. Be direct. Avoid tentative language. (Here is an actual example of the way one student presented the thesis of her essay: "We may perhaps wish to consider the possibility that Lear was vain." Beware of trying so hard not to commit yourself to one side of an argument that you overqualify what you say.)

4. Don't manipulate the emotions of your reader in unfair ways. Clever uses of language and wit are useful and welcome—as long as they are not used as substitutes for evidence or clear thinking.

5. Deal fairly with opposing viewpoints. Most often there is a legitimate counterargument to be made against your idea. Don't ignore it. Accommodate it. Challenge it. Your argument is more likely to be convincing if you make it clear that you have considered the opposing points of view and show the reader why you have rejected them.

5

Writing about Essays

As part of your education you will probably write many essays to satisfy course requirements. The essays in this anthology have much in common with your own work: they are short prose compositions; they are the beginnings of an exploration of a subject, not the final word. (The word *essay* comes from a French verb meaning "to try" or "to attempt.") The essays we have included were written for various reasons—to persuade, to entertain, to inform, to describe—and they vary widely in both subject and style. A scientist muses in nontechnical language about the way cells divide to form an embryo. A waitress talks informally about the dignity she finds in her work. A psychoanalyst describes and explains his theories about family life. A woman reminisces about her grade school graduation.

In this anthology we include under the heading "Essays" not only the kind of essay that you normally write for your courses but also various pieces of prose nonfiction that do not fit the conventional form of the essay. For example, Martin Luther King, Jr.'s "Letter from Birmingham Jail" is, as the title suggests, written in the form of a letter. King is writing to eight white clergymen, arguing that supporting the civil rights movement is an obligation of their profession. When reading this essay we can see how its impact would be different if it were not written as a letter to a specific group of people. We can also see that King intended to persuade not only the eight original recipients but a much wider audience.

We also include under "Essays" excerpts from diaries and journals. Diaries and journals are usually not intended to be shared with the public. Thoreau, who kept a journal to use as a source for writing books and articles, once wrote, "'Says I to myself' should be the motto of my journal." Nevertheless, private journals are often of great interest to outside readers. Anne Frank did not keep her diary for the purpose of publication, and yet it has fascinated generations of readers. The diary is an account of her daily life: her conflicts with her family, the progress of the war as she learned about it, her growing love for the boy who was in hiding with her in the "Secret Annex." Her talent as a writer and her ability to put her personality down on paper, along with the tragic circumstances under which she wrote, make her private reflections a significant work of literature.

Some journals *are* intended to be shared with other readers. The work entitled "Leningrad" in this anthology is a section from a book called *Russian Journal,* in which American Andrea Lee describes the year she spent in the Soviet Union.

We also include a number of speeches and interviews: for example, Chief Seattle's "Reply to the U.S. Government," Virginia Woolf's "Professions for Women," and Studs Terkel's interview "Waitress." It is interesting to compare these with conventionally written essays. In the case of speeches the speechmaker is highly conscious of the audience and the occasion, and yet, as with "Letter from Birmingham Jail," this does not seem to lessen the impact of the essay on later readers.

Types of Essays

King's "Letter from Birmingham Jail" was intended to persuade his readers. Other essays are written with different aims in mind. We have divided essays into four main categories: exposition, persuasion, description, and narration. Of course, many essays do several things at once: A descriptive essay may intend to persuade; a narration may also describe. For the purpose of discussion, however, we will examine each of these categories separately.

Exposition

The purpose of an expository essay is to explain either a process or the nature of an object or idea. A good deal of what we read from day to day is expository writing: directions for washing a new shirt, articles in news magazines, textbooks, and so on. There are several types of expository essays, each of which uses a different method. Two of the more common methods are showing a process and making comparisons.

The *process* essay explains how to do something one step at a time. This type of essay usually calls for an uncluttered, "cookbook" style of writing. Yet some process writing is remarkably literary. Thoreau's essay "The Bean-Field" is more than a set of directions for cultivating beans; Thoreau is simultaneously discussing the process of writing.

Another way of explaining something is to *compare* it to something else. In explaining how a steam engine works, we might point to a boiling kettle. In "Letter from Birmingham Jail" King uses comparison to answer the charge that desegregationists should be condemned because their actions, although peaceful, precipitate violence:

> Isn't this like condemning a robbed man because his possession of money precipitated the evil act of robbery? Isn't this like condemning Socrates because his unswerving commitment to truth and his philosophical inquiries precipitated the act by the misguided populace in which they made him drink hemlock? Isn't this like condemning Jesus because his unique God-consciousness and never-ceasing devotion to God's will precipitated the evil act of crucifixion?

Of course, King's comparisons are intended not only to explain but also to persuade.

Persuasion

In a persuasive essay the author seeks to persuade the reader to accept a particular opinion. The persuasion, or argument, in an essay can be obvious, like Emma Goldman's vigorous argument in "Marriage and Love" that the institution of marriage is inimical to love and should be abolished. Sometimes an argument is less overt. In "The Bean-Field" Thoreau makes a case for certain values, but he does it so subtly that we may not immediately be aware of the argument.

When you read a persuasive essay, you should look at how the author is making his or her case. Is the author giving objective evidence or describing personal experiences? Is the author using wit and rhetoric, or is it the impression of his or her sincerity that convinces us?

Suppose two authors both want to persuade readers to send help to victims of a drought in Africa. They could go about this in very different ways. One might portray the struggle of a woman to find food and shelter for her family in the midst of poverty and drought. The other might quote statistics on the number of persons who are homeless or starving without ever mentioning any specific victim. Both these writers could be very persuasive. Look at the difference between the Declaration of Independence and Margaret Sanger's "The Turbid Ebb and Flow of Misery." Jefferson makes no reference to individuals among the colonists or to himself; he builds a logical case, impersonally. Sanger, on the other hand, makes her argument by describing her first-hand experiences with specific persons.

Description

The aim of a descriptive essay is to depict something—a place, an event, a piece of music—so that the reader will be able to imagine what it would be like to experience the thing described. Descriptive writing appeals to the senses. The fact that descriptive essays as a rule do not attempt to persuade or explain does not mean they are simplistic or unchallenging. Descriptive essays must be well organized, with their details presented in a carefully chosen order.

Many of the essays in the section of this book entitled "Places" are descriptive. Look at this passage from Andrea Lee's "Leningrad":

> The stores are filled with crowds, strong smells, and puddles of soupy mud near the doors. Entering the *gastro-nom* on Malyi Prospekt, where I shop almost daily, one is assailed with the stink of stale meat and turning milk, of crowds who eat too much sausage and wash infrequently. Behind the counters, big slatternly women—who usually have crudely bleached hair above exhausted faces shining with grease and perspiration, faces whose fine-textured skin is a startling reminder that these women are quite young, perhaps thirty or thirty-five—slice kilos of cheese, weigh butter, and bring out the greenish bottles of *kefir* and acidophilus milk. The people in the endless jostling lines are constantly shouting orders and thrusting out their cashier slips, but these women in their bedraggled white coats do everything with an insolent slowness.

Notice that Lee tells us not only how things look but also how they sound and even how they smell. She is in effect transporting us to Leningrad.

Narration

A narrative essay relates a sequence of events. A narrative can be autobiographical, like Lincoln Steffens' "A Miserable, Merry Christmas." Steffens gives an account of a particular Christmas day, relating the events chronologically, allowing his story to unfold gradually. He writes in a lively, vivid style, introducing his family and his younger self almost as if they were characters in fiction.

Not all narrative essays bear this close resemblance to fiction; nor do they have to be autobiographical. In "Union Organizer" Pauline Newman recounts her life as an immigrant, a factory worker, and a union organizer. Her narrative spans several decades and relates an important part of history from her point of view. Unlike Steffens, she does not put herself at the center of the narrative, and her essay does not feel like a story.

Thesis and Theme

When you write an essay, your instructor will often ask what point you are trying to make, that is, what your thesis is. Most often you will be expected to write essays in which the thesis is clearly stated. When you read the essays in this book, however, you will see that not all of them have an explicit thesis. In some cases you will have to read carefully to work out the author's thesis. In other cases, you may decide that the author doesn't really have a thesis.

Here is the first paragraph of Freud's "Family Romance."

> The freeing of an individual, as he grows up, from the authority of his parents is one of the most necessary though one of the most painful results brought about by the course of his development. It is quite essential that that liberation should occur and it may be presumed that it has been to some extent achieved by

everyone who has reached a normal state. Indeed, the whole progress of society rests upon the opposition between successive generations. On the other hand, there is a class of neurotics whose condition is recognizably determined by their having failed in this task.

In this paragraph, Freud clearly states his thesis: that although it is necessary for children to free themselves from their parents as they grow up, certain people fail to do it. Compare this direct approach with the opening paragraph of N. Scott Momaday's "A Kiowa Grandmother."

A single knoll rises out of the plain in Oklahoma, north and west of the Wichita Range. For my people, the Kiowas, it is an old landmark, and they gave it the name Rainy Mountain. The hardest weather in the world is there. Winter brings blizzards, hot tornadic winds arise in the spring, and in summer the prairie is an anvil's edge. The grass turns brittle and brown, and it cracks beneath your feet. There are green belts along the rivers and creeks, linear groves of hickory and pecan, willow and witch hazel. At a distance in July or August the steaming foliage seems almost to writhe in fire. Great green and yellow grasshoppers are everywhere in the tall grass, popping up like corn to sting the flesh, and tortoises crawl about on the red earth, going nowhere in the plenty of time. Loneliness is an aspect of the land. All things in the plain are isolate; there is no confusion of objects in the eye, but *one* hill or *one* tree or *one* man. To look upon that landscape in the early morning, with the sun at your back, is to lose the sense of proportion. Your imagination comes to life, and this, you think, is where Creation was begun.

Momaday does not state his thesis explicitly either in this paragraph or elsewhere in the essay, but reading carefully we realize that he is not only describing the unique relationship between the Kiowas and Rainy Mountain but also showing us that it is irreplaceable.

If we compare both of these essays with Andrea Lee's "Leningrad," we can see that Lee does not really have a thesis. The aim of her essay is not to make a point but to give us a picture of life in Leningrad. Hers is a descriptive essay; the absence of a thesis is more common in descriptive essays than in any other kind.

Like fiction, poetry, and drama, an essay can have a theme. In the case of essays that are direct in their approach, it may not be necessary or appropriate to explore the theme, the deeper meaning. For example, in Gandhi's "Nonviolence and Civil Disobedience" it is immediately clear that Gandhi is explicitly urging the need for nonviolence. In an essay like Lee's "Leningrad," however, where there is not an overt thesis, you might argue that there is an underlying theme—in this case, perhaps the contrast between the beauty and the poverty of life in Russia.

The Use of Words

The authors of the essays we have included in this anthology choose their words with care. If you look back at the opening paragraph of Momaday's essay, you will see that right from the beginning he has the main idea of the paragraph (indeed of the whole essay) in mind. He begins by describing the knoll as "a single knoll." Later in the paragraph, he tells us that "all things in the plain are isolate." The idea of singleness, begun with the knoll, is amplified. It now includes isolation and at the same time the suggestion that each of these single things is irreplaceable, like Momaday's grandmother, like the life of the Kiowa tribe.

Choosing the right word does not mean simply choosing the literally correct word but also the word that evokes the right feelings. Words not only have different explicit meanings, or denotations; they also have different associations or suggestions—that is, they have different connotations. *Spinster, old maid, single woman, unmarried woman* are all terms, sexist though they may be, that could be used to refer to the same person, but each gives a very different sense of that person; they have very different connotations. Momaday could have described the knoll as *solitary* or *lone,* either of which would have evoked a different feeling in the reader from *single.*

It is not enough for a writer to choose the best possible words; it is also necessary to arrange them in the best possible order. When Jefferson lists as unalienable rights "Life, Liberty and the pursuit of Happiness," the phrase is memorable not only because of the words he uses but also because of their order. The ideas are presented logically: Life is a prerequisite of liberty and liberty is a prerequisite of the pursuit of happiness. But it is more than logic that makes the phrase memorable. The sound of the words, their rhythm, the alliteration between *life* and *liberty,* the increasing lengths of the phrases that make up the longer phrase, all reinforce the logic and make Jefferson's order the best one possible.

Subjectivity and Objectivity

In some essays the author is a strong presence. In "Venice" Henry James not only describes the city but also gives us a keen sense of his own personality. He makes no pretense of objectivity; he is writing subjectively, and part of what we as readers enjoy is getting a glimpse of James's personality. In the Declaration of Independence, Thomas Jefferson is writing objectively; he himself is not part of the subject of the essay. Although we can speculate after reading the Declaration of Independence what kind of man he must have been, he does not give us a great deal of information. As you read the essays in this book, pay attention to how subjectively or objectively the author writes.

Tone

Not understanding or being aware of the tone of a work is like not getting a joke—or like not even being aware that someone is telling a joke. Although you understand the words literally, you are missing the speaker's point. Recognizing the tone of a work is essential to understanding it. An author can write seriously or humorously, ironically or straightforwardly, and many other ways besides. Each of these tones expresses a different attitude toward the subject and the reader. The tone of an essay does not have to be constant; for example, an author may use a humorous tone when writing about him- or herself, but a serious one when writing about other people.

Humor

It is important to recognize when an author is being humorous if we are not to miss some part of the meaning of the essay. For example, consider the following paragraph by Lincoln Steffens about his childhood:

> As the store made money and I was getting through the primary school, my father bought a lot uptown, at Sixteenth and K Streets, and built us a "big" house. It was off the line of the city's growth, but it was near a new grammar school for me and my sisters, who were coming along fast after me. This interested the family, not me. They were always talking about school; they had not had much of it themselves, and they thought they had missed something. . . . They agreed, therefore, that their children's gifts should have all the schooling there was. My view, then, was that I had had a good deal of it already, and I was not interested at all. It interfered with my own business, with my own education.

Reading this paragraph with awareness of Steffens' tone, we understand that he is humorously portraying the attitudes of his younger self. We realize that this is not intended to represent his mature attitude toward education.

Irony

Being aware of the use of irony in an essay is essential to understanding the author's attitude to his or her subject. Like humor, irony often seems to involve saying something other than what one actually means. A statement is ironic when the intended meaning is the opposite of the literal. For example, a doctor may say, "My, what a lovely case of measles you have." Maya Angelou is being ironic when she describes her school as "distinguished" by "having neither lawn, nor hedges, nor tennis court, nor climbing ivy"; the word *distinguished* implies that she is going to draw attention to the good points of her school rather than to its lack of amenities.

In "A Modest Proposal" Jonathan Swift has his speaker advocate that the English eat the babies of the starving Irish in order to solve social and economic problems. The irony arises from the reasonable, straight-faced manner with which Swift's speaker offers his extreme solution and from our understanding that Swift's own view is not the same as the speaker's.

In addition to deliberate irony, an essay may also include unintentional irony. When Lincoln said in the Gettysburg Address that it was the soldiers who fought at Gettysburg who were important and that "the world will little note nor long remember what we say here," he was not being ironic. A century later, however, this remark has a kind of irony, because few people remember the details of the battle or the names of the men who fought in it, while Lincoln's address is one of the most famous texts in American history.

Suggestions for Writing about Essays

What is the essay about? A simple answer to this question is usually fairly obvious. For example, Martha Weinman Lear's "Mother's Day" is about Lear's relationship with her mother. But to write a good essay you will need to find a deeper answer to the question. What does Lear tell us about the relationship? She tells us that things are difficult between the two women. Why? What is the history of their relationship? What are the implications of the difficulties between them? Keep asking questions and then questioning your answers until you feel you are giving the fullest possible account of the essay. Writing about an essay's subject does not mean simply paraphrasing the original work; it means understanding every part of the essay, seeing the connections among them, and being aware of the implications of what the author is saying.

Do you agree or disagree with the author? Why? Do you agree with Emma Goldman's claim that love and marriage can never be combined? Why? Because of the arguments Goldman gives? Which of her arguments are most convincing? Are there additional arguments that support her position? Do you think Gandhi is wrong when he claims that Red Cross workers are just as much to blame for the violence of war as armed combatants? How does he support his position? How would you argue against it? Either agreeing or disagreeing with an author and showing why you do so can be the basis of a lively essay.

This question about agreeing or disagreeing does not apply equally well to all essays. It would be odd to ask it about Lee's descriptions of Leningrad, for example, unless you know enough about Leningrad to agree or disagree with specific details of her account.

Will background information help you to evaluate the work? For essays, perhaps more than for any of the other genres, the answer to this question is yes. Information about the author may affect your reaction to an essay. In "On Embryology," Lewis Thomas celebrates the multiplication of cells by which an embryo grows. Does it make the essay more convincing to learn that Thomas has spent much of his professional life involved with cancer research, a field in which the multiplication of cells has a far more sinister meaning?

Knowing what literary works influenced an author can also be illuminating. Thoreau wrote that he was greatly influenced by *Antigone*; knowing this gives us insight into his attitude toward civil disobedience. Reading about Gandhi, we find that he studied Thoreau. And Martin Luther King, Jr., wrote that he was most influenced by the teachings of Gandhi. This kind of information helps us to appreciate the relationship of one work to another or to several others. We recognize that writers are also readers. The literary background of an essay might be a good topic for a paper.

What is the tone of the essay? As we have said, an author may write subjectively or objectively, humorously or seriously, ironically or straightforwardly. For example, Jonathan Swift's "A Modest Proposal" relies heavily on irony. If Swift had written a solemn treatise stating facts and figures about poverty in Ireland, he might have been as persuasive, but it seems unlikely that such an essay would still be widely read today. Swift's carefully considered use of irony and satire makes the essay memorable.

Focusing on the tone of an essay can give you an interesting topic. For example, you might look at Virginia Woolf's "Professions for Women" and write about the different tones Woolf adopts at different moments in the piece. The overall tone is light and mildly humorous, clearly intended to entertain her audience; when she writes specifically about herself, the tone becomes almost mocking or self-deprecating; when she writes about the position of women in general, she is much more serious. Analyzing these shifts in tone and the reasons for them would make a strong essay.

What is the significance of the title? A title is part of the work, not merely a means of distinguishing one work from another. Certainly "Declaration of Independence" is not too pompous a title considering what the document was intended to do. Lincoln Steffens' "A Miserable, Merry Christmas" is immediately intriguing. After reading Swift's "A Modest Proposal," we see how ironic the title is. You may be able to build your own essay around the question of how the title is related to the essay as a whole and what it contributes to the work.

We include here an example of a narrative essay: " Graduation" by Maya Angelou. Thematically this essay belongs in "Struggles," and you may want to compare it to other works in that section. It is followed by an essay about it, written by a student.

Maya Angelou (American, 1928–   )

Graduation

The children in Stamps trembled visibly with anticipation. Some adults were excited too, but to be certain the whole young population had come down with graduation epidemic. Large classes were graduating from both the grammar school and the high school. Even those who were years removed from their own day of glorious release were anxious to help with preparations as a kind of dry run. The junior students who were moving into the vacating classes' chairs were tradition-bound to show their talents for leadership and management. They strutted through the school and around the campus exerting pressure on the lower grades. Their authority was so new that occasionally if they pressed a little too hard it had to be overlooked. After all, next term was coming, and it never hurt a sixth grader to have a play sister in the eighth grade, or a tenth-year student to be able to call a twelfth grader Bubba. So all was endured in a spirit of shared understanding. But the graduating classes themselves were the nobility. Like travelers with exotic destinations on their minds, the graduates were remarkably forgetful. They came to school without their books, or tablets or even pencils. Volunteers fell over themselves to secure replacements for the missing equipment. When accepted, the willing workers might or might not be thanked, and it was of no importance to the pregraduation rites. Even teachers were respectful of the now quiet and aging seniors, and tended to speak to them, if not as equals, as beings only slightly lower than themselves. After tests were returned and grades given, the student body, which acted like an extended family, knew who did well, who excelled, and what piteous ones had failed.

Unlike the white high school, Lafayette County Training School distinguished itself by having neither lawn, nor hedges, nor tennis court, nor climbing ivy. Its two buildings (main classrooms, the grade school and home economics) were set on a dirt hill with no fence to limit either its boundaries or those of bordering farms. There was a large expanse to the left of the school which was used alternately as a baseball diamond or a basketball court. Rusty hoops on the swaying poles represented the permanent recreational equipment, although bats and balls could be borrowed from the P.E. teacher if the borrower was qualified and if the diamond wasn't occupied.

Over this rocky area relieved by a few shady tall persimmon trees the graduating class walked. The girls often held hands and no longer bothered to speak to the lower students. There was a sadness about them, as if this old world was not their home and they were bound for higher ground. The boys, on the other hand, had become more friendly, more outgoing. A decided change from the closed attitude they projected while studying for finals. Now they seemed not ready to give up the old school, the familiar paths and classrooms. Only a small percentage would be continuing on to college—one of the South's A & M (agricultural and mechanical) schools, which trained Negro youths to be carpenters, farmers, handymen, masons, maids, cooks and baby nurses. Their future rode heavily on their shoulders, and blinded them to the collective joy that had pervaded the lives of the boys and girls in the grammar school graduating class.

Parents who could afford it had ordered new shoes and ready-made clothes for themselves from Sears and Roebuck or Montgomery Ward. They also engaged the best seamstresses to make the floating graduating dresses and to cut down secondhand pants which would be pressed to a military slickness for the important event.

Oh, it was important, all right. Whitefolks would attend the ceremony, and two or three would speak of God and home, and the Southern way of life, and Mrs. Parsons, the principal's wife, would play the graduation march while the lower-grade graduates paraded down the aisles and took their seats below the platform. The high school seniors would wait in empty classrooms to make their dramatic entrance.

In the Store I was the person of the moment. The birthday girl. The center. Bailey had graduated the year before, although to do so he had had to forfeit all pleasures to make up for his time lost in Baton Rouge.

My class was wearing butter-yellow piqué dresses, and Momma launched out on mine. She smocked the yoke into tiny crisscrossing puckers, then shirred the rest of the bodice. Her dark fingers ducked in and out of the lemony cloth as she embroidered raised daisies around the hem. Before she considered herself finished she had added a crocheted cuff on the puff sleeves, and a pointy crocheted collar.

I was going to be lovely. A walking model of all the various styles of fine hand sewing and it didn't worry me that I was only twelve years old and merely graduating from the eighth grade. Besides, many teachers in Arkansas Negro schools had only that diploma and were licensed to impart wisdom.

The days had become longer and more noticeable. The faded beige of former times had been replaced with strong and sure colors. I began to see my classmates' clothes, their skin tones, and the dust that waved off pussy willows. Clouds that lazed across the sky were objects of great concern to me. Their shiftier shapes might have held a message that in my new happiness and with a little bit of time I'd soon decipher. During that period I looked at the arch of heaven so religiously my neck kept a steady ache. I had taken to smiling more often, and my jaws hurt from the unaccustomed activity. Between the two physical sore spots, I suppose I could have been uncomfortable, but that was not the case. As a member of the winning team (the graduating class of 1940) I had outdistanced unpleasant sensations by miles. I was headed for the freedom of open fields.

Youth and social approval allied themselves with me and we trammeled memories of slights and insults. The wind of our swift passage remodeled my features. Lost tears were pounded to mud and then to dust. Years of withdrawal were brushed aside and left behind, as hanging ropes of parasitic moss.

My work alone had awarded me a top place and I was going to be one of the first called in the graduating ceremonies. On the classroom blackboard, as well as on the bulletin board in the auditorium, there were blue stars and white stars and red stars. No absences, no tardinesses, and my academic work was among the best of the year. I could say the preamble to the Constitution even faster than Bailey. We timed ourselves often: ``WethepeopleoftheUnitedStatesinordertoformamoreperfectunion . . .'' I had memorized the Presidents of the United States from Washington to Roosevelt in chronological as well as alphabetical order.

My hair pleased me too. Gradually the black mass had lengthened and thickened, so that it kept at last to its braided pattern, and I didn't have to yank my scalp off when I tried to comb it.

Louise and I had rehearsed the exercises until we tired out ourselves. Henry Reed was class valedictorian. He was a small, very black boy with hooded eyes, a long, broad nose and an oddly shaped head. I had admired him for years because each term he and I vied for the best grades in our class. Most often he bested me, but instead of being disappointed I was pleased that we shared top places between us. Like many Southern Black children, he lived with his grandmother, who was as strict as Momma and as kind as she knew how to be. He was courteous, respectful and soft-spoken to elders, but on the playground he chose to play the roughest games. I admired him. Anyone, I reckoned, sufficiently afraid or sufficiently dull could be polite. But to be able to operate at a top level with both adults and children was admirable.

His valedictory speech was entitled "To Be or Not to Be." The rigid tenth-grade teacher had helped him to write it. He'd been working on the dramatic stresses for months.

The weeks until graduation were filled with heady activities. A group of small children were to be presented in a play about buttercups and daisies and bunny rabbits. They could be heard throughout the building practicing their hops and their little songs that sounded like silver bells. The older girls (non-graduates, of course) were assigned the task of making refreshments for the night's festivities. A tangy scent of ginger, cinnamon, nutmeg and chocolate wafted around the home economics building as the budding cooks made samples for themselves and their teachers.

In every corner of the workshop, axes and saws split fresh timber as the woodshop boys made sets and stage scenery. Only the graduates were left out of the general bustle. We were free to sit in the library at the back of the building or look in quite detachedly, naturally, on the measures being taken for our event.

Even the minister preached on graduation the Sunday before. His subject was, "Let your light so shine that men will see your good works and praise your Father, Who is in Heaven." Although the sermon was purported to be addressed to us, he used the occasion to speak to backsliders, gamblers, and general ne'er-do-wells. But since he had called our names at the beginning of the service we were mollified.

Among Negroes the tradition was to give presents to children going only from one grade to another. How much more important this was when the person was graduating at the top of the class. Uncle Willie and Momma had sent away for a Mickey Mouse watch like Bailey's. Louise gave me four embroidered handkerchiefs. (I gave her three crocheted doilies.) Mrs. Sneed, the minister's wife, made me an undershirt to wear for graduation, and nearly every customer gave me a nickel or maybe even a dime with the instruction "Keep on moving to higher ground," or some such encouragement.

Amazingly the great day finally dawned and I was out of bed before I knew it. I threw open the back door to see it more clearly, but Momma said, "Sister, come away from that door and put your robe on."

I hoped the memory of that morning would never leave me. Sunlight was itself still young, and the day had none of the insistence maturity would bring it in a few hours. In my robe and barefoot in the backyard, under cover of going to see about my new beans, I gave myself up to the gentle warmth and thanked God that no matter what evil I had done in my life He had allowed me to live to see this day. Somewhere in my fatalism I had expected to die, accidentally, and never have the chance to walk up the stairs in the auditorium and gracefully receive my hard-earned diploma. Out of God's merciful bosom I had won reprieve.

Bailey came out in his robe and gave me a box wrapped in Christmas paper. He said he had saved his money for months to pay for it. It felt like a box of chocolates, but I knew Bailey wouldn't save money to buy candy when we had all we could want under our noses.

He was as proud of the gift as I. It was a soft-leather-bound copy of a collection of poems by Edgar Allan Poe, or, as Bailey and I called him, "Eap." I turned to "Annabel Lee" and we walked up and down the garden rows, the cool dirt between our toes, reciting the beautifully sad lines.

Momma made a Sunday breakfast although it was only Friday. After we finished the blessing, I opened my eyes to find the watch on my plate. It was a dream of a day. Everything went smoothly and to my credit. I didn't have to be reminded or scolded for anything. Near evening I was too jittery to attend to chores, so Bailey volunteered to do all before his bath.

Days before, we had made a sign for the Store and as we turned out the lights Momma hung the cardboard over the doorknob. It read clearly: CLOSED. GRADUATION.

My dress fitted perfectly and everyone said that I looked like a sunbeam in it. On the hill, going toward the school, Bailey walked behind with Uncle Willie, who muttered, "Go on, Ju." He wanted him to walk ahead with us because it embarrassed him to have to walk so slowly. Bailey said he'd let the ladies walk together, and the men would bring up the rear. We all laughed, nicely.

Little children dashed by out of the dark like fireflies. Their crepe-paper dresses and butterfly wings were not made for running and we heard more than one rip, dryly, and the regretful "uh uh" that followed.

The school blazed without gaiety. The windows seemed cold and unfriendly from the lower hill. A sense of ill-fated timing crept over me, and if Momma hadn't reached for my hand I would have drifted back to Bailey and Uncle Willie, and possibly beyond. She made a few slow jokes about my feet getting cold, and tugged me along to the now-strange building.

Around the front steps, assurance came back. There were my fellow "greats," the graduating class. Hair brushed back, legs oiled, new dresses and pressed pleats, fresh pocket handkerchiefs and little hand-

bags, all home-sewn. Oh, we were up to snuff, all right. I joined my comrades and didn't even see my family go in to find seats in the crowded
auditorium.

The school band struck up a march and all classes filed in as had
been rehearsed. We stood in front of our seats, as assigned, and on a
signal from the choir director, we sat. No sooner had this been accomplished than the band started to play the national anthem. We rose again
and sang the song, after which we recited the pledge of allegiance. We
remained standing for a brief minute before the choir director and the
principal signaled to us, rather desperately I thought, to take our seats.
The command was so unusual that our carefully rehearsed and smooth-
running machine was thrown off. For a full minute we fumbled for our
chairs and bumped into each other awkwardly. Habits change or solidify
under pressure, so in our state of nervous tension we had been ready to
follow our usual assembly pattern: the American National Anthem, then
the pledge of allegiance, then the song every Black person I knew called
the Negro National Anthem. All done in the same key, with the same passion and most often standing on the same foot.

Finding my seat at last, I was overcome with a presentiment of worse
things to come. Something unrehearsed, unplanned, was going to happen, and we were going to be made to look bad. I distinctly remember
being explicit in the choice of pronoun. It was "we," the graduating class,
the unit, that concerned me then.

The principal welcomed "parents and friends" and asked the Baptist
minister to lead us in prayer. His invocation was brief and punchy, and for
a second I thought we were getting back on the high road to right action.
When the principal came back to the dais, however, his voice had
changed. Sounds always affected me profoundly and the principal's voice
was one of my favorites. During assembly it melted and lowed weakly into
the audience. It had not been in my plan to listen to him, but my curiosity
was piqued and I straightened up to give him my attention.

He was talking about Booker T. Washington, our "late great leader,"
who said we can be as close as the fingers on the hand, etc. . . . Then he
said a few vague things about friendship and the friendship of kindly people to those less fortunate than themselves. With that his voice nearly
faded, thin, away. Like a river diminishing to a stream and then to a
trickle. But he cleared his throat and said, "Our speaker tonight, who is
also our friend, came from Texarkana to deliver the commencement
address, but due to the irregularity of the train schedule, he's going to,
as they say, 'speak and run.'" He said that we understood and wanted
the man to know that we were most grateful for the time he was able to
give us and then something about how we were willing always to adjust
to another's program, and without more ado—"I give you Mr. Edward
Donleavy."

Not one but two white men came through the door offstage. The
shorter one walked to the speaker's platform, and the tall one moved

over to the center seat and sat down. But that was our principal's seat, and already occupied. The dislodged gentleman bounced around for a long breath or two before the Baptist minister gave him his chair, then with more dignity than the situation deserved, the minister walked off the stage.

Donleavy looked at the audience once (on reflection, I'm sure that he wanted only to reassure himself that we were really there), adjusted his glasses and began to read from a sheaf of papers.

He was glad "to be here and to see the work going on just as it was in the other schools."

At the first "Amen" from the audience I willed the offender to immediate death by choking on the word. But Amens and Yes, sir's began to fall around the room like rain through a ragged umbrella.

He told us of the wonderful changes we children in Stamps had in store. The Central School (naturally, the white school was Central) had already been granted improvements that would be in use in the fall. A well-known artist was coming from Little Rock to teach art to them. They were going to have the newest microscopes and chemistry equipment for their laboratory. Mr. Donleavy didn't leave us long in the dark over who made these improvements available to Central High. Nor were we to be ignored in the general betterment scheme he had in mind.

He said that he had pointed out to people at a very high level that one of the first-line football tacklers at Arkansas Agricultural and Mechanical College had graduated from good old Lafayette County Training School. Here fewer Amen's were heard. Those few that did break through lay dully in the air with the heaviness of habit.

He went on to praise us. He went on to say how he had bragged that "one of the best basketball players at Fisk sank his first ball right here at Lafayette County Training School."

The white kids were going to have a chance to become Galileos and Madame Curies and Edisons and Gauguins, and our boys (the girls weren't even in on it) would try to be Jesse Owenses and Joe Louises.

Owens and the Brown Bomber were great heroes in our world, but what school official in the white-goddom of Little Rock had the right to decide that those two men must be our only heroes? Who decided that for Henry Reed to become a scientist he had to work like George Washington Carver, as a bootblack, to buy a lousy microscope? Bailey was obviously always going to be too small to be an athlete, so which concrete angel glued to what country seat had decided that if my brother wanted to become a lawyer he had to first pay penance for his skin by picking cotton and hoeing corn and studying correspondence books at night for twenty years?

The man's dead words fell like bricks around the auditorium and too many settled in my belly. Constrained by hard-learned manners I couldn't look behind me, but to my left and right the proud graduating class of 1940 had dropped their heads. Every girl in my row had found something new to do with her handkerchief. Some folded the tiny squares into love knots, some into triangles, but most were wadding them, then pressing them flat on their yellow laps.

On the dais, the ancient tragedy was being replayed. Professor Parsons sat, a sculptor's reject, rigid. His large, heavy body seemed devoid of will or willingness, and his eyes said he was no longer with us. The other teachers examined the flag (which was draped stage right) or their notes, or the windows which opened on our now-famous playing diamond.

Graduation, the hush-hush magic time of frills and gifts and congratulations and diplomas, was finished for me before my name was called. The accomplishment was nothing. The meticulous maps, drawn in three colors of ink, learning and spelling decasyllabic words, memorizing the whole of *The Rape of Lucrece*—it was nothing. Donleavy had exposed us.

We were maids and farmers, handymen and washerwomen, and anything higher that we aspired to was farcical and presumptuous. Then I wished that Gabriel Prosser and Nat Turner had killed all whitefolks in their beds and that Abraham Lincoln had been assassinated before the signing of the Emancipation Proclamation, and that Harriet Tubman had been killed by that blow on her head and Christopher Columbus had drowned in the *Santa Maria.*

It was awful to be Negro and have no control over my life. It was brutal to be young and already trained to sit quietly and listen to charges brought against my color with no chance of defense. We should all be dead. I thought I should like to see us all dead, one on top of the other. A pyramid of flesh with the whitefolks on the bottom, as the broad base, then the Indians with their silly tomahawks and teepees and wigwams and treaties, the Negroes with their mops and recipes and cotton sacks and spirituals sticking out of their mouths. The Dutch children should all stumble in their wooden shoes and break their necks. The French should choke to death on the Louisiana Purchase (1803) while silkworms ate all the Chinese with their stupid pigtails. As a species, we were an abomination. All of us.

Donleavy was running for election, and assured our parents that if he won we could count on having the only colored paved playing field in that part of Arkansas. Also—he never looked up to acknowledge the grunts of acceptance—also, we were bound to get some new equipment for the home economics building and the workshop.

He finished, and since there was no need to give any more than the most perfunctory thank-you's, he nodded to the men on the stage, and the tall white man who was never introduced joined him at the door. They left with the attitude that now they were off to something really important. (The graduation ceremonies at Lafayette County Training School had been a mere preliminary.)

The ugliness they left was palpable. An uninvited guest who wouldn't leave. The choir was summoned and sang a modern arrangement of ''Onward, Christian Soldiers,'' with new words pertaining to graduates seeking their place in the world. But it didn't work. Elouise, the daughter of the Baptist minister, recited ''Invictus,'' and I could have cried at the impertinence of ''I am the master of my fate, I am the captain of my soul.''

My name had lost its ring of familiarity and I had to be nudged to go and receive my diploma. All my preparations had fled. I neither marched up to the stage like a conquering Amazon, nor did I look in the audience for Bailey's nod of approval. Marguerite Johnson. I heard the name again, my honors were read, there were noises in the audience of appreciation, and I took my place on the stage as rehearsed.

I thought about colors I hated: ecru, puce, lavender, beige and black.

There was shuffling and rustling around me, then Henry Reed was giving his valedictory address, ''To Be or Not to Be.'' Hadn't he heard the whitefolks? We couldn't *be*, so the question was a waste of time. Henry's voice came out clear and strong. I feared to look at him. Hadn't he got the message? There was no ''nobler in the mind'' for Negroes because the world didn't think we had minds, and they let us know it. ''Outrageous fortune''? Now, that was a joke. When the ceremony was over I had to tell Henry Reed some things. That is, if I still cared. Not ''rub,'' Henry, ''erase.'' ''Ah, there's the erase.'' Us.

Henry had been a good student in elocution. His voice rose on tides of promise and fell on waves of warnings. The English teacher had helped him to create a sermon winging through Hamlet's soliloquy. To be a man, a doer, a builder, a leader, or to be a tool, an unfunny joke, a crusher of funky toadstools. I marveled that Henry could go through with the speech as if we had a choice.

I had been listening and silently rebutting each sentence with my eyes closed; then there was a hush, which in an audience warns that something unplanned is happening. I looked up and saw Henry Reed, the conservative, the proper, the A student, turn his back to the audience and turn to us (the proud graduating class of 1940) and sing, nearly speaking,

Lift ev'ry voice and sing
Till earth and heaven ring
Ring with the harmonies of Liberty . . .

It was the poem written by James Weldon Johnson. It was the music composed by J. Rosamond Johnson. It was the Negro National Anthem. Out of habit we were singing it.

Our mothers and fathers stood in the dark hall and joined the hymn of encouragement. A kindergarten teacher led the small children onto the stage and the buttercups and daisies and bunny rabbits marked time and tried to follow:

> Stony the road we trod
> Bitter the chastening rod
> Felt in the days when hope, unborn, had died.
> Yet with a steady beat
> Have not our weary feet
> Come to the place for which our fathers sighed?

Every child I knew had learned that song with his ABC's and along with ''Jesus Loves Me This I Know.'' But I personally had never heard it before. Never heard the words, despite the thousands of times I had sung them. Never thought they had anything to do with me.

On the other hand, the words of Patrick Henry had made such an impression on me that I had been able to stretch myself tall and trembling and say, ''I know not what course others may take, but as for me, give me liberty or give me death.''

And now I heard, really for the first time:

> We have come over a way that with tears has been watered,
> We have come, treading our path through the blood of the slaughtered.

While echoes of the song shivered in the air, Henry Reed bowed his head, said ''Thank you,'' and returned to his place in the line. The tears that slipped down many faces were not wiped away in shame.

We were on top again. As always, again. We survived. The depths had been icy and dark, but now a bright sun spoke to our souls. I was no longer simply a member of the proud graduating class of 1940; I was a proud member of the wonderful, beautiful Negro race.

Oh, Black known and unknown poets, how often have your auctioned pains sustained us? Who will compute the lonely nights made less lonely by your songs, or the empty pots made less tragic by your tales?

If we were a people much given to revealing secrets, we might raise monuments and sacrifice to the memories of our poets, but slavery cured us of that weakness. It may be enough, however, to have it said that we survive in exact relationship to the dedication of our poets (include preachers, musicians and blues singers).

SUGGESTIONS FOR WRITING AND DISCUSSION

1. Throughout this essay Angelou describes graduation from the point of view of a child. As adult readers, however, we can see that things were not always quite as they appeared to her. Discuss how Angelou allows her readers to see events from the point of view of an adult and a child simultaneously.
2. What does Angelou mean by the phrase ''we should all be dead''?
3. Discuss the multiple meanings of the word *graduation* in this essay.

4. Has there ever been an experience in your life that did not live up to your fantasy? Write a two- to three-page account of it.
5. Angelou quotes a poem by James Weldon Johnson. Write a three- to five-page essay about Angelou's graduation, quoting two or more lines of the poem at the beginning—having them become, in effect, the thesis of your paper.

SAMPLE STUDENT ESSAY

Assignment: In a two- to three-page essay analyze the changes that occur in Maya Angelou's "Graduation."

Coming of Age

The events in "Graduation" take place more than thirty years ago in the small town of Stamps, Arkansas. At the beginning of the essay Maya Angelou vividly describes the happiness of her graduating class at an all-black school. In the course of the actual ceremony, however, the class is crushed by the attitude of the white graduation speaker. Although the students recover, their happiness is tinged with a new knowledge. In this essay Angelou describes not just graduation but growth.

In the first part of the essay the preparations for graduation are described in great detail. Women are sewing lovely butter-yellow dresses for the girls to wear; boys are making sets of scenery in the workshop. The graduates themselves are free of these labors and Angelou uses this as a time to ponder her "new happiness." She calls herself a "member of the winning team." For the first time she is pleased with her physical appearance, and her academic achievements have been recognized. As a graduate she is the center of attention; family and friends give her presents.

Yet throughout these descriptions of a dreamlike time, there runs an undercurrent of injustice. Angelou comments ironically that her segregated high school "distinguished itself by having neither lawn, nor hedges, nor tennis court, nor climbing ivy." We begin to think that the title of the valedictory speech—"To Be or Not to Be"—might become ironic.

The pride and well-being described in the first part of the essay change dramatically on the night of graduation. Though the ceremony has been well-rehearsed, the principal cuts the beginning short, throwing the timing off and making the graduates seem awkward, and his voice changes as he introduces the speaker, Mr. Donleavy, a white man. Donleavy begins his speech by listing the improvements that have occurred, not at their school, but at the white school.

As he continues, the graduates become more and more downcast and self-conscious. Angelou emphasizes that it was not just she who had this reaction but the whole class. Even worse perhaps is that their parents greet Donleavy's words with "Amens" and "Yes, sirs." In this school-hall, centuries of tradition are being reenacted as the white man oppresses the crowd of black people. Angelou begins to wish not only that the position was different, that history could be undone, but that everyone, the whole species, was dead. Although earlier she was pleased with her appearance, she now lists black among the colors she hates. Donleavy has changed the meaning of graduation; the students are graduating into the world of racism, prejudice, and limited opportunities.

After Donleavy leaves, the class valedictorian, Henry Reed, delivers a stirring speech entitled "To Be or Not to Be." His optimism strikes Angelou as absurd. After all, hasn't Donleavy's speech made it perfectly clear that they have no choice about their future? Reed, who is described as quiet and conservative, senses the audience's mood; suddenly he does something startling. He leads the class in singing the James Weldon Johnson poem "Lift ev'ry voice and sing," also known as the "Negro National Anthem." Everyone knows the anthem and at first they sing "out of habit," but gradually they begin to realize the real meaning of the familiar words. Graduation is once again transformed into a triumphant event.

It is no longer the horror that Donleavy's presence created, nor is it the dreamlike occasion Angelou first anticipated. The anthem is about the survival of blacks. Despite a history of physical and emotional suffering, they have survived and will continue to do so. In recognizing the truth of Johnson's words, Angelou and her fellow graduates have lost their innocence and learned what kind of world awaits them after graduation. Their knowledge is their strength. In the process of graduating, they have begun to grow up.

The author of this essay paid careful attention to Angelou's tone and by doing so arrived at a thesis. She uses the skills of analysis (see Chapter 4) to show the significance of the changes Angelou describes.

6

Writing about Fiction

You complain to a friend that you spent all day yesterday waiting for someone to come to repair your telephone line. You had to stay home from work, and because your phone was broken you couldn't call in to explain. Your boss tried to call you to find out if you were sick, but all she heard was ringing, while you heard nothing. What will she think you were doing? How will you explain things to her? And on top of everything else the person from the telephone company never showed up.

You have just told your friend a story. Each day we tell stories—ones about our own experiences as well as ones we have heard about other people. Fiction is close to us, perhaps more than the other three genres, because storytelling is so much a part of the way we reveal ourselves to others and the way others reveal themselves to us. As we tell these real-life stories, we do what writers of fiction do: enhance our tales with language, distill important elements from the mundane ones, and usually imply a larger point than the details of the story convey in themselves.

Stories usually revolve around a conflict. This conflict is acted out by *characters.* The *plot* is the series of actions that reveal the conflict and its resolution. The deeper meaning of the events in the story is the *theme.*

Plot and Theme

The story about waiting to get your phone repaired has a plot: One thing happened, the phone broke; and then another, you stayed home to get it repaired; and this led to something else, your getting into trouble. It also has a theme: Troubles never come one at a time; one problem often leads to another. This is the deeper meaning that these events suggest or illustrate.

The plot of a story is what happens in it, the sequence of events. The connections between the events—why things happen in the way they do and what motivates the characters—are part of the plot. The story's theme is what those events mean. It is usually not too difficult to summarize what happens to whom in a story; when we do this we are recounting the plot. Finding and expressing the story's deeper meaning is often more difficult.

Here is a student's account of the plot of E. M. Forster's story "The Road from Colonus."

> Mr. Lucas, an elderly, middle-class Englishman, is on vacation in Greece for the first time. He is traveling with a group of people, including his daughter, Ethel. They visit a tiny shrine, where Mr. Lucas experiences a sense of enlightenment. He wants very much to stay at the inn next to the shrine, but after having lunch there, Ethel and the other members of his party insist that he continue the journey.
>
> Several months later, Mr. Lucas and Ethel are having breakfast at home in London when a package arrives from Greece. It contains some bulbs wrapped in a Greek newspaper. Looking at the paper, Ethel discovers that almost immediately after their visit to the shrine everyone staying at the inn was killed by a falling tree. She tells her father about his lucky escape, but he has forgotten all about the shrine.

This account does provide an answer to the question of what happens in the story. The student tells his readers about Mr. Lucas' conflict—he wants to stay at the shrine but is unable to insist on it. The conflict is both internal, within Mr. Lucas, and external, between him and the other members of his party. Still, there is more to this story than these conflicts. There is a deeper meaning to plot: the theme.

"The Road from Colonus" is a complex story, and its theme is not immediately easy to state. Here is a student's first attempt.

> An elderly gentleman visits Greece for the first time, discovers the meaning of life, and narrowly escapes death.

This statement is more like a very brief summary of the plot than an account of the theme. It gives no indication of how the three events mentioned are connected: Did discovering the meaning of life help the man to escape death? Also, phrases like "the meaning of life" are too vague to convey much information. The theme of a story should be stated in general terms. It should be a meaning that can apply to people in general, not just to one elderly gentleman. Here is a second attempt.

> Middle-aged people who have devoted their lives to doing the right thing cannot suddenly change their ways, even if they want to.

This is a better statement of theme, but like its predecessor it ignores the literary allusion that is central to the story. Forster links Mr. Lucas' experiences with those of Oedipus. Oedipus was warned by an oracle that he would kill his father and marry his mother; in seeking to avoid this terrible fate, he instead fulfilled the prophecy. The Greek setting of the Forster story is one link with Oedipus, as is the story's title, which refers to Sophocles' play *Oedipus at Colonus*. In the play Oedipus' daughter Antigone guides her father in his wanderings after he has discovered what he has done and has blinded himself in remorse. When they come to a shrine, Oedipus sits down and refuses to leave. Eventually, the gods come and carry him off to his rest. In Forster's story, Mr. Lucas' daughter is referred to as Antigone. Mr. Lucas does not die at the shrine, but in the second part of the story he has become an irritable old man full of trivial concerns. Perhaps Forster is suggesting, through the allusions to Oedipus, that it would have been better if Mr. Lucas had stayed at the inn and been killed. These ideas might be condensed into something like the following:

> Self-knowledge often carries a high price, but the failure to embrace it leads inevitably to a diminished life.

This, too, is by no means the final word. There is no single correct way to state the theme. Another student might argue that in "The Road from Colonus" Forster is making fun of the educated Englishman's obsession with Greece, that Mr. Lucas' experience at the shrine was illusory and that self-knowledge was never within his grasp. Obviously, your interpretation of the events of a story will govern your view of the theme.

Understanding the theme of a story is a prerequisite for any essay you will write about fiction: a character study, an analysis of symbols, an account of the use of setting. Of course, the thematic analysis of a story is itself a good topic for an essay. It is helpful to begin an essay on theme by asking yourself a question, for example, "Does Mr. Lucas miss anything besides an immediate death by not staying at the shrine?" Answering this question will help you ascertain the theme.

Character

An author of fiction creates a character or characters. The conflict in a story happens within a character or between characters. In good fiction, characters and events are closely linked. The events have effects on the characters, and the personalities and behavior of the characters often bring about the events. In Flannery O'Connor's "Everything That Rises Must Converge," Julian's mother's choice of an extraordinary hat and her distress at meeting a black woman wearing an identical one lead directly to the climax of the story. As a rule, short stories do not show characters confronted by random events like earthquakes or airplane crashes; instead, plots rely on events that are brought about by the characters.

In stories, as in real life, we should avoid believing everything we are told. Other characters may not understand the main character; they may gossip, or speak maliciously. In "Everything that Rises Must Converge" Julian condemns his mother for being bigoted. As readers we can see both why he makes this judgment and that the judgment does not fully define her character; it is too severe. Even when we are overhearing the characters' thoughts, we should be prepared for the possibility that they may be deceiving themselves. To make a judgment about a character we must put together everything we are told and shown, taking into account the tone of the story. Investigating to what extent a character's opinion of him- or herself or of another character is justified makes an excellent writing topic.

Not all the characters in a story are given equal space. As a rule, an author will concentrate on one or two while describing others only briefly. In John Cheever's "The Swimmer" the central character, Ned, meets a number of friends and neighbors as he swims through their pools on his way home. Cheever could not possibly describe all these people in the same detail as Ned. Instead, he characterizes them briefly by their names, their possessions, a few details, or sometimes a short speech. Mrs. Hammer is tending her roses. Mrs. Levy has decorated her gazebo with Japanese lanterns that she "bought in Kyoto the year before last." Enid Bunker screams with enthusiasm when she sees Ned.

E. M. Forster made a distinction between two types of fictional characters: *Flat characters* are described only briefly, in terms of a single characteristic, and do not develop in the course of the story. *Round characters* are described in considerable depth and do develop in the course of the story. In these terms Ned is a round character, and his neighbors are flat. Other critics, however, have pointed out that the categories are not as clear-cut as Forster suggested. Flat characters are not necessarily simple; their single characteristic may be quite complicated. And flat characters sometimes change in the course of a story, while round characters occasionally stay the same. It is more accurate to think of a continuum, with gradations rather than sharp distinctions, from extremely complex characters to extremely simple ones. If you plan to write a character study, you should choose a complex character whom you can explore in depth. It is also possible to write about the parts several minor characters play in a story.

A third kind of character is worth mentioning: the *stock character.* A stock character represents a certain familiar type, such as the absentminded professor, the obnoxiously precocious child, the harassed housewife. Some of the minor characters in "The Swimmer" are stock characters; for example, Enid Bunker is easily recognizable as an insincere society hostess. Flat characters are sometimes stock characters. Charles Dickens had a talent for making flat characters so vivid and memorable that they have become part of our literary repertoire of stock characters. An example is Scrooge in "A Christmas Carol," whose name has become synonymous with miserliness. Any subsequent writer who portrays a miser has to take account of this well-known predecessor.

Point of View

Think how different the story of Jack and the beanstalk would be if it were told by the Giant. It might not even seem to be the same story. The point of view an author uses—that is, who tells the story—is an integral part of the story.

In fiction point of view can be divided into two large classes: *first person* and *third person.* When an author writes a story in the first person, the story is told by one of the major or minor characters. A story told in the third person has no easily identifiable narrator. Within these two categories, there are many possible variations, as we will discuss later in this section. Whatever point of view an author chooses, he or she creates a narrative voice in which to tell the story.

We learn about fictional characters in much the same way we learn about people in real life. We look at their environment, listen to their talk, watch their reactions to various situations, and examine what other people say about them. What we learn about a particular character depends in large measure on the way in which the story is told. In stories that are told in the first person by the central character, like James Joyce's "Araby" or Ernest Hemingway's "In Another Country," we learn how the narrators think and feel by listening to them; it is as if we are inside their heads. In such cases we may not be able to see the main character from outside; we may not know how the character looks unless the narrator or another character remarks on the narrator's appearance. In a story that is told in the third person, like Nikolai Gogol's "The Overcoat," we will probably learn more external facts about the character, but we may not always know what he or she is thinking.

First Person

When writing in the first person, an author is simultaneously creating a character and using the character's voice to narrate the story. In the most direct and immediate use of the first person, a character tells a story about him- or herself. Two examples are Hemingway's "In Another Country" and Hilma Wolitzer's "No Pictures." A comparison of these two stories makes it clear that even within this category of first-person narrative, authors can achieve very different effects. Wolitzer uses the natural speech of her character, Paulette:

> I planned to go on a diet right after the baby was born. In the meantime I was growing bigger, becoming bigger than life. I might have been a stand-in for the Russian Women's Decathlon champ—a thing of beauty and power.

We imagine that if we could meet Paulette this is how she would speak, and reading the story is like having a conversation with the character.

Hemingway also uses simple language, but the effect is more formal. Reading the first paragraph of his story, we never imagine that this is how a young American soldier would talk:

> In the fall the war was always there, but we did not go to it any more. It was cold in the fall in Milan and the dark came very early. Then the electric lights came on, and it was pleasant along the streets looking in the windows. There was much game hanging outside the shops, and the snow powdered in the fur of the foxes and the wind blew their tails.

Instead, Hemingway's carefully crafted sentences seem to represent a kind of inner speech, as if we were listening to the mind of the character, a sort of secret voice.

The firts person narrator can describe events as they occur, or after some time has elapsed. Sometimes—as in James Joyce's "Araby"—a narrator looking back on his or her younger self will show us not only how events seemed at the time but also how they appear in retrospect, thereby offering an additional perspective.

In one variation of the use of the first person, the narrator plays a major part in the story but does not fully understand the events he or she is recounting. Frank O'Connor's "My Oedipus Complex" is narrated from the point of view of a small boy, Larry. Near the beginning of the story Larry says,

> Ours was the only house in the terrace without a new baby, and mother said we couldn't afford one till Father came back from the war because they cost seventeen and six. That showed how simple she was. The Geneys up the road had a baby, and everyone knew they couldn't afford seventeen and six.

Reading this, we are delighted both by Larry's innocence and by his assumption of superiority. Larry's naivete makes him a credible character and at the same time draws us into the story. A narrator like Larry is called a *naive narrator*. We might also call Larry an *unreliable narrator* because in the course of the story we come to understand that he distorts things, such as the relationship between his parents. We cannot always trust his descriptions.

A first-person narrator is not always the main character. In Ursula K. Le Guin's "Sur" the narrator is one of a group of women who make a journey to the South Pole. She is not by any means the principal character; in fact this story does not have a main protagonist. The narrator speaks as a member of the group rather than as an individual.

There are many first-person stories in which, although we as readers supposedly get all our information from the narrator, the author manages to let us know more than the narrator knows. This can be a source of pleasure for us. It might also be a topic for a paper: you might show how, in a particular story, the author gives us clues that the narrator misses.

Third Person

When a story is told in the third person, no narrator is present as a character. We can still think of such a story as having a narrator, however, because the author is creating a voice in which to narrate the story.

When the author describes the thoughts and feelings of several characters, we say that the story is written from the omniscient point of view. The author knows everything about his or her characters. In "The Rocking-Horse Winner" D. H. Lawrence uses the third person in this way. He describes the thoughts and feelings not only of the main character, the boy Paul, but also of Paul's mother and other relatives.

Other stories are told in the third person but from the point of view of one character, so that we as readers have insight into only that character's thoughts and feelings. The effect of this technique can be similar to that of the first person, or it can provide a more distant or objective view of the character's world. This kind of point of view is called *limited omniscience*. In "The Swimmer" we see and hear everything from Ned's point of view: We see the swimming pools and the neighbors only when Ned sees them; we hear only the conversations he hears. But the story is not simply a translation from the first person into the third. Throughout the story, by his use of language, the tone he adopts, and the details he selects, Cheever gives his readers a larger view of the situation than Ned himself could possibly have.

Remember that in fiction the author has chosen who will tell the story. After reading a story, ask yourself why the author chose to tell it from a particular point of view. Each point of view serves certain purposes better than others. A first-person narrative can give us, as readers, a thorough understanding of one character, but our view of events is restricted to that character's perceptions. With limited omniscience we get a larger perspective on the character and the situation, but we may lose the immediacy and the autobiographical quality that are possible in the first person. When using the omniscient point of view, an author can tell us the thoughts and feelings of any of the characters and can also comment on them from outside, but usually cannot fully explore any single character's perspective on the events of the story.

Setting

Characters cannot exist without surroundings; they must have a place in the world. The kind of house they live in, the sort of town or landscape through which they move, contribute to the overall theme of the story and at the same time make the characters and the story seem more credible. These are part of the setting. The setting also includes the season or the time of day when a story takes place. Recall the beginning of "In Another Country":

> In the fall the war was always there, but we did not go to it any more. It was cold in the fall in Milan and the dark came very early.

In this story it is important not only that the events are taking place in Milan but also that they are taking place in the fall. Similarly, in Joyce's "Araby" most of the action occurs in the early evening. Dusk is part of the setting.

The setting of a story not only makes the characters live in the reader's imagination but also can govern the action and play an important part in the plot. In Richard Wright's "The Man Who Saw the Flood," the flood itself creates the conflict in the story. In "The Road from Colonus" the atmosphere of the Greek shrine dramatically, if temporarily, changes Mr. Lucas. In "The Rocking-Horse Winner" a woman's need for money transforms her home, so that to her children it seems as if the house itself is clamoring for money.

The way the author describes the setting of a story often prepares us for what is going to happen; that is, the author uses the setting to foreshadow the rest of the story. This is how Joseph Conrad describes the jungle in "The Lagoon":

> Here and there, near the glistening blackness of the water, a twisted root of some tall tree showed amongst the tracery of small ferns, black and dull, writhing and motionless, like an arrested snake. The short words of the paddlers reverberated loudly between the thick and sombre walls of vegetation. Darkness oozed out from between the trees, through the tangled maze of the creepers, from behind the great fantastic and unstirring leaves; the darkness mysterious and invincible; the darkness scented and poisonous of impenetrable forests.

Reading this sinister description, we cannot help feeling that something terrible is about to happen. If an author describes a house in a way that makes it sound haunted, this alerts us to the possibility that ghosts may appear and makes their appearance more credible. In the same way, Conrad prepares his readers for the awful events of his story and makes these events seem more plausible. He uses the setting to foreshadow the tale he is about to tell.

Symbols

A symbol is something that represents or suggests something else. It works within the context of the story as a whole to suggest meanings on a number of levels.

In Guy de Maupassant's "The Necklace," Mathilde loses the diamond necklace that she has borrowed from a friend. She and her husband borrow money to replace it and then slave for ten years to repay the loan—only to discover at the end of that time that the original necklace was an inexpensive fake. The necklace plays an important part in the plot of the story, and at the same time it is a symbol that helps to convey the theme. The falseness of the original necklace suggests Mathilde's vanity and pretentiousness. The replacement of this false necklace by a true one symbolizes Mathilde's transformation, through hard work, into a much worthier person. It has other symbolic meanings as well; this brief analysis does not do justice to the richness of the story.

Almost anything can be used as a symbol: a person, an object, a gesture, an event, a setting, a situation. How can we recognize when something in a story has symbolic meaning? When we sense that we are not meant to take it only at face value. For something to be a symbol, it must have more meaning in the context of the story than it would have if considered by itself. Further, this additional meaning must be distinct from the original meaning. It would not be correct to say that the necklace in Maupassant's story symbolizes jewelry—this would be like saying that it symbolizes itself. In this story the title draws attention to the necklace; it would be hard not to notice it or the part it plays in the story. Not all symbols are this obvious. Often an author will signal that something is a symbol by calling our attention to it in some way: by repetition, by description, by the use of figurative language. But there are no rules that will enable you to recognize all symbols.

In Raymond Barrio's "The Campesinos" there are many descriptions of the golden apricots that Manuel, a poor migrant worker, is picking. "The plump orange balls plopped pitter patter like heavy drops of golden rain into his swaying sweaty canvas bucket." The goldenness of the fruit symbolizes the wealth it will bring to the owners of the orchards; it also symbolizes a kind of natural wealth, the richness of the earth, which should be available to everyone but isn't. The fruit is crucial to the plot of the story, and at the same time the descriptions of it help to convey the theme.

Symbols do not have to appear several times in a story. In Tillie Olsen's "I Stand Here Ironing," there is a brief description of little girls in a convalescent home wearing gigantic red bows. The one mention is enough to call the reader's attention to the irony of sick little girls wearing cheerful red bows.

Symbols do not have to be objects. Sometimes an author will use a minor character as a symbol. The four young soldiers who befriend the narrator of "In Another Country" have a symbolic effect. They are only briefly described, and in each case what is emphasized is how the war has affected their lives. In "The Road from Colonus" Greece is a symbol, both to Mr. Lucas and, in a rather different way, to the reader. Recognizing when an author is using symbols and what these symbols mean is an important part of understanding the deeper meaning of a story. Symbols suggest what plot does not explicitly reveal.

Suggestions for Writing about Fiction

What is the main theme of the story? Always, when thinking about fiction, you should be concerned with theme. In our discussion of "The Road from Colonus" we showed how you might come closer to understanding a story's theme. Remember that how you interpret the events of the story, the plot, will influence what you judge the theme to be.

Why do the characters behave as they do? How do the characters relate to each other? Do they change in the course of the story? How would you describe Gurov and Anne, the two main characters in Chekhov's story "A Lady with a Dog"? Does their love change them?

How would a different point of view change the story? We have discussed how the point of view from which a story is told shapes the story. "My Oedipus Complex" would be quite different if it had been written from the point of view of the father rather than the son. You might discuss how the author's choice of narrator or narrative voice shapes or affects a particular story.

What is the significance of the symbols in the story? The author of "The Campesinos" writes in vivid detail about the fruit the workers pick. In "The Necklace" and "The Overcoat" the plots revolve around the two objects in the titles, and at the same time these objects have rich symbolic significance. How does understanding these symbols and their meanings help you interpret the story?

What does the setting contribute? Where and when a story takes place are extremely important in creating the world of the story. In Ursula K. Le Guin's

"Sur" a group of women discover the South Pole. How do the snow, cold, and silence of the Antarctic affect the characters and what happens to them?

How do two stories compare? You can compare what happens in two stories, what the characters do, how they react to certain situations. You can compare the ways two authors use symbols, setting, or language.

We include here two short stories: "Araby" by James Joyce and "The Swimmer" by John Cheever. Thematically both belong in "Places," and you may want to compare them to other works in that section. The stories are followed by an essay comparing the two, written by a student.

James Joyce (Irish, 1882–1941)

Araby

North Richmond Street, being blind, was a quiet street except at the hour when the Christian Brothers' School set the boys free. An uninhabited house of two storeys stood at the blind end, detached from its neighbours in a square ground. The other houses of the street, conscious of decent lives within them, gazed at one another with brown imperturbable faces.

The former tenant of our house, a priest, had died in the back drawing-room. Air, musty from having been long enclosed, hung in all the rooms, and the waste room behind the kitchen was littered with old useless papers. Among these I found a few paper-covered books, the pages of which were curled and damp: *The Abbot,* by Walter Scott, *The Devout Communicant* and *The Memoirs of Vidocq.* I liked the last best because its leaves were yellow. The wild garden behind the house contained a central apple-tree and a few straggling bushes under one of which I found the late tenant's rusty bicycle-pump. He had been a very charitable priest; in his will he had left all his money to institutions and the furniture of his house to his sister.

When the short days of winter came dusk fell before we had well eaten our dinners. When we met in the street the houses had grown sombre. The space of sky above us was the colour of ever-changing violet and towards it the lamps of the street lifted their feeble lanterns. The cold air stung us and we played till our bodies glowed. Our shouts echoed in the silent street. The career of our play brought us through the dark muddy lanes behind the houses where we ran the gantlet of the rough tribes from the cottages, to the back doors of the dark dripping gardens where odours arose from the ashpits, to the dark odorous stables where a coachman smoothed and combed the horse or shook music from the buckled harness. When we returned to the street light from the kitchen windows had filled the areas. If my uncle was seen turning the corner we hid in the shadow until we had seen him safely housed. Or if Mangan's sister came out on the doorstep to call her brother in to his tea we watched her from our shadow peer up and down the street. We waited to see whether she would remain or go in and, if she remained, we left our shadow and walked up to Mangan's steps resignedly. She was waiting for us, her figure defined by the light from the half-opened door. Her brother always teased her before he obeyed and I stood by the railings looking at her. Her dress swung as she moved her body and the soft rope of her hair tossed from side to side.

Every morning I lay on the floor in the front parlour watching her door. The blind was pulled down to within an inch of the sash so that I could not be seen. When she came out on the doorstep my heart leaped. I ran to the hall, seized my books and followed her. I kept her brown figure always in my eye and, when we came near the point at which our ways diverged, I quickened my pace and passed her. This happened morning after morning. I had never spoken to her, except for a few casual words, and yet her name was like a summons to all my foolish blood.

Her image accompanied me even in places the most hostile to romance. On Saturday evenings when my aunt went marketing I had to go to carry some of the parcels. We walked through the flaring streets, jostled by drunken men and bargaining women, amid the curses of labourers, the shrill litanies of shop-boys who stood on guard by the barrels of pigs' cheeks, the nasal chanting of street-singers, who sang a *come-all-you* about O'Donovan Rossa, or a ballad about the troubles in our native land. These noises converged in a single sensation of life for me: I imagined that I bore my chalice safely through a throng of foes. Her name sprang to my lips at moments in strange prayers and praises which I myself did not understand. My eyes were often full of tears (I could not tell why) and at times a flood from my heart seemed to pour itself out into my bosom. I thought little of the future. I did not know whether I would ever speak to her or not or, if I spoke to her, how I could tell her of my confused adoration. But my body was like a harp and her words and gestures were like fingers running upon the wires.

One evening I went into the back drawing-room in which the priest had died. It was a dark rainy evening and there was no sound in the house. Through one of the broken panes I heard the rain impinge upon the earth, the fine incessant needles of water playing in the sodden beds. Some distant lamp or lighted window gleamed below me. I was thankful that I could see so little. All my senses seemed to desire to veil themselves and, feeling that I was about to slip from them, I pressed the palms of my hands together until they trembled, murmuring: *O love! O love!* many times.

At last she spoke to me. When she addressed the first words to me I was so confused that I did not know what to answer. She asked me was I going to *Araby*. I forget whether I answered yes or no. It would be a splendid bazaar, she said; she would love to go.

—And why can't you? I asked.

While she spoke she turned a silver bracelet round and round her wrist. She could not go, she said, because there would be a retreat that week in her convent. Her brother and two other boys were fighting for their caps and I was alone at the railings. She held one of the spikes, bowing her head towards me. The light from the lamp opposite our door caught the white curve of her neck, lit up her hair that rested there and, falling, lit up the hand upon the railing. It fell over one side of her dress and caught the white border of a petticoat, just visible as she stood at ease.

—It's well for you, she said.

—If I go, I said, I will bring you something.

What innumerable follies laid waste my waking and sleeping thoughts after that evening! I wished to annihilate the tedious intervening days. I chafed against the work of school. At night in my bedroom and by day in the classroom her image came between me and the page I strove to read. The syllables of the word *Araby* were called to me through the silence in which my soul luxuriated and cast an Eastern enchantment over me. I asked for leave to go to the bazaar on Saturday night. My aunt was surprised and hoped it was not some Freemason affair. I answered few questions in class. I watched my master's face pass from amiability to sternness; he hoped I was not beginning to idle. I could not call my wandering thoughts together. I had hardly any patience with the serious work of life which, now that it stood between me and my desire, seemed to me child's play, ugly monotonous child's play.

On Saturday morning I reminded my uncle that I wished to go to the bazaar in the evening. He was fussing at the hallstand, looking for the hat-brush, and answered me curtly:

—Yes, boy, I know.

As he was in the hall I could not go into the front parlour and lie at the window. I left the house in bad humour and walked slowly towards the school. The air was pitilessly raw and already my heart misgave me.

When I came home to dinner my uncle had not yet been home. Still it was early. I sat staring at the clock for some time and, when its ticking began to irritate me, I left the room. I mounted the staircase and gained the upper part of the house. The high cold empty gloomy rooms liberated me and I went from room to room singing. From the front window I saw my companions playing below in the street. Their cries reached me weakened and indistinct and, leaning my forehead against the cool glass, I looked over at the dark house where she lived. I may have stood there for an hour, seeing nothing but the brown-clad figure cast by my imagination, touched discreetly by the lamplight at the curved neck, at the hand upon the railings and at the border below the dress.

When I came downstairs again I found Mrs. Mercer sitting at the fire. She was an old garrulous woman, a pawnbroker's widow, who collected used stamps for some pious purpose. I had to endure the gossip of the tea-table. The meal was prolonged beyond an hour and still my uncle did not come. Mrs. Mercer stood up to go: she was sorry she couldn't wait any longer, but it was after eight o'clock and she did not like to be out late, as the night air was bad for her. When she had gone I began to walk up and down the room, clenching my fists. My aunt said:

—I'm afraid you may put off your bazaar for this night of Our Lord.

At nine o'clock I heard my uncle's latchkey in the halldoor. I heard him talking to himself and heard the hallstand rocking when it had received the weight of his overcoat. I could interpret these signs. When he was midway through his dinner I asked him to give me the money to go to the bazaar. He had forgotten.

—The people are in bed and after their first sleep now, he said.

I did not smile. My aunt said to him energetically:

—Can't you give him the money and let him go? You've kept him late enough as it is.

My uncle said he was very sorry he had forgotten. He said he believed in the old saying: *All work and no play makes Jack a dull boy.* He asked me where I was going and, when I had told him a second time he asked me did I know *The Arab's Farewell to his Steed.* When I left the kitchen he was about to recite the opening lines of the piece to my aunt.

I held a florin tightly in my hand as I strode down Buckingham Street towards the station. The sight of the streets thronged with buyers and glaring with gas recalled to me the purpose of my journey. I took my seat in a third-class carriage of a deserted train. After an intolerable delay the train moved out of the station slowly. It crept onward among ruinous houses and over the twinkling river. At Westland Row Station a crowd of people pressed to the carriage doors; but the porters moved them back, saying that it was a special train for the bazaar. I remained alone in the bare carriage. In a few minutes the train drew up beside an improvised wooden platform. I passed out on to the road and saw by the lighted dial of a clock that it was ten minutes to ten. In front of me was a large building which displayed the magical name.

I could not find any sixpenny entrance and, fearing that the bazaar would be closed, I passed in quickly through a turnstile, handing a shilling to a weary-looking man. I found myself in a big hall girdled at half its height by a gallery. Nearly all the stalls were closed and the greater part of the hall was in darkness. I recognised a silence like that which pervades a church after a service. I walked into the centre of the bazaar timidly. A few people were gathered about the stalls which were still open. Before a curtain, over which the words *Café Chantant* were written in coloured lamps, two men were counting money on a salver. I listened to the fall of the coins.

Remembering with difficulty why I had come I went over to one of the stalls and examined porcelain vases and flowered tea-sets. At the door of the stall a young lady was talking and laughing with two young gentlemen. I remarked their English accents and listened vaguely to their conversation.

—O, I never said such a thing!

—O, but you did!

—O, but I didn't!

—Didn't she say that?

—Yes. I heard her.

—O, there's a . . . fib!

Observing me the young lady came over and asked me did I wish to buy anything. The tone of her voice was not encouraging; she seemed to have spoken to me out of a sense of duty. I looked humbly at the great jars that stood like eastern guards at either side of the dark entrance to the stall and murmured:

—No, thank you.

The young lady changed the position of one of the vases and went back to the two young men. They began to talk of the same subject. Once or twice the young lady glanced at me over her shoulder.

I lingered before her stall, though I knew my stay was useless, to make my interest in her wares seem the more real. Then I turned away slowly and walked down the middle of the bazaar. I allowed the two pennies to fall against the sixpence in my pocket. I heard a voice call from one end of the gallery that the light was out. The upper part of the hall was now completely dark.

Gazing up into the darkness I saw myself as a creature driven and derided by vanity; and my eyes burned with anguish and anger.

SUGGESTIONS FOR WRITING AND DISCUSSION

1. How long after the events described is the narrator telling the story? Give evidence to support your answer. How does he now regard his younger self? What do you think the story gains by being told from this point of view?
2. Look at the many references in the story to darkness and light. What do these images suggest? How do they combine with religious imagery in the final scene?
3. The narrator's home is described in great detail. How do these descriptions help to foreshadow the ending of the story?
4. Write a two- to three-page essay discussing the changes the narrator goes through.
5. This story takes place in Catholic Dublin, and throughout the story there are many references to religion. For example, the former tenant of the boy's home is a priest and Mangan's sister attends a convent school. Write a three- to five-page essay analyzing the use of religious imagery and symbolism in this story.

John Cheever (American, 1912–1982)

The Swimmer

It was one of those midsummer Sundays when everyone sits around saying, "I *drank* too much last night." You might have heard it whispered by the parishioners leaving church, heard it from the lips of the priest himself, struggling with his cassock in the *vestiarium,* heard it from the golf links and the tennis courts, heard it from the wildlife preserve where the leader of the Audubon group was suffering from a terrible hangover. ``I *drank* too much,'' said Donald Westerhazy. ``We all *drank* too much,'' said Lucinda Merrill. ``It must have been the wine,'' said Helen Westerhazy. ``I *drank* too much of that claret.''

This was at the edge of the Westerhazys' pool. The pool, fed by an artesian well with a high iron content, was a pale shade of green. It was a fine day. In the west there was a massive stand of cumulus cloud so like a city seen from a distance—from the bow of an approaching ship—that it might have had a name. Lisbon. Hackensack. The sun was hot. Neddy Merrill sat by the green water, one hand in it, one around a glass of gin. He was a slender man—he seemed to have the especial slenderness of youth—and while he was far from young he had slid down his banister that morning and given the bronze backside of Aphrodite on the hall table a smack, as he jogged toward the smell of coffee in his dining room. He might have been compared to a summer's day, particularly the last hours of one, and while he lacked a tennis racket or a sail bag the impression was definitely one of youth, sport, and clement weather. He had been swimming and now he was breathing deeply, stertorously as if he could gulp into his lungs the components of that moment, the heat of the sun, the intenseness of his pleasure. It all seemed to flow into his chest. His own house stood in Bullet Park, eight miles to the south, where his four beautiful daughters would have had their lunch and might be playing tennis. Then it occurred to him that by taking a dogleg to the southwest he could reach his home by water.

His life was not confining and the delight he took in this observation could not be explained by its suggestion of escape. He seemed to see, with a cartographer's eye, that string of swimming pools, that quasi-subterranean stream that curved across the county. He had made a discovery, a contribution to modern geography; he would name the stream Lucinda after his wife. He was not a practical joker nor was he a fool but he was determinedly original and had a vague and modest idea of himself as a legendary figure. The day was beautiful and it seemed to him that a long swim might enlarge and celebrate its beauty.

He took off a sweater that was hung over his shoulders and dove in. He had an inexplicable contempt for men who did not hurl themselves into pools. He swam a choppy crawl, breathing either with every stroke or every fourth stroke and counting somewhere well in the back of his mind the one-two one-two of a flutter kick. It was not a serviceable stroke for long distances but the domestication of swimming had saddled the sport with some customs and in his part of the world a crawl was customary. To be embraced and sustained by the light green water was less a pleasure, it seemed, than the resumption of a natural condition, and he would have liked to swim without trunks, but this was not possible, considering his project. He hoisted himself up on the far curb—he never used the ladder—and started across the lawn. When Lucinda asked where he was going he said he was going to swim home.

The only maps and charts he had to go by were remembered or imaginary but these were clear enough. First there were the Grahams, the Hammers, the Lears, the Howlands, and the Crosscups. He would cross Ditmar Street to the Bunkers and come, after a short portage, to the Levys, the Welchers, and the public pool in Lancaster. Then there were the Hallorans, the Sachses, the Biswangers, Shirley Adams, the Gilmartins, and the Clydes. The day was lovely, and that he lived in a world so generously supplied with water seemed like a clemency, a beneficence. His heart was high and he ran across the grass. Making his way home by an uncommon route gave him the feeling that he was a pilgrim, an explorer, a man with a destiny, and he knew that he would find friends all along the way; friends would line the banks of the Lucinda River.

He went through a hedge that separated the Westerhazys' land from the Grahams', walked under some flowering apple trees, passed the shed that housed their pump and filter, and came out at the Grahams' pool. "Why, Neddy," Mrs. Graham said, "what a marvelous surprise. I've been trying to get you on the phone all morning. Here, let me get you a drink." He saw then, like any explorer, that the hospitable customs and traditions of the natives would have to be handled with diplomacy if he was ever going to reach his destination. He did not want to mystify or seem rude to the Grahams nor did he have the time to linger there. He swam the length of their pool and joined them in the sun and was rescued, a few minutes later, by the arrival of two carloads of friends from Connecticut. During the uproarious reunions he was able to slip away. He went down by the front of the Grahams' house, stepped over a thorny hedge, and crossed a vacant lot to the Hammers'. Mrs. Hammer, looking up from her roses, saw him swim by although she wasn't quite sure who it was. The Lears heard him splashing past the open windows of their living room. The Howlands and the Crosscups were away. After leaving the Howlands' he crossed Ditmar Street and started for the Bunkers', where he could hear, even at that distance, the noise of a party.

The water refracted the sound of voices and laughter and seemed to suspend it in midair. The Bunkers' pool was on a rise and he climbed some stairs to a terrace where twenty-five or thirty men and women were drinking. The only person in the water was Rusty Towers, who floated there on a rubber raft. Oh, how bonny and lush were the banks of the Lucinda River! Prosperous men and women gathered by the sapphire-colored waters while caterer's men in white coats passed them cold gin. Overhead a red de Haviland trainer was circling around and around and around in the sky with something like the glee of a child in a swing. Ned felt a passing affection for the scene, a tenderness for the gathering, as if it was something he might touch. In the distance he heard thunder. As soon as Enid Bunker saw him she began to scream: "Oh, look who's here! What a marvelous surprise! When Lucinda said that you couldn't come I thought I'd *die*." She made her way to him through the crowd, and when they had finished kissing she led him to the bar, a progress that was slowed by the fact that he stopped to kiss eight or ten other women and shake the hands of as many men. A smiling bartender he had seen at a hundred parties gave him a gin and tonic and he stood by the bar for a moment, anxious not to get stuck in any conversation that would delay his voyage. When he seemed about to be surrounded he dove in and swam close to the side to avoid colliding with Rusty's raft. At the far end of the pool he bypassed the Tomlinsons with a broad smile and jogged up the garden path. The gravel cut his feet but this was the only unpleasantness. The party was confined to the pool, and as he went toward the house he heard the brilliant, watery sound of voices fade, heard the noise of a radio from the Bunkers' kitchen, where someone was listening to a ball game. Sunday afternoon. He made his way through the parked cars and down the grassy border of their driveway to Alewives Lane. He did not want to be seen on the road in his bathing trunks but there was no traffic and he made the short distance to the Levys' driveway, marked with a PRIVATE PROPERTY sign and a green tube for *The New York Times.* All the doors and windows of the big house were open but there were no signs of life; not even a dog barked. He went around the side of the house to the pool and saw that the Levys had only recently left. Glasses and bottles and dishes of nuts were on a table at the deep end, where there was a bathhouse or gazebo, hung with Japanese lanterns. After swimming the pool he got himself a glass and poured a drink. It was his fourth or fifth drink and he had swum nearly half the length of the Lucinda River. He felt tired, clean, and pleased at that moment to be alone; pleased with everything.

It would storm. The stand of cumulus cloud—that city—had risen and darkened, and while he sat there he heard the percussiveness of thunder again. The de Haviland trainer was still circling overhead and it seemed to Ned that he could almost hear the pilot laugh with pleasure in the afternoon; but when there was another peal of thunder he took off for home. A train whistle blew and he wondered what time it had gotten to be. Four? Five? He thought of the provincial station at that hour, where a waiter, his tuxedo concealed by a raincoat, a dwarf with some flowers wrapped in newspaper, and a woman who had been crying would be waiting for the local. It was suddenly growing dark; it was that moment when the pin-headed birds seem to organize their song into some acute and knowledgeable recognition of the storm's approach. Then there was a fine noise of rushing water from the crown of an oak at his back, as if a spigot there had been turned. Then the noise of fountains came from the crowns of all the tall trees. Why did he love storms, what was the meaning of his excitement when the door sprang open and the rain wind fled rudely up the stairs, why had the simple task of shutting the windows of an old house seemed fitting and urgent, why did the first watery notes of a storm wind have for him the unmistakable sound of good news, cheer, glad tidings? Then there was an explosion, a smell of cordite, and rain lashed the Japanese lanterns that Mrs. Levy had bought in Kyoto the year before last, or was it the year before that?

He stayed in the Levys' gazebo until the storm had passed. The rain had cooled the air and he shivered. The force of the wind had stripped a maple of its red and yellow leaves and scattered them over the grass and the water. Since it was midsummer the tree must be blighted, and yet he felt a peculiar sadness at this sign of autumn. He braced his shoulders, emptied his glass, and started for the Welchers' pool. This meant cross- ing the Lindleys' riding ring and he was surprised to find it overgrown with grass and all the jumps dismantled. He wondered if the Lindleys had sold their horses or gone away for the summer and put them out to board. He seemed to remember having heard something about the Lindleys and their horses but the memory was unclear. On he went, barefoot through the wet grass, to the Welchers', where he found their pool was dry.

This breach in his chain of water disappointed him absurdly, and he felt like some explorer who seeks a torrential headwater and finds a dead stream. He was disappointed and mystified. It was common enough to go away for the summer but no one ever drained his pool. The Welchers had definitely gone away. The pool furniture was folded, stacked, and covered with a tarpaulin. The bathhouse was locked. All the windows of the house were shut, and when he went around to the driveway in front he saw a FOR SALE sign nailed to a tree. When had he last heard from the Welchers— when, that is, had he and Lucinda last regretted an invitation to dine with them? It seemed only a week or so ago. Was his memory failing or had he so disciplined it in the repression of unpleasant facts that he had dam- aged his sense of the truth? Then in the distance he heard the sound of a tennis game. This cheered him, cleared away all his apprehensions and let him regard the overcast sky and the cold air with indifference. This was the day that Neddy Merrill swam across the county. That was the day! He started off then for his most difficult portage.

Had you gone for a Sunday afternoon ride that day you might have seen him, close to naked, standing on the shoulders of Route 424, wait- ing for a chance to cross. You might have wondered if he was the victim of foul play, had his car broken down, or was he merely a fool. Standing barefoot in the deposits of the highway—beer cans, rags, and blowout patches—exposed to all kinds of ridicule, he seemed pitiful. He had known when he started that this was a part of his journey—it had been on his maps—but confronted with the lines of traffic, worming through the summery light, he found himself unprepared. He was laughed at, jeered at, a beer can was thrown at him, and he had no dignity or humor to bring to the situation. He could have gone back, back to the Wester- hazys', where Lucinda would still be sitting in the sun. He had signed nothing, vowed nothing, pledged nothing, not even to himself. Why, believing as he did, that all human obduracy was susceptible to common sense, was he unable to turn back? Why was he determined to complete his journey even if it meant putting his life in danger? At what point had this prank, this joke, this piece of horseplay become serious? He could not go back, he could not even recall with any clearness the green water at the Westerhazys', the sense of inhaling the day's components, the friendly and relaxed voices saying that they had *drunk* too much. In the space of an hour, more or less, he had covered a distance that made his return impossible.

An old man, tooling down the highway at fifteen miles an hour, let him get to the middle of the road, where there was a grass divider. Here he was exposed to the ridicule of the northbound traffic, but after ten or fifteen minutes he was able to cross. From here he had only a short walk to the Recreation Center at the edge of the village of Lancaster, where there were some handball courts and a public pool.

The effect of the water on voices, the illusion of brilliance and suspense, was the same here as it had been at the Bunkers' but the sounds here were louder, harsher, and more shrill, and as soon as he entered the crowded enclosure he was confronted with regimentation. ''ALL SWIMMERS MUST TAKE A SHOWER BEFORE USING THE POOL. ALL SWIMMERS MUST USE THE FOOTBATH. ALL SWIMMERS MUST WEAR THEIR IDENTIFICATION DISKS.'' He took a shower, washed his feet in a cloudy and bitter solution, and made his way to the edge of the water. It stank of chlorine and looked to him like a sink. A pair of lifeguards in a pair of towers blew police whistles at what seemed to be regular intervals and abused the swimmers through a public address system. Neddy remembered the sapphire water at the Bunkers' with longing and thought that he might contaminate himself—damage his own prosperousness and charm—by swimming in this murk, but he reminded himself that he was an explorer, a pilgrim, and that this was merely a stagnant bend in the Lucinda River. He dove, scowling with distaste, into the chlorine and had to swim with head above water to avoid collisions, but even so he was bumped into, splashed, and jostled. When he got to the shallow end both lifeguards were shouting at him: ''Hey, you, you without the identification disk, get outa the water.'' He did, but they had no way of pursuing him and he went through the reek of suntan oil and chlorine out through the hurricane fence and passed the handball courts. By crossing the road he entered the wooded part of the Halloran estate. The woods were not cleared and the footing was treacherous and difficult until he reached the lawn and the clipped beech hedge that encircled their pool.

The Hallorans were friends, an elderly couple of enormous wealth who seemed to bask in the suspicion that they might be Communists. They were zealous reformers but they were not Communists, and yet when they were accused, as they sometimes were, of subversion, it seemed to gratify and excite them. Their beech hedge was yellow and he guessed this had been blighted like the Levys' maple. He called hullo, hullo, to warn the Hallorans of his approach, to palliate his invasion of their privacy. The Hallorans, for reasons that had never been explained to him, did not wear bathing suits. No explanations were in order, really. Their nakedness was a detail in their uncompromising zeal for reform and he stepped politely out of his trunks before he went through the opening in the hedge.

Mrs. Halloran, a stout woman with white hair and a serene face, was reading the *Times.* Mr. Halloran was taking beech leaves out of the water with a scoop. They seemed not surprised or displeased to see him. Their pool was perhaps the oldest in the country, a fieldstone rectangle, fed by a brook. It had no filter or pump and its waters were the opaque gold of the stream.

"I'm swimming across the county," Ned said.

"Why, I didn't know one could," exclaimed Mrs. Halloran.

"Well, I've made it from the Westerhazys'," Ned said. "That must be about four miles."

He left his trunks at the deep end, walked to the shallow end, and swam this stretch. As he was pulling himself out of the water he heard Mrs. Halloran say, "We've been *terribly* sorry to hear about all your misfortunes, Neddy."

"My misfortunes?" Ned asked. "I don't know what you mean."

"Why, we heard that you'd sold the house and that your poor children . . ."

"I don't recall having sold the house," Ned said, "and the girls are at home."

"Yes," Mrs. Halloran sighed. "Yes . . ." Her voice filled the air with an unseasonable melancholy and Ned spoke briskly. "Thank you for the swim."

"Well, have a nice trip," said Mrs. Halloran.

Beyond the hedge he pulled on his trunks and fastened them. They were loose and he wondered if, during the space of an afternoon, he could have lost some weight. He was cold and he was tired and the naked Hallorans and their dark water had depressed him. The swim was too much for his strength but how could he have guessed this, sliding down the banister that morning and sitting in the Westerhazys' sun? His arms were lame. His legs felt rubbery and ached at the joints. The worst of it was the cold in his bones and the feeling that he might never be warm again. Leaves were falling down around him and he smelled wood smoke on the wind. Who would be burning wood at this time of year?

He needed a drink. Whiskey would warm him, pick him up, carry him through the last of his journey, refresh his feeling that it was original and valorous to swim across the county. Channel swimmers took brandy. He needed a stimulant. He crossed the lawn in front of the Hallorans' house and went down a little path to where they had built a house for their only daughter, Helen, and her husband, Eric Sachs. The Sachses' pool was small and he found Helen and her husband there.

"Oh, *Neddy*," Helen said. "Did you lunch at Mother's?"

"Not *really*," Ned said. "I *did* stop to see your parents." This seemed to be explanation enough. "I'm terribly sorry to break in on you like this but I've taken a chill and I wonder if you'd give me a drink."

``Why, I'd *love* to,'' Helen said, ``but there hasn't been anything in this house to drink since Eric's operation. That was three years ago.''

Was he losing his memory, had his gift for concealing painful facts let him forget that he had sold his house, that his children were in trouble, and that his friend had been ill? His eyes slipped from Eric's face to his abdomen, where he saw three pale, sutured scars, two of them at least a foot long. Gone was his navel, and what, Neddy thought, would the roving hand, bed-checking one's gifts at 3 A.M., make of a belly with no navel, no link to birth, this breach in the succession?

``I'm sure you can get a drink at the Biswangers','' Helen said. ``They're having an enormous do. You can hear it from here. Listen!''

She raised her head and from across the road, the lawns, the gardens, the woods, the fields, he heard again the brilliant noise of voices over water. ``Well, I'll get wet,'' he said, still feeling that he had no freedom of choice about his means of travel. He dove into the Sachses' cold water and, gasping, close to drowning, made his way from one end of the pool to the other. ``Lucinda and I want *terribly* to see you,'' he said over his shoulder, his face set toward the Biswangers'. ``We're sorry it's been so long and we'll call you *very* soon.''

He crossed some fields to the Biswangers' and the sounds of revelry there. They would be honored to give him a drink, they would be happy to give him a drink. The Biswangers invited him and Lucinda for dinner four times a year, six weeks in advance. They were always rebuffed and yet they continued to send out their invitations, unwilling to comprehend the rigid and undemocratic realities of their society. They were the sort of people who discussed the price of things at cocktails, exchanged market tips during dinner, and after dinner told dirty stories to mixed company. They did not belong to Neddy's set—they were not even on Lucinda's Christmas-card list. He went toward their pool with feelings of indifference, charity, and some unease, since it seemed to be getting dark and these were the longest days of the year. The party when he joined it was noisy and large. Grace Biswanger was the kind of hostess who asked the optometrist, the veterinarian, the real-estate dealer, and the dentist. No one was swimming and the twilight, reflected on the water of the pool, had a wintry gleam. There was a bar and he started for this. When Grace Biswanger saw him she came toward him, not affectionately as he had every right to expect, but bellicosely.

``Why, this party has everything,'' she said loudly, ``including a gate crasher.''

She could not deal him a social blow—there was no question about this and he did not flinch. ``As a gate crasher,'' he asked politely, ``do I rate a drink?''

``Suit yourself,'' she said. ``You don't seem to pay much attention to invitations.''

She turned her back on him and joined some guests, and he went to the bar and ordered a whiskey. The bartender served him but he served him rudely. His was a world in which the caterer's men kept the social score, and to be rebuffed by a part-time barkeep meant that he had suffered some loss of social esteem. Or perhaps the man was new and uninformed. Then he heard Grace at his back say: "They went for broke overnight—nothing but income—and he showed up drunk one Sunday and asked us to loan him five thousand dollars. . . . " She was always talking about money. It was worse than eating your peas off a knife. He dove into the pool, swam its length and went away.

The next pool on his list, the last but two, belonged to his old mistress, Shirley Adams. If he had suffered any injuries at the Biswangers' they would be cured here. Love—sexual roughhouse in fact—was the supreme elixir, the pain killer, the brightly colored pill that would put the spring back into his step, the joy of life in his heart. They had had an affair last week, last month, last year. He couldn't remember. It was he who had broken it off, his was the upper hand, and he stepped through the gate of the wall that surrounded her pool with nothing so considered as self-confidence. It seemed in a way to be his pool, as the lover, particularly the illicit lover, enjoys the possessions of his mistress with an authority unknown to holy matrimony. She was there, her hair the color of brass, but her figure, at the edge of the lighted, cerulean water, excited in him no profound memories. It had been, he thought, a lighthearted affair, although she had wept when he broke it off. She seemed confused to see him and he wondered if she was still wounded. Would she, God forbid, weep again?

"What do you want?" she asked.

"I'm swimming across the county."

"Good Christ. Will you ever grow up?"

"What's the matter?"

"If you've come here for money," she said, "I won't give you another cent."

"You could give me a drink."

"I could but I won't. I'm not alone."

"Well, I'm on my way."

He dove in and swam the pool, but when he tried to haul himself up onto the curb he found that the strength in his arms and shoulders had gone, and he paddled to the ladder and climbed out. Looking over his shoulder he saw, in the lighted bathhouse, a young man. Going out onto the dark lawn he smelled chrysanthemums or marigolds—some stubborn autumnal fragrance—on the night air, strong as gas. Looking overhead he saw that the stars had come out, but why should he seem to see Andromeda, Cepheus, and Cassiopeia? What had become of the constellations of midsummer? He began to cry.

It was probably the first time in his adult life that he had ever cried, certainly the first time in his life that he had ever felt so miserable, cold, tired, and bewildered. He could not understand the rudeness of the caterer's barkeep or the rudeness of a mistress who had come to him on her knees and showered his trousers with tears. He had swum too long, he had been immersed too long, and his nose and his throat were sore from the water. What he needed then was a drink, some company, and some clean, dry clothes, and while he could have cut directly across the road to his home he went on to the Gilmartins' pool. Here, for the first time in his life, he did not dive but went down the steps into the icy water and swam a hobbled sidestroke that he might have learned as a youth. He staggered with fatigue on his way to the Clydes' and paddled the length of their pool, stopping again and again with his hand on the curb to rest. He climbed up the ladder and wondered if he had the strength to get home. He had done what he wanted, he had swum the county, but he was so stupefied with exhaustion that his triumph seemed vague. Stooped, holding on to the gateposts for support, he turned up the driveway of his own house.

The place was dark. Was it so late that they had all gone to bed? Had Lucinda stayed at the Westerhazys' for supper? Had the girls joined her there or gone someplace else? Hadn't they agreed, as they usually did on Sunday, to regret all their invitations and stay at home? He tried the garage doors to see what cars were in but the doors were locked and rust came off the handles onto his hands. Going toward the house, he saw that the force of the thunderstorm had knocked one of the rain gutters loose. It hung down over the front door like an umbrella rib, but it could be fixed in the morning. The house was locked, and he thought that the stupid cook or the stupid maid must have locked the place up until he remembered that it had been some time since they had employed a maid or a cook. He shouted, pounded on the door, tried to force it with his shoulder, and then, looking in at the windows, saw that the place was empty.

SUGGESTIONS FOR WRITING AND DISCUSSION

1. Each encounter at a pool illustrates an aspect of Ned's life. Choose one encounter and discuss what it shows us about Ned.
2. What is the significance of the storm?
3. What details foreshadow the end of the story?
4. By the end of the story we must reevaluate everything Ned has said to the other characters. On rereading, what do you still think is true? What is not? How much of what he says is fantasy?
5. Write a two- to three-page essay in which you construct hypothetical events leading to the desertion of Ned by Lucinda and her daughters.
6. Look at the section on setting in the chapter "Writing about Fiction." What is the importance of setting in this story? How would this story be different if it took place in a less affluent community? How do each of the pools reveal Ned's state of mind? Write a three- to five-page essay.

SAMPLE STUDENT ESSAY

Assignment: In a three- to four-page essay compare "Araby" and "The Swimmer," paying particular attention to setting.

"Araby" and "The Swimmer":

Two Journeys of Disillusionment

There are great differences between the Dublin James Joyce portrays in his story "Araby" and the upper-class American suburbs of John Cheever's "The Swimmer." Nevertheless, the two stories have certain similarities. In each of them the main character tries to protect himself from everyday life by spinning a cocoon of fantasies, and in each it is only at the end of the story that these characters give up their illusions. Also, both Joyce and Cheever use description of the setting to convey their characters' thoughts, fantasies, and feelings.

"Araby" opens with a description of the street where the narrator lives. It is a quiet, decent street, noisy only when the boys get out of the Christian Brothers' School. In the very short opening paragraph, the narrator twice refers to the street as blind, meaning that it is a dead end. This repetition suggests his own myopia and at the same time foreshadows a scene later in the story where he hides behind a window blind to watch the sister of his friend Mangan.

On the short winter evenings, the narrator and his school friends, including Mangan, meet in the street to play. Night after night, Mangan's sister comes out to call her brother in, and gradually the narrator becomes infatuated with her. He begins to watch her in secret and is haunted by her image, although he admits, "I had never spoken to her, except for a few casual words, and yet her name was like a summons to all my foolish blood." It is apparent to the reader how little this passion has to do with Mangan's sister herself.

Finally, the narrator manages to initiate an awkward conversation with her, and he invites her to go to the bazaar, Araby. When she says she is unable to go he impulsively says he will go to the bazaar and bring something back for her. The reader sees that he is struggling to maintain whatever interest she might have in him, and Araby comes to symbolize the possibility of something wonderful in his future.

On the day of the bazaar family difficulties almost prevent him from going. Finally, however, he manages to get away. When other people try to get on the train, the porters refuse to let them, and the narrator is carried toward Araby in ambivalent, solitary triumph. When he arrives it is so late that already many of the stalls are closed and much of the building is dark. He recognizes "a silence like that which pervades a church after service." This religious image recalls other references to religion throughout the story. Araby, however, turns out to be a false temple. The narrator is about to purchase his gift when he overhears a playful argument between a woman and two men. The everyday unromantic conversation rouses the narrator from his fantasies. He realizes that he is nothing to Mangan's sister, the fair is tawdry and second-rate, and any gift he bought would be merely a gift.

In "The Swimmer" the fantasies of the main character, Ned, have quite a different source. For most of the story the reader does not realize that Ned is trying to forget that he has lost all his money and his family. As in "Araby," nightfall and the darkening sky are a metaphor for the main character's impending collision with reality.

One sunny afternoon Ned decides to swim home from a friend's pool, through the various pools of his neighbors. Swimming seems to symbolize a desire to escape, although the narrator denies this motive, and also for purification, an attempt to wash away or eradicate something. Just as the narrator in "Araby" glorifies the bazaar, so Ned glorifies his journey. He imagines that he is an explorer, and he ironically names the line of swimming pools the "Lucinda River" after his wife. He swims from house to house, stopping briefly to drink and socialize, but never letting these pauses interfere with his pilgrimage.

It is at the height of Ned's pleasure that the turning point of the story occurs. There is a storm. Like the narrator in "Araby," Ned begins to encounter a series of difficulties and disappointments. The Welchers' pool has been drained. Then he comes to the public swimming pool. The water in it is cloudy and dirty, similar to Ned's mind, which is clouded with confusion. He dives in and swims a length. When he gets out the lifeguards are yelling at him for not having an identification tag. This incident suggests Ned's deeper loss of identity.

The descriptions of the various pools and their owners become increasingly revealing of Ned's true situation. He finds the Hallorans, an elderly couple, sitting naked beside their pool and to be polite removes his own bathing trunks. The water in their pool is a clear, natural color, and it seems perfectly appropriate that the Hallorans are the first people who attempt something other than superficial conversation. However, although he is completely naked, Ned still clings to his illusions and refuses to listen to them. With each successive pool, Ned is brought closer to remembering the truth, but not until he gazes through the windows of his former home and finds it empty and deserted does he fully acknowledge what has happened to him. Like the bazaar in "Araby," his house is in darkness. And that darkness, where there should be light, breaks the spell of the illusion and suggests the unenlightened state of Ned's mind.

For the narrator of "Araby" it is painful to realize that he has been living in a fantasy world. For Ned, however, reality is so painful that he desperately embraces a fantasy world. For both these characters, it is their environment that finally pierces the darkness of their illusions.

Notice how the author of this essay kept the comparison of the two stories vital throughout by consistently making connections between the two works. Although the two stories might not seem to have much in common on first reading, the comparison does not seem contrived. (See Chapter 4 for methods of organizing a comparison.)

7

Writing about Poetry

If asked to define or describe poetry, most people would probably say something about form: words arranged in lines that end in rhymes. When poets themselves try to describe poetry, however, they usually do so in terms of emotions:

> Poetry is the spontaneous overflow of powerful feelings: it takes its origin from emotion recollected in tranquility.
>
> *William Wordsworth*

> If I read a book and it makes my whole body so cold no fire can ever warm me, I know that it is poetry. If I feel physically as if the top of my head were taken off, I know that it's poetry. Is there any other way?
>
> *Emily Dickinson*

> Poetry is a way of taking life by the throat.
>
> *Robert Frost*

> Poetry is not a turning loose of emotion, but an escape from emotion; it is not the expression of personality, but an escape from personality.
>
> *T. S. Eliot*

This emphasis on emotion says something important about the nature of poetry. As both Wordsworth's and Eliot's descriptions make clear, however, poetry is more than simply the outpouring of emotion. The expression of emotion is carefully controlled to fit the formal requirements of poetry. It is by use of these formal restraints that poets transform the purely personal—their own feelings or experiences—into something public or universal. Paradoxically, poetry is at the same time the most personal and the most formal of the four genres.

This formal quality sometimes makes poetry seem complicated or obscure. In this chapter we will introduce you to a critical vocabulary that will help to make poetry more accessible.

Lyric and Narrative Poetry

Poetry can be divided into lyric and narrative poetry. The term *lyric* was originally applied to poems that were intended to be sung to the accompaniment of the lyre. Now the term has come to embrace a wider variety of poems. Any relatively short poem that expresses the emotions and thoughts of a single speaker can be described as a lyric poem.

A *narrative* poem is one that tells a story. Very long narrative poems in which the adventures of the hero border on the mythic are called *epics*. Homer's *Odyssey* and Milton's *Paradise Lost* are epic poems. Another traditional type of the narrative poem is the *ballad:* a short narrative poem usually written in song-like stanzas with a repeating refrain. Traditionally ballads were preserved through an oral tradition rather than written down.

How to Read a Poem

The poet Ezra Pound described poetry as language charged with meaning to the highest degree. To be appreciated, poetry must be read slowly and thoroughly. You should never begin to write about a poem without first reading it several times. When working a short poem, you may also find it helpful to copy it out.

Another effective way to get acquainted with a poem is to read it aloud. The sounds and rhythms of the words contribute to the poem's meaning, and we hear them more easily when we read aloud. To do this properly, you should have an audience, real or imaginary; a tape recorder or a cat will do. When you are reading, try to take account of both the line breaks and the punctuation of the poem. Sometimes the two will coincide, but not always. A sentence or phrase may stretch across several lines. (You should also consider the rhythm of the poem; we will discuss this later in the chapter.)

The exact choice and arrangement of words carry so much of a poem's meaning that it is not usually possible to capture that meaning in a paraphrase. Nevertheless, you may find it helpful to write a one- or two-sentence paraphrase of each stanza of the poem. Paying attention to the literal meaning of each part will help you to understand and appreciate the poem as a whole. A dictionary may be useful at this stage. The meanings and connotations of words change from century to century; in reading a poem written long ago, be on the lookout for any changes in meaning. In "My mistress' eyes are nothing like the sun," Shakespeare compares women's hair to wires. The *Oxford English Dictionary* makes clear that in Shakespeare's time *wire* had a more romantic connotation than it does today.

The Speaker of the Poem

When a poem is written in the first person and has no obvious fictitious speaker, it is tempting to assume that the poem is autobiographical. Almost inevitably we take the speaker to be the poet. Let us look at A. E. Housman's "When I Was One-and-Twenty":

> When I was one-and-twenty
>   I heard a wise man say,
> "Give crowns and pounds and guineas
>   But not your heart away;
>
> Give pearls away and rubies
>   But keep your fancy free."
> But I was one-and-twenty,
>   No use to talk to me.
>
> When I was one-and-twenty
>   I heard him say again,
> "The heart out of the bosom
>   Was never given in vain;
>
> 'Tis paid with sighs a plenty
>   And sold for endless rue."
> And I am two-and-twenty,
>   And oh, 'tis true, 'tis true.

It would be easy to assume from reading this poem that Housman wrote it at the age of twenty-two. Actually he was in his midthirties when he wrote it. We would be wrong to read the poem as being literally about Housman. When we look at the poem closely we discover additional reasons for not reading it autobiographically. Housman presents the events of the poem in such a way that we do not regard them in exactly the same manner as does the twenty-two-year-old speaker: There is a note of irony in the last two lines that makes this distinction fairly clear. In fact, Houseman shapes the poem so that we will view the speaker with some detachment.

This example from Housman makes clear something that is true of all poems. However autobiographical a poem may appear to be, the poet, like the writer of fiction, is always creating a voice or a persona. As William Butler Yeats said, the writer of the poem is not the same as "that bundle of accident and incoherence that sits down to breakfast." The first act of the poet is to create the persona that speaks the poem. When you are writing about the feelings or opinions expressed in a poem, it is always more accurate to attribute them to the speaker of the poem than to the poet. Sometimes, as in the Housman poem, it is possible to differentiate the sentiments of the speaker from those of the poet. The difference is conveyed not overtly, but by the overall tone of the poem.

In some first-person poems, it is immediately clear that the speaker is someone other than the poet. Look at the opening lines of Robert Browning's "My Last Duchess":

> That's my last duchess painted on the wall,
> Looking as if she were alive. I call
> That piece a wonder, now: Fra Pandolf's hands
> Worked busily a day, and there she stands.

Here Browning has created a fictitious character, the Duke, and given him a voice in the same way that an author would in a short story. There is no chance of our mistaking the "I" for Browning.

You should be alert not only to who is speaking the poem but also to whether it is addressed to someone specific. In some poems the speaker is addressing a general audience, as for example in "When I Was One-and-Twenty." In others, there is a very specific audience, as for instance in a love poem addressed to the poet's beloved. In yet a third kind of poem, the poet creates both a speaker and a specific listener: In "My Last Duchess" the Duke is speaking to a messenger from the father of his future second wife. This information is important to our interpretation of the poem. Working out who is speaking, to whom, and on what occasion is part of understanding a poem.

Imagery

We see clouds in the sky, we hear traffic noise and birdsong, we smell the earth after rain, we feel the roughness of a stone. In large measure we learn about the world and experience life through our senses. Poets use words to paint pictures and to reproduce the experiences of the senses; that is, they make images. Images enable us as readers to share in the poet's experiences. In the following stanzas Wordsworth creates an image of daffodils:

> I wander'd lonely as a cloud
> That floats on high o'er vales and hills,
> When all at once I saw a crowd,
> A host of golden daffodils,
> Beside the lake, beneath the trees
> Fluttering and dancing in the breeze.
>
> Continuous as the stars that shine
> And twinkle in the milky way,

They stretched in never-ending line
Along the margin of a bay:
Ten thousand saw I at a glance
Tossing their heads in sprightly dance.

Here Wordsworth is helping us visualize what the speaker saw, the innumerable daffodils fluttering in the breeze on the shore of a lake. At the same time he is conveying through this description not only what the daffodils looked like but also what feelings they evoked in the speaker, thus enabling us as readers to share these feelings. For instance, he does not simply tell us that there were a great many daffodils, more than one could count; rather he gives us a feeling of their infinite number by comparing them to something we are all familiar with, the stars in the Milky Way.

Look at another kind of image, one that conjures up the sound of a voice:

Upon Julia's Voice

So smoothe, so sweet, so silvery is thy voice,
As, could they hear, the Damned would make no noise,
But listen to thee (walking in thy chamber)
Melting melodious words to Lutes of Amber.

Robert Herrick

The speaker describes Julia's voice both literally as smooth, sweet, and melodious and more figuratively as silvery and melting. It is not only through description, however, that an image of Julia's voice is conveyed; the actual sound of the poet's words, soft and mellifluous, imitates what is being described and helps to give us a sense of what it would be like to hear Julia speak, of what effect her voice might have on us.

Figurative Language

We all use figures of speech more often than we realize. "It's raining cats and dogs." "He's green with envy." "I'm bowled over." Expressions like these are so familiar that we usually are not even aware of them as figures of speech. When a figure of speech is used too often, it becomes a cliché and no longer evokes an image. New figures of speech, however, can help us look at familiar subjects with fresh awareness; they can also be used to make abstract qualities, such as peace and justice, more concrete. In this section we will talk about the more common types of figures of speech. For definitions of less common ones, consult the Glossary.

Metaphor

Metaphors help us to see something in a new way by comparing two things that are not obviously similar. When Shakespeare says love "is the star to every wandering bark," he is using a metaphor to tell us that love is as constant as the star by which sailors reckon to steer the course of their ships. Note that Shakespeare does not say that love is *like* the star; in a metaphor the two things are compared not by saying that one is similar to the other but by claiming that one *is* the other: Love "is the star."

In this example both terms in the metaphor are named, but metaphors do not always have to be this explicit. One, or occasionally both, terms in the comparison may be implied without being named. For an example of a less explicit metaphor see the Langston Hughes poem "Dream Deferred" (page 98). The last line is "Or does it explode?" *It* is the dream deferred, but the other term in this metaphor is never named. Instead Hughes uses the verb *explode* to compare the dream to a bomb.

A metaphor that is sustained through several lines, or through a whole poem, is called an *extended metaphor*. In the following stanza by Thomas Campion, the speaker of the poem describes his mistress in terms of the flowers and fruits found in a garden.

> There is a garden in her face,
>   Where roses and white lilies grow;
> A heavenly paradise is that place,
>   Wherein all pleasant fruits do flow.
> There cherries grow, which none may buy
>   Till "Cherry ripe!" themselves do cry.

Campion does not tell us exactly what the roses, lilies, and cherries represent but leaves the reader to decipher the implied meaning. In the other two verses of the poem he sustains the metaphor.

Simile

A simile is a figure of speech in which one thing is overtly compared to another. The comparison is signaled by the prepositions *as* or *like*.

> She is *as* in a field a silken tent.
>   *Robert Frost*

> Now, therefore, while the youthful hue
> Sits on thy skin *like* morning dew,
>   *Andrew Marvell*

> O my luve's *like* a red, red rose,
>   *Robert Burns*

Like metaphors, similes can be extended through several lines or even through a whole poem.

To see the difference between similes and metaphors look at the following poem, "Dream Deferred," by Langston Hughes.

What happens to a dream deferred?

Does it dry up
like a raisin in the sun?
Or fester like a sore—
And then run?
Does it stink like rotten meat?
Or crust and sugar over—
like a syrupy sweet?

Maybe it just sags
like a heavy load.

Or does it explode?

The first five figures of speech in the poem are similes. The speaker asks if a dream deferred is *like* a raisin, a sore, rotten meat, a sweet, or maybe a heavy load. In each case we are told the names of the two things being compared and in what respect they are being compared. The last line of the poem is not a simile but a metaphor. The speaker does not say that the dream is like a bomb, but by using the word *explode* he implies that it is. This is an implicit metaphor. The dream deferred is identified with the bomb by its potential for explosion. Because of the way one thing is identified with another in metaphors, metaphors are often more compressed than similes, in which the comparison is overt. This quality of compression gives a greater sense of urgency to the final line of this poem and makes it more effective than it would be if it had been phrased as a simile.

Personification

Another common figure of speech is personification. We personify animals, objects, or concepts when we attribute human qualities to them. In his ode "To Autumn" John Keats personifies the season by describing autumn as a young woman:

Who hath not seen thee oft amid thy store?
   Sometimes whoever seeks abroad may find
Thee sitting careless on a granary floor,
   Thy hair soft-lifted by the winnowing wind;
Or on a half-reaped furrow sound asleep,
   Drowsed with the fume of poppies, while thy hook
      Spares the next swath and all its twined flowers

We get a clear picture of a young woman present among the barns and fields of a farm. Autumn is as vivid as this young woman. Like other figures of speech, personification can make the abstract concrete, as it does in this case, and make the overly familiar seem new again.

Being aware of a poet's use of figures of speech is essential to understanding a poem. Analyzing what figures of speech contribute to a particular poem often makes a good topic for an essay.

Rhyme, Musical Effects, and Meter

The total effect of a poem depends not only on what the words mean, literally and figuratively, but also on how they sound. We can think of the sound of a poem as having three aspects: *rhyme, musical effects,* and *meter.* These three are inextricably entwined. Together they work to reinforce or heighten the meaning of a poem. A poet uses rhyme and meter to give certain words and phrases more emphasis and to convey the connections between them. The musical effect of the words also helps to reinforce meaning by mirroring or mimicking the literal meaning of the words; to convey anger, for example, a poet may choose words that contain many hard consonants so that the line will have a harsh sound.

Rhyme

Rhyme depends on the repetition of sounds. When we think of rhyme we commonly think of *end rhymes,* that is, rhyming words appearing at the end of lines—as in "Hickory, dickory, dock/the mouse ran up the clock." Rhymes can also occur in the middle of a line, like "Hickory, dickory"; this is called *internal rhyme.* Almost all poems contain rhyme of some kind. We will begin by discussing end rhyme, which is used in many traditional forms of poetry. Look at Shakespeare's Sonnet 116:

Let me not to the marriage of true minds	*a*
Admit impediments. Love is not love	*b*
Which alters when it alteration finds,	*a*
Or bends with the remover to remove.	*b*
O no! it is an ever-fixèd mark	*c*
That looks on tempests and is never shaken;	*d*
It is the star to every wand'ring bark,	*c*
Whose worth's unknown, although his height be taken.	*d*
Love's not Time's fool, though rosy lips and cheeks	*e*
Within his bending sickle's compass come;	*f*
Love alters not with his brief hours and weeks,	*e*
But bears it out even to the edge of doom.	*f*
If this be error, and upon me proved,	*g*
I never writ, nor no man ever loved.	*g*

As its title indicates, this poem is a sonnet, one of the most widely used traditional forms. A sonnet is a fourteen-line poem, usually written in iambic pentameter (see the section on meter). A sonnet often follows a strict *rhyme scheme.* The rhyme scheme of a poem is the pattern in which end rhymes recur. We refer to the rhyme scheme by using letters of the alphabet, as shown to the right of the sonnet. The rhyme scheme of Sonnet 116 identifies it as being what is called a *Shakespearian* or *English sonnet.* It can be divided into three groups of four lines, called *quatrains,* and two concluding lines, called a *couplet.* The first quatrain in a Shakespearian sonnet rhymes *abab,* the second *cdcd,* the third *efef,* and the couplet *gg.* Another widely used form is the *Italian sonnet.* An Italian sonnet is divided into an eight-line stanza or *octave,* which is rhymed *abbaabba,* and a six-line stanza or *sestet,* rhymed *cdecde, cdcdcd,* or *cdedce.* (The terms *octave* and *sestet* can also be used to apply to the first eight lines and the last six lines in an English sonnet.) For an example of an Italian sonnet see Milton's "On the Late Massacre in Piedmont." In both the Shakespearian and the Italian sonnet the first eight lines develop a theme that the last six lines then comment on or modify.

Even when two poems have similar rhyme schemes, the effect of the rhymes can be quite different. If the lines of a poem are end-stopped—that is, if they end with a pause, usually indicated by punctuation—this makes the rhyme more noticeable. We cannot help being aware of the couplet with which Shakespeare ends Sonnet 18:

> So long as men can breathe or eyes can see,
> So long lives this, and this gives life to thee.

However, if a sentence or a phrase continues from one line into the next without a pause, the rhymes become less noticeable. Browning's use of rhyming couplets in "My Last Duchess" may not be immediately obvious because most of the lines are not end-stopped:

> That's my last duchess painted on the wall,
> Looking as if she were alive. I call
> That piece a wonder, now: Fra Pandolf's hands
> Worked busily a day, and there she stands.

The continuation of a sentence or phrase from one line into the next, without punctuation or pause, is called *enjambment.* When you are marking the rhyme scheme of a poem, you should take careful note of whether the lines are end-stopped or enjambed.

In the examples we have just given, both Browning and Shakespeare are using *exact* rhymes; except for the initial consonants, the rhyming words have exactly the same sound. Another type of end rhyme is a *slant* rhyme or *half* rhyme, in which the rhyming words have approximately the same sound. Philip Larkin's poem "Toads" contains many examples of this kind of rhyme.

> Why should I let the toad *work*
> Squat on my life?
> Can't I use my wit as a pitchfork
> And drive the brute off?

> Six days of the week it soils
> > With its sickening poison—
> Just for paying a few bills!
> > That's out of proportion.

The words in the pairs *work* and *fork, life* and *off, poison* and *proportion,* do not have exactly the same sound but do have a close resemblance. They are *slant rhymes.*

Slant rhymes are often created by the use of one of two kinds of rhyme, *assonance* and *consonance.* Both of these can also be used to create internal rhymes as well as end rhymes.

Assonance is the repetition of the same stressed vowel sound in words in which the consonants differ: for example, c*a*t, m*a*n; p*a*le, gr*a*in.

> Bind up, bind up your yellow hair,
> And tie it on your n*e*ck;
> And see you look as maiden-like
> As the day that first we m*e*t.
> > "Fair Annie" *(Anonymous)*

The assonance between "n*e*ck" and "m*e*t" creates a slant rhyme.

> At midday in a s*u*nny s*u*mmer breeze
> > *Robert Frost*

In the line from Frost the assonance of the repeated *u* sound reinforces the alliteration of the repeated *s* sound of *sunny* and *summer,* and creates internal rhyme.

Consonance is the repetition of the same final consonant sound in words with different main vowels: for example, sta*mp*, tru*mp*; groa*n*, pai*n.*

> Lots of folks live on their w*its*:
> > Lecturers, lispers,
> Losels, loblolly-men, l*outs*—
> > They don't end up as paupers
> > *Philip Larkin*

The consonance between "w*its*" and "l*outs*" creates a slant rhyme. Here is an example of consonance creating internal rhyme.

> And wake to the farm forever fle*d* from the chil*d*less lan*d.*
> > *Dylan Thomas*

Note that consonance can occur not only in the final letters of words but also in the final stressed syllable, as in *childless.*

Alliteration is the repetition of sounds in initial or stressed syllables. It is also called *head rhyme.* Alliteration is usually, but not always, used to refer to consonants: for example, *b*ig, *b*ad; *d*azzling, *d*ew. Because it applies to the beginnings of words, alliteration is used in creating internal rhyme rather than end rhyme.

> The *p*lowman homeward *p*lods his *w*eary *w*ay
> *Thomas Gray*

Here the repeated *p* emphasizes the connection between the plowman and his plodding. In the same way the repeated *w* links *weary* and *way*.

Alliteration may also include the repetition of sounds other than initial ones.

> In *h*abite as an *h*eremite   Un*h*oly of workes
> *Piers Plowman*

Here the *h* in *habite, heremite,* and *Unholy* creates alliteration. Note that all the syllables in question are stressed syllables.

Musical Effects

Onomatopoeia is the use of words whose sound resembles either the object or the action they describe: for example, *cuckoo, hiss, murmur, twitter.*

> I hear lake water lapping with low sounds by the shore
> *William Butler Yeats*

Strictly speaking, the only onomatopoetic word in this line is *lapping*, where the *la* sound may be said to imitate the sound of water on the shore of the lake. However, the alliterative *l* sound in *lake* and *low* as well as *lapping* reinforces this effect, so we describe the entire line as onomatopoetic.

Two more general terms to describe sound are *euphony* and *cacophony*. *Euphonious* means "sweet sounding" or "harmonious."

> And I shall have some peace there, for peace comes dropping slow,
> Dropping from the veils of morning to where the cricket sings;
> There midnight's all a glimmer, and noon a purple glow,
> And evening full of the linnet's wings.
> *William Butler Yeats*

Here the long vowel sounds in "peace" and "noon" and the repetition of words and sounds help to create a harmonious effect that reinforces the sense of the peace the poet is describing.

Cacophony is the opposite of euphony. *Cacophonous* means discordant or harsh sounding.

> I have seen roses damasked, red and white,
> But no such roses see I in her cheeks;
> And in some perfumes is there more delight
> Than in the breath that from my mistress reeks.
> *William Shakespeare*

The sharp consonants in "dama*sk*ed," "re*d*," "whi*t*e," "chee*ks*," "deli*ght*," "ree*ks*," create a harsh sound, which helps to emphasize the harshness of the sentiments toward his mistress that the speaker is expressing.

You should note that however sweet sounding a word, we would not call it euphonious if its meaning is harsh or unpleasant. Euphony and cacophony work in conjunction with the meaning, not independently of it.

Meter

You do not need any special training to recognize the presence of meter. When you say a children's nursery rhyme you automatically emphasize certain words and syllables according to the meter:

> Ride a cock-horse to Banbury Cross
> To see a fine lady upon a fine horse
> With rings on her fingers and bells on her toes
> She shall have music wherever she goes.

Meter is the rhythmic pattern of sound formed by stressed and unstressed syllables. How a word is stressed in a line of poetry usually coincides with the way the word is accented in normal speech. When a poem is written in meter, the words in each line are arranged so that the stressed and unstressed syllables form a repeating pattern. Each unit of the pattern is called a *foot*. The meter of a poem is described by naming the kind of foot and saying how many feet there are in a line.

The most common kind of meter in English poetry is *iambic pentameter*. An iamb is a kind of foot in which an unstressed syllable is followed by a stressed syllable: for example, to-dáy. A pentameter is a line with five feet. A line written in iambic pentameter has ten syllables, with unstressed and stressed syllables alternating. This is the meter in which Shakespeare wrote. Unrhymed iambic pentameter is called *blank verse*. Here is an example:

> For I have learned
> To look on nature, not as in the hour
> Of thoughtless youth; but hearing oftentimes
> The still, sad music of humanity
> *William Wordsworth*

Note that although the basic meter of these lines is iambic pentameter, Words-worth does not hesitate to break the meter for greater effect. In the line "The still, sad music of humanity," the unexpected stress on *sad* gives the word additional emphasis.

You should not confuse blank verse with *free verse*. Blank verse, although free of rhyme, is carefully controlled by meter. Free verse, in contrast, may be rhymed but does not follow a regular rhythm, and its lines are often of very different lengths. Walt Whitman's "The Dalliance of Eagles" is a fine example of unrhymed free verse. Here is an example of free verse that does use rhyme.

> He was my father. I was his son.
> On our yearly autumn get-aways from Boston

to the family graveyard in Dunbarton,
he took the wheel himself—. . .

Robert Lowell

If you say these lines aloud, you will immediately hear that they do not fall into any regular rhythm.

Here is a list of the different kinds of feet:

Name of Foot/Adjective	Example
iamb/iambic	em-bráce
trochee/trochaic	sún-ny
anapest/anapestic	un-em-plóyed
dactyl/dactylic	yés-ter-day
spondee/spondaic	reál coól

We have already mentioned the term *pentameter,* meaning a line with five feet. The other terms are

monometer: one foot

dimeter: two feet

trimeter: three feet

tetrameter: four feet

hexameter: six feet

heptameter: seven feet

octameter: eight feet

When we *scan* a poem we divide each line into feet and mark in the stressed and unstressed syllables. We can then describe the meter of the poem. Here is an example of scansion:

The land/ was ours/ before/ we were/ the land's.
She was/ our land/ more than/ a hun/ dred years
Before/ we were/ her peo/ ple. She/ was ours
In Mass/ achu/ setts, in/ Virgin/ ia,
But we/ were Eng/ land's, still/ colon/ ials,
Possess/ing what/ we still/ were un/possessed/ by.

Robert Frost

We have scanned the poem in such a way as to make it seem like extremely regular iambic pentameter. According to this scansion, Frost breaks the meter only at the end of lines 4 and 6. But if you try to say the poem according to this scansion, you will quickly feel that you are distorting the sense and feeling of the words. There is another way to scan this poem, by marking the syllables and words that a speaker would naturally emphasize:

The land/ was ours/ before/ we were/ the land's.
She was/ our land/ more than/ a hundred years
Before/ we were/ her peo/ ple. She/ was ours
In Mass/ achu/ setts, in/ Vir/ gin/ ia,
But we/ were Eng/ land's, still/ colon/ ials,
Possess/ing what/ we still/ were un/possessed/ by.

As you can see, the two scansions stress many, but not all, of the same syllables. A different reader, emphasizing different words when reading aloud, might produce yet another pattern of stressed and unstressed syllables.

Given all these possible permutations, what is the point of scanning a poem? You know from your own experience that you can change the meaning of a sentence considerably by pausing in certain places, by emphasizing certain words. The same is true for poetry. Scanning a poem is a way to discover which words the poet wishes to stress and where you should pause, and thus a way to understand the meaning of the poem more fully. This is true even though there may be several ways to scan a poem; scanning narrows down the number of possible readings, and combined with other evidence it helps us to understand the tone of a poem and to clarify its meaning.

Interpreting a Poem

Both the meaning of the words and their sound contribute to our understanding of a poem as a whole. When interpreting a poem it is important to take into account all the elements of poetry we have discussed in this chapter. Who is speaking, on what occasion, and to whom? What images is the poet creating? Are figures of speech being used, and if so, what is their effect? Is the poem written in a traditional form? Does the poet use end rhyme? Internal rhyme? Both? How does the sound of the words reinforce the meaning? Is the poem written in meter? If so, what kind, and what is its effect? Are there places where the poet breaks the meter? What is the effect of that? You must also be sensitive to something we have not discussed, namely, the overall tone of the poem.

Keeping all these things in mind, let us look closely at Shakespeare's sonnet "My mistress' eyes are nothing like the sun."

My mistress' eyes are nothing like the sun;	*a*
Coral is far more red than her lips' red:	*b*
If snow be white, why then her breasts are dun;	*a*
If hairs be wires, black wires grow on her head.	*b*
I have seen roses damasked, red and white,	*c*
But no such roses see I in her cheeks;	*d*
And in some perfumes is there more delight	*c*
Than in the breath that from my mistress reeks.	*d*
I love to hear her speak, yet well I know	*e*
That music hath a far more pleasing sound:	*f*
I grant I never saw a goddess go,—	*e*
My mistress, when she walks, treads on the ground.	*f*
And yet, by heaven, I think my love as rare	*g*
As any she belied with false compare.	*g*

The speaker of this poem begins brusquely. He is speaking about his mistress, but the poem is not addressed to her. Rather he seems to be addressing other men, reproaching them for their stale, outworn flattery and explaining that although he himself does not praise his mistress exorbitantly, he does not love her any the less.

Rather than creating images, the speaker of this poem destroys them. The comparisons are negative—things are not like, but unlike. The speaker is not using figurative language; in fact, he is criticizing the use of such language: No skin is really white as snow; no woman's complexion really bears a close resemblance to roses.

The poem is written in the form of a sonnet, with three groups of four rhyming lines and a final couplet. In the first eight lines the speaker seems to be expressing displeasure not only with hackneyed compliments but also with his mistress, who unlike other women, he implies, is not worthy of these elevated compliments. In the line "If snow be white, why then her breasts are dun," the rhyming of *dun* with *sun* in the first line underscores the meaning: Not only are her breasts much less white than snow but they also, like her eyes, compare unfavorably with the sun. In the last line of the octave the speaker's disaffection reaches a new level. Using the word *reeks* to refer to his mistress' breath is harsh criticism in itself; in addition, the rhyming of *reeks* with *cheeks* makes some of the condemnation of the former spill over to the latter.

In the sestet, the rhyming words are softer and less brusque. The alliteration in the line "I grant I never saw a goddess go" creates internal rhyme. The speaker seems to realize that the proper object of his scorn is not his mistress but rather the men who offer women such foolish praise. The final couplet confirms this view.

The change in tone between the octave and the sestet makes it hard to pin down the speaker's attitude in this sonnet. We may argue that we were not mistaken in our understanding of the first eight lines: that initially the speaker of the poem is wondering if his mistress is inferior to other women who are apparently worthy of such superlative compliments. Gradually he comes to see that other women are not really superior to her but only seem so because other men are false and excessive in their praise. The change in tone indicates a growth in understanding on the part of the speaker.

Another way to read the poem, however, is to interpret the first eight lines as a strategy. Right from the beginning the speaker intends to praise his mistress by showing how false is the conventional praise offered to women. We might comment that this reading does not entirely explain the harshness of the first eight lines, which surely goes beyond the needs of any strategy. Perhaps there is a bitterness in the speaker's feelings, of which he may be unaware, that shows through his strategy.

In comparing these different ways of reading the poem, we are discussing the overall *tone*. That is, we are taking into account not only how the speaker says the lines and what kind of feeling is conveyed by them but also the attitudes of the poet that we sense behind the attitude of the speaker. All this is part of the meaning of the poem.

In writing about a poem it may not be possible to reach a firm conclusion; in fact, showing the range of alternative readings will often be preferable. One reason poems continue to be read and reread is that they cannot be paraphrased or reduced to any one interpretation.

Suggestions for Writing about Poetry

The kinds of questions you can usefully ask about a poem depend very much on the individual poem: Some poems tell a story, like Browning's "My Last Duchess"; others, like H. D.'s "Never More Will the Wind," are simply reflective. Some poems, such as John Donne's "A Valediction: Forbidding Mourning," use many figures of speech; others, such as Elizabeth Bishop's "One Art," are plain-spoken and direct. Some poems are written in meter and rhyme, like Shakespeare's sonnets; others are written in free verse, like Whitman's "The Dalliance of Eagles." For suggestions for writing about specific poems, see the questions that follow each poem. Here is a list of general questions. Some of them will apply to the poem (or poems) you have decided to write about; after reading the poem carefully you will know which ones are useful to you.

What is the poem about? What is the theme of the poem? Is it similar in subject or theme to other poems you have read? Could it be compared with them?

Who is the speaker of the poem? Is the speaker addressing a particular person? On a particular occasion?

What is the tone of the poem? Does it change in the course of the poem?

How would you describe the language of the poem? Is it figurative or literal? Is the poet using figures of speech? What kind and to what effect? Does the poem contain images? Can the poem be read in more than one way?

Does the poem contain rhymes? If so, what kinds? Are the lines end-stopped or enjambed? How does the rhyme serve to emphasize the meaning? The connections between certain words? What other notable features are there about the sound of the poem?

Is the poem written in meter? If so, what meter? Is it regular or irregular? What is its effect? What is the effect of any irregularities? Is there more than one way to scan the poem? What different meanings do these different scansions suggest?

Does the poem contain any literary allusions? Is it influenced by earlier poems? Could it be compared to other poems you have read by the same author or different authors?

We include here a sonnet "The Silken Tent" by Robert Frost. Thematically this poem belongs in the "Varieties of Love," and you may want to compare it to other works in this section. It is followed by an explication written by a student.

Robert Frost (American, 1874–1963)

The Silken Tent

She is as in a field a silken tent
At midday when a sunny summer breeze
Has dried the dew and all its ropes relent,
So that in guys it gently sways at ease,
And its supporting central cedar pole,
That is its pinnacle to heavenward
And signifies the sureness of the soul,
Seems to owe naught to any single cord,
But strictly held by none, is loosely bound
By countless silken ties of love and thought
To everything on earth the compass round,
And only by one's going slightly taut
In the capriciousness of summer air
Is of the slightest bondage made aware.

SAMPLE STUDENT ESSAY

Assignment: Write a two-page explication of Robert Frost's "The Silken Tent."

The Silken Tent

What is immediately striking about this Shakespearian sonnet is that the poet sustains throughout the poem a single analogy: a woman, mentioned only in the first line, is compared to a silken tent. This comparison is made in one continuous sentence, and it is a real sentence, not one in which several independent parts are linked by colons or semicolons.

In the first four lines of the poem the tent is described at midday on a sunny summer day. Midday suggests middle age, a time of life when the immediate cares and fiercer demands of raising a family are past. If the woman of the poem is a mother, we imagine that she offers shelter to her friends and children. Shelter is the main function of a tent. The dew has dried on the ropes (guy ropes that support the tent); they are somewhat slack, and the material sways gently in the breeze. We imagine the tent bell-

like, resembling the voluminous skirts that women used to wear. The
repeated s sounds in these lines suggest the swishing of skirts and the
rustling of the tent.

Frost goes on to look more closely at the tent's means of support. He
tells us that the upright cedar center pole is analogous to the soul. His
choice of the wood—cedar—reinforces this comparison because cedar wood
has biblical connotations. The pole is supported by all the guy ropes
simultaneously rather than by any particular one.

The next four lines present the third analogy of the poem. Just as the
woman is like a tent and the cedar pole is like her soul, so now we learn
that the guy ropes are "silken ties of love and thought," which bind the
tent to "everything on earth the compass round." Like the world, the tent
is round. These lines are not easy to paraphrase. The cedar pole both
supports and is supported by the guy ropes. The guy ropes suggest both the
bonds of human relationships and the bonds that connect the soul of the
woman to earth. There is something intangible or ineffable about these
bonds. Like the tent, they are made of silk and are both delicate and strong.

Throughout the first twelve lines of the poem, there is a feeling of ease
and contentment—the ties are pleasantly reciprocal relationships. In the
final couplet, however, the words capriciousness and bondage stand out and
suggest a sense of chafing or constraint in human relationships: a
dimension of feeling that has not been present in the rest of the poem.

This explication is more than simply a paraphrase. The author examines
in detail Frost's choice of words and images in order to interpret the poem.

Writing about Drama

Drama is entertainment, the acting out of a story. The fact that plays are written to be performed on a stage means that the story is presented with a kind of immediacy: We experience what the characters experience; we are part of the action. In reading a play we miss seeing the characters portrayed by actors, but there are compensations. We can pause and consider the dialogue; we can look back and see what a character really said; best of all we are free to imagine what the characters are like.

As a genre, plays are immediately distinctive because of their structure and format; however, they have many elements in common with fiction, including characters, plot, and conflict. Some of the qualities of poetry and essays may be present as well. Some dramatists, most notably Shakespeare, wrote their plays in verse. Often a speech in a play, taken out of context, uses the same methods of persuasion, description, or narration as an essay. We will look at some of these common elements, and also at others that are unique to drama. Toward the end of the chapter, we include a very short play by David Mamet and discuss how some of these terms apply to it.

Broadly speaking, plays are categorized as either tragedies, comedies, or tragicomedies. In practice, these terms are not as easy to distinguish as one might think. They are useful distinctions, however, and knowing the characteristics of each will help you to understand a play before you write about it.

Tragedy

One definition says that tragedy is the gulf between expectation and what actually happens. Another definition calls tragedy the struggle between a character and the limits of society. Aristotle, in *The Poetics,* said, "Tragedy should, moreover, imitate actions which excite pity and fear, this being the distinctive mark of tragic imitation." One element of tragedy is constant in the various definitions: All tragedy involves struggle.

A tragic character may have to struggle against external circumstances, but most often the seeds of the tragedy exist within the characters themselves. We might say that since Tennessee Williams' *The Glass Menagerie* takes place during the Depression, external economic conditions are responsible for the struggle Tom Wingfield faces between self-fulfillment and the need to support his family. Yet it becomes clear, as we learn more about the Wingfields, that the Depression is only one reason for Tom's problems. His mother, Amanda, would probably lack insight about herself and her children whether or not she had money.

Often the hero of the tragedy has a "tragic fault" or "tragic flaw," which brings about his downfall. In classical tragedy the flaw of excessive pride is called *hubris.* Creon in *Antigone,* like many of Sophocles' tragic heroes, suffers from this flaw. He arrogantly insists that the laws he himself has made take precedence over the laws of the gods. External circumstances—in this case, political unrest and family troubles—create the conflict of the play, and Creon's hubris leads to the downfall of both himself and those close to him. In tragedy, as in real life, when people are faced with important decisions, or conflicts, their strengths and weaknesses surface.

Another part of the classical definition of tragedy is that what happens to the main characters changes the world in which they live. In *Antigone* what happens to Creon affects the state he rules. This is also true in *King Lear.* Lear's personal downfall causes upheaval in his kingdom. This classical definition seldom applies to contemporary tragedies, however. When Tom Wingfield leaves home, the lives of most people in St. Louis are not greatly changed.

What *The Glass Menagerie* has in common with classical tragedies is that, like Creon and Lear, Tom is in an unbearable situation: Remaining loyal to his family means abandoning his own ambitions. The two alternatives cannot be reconciled; Tom is forced to choose, and the outcome is tragic for him and his family. At the same time—and this is another common element of tragedy— given the situation the ending seems inevitable. Whatever choice Tom had made, things would have ended badly.

Note that there is a difference between what is tragic and what is pathetic. *Pathos* is a condition or situation that evokes pity. Pathetic characters are more often innocent victims than active participants. If a tree falls on a man and he dies, the man is not a participant in his own demise. This is a pathetic situation; though it evokes our sympathy, pathos rarely has the complex characteristics of tragedy.

A central characteristic of most tragedy is *irony.* A character's actions are ironic when they bring about the opposite result of what the character intended. In *Antigone* Creon believes that the only way to ensure political stability is to enforce a law that eventually destroys his family. King Lear drives away his only loyal daughter by demanding proof of her affection. In Arthur Miller's *Death of a Salesman*, Willy Loman's belief in the American dream of success leads to a nightmare of disillusionment.

There can also be verbal irony; individual speeches can be ironic in themselves, given their context and what occurs in the play. Creon's first speech in *Antigone*, for example, could not be further from an accurate account of the situation:

> Gentlemen: I have the honor to inform you that our Ship of State, which recent storms have threatened to destroy, has come safely to harbor at last, guided by the merciful wisdom of heaven.

Although Creon may not perceive the irony of his words, the audience is in a position to understand it, being already aware that the Ship of State is still in danger.

Comedy

Comedy is no less complex than tragedy. Most comedies begin in a world that is in disorder and confusion, but by the end of the play events have occurred that create, if not an orderly world, usually a more sympathetic or genial one. There is struggle or conflict, but it is less likely than in tragedy to be caused by the complex psychological makeup of the characters; and instead of destroying the main character the conflict is resolved happily in the end. A rich father may try to prevent his daughter from marrying a poor young man. If the couple are united at the end of the play with no real harm done to any of the major characters, the play is a comedy.

There are several types of comedies. The *comedy of manners* relies on the witty use of language. Characters give unexpected replies to questions; the pace of the speeches is quick. The characters in these plays are often aristocratic, and they may represent values that the play holds up to ridicule. In George Bernard Shaw's *Pygmalion*, for example, Professor Henry Higgins sneers at people who, he believes, abuse the English language. He jokes about these people with his friends, and he has a high opinion of his own intellect and wit. Yet he receives his comeuppance from Eliza Doolittle, the Cockney flower girl whom he decides to turn into a "lady" by teaching her to speak like him. She proves to be wiser and more capable than he. *Pygmalion* is also referred to as a *satiric* comedy because the playwright mocks an "establishment" character, in this case the arrogant, upper-class intellectual.

A *romantic comedy* usually has as its protagonists a young couple who are likeable and often a bit naive. They are in love, but some obstacle seems to prevent their union. We are sympathetic to the couple and their plight. In Shakespeare's *A Midsummer Night's Dream*, Lysander and Hermia are in love; but Demetrius also loves Hermia, and Hermia's father insists that she either marry Demetrius or enter a convent. Numerous complications occur—the two lovers plan to escape; Demetrius' former lover reappears; fairies play tricks on Lysander, Hermia, and Demetrius. By the end of the play the conflict is resolved, and Hermia and Lysander are married, with her father's blessing.

Comedies that depend more on action than on character are usually referred to as *farce*. Farce relies on surprise and physical action rather than on the emotional and intellectual depth of the characters. The plot is highly complicated but not necessarily sophisticated. In Chekhov's *The Marriage Proposal*, for example, what begins as a fairly straightforward exchange between Chubukov and Lomov, who has come to ask for Chubukov's daughter's hand in marriage, becomes quickly and absurdly complicated.

Comedies, like tragedies, contain irony. In *The Marriage Proposal*, Lomov cannot manage to propose to Natasha even though it is what they both want; instead they keep falling into new quarrels.

Tragicomedy

As its name suggests, *tragicomedy* includes elements of both tragedy and comedy. It is not precisely tragedy because the central character is not completely destroyed. The characters may say witty things to each other, but the play often has a strong undercurrent of sadness, so it is not a comedy. Some critics argue that tragicomedy mirrors contemporary life better than either tragedy or comedy because it allows for the complexities of the world and does not assume an inevitably tragic or happy outcome. Some of the best-known examples of tragicomedy are Samuel Beckett's *Waiting for Godot*, Anton Chekhov's *The Cherry Orchard*, and Luigi Pirandello's *Six Characters in Search of an Author*.

These definitions of types of drama can help you decide how to approach a play when you write about it. If you were writing about *Antigone*, for example, you might focus on Creon as a tragic hero or Antigone as a tragic heroine. How do these characters contribute to their own downfall?

Character

Plays, like fiction, have characters. The major character in a play is the *protagonist*. The character or force that opposes the protagonist is the *antagonist*. Many plays also include a *foil*, whose characteristics illuminate those of one of the major characters through contrast. Often these distinctions are not clear-cut. The protagonist may not be entirely likeable. The antagonist may have at least one endearing quality. In *The Glass Menagerie* we assume Tom is the protagonist, because the play is mainly about his situation and how he resolves it. We could say that Amanda is the antagonist, because her behavior contributes to driving Tom away. Yet Tom's behavior is not always honorable, and Amanda is not without a sense of humor or duty. Jim, the gentleman caller, can be seen as a foil to Tom's sister, Laura: his easy-going, extroverted personality points up just how shy and ill at ease she is.

Stock characters appear mainly in comedies. We have an immediate sense of having met these characters before; they are familiar to us as types, rather than as individuals. The three characters in *The Marriage Proposal* verge on being stock characters: Lomov's hypochondria and Natasha's shrewishness already seem familiar to us. It is unlikely that such characters could sustain our interest in a longer play or one in which characterization is more important than physical action.

The playwright can convey the essence of a character through what the character *says*, what the character *does*, and what other characters say about the character in question. When you read a play it is up to you to interpret what these words and deeds mean and to decide with what expression the characters are saying their lines. As in fiction, you should not believe everything you read. Some characters may be lying to others or deceiving themselves. A reader of *Death of a Salesman* who takes Willy Loman's pronouncements about success to be reliable, rather than seeing them as the fantasies they are, will seriously misinterpret the play.

When you watch a play in performance rather than reading it, less of the interpretation is up to you. The director and the actors present their own interpretations of the characters, and these may vary from production to production. In a recent production of *Death of a Salesman* Willy Loman was portrayed as an almost meek character. If you go to a performance of a play you have already read, you may find the characters portrayed quite differently from the way you imagined them. When writing about the characters of a play, remember that the interpretation of a character can vary.

Plot and Conflict

The conflict or plot in a play is literally "acted out" rather than expressed through the variety of narrative devices available to the writer of fiction. When reading a play, we have to imagine how the characters say their lines and what physical characteristics or gestures they may use to create meaning. The dramatist must use dialogue to convey the conflict and the changes the characters undergo in response to the conflict.

Most plays written before the twentieth century use a formal structure to create dramatic tension. The conflict of the play is presented during the *exposition,* a term we will examine in more detail shortly. The exposition is followed by a *complication,* also known as the *rising action.* This is the stage when the protagonist encounters opposition. Next comes the crisis, or *climax,* when the tension or conflict of the play comes to a peak. The climax is often referred to as the turning point of the play. What follows it is the *falling action.* In a tragedy this is the part when the protagonist is weakened. The formally structured play ends with the *denouement,* a word that means "unknotting"; this is also often called the *resolution.* These terms could be shown on a graph, the climax being the high point.

Many plays also contain *subplots.* A subplot is a secondary plot that in some way reflects the major plot and enlarges the theme and content of the play. In *King Lear* Gloucester punishes his dutiful son and promotes his wicked son to power. This conflict mirrors the major conflict between Lear and his daughters, and contributes to the overall plot of the play as well.

Many contemporary plays do not use a structure as rigid as this. Ionesco's short play *The Gap,* for example, would be difficult to break into these divisions. But the play nevertheless has dramatic tension. Ionesco has said that plays cannot end when the curtain falls; we must feel that life continues for the characters. He claims that this need makes formal structures seem artificial.

Most plays are broken into *acts* and *scenes.* The acts are the major divisions. At the end of an act the stage is usually darkened or the curtain lowered; there is a pause that invites us to contemplate the part of the play we have just seen. After Act I of *Death of a Salesman* we know that Willy's fantasies are going to collide with reality, but we do not know when or how. We await the result in the next act.

Acts are divided into scenes. A change of scene usually indicates a shift in time or place. When you are reading a play the stage directions usually tell you when the scene changes and where or when the new scene takes place. In older plays, such as *Antigone* and *King Lear,* the division into acts and scenes did not exist in the original versions but was added later by editors. These plays are not explicit about the changes in time or place the scene changes represent.

Not all plays have these divisions. Some plays, such as *The Marriage Proposal, The Gap,* and Eugene O'Neill's *Ile,* are only one act. Although short, *Ile* has a fully developed plot with a climax and a resolution. *The Gap* is only one scene, but it is still complex, moving subtly from the realistic to the absurd.

Scene changes do not always represent the occurrence of events in chronological order. *Death of a Salesman,* for example, uses scene changes to switch not just from place to place but also from present to past and back again.

It is worth noting how the exposition in a play is different from exposition in fiction. It is always a challenge for the playwright to find a way to convey essential information. Most plays present their exposition almost entirely through dialogue; there is generally no narrator to tell us what events led up to the play or to describe the characters and the relationships among them. Stage directions often do not provide this kind of information either. Except for entrances and exits, Shakespeare has provided no stage directions at all. In reading a play such as *King Lear* we come to know the setting, the characters, and their conflicts solely through the dialogue.

There are other, less common, methods of exposition. Sometimes a narrator is used, such as Tom in *The Glass Menagerie.* But Tom only gives the play its basic framework; the dialogue creates the rest of the exposition. The ancient Greek dramatists relied on a chorus. In *Antigone,* the chorus comments on the action, much as a narrator might in a story or a novel.

To help you understand the terms that are used to describe the plot of a play, we will trace them through the plot of *Death of a Salesman.*

In this play the *exposition* is immediate. The playwright provides detailed stage directions about the interior of the Loman house. In the first exchange of dialogue Linda is already worried that something has happened to Willy. We get the suggestion that there is an uneasy relationship between Willy and Biff, and we learn that Willy is having trouble at work.

The *rising action* occurs when we start to see the gap between Willy and his sons. We learn that Happy and Biff regard Willy as a pathetic man. Meanwhile Willy tries desperately to prove he is a success. We get a sense that Willy and his sons are moving toward a confrontation.

The *climax* occurs in Act II. Willy gets fired. He meets his sons in a restaurant, and Biff tries to tell him the truth about Biff's failure. Willy's dreams collapse.

The *falling action* is the confrontation between Biff and Willy at home. Willy now seems disoriented and confused. He has been forced to see his life as it is, not as he wishes it were.

The *denouement* is Willy's offstage suicide and Linda's final speech at his grave, in which she declares that the family is free.

It may seem surprising that Willy's suicide is not the climax of the play. But for Willy, disaster strikes well before the suicide, first when he is fired and then in the scene in the restaurant, when he can no longer even pretend to be a success. He gets weaker and weaker as he realizes that his sons do not respect him and that they too are unsuccessful. By killing himself, Willy allows his family to pursue their own lives without having to support his fantasies. So the suicide is not the great tragic moment in the play; it is the denouement, the unknotting of the plot.

Like fiction, a play has a theme or themes. Although the plot of *Death of a Salesman* is fairly easy to relate, arriving at a single theme for the play is harder: the elusive quality of the American dream; the high price one pays to be well liked; the difficulty parents have in seeing their children realistically. Often a play does not have a single clear-cut theme. As a paper topic, you might explore the theme or themes of a play.

Setting

In any production of a play the director and the designer create an environment for the characters. This is the *set.* In reading a play, we must create the set for ourselves out of the author's stage directions and from what the characters say. Even where an author gives copious stage directions, as Arthur Miller does in *Death of a Salesman,* our most vivid impression of the setting comes from what the characters themselves say about their environment, how they feel about it.

We have already mentioned that the setting can contribute to the exposition of a play. Arthur Miller writes six paragraphs about the setting in which we are going to meet Willy and Linda. There is a detailed account of where the rooms in the Loman house are—a floor plan. This technical detail allows us as readers to visualize where the action occurs. We imagine the bedroom Biff and Happy retreat to. Miller tells us that a flute is playing in the background. Do we imagine that the melody it plays makes the scene melancholy? Joyful? Remote? The flute is part of the setting, and it evokes certain emotions from us. Miller makes a point of telling us that there is a silver athletic trophy on the shelf. We become curious. Such a trophy represents achievement. Whose achievement is it, and why is the trophy placed so prominently? Later this trophy becomes a symbol of failure rather than of success.

As in fiction, the setting of a play often contributes to the plot or acts as a catalyst for the action. The storm on the heath in *King Lear* mirrors the king's inner turbulence and at the same time helps him to recognize his own true nature.

Arthur Miller and Tennessee Williams describe the settings of their plays in meticulous detail, even telling us what kind of music is playing. These realistic descriptions have no counterpart in the plays of Sophocles and Shakespeare—but their absence in no way diminishes the impact of *Antigone* or *King Lear*. Each production of these plays portrays the settings differently. Successful productions of *Antigone* and *King Lear* have, in fact, taken place on bare stages. Just as actors and directors interpret characters, set designers create settings for different productions of a play.

Reading David Mamet's *The Hat*

David Mamet's plays include *American Buffalo, Sexual Perversity in Chicago,* and *Glengarry Glen Ross,* for which Mamet won the 1984 Pulitzer Prize for drama. *The Hat,* though only three pages long, represents Mamet's style well: The scene itself appears to be quite ordinary and the characters seem to be speaking the words we hear in everyday conversations. Yet there is also a deep underlying tension and sense of urgency in this play.

The Hat

CUSTOMER. What do you think?

SALESWOMAN. You look wonderful. (*Pause.*)

CUSTOMER. Do you think so?

SALESWOMAN. I do.

CUSTOMER. With the veil?

SALESWOMAN. I don't know. Let's see. Let's try it on.

CUSTOMER. With this coat, though.

SALESWOMAN. Yes. Absolutely. (*Pause.*)

CUSTOMER. I'm going out tomorrow on this *interview?*

SALESWOMAN. Uh huh.

CUSTOMER. No. I don't like the veil. This hat, though, with this coat. (*Saleswoman nods.*) Yes.

SALESWOMAN. I think that's the nicest coat this season.

CUSTOMER. Do you think so?

SALESWOMAN. Far and away. Far and away.

CUSTOMER. Alright. I need the hat. This hat, this coat. (*Pause.*) This bag? (*Pause.*)

SALESWOMAN. For an interview?

CUSTOMER. Yes.

SALESWOMAN. I'm going to say ``no.''

CUSTOMER. No. I knew you would say that. No. You're right. Alright. The hat, the coat . . . oh, this is going to cost me, I know . . . not these boots, though?

SALESWOMAN. No.

CUSTOMER. Too casual.

SALESWOMAN. Yes.

CUSTOMER. Alright. Boots. Something dark. Black.

SALESWOMAN. . . . You have those ankle boots . . . ?

CUSTOMER. No, no, I want real boots. Dark. Long.

SALESWOMAN. Severe.

CUSTOMER. Very severe . . . alright. I need the boots. (*Pause.*) Pants?

SALESWOMAN. Or a skirt.

CUSTOMER. I thought pants. Something in dark green. You know? (*Pause.*)

SALESWOMAN. Well, you would have to be careful.

CUSTOMER. I know, I know. No, I know I would. And I thought a shawl-neck sweater. Something soft.

SALESWOMAN. Uh huh.

CUSTOMER. In white. (*Pause.*) In off-white. In eggshell.

SALESWOMAN. Good. Sure.

CUSTOMER. This is going to cost me. But I *want* . . . do you know?

SALESWOMAN. Yes.

CUSTOMER. I *want.* When I walk *in* there . . .

SALESWOMAN. Yes.

CUSTOMER. I *want.* (*Pause.*) What do you think? Pants?

SALESWOMAN. Well, if you feel comfortable . . .

CUSTOMER. I would, I would. You know why? 'Cause it says something.

SALESWOMAN. Uh huh.

CUSTOMER. And it holds me in. It makes me stand up. I saw the ones that I want.

SALESWOMAN. Here?

CUSTOMER. Upstairs. Yes. A hundred-twenty dollars. (*Pause.*) What do you think on top?

SALESWOMAN. You've got the *sweater* . . .

CUSTOMER. Underneath.

SALESWOMAN. . . . Well . . .

CUSTOMER. Oh, oh! You know what? I saw it last month. You know, you know, underthings, an undergarment. (*Pause.*) One piece, you know, like a camisole.

SALESWOMAN. A teddy.

CUSTOMER. Yes. Yes. Just a little lace.

SALESWOMAN. That would be nice.

CUSTOMER. Silk. (*Pause.*) A teddy. Just a little *off.* A little *flush,* what do they call it, *beige* . . .

SALESWOMAN. Uh huh.

CUSTOMER. Not really beige. A little blusher. (*Smiles.*) I put a little blusher underneath. (*Pause.*) Just beneath the lace. Mmm? (*Saleswoman nods.*)

CUSTOMER. Alright. The slacks, the teddy, not the bag, the boots, the sweater. (*Pause.*) This is going to cost five hundred dollars.

SALESWOMAN. No.

CUSTOMER. Yes. With a new bag. Yes. (*Pause.*) But it's worth it, right? If I know when I walk in there?

SALESWOMAN. Yes.

CUSTOMER. Look! Look! Oh, look, look what she's got. The clutch bag. Yes. That bag. Yes. Do you think? With this coat.

SALESWOMAN. Yes.

CUSTOMER. 'Cause, 'cause, you know why? You've *got* it. Under *here.* (*Clutches imaginary bag under her arm.*) You know? So when you walk in there . . . you know? Just . . . just a small . . . just . . . just the perfect . . . you know? (*Pause.*) I have to have that bag. (*Pause. Shrugs.*) Yes, that bag. The slacks, the teddy, sweater . . . I couldn't get by with these boots, huh?

SALESWOMAN. No.

CUSTOMER. I know. They're great, though.

SALESWOMAN. Yes. They are.

CUSTOMER. (*Sighs.*) That bag's got to be two hundred dollars. (*Pause.*) How much is the hat?

SALESWOMAN. With or without the veil? (*Pause.*)

CUSTOMER. Without.

SALESWOMAN. Fifty-eight dollars.

CUSTOMER. And you're sure that you like it.

SALESWOMAN. You look lovely in it.

CUSTOMER. With this coat.

SALESWOMAN. With that coat. Absolutely.

CUSTOMER. (*Pause.*) I think so. (*Pause.*) I'll take it. Thank you. Thank you. You've been very . . .

SALESWOMAN. Not at all.

CUSTOMER. No, no. You have. You have been very gracious.

SALESWOMAN. Not at all.

CUSTOMER. Because I want to look nice for tomorrow.

SALESWOMAN. Well, you will.

CUSTOMER. (*Nods.*) Yes. Thank you. (*To self.*) With this hat.

SALESWOMAN. Anything else?

CUSTOMER. No.

This play illustrates a number of points about both conventional and unconventional drama. Its conventional elements include a plot: A woman is going to a job interview and it is apparent that getting this job is of great importance to her. Most of the external plot is the ongoing question of what clothes and accessories the woman should buy to wear at the interview. Each decision about an item of clothing seems to be of major consequence. Although the elements of plot (rising action, climax, denouement) are perhaps not as obvious here as in other plays, there is nevertheless an increasing tension. The customer's insecurity seems to increase with every choice she makes.

But this play is probably more easily defined by what it does not share with conventional drama. First, it is neither strictly tragic nor comic. Also, both the Saleswoman and the Customer appear to be protagonists. The job interview itself is the antagonist, and our imaginations supply some of the details: What is the job? How will the woman do at the interview? Is she always this nervous? Why does the Saleswoman have so much confidence in her ability to help the Customer?

While the dialogue sounds much like an ordinary conversation, notice how much we infer from it. Much of what this play is about is what people *don't* say to each other.

Suggestions for Writing about Drama

Is the main character of a play basically tragic? Pathetic? Both? It is possible to view Willy Loman as a character who essentially controls his own destiny, and therefore, as tragic. It is also possible to see him as a victim of his circumstances, and therefore, more pathetic than tragic. You might want to examine this question with a character like Antigone or Lear.

What generates the conflict? Is the conflict generated by flaws in the characters? Is the momentum generated by external circumstances, such as economic conditions or politics? If so, how do the major characters respond to these circumstances? When writing this kind of essay, you might want to look at a character like Dr. Stockmann in Ibsen's *An Enemy of the People*. How much of the conflict arises from his stubborness and how much from the political conflicts in his town?

What are some of the contradictions between a character's words and actions? In *The Glass Menagerie* Amanda Wingfield tells her daughter, Laura, that her only hope for the future lies in marriage. When a gentleman caller finally comes to dinner, however, Amanda becomes so overpowering that Laura is all but invisible. Looking at the difference between what a character says and what he or she does often makes a good topic.

What is the function of some of the minor characters? We assume that each character is included in a play for a reason. You might look closely at one or two minor characters in a particular play to see how they move the plot along, generate a conflict or its resolution, or act as foils.

How are symbols used? Another type of essay about plays might involve an analysis of the playwright's use of symbols. What does the use of a particular object mean? What does the setting represent? Should physical descriptions be interpreted in any other way than literally? Sometimes looking at obvious symbols, such as the glass unicorn in *The Glass Menagerie,* can produce insightful essays. Other plays may present more of a challenge because the significance of a symbol or symbols may not be so apparent. (See the sample essay at the end of this chapter.)

How was the play first regarded? How have interpretations changed through the years? In Chapter 9 we have included a review of the opening night performance of *Death of a Salesman.* It shows what was immediately appreciated about this play in 1949. There have been many subsequent productions, some meeting with considerably less enthusiasm. You could research the background of a play, looking to see how it was first regarded and how reactions to it have changed.

This need not apply only to contemporary plays. You could write a paper about the history of productions of Sophocles' plays. Or you could compare translations and adaptations of a single play. For example, you could compare the translation of Sophocles' *Antigone* that appears in this anthology with an updated version of the play by the French playwright Jean Anouilh.

SAMPLE STUDENT ESSAY

Assignment: In a three-page essay analyze the use of setting in *Death of a Salesman.*

Willy Loman's Dream House

In his stage directions at the beginning of Death of a Salesman, Miller describes the set in terms that suggest the strongly symbolic nature of the Lomans' home. It is "fragile-seeming" and an "air of the dream clings to the place." The term "dream house" seems ironically apt. Everyone who lives here seems to daydream incessantly, as if the house prompted and fostered certain kinds of self-delusion. In the course of the play Miller uses the house to help reveal the "terrible thing" that is happening to Willy.

On the purely physical level, the house is described as flimsy and faulty. Charley, the next-door neighbor, says, "You only have to sneeze in here, and in my house hats blow off." Willy complains bitterly that he has never bought anything that wasn't broken by the time he finished paying for it, and throughout the play we hear about various problems the house and its contents have—the plumbing he just fixed needs to be repaired again; the roof has been leaking.

The house is not presented only in a negative light. It is also described as a place in which Willy has invested a considerable amount of himself. In spite of his complaints he fixes it up skillfully and derives considerable pleasure from doing so. Even though more repairs are needed, working on the house still gives him more satisfaction than his job. Being good at manual labor is important to Willy. He prides himself on the fact that both his sons are skilled at carpentry, and when he wants to impress his brother, Ben, he orders Biff and Happy to rebuild the stoop. What Willy fails to realize is that in modern society these skills are not necessarily of value. He persists in regarding Charley and his son Bernard as failures because they have no talent for manual work. Only toward the end of the play does he realize that physical prowess, like being well liked, is no guarantee of success.

Since Willy and Linda bought the house, apartment buildings have sprung up on all sides. The buildings reinforce the idea that the house is a bastion of nostalgia. Unlike the house, these buildings have nothing to do with the individual. As these anonymous tall buildings diminish Willy's house, so we feel that Willy's life is being diminished as well. They also convey the feeling that life is closing in on willy Loman. You can't see a star without "breaking your neck," according to Willy, and nothing will grow in the garden because the tall buildings block out all the light. These images help to create a sense of claustrophobia and stagnation. The people who live in this house are no longer capable of keeping up with the times.

Willy is a man of contrasts. He sees being a salesman as one of life's highest callings, but at the same time he is temperamentally unsuited to being a salesman because he is out of step with modern society. The house embodies this contrast. It is the one substantial thing that Willy owns, but it is falling apart, in spite of his endless repairs, and the apartment buildings are creeping closer. In the same way that Willy devotes himself to a company that will fire him after thirty years, so too does his dream house betray him. In fact Willy kills himself just before the mortgage is paid off. Willy is a man with the wrong dreams.

The writer of this essay has dealt successfully with the problem of finding a subject that will be manageable in such a long play The writer makes us aware of the fact that this is a play by drawing on the stage directions and Miller's notes about the set. This essay also uses the information about *analysis* that we presented in Chapter 4 as it explores the significance of the house.

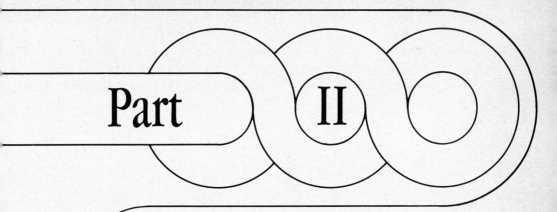

Part II

Thematic Anthology

Generation to Generation

The storks have a great many stories which they tell their little ones, all about the bogs and the marshes. They suit them to their ages and capacities. The youngest ones are quite satisfied with "Kribble krabble," or some such nonsense, but the older ones want something with more meaning in it, or at any rate something about the family. We all know one of the two oldest and longest tales which have been kept up among the storks: the one about Moses, who was placed by his mother on the waters of the Nile and found there by the King's daughter. How she reared him and how he became a great man whose burial place nobody to this day knows. This is all common knowledge.

The other story is not known yet because the storks have kept it among themselves.

—HANS CHRISTIAN ANDERSEN
"THE MARSH KING'S DAUGHTER"

Essays

Lewis Thomas (American, 1913–   )

On Embryology

A short while ago, in mid-1978, the newest astonishment in medicine, covering all the front pages, was the birth of an English baby nine months after conception in a dish. The older surprise, which should still be fazing us all, is that a solitary sperm and a single egg can fuse and become a human being under any circumstance, and that, however implanted, a mere cluster of the progeny of this fused cell affixed to the uterine wall will grow and differentiate into eight pounds of baby; this has been going on under our eyes for so long a time that we've gotten used to it; hence the outcries of amazement at this really minor technical modification of the general procedure—nothing much, really, beyond relocating the beginning of the process from the fallopian tube to a plastic container and, perhaps worth mentioning, the exclusion of the father from any role likely to add, with any justification, to his vanity.

There is, of course, talk now about extending the technology beyond the act of conception itself, and predictions are being made that the whole process of embryonic development, all nine months of it, will ultimately be conducted in elaborate plastic flasks. When this happens, as perhaps it will someday, it will be another surprise, with more headlines. Everyone will say how marvelously terrifying is the new power of science, and arguments over whether science should be stopped in its tracks will preoccupy senatorial subcommittees, with more headlines. Meanwhile, the sheer incredibility of the process itself, whether it occurs in the uterus or *in* some sort of *vitro*, will probably be overlooked as much as it is today.

For the real amazement, if you want to be amazed, is the process. You start out as a single cell derived from the coupling of a sperm and an egg, this divides into two, then four, then eight, and so on, and at a certain stage there emerges a single cell which will have as all its progeny the human brain. The mere existence of that cell should be one of the great astonishments of the earth. People ought to be walking around all day, all through their waking hours, calling to each other in endless wonderment, talking of nothing except that cell. It is an unbelievable thing, and yet there it is, popping neatly into its place amid the jumbled cells of every one of the several billion human embryos around the planet, just as if it were the easiest thing in the world to do.

If you like being surprised, there's the source. One cell is switched on to become the whole trillion-cell, massive apparatus for thinking and imagining and, for that matter, being surprised. All the information needed for learning to read and write, playing the piano, arguing before senatorial subcommittees, walking across a street through traffic, or the marvelous human act of putting out one hand and leaning against a tree, is contained in that first cell. All of grammar, all syntax, all arithmetic, all music.

It is not known how the switching on occurs. At the very beginning of an embryo, when it is still nothing more than a cluster of cells, all of this information and much more is latent inside every cell in the cluster. When the stem cell for the brain emerges, it could be that the special quality of brainness is simply switched on. But it could as well be that everything else, every other potential property, is switched off, so that this most specialized of all cells no longer has its precursors' option of being a thyroid or a liver or whatever, only a brain.

No one has the ghost of an idea how this works, and nothing else in life can ever be so puzzling. If anyone does succeed in explaining it, within my lifetime, I will charter a skywriting airplane, maybe a whole fleet of them, and send them aloft to write one great exclamation point after another, around the whole sky, until all my money runs out.

SUGGESTIONS FOR WRITING AND DISCUSSION

1. The author of this piece is a scientist in the field of cancer research. Does this information change the way we read this essay? Why?
2. At the end of the first paragraph Thomas says that the fact that the baby was conceived in a dish excludes the father "from any role likely to add, with any justification, to his vanity." Discuss the implications of this scientific advance to our ideas of parenthood.
3. In his discussion of the multiplication of cells, why does Thomas focus attention on the development of the brain?
4. The first paragraph is made up of one short sentence and one very long sentence. What effect does this have? Why do you feel Thomas did this?
5. Thomas is expressing wonder at something we take for granted. Choose something ordinary and in a two- to three-page essay describe it in a way that shows how amazing it really is.

Sigmund Freud (Austrian, 1856–1939)

Family Romances

The freeing of an individual, as he grows up, from the authority of his parents is one of the most necessary though one of the most painful results brought about by the course of his development. It is quite essential that that liberation should occur and it may be presumed that it has been to some extent achieved by everyone who has reached a normal state. Indeed, the whole progress of society rests upon the opposition between successive generations. On the other hand, there is a class of neurotics whose condition is recognizably determined by their having failed in this task.

For a small child his parents are at first the only authority and the source of all belief. The child's most intense and most momentous wish during these early years is to be like his parents (that is, the parent of his own sex) and to be big like his father and mother. But as intellectual growth increases, the child cannot help discovering by degrees the category to which his parents belong. He gets to know other parents and compares them with his own, and so comes to doubt the incomparable and unique quality which he has attributed to them. Small events in the child's life which make him feel dissatisfied afford him provocation for beginning to criticize his parents, and for using, in order to support his critical attitude, the knowledge which he has acquired that other parents are in some respects preferable to them. The psychology of the neuroses teaches us that, among other factors, the most intense impulses of sexual rivalry contribute to this result. A feeling of being slighted is obviously what constitutes the subject-matter of such provocations. There are only too many occasions on which a child is slighted, or at least *feels* he has been slighted, on which he feels he is not receiving the whole of his parents' love, and, most of all, on which he feels regrets at having to share it with brothers and sisters. His sense that his own affection is not being fully reciprocated then finds a vent in the idea, which is often consciously recollected from early childhood, of being a step-child or an adopted child. People who have not developed neuroses very frequently remember occasions of this kind on which—usually as a result of something they have read—they thus interpreted and responded to their parents' hostile behaviour. But at this point the influence of sex is already in evidence, for a boy is far more inclined to feel hostile impulses towards his father than towards his mother and has a far more intense desire to get free from *him* than from *her*. In this respect the imagination of girls is apt to show itself much weaker. These consciously remembered mental impulses of childhood embody the factor which enables us to understand the nature of hero-myths.

The later stage in the development of the neurotic's estrangement from his parents, begun in this manner, might be described as 'the neurotic's family romance'. It is seldom remembered consciously but can almost always be revealed by psycho-analysis. For a quite specific form of imaginative activity is one of the essential characteristics of neurotics and also of all comparatively highly gifted people. This activity emerges first in children's play, and then, starting roughly from the period before puberty, takes over the topic of family relations. A characteristic example of this particular kind of phantasy is to be seen in the familiar day-dreams which persist far beyond puberty. If these day-dreams are carefully examined, they are found to serve as the fulfillment of wishes and as a correction of actual life. They have two principal aims, erotic and ambitious— though an erotic aim is usually concealed behind the latter too. At about the period I have mentioned, then, the child's imagination becomes engaged in the task of getting free from the parents of whom he now has such a low opinion and of replacing them by others, occupying, as a rule, a higher social station. He will make use in this connection of any opportune coincidences from his actual experience, such as his becoming acquainted with the Lord of the Manor or some landed proprietor if he lives in the country or with some member of the aristocracy if he lives in town. Chance occurrences of this kind arouse the child's envy, which finds expression in a phantasy in which both his parents are replaced by others of better birth. The technique used in carrying out phantasies like this (which are, of course, conscious at this period) depends upon the ingenuity and the material which the child has at his disposal. There is also the question of whether the phantasies are worked out with greater or less effort to obtain verisimilitude. This stage is reached at a time at which the child is still in ignorance of the sexual determinants of procreation.

When presently the child comes to know of the various kinds of sexual relations between fathers and mothers and realizes that `pater semper incertus est' (paternity is always uncertain), while the mother is `certissima' (very certain), the family romance undergoes a peculiar curtailment: it contents itself with exalting the child's father, but no longer casts any doubts on his maternal origin, which is regarded as something unalterable. This second (sexual) stage of the family romance is actuated by another motive as well, which is absent in the first (asexual) stage. The child, having learnt about sexual processes, tends to picture to himself erotic situations and relations, the motive force behind this being his desire to bring his mother (who is the subject of the most intense sexual curiosity) into situations of secret infidelity and into secret love-affairs. In this way the child's phantasies, which started by being, as it were, asexual, are brought up to the level of his later knowledge.

Moreover the motive of revenge and retaliation, which was in the background at the earlier stage, is also to be found at the later one. It is, as a rule, precisely these neurotic children who were punished by their parents for sexual naughtiness and who later revenge themselves on their parents by means of phantasies of this kind.

A younger child is very specially inclined to use imaginative stories such as these in order to rob those born before him of their prerogatives—in a way which reminds one of historical intrigues; and he often has no hesitation in attributing to his mother as many fictitious love-affairs as he himself has competitors. An interesting variant of the family romance may then appear, in which the hero and author returns to legitimacy himself while his brothers and sisters are got out of the way by being bastardized. So too if there are any other particular interests at work they can direct the course to be taken by the family romance; for its many-sidedness and its great range of applicability enable it to meet every sort of requirement. In this way, for instance, the young phantasy-builder can get rid of his forbidden degree of kinship with one of his sisters if he finds himself sexually attracted by her.

If anyone is inclined to turn away in horror from this depravity of the childish heart or feels tempted, indeed, to dispute the possibility of such things, he should observe that these works of fiction, which seem so full of hostility, are none of them really so badly intended, and that they still preserve, under a slight disguise, the child's original affection for his parents. The faithlessness and ingratitude are only apparent. If we examine in detail the commonest of these imaginative romances, the replacement of both parents or of the father alone by grander people, we find that these new and aristocratic parents are equipped with attributes that are derived entirely from real recollections of the actual and humble ones; so that in fact the child is not getting rid of his father but exalting him. Indeed the whole effort at replacing the real father by a superior one is only an expression of the child's longing for the happy, vanished days when his father seemed to him the noblest and strongest of men and his mother the dearest and loveliest of women. He is turning away from the father whom he knows to-day to the father in whom he believed in the earlier years of his childhood; and his phantasy is no more than the expression of a regret that those happy days have gone. Thus in these phantasies the over-valuation that characterizes a child's earliest years comes into its own again. An interesting contribution to this subject is afforded by the study of dreams. We learn from their interpretation that even in later years, if the Emperor and Empress appear in dreams, those exalted personages stand for the dreamer's father and mother. So that the child's over-valuation of his parents also survives in the dreams of normal adults.

SUGGESTIONS FOR WRITING AND DISCUSSION

1. This essay gives an account of how children come to have certain kinds of fantasies about their parents and how these fantasies evolve. Go through this essay paragraph by paragraph, making an outline of the different stages in these fantasies and the reasons Freud gives for them.
2. Look up the definitions of *neurosis* and *psychosis*. How do you interpret Freud's thesis that imaginative activity is an essential characteristic not only of neurotics but also of highly gifted people?
3. In the first paragraph Freud describes how necessary it is for children to free themselves from their parents: "Indeed the whole process of society rests upon the opposition between successive generations." Apply this remark to one of the stories. Read Flannery O'Connor's "Everything That Rises Must Converge" (pp. 155–167) and write a three- to five-page analysis of the story in view of Freud's remark.
4. Do you recall an incident in your childhood when you became aware of the fallibility of your parents? Discuss this in a one- to two-page essay.

Wolfgang Amadeus Mozart (Austrian, 1756–1791)

Letter to His Father

Mozart was born in Salzburg. His father, Leopold, taught him to play the harp-sichord, violin, and piano, and the younger Mozart began composing at the

age of five. Leopold was employed by Hieronymous von Colloredo, arch-
bishop of Salzburg, and in 1771 Mozart began his employment with the arch-
bishop, becoming concertmaster. In 1781, while visiting Vienna in the service
of the archbishop, Mozart had an argument with his employer about being
allowed to play only at the palace.

Mozart knew that his father was opposed to his leaving the security of
his position with the archbishop. The following letter was written in an
attempt to win his father's support to do just that. Once Mozart did leave his
position he never again had financial security, although he continued to com-
pose and perform. Despite his brilliance, Mozart died, impoverished, of mal-
nutrition and exhaustion at the age of thirty-five.

Vienna, May 9, 1781

My Very Dear Father:

I am still seething with rage! And you, my dearest and most beloved father, are doubtless in the same condition. My patience has been so long tried that at last it has given out. I am no longer so unfortunate as to be in Salzburg service. Today is a happy day for me. Just listen.

Twice already that—I don't know what to call him—has said to my face the greatest *sottises* and *impertinences*, which I have not repeated to you, as I wished to spare your feelings, and for which I only refrained from taking my revenge on the spot because you, my most beloved father, were ever before my eyes. He called me a rascal and a dissolute fellow and told me to be off. And I—endured it all, although I felt that not only my honor but yours also was being attacked. But, as you would have it so, I was silent. Now listen to this. A week ago the footman came up unexpectedly and told me to clear out that very instant. All the others had been informed of the day of their departure, but not I. Well, I shoved everything into my trunk in haste, and old Madame Weber has been good enough to take me into her house, where I have a pretty room. Moreover, I am living with people who are obliging and who supply me with all the things which one often requires in a hurry and which one cannot have when one is living alone. I decided to travel home by the *ordinaire* on Wednesday, that is, today, May 9th. But as I could not collect the money still due to me within that time, I postponed my departure until Saturday.

When I presented myself today, the valets informed me that the Archbishop wanted to give me a parcel to take charge of. I asked whether it was urgent. They told me, "Yes, it is of the greatest importance." "Well," said I, "I am sorry that I cannot have the privilege of serving His Grace, for (on account of the reason mentioned above) I cannot leave before Saturday. I have left this house, and must live at my own expense. So it is evident that I cannot leave Vienna until I am in a position to do so. For surely no one will ask me to ruin myself." Kleinmayr, Moll, Bönike and the two valets all said that I was perfectly right. When I went in to the Archbishop—that reminds me, I must tell you first of all that Schlauka advised me to make the excuse that the *ordinaire* was already full, a reason which would carry more weight with him than if I gave him the true one—well, when I entered the room, his first words were:—*Archbishop:*

"Well, young fellow, when are you going off?" *I:* "I intended to go tonight, but all the seats were already engaged." Then he rushed full steam ahead, without pausing for breath—I was the most dissolute fellow he knew—no one served him so badly as I did—I had better leave today or else he would write home and have my salary stopped.

I couldn't get a word in edgeways, for he blazed away like a fire. I listened to it all very calmly. He lied to my face that my salary was five hundred gulden, called me a scoundrel, a rascal, a vagabond. Oh, I really cannot tell you all he said. At last my blood began to boil, I could no longer contain myself and I said, "So Your Grace is not satisfied with me?" "What, you dare to threaten me—you scoundrel? There is the door! Look out, for I will have nothing more to do with such a miserable wretch." At last I said: "Nor I with you!" "Well, be off!" When leaving the room, I said, "This is final. You shall have it tomorrow in writing."

Tell me now, most beloved father, did I not say the word too late rather than too soon? Just listen for a moment. My honor is more precious to me than anything else and I know that it is so to you also. Do not be the least bit anxious about me. I am so sure of my success in Vienna that I would have resigned even without the slightest reason; and now that I have a very good reason—and that too thrice over—I cannot make a virtue of it. *Au contraire,* I had twice played the coward and I could not do so a third time.

As long as the Archbishop remains here, I shall not give a concert. You are altogether mistaken if you think that I shall get a bad name with the Emperor and the nobility, for the Archbishop is detested here and most of all by the Emperor. In fact, he is furious because the Emperor did not invite him to Laxenburg. By the next post I shall send you a little money to show you that I am not starving. Now please be cheerful, for my good luck is just beginning, and I trust that my good luck will be yours also. Write to me in cipher that you are pleased—and indeed you may well be so—but in public rail at me as much as you like, so that none of the blame may fall on you. But if, in spite of this, the Archbishop should be the slightest bit impertinent to you, come at once with my sister to Vienna, for I give you my word of honor that there is enough for all three of us to live on. Still, I should prefer it if you could hold out for another year. Do not send any more letters to the Deutsches Haus, nor enclose them in their parcels—I want to hear nothing more about Salzburg. I hate the Archbishop to madness.

Adieu. I kiss your hands a thousand times and embrace my dear sister with all my heart and am ever your obedient son

W. A. Mozart

Just address your letters:
To be delivered Auf dem Peter, im Auge Gottes, 2nd Floor.
Please inform me soon of your approval, for that is the only thing which is still wanting to my present happiness. Adieu.

SUGGESTIONS FOR WRITING AND DISCUSSION

1. In the first paragraph Mozart says, "I am seething with rage" and "Today is a happy day for me." What is suggested by these contradictory feelings?
2. What is Mozart's attitude toward his father?
3. Mozart writes, "My honor is more precious to me than anything else . . . and I know it is so to you." What does he hope to accomplish by comparing his values with those of his father?
4. What is suggested by the tone of the last three lines of the letter?
5. Write a letter as either a parent or a child, explaining why you made a particular decision.

John Gregory Dunne (American, 1932–   )

Quintana

Quintana will be eleven this week. She approaches adolescence with what I can only describe as panache, but then watching her journey from infancy has always been like watching Sandy Koufax pitch or Bill Russell play basketball. There is the same casual arrogance, the implicit sense that no one has ever done it any better. And yet it is difficult for a father to watch a daughter grow up. With each birthday she becomes more like us, an adult, and what we cling to is the memory of the child. I remember the first time I saw her in the nursery at Saint John's Hospital. It was after visiting hours and my wife and I stood staring through the soundproof glass partition at the infants in their cribs, wondering which was ours. Then a nurse in a surgical mask appeared from a back room carrying a fierce, black-haired baby with a bow in her hair. She was just seventeen hours old and her face was still wrinkled and red and the identification beads on her wrist had not our name but only the letters "NI." "NI" stood for "No Information," the hospital's code for an infant to be placed for adoption. Quintana is adopted.

It has never been an effort to say those three words, even when they occasion the well-meaning but insensitive compliment, "You couldn't love her more if she were your own." At moments like that, my wife and I say nothing and smile through gritted teeth. And yet we are not unaware that sometime in the not too distant future we face a moment that only those of us who are adoptive parents will ever have to face—our daughter's decision to search or not to search for her natural parents.

I remember that when I was growing up a staple of radio drama was the show built around adoption. Usually the dilemma involved a child who had just learned by accident that it was adopted. This information could only come accidentally, because in those days it was considered a radical departure from the norm to inform your son or daughter that he or she was not your own flesh and blood. If such information had to be revealed, it was often followed by the specious addendum that the natu-

ral parents had died when the child was an infant. An automobile accident was viewed as the most expeditious and efficient way to get rid of
both parents at once. One of my contemporaries, then a young actress,
was not told that she was adopted until she was twenty-two and the ben-
eficiary of a small inheritance from her natural father's will. Her adoptive
mother could not bring herself to tell her daughter the reason behind the
bequest and entrusted the task to an agent from the William Morris office.

Today we are more enlightened, aware of the psychological evidence that such barbaric secrecy can only inflict hurt. When Quintana
was born, she was offered to us privately by the gynecologist who delivered her. In California, such private adoptions are not only legal but in
the mid-sixties, before legalized abortion and before the sexual revolution made it acceptable for an unwed mother to keep her child, were quite
common. The night we went to see Quintana for the first time at Saint
John's, there was a tacit agreement between us that ''No Information''
was only a bracelet. It was quite easy to congratulate ourselves for agreeing to be so open when the only information we had about her mother
was her age, where she was from and a certified record of her good
health. What we did not realize was that through one bureaucratic slipup
we would learn her mother's name and that through another she would
learn ours, and Quintana's.

From the day we brought Quintana home from the hospital, we tried
never to equivocate. When she was little, we always had Spanish-speak-
ing help and one of the first words she learned, long before she understood its import, was *adoptada*. As she grew older, she never tired of asking us how we happened to adopt her. We told her that we went to the
hospital and were given our choice of any baby in the nursery. ''No, not
that baby,'' we had said, ''not that baby, not that baby . . .'' All this with
full gestures of inspection, until finally: ''That baby!'' Her face would
always light up and she would say: ''Quintana.'' When she asked a question about her adoption, we answered, never volunteering more than she
requested, convinced that as she grew her questions would become
more searching and complicated. In terms I hoped she would understand, I tried to explain that adoption offered to a parent the possibility
of escaping the prison of genes, that no matter how perfect the natural
child, the parent could not help acknowledging in black moments that
some of his or her bad blood was bubbling around in the offspring; with
an *adoptada,* we were innocent of any knowledge of bad blood.

In time Quintana began to intuit that our simple parable of free
choice in the hospital nursery was somewhat more complex than we had
indicated. She now knew that being adopted meant being born of another
mother, and that person she began referring to as ''my other mommy.''
How old, she asked, was my other mommy when I was born? Eighteen,
we answered, and on her stubby little fingers she added on her own age,
and with each birthday her other mommy became twenty-three, then
twenty-five and twenty-eight. There was no obsessive interest, just occa-

sional queries, some more difficult to answer than others. Why had her other mother given her up? We said that we did not know—which was true—and could only assume that it was because she was little more than a child herself, alone and without the resources to bring up a baby. The answer seemed to satisfy, at least until we became close friends with a young woman, unmarried, with a small child of her own. The contradiction was, of course, apparent to Quintana, and yet she seemed to understand, in the way that children do, that there had been a millennium's worth of social change in the years since her birth, that the pressures on a young unmarried mother were far more in 1966 than they were in 1973. (She did, after all, invariably refer to the man in the White House as President Nixon Vietnam Watergate, almost as if he had a three-tiered name like John Quincy Adams.) We were sure that she viewed her status with equanimity, but how much so we did not realize until her eighth birthday party. There were twenty little girls at the party, and as little girls do, they were discussing things gynecological, specifically the orifice in their mothers' bodies from which they had emerged at birth. ''I didn't,'' Quintana said matter-of-factly. She was sitting in a large wicker fan chair and her pronouncement impelled the other children to silence. ''I was adopted.'' We had often wondered how she would handle this moment with her peers, and we froze, but she pulled it off with such élan and aplomb that in moments the other children were bemoaning their own misfortune in not being adopted, one even claiming, ''Well, I was almost adopted.''

Because my wife and I both work at home, Quintana has never had any confusion about how we make our living. Our mindless staring at our respective typewriters means food on the table in a way the mysterious phrase ''going to the office'' never can. From the time she could walk, we have taken her to meetings whenever we were without help, and she has been a quick study on the nuances of our life. ''She's remarkably well adjusted,'' my brother once said about her. ''Considering that every time I see her she's in a different city.'' I think she could pick an agent out of a police lineup, and out of the blue one night at dinner she offered that all young movie directors were short and had frizzy hair and wore Ditto pants and wire glasses and shirts with three buttons opened. (As far as I know, she had never laid eyes on Bogdanovich, Spielberg or Scorsese.) Not long ago an actress received an award for a picture we had written for her. The actress's acceptance speech at the televised award ceremony drove Quintana into an absolute fury. ''She never,'' Quintana reported, ''thanked *us*.'' Since she not only identifies with our work but at times even considers herself an equal partner, I of course discussed this piece with her before I began working on it. I told her what it was about and said I would drop it if she would be embarrassed or if she thought the subject was too private. She gave it some thought and finally said she wanted me to write it.

I must, however, try to explain and perhaps even try to justify my own motives. The week after *Roots* was televised, each child in

Quintana's fifth-grade class was asked to trace a family tree. On my side Quintana went back to her great-grandfather Burns, who arrived from Ireland shortly after the Civil War, a ten-year-old refugee from the potato famine, and on her mother's side to her great-great-great-great-grandmother Cornwall, who came west in a wagon train in 1846. As it happens, I have little interest in family beyond my immediate living relatives. (I can never remember the given names of my paternal grandparents and have never known my paternal grandmother's maiden name. This lack of interest mystifies my wife.) Yet I wanted Quintana to understand that if she wished, there were blood choices other than Dominick Burns and Nancy Hardin Cornwall. Over the past few years, there has been a growing body of literature about adoptees seeking their own roots. I am in general sympathetic to this quest, although not always to the dogged absolutism of the more militant seekers. But I would be remiss if I did not say that I am more than a little sensitive to the way the literature presents adoptive parents. We are usually shown as frozen in the postures of radio drama, untouched by the changes in attitudes of the last several generations. In point of fact we accept that our children might seek out their roots, even encourage it; we accept it as an adventure like life itself—perhaps painful, one hopes enriching. I know not one adoptive parent who does not feel this way. Yet in the literature there is the implicit assumption that we are threatened by the possibility of search, that we would consider it an act of disloyalty on the part of our children. The patronizing nature of this assumption is never noted in the literature. It is as if we were Hudson and Mrs. Bridges, below-stairs surrogates taking care of the wee one, and I don't like it one damn bit.

Often these days I find myself thinking of Quintana's natural mother. Both my wife and I admit more than a passing interest in the woman who produced this extraordinary child. (As far as we know, she never named the father, and even more interesting, Quintana has never asked about him.) When Quintana was small, and before the legalities of adoption were complete, we imagined her mother everywhere, a wraithlike presence staring through the chain-link fence at the blond infant sunbathing in the crib. Occasionally today we see a photograph of a young woman in a magazine—the mother as we imagine her to look—and we pass it to each other without comment. Once we even checked the name of a model in *Vogue* through her modeling agency; she turned out to be a Finn. I often wonder if she thinks of Quintana, or of us. (Remember, we know each other's names.) There is the possibility that having endured the twin traumas of birth and the giving up of a child, she blocked out the names the caseworker gave her, but I don't really believe it. I consider it more likely that she has followed the fairly well-documented passage of Quintana through childhood into adolescence. Writers are at least semi-public figures, and in the interest of commerce or selling a book or a movie, or even out of simple vanity, we allow interviews and photo layouts and look into television cameras; we even write about ourselves, and our children. I recall wondering how this sentient young woman of our imagination had reacted to four pages in *People*. It is possible, even likely, that she will read this piece. I know that it is an almost intolerable invasion of her privacy. I think it probable, however, that in the dark reaches of night she has considered the possibility of a further incursion, of opening a door one day and seeing a young woman who says, "Hello, Mother, I am your daughter."

Perhaps this is romantic fantasy. We know none of the circumstances of the woman's life, or even if she is still alive. We once suggested to our lawyer that we make a discreet inquiry and he quite firmly said that this was a quest that belonged only to Quintana, if she wished to make it, and not to us. What is not fantasy is that for the past year, Quintana has known the name of her natural mother. It was at dinner and she said that she would like to meet her one day, but that it would be hard, not knowing her name. There finally was the moment: we had never equivocated; did we begin now? We took a deep breath and told Quintana, then age ten, her mother's name. We also said that if she decided to search her out, we would help her in any way we could. (I must allow, however, that we would prefer she wait to make this decision until the Sturm and Drang of adolescence is past.) We then considered the possibility that her mother, for whatever good or circumstantial reasons of her own, might prefer not to see her. I am personally troubled by the militant contention that the natural mother has no right of choice in this matter. "I did not ask to be born," an adoptee once was quoted in a news story I read. "She has to see me." If only life were so simple, if only pain did not hurt. Yet we would never try to influence Quintana on this point. How important it is to know her parentage is a question only she can answer; it is her decision to make.

All parents realize, or should realize, that children are not possessions, but are only lent to us, angel boarders, as it were. Adoptive parents realize this earlier and perhaps more poignantly than others. I do not know the end of this story. It is possible that Quintana will find more reality in family commitment and cousins across the continent and heirloom orange spoons and pictures in an album and faded letters from Dominick Burns and diary entries from Nancy Hardin Cornwall than in the uncertainties of blood. It is equally possible that she will venture into the unknown. I once asked her what she would do if she met her natural mother. "I'd put one arm around Mom," she said, "and one arm around my other mommy, and I'd say, 'Hello, Mommies.'"

If that's the way it turns out, that is what she will do.

SUGGESTIONS FOR WRITING AND DISCUSSION

1. Throughout this essay Dunne compares Quintana's biological parents with her adoptive parents. In doing so he raises the question of what a parent really is and what constitutes a family. How does he define these terms? How would you define these terms?

2. What does Dunne show as the main characteristics of Quintana's personality?
3. What are Dunne's views on the rights of adoptive children? Do you agree? Do you think that biological parents have rights once they have let their children be adopted? Are the rights of these two groups in conflict?
4. There are many different kinds of families. Write a two- to three-page essay in which you define the word *family*.

Martha Weinman Lear (American, 1930–   )

Mother's Day

My mother's mother lived with us, with my parents and my brother and me, from the time she was widowed until her death a quarter-century later. It was the last generation that pretended to any natural feel for extended-family life. She sensed that the divine right of parents was slipping, that she lived in this household by the largess of hosts, and she strove to keep their goodwill by being invisible.

When my father came home from work she murmured good evening and disappeared immediately, so that he and his wife might have their privacy. She never trespassed in any way upon our nuclear circle: When a quarrel arose between husband and wife, or parent and child, she fled to her room. She cooked, insisted upon cooking, but rarely joined us at the dinner table (on Mother's Day, yes). Instead, well before we sat down to eat, she would take a small plate of food, finish it quickly, clean up after herself, and disappear. "Why don't you eat with us?" I once asked. "I don't have all my teeth," she said. "It doesn't look nice." I never realized until my own adulthood that she seemed, in some dim way that she herself may not have perceived at all, to want my mother to realize the burden of her own invisibility. See how much I love you.

When she was very old, about 90, she suffered a stroke and lost her speech but began to scream—strange, high, sudden caws, as though she were in the most unbearable pain. The doctor assured my mother that she was in no pain at all; it was an involuntary sound caused, he said, by vocal chords in spasm. I was by this time no longer living at home, but I came to visit on a weekend. She knew no one, which shook my mother's soul and even mine—that ghastly threat, that childhood nightmare materialized, when our parents do not know us!—and the sound she made was terrifying. It racked our nerves. It broke our sleep. And she could tend to none of her bodily functions, and her daughter had become her anxious, bitter keeper.

My father, dangling finally at the end of a quarter-century's tether of patience, insisted that she be placed in a nursing home. My mother at first said no, then relented. A week later I went with her to see the old woman. It was an awful place, dour and dirty, with those wretched elders sitting and lying about, catatonic, and my grandmother struggling down a corridor with the aid of a walker and emitting those terrible caws. I cried. My mother said, ``No, I can't stand it. I'm taking her out,'' and transferred her to a hospital, where she died within days. To this time, a dozen years later, my mother weeps on Mother's Day with the most bitter remorse and intones: ``I shouldn't have let her go to that place.''

What I remember vividly is that in my late adolescence, my mother bought a fine big white stove. It was her pride, replacing a despised cast-iron model, and she cleaned it carefully after each meal. My grandmother, whose sight by then had gone quite bad, would drop food on the stove and leave greasy finger marks, and I can remember my mother cleaning up after her, scrubbing and rubbing and muttering angrily to herself.

Now my mother is widowed and lives alone in another city. Sometimes she comes to visit. She comes for two weeks and stays for a week, and in that time she lives like a shadow, silent and fleeting. Her self-effacement infuriates me. It fills me with guilt, and I can't cope with the guilt, and what comes out is rage. She is blameless, almost. So am I, almost. We are locked into one another, dancing that ineffably sad old mother-daughter waltz. Who leads?

She tries to help in the kitchen, paying her dues, as her mother used to. And her sight is not good, and sometimes she takes dirty dishes out of the dishwasher and stacks them up on the shelves, and she leaves charred bits of food and grease on my fine copper-colored stove, and I find myself standing there scrubbing and rubbing, muttering angrily.

She is arthritic. Sometimes we talk, cautiously, about what will happen if the time comes when she can no longer maintain her own home. ``Mothers cannot live with daughters,'' she says. And: ``I will never go to a nursing home. It is better to die.'' ``You will never have to worry. We will take care of you,'' I say. ``May I never need you,'' she says.

It astonishes me how often, in my women's group, we talk about our mothers. ``What shall we talk about tonight?'' we say. And the topic, most often, is ourselves in relation to men, or our sexuality; or our children; or our work, our ambitions, our struggles with sex roles. But so often, wherever we set out, we end up talking about our mothers. Bittersweet. Love-hate. We are in our thirties and forties and fifties, some of us with grown daughters of our own. But we cannot excape that vise, and possibly we never will.

One of our group, a woman who manages so intelligently a complex and creative life, tells us that the worst hours of her week have been spent shopping for a birthday present for her mother. Imagine it: She has work deadlines to meet, a household, a husband, three children, and she has spent two days wandering anxiously from store to store, in search of the perfect gift. The perfect gift from the perfect daughter. A gift (a daughter) so *good* as to insure love, recognition, approval. Where do you buy such a thing? The despair of having to settle for something as imperfect as herself, and then the day-long wait, tense as a hospital vigil, to learn how it had been received. And then, finally, that preposterous sense of relief and reprieve: Her mother *liked* it.

As she told the story she laughed a little, near-cried a little. We all did. Who could understand such a *madness?* she said. We all could.

Liberation. Extrication. Our mothers grow old and we watch them becoming us, and ourselves becoming them, and whom do we extricate from what? And how? And do we pass this dear, murderous entanglement on to our daughters with the family silver? Often I wonder if this is not some ultimate form of liberation: the most painful, and the most elusive. . . .

SUGGESTIONS FOR WRITING AND DISCUSSION

1. This essay moves from specific examples to a more general thesis about the relationship between parents and children. How would you summarize this thesis? Does it apply equally to both sexes?
2. What point is Lear making in the anecdote about the stove?
3. Lear's mother feels guilty for allowing her mother to be put in a nursing home. At the same time she is adamant that Lear should never have to take care of *her.* How does this ambivalence echo in Lear's mother's behavior? Analyze this in a two- to three-page essay.
4. The question of what obligations children have to their aging parents is often a thorny one. Discuss this issue in relation to a specific family you know.

Lincoln Steffens (American, 1866–1936)

A Miserable, Merry Christmas

My father's business seems to have been one of slow but steady growth. He and his local partner, Llewelen Tozer, had no vices. They were devoted to their families and to ''the store,'' which grew with the town, which, in turn, grew and changed with the State from a gambling, mining, and ranching community to one of farming, fruit-raising, and building. Immigration poured in, not gold-seekers now, but farmers, business men and home-builders, who settled, planted, reaped and traded in the natural riches of the State, which prospered greatly, ''making'' the people who will tell you that they ''made the State.''

As the store made money and I was getting through the primary school, my father bought a lot uptown, at Sixteenth and K Streets, and built us a ''big'' house. It was off the line of the city's growth, but it was near a new grammar school for me and my sisters, who were coming along fast after me. This interested the family, not me. They were always talking about school; they had not had much of it themselves, and they thought they had missed something. My father used to write speeches, my mother verses, and their theory seems to have been that they had talents which a school would have brought to flower. They agreed, therefore, that their children's gifts should have all the schooling there was. My view, then, was that I had had a good deal of it already, and I was not interested at all. It interfered with my own business, with my own education.

And indeed I remember very little of the primary school. I learned to read, write, spell, and count, and reading was all right. I had a practical use for books, which I searched for ideas and parts to play with, characters to be, lives to live. The primary school was probably a good one, but I cannot remember learning anything except to read aloud ''perfectly'' from a teacher whom I adored and who was fond of me. She used to embrace me before the whole class and she favored me openly to the scandal of the other pupils, who called me ''teacher's pet.'' Their scorn did not trouble me; I saw and I said that they envied me. I paid for her favor, however. When she married I had queer, unhappy feelings of resentment; I didn't want to meet her husband, and when I had to I wouldn't speak to him. He laughed, and she kissed me—happily for her, to me offensively. I never would see her again. Through with her, I fell in love immediately with Miss Kay, another grown young woman who wore glasses and had a fine, clear skin. I did not know her, I only saw her in the street, but once I followed her, found out where she lived, and used to pass her house, hoping to see her, and yet choking with embarrassment if I did. This fascination lasted for years; it was still a sort of super-romance to me when later I was ''going with'' another girl nearer my own age.

What interested me in our new neighborhood was not the school, nor the room I was to have in the house all to myself, but the stable which was built back of the house. My father let me direct the making of a stall, a little smaller than the other stalls, for my pony, and I prayed and hoped and my sister Lou believed that that meant that I would get the pony, perhaps for Christmas. I pointed out to her that there were three other stalls and no horses at all. This I said in order that she should answer it. She could not. My father, sounded, said that some day we might have horses and a cow; meanwhile a stable added to the value of a house. ''Some day'' is a pain to a boy who lives in and knows only ''now.'' My good little sisters, to comfort me, remarked that Christmas was coming, but Christmas was always coming and grown-ups were always talking about it, asking you what you wanted and then giving you what they wanted you to have. Though everybody knew what I wanted, I told them all again. My mother knew that I told God, too, every night. I wanted a pony, and to make sure that they understood, I declared that I wanted nothing else.

"Nothing but a pony?" my father asked.

"Nothing," I said.

"Not even a pair of high boots?"

That was hard. I did want boots, but I stuck to the pony. "No, not even boots."

"Nor candy? There ought to be something to fill your stocking with, and Santa Claus can't put a pony into a stocking."

That was true, and he couldn't lead a pony down the chimney either. But no. "All I want is a pony," I said. "If I can't have a pony, give me nothing, nothing."

Now I had been looking myself for the pony I wanted, going to sales stables, inquiring of horsemen, and I had seen several that would do. My father let me "try" them. I tried so many ponies that I was learning fast to sit a horse. I chose several, but my father always found some fault with them. I was in despair. When Christmas was at hand I had given up all hope of a pony, and on Christmas Eve I hung up my stocking along with my sisters', of whom, by the way, I now had three. I haven't mentioned them or their coming because, you understand, they were girls, and girls, young girls, counted for nothing in my manly life. They did not mind me either; they were so happy that Christmas Eve that I caught some of their merriment. I speculated on what I'd get; I hung up the biggest stocking I had, and we all went reluctantly to bed to wait till morning. Not to sleep; not right away. We were told that we must not only sleep promptly, we must not wake up till seven-thirty the next morning—or if we did, we must not go to the fireplace for our Christmas. Impossible.

We did sleep that night, but we woke up at six A.M. We lay in our beds and debated through the open doors whether to obey till, say, half-past six. Then we bolted. I don't know who started it, but there was a rush. We all disobeyed; we raced to disobey and get first to the fireplace in the front room downstairs. And there they were, the gifts, all sorts of wonderful things, mixed-up piles of presents; only, as I disentangled the mess, I saw that my stocking was empty; it hung limp; not a thing in it; and under and around it—nothing. My sisters had knelt down, each by her pile of gifts; they were squealing with delight, till they looked up and saw me standing there in my nightgown with nothing. They left their piles to come to me and look with me at my empty place. Nothing. They felt my stocking: nothing.

I don't remember whether I cried at that moment, but my sisters did. They ran with me back to my bed, and there we all cried till I became indignant. That helped some. I got up, dressed, and driving my sisters away, I went alone out into the yard, down to the stable, and there, all by myself, I wept. My mother came out to me by and by; she found me in my pony stall, sobbing on the floor, and she tried to comfort me. But I heard my father outside; he had come part way with her, and she was having some sort of angry quarrel with him. She tried to comfort me; besought me to come to breakfast. I could not; I wanted no comfort and no break-fast. She left me and went on into the house with sharp words for my father.

I don't know what kind of a breakfast the family had. My sisters said it was "awful." They were ashamed to enjoy their own toys. They came to me, and I was rude. I ran away from them. I went around to the front of the house, sat down on the steps, and, the crying over, I ached. I was wronged, I was hurt—I can feel now what I felt then, and I am sure that if one could see the wounds upon our hearts, there would be found still upon mine a scar from that terrible Christmas morning. And my father, the practical joker, he must have been hurt, too, a little. I saw him looking out of the window. He was watching me or something for an hour or two, drawing back the curtain ever so little lest I catch him, but I saw his face, and I think I can see now the anxiety upon it, the worried impatience.

After—I don't know how long—surely an hour or two—I was brought to the climax of my agony by the sight of a man riding a pony down the street, a pony and a brand-new saddle; the most beautiful sad-dle I ever saw, and it was a boy's saddle; the man's feet were not in the stirrups; his legs were too long. The outfit was perfect; it was the realiza-tion of all my dreams, the answer to all my prayers. A fine new bridle, with a light curb bit. And the pony! As he drew near, I saw that the pony was really a small horse, what we called an Indian pony, a bay, with black mane and tail, and one white foot and a white star on his forehead. For such a horse as that I would have given, I could have forgiven, anything.

But the man, a disheveled fellow with a blackened eye and a fresh-cut face, came along, reading the numbers on the houses, and, as my hopes—my impossible hopes—rose, he looked at our door and passed by, he and the pony, and the saddle and the bridle. Too much. I fell upon the steps, and having wept before, I broke now into such a flood of tears that I was a floating wreck when I heard a voice.

"Say, kid," it said, "do you know a boy named Lennie Steffens?"

I looked up. It was the man on the pony, back again, at our horse block.

"Yes," I spluttered through my tears. "That's me."

"Well," he said, "then this is your horse. I've been looking all over for you and your house. Why don't you put your number where it can be seen?"

"Get down," I said, running out to him.

He went on saying something about "ought to have got here at seven o'clock; told me to bring the nag here and tie him to your post and leave him for you. But, hell, I got into a drunk—and a fight—and a hos-pital, and—"

"Get down," I said.

He got down, and he boosted me up to the saddle. He offered to fit the stirrups to me, but I didn't want him to. I wanted to ride.

"What's the matter with you?" he said, angrily. "What you crying for? Don't you like the horse? He's a dandy, this horse. I know him of old. He's fine at cattle; he'll drive 'em alone."

I hardly heard, I could scarcely wait, but he persisted. He adjusted the stirrups, and then, finally, off I rode, slowly, at a walk, so happy, so thrilled, that I did not know what I was doing. I did not look back at the house or the man, I rode off up the street, taking note of everything—of the reins, of the pony's long mane, of the carved leather saddle. I had never seen anything so beautiful. And mine! I was going to ride up past Miss Kay's house. But I noticed on the horn of the saddle some stains like rain-drops, so I turned and trotted home, not to the house but to the stable. There was the family, father, mother, sisters, all working for me, all happy. They had been putting in place the tools of my new business: blankets, currycomb, brush, pitchfork—everything, and there was hay in the loft.

"What did you come back so soon for?" somebody asked. "Why didn't you go on riding?"

I pointed to the stains. "I wasn't going to get my new saddle rained on," I said. And my father laughed. "It isn't raining," he said. "Those are not rain-drops."

"They are tears," my mother gasped, and she gave my father a look which sent him off to the house. Worse still, my mother offered to wipe away the tears still running out of my eyes. I gave her such a look as she had given him, and she went off after my father, drying her own tears. My sisters remained and we all unsaddled the pony, put on his halter, led him to his stall, tied and fed him. It began really to rain; so all the rest of that memorable day we curried and combed that pony. The girls plaited his mane, forelock, and tail, while I pitchforked hay to him and curried and brushed, curried and brushed. For a change we brought him out to drink; we led him up and down, blanketed like a race-horse; we took turns at that. But the best, the most inexhaustible fun, was to clean him. When we went reluctantly to our midday Christmas dinner, we all smelt of horse, and my sisters had to wash their faces and hands. I was asked to, but I wouldn't, till my mother bade me look in the mirror. Then I washed up—quick. My face was caked with the muddy lines of tears that had coursed over my cheeks to my mouth. Having washed away that shame, I ate my dinner, and as I ate I grew hungrier and hungrier. It was my first meal that day, and as I filled up on the turkey and the stuffing, the cranberries and the pies, the fruit and the nuts—as I swelled, I could laugh. My mother said I still choked and sobbed now and then, but I laughed, too; I saw and enjoyed my sisters' presents till—I had to go out and attend to my pony, who was there, really and truly there, the promise, the beginning, of a happy double life. And—I went and looked to make sure—there was the saddle, too, and the bridle.

But that Christmas, which my father had planned so carefully, was it the best or the worst I ever knew? He often asked me that; I never could answer as a boy. I think now that it was both. It covered the whole distance from broken-hearted misery to bursting happiness—too fast. A grown-up could hardly have stood it.

SUGGESTIONS FOR WRITING AND DISCUSSION

1. What do Steffens' persistent tears show about his feelings?
2. How do the adjectives *miserable* and *merry* apply to other people in this essay besides the author?
3. What details in this essay make you feel that you are being shown events from a child's point of view?
4. How does Steffens characterize his father? Why does his father play this trick on him? When the pony doesn't arrive why doesn't his father confess? Write a two- to three-page essay analyzing the father's behavior.

Fiction

Hilma Wolitzer (American, 1930–   )

No Pictures

> Being born is something
> like showing up without
> cash in a small town.
> Try pretending vagrancy
> is only innocence.
> Learn the local lingo
> in a crash course,
> and make one good friend.
> PAULETTE F.
January 5, 1958

I planned to go on a diet right after the baby was born. In the meantime I was growing, becoming bigger than life. I might have been a stand-in for the Russian Women's Decathlon champ—a thing of beauty and power.

Howard assured me that he loved me this way, statuesque, he called it, a word borrowed from false novels. He claimed that I was the first woman he could really *sleep* with, in the literal sense of the word. Renee, his first wife, had been scrawny and pale, poor thing. The knobs of her hips and elbows had poked him abruptly from dreams, reminding him of the skeletal frame underneath.

"Everyone is big nowadays," my mother said, *her* hands and feet like tiny blunt instruments.

"Ah, beautiful," Howard murmured, in the sleepy voice of sex, as he burrowed in.

But I'm nobody's fool. On Sundays I saw him look through the magazine section of *The Times* and pause with wistful concentration at those slender models in the brassiere ads. There is desire beyond mere lust in that, I thought. He might have looked at girls in centerfolds instead, at the opulent ones, who were there to inspire a different and simpler kind of longing.

If, in his secret heart, he wanted me to be slim and trim, I would be. The women's magazines were full of easy formulas I could follow: the thinking woman's diet, the drinking woman's diet, the shrinking woman's diet. It would be a cinch.

But there had always been more to me than meets the eye, more than can be seen on the wide screen. More than those breasts weighting their hammock or the frizzy-haired head ducking in doorways. Underneath there was a domestic heart with the modest beat of a ladies' wristwatch. And inside my bulk, the future me stepped daintily, waiting for release.

The baby grew too, floated in its confinement, pulsed and sounded its limits.

And Howard was madly in love with it. It was a romance he had never experienced before. He had been married once and of course he had always had women. They would have followed him from Hamelin without even a note. They still sought him out. I watched, narrow-eyed, as new ones came up, threatened and disappeared. Howard was inviolate, he was a family man now. When he embraced me, he said, "I feel as if I'm embracing the world."

Confident, a veritable monument to his new life, I stretched and sighed in his arms. "I'm going to diet when this is all over. Become très chic."

"No," he protested. "Don't."

I did a little pirouette. "This stuff is going to fall off like snakeskins."

"Don't lose my favorite parts," Howard warned.

We went to visit other couples who nested in their apartments. Judy and Lenny Miller had a little girl named Roberta. Her toys were always in evidence; a vaporizer was her constant bedside companion.

Howard and I tiptoed in to admire her. When she was awake she was a fresh kid, the kind who screams whenever she speaks, and who answers civil, friendly questions with "No, *silly*," or "No, *stupid*," a miserable kid who makes nose-picking a public pleasure.

But now the steam curled her hair into heartbreaking tendrils. The hiss of the vaporizer and the sweet rush of breath. We whispered in this shrine, made reverent by the miracle.

When we tiptoed back to the living room, I thought: Howard doesn't even feel trapped. He actually *wants* a baby, wants this whole homely scene for his own. And I hadn't really trapped him anyway, had I? Isn't the sperm the true aggressor, those little Weissmullers breaststroking to their destiny? Or is it the egg after all, waiting in ambush, ready to grab the first innocent stray? "Who really did this?" I once asked Howard. But he thought it was a theological poser. "God, I suppose, if you believe in Him," he said. "Or else the life-force of nature."

We sat in the Millers' living room among the debris and leavings of playtime. Howard rested a proprietary hand on my belly. All conversation came back to the inevitable subject.

"My doctor said he never saw anything like it," Judy said. "He had real tears in his eyes when he held Roberta up."

It might have been sweat, I thought. Judy tended to idealize things.

She was talking about the natural childbirth course they had taken, where she had learned to breathe the right way during labor, so that she was able to be an active member of the delivery team.

Lenny had been there too. Now he picked up a baby shoe and allowed us to observe the wonder of its size in the width of his palm. "It was a beautiful experience," he said. "Most of the time we're working against nature in the births of our children. It's hypocrisy to keep the father outside, a stranger at the gates, so to speak.''

What a metaphor! Lenny, who was a teacher in the city school system, was a pushover for any innovation in education. I imagined him whispering tips to his unborn daughter on the phonic method of reading.

Now he advised Howard not to be that notorious slacker, the biological father who drops his seed and runs. Lenny had been right there, rubbing Judy's back, speaking encouragement, talking and stroking his child into the world. I could sense Howard's excitement.

Then Judy brought out the photographs. We had seen them before, of course, but it seemed particularly appropriate to see them once again. Lenny was careful to hand them to us in proper chronological sequence. Judy, huge, horizontal on the delivery table. Himself, the masked robber of innocence, smiling at her with his eyes. The doctor, glistening with sweat/tears, his hand upward and lost to view. Oh, God, what was I doing? The evidence was all there. Judy, grimacing, clenching, contracting, her every expression reflected in the other faces.

''See,'' Lenny pointed out. ''*I* was in labor, too.'' Then, ''Here she comes!'' handing us the one with the emerging head, a small, bloodied, determined ball. Judy's own head was lifted in an effort to watch, and she was smiling.

Then, triumph! The whole family united at last on this shore. Mortal, tender, exquisite.

They were winning photos, there was no denying that. Howard was speechless with emotion.

''I thought I was dying, that's all,'' my mother said. ''You were ripping me to shreds.''

My father left the room.

''He can't stand to hear about it,'' my mother whispered. ''They feel guilty, you know.''

''Howard and I are taking a course,'' I said.

''A course! What are they going to teach you—how to scream? *You* were feet first,'' she said accusingly.

But I wasn't put off by her. She had lied about everything else most of my life. ''God helps those who help themselves,'' she used to say. And, ''All cats are gray in the dark.'' That, about lovemaking!

Howard and I went to school where I learned to breathe. We saw films on the development of the embryo and the benefits of nursing. I could picture that small silvery fish already endowed with my genes and Howard's, already bound to us by far more than the nourishing cord. I continued to grow, stretching my skin to translucency, to a new iridescent glow. Howard fed me tidbits from his plate to support my image and keep up my strength, and I took a vitamin supplement that came in little pink and blue capsules.

I learned to pant, little doglike huffs and puffs for the last stages of labor. I practiced smiling into the bathroom mirror while I panted, in imitation of Judy's Madonna smile of the last photograph. She had looked radiant, more beautiful even than in her wedding pictures.

We had decided against delivery photographs for ourselves. Everything would be recorded perfectly in the darkroom of the heart.

Howard and I cherished our new vocabulary. *Term.* I was carrying to full *term. Dilation. Presentation. Lactation.* Gorgeous words from a superior language.

Our lovemaking took on the excitement of imposed restraint. "Are you all right?" Howard would ask. What a paradox!—to be so powerful and fragile at once.

We played with names for the baby, from the biblical to the historical to the mythical. Nothing seemed good enough or suitably original.

We waited. I went for monthly checkups. Other pregnant women in the doctor's waiting room and I smiled knowingly at one another. We found ourselves united in a vast and ancient sorority without the rituals of pledging. Reducing us to girlish dependence, Dr. Marvin Kramer called us by our first names. We called him Dr. Kramer.

Opening my legs on the examining table while his cheerless nurse laid a sheet across my knees for the sake of discretion, I could just make out the blond crown of his head, halo-lit by his miner's lamp. But I could hear his voice as it tunneled through me. "You're coming along fine, Paulette. Good girl, good girl."

"Well, if you can't be good, be careful." That wasn't one of my mother's chestnuts, though it could have been. But I had been carried away, lost forever to common sense and practical advice. In the back seat of a car, so many destinies irrevocably set. It was astonishing.

"I can hardly move anymore," I complained to Howard one day. He crawled to a corner of the bed and folded himself to give me the most possible room.

The gestation of an elephant is almost two years. Mindless hamsters pop out in sixteen days.

"It will be over soon, love," Howard said, and he reached across the bed and touched my hair.

Then what? I wondered. Was that when my magic would lose its potency?

"Do the breathing," Howard suggested.

"Take gas when the time comes," my mother said. "I wouldn't lead you astray."

Judy and Lenny came to visit with Roberta, who whined and tap-danced on our coffee table.

"I'm going on five hundred calories a day," I said, "as soon as I drop this load."

"Try to sound more maternal," Howard whispered.

"Short skirts are coming back," I said in a threatening voice. "And those skimpy little blouses."

"Oh, just breathe," he begged.

"I'm sick of breathing," I said.

Labor began in the afternoon. It was a dispirited Sunday and we were listening to a melancholy Ethical Culture sermon on the radio.

The elevator stopped five times for other passengers on our way down to the lobby of our building. Neighbors smiled at us and looked away, pretending they didn't know where we were going with my swollen belly and little overnight case. Inside their pockets they counted on their fingers and were satisfied.

When we came to the hospital, Howard immediately notified the admitting secretary that he was a Participating Father, and that he was going up with me.

She laughed out loud and continued to type information on the insurance forms.

"It's not too bad, so far," I told Howard, wondering why my mother had to dramatize everything.

"I'll be with you," Howard promised.

They made him wait downstairs, despite his protests. "We won't be needing *you* for a while," the secretary told him, and she winked at me.

"Good-bye," I said at the elevator. I wished we had decided in favor of pictures, after all. I would have started right there with a record of his poor face as the elevator doors slid shut and the nurse and I went up.

"Primapara!" she shouted to someone I couldn't see, as soon as we left the elevator.

Well, *that* sounds nice, I thought. Like prima donna or prima ballerina. We went swiftly down a corridor past little rooms. Other women looked out at me.

What's all this? I wondered, everything unlearned in that first bolt of fear.

I had my own room. A Room of One's Own, I thought. But *this* certainly wasn't what Woolf had meant. The minute this was over, the first chance I could get to concentrate, I would start writing again. It was only a biological pause; just so much psychic energy to go around, one thing at a time. I climbed into the high bed like a tired and obedient child.

The new doctors who came to examine me all seemed so short. And they smiled as they dug in and announced their findings. "Two fingers. Three fingers."

Why didn't they use some secret medical jargon for what they were doing? It sounded suspiciously like a juvenile sex game to me, as if they were only *playing* doctor.

It was such a quiet place. There was none of my mother's famous screaming. Things must have changed, I decided, since her day.

After a while I was shaved, for collaborating with the enemy, I supposed. More silence. Then a shriek! I sat up, alerted, but it was only some horseplay among the nurses. ``What's going on?'' I asked someone who came in and went out again without answering. ``Hello?''

It was lonely. Where was Howard anyway?

And then he was there. When had he grown that shadowed jowl? And why were his eyes so dark with sympathy?

``It's nothing,'' I said severely. ``Stop looking like that.'' Lenny had seemed magnificent. Howard only looked mournful and terrified. So *this* was where his life had led him.

Things didn't get better. Howard rubbed my back and jerked me from the haven of short dozes with his murmurs, his restlessness. There were noises now from other rooms as well. Voices rose in wails of protest.

But I had my own troubles. The contractions were coming so damn fast. I was thirsty, but water wasn't permitted—only the rough swipe of the washcloth across my tongue. I caught it with my teeth and tried to suck on it, cheating.

There was no discreet examination sheet in this place. Strangers peered at me in full view. They measured, probed and went away. A nurse pushed a hypodermic into my thigh when I wasn't looking.

``Hey, what's that?'' I demanded. ``I'm not supposed to have anything. This is a *natural* case, you know.''

``Dr. Kramer is on his way,'' she said, evading the issue.

``Taking his own sweet time,'' I snarled.

Howard seemed shocked by my rudeness and the abrupt shift of mood.

``This is getting *bad*,'' I told him, but it wasn't what he wanted to hear. In the distance a Greek chorus warned—too late, too late.

They wheeled me dizzingly fast to the delivery room. Howard ran alongside like a winded trainer trying to keep up with his fighter. ``Almost there,'' he said, breathless.

How would *he* know? It was miles and miles.

Despite everything, they strapped me down. ``This is barbaric!'' I shouted. ``Women in primitive places squat in the fields!''

``Oh God, *that* bullshit again,'' a black nurse said.

``You trapped me into this,'' I told Howard. ``I'll never forgive you. Never!''

He was wearing a green surgical mask and now he stood as poised and eager as an outfielder waiting for the long ball.

``Imposter!'' I cried.

``Paulette!'' Dr. Kramer called. ``How is my big girl?''

``Just tell me what to do,'' Howard said.

``Why don't you hold her? There. Lift her a little and support her sternum.''

Sternum, sternum, what were they *talking* about?

I yowled and Howard said, ``My love, I'm here!'' His eyes were brilliant with tears.

The whole room shuddered with pain. And I was the center of it, the spotlit star of the universe. Who was trying to be born here anyway—Moby Dick?

Oh, all the good, wise things I had done in my life. I might have done anything and still come to this. In school the teacher rolled down charts on nutrition. We saw the protein groups, the grain groups. Green leafy vegetables. Lack of vitamin C leads to scurvy.

Liars! The charts ought to show *this*, the extraordinary violence of birth, worse than mob violence, worse than murder. FUCKING LEADS TO THIS! those charts ought to say.

"A few more pushes and you'll have your baby," Dr. Kramer said.

Ah, who wanted a baby? For once in her whole rotten life, my mother was right. "Dr. Kramer! Marvin! Give me gas!" I cried, using his first name for equal footing.

But instead he caught the baby who had shouldered through in the excitement.

And I had forgotten to smile, had greeted my child with the face of a madwoman.

Somewhere else in the room, a nurse pressed Howard's head down between his knees.

"No pictures. No pictures," I said.

SUGGESTIONS FOR WRITING AND DISCUSSION

1. Using specific examples, describe the relationship between Paulette and her mother.
2. What are the implications of the line "I . . . had greeted my child with the face of a madwoman"?
3. Compare this story with the poem "Labor Pains" on page 200. What do the two narrators share?
4. Do Paulette and Howard have a realistic view of each other? What evidence supports your answer?
5. Contrast the tone of this story with Lewis Thomas' essay "On Embryology."
6. Why does Paulette spend so much time discussing the evening at the Millers'?
7. What is Paulette's attitude toward her pregnancy? Does this change in the course of the story? Analyze her attitude in a two- to three-page essay.

Flannery O'Connor (American, 1925–1964)

Everything That Rises Must Converge

Her doctor had told Julian's mother that she must lose twenty pounds on account of her blood pressure, so on Wednesday nights Julian had to take her downtown on the bus for a reducing class at the Y. The reducing class was designed for working girls over fifty, who weighed from 165 to

200 pounds. His mother was one of the slimmer ones, but she said ladies did not tell their age or weight. She would not ride the buses by herself at night since they had been integrated, and because the reducing class was one of her few pleasures, necessary for her health, and *free,* she said Julian could at least put himself out to take her, considering all she did for him. Julian did not like to consider all she did for him, but every Wednesday night he braced himself and took her.

She was almost ready to go, standing before the hall mirror, putting on her hat, while he, his hands behind him, appeared pinned to the door frame, waiting like Saint Sebastian for the arrows to begin piercing him. The hat was new and had cost her seven dollars and a half. She kept saying, "Maybe I shouldn't have paid that for it. No, I shouldn't have. I'll take it off and return it tomorrow. I shouldn't have bought it."

Julian raised his eyes to heaven. "Yes, you should have bought it," he said. "Put it on and let's go." It was a hideous hat. A purple velvet flap came down on one side of it and stood up on the other; the rest of it was green and looked like a cushion with the stuffing out. He decided it was less comical than jaunty and pathetic. Everything that gave her pleasure was small and depressed him.

She lifted the hat one more time and set it down slowly on top of her head. Two wings of gray hair protruded on either side of her florid face, but her eyes, sky-blue, were as innocent and untouched by experience as they must have been when she was ten. Were it not that she was a widow who had struggled fiercely to feed and clothe and put him through school and who was supporting him still, "until he got on his feet," she might have been a little girl that he had to take to town.

"It's all right, it's all right," he said. "Let's go." He opened the door himself and started down the walk to get her going. The sky was a dying violet and the houses stood out darkly against it, bulbous liver-colored monstrosities of a uniform ugliness though no two were alike. Since this had been a fashionable neighborhood forty years ago, his mother persisted in thinking they did well to have an apartment in it. Each house had a narrow collar of dirt around it in which sat, usually, a grubby child. Julian walked with his hands in his pockets, his head down and thrust forward and his eyes glazed with the determination to make himself completely numb during the time he would be sacrificed to her pleasure.

The door closed and he turned to find the dumpy figure, surmounted by the atrocious hat, coming toward him. "Well," she said, "you only live once and paying a little more for it, I at least won't meet myself coming and going."

"Some day I'll start making money," Julian said gloomily—he knew he never would—"and you can have one of those jokes whenever you take the fit." But first they would move. He visualized a place where the nearest neighbors would be three miles away on either side.

"I think you're doing fine," she said, drawing on her gloves. "You've only been out of school a year. Rome wasn't built in a day."

She was one of the few members of the Y reducing class who arrived in hat and gloves and who had a son who had been to college. "It takes time," she said, "and the world is in such a mess. This hat looked better on me than any of the others, though when she brought it out I said, 'Take that thing back. I wouldn't have it on my head,' and she said, 'Now wait till you see it on,' and when she put it on me, I said, 'We-ull,' and she said, 'If you ask me, that hat does something for you and you do something for the hat, and besides,' she said, 'with that hat, you won't meet yourself coming and going.'"

Julian thought he could have stood his lot better if she had been selfish, if she had been an old hag who drank and screamed at him. He walked along, saturated in depression, as if in the midst of his martyrdom he had lost his faith. Catching sight of his long, hopeless, irritated face, she stopped suddenly with a grief-stricken look, and pulled back on his arm. "Wait on me," she said. "I'm going back to the house and take this thing off and tomorrow I'm going to return it. I was out of my head. I can pay the gas bill with that seven-fifty."

He caught her arm in a vicious grip. "You are not going to take it back," he said, "I like it."

"Well," she said, "I don't think I ought . . . "

"Shut up and enjoy it," he muttered, more depressed than ever.

"With the world in the mess it's in," she said, "it's a wonder we can enjoy anything. I tell you, the bottom rail is on the top."

Julian sighed.

"Of course," she said, "if you know who you are, you can go anywhere." She said this every time he took her to the reducing class. "Most of them in it are not our kind of people," she said, "but I can be gracious to anybody. I know who I am."

"They don't give a damn for your graciousness," Julian said savagely. "Knowing who you are is good for one generation only. You haven't the foggiest idea where you stand now or who you are."

She stopped and allowed her eyes to flash at him. "I most certainly do know who I am," she said, "and if you don't know who you are, I'm ashamed of you."

"Oh hell," Julian said.

"Your great-grandfather was a former governor of this state," she said. "Your grandfather was a prosperous land-owner. Your grandmother was a Godhigh."

"Will you look around you," he said tensely, "and see where you are now?" and he swept his arm jerkily out to indicate the neighborhood, which the growing darkness at least made less dingy.

"You remain what you are," she said. "Your great-grandfather had a plantation and two hundred slaves."

"There are no more slaves," he said irritably.

"They were better off when they were," she said. He groaned to see that she was off on that topic. She rolled onto it every few days like a train on an open track. He knew every stop, every junction, every swamp along the way, and knew the exact point at which her conclusion would roll majestically into the station: "It's ridiculous. It's simply not realistic. They should rise, yes, but on their own side of the fence."

"Let's skip it," Julian said.

"The ones I feel sorry for," she said, "are the ones that are half white. They're tragic."

"Will you skip it?"

"Suppose we were half white. We would certainly have mixed feelings."

"I have mixed feelings now," he groaned.

"Well let's talk about something pleasant," she said. "I remember going to Grandpa's when I was a little girl. Then the house had double stairways that went up to what was really the second floor—all the cooking was done on the first. I used to like to stay down in the kitchen on account of the way the walls smelled. I would sit with my nose pressed against the plaster and take deep breaths. Actually the place belonged to the Godhighs but your grandfather Chestny paid the mortgage and saved it for them. They were in reduced circumstances," she said, "but reduced or not, they never forgot who they were."

"Doubtless that decayed mansion reminded them," Julian muttered. He never spoke of it without contempt or thought of it without longing. He had seen it once when he was a child before it had been sold. The double stairways had rotted and been torn down. Negroes were living in it. But it remained in his mind as his mother had known it. It appeared in his dreams regularly. He would stand on the wide porch, listening to the rustle of oak leaves, then wander through the high-ceilinged hall into the parlor that opened onto it and gaze at the worn rugs and faded draperies. It occurred to him that it was he, not she, who could have appreciated it. He preferred its threadbare elegance to anything he could name and it was because of it that all the neighborhoods they had lived in had been a torment to him—whereas she had hardly known the difference. She called her insensitivity "being adjustable."

"And I remember the old darky who was my nurse, Caroline. There was no better person in the world. I've always had a great respect for my colored friends," she said. "I'd do anything in the world for them and they'd . . ."

"Will you for God's sake get off that subject?" Julian said. When he got on a bus by himself, he made it a point to sit down beside a Negro, in reparation as it were for his mother's sins.

"You're mighty touchy tonight," she said. "Do you feel all right?"

"Yes I feel all right," he said. "Now lay off."

She pursed her lips. "Well, you certainly are in a vile humor," she observed. "I just won't speak to you at all."

They had reached the bus stop. There was no bus in sight and Julian, his hands still jammed in his pockets and his head thrust forward, scowled down the empty street. The frustration of having to wait on the bus as well as ride on it began to creep up his neck like a hot hand. The presence of his mother was borne in upon him as she gave a pained sigh. He looked at her bleakly. She was holding herself very erect under the preposterous hat, wearing it like a banner of her imaginary dignity. There was in him an evil urge to break her spirit. He suddenly unloosened his tie and pulled it off and put it in his pocket.

She stiffened. "Why must you look like *that* when you take me to town?" she said. "Why must you deliberately embarrass me?"

"If you'll never learn where you are," he said, "you can at least learn where I am."

"You look like a —thug," she said.

"Then I must be one," he murmured.

"I'll just go home," she said. "I will not bother you. If you can't do a little thing like that for me . . ."

Rolling his eyes upward, he put his tie back on. "Restored to my class," he muttered. He thrust his face toward her and hissed, "True culture is in the mind, the *mind*," he said, and tapped his head, "the mind."

"It's in the heart," she said, "and in how you do things and how you do things is because of who you *are*."

"Nobody in the damn bus cares who you are."

"I care who I am," she said icily.

The lighted bus appeared on top of the next hill and as it approached, they moved out into the street to meet it. He put his hand under her elbow and hoisted her up on the creaking step. She entered with a little smile, as if she were going into a drawing room where everyone had been waiting for her. While he put in the tokens, she sat down on one of the broad front seats for three which faced the aisle. A thin woman with protruding teeth and long yellow hair was sitting on the end of it. His mother moved up beside her and left room for Julian beside herself. He sat down and looked at the floor across the aisle where a pair of thin feet in red and white canvas sandals were planted.

His mother immediately began a general conversation meant to attract anyone who felt like talking. "Can it get any hotter?" she said and removed from her purse a folding fan, black with a Japanese scene on it, which she began to flutter before her.

"I reckon it might could," the woman with the protruding teeth said, "but I know for a fact my apartment couldn't get no hotter."

"It must get the afternoon sun," his mother said. She sat forward and looked up and down the bus. It was half filled. Everybody was white. "I see we have the bus to ourselves," she said. Julian cringed.

"For a change," said the woman across the aisle, the owner of the red and white canvas sandals. "I come on one the other day and they were thick as fleas—up front and all through."

"The world is in a mess everywhere," his mother said. "I don't know how we've let it get in this fix."

``What gets my goat is all those boys from good families stealing automobile tires,'' the woman with the protruding teeth said. ``I told my boy, I said you may not be rich but you been raised right and if I ever catch you in any such mess, they can send you on to the reformatory. Be exactly where you belong.''

``Training tells,'' his mother said. ``Is your boy in high school?''

``Ninth grade,'' the woman said.

``My son just finished college last year. He wants to write but he's selling typewriters until he gets started,'' his mother said.

The woman leaned forward and peered at Julian. He threw her such a malevolent look that she subsided against the seat. On the floor across the aisle there was an abandoned newspaper. He got up and got it and opened it out in front of him. His mother discreetly continued the conversation in a lower tone but the woman across the aisle said in a loud voice, ``Well that's nice. Selling typewriters is close to writing. He can go right from one to the other.''

``I tell him,'' his mother said, ``that Rome wasn't built in a day.''

Behind the newspaper Julian was withdrawing into the inner compartment of his mind where he spent most of his time. This was a kind of mental bubble in which he established himself when he could not bear to be a part of what was going on around him. From it he could see out and judge but in it he was safe from any kind of penetration from without. It was the only place where he felt free of the general idiocy of his fellows. His mother had never entered it but from it he could see her with absolute clarity.

The old lady was clever enough and he thought that if she had started from any of the right premises, more might have been expected of her. She lived according to the laws of her own fantasy world, outside of which he had never seen her set foot. The law of it was to sacrifice herself for him after she had first created the necessity to do so by making a mess of things. If he had permitted her sacrifices, it was only because her lack of foresight had made them necessary. All of her life had been a struggle to act like a Chestny without the Chestny goods, and to give him everything she thought a Chestny ought to have; but since, said she, it was fun to struggle, why complain? And when you had won, as she had won, what fun to look back on the hard times! He could not forgive her that she had enjoyed the struggle and that she thought *she* had won.

What she meant when she said she had won was that she had brought him up successfully and had sent him to college and that he had turned out so well—good looking (her teeth had gone unfilled so that his could be straightened), intelligent (he realized he was too intelligent to be a success), and with a future ahead of him (there was of course no future ahead of him). She excused his gloominess on the grounds that he was still growing up and his radical ideas on his lack of practical experience. She said he didn't yet know a thing about ``life,'' that he hadn't even entered the real world—when already he was as disenchanted with it as a man of fifty.

The further irony of all this was that in spite of her, he had turned out so well. In spite of going to only a third-rate college, he had, on his own initiative, come out with a first-rate education; in spite of growing up dominated by a small mind, he had ended up with a large one; in spite of all her foolish views, he was free of prejudice and unafraid to face facts. Most miraculous of all, instead of being blinded by love for her as she was for him, he had cut himself emotionally free of her and could see her with complete objectivity. He was not dominated by his mother.

The bus stopped with a sudden jerk and shook him from his meditation. A woman from the back lurched forward with little steps and barely escaped falling in his newspaper as she righted herself. She got off and a large Negro got on. Julian kept his paper lowered to watch. It gave him a certain satisfaction to see injustice in daily operation. It confirmed his view that with a few exceptions there was no one worth knowing within a radius of three hundred miles. The Negro was well dressed and carried a briefcase. He looked around and then sat down on the other end of the seat where the woman with the red and white canvas sandals was sitting. He immediately unfolded a newspaper and obscured himself behind it. Julian's mother's elbow at once prodded insistently into his ribs. "Now you see why I won't ride on these buses by myself," she whispered.

The woman with the red and white canvas sandals had risen at the same time the Negro sat down and had gone further back in the bus and taken the seat of the woman who had got off. His mother leaned forward and cast her an approving look.

Julian rose, crossed the aisle, and sat down in the place of the woman with the canvas sandals. From this position, he looked serenely across at his mother. Her face had turned an angry red. He stared at her, making his eyes the eyes of a stranger. He felt his tension suddenly lift as if he had openly declared war on her.

He would have liked to get in conversation with the Negro and to talk with him about art or politics or any subject that would be above the comprehension of those around them, but the man remained entrenched behind his paper. He was either ignoring the change of seating or had never noticed it. There was no way for Julian to convey his sympathy.

His mother kept her eyes fixed reproachfully on his face. The woman with the protruding teeth was looking at him avidly as if he were a type of monster new to her.

"Do you have a light?" he asked the Negro.

Without looking away from his paper, the man reached in his pocket and handed him a packet of matches.

"Thanks," Julian said. For a moment he held the matches foolishly. A NO SMOKING sign looked down upon him from over the door. This alone would not have deterred him: he had no cigarettes. He had quit smoking some months before because he could not afford it. "Sorry," he muttered and handed back the matches. The Negro lowered the paper and gave him an annoyed look. He took the matches and raised the paper again.

His mother continued to gaze at him but she did not take advantage of his momentary discomfort. Her eyes retained their battered look. Her face seemed to be unnaturally red, as if her blood pressure had risen. Julian allowed no glimmer of sympathy to show on his face. Having got the advantage, he wanted desperately to keep it and carry it through. He would have liked to teach her a lesson that would last her a while, but there seemed no way to continue the point. The Negro refused to come out from behind his paper.

Julian folded his arms and looked stolidly before him, facing her but as if he did not see her, as if he had ceased to recognize her existence. He visualized a scene in which, the bus having reached their stop, he would remain in his seat and when she said, "Aren't you going to get off?" he would look at her as a stranger who had rashly addressed him. The corner they got off on was usually deserted, but it was well lighted and it would not hurt her to walk by herself the four blocks to the Y. He decided to wait until the time came and then decide whether or not he would let her get off by herself. He would have to be at the Y at ten to bring her back, but he could leave her wondering if he was going to show up. There was no reason for her to think she could always depend on him.

He retired again into the high-ceilinged room sparsely settled with large pieces of antique furniture. His soul expanded momentarily but then he became aware of his mother across from him and the vision shriveled. He studied her coldly. Her feet in little pumps dangled like a child's and did not quite reach the floor. She was training on him an exaggerated look of reproach. He felt completely detached from her. At that moment he could with pleasure have slapped her as he would have slapped a particularly obnoxious child in his charge.

He began to imagine various unlikely ways by which he could teach her a lesson. He might make friends with some distinguished Negro professor or lawyer and bring him home to spend the evening. He would be entirely justified but her blood pressure would rise to 300. He could not push her to the extent of making her have a stroke, and moreover, he had never been successful at making any Negro friends. He had tried to strike up an acquaintance on the bus with some of the better types, with ones that looked like professors or ministers or lawyers. One morning he had sat down next to a distinguished-looking dark brown man who had answered his questions with a sonorous solemnity but who had turned out to be an undertaker. Another day he had sat down beside a cigar-smoking Negro with a diamond ring on his finger, but after a few stilted pleasantries, the Negro had rung the buzzer and risen, slipping two lottery tickets into Julian's hand as he climbed over him to leave.

He imagined his mother lying desperately ill and his being able to

secure only a Negro doctor for her. He toyed with that idea for a few minutes and then dropped it for a momentary vision of himself participating
as a sympathizer in a sit-in demonstration. This was possible but he did
not linger with it. Instead, he approached the ultimate horror. He brought
home a beautiful suspiciously Negroid woman. Prepare yourself, he said.
There is nothing you can do about it. This is the woman I've chosen.
She's intelligent, dignified, even good, and she's suffered and she hasn't
thought it *fun.* Now persecute us, go ahead and persecute us. Drive her
out of here, but remember, you're driving me too. His eyes were narrowed
and through the indignation he had generated, he saw his mother across
the aisle, purple-faced, shrunken to the dwarf-like proportions of her
moral nature, sitting like a mummy beneath the ridiculous banner of her
hat.

He was tilted out of his fantasy again as the bus stopped. The door
opened with a sucking hiss and out of the dark a large, gaily dressed,
sullen-looking colored woman got on with a little boy. The child, who
might have been four, had on a short plaid suit and a Tyrolean hat with
a blue feather in it. Julian hoped that he would sit down beside him and
that the woman would push in beside his mother. He could think of no
better arrangement.

As she waited for her tokens, the woman was surveying the seating
possibilities—he hoped with the idea of sitting where she was least
wanted. There was something familiar-looking about her but Julian could
not place what it was. She was a giant of a woman. Her face was set not
only to meet opposition but to seek it out. The downward tilt of her large
lower lip was like a warning sign: DON'T TAMPER WITH ME. Her bulging figure
was encased in a green crepe dress and her feet overflowed in red shoes.
She had on a hideous hat. A purple velvet flap came down on one side
of it and stood up on the other; the rest of it was green and looked like a
cushion with the stuffing out. She carried a mammoth red pocketbook
that bulged throughout as if it were stuffed with rocks.

To Julian's disappointment, the little boy climbed up on the empty
seat beside his mother. His mother lumped all children, black and white,
into the common category, "cute," and she thought little Negroes were
on the whole cuter than little white children. She smiled at the littly boy
as he climbed on the seat.

Meanwhile the woman was bearing down upon the empty seat
beside Julian. To his annoyance, she squeezed herself into it. He saw his
mother's face change as the woman settled herself next to him and he
realized with satisfaction that this was more objectionable to her than it
was to him. Her face seemed almost gray and there was a look of dull
recognition in her eyes, as if suddenly she had sickened at some awful
confrontation. Julian saw that it was because she and the woman had, in
a sense, swapped sons. Though his mother would not realize the symbolic significance of this, she would feel it. His amusement showed plainly
on his face.

The woman next to him muttered something unintelligible to herself. He was conscious of a kind of bristling next to him, a muted growling like that of an angry cat. He could not see anything but the red pocketbook upright on the bulging green thighs. He visualized the woman as she had stood waiting for her tokens—the ponderous figure, rising from the red shoes upward over the solid hips, the mammoth bosom, the haughty face, to the green and purple hat.

His eyes widened.

The vision of the two hats, identical, broke upon him with the radiance of a brilliant sunrise. His face was suddenly lit with joy. He could not believe that Fate had thrust upon his mother such a lesson. He gave a loud chuckle so that she would look at him and see that he saw. She turned her eyes on him slowly. The blue in them seemed to have turned a bruised purple. For a moment he had an uncomfortable sense of her innocence, but it lasted only a second before principle rescued him. Justice entitled him to laugh. His grin hardened until it said to her as plainly as if he were saying aloud: Your punishment exactly fits your pettiness. This should teach you a permanent lesson.

Her eyes shifted to the woman. She seemed unable to bear looking at him and to find the woman preferable. He became conscious again of the bristling presence at his side. The woman was rumbling like a volcano about to become active. His mother's mouth began to twitch slightly at one corner. With a sinking heart, he saw incipient signs of recovery on her face and realized that this was going to strike her suddenly as funny and was going to be no lesson at all. She kept her eyes on the woman and an amused smile came over her face as if the woman were a monkey that had stolen her hat. The little Negro was looking up at her with large fascinated eyes. He had been trying to attract her attention for some time.

''Carver!'' the woman said suddenly. ''Come heah!''

When he saw that the spotlight was on him at last, Carver drew his feet up and turned himself toward Julian's mother and giggled.

''Carver!'' the woman said. ''You heah me? Come heah!''

Carver slid down from the seat but remained squatting with his back against the base of it, his head turned slyly around toward Julian's mother, who was smiling at him. The woman reached a hand across the aisle and snatched him to her. He righted himself and hung backwards on her knees, grinning at Julian's mother. ''Isn't he cute?'' Julian's mother said to the woman with the protruding teeth.

''I reckon he is,'' the woman said without conviction.

The Negress yanked him upright but he eased out of her grip and shot across the aisle and scrambled, giggling wildly, onto the seat beside his love.

''I think he likes me,'' Julian's mother said, and smiled at the woman. It was the smile she used when she was being particularly gracious to an inferior. Julian saw everything lost. The lesson had rolled off her like rain on a roof.

The woman stood up and yanked the little boy off the seat as if she were snatching him from contagion. Julian could feel the rage in her at having no weapon like his mother's smile. She gave the child a sharp slap across his leg. He howled once and then thrust his head into her stomach and kicked his feet against her shins. "Behave," she said vehemently.

The bus stopped and the Negro who had been reading the newspaper got off. The woman moved over and set the little boy down with a thump between herself and Julian. She held him firmly by the knee. In a moment he put his hands in front of his face and peeped at Julian's mother through his fingers.

"I see yoooooooo!" she said and put her hand in front of her face and peeped at him.

The woman slapped his hand down. "Quit yo' foolishness," she said, "before I knock the living Jesus out of you!"

Julian was thankful that the next stop was theirs. He reached up and pulled the cord. The woman reached up and pulled it at the same time. Oh my God, he thought. He had the terrible intuition that when they got off the bus together, his mother would open her purse and give the little boy a nickel. The gesture would be as natural to her as breathing. The bus stopped and the woman got up and lunged to the front, dragging the child, who wished to stay on, after her. Julian and his mother got up and followed. As they neared the door, Julian tried to relieve her of her pocketbook.

"No," she murmured, "I want to give the little boy a nickel."

"No!" Julian hissed. "No!"

She smiled down at the child and opened her bag. The bus door opened and the woman picked him up by the arm and descended with him, hanging at her hip. Once in the street she set him down and shook him.

Julian's mother had to close her purse while she got down the bus step but as soon as her feet were on the ground, she opened it again and began to rummage inside. "I can't find but a penny," she whispered, "but it looks like a new one."

"Don't do it!" Julian said fiercely between his teeth. There was a streetlight on the corner and she hurried to get under it so that she could better see into her pocketbook. The woman was heading off rapidly down the street with the child still hanging backward on her hand.

"Oh little boy!" Julian's mother called and took a few quick steps and caught up with them just beyond the lamppost. "Here's a bright new penny for you," and she held out the coin, which shone bronze in the dim light.

The huge woman turned and for a moment stood, her shoulders lifted and her face frozen with frustrated rage, and stared at Julian's mother. Then all at once she seemed to explode like a piece of machinery that had been given one ounce of pressure too much. Julian saw the black fist swing out with the red pocketbook. He shut his eyes and cringed as he heard the woman shout, ''He don't take nobody's pennies!'' When he opened his eyes, the woman was disappearing down the street with the little boy staring wide-eyed over her shoulder. Julian's mother was sitting on the sidewalk.

''I told you not to do that,'' Julian said angrily. ''I told you not to do that!''

He stood over her for a minute, gritting his teeth. Her legs were stretched out in front of her and her hat was on her lap. He squatted down and looked her in the face. It was totally expressionless. ''You got exactly what you deserved,'' he said. ''Now get up.''

He picked up her pocketbook and put what had fallen out back in it. He picked the hat up off her lap. The penny caught his eye on the sidewalk and he picked that up and let it drop before her eyes into the purse. Then he stood up and leaned over and held his hands out to pull her up. She remained immobile. He sighed. Rising above them on either side were black apartment buildings, marked with irregular rectangles of light. At the end of the block a man came out of a door and walked off in the opposite direction. ''All right,'' he said, ''suppose somebody happens by and wants to know why you're sitting on the sidewalk?''

She took the hand and, breathing hard, pulled heavily up on it and then stood for a moment, swaying slightly as if the spots of light in the darkness were circling around her. Her eyes, shadowed and confused, finally settled on his face. He did not try to conceal his irritation. ''I hope this teaches you a lesson,'' he said. She leaned forward and her eyes raked his face. She seemed trying to determine his identity. Then, as if she found nothing familiar about him, she started off with a headlong movement in the wrong direction.

''Aren't you going on to the Y?'' he asked.

''Home,'' she muttered.

''Well, are we walking?''

For answer she kept going. Julian followed along, his hands behind him. He saw no reason to let the lesson she had had go without backing it up with an explanation of its meaning. She might as well be made to understand what had happened to her. ''Don't think that was just an up-pity Negro woman,'' he said. ''That was the whole colored race which will no longer take your condescending pennies. That was your black double. She can wear the same hat as you, and to be sure,'' he added gratuitously (because he thought it was funny), ''it looked better on her than it did on you. What all this means,'' he said, ''is that the old world is gone. The old manners are obsolete and your graciousness is not worth a damn.'' He thought bitterly of the house that had been lost for him. ''You aren't who you think you are,'' he said.

She continued to plow ahead, paying no attention to him. Her hair had come undone on one side. She dropped her pocketbook and took no notice. He stooped and picked it up and handed it to her but she did not take it.

"You needn't act as if the world had come to an end," he said, "because it hasn't. From now on you've got to live in a new world and face a few realities for a change. Buck up," he said, "it won't kill you."

She was breathing fast.

"Let's wait on the bus," he said.

"Home," she said thickly.

"I hate to see you behave like this," he said. "Just like a child. I should be able to expect more of you." He decided to stop where he was and make her stop and wait for a bus. "I'm not going any farther," he said, stopping. "We're going on the bus."

She continued to go on as if she had not heard him. He took a few steps and caught her arm and stopped her. He looked into her face and caught his breath. He was looking into a face he had never seen before. "Tell Grandpa to come get me," she said.

He stared, stricken.

"Tell Caroline to come get me," she said.

Stunned, he let her go and she lurched forward again, walking as if one leg were shorter than the other. A tide of darkness seemed to be sweeping her from him. "Mother!" he cried. "Darling, sweetheart, wait!" Crumpling, she fell to the pavement. He dashed forward and fell at her side, crying, "Mamma, Mamma!" He turned her over. Her face was fiercely distorted. One eye, large and staring, moved slightly to the left as if it had become unmoored. The other remained fixed on him, raked his face again, found nothing and closed.

"Wait here, wait here!" he cried and jumped up and began to run for help toward a cluster of lights he saw in the distance ahead of him. "Help, help!" he shouted, but his voice was thin, scarcely a thread of sound. The lights drifted farther away the faster he ran and his feet moved numbly as if they carried him nowhere. The tide of darkness seemed to sweep him back to her, postponing from moment to moment his entry into the world of guilt and sorrow.

SUGGESTIONS FOR WRITING AND DISCUSSION

1. Does Julian manipulate his mother or does she manipulate him?
2. Julian and his mother each claim to have a set of principles. How would you describe these? How consistent is their behavior with these principles?
3. O'Connor describes the eyes of either Julian or his mother at several crucial points in this story. Analyze this in a two- to three-page essay.
4. Are there similarities between Julian's mother and the woman on the bus other than their hats?
5. How does O'Connor suggest that Julian will be unhappy after his mother's death? Explicate the final lines of the story to show what you think Julian's

life will be like. Write one- to two-page essay about Julian's life after his mother's death.

6. Write a two- to three-page essay showing how O'Connor foreshadows the conclusion of this story.

7. In discussing her work, O'Connor frequently emphasized the fact that her stories reflected her strong beliefs as a Catholic. What evidence of her religious beliefs can you find in "Everything That Rises Must Converge"?

Howard Norman, translator (American, 1949–   )

The Orphan Doll

Eskimo tales such as "The Orphan Doll" are told for enjoyment and educa-tion—and they are believed. As the ethnologist Bronislaw Malinowski wrote, "Myth in its living, primitive form is not merely a story but a reality lived." "The Orphan Doll" is one variation on a Greenland Eskimo tale that is cen-turies old. This version was told by Isaac Uliviuk, age sixty-eight, in the sum-mer of 1971.

Although specific events may enter a folktale obliquely, each tale reflects the collective experience of a particular village or tribe. In "The Orphan Doll," for example, several popular motifs are present: the hazards of breaking a taboo, that is, forcing someone from the period of mourning following the death of a child; travel between the spirit and human worlds; tampering with basic cycles of nature, the moon and tides; killing more food animals (walrus) than is necessary; the need to go on a journey in order finally to live at home with more psychological calm; communal intuition triumphing over individual greed.

The literature of the North—folktales to explorers' journals, hermits' jottings to memoirs of missionaries—is generous for many reasons, not the least of which is that it takes readers through the paradoxes of isolated life in a harsh climate and fine-tunes their senses to the inexplicable. Typical of Eskimo tales is the underlying paradox that runs throughout "The Orphan Doll": The more Uteritsoq himself battles his fate as a father, the more chil-dren he eventually has. (Translator's note.)

There once was an obstinate man—no one in the world could be as obsti-nate as he: no one argued with him anymore. Because here is how an argument with him went:

"Uteritsoq, look, over there, aren't those Northern Lights here to give us good luck?"

"No," he would say, even if good luck things happened all that night to prove him wrong. Even if the sled dogs grew stronger, and seals appeared at everyone's door.

"No, no."

Even if it was the most luck-filled night in memory.

"No, no."

"O.K., you are always right," someone said.

"No," Uteritsoq replied.

He was that way. He was his own self caught under the ice, trying to find a way through into the air, as we say. He was made of angers and blames.

Sometimes you could trick Uteritsoq. One day his wife said, "Let's not have a child." Later they had a child.

"No, I was not tricked," he said.

One day his wife was in mourning. Her little child had died, and according to the rules of her village she had to remain idle at home for a while.

And while she was at home, Uteritsoq, her husband, came in and said:

"You must sew and repair the skin of my kayak."

"You know full well that I am not permitted to do any kind of work while I am in mourning," said the wife.

"You must sew and repair the skin of my kayak!" he said again. "Bring it down to the shore and do the work there."

And so his wife, for all her mourning, was forced to go down to the shore, and sew the skin of her husband's kayak. But when she had sewn a little, suddenly her thread began to make a sound, and the sound grew to a muttering, louder and louder. And then a monster came up out of the sea! It was a monster in the shape of a dog, and it said:

"Why do you sew, you who are in mourning?"

"My husband will not listen to me, for he is so obstinate," she said.

And then the powerful dog sprang ashore and fell upon Uteritsoq.

But Uteritsoq was not worried by this; as usual, he thought he would get his own way, and his own way was to kill this monster dog. They fought together, and the dog was killed!

But just then the owner of the monster dog appeared, who turned out to be Moon Man.

He fell upon Uteritsoq, and in turn Uteritsoq fought back. He caught the Moon Man by the throat, and was choking him. He clenched and clenched, and the Moon Man was nearly choked to death.

"There will be no more ebb-tide or flood if you throttle me," the Moon Man said.

But Uteritsoq, the obstinate one, cared little about that; he clutched tighter, and there was an unusual sound in the sky, as though—and people spoke of this for years—the moon itself was choking. They expected an eclipse!

"The seal will never breed again if you throttle me," screamed the Moon Man.

But the obstinate one cared about none of those things, and still the Moon Man threatened some more:

"There will never again be dawn of any day if you work my death," said the Moon Man at last.

And with this, Uteritsoq began to hesitate; he did not like the thought of living in the ceaseless dark. And he let the Moon Man go.

Then the Moon Man called his dead dog to life again. He took his sled dog team and cast them all into the air one by one, and they did not come down again; at last there was the whole team hovering in the air.

''Can I come visit you on the moon?'' Uteritsoq said. He felt a strong desire to do so.

''Yes, all right, visit if you want,'' the Moon Man said. ''But when you see a high rock in your way, take great care to drive your sled around it. Do not pass it on the sunny side, for if you do you will lose your guts.''

And then the Moon Man cracked his whip and drove off through the high air.

Now Uteritsoq, the obstinate one, began to prepare for his journey. It had been his custom to keep his dogs inside the house, and therefore they had a thick layer of ingrown filth in their coats. Now he took them and cast them out into the sea so that they might get clean again. The dogs, little used to going out at all, nearly froze to death after their cold bath; they ran about, shivering, shivering.

Then Uteritsoq took one dog and cast it up into the air, but it fell down heavily to earth again. He took another, then a third, but they all fell down again. They were still too dirty.

But the obstinate one would not give in, and so he cast them into the sea once more.

A second time he tried casting a dog up into the air, and this time it stayed there! Now he made himself a sledge, threw his team up into the air, and drove off.

When he came to the rock he was supposed to drive around, Uteritsoq thought to himself:

''Why should I drive around this rock at all? I will go by the sunny side!''

When he came up alongside the rock, he heard a woman singing drum songs and whetting her knife; she kept on singing, and he could hear how the steel hummed as she worked.

Now Uteritsoq tried to fight this old woman, but he soon lost his senses. And when he woke up, his guts were gone.

''I had better go around the rock after all,'' he thought. He went around the rock, he went around by the shady side.

Then he arrived at the moon, and told how he had lost his guts by trying to drive around the sunny side.

The Moon Man said, ''Lie down.''

Uteritsoq lay down at full length on his back, with a black sealskin under him, which he had spread on the floor. Uteritsoq did that, and then the Moon Man fetched his guts from the old woman and stuffed them into Uteritsoq again.

The two spoke for a while. Then the Moon Man took up one of the stones from the floor and let Uteritsoq look through it back to the earth. And there he saw his wife sitting at her bench, plaiting sinews for thread—even though she was still in mourning! A thick smoke rose from her body; the smoke of her evil thoughts, and her thoughts were evil because Uteritsoq had started her working while she was in mourning and she could not stop.

"She's plaiting sinews!" Uteritsoq said.

"No, look closer," the Moon Man said.

Uteritsoq looked closer.

It became clear to Uteritsoq that his wife was fashioning orphan dolls. Their entire house was full of them. Those are the kind of dolls that keep your hands awake night and day, they are so insistent. First you hear a weeping sound. You look around but see nothing; but you find yourself starting to sew. Then you hear, "food," and you sew a mouth. So it goes, night and day. Until one after the other orphan dolls are living with you. Uteritsoq watched all this from the moon.

But all he could say was, "How will I feed them all! I'll have to hunt night and day." He had forgotten that he had made his wife work while she was in mourning. He grew angry.

After a while, Moon Man opened another stone and Uteritsoq looked through that stone. He saw that the water below was full of walrus! There were so many they had to lie on top of each other. "Plenty of food, blubber and fur!" Uteritsoq said.

"It is a joy to catch such beasts!" the Moon Man said.

Uteritsoq felt a great desire to harpoon a walrus then.

"But you must not, you cannot!" said the Moon Man. "I'll share what I already have here!"

But Uteritsoq, the obstinate one, was too overpowered by the sight of all those walrus. He took harpoons from the Moon Man and harpooned a walrus. He held it on the line—he was a man of great strength, Uteritsoq—and managed to kill it. Then he harpooned another one.

He returned from the Moon Man's place; when he arrived at his own house, he saw that it was filled not only with human orphan dolls but also walrus orphan dolls.

"What's this?" he cried out.

"I know what has happened up on the moon!" his wife said. "Your obstinance has at least brought us food."

After this, Uteritsoq stopped being obstinate except when it came to finding food for his family. He never again afterwards forced his wife to work while she was in mourning.

Still later, the orphan dolls awoke and became his daughters.

SUGGESTIONS FOR WRITING AND DISCUSSION

1. In his preface the translator says the story is about several traditional Eskimo beliefs. Choose one and discuss the part it plays in the story.
2. Does Uteritsoq's obstinacy always cause trouble? Does it ever have good results?

3. Why do you think Uteritsoq changes his ways after visiting the Moon Man? There are several possible interpretations. Discuss some of them.
4. What do you feel is the theme of this tale? Answer in a two- to three-page essay.

D. H. Lawrence (British, 1885–1930)

The Rocking-Horse Winner

There was a woman who was beautiful, who started with all the advantages, yet she had no luck. She married for love, and the love turned to dust. She had bonny children, yet she felt they had been thrust upon her, and she could not love them. They looked at her coldly, as if they were finding fault with her. And hurriedly she felt she must cover up some fault in herself. Yet what it was that she must cover up she never knew. Nevertheless, when her children were present, she always felt the centre of her heart go hard. This troubled her, and in her manner she was all the more gentle and anxious for her children, as if she loved them very much. Only she herself knew that at the centre of her heart was a hard little place that could not feel love, no, not for anybody. Everybody else said of her: "She is such a good mother. She adores her children." Only she herself, and her children themselves, knew it was not so. They read it in each other's eyes.

There were a boy and two little girls. They lived in a pleasant house, with a garden, and they had discreet servants, and felt themselves superior to anyone in the neighbourhood.

Although they lived in style, they felt always an anxiety in the house. There was never enough money. The mother had a small income, and the father had a small income, but not nearly enough for the social position which they had to keep up. The father went in to town to some office. But though he had good prospects, these prospects never materialized. There was always the grinding sense of the shortage of money, though the style was always kept up.

At last the mother said: "I will see if *I* can't make something." But she did not know where to begin. She racked her brains, and tried this thing and the other, but could not find anything successful. The failure made deep lines come into her face. Her children were growing up, they would have to go to school. There must be more money, there must be more money. The father, who was always very handsome and expensive in his tastes, seemed as if he never *would* be able to do anything worth doing. And the mother, who had a great belief in herself, did not succeed any better, and her tastes were just as expensive.

And so the house came to be haunted by the unspoken phrase: *There must be more money! There must be more money!* The children could hear it all the time, though nobody said it aloud. They heard it at

Christmas, when the expensive and splendid toys filled the nursery. Behind the shining modern rocking horse, behind the smart doll's-house, a voice would start whispering: "There *must* be more money! There *must* be more money!" And the children would stop playing, to listen for a moment. They would look into each other's eyes, to see if they had all heard. And each one saw in the eyes of the other two that they had heard. "There *must* be more money! There *must* be more money!"

It came whispering from the springs of the still-swaying rocking horse, and even the horse, bending his wooden, champing head, heard it. The big doll, sitting so pink and smirking in her new pram, could hear it quite plainly, and seemed to be smirking all the more self-consciously because of it. The foolish puppy, too, that took the place of the Teddy bear, he was looking so extraordinarily foolish for no other reason but that he heard the secret whisper all over the house: "There must be more money!"

Yet nobody ever said it aloud. The whisper was everywhere, and therefore no one spoke it. Just as no one ever says: "We are breathing!" in spite of the fact that breath is coming and going all the time.

"Mother," said the boy Paul one day, "Why don't we keep a car of our own? Why do we always use uncle's, or else a taxi?"

"Because we're the poor members of the family," said the mother.

"But why are we, mother?"

"Well—I suppose," she said slowly and bitterly, "it's because your father has no luck."

The boy was silent for some time.

"Is luck money, mother?" he asked, rather timidly.

"No, Paul. Not quite. It's what causes you to have money."

"Oh!" said Paul vaguely. "I thought when Uncle Oscar said filthy lucker, it meant money."

"Filthy lucre does mean money," said the mother. "But it's lucre, not luck."

"Oh!" said the boy. "Then what is luck, mother?"

"It's what causes you to have money. If you're lucky you have money. That's why it's better to be born lucky than rich. If you're rich, you may lose your money. But if you're lucky, you will always get more money."

"Oh! Will you? And is father not lucky?"

"Very unlucky, I should say," she said bitterly.

The boy watched her with unsure eyes.

"Why?" he asked.

"I don't know. Nobody ever knows why one person is lucky and another unlucky."

"Don't they? Nobody at all? Does nobody know?"

"Perhaps God. But He never tells."

"He ought to, then. And aren't you lucky either, mother?"

"I can't be, if I married an unlucky husband."

"But by yourself, aren't you?"

"I used to think I was, before I married. Now I think I am very unlucky indeed."

"Why?"

"Well—never mind! Perhaps I'm not really," she said.

The child looked at her, to see if she meant it. But he saw, by the lines of her mouth, that she was only trying to hide something from him.

"Well, anyhow," he said stoutly, "I'm a lucky person."

"Why?" said his mother, with a sudden laugh.

He stared at her. He didn't even know why he had said it.

"God told me," he asserted, brazening it out.

"I hope He did, dear!" she said, again with a laugh, but rather bitter.

"He did, mother!"

"Excellent!" said the mother, using one of her husband's exclamations.

The boy saw she did not believe him; or, rather, that she paid no attention to his assertion. This angered him somewhat, and made him want to compel her attention.

He went off by himself, vaguely, in a childish way, seeking for the clue to "luck." Absorbed, taking no heed of other people, he went about with a sort of stealth, seeking inwardly for luck. He wanted luck, he wanted it, he wanted it. When the two girls were playing dolls in the nursery, he would sit on his big rocking horse, charging madly into space, with a frenzy that made the little girls peer at him uneasily. Wildly the horse careened, the waving dark hair of the boy tossed, his eyes had a strange glare in them. The little girls dared not speak to him.

When he had ridden to the end of his mad little journey, he climbed down and stood in front of his rocking horse, staring fixedly into its lowered face. Its red mouth was slightly open, its big eye was wide and glassy-bright.

"Now!" he would silently command the snorting steed. "Now, take me to where there is luck! Now take me!"

And he would slash the horse on the neck with the little whip he had asked Uncle Oscar for. He knew the horse could take him to where there was luck, if only he forced it. So he would mount again, and start on his furious ride, hoping at last to get there. He knew he could get there.

"You'll break your horse, Paul!" said the nurse.

"He's always riding like that! I wish he'd leave off!" said his elder sister Joan.

But he only glared down on them in silence. Nurse gave him up. She could make nothing of him. Anyhow he was growing beyond her.

One day his mother and his Uncle Oscar came in when he was on one of his furious rides. He did not speak to them.

"Hallo, you young jockey! Riding a winner?" said his uncle.

"Aren't you growing too big for a rocking horse? You're not a very little boy any longer, you know," said his mother.

But Paul only gave a blue glare from his big, rather close-set eyes. He would speak to nobody when he was in full tilt. His mother watched him with an anxious expression on her face.

At last he suddenly stopped forcing his horse into the mechanical gallop, and slid down.

"Well, I got there!" he announced fiercely, his blue eyes still flaring, and his sturdy long legs straddling apart.

"Where did you get to?" asked his mother.

"Where I wanted to go," he flared back at her.

"That's right, son!" said Uncle Oscar. "Don't you stop till you get there. What's the horse's name?"

"He doesn't have a name," said the boy.

"Gets on without all right?" asked the uncle.

"Well, he has different names. He was called Sansovino last week."

"Sansovino, eh? Won the Ascot. How did you know his name?"

"He always talks about horse races with Bassett," said Joan.

The uncle was delighted to find that his small nephew was posted with all the racing news. Bassett, the young gardener, who had been wounded in the left foot in the war and had got his present job through Oscar Cresswell, whose batman he had been, was a perfect blade of the "turf." He lived in the racing events, and the small boy lived with him.

Oscar Cresswell got it all from Bassett.

"Master Paul comes and asks me, so I can't do more than tell him, sir," said Bassett, his face terribly serious, as if he were speaking of religious matters.

"And does he ever put anything on a horse he fancies?"

"Well—I don't want to give him away—he's a young sport, a fine sport, sir. Would you mind asking him yourself? He sort of takes a pleasure in it, and perhaps he'd feel I was giving him away, sir, if you don't mind."

Bassett was serious as a church.

The uncle went back to his nephew, and took him off for a ride in the car.

"Say, Paul, old man, do you ever put anything on a horse?" the uncle asked.

The boy watched the handsome man closely.

"Why, do you think I oughtn't to?" he parried.

"Not a bit of it! I thought perhaps you might give me a tip for the Lincoln."

The car sped on into the country, going down to Uncle Oscar's place in Hampshire.

"Honour bright?" said the nephew.

"Honour bright, son!" said the uncle.

"Well, then, Daffodil."

"Daffodil! I doubt it, sonny. What about Mirza?"

"I only know the winner," said the boy. "That's Daffodil."

"Daffodil, eh?"

There was a pause. Daffodil was an obscure horse comparatively.

"Uncle!"

"Yes, son?"

"You won't let it go any further, will you? I promised Bassett."

"Bassett be damned, old man! What's he got to do with it?"

"We're partners. We've been partners from the first. Uncle, he lent me my first five shillings, which I lost. I promised him, honour bright, it was only between me and him; only you gave me that ten-shilling note I started winning with, so I thought you were lucky. You won't let it go any further, will you?"

The boy gazed at his uncle from those big, hot, blue eyes, set rather close together. The uncle stirred and laughed uneasily.

"Right you are, son! I'll keep your tip private. Daffodil, eh? How much are you putting on him?"

"All except twenty pounds," said the boy. "I keep that in reserve."

The uncle thought it a good joke.

"You keep twenty pounds in reserve, do you, you young romancer? What are you betting, then?"

"I'm betting three hundred," said the boy gravely. "But it's between you and me, Uncle Oscar! Honour bright?"

The uncle burst into a roar of laughter.

"It's between you and me all right, you young Nat Gould," he said, laughing. "But where's your three hundred?"

"Bassett keeps it for me. We're partners."

"You are, are you! And what is Bassett putting on Daffodil?"

"He won't go quite as high as I do, I expect. Perhaps he'll go a hundred and fifty."

"What, pennies?" laughed the uncle.

"Pounds," said the child, with a surprised look at his uncle. "Bassett keeps a bigger reserve than I do."

Between wonder and amusement Uncle Oscar was silent. He pursued the matter no further, but he determined to take his nephew with him to the Lincoln races.

"Now, son," he said, "I'm putting twenty on Mirza, and I'll put five for you on any horse you fancy. What's your pick?"

"Daffodil, uncle."

"No, not the fiver on Daffodil!"

"I should if it was my own fiver," said the child.

"Good! Good! Right you are! A fiver for me and a fiver for you on Daffodil."

The child had never been to a race meeting before, and his eyes were blue fire. He pursed his mouth tight, and watched. A Frenchman just in front had put his money on Lancelot. Wild with excitement, he flayed his arms up and down, yelling, "Lancelot! Lancelot!" in his French accent.

Daffodil came in first, Lancelot second, Mirza third. The child, flushed and with eyes blazing, was curiously serene. His uncle brought him four five-pound notes, four to one.

"What am I to do with these?" he cried, waving them before the boy's eyes.

"I suppose we'll talk to Bassett," said the boy. "I expect I have fifteen hundred now; and twenty in reserve; and this twenty."

His uncle studied him for some moments.

"Look here, son!" he said. "You're not serious about Bassett and that fifteen hundred, are you?"

"Yes, I am. But it's between you and me, uncle. Honour bright!"

"Honour bright all right, son! But I must talk to Bassett."

"If you'd like to be a partner, uncle, with Bassett and me, we could all be partners. Only, you'd have to promise, honour bright, uncle, not to let it go beyond us three. Bassett and I are lucky, and you must be lucky, because it was your ten shillings I started winning with. . . ."

Uncle Oscar took both Bassett and Paul into Richmond Park for an afternoon, and there they talked.

"It's like this, you see, sir," Bassett said. "Master Paul would get me talking about racing events, spinning yarns, you know, sir. And he was always keen on knowing if I'd made or if I'd lost. It's about a year since, now, that I put five shillings on Blush of Dawn for him—and we lost. Then the luck turned, with that ten shillings he had from you, that we put on Singhalese. And since that time, it's been pretty steady, all things considering. What do you say, Master Paul?"

"We're all right when we're sure," said Paul. "It's when we're not quite sure that we go down."

"Oh, but we're careful then," said Bassett.

"But when are you sure?" smiled Uncle Oscar.

"It's Master Paul, sir," said Bassett, in a secret, religious voice. "It's as if he had it from heaven. Like Daffodil, now, for the Lincoln. That was as sure as eggs."

"Did you put anything on Daffodil?" asked Oscar Cresswell.

"Yes, sir, I made my bit."

"And my nephew?"

Bassett was obstinately silent, looking at Paul.

"I made twelve hundred, didn't I, Bassett? I told uncle I was putting three hundred on Daffodil."

"That's right," said Bassett, nodding.

"But where's the money?" asked the uncle.

"I keep it safe locked up, sir. Master Paul he can have it any minute he likes to ask for it."

"What, fifteen hundred pounds?"

"And twenty! and forty, that is, with the twenty he made on the course."

"It's amazing!" said the uncle.

"If Master Paul offers you to be partners, sir, I would, if I were you; if you'll excuse me," said Bassett.

Oscar Cresswell thought about it.

"I'll see the money," he said.

They drove home again, and sure enough, Bassett came round to the garden-house with fifteen hundred pounds in notes. The twenty pounds reserve was left with Joe Glee, in the Turf Commission deposit.

"You see, it's all right, uncle, when I'm sure! Then we go strong, for all we're worth. Don't we, Bassett?"

"We do that, Master Paul."

"And when are you sure?" said the uncle, laughing.

"Oh, well, sometimes I'm absolutely sure, like about Daffodil," said the boy; "and sometimes I have an idea; and sometimes I haven't even an idea, have I, Bassett? Then we're careful, because we mostly go down."

"You do, do you? And when you're sure, like about Daffodil, what makes you sure, sonny?"

"Oh, well, I don't know," said the boy uneasily. "I'm sure, you know, uncle; that's all."

"It's as if he had it from heaven, sir," Bassett reiterated.

"I should say so!" said the uncle.

But he became a partner. And when the Leger was coming on, Paul was "sure" about Lively Spark, which was a quite inconsiderable horse. The boy insisted on putting a thousand on the horse, Bassett went for five hundred, and Oscar Cresswell two hundred. Lively Spark came in first, and the betting had been ten to one against him. Paul had made ten thousand.

"You see," he said, "I was absolutely sure of him."

Even Oscar Cresswell had cleared two thousand.

"Look here, son," he said, "this sort of thing makes me nervous."

"It needn't, uncle! Perhaps I shan't be sure again for a long time."

"But what are you going to do with your money?" asked the uncle.

"Of course," said the boy, "I started it for mother. She said she had no luck, because father is unlucky, so I thought If I was lucky, it might stop whispering."

"What might stop whispering?"

"Our house. I hate our house for whispering."

"What does it whisper?"

"Why—why"—the boy fidgeted—"why, I don't know. But it's always short of money, you know, uncle."

"I know it, son, I know it."

"You know people send mother writs, don't you, uncle?"

"I'm afraid I do," said the uncle.

"And then the house whispers, like people laughing at you behind your back, it's awful, that is! I thought if I was lucky. . . ."

"You might stop it," added the uncle.

The boy watched him with big blue eyes that had an uncanny cold fire in them, and he said never a word.

"Well, then!" said the uncle. "What are we doing?"

"I shouldn't like mother to know I was lucky," said the boy.

"Why not, son?"

"She'd stop me."

"I don't think she would."

"Oh!"—and the boy writhed in an odd way—"I don't want her to know, uncle."

"All right, son! We'll manage it without her knowing."

They managed it very easily. Paul, at the other's suggestion, handed over five thousand pounds to his uncle, who deposited it with the family lawyer, who was then to inform Paul's mother that a relative had put five thousand pounds into his hands, which sum was to be paid out a thousand pounds at a time, on the mother's birthday, for the next five years.

"So she'll have a birthday present of a thousand pounds for five successive years," said Uncle Oscar. "I hope it won't make it all the harder for her later."

Paul's mother had her birthday in November. The house had been "whispering" worse than ever lately, and, even in spite of his luck, Paul could not bear up against it. He was very anxious to see the effect of the birthday letter, telling his mother about the thousand pounds.

When there were no visitors, Paul now took his meals with his parents, as he was beyond the nursery control. His mother went into town nearly every day. She had discovered that she had an odd knack of sketching furs and dress materials, so she worked secretly in the studio of a friend who was the chief "artist" for the leading drapers. She drew the figures of ladies in furs and ladies in silk and sequins for the newspaper advertisements. This young woman artist earned several thousand pounds a year, but Paul's mother only made several hundreds, and she was again dissatisfied. She so wanted to be first in something, and she did not succeed, even in making sketches for drapery advertisements.

She was down to breakfast on the morning of her birthday. Paul watched her face as she read her letters. He knew the lawyer's letter. As his mother read it, her face hardened and became more expressionless. Then a cold, determined look came on her mouth. She hid the letter under the pile of others and said not a word about it.

"Didn't you have anything nice in the post for your birthday, mother?" said Paul.

"Quite moderately nice," she said, her voice cold and absent.

She went away to town without saying more.

But in the afternoon Uncle Oscar appeared. He said Paul's mother had had a long interview with the lawyer, asking if the whole five thousand could be advanced at once, as she was in debt.

"What do you think, uncle?" said the boy.

"I leave it to you, son."

"Oh, let her have it, then! We can get some more with the other," said the boy.

"A bird in the hand is worth two in the bush, laddie!" said Uncle Oscar.

"But I'm sure to know for the Grand National; or the Lincolnshire; or else the Derby. I'm sure to know for one of them," said Paul.

So Uncle Oscar signed the agreement, and Paul's mother touched the whole five thousand. Then something very curious happened. The voice in the house suddenly went mad, like a chorus of frogs on a spring evening. There were certain new furnishings, and Paul had a tutor. He was really going to Eton, his father's school, in the following autumn. There were flowers in the winter, and a blossoming of the luxury Paul's mother had been used to. And yet the voices in the house, behind the sprays of mimosa and almond blossom, and from under the piles of iridescent cushions, simply trilled and screamed in a sort of ecstasy: "There must be more money! Oh-h, there must be more money. Oh, now, now-w! Now-w-w—there must be more money!—more than ever! More than ever!"

It frightened Paul terribly. He studied away at his Latin and Greek with his tutors. But his intense hours were spent with Bassett. The Grand National had gone by; he had not "known," and had lost a hundred pounds. Summer was at hand. He was in agony for the Lincoln. But even for the Lincoln he didn't "know" and he lost fifty pounds. He became wild-eyed and strange, as if something were going to explode in him.

"Let it alone, son! Don't you bother about it!" urged Uncle Oscar. But it was as if the boy couldn't really hear what his uncle was saying.

"I've got to know for the Derby! I've got to know for the Derby!" the child reiterated, his big eyes blazing with a sort of madness.

His mother noticed how overwrought he was.

"You'd better go to the seaside. Wouldn't you like to go now to the seaside, instead of waiting? I think you'd better," she said, looking down at him anxiously, her heart curiously heavy because of him.

But the child lifted his uncanny blue eyes.

"I couldn't possibly go before the Derby, mother!" he said. "I couldn't possibly!"

"Why not?" she said, her voice becoming heavy when she was opposed. "Why not? You can still go from the seaside to see the Derby with your Uncle Oscar, if that's what you wish. No need for you to wait here. Besides, I think you care too much about these races. It's a bad sign. My family has been a gambling family, and you won't know till you grow up how much damage it has done. But it has done damage. I shall have to send Bassett away, and ask Uncle Oscar not to talk racing to you, unless you promise to be reasonable about it; go away to the seaside and forget it. You're all nerves!"

"I'll do what you like, mother, so long as you don't send me away till after the Derby," the boy said.

"Send you away from where? Just from this house?"

"Yes," he said, gazing at her.

"Why, you curious child, what makes you care about this house so much, suddenly? I never knew you loved it."

He gazed at her without speaking. He had a secret within a secret, something he had not divulged, even to Bassett or to his Uncle Oscar.

But his mother, after standing undecided and a little bit sullen for some moments, said:

"Very well, then! Don't go to the seaside till after the Derby, if you don't wish it. But promise me you won't let your nerves go to pieces. Promise you won't think so much about horse racing and events, as you call them!"

"Oh, no," said the boy casually. "I won't think much about them, mother. You needn't worry. I wouldn't worry, mother, if I were you."

"If you were me and I were you," said his mother, "I wonder what we should do!"

"But you know you needn't worry, mother, don't you?" the boy repeated.

"I should be awfully glad to know it," she said wearily.

"Oh, well, you can, you know. I mean, you ought to know you needn't worry," he insisted.

"Ought I? Then I'll see about it," she said.

Paul's secret of secrets was his wooden horse, that which had no name. Since he was emancipated from a nurse and a nursery-governess, he had had his rocking horse removed to his own bedroom at the top of the house.

"Surely, you're too big for a rocking horse!" his mother had remonstrated.

"Well, you see, mother, till I can have a real horse, I like to have some sort of animal about," had been his quaint answer.

"Do you feel he keeps you company?" she laughed.

"Oh yes! He's very good, he always keeps me company, when I'm there," said Paul.

So the horse, rather shabby, stood in an arrested prance in the boy's bedroom.

The Derby was drawing near, and the boy grew more and more tense. He hardly heard what was spoken to him, he was very frail, and his eyes were really uncanny. His mother had sudden seizures of uneasiness about him. Sometimes, for half-an-hour, she would feel a sudden anxiety about him that was almost anguish. She wanted to rush to him at once, and know he was safe.

Two nights before the Derby, she was at a big party in town, when one of her rushes of anxiety about her boy, her first-born, gripped her heart till she could hardly speak. She fought with the feeling, might and main, for she believed in common sense. But it was too strong. She had to leave the dance and go downstairs to telephone to the country. The children's nursery-governess was terribly surprised and startled at being rung up in the night.

"Are the children all right, Miss Wilmot?"

"Oh, yes, they are quite all right."

"Master Paul? Is he all right?"

"He went to bed as right as a trivet. Shall I run up and look at him?"

"No," said Paul's mother reluctantly. "No! Don't trouble. It's all right. Don't sit up. We shall be home fairly soon." She did not want her son's privacy intruded upon.

"Very good," said the governess.

It was about one o'clock when Paul's mother and father drove up to their house. All was still. Paul's mother went to her room and slipped off her white fur coat. She had told her maid not to wait up for her. She heard her husband downstairs, mixing a whisky-and-soda.

And then, because of the strange anxiety at her heart, she stole upstairs to her son's room. Noiselessly she went along the upper corridor. Was there a faint noise? What was it?

She stood, with arrested muscles, outside his door, listening. There was a strange, heavy, and yet not loud noise. Her heart stood still. It was a soundless noise, yet rushing and powerful. Something huge, in violent, hushed motion. What was it? What in God's name was it? She ought to know. She felt that she knew the noise. She knew what it was.

Yet she could not place it. She couldn't say what it was. And on and on it went, like a madness.

Softly, frozen with anxiety and fear, she turned the door handle.

The room was dark. Yet in the space near the window, she heard and saw something plunging to and fro. She gazed in fear and amazement.

Then suddenly she switched on the light, and saw her son, in his green pyjamas, madly surging on the rocking horse. The blaze of light suddenly lit him up, as he urged the wooden horse, and lit her up, as she stood, blonde, in her dress of pale green and crystal, in the doorway.

"Paul!" she cried. "Whatever are you doing?"

"It's Malabar!" he screamed, in a powerful, strange voice. "It's Malabar."

His eyes blazed at her for one strange and senseless second, as he ceased urging his wooden horse. Then he fell with a crash to the ground, and she, all her tormented motherhood flooding upon her, rushed to gather him up.

But he was unconscious, and unconscious he remained, with some brain-fever. He talked and tossed, and his mother sat stonily by his side.

"Malabar! It's Malabar! Bassett, Bassett, I know! It's Malabar!"

So the child cried, trying to get up and urge the rocking horse that gave him his inspiration.

"What does he mean by Malabar?" asked the heart-frozen mother.

"I don't know," said the father stonily.

"What does he mean by Malabar?" she asked her brother Oscar.

"It's one of the horses running for the Derby," was the answer.

And, in spite of himself, Oscar Cresswell spoke to Bassett, and himself put a thousand on Malabar: at fourteen to one.

The third day of the illness was critical: they were waiting for a change. The boy, with his rather long, curly hair, was tossing ceaselessly on the pillow. He neither slept nor regained consciousness, and his eyes were like blue stones. His mother sat, feeling her heart had gone, turned actually into stone.

In the evening, Oscar Cresswell did not come, but Bassett sent a message, saying could he come up for one moment, just one moment? Paul's mother was very angry at the intrusion, but on second thought she agreed. The boy was the same. Perhaps Bassett might bring him to consciousness.

The gardener, a shortish fellow with a little brown moustache, and sharp little brown eyes, tiptoed into the room, touched his imaginary cap to Paul's mother, and stole to the bedside, staring with glittering, smallish eyes, at the tossing, dying child.

"Master Paul!" he whispered. "Master Paul! Malabar came in first all right, a clean win. I did as you told me. You've made over seventy thousand pounds, you have; you've got over eighty thousand. Malabar came in all right, Master Paul."

"Malabar! Malabar! Did I say Malabar, mother? Did I say Malabar? Do you think I'm lucky, mother? I knew Malabar, didn't I? Over eighty thousand pounds! I call that lucky, don't you, mother? Over eighty thousand pounds! I knew, didn't I know I knew? Malabar came in all right. If I ride my horse till I'm sure, then I tell you, Bassett, you can go as high as you like. Did you go for all you were worth, Bassett?"

"I went a thousand on it, Master Paul."

"I never told you, mother, that if I can ride my horse, and get there, then I'm absolutely sure—oh, absolutely! Mother, did I ever tell you? I am lucky."

"No, you never did," said the mother.

But the boy died in the night.

And even as he lay dead, his mother heard her brother's voice saying to her: "My God, Hester, you're eighty-odd thousand to the good and a poor devil of a son to the bad. But, poor devil, poor devil, he's best gone out of a life where he rides his rocking horse to find a winner."

SUGGESTIONS FOR WRITING AND DISCUSSION

1. In this story it is the child, rather than the adult, who is burdened by a sense of responsibility. What special circumstances bring this about?

2. Do you interpret the events in this story as supernatural?
3. What do you think the word *luck* means to the various characters in this story?
4. In a two- to three-page essay analyze the rocking-horse as a symbol.
5. Write a one-page character sketch of Paul's mother.
6. What is the theme of this story? What, if anything, is Lawrence trying to teach the reader? Discuss this in a two- to three-page essay.
7. The family in this story is by no means poor. The extra money Paul provides is spent on things like flowers in winter, a tutor, and new furniture. How would your interpretation of this story change if Paul were providing basic necessities? Discuss this in a three- to five-page essay.

Frank O'Connor (Irish, 1903–1966)

My Oedipus Complex

Father was in the army all through the war—the first war, I mean—so, up to the age of five, I never saw much of him, and what I saw did not worry me. Sometimes I woke and there was a big figure in khaki peering down at me in the candlelight. Sometimes in the early morning I heard the slamming of the front door and the clatter of nailed boots down the cobbles of the lane. These were Father's entrances and exits. Like Santa Claus he came and went mysteriously.

In fact, I rather liked his visits, though it was an uncomfortable squeeze between Mother and him when I got into the big bed in the early morning. He smoked, which gave him a pleasant musty smell, and shaved, an operation of astounding interest. Each time he left a trail of souvenirs—model tanks and Gurkha knives with handles made of bullet cases, and German helmets and cap badges and button-sticks, and all sorts of military equipment—carefully stowed away in a long box on top of the wardrobe, in case they ever came in handy. There was a bit of the magpie about Father; he expected everything to come in handy. When his back was turned, Mother let me get a chair and rummage through his treasures. She didn't seem to think so highly of them as he did.

The war was the most peaceful period of my life. The window of my attic faced southeast. My mother had curtained it, but that had small effect. I always woke with the first light and, with all the responsibilities of the previous day melted, feeling myself rather like the sun, ready to illumine and rejoice. Life never seemed so simple and clear and full of possibilities as then. I put my feet out from under the clothes—I called them Mrs. Left and Mrs. Right—and invented dramatic situations for them in which they discussed the problems of the day. At least Mrs. Right did; she was very demonstrative, but I hadn't the same control of Mrs. Left, so she mostly contented herself with nodding agreement.

They discussed what Mother and I should do during the day, what Santa Claus should give a fellow for Christmas, and what steps should be taken to brighten the home. There was that little matter of the baby, for instance. Mother and I could never agree about that. Ours was the only house in the terrace without a new baby, and Mother said we couldn't afford one till Father came back from the war because they cost seventeen and six. That showed how simple she was. The Geneys up the road had a baby, and everyone knew they couldn't afford seventeen and six. It was probably a cheap baby, and Mother wanted something really good, but I felt she was too exclusive. The Geneys' baby would have done us fine.

Having settled my plans for the day, I got up, put a chair under the attic window, and lifted the frame high enough to stick out my head. The window overlooked the front gardens of the terrace behind ours, and beyond these it looked over a deep valley to the tall, red-brick houses terraced up the opposite hillside, which were all still in shadow, while those at our side of the valley were all lit up, though with long strange shadows that made them seem unfamiliar; rigid and painted.

After that I went into Mother's room and climbed into the big bed. She woke and I began to tell her of my schemes. By this time, though I never seem to have noticed it, I was petrified in my nightshirt, and I thawed as I talked until, the last frost melted, I fell asleep beside her and woke again only when I heard her below in the kitchen, making the breakfast.

After breakfast we went into town; heard Mass at St. Augustine's and said a prayer for Father, and did the shopping. If the afternoon was fine we either went for a walk in the country or a visit to Mother's great friend in the convent, Mother St. Dominic. Mother had them all praying for Father, and every night, going to bed, I asked God to send him back safe from the war to us. Little, indeed, did I know what I was praying for!

One morning, I got into the big bed, and there, sure enough, was Father in his usual Santa Claus manner, but later, instead of uniform, he put on his best blue suit, and Mother was as pleased as anything. I saw nothing to be pleased about, because, out of uniform, Father was altogether less interesting, but she only beamed, and explained that our prayers had been answered, and off we went to Mass to thank God for having brought Father safely home.

The irony of it! That very day when he came in to dinner he took off his boots and put on his slippers, donned the dirty old cap he wore about the house to save him from colds, crossed his legs, and began to talk gravely to Mother, who looked anxious. Naturally, I disliked her looking anxious, because it destroyed her good looks, so I interrupted him.

"Just a moment, Larry!" she said gently.

This was only what she said when we had boring visitors, so I attached no importance to it and went on talking.

"Do be quiet, Larry!" she said impatiently. "Don't you hear me talking to Daddy?"

This was the first time I had heard those ominous words, "talking to Daddy," and I couldn't help feeling that if this was how God answered prayers, he couldn't listen to them very attentively.

"Why are you talking to Daddy?" I asked with as great a show of indifference as I could muster.

"Because Daddy and I have business to discuss. Now, don't interrupt again!"

In the afternoon, at Mother's request, Father took me for a walk. This time we went into town instead of out the country, and I thought at first, in my usual optimistic way, that it might be an improvement. It was nothing of the sort. Father and I had quite different notions of a walk in town. He had no proper interest in trams, ships, and horses, and the only thing that seemed to divert him was talking to fellows as old as himself. When I wanted to stop he simply went on, dragging me behind him by the hand; when he wanted to stop I had no alternative but to do the same. I noticed that it seemed to be a sign that he wanted to stop for a long time whenever he leaned against a wall. The second time I saw him do it I got wild. He seemed to be settling himself forever. I pulled him by the coat and trousers, but, unlike Mother who, if you were too persistent, got into a wax and said: "Larry, if you don't behave yourself, I'll give you a good slap," Father had an extraordinary capacity for amiable inattention. I sized him up and wondered would I cry, but he seemed to be too remote to be annoyed even by that. Really, it was like going for a walk with a mountain! He either ignored the wrenching and pummeling entirely, or else glanced down with a grin of amusement from his peak. I had never met anyone so absorbed in himself as he seemed.

At teatime, "talking to Daddy" began again, complicated this time by the fact that he had an evening paper, and every few minutes he put it down and told Mother something new out of it. I felt this was foul play. Man for man, I was prepared to compete with him any time for Mother's attention, but when he had it all made up for him by other people it left me no chance. Several times I tried to change the subject without success.

"You must be quiet while Daddy is reading, Larry," Mother said impatiently.

It was clear that she either genuinely liked talking to Father better than talking to me, or else that he had some terrible hold on her which made her afraid to admit the truth.

"Mummy," I said that night when she was tucking me up, "do you think if I prayed hard God would send Daddy back to the war?"

She seemed to think about that for a moment.

"No, dear," she said with a smile. "I don't think he would."

"Why wouldn't he, Mummy?"

"Because there isn't a war any longer, dear."

"But, Mummy, couldn't God make another war, if He liked?"

"He wouldn't like to, dear. It's not God who makes wars, but bad people."

"Oh!" I said.

I was disappointed about that. I began to think that God wasn't quite what he was cracked up to be.

Next morning I woke at my usual hour, feeling like a bottle of champagne. I put out my feet and invented a long conversation in which Mrs. Right talked of the trouble she had with her own father till she put him in the Home. I didn't quite know what the Home was but it sounded like the right place for Father. Then I got my chair and stuck my head out of the attic window. Dawn was just breaking, with a guilty air that made me feel I had caught it in the act. My head bursting with stories and schemes, I stumbled in next door, and in the half-darkness scrambled into the big bed. There was no room at Mother's side so I had to get between her and Father. For the time being I had forgotten about him, and for several minutes I sat bolt upright, racking my brains to know what I could do with him. He was taking up more than his fair share of the bed, and I couldn't get comfortable, so I gave him several kicks that made him grunt and stretch. He made room all right, though. Mother waked and felt for me. I settled back comfortably in the warmth of the bed with my thumb in my mouth.

"Mummy!" I hummed, loudly and contentedly.

"Sssh! dear," she whispered. "Don't wake Daddy!"

This was a new development, which threatened to be even more serious than "talking to Daddy." Life without my early-morning conferences was unthinkable.

"Why?" I asked severely.

"Because poor Daddy is tired."

This seemed to me a quite inadequate reason, and I was sickened by the sentimentality of her "poor Daddy." I never liked that sort of gush; it always struck me as insincere.

"Oh!" I said lightly. Then in my most winning tone: "Do you know where I want to go with you today, Mummy?"

"No, dear," she sighed.

"I want to go down the Glen and fish for thornybacks with my new net, and then I want to go out to the Fox and Hounds, and—"

"Don't-wake-Daddy!" she hissed angrily, clapping her hand across my mouth.

But it was too late. He was awake, or nearly so. He grunted and reached for the matches. Then he stared incredulously at his watch.

"Like a cup of tea, dear?" asked Mother in a meek, hushed voice I had never heard her use before. It sounded almost as though she were afraid.

"Tea?" he exclaimed indignantly. "Do you know what the time is?"

"And after that I want to go up the Rathcooney Road," I said loudly, afraid I'd forget something in all those interruptions.

"Go to sleep at once, Larry!" she said sharply.

I began to snivel. I couldn't concentrate, the way that pair went on, and smothering my early-morning schemes was like burying a family from the cradle.

Father said nothing, but lit his pipe and sucked it, looking out into the shadows without minding Mother or me. I knew he was mad. Every time I made a remark Mother hushed me irritably. I was mortified. I felt it wasn't fair; there was even something sinister in it. Every time I had pointed out to her the waste of making two beds when we could both sleep in one, she had told me it was healthier like that, and now here was this man, this stranger sleeping with her without the least regard for her health!

He got up early and made tea but though he brought Mother a cup he brought none for me.

"Mummy," I shouted, "I want a cup of tea, too."

"Yes, dear," she said patiently. "You can drink from Mummy's saucer."

That settled it. Either Father or I would have to leave the house. I didn't want to drink from Mother's saucer; I wanted to be treated as an equal in my own home, so, just to spite her, I drank it all and left none for her. She took that quietly, too.

But that night when she was putting me to bed she said gently:

"Larry, I want you to promise me something."

"What is it?" I asked.

"Not to come in and disturb poor Daddy in the morning. Promise?"

"Poor Daddy" again! I was becoming suspicious of everything involving that quite impossible man.

"Why?" I asked.

"Because poor Daddy is worried and tired and he doesn't sleep well."

"Why doesn't he, Mummy?"

"Well, you know, don't you, that while he was at the war Mummy got the pennies from the Post Office?"

"From Miss MacCarthy?"

"That's right. But now, you see, Miss MacCarthy hasn't any more pennies, so Daddy must go out and find us some. You know what would happen if he couldn't?"

"No," I said, "tell us."

"Well, I think we might have to go out and beg for them like the poor old woman on Fridays. We wouldn't like that, would we?"

"No," I agreed. "We wouldn't."

"So you'll promise not to come in and wake him?"

"Promise."

Mind you, I meant that. I knew pennies were a serious matter, and I was all against having to go out and beg like the old woman on Fridays. Mother laid out all my toys in a complete ring round the bed so that, whatever way I got out, I was bound to fall over one of them.

When I woke I remembered my promise all right. I got up and sat on the floor and played—for hours, it seemed to me. Then I got my chair and looked out the attic window for more hours. I wished it was time for Father to wake; I wished someone would make me a cup of tea. I didn't feel in the least like the sun; instead, I was bored and so very, very cold! I simply longed for the warmth and depth of the big featherbed.

At last I could stand it no longer. I went into the next room. As there was still no room at Mother's side I climbed over her and she woke with a start.

"Larry," she whispered, gripping my arm very tightly, "what did you promise?"

"But I did, Mummy," I wailed, caught in the very act. "I was quiet for ever so long."

"Oh, dear, and you're perished!" she said sadly, feeling me all over. "Now, if I let you stay will you promise not to talk?"

"But I want to talk, Mummy," I wailed.

"That has nothing to do with it," she said with a firmness that was new to me. "Daddy wants to sleep. Now, do you understand that?"

I understood it only too well. I wanted to talk, he wanted to sleep—whose house was it, anyway?

"Mummy," I said with equal firmness, "I think it would be healthier for Daddy to sleep in his own bed."

That seemed to stagger her, because she said nothing for a while.

"Now, once for all," she went on, "you're to be perfectly quiet or go back to your own bed. Which is it to be?"

The injustice of it got me down. I had convicted her out of her own mouth of inconsistency and unreasonableness, and she hadn't even attempted to reply. Full of spite, I gave Father a kick, which she didn't notice but which made him grunt and open his eyes in alarm.

"What time is it?" he asked in a panic-stricken voice, not looking at Mother but at the door, as if he saw someone there.

"It's early yet," she replied soothingly. "It's only the child. Go to sleep again. . . . Now, Larry," she added, getting out of bed, "you've wakened Daddy and you must go back."

This time, for all her quiet air, I knew she meant it, and knew that my principal rights and privileges were as good as lost unless I asserted them at once. As she lifted me, I gave a screech, enough to wake the dead, not to mind Father. He groaned.

"That damn child! Doesn't he ever sleep?"

"It's only a habit, dear," she said quietly, though I could see she was vexed.

"Well, it's time he got out of it," shouted Father, beginning to heave in the bed. He suddenly gathered all the bedclothes about him, turned to the wall, and then looked back over his shoulder with nothing showing only two small, spiteful, dark eyes. The man looked very wicked.

To open the bedroom door, Mother had to let me down, and I broke free and dashed for the farthest corner, screeching. Father sat bolt upright in bed.

"Shut up, you little puppy!" he said in a choking voice.

I was so astonished that I stopped screeching. Never, never had anyone spoken to me in that tone before. I looked at him incredulously and saw his face convulsed with rage. It was only then that I fully realized how God had codded me, listening to my prayers for the safe return of this monster.

"Shut up, you!" I bawled, beside myself.

"What's that you said?" shouted Father, making a wild leap out of the bed.

"Mick, Mick!" cried Mother. "Don't you see the child isn't used to you?"

"I see he's better fed than taught," snarled Father, waving his arms wildly. "He wants his bottom smacked."

All his previous shouting was as nothing to these obscene words referring to my person. They really made my blood boil.

"Smack your own!" I screamed hysterically. "Smack your own! Shut up! Shut up!"

At this he lost his patience and let fly at me. He did it with the lack of conviction you'd expect of a man under Mother's horrified eyes, and it ended up as a mere tap, but the sheer indignity of being struck at all by a stranger, a total stranger who had cajoled his way back from the war into our big bed as a result of my innocent intercession, made me completely dotty. I shrieked and shrieked, and danced in my bare feet, and Father, looking awkward and hairy in nothing but a short grey army shirt, glared down at me like a mountain out for murder. I think it must have been then that I realized he was jealous too. And there stood Mother in her nightdress, looking as if her heart was broken between us. I hoped she felt as she looked. It seemed to me that she deserved it all.

From that morning out my life was a hell. Father and I were enemies, open and avowed. We conducted a series of skirmishes against one another, he trying to steal my time with Mother and I his. When she was sitting on my bed, telling me a story, he took to looking for some pair of old boots which he alleged he had left behind him at the beginning of the war. While he talked to Mother I played loudly with my toys to show my total lack of concern. He created a terrible scene one evening when he came in from work and found me at his box, playing with his regimental badges, Gurkha knives and button-sticks. Mother got up and took the box from me.

"You mustn't play with Daddy's toys unless he lets you, Larry," she said severely. "Daddy doesn't play with yours."

For some reason Father looked at her as if she had struck him and then turned away with a scowl.

"Those are not toys," he growled, taking down the box again to see had I lifted anything. "Some of those curios are very rare and valuable."

But as time went on I saw more and more how he managed to alienate Mother and me. What made it worse was that I couldn't grasp his method or see what attraction he had for Mother. In every possible way he was less winning than I. He had a common accent and made noises at his tea. I thought for a while that it might be the newspapers she was interested in, so I made up bits of news of my own to read to her. Then I thought it might be the smoking, which I personally thought attractive, and took his pipes and went round the house dribbling into them till he caught me. I even made noises at my tea, but Mother only told me I was disgusting. It all seemed to hinge round that unhealthy habit of sleeping together, so I made a point of dropping into their bedroom and nosing round, talking to myself, so that they wouldn't know I was watching them, but they were never up to anything that I could see. In the end it beat me. It seemed to depend on being grown-up and giving people rings, and I realized I'd have to wait.

But at the same time I wanted him to see that I was only waiting, not giving up the fight. One evening when he was being particularly obnoxious, chattering away well above my head, I let him have it.

"Mummy," I said, "do you know what I'm going to do when I grow up?"

"No, dear," she replied. "What?"

"I'm going to marry you," I said quietly.

Father gave a great guffaw out of him, but he didn't take me in. I knew it must only be pretence. And Mother, in spite of everything, was pleased. I felt she was probably relieved to know that one day Father's hold on her would be broken.

"Won't that be nice?" she said with a smile.

"It'll be very nice," I said confidently. "Because we're going to have lots and lots of babies."

"That's right, dear," she said placidly. "I think we'll have one soon, and then you'll have plenty of company."

I was no end pleased about that because it showed that in spite of the way she gave in to Father she still considered my wishes. Besides, it would put the Geneys in their place.

It didn't turn out like that, though. To begin with, she was very preoccupied—I suppose about where she would get the seventeen and six—and though Father took to staying out late in the evenings it did me no particular good. She stopped taking me for walks, became as touchy as blazes, and smacked me for nothing at all. Sometimes I wished I'd never mentioned the confounded baby—I seemed to have a genius for bringing calamity on myself.

And calamity it was! Sonny arrived in the most appalling hullabaloo—even that much he couldn't do without a fuss—and from the first moment I disliked him. He was a difficult child—so far as I was concerned he was always difficult—and demanded far too much attention. Mother was simply silly about him, and couldn't see when he was only showing off. As company he was worse than useless. He slept all day, and I had to go round the house on tiptoe to avoid waking him. It wasn't any longer a question of not waking Father. The slogan now was ''Don't-wake-Sonny!'' I couldn't understand why the child wouldn't sleep at the proper time, so whenever Mother's back was turned I woke him. Sometimes to keep him awake I pinched him as well. Mother caught me at it one day and gave me a most unmerciful flaking.

One evening, when Father was coming in from work, I was playing trains in the front garden. I let on not to notice him; instead, I pretended to be talking to myself, and said in a loud voice: ''If another bloody baby comes into this house, I'm going out.''

Father stopped dead and looked at me over his shoulder.

''What's that you said?'' he asked sternly.

''I was only talking to myself,'' I replied, trying to conceal my panic. ''It's private.''

He turned and went in without a word. Mind you, I intended it as a solemn warning, but its effect was quite different. Father started being quite nice to me. I could understand that, of course. Mother was quite sickening about Sonny. Even at mealtimes she'd get up and gawk at him in the cradle with an idiotic smile, and tell Father to do the same. He was always polite about it, but he looked so puzzled you could see he didn't know what she was talking about. He complained of the way Sonny cried at night but she only got cross and said that Sonny never cried except when there was something up with him—which was a flaming lie, because Sonny never had anything up with him, and only cried for attention. It was really painful to see how simple-minded she was. Father wasn't attractive, but he had a fine intelligence. He saw through Sonny, and now he knew that I saw through him as well.

One night I woke with a start. There was someone beside me in the bed. For one wild moment I felt sure it must be Mother, having come to her senses and left Father for good, but then I heard Sonny in convulsions in the next room, and Mother saying: ''There! There! There!'' and I knew it wasn't she. It was Father. He was lying beside me, wide awake, breathing hard and apparently as mad as hell.

After a while it came to me what he was mad about. It was his turn now. After turning me out of the big bed, he had been turned out himself. Mother had no consideration now for anyone but that poisonous pup, Sonny. I couldn't help feeling sorry for Father. I had been through it all myself, and even at that age I was magnanimous. I began to stroke him down and say: ''There! There!'' He wasn't exactly responsive.

''Aren't you asleep either?'' he snarled.

''Ah, come on and put your arm around us, can't you?'' I said, and he did, in a sort of way. Gingerly, I suppose, is how you'd describe it. He was very bony but better than nothing.

At Christmas he went out of his way to buy me a really nice model railway.

SUGGESTIONS FOR WRITING AND DISCUSSION

1. Discuss the meaning of the title. Is it serious or facetious?
2. Part of the charm of this story is that we see things two ways at once: as the child Larry sees them, and from an adult's perspective. Find one example and discuss the effect.
3. Does the narrator change or mature during the course of the story?
4. What do we learn about the narrator's parents during the course of the story? Write a short character sketch of each.
5. This story deals with a serious, potentially tragic subject in a lighthearted manner. Why do you think O'Connor does this? What is the effect?
6. After reading Freud's "Family Romances" (pages 130–133), discuss the ways in which the narrator of this story seems to prove Freud's theory. Does he romanticize his parents? If so, how? Discuss this in a two- to three-page essay.

Tillie Olsen (American, 1913–   )

I Stand Here Ironing

I stand here ironing, and what you asked me moves tormented back and forth with the iron.

"I wish you would manage the time to come in and talk with me about your daughter. I'm sure you can help me understand her. She's a youngster who needs help and whom I'm deeply interested in helping."

"Who needs help." . . . Even if I came, what good would it do? You think because I am her mother I have a key, or that in some way you could use me as a key? She has lived for nineteen years. There is all that life that has happened outside of me, beyond me.

And when is there time to remember, to sift, to weigh, to estimate, to total? I will start and there will be an interruption and I will have to gather it all together again. Or I will become engulfed with all I did or did not do, with what should have been and what cannot be helped.

She was a beautiful baby. The first and only one of our five that was beautiful at birth. You do not guess how new and uneasy her tenancy in her now-loveliness. You did not know her all those years she was thought homely, or see her poring over her baby pictures, making me tell her over and over how beautiful she had been—and would be, I would tell her— and was now, to the seeing eye. But the seeing eyes were few or nonexistent. Including mine.

I nursed her. They feel that's important nowadays. I nursed all the children, but with her, with all the fierce rigidity of first motherhood, I did like the books then said. Though her cries battered me to trembling and my breasts ached with swollenness, I waited till the clock decreed.

Why do I put that first? I do not even know if it matters, or if it explains anything.

She was a beautiful baby. She blew shining bubbles of sound. She loved motion, loved light, loved color and music and textures. She would lie on the floor in her blue overalls patting the surface so hard in ecstasy her hands and feet would blur. She was a miracle to me, but when she was eight months old I had to leave her daytimes with the woman downstairs to whom she was no miracle at all, for I worked or looked for work and for Emily's father, who ``could no longer endure'' (he wrote in his good-bye note) ``sharing want with us.''

I was nineteen. It was the pre-relief, pre-WPA world of the depression. I would start running as soon as I got off the streetcar, running up the stairs, the place smelling sour, and awake or asleep to startle awake, when she saw me she would break into a clogged weeping that could not be comforted, a weeping I can hear yet.

After a while I found a job hashing at night so I could be with her days, and it was better. But it came to where I had to bring her to his family and leave her.

It took a long time to raise the money for her fare back. Then she got chicken pox and I had to wait longer. When she finally came, I hardly knew her, walking quick and nervous like her father, looking like her father, thin, and dressed in a shoddy red that yellowed her skin and glared at the pockmarks. All the baby loveliness gone.

She was two. Old enough for nursery school they said, and I did not know then what I know now—the fatigue of the long day, and the lacerations of group life in the kinds of nurseries that are only parking places for children.

Except that it would have made no difference if I had known. It was the only place there was. It was the only way we could be together, the only way I could hold a job.

And even without knowing, I knew. I knew the teacher that was evil because all these years it has curdled into my memory, the little boy hunched in the corner, her rasp, ``why aren't you outside, because Alvin hits you? that's no reason, go out, scaredy.'' I knew Emily hated it even if she did not clutch and implore ``don't go Mommy'' like the other children, mornings.

She always had a reason why we should stay home. Momma, you look sick. Momma, I feel sick. Momma, the teachers aren't there today, they're sick. Momma, we can't go, there was a fire there last night. Momma, it's a holiday today, no school, they told me.

But never a direct protest, never rebellion. I think of our others in their three-, four-year-oldness—the explosions, the tempers, the denunciations, the demands—and I feel suddenly ill. I put the iron down. What in me demanded that goodness in her? And what was the cost, the cost to her of such goodness?

The old man living in the back once said in his gentle way: "You should smile at Emily more when you look at her." What *was* in my face when I looked at her? I loved her. There were all the acts of love.

It was only with the others I remembered what he said, and it was the face of joy, and not of care or tightness or worry I turned to them—too late for Emily. She does not smile easily, let alone almost always as her brothers and sisters do. Her face is closed and sombre, but when she wants, how fluid. You must have seen it in her pantomimes, you spoke of her rare gift for comedy on the stage that rouses a laughter out of the audience so dear they applaud and applaud and do not want to let her go.

Where does it come from, that comedy? There was none of it in her when she came back to me that second time, after I had had to send her away again. She had a new daddy now to learn to love, and I think perhaps it was a better time.

Except when we left her alone nights, telling ourselves she was old enough.

"Can't you go some other time, Mommy, like tomorrow?" she would ask. "Will it be just a little while you'll be gone? Do you promise?"

The time we came back, the front door open, the clock on the floor in the hall. She rigid awake. "It wasn't just a little while. I didn't cry. Three times I called you, just three times, and then I ran downstairs to open the door so you could come faster. The clock talked loud. I threw it away, it scared me what it talked."

She said the clock talked loud again that night I went to the hospital to have Susan. She was delirious with the fever that comes before red measles, but she was fully conscious all the week I was gone and the week after we were home when she could not come near the new baby or me.

She did not get well. She stayed skeleton thin, not wanting to eat, and night after night she had nightmares. She would call for me, and I would rouse from exhaustion to sleepily call back: "You're all right, darling, go to sleep, it's just a dream," and if she still called, in a sterner voice, "now go to sleep, Emily, there's nothing to hurt you." Twice, only twice, when I had to get up for Susan anyhow, I went in to sit with her.

Now when it is too late (as if she would let me hold and comfort her like I do the others) I get up and go to her at once at her moan or restless stirring. "Are you awake, Emily? Can I get you something?" And the answer is always the same: "No, I'm all right, go back to sleep, Mother."

They persuaded me at the clinic to send her away to a convalescent home in the country where "she can have the kind of food and care you can't manage for her, and you'll be free to concentrate on the new baby." They still send children to that place. I see pictures on the society page of sleek young women planning affairs to raise money for it, or dancing at the affairs, or decorating Easter eggs or filling Christmas stockings for the children.

They never have a picture of the children so I do not know if the girls still wear those gigantic red bows and the ravaged looks on the every other Sunday when parents can come to visit "unless otherwise notified"—as we were notified the first six weeks.

Oh it is a handsome place, green lawns and tall trees and fluted flower beds. High up on the balconies of each cottage the children stand, the girls in their red bows and white dresses, the boys in white suits and giant red ties. The parents stand below shrieking up to be heard and the children shriek down to be heard, and between them the invisible wall "Not To Be Contaminated by Parental Germs or Physical Affection."

There was a tiny girl who always stood hand in hand with Emily. Her parents never came. One visit she was gone. "They moved her to Rose Cottage," Emily shouted in explanation. "They don't like you to love anybody here."

She wrote once a week, the labored writing of a seven-year-old. "I am fine. How is the baby. If I write my leter nicly I will have a star. Love." There never was a star. We wrote every other day, letters she could never hold or keep but only hear read—once. "We simply do not have room for children to keep any personal possessions," they patiently explained when we pieced one Sunday's shrieking together to plead how much it would mean to Emily, who loved so to keep things, to be allowed to keep her letters and cards.

Each visit she looked frailer. "She isn't eating," they told us.

(They had runny eggs for breakfast or mush with lumps, Emily said later, I'd hold it in my mouth and not swallow. Nothing ever tasted good, just when they had chicken.)

It took us eight months to get her released home, and only the fact that she gained back so little of her seven lost pounds convinced the social worker.

I used to try to hold and love her after she came back, but her body would stay stiff, and after a while she'd push away. She ate little. Food sickened her, and I think much of life too. Oh she had physical lightness and brightness, twinkling by on skates, bouncing like a ball up and down up and down over the jump rope, skimming over the hill; but these were momentary.

She fretted about her appearance, thin and dark and foreign-looking at a time when every little girl was supposed to look or thought she should look a chubby blonde replica of Shirley Temple. The doorbell sometimes rang for her, but no one seemed to come and play in the house or be a best friend. Maybe because we moved so much.

There was a boy she loved painfully through two school semesters. Months later she told me how she had taken pennies from my purse to buy him candy. "Licorice was his favorite and I brought him some every day, but he still liked Jennifer better'n me. Why, Mommy?'' The kind of question for which there is no answer.

School was a worry to her. She was not glib or quick in a world where glibness and quickness were easily confused with ability to learn. To her overworked and exasperated teachers she was an overconscientious ''slow learner'' who kept trying to catch up and was absent entirely too often.

I let her be absent, though sometimes the illness was imaginary. How different from my now-strictness about attendance with the others. I wasn't working. We had a new baby, I was home anyhow. Sometimes, after Susan grew old enough, I would keep her home from school, too, to have them all together.

Mostly Emily had asthma, and her breathing, harsh and labored, would fill the house with a curiously tranquil sound. I would bring the two old dresser mirrors and her boxes of collections to her bed. She would select beads and single earrings, bottle tops and shells, dried flowers and pebbles, old postcards and scraps, all sorts of oddments; then she and Susan would play Kingdom, setting up landscapes and furniture, peopling them with action.

Those were the only times of peaceful companionship between her and Susan. I have edged away from it, that poisonous feeling between them, that terrible balancing of hurts and needs I had to do between the two, and did so badly, those earlier years.

Oh there are conflicts between the others too, each one human, needing, demanding, hurting, taking—but only between Emily and Susan, no, Emily toward Susan that corroding resentment. It seems so obvious on the surface, yet it is not obvious. Susan, the second child, Susan, golden- and curly-haired and chubby, quick and articulate and assured, everything in appearance and manner Emily was not; Susan, not able to resist Emily's precious things, losing or sometimes clumsily breaking them; Susan telling jokes and riddles to company for applause while Emily sat silent (to say to me later: that was *my* riddle, Mother, I told it to Susan); Susan, who for all the five years' difference in age, was just a year behind Emily in developing physically.

I am glad for that slow physical development that widened the difference between her and her contemporaries, though she suffered over it. She was too vulnerable for that terrible world of youthful competition, of preening and parading, of constant measuring of yourself against every other, of envy, ''If I had that copper hair,'' ''If I had that skin. . . . '' She tormented herself enough about not looking like the others, there was enough of the unsureness, the having to be conscious of words before you speak, the constant caring—what are they thinking of me? without having it all magnified by the merciless physical drives.

Ronnie is calling. He is wet and I change him. It is rare there is such a cry now. That time of motherhood is almost behind me when the ear is not one's own but must always be racked and listening for the child cry, the child call. We sit for a while and I hold him, looking out over the city spread in charcoal with its soft aisles of light. *"Shoogily,"* he breathes and curls closer. I carry him back to bed, asleep. *Shoogily.* A funny word, a family word, inherited from Emily, invented by her to say: *comfort.*

In this and other ways she leaves her seal, I say aloud. And startle at my saying it. What do I mean? What did I start to gather together, to try and make coherent? I was at the terrible, growing years. War years. I do not remember them well. I was working, there were four smaller ones now, there was not time for her. She had to help be a mother, and house-keeper, and shopper. She had to set her seal. Mornings of crisis and near hysteria trying to get lunches packed, hair combed, coats and shoes found, everyone to school or Child Care on time, the baby ready for trans-portation. And always the paper scribbled on by a smaller one, the book looked at by Susan then mislaid, the homework not done. Running out to that huge school where she was one, she was lost, she was a drop; suffering over the unpreparedness, stammering and unsure in her classes.

There was so little time left at night after the kids were bedded down. She would struggle over books, always eating (it was in those years she developed her enormous appetite that is legendary in our family) and I would be ironing, or preparing food for the next day, or writing V-mail to Bill, or tending the baby. Sometimes, to make me laugh, or out of her despair, she would imitate happenings or types at school.

I think I said once: "Why don't you do something like this in the school amateur show?" One morning she phoned me at work, hardly understandable through the weeping: "Mother, I did it. I won, I won; they gave me first prize; they clapped and clapped and wouldn't let me go."

Now suddenly she was Somebody, and as imprisoned in her differ-ence as she had been in anonymity.

She began to be asked to perform at other high schools, even in colleges, then at city and statewide affairs. The first one we went to, I only recognized her that first moment when thin, shy, she almost drowned herself into the curtains. Then: Was this Emily? The control, the com-mand, the convulsing and deadly clowning, the spell, then the roaring, stamping audience, unwilling to let this rare and precious laughter out of their lives.

Afterwards: You ought to do something about her with a gift like that—but without money or knowing how, what does one do? We have left it all to her, and the gift has as often eddied inside, clogged and clot-ted, as been used and growing.

She is coming. She runs up the stairs two at a time with her light graceful step, and I know she is happy tonight. Whatever it was that occa-sioned your call did not happen today.

"Aren't you ever going to finish the ironing, Mother? Whistler painted his mother in a rocker. I'd have to paint mine standing over an ironing board." This is one of her communicative nights and she tells me everything and nothing as she fixes herself a plate of food out of the icebox.

She is so lovely. Why did you want me to come in at all? Why were you concerned? She will find her way.

She starts up the stairs to bed. "Don't get me up with the rest in the morning." "But I thought you were having midterms." "Oh, those," she comes back in, kisses me, and says quite lightly, "in a couple of years when we'll all be atom-dead they won't matter a bit."

She has said it before. She *believes* it. But because I have been dredging the past, and all that compounds a human being is so heavy and meaningful in me, I cannot endure it tonight.

I will never total it all. I will never come in to say: She was a child seldom smiled at. Her father left me before she was a year old. I had to work her first six years when there was work, or I sent her home and to his relatives. There were years she had care she hated. She was dark and thin and foreign-looking in a world where the prestige went to blondeness and curly hair and dimples, she was slow where glibness was prized. She was a child of anxious, not proud, love. We were poor and could not afford for her the soil of easy growth. I was a young mother, I was a distracted mother. There were the other children pushing up, demanding. Her younger sister seemed all that she was not. There were years she did not want me to touch her. She kept too much in herself, her life was such she had to keep too much in herself. My wisdom came too late. She has much to her and probably little will come of it. She is a child of her age, of depression, of war, of fear.

Let her be. So all that is in her will not bloom—but in how many does it? There is still enough left to live by. Only help her to know—help make it so there is cause for her to know—that she is more than this dress on the ironing board, helpless before the iron.

SUGGESTIONS FOR WRITING AND DUSCUSSION

1. To whom is the narrator speaking?
2. Do you feel Emily's life would have been substantially different if her family had been wealthy?
3. Does it seem improbable that Emily becomes an entertainer, or is there a certain logic to it? Discuss this in a one- to two-page paper.
4. One of the questions that social scientists have been asking for years is which is more influential in the development of a child, nature or nurture. How much of a person's character is determined by genes and how much is determined by environment? In a three- to five-page paper, argue for one or the other being the dominant force in a child's life. Illustrate with examples of people you know.

Poetry

Yosano Akiko (Japanese, 1878–1942)

Labor Pains

I am sick today,
sick in my body,
eyes wide open, silent,
I lie on the bed of childbirth.

Why do I,
so used to the nearness of death,
to pain and blood and screaming,
now uncontrollably tremble with dread?

A nice young doctor tried to comfort me,
and talked about the joy of giving birth.
Since I know better than he about this matter,
what good purpose can his prattle serve?

Knowledge is not reality.
Experience belongs to the past.
Let those who lack immediacy be silent.
Let observers be content to observe.

I am all alone,
totally, utterly, entirely on my own,
gnawing my lips, holding my body rigid,
waiting on inexorable fate.

There is only one truth.
I shall give birth to a child,
truth driving outward from my inwardness.

Neither good nor bad; real, no sham about it.
With the first labor pains,
suddenly the sun goes pale.
The indifferent world goes strangely calm.
I am alone.
It is alone I am.

SUGGESTIONS FOR WRITING AND DISCUSSION

1. In the first stanza the speaker says she is sick because she is about to give
   birth. Does her attitude to childbirth change in the course of the poem? Support your answer.

2. In the second stanza the speaker describes herself as being "used to the nearness of death." This description could also apply to the doctor. Why is it
then, given this similarity, that his words seem to her like prattle?
3. Hilma Wolitzer's story "No Pictures" is also an account of childbirth. What
do the two women have in common? Compare them in a two- to three-page
essay.

William Butler Yeats (Irish, 1865–1939)

A Prayer for My Daughter

Once more the storm is howling, and half hid
Under this cradle-hood and coverlid
My child sleeps on. There is no obstacle
But Gregory's wood and one bare hill
Whereby the haystack- and roof-levelling wind,
Bred on the Atlantic, can be stayed;
And for an hour I have walked and prayed
Because of the great gloom that is in my mind.

I have walked and prayed for this young child an hour
And heard the sea-wind scream upon the tower,
And under the arches of the bridge, and scream
In the elms above the flooded stream;
Imagining in excited reverie
That the future years had come,
Dancing to a frenzied drum,
Out of the murderous innocence of the sea.

May she be granted beauty and yet not
Beauty to make a stranger's eye distraught,
Or hers before a looking-glass, for such,
Being made beautiful overmuch,
Consider beauty a sufficient end,
Lose natural kindness and maybe
The heart-revealing intimacy
That chooses right, and never find a friend.

Helen being chosen found life flat and dull
And later had much trouble from a fool,
While that great Queen, that rose out of the spray,
Being fatherless could have her way
Yet chose a bandy-legged smith for man.
It's certain that fine women eat
A crazy salad with their meat
Whereby the Horn of Plenty is undone.

In courtesy I'd have her chiefly learned;
Hearts are not had as a gift but hearts are earned
By those that are not entirely beautiful;
Yet many, that have played the fool
For beauty's very self, has charm made wise,
And many a poor man that has roved,
Loved and thought himself beloved,
From a glad kindness cannot take his eyes.

May she become a flourishing hidden tree
That all her thoughts may like the linnet be,
And have no business but dispensing round
Their magnanimities of sound,
Nor but in merriment begin a chase,
Nor but in merriment a quarrel.
O may she live like some green laurel
Rooted in one dear perpetual place.

My mind, because the minds that I have loved,
The sort of beauty that I have approved,
Prosper but little, has dried up of late,
Yet knows that to be choked with hate
May well be of all evil chances chief.
If there's no hatred in a mind
Assault and battery of the wind
Can never tear the linnet from the leaf.

An intellectual hatred is the worst,
So let her think opinions are accursed.
Have I not seen the loveliest woman born
Out of the mouth of Plenty's horn,
Because of her opinionated mind
Barter that horn and every good
By quiet natures understood
For an old bellows full of angry wind?

Considering that, all hatred driven hence,
The soul recovers radical innocence
And learns at last that it is self-delighting,
Self-appeasing, self-affrighting,
And that its own sweet will is Heaven's will;
She can, though every face should scowl
And every windy quarter howl
Or every bellows burst, be happy still.

And may her bridegroom bring her to a house
Where all's accustomed, ceremonious;

For arrogance and hatred are the wares
Peddled in the thoroughfares.
How but in custom and in ceremony
Are innocence and beauty born?
Ceremony's a name for the rich horn,
And custom for the spreading laurel tree.

SUGGESTIONS FOR WRITING AND DISCUSSION

1. This poem was written for Yeats's daughter, Anne Butler Yeats, who was born on February 24, 1919. In the first stanza a storm is raging over the Atlantic while the baby sleeps. The speaker tells us he is in "great gloom." What do we learn about the reasons for his gloom in the second stanza? How does the nature of the storm change?
2. "Helen" is Helen of Troy and "that great Queen" is Venus. In a two- to three-page essay analyze the speaker's attitude to beauty and what kind of beauty it is that he wishes for his daughter.
3. The Horn of Plenty and the laurel tree are both images of what the speaker hopes for his daughter. The Horn of Plenty stands for courtesy and ceremony; the laurel tree represents the virtues of custom and tradition. Trace the way Yeats uses these two images in the course of the poem. How is the laurel tree linked with the storm of the first stanza?

Weldon Kees (American, 1914–1955?)

For My Daughter

Looking into my daughter's eyes I read
Beneath the innocence of morning flesh
Concealed, hintings of death she does not heed.
Coldest of winds have blown this hair, and mesh
Of seaweed snarled these miniatures of hands;
The night's slow poison, tolerant and bland,
Has moved her blood. Parched years that I have seen
That may be hers appear: foul, lingering
Death in certain war, the slim legs green.
Or, fed on hate, she relishes the sting
Of others' agony; perhaps the cruel
Bride of a syphilitic or a fool.
These speculations sour in the sun.
I have no daughter. I desire none.

SUGGESTIONS FOR WRITING AND DISCUSSION

1. Does the bitter tone of this poem come from the speaker's genuine desire not to have a daughter or from his distress at not having one? What reasons does the speaker give for not wanting a daughter? Do you think it might be wrong to bring a child into the world, if the world is full of evils?

2. Compare this poem with Ben Jonson's "On My First Son." Both poems deal with a parent's loss of a child, either to the dangers of the world, or to death. In a two- to three-page essay compare the attitudes of the two speakers to a father's lack of control over his child's fate.

Ben Jonson (British, 1573?–1637)

On My First Daughter

Here lies, to each her parents' ruth,
Mary, the daughter of their youth;
Yet all heaven's gifts being heaven's due,
It makes the father less to rue.
At six months' end she parted hence
With safety of her innocence;
Whose soul heaven's queen, whose name she bears,
In comfort of her mother's tears.
Hath placed amongst her virgin-train:
Where, while that severed doth remain,
This grave partakes the fleshly birth;
Which cover lightly, gentle earth!

On My First Son

Farewell, thou child of my right hand, and joy;
My sin was too much hope of thee, loved boy:
Seven years thou 'wert lent to me, and I thee pay,
Exacted by thy fate, on the just day.
O could I lose all father now! for why
Will man lament the state he should envy,
To have so soon 'scaped world's and flesh's rage,
And, if no other misery, yet age?
Rest in soft peace, and asked, say, "Here doth lie
Ben Jonson his best piece of poetry."
For whose sake henceforth all his vows be such
As what he loves may never like too much.

SUGGESTIONS FOR WRITING AND DISCUSSION

1. By describing Mary as "the daughter of their youth," the poet reminds us of the parents' mortality and helps to prepare us for the religious consolation that the poem offers. How does religion console each of the parents?
2. Are the parents resigned to the death of their daughter? In a one- to two-page essay make an argument and support your answer.
3. In comparing these two poems it is important to remember that Mary died at the age of six months and Benjamin died at the age of seven. As in "On

My First Daughter" the speaker tries to console himself by reminding himself that a good Christian should welcome death, "For why/Will man lament the state he should envy." How successful is he in resolving the tension between his love for his son and his duty as a Christian?
4. In a four-page essay explicate and compare these two poems.

Theodore Roethke (American, 1908–1963)

My Papa's Waltz

The whiskey on your breath
Could make a small boy dizzy;
But I hung on like death:
Such waltzing was not easy.

We romped until the pans
Slid from the kitchen shelf;
My mother's countenance
Could not unfrown itself.

The hand that held my wrist
Was battered on one knuckle;
At every step you missed
My right ear scraped a buckle.

You beat time on my head
With a palm caked hard by dirt,
Then waltzed me off to bed
Still clinging to your shirt.

SUGGESTIONS FOR WRITING AND DISCUSSION

1. How does the speaker of this poem feel about his father? How would you describe the father? In a one-page essay support both your answers by referring to the text.
2. As the title suggests the poem mimics the rhythm of a dance. Why do you think the poet chose to do this?

Robert Hayden (American, 1913–1980)

Those Winter Sundays

Sundays too my father got up early
and put his clothes on in the blueblack cold,
then with cracked hands that ached

from labor in the weekday weather made
banked fires blaze. No one ever thanked him.

I'd wake and hear the cold splintering, breaking.
When the rooms were warm, he'd call,
and slowly I would rise and dress,
fearing the chronic angers of that house,

Speaking indifferently to him,
who had driven out the cold
and polished my good shoes as well.
What did I know, what did I know
of love's austere and lonely offices?

SUGGESTIONS FOR WRITING AND DISCUSSION

1. The word *cold* appears in each stanza. Examine the way in which the speaker
   characterizes the cold. What else, besides the weather, do these descriptions
   suggest?
2. What was the speaker's attitude to his father and family at the time
   described in the poem? How has his attitude changed? Compare this aspect
   of the poem with Theodore Roethke's "My Papa's Waltz."
3. Using your answers to the first two questions, write an explication of the
   poem (two to three pages). Before you begin, look up the word *offices* in a
   good dictionary.

Robert Lowell (American, 1917–1980)

Dunbarton

My Grandfather found
his grandchild's fogbound solitudes
sweeter than human society.

When Uncle Devereux died,
Daddy was still on sea-duty in the Pacific;
it seemed spontaneous and proper
for Mr. MacDonald, the farmer,
Karl, the chauffeur, and even my Grandmother
to say, ``your Father.'' They meant my Grandfather.

He was my Father. I was his son.
On our yearly autumn get-aways from Boston
to the family graveyard in Dunbarton,

he took the wheel himself—
like an admiral at the helm.
Freed from Karl and chuckling over the gas he was saving,
he let his motor roller-coaster
out of control down each hill.
We stopped at the *Priscilla* in Nashua
for brownies and root-beer,
and later ``pumped ship'' together in the Indian Summer. . . .

At the graveyard, a suave Venetian Christ
gave a sheepdog's nursing patience
to Grandfather's Aunt Lottie,
his Mother, the stone but not the bones
of his Father, Francis.
Failing as when Francis Winslow could count
them on his fingers,
the clump of virgin pine still stretched patchy ostrich necks
over the disused millpond's fragrantly woodstained water,
a reddish blur,
like the ever-blackening wine-dark coat
in our portrait of Edward Winslow
once sheriff for George the Second,
the sire of bankrupt Tories.

Grandfather and I
raked leaves from our dead forebears,
defied the dank weather
with ``dragon'' bonfires.

Our helper, Mr. Burroughs,
had stood with Sherman at Shiloh—
his thermos of shockless coffee
was milk and grounds;
his illegal home-made claret
was as sugary as grape jelly
in a tumbler capped with paraffin.

I borrowed Grandfather's cane
carved with the names and altitudes
of Norwegian mountains he had scaled—
more a weapon than a crutch.
I lanced it in the fauve ooze for newts.
In a tobacco tin after capture, the umber yellow mature newts
lost their leopard spots,
lay grounded as numb

as scrolls of candied grapefruit peel.
I saw myself as a young newt,
neurasthenic, scarlet
and wild in the wild coffee-colored water.

In the mornings I cuddled like a paramour
in my Grandfather's bed,
while he scouted about the chattering greenwood stove.

SUGGESTIONS FOR WRITING AND DISCUSSION

1. What kind of portrait does this poem paint of the grandfather?
2. In what ways is the grandfather a father to the boy?
3. There is a great deal of description in this poem. What is the mood of the description? What does it convey?
4. In this poem there are many references to the past: Edward Winslow was "once sheriff for George the Second"; "Mr. Burroughs, had stood with Sherman at Shiloh." In a two-page essay discuss the speaker's attitude to the past and the importance of these references to the theme of the poem.
5. Write a one-page explication of the last three lines of the poem.

Sylvia Plath (American, 1932–1963)

Daddy

You do not do, you do not do
Any more, black shoe
In which I have lived like a foot
For thirty years, poor and white,
Barely daring to breathe or Achoo.

Daddy, I have had to kill you.
You died before I had time—
Marble-heavy, a bag full of God,
Ghastly statue with one grey toe
Big as a Frisco seal

And a head in the freakish Atlantic
Where it pours bean green over blue
In the waters off beautiful Nauset.
I used to pray to recover you.
Ach, du.

In the German tongue, in the Polish town
Scraped flat by the roller

Of wars, wars, wars.
But the name of the town is common.
My Polack friend

Says there are a dozen or two.
So I never could tell where you
Put your foot, your root,
I never could talk to you.
The tongue stuck in my jaw.

It stuck in a barb wire snare.
Ich, ich, ich, ich,
I could hardly speak.
I thought every German was you.
And the language obscene

An engine, an engine
Chuffing me off like a Jew.
A Jew to Dachau, Auschwitz, Belsen.
I began to talk like a Jew.
I think I may well be a Jew.

The snows of the Tyrol, the clear beer of Vienna
Are not very pure or true.
With my gypsy ancestress and my weird luck
And my Taroc pack and my Taroc pack
I may be a bit of a Jew.

I have always been scared of *you.*
With your Luftwaffe, your gobbledygoo.
And your neat moustache
And your Aryan eye, bright blue.
Panzer-man, panzer-man, O You—

Not God but a swastika
So black no sky could squeak through.
Every woman adores a Fascist,
The boot in the face, the brute
Brute heart of a brute like you.

You stand at the blackboard, daddy,
In the picture I have of you,
A cleft in your chin instead of your foot
But no less a devil for that, no not
Any less the black man who

Bit my pretty red heart in two.
I was ten when they buried you.
At twenty I tried to die
And get back, back, back at you.
I thought even the bones will do.

But they pulled me out of the sack,
And they stuck me together with glue.
And then I knew what to do.
I made a model of you,
A man in black with a Meinkampf look

And a love of the rack and the screw.
And I said I do, I do.
So daddy, I'm finally through.
The black telephone's off at the root,
The voices just can't worm through.

If I've killed one man, I've killed two—
The vampire who said he was you
And drank my blood for a year,
Seven years, if you want to know.
Daddy, you can lie back now.

There's a stake in your fat black heart
And the villagers never liked you.
They are dancing and stamping on you.
They always *knew* it was you.
Daddy, daddy, you bastard, I'm through.

SUGGESTIONS FOR WRITING AND DISCUSSION

1. At a reading Plath introduced "Daddy" with the following remarks:

> The poem is spoken by a girl with an Electra complex. Her father died while she thought he was God. Her case is complicated by the fact that her father was also a Nazi and her mother very possibly part Jewish. In the daughter the two strains marry and paralyze each other—she has to act out the awful little allegory before she is free of it.

   An "Electra complex" is Freud's name for the unconscious desire of a daughter to murder her mother. What effect does the fact that the speaker had an Electra complex as a child now have on her attitudes to her father and to herself? What is "the awful little allegory" she now has to act out in order to get rid of it? What does she have to do to her father? To herself?

2. *Ach, du* means "Oh, you" in German; *Ich* means "I"; Dachau, Auschwitz, and Belsen are the names of concentration camps where Jews were imprisoned and murdered during World War II; *Mein Kampf* means *My Life* and is

the title of Adoph Hitler's autobiography. In a two- to three-page essay analyze Plath's use of Nazi imagery.

William Carlos Williams (American, 1883–1963)

The Horse Show

Constantly near you, I never in my entire
sixty four years knew you so well as yesterday
or half so well. We talked. You were never
so lucid, so disengaged from all exigencies
of place and time. We talked of ourselves,
intimately, a thing never heard of between us.
How long have we waited? almost a hundred years.

You said, Unless there is some spark, some
spirit we keep within ourselves, life, a
continuing life's impossible—and it is all
we have. There is no other life, only the one.
The world of the spirits that comes afterward
is the same as our own, just like you sitting
there they come and talk to me, just the same.

They come to bother us. Why? I said. I don't
know. Perhaps to find out what we are doing.
Jealous, do you think? I don't know. I
don't know why they should want to come back.
I was reading about some men who had been
buried under a mountain, I said to her, and
one of them came back after two months,

digging himself out. It was in Switzerland,
you remember? Of course I remember. The
villagers tho't it was a ghost coming down
to complain. They were frightened. They
do come, she said, what you call
my ``visions.'' I talk to them just as I
am talking to you. I see them plainly.

Oh if I could only read! You don't know
what adjustments I have made. All
I can do is to try to live over again
what I knew when your brother and you
were children—but I can't always succeed.
Tell me about the horse show. I have
been waiting all week to hear about it.

Mother darling, I wasn't able to get away.
Oh that's too bad. It was just a show;
they make the horses walk up and down
to judge them by their form. Oh is that
all? I tho't it was something else. Oh
they jump and run too. I wish you had been
there, I was so interested to hear about it.

SUGGESTIONS FOR WRITING AND DISCUSSION

1. The speaker relates a conversation he has had with his mother. Go through
   the poem making sure that you know who is saying what. Why does the
   speaker describe this conversation as one of peculiar intimacy and how does
   the theme of their conversation show this?
2. What do we learn about the mother from the speaker's descriptions of her
   and how does this influence the way we understand her conversation?
3. Why does the speaker discuss the horse show? What does it indicate about
   his relationship with his mother?
4. Write a two-page essay analyzing the speaker's attitude toward his mother
   and toward what she says. Does he share her views? Support your answer.

Donald Justice (American, 1925–   )

Men at Forty

Men at forty
Learn to close softly
The doors to rooms they will not be
Coming back to.

At rest on a stair landing,
They feel it moving
Beneath them now like the deck of a ship,
Though the swell is gentle.

And deep in mirrors
They rediscover
The face of the boy as he practices tying
His father's tie there in secret

And the face of that father,
Still warm with the mystery of lather.
They are more fathers than sons themselves now.
Something is filling them, something

That is like the twilight sound
Of the crickets, immense,
Filling the woods at the foot of the slope
Behind their mortgaged houses.

SUGGESTIONS FOR WRITING AND DISCUSSION

1. Write a paraphrase of each stanza of the poem. What is the connection
    between each stanza and the preceding one? How does the fact that the
    houses in the last stanza are "mortgaged" reflect the theme of the poem?
2. What is the "something" that is filling the men?
3. In stanzas three and four the poet mentions that "men at forty" are simul-
    taneously both parents and children. Read Martha Weinman Lear's essay
    "Mother's Day" and compare the way the two works present this idea. Are
    these accounts of family relationships optimistic or pessimistic? Answer in
    a two- to three-page essay.

Robert Mezey (American, 1935–   )

My Mother

My mother writes from Trenton,
a comedian to the bone
but underneath serious
and all heart. 'Honey,' she says,
'be a mensch and Mary too,
its no good, to worry, you
are doing the best you can
your Dad and everyone
thinks you turned out very well
as long as you pay your bills
nobody can say a word
you can tell them to drop dead
so save a dollar it can't
hurt—remember Frank you went
to highschool with? he still lives
with his wife's mother, his wife
works while he writes his books and
did he ever sell a one
the four kids run around naked
36, and he's never had,
you'll forgive my expression
even a pot to piss in
or a window to throw it,
such a smart boy he couldn't

read the footprints on the wall
honey you think you know all
the answers you dont, please try
to put some money away
believe me it wouldn't hurt
artist shmartist life's too short
for that kind of, forgive me,
horseshit, I know what you want
better than you, all that counts
is to make a good living
and the best of everything,
as Sholem Aleichem said,
he was a great writer did
you ever read his books dear,
you should make what he makes a year
anyway he says some place
Poverty is no disgrace
but its no honor either
that's what I say,
     love,
      Mother'

SUGGESTIONS FOR WRITING AND DISCUSSION

1. What attitude does the speaker of the poem have to his mother? What can you deduce about the speaker and his mother from her letter? Do you think he will follow her advice?

2. In a one- to two-page essay discuss the use of colloquial language in this poem. What effect does this kind of language have?

Drama

Tennessee Williams (American, 1914–1982)

The Glass Menagerie

CHARACTERS

AMANDA WINGFIELD, *the mother.*

A little woman of great but confused vitality clinging frantically to another time and place. Her characterization must be carefully created, not copied from type. She is not paranoiac, but her life is paranoia. There is much to admire in AMANDA, *and as much to love and pity as there is to laugh at. Certainly she has endurance and a kind of heroism, and though her foolishness makes her unwittingly cruel at times, there is tenderness in her slight person.*

LAURA WINGFIELD, *her daughter.*

AMANDA, *having failed to establish contact with reality, continues to live vitally in her illusions, but*

LAURA'S *situation is even graver. A childhood illness has left her crippled, one leg slightly shorter than the other, and held in a brace. This defect need not be more than suggested on the stage. Stemming from this,* LAURA'S *separation increases till she is like a piece of her own glass collection, too exquisitely fragile to move from the shelf.*

TOM WINGFIELD, *her son, and the narrator of the play.*

A poet with a job in a warehouse. His nature is not remorseless, but to escape from a trap he has to act without pity.

JIM O'CONNOR, *the gentleman caller. A nice, ordinary, young man.*

SCENE: *An alley in St. Louis.*
PART I: *Preparation for a Gentleman Caller.*
PART II: *The Gentleman Calls.*
TIME: *Now and the Past.*

Scene I

The Wingfield apartment is in the rear of the building, one of those vast hive-like conglomerations of cellular living-units that flower as warty growths in overcrowded urban centers of lower middle-class population and are symptomatic of the impulse of this largest and fundamentally enslaved section of American society to avoid fluidity and differentiation and to exist and function as one interfused mass of automatism.

The apartment faces an alley and is entered by a fire-escape, a structure whose name is a touch of accidental poetic truth, for all of these huge buildings are always burning with the slow and implacable fires of human desperation. The fire-escape is included in the set—that is, the landing of it and steps descending from it.

The scene is memory and is therefore nonrealistic. Memory takes a lot of poetic license. It omits some details; others are exaggerated, according to the emotional value of the articles it touches, for memory is seated predominantly in the heart. The interior is therefore rather dim and poetic.

At the rise of the curtain, the audience is faced with the dark, grim rear wall of the Wingfield tenement. This building, which runs parallel to the footlights, is flanked on both sides by dark, narrow alleys which run into murky canyons of tangled clotheslines, garbage cans and the sinister latticework of neighboring fire-escapes. It is up and down these side alleys that exterior entrances and exits are made, during the play. At the end of TOM's *opening commentary, the dark tenement wall slowly reveals (by means of a transparency) the interior of the ground floor Wingfield apartment.*

Downstage is the living room, which also serves as a sleeping room for LAURA, *the sofa unfolding to make her bed. Upstage, center, and divided by a wide arch or second proscenium with transparent faded portieres (or second curtain), is the dining room. In an old-fashioned what-not in the living room are seen scores of transparent glass animals. A blown-up photograph of the father hangs on the wall of the living room, facing the audience, to the left of the archway. It is the face of a very handsome young man in a doughboy's First World War cap. He is gallantly smiling, ineluctably smiling, as if to say, ``I will be smiling forever.''*

The audience hears and sees the opening scene in the dining room through both the transparent fourth wall of the building and the transparent gauze portieres of the dining-room arch. It is during this revealing scene that the fourth wall slowly ascends, out of sight. This transparent exterior wall is not brought down again until the very end of the play, during TOM's *final speech.*

The narrator is an undisguised convention of the play. He takes whatever license with dramatic convention as is convenient to his purposes.

TOM enters dressed as a merchant sailor from alley, stage left, and strolls across the front of the stage to the fire-escape. There he stops and lights a cigarette. He addresses the audience.

TOM. Yes, I have tricks in my pocket, I have things up my sleeve. But I am the opposite of a stage magician. He gives you illusion that has the appearance of truth. I give you truth in the pleasant disguise of illusion. To begin with, I turn back time. I reverse it to that quaint period, the thirties, when the huge middle class of America was matriculating in a school for the blind. Their eyes had failed them, or they had failed their eyes, and so they were having their fingers pressed forcibly down on the fiery Braille alphabet of a dissolving economy. In Spain there was revolution. Here there was only shouting and confusion. In Spain there was Guernica. Here there were disturbances of labor, sometimes pretty violent, in otherwise peaceful cities such as Chicago, Cleveland, Saint Louis. . . . This is the social background of the play.

(MUSIC.)

The play is memory. Being a memory play, it is dimly lighted, it is sentimental, it is not realistic. In memory everything seems to happen to music. That explains the fiddle in the wings. I am the narrator of the play, and also a character in it. The other characters are my mother, Amanda, my sister, Laura, and a gentleman caller who appears in the final scenes. He is the most realistic character in the play, being an emissary from a world of reality that we were somehow set apart from. But since I have a poet's weakness for symbols, I am using this character also as a symbol; he is the long delayed but always expected something that we live for. There is a fifth character who doesn't appear except in this larger-than-life photograph over the mantel. This is our father who left us a long time ago. He was a telephone man who fell in love with long distances; he gave up his job with the telephone company and skipped the light fantastic out of town . . . The last we heard of him was a picture post-card from Mazatlan, on the Pacific coast of Mexico, containing a message of two words—"Hello—Goodbye!" and an address. I think the rest of the play will explain itself. . . .

AMANDA's *voice becomes audible through the portieres.*

(LEGEND ON SCREEN: "OÙ SONT LES NEIGES.")

He divides the portieres and enters the upstage area.

AMANDA *and* LAURA *are seated at a drop-leaf table. Eating is indicated by gestures without food or utensils.* AMANDA *faces the audience.* TOM *and* LAURA *are seated in profile.*

The interior has lit up softly and through the scrim we see AMANDA *and* LAURA *seated at the table in the upstage area.*

AMANDA *(calling)*. Tom?

TOM. Yes, Mother.

AMANDA. We can't say grace until you come to the table!

TOM. Coming, Mother. *(He bows slightly and withdraws, reappearing a few moments later in his place at the table.)*

AMANDA *(to her son)*. Honey, don't *push* with your *fingers*. If you have to push with something, the thing to push with is a crust of bread. And chew—chew! Animals have sections in their stomachs which enable them to digest food without mastication, but human beings are supposed to chew their food before they swallow it down. Eat food leisurely, son, and really enjoy it. A well-cooked meal has lots of delicate flavors that have to be held in the mouth for appreciation. So chew your food and give your salivary glands a chance to function!

TOM *deliberately lays his imaginary fork down and pushes his chair back from the table.*

TOM. I haven't enjoyed one bite of this dinner because of your constant directions on how to eat it. It's you that makes me rush through meals with your hawk-like attention to every bite I take. Sickening—spoils my appetite—all this discussion of animals' secretion—salivary glands—mastication!

AMANDA *(lightly)*. Temperament like a Metropolitan star! *(He rises and crosses downstage.)* You're not excused from the table.

TOM. I am getting a cigarette.

AMANDA. You smoke too much.

LAURA *rises.*

LAURA. I'll bring in the blanc mange.

He remains standing with his cigarette by the portieres during the following.

AMANDA *(rising)*. No, sister, no, sister—you be the lady this time and I'll be the darky.

LAURA. I'm already up.

AMANDA. Resume your seat, little sister—I want you to stay fresh and pretty—for gentlemen callers!

LAURA. I'm not expecting any gentlemen callers.

AMANDA *(crossing out to kitchenette. Airily)*. Sometimes they come when they are least expected! Why, I remember one Sunday afternoon in Blue Mountain—*(Enters kitchenette.)*

TOM. I know what's coming!

LAURA. Yes. But let her tell it.

TOM. Again?

LAURA. She loves to tell it.

AMANDA *returns with bowl of dessert.*

AMANDA. One Sunday afternoon in Blue Mountain—your mother received—*seventeen!*—gentlemen callers! Why, sometimes there weren't chairs enough to accommodate them all. We had to send the nigger over to bring in folding chairs from the parish house.

TOM *(remaining at portieres)*. How did you entertain those gentlemen callers?

AMANDA. I understood the art of conversation!

TOM. I bet you could talk.

AMANDA. Girls in those days *knew* how to talk, I can tell you.

TOM. Yes?

(IMAGE: AMANDA AS A GIRL ON A PORCH GREETING CALLERS.)

AMANDA. They knew how to entertain their gentlemen callers. It wasn't enough for a girl to be possessed of a pretty face and a graceful figure—although I wasn't slighted in either respect. She also needed to have a nimble wit and a tongue to meet all occasions.

TOM. What did you talk about?

AMANDA. Things of importance going on in the world! Never anything coarse or common or vulgar. *(She addresses* TOM *as though he were seated in the vacant chair at the table though he remains by portieres. He plays this scene as though he held the book.)* My callers were gentlemen—all! Among my callers were some of the most prominent young planters of the Mississippi Delta—planters and sons of planters!

TOM *motions for music and a spot of light on* AMANDA.
Her eyes lift, her face glows, her voice becomes rich and elegiac.

(SCREEN LEGEND: "OÙ SONT LES NEIGES.")

There was young Champ Laughlin who later became vice-president of the Delta Planters Bank. Hadley Stevenson who was drowned in Moon Lake and left his widow one hundred and fifty thousand in Government bonds. There were the Cutrere brothers, Wesley and Bates. Bates was one of my bright particular beaux! He got in a quarrel with that wild Wainright boy. They shot it out on the floor of Moon Lake Casino. Bates was shot through the stomach. Died in the ambulance on his way to Memphis. His widow was also well-provided for, came into eight or ten thousand acres, that's all. She married him on the rebound—never loved her—carried my picture on him the night he died! And there was that boy that every girl in the Delta had set her cap for! That beautiful, brilliant young Fitzhugh boy from Green County!

TOM. What did he leave his widow?

AMANDA. He never married! Gracious, you talk as though all of my old admirers had turned up their toes to the daisies!

TOM. Isn't this the first you mentioned that still survives?

AMANDA. That Fitzhugh boy went North and made a fortune—came to be known as the Wolf of Wall Street! He had the Midas touch, whatever he touched turned to gold! And I could have been Mrs. Duncan J. Fitzhugh, mind you! But—I picked your *father!*

LAURA *(rising).* Mother, let me clear the table.

AMANDA. No, dear, you go in front and study your typewriter chart. Or practice your shorthand a little. Stay fresh and pretty—It's almost time for our gentlemen callers to start arriving. *(She flounces girlishly toward the kitchenette.)* How many do you suppose we're going to entertain this afternoon?

TOM *throws down the paper and jumps up with a groan.*

LAURA *(alone in the dining room).* I don't believe we're going to receive any, Mother.

AMANDA *(reappearing, airily).* What? No one—not one? You must be joking! *(*LAURA *nervously echoes her laugh. She slips in a fugitive manner through the half-open portieres and draws them gently behind her. A shaft of very clear light is thrown on her face against the faded tapestry of the curtains.* MUSIC: ''THE GLASS MENAGERIE'' UNDER FAINTLY. *Lightly.)* Not one gentleman caller? It can't be true! There must be a flood, there must have been a tornado!

LAURA. It isn't a flood, it's not a tornado, Mother. I'm just not popular like you were in Blue Mountain. . . . *(*TOM *utters another groan.* LAURA *glances at him with a faint, apologetic smile. Her voice catching a little.)* Mother's afraid I'm going to be an old maid.

(THE SCENE DIMS OUT WITH ''GLASS MENAGERIE'' MUSIC.)

Scene II

''*Laura, Haven't You Ever Liked Some Boy?*''

> *On the dark stage the screen is lighted with the image of blue roses. Gradually* LAURA*'s figure becomes apparent and the screen goes out. The music subsides.*
> LAURA *is seated in the delicate ivory chair at the small clawfoot table. She wears a dress of soft violet material for a kimono—her hair tied back from her forehead with a ribbon.*
> *She is washing and polishing her collection of glass.*
> AMANDA *appears on the fire-escape steps. At the sound of her ascent,* LAURA *catches her breath, thrusts the bowl of ornaments away and seats herself stiffly before the diagram of the typewriter keyboard as though it held her spellbound. Something has happened to* AMANDA. *It is written in her face as she climbs to the landing: a look that is grim and hopeless and a little absurd.*
> *She has on one of those cheap or imitation velvety-looking cloth coats with imitation fur collar. Her hat is five or six years old, one of those dreadful cloche hats that were worn in the late twenties and she is clasping an enormous black patent-leather pocket-book with nickel clasp and initials. This is her full-dress outfit, the one she usually wears to the D.A.R.*
> *Before entering she looks through the door.*
> *She purses her lips, opens her eyes wide, rolls them upward, and shakes her head.*
> *Then she slowly lets herself in the door. Seeing her mother's expression* LAURA *touches her lips with a nervous gesture.*

LAURA. Hello, Mother, I was—*(She makes a nervous gesture toward the chart on the wall.* AMANDA *leans against the shut door and stares at* LAURA *with a martyred look.)*

AMANDA. Deception? Deception? *(She slowly removes her hat and gloves, continuing the swift suffering stare. She lets the hat and gloves fall on the floor—a bit of acting.)*

LAURA *(shakily).* How was the D.A.R. meeting? *(AMANDA slowly opens her purse and removes a dainty white handkerchief which she shakes out delicately and delicately touches to her lips and nostrils.)* Didn't you go to the D.A.R. meeting, Mother?

AMANDA *(faintly, almost inaudibly).* —No.—No. *(Then more forcibly.)* I did not have the strength—to go to the D.A.R. In fact, I did not have the courage! I wanted to find a hole in the ground and hide myself in it forever! *(She crosses slowly to the wall and removes the diagram of the typewriter keyboard. She holds it in front of her for a second, staring at it sweetly and sorrowfully—then bites her lips and tears it in two pieces.)*

LAURA *(faintly).* Why did you do that, Mother? *(AMANDA repeats the same procedure with the chart of the Gregg Alphabet.)* Why are you—

AMANDA. Why? Why? How old are you, Laura?

LAURA. Mother, you know my age.

AMANDA. I thought that you were an adult; it seems that I was mistaken. *(She crosses slowly to the sofa and sinks down and stares at* LAURA.*)*

LAURA. Please don't stare at me, Mother.

AMANDA *closes her eyes and lowers her head. Count ten.*

AMANDA. What are we going to do, what is going to become of us, what is the future?

Count ten.

LAURA. Has something happened, Mother? *(AMANDA draws a long breath and takes out the handkerchief again. Dabbing process.)* Mother, has—something happened?

AMANDA. I'll be all right in a minute. I'm just bewildered—*(Count five.)*—by life. . . .

LAURA. Mother, I wish that you would tell me what's happened.

AMANDA. As you know, I was supposed to be inducted into my office at the D.A.R. this afternoon. (IMAGE: A SWARM OF TYPEWRITERS.) But I stopped off at Rubicam's Business College to speak to your teachers about your having a cold and ask them what progress they thought you were making down there.

LAURA. Oh. . . .

AMANDA. I went to the typing instructor and introduced myself as your mother. She didn't know who you were. Wingfield, she said. We don't have any such student enrolled at the school! I assured her she did, that you had been going to classes since early in January. "I wonder," she said, "if you could be talking about that terribly shy little girl who dropped out of school after only a few days' attendance?" "No," I said, "Laura, my daughter, has been going to school every day for the past six weeks!" "Excuse me," she said. She took the attendance book out and there was your name, unmistakably printed, and all the dates you were absent until they decided that you had dropped out of school. I still said, "No, there must have been some mistake! There must have been some mix-up in the records!" And she said, "No—I remember her perfectly now. Her hand shook so that she couldn't hit the right keys! The first time we gave a speed-test, she broke down completely—was sick at the stomach and almost had to be carried into the wash-room! After that morning she never showed up any more. We phoned the house but never got any answer"—while I was working at Famous and Barr, I suppose, demonstrating those—Oh! I felt so weak I could barely keep on my feet! I had to sit down while they got me a glass of water! Fifty dollars' tuition, all of our plans—my hopes and ambitions for you—just gone up the spout, just gone up the spout like that. *(LAURA draws a long breath and gets awkwardly to her feet. She crosses to the victrola and winds it up.)* What are you doing?

LAURA. Oh! *(She releases the handle and returns to her seat.)*

AMANDA. Laura, where have you been going when you've gone out pretending that you were going to business college?

LAURA. I've just been going out walking.

AMANDA. That's not true.

LAURA. It is. I just went walking.

AMANDA. Walking? Walking? In winter? Deliberately courting pneumonia in that light coat? Where did you walk to, Laura?

LAURA. All sorts of places—mostly in the park.

AMANDA. Even after you'd started catching that cold?

LAURA. It was the lesser of two evils, Mother. (IMAGE: WINTER SCENE IN PARK.) I couldn't go back up. I—threw up—on the floor!

AMANDA. From half past seven till after five every day you mean to tell me you walked around in the park, because you wanted to make me think that you were still going to Rubicam's Business College?

LAURA. It wasn't as bad as it sounds. I went inside places to get warmed up.

AMANDA. Inside where?

LAURA. I went in the art museum and the bird-houses at the Zoo. I visited the penguins every day! Sometimes I did without lunch and went to the movies. Lately I've been spending most of my afternoons in the Jewel-box, that big glass house where they raise the tropical flowers.

AMANDA. You did all this to deceive me, just for the deception? (LAURA *looks down.*) Why?

LAURA. Mother, when you're disappointed, you get that awful suffering look on your face, like the picture of Jesus' mother in the museum!

AMANDA. Hush!

LAURA. I couldn't face it.

Pause. A whisper of strings.

(LEGEND: ``THE CRUST OF HUMILITY.'')

AMANDA (*hopelessly fingering the huge pocketbook*). So what are we going to do the rest of our lives? Stay home and watch the parades go by? Amuse ourselves with the glass menagerie, darling? Eternally play those worn-out phonograph records your father left as a painful reminder of him? We won't have a business career—we've given that up because it gave us nervous indigestion! (*Laughs wearily.*) What is there left but dependency all our lives? I know so well what becomes of unmarried women who aren't prepared to occupy a position. I've seen such pitiful cases in the South—barely tolerated spinsters living upon the grudging patronage of sister's husband or brother's wife!—stuck away in some little mouse-trap of a room— encouraged by one in-law to visit another—little birdlike women without any nest—eating the crust of humility all their life! Is that the future that we've mapped out for ourselves? I swear it's the only alternative I can think of! It isn't a very pleasant alternative, is it? Of course—some girls *do* marry. (LAURA *twists her hands nervously.*) Haven't you ever liked some boy?

LAURA. Yes. I liked one once. (*Rises.*) I came across his picture a while ago.

AMANDA (*with some interest*). He gave you his picture?

LAURA. No, it's in the year-book.

AMANDA (*disappointed*). Oh—a high-school boy.

(SCREEN IMAGE: JIM AS A HIGH-SCHOOL HERO BEARING A SILVER CUP.)

LAURA. Yes. His name was Jim. (LAURA *lifts the heavy annual from the claw-foot table.*) Here he is in *The Pirates of Penzance*.

AMANDA (*absently*). The what?

LAURA. The operetta the senior class put on. He had a wonderful voice and we sat across the aisle from each other Mondays, Wednesdays and Fridays in the Aud. Here he is with the silver cup for debating! See his grin?

AMANDA *(absently)*. He must have had a jolly disposition.

LAURA. He used to call me—Blue Roses.

(IMAGE: BLUE ROSES.)

AMANDA. Why did he call you such a name as that?

LAURA. When I had that attack of pleurosis—he asked me what was the matter when I came back. I said pleurosis—he thought that I said Blue Roses! So that's what he always called me after that. Whenever he saw me, he'd holler, "Hello, Blue Roses!" I didn't care for the girl that he went out with. Emily Meisenbach. Emily was the best-dressed girl at Soldan. She never struck me, though, as being sincere . . . It says in the Personal Section—they're engaged. That's—six years ago! They must be married by now.

AMANDA. Girls that aren't cut out for business careers usually wind up married to some nice man. *(Gets up with a spark of revival.)* Sister, that's what you'll do!

LAURA *utters a startled, doubtful laugh. She reaches quickly for a piece of glass.*

LAURA. But, Mother—

AMANDA. Yes? *(Crossing to photograph.)*

LAURA *(in a tone of frightened apology)*. I'm—crippled!

(IMAGE: SCREEN.)

AMANDA. Nonsense! Laura, I've told you never, never to use that word. Why, you're not crippled, you just have a little defect—hardly noticeable, even! When people have some slight disadvantage like that, they cultivate other things to make up for it—develop charm—and vivacity—and—*charm!* That's all you have to do! *(She turns again to the photograph.)* One thing your father had *plenty of*—was *charm!*

TOM *motions to the fiddle in the wings.*

(THE SCENE FADES OUT WITH MUSIC.)

Scene III

(LEGEND ON SCREEN: "AFTER THE FIASCO—")

TOM *speaks from the fire-escape landing.*

TOM. After the fiasco at Rubicam's Business College, the idea of getting a gentleman caller for Laura began to play a more important part in Mother's calculations. It became an obsession. Like some archetype of the universal unconscious, the image of the gentleman caller haunted our small apartment. . . . (IMAGE: YOUNG MAN AT DOOR WITH FLOW-

ERS.) An evening at home rarely passed without some allusion to this image, this spectre, this hope. . . . Even when he wasn't mentioned, his presence hung in Mother's preoccupied look and in my sister's frightened, apologetic manner—hung like a sentence passed upon the Wingfields! Mother was a woman of action as well as words. She began to take logical steps in the planned direction. Late that winter and in the early spring—realizing that extra money would be needed to properly feather the nest and plume the bird—she conducted a vigorous campaign on the telephone, roping in subscribers to one of those magazines for matrons called *The Home-maker's Companion,* the type of journal that features the serialized sublimations of ladies of letters who think in terms of delicate cup-like breasts, slim, tapering waists, rich, creamy thighs, eyes like woodsmoke in autumn, fingers that soothe and caress like strains of music, bodies as powerful as Etruscan sculpture.

(SCREEN IMAGE: GLAMOR MAGAZINE COVER.)

AMANDA *enters with phone on long extension cord. She is spotted in the dim stage.*

AMANDA. Ida Scott? This is Amanda Wingfield! We *missed* you at the D.A.R. last Monday! I said to myself: She's probably suffering with that sinus condition! How is that sinus condition? Horrors! Heaven have mercy!—You're a Christian martyr, yes, that's what you are, a Christian martyr! Well, I just now happened to notice that your subscription to the *Companion*'s about to expire! Yes, it expires with the next issue, honey!—just when that wonderful new serial by Bessie Mae Hopper is getting off to such an exciting start. Oh, honey, it's something that you can't miss! You remember how *Gone With the Wind* took everybody by storm? You simply couldn't go out if you hadn't read it. All everybody *talked* was Scarlett O'Hara. Well, this is a book that critics already compare to *Gone With the Wind.* It's the *Gone With the Wind* of the post-World War generation!—What?—Burning?—Oh, honey, don't let them burn, go take a look in the oven and I'll hold the wire! Heavens—I think she's hung up!

(DIM OUT.)

(LEGEND ON SCREEN: "YOU THINK I'M IN LOVE WITH CONTINENTAL SHOEMAKERS?")

Before the stage is lighted, the violent voices of TOM *and* AMANDA *are heard.*
    They are quarreling behind the portieres. In front of them stands LAURA *with clenched hands and panicky expression.*
    A clear pool of light on her figure throughout this scene.

TOM. What in Christ's name am I—

AMANDA *(shrilly).* Don't you use that—

Toм. Supposed to do!

Amanda. Expression! Not in my—

Toм. Ohhh!

Amanda. Presence! Have you gone out of your senses?

Toм. I have, that's true, *driven* out!

Amanda. What is the matter with you, you—big—big—IDIOT!

Toм. Look—I've got *no thing,* no single thing—

Amanda. Lower your voice!

Toм. In my life here that I can call my OWN! Everything is—

Amanda. Stop that shouting!

Toм. Yesterday you confiscated my books! You had the nerve to—

Amanda. I took that horrible novel back to the library—yes! That hideous book by that insane Mr. Lawrence. *(*Toм *laughs wildly.)* I cannot control the output of diseased minds or people who cater to them— *(*Toм *laughs still more wildly.)* BUT I WON'T ALLOW SUCH FILTH BROUGHT INTO MY HOUSE! No, no, no, no, no!

Toм. House, house! Who pays rent on it, who makes a slave of himself to—

Amanda *(fairly screeching).* Don't you DARE to—

Toм. No, no, *I* mustn't say things! *I've* got to just—

Amanda. Let me tell you—

Toм. I don't want to hear any more! *(He tears the portieres open. The upstage area is lit with a turgid smoky red glow.)*

Amanda*'s hair is in metal curlers and she wears a very old bathrobe, much too large for her slight figure, a relic of the faithless Mr. Wingfield.*

An upright typewriter and a wild disarray of manuscripts is on the dropleaf table. The quarrel was probably precipitated by Amanda*'s interruption of his creative labor. A chair lying overthrown on the floor.*

Their gesticulating shadows are cast on the ceiling by the fiery glow.

Amanda. You *will* hear more, you—

Toм. No, I won't hear more, I'm going out!

Amanda. You come right back in—

Toм. Out, out, out! Because I'm—

Amanda. Come back here, Tom Wingfield! I'm not through talking to you!

Toм. Oh, go—

Laura *(desperately).* —Tom!

Amanda. You're going to listen, and no more insolence from you! I'm at the end of my patience! *(He comes back toward her.)*

Toм. What do you think I'm at? Aren't I supposed to have any patience to reach the end of, Mother? I know, I know. It seems unimportant to you, what I'm *doing*—what I *want* to do—having a little *difference* between them! You don't think that—

AMANDA. I think you've been doing things that you're ashamed of. That's why you act like this. I don't believe that you go every night to the movies. Nobody goes to the movies night after night. Nobody in their right minds goes to the movies as often as you pretend to. People don't go to the movies at nearly midnight, and movies don't let out at two A.M. Come in stumbling. Muttering to yourself like a maniac! You get three hours sleep and then go to work. Oh, I can picture the way you're doing down there. Moping, doping, because you're in no condition.

TOM *(wildly)*. No, I'm in no condition!

AMANDA. What right have you got to jeopardize your job? Jeopardize the security of us all? How do you think we'd manage if you were—

TOM. Listen! You think I'm crazy *about* the *warehouse? (He bends fiercely toward her slight figure.)* You think I'm in love with the Continental Shoemakers? You think I want to spend fifty-five *years* down there in that—*celotex interior!* with—*fluorescent*—*tubes!* Look! I'd rather somebody picked up a crowbar and battered out my brains—than go back mornings! I *go!* Every time you come in yelling that God damn ``*Rise and Shine!*'' ``*Rise and Shine!*'' I say to myself ``How *lucky dead* people are!'' But I get up. I *go!* For sixty-five dollars a month I give up all that I dream of doing and being *ever!* And you say self—*self*'s all I ever think of. Why, listen, if self is what I thought of, Mother, I'd be where he is—GONE! *(Pointing to father's picture.)* As far as the system of transportation reaches! *(He starts past her. She grabs his arm.)* Don't grab me, Mother!

AMANDA. Where are you going?

TOM. I'm going to the *movies!*

AMANDA. I don't believe that lie!

TOM *(crouching toward her, overtowering her tiny figure. She backs away, gasping)*. I'm going to opium dens! Yes, opium dens, dens of vice and criminals' hang-outs, Mother. I've joined the Hogan gang, I'm a hired assassin, I carry a tommy-gun in a violin case! I run a string of cat-houses in the Valley! They call me Killer, Killer Wingfield, I'm leading a double-life, a simple, honest warehouse worker by day, by night, a dynamic *czar* of the *underworld, Mother.* I go to gambling casinos, I spin away fortunes on the roulette table! I wear a patch over one eye and a false mustache, sometimes I put on green whiskers. On those occasions they call me—*El Diablo!* Oh, I could tell you things to make you sleepless! My enemies plan to dynamite this place. They're going to blow us all sky-high some night! I'll be glad, very happy, and so will you! You'll go up, up on a broomstick, over

Blue Mountain with seventeen gentlemen callers! You ugly—babbling old—*witch*. . . . *(He goes through a series of violent, clumsy movements, seizing his overcoat, lunging to the door, pulling it fiercely open. The women watch him, aghast, his arm catches in the sleeve of the coat as he struggles to pull it on. For a moment he is pinioned by the bulky garment. With an outraged groan he tears the coat off again, splitting the shoulders of it, and hurls it across the room. It strikes against the shelf of* LAURA's *glass collection, there is a tinkle of shattering glass.* LAURA *cries out as if wounded.)*

(MUSIC LEGEND: ``THE GLASS MENAGERIE.'')

LAURA *(shrilly).* My glass!—menagerie. . . . *(She covers her face and turns away.)*

But AMANDA *is still stunned and stupefied by the ``ugly witch'' so that she barely notices this occurrence. Now she recovers her speech.*

AMANDA *(in an awful voice).* I won't speak to you—until you apologize! *(She crosses through portieres and draws them together behind her.* TOM *is left with* LAURA. LAURA *clings weakly to the mantel with her face averted.* TOM *stares at her stupidly for a moment. Then he crosses to shelf. Drops awkwardly to his knees to collect the fallen glass, glancing at* LAURA *as if he would speak but couldn't.)*

``The Glass Menagerie'' steals in as

(THE SCENE DIMS OUT.)

Scene IV

The interior is dark. Faint light in the alley.

A deep-voiced bell in a church is tolling the hour of five as the scene commences.

TOM *appears at the top of the alley. After each solemn boom of the bell in the tower, he shakes a little noise-maker or rattle as if to express the tiny spasm of man in contrast to the sustained power and dignity of the Almighty. This and the unsteadiness of his advance make it evident that he has been drinking.*

As he climbs the few steps to the fire-escape landing light steals up inside. LAURA *appears in night-dress, observing* TOM's *empty bed in the front room.*

TOM *fishes in his pockets for the door-key, removing a motley assortment of articles in the search, including a perfect shower of movie-ticket stubs and an empty bottle. At last he finds the key, but just as he is about to insert it, it slips from his fingers. He strikes a match and crouches below the door.*

TOM *(bitterly).* One crack—and it falls through!

LAURA *opens the door.*

LAURA. Tom! Tom, what are you doing?

TOM. Looking for a door-key.

LAURA. Where have you been all this time?

TOM. I have been to the movies.

LAURA. All this time at the movies?

TOM. There was a very long program. There was a Garbo picture and a Mickey Mouse and a travelogue and a newsreel and a preview of coming attractions. And there was an organ solo and a collection for the milk-fund—simultaneously—which ended up in a terrible fight between a fat lady and an usher!

LAURA *(innocently)*. Did you have to stay through everything?

TOM. Of course! And, oh, I forgot! There was a big stage show! The head-liner on this stage show was Malvolio the Magician. He performed wonderful tricks, many of them, such as pouring water back and forth between pitchers. First it turned to wine and then it turned to beer and then it turned to whiskey. I know it was whiskey it finally turned into because he needed somebody to come up out of the audience to help him, and I came up—both shows! It was Kentucky Straight Bourbon. A very generous fellow, he gave souvenirs. *(He pulls from his back pocket a shimmering rainbow-colored scarf.)* He gave me this. This is his magic scarf. You can have it, Laura. You wave it over a canary cage and you get a bowl of gold-fish. You wave it over the gold-fish bowl and they fly away canaries. . . . But the won-derfullest trick of all was the coffin trick. We nailed him into a coffin and he got out of the coffin without removing one nail. *(He has come inside.)* There is a trick that would come in handy for me—get me out of this 2 by 4 situation! *(Flops onto bed and starts removing shoes.)*

LAURA. Tom—Shhh!

TOM. What you shushing me for?

LAURA. You'll wake up Mother.

TOM. Goody, goody! Pay 'er back for all those "Rise an' Shines." *(Lies down, groaning.)* You know it don't take much intelligence to get yourself into a nailed-up coffin, Laura. But who in hell ever got him-self out of one without removing one nail?

As if in answer, the father's grinning photograph lights up.

(SCENE DIMS OUT.)

Immediately following: The church bell is heard striking six. At the sixth stroke the alarm clock goes off in AMANDA*'s room, and after a few moments we hear her calling: "Rise and Shine! Rise and Shine! Laura, go tell your brother to rise and shine!"*

Tom *(sitting up slowly)*. I'll rise—but I won't shine.

The light increases.

AMANDA. Laura, tell your brother his coffee is ready.

LAURA *slips into front room.*

LAURA. Tom! it's nearly seven. Don't make Mother nervous. *(He stares at her stupidly. Beseechingly.)* Tom, speak to Mother this morning. Make up with her, apologize, speak to her!

TOM. She won't to me. It's her that started not speaking.

LAURA. If you just say you're sorry she'll start speaking.

TOM. Her not speaking—is that such a tragedy?

LAURA. Please—please!

AMANDA *(calling from kitchenette)*. Laura, are you going to do what I asked you to do, or do I have to get dressed and go out myself?

LAURA. Going, going—soon as I get on my coat! *(She pulls on a shapeless felt hat with nervous, jerky movement, pleadingly glancing at* TOM. *Rushes awkwardly for coat. The coat is one of* AMANDA *'s, inaccurately made-over, the sleeves too short for* LAURA.*)* Butter and what else?

AMANDA *(entering upstage)*. Just butter. Tell them to charge it.

LAURA. Mother, they make such faces when I do that.

AMANDA. Sticks and stones may break my bones, but the expression on Mr. Garfinkel's face won't harm us! Tell your brother his coffee is getting cold.

LAURA *(at door)*. Do what I asked you, will you, will you, Tom?

He looks sullenly away.

AMANDA. Laura, go now or just don't go at all!

LAURA *(rushing out)*. Going—going! *(A second later she cries out.* TOM *springs up and across to the door.* AMANDA *rushes anxiously in.* TOM *opens the door.)*

TOM. Laura?

LAURA. I'm all right. I slipped, but I'm all right.

AMANDA *(peering anxiously after her)*. If anyone breaks a leg on those fire-escape steps, the landlord ought to be sued for every cent he possesses! *(She shuts door. Remembers she isn't speaking and returns to other room.)*

As TOM *enters listlessly for his coffee, she turns her back to him and stands rigidly facing the window on the gloomy gray vault of the areaway. Its light on her face with its aged but childish features is cruelly sharp, satirical as a Daumier print.*

(MUSIC UNDER: ``AVE MARIA.'')

TOM *glances sheepishly but sullenly at her averted figure and slumps at the table. The coffee is scalding hot; he sips it and gasps and spits it back in the cup. At his gasp,* AMANDA *catches her breath and half turns. Then catches herself and turns back to window.*

TOM *blows on his coffee, glancing sidewise at his mother. She clears her throat.* TOM *clears his. He starts to rise. Sinks back down again, scratches his head, clears his throat again.* AMANDA *coughs.* TOM *raises his cup in both hands to blow on it, his eyes staring over the rim of it at his mother for several moments. Then he slowly sets the cup down and awkwardly and hesitantly rises from the chair.*

TOM (*hoarsely*). Mother. I—I apologize. Mother. (AMANDA *draws a quick, shuddering breath. Her face works grotesquely. She breaks into child-like tears.*) I'm sorry for what I said, for everything that I said, I didn't mean it.

AMANDA (*sobbingly*). My devotion has made me a witch and so I make myself hateful to my children!

TOM. No, you *don't*.

AMANDA. I worry so much, don't sleep, it makes me nervous!

TOM (*gently*). I understand that.

AMANDA. I've had to put up a solitary battle all these years. But you're my right-hand bower! Don't fall down, don't fail!

TOM (*gently*). I try, Mother.

AMANDA (*with great enthusiasm*). Try and you will SUCCEED! (*The notion makes her breathless.*) Why, you—you're just *full* of natural endowments! Both of my children—they're *unusual* children! Don't you think I know it? I'm so—*proud!* Happy and—feel I've—so much to be thankful for but—Promise me one thing, son!

TOM. What, Mother?

AMANDA. Promise, son, you'll—never be a drunkard!

TOM (*turns to her grinning*). I will never be a drunkard, Mother.

AMANDA. That's what frightened me so, that you'd be drinking! Eat a bowl of Purina!

TOM. Just coffee, Mother.

AMANDA. Shredded wheat biscuit?

TOM. No. No, Mother, just coffee.

AMANDA. You can't put in a day's work on an empty stomach. You've got ten minutes—don't gulp! Drinking too-hot liquids makes cancer of the stomach. . . . Put cream in.

TOM. No, thank you.

AMANDA. To cool it.

TOM. No! No, thank you, I want it black.

AMANDA. I know, but it's not good for you. We have to do all that we can to build ourselves up. In these trying times we live in, all that we have to cling to is—each other. . . . that's why it's so important to— Tom, I—I sent out your sister so I could discuss something with you. If you hadn't spoken I would have spoken to you. *(Sits down.)*

TOM *(gently)*. What is it, Mother, that you want to discuss?

AMANDA. Laura!

TOM *puts his cup down slowly.*

> (LEGEND ON SCREEN: ``LAURA.'')

> (MUSIC: ``THE GLASS MENAGERIE.'')

TOM. —Oh.—Laura . . .

AMANDA *(touching his sleeve)*. You know how Laura is. So quiet but—still water runs deep! She notices things and I think she—broods about them. *(TOM looks up.)* A few days ago I came in and she was crying.

TOM. What about?

AMANDA. You.

TOM. Me?

AMANDA. She has an idea that you're not happy here.

TOM. What gave her that idea?

AMANDA. What gives her any idea? However, you do act strangely. I—I'm not criticizing, understand *that!* I know your ambitions do not lie in the warehouse, that like everybody in the whole wide world—you've had to—make sacrifices, but—Tom—Tom—life's not easy, it calls for—Spartan endurance! There's so many things in my heart that I cannot describe to you! I've never told you but I—*loved* your father. . . .

TOM *(gently)*. I know that, Mother.

AMANDA. And you—when I see you taking after his ways! Staying out late—and—well, you *had* been drinking the night you were in that— terrifying condition! Laura says that you hate the apartment and that you go out nights to get away from it! Is that true, Tom?

TOM. No. You say there's so much in your heart that you can't describe to me. That's true of me, too. There's so much in my heart that I can't describe to *you!* So let's respect each other's—

AMANDA. But, why—*why,* Tom—are you always so *restless?* Where do you go to, nights?

TOM. I—go to the movies.

AMANDA. Why do you go to the movies so much, Tom?

TOM. I go to the movies because—I like adventure. Adventure is something I don't have much of at work, so I go to the movies.

AMANDA. But, Tom, you go to the movies *entirely* too *much!*

TOM. I like a lot of adventure.

AMANDA *looks baffled, then hurt. As the familiar inquisition resumes he becomes hard and impatient again.* AMANDA *slips back into her querulous attitude toward him.*

(IMAGE ON SCREEN: SAILING VESSEL WITH JOLLY ROGER.)

AMANDA. Most young men find adventure in their careers.

TOM. Then most young men are not employed in a warehouse.

AMANDA. The world is full of young men employed in warehouses and offices and factories.

TOM. Do all of them find adventure in their careers?

AMANDA. They do or they do without it! Not everybody has a craze for adventure.

TOM. Man is by instinct a lover, a hunter, a fighter, and none of those instincts are given much play at the warehouse!

AMANDA. Man is by instinct! Don't quote instinct to me! Instinct is something that people have got away from! It belongs to animals! Christian adults don't want it!

TOM. What do Christian adults want, then, Mother?

AMANDA. Superior things! Things of the mind and the spirit! Only animals have to satisfy instincts! Surely your aims are somewhat higher than theirs! Than monkeys—pigs—

TOM. I reckon they're not.

AMANDA. You're joking. However, that isn't what I wanted to discuss.

TOM *(rising).* I haven't much time.

AMANDA *(pushing his shoulders).* Sit down.

TOM. You want me to punch in red at the warehouse, Mother?

AMANDA. You have five minutes. I want to talk about Laura.

(LEGEND: ``PLANS AND PROVISIONS.'')

TOM. All right! What about Laura?

AMANDA. We have to be making plans and provisions for her. She's older than you, two years, and nothing has happened. She just drifts along doing nothing. It frightens me terribly how she just drifts along.

TOM. I guess she's the type that people call home-girls.

AMANDA. There's no such type, and if there is, it's a pity! That is unless the home is hers, with a husband!

TOM. What?

AMANDA. Oh, I can see the handwriting on the wall as plain as I see the nose in front of my face! It's terrifying! More and more you remind me of your father! He was out all hours without explanation—Then *left! Goodbye!* And me with a bag to hold. I saw that letter you got from the Merchant Marine. I know what you're dreaming of. I'm not standing here blindfolded. Very well, then. Then *do* it! But not till there's somebody to take your place.

Tom. What do you mean?

Amanda. I mean that as soon as Laura has got somebody to take care of her, married, a home of her own, independent—why, then you'll be free to go wherever you please, on land, on sea, whichever way the wind blows! But until that time you've got to look out for your sister. I don't say me because I'm old and don't matter! I say for your sister because she's young and dependent. I put her in business college— a dismal failure! Frightened her so it made her sick to her stomach. I took her over to the Young People's League at the church. Another fiasco. She spoke to nobody, nobody spoke to her. Now all she does is fool with those pieces of glass and play those worn-out records. What kind of a life is that for a girl to lead?

Tom. What can I do about it?

Amanda. Overcome selfishness! Self, self, self is all that you ever think of! (*Tom springs up and crosses to get his coat. It is ugly and bulky. He pulls on a cap with earmuffs.*) Where is your muffler? Put your wool muffler on! (*He snatches it angrily from the closet and tosses it around his neck and pulls both ends tight.*) Tom! I haven't said what I had in mind to ask you.

Tom. I'm too late to—

Amanda (*catching his arm.—very importunately. Then shyly*). Down at the warehouse, aren't there some—nice young men?

Tom. No!

Amanda. There *must* be—*some* . . .

Tom. Mother—

Gesture.

Amanda. Find out one that's clean-living—doesn't drink and—ask him out for sister!

Tom. What?

Amanda. For *sister!* To *meet!* Get *acquainted!*

Tom (*stamping to door*). Oh, my *go-osh!*

Amanda. Will you? (*He opens door. Imploringly.*) Will you? (*He starts down.*) Will you? *Will* you, dear?

Tom (*calling back*). YES!

Amanda *closes the door hesitantly and with a troubled but faintly hopeful expression.*

(SCREEN IMAGE: GLAMOR MAGAZINE COVER.)

Spot AMANDA *at phone.*

AMANDA. Ella Cartwright? This is Amanda Wingfield! How are you, honey? How is that kidney condition? *(Count five.)* Horrors! *(Count five.)* You're a Christian martyr, yes, honey, that's what you are, a Christian martyr! Well, I just happened to notice in my little red book that your subscription to the *Companion* has just run out! I know that you wouldn't want to miss out on the wonderful serial starting in this new issue. It's by Bessie Mae Hopper, the first thing she's written since *Honeymoon for Three.* Wasn't that a strange and interesting story? Well, this one is even lovelier, I believe. It has a sophisticated society background. It's all about the horsey set on Long Island!

(FADE OUT.)

Scene V

(LEGEND ON SCREEN: ``ANNUNCIATION.'')

Fade with music.

It is early dusk of a spring evening. Supper has just been finished in the Wingfield apartment. AMANDA *and* LAURA *in light colored dresses are removing dishes from the table, in the upstage area, which is shadowy, their movements formalized almost as a dance or ritual, their moving forms as pale and silent as moths.*

TOM, *in white shirt and trousers, rises from the table and crosses toward the fire-escape.*

AMANDA *(as he passes her).* Son, will you do me a favor?

TOM. What?

AMANDA. Comb your hair! You look so pretty when your hair is combed! *(*TOM *slouches on sofa with evening paper. Enormous caption ``Franco Triumphs.'')* There is only one respect in which I would like you to emulate your father.

TOM. What respect is that?

AMANDA. The care he always took of his appearance. He never allowed himself to look untidy. *(He throws down the paper and crosses to fire-escape.)* Where are you going?

TOM. I'm going out to smoke.

AMANDA. You smoke too much. A pack a day at fifteen cents a pack. How much would that amount to in a month? Thirty times fifteen is how much, Tom? Figure it out and you will be astounded at what you could save. Enough to give you a night-school course in accounting at Washington U! Just think what a wonderful thing that would be for you, son!

TOM *is unmoved by the thought.*

Tom. I'd rather smoke. *(He steps out on landing, letting the screen door slam.)*

Amanda *(sharply)*. I know! That's the tragedy of it. . . . *(Alone, she turns to look at her husband's picture.)*

(DANCE MUSIC: ``ALL THE WORLD IS WAITING FOR THE SUNRISE!'')

Tom *(to the audience)*. Across the alley from us was the Paradise Dance Hall. On evenings in spring the windows and doors were open and the music came outdoors. Sometimes the lights were turned out except for a large glass sphere that hung from the ceiling. It would turn slowly about and filter the dusk with delicate rainbow colors. Then the orchestra played a waltz or a tango, something that had a slow and sensuous rhythm. Couples would come outside, to the relative privacy of the alley. You could see them kissing behind ash-pits and telephone poles. This was the compensation for lives that passed like mine, without any change or adventure. Adventure and change were imminent in this year. They were waiting around the corner for all these kids. Suspended in the mist over Berchtesgaden, caught in the folds of Chamberlain's umbrella—In Spain there was Guernica! But here there was only hot swing music and liquor, dance halls, bars, and movies, and sex that hung in the gloom like a chandelier and flooded the world with brief, deceptive rainbows. . . . All the world was waiting for bombardments!

Amanda *turns from the picture and comes outside.*

Amanda *(sighing)*. A fire-escape landing's a poor excuse for a porch. *(She spreads a newspaper on a step and sits down, gracefully and demurely as if she were settling into a swing on a Mississippi veranda.)* What are you looking at?

Tom. The moon.

Amanda. Is there a moon this evening?

Tom. It's rising over Garfinkel's Delicatessen.

Amanda. So it is! A little silver slipper of a moon. Have you made a wish on it yet?

Tom. Um-hum.

Amanda. What did you wish for?

Tom. That's a secret.

Amanda. A secret, huh? Well, I won't tell mine either. I will be just as mysterious as you.

Tom. I bet I can guess what yours is.

Amanda. Is my head so transparent?

Tom. You're not a sphinx.

Amanda. No, I don't have secrets. I'll tell you what I wished for on the moon. Success and happiness for my precious children! I wish for that whenever there's moon, and when there isn't a moon, I wish for it, too.

TOM. I thought perhaps you wished for a gentleman caller.

AMANDA. Why do you say that?

TOM. Don't you remember asking me to fetch one?

AMANDA. I remember suggesting that it would be nice for your sister if you brought home some nice young man from the warehouse. I think I've made that suggestion more than once.

TOM. Yes, you have made it repeatedly.

AMANDA. Well?

TOM. We are going to have one.

AMANDA. *What?*

TOM. A gentleman caller!

(THE ANNUNCIATION IS CELEBRATED WITH MUSIC.)

AMANDA *rises.*

(IMAGE ON SCREEN: CALLER WITH BOUQUET.)

AMANDA. You mean you have asked some nice young man to come over?

TOM. Yep. I've asked him to dinner.

AMANDA. You really did?

TOM. I did!

AMANDA. You did, and did he—*accept?*

TOM. He did!

AMANDA. Well, well—well, well! That's—lovely!

TOM. I thought that you would be pleased.

AMANDA. It's definite, then?

TOM. Very definite.

AMANDA. Soon?

TOM. Very soon.

AMANDA. For heaven's sake, stop putting on and tell me some things, will you?

TOM. What things do you want me to tell you?

AMANDA. *Naturally* I would like to know when he's *coming!*

TOM. He's coming tomorrow.

AMANDA. *Tomorrow?*

TOM. Yep. Tomorrow.

AMANDA. But, Tom!

Tom. Yes, Mother?

Amanda. Tomorrow gives me no time!

Tom. Time for what?

Amanda. Preparations! Why didn't you phone me at once, as soon as you asked him, the minute that he accepted? Then, don't you see, I could have been getting ready!

Tom. You don't have to make any fuss.

Amanda. Oh, Tom, Tom, Tom, of course I have to make a fuss! I want things nice, not sloppy! Not thrown together. I'll certainly have to do some fast thinking, won't I?

Tom. I don't see why you have to think at all.

Amanda. You just don't know. We can't have a gentleman caller in a pig-sty! All my wedding silver has to be polished, the monogrammed table linen ought to be laundered! The windows have to be washed and fresh curtains put up. And how about clothes? We have to *wear* something, don't we?

Tom. Mother, this boy is no one to make a fuss over!

Amanda. Do you realize he's the first young man we've introduced to your sister? It's terrible, dreadful, disgraceful that poor little sister has never received a single gentleman caller! Tom, come inside! *(She opens the screen door.)*

Tom. What for?

Amanda. I want to ask you some things.

Tom. If you're going to make such a fuss, I'll call it off, I'll tell him not to come.

Amanda. You certainly won't do anything of the kind. Nothing offends people worse than broken engagements. It simply means I'll have to work like a Turk! We won't be brilliant, but we'll pass inspection. Come on inside. *(Tom follows, groaning.)* Sit down.

Tom. Any particular place you would like me to sit?

Amanda. Thank heavens I've got that new sofa! I'm also making payments on a floor lamp I'll have sent out! And put the chintz covers on, they'll brighten things up! Of course I'd hoped to have these walls re-papered. . . . What is the young man's name?

Tom. His name is O'Connor.

Amanda. That, of course, means fish—tomorrow is Friday! I'll have that salmon loaf—with Durkee's dressing! What does he do? He works at the warehouse?

Tom. Of course! How else would I—

Amanda. Tom, he—doesn't drink?

Tom. Why do you ask me that?

AMANDA. Your father *did!*

TOM. Don't get started on that!

AMANDA. He *does* drink, then?

TOM. Not that I know of!

AMANDA. Make sure, be certain! The last thing I want for my daughter's a boy who drinks!

TOM. Aren't you being a little premature? Mr. O'Connor has not yet appeared on the scene!

AMANDA. But will tomorrow. To meet your sister, and what do I know about his character? Nothing! Old maids are better off than wives of drunkards!

TOM. Oh, my God!

AMANDA. Be still!

TOM *(leaning forward to whisper).* Lots of fellows meet girls whom they don't marry!

AMANDA. Oh, talk sensibly, Tom—and don't be sarcastic! *(She has gotten a hairbrush.)*

TOM. What are you doing?

AMANDA. I'm brushing that cow-lick down! What is this young man's position at the warehouse?

TOM *(submitting grimly to the brush and the interrogation).* This young man's position is that of a shipping clerk, Mother.

AMANDA. Sounds to me like a fairly responsible job, the sort of a job *you* would be in if you just had more *get-up.* What is his salary? Have you got any idea?

TOM. I would judge it to be approximately eighty-five dollars a month.

AMANDA. Well—not princely, but—

TOM. Twenty more than I make.

AMANDA. Yes, how well I know! But for a family man, eighty-five dollars a month is not much more than you can just get by on. . . .

TOM. Yes, but Mr. O'Connor is not a family man.

AMANDA. He might be, mightn't he? Some time in the future?

TOM. I see. Plans and provisions.

AMANDA. You are the only young man that I know of who ignores the fact that the future becomes the present, the present the past, and the past turns into everlasting regret if you don't plan for it!

TOM. I will think that over and see what I can make of it.

AMANDA. Don't be supercilious with your mother! Tell me some more about this—what do you call him?

TOM. James D. O'Connor. The D. is for Delaney.

AMANDA. Irish on *both* sides! *Gracious!* And doesn't drink?

TOM. Shall I call him up and ask him right this minute?

AMANDA. The only way to find out about those things is to make discreet inquiries at the proper moment. When I was a girl in Blue Mountain and it was suspected that a young man drank, the girl whose attentions he had been receiving, if any girl *was,* would sometimes speak to the minister of his church, or rather her father would if her father was living, and sort of feel him out on the young man's character. That is the way such things are discreetly handled to keep a young woman from making a tragic mistake!

TOM. Then how did you happen to make a tragic mistake?

AMANDA. That innocent look of your father's had everyone fooled! He *smiled*—the world was *enchanted!* No girl can do worse than put herself at the mercy of a handsome appearance! I hope that Mr. O'Connor is not too good-looking.

TOM. No, he's not too good-looking. He's covered with freckles and hasn't too much of a nose.

AMANDA. He's not right-down homely, though?

TOM. Not right-down homely. Just medium homely. I'd say.

AMANDA. Character's what to look for in a man.

TOM. That's what I've always said, Mother.

AMANDA. You've never said anything of the kind and I suspect you would never give it a thought.

TOM. Don't be suspicious of me.

AMANDA. At least I hope he's the type that's up and coming.

TOM. I think he really goes in for self-improvement.

AMANDA. What reason have you to think so?

TOM. He goes to night school.

AMANDA *(beaming).* Splendid! What does he do, I mean study?

TOM. Radio engineering and public speaking!

AMANDA. Then he has visions of being advanced in the world! Any young man who studies public speaking is aiming to have an executive job some day! And radio engineering? A thing for the future! Both of these facts are very illuminating. Those are the sort of things that a mother should know concerning any young man who comes to call on her daughter. Seriously or—not.

TOM. One little warning. He doesn't know about Laura. I didn't let on that we had dark ulterior motives. I just said, why don't you come have dinner with us? He said okay and that was the whole conversation.

AMANDA. I bet it was! You're eloquent as an oyster. However, he'll know about Laura when he gets here. When he sees how lovely and sweet and pretty she is, he'll thank his lucky stars he was asked to dinner.

Tom. Mother, you mustn't expect too much of Laura.

Amanda. What do you mean?

Tom. Laura seems all those things to you and me because she's ours and we love her. We don't even notice she's crippled any more.

Amanda. Don't say crippled! You know that I never allow that word to be used!

Tom. But face facts, Mother. She is and—that's not all—

Amanda. What do you mean "not all"?

Tom. Laura is very different from other girls.

Amanda. I think the difference is all to her advantage.

Tom. Not quite all—in the eyes of others—strangers—she's terribly shy and lives in a world of her own and those things make her seem a little peculiar to people outside the house.

Amanda. Don't say peculiar.

Tom. Face the facts. She is.

(THE DANCE-HALL MUSIC CHANGES TO A TANGO THAT HAS A MINOR AND SOMEWHAT OMINOUS TONE.)

Amanda. In what way is she peculiar—may I ask?

Tom (gently). She lives in a world of her own—a world of—little glass ornaments, Mother. . . . (Gets up. AMANDA remains holding brush, looking at him, troubled.) She plays old phonograph records and—that's about all—(He glances at himself in the mirror and crosses to door.)

Amanda (sharply). Where are you going?

Tom. I'm going to the movies. (Out screen door.)

Amanda. Not to the movies, every night to the movies! (Follows quickly to screen door.) I don't believe you always go to the movies! (He is gone. AMANDA looks worriedly after him for a moment. Then vitality and optimism return and she turns from the door. Crossing to portieres.) Laura! Laura! (LAURA answers from kitchenette.)

Laura. Yes, Mother.

Amanda. Let those dishes go and come in front! (LAURA appears with dish towel. Gaily.) Laura, come here and make a wish on the moon!

Laura (entering). Moon—moon?

Amanda. A little silver slipper of a moon. Look over your left shoulder, Laura, and make a wish! (LAURA looks faintly puzzled as if called out *of sleep.* AMANDA *seizes her shoulders and turns her at an angle by the door.)* No! Now, darling, *wish!*

LAURA. What shall I wish for, Mother?

AMANDA *(her voice trembling and her eyes suddenly filling with tears).* Happiness! Good Fortune!

The violin rises and the stage dims out.

Scene VI

(IMAGE: HIGH-SCHOOL HERO.)

TOM. And so the following evening I brought Jim home to dinner. I had known Jim slightly in high school. In high school Jim was a hero. He had tremendous Irish good nature and vitality with the scrubbed and polished look of white chinaware. He seemed to move in a continual spotlight. He was a star in basketball, captain of the debating club, president of the senior class and the glee club and he sang the male lead in the annual light operas. He was always running or bounding, never just walking. He seemed always at the point of defeating the law of gravity. He was shooting with such velocity through his adolescence that you would logically expect him to arrive at nothing short of the White House by the time he was thirty. But Jim apparently ran into more interference after his graduation from Soldan. His speed had definitely slowed. Six years after he left high school he was holding a job that wasn't much better than mine.

(IMAGE: CLERK.)

He was the only one at the warehouse with whom I was on friendly terms. I was valuable to him as someone who could remember his former glory, who had seen him win basketball games and the silver cup in debating. He knew of my secret practice of retiring to a cabinet of the washroom to work on poems when business was slack in the warehouse. He called me Shakespeare. And while the other boys in the warehouse regarded me with suspicious hostility, Jim took a humorous attitude toward me. Gradually his attitude affected the others, their hostility wore off and they also began to smile at me as people smile at an oddly fashioned dog who trots across their path at some distance.

I knew that Jim and Laura had known each other at Soldan, and I had heard Laura speak admiringly of his voice. I didn't know if Jim remembered her or not. In high school Laura had been as unobtrusive as Jim had been astonishing. If he did remember Laura, it was not as my sister, for when I asked him to dinner, he grinned and said, "You know, Shakespeare, I never thought of you as having folks!"

He was about to discover that I did. . . .

(LIGHT UP STAGE.)

(LEGEND ON SCREEN: "THE ACCENT OF A COMING FOOT.")

Friday evening. It is about five o'clock of a late spring evening which comes "scattering poems in the sky."

A delicate lemony light is in the Wingfield apartment.

AMANDA *has worked like a Turk in preparation for the gentleman caller. The results are astonishing. The new floor lamp with its rose-silk shade is in place, a colored paper lantern conceals the broken light fixture in the ceiling, new billowing white curtains are at the windows, chintz covers are on chairs and sofa, a pair of new sofa pillows make their initial appearance.*

Open boxes and tissue paper are scattered on the floor.

LAURA *stands in the middle with lifted arms while* AMANDA *crouches before her, adjusting the hem of the new dress, devout and ritualistic. The dress is colored and designed by memory. The arrangement of* LAURA*'s hair is changed; it is softer and more becoming. A fragile, unearthly prettiness has come out in* LAURA*: she is like a piece of translucent glass touched by light, given a momentary radiance, not actual, not lasting.*

AMANDA *(impatiently).* Why are you trembling?

LAURA. Mother, you've made me so nervous!

AMANDA. How have I made you nervous?

LAURA. By all this fuss! You make it seem so important!

AMANDA. I don't understand you, Laura. You couldn't be satisfied with just sitting home, and yet whenever I try to arrange something for you, you seem to resist it. *(She gets up.)* Now take a look at yourself. No, wait! Wait just a moment—I have an idea!

LAURA. What is it now?

AMANDA *produces two powder puffs which she wraps in handkerchiefs and stuffs in* LAURA*'s bosom.*

LAURA. Mother, what are you doing?

AMANDA. They call them "Gay Deceivers"!

LAURA. I won't wear them!

AMANDA. You will!

LAURA. Why should I?

AMANDA. Because, to be painfully honest, your chest is flat.

LAURA. You make it seem like we were setting a trap.

AMANDA. All pretty girls are a trap, a pretty trap, and men expect them to be. (LEGEND: ``A PRETTY TRAP.'') Now look at yourself, young lady. This is the prettiest you will ever be! I've got to fix myself now! You're going to be surprised by your mother's appearance! *(She crosses through portieres, humming gaily.)*

LAURA *moves slowly to the long mirror and stares solemnly at herself.*

A wind blows the white curtains inward in a slow, graceful motion and with a faint, sorrowful sighing.

AMANDA *(off stage).* It isn't dark enough yet. *(She turns slowly before the mirror with a troubled look.)*

(LEGEND ON SCREEN: ``THIS IS MY SISTER: CELEBRATE HER WITH STRINGS!'' MUSIC.)

AMANDA *(laughing, off).* I'm going to show you something. I'm going to make a spectacular appearance!

LAURA. What is it, mother?

AMANDA. Possess your soul in patience—you will see! Something I've res-urrected from that old trunk! Styles haven't changed so terribly much after all. . . . *(She parts the portieres.)* Now just look at your mother! *(She wears a girlish frock of yellowed voile with a blue silk sash. She carries a bunch of jonquils—the legend of her youth is nearly revived. Feverishly.)* This is the dress in which I led the cotil-lion. Won the cakewalk twice at Sunset Hill, wore one spring to the Governor's ball in Jackson! See how I sashayed around the ball-room, Laura? *(She raises her skirt and does a mincing step around the room.)* I wore it on Sundays for my gentlemen callers! I had it on the day I met your father—I had malaria fever all that spring. The change of climate from East Tennessee to the Delta—weakened resistance—I had a little temperature all the time—not enough to be serious—just enough to make me restless and giddy! Invitations poured in—parties all over the Delta!—``Stay in bed,'' said Mother, ``you have fever!''—but I just wouldn't.—I took quinine but kept on going, going!—Evenings, dances!—Afternoons, long, long rides! Picnics—lovely!—So lovely, that country in May.—All lacy with dog-wood, literally flooded with jonquils!—That was the spring I had the craze for jonquils. Jonquils became an absolute obsession. Mother said, ``Honey, there's no more room for jonquils.'' And still I kept bringing in more jonquils. Whenever, wherever I saw them, I'd say, ``Stop! Stop! I see jonquils!'' I made the young men help me gather the jonquils! It was a joke, Amanda and her jonquils! Finally there were no more vases to hold them, every available space was filled with jonquils. No vases to hold them? All right, I'll hold them myself! And then I—*(She stops in front of the picture.* MUSIC.*)* met your father! Malaria fever and jonquils and then—this—boy. . . . *(She switches on the rose-colored lamp.)* I hope they get here before it starts to rain. *(She crosses upstage and places the jonquils in bowl on table.)*

I gave your brother a little extra change so he and Mr. O'Connor could take the service car home.

LAURA *(with altered look)*. What did you say his name was?

AMANDA. O'Connor.

LAURA. What is his first name?

AMANDA. I don't remember. Oh, yes, I do. It was—Jim!

LAURA *sways slightly and catches hold of a chair.*

(LEGEND ON SCREEN: ``NOT JIM!'')

LAURA *(faintly)*. Not—Jim!

AMANDA. Yes, that was it, it was Jim! I've never known a Jim that wasn't nice!

(MUSIC: OMINOUS.)

LAURA. Are you sure his name is Jim O'Connor?

AMANDA. Yes. Why?

LAURA. Is he the one that Tom used to know in high school?

AMANDA. He didn't say so. I think he just got to know him at the warehouse.

LAURA. There was a Jim O'Connor we both knew in high school— *(Then, with effort.)* If that is the one that Tom is bringing to dinner—you'll have to excuse me, I won't come to the table.

AMANDA. What sort of nonsense is this?

LAURA. You asked me once if I'd ever liked a boy. Don't you remember I showed you this boy's picture?

AMANDA. You mean the boy you showed me in the year-book?

LAURA. Yes, that boy.

AMANDA. Laura, Laura, were you in love with that boy?

LAURA. I don't know, Mother. All I know is I couldn't sit at the table if it was him!

AMANDA. It won't be him! It isn't the least bit likely. But whether it is or not, you will come to the table. You will not be excused.

LAURA. I'll have to be, Mother.

AMANDA. I don't intend to humor your silliness, Laura. I've had too much from you and your brother, both! So just sit down and compose yourself till they come. Tom has forgotten his key so you'll have to let them in, when they arrive.

LAURA *(panicky)*. Oh, Mother—*you* answer the door!

AMANDA *(lightly)*. I'll be in the kitchen—busy!

LAURA. Oh, Mother, please answer the door, don't make me do it!

AMANDA *(crossing into kitchenette).* I've got to fix the dressing for the salmon. Fuss, fuss—silliness!—over a gentleman caller!

Door swings shut. LAURA *is left alone.*

(LEGEND: ``TERROR!'')

She utters a low moan and turns off the lamp—sits stiffly on the edge of the sofa, knotting her fingers together.

(LEGEND ON SCREEN: ``THE OPENING OF A DOOR!'')

TOM *and* JIM *appear on the fire-escape steps and climb to landing. Hearing their approach,* LAURA *rises with a panicky gesture. She retreats to the portieres.*

The doorbell. LAURA *catches her breath and touches her throat. Low drums.*

AMANDA *(calling).* Laura, sweetheart! The door!

LAURA *stares at it without moving.*

JIM. I think we just beat the rain.

TOM. Uh-huh. *(He rings again, nervously.* JIM *whistles and fishes for a cigarette.)*

AMANDA *(very, very gaily).* Laura, that is your brother and Mr. O'Connor! Will you let them in, darling?

LAURA *crosses toward kitchenette door.*

LAURA *(breathlessly).* Mother—you go to the door!

AMANDA *steps out of kitchenette and stares furiously at* LAURA. *She points imperiously at the door.*

LAURA. Please, please!

AMANDA *(in a fierce whisper).* What is the matter with you, you silly thing?

LAURA *(desperately).* Please, you answer it, *please!*

AMANDA. I told you I wasn't going to humor you, Laura. Why have you chosen this moment to lose your mind?

LAURA. Please, please, please, you go!

AMANDA. You'll have to go the door because I can't!

LAURA *(despairingly).* I can't either!

AMANDA. Why?

LAURA. I'm *sick!*

AMANDA. I'm sick, too—of your nonsense! Why can't you and your brother be normal people? Fantastic whims and behavior! *(TOM gives a long ring.)* Preposterous goings on! Can you give me one reason—*(Calls out lyrically.)* COMING! JUST ONE SECOND!—why should you be afraid to open a door? Now you answer it, Laura!

Laura. Oh, oh, oh . . . *(She returns through the portieres. Darts to the victrola and winds it frantically and turns it on.)*

Amanda. Laura Wingfield, you march right to that door!

Laura. Yes—yes, Mother!

A faraway, scratchy rendition of ``Dardanella'' softens the air and gives her strength to move through it. She slips to the door and draws it cautiously open.

 Tom *enters with the caller,* Jim O'Connor.

Tom. Laura, this is Jim. Jim, this is my sister, Laura.

Jim *(stepping inside).* I didn't know that Shakespeare had a sister!

Laura *(retreating stiff and trembling from the door).* How—how do you do?

Jim *(heartily extending his hand).* Okay!

Laura *touches it hesitantly with hers.*

Jim. Your hand's *cold,* Laura!

Laura. Yes, well—I've been playing the victrola. . . .

Jim. Must have been playing classical music on it! You ought to play a little hot swing music to warm you up!

Laura. Excuse me—I haven't finished playing the victrola. . . .

She turns awkwardly and hurries into the front room. She pauses a second by the victrola. Then catches her breath and darts through the portieres like a frightened deer.

Jim *(grinning).* What was the matter?

Tom. Oh—with Laura? Laura is—terribly shy.

Jim. Shy, huh? It's unusual to meet a shy girl nowadays. I don't believe you ever mentioned you had a sister.

Tom. Well, now you know. I have one. Here is the *Post Dispatch.* You want a piece of it?

Jim. Uh-huh.

Tom. What piece? The comics?

Jim. Sports! *(Glances at it.)* Ole Dizzy Dean is on his bad behavior.

Tom *(disinterest).* Yeah? *(Lights cigarette and crosses back to fire-escape door.)*

Jim. Where are *you* going?

Tom. I'm going out on the terrace.

Jim *(goes after him).* You know, Shakespeare—I'm going to sell you a bill of goods!

Tom. What goods?

Jim. A course I'm taking.

Tom. Huh?

JIM. In public speaking! You and me, we're not the warehouse type.

TOM. Thanks—that's good news. But what has public speaking got to do with it?

JIM. It fits you for—executive positions!

TOM. Awww.

JIM. I tell you it's done a helluva lot for me.

(IMAGE: EXECUTIVE AT DESK.)

TOM. In what respect?

JIM. In every! Ask yourself what is the difference between you an' me and men in the office down front? Brains?—No!—Ability?—No! Then what? Just one little thing—

TOM. What is that one little thing?

JIM. Primarily it amounts to—social poise! Being able to square up to people and hold your own on any social level!

AMANDA (off stage). Tom?

TOM. Yes, Mother?

AMANDA. Is that you and Mr. O'Connor?

TOM. Yes, Mother.

AMANDA. Well, you just make yourselves comfortable in there.

TOM. Yes, Mother.

AMANDA. Ask Mr. O'Connor if he would like to wash his hands.

JIM. Aw—no—no—thank you—I took care of that at the warehouse. Tom.—

TOM. Yes?

JIM. Mr. Mendoza was speaking to me about you.

TOM. Favorably?

JIM. What do you think?

TOM. Well—

JIM. You're going to be out of a job if you don't wake up.

TOM. I am waking up—

JIM. You show no signs.

TOM. The signs are interior.

(IMAGE ON SCREEN: THE SAILING VESSEL WITH JOLLY ROGER AGAIN.)

TOM. I'm planning to change. (He leans over the rail speaking with quiet exhilaration. The incandescent marquees and signs of the first-run movie houses light his face from across the alley. He looks like a voyager.) I'm right at the point of committing myself to a future that doesn't include the warehouse and Mr. Mendoza or even a night-school course in public speaking.

JIM. What are you gassing about?

TOM. I'm tired of the movies.

JIM. Movies!

TOM. Yes, movies! Look at them—*(A wave toward the marvels of Grand Avenue.)* All of those glamorous people—having adventures—hogging it all, gobbling the whole thing up! You know what happens? People go to the *movies* instead of *moving!* Hollywood characters are supposed to have all the adventures for everybody in America, while everybody in America sits in a dark room and watches them have them! Yes, until there's a war. That's when adventure becomes available to the masses! *Everyone's* dish, not only Gable's! Then the people in the dark room come out of the dark room to have some adventures themselves—Goody, goody!—It's our turn now, to go to the South Sea Island—to make a safari—to be exotic, far-off!—But I'm not patient. I don't want to wait till then. I'm tired of the *movies* and I am *about* to *move!*

JIM *(incredulously).* Move?

TOM. Yes.

JIM. When?

TOM. Soon!

JIM. Where? Where?

> (THEME THREE MUSIC SEEMS TO ANSWER THE QUESTION, WHILE TOM THINKS IT OVER. HE SEARCHES AMONG HIS POCKETS.)

TOM. I'm starting to boil inside. I know I seem dreamy, but inside—well, I'm boiling! Whenever I pick up a shoe, I shudder a little thinking how short life is and what I am doing!—Whatever that means. I know it doesn't mean shoes—except as something to wear on a traveler's feet! *(Finds paper.)* Look—

JIM. What?

TOM. I'm a member.

JIM *(reading).* The Union of Merchant Seamen.

TOM. I paid my dues this month, instead of the light bill.

JIM. You will regret it when they turn the lights off.

TOM. I won't be here.

JIM. How about your mother?

TOM. I'm like my father. The bastard son of a bastard! See how he grins? And he's been absent going on sixteen years!

JIM. You're just talking, you drip. How does your mother feel about it?

TOM. Shhh!—Here comes Mother! Mother is not acquainted with my plans!

AMANDA *(enters portieres).* Where are you all?

TOM. On the terrace, Mother.

They start inside. She advances to them. Tom is distinctly shocked at her appearance. Even Jim blinks a little. He is making his first contact with girlish Southern vivacity and in spite of the high-school course in public speaking is somewhat thrown off the beam by the unexpected outlay of social charm.

Certain responses are attempted by Jim but are swept aside by Amanda's gay laughter and chatter. Tom is embarrassed but after the first shock Jim reacts very warmly. Grins and chuckles, is altogether won over.

(IMAGE: AMANDA AS A GIRL.)

Amanda *(coyly smiling, shaking her girlish ringlets).* Well, well, well, so this is Mr. O'Connor. Introductions entirely unnecessary. I've heard so much about you from my boy. I finally said to him, Tom—good gracious!—why don't you bring this paragon to supper! I'd like to meet this nice young man at the warehouse!—Instead of just hearing him sing your praises so much! I don't know why my son is so standoffish—that's not Southern behavior! Let's sit down and—I think we could stand a little more air in here! Tom, leave the door open. I felt a nice fresh breeze a moment ago. Where has it gone? Mmm, so warm already! And not quite summer, even. We're going to burn up when summer really gets started. However, we've having a very light supper. I think light things are better fo' this time of year. The same as light clothes are. Light clothes an' light food are what warm weather calls fo'. You know our blood gets so thick during th' winter—it takes a while fo' us to *adjust* ou'selves!—when the season changes . . . It's come so quick this year. I wasn't prepared. All of a sudden—heavens! Already summer!—I ran to the trunk an' pulled out this light dress—Terribly old! Historical almost! But feels so good—so good an' co-ol, y'know . . . .

Tom. Mother—

Amanda. Yes, honey?

Tom. How about—supper?

Amanda. Honey, you go ask Sister if supper is ready! You know that Sister is in full charge of supper! Tell her you hungry boys are waiting for it. *(To Jim.)* Have you met Laura?

Jim. She—

Amanda. Let you in? Oh, good, you've met already! It's rare for a girl as sweet an' pretty as Laura to be domestic! But Laura is, thank heavens, not only pretty but also very domestic. I'm not at all. I never was a bit. I never could make a thing but angel-food cake. Well, in the South we had so many servants. Gone, gone, gone. All vestige of gracious living! Gone completely! I wasn't prepared for what the future brought me. All of my gentlemen callers were sons of planters and so of course I assumed that I would be married to one and raise my family on a large piece of land with plenty of servants. But man proposes—and woman accepts the proposal!—To vary that old, old saying a little bit—I married no planter! I married a man who worked for the telephone company!—That gallantly smiling gentleman over there! *(Points to the picture.)* A telephone man who—fell in love with long-distance!—Now he travels and I don't even know where!—But what am I going on for about my—tribulations? Tell me yours—I hope you don't have any! Tom?

TOM *(returning)*. Yes, Mother?

AMANDA. Is supper nearly ready?

TOM. It looks to me like supper is on the table.

AMANDA. Let me look—*(She rises prettily and looks through portieres.)* Oh, lovely!—But where is Sister?

TOM. Laura is not feeling well and she says that she thinks she'd better not come to the table.

AMANDA. What?—Nonsense!—Laura? Oh, Laura!

LAURA *(off stage, faintly)*. Yes, Mother.

AMANDA. You really must come to the table. We won't be seated until you come to the table? Come in, Mr. O'Connor. You sit over there and I'll—Laura? Laura Wingfield! You're keeping us waiting, honey! We can't say grace until you come to the table!

The back door is pushed weakly open and LAURA *comes in. She is obviously quite faint, her lips trembling, her eyes wide and staring. She moves unsteadily toward the table.*

(LEGEND: ``TERROR!'')

Outside a summer storm is coming abruptly. The white curtains billow inward at the windows and there is a sorrowful murmur and deep blue dusk.

LAURA *suddenly stumbles—she catches at a chair with a faint moan.*

TOM. Laura!

AMANDA. Laura! *(There is a clap of thunder.)* (LEGEND: ``AH!'') *(Despairingly.)* Why, Laura, you *are* sick, darling! Tom, help your sister into the living room, dear! Sit in the living room, Laura—rest on the sofa. Well! *(To the gentleman caller.)* Standing over the hot stove made her ill!— I told her that it was just too warm this evening, but—*(*TOM *comes back in.* LAURA *is on the sofa.)* Is Laura all right now?

TOM. Yes.

AMANDA. What *is* that? Rain? A nice cool rain has come up! *(She gives the gentleman caller a frightened look.)* I think we may—have grace— now . . . *(*TOM *looks at her stupidly.)* Tom, honey—you say grace!

TOM. Oh . . . ``For these and all thy mercies—'' *(They bow their heads,* AMANDA *stealing a nervous glance at* JIM. *In the living room* LAURA, *stretched on the sofa, clenches her hand to her lips, to hold back a shuddering sob.)* God's Holy Name be praised—

(THE SCENE DIMS OUT.)

Scene VII

(LEGEND: ``A SOUVENIR.'')

Half an hour later. Dinner is just being finished in the upstage area which is concealed by the drawn portieres.

As the curtain rises LAURA *is still huddled upon the sofa, her feet drawn under her, her head resting on a pale blue pillow, her eyes wide and mysteriously watchful. The new floor lamp with its shade of rose-colored silk gives a soft, becoming light to her face, bringing out the fragile, unearthly prettiness which usually escapes attention. There is a steady murmur of rain, but it is slackening and stops soon after the scene begins; the air outside becomes pale and luminous as the moon breaks out.*

A moment after the curtain rises, the lights in both rooms flicker and go out.

JIM. Hey, there, Mr. Light Bulb!

AMANDA *laughs nervously.*

(LEGEND: ``SUSPENSION OF A PUBLIC SERVICE.'')

AMANDA. Where was Moses when the lights went out? Ha-ha. Do you know the answer to that one, Mr. O'Connor?

JIM. No, Ma'am, what's the answer?

AMANDA. In the dark! *(JIM laughs appreciatively.)* Everybody sit still. I'll light the candles. Isn't it lucky we have them on the table? Where's a match? Which of you gentlemen can provide a match?

JIM. Here.

AMANDA. Thank you, sir.

JIM. Not at all, Ma'am!

AMANDA. I guess the fuse has burnt out. Mr. O'Connor, can you tell a burnt-out fuse? I know I can't and Tom is a total loss when it comes to mechanics. (SOUND: GETTING UP: VOICES RECEDE A LITTLE TO KITCHENETTE.) Oh, be careful you don't bump into something. We don't want our gentleman caller to break his neck. Now wouldn't that be a fine howdy-do?

JIM. Ha-ha! Where is the fuse-box?

AMANDA. Right here next to the stove. Can you see anything?

JIM. Just a minute.

AMANDA. Isn't electricity a mysterious thing? Wasn't it Benjamin Franklin who tied a key to a kite? We live in such a mysterious universe, don't we? Some people say that science clears up all the mysteries for us. In my opinion it only creates more! Have you found it yet?

JIM. No, Ma'am. All these fuses look okay to me.

AMANDA. Tom!

TOM. Yes, Mother?

AMANDA. That light bill I gave you several days ago. The one I told you we got the notices about?

TOM. Oh.—Yeah.

(LEGEND: ``HA!'')

AMANDA. You didn't neglect to pay it by any chance?

TOM. Why, I—

AMANDA. Didn't! I might have known it!

JIM. Shakespeare probably wrote a poem on that light bill, Mrs. Wingfield.

AMANDA. I might have known better than to trust him with it! There's such a high price for negligence in this world!

JIM. Maybe the poem will win a ten-dollar prize.

AMANDA. We'll just have to spend the remainder of the evening in the nineteenth century, before Mr. Edison made the Mazda lamp!

JIM. Candlelight is my favorite kind of light.

AMANDA. That shows you're romantic! But that's no excuse for Tom. Well, we got through dinner. Very considerate of them to let us get through dinner before they plunged us into everlasting darkness, wasn't it, Mr. O'Connor?

JIM. Ha-ha!

AMANDA. Tom, as a penalty for your carelessness you can help me with the dishes.

JIM. Let me give you a hand.

AMANDA. Indeed you will not!

JIM. I ought to be good for something.

AMANDA. Good for something? (Her tone is rhapsodic.) You? Why, Mr. O'Connor, nobody, *nobody's* given me this much entertainment in years—as you have!

JIM. Aw, now, Mrs. Wingfield!

AMANDA. I'm not exaggerating, not one bit! But Sister is all by her lonesome. You go keep her company in the parlor! I'll give you this lovely old candelabrum that used to be on the altar at the church of the Heavenly Rest. It was melted a little out of shape when the church burnt down. Lightning struck it one spring. Gypsy Jones was holding a revival at the time and he intimated that the church was destroyed because the Episcopalians gave card parties.

JIM. Ha-ha.

AMANDA. And how about coaxing Sister to drink a little wine? I think it would be good for her! Can you carry both at once?

JIM. Sure. I'm Superman!

AMANDA. Now, Thomas, get into this apron!

The door of kitchenette swings closed on AMANDA*'s gay laughter; the flickering light approaches the portieres.*

LAURA sits up nervously as he enters. Her speech at first is low and breathless from the almost intolerable strain of being alone with a stranger.*

    (THE LEGEND: ''I DON'T SUPPOSE YOU REMEMBER ME AT ALL!'')

In her first speeches in this scene, before JIM*'s warmth overcomes her paralyzing shyness,* LAURA*'s voice is thin and breathless as though she has just run up a steep flight of stairs.*

    JIM's attitude is gently humorous. In playing this scene it should be stressed that while the incident is apparently unimportant, it is to* LAURA *the climax of her secret life.*

JIM. Hello, there, Laura.

LAURA *(faintly).* Hello. *(She clears her throat.)*

JIM. How are you feeling now? Better?

LAURA. Yes. Yes, thank you.

JIM. This is for you. A little dandelion wine. *(He extends it toward her with extravagant gallantry.)*

LAURA. Thank you.

JIM. Drink it—but don't get drunk! *(He laughs heartily.* LAURA *takes the glass uncertainly; laughs shyly.)* Where shall I set the candles?

LAURA. Oh—oh, anywhere . . .

JIM. How about here on the floor? Any objections?

LAURA. No.

JIM. I'll spread a newspaper under to catch the drippings. I like to sit on the floor. Mind if I do?

LAURA. Oh, no.

JIM. Give me a pillow?

LAURA. What?

JIM. A pillow!

LAURA. Oh . . . *(Hands him one quickly.)*

JIM. How about you? Don't you like to sit on the floor?

LAURA. Oh—yes.

JIM. Why don't you, then?

LAURA. I—will.

JIM. Take a pillow! *(LAURA does. Sits on the other side of the candelabrum. JIM crosses his legs and smiles engagingly at her.)* I can't hardly see you sitting way over there.

LAURA. I can—see you.

JIM. I know, but that's not fair, I'm in the limelight. *(LAURA moves her pillow closer.)* Good! Now I can see you! Comfortable?

LAURA. Yes.

JIM. So am I. Comfortable as a cow. Will you have some gum?

LAURA. No, thank you.

JIM. I think that I will indulge, with your permission. *(Musingly unwraps it and holds it up.)* Think of the fortune made by the guy that invented the first piece of chewing gum. Amazing, huh? The Wrigley Building is one of the sights of Chicago.—I saw it summer before last when I went up to the Century of Progress. Did you take in the Century of Progress?

LAURA. No, I didn't.

JIM. Well, it was quite a wonderful exposition. What impressed me most was the Hall of Science. Gives you an idea of what the future will be in America, even more wonderful than the present time is! *(Pause. Smiling at her.)* Your brother tells me you're shy. Is that right, Laura?

LAURA. I—don't know.

JIM. I judge you to be an old-fashioned type of girl. Well, I think that's a pretty good type to be. Hope you don't think I'm being too per-sonal—do you?

LAURA *(hastily, out of embarrassment)*. I believe I *will* take a piece of gum, if you—don't mind. *(Clearing her throat.)* Mr. O'Connor, have you—kept up with your singing?

JIM. Singing? Me?

LAURA. Yes. I remember what a beautiful voice you had.

JIM. When did you hear me sing?

(VOICE OFF STAGE IN THE PAUSE.)

VOICE *(off stage)*

> O blow, ye winds, heigh-ho,
> A-roving I will go!
> I'm off to my love
> With a boxing glove—
> Ten thousand miles away!

JIM. You say you've heard me sing?

LAURA. Oh, yes! Yes, very often . . . I—don't suppose you remember me—at all?

JIM *(smiling doubtfully)*. You know I have an idea I've seen you before. I had that idea soon as you opened the door. It seemed almost like I was about to remember your name. But the name that I started to call you—wasn't a name! And so I stopped myself before I said it.

LAURA. Wasn't it—Blue Roses?

JIM *(springs up, grinning)*. Blue Roses! My gosh, yes—Blue Roses! That's what I had on my tongue when you opened the door! Isn't it funny what tricks your memory plays? I didn't connect you with the high school somehow or other. But that's where it was; it was high school. I didn't even know you were Shakespeare's sister! Gosh, I'm sorry.

LAURA. I didn't expect you to. You—barely knew me!

JIM. But we did have a speaking acquaintance, huh?

LAURA. Yes, we—spoke to each other.

JIM. When did you recognize me?

LAURA. Oh, right away!

JIM. Soon as I came in the door?

LAURA. When I heard your name I thought it was probably you. I knew that Tom used to know you a little in high school. So when you came in the door—Well, then I was—sure.

JIM. Why didn't you *say* something, then?

LAURA *(breathlessly)*. I didn't know what to say, I was—too surprised!

JIM. For goodness' sakes! You know, this sure is funny!

LAURA. Yes! Yes, isn't it, though . . .

JIM. Didn't we have a class in something together?

LAURA. Yes, we did.

JIM. What class was that?

LAURA. It was—singing—Chorus!

JIM. Aw!

LAURA. I sat across the aisle from you in the Aud.

JIM. Aw.

LAURA. Monday, Wednesdays and Fridays.

JIM. Now I remember—you always came in late.

LAURA. Yes, it was so hard for me, getting upstairs. I had that brace on my leg—it clumped so loud!

JIM. I never heard any clumping.

LAURA *(wincing at the recollection)*. To me it sounded like—thunder!

JIM. Well, well, well. I never even noticed.

LAURA. And everybody was seated before I came in. I had to walk in front

of all those people. My seat was in the back row. I had to go clumping all the way up the aisle with everyone watching!

JIM. You shouldn't have been self-conscious.

LAURA. I know, but I was. It was always such a relief when the singing
started.

JIM. Aw, yes. I've placed you now! I used to call you Blue Roses. How was
it that I got started calling you that?

LAURA. I was out of school a little while with pleurosis. When I came back
you asked me what was the matter. I said I had pleurosis—you
thought I said Blue Roses. That's what you always called me after
that!

JIM. I hope you didn't mind.

LAURA. Oh, no—I liked it. You see, I wasn't acquainted with many—
people. . . .

JIM. As I remember you sort of stuck by yourself.

LAURA. I—I—never had much luck at—making friends.

JIM. I don't see why you wouldn't.

LAURA. Well, I—started out badly.

JIM. You mean being—

LAURA. Yes, it sort of—stood between me—

JIM. You shouldn't have let it!

LAURA. I know, but it did, and—

JIM. You were shy with people!

LAURA. I tried not to be but never could—

JIM. Overcome it?

LAURA. No, I—I never could!

JIM. I guess being shy is something you have to work out of kind of
gradually.

LAURA *(sorrowfully)*. Yes—I guess it—

JIM. Takes time!

LAURA. Yes—

JIM. People are not so dreadful when you know them. That's what you
have to remember! And everybody has problems, not just you, but
practically everybody has got some problems. You think of yourself
as having the only problems, as being the only one who is disappointed. But just look around you and you will see lots of people
disappointed as you are. For instance, I hoped when I was going to
high school that I would be further along at this time, six years later,
than I am now—You remember that wonderful write-up I had in *The
Torch?*

LAURA. Yes! *(She rises and crosses to table.)*

JIM. It said I was bound to succeed in anything I went into! *(LAURA returns with the annual.)* Holy Jeez! *The Torch! (He accepts it reverently. They smile across it with mutual wonder. LAURA crouches beside him and they begin to turn through it. LAURA's shyness is dissolving in his warmth.)*

LAURA. Here you are in *Pirates of Penzance!*

JIM *(wistfully).* I sang the baritone lead in that operetta.

LAURA *(rapidly).* So—*beautifully!*

JIM *(protesting).* Aw—

LAURA. Yes, yes—beautifully—beautifully!

JIM. You heard me?

LAURA. All three times!

JIM. No!

LAURA. Yes!

JIM. All three performances?

LAURA *(looking down).* Yes.

JIM. Why?

LAURA. I—wanted to ask you to—autograph my program.

JIM. Why didn't you ask me to?

LAURA. You were always surrounded by your own friends so much that I never had a chance to.

JIM. You should have just—

LAURA. Well, I—thought you might think I was—

JIM. Thought I might think you was—what?

LAURA. Oh—

JIM *(with reflective relish).* I was beleaguered by females in those days.

LAURA. You were terribly popular!

JIM. Yeah—

LAURA. You had such a —friendly way—

JIM. I was spoiled in high school.

LAURA. Everybody—liked you!

JIM. Including you?

LAURA. I—yes, I—I did, too—*(She gently closes the book in her lap.)*

JIM. Well, well, well!—Give me that program, Laura. *(She hands it to him. He signs it with a flourish.)* There you are—better late than never!

LAURA. Oh, I—what a—surprise!

JIM. My signature isn't worth very much right now. But some day—

maybe—it will increase in value! Being disappointed is one thing and being discouraged is something else. I am disappointed but I am not discouraged. I'm twenty-three years old. How old are you?

LAURA. I'll be twenty-four in June.

JIM. That's not old age!

LAURA. No, but—

JIM. You finished high school?

LAURA *(with difficulty).* I didn't go back.

JIM. You mean you dropped out?

LAURA. I made bad grades in my final examinations. *(She rises and replaces the book and the program. Her voice strained.)* How is— Emily Meisenbach getting along?

JIM. Oh, that kraut-head!

LAURA. Why do you call her that?

JIM. That's what she was.

LAURA. You're not still—going with her?

JIM. I never see her.

LAURA. It said in the Personal Section that you were—engaged!

JIM. I know, but I wasn't impressed by that—propaganda!

LAURA. It wasn't—the truth?

JIM. Only in Emily's optimistic opinion!

LAURA. Oh—

(LEGEND: ``WHAT HAVE YOU DONE SINCE HIGH SCHOOL?'')

JIM. *lights a cigarette and leans indolently back on his elbows smiling at* LAURA *with a warmth and charm which lights her inwardly with altar candles. She remains by the table and turns in her hands a piece of glass to cover her tumult.*

JIM *(after several reflective puffs on a cigarette).* What have you done since high school? *(She seems not to hear him.)* Huh? *(*LAURA *looks up.)* I said what have you done since high school, Laura?

LAURA. Nothing much.

JIM. You must have been doing something these six long years.

LAURA. Yes.

JIM. Well, then, such as what?

LAURA. I took a business course at business college—

JIM. How did that work out?

LAURA. Well, not very—well—I had to drop out, it gave me—indigestion—

JIM *laughs gently.*

JIM. What are you doing now?

LAURA. I don't do anything—much. Oh, please don't think I sit around doing nothing! My glass collection takes up a good deal of my time. Glass is something you have to take good care of.

JIM. What did you say—about glass?

LAURA. Collection I said—I have one—*(She clears her throat and turns away again, acutely shy.)*

JIM *(abruptly).* You know what I judge to be the trouble with you? Inferiority complex! Know what that is? That's what they call it when someone low-rates himself! I understand it because I had it, too. Although my case was not so aggravated as yours seems to be. I had it until I took up public speaking, developed my voice, and learned that I had an aptitude for science. Before that time I never thought of myself as being outstanding in any way whatsoever! Now I've never made a regular study of it, but I have a friend who says I can analyze people better than doctors that make a profession of it. I don't claim that to be necessarily true, but I can sure guess a person's psychology, Laura! *(Takes out his gum.)* Excuse me, Laura. I always take it out when the flavor is gone. I'll use this scrap of paper to wrap it in. I know how it is to get it stuck on a shoe. Yep—that's what I judge to be your principal trouble. A lack of confidence in yourself as a person. You don't have the proper amount of faith in yourself. I'm basing that fact on a number of your remarks and also on certain observations I've made. For instance that clumping you thought was so awful in high school. You say that you even dreaded to walk into class. You see what you did? You dropped out of school, you gave up an education because of a clump, which as far as I know was practically non-existent! A little physical defect is what you have. Hardly noticeable even! Magnified thousands of times by imagination! You know what my strong advice to you is? Think of yourself as *superior* in some way!

LAURA. In what way would I think?

JIM. Why, man alive, Laura! Just look about you a little. What do you see? A world full of common people! All of 'em born and all of 'em going to die! Which of them has one-tenth of your good points! Or mine! Or anyone else's, as far as that goes—Gosh! Everybody excels in some one thing. Some in many! *(Unconsciously glances at himself in the mirror.)* All you've got to do is discover in *what!* Take me, for instance. *(He adjusts his tie at the mirror.)* My interest happens to lie in electro-dynamics. I'm taking a course in radio engineering at night school, Laura, on top of a fairly responsible job at the warehouse. I'm taking that course and studying public speaking.

LAURA. Ohhhh.

JIM. Because I believe in the future of television! *(Turning back to her.)* I wish to be ready to go up right along with it. Therefore I'm planning to get in on the ground floor. In fact, I've already made the right connections and all that remains is for the industry itself to get under way! Full steam—*(His eyes are starry.)* Knowledge—Zzzzzp! Money—Zzzzzp!—Power! That's the cycle democracy is built on! *(His attitude is convincingly dynamic.* LAURA *stares at him, even her shyness eclipsed in her absolute wonder. He suddenly grins.)* I guess you think I think a lot of myself!

LAURA. No—o-o-o, I—

JIM. Now how about you? Isn't there something you take more interest in than anything else?

LAURA. Well, I do—as I said—have my—glass collection—

A peal of girlish laughter from the kitchen.

JIM. I'm not right sure I know what you're talking about. What kind of glass is it?

LAURA. Little articles of it, they're ornaments mostly! Most of them are little animals made out of glass, the tiniest little animals in the world. Mother calls them a glass menagerie! Here's an example of one, if you'd like to see it! This one is the oldest. It's nearly thirteen. *(He stretches out his hand.)* (MUSIC: ``THE GLASS MENAGERIE.'') Oh, be careful—if you breathe, it breaks!

JIM. I'd better not take it. I'm pretty clumsy with things.

LAURA. Go on, I trust you with him! *(Places it in his palm.)* There now—you're holding him gently! Hold him over the light, he loves the light! You see how the light shines through him?

JIM. It sure does shine!

LAURA. I shouldn't be partial, but he is my favorite one.

JIM. What kind of a thing is this one supposed to be?

LAURA. Haven't you noticed the single horn on his forehead?

JIM. A unicorn, huh?

LAURA. Mmm-hmmm!

JIM. Unicorns, aren't they extinct in the modern world?

LAURA. I know!

JIM. Poor little fellow, he must feel sort of lonesome.

LAURA *(smiling)*. Well, if he does he doesn't complain about it. He stays on a shelf with some horses that don't have horns and all of them seem to get along nicely together.

JIM. How do you know?

Laura *(lightly)*. I haven't heard any arguments among them!

Jim *(grinning)*. No arguments, huh? Well, that's a pretty good sign! Where shall I set him?

Laura. Put him on the table. They all like a change of scenery once in a while!

Jim *(stretching)*. Well, well, well, well—Look how big my shadow is when I stretch!

Laura. Oh, oh, yes—it stretches across the ceiling!

Jim *(crossing to door)*. I think it's stopped raining. *(Opens fire-escape door.)* Where does the music come from?

Laura. From the Paradise Dance Hall across the alley.

Jim. How about cutting the rug a little, Miss Wingfield?

Laura. Oh, I—

Jim. Or is your program filled up? Let me have a look at it. *(Grasps imaginary card.)* Why, every dance is taken! I'll just have to scratch some out. (WALTZ MUSIC: ``LA GOLONDRINA.'') Ahhh, a waltz! *(He executes some sweeping turns by himself, then holds his arms toward* Laura.*)*

Laura *(breathlessly)*. I—can't dance!

Jim. There you go, that inferiority stuff!

Laura. I've never danced in my life!

Jim. Come on, try!

Laura. Oh, but I'd step on you!

Jim. I'm not made out of glass.

Laura. How—how—how do we start?

Jim. Just leave it to me. You hold your arms out a little.

Laura. Like this?

Jim. A little bit higher. Right. Now don't tighten up, that's the main thing about it—relax.

Laura *(laughing breathlessly)*. It's hard not to.

Jim. Okay.

Laura. I'm afraid you can't budge me.

Jim. What do you bet I can't? *(He swings her into motion.)*

Laura. Goodness, yes, you can!

Jim. Let yourself go, now, Laura, just let yourself go.

Laura. I'm—

Jim. Come on!

Laura. Trying!

Jim. Not so stiff—Easy does it!

LAURA. I know but I'm—

JIM. Loosen th' backbone! There now, that's a lot better.

LAURA. Am I?

JIM. Lots, lots better! *(He moves her about the room in a clumsy waltz.)*

LAURA. Oh, my!

JIM. Ha-ha!

LAURA. Goodness, yes you can!

JIM. Ha-ha-ha! *(They suddenly bump into the table. JIM stops.)* What did we hit on?

LAURA. Table.

JIM. Did something fall off it? I think—

LAURA. Yes.

JIM. I hope that it wasn't the little glass horse with the horn!

LAURA. Yes.

JIM. Aw, aw, aw. Is it broken?

LAURA. Now it is just like all the other horses.

JIM. It's lost its—

LAURA. Horn! It doesn't matter. Maybe it's a blessing in disguise.

JIM. You'll never forgive me. I bet that that was your favorite piece of glass.

LAURA. I don't have favorites much. It's no tragedy, Freckles. Glass breaks so easily. No matter how careful you are. The traffic jars the shelves and things fall off them.

JIM. Still I'm awfully sorry that I was the cause.

LAURA *(smiling).* I'll just imagine he had an operation. The horn was removed to make him feel less—freakish! *(They both laugh.)* Now he will feel more at home with the other horses, the ones that don't have horns . . .

JIM. Ha-ha, that's very funny! *(Suddenly serious.)* I'm glad to see that you have a sense of humor. You know—you're—well—very different! Surprisingly different from anyone else I know! *(His voice becomes soft and hesitant with a genuine feeling.)* Do you mind me telling you that? *(LAURA is abashed beyond speech.)* You make me feel sort of— I don't know how to put it! I'm usually pretty good at expressing things, but—This is something that I don't know how to say! *(LAURA touches her throat and clears it—turns the broken unicorn in her hands.) (Even softer.)* Has anyone ever told you that you were pretty? *(PAUSE: MUSIC.) (LAURA looks up slowly, with wonder, and shakes her head.)* Well, you are! In a very different way from anyone else. And all the nicer because of the difference, too. *(His voice becomes low and husky. LAURA turns away, nearly faint with the novelty of her emo-*

tions.) I wish that you were my sister. I'd teach you to have some confidence in yourself. The different people are not like other people, but being different is nothing to be ashamed of. Because other people are not such wonderful people. They're one hundred times one thousand. You're one times one! They walk all over the earth. You just stay here. They're common as—weeds, but—you—well, you're—*Blue Roses!*

(IMAGE ON SCREEN: BLUE ROSES.)

(MUSIC CHANGES.)

LAURA. But blue is wrong for—roses . . .

JIM. It's right for you—You're—pretty!

LAURA. In what respect am I pretty?

JIM. In all respects—believe me! Your eyes—your hair—are pretty! Your hands are pretty! *(He catches hold of her hand.)* You think I'm making this up because I'm invited to dinner and have to be nice. Oh, I could do that! I could put on an act for you, Laura, and say lots of things without being very sincere. But this time I am. I'm talking to you sincerely. I happened to notice you had this inferiority complex that keeps you from feeling comfortable with people. Somebody needs to build your confidence up and make you proud instead of shy and turning away and—blushing—Somebody ought to—Ought to— kiss you, Laura! *(His hand slips slowly up her arm to her shoulder.)* (MUSIC SWELLS TUMULTUOUSLY.) *(He suddenly turns her about and kisses her on the lips. When he releases her* LAURA *sinks on the sofa with a bright, dazed look.* JIM *backs away and fishes in his pocket for a cigarette.)* (LEGEND ON SCREEN: "SOUVENIR.") Stumble-john! *(He lights the cigarette, avoiding her look. There is a peal of girlish laughter from* AMANDA *in the kitchen.* LAURA *slowly raises and opens her hand. It still contains the little broken glass animal. She looks at it with a tender, bewildered expression.)* Stumble-john! I shouldn't have done that— That was way off the beam. You don't smoke, do you? *(She looks up, smiling, not hearing the question. He sits beside her a little gingerly. She looks at him speechlessly—waiting. He coughs decorously and moves a little farther aside as he considers the situation and senses her feelings, dimly, with perturbation. Gently.)* Would you—care for a—mint? *(She doesn't seem to hear him but her look grows brighter even.)* Peppermint—Life Saver? My pocket's a regular drug store— wherever I go . . . *(He pops a mint in his mouth. Then gulps and decides to make a clean breast of it. He speaks slowly and gingerly.)* Laura, you know, if I had a sister like you, I'd do the same thing as Tom. I'd bring out fellows—introduce her to them. The right type of boys of a type to—appreciate her. Only—well—he made a mistake about me. Maybe I've got no call to be saying this. That may not have been the idea in having me over. But what if it was? There's nothing wrong about that. The only trouble is that in my case—I'm not in a situation to—do the right thing. I can't take down your number and say I'll phone. I can't call up next week and—ask for a date. I thought I had better explain the situation in case you misunderstood it and—hurt your feelings. . . . *(Pause. Slowly, very slowly,* LAURA*'s look changes, her eyes returning slowly from his to the ornament in her palm.)*

AMANDA *utters another gay laugh in the kitchen.*

LAURA *(faintly).* You—won't—call again?

JIM. No, Laura, I can't. *(He rises from the sofa.)* As I was just explaining, I've—got strings on me, Laura, I've—been going steady! I go out all the time with a girl named Betty. She's a home-girl like you, and Catholic, and Irish, and in a great many ways we—get along fine. I met her last summer on a moonlight boat trip up the river to Alton, on the *Majestic.* Well—right away from the start it was—love! (LEGEND: LOVE!) *(*LAURA *sways slightly forward and grips the arm of the sofa. He fails to notice, now enrapt in his own comfortable being.)* Being in love has made a new man of me! *(Leaning stiffly forward, clutching the arm of the sofa,* LAURA *struggles visibly with her storm. But* JIM *is oblivious, she is a long way off.)* The power of love is really pretty tremendous! Love is something that—changes the whole world, Laura! *(The storm abates a little and* LAURA *leans back. He notices her again.)* It happened that Betty's aunt took sick, she got a wire and had to go to Centralia. So Tom—when he asked me to dinner—I naturally just accepted the invitation, not knowing that you—that he—that I—*(He stops awkwardly.)* Huh—I'm a stumble-john! *(He flops back on the sofa. The holy candles in the altar of* LAURA*'s face have been snuffed out! There is a look of almost infinite desolation.* JIM *glances at her uneasily.)* I wish that you would—say something. *(She bites her lip which was trembling and then bravely smiles. She opens her hand again on the broken glass ornament. Then she gently takes his hand and raises it level with her own. She carefully places the unicorn in the palm of his hand, then pushes his fingers closed upon it.)* What are you—doing that for? You want me to have him?—Laura? *(She nods.)* What for?

LAURA. A—souvenir . . .

She rises unsteadily and crouches beside the victrola to wind it up.

(LEGEND ON SCREEN: "THINGS HAVE A WAY OF TURNING OUT SO BADLY.")

(OR IMAGE: "GENTLEMAN CALLER WAVING GOODBYE!—GAILY.")

At this moment AMANDA *rushes brightly back in the front room. She bears a pitcher of fruit punch in an old-fashioned cut-glass pitcher and a plate of macaroons. The plate has a gold border and poppies painted on it.*

AMANDA. Well, well, well! Isn't the air delightful after the shower? I've made you children a little liquid refreshment. *(Turns gaily to the gentleman caller.)* Jim, do you know that song about lemonade?

> "Lemonade, lemonade
> Made in the shade and stirred with a spade—
> Good enough for any old maid!"

JIM *(uneasily)*. Ha-ha! No—I never heard it.

AMANDA. Why, Laura! You look so serious!

JIM. We were having a serious conversation.

AMANDA. Good! Now you're better acquainted!

JIM *(uncertainly)*. Ha-ha! Yes.

AMANDA. You modern young people are much more serious-minded than my generation. I was so gay as a girl!

JIM. You haven't changed, Mrs. Wingfield.

AMANDA. Tonight I'm rejuvenated! The gaiety of the occasion, Mr. O'Connor! *(She tosses her head with a peal of laughter. Spills lemonade.)* Oooo! I'm baptizing myself!

JIM. Here—let me—

AMANDA *(setting the pitcher down)*. There now. I discovered we had some maraschino cherries. I dumped them in, juice and all!

JIM. You shouldn't have gone to that trouble, Mrs. Wingfield.

AMANDA. Trouble, trouble? Why it was loads of fun! Didn't you hear me cutting up in the kitchen? I bet your ears were burning! I told Tom how outdone with him I was for keeping you to himself so long a time! He should have brought you over much, much sooner! Well, now that you've found your way, I want you to be a very frequent caller! Not just occasional but all the time. Oh, we're going to have a lot of gay times together! I see them coming! Mmm, just breathe that air! So fresh, and the moon's so pretty! I'll skip back out—I know where my place is when young folks are having a—serious conversation!

JIM. Oh, don't go out, Mrs. Wingfield. The fact of the matter is I've got to be going.

AMANDA. Going, now? You're joking! Why, it's only the shank of the evening, Mr. O'Connor!

JIM. Well, you know how it is.

AMANDA. You mean you're a young workingman and have to keep workingmen's hours. We'll let you off early tonight. But only on the condition that next time you stay later. What's the best night for you? Isn't Saturday night the best night for you workingmen?

JIM. I have a couple of time-clocks to punch, Mrs. Wingfield. One at morning, another one at night!

AMANDA. My, but you *are* ambitious! You work at night, too?

JIM. No, Ma'am, not work but—Betty! *(He crosses deliberately to pick up his hat. The band at the Paradise Dance Hall goes into a tender waltz.)*

AMANDA. Betty? Betty? Who's—Betty! *(There is an ominous cracking sound in the sky.)*

JIM. Oh, just a girl. The girl I go steady with! *(He smiles charmingly. The sky falls.)*

(LEGEND: ''THE SKY FALLS.'')

AMANDA *(a long-drawn exhalation)*. Ohhhh . . . Is it a serious romance, Mr. O'Connor?

JIM. We're going to be married the second Sunday in June.

AMANDA. Ohhhh—how nice! Tom didn't mention that you were engaged to be married.

JIM. The cat's not out of the bag at the warehouse yet. You know how they are. They call you Romeo and stuff like that. *(He stops at the oval mirror to put on his hat. He carefully shapes the brim and the crown to give a discreetly dashing effect.)* It's been a wonderful evening, Mrs. Wingfield. I guess this is what they mean by Southern hospitality.

AMANDA. It really wasn't anything at all.

JIM. I hope it don't seem like I'm rushing off. But I promised Betty I'd pick her up at the Wabash depot, an' by the time I get my jalopy down there her train'll be in. Some women are pretty upset if you keep 'em waiting.

AMANDA. Yes, I know—The tyranny of women! *(Extends her hand.)* Good-bye, Mr. O'Connor. I wish you luck—and happiness—and success! All three of them, and so does Laura!—Don't you, Laura?

LAURA. Yes!

JIM *(taking her hand)*. Good-bye, Laura. I'm certainly going to treasure that souvenir. And don't you forget the good advice I gave you. *(Raises his voice to a cheery shout.)* So long, Shakespeare! Thanks again, ladies—Good night!

He grins and ducks jauntily out.

 Still bravely grimacing, AMANDA *closes the door on the gentleman caller. Then she turns back to the room with a puzzled expression. She and* LAURA *don't dare to face each other.* LAURA *crouches beside the victrola to wind it.*

AMANDA *(faintly)*. Things have a way of turning out so badly. I don't believe that I would play the victrola. Well, well—well—Our gentleman caller was engaged to be married! Tom!

TOM *(from back)*. Yes, Mother?

AMANDA. Come in here a minute. I want to tell you something awfully funny.

Tom *(enters with a macaroon and a glass of the lemonade).* Has the gentleman caller gotten away already?

Amanda. The gentleman caller has made an early departure. What a wonderful joke you played on us!

Tom. How do you mean?

Amanda. You didn't mention that he was engaged to be married.

Tom. Jim? Engaged?

Amanda. That's what he just informed us.

Tom. I'll be jiggered! I didn't know about that.

Amanda. That seems very peculiar.

Tom. What's peculiar about it?

Amanda. Didn't you call him your best friend down at the warehouse?

Tom. He is, but how did I know?

Amanda. It seems extremely peculiar that you wouldn't know your best friend was going to be married!

Tom. The warehouse is where I work, not where I know things about people!

Amanda. You don't know things anywhere! You live in a dream; you manufacture illusions! *(He crosses to door.)* Where are you going?

Tom. I'm going to the movies.

Amanda. That's right, now that you've had us make such fools of ourselves. The effort, the preparations, all the expense! The new floor lamp, the rug, the clothes for Laura! All for what? To entertain some other girl's fiancé! Go to the movies, go! Don't think about us, a mother deserted, an unmarried sister who's crippled and has no job! Don't let anything interfere with your selfish pleasure! Just go, go, go—to the movies!

Tom. All right, I will! The more you shout about my selfishness to me the quicker I'll go, and I won't go to the movies!

Amanda. Go, then! Then go to the moon—you selfish dreamer!

Tom *smashes his glass on the floor. He plunges out on the fire-escape, slamming the door,* Laura *screams—cut off by the door.*

Dance-hall music up. Tom *goes to the rail and grips it desperately, lifting his face in the chill white moonlight penetrating the narrow abyss of the alley.*

(LEGEND ON SCREEN: ``AND SO GOOD-BYE . . .'')

Tom*'s closing speech is timed with the interior pantomime. The interior scene is played as though viewed through soundproof glass.* Amanda *appears to be making a comforting speech to* Laura *who is huddled upon the sofa. Now that we cannot hear the mother's speech, her silliness is* *gone and she has dignity and tragic beauty.* LAURA*'s dark hair hides her face until at the end of the speech she lifts it to smile at her mother.* AMANDA*'s gestures are slow and graceful, almost dancelike, as she comforts the daughter. At the end of her speech she glances a moment at the father's picture—then withdraws through the portieres. At close of* TOM*'s speech,* LAURA *blows out the candles, ending the play.*

TOM. I didn't go to the moon, I went much further—for time is the longest distance between two places—Not long after that I was fired for writing a poem on the lid of a shoe-box. I left Saint Louis. I descended the steps of this fire-escape for a last time and followed, from then on, in my father's footsteps, attempting to find in motion what was lost in space—I traveled around a great deal. The cities swept about me like dead leaves, leaves that were brightly colored but torn away from the branches. I would have stopped, but I was pursued by something. It always came upon me unawares, taking me altogether by surprise. Perhaps it was a familiar bit of music. Perhaps it was only a piece of transparent glass—Perhaps I am walking along a street at night, in some strange city, before I have found companions. I pass the lighted window of a shop where perfume is sold. The window is filled with pieces of colored glass, tiny transparent bottles in delicate colors, like bits of a shattered rainbow. Then all at once my sister touches my shoulder. I turn around and look into her eyes . . . Oh, Laura, Laura, I tried to leave you behind me, but I am more faithful than I intended to be! I reach for a cigarette, I cross the street, I run into the movies or a bar, I buy a drink, I speak to the nearest stranger—anything that can blow your candles out! *(*LAURA *bends over the candles.)*—for nowadays the world is lit by lightning! Blow out your candles, Laura—and so good-bye. . . .

She blows the candles out.

(THE SCENE DISSOLVES.)

SUGGESTIONS FOR WRITING AND DISCUSSION

1. In his opening speech Tom tells us that the play is not realistic; it is a memory play. Write a two- to three-page essay showing how this is true.
2. Look at the speeches that Tom as the narrator addresses to the audience. Does Tom use the same kind of language when he talks to other characters as when he addresses the audience? In a two- to three-page essay explicate and discuss several of his speeches of both types.
3. Discuss how the play would change if narrated by any of the other characters.
4. In the stage directions Tom is described as "not remorseless, but to escape from a trap he has to act without pity." This suggests that he had no choice but to act as he did. Is this really true or are there alternatives?
5. In his production notes Williams said that the purpose of the screen device

was "to give accent to certain values in each scene" which might otherwise "be obscured from the audience." Make a list of the screen legends and explain why you think Williams chose each of them. Write an analysis of one scene in terms of the legend.

6. Amanda wishes on the moon for "success and happiness for my precious children." In what ways do we see her pursuing this wish in the course of the play? How does she herself prevent this wish from coming true? Discuss these questions in a two- to three-page essay.

7. What is so attractive about the past to Amanda, Laura, and Jim?

8. What do we learn about Laura from the way Jim remembers her at high school? Does she appear to have changed?

9. Why is Jim so important to Laura?

10. Jim lectures Laura about having an inferiority complex. Do you think he is as self-confident as he claims? How does he act as a foil to each of the Wingfields?

11. When Jim breaks the unicorn, Laura reassures him by saying "now it is just like all the other horses." In a three- to four-page essay discuss what the unicorn and the glass menagerie mean to Laura and how they are used as symbols.

12. Most of the action of the play centers on Laura. This being the case, what is the climax? Explain why.

13. Initially Tom seems to be the more difficult of Amanda's children. Is this true?

14. Write a brief description of the life you imagine Amanda and Laura leading ten years after Tom leaves.

15. What part does the father play in the lives of each of the characters? Write a paragraph about the attitude of each of the Wingfields toward him.

16. In this play the question of what duties parents owe their children and vice versa is a central one. Does Laura have an obligation to go to typing school? Does Tom have an obligation to work in a shoe factory? Does Amanda have an obligation to care for Laura and sell magazine subscriptions? In a three- to four-page essay make an argument for the obligations of one of the Wingfields.

17. In his final speech Tom says "I didn't go to the moon, I went much further—for time is the longest distance between two places." What does he mean by this, and is it true? Explicate the rest of his speech in the light of this remark.

William Shakespeare (British, 1564–1616)

Shakespeare's plays were performed on a platform stage in a wooden theater which was probably circular or polygonal in shape. Plays had to be performed in the afternoon to make use of daylight, and changes in the time of day in the play were announced by actors. There was a certain amount of scenery: In 1598 the Rose Theater drew up an inventory of stage props.

These included a tree, an altar, a bedstead, and two moss banks. Plays were probably acted without any intermission or pause for scene changes.

Estimates of the size of Elizabethan audiences vary considerably. One well-known theater, the Swan, is said to have seated up to 3,000 people; another, the Rose, had an average attendance of 1,000. All kinds of people attended the theater—from aristocrats and prosperous merchants to pickpockets and prostitutes. The poorer members of the audience, those who could not afford to pay for their seats, were called groundlings. *So varied an audience helps to account for the breadth and tone of Shakespeare's plays.*

William Shakespeare was born in Stratford-on-Avon. Literary historians know little of his early life; he was first heard of in London in 1592. He was not only a dramatist but also an actor and producer. He was involved in the Lord Chamberlain's Theater Company, and he had particular actors—members of the company—in mind as he wrote. His company eventually moved into the Globe Theater, in which Shakepeare was one of the shareholders. By 1611, the year of his retirement, Shakespeare had written thirty-six plays, well over a hundred sonnets (two of which appear in this anthology) and two long epic poems.

King Lear is based on the legend of Lear, an early British king, but Shakespeare also borrowed material from a number of Elizabethan sources. In the first production, as with all Elizabethan plays, the characters were played by men, with adolescent boys portraying women. (L.K./M.L.)

The Tragedy of King Lear

Edited by Russell Fraser

DRAMATIS PERSONAE

LEAR, *King of Britain*
KING OF FRANCE
DUKE OF BURGUNDY
DUKE OF CORNWALL, *husband to* REGAN
DUKE OF ALBANY, *husband to* GONERIL
EARL OF KENT
EARL OF GLOUCESTER
EDGAR, *son to* GLOUCESTER
EDMUND, *bastard son to* GLOUCESTER
CURAN, *a courtier*
OSWALD, *steward to* GONERIL
OLD MAN, *tenant to* GLOUCESTER
DOCTOR
LEAR'S FOOL
A CAPTAIN, *subordinate to* EDMUND
GENTLEMEN, *attending on* CORDELIA
A HERALD
SERVANTS TO CORNWALL
GONERIL ⎫
REGAN ⎬ *daughters to* LEAR
CORDELIA ⎭
KNIGHTS *attending on* LEAR, OFFICERS, MESSENGERS, SOLDIERS, ATTENDANTS

Scene: [*Britain*]

ACT I

Scene I. [*King Lear's palace.*]

Enter Kent, Gloucester, and Edmund.

KENT. I thought the King had more affected°[1] the Duke of Albany°
than Cornwall.

GLOUCESTER. It did always seem so to us; but now, in the division of
the kingdom, it appears not which of the dukes he values most,
for equalities are so weighed that curiosity in neither can make   5
choice of either's moiety.°

KENT. Is not this your son, my lord?

GLOUCESTER. His breeding,° sir, hath been at my charge. I have so
often blushed to acknowledge him that now I am brazed° to't.

KENT. I cannot conceive° you.   10

GLOUCESTER. Sir, this young fellow's mother could; whereupon she
grew round-wombed, and had indeed, sir, a son for her cradle
ere she had a husband for her bed. Do you smell a fault?

KENT. I cannot wish the fault undone, the issue° of it being so proper.°

GLOUCESTER. But I have a son, sir, by order of law, some year elder   15
than this, who yet is no dearer in my account:° though this
knave° came something saucily° to the world before he was
sent for, yet was his mother fair, there was good sport at his
making, and the whoreson° must be acknowledged. Do you
know this noble gentleman, Edmund?   20

EDMUND. No, my lord.

GLOUCESTER. My Lord of Kent. Remember him hereafter as my honorable friend.

EDMUND. My services to your lordship.

KENT. I must love you, and sue° to know you better.   25

EDMUND. Sir, I shall study deserving.

GLOUCESTER. He hath been out° nine years, and away he shall again.
The King is coming.

---

[1] The degree sign (°) indicates a footnote, which is keyed to the text by line number. Text
references are printed in *italic* type; the annotation follows in roman type.

I.i. [1] *affected* loved   [1] *Albany* Albanacte, whose domain extended ``from the river Humber
to the point of Caithness'' (Holinshed) [5-6] *equalities . . . moiety* i.e., shares are so balanced against one another that careful examination by neither can make him wish the
other's portion   [8] *breeding* upbringing   [9] *brazed* made brazen, hardened
[10] *conceive* understand (pun follows)   [14] *issue* result (child)   [14] *proper* handsome
[16] *account* estimation   [17] *knave* fellow (without disapproval)   [17] *saucily* (1) insolently (2)
lasciviously   [19] *whoreson* fellow (lit., son of a whore)   [25] *sue* entreat   [27] *out* away,
abroad

    Sound a sennet.° Enter one bearing a coronet,° then King Lear,
    then the Dukes of Cornwall and Albany, next Goneril, Regan, Cor-
    delia, and Attendants.

LEAR. Attend the lords of France and Burgundy, Gloucester.

GLOUCESTER. I shall, my lord. *Exit [with Edmund].*   30

LEAR. Meantime we shall express our darker purpose.°
    Give me the map there. Know that we have divided
    In three our kingdom; and 'tis our fast° intent
    To shake all cares and business from our age,
    Conferring them on younger strengths, while we   35
    Unburthened crawl toward death. Our son of Cornwall,
    And you our no less loving son of Albany,
    We have this hour a constant will to publish°
    Our daughters' several° dowers, that future strife
    May be prevented° now. The Princes, France and Burgundy,   40
    Great rivals in our youngest daughter's love,
    Long in our court have made their amorous sojourn,
    And here are to be answered. Tell me, my daughters
    (Since now we will divest us both of rule,
    Interest° of territory, cares of state),   45
    Which of you shall we say doth love us most,
    That we our largest bounty may extend
    Where nature doth with merit challenge.° Goneril,
    Our eldest-born, speak first.

GONERIL. Sir, I love you more than word can wield° the matter;   50
    Dearer than eyesight, space° and liberty;
    Beyond what can be valued, rich or rare;
    No less than life, with grace, health, beauty, honor;
    As much as child e'er loved, or father found;
    A love that makes breath° poor, and speech unable:°   55
    Beyond all manner of so much° I love you.

CORDELIA. *[Aside]* What shall Cordelia speak? Love, and be silent.

LEAR. Of all these bounds, even from this line to this,
    With shadowy forests, and with champains riched,°
    With plenteous rivers, and wide-skirted meads,°   60
    We make thee lady. To thine and Albany's issues°

---

29 s.d. *sennet* set of notes played on a trumpet, signalizing the entrance or departure of a procession   29 s.d. *coronet* small crown, intended for Cordelia   31 *darker purpose* hidden intention   33 *fast* fixed   38 *constant will to publish* fixed intention to proclaim   39 *several* separate   40 *prevented* forestalled   45 *Interest* legal right   48 *nature . . . challenge* i.e., natural affection contends with desert for (or lays claim to) bounty   50 *wield* handle   51 *space* scope   55 *breath* language   55 *unable* impotent   56 *Beyond . . . much* beyond all these comparisons   59 *champains riched* enriched plains   60 *wideskirted meads* extensive grasslands   61 *issues* descendants

Be this perpetual.° What says our second daughter,
Our dearest Regan, wife of Cornwall? Speak.

REGAN. I am made of that self mettle° as my sister,
And prize me at her worth.° In my true heart   65
I find she names my very deed of love;°
Only she comes too short, that° I profess
Myself an enemy to all other joys
Which the most precious square of sense professes,°
And find I am alone felicitate°   70
In your dear Highness' love.

CORDELIA.   [*Aside*] Then poor Cordelia!
And yet not so, since I am sure my love's
More ponderous° than my tongue.

LEAR. To thee and thine hereditary ever
Remain this ample third of our fair kingdom,   75
No less in space, validity,° and pleasure
Than that conferred on Goneril. Now, our joy,
Although our last and least;° to whose young love
The vines of France and milk° of Burgundy
Strive to be interest;° what can you say to draw   80
A third more opulent than your sisters? Speak.

CORDELIA. Nothing, my lord.

LEAR. Nothing?

CORDELIA. Nothing.

LEAR. Nothing will come of nothing. Speak again.   85

CORDELIA. Unhappy that I am, I cannot heave
My heart into my mouth. I love your Majesty
According to my bond,° no more nor less.

LEAR. How, how, Cordelia? Mend your speech a little,
Lest you may mar your fortunes.

CORDELIA.   Good my lord,   90
You have begot me, bred me, loved me. I
Return those duties back as are right fit,°
Obey you, love you, and most honor you.
Why have my sisters husbands, if they say
They love you all? Haply,° when I shall wed,   95
That lord whose hand must take my plight° shall carry

---

⁶² *perpetual* in perpetuity   ⁶⁴ *self mettle* same material or temperament   ⁶⁵ *prize . . . worth*
value me the same (imperative)   ⁶⁶ *my . . . love* what my love really is (a legalism)
⁶⁷ *that* in that   ⁶⁹ *Which . . . professes* which the choicest estimate of sense avows
⁷⁰ *felicitate* made happy   ⁷⁴ *ponderous* weighty   ⁷⁶ *validity* value   ⁷⁸ *least* youngest,
smallest   ⁷⁹ *milk* i.e., pastures   ⁸⁰ *interest* closely connected, as interested parties
⁸⁸ *bond* i.e., filial obligation   ⁹² *Return . . . fit* i.e., am correspondingly dutiful   ⁹⁵ *Haply*
perhaps   ⁹⁶ *plight* troth plight

Half my love with him, half my care and duty.
Sure I shall never marry like my sisters,
To love my father all.

LEAR. But goes thy heart with this?

CORDELIA.   Ay, my good lord.   100

LEAR. So young, and so untender?

CORDELIA. So young, my lord, and true.

LEAR. Let it be so, thy truth then be thy dower!
     For, by the sacred radiance of the sun,
     The mysteries of Hecate° and the night,   105
     By all the operation of the orbs°
     From whom we do exist and cease to be,
     Here I disclaim all my paternal care,
     Propinquity and property of blood,°
     And as a stranger to my heart and me   110
     Hold thee from this for ever. The barbarous Scythian,°
     Or he that makes his generation messes°
     To gorge his appetite, shall to my bosom
     Be as well neighbored, pitied, and relieved,
     As thou my sometime° daughter.

KENT.   Good my liege—   115

LEAR. Peace, Kent!
     Come not between the Dragon° and his wrath.
     I loved her most, and thought to set my rest°
     On her kind nursery.° Hence and avoid my sight!
     So be my grave my peace, as here I give   120
     Her father's heart from her! Call France. Who stirs?
     Call Burgundy. Cornwall and Albany,
     With my two daughters' dowers digest° the third;
     Let pride, which she calls plainness, marry her.°
     I do invest you jointly with my power,   125
     Pre-eminence, and all the large effects
     That troop with majesty.° Ourself,° by monthly course,
     With reservation° of an hundred knights,
     By you to be sustained, shall our abode

---

[105] *mysteries of Hecate* secret rites of Hecate (goddess of the infernal world, and of witchcraft)   [106] *operation of the orbs* astrological influence   [109] *Propinquity and property of blood* relationship and common blood   [111] *Scythian* (type of the savage)   [112] *makes his generation messes* eats his own offspring   [115] *sometime* former   [117] *Dragon* (1) heraldic device of Britain (2) emblem of ferocity   [118] *set my rest* (1) stake my all (a term from the card game of primero) (2) find my rest   [119] *nursery* care, nursing   [123] *digest* absorb   [124] *Let . . . her* i.e., let her pride be her dowry and gain her a husband   [126–27] *effects/That troop with majesty* accompaniments that go with kingship   [127] *Ourself* (the royal "we")   [128] *reservation* the action of reserving a privilege (a legalism)

Make with you by due turn. Only we shall retain   130
The name, and all th' addition° to a king. The sway,
Revènue, execution of the rest,
Belovèd sons, be yours; which to confirm,
This coronet° part between you.

KENT.   Royal Lear,
Whom I have ever honored as my king,   135
Loved as my father, as my master followed,
As my great patron thought on in my prayers—

LEAR. The bow is bent and drawn; make from the shaft.°

KENT. Let it fall° rather, though the fork° invade
The region of my heart. Be Kent unmannerly   140
When Lear is mad. What wouldst thou do, old man?
Think'st thou that duty shall have dread to speak
When power to flattery bows? To plainness honor's bound
When majesty falls to folly. Reserve thy state,°
And in thy best consideration° check   145
This hideous rashness. Answer my life my judgment,°
Thy youngest daughter does not love thee least,
Nor are those empty-hearted whose low sounds
Reverb° no hollowness.°

LEAR.   Kent, on thy life, no more!

KENT. My life I never held but as a pawn°   150
To wage° against thine enemies; nor fear to lose it,
Thy safety being motive.°

LEAR.   Out of my sight!

KENT. See better, Lear, and let me still° remain
The true blank° of thine eye.

LEAR. Now by Apollo—

KENT.   Now by Apollo, King,   155
Thou swear'st thy gods in vain.

LEAR.   O vassal! Miscreant!°
                                 [*Laying his hand on his sword.*]

ALBANY, CORNWALL. Dear sir, forbear!

KENT. Kill thy physician, and the fee bestow
Upon the foul disease. Revoke thy gift,

---

[131] *addition* titles and honors   [134] *coronet* (the crown which was to have been Cordelia's)   [138] *make from the shaft* avoid the arrow   [139] *fall* strike   [139] *fork* forked head of the arrow   [144] *Reserve thy state* retain your kingly authority   [145] *best consideration* most careful reflection   [146] *Answer . . . judgment* I will stake my life on my opinion   [149] *Reverb* reverberate   [149] *hollowness* (1) emptiness (2) insincerity   [150] *pawn* stake in a wager   [151] *wage* (1) wager (2) carry on war   [152] *motive* moving cause   [153] *still* always   [154] *blank* the white spot in the center of the target (at which Lear should aim)   [156] *vassal! Miscreant!* base wretch! Misbeliever!

Or, whilst I can vent clamor° from my throat,   160
I'll tell thee thou dost evil.

LEAR.   Hear me, recreant!°
On thine allegiance,° hear me!
That thou hast sought to make us break our vows,
Which we durst never yet, and with strained° pride
To come betwixt our sentence° and our power,   165
Which nor our nature nor our place can bear,
Our potency made good,° take thy reward.
Five days we do allot thee for provision°
To shield thee from diseases° of the world,
And on the sixth to turn thy hated back   170
Upon our kingdom. If, on the tenth day following,
Thy banished trunk° be found in our dominions,
The moment is thy death. Away! By Jupiter,
This shall not be revoked.

KENT. Fare thee well, King. Sith° thus thou wilt appear,   175
Freedom lives hence, and banishment is here.
[*To Cordelia*] The gods to their dear shelter take thee, maid,
That justly think'st, and hast most rightly said.
[*To Regan and Goneril*] And your large speeches may your
    deeds approve,°
That good effects° may spring from words of love.   180
Thus Kent, O Princes, bids you all adieu;
He'll shape his old course° in a country new.   *Exit.*

          Flourish.° Enter Gloucester, with France and Burgundy;
                              Attendants.

GLOUCESTER. Here's France and Burgundy, my noble lord.

LEAR. My Lord of Burgundy,
We first address toward you, who with this king   185
Hath rivaled for our daughter. What in the least
Will you require in present° dower with her,
Or cease your quest of love?

BURGUNDY.   Most royal Majesty,
I crave no more than hath your Highness offered,
Nor will you tender° less.

LEAR.   Right noble Burgundy,   190
When she was dear° to us, we did hold her so;

---

¹⁶⁰ *vent clamor* utter a cry   ¹⁶¹ *recreant* traitor   ¹⁶² *On thine allegiance* (to forswear, which
is to commit high treason)   ¹⁶⁴ *strained* forced (and so excessive)   ¹⁶⁵ *sentence* judgment, decree   ¹⁶⁷ *Our potency made good* my royal authority being now asserted
¹⁶⁸ *for provision* for making preparation   ¹⁶⁹ *diseases* troubles   ¹⁷² *trunk* body
¹⁷⁵ *Sith* since   ¹⁷⁹ *approve* prove true   ¹⁸⁰ *effects* results   ¹⁸² *shape . . . course* pursue
his customary way   ¹⁸³ s.d. *Flourish* trumpet fanfare ¹⁸⁷ *present* immediate   ¹⁹⁰ *tender*
offer   ¹⁹¹ *dear* (1) beloved (2) valued at a high price

But now her price is fallen. Sir, there she stands.
If aught within the little seeming substance,°
Or all of it, with our displeasure pieced,°
And nothing more, may fitly like° your Grace,   195
She's there, and she is yours.

BURGUNDY.   I know no answer.

LEAR. Will you, with those infirmities she owes,°
     Unfriended, new adopted to our hate,
     Dow'red with our curse, and strangered° with our oath,
     Take her, or leave her?

BURGUNDY.   Pardon me, royal sir.   200
     Election makes not up° on such conditions.

LEAR. Then leave her, sir; for, by the pow'r that made me,
     I tell you all her wealth. [*To France.*] For you, great King,
     I would not from your love make such a stray
     To° match you where I hate; therefore beseech° you   205
     T' avert your liking a more worthier way°
     Than on a wretch whom nature is ashamed
     Almost t' acknowledge hers.

FRANCE.   This is most strange,
     That she whom even but now was your best object,°
     The argument° of your praise, balm of your age,   210
     The best, the dearest, should in this trice of time
     Commit a thing so monstrous to dismantle°
     So many folds of favor. Sure her offense
     Must be of such unnatural degree
     That monsters it,° or your fore-vouched° affection   215
     Fall into taint;° which to believe of her
     Must be a faith that reason without miracle
     Should never plant in me.°

CORDELIA.   I yet beseech your Majesty,
     If for° I want that glib and oily art
     To speak and purpose not,° since what I well intend   220
     I'll do't before I speak, that you make known
     It is no vicious blot, murder, or foulness,

No unchaste action or dishonored step,
That hath deprived me of your grace and favor;
But even for want of that for which I am richer,   225
A still-soliciting° eye, and such a tongue
That I am glad I have not, though not to have it
Hath lost° me in your liking.

LEAR.   Better thou
Hadst not been born than not t' have pleased me better.

FRANCE. Is it but this? A tardiness in nature°   230
Which often leaves the history unspoke°
That it intends to do. My Lord of Burgundy,
What say you° to the lady? Love's not love
When it is mingled with regards° that stands
Aloof from th' entire point.° Will you have her?   235
She is herself a dowry.

BURGUNDY.   Royal King,
Give but that portion which yourself proposed,
And here I take Cordelia by the hand,
Duchess of Burgundy.

LEAR. Nothing. I have sworn. I am firm.   240

BURGUNDY. I am sorry then you have so lost a father
That you must lose a husband.

CORDELIA.   Peace be with Burgundy.
Since that respects of fortune° are his love,
I shall not be his wife.

FRANCE. Fairest Cordelia, that art most rich being poor,   245
Most choice forsaken, and most loved despised,
Thee and thy virtues here I seize upon.
Be it lawful I take up what's cast away.
Gods, gods! 'Tis strange that from their cold'st neglect
My love should kindle to inflamed respect.°   250
Thy dow'rless daughter, King, thrown to my chance,°
Is Queen of us, of ours, and our fair France.
Not all the dukes of wat'rish° Burgundy
Can buy this unprized precious° maid of me.
Bid them farewell, Cordelia, though unkind.   255
Thou losest here, a better where° to find.

---

[226] *still-soliciting* always begging   [228] *lost* ruined   [230] *tardiness in nature* natural reticence   [231] *leaves the history unspoke* does not announce the action   [233] *What say you* i.e., will you have   [234] *regards* considerations (the dowry)   [234–35] *stands . . . point* have nothing to do with the essential question (love)   [243] *respects of fortune* mercenary considerations   [250] *inflamed respect* more ardent affection   [251] *chance* lot   [253] *wat'rish* (1) with many rivers (2) weak, diluted   [254] *unprized precious* unappreciated by others, and yet precious   [256] *here . . . where* in this place, in another place

LEAR. Thou hast her, France; let her be thine, for we
Have no such daughter, nor shall ever see
That face of hers again. Therefore be gone,
Without our grace, our love, our benison.° 260
Come, noble Burgundy.

> *Flourish. Exeunt (Lear, Burgundy, Cornwall, Albany,*
> *Gloucester, and Attendants).*

FRANCE. Bid farewell to your sisters.

CORDELIA. The jewels of our father,° with washed° eyes
Cordelia leaves you. I know you what you are,
And, like a sister,° am most loath to call 265
Your faults as they are named.° Love well our father.
To your professèd° bosoms I commit him.
But yet, alas, stood I within his grace,
I would prefer° him to a better place.
So farewell to you both. 270

REGAN. Prescribe not us our duty.

GONERIL.   Let your study
Be to content your lord, who hath received you
At Fortune's alms.° You have obedience scanted,°
And well are worth the want that you have wanted.°

CORDELIA. Time shall unfold what plighted° cunning hides, 275
Who covers faults, at last shame them derides.°
Well may you prosper.

FRANCE.   Come, my fair Cordelia.
> *Exit France and Cordelia.*

GONERIL. Sister, it is not little I have to say of what most nearly apper-
tains to us both. I think our father will hence tonight.

REGAN. That's most certain, and with you; next month with us. 280

GONERIL. You see how full of changes his age is. The observation we
have made of it hath not been little. He always loved our sister
most, and with what poor judgment he hath now cast her off
appears too grossly.°

REGAN. 'Tis the infirmity of his age; yet he hath ever but slenderly 285
known himself.

---

[260] *benison* blessing   [263] *The jewels of our father* you creatures prized by our father   [263] *washed* (1) weeping (2) clear-sighted   [265] *like a sister* because I am a sister i.e., loyal, affectionate   [266] *as they are named* i.e., by their right and ugly names   [267] *professèd* pretending to love   [269] *prefer* recommend   [273] *At Fortune's alms* as a charitable bequest from Fortune (and so, by extension, as one beggared or cast down by Fortune)   [273] *scanted* stinted   [274] *worth . . . wanted* deserve to be denied, even as you have denied   [275] *plighted* pleated, enfolded   [276] *Who . . . derides* those who hide their evil are finally exposed and shamed ("He that hideth his sins, shall not prosper")   [284] *grossly* obviously

GONERIL. The best and soundest of his time° hath been but rash; then must we look from his age to receive not alone the imperfections of long-ingrafted° condition,° but therewithal° the unruly waywardness that infirm and choleric years bring with them. 290

REGAN. Such unconstant starts° are we like to have from him as this of Kent's banishment.

GONERIL. There is further compliment° of leave-taking between France and him. Pray you, let's hit° together; if our father carry authority with such disposition as he bears,° this last surren- 295 der° of his will but offend° us.

REGAN. We shall further think of it.

GONERIL. We must do something, and i' th' heat.°

Exeunt.

Scene II. [*The Earl of Gloucester's castle.*]

Enter Edmund (with a letter).

EDMUND. Thou, Nature,° art my goddess; to thy law
My services are bound. Wherefore should I
Stand in the plague of custom,° and permit
The curiosity° of nations to deprive me,
For that° I am some twelve or fourteen moonshines°   5
Lag of° a brother? Why bastard? Wherefore base?
When my dimensions are as well compact,°
My mind as generous,° and my shape as true,
As honest° madam's issue? Why brand they us
With base? With baseness? Bastardy? Base? Base?   10
Who, in the lusty stealth of nature, take
More composition° and fierce° quality
Than doth, within a dull, stale, tired bed,
Go to th' creating a whole tribe of fops°
Got° 'tween asleep and wake? Well then,   15
Legitimate Edgar, I must have your land.
Our father's love is to the bastard Edmund
As to th' legitimate. Fine word, ``legitimate.''

---

[287] *of his time* period of his life up to now   [289] *long-ingrafted* implanted for a long time   [289] *condition* disposition   [289] *therewithal* with them   [291] *unconstant starts* impulsive whims   [293] *compliment* formal courtesy   [294] *hit* agree   [294–95] *carry . . .bears* continues, and in such frame of mind, to wield the sovereign power   [296] *last surrender* recent abdication   [296] *offend* vex   [298] *i' th' heat* while the iron is hot   I.ii.   [1] *Nature* (Edmund's conception of Nature accords with our description of a bastard as a natural child)   [3] *Stand . . . custom* respect hateful convention   [4] *curiosity* nice distinctions   [5] *For that* because   [5] *moonshines* months   [6] *Lag of* short of being (in age)   [7] *compact* framed   [8] *generous* gallant   [9] *honest* chaste   [12] *composition* completeness   [12] *fierce* energetic   [14] *fops* fools   [15] *Got* begot

Well, my legitimate, if this letter speed,°
And my invention° thrive, Edmund the base   20
Shall top th' legitimate. I grow, I prosper.
Now, gods, stand up for bastards.

Enter Gloucester.

GLOUCESTER. Kent banished thus? and France in choler parted?
And the King gone tonight? prescribed° his pow'r?
Confined to exhibition?° All this done   25
Upon the gad?° Edmund, how now? What news?

EDMUND. So please your lordship, none.

GLOUCESTER. Why so earnestly seek you to put up° that letter?

EDMUND. I know no news, my lord.

GLOUCESTER. What paper were you reading?   30

EDMUND. Nothing, my lord.

GLOUCESTER. No? What needed then that terrible dispatch° of it into
your pocket? The quality of nothing hath not such need to hide
itself. Let's see. Come, if it be nothing, I shall not need
spectacles.   35

EDMUND. I beseech you, sir, pardon me. It is a letter from my brother
that I have not all o'er-read; and for so much as I have perused,
I find it not fit for your o'erlooking.°

GLOUCESTER. Give me the letter,sir.

EDMUND. I shall offend, either to detain or give it. The contents, as in   40
part I understand them, are to blame.°

GLOUCESTER. Let's see, let's see.

EDMUND. I hope, for my brother's justification, he wrote this but as an
essay or taste° of my virtue.

GLOUCESTER. *(Reads)* "This policy and reverence° of age makes the   45
world bitter to the best of our times;° keeps our fortunes from
us till our oldness cannot relish° them. I begin to find an idle
and fond° bondage in the oppression of aged tyranny, who
sways, not as it hath power, but as it is suffered.° Come to me,
that of this I may speak more. If our father would sleep till I   50
waked him, you should enjoy half his revenue° for ever, and live
the beloved of your brother,   EDGAR.''

---

¹⁹ *speed* prosper   ²⁰ *invention* plan   ²⁴ *prescribed* limited   ²⁵ *exhibition* an allowance or
pension   ²⁶ *Upon the gad* on the spur of the moment (as if pricked by a gad or goad)
²⁸ *put up* put away, conceal   ³² *terrible dispatch* hasty putting away   ³⁸ *o'erlooking*
inspection   ⁴¹ *to blame* blameworthy   ⁴⁴ *essay or taste* test   ⁴⁵ *policy and reverence*
policy of reverencing (hendiadys)   ⁴⁶ *best of our times* best years of our lives (i.e., our
youth)   ⁴⁷ *relish* enjoy   ^{47–48} *idle and fond* foolish   ^{48–49} *who . . . suffered* which rules,
not from its own strength, but from our allowance   ⁵¹ *revenue* income

Hum! Conspiracy? "Sleep till I waked him, you should enjoy
half his revenue." My son Edgar! Had he a hand to write this?
A heart and brain to breed it in? When came you to this? Who 　55
brought it?

EDMUND. It was not brought me, my lord; there's the cunning of it. I
found it thrown in at the casement of my closet.°

GLOUCESTER. You know the character° to be your brother's?

EDMUND. If the matter were good, my lord, I durst swear it were his; 　60
but in respect of that,° I would fain° think it were not.

GLOUCESTER. It is his.

EDMUND. It is his hand, my lord; but I hope his heart is not in the
contents.

GLOUCESTER. Has he never before sounded° you in this business? 　65

EDMUND. Never, my lord. But I have heard him oft maintain it to be fit
that, sons at perfect° age, and fathers declined, the father
should be as ward to the son, and the son manage his revenue.

GLOUCESTER. O villain, villain! His very opinion in the letter. Abhorred
villain, unnatural, detested,° brutish villain; worse than brutish! 　70
Go, sirrah,° seek him. I'll apprehend him. Abominable villain!
Where is he?

EDMUND. I do not well know, my lord. If it shall please you to suspend
your indignation against my brother till you can derive from
him better testimony of his intent, you should run a certain 　75
course;° where, if you violently proceed against him, mistaking
his purpose, it would make a great gap° in your own honor and
shake in pieces the heart of his obedience. I dare pawn down°
my life for him that he hath writ this to feel° my affection to your
honor, and to no other pretense of danger.° 　80

GLOUCESTER. Think you so?

EDMUND. If your honor judge it meet,° I will place you where you shall
hear us confer of this, and by an auricular assurance° have your
satisfaction, and that without any further delay than this very
evening. 　85

GLOUCESTER. He cannot be such a monster.

EDMUND. Nor is not, sure.

GLOUCESTER. To his father, that so tenderly and entirely loves him.

---

[58] *casement of my closet* window of my room　　[59] *character* handwriting　　[61] *in respect of that*
in view of what it is　　[61] *fain* prefer to　　[65] *sounded* sounded you out　　[67] *perfect*
mature　　[70] *detested* detestable　　[71] *sirrah* sir (familiar form of address)　　[75-76] *run a
certain course* i.e., proceed safely, know where you are going　　[77] *gap* breach　　[78] *pawn
down* stake　　[79] *feel* test　　[80] *pretense of danger* dangerous purpose　　[82] *meet* fit
[83] *auricular assurance* proof heard with your own ears

Heaven and earth! Edmund, seek him out; wind me into him,° I
pray you; frame° the business after your own wisdom. I would   90
unstate myself to be in a due resolution.°

EDMUND. I will seek him, sir, presently;° convey° the business as I shall
find means, and acquaint you withal.°

GLOUCESTER. These late° eclipses in the sun and moon portend no
good to us. Though the wisdom of Nature° can reason° it thus   95
and thus, yet Nature finds itself scourged by the sequent
effects.° Love cools, friendship falls off,° brothers divide. In cities, mutinies;° in countries, discord; in palaces, treason; and
the bond cracked 'twixt son and father. This villain of mine
comes under the prediction,° there's son against father; the   100
King falls from bias of nature,° there's father against child. We
have seen the best of our time.° Machinations, hollowness,°
treachery, and all ruinous disorders follow us disquietly° to our
graves. Find out this villain, Edmund; it shall lose thee nothing.° Do it carefully. And the noble and true-hearted Kent ban-   105
ished; his offense, honesty. 'Tis strange.

Exit.

EDMUND. This is the excellent foppery° of the world, that when we are
sick in fortune, often the surfeits of our own behavior,° we make
guilty of our disasters the sun, the moon, and stars; as if we
were villains on° necessity; fools by heavenly compulsion;   110
knaves, thieves, and treachers by spherical predominance;°
drunkards, liars, and adulterers by an enforced obedience of
planetary influence;° and all that we are evil in, by a divine
thrusting on.° An admirable evasion of whoremaster° man, to
lay his goatish° disposition on the charge of a star. My father   115
compounded° with my mother under the Dragon's Tail,° and my
nativity° was under Ursa Major,° so that it follows I am rough
and lecherous. Fut!° I should have been that° I am, had the mai-
denliest star in the firmament twinkled on my bastardizing.
Edgar—   120

---

[89] *wind me into him* insinuate yourself into his confidence for me   [90] *frame* manage
[91] *unstate . . . resolution* forfeit my earldom to know the truth   [92] *presently* at once
[92] *convey* manage   [93] *withal* with it   [94] *late* recent   [95] *wisdom of Nature* scientific
learning   [95] *reason* explain   [96–97] *yet . . . effects* nonetheless our world is punished
with subsequent disasters   [97] *falls off* revolts   [98] *mutinies* riots   [99–100] *This . . . prediction* i.e., my son's villainous behavior is included in these portents, and bears them
out   [101] *bias of nature* natural inclination (the metaphor is from the game of bowls)
[102] *best of our time* our best days   [102] *hollowness* insincerity   [103] *disquietly* unquietly
[104–105] *it . . . nothing* you will not lose by it   [107] *foppery* folly   [108] *often . . . behavior*
often caused by our own excesses   [110] *on* of   [111] *treachers . . . predominance* traitors
because of the ascendancy of a particular star at our birth   [112–13] *by . . . influence*
because we had to submit to the influence of our star   [113–114] *divine thrusting on*
supernatural   compulsion   [114] *whoremaster*   lecherous   [115] *goatish*   lascivious
[116] *compounded* (1) made terms (2) formed (a child)   [116] *Dragon's Tail* the constella-
tion Draco   [117] *nativity* birthday   [117] *Ursa Major* the Great Bear   [118] *Fut!* 's foot (an
impatient oath)   [118] *that* what

Enter Edgar.

and pat he comes, like the catastrophe° of the old comedy. My
cue is villainous melancholy, with a sigh like Tom o' Bedlam.°—O, these eclipses do portend these divisions. Fa, sol, la,
mi.°

EDGAR. How now, brother Edmund; what serious contemplation are
you in?   125

EDMUND. I am thinking, brother, of a prediction I read this other day,
what should follow these eclipses.

EDGAR. Do you busy yourself with that?

EDMUND. I promise you, the effects he writes of succeed° unhappily:
as of unnaturalness° between the child and the parent, death,   130
dearth, dissolutions of ancient amities,° divisions in state, men-
aces and maledictions against King and nobles, needless diffidences,° banishment of friends, dissipation of cohorts,° nuptial
breaches, and I know not what.

EDGAR. How long have you been a sectary astronomical?°   135

EDMUND. Come, come, when saw you my father last?

EDGAR. Why, the night gone by.

EDMUND. Spake you with him?

EDGAR. Ay, two hours together.

EDMUND. Parted you in good terms? Found you no displeasure in him   140
by word nor countenance?°

EDGAR. None at all.

EDMUND. Bethink yourself wherein you may have offended him; and
at my entreaty forbear his presence° until some little time hath
qualified° the heat of his displeasure, which at this instant so   145
rageth in him that with the mischief of your person it would
scarcely allay.°

EDGAR. Some villain hath done me wrong.

EDMUND. That's my fear, brother I pray you have a continent forbear-
ance° till the speed of his rage goes slower; and, as I say, retire   150
with me to my lodging, from whence I will fitly° bring you to hear

---

¹²¹ *catastrophe* conclusion   ¹²¹⁻²² *My . . . Bedlam* I must be doleful, like a lunatic beggar
out of Bethlehem (Bedlam) Hospital, the London madhouse   ¹²³ *Fa, sol, la, mi*
(Edmund's humming of the musical notes is perhaps prompted by his use of the word
"divison," which describes a musical variation)   ¹²⁹ *succeed* follow   ¹³⁰ *unnaturalness*
unkindness   ¹³¹ *amities* friendships   ¹³²⁻³³ *diffidences* distrusts   ¹³³ *dissipation of
cohorts* falling away of supporters   ¹³⁵ *sectary astronomical* believer in astrology
¹⁴¹ *countenance* expression   ¹⁴⁴ *forbear his presence* keep away from him   ¹⁴⁵ *qualified*
lessened   ¹⁴⁶⁻⁴⁷ *with . . . allay* even an injury to you would not appease his anger
¹⁴⁹⁻⁵⁰ *have a continent forebearance* be restrained and keep yourself withdrawn   ¹⁵¹ *fitly*
at a fit time

, my lord speak. Pray ye, go; there's my key. If you do stir
abroad, go armed.

EDGAR. Armed, brother?

EDMUND. Brother, I advise you to the best. Go armed. I am no honest   155
man if there be any good meaning toward you. I have told you
what I have seen and heard; but faintly, nothing like the image
and horror° of it. Pray you, away.

EDGAR. Shall I hear from you anon?°

EDMUND. I do serve you in this business.   160

Exit Edgar.

A credulous father, and a brother noble,
Whose nature is so far from doing harms
That he suspects none; on whose foolish honesty
My practices° ride easy. I see the business.
Let me, if not by birth, have lands by wit.   165
All with me's meet° that I can fashion fit.°   *Exit.*

Scene III. [*The Duke of Albany's palace.*]

Enter Goneril, and [Oswald, her] Steward.

GONERIL. Did my father strike my gentleman for chiding of his Fool?°

OSWALD. Ay, madam.

GONERIL. By day and night he wrongs me. Every hour
He flashes into one gross crime° or other
That sets us all at odds. I'll not endure it.   5
His knights grow riotous,° and himself upbraids us
On every trifle. When he returns from hunting,
I will not speak with him. Say I am sick.
If you come slack of former services,°
You shall do well; the fault of it I'll answer.°   10

[*Horns within.*]

OSWALD. He's coming, madam; I hear him.

GONERIL. Put on what weary negligence you please,
You and your fellows. I'd have it come to question.°
If he distaste° it, let him to my sister,
Whose mind and mine I know in that are one,   15
Not to be overruled. Idle° old man,

---

¹⁵⁷⁻⁵⁸ *image and horror* true horrible picture   ¹⁵⁹ *anon* in a little while   ¹⁶⁴ *practices* plots
¹⁶⁶ *meet* proper   ¹⁶⁶ *fashion fit* shape to my purpose   I.iii.   ¹ *Fool* court jester
⁴ *crime* offense   ⁶ *riotous* dissolute   ⁹ *come . . . services* are less serviceable to him
than formerly   ¹⁰ *answer* answer for   ¹³ *come to question* be discussed openly
¹⁴ *distaste* dislike   ¹⁶ *Idle* foolish

That still would manage those authorities
That he hath given away. Now, by my life,
Old fools are babes again, and must be used
With checks as flatteries, when they are seen abused.°   20
Remember what I have said.

OSWALD.   Well, madam.

GONERIL. And let his knights have colder looks among you.
What grows of it, no matter; advise your fellows so.
I would breed from hence occasions, and I shall,
That I may speak.° I'll write straight° to my sister   25
To hold my course. Go, prepare for dinner.

Exeunt.

Scene IV. [*A hall in the same.*]

Enter Kent [disguised].

KENT. If but as well I other accents borrow
That can my speech defuse,° my good intent
May carry through itself to that full issue°
For which I razed my likeness.° Now, banished Kent,
If thou canst serve where thou dost stand condemned,   5
So may it come,° thy master whom thou lov'st
Shall find thee full of labors.

Horns within.° Enter Lear, [Knights] and Attendants.

LEAR. Let me not stay° a jot for dinner; go, get it ready. [*Exit an Attendant.*] How now, what art thou?

KENT. A man, sir.   10

LEAR. What dost thou profess?° What wouldst thou with us?

KENT. I do profess° to be no less than I seem, to serve him truly that
will put me in trust, to love him that is honest, to converse with
him that is wise and says little, to fear judgment,° to fight when
I cannot choose, and to eat no fish.°   15

LEAR. What art thou?

KENT. A very honest-hearted fellow, and as poor as the King.

---

²⁰ *With . . . abused* with restraints as well as soothing words when they are misguided
^{24–25} *breed . . . speak* find in this opportunities for speaking out   ²⁵ *straight* at once
I.iv.   ² *defuse* disguise   ³ *full issue* perfect result   ⁴ *razed my likeness* shaved off, disguised my natural appearance   ⁶ *So may it come* so may it fall out   ⁸ s.d. *within*
offstage   ⁸ *stay* wait   ¹¹ *What dost thou profess* what do you do   ¹² *profess* claim
¹⁴ *judgment* (by a heavenly or earthly judge)   ¹⁵ *eat no fish* i.e., (1) I am no Catholic,
but a loyal Protestant (2) I am no weakling (3) I use no prostitutes

LEAR. If thou be'st as poor for a subject as he's for a king, thou art poor enough. What wouldst thou?

KENT. Service.   20

LEAR. Who wouldst thou serve?

KENT. You.

LEAR. Dost thou know me, fellow?

KENT. No, sir, but you have that in your countenance° which I would fain° call master.   25

LEAR. What's that?

KENT. Authority.

LEAR. What services canst thou do?

KENT. I can keep honest counsel,° ride, run, mar a curious tale in telling it,° and deliver a plain message bluntly. That which ordi-   30
nary men are fit for, I am qualified in, and the best of me is diligence.

LEAR. How old art thou?

KENT. Not so young, sir, to love a woman for singing, nor so old to dote on her for anything. I have years on my back forty-   35
eight.

LEAR. Follow me; thou shalt serve me. If I like thee no worse after dinner, I will not part from thee yet. Dinner, ho, dinner! Where's my knave?° my Fool? Go you and call my Fool hither.

[*Exit an Attendant.*]

Enter Oswald.

You, you, sirrah, where's my daughter?   40

OSWALD. So please you—   *Exit.*

LEAR. What says the fellow there? Call the clotpoll° back. [*Exit a Knight.*] Where's my Fool? Ho, I think the world's asleep.

[*Re-enter Knight.*]

How now? Where's that mongrel?

KNIGHT. He says, my lord, your daughter is not well.   45

LEAR. Why came not the slave back to me when I called him?

KNIGHT. Sir, he answered me in the roundest° manner, he would not.

LEAR. He would not?

---

[24] *countenance* bearing   [25] *fain* like to   [29] *honest counsel* honorable secrets   [29-30] *mar . . . it* i.e., I cannot speak like an affected courtier ("curious" = "elaborate," as against "plain")   [38] *knave* boy   [41] *clotpoll* clodpoll, blockhead   [47] *roundest* rudest

KNIGHT. My lord, I know not what the matter is; but to my judgment
your Highness is not entertained° with that ceremonious affec-　　50
tion as you were wont. There's a great abatement of kindness
appears as well in the general dependants° as in the Duke himself also and your daughter.

LEAR. Ha? Say'st thou so?

KNIGHT. I beseech you pardon me, my lord, if I be mistaken; for my　　55
duty cannot be silent when I think your Highness wronged.

LEAR. Thou but rememb'rest° me of mine own conception.° I have
perceived a most faint neglect° of late, which I have rather
blamed as mine own jealous curiosity° than as a very pretense°
and purpose of unkindness. I will look further into't. But　　60
where's my Fool? I have not seen him this two days.

KNIGHT. Since my young lady's going into France, sir, the Fool hath
much pined away.

LEAR. No more of that; I have noted it well. Go you and tell my daughter I would speak with her. Go you, call hither my Fool.　　65

[Exit an Attendant.]

Enter Oswald.

O, you, sir, you! Come you hither, sir. Who am I, sir?

OSWALD. My lady's father.

LEAR. "My lady's father?" My lord's knave, you whoreson dog, you
slave, you cur!

OSWALD. I am none of these, my lord; I beseech your pardon.　　70

LEAR. Do you bandy° looks with me, you rascal?　　*[Striking him.]*

OSWALD. I'll not be strucken,° my lord.

KENT. Nor tripped neither, you base football° player.

[Tripping up his heels.]

LEAR. I thank thee, fellow. Thou serv'st me, and I'll love thee.

KENT. Come, sir, arise, away. I'll teach you differences.° Away, away.　　75
If you will measure your lubber's° length again, tarry; but away.
Go to!° Have you wisdom?° So.°　　*[Pushes Oswald out.]*

LEAR. Now, my friendly knave, I thank thee. There's earnest° of thy
service.　　*[Giving Kent money.]*

---

⁵⁰ *entertained* treated　⁵² *dependants* servants　⁵⁷ *rememb'rest* remindest　⁵⁷ *conception*
idea　⁵⁸ *faint neglect* i.e., "weary negligence" (I.iii.12)　⁵⁸ *mine own jealous curiosity*
suspicious concern for my own dignity　⁵⁹ *very pretense* actual intention　⁷¹ *bandy*
exchange insolently (metaphor from tennis)　⁷² *strucken* struck　⁷³ *football* (a low
game played by idle boys to the scandal of sensible men)　⁷⁵ *differences* (of rank)
⁷⁶ *lubber's* lout's　⁷⁷ *Go to* (expression of derisive incredulity)　⁷⁷ *Have you wisdom*
i.e., do you know what's good for you　⁷⁷ *So* good　⁷⁸ *earnest* money for services
rendered

Enter Fool.

Fool. Let me hire him too. Here's my coxcomb.°   80

> [*Offering Kent his cap.*]

Lear. How now, my pretty knave? How dost thou?

Fool. Sirrah, you were best° take my coxcomb.

Kent. Why, Fool?

Fool. Why? For taking one's part that's out of favor. Nay, an° thou
   canst not smile as the wind sits,° thou'lt catch cold shortly.   85
   There, take my coxcomb. Why, this fellow has banished° two
   on's daughters, and did the third a blessing against his will. If
   thou follow him, thou must needs wear my coxcomb. —How
   now, Nuncle?° Would I had two coxcombs and two daughters.

Lear. Why, my boy?   90

Fool. If I gave them all my living,° I'd keep my coxcombs myself.
   There's mine; beg another of thy daughters.

Lear. Take heed, sirrah—the whip.

Fool. Truth's a dog must to kennel; he must be whipped out, when
   Lady the Brach° may stand by th' fire and stink.   95

Lear. A pestilent gall° to me.

Fool. Sirrah, I'll teach thee a speech.

Lear. Do.

Fool. Mark it, Nuncle.

> Have more than thou showest,
> Speak less than thou knowest,   100
> Lend less than thou owest,°
> Ride more than thou goest,°
> Learn more than thou trowest,°
> Set less than thou throwest;°
> Leave thy drink and thy whore,   105
> And keep in-a-door,
> And thou shalt have more
> Than two tens to a score.°

Kent. This is nothing, Fool.

---

80 *coxcomb* professional fool's cap, shaped like a coxcomb   82 *you were best* you had
better   84 *an* if   85 *smile . . . sits* ingratiate yourself with those in power   86 *banished*
alienated (by making them independent)   89 *Nuncle* (contraction of "mine uncle")
91 *living* property   95 *Brach* bitch   96 *gall* sore   101 *owest* ownest   102 *goest* walkest
103 *trowest* knowest   104 *Set . . . throwest* bet less than you play for (get odds from your
opponent)   107–8 *have . . . score* i.e., come away with more than you had (two tens, or
twenty shillings, make a score, or one pound)

FOOL. Then 'tis the breath of an unfeed° lawyer —you gave me noth-   110
    ing for't. Can you make no use of nothing, Nuncle?

LEAR. Why, no, boy. Nothing can be made out of nothing.

FOOL. [*To Kent*] Prithee tell him, so much the rent of his land comes
    to; he will not believe a Fool.

LEAR. A bitter° Fool.   115

FOOL. Dost thou know the difference, my boy, between a bitter Fool
    and a sweet one?

LEAR. No, lad; teach me.

FOOL.

            That lord that counseled thee
               To give away thy land,   120
            Come place him here by me,
               Do thou for him stand.
            The sweet and bitter fool
               Will presently appear;
            The one in motley° here,   125
               The other found out° there.°

LEAR. Dost thou call me fool, boy?

FOOL. All thy other titles thou hast given away; that thou wast born
    with.

KENT. This is not altogether fool, my lord.   130

FOOL. No, faith; lords and great men will not let me.° If I had a monop-
    oly° out, they would have part on't. And ladies too, they will not
    let me have all the fool to myself; they'll be snatching. Nuncle,
    give me an egg, and I'll give thee two crowns.

LEAR. What two crowns shall they be?   135

FOOL. Why, after I have cut the egg i' th' middle and eat up the meat,
    the two crowns of the egg. When thou clovest thy crown i' th'
    middle and gav'st away both parts, thou bor'st thine ass on thy
    back o'er the dirt.° Thou hadst little wit in thy bald crown when
    thou gav'st thy golden one away. If I speak like myself° in this,   140
    let him be whipped° that first finds it so.
    [*Singing*]   Fools had ne'er less grace in a year,
                     For wise men are grown foppish,

---

110 *unfeed* unpaid for   115 *bitter* satirical   125 *motley* the drab costume of the professional
jester   126 *found out* revealed   126 *there* (the Fool points at Lear, as a fool in the
grain)   131 *let me* (have all the folly to myself)   131–32 *monopoly* (James I gave great
scandal by granting to his ''snatching'' courtiers royal patents to deal exclusively in
some commodity)   138–39 *bor'st . . . dirt* (like the foolish and unnatural countryman in
Aesop's fable)   140 *like myself* like a Fool   141 *let him be whipped* i.e., let the man be
whipped for a Fool who thinks my true saying to be foolish

And know not how their wits to wear,
　　　Their manners are so apish.°   145

LEAR. When were you wont to be so full of songs, sirrah?

FOOL. I have used° it, Nuncle, e'er since thou mad'st thy daughters
thy mothers; for when thou gav'st them the rod, and put'st
down thine own breeches,
　　[*Singing*]Then they for sudden joy did weep,   150
　　　　And I for sorrow sung,
　　　That such a king should play bo-peep°
　　　And go the fools among.
Prithee, Nuncle, keep a schoolmaster that can teach thy Fool
to lie. I would fain learn to lie.   155

LEAR. And° you lie, sirrah, we'll have you whipped.

FOOL. I marvel what kin thou and thy daughters are. They'll have me
whipped for speaking true; thou'lt have me whipped for lying;
and sometimes I am whipped for holding my peace. I had
rather be any kind o' thing than a Fool, and yet I would not be   160
thee, Nuncle; thou hast pared thy wit o' both sides and left
nothing i' th' middle. Here comes one o' the parings.

Enter Goneril.

LEAR. How now, daughter? What makes that frontlet° on? Methinks
you are too much of late i' th' frown.

FOOL. Thou wast a pretty fellow when thou hadst no need to care for   165
her frowning. Now thou art an O without a figure.° I am better
than thou art now: I am a Fool, thou art nothing. [*To Goneril.*]
Yes, forsooth, I will hold my tongue. So your face bids me,
though you say nothing. Mum, mum,
　　　　He that keeps nor crust nor crum,°   170
　　　　Weary of all, shall want° some.
　　[*Pointing to Lear*] That's a shealed peascod.°

GONERIL. Not only, sir, this your all-licensed° Fool,
But other° of your insolent retinue
Do hourly carp and quarrel, breaking forth   175
In rank° and not-to-be-endurèd riots. Sir,
I had thought by making this well known unto you

---

^{142–45} *Fools . . . apish* i.e., fools were never in less favor than now, and the reason is that
wise men, turning foolish, and not knowing how to use their intelligence, imitate the
professional fools and so make them unnecessary   ¹⁴⁷ *used* practiced   ¹⁵² *play bo-
peep* (1) act like a child (2) blind himself   ¹⁵⁶ *And* if   ¹⁶³ *frontlet* frown (lit., ornamental
band)   ¹⁶⁶ *figure* digit, to give value to the cipher (Lear is a nought)   ¹⁷⁰ *crum* soft
bread inside the loaf   ¹⁷¹ *want* lack   ¹⁷² *shealed peascod* empty pea pod   ¹⁷³ *all-
licensed* privileged to take any liberties   ¹⁷⁴ *other* others   ¹⁷⁶ *rank* gross

To have found a safe° redress, but now grow fearful,
By what yourself too late° have spoke and done,
That you protect this course, and put it on   180
By your allowance;° which if you should, the fault
Would not 'scape censure, nor the redresses sleep,°
Which, in the tender of° a wholesome weal,°
Might in their working do you that offense,
Which else were shame, that then necessity   185
Will call discreet proceeding.°

FOOL. For you know, Nuncle,
            The hedge-sparrow fed the cuckoo° so long
            That it had it head bit off by it° young.
So out went the candle, and we were left darkling.°   190

LEAR. Are you our daughter?

GONERIL. Come, sir,
I would you would make use of your good wisdom
Whereof I know you are fraught° and put away
These dispositions° which of late transport you   195
From what you rightly are.

FOOL. May not an ass know when the cart draws the horse? Whoop,
    Jug,° I love thee!

LEAR. Does any here know me? This is not Lear.
Does Lear walk thus? Speak thus? Where are his eyes?   200
Either his notion° weakens, or his discernings°
Are lethargied°—Ha! Waking? 'Tis not so.
Who is it that can tell me who I am?

FOOL. Lear's shadow.

LEAR. I would learn that; for, by the marks of sovereignty,° knowl-   205
    edge, and reason, I should be false° persuaded I had
    daughters.

FOOL. Which° they will make an obedient father.

LEAR. Your name, fair gentlewoman?

GONERIL. This admiration,° sir, is much o' th' savor°   210

---

[178] *safe* sure   [179] *too late* lately   [180-81] *put . . . allowance* promote it by your approval   [181] *allowance* approval   [182] *redresses sleep* correction fail to follow   [183] *tender of* desire for   [183] *weal* state   [184-86] *Might . . . proceeding* as I apply it, the correction might humiliate you; but the need to take action cancels what would otherwise be unfilial conduct in me   [188] *cuckoo* (who lays its eggs in the nests of other birds)   [189] *it* its   [190] *darkling* in the dark   [194] *fraught* endowed   [195] *dispositions* moods   [198] *Jug* Joan (? a quotation from a popular song)   [201] *notion* understanding   [201] *discernings* faculties   [202] *lethargied* paralyzed   [205] *marks of sovereignty* i.e., tokens that Lear is king, and hence father to his daughters   [206] *false* falsely   [208] *Which* whom (Lear)   [210] *admiration* (affected) wonderment   [210] *is much o' th' savor* smacks much

Of other your° new pranks. I do beseech you
To understand my purposes aright.
As you are old and reverend, should be wise.
Here do you keep a hundred knights and squires,
Men so disordered, so deboshed,° and bold,   215
That this our court, infected with their manners,
Shows° like a riotous inn. Epicurism° and lust
Makes it more like a tavern or a brothel
Than a graced° palace. The shame itself doth speak
For instant remedy. Be then desired°   220
By her, that else will take the thing she begs,
A little to disquantity your train,°
And the remainders° that shall still depend,°
To be such men as may besort° your age,
Which know themselves, and you.

LEAR.   Darkness and devils!   225
Saddle my horses; call my train together.
Degenerate° bastard, I'll not trouble thee:
Yet have I left a daughter.

GONERIL. You strike my people, and your disordered rabble
Make servants of their betters.   230

Enter Albany.

LEAR. Woe, that too late repents. O, sir, are you come?
Is it your will? Speak, sir. Prepare my horses.
Ingratitude! thou marble-hearted fiend,
More hideous when thou show'st thee in a child
Than the sea-monster.

ALBANY.   Pray, sir, be patient.   235

LEAR. Detested kite,° thou liest.
My train are men of choice and rarest parts,°
That all particulars of duty know,
And, in the most exact regard,° support
The worships° of their name. O most small fault,   240
How ugly didst thou in Cordelia show!
Which, like an engine,° wrenched my frame of nature
From the fixed place;° drew from my heart all love,

---

²¹¹ *other your* others of your   ²¹⁵ *deboshed* debauched   ²¹⁷ *Shows* appears   ²¹⁷ *Epicurism*
riotous living   ²¹⁹ *graced* dignified   ²²⁰ *desired* requested   ²²² *disquantity your train*
reduce the number of your dependents   ²²³ *remainders* those who remain   ²²³ *depend*
attend on you   ²²⁴ *besort* befit   ²²⁸ *Degenerate* unnatural   ²³⁶ *kite* scavenging bird of
prey   ²³⁷ *parts* accomplishments   ²³⁹ *exact regard* strict attention to detail
²⁴⁰ *worships* honor   ²⁴² *engine* destructive contrivance   ²⁴²⁻⁴³ *wrenched . . . place* i.e.,
disordered my natural self

And added to the gall.° O Lear, Lear, Lear!
Beat at this gate that let thy folly in [*Striking his head.*]   245
And thy dear judgment out. Go, go, my people.

ALBANY. My lord, I am guiltless, as I am ignorant
Of what hath moved you.

LEAR.   It may be so, my lord.
Hear, Nature, hear; dear Goddess, hear:
Suspend thy purpose if thou didst intend   250
To make this creature fruitful.
Into her womb convey sterility,
Dry up in her the organs of increase,°
And from her derogate° body never spring
A babe to honor her. If she must teem,°   255
Create her child of spleen,° that it may live
And be a thwart disnatured° torment to her.
Let it stamp wrinkles in her brow of youth,
With cadent° tears fret° channels in her cheeks,
Turn all her mother's pains and benefits°   260
To laughter and contempt, that she may feel
How sharper than a serpent's tooth it is
To have a thankless child. Away, away!   *Exit.*

ALBANY. Now, gods that we adore, whereof comes this?

GONERIL. Never afflict yourself to know the cause,   265
But let his disposition° have that scope
As° dotage gives it.

Enter Lear.

LEAR. What, fifty of my followers at a clap?°
Within a fortnight?

ALBANY.   What's the matter, sir?

LEAR. I'll tell thee. [*To Goneril*] Life and death, I am ashamed   270
That thou hast power to shake my manhood° thus!
That these hot tears, which break from me perforce,°
Should make thee worth them. Blasts and fogs upon thee!
Th' untented woundings° of a father's curse
Pierce every sense about thee! Old fond° eyes,   275
Beweep° this cause again, I'll pluck ye out

---

²⁴⁴ *gall* bitterness   ²⁵³ *increase* childbearing   ²⁵⁴ *derogate* degraded   ²⁵⁵ *teem* conceive   ²⁵⁶ *spleen* ill humor   ²⁵⁷ *thwart disnatured* perverse unnatural   ²⁵⁹ *cadent* falling   ²⁵⁹ *fret* wear   ²⁶⁰ *benefits* the mother's beneficent care of her child   ²⁶⁶ *disposition* mood   ²⁶⁷ *As* that   ²⁶⁸ *at a clap* at one stroke   ²⁷¹ *shake my manhood* i.e., with tears   ²⁷² *perforce* involuntarily, against my will   ²⁷⁴ *untented woundings* wounds too deep to be probed with a tent (a roll of lint)   ²⁷⁵ *fond* foolish   ²⁷⁶ *Beweep* if you weep over

And cast you, with the waters that you loose,°
To temper° clay. Yea, is it come to this?
Ha! Let it be so. I have another daughter,
Who I am sure is kind and comfortable.° 280
When she shall hear this of thee, with her nails
She'll flay thy wolvish visage. Thou shalt find
That I'll resume the shape° which thou dost think
I have cast off for ever.

Exit (Lear with Kent and Attendants.)

GONERIL.   Do you mark that?

ALBANY. I cannot be so partial, Goneril, 285
To the great love I bear you°—

GONERIL. Pray you, content. What, Oswald, ho!
    (*To the Fool*) You, sir, more knave than fool, after your
      master!

FOOL. Nuncle Lear, Nuncle Lear, tarry. Take the Fool° with thee.
          A fox, when one has caught her, 290
          And such a daughter,
          Should sure to the slaughter,
          If my cap would buy a halter.°
          So the Fool follows after.°   *Exit.*

GONERIL. This man hath had good counsel. A hundred knights! 295
    'Tis politic° and safe to let him keep
    At point° a hundred knights: yes, that on every dream,
    Each buzz,° each fancy, each complaint, dislike,
    He may enguard° his dotage with their pow'rs
    And hold our lives in mercy.° Oswald, I say! 300

ALBANY. Well, you may fear too far.

GONERIL.   Safer than trust too far.
    Let me still take away the harms I fear,
    Not fear still to be taken.° I know his heart.
    What he hath uttered I have writ my sister.
    If she sustain him and his hundred knights, 305
    When I have showed th' unfitness—

---

²⁷⁷ *loose* (1) let loose (2) lose, as of no avail   ²⁷⁸ *temper* mix with and soften ²⁸⁰ *comfortable* ready to comfort   ²⁸³ *shape* i.e., kingly role   ²⁸⁵⁻⁸⁶ *I cannot . . . you* i.e., even though my love inclines me to you, I must protest   ²⁸⁹ *Fool* (1) the Fool himself (2) the epithet or character of "fool"   ²⁹³⁻⁹⁴ *halter, after* pronounced "hauter," "auter"   ²⁹⁶ *politic* good policy   ²⁹⁷ *At point* armed   ²⁹⁸ *buzz* rumor   ²⁹⁹ *enguard* protect   ³⁰⁰ *in mercy* at his mercy   ³⁰³ *Not . . . taken* rather than remain fearful of being overtaken by them

Enter Oswald.

How now, Oswald?
What, have you writ that letter to my sister?

OSWALD. Ay, madam.

GONERIL. Take you some company,° and away to horse.
Inform her full of my particular° fear,   310
And thereto add such reasons of your own
As may compact° it more. Get you gone,
And hasten your return. [*Exit Oswald.*] No, no, my lord,
This milky gentleness and course° of yours,
Though I condemn not,° yet under pardon,   315
You are much more attasked° for want of wisdom
Than praised for harmful mildness.°

ALBANY. How far your eyes may pierce I cannot tell;
Striving to better, oft we mar what's well.

GONERIL. Nay then—   320

ALBANY. Well, well, th' event.°   *Exeunt.*

Scene V. [*Court before the same.*]

Enter Lear, Kent, and Fool.

LEAR. Go you before to Gloucester with these letters. Acquaint my
daughter no further with anything you know than comes from
her demand out of the letter.° If your diligence be not speedy, I
shall be there afore you.

KENT. I will not sleep, my lord, till I have delivered your letter.   5

Exit.

FOOL. If a man's brains were in's heels, were't° not in danger of
kibes?°

LEAR. Ay, boy.

FOOL. Then I prithee be merry. Thy wit shall not go slipshod.°

LEAR. Ha, ha, ha.   10

---

[309] *company* escort   [310] *particular* own   [312] *compact* strengthen   [314] *milky . . . course* mild
and gentle way (hendiadys)   [315] *condemn not* condemn it not   [316] *attasked* taken to
task, blamed   [317] *harmful mildness* dangerous indulgence   [321] *th' event* i.e., we'll see
what happens   I.v.   [2-3] *than . . . letter* than her reading of the letter brings her to
ask   [6] *were't* i.e., the brains   [7] *kibes* chilblains   [9] *Thy . . . slipshod* your brains shall
not go in slippers (because you have no brains to be protected from chilblains)

Fool. Shalt° see thy other daughter will use thee kindly;° for though
    she's as like this as a crab's° like an apple, yet I can tell what I
    can tell.

Lear. Why, what canst thou tell, my boy?

Fool. She will taste as like this as a crab does to a crab. Thou canst   15
    tell why one's nose stands i' th' middle on's° face?

Lear. No.

Fool. Why, to keep one's eyes of° either side's nose, that what a man
    cannot smell out, he may spy into.

Lear. I did her wrong.   20

Fool. Canst tell how an oyster makes his shell?

Lear. No.

Fool. Nor I neither; but I can tell why a snail has a house.

Lear. Why?

Fool. Why, to put 's head in; not to give it away to his daughters, and   25
    leave his horns° without a case.

Lear. I will forget my nature.° So kind a father! Be my horses ready?

Fool. Thy asses are gone about 'em. The reason why the seven
    stars° are no moe° than seven is a pretty° reason.

Lear. Because they are not eight.   30

Fool. Yes indeed. Thou wouldst make a good Fool.

Lear. To take't again perforce!° Monster ingratitude!

Fool. If thou wert my Fool, Nuncle, I'd have thee beaten for being
    old before thy time.

Lear. How's that?   35

Fool. Thou shouldst not have been old till thou hadst been wise.

Lear. O, let me not be mad, not mad, sweet heaven! Keep me in tem-
    per;° I would not be mad!

[Enter Gentleman.]

    How now, are the horses ready?

Gentleman. Ready, my lord.   40

Lear. Come, boy.

---

[11] *Shalt* thou shalt   [11] *kindly* (1) affectionately (2) after her kind or nature   [12] *crab* crab
apple   [16] *on's* of his   [18] *of* on   [26] *horns* (1) snail's horns (2) cuckold's horns
[27] *nature* paternal instincts   [28-29] *seven stars* the Pleiades   [29] *moe* more   [29] *pretty*
apt   [32] *To . . . perforce* (1) of Goneril, who has forcibly taken away Lear's privileges; or
(2) of Lear, who meditates a forcible resumption of authority   [37-38] *in temper* sane

FOOL. She that's a maid now, and laughs at my departure,
     Shall not be a maid long, unless things be cut shorter.°*Exeunt.*

ACT II

Scene I. [*The Earl of Gloucester's castle.*]

Enter Edmund and Curan, severally.°

EDMUND. Save° thee, Curan.

CURAN. And you, sir. I have been with your father, and given him
     notice that the Duke of Cornwall and Regan his duchess will be
     here with him this night.

EDMUND. How comes that?   5

CURAN. Nay, I know not. You have heard of the news abroad? I mean
     the whispered ones, for they are yet but ear-kissing arguments.°

EDMUND. Not I. Pray you, what are they?

CURAN. Have you heard of no likely° wars toward,° 'twixt the Dukes of
     Cornwall and Albany?   10

EDMUND. Not a word.

CURAN. You may do, then, in time. Fare you well, sir.   *Exit.*

EDMUND. The Duke be here tonight? The better!° best!
     This weaves itself perforce° into my business.
     My father hath set guard to take my brother,   15
     And I have one thing of a queasy question°
     Which I must act. Briefness° and Fortune, work!
     Brother, a word; descend. Brother, I say!

Enter Edgar.

My father watches. O sir, fly this place.
     Intelligence° is given where you are hid.   20
     You have now the good advantage of the night.
     Have you not spoken 'gainst the Duke of Cornwall?
     He's coming hither, now i' th' night, i' th' haste,°

42–43 *She . . . shorter* the maid who laughs, missing the tragic implications of this quarrel,
will not have sense enough to preserve her virginity ("things" = penises) II.i.
1 s.d.*severally* separately (from different entrances on stage)   1 *Save* God save   7 *ear-
kissing arguments* subjects whispered in the ear   9 *likely* probable   9 *toward*
impending   13 *The better* so much the better   14 *perforce* necessarily   16 *of a queasy
question* that requires delicate handling (to be "queasy" is to be on the point of
vomiting)   17 *Briefness* speed   20 *Intelligence* information   23 *i' th' haste* in great
haste

And Regan with him. Have you nothing said
Upon his party° 'gainst the Duke of Albany?   25
Advise yourself.°

EDGAR. I am sure on't,° not a word.

EDMUND. I hear my father coming. Pardon me:
In cunning° I must draw my sword upon you.
Draw, seem to defend yourself; now quit you° well.   30
Yield! Come before my father! Light ho, here!
Fly, brother. Torches, torches!—So farewell.

                                        Exit Edgar.

Some blood drawn on me would beget opinion°

                              (*Wounds his arm*)

Of my more fierce endeavor. I have seen drunkards
Do more than this in sport. Father, father!   35
Stop, stop! No help?

            Enter Gloucester, and Servants with torches.

GLOUCESTER. Now, Edmund, where's the villain?

EDMUND. Here stood he in the dark, his sharp sword out,
Mumbling of wicked charms, conjuring the moon
To stand auspicious mistress.

GLOUCESTER.   But where is he?   40

EDMUND. Look, sir, I bleed.

GLOUCESTER.   Where is the villain, Edmund?

EDMUND. Fled this way, sir, when by no means he could—

GLOUCESTER. Pursue him, ho! Go after.

                              (*Exeunt some Servants.*)

By no means what?

EDMUND. Persuade me to the murder of your lordship;
But that I told him the revenging gods   45
'Gainst parricides did all the thunder bend;°
Spoke with how manifold and strong a bond
The child was bound to th' father. Sir, in fine,°
Seeing how loathly opposite° I stood
To his unnatural purpose, in fell° motion°   50
With his preparèd sword he charges home
My unprovided° body, latched° mine arm;
But when he saw my best alarumed° spirits

---

²⁵ *Upon his party* censuring his enmity   ²⁶ *Advise yourself* reflect   ²⁷ *on't* of it   ²⁹ *In cunning* as a pretense   ³⁰ *quit you* acquit yourself   ³³ *beget opinion* create the impression   ⁴⁶ *bend* aim   ⁴⁸ *in fine* finally   ⁴⁹ *loathly opposite* bitterly opposed   ⁵⁰ *fell* deadly   ⁵⁰ *motion* thrust (a term from fencing)   ⁵² *unprovided* unprotected   ⁵² *latched* wounded (lanced)   ⁵³ *best alarumed* wholly aroused

Bold in the quarrel's right,° roused to th' encounter,
Or whether gasted° by the noise I made,   55
Full suddenly he fled.

GLOUCESTER.   Let him fly far.
Not in this land shall he remain uncaught;
And found—dispatch.° The noble Duke my master,
My worthy arch° and patron, comes tonight.
By his authority I will proclaim it,   60
That he which finds him shall deserve our thanks,
Bringing the murderous coward to the stake.
He that conceals him, death.°

EDMUND. When I dissuaded him from his intent,
And found him pight° to do it, with curst° speech   65
I threatened to discover° him. He replied,
"Thou unpossessing° bastard, dost thou think,
If I would stand against thee, would the reposal°
Of any trust, virtue, or worth in thee
Make thy words faithed?° No. What I should deny—   70
As this I would, ay, though thou didst produce
My very character°—I'd turn it all
To thy suggestion,° plot, and damnèd practice.°
And thou must make a dullard of the world,°
If they not thought° the profits of my death   75
Were very pregnant° and potential spirits°
To make thee seek it."

GLOUCESTER.   O strange and fastened° villain!
Would he deny his letter, said he? I never got° him.
                                   Tucket° within.
Hark, the Duke's trumpets. I know not why he comes.
All ports° I'll bar; the villain shall not 'scape;   80
The Duke must grant me that. Besides, his picture
I will send far and near, that all the kingdom
May have due note of him; and of my land,
Loyal and natural° boy, I'll work the means
To make thee capable.°   85

---

[54] *Bold ... right* confident in the rightness of my cause   [55] *gasted* struck aghast
[58] *dispatch* i.e., he will be killed   [59] *arch* chief   [67] *death* (the same elliptical form that
characterizes "dispatch," l. 62)   [65] *pight* determined   [65] *curst* angry   [66] *discover*
expose   [67] *unpossessing* beggarly (landless)   [68] *reposal* placing   [70] *faithed* believed
[72] *character* handwriting   [73] *suggestion* instigation   [73] *practice* device   [74] *make ...
world* think everyone stupid   [75] *not thought* did not think   [76] *pregnant* teeming with
incitement   [76] *potential spirits* powerful evil spirits   [77] *fastened* hardened   [78] *got*
begot   [79] s.d. *Tucket* (Cornwall's special trumpet call)   [80] *ports* exits, of whatever
sort   [84] *natural* (1) kind (filial) (2) illegitimate   [85] *capable* able to inherit

Enter Cornwall, Regan, and Attendants.

CORNWALL. How now, my noble friend! Since I came hither,
    Which I can call but now, I have heard strange news.

REGAN. If it be true, all vengeance comes too short
    Which can pursue th' offender. How dost, my lord?

GLOUCESTER. O madam, my old heart is cracked, it's cracked.   90

REGAN. What, did my father's godson seek your life?
    He whom my father named, your Edgar?

GLOUCESTER. O lady, lady, shame would have it hid.

REGAN. Was he not companion with the riotous knights
    That tended upon my father?   95

GLOUCESTER. I know not, madam. 'Tis too bad, too bad.

EDMUND. Yes, madam, he was of that consort.°

REGAN. No marvel then, though he were ill affected.°
    'Tis they have put° him on the old man's death,
    To have th' expense and waste° of his revenues.   100
    I have this present evening from my sister
    Been well informed of them, and with such cautions
    That, if they come to sojourn at my house,
    I'll not be there.

CORNWALL.   Nor I, assure thee, Regan.   105
    Edmund, I hear that you have shown your father
    A childlike° office.

EDMUND. It was my duty, sir.

GLOUCESTER. He did bewray his practice,° and received
    This hurt you see, striving to apprehend him.

CORNWALL. Is he pursued?

GLOUCESTER.   Ay, my good lord.   110

CORNWALL. If he be taken, he shall never more
    Be feared of doing° harm. Make your own purpose,
    How in my strength you please.° For you, Edmund,
    Whose virtue and obedience° doth this instant
    So much commend itself, you shall be ours.   115
    Natures of such deep trust we shall much need;
    You we first seize on.

EDMUND.   I shall serve you, sir,
    Truly, however else.

---

[97] *consort* company   [98] *ill affected* disposed to evil   [99] *put* set   [100] *expense and waste*
squandering   [106] *childlike* filial   [108] *bewray his practice* disclose his plot   [112] *of doing*
because he might do   [112–13] *Make . . . please* use my power freely, in carrying out your
plans for his capture   [114] *virtue and obedience* virtuous obedience

GLOUCESTER. For him I thank your Grace.

CORNWALL. You know not why we came to visit you?

REGAN. Thus out of season, threading dark-eyed night. 120
    Occasions, noble Gloucester, of some prize,°
    Wherein we must have use of your advice.
    Our father he hath writ, so hath our sister,
    Of differences,° which ° I best thought it fit
    To answer from° our home. The several messengers 125
    From hence attend dispatch.° Our good old friend,
    Lay comforts to your bosom,° and bestow
    Your needful° counsel to our businesses,
    Which craves the instant use.°

GLOUCESTER. I serve you, madam.
    Your Graces are right welcome. 130

Exeunt. Flourish.

Scene II. [*Before Gloucester's castle.*]

Enter Kent and Oswald, severally.

OSWALD. Good dawning° to thee, friend. Art of this house?°

KENT. Ay.

OSWALD. Where may we set our horses?

KENT. I' th' mire.

OSWALD. Prithee, if thou lov'st me, tell me. 5

KENT. I love thee not.

OSWALD. Why then, I care not for thee.

KENT. If I had thee in Lipsbury Pinfold,° I would make thee care for
    me.

OSWALD. Why dost thou use me thus? I know thee not. 10

KENT. Fellow, I know thee.

OSWALD. What dost thou know me for?

KENT. A knave, a rascal, an eater of broken meats;° a base, proud,
    shallow, beggarly, three-suited,° hundred-pound,° filthy wor-

---

[121] *prize* importance [124] *differences* quarrels [124] *which* (referring not to "differences," but
to the letter Lear has written) [125] *from* away from [126] *attend dispatch* are waiting to
be sent off [127] *Lay . . . bosom* console yourself (about Edgar's supposed treason)
[128] *needful* needed [129] *craves the instant use* demands immediate transaction
II.ii. [1] *dawning* (dawn is impending, but not yet arrived) [1] *Art of this house* i.e., do
you live here [8] *Lipsbury Pinfold* a pound or pen in which strayed animals are enclosed
("Lipsbury" may denote a particular place, or may be slang for "between my teeth")
[13] *broken meats* scraps of food [14] *three-suited* (the wardrobe permitted to a servant or
"knave") [14] *hundred-pound* (the extent of Oswald's wealth, and thus a sneer at his
aspiring to gentility)

sted-stocking° knave; a lily-livered, action-taking,° whoreson,   15
glass-gazing,° superserviceable,° finical° rogue; one-trunk-
inheriting° slave; one that wouldst be a bawd in way of good
service,° and art nothing but the composition° of a knave, beggar, coward, pander, and the son and heir of a mongrel bitch;
one whom I will beat into clamorous whining if thou deniest the   20
least syllable of thy addition.°

OSWALD. Why, what a monstrous fellow art thou, thus to rail on one
that is neither known of thee nor knows thee!

KENT. What a brazen-faced varlet art thou to deny thou knowest me!
Is it two days since I tripped up thy heels and beat thee before   25
the King? (*Drawing his sword*) Draw, you rogue, for though it be
night, yet the moon shines. I'll make a sop o' th' moonshine°
of you. You whoreson cullionly barbermonger,° draw!

OSWALD. Away, I have nothing to do with thee.

KENT. Draw, you rascal. You come with letters against the King, and   30
take Vanity the puppet's° part against the royalty of her father.
Draw, you rogue, or I'll so carbonado° your shanks. Draw, you
rascal. Come your ways!°

OSWALD. Help, ho! Murder! Help!

KENT. Strike, you slave! Stand, rogue! Stand, you neat° slave! Strike!   35
(*Beating him*)

OSWALD. Help, ho! Murder, murder!

Enter Edmund, with his rapier drawn, Cornwall, Regan, Gloucester,
Servants

EDMUND. How now? What's the matter? Part!

KENT. With you,° goodman boy,° if you please! Come, I'll flesh° ye,
come on, young master.

GLOUCESTER. Weapons? Arms? What's the matter here?   40

CORNWALL. Keep peace, upon your lives.
He dies that strikes again. What is the matter?

---

¹⁴⁻¹⁵ *worsted-stocking* (worn by servants)   ¹⁵ *action-taking* one who refuses a fight and goes
to law instead   ¹⁶ *glass-gazing* conceited   ¹⁶ *superserviceable* sycophantic, serving
without principle   ¹⁶ *finical* overfastidious   ¹⁶⁻¹⁷ *one-trunk-inheriting* possessing only
a trunkful of goods   ¹⁷⁻¹⁸ *bawd . . . service* pimp, to please his master   ¹⁸ *composition*
compound   ²¹ *addition* titles   ²⁷ *sop o' th' moonshine* i.e., Oswald will admit the
moonlight, and so sop it up, through the open wounds Kent is preparing to give him
²⁸ *cullionly barbermonger* base patron of hairdressers (effeminate man)   ³¹ *Vanity the*
puppet's Goneril, here identified with one of the personified characters in the morality
plays, which were sometimes put on as puppet shows   ³² *carbonado* cut across, like a
piece of meat before cooking   ³³ *Come your ways* get along   ³⁵ *neat* (1) foppish (2)
unmixed, as in "neat wine"   ³⁸ *With you* i.e., the quarrel is with you   ³⁸ *goodman boy*
young man (peasants are "goodmen"; "boy" is a term of contempt)   ³⁸ *flesh* introduce
to blood (term from hunting)

Regan. The messengers from our sister and the King.

Cornwall. What is your difference?° Speak.

Oswald. I am scarce in breath, my lord.　　　　　　　　　　　45

Kent. No marvel, you have so bestirred° your valor. You cowardly
　　rascal, nature disclaims in thee.° A tailor made thee.°

Cornwall. Thou art a strange fellow. A tailor make a man?

Kent. A tailor, sir. A stonecutter or a painter could not have made
　　him so ill, though they had been but two years o' th' trade.　　50

Cornwall. Speak yet, how grew your quarrel?

Oswald. This ancient ruffian, sir, whose life I have spared at suit of°
　　his gray beard—

Kent. Thou whoreson zed,° thou unnecessary letter! My lord, if you
　　will give me leave, I will tread this unbolted° villain into mortar　　55
　　and daub the wall of a jakes° with him. Spare my gray beard,
　　you wagtail!°

Cornwall. Peace, sirrah!
　　You beastly° knave, know you no reverence?

Kent. Yes, sir, but anger hath a privilege.　　　　　　　　　60

Cornwall. Why art thou angry?

Kent. That such a slave as this should wear a sword,
　　Who wears no honesty. Such smiling rogues as these,
　　Like rats, oft bite the holy cords° atwain
　　Which are too intrince° t' unloose; smooth° every passion　　65
　　That in the natures of their lords rebel,
　　Being oil to fire, snow to the colder moods;
　　Renege,° affirm, and turn their halcyon beaks°
　　With every gale and vary° of their masters,
　　Knowing naught, like dogs, but following.　　　　　　　70
　　A plague upon your epileptic° visage!
　　Smile you° my speeches, as I were a fool?
　　Goose, if I had you upon Sarum Plain,°
　　I'd drive ye cackling home to Camelot.°

---

⁴⁴ *difference* quarrel　⁴⁶ *bestirred* exercised　⁴⁷ *nature disclaims in thee* nature renounces
any part in you　⁴⁷ *A tailor made thee* (from the proverb "The tailor makes the man")
⁵² *at suit of* out of pity for　⁵⁴ *zed* the letter *Z*, generally omitted in contemporary
dictionaries　⁵⁵ *unbolted* unsifted, i.e., altogether a villain　⁵⁶ *jakes* privy　⁵⁷ *wagtail* a
bird that bobs its tail up and down, and thus suggests obsequiousness　⁵⁹ *beastly*
irrational　⁶⁴ *holy cords* sacred bonds of affection (as between husbands and wives,
parents and children)　⁶⁵ *intrince* entangled, intricate　⁶⁵ *smooth* appease　⁶⁸ *Renege*
deny　⁶⁸ *halcyon beaks* (the halcyon or kingfisher serves here as a type of the oppor-
tunist because, when hung up by the tail or neck, it was supposed to turn with the wind,
like a weathervane)　⁶⁹ *gale and vary* varying gale (hendiadys)　⁷¹ *epileptic* distorted
by grinning　⁷² *Smile you* do you smile at　⁷³ *Sarum Plain* Salisbury Plain　⁷⁴ *Camelot*
the residence of King Arthur (presumably a particular point, now lost, is intended here)

CORNWALL. What, art thou mad, old fellow?   75

GLOUCESTER. How fell you out? Say that.

KENT. No contraries° hold more antipathy
    Than I and such a knave.

CORNWALL. Why dost thou call him knave? What is his fault?

KENT. His countenance likes° me not.   80

CORNWALL. No more perchance does mine, nor his, nor hers.

KENT. Sir, 'tis my occupation to be plain:
    I have seen better faces in my time
    Than stands on any shoulder that I see
    Before me at this instant.

CORNWALL.   This is some fellow   85
    Who, having been praised for bluntness, doth affect
    A saucy roughness, and constrains the garb
    Quite from his nature.° He cannot flatter, he;
    An honest mind and plain, he must speak truth.
    And° they will take it, so; if not, he's plain.   90
    These kind of knaves I know, which in this plainness
    Harbor more craft and more corrupter ends
    Than twenty silly-ducking observants°
    That stretch their duties nicely.°

KENT. Sir, in good faith, in sincere verity,   95
    Under th' allowance° of your great aspect,°
    Whose influence,° like the wreath of radiant fire
    On flick'ring Phoebus' front°—

CORNWALL.   What mean'st by this?

KENT. To go out of my dialect,° which you discommend so much. I
    know, sir, I am no flatterer. He° that beguiled you in a plain   100
    accent was a plain knave, which, for my part, I will not be,
    though I should win your displeasure to entreat me to't.°

CORNWALL. What was th' offense you gave him?

OSWALD. I never gave him any.
    It pleased the King his master very late°   105

°⁷⁷ *contraries* opposites   °⁸⁰ *likes* pleases   °⁸⁷⁻⁸⁸ *constrains . . . nature* forces the manner of
candid speech to be a cloak, not for candor but for craft   °⁹⁰ *And* if   °⁹³ *silly-ducking
observants* ridiculously obsequious attendants   °⁹⁴ *nicely* punctiliously   °⁹⁶ *allowance*
approval   °⁹⁶ *aspect* (1) appearance (2) position of the heavenly bodies   °⁹⁷ *influence*
astrological power   °⁹⁸ *Phoebus' front* forehead of the sun   °⁹⁹ *dialect* customary manner of speaking   °¹⁰⁰ *He* i.e., the sort of candid-crafty man Cornwall has been
describing   °¹⁰² *though . . . to't* even if I were to succeed in bringing your graceless person (``displeasure'' personified, and in lieu of the expected form, ``your grace'') to beg
me to be a plain knave   °¹⁰⁵ *very late* recently

To strike at me, upon his misconstruction;°
When he, compact,° and flattering his displeasure,
Tripped me behind; being down, insulted, railed,
And put upon him such a deal of man°
That worthied him,° got praises of the King　　　　　　　110
For him attempting who was self-subdued;°
And, in the fleshment° of this dread exploit,
Drew on me here again.

KENT.　　　　　　　　　　　None of these rogues and cowards
But Ajax is their fool.°

CORNWALL.　　　　　　　　Fetch forth the stocks!　　　　　115
You stubborn° ancient knave, you reverent° braggart,
We'll teach you.

KENT.　　　　　　　　Sir, I am too old to learn.
Call not your stocks for me, I serve the King,
On whose employment I was sent to you.
You shall do small respect, show too bold malice　　　120
Against the grace and person° of my master,
Stocking his messenger.

CORNWALL. Fetch forth the stocks. As I have life and honor,
There shall he sit till noon.

REGAN. Till noon? Till night, my lord, and all night too.　　125

KENT. Why, madam, if I were your father's dog,
You should not use me so.

REGAN.　　　　　　　　　　Sir, being his knave, I will.

CORNWALL. This is a fellow of the selfsame color°
Our sister speaks of. Come, bring away° the stocks.

　　　　　　　　　　　　　　　Stocks brought out.

GLOUCESTER. Let me beseech your Grace not to do so.　　130
His fault is much, and the good King his master
Will check° him for't. Your purposed° low correction
Is such as basest and contemnèd'st° wretches
For pilf'rings and most common trespasses
Are punished with.　　　　　　　　　　　　　　　135
The King his master needs must take it ill

---

[106] *misconstruction* misunderstanding　[107] *compact* in league with the king　[109] *put . . . man* pretended such manly behavior　[110] *worthied him* made him seem heroic　[111] *For . . . self-subdued* for attacking a man (Oswald) who offered no resistance　[112] *fleshment* the bloodthirstiness excited by his first success or "fleshing"　[114–15] *None . . . fool* i.e., cowardly rogues like Oswald always impose on fools like Cornwall (who is likened to Ajax: (1) the braggart Greek warrior (2) a jakes or privy)　[116] *stubborn* rude　[116] *reverent* old　[121] *grace and person* i.e., Lear as sovereign and in his personal character　[128] *color* kind　[129] *away* out　[132] *check* correct　[132] *purposed* intended　[133] *contemnèd'st* most despised

That he, so slightly valued in° his messenger,
Should have him thus restrained.

CORNWALL.   I'll answer° that.

REGAN. My sister may receive it much more worse,
To have her gentleman abused, assaulted,   140
For following her affairs. Put in his legs.
                              [*Kent is put in the stocks.*]
     Come, my good lord, away!
                    [*Exeunt all but Gloucester and Kent.*]

GLOUCESTER. I am sorry for thee, friend. 'Tis the Duke's pleasure,
Whose disposition° all the world well knows
Will not be rubbed° nor stopped. I'll entreat for thee.   145

KENT. Pray do not, sir. I have watched° and traveled hard.
Some time I shall sleep out, the rest I'll whistle.
A good man's fortune may grow out at heels.°
Give° you good morrow.

GLOUCESTER. The Duke's to blame in this. 'Twill be ill taken.°   *Exit.*   150

KENT. Good King, that must approve° the common saw,°
Thou out of Heaven's benediction com'st
To the warm sun.°
Approach, thou beacon to this under globe,°
That by thy comfortable° beams I may   155
Peruse this letter. Nothing almost sees miracles
But misery.° I know 'tis from Cordelia,
Who hath most fortunately been informed
Of my obscurèd° course. And shall find time
From this enormous state, seeking to give   160
Losses their remedies.° All weary and o'erwatched,
Take vantage,° heavy eyes, not to behold
This shameful lodging. Fortune, good night;
Smile once more, turn thy wheel.°
                                                        Sleeps.

---

¹³⁶ *slightly valued in* little honored in the person of   ¹³⁷ *answer* answer for   ¹⁴⁴ *disposition* inclination   ¹⁴⁵ *rubbed* diverted (metaphor from the game of bowls)   ¹⁴⁶ *watched* gone without sleep   ¹⁴⁸ *A . . . heels* even a good man may have bad fortune   ¹⁴⁹ *Give* God give   ¹⁵⁰ *taken* received   ¹⁵¹ *approve* confirm   ¹⁵¹ *saw* proverb   ¹⁵²⁻⁵³ *Thou . . . sun* i.e., Lear goes from better to worse, from Heaven's blessing or shelter to lack of shelter   ¹⁵⁴ *beacon . . . globe* i.e., the sun, whose rising Kent anticipates   ¹⁵⁵ *comfortable* comforting   ¹⁵⁶⁻⁵⁷ *Nothing . . . misery* i.e., true perception belongs only to the wretched   ¹⁵⁹ *obscurèd* disguised   ¹⁵⁹⁻⁶¹ *shall . . . remedies* (a possible reading: Cordelia, away from this monstrous state of things, will find occasion to right the wrongs we suffer)   ¹⁶² *vantage* advantage (of sleep)   ¹⁶⁴ *turn thy wheel* i.e., so that Kent, who is at the bottom, may climb upward

[Scene III. *A wood.*]

Enter Edgar.

EDGAR. I heard myself proclaimed,
  And by the happy° hollow of a tree
  Escaped the hunt. No port is free, no place
  That guard and most unusual vigilance
  Does not attend my taking.° Whiles I may 'scape,   5
  I will preserve myself; and am bethought°
  To take the basest and most poorest shape
  That ever penury, in contempt of man,
  Brought near to beast;° my face I'll grime with filth,
  Blanket° my loins, elf° all my hairs in knots,   10
  And with presented° nakedness outface°
  The winds and persecutions of the sky.
  The country gives me proof° and precedent
  Of Bedlam° beggars, who, with roaring voices,
  Strike° in their numbed and mortified° bare arms   15
  Pins, wooden pricks,° nails, sprigs of rosemary;
  And with this horrible object,° from low° farms,
  Poor pelting° villages, sheepcotes, and mills,
  Sometimes with lunatic bans,° sometime with prayers,
  Enforce their charity. Poor Turlygod, Poor Tom,°   20
  That's something yet: Edgar I nothing am.°

                                                              Exit.

[Scene IV. *Before Gloucester's castle. Kent in the stocks.*]

Enter Lear, Fool, and Gentleman.

LEAR. 'Tis strange that they should so depart from home,
  And not send back my messenger.

GENTLEMAN.   As I learned,
  The night before there was no purpose° in them
  Of this remove.°

KENT.   Hail to thee, noble master.

II.iii.   ² *happy* lucky   ⁵ *attend my taking* watch to capture me   ⁶ *am bethought* have
decided   ⁸⁻⁹ *penury . . . beast* poverty, to show how contemptible man is, reduced to
the level of a beast   ¹⁰ *Blanket* cover only with a blanket   ¹⁰ *elf* tangle (into "elflocks,"
supposed to be caused by elves)   ¹¹ *presented* the show of   ¹¹ *outface* brave
¹³ *proof* example   ¹⁴ *Bedlam* (see I.ii.r.¹²¹⁻²²)   ¹⁵ *strike* stick   ¹⁵ *mortified* not alive to
pain   ¹⁶ *pricks* skewers   ¹⁷ *object* spectacle   ¹⁷ *low* humble   ¹⁸ *pelting* paltry
¹⁹ *bans* curses   ²⁰ *Poor . . . Tom* (Edgar recites the names a Bedlam beggar gives
himself)   ²¹ *That's . . . am* there's a chance for me in that I am no longer known for
myself   II.iv.   ⁴ *purpose* intention   ⁵ *remove* removal

LEAR. Ha!   5
  Mak'st thou this shame thy pastime?°

KENT.   No, my lord.

FOOL. Ha, ha, he wears cruel° garters. Horses are tied by the heads,
  dogs and bears by th' neck, monkeys by th' loins, and man by
  th' legs. When a man's overlusty at legs,° then he wears
  wooden netherstocks.°   10

LEAR. What's he that hath so much thy place mistook
  To set thee here?

KENT.   It is both he and she,
  Your son and daughter.

LEAR. No.

KENT. Yes.   15

LEAR. No, I say.

KENT. I say yea.

LEAR. No, no, they would not.

KENT. Yes, they have.

LEAR. By Jupiter, I swear no!   20

KENT. By Juno, I swear ay!

LEAR.   They durst not do't;
  They could not, would not do't. 'Tis worse than murder
  To do upon respect° such violent outrage.
  Resolve° me with all modest° haste which way
  Thou mightst deserve or they impose this usage,   25
  Coming from us.

KENT.   My lord, when at their home
  I did commend° your Highness' letters to them,
  Ere I was risen from the place that showed
  My duty kneeling, came there a reeking post,°
  Stewed° in his haste, half breathless, panting forth   30
  From Goneril his mistress salutations,
  Delivered letters, spite of intermission,°
  Which presently° they read; on° whose contents
  They summoned up their meiny,° straight took horse,

---

⁶ *Mak'st . . . pastime* i.e., are you doing this to amuse yourself   ⁷ *cruel* (1) painful (2)
"crewel," a worsted yarn used in garters   ⁹ *overlusty at legs* (1) a vagabond (2) ? sexually promiscuous   ¹⁰ *netherstocks* stockings (as opposed to knee breeches or
upperstocks)   ²³ *upon respect* (1) on the respect due to the King (2) deliberately
²⁴ *Resolve* inform   ²⁴ *modest* becoming   ²⁷ *commend* deliver   ²⁹ *reeking post* sweat-
ing messenger   ³⁰ *stewed* steaming   ³² *spite of intermission* in spite of the interrupting
of my business   ³³ *presently* at once   ³³ *on* on the strength of   ³⁴ *meiny* retinue

Commanded me to follow and attend   35
The leisure of their answer, gave me cold looks,
And meeting here the other messenger,
Whose welcome I perceived had poisoned mine,
Being the very fellow which of late
Displayed° so saucily against your Highness,   40
Having more man than wit° about me, drew;
He raised° the house, with loud and coward cries.
Your son and daughter found this trespass worth°
The shame which here it suffers.

Fool. Winter's not gone yet, if the wild geese fly that way.°   45
          Fathers that wear rags
             Do make their children blind,°
          But fathers that bear bags°
             Shall see their children kind.
          Fortune, that arrant whore,   50
             Ne'er turns the key° to th' poor.
But for all this, thou shalt have as many dolors° for thy daughters as thou canst tell° in a year.

Lear. O, how this mother° swells up toward my heart!
Hysterica passio,° down, thou climbing sorrow,   55
Thy element's° below. Where is this daughter?

Kent. With the Earl, sir, here within.

Lear.   Follow me not;
Stay here.   *Exit.*

Gentleman. Made you no more offense but what you speak of?

Kent. None.   60
How chance° the King comes with so small a number?

Fool. And° thou hadst been set i' th' stocks for that question,
thou'dst well deserved it.

Kent. Why, Fool?

Fool. We'll set thee to school to an ant, to teach thee there's no   65
laboring i' th' winter.° All that follow their noses are led by their

---

[40] *Displayed* showed off   [41] *more man than wit* more manhood than sense   [42] *raised* aroused   [43] *worth* deserving   [45] *Winter's . . . way* i.e., more trouble is to come, since Cornwall and Regan act so ("geese" is used contemptuously, as in Kent's quarrel with Oswald, II.ii. 85–6)   [47] *blind* i.e., indifferent   [48] *bags* money-bags   [51] *turns the key* i.e., opens the door   [52] *dolors* (1) sorrows (2) dollars (English name for Spanish and German coins)   [53] *tell* (1) tell about (2) count   [54–55] *mother . . . Hysterica passio* hysteria, causing suffocation or choking   [56] *element* proper place   [61] *How chance* how does it happen that   [62] *And* if   [65–66] *We'll . . . winter* (in the popular fable the ant, unlike the improvident grasshopper, anticipates the winter when none can labor by laying up provisions in the summer. Lear, trusting foolishly to summer days, finds himself unprovided for, and unable to provide, now that "winter" has come)

eyes but blind men, and there's not a nose among twenty but
can smell him that's stinking.° Let go thy hold when a great
wheel runs down a hill, lest it break thy neck with following. But
the great one that goes upward, let him draw thee after. When   70
a wise man gives thee better counsel, give me mine again. I
would have none but knaves follow it since a Fool gives it.
>   That sir, which serves and seeks for gain,
>   And follows but for form,°
>   Will pack,° when it begins to rain,   75
>   And leave thee in the storm.
>   But I will tarry; the Fool will stay,
>   And let the wise man fly.
>   The knave turns Fool that runs away,
>   The Fool no knave,° perdy.°   80

KENT. Where learned you this, Fool?

FOOL. Not i' th' stocks, fool.

Enter Lear and Gloucester.

LEAR. Deny° to speak with me? They are sick, they are weary,
They have traveled all the night? Mere fetches,°
The images° of revolt and flying off!°   85
Fetch me a better answer.

GLOUCESTER.   My dear lord,
You know the fiery quality° of the Duke,
How unremovable and fixed he is
In his own course.

LEAR.   Vengeance, plague, death, confusion!
Fiery? What quality? Why, Gloucester, Gloucester,   90
I'd speak with the Duke of Cornwall and his wife.

GLOUCESTER. Well, my good lord, I have informed them so.

LEAR. Informed them? Dost thou understand me, man?

GLOUCESTER. Ay, my good lord.

LEAR. The King would speak with Cornwall. The dear father   95
Would with his daughter speak, commands—tends° —
    service.
Are they informed of this? My breath and blood!
Fiery? The fiery Duke, tell the hot Duke that—
No, but not yet. May be he is not well.

66–68 *All . . . stinking* i.e., all can smell out the decay of Lear's fortunes   74 *form* show
75 *pack* be off   79–80 *The . . . knave* i.e., the faithless man is the true fool, for wisdom
requires fidelity. Lear's Fool, who remains faithful, is at least no knave   80 *perdy* by God
(Fr. *par Dieu*)   83 *Deny* refuse   84 *fetches* subterfuges, acts of tacking (nautical
metaphor)   85 *images* exact likenesses   85 *flying off* desertion   87 *quality*
temperament   96 *tends* attends (i.e., awaits); with, possibly, an ironic second meaning,
"tenders," or "offers"

Infirmity doth still neglect all office   100
Whereto our health is bound.° We are not ourselves
When nature, being oppressed, commands the mind
To suffer with the body. I'll forbear;
And am fallen out° with my more headier will°
To take the indisposed and sickly fit   105
For the sound man. [*Looking on Kent*] Death on my state!°
  Wherefore
Should he sit here? This act persuades me
That this remotion° of the Duke and her
Is practice° only. Give me my servant forth.°
Go tell the Duke and's wife I'd speak with them!   110
Now, presently!° Bid them come forth and hear me,
Or at their chamber door I'll beat the drum
Till it cry sleep to death.°

GLOUCESTER. I would have all well betwixt you.

                                                                          Exit.

LEAR. O me, my heart, my rising heart! But down!   115

FOOL. Cry to it, Nuncle, as the cockney° did to the eels when she put
'em i' th' paste° alive. She knapped° 'em o' th' coxcombs° with
a stick and cried, "Down, wantons,° down!" 'Twas her brother
that, in pure kindness to his horse, buttered his hay.°

Enter Cornwall, Regan, Gloucester, Servants.

LEAR. Good morrow to you both.

CORNWALL.   Hail to your Grace.   120

                              Kent here set at liberty.

REGAN. I am glad to see your Highness.

LEAR. Regan, I think you are. I know what reason
I have to think so. If thou shouldst not be glad,
I would divorce me from thy mother's tomb,
Sepulchring an adultress.° [*To Kent*] O, are you free?   125
Some other time for that. Beloved Regan,
Thy sister's naught.° O Regan, she hath tied
Sharp-toothed unkindness, like a vulture, here.

                              [*Points to his heart.*]

---

[101] *Whereto . . . bound* duties which we are required to perform, when in health   [104] *fallen out* angry   [104] *headier will* headlong inclination   [106] *state* royal condition   [108] *remotion* (1) removal (2) remaining aloof   [109] *practice* pretense   [109] *forth* i.e., out of the stocks   [111] *presently* at once   [113] *cry . . . death* follow sleep, like a cry or pack of hounds, until it kills it   [116] *cockney* Londoner (ignorant city dweller)   [117] *paste* pastry pie   [117] *knapped* rapped   [117] *coxcombs* heads   [118] *wantons* i.e., playful things (with a sexual implication)   [119] *buttered his hay* i.e., the city dweller does from ignorance what the dishonest ostler does from craft: greases the hay the traveler has paid for, so that the horse will not eat   [124-25] *divorce . . . adultress* i.e., repudiate your dead mother as having conceived you by another man   [127] *naught* wicked

I can scarce speak to thee. Thou'lt not believe
With how depraved a quality°—O Regan!   130

REGAN. I pray you, sir, take patience. I have hope
You less know how to value her desert
Than she to scant her duty.°

LEAR.   Say? how is that?

REGAN. I cannot think my sister in the least
Would fail her obligation. If, sir, perchance   135
She have restrained the riots of your followers,
'Tis on such ground, and to such wholesome end,
As clears her from all blame.

LEAR. My curses on her!

REGAN.   O, sir, you are old,
Nature in you stands on the very verge   140
Of his confine.° You should be ruled, and led
By some discretion that discerns your state
Better than you yourself.° Therefore I pray you
That to our sister you do make return,
Say you have wronged her.

LEAR.   Ask her forgiveness?   145
Do you but mark how this becomes the house:°
"Dear daughter, I confess that I am old.

                                                            [*Kneeling.*]

Age is unnecessary. On my knees I beg
That you'll vouchsafe me raiment, bed, and food."

REGAN. Good sir, no more. These are unsightly tricks.   150
Return you to my sister.

LEAR.   [*Rising*] Never, Regan.
She hath abated° me of half my train,
Looked black upon me, struck me with her tongue,
Most serpentlike, upon the very heart.
All the stored vengeances of heaven fall   155
On her ingrateful top!° Strike her young bones,°
You taking° airs, with lameness.

CORNWALL.   Fie, sir, fie!

---

[130] *quality* nature   [131–33] *I . . . duty* (despite the double negative, the passage means, "I believe that you fail to give Goneril her due, rather than that she fails to fulfill her duty")   [140–41] *Nature . . . confine* i.e., you are nearing the end of your life   [142–43] *some . . . yourself* some discreet person who understands your condition more than you do   [146] *becomes the house* suits my royal and paternal position   [152] *abated* curtailed   [156] *top* head   [156] *young bones* (the reference may be to unborn children, rather than to Goneril herself)   [157] *taking* infecting

LEAR. You nimble lightnings, dart your blinding flames
　　　Into her scornful eyes! Infect her beauty,
　　　You fen-sucked° fogs, drawn by the pow'rful sun,　　　160
　　　To fall and blister° her pride.

REGAN.　　　　　　　　　　　O the blest gods!
　　　So will you wish on me when the rash mood is on.

LEAR. No, Regan, thou shalt never have my curse.
　　　Thy tender-hefted° nature shall not give
　　　Thee o'er to harshness. Her eyes are fierce, but thine　　　165
　　　Do comfort, and not burn. 'Tis not in thee
　　　To grudge my pleasures, to cut off my train,
　　　To bandy° hasty words, to scant my sizes,°
　　　And, in conclusion, to oppose the bolt°
　　　Against my coming in. Thou better know'st　　　170
　　　The offices of nature, bond of childhood,°
　　　Effects° of courtesy, dues of gratitude.
　　　Thy half o' th' kingdom hast thou not forgot,
　　　Wherein I thee endowed.

REGAN.　　　　　　　　　　　Good sir, to th' purpose.°
　　　　　　　　　　　　　　Tucket within.

LEAR. Who put my man i' th' stocks?

CORNWALL.　　　　　　　　　What trumpet's that?　　　175

REGAN. I know't—my sister's. This approves° her letter,
　　　That she would soon be here.
　　　　　　　　　Enter Oswald.
　　　　　　　　　Is your lady come?

LEAR. This is a slave, whose easy borrowed° pride
　　　Dwells in the fickle grace° of her he follows.
　　　Out, varlet,° from my sight.

CORNWALL.　　　　　　　　What means your Grace?　　　180

LEAR. Who stocked my servant? Regan, I have good hope
　　　Thou didst not know on't.
　　　　　　　　　Enter Goneril.
　　　　　　　　　Who comes here? O heavens!
　　　If you do love old men, if your sweet sway

---

[160] *fen-sucked* drawn up from swamps by the sun　[161] *fall and blister* fall upon and raise blisters　[164] *tender-hefted* gently framed　[168] *bandy* volley (metaphor from tennis)　[168] *scant my sizes* reduce my allowances　[169] *oppose the bolt* i.e., bar the door　[171] *offices . . . childhood* natural duties, a child's duty to its parent　[172] *Effects* manifestations　[174] *to th' purpose* come to the point　[176] *approves* confirms　[178] *easy borrowed* (1) facile and taken from another (2) acquired without anything to back it up (like money borrowed without security)　[179] *grace* favor　[180] *varlet* base fellow

Allow° obedience, if you yourselves are old,
Make it° your cause. Send down, and take my part.   185
[*To Goneril*] Art not ashamed to look upon this beard?
O Regan, will you take her by the hand?

GONERIL. Why not by th' hand, sir? How have I offended?
All's not offense that indiscretion finds°
And dotage terms so.

LEAR.   O sides,° you are too tough!   190
Will you yet hold? How came my man i' th' stocks?

CORNWALL. I set him there, sir; but his own disorders°
Deserved much less advancement.°

LEAR.   You? Did you?

REGAN. I pray you, father, being weak, seem so.°
If till the expiration of your month   195
You will return and sojourn with my sister,
Dismissing half your train, come then to me.
I am now from home, and out of that provision
Which shall be needful for your entertainment.°

LEAR. Return to her, and fifty men dismissed?   200
No, rather I abjure all roofs, and choose
To wage° against the enmity o' th' air,
To be a comrade with the wolf and owl,
Necessity's sharp pinch.° Return with her?
Why, the hot-blooded° France, that dowerless took   205
Our youngest born, I could as well be brought
To knee° his throne, and squirelike,° pension beg
To keep base life afoot. Return with her?
Persuade me rather to be slave and sumpter°
To this detested groom. [*Pointing at Oswald.*]

GONERIL.   At your choice, sir.   210

LEAR. I prithee, daughter, do not make me mad.
I will not trouble thee, my child; farewell.
We'll no more meet, no more see one another.
But yet thou art my flesh, my blood, my daughter,
Or rather a disease that's in my flesh,   215
Which I must needs call mine. Thou art a boil,
A plague-sore, or embossèd carbuncle°
In my corrupted blood. But I'll not chide thee.

---

¹⁸⁴ *Allow* approve of   ¹⁸⁵ *it* i.e., my cause   ¹⁸⁹ *finds* judges   ¹⁹⁰ *sides* breast   ¹⁹² *disorders* misconduct   ¹⁹³ *advancement* promotion   ¹⁹⁴ *seem so* i.e., act weak   ²¹⁹ *entertainment* maintenance   ²⁰² *wage* fight   ²⁰⁴ *Necessity's sharp pinch* (a summing up of the hard choice he has just announced)   ²⁰⁵ *hot-blooded* passionate   ²⁰⁷ *knee* kneel before   ²⁰⁷ *squirelike* like a retainer   ²⁰⁹ *sumpter* pack horse   ²¹⁷ *embossèd carbuncle* swollen boil

Let shame come when it will, I do not call it.　　　　　220
I do not bid the Thunder-bearer° shoot,
Nor tell tales of thee to high-judging° Jove.
Mend when thou canst, be better at thy leisure,
I can be patient, I can stay with Regan,
I and my hundred knights.

REGAN.　　　　　　　　　　Not altogether so.
I looked not for you yet, nor am provided　　　　　225
For your fit welcome. Give ear, sir, to my sister,
For those that mingle reason with your passion°
Must be content to think you old, and so—
But she knows what she does.

LEAR.　　　　　　　　　　Is this well spoken?

REGAN. I dare avouch° it, sir. What, fifty followers?　　　　　230
Is it not well? What should you need of more?
Yea, or so many, sith that° both charge° and danger
Speak 'gainst so great a number? How in one house
Should many people, under two commands,
Hold° amity? 'Tis hard, almost impossible.　　　　　235

GONERIL. Why might not you, my lord, receive attendance
From those that she calls servants, or from mine?

REGAN. Why not, my lord? If then they chanced to slack° ye,
We could control them. If you will come to me
(For now I spy a danger), I entreat you　　　　　240
To bring but five-and-twenty. To no more
Will I give place or notice.°

LEAR. I gave you all.

REGAN.　　　　　　　　And in good time you gave it.

LEAR. Made you my guardians, my depositaries,°
But kept a reservation° to be followed　　　　　245
With such a number. What, must I come to you
With five-and-twenty? Regan, said you so?

REGAN. And speak't again, my lord. No more with me.

LEAR. Those wicked creatures yet do look well-favored°
When others are more wicked; not being the worst　　　　　250
Stands in some rank of praise.° [*To Goneril*] I'll go with thee.

---

²²⁰*Thunder-bearer* i.e., Jupiter　²²¹ *high-judging* (1) supreme (2) judging from heaven
²²⁷ *mingle . . . passion* i.e., consider your turbulent behavior coolly and reasonably
²³⁰ *avouch* swear by　²³² *sith that* since　²³² *charge* expense　²³⁵ *hold* preserve
²³⁸ *slack* neglect　²⁴² *notice* recognition　²⁴⁴ *depositaries* trustees　²⁴⁵ *reservation*
condition　²⁴⁹ *well-favored* handsome　²⁵⁰⁻⁵⁴ *not . . . praise* i.e., that Goneril is not so
bad as Regan is one thing in her favor

Thy fifty yet doth double five-and-twenty,
And thou art twice her love.°

GONERIL.   Hear me, my lord.
What need you five-and-twenty? ten? or five?
To follow° in a house where twice so many   255
Have a command to tend you?

REGAN.   What need one?

LEAR. O reason° not the need! Our basest beggars
Are in the poorest thing superfluous.°
Allow not nature more than nature needs,°
Man's life is cheap as beast's. Thou art a lady: 260
If only to go warm were gorgeous,
Why, nature needs not what thou gorgeous wear'st,
Which scarcely keeps thee warm.° But, for true need—
You heavens, give me that patience, patience I need.
You see me here, you gods, a poor old man,   265
As full of grief as age, wretched in both.
If it be you that stirs these daughters' hearts
Against their father, fool° me not so much
To bear° it tamely; touch me with noble anger,
And let not women's weapons, water drops,   270
Stain my man's cheeks. No, you unnatural hags!
I will have such revenges on you both
That all the world shall—I will do such things—
What they are, yet I know not; but they shall be
The terrors of the earth. You think I'll weep.   275
No, I'll not weep.

                                   Storm and tempest.

I have full cause of weeping, but this heart
Shall break into a hundred thousand flaws°
Or ere° I'll weep. O Fool, I shall go mad!

                    Exeunt Lear, Gloucester, Kent, and Fool.

CORNWALL. Let us withdraw, 'twill be a storm.   280

REGAN. This house is little; the old man and's people
Cannot be well bestowed.°

GONERIL. 'Tis his own blame; hath° put himself from rest°
And must needs taste his folly.

---

[253] *her love* i.e., as loving as she   [255] *follow* attend on you   [257] *reason* scrutinize   [258] *Are . . . superfluous* i.e., have some trifle not absolutely necessary   [259] *needs* i.e., to sustain life   [261–263] *If . . .warm* i.e., if to satisfy the need for warmth were to be gorgeous, you would not need the clothing you wear, which is worn more for beauty than warmth   [268] *fool* humiliate   [269] *To bear* as to make me bear   [278] *flaws* (1) pieces (2) cracks (3) gusts of passion   [279] *Or ere* before   [282] *bestowed* lodged   [283] *hath* he hath   [283] *rest* (1) place of residence (2) repose of mind

REGAN. For his particular,° I'll receive him gladly,   285
    But not one follower.

GONERIL.   So am I purposed.°
    Where is my Lord of Gloucester?

CORNWALL. Followed the old man forth.

Enter Gloucester.

                    He is returned.

GLOUCESTER. The King is in high rage.

CORNWALL.   Whither is he going?

GLOUCESTER. He calls to horse, but will I know not whither.   290

CORNWALL. 'Tis best to give him way, he leads himself.°

GONERIL. My lord, entreat him by no means to stay.

GLOUCESTER. Alack, the night comes on, and the high winds
    Do sorely ruffle.° For many miles about
    There's scarce a bush.

REGAN.   O, sir, to willful men   295
    The injuries that they themselves procure
    Must be their schoolmasters. Shut up your doors.
    He is attended with a desperate train,
    And what they may incense° him to, being apt
    To have his ear abused,° wisdom bids fear.   300

CORNWALL. Shut up your doors, my lord; 'tis a wild night.
    My Regan counsels well. Come out o' th' storm.

                        Exeunt.

ACT III

Scene I. [*A heath.*]

Storm still.° Enter Kent and a Gentleman severally.

KENT. Who's there besides foul weather?

GENTLEMAN. One minded like the weather most unquietly.°

KENT. I know you. Where's the King?

GENTLEMAN. Contending with the fretful elements;
    Bids the wind blow the earth into the sea,   5
    Or swell the curlèd waters 'bove the main,°
    That things might change,° or cease; tears his white hair,

---

[285] *his particular* himself personally   [286] *purposed* determined   [291] *give . . . himself* let him go; he insists on is own way   [249] *ruffle* rage   [299] *incense* incite   [299–300] *being . . . abused* he being inclined to harken to bad counsel   III.i.s.d. *still* continually   [2] *minded . . . unquietly* disturbed in mind, like the weather   [6]*main* land   [7] *change* (1) be destroyed (2) be exchanged (i.e., turned upside down) (3) change for the better

Which the impetuous blasts, with eyeless° rage,
Catch in their fury, and make nothing of;
Strives in his little world of man° to outscorn   10
The to-and-fro-conflicting wind and rain.
This night, wherein the cub-drawn° bear would couch,°
The lion, and the belly-pinchèd° wolf
Keep their fur dry, unbonneted° he runs,
And bids what will take all.°   15

KENT. But who is with him?

GENTLEMAN. None but the Fool, who labors to outjest
His heart-struck injuries.

KENT.   Sir, I do know you,
And dare upon the warrant of my note°
Commend a dear thing° to you. There is division,   20
Although as yet the face of it is covered
With mutual cunning, 'twixt Albany and Cornwall;
Who have—as who have not, that° their great stars
Throned° and set high?—servants, who seem no less,°
Which are to France the spies and speculations   25
Intelligent° of our state. What hath been seen,
Either in snuffs and packings° of the Dukes,
Or the hard rein which both of them hath borne°
Against the old kind King, or something deeper,
Whereof, perchance, these are but furnishings°—   30
But, true it is, from France there comes a power°
Into this scattered° kingdom, who already,
Wise in our negligence, have secret feet
In some of our best ports, and are at point°
To show their open banner. Now to you: 35
If on my credit you dare build° so far
To° make your speed to Dover, you shall find
Some that will thank you, making° just° report
Of how unnatural and bemadding° sorrow
The King hath cause to plain.°   40

---

8 *eyeless* (1)blind (2) invisible   10 *little world of man* (the microcosm, as opposed to the universe or macrocosm, which it copies in little)   12 *cub-drawn* sucked dry by her cubs, and so ravenously hungry   12 *couch* take shelter in its lair   13 *belly-pinchèd* starved   14 *unbonneted* hatless   15 *take all* (like the reckless gambler, staking all he has left)   19 *warrant of my note* strength of what I have taken note (of you)   20 *Commend . . . thing* entrust important business   23 *that* whom   23–24 *stars/Throned* destinies have throned   24 *seem no less* seem to be so   25–26 *speculations/Intelligent* giving intelligence   27 *snuffs and packings* quarrels and plots   28 *hard . . . borne* close and cruel control they have exercised   30 *furnishings* excuses   31 *power* army   32 *scattered* disunited   34 *at point* ready   36 *If . . . build* if you can trust me, proceed   37 *To* as to   38 *making* for making   38 *just* accurate   39 *bemadding* maddening   40 *plain* complain of

I am a gentleman of blood and breeding,°
And from some knowledge and assurance° offer
This office° to you.

GENTLEMAN. I will talk further with you.

KENT.   No, do not.
    For confirmation that I am much more   45
    Than my out-wall,° open this purse and take
    What it contains. If you shall see Cordelia,
    As fear not but you shall, show her this ring,
    And she will tell you who that fellow° is
    That yet you do not know. Fie on this storm!   50
    I will go seek the King.

GENTLEMAN. Give me your hand. Have you no more to say?

KENT. Few words, but, to effect,° more than all yet:
    That when we have found the King—in which your pain°
    That way, I'll this—he that first lights on him,   55
    Holla the other.   *Exeunt (severally).*

Scene II. [*Another part of the heath.*]
Storm still.

Enter Lear and Fool.

LEAR. Blow, winds, and crack your cheeks. Rage, blow!
    You cataracts and hurricanoes,° spout
    Till you have drenched our steeples, drowned the cocks.°
    You sulph'rous and thought-executing° fires,
    Vaunt-couriers° of oak-cleaving thunderbolts,   5
    Singe my white head. And thou, all-shaking thunder,
    Strike flat the thick rotundity° o' th' world,
    Crack Nature's molds,° all germains spill° at once,
    That makes ingrateful° man.

FOOL. O Nuncle, court holy-water° in a dry house is better than this   10
    rain water out o' door. Good Nuncle, in; ask thy daughters
    blessing. Here's a night pities neither wise man nor fools.

---

[41] *blood and breeding* noble family   [42] *knowledge and assurance* sure and trustworthy information   [43] *office* service (i.e., the trip to Dover)   [46] *out-wall* superficial appearance   [49] *fellow* companion   [53] *to effect* in their importance   [54] *pain* labor III.ii.   [2] *hurricanoes* waterspouts   [3] *cocks* weathercocks   [4] *thought-executing* (1) doing execution as quick as thought (2) executing or carrying out the thought of him who hurls the lightning   [5] *Vaunt-couriers* heralds, scouts who range before the main body of the army   [7] *rotundity* i.e., not only the sphere of the globe, but the roundness of gestation (Delius)   [8] *Nature's molds* the molds or forms in which men are made   [8] *all germains spill* destroy the basic seeds of life   [9] *ingrateful* ungrateful   [10] *court holy-water* flattery

LEAR. Rumble thy bellyful. Spit, fire. Spout, rain!
      Nor rain, wind, thunder, fire are my daughters.
      I tax° not you, you elements, with unkindness.   15
      I never gave you kingdom, called you children,
      You owe me no subscription.° Then let fall
      Your horrible pleasure.° Here I stand your slave,
      A poor, infirm, weak, and despised old man.
      But yet I call you servile ministers,°   20
      That will with two pernicious daughters join
      Your high-engendered battles° 'gainst a head
      So old and white as this. O, ho! 'tis foul.

FOOL. He that has a house to put 's head in has a good headpiece.°
               The codpiece° that will house   25
                  Before the head has any,
               The head and he° shall louse:
                  So beggars marry many.°
               The man that makes his toe
                  What he his heart should make   30
               Shall of a corn cry woe,
                  And turn his sleep to wake.°
      For there was never yet fair woman but she made mouths in a
      glass.°

                    Enter Kent.

LEAR. No, I will be the pattern of all patience,   35
      I will say nothing.

KENT. Who's there?

FOOL. Marry,° here's grace and a codpiece; that's a wise man and a
      fool.°

KENT. Alas, sir, are you here? Things that love night   40
      Love not such nights as these. The wrathful skies
      Gallow° the very wanderers of the dark
      And make them keep° their caves. Since I was man,

---

[15] *tax* accuse   [17] *subscription* allegiance, submission   [18] *pleasure* will   [20] *ministers* agents
   [22] *high-engendered battles* armies formed in the heavens   [24] *headpiece* (1) helmet (2)
brain   [25] *codpiece* penis (lit., padding worn at the crotch of a man's hose)   [27] *he* it
[28] *many* i.e., lice   [29–32] *The . . . many* i.e., the man who gratifies his sexual appetites
before he has a roof over his head will end up a lousy beggar   [29–32] *The . . . wake* i.e.,
the man who, ignoring the fit order of things, elevates what is base above what is noble,
will suffer for it as Lear has, in banishing Cordelia and enriching her sisters   [33–34] *made
mouths in a glass* posed before a mirror (irrelevant nonsense, except that it calls to
mind the general theme of vanity and folly)   [38] *Marry* by the Virgin Mary   [38–39] *here's
. . . fool* (Kent's question is answered: The King ("grace") is here, and the Fool—who
customarily wears an exaggerated codpiece. But which is which is left ambiguous, since
Lear has previously been called a codpiece)   [42] *Gallow* frighten   [43] *keep* remain inside

Such sheets of fire, such bursts of horrid° thunder,
Such groans of roaring wind and rain, I never　　　　　　　45
Remember to have heard. Man's nature cannot carry°
Th' affliction nor the fear.

LEAR.　　　　　　　　　　Let the great gods
That keep this dreadful pudder° o'er our heads
Find out their enemies now.° Tremble, thou wretch,
That hast within thee undivulgèd crimes　　　　　　　50
Unwhipped of justice. Hide thee, thou bloody hand,
Thou perjured,° and thou simular° of virtue
That art incestous, Caitiff,° to pieces shake,
That under covert and convenient seeming°
Has practiced on° man's life. Close° pent-up guilts,　　　55
Rive° your concealing continents° and cry
These dreadful summoners grace.° I am a man
More sinned against than sinning.

KENT.　　　　　　　　　　Alack, bareheaded?
Gracious my lord,° hard by here is a hovel;
Some friendship will it lend you 'gainst the tempest.　　　60
Repose you there, while I to this hard house
(More harder than the stones whereof 'tis raised,
Which even but now, demanding after° you,
Denied me to come in) return, and force
Their scanted° courtesy.

LEAR.　　　　　　　　　　My wits begin to turn.　　　65
Come on, my boy. How dost, my boy? Art cold?
I am cold myself. Where is this straw, my fellow?
The art° of our necessities is strange,
That can make vile things precious. Come, your hovel.
Poor Fool and knave, I have one part in my heart　　　70
That's sorry yet for thee.

FOOL. [*Singing*]

　　　He that has and a little tiny wit,
　　　　With heigh-ho, the wind and the rain,
　　　Must make content with his fortunes fit,°
　　　　Though the rain it raineth every day.　　　75

---

[44] *horrid* horrible　[46] *carry* endure　[48] *pudder* turmoil　[49] *Find . . . now* i.e., discover sinners by the terror they reveal　[52] *perjured* perjurer　[52] *simular* counterfeiter　[53] *Caitiff* wretch　[54] *seeming* hypocrisy　[55] *practiced on* plotted against　[55] *Close* hidden　[56] *Rive* split open　[56] *continents* containers　[56–57] *cry . . . grace* beg mercy from the vengeful gods (here figured as officers who summoned a man charged with immorality before the ecclesiastical court)　[59] *Gracious my lord* my gracious lord　[63] *demanding after* asking for　[65] *scanted* stinted　[78] *art* magic powers of the alchemists, who sought to transmute base metals into precious　[74] *Must . . . fit* must be satisfied with a fortune as tiny as his wit

LEAR. True, my good boy. Come, bring us to this hovel.

Exit [with Kent].

FOOL. This is a brave° night to cool a courtesan. I'll speak a prophecy
ere I go:
> When priests are more in word than matter;
> When brewers mar their malt with water;   80
> When nobles are their tailors' tutors.
> No heretics burned, but wenches' suitors;°
> When every case in law is right,
> No squire in debt nor no poor knight;
> When slanders do not live in tongues;   85
> Nor cutpurses come not to throngs;
> When usurers tell their gold i' th' field,°
> And bawds and whores do churches build,°
> Then shall the realm of Albion°
> Come to great confusion.   90
> Then comes the time, who lives to see't,
> That going shall be used with feet.°

This prophecy Merlin° shall make, for I live before his time.

Exit.

Scene III. [*Gloucester's castle.*]

Enter Gloucester and Edmund.

GLOUCESTER. Alack, alack, Edmund, I like not this unnatural dealing.
When I desired their leave that I might pity° him, they took from
me the use of mine own house, charged me on pain of perpetual displeasure neither to speak of him, entreat for him, or any
way sustain° him.   5

EDMUND. Most savage and unnatural.

GLOUCESTER. Go to; say you nothing. There is division° between the
Dukes, and a worse° matter than that. I have received a letter
this night—'tis dangerous to be spoken°—I have locked the
letter in my closet.° These injuries the King now bears will be   10

---

[77] *brave* fine   [81–83] *When . . . suitors* (the first four prophecies are fulfilled already, and
hence "confusion" has come to England. The priest does not suit his action to his
words. The brewer adulterates his beer. The nobleman is subservient to his tailor (i.e.,
cares only for fashion). Religious heretics escape, and only those burn (i.e., suffer) who
are afflicted with veneral disease)   [87] *tell . . . field* count their money in the open
[85–88] *When . . . build* (the last six prophecies, as they are Utopian, are meant ironically.
They will never be fulfilled)   [89] *Albion* England   [92] *going . . . feet* people will walk on
their feet   [93] *Merlin* King Arthur's great magician who, according to Holinshed's *Chron-
icles,* lived later than Lear   III.iii.   [2] *pity* show pity to   [5] *sustain* care for   [7] *division*
falling out   [8] *worse* more serious (i.e., the French invasion)   [9] *spoken* spoken of
[10] *closet* room

revenged home;° there is part of a power° already footed;° we
must incline to° the King. I will look° him and privily° relieve
him. Go you and maintain talk with the Duke, that my charity
be not of° him perceived. If he ask for me, I am ill and gone to
bed. If I die for it, as no less is threatened me, the King my old   15
master must be relieved. There is strange things toward,°
Edmund; pray you be careful.   *Exit.*

EDMUND. This courtesy forbid° thee shall the Duke
    Instantly know, and of that letter too.
    This seems a fair deserving,° and must draw me   20
    That which my father loses—no less than all.
    The younger rises when the old doth fall.

                                       Exit.

Scene IV. [*The heath. Before a hovel.*]

Enter Lear, Kent, and Fool.

KENT. Here is the place, my lord. Good my lord, enter.
    The tyranny of the open night's too rough
    For nature to endure.

                                       Storm still.

LEAR.   Let me alone.

KENT. Good my lord, enter here.

LEAR.   Wilt break my heart?°

KENT. I had rather break mine own. Good my lord, enter.   5

LEAR. Thou think'st 'tis much that this contentious storm
    Invades us to the skin: so 'tis to thee;
    But where the greater malady is fixed,°
    The lesser is scarce felt. Thou'dst shun a bear;
    But if thy flight lay toward the roaring sea,   10
    Thou'dst meet the bear i' th' mouth.° When the mind's free,°
    The body's delicate. The tempest in my mind
    Doth from my senses take all feeling else,
    Save what beats there. Filial ingratitude,
    Is it not as° this mouth should tear this hand   15
    For lifting food to't? But I will punish home.°
    No, I will weep no more. In such a night
    To shut me out! Pour on, I will endure.

---

[11] *home* to the utmost [11] *power* army [11] *footed* landed [12] *incline to* take the side of [12] *look* search for [12] *privily* secretly [14] *of* by [16] *toward* impending [18] *courtesy forbid* kindness forbidden (i.e., to Lear) [20] *fair deserving* an action deserving reward III.iv. [4] *break my heart* i.e., by shutting out the storm which distracts me from thinking [8] *fixed* lodged (in the mind) [11] *i' th' mouth* in the teeth [11] *free* i.e., from care [15] *as* as if [16] *home* to the utmost

In such a night as this! O Regan, Goneril,
Your old kind father, whose frank° heart gave all—   20
O, that way madness lies; let me shun that.
No more of that.

KENT.   Good my lord, enter here.

LEAR. Prithee go in thyself; seek thine own ease.
This tempest will not give me leave to ponder
On things would hurt me more, but I'll go in.   25
[*To the Fool*] In, boy; go first; You houseless poverty°—
Nay, get thee in. I'll pray, and then I'll sleep.

                                  Exit [*Fool*].

Poor naked wretches, wheresoe'er you are,
That bide° the pelting of this pitiless storm,
How shall your houseless heads and unfed sides,   30
Your looped and windowed° raggedness, defend you
From seasons such as these? O, I have ta'en
Too little care of this! Take physic, pomp,°
Expose thyself to feel what wretches feel,
That thou mayst shake the superflux° to them,   35
And show the heavens more just.

EDGAR. [*Within*] Fathom and half, fathom and half!° Poor Tom!

                   Enter Fool.

FOOL. Come not in here, Nuncle, here's a spirit. Help me, help me!

KENT. Give me thy hand. Who's there?

FOOL. A spirit, a spirit. He says his name's Poor Tom.   40

KENT. What art thou that dost grumble there i' th' straw?
Come forth.

        Enter Edgar [*disguised as a madman*].

EDGAR. Away! the foul fiend follows me. Through the sharp hawthorn
blows the cold wind.° Humh! Go to thy cold bed, and warm
thee.°   45

LEAR. Didst thou give all to thy daughters? And art thou come to
this?

EDGAR. Who gives anything to Poor Tom? Whom the foul fiend hath
led through fire and through flame, through ford and whirlpool,

---

²⁰ *frank* liberal (magnanimous)   ²⁶ *houseless poverty* (the unsheltered poor, abstracted)
  ²⁹ *bide* endure   ³¹ *looped and windowed* full of holes   ³³ *Take physic, pomp* take medicine to cure yourselves, you great men   ³⁵ *superflux* superfluity   ³⁷ *Fathom and half*
(Edgar, because of the downpour, pretends to take soundings) ⁴³⁻⁴⁴ *Through . . . wind*
(a line from the ballad of "The Friar of Orders Gray")   ⁴⁴⁻⁴⁵ *go . . . thee* (a reminiscence of *The Taming of the Shrew*, Induction, 1.10)

o'er bog and quagmire; that hath laid knives under his pillow   50
and halters in his pew,° set ratsbane by his porridge,° made
him proud of heart, to ride on a bay trotting horse over four-
inched bridges,° to course° his own shadow for° a traitor. Bless
thy five wits,° Tom's a-cold. O, do, de, do, de, do, de. Bless thee
from whirlwinds, star-blasting,° and taking.° Do Poor Tom some   55
charity, whom the foul fiend vexes. There could I have him
now—and there—and there again—and there.

Storm still.

LEAR. What, has his daughters brought him to this pass?°
Couldst thou save nothing? Wouldst thou give 'em all?

FOOL. Nay, he reserved a blanket,° else we had been all shamed.   60

LEAR. Now all the plagues that in the pendulous° air
Hang fated o'er° men's faults light on thy daughters!

KENT. He hath no daughters, sir.

LEAR. Death, traitor; nothing could have subdued° nature
To such a lowness but his unkind daughters.   65
Is it the fashion that discarded fathers
Should have thus little mercy on° their flesh?
Judicious punishment—'twas this flesh begot
Those pelican° daughters.

EDGAR. Pillicock sat on Pillicock Hill.° Alow, alow, loo, loo!°   70

FOOL. This cold night will turn us all to fools and madmen.

EDGAR. Take heed o' th' foul fiend; obey thy parents; keep thy word's
justice;° swear not; commit not° with man's sworn spouse; set
not thy sweet heart on proud array. Tom's a-cold.

LEAR. What hast thou been?   75

EDGAR. A servingman, proud in heart and mind; that curled my hair,
wore gloves in my cap;° served the lust of my mistress' heart,
and did the act of darkness with her; swore as many oaths as I
spake words, and broke them in the sweet face of heaven. One
that slept in the contriving of lust, and waked to do it. Wine   80

---

⁵⁰⁻⁵¹ *knives . . . halters . . . ratsbane* (the fiend tempts Poor Tom to suicide)   ⁵¹ *pew* gallery
or balcony outside a window   ⁵¹ *porridge* broth   ⁵²⁻⁵³ *ride . . . bridges* i.e., risk his life
⁵³ *course* chase   ⁵³ *for* as   ⁵⁴ *five wits* i.e., common wit, imagination, fantasy, estima-
tion, memory   ⁵⁵ *star-blasting* the evil caused by malignant stars   ⁵⁵ *taking* pernicious
influences   ⁵⁸ *pass* wretched condition   ⁶⁰ *blanket* i.e., to cover his nakedness
⁶¹ *pendulous* overhanging   ⁶² *fated o'er* destined to punish   ⁶⁴ *subdued* reduced
⁶⁷ *on* i.e., shown to   ⁶⁹ *pelican* (supposed to feed on its parent's blood)   ⁷⁰ *Pillicock . . .
Hill* (probably quoted from a nursery rhyme, and suggested by "pelican." *Pillicock* is a
term of endearment and the phallus)   ⁷⁰ *Alow . . . loo* (? a hunting call, or the refrain
of the song)   ⁷²⁻⁷³ *keep . . . justice* i.e., do not break thy word   ⁷³ *commit not* i.e., adultery
⁷⁷ *gloves in my cap* i.e., as a pledge from his mistress

loved I deeply, dice dearly; and in woman out-paramoured the
Turk.° False of heart, light of ear,° bloody of hand; hog in sloth,
fox in stealth, wolf in greediness, dog in madness, lion in prey.°
Let not the creaking° of shoes nor the rustling of silks betray
thy poor heart to woman. Keep thy foot out of brothels, thy   85
hand out of plackets,° thy pen from lenders' books,° and defy
the foul fiend. Still through the hawthorn blows the cold wind;
says suum, mun, nonny° Dolphin° my boy, boy, sessa!° let him
trot by.

Storm still.

LEAR. Thou wert better in a grave than to answer° with thy uncovered   90
body this extremity° of the skies. Is man no more than this?
Consider him well. Thou ow'st° the worm no silk, the beast no
hide, the sheep no wool, the cat° no perfume. Ha! here's three
on's° are sophisticated.° Thou art the thing itself; unaccom-
modated° man is no more but such a poor, bare, forked° animal   95
as thou art. Off, Off, you lendings!° Come, unbutton here.

[*Tearing off his clothes.*]

FOOL. Prithee, Nuncle, be contented, 'tis a naughty° night to swim in.
Now a little fire in a wild° field were like an old lecher's heart—
a small spark, all the rest on's body, cold. Look, here comes a
walking fire.   100

Enter Gloucester, with a torch.

EDGAR. This is the foul fiend Flibbertigibbet.° He begins at curfew,°
and walks till the first cock.° He gives the web and the pin,°
squints° the eye, and makes the harelip; mildews the white°
wheat, and hurts the poor creature of earth.

Swithold footed thrice the old;°   105
He met the nightmare,° and her nine fold;°

> Bid her alight°
> And her troth plight,°
> And aroint° thee, witch, aroint thee!

KENT. How fares your Grace?   110

LEAR. What's he?

KENT. Who's there? What is't you seek?

GLOUCESTER. What are you there? Your names?

EDGAR. Poor Tom, that eats the swimming frog, the toad, the todpole, the wall-newt and the water;° that in the fury of his heart,   115
when the foul fiend rages, eats cow-dung for sallets,° swallows
the old rat and the ditch-dog,° drinks the green mantle° of the
standing° pool; who is whipped from tithing° to tithing, and
stocked, punished, and imprisoned; who hath had three suits
to his back, six shirts to his body,   120
> Horse to ride, and weapon to wear,
> But mice and rats, and such small deer,°
> Have been Tom's food for seven long year.°
Beware my follower!° Peace, Smulkin,° peace, thou fiend!

GLOUCESTER. What, hath your Grace no better company?   125

EDGAR. The Prince of Darkness is a gentleman.
> Modo° he's called, and Mahu.°

GLOUCESTER. Our flesh and blood, my Lord, is grown so vile
> That it doth hate what gets° it.

EDGAR. Poor Tom's a-cold.   130

GLOUCESTER. Go in with me. My duty cannot suffer°
> T' obey in all your daughters' hard commands.
> Though their injunction be to bar my doors
> And let this tyrannous night take hold upon you,
> Yet have I ventured to come seek you out   135
> And bring you where both fire and food is ready.

LEAR. First let me talk with this philosopher.
> What is the cause of thunder?

KENT. Good my lord, take his offer; go into th' house.

---

107 *alight* i.e., from the horse she had possessed   108 *her troth plight* pledge her word
109 *aroint* be gone   114–115 *todpole . . . water* tadpole, wall lizard, water newt   116 *sallets*
salads   117 *ditch-dog* dead dog in a ditch   117 *mantle* scum   118 *standing* stagnant
118 *tithing* a district comprising ten families   122 *deer* game   122–123 *But . . . year*
(adapted from a popular romance, "Bevis of Hampton")   124 *follower* familiar
124,127 *Smulkin, Modo, Mahu* (Elizabethan devils, from Samuel Harsnett's *Declaration* of
1603)   129 *gets* begets   131 *suffer* permit me

LEAR. I'll talk a word with this same learnèd Theban.° What is your   140
study?°

EDGAR. How to prevent° the fiend, and to kill vermin.

LEAR. Let me ask you one word in private.

KENT. Importune him once more to go, my lord.
His wits begin t' unsettle.   145

GLOUCESTER. Canst thou blame him?

Storm still.

His daughters seek his death. Ah, that good Kent,
He said it would be thus, poor banished man!
Thou say'st the King grows mad—I'll tell thee, friend,
I am almost mad myself. I had a son,   150
Now outlawed from my blood,° he sought my life
But lately, very late° I loved him, friend,
No father his son dearer. True to tell thee,
The grief hath crazed my wits. What a night's this!
I do beseech your Grace—

LEAR.   O, cry you mercy,° sir.   155
Noble philosopher, your company.

EDGAR. Tom's a-cold.

GLOUCESTER. In, fellow, there, into th' hovel; keep thee warm.

LEAR. Come, let's in all.

KENT.   This way, my lord

LEAR.   With him!
I will keep still with my philosopher.   160

KENT. Good my lord, soothe° him; let him take the fellow.

GLOUCESTER. Take him you on.°

KENT. Sirrah, come on; go along with us.

LEAR. Come, good Athenian.°

GLOUCESTER. No words, no words! Hush.   165

EDGAR. Child Rowland to the dark tower came;°
His word was still,° ``Fie, foh, and fum,
I smell the blood of a British man.''°   *Exeunt.*

---

¹⁴⁰ *Theban* i.e., Greek philosopher   ¹⁴¹ *study* particular scientific study   ¹⁴² *prevent* balk   ¹⁵¹ *outlawed from my blood* disowned and tainted, like a carbuncle in the corrupted blood   ¹⁵² *late* recently   ¹⁵⁵ *cry you mercy* I beg your pardon   ¹⁶¹ *soothe* humor   ¹⁶² *you on* with you   ¹⁶⁴ *Athenian* i.e., philosopher (like ``Theban'')   ¹⁶⁶ *Child . . . came* (? from a lost ballad; ``child'' = a candidate for knighthood; *Rowland* was Charlemagne's nephew, the hero of *The Song of Roland*)   ¹⁶⁷ *His . . . still* his motto was always   ¹⁶⁷⁻¹⁶⁸ *Fie . . . man* (a deliberately absurd linking of the chivalric hero with the nursery tale of Jack the Giant-Killer)

Scene V. [*Gloucester's castle.*]

Enter Cornwall and Edmund.

CORNWALL. I will have my revenge ere I depart his house.

EDMUND. How, my lord, I may be censured,° that nature thus gives
   way to loyalty, something fears° me to think of.

CORNWALL. I now perceive it was not altogether your brother's evil
   disposition made him seek his death; but a provoking merit,   5
   set a-work by a reprovable badness in himself.°

EDMUND. How malicious is my fortune that I must repent to be just!
   This is the letter which he spoke of, which approves° him an
   intelligent party° to the advantages° of France. O heavens, that
   his treason were not! or not I the detector!   10

CORNWALL. Go with me to the Duchess.

EDMUND. If the matter of this paper be certain, you have mighty business in hand.

CORNWALL. True or false, it hath made thee Earl of Gloucester. Seek
   out where thy father is, that he may be ready for our   15
   apprehension.°

EDMUND. [*Aside*] If I find him comforting° the King, it will stuff his suspicion more fully.—I will persever° in my course of loyalty,
   though the conflict be sore between that and my blood.°

CORNWALL. I will lay trust upon° thee, and thou shalt find a dearer   20
   father in my love.   *Exeunt.*

Scene VI. [*A chamber in a farmhouse adjoining the castle.*]

Enter Kent and Gloucester.

GLOUCESTER. Here is better than the open air; take it thankfully. I will
   piece out the comfort with what addition I can. I will not be long
   from you.

KENT. All the power of his wits have given way to his impatience.° The
   gods reward your kindness.   5

          Exit [*Gloucester*].

III.v.   ² *censured* judged   ³ *something fears* somewhat frightens   ⁵⁻⁶ *a provoking . . . him-*
   self a stimulating goodness in Edgar, brought into play by a blamable badness in
   Gloucester   ⁸ *approves* proves   ⁹ *intelligent party* (1) spy (2) well-informed person
   ⁹ *to the advantages* on behalf of   ¹⁶ *apprehension* arrest   ¹⁷ *comforting* supporting (a
   legalism)   ¹⁸ *persever* persevere   ¹⁹ *blood* natural feelings   ²⁰ *lay trust upon* (1) trust
   (2) advance   III.vi.   ⁴ *impatience* raging

Enter Lear, Edgar, and Fool.

EDGAR. Frateretto° calls me, and tells me Nero° is an angler in the
lake of darkness. Pray, innocent,° and beware the foul fiend.

FOOL. Prithee, Nuncle, tell me whether a madman be a gentleman or
a yeoman.°

LEAR. A king, a king.   10

FOOL. No, he's a yeoman that has a gentleman to his son; for he's a
mad yeoman that sees his son a gentleman before him.

LEAR. To have a thousand with red burning spits
Come hizzing° in upon 'em—

EDGAR. The foul fiend bites my back.   15

FOOL. He's mad that trusts in the tameness of a wolf, a horse's
health, a boy's love, or a whore's oath.

LEAR. It shall be done; I will arraign° them straight.°
[*To Edgar*] Come, sit thou here, most learned justice.°
[*To the Fool*] Thou, sapient° sir, sit here. Now, you she-foxes—   20

EDGAR. Look, where he° stands and glares. Want'st thou eyes at trial,
madam?°
Come o'er the bourn,° Bessy, to me.

FOOL. Her boat hath a leak,
And she must not speak   25
Why she dares not come over to thee.°

EDGAR. The foul fiend haunts Poor Tom in the voice of a nightingale.°
Hoppedance° cries in Tom's belly for two white herring.° Croak°
not, black angel; I have no food for thee.

KENT. How do you, sir? Stand you not so amazed.° Will you lie down   30
and rest upon the cushions?

LEAR. I'll see their trial first. Bring in their evidence.°
[*To Edgar*] Thou, robèd man of justice, take thy place.
[*To the Fool*] And thou, his yokefellow of equity,°

---

⁶ *Frateretto* Elizabethan devil, from Harsnett's *Declaration*   ⁶ *Nero* (who is mentioned by
Harsnett, and whose angling is reported by Chaucer in "The Monk's Tale")   ⁷ *innocent*
fool   ⁹ *yeoman* farmer (just below a gentleman in rank. The Fool asks what class of
man has most indulged his children, and thus been driven mad)   ¹³ *hizzing* hissing
¹⁸ *arraign* bring to trial   ¹⁸ *straight* straightaway   ¹⁹ *justice* justicer, judge   ²⁰ *sapient*
wise   ²¹ *he* i.e., a fiend   ²¹⁻²² *Want'st . . . madam* (to Goneril) i.e., do you want eyes to
look at you during your trial? The fiend serves that purpose   ²³ *bourn* brook (Edgar
quotes from a popular ballad)   ²⁴⁻²⁶ *Her . . . thee* (the Fool parodies the ballad)
²⁷ *nightingale* i.e., the Fool's singing   ²⁸ *Hoppedance* Hoberdidance (another devil from
Harsnett's *Declaration*)   ²⁸ *white herring* unsmoked (? as against the black and sulfur-
ous devil)   ²⁸ *Croak* rumble (because his belly is empty)   ³⁰ *amazed* astonished
³² *evidence* the evidence of witnesses against them   ³⁴ *yokefellow of equity* partner in
justice

Bench° by his side. [*To Kent*] You are o' th' commission;°   35
Sit you too.

EDGAR. Let us deal justly.
> Sleepest or wakest thou, jolly shepherd?
>   Thy sheep be in the corn;°
> And for one blast of thy minikin° mouth   40
>   Thy sheep shall take no harm.°

Purr, the cat is gray.°

LEAR. Arraign her first. 'Tis Goneril, I here take my oath before this
honorable assembly, she kicked the poor King her father.

FOOL. Come hither, mistress. Is your name Goneril?   45

LEAR. She cannot deny it.

FOOL. Cry you mercy, I took you for a joint stool.°

LEAR. And here's another, whose warped looks proclaim
What store° her heart is made on. Stop here there!
Arms, arms, sword, fire! Corruption in the place!°   50
False justicer, why hast thou let her 'scape?

EDGAR. Bless thy five wits!

KENT. O pity! Sir, where is the patience now
That you so oft have boasted to retain?

EDGAR. [*Aside*] My tears begin to take his part so much   55
They mar my counterfeiting.°

LEAR. The little dogs and all,
Tray, Blanch, and Sweetheart—see, they bark at me.

EDGAR. Tom will throw his head at them. Avaunt, you curs.
> Be thy mouth or black or° white,   60
> Tooth that poisons if it bite;
> Mastiff, greyhound, mongrel grim,
> Hound or spaniel, brach° or lym,°
> Or bobtail tike, or trundle-tail°—
> Tom will make him weep and wail;   65

---

[35] *Bench* sit on the bench   [35]*commission* those commissioned as king's justices [38-41] *Sleepest . . . harm* (probably quoted or adapted from an Elizabethan song) [39] *corn* wheat   [40] *minikin* shrill   [42] *gray* (devils were thought to assume the shape of a gray cat)   [47] *Cry . . . joint stool* (proverbial and deliberately impudent apology for overlooking a person. A joint stool was a low stool made by a joiner, perhaps here a stage property to represent Goneril and in line 52, Regan. "Joint stool" can also suggest the judicial bench; hence Goneril may be identified by the Fool, ironically, with those in power, who judge)   [49] *store* stuff   [50] *Corruption . . . place* bribery in the court [56] *counterfeiting* i.e., feigned madness   [60] *or . . . or* either . . . or   [63] *brach* bitch [63] *lym* bloodhound (from the liam or leash with which he was led)   [64] *bobtail . . . trundle-tail* short-tailed or long-tailed cur

> For, with throwing° thus my head,
> Dogs leaped the hatch,° and all are fled.
>
> Do, de, de, de. Sessa!° Come, march to wakes° and fairs and
> market towns. Poor Tom, thy horn° is dry.

LEAR. Then let them anatomize Regan. See what breeds about her   70
heart.° Is there any cause in nature that make° these hard
hearts? [*To Edgar*] You, sir, I entertain° for one of my hundred;°
only I do not like the fashion of your garments. You will say they
are Persian;° but let them be changed.

KENT. Now, good my lord, lie here and rest awhile.   75

LEAR. Make no noise, make no noise; draw the curtains.°
So, so. We'll go to supper i' th' morning.

FOOL. And I'll go to bed at noon.°

Enter Gloucester.

GLOUCESTER. Come hither, friend. Where is the King my master?

KENT. Here, sir, but trouble him not; his wits are gone.   80

GLOUCESTER. Good friend, I prithee take him in thy arms.
I have o'erheard a plot of death upon him.
There is a litter ready; lay him in't
And drive toward Dover, friend, where thou shalt meet
Both welcome and protection. Take up thy master.   85
If thou shouldst dally half an hour, his life,
With thine and all that offer to defend him,
Stand in assurèd loss. Take up, take up,
And follow me, that will to some provision°
Give thee quick conduct.°

KENT.   Oppressèd nature sleeps.
This rest might yet have balmed thy broken sinews,°   90
Which, if convenience° will not allow,
Stand in hard cure.° [*To the Fool*] Come, help to bear thy
master.
Thou must not stay behind.

GLOUCESTER.   Come, come, away!

Exeunt [all but Edgar].

---

⁶⁶ *throwing* jerking (as a hound lifts its head from the ground, the scent having been lost)
⁶⁷ *leaped the hatch* leaped over the lower half of a divided door (i.e., left in a hurry)
⁶⁸ *Sessa* be off   ⁶⁸ *wakes* feasts attending the dedication of a church   ⁶⁹ *horn* horn bottle which the Bedlam used in begging a drink (Edgar is suggesting that he is unable to play his role any longer)   ⁷⁰⁻⁷¹ *Then . . . heart* i.e., if the Bedlam's horn is dry, let Regan, whose heart has become as hard as horn, be dissected   ⁷¹ *make* (subjunctive)   ⁷² *entertain* engage   ⁷² *hundred* i.e., Lear's hundred knights   ⁷⁴ *Persian* gorgeous (ironically of Edgar's rags)   ⁷⁶ *curtains* (Lear imagines himself in bed)   ⁷⁸ *And . . . noon* (the Fool's last words)   ⁸⁹ *provision* maintenance   ⁹⁰ *conduct* direction   ⁹⁰ *balmed thy broken sinews* soothed thy racked nerves   ⁹¹ *convenience* fortunate occasion   ⁹² *Stand . . . cure* will be hard to cure

EDGAR. When we our betters see bearing our woes,　　　　　　　　　95
　　We scarcely think our miseries our foes.°
　　Who alone suffers suffers most i' th' mind,
　　Leaving free° things and happy shows° behind;
　　But then the mind much sufferance° doth o'erskip
　　When grief hath mates, and bearing fellowship.°
　　How light and portable° my pain seems now,　　　　　　　　　100
　　When that which makes me bend makes the King bow.
　　He childed as I fathered. Tom away.
　　Mark the high noises,° and thyself bewray°
　　When false opinion, whose wrong thoughts° defile thee,　　　　　105
　　In thy just proof repeals and reconciles thee.°
　　What will hap more° tonight, safe 'scape the King!
　　Lurk,° lurk.　　　　　　　　　　　　　　　　　　　　　　　[*Exit.*]

Scene VII. [*Gloucester's castle.*]

Enter Cornwall, Regan, Goneril, Edmund, and Servants.

CORNWALL. [*To Goneril*] Post speedily to my Lord your husband; show
　　him this letter. The army of France is landed. [*To Servants*] Seek
　　out the traitor Gloucester. [*Exeunt some of the Servants.*]

REGAN. Hang him instantly.

GONERIL. Pluck out his eyes.　　　　　　　　　　　　　　　　　　5

CORNWALL. Leave him to my displeasure. Edmund, keep you our sis-
　　ter company. The revenges we are bound° to take upon your
　　traitorous father are not fit for your beholding. Advise the Duke
　　where you are going, to a most festinate° preparation. We are
　　bound to the like. Our posts° shall be swift and intelligent°　　　10
　　betwixt us. Farewell, dear sister; farewell, my Lord of
　　Gloucester.°

Enter Oswald.

　　How now? Where's the King?

OSWALD. My Lord of Gloucester hath conveyed him hence.
　　Some five or six and thirty of his knights,　　　　　　　　　　15
　　Hot questrists° after him, met him at gate;

---

⁹⁶ *our foes* enemies peculiar to ourselves　⁹⁸ *free* carefree　⁹⁸ *shows* scenes
⁹⁹ *sufferance* suffering　¹⁰⁰ *bearing fellowship* suffering has company　¹⁰¹ *portable* able
to be supported or endured　¹⁰⁴ *Mark the high noises* observe the rumors of strife
among those in power　¹⁰⁴ *bewray* reveal　¹⁰⁵ *wrong thoughts* misconceptions　¹⁰⁶*In
. . . thee* on the manifesting of your innocence recalls you from outlawry and restores
amity between you and your father　¹⁰⁷ *What . . . more* whatever else happens
¹⁰⁸ *Lurk* hide III.vii.　⁷ *bound* (1) forced (2) purposing to　⁹ *festinate* speedy　¹⁰ *posts*
messengers　¹⁰ *intelligent* full of information　^{11–12} *Lord of Gloucester* i.e., Edmund,
now elevated to the title　¹⁶ *questrists* searchers

Who, with some other of the lords dependants,°
Are gone with him toward Dover, where they boast
To have well-armèd friends.

CORNWALL.   Get horses for your mistress.

[*Exit Oswald.*]

GONERIL. Farewell, sweet lord, and sister.   20

CORNWALL. Edmund, farewell.

[*Exeunt Goneril and Edmund.*]

Go seek the traitor Gloucester,
Pinion him like a thief, bring him before us.

[*Exeunt other Servants.*]

Though well we may not pass upon° his life
Without the form of justice, yet our power
Shall do a court'sy to° our wrath, which men   25
May blame, but not control.

Enter Gloucester, brought in by two or three.

Who's there, the traitor?

REGAN. Ingrateful fox, 'tis he.

CORNWALL. Bind fast his corky° arms.

GLOUCESTER. What means your Graces? Good my friends, consider
You are my guests. Do me no foul play, friends.   30

CORNWALL. Bind him, I say.

[*Servants bind him.*]

REGAN.   Hard, hard! O filthy traitor.

GLOUCESTER. Unmerciful lady as you are, I'm none.

CORNWALL. To this chair bind him. Villain, thou shalt find—

[*Regan plucks his beard.°*]

GLOUCESTER. By the kind gods, 'tis mostly ignobly done
To pluck me by the beard.   35

REGAN. So white, and such a traitor?

GLOUCESTER.   Naughty° lady,
These hairs which thou dost ravish from my chin
Will quicken° and accuse thee. I am your host.
With robber's hands my hospitable favors°
You should not ruffle° thus. What will you do?   40

CORNWALL. Come, sir, what letters had you late° from France?

---

[17] *lords dependants* attendant lords (members of Lear's retinue)   [23] *pass upon* pass judgment on   [25] *do a court'sy to* indulge   [28] *corky* sapless (because old)   [34] s.d. *plucks
his beard* (a deadly insult)   [36] *Naughty* wicked   [38] *quicken* come to life   [39] *hospitable
favors* face of your host   [40] *ruffle* tear at violently   [41] *late* recently

REGAN. Be simple-answered,° for we know the truth,

CORNWALL. And what confederacy have you with the traitors
    Late footed in the kingdom?

REGAN. To whose hands you have sent the lunatic King: 45
    Speak.

GLOUCESTER. I have a letter guessingly° set down,
    Which came from one that's of a neutral heart,
    And not from one opposed.

CORNWALL.   Cunning.

REGAN.   And false.   50

CORNWALL. Where hast thou sent the King?

GLOUCESTER. To Dover.

REGAN. Wherefore to Dover? Wast thou not charged at peril°—

CORNWALL. Wherefore to Dover? Let him answer that.

GLOUCESTER. I am tied to th' stake, and I must stand the course,°   55

REGAN. Wherefore to Dover?

GLOUCESTER. Because I would not see thy cruel nails
    Pluck out his poor old eyes; nor thy fierce sister
    In his anointed° flesh rash° boarish fangs.
    The sea, with such a storm as his bare head   60
    In hell-black night endured, would have buoyed° up
    And quenched the stellèd° fires.
    Yet, poor old heart, he holp° the heavens to rain.
    If wolves had at thy gate howled that dearn° time,
    Thou shouldst have said, ``Good porter, turn the key.''°   65
    All cruels else subscribe.° But I shall see
    The wingèd° vengeance overtake such children.

CORNWALL. See't shalt thou never. Fellows, hold the chair.
    Upon these eyes of thine I'll set my foot.

GLOUCESTER. He that will think° to live till he be old,   70
    Give me some help.—O cruel! O you gods!

REGAN. One side will mock° another. Th' other too.

CORNWALL. If you see vengeance—

---

⁴² *simple-answered* straightforward in answering   ⁴⁷ *guessingly* without certain knowledge
   ⁵³ *charged at peril* ordered under penalty   ⁵⁵ *course* coursing (in which a relay of dogs
baits a bull or bear tied in the pit)   ⁵⁹ *anointed* holy (because king)   ⁵⁹ *rash* strike with
the tusk, like a boar   ⁶¹ *buoyed* risen   ⁶² *stellèd* (1) fixed (as opposed to the planets
or wandering stars) (2) starry   ⁶³ *holp* helped   ⁶⁴ *dearn* dread   ⁶⁵ *turn the key* i.e.,
unlock the gate   ⁶⁶ *All cruels else subscribe* all cruel creatures but man are
compassionate   ⁶⁷ *wingèd* (1) heavenly (2) swift   ⁷⁰ *will think* expects   ⁷² *mock* make
ridiculous (because of the contrast)

FIRST SERVANT.   Hold your hand, my lord!
  I have served you ever since I was a child;
  But better service have I never done you   75
  Than now to bid you hold.

REGAN.   How now, you dog?

FIRST SERVANT. If you did wear a beard upon your chin,
  I'd shake it° on this quarrel. What do you mean!°

CORNWALL. My villain!°

                                        Draw and fight.

FIRST SERVANT. Nay, then, come on, and take the chance of anger.   80

REGAN. Give me thy sword. A peasant stand up thus?

            She takes a sword and runs at him behind, kills him.

FIRST SERVANT. O, I am slain! my lord, you have one eye left
  To see some mischief° on him. O!

CORNWALL. Lest it see more, prevent it. Out, vile jelly.
  Where is thy luster now?   85

GLOUCESTER. All dark and comfortless. Where's my son Edmund?
  Edmund, enkindle all the sparks of nature°
  To quit° this horrid act.

REGAN.   Out, treacherous villain,
  Thou call'st on him that hates thee. It was he
  That made the overture° of thy treasons to us;   90
  Who is too good to pity thee.

GLOUCESTER. O my follies! Then Edgar was abused.°
  Kind gods, forgive me that, and prosper him.

REGAN. Go thrust him out at gates, and let him smell
  His way to Dover.   *Exit (one) with Gloucester.*
            How is't, my lord? How look you?°   95

CORNWALL. I have received a hurt. Follow me, lady.
  Turn out that eyeless villain. Throw this slave
  Upon the dunghill. Regan, I bleed apace.
  Untimely comes this hurt. Give me your arm.

                                        Exeunt.

SECOND SERVANT. I'll never care what wickedness I do,   100
  If this man come to good.

---

⁸⁶ *shake it* (an insult comparable to Regan's plucking of Gloucester's beard)   ⁸⁶ *What . . . mean* i.e., what terrible thing are you doing   ⁸⁷ *villain* serf (with a suggestion of the modern meaning)   ⁹¹ *mischief* injury   ⁹⁵ *enkindle . . . nature* fan your natural feeling into flame   ⁹⁶ *quit* requite   ⁹⁹ *overture* disclosure   ¹⁰¹ *abused* wronged   ¹⁰⁵ *How look you* how are you

THIRD SERVANT.   If she live long,
    And in the end meet the old course of death,°
    Women will all turn monsters.

SECOND SERVANT. Let's follow the old Earl, and get the Bedlam
    To lead him where he would. His roguish madness   105
    Allows itself to anything.°

THIRD SERVANT. Go thou. I'll fetch some flax and whites of eggs
    To apply to his bleeding face. Now heaven help him.

                                [Exeunt severally.]

ACT IV

Scene I. [*The heath.*]

Enter Edgar.

EDGAR. Yet better thus, and known to be contemned,°
    Than still contemned and flattered. To be worst,
    The lowest and most dejected° thing of fortune,
    Stands still in esperance,° lives not in fear:
    The lamentable change is from the best,   5
    The worst returns to laughter.° Welcome then,
    Thou unsubstantial air that I embrace!
    The wretch that thou hast blown unto the worst
    Owes° nothing to thy blasts.

              Enter Gloucester, led by an Old Man.

              But who comes here?
    My father, poorly led?° World, world, O world!   10
    But that thy strange mutations make us hate thee,
    Life would not yield to age.°

OLD MAN. O, my good lord, I have been your tenant, and your father's
    tenant, these fourscore years.

GLOUCESTER. Away, get thee away; good friend, be gone: 15
    Thy comforts° can do me no good at all;
    Thee they may hurt,°

OLD MAN.   You cannot see your way.

---

[113] *meet . . . death* die the customary death of old age   [116–17] *His . . . anything* his lack of all self-control leaves him open to any suggestion   IV.i.   [1] *known to be contemned* conscious of being despised   [3] *dejected* abased   [4] *esperance* hope   [6] *returns to laughter* changes for the better   [9] *Owes* is in debt for   [11] *poorly led* (1) led like a poor man, with only one attendant (2) led by a poor man   [12–13] *But . . . age* we should not agree to grow old and hence die, except for the hateful mutability of life   [17] *comforts* ministrations   [18] *hurt* injure

GLOUCESTER. I have no way and therefore want° no eyes;
    I stumbled when I saw. Full oft 'tis seen,
    Our means secure us, and our mere defects
    Prove our commodities.° Oh, dear son Edgar,   20
    The food° of thy abusèd° father's wrath!
    Might I but live to see thee in° my touch,
    I'd say I had eyes again!

OLD MAN.   How now! Who's there?

EDGAR. [*Aside*] O gods! Who is 't can say "I am at the worst"?   25
    I am worse than e'er I was.

OLD MAN.   'Tis poor mad Tom.

EDGAR. [*Aside*] And worse I may be yet: the worst is not
    So long as we can say "This is the worst."°

OLD MAN. Fellow, where goest?

GLOUCESTER.   Is it a beggar-man?

OLD MAN. Madman and beggar too.   30

GLOUCESTER. He has some reason,° else he could not beg.
    I' th' last night's storm I such a fellow saw,
    Which made me think a man a worm. My son
    Came then into my mind, and yet my mind
    Was then scarce friends with him. I have heard more since.   35
    As flies to wanton° boys, are we to th' gods,
    They kill us for their sport.

EDGAR. [*Aside*]   How should this be?°
    Bad is the trade that must play fool to sorrow,
    Ang'ring° itself and others. Bless thee, master!

GLOUCESTER. Is that the naked fellow?

OLD MAN.   Ay, my lord.   40

GLOUCESTER. Then, prithee, get thee gone: if for my sake
    Thou wilt o'ertake us hence a mile or twain
    I' th' way toward Dover, do it for ancient° love,
    And bring some covering for this naked soul,
    Which I'll entreat to lead me.

---

[18] *want* require   [21] *Our . . . commodities* our resources make us overconfident, while our afflictions make for our advantage   [22] *food* i.e., the object on which Gloucester's anger fed   [22] *abusèd* deceived   [23] *In* i.e., with, by means of   [27–28] *the . . . worst* so long as a man continues to suffer (i.e., is still alive), even greater suffering may await him   [31] *reason* faculty of reasoning   [36] *wanton* (1) playful (2) reckless   [37] *How should this be* i.e., how can this horror be?   [39] *Ang'ring* offending   [43] *ancient* (1) the love the Old Man feels, by virtue of his long tenancy (2) the love that formerly obtained between master and man

OLD MAN. Alack, sir, he is mad. 45

GLOUCESTER. 'Tis the times' plague,° when madmen lead the blind.
  Do as I bid thee, or rather do thy pleasure;°
  Above the rest,° be gone.

OLD MAN. I'll bring him the best 'parel° that I have,
  Come on 't what will. *Exit.* 50

GLOUCESTER. Sirrah, naked fellow—

EDGAR. Poor Tom's a-cold. [*Aside*] I cannot daub it° further.

GLOUCESTER. Come hither, fellow.

EDGAR. [*Aside*] And yet I must.—Bless thy sweet eyes, they bleed.

GLOUCESTER. Know'st thou the way to Dover? 55

EDGAR. Both stile and gate, horse-way and footpath. Poor Tom hath
  been scared out of his good wits. Bless thee, good man's son,
  from the foul fiend! Five fiends have been in Poor Tom at once;
  of lust, as Obidicut;° Hobbididence, prince of dumbness;° Mahu,
  of stealing; Modo, of murder; Flibbertigibbet, of mopping and 60
  mowing;° who since possesses chambermaids and waiting-
  women. So, bless thee, master!

GLOUCESTER. Here, take this purse, thou whom the heavens' plagues
  Have humbled to all strokes:° that I am wretched
  Makes thee the happier. Heavens, deal so still! 65
  Let the superfluous° and lust-dieted° man,
  That slaves° your ordinance,° that will not see
  Because he does not feel, feel your pow'r quickly;
  So distribution should undo excess,°
  And each man have enough. Dost thou know Dover? 70

EDGAR. Ay, master.

GLOUCESTER. There is a cliff whose high and bending° head
  Looks fearfully° in the confinèd deep:°
  Bring me but to the very brim of it,
  And I'll repair the misery thou dost bear 75

---

[46] *times' plague* characteristic disorder of this time [47] *thy pleasure* as you like [48] *the rest* all [49] *'parel* apparel [52] *daub it* lay it on (figure from plastering mortar) [59] *Obidicut* Hoberdicut, a devil (like the four that follow, from Harsnett's *Declaration*) [59] *dumbness* muteness (like the crimes and afflictions in the next lines, the result of diabolic possession) [60–61] *mopping and mowing* grimacing and making faces [64] *humbled to all strokes* brought so low as to bear anything humbly [66] *superfluous* possessed of superfluities [66] *lust-dieted* whose lust is gratified (like Gloucester's) [67] *slaves* (1) tramples, spurns like a slave (2) ? tears, rends (Old English *slaefan*) [67] *ordinance* law [69] *So . . . excess* then the man with too much wealth would distribute it among those with too little [72] *bending* overhanging [73] *fearfully* occasioning fear [73] *confinèd deep* the sea, hemmed in below

With something rich about me: from that place
I shall no leading need.

EDGAR. Give me thy arm:
Poor Tom shall lead thee. *Exeunt.*

Scene II. [*Before the Duke of Albany's palace.*]

Enter Goneril and Edmund.

GONERIL. Welcome, my lord: I marvel our mild husband
Not met° us on the way.
Enter Oswald.
Now, where's your master?

OSWALD. Madam, within; but never man so changed.
I told him of the army that was landed:
He smiled at it. I told him you were coming;
His answer was, "The worse." Of Gloucester's treachery,   5
And of the loyal service of his son
When I informed him, then he called me sot,°
And told me I had turned the wrong side out:
What most he should dislike seems pleasant to him;   10
What like,° offensive.

GONERIL. (*To Edmund*) Then shall you go no further.
It is the cowish° terror of his spirit,
That dares not undertake:° he'll not feel wrongs,
Which tie him to an answer.° Our wishes on the way
May prove effects.° Back, Edmund, to my brother;   15
Hasten his musters° and conduct his pow'rs.°
I must change names° at home and give the distaff°
Into my husband's hands. This trusty servant
Shall pass between us: ere long you are like to hear,
If you dare venture in your own behalf,   20
A mistress's° command. Wear this; spare speech;

(*Giving a favor*)

Decline your head.° This kiss, if it durst speak,
Would stretch thy spirits up into the air:
Conceive,° and fare thee well.

IV.ii.   ² *Not met* did not meet   ⁷ *sot* fool   ¹¹ *What like* what he should like   ¹³ *cowish*
cowardly   ¹³ *undertake* venture   ¹⁴ *tie him to an answer* oblige him to retaliate
¹⁴⁻¹⁵ *Our . . . effects* our desires (that you might be my husband), as we journeyed here,
may be fulfilled   ¹⁶ *musters* collecting of troops   ¹⁶ *conduct his pow'rs* lead his army
¹⁷ *change names* i.e., exchange the name of "mistress" for that of "master"   ¹⁷ *distaff*
spinning stick (wifely symbol)   ²¹ *mistress's* lover's (and also, Albany having been disposed of, lady's or wife's)   ²² *Decline your head* i.e., that Goneril may kiss him
²⁴ *Conceive* understand (with a sexual implication, that includes "stretch thy spirits,"
l.25; and "death," l.27: "to die," meaning "to experience sexual intercourse")

EDMUND. Yours in the ranks of death.   25

GONERIL.   My most dear Gloucester!

                                        Exit (Edmund).

O, the difference of man and man!
To thee a woman's services are due:
My fool usurps my body.°

OSWALD.   Madam, here comes my lord.

                                              Exit.

                    Enter Albany.

GONERIL. I have been worth the whistle.°

ALBANY.   O Goneril!
You are not worth the dust which the rude wind   30
Blows in your face. I fear your disposition:°
That nature which contemns° its origin
Cannot be bordered certain in itself;°
She that herself will sliver and disbranch°
From her material sap,° perforce must wither   35
And come to deadly use.°

GONERIL. No more; the text° is foolish.

ALBANY. Wisdom and goodness to the vile seem vile:
Filths savor but themselves.° What have you done?
Tigers, not daughters, what have you performed?   40
A father, and a gracious agèd man,
Whose reverence even the head-lugged bear° would lick,
Most barbarous, most degenerate, have you madded°
Could my good brother suffer you to do it?
A man, a prince, by him so benefited!   45
If that the heavens do not their visible spirits°
Send quickly down to tame these vile offenses,
It will come,
Humanity must perforce prey on itself,
Like monsters of the deep.

GONERIL.   Milk-livered° man!   50
That bear'st a cheek for blows, a head for wrongs;

---

²⁸ *My fool usurps body* my husband wrongfully enjoys me   ²⁹ *I . . . whistle* i.e., once you valued me (the proverb is implied, "It is a poor dog that is not worth the whistling") ³¹ *disposition* nature   ³² *contemns* despises   ³³ *bordered . . . itself* kept within its normal bounds   ³⁴ *sliver and disbranch* cut off   ³⁵ *material sap* essential and life-giving sustenance   ³⁶ *come to deadly use* i.e., be as a dead branch for the burning   ³⁷ *text* i.e., on which your sermon is based   ³⁹ *Filths savor but themselves* the filthy relish only the taste of filth   ⁴² *head-lugged bear* bear-baited by the dogs, and hence enraged   ⁴³ *madded* made mad   ⁴⁵ *visible spirits* avenging spirits in material form   ⁵⁰ *Milk-livered* lily-livered (hence cowardly, the liver being regarded as the seat of courage)

Who hast not in thy brows an eye discerning
Thine honor from thy suffering;° that not know'st
Fools do those villains pity who are punished
Ere they have done their mischief.° Where's thy drum?   55
France spreads his banners in our noiseless° land,
With plumèd helm° thy state begins to threat,°
Whilst thou, a moral° fool, sits still and cries
"Alack, why does he so?"

ALBANY.   See thyself, devil!
Proper° deformity seems not in the fiend   60
So horrid as in woman.

GONERIL.   O vain fool!

ALBANY. Thou changèd and self-covered° thing, for shame,
Be-monster not thy feature.° Were't my fitness°
To let these hands obey my blood,°
They are apt enough to dislocate and tear   65
Thy flesh and bones: howe'er° thou art a fiend,
A woman's shape doth shield thee.

GONERIL. Marry,° your manhood mew°—

                        Enter a Messenger.

ALBANY. What news?

MESSENGER. O, my good lord, the Duke of Cornwall's dead,   70
Slain by his servant, going to° put out
The other eye of Gloucester.

ALBANY.   Gloucester's eyes!

MESSENGER. A servant that he bred,° thrilled with remorse.°
Opposed against the act, bending his sword
To his great master, who thereat enraged
Flew on him, and amongst them felled° him dead,   75

---

⁵²⁻⁵³ *discerning . . . suffering* able to distinguish between insults that ought to be resented, and ordinary pain that is to be borne   ⁵⁴⁻⁵⁵ *Fools . . . mischief* only fools are sorry for criminals whose intended criminality is prevented by punishment   ⁵⁶ *noiseless* i.e., the drum, signifying preparation for war, is silent   ⁵⁷ *helm* helmet   ⁵⁷ *thy . . . threat* France begins to threaten Albany's realm   ⁵⁸ *moral* moralizing; but also with the implication that morality and folly are one   ⁶⁰ *Proper* (1) natural (to a fiend) (2) fair-appearing   ⁶² *changèd and self-covered* i.e., transformed, by the contorting of her woman's face, on which appears the fiendish behavior she has allowed herself. (Goneril has disguised nature by wickedness)   ⁶³ *Be-monster not thy feature* do not change your appearance into a fiend's   ⁶³ *my fitness* appropriate for me   ⁶⁴ *blood* passion   ⁶⁶ *howe'er* but even if   ⁶⁸ *Marry* by the Virgin Mary   ⁶⁸ *your manhood mew* (1) coop up or confine your (pretended) manhood (2) molt or shed it, if that is what is supposed to "shield" me from you   ⁷¹ *going to* as he was about to   ⁷³ *bred* reared   ⁷³ *thrilled with remorse* pierced by compassion   ⁷⁶ *amongst them felled* others assisting, they felled

But not without that harmful stroke which since
Hath plucked him after.°

ALBANY.   This shows you are above,
You justicers,° that these our nether° crimes
So speedily can venge.° But, O poor Gloucester!   80
Lost he his other eye?

MESSENGER.   Both, both, my lord.
This letter, madam, craves° a speedy answer;
'Tis from your sister.

GONERIL.   [*Aside*] One way I like this well;
But being widow, and my Gloucester with her,
May all the building in my fancy pluck   85
Upon my hateful life.° Another way,°
The news is not so tart.°—I'll read, and answer.

                                                            Exit.

ALBANY. Where was his son when they did take his eyes?

MESSENGER. Come with my lady hither.

ALBANY.   He is not here.

MESSENGER. No, my good lord; I met him back° again.   90

ALBANY. Knows he the wickedness?

MESSENGER. Ay, my good lord; 'twas he informed against him,
And quit the house on purpose, that their punishment
Might have the freer course.

ALBANY.   Gloucester, I live
To thank thee for the love thou showed'st the King,   95
And to revenge thine eyes. Come hither, friend:
Tell me what more thou know'st.   *Exeunt.*

[Scene III. *The French camp near Dover.*]

Enter Kent and a Gentleman.

KENT. Why the King of France is so suddenly gone back, know you
  no reason?

GENTLEMAN. Something he left imperfect in the state,° which since his
  coming forth is thought of, which imports° to the kingdom so

---

[78] *plucked him after* i.e., brought Cornwall to death with his servant [79] *justicers* judges
  [79] *nether* committed below (on earth) [80] *venge* avenge [82] *craves* demands
  [85-86] *May . . . life* these things (l.84) may send my future hopes, my castles in air, crash-
ing down upon the hateful (married) life I lead now [86] *Another way* looked at another
way [87] *tart* sour [90] *back* going back IV.iii. [3] *imperfect in the state* unsettled in his
own kingdom [4] *imports* portends

much fear and danger that his personal return was most   5
required and necessary.

KENT. Who hath he left behind him general?

GENTLEMAN. The Marshal of France, Monsieur La Far.

KENT. Did your letters pierce° the queen to any demonstration of
grief?   10

GENTLEMAN. Ay, sir; she took them, read them in my presence,
And now and then an ample tear trilled° down
Her delicate cheek: it seemed she was a queen
Over her passion, who most rebel-like
Sought to be king o'er her.

KENT.   O, then it moved her.   15

GENTLEMAN. Not to a rage: patience and sorrow strove
Who should express her goodliest.° You have seen
Sunshine and rain at once: her smiles and tears
Were like a better way:° those happy smilets°
That played on her ripe lip seemed not to know   20
What guests were in her eyes, which parted thence
As pearls from diamonds dropped. In brief,
Sorrow would be a rarity most belovèd,
If all could so become it.°

KENT.   Made she no verbal question?

GENTLEMAN. Faith, once or twice she heaved° the name of "father"   25
Pantingly forth, as if it pressed her heart;
Cried "Sisters! Sisters! Shame of ladies! Sisters!
Kent! Father! Sisters! What, i' th' storm? i' th' night?
Let pity not be believed!"° There she shook
The holy water from her heavenly eyes,   30
And clamor moistened:° then away she started
To deal with grief alone.

KENT.   It is the stars,
The stars above us, govern our conditions;°
Else one self mate and make could not beget
Such different issues.° You spoke not with her since?   35

GENTLEMAN. No.

---

⁹ *pierce* impel   ¹² *trilled* trickled   ¹⁸ *Who . . . goodliest* which should give her the most
becoming expression   ¹⁹ *Were like a better way* i.e., improved on that spectacle
¹⁹*smilets* little smiles   ²³⁻²⁴ *Sorrow . . . it* sorrow would be a coveted jewel if it became
others as it does her   ²⁵ *heaved* expressed with difficulty   ²⁹ *Let pity not be believed*
let it not be believed for pity   ³¹ *clamor moistened* moistened clamor, i.e., mixed (and
perhaps assuaged) her outcries with tears   ³³ *govern our conditions* determine what
we are   ³⁴⁻³⁵ *Else . . . issues* otherwise the same husband and wife could not produce
such different children

KENT. Was this before the King returned?

GENTLEMAN.   No, since.

KENT. Well, sir, the poor distressèd Lear's i' th' town;
　　Who sometime in his better tune° remembers
　　What we are come about, and by no means   40
　　Will yield to see his daughter.

GENTLEMAN.   Why, good sir?

KENT. A sovereign° shame so elbows° him: his own unkindness
　　That stripped her from his benediction, turned her
　　To foreign casualties,° gave her dear rights
　　To his dog-hearted daughters: these things sting   45
　　His mind so venomously that burning shame
　　Detains him from Cordelia.

GENTLEMAN.   Alack, poor gentleman!

KENT. Of Albany's and Cornwall's powers you heard not?

GENTLEMAN. 'Tis so;° they are afoot.

KENT. Well, sir, I'll bring you to our master Lear,   50
　　And leave you to attend him: some dear cause°
　　Will in concealment wrap me up awhile;
　　When I am known aright, you shall not grieve
　　Lending me this acquaintance, I pray you, go
　　Along with me.   [*Exeunt.*]   55

[Scene IV. *The same. A tent.*]

Enter, with drum and colors, Cordelia, Doctor, and Soldiers.

CORDELIA. Alack, 'tis he: why, he was met even now
　　As mad as the vexed sea; singing aloud;
　　Crowned with rank femiter and furrow-weeds,
　　With hardocks, hemlock, nettles, cuckoo-flow'rs,
　　Darnel,° and all the idle weeds that grow   5
　　In our sustaining corn.° A century° send forth;
　　Search every acre in the high-grown field,
　　And bring him to our eye [*Exit an Officer.*] What can man's
　　wisdom°

---

[39] *better tune* composed, less jangled intervals [42] *soverign* overpowering [42] *elbows* jogs
his elbow i.e., reminds him [44] *casualties* chances [49] *'Tis so* i.e., I have heard of
them [51] *dear cause* important reason IV.iv. [3-5] *femiter . . . Darnel: femiter* fumi-
tory, whose leaves and juice are bitter; *furrow-weeds* weeds that grow in the furrow; or
plowed land; *hardocks?* hoar or white docks, burdocks, harlocks; *hemlock* a poison;
nettles plants which sting and burn; *cuckoo-flow'rs* identified with a plant employed to
remedy diseases of the brain; *Darnel* tares, noisome weeds [6] *sustaining corn* life-main-
taining wheat [6] *century* ? sentry; troop of a hundred soldiers [9] *What can man's wisdom* what can science accomplish

In the restoring his bereavèd° sense?   10
He that helps him take all my outward° worth.

DOCTOR. There is means, madam:
Our foster-nurse° of nature is repose,
The which he lacks: that to provoke° in him,
Are many simples operative,° whose power   15
Will close the eye of anguish.

CORDELIA.   All blest secrets,
All you unpublished virtues° of the earth,
Spring with my tears! be aidant and remediate°
In the good man's distress! Seek, seek for him,
Lest his ungoverned rage dissolve the life   20
That wants the means to lead it.°

                    Enter Messenger.

MESSENGER.   News, madam;
The British pow'rs are marching hitherward.

CORDELIA. 'Tis known before. Our preparation stands
In expectation of them. O dear father,
It is thy business that I go about;   25
Therefore° great France
My mourning and importuned° tears hath pitied.
No blown° ambition doth our arms incite,
But love, dear love, and our aged father's right:
Soon may I hear and see him!   *Exeunt.*   30

[Scene V. *Gloucester's castle.*]

                    Enter Regan and Oswald.

REGAN. But are my brother's pow'rs set forth?

OSWALD.   Ay, madam.

REGAN. Himself in person there?

OSWALD.   Madam, with much ado:°
Your sister is the better soldier.

REGAN. Lord Edmund spake not with your lord at home?

OSWALD. No, madam.   5

REGAN. What might import° my sister's letter to him?

OSWALD. I know not, lady.

---

[10] *bereavèd* impaired   [11] *outward* material   [13] *foster-nurse* fostering nurse   [14] *provoke* induce   [15] *simples operative* efficacious medicinal herbs   [17] *unpublished virtues* i.e., secret remedial herbs   [18] *remediate* remedial   [21] *wants . . . it* i.e., lacks the reason to control the rage   [26] *Therefore* because of that   [27] *importuned* importunate   [28] *blown* puffed up   IV.v.   [2] *ado* bother and persuasion   [6] *import* purport, carry as its message

REGAN. Faith, he is posted° hence on serious matter.
　　It was great ignorance,° Gloucester's eyes being out,
　　To let him live. Where he arrives he moves　　　　　　　10
　　All hearts against us: Edmund, I think, is gone,
　　In pity of his misery, to dispatch
　　His nighted° life; moreover, to descry
　　The strength o' th' enemy.

OSWALD. I must needs after him, madam, with my letter.　　15

REGAN. Our troops set forth tomorrow: stay with us;
　　The ways are dangerous.

OSWALD.　　　　　　　　　　I may not, madam:
　　My lady charged my duty° in this business.

REGAN. Why should she write to Edmund? Might not you
　　Transport her purposes° by word? Belike,°　　　　　　20
　　Some things I know not what. I'll love thee much,
　　Let me unseal the letter.

OSWALD.　　　　　　　　　　Madam, I had rather—

REGAN. I know your lady does not love her husband;
　　I am sure of that: and at her late° being here
　　She gave strange eliads° and most speaking looks　　　25
　　To noble Edmund. I know you are of her bosom.°

OSWALD. I, madam?

REGAN. I speak in understanding: y'are; I know't:
　　Therefore I do advise you, take this note:°
　　My lord is dead; Edmund and I have talked;　　　　　30
　　And more convenient° is he for my hand
　　Than for your lady's: you may gather more.°
　　If you do find him, pray you, give him this;°
　　And when your mistress hears thus much from you,
　　I pray, desire her call° her wisdom to her.　　　　　35
　　So, fare you well.
　　If you do chance to hear of that blind traitor,
　　Preferment° falls on him that cuts him off.

OSWALD. Would I could meet him, madam! I should show
　　What party I do follow.

REGAN.　　　　　　　　　　Fare thee well.　　　　　40

　　　　　　　　　　　　　　　　　Exeunt.

---

[8] *is posted* has ridden speedily　[9] *ignorance* folly　[13] *nighted* (1) darkened, because blinded (2) benighted　[18] *charged my duty* ordered me as a solemn duty　[20] *Transport her purposes* convey her intentions　[20] *Belike* probably　[24] *late* recently　[25] *eliads* amorous looks　[26] *of her bosom* in her confidence　[29] *take this note* take note of this　[31] *convenient* fitting　[32] *gather more* surmise more yourself　[33] *this* this advice　[35] *call* recall　[38] *Preferment* promotion

[Scene VI. *Fields near Dover.*]

Enter Gloucester and Edgar.

GLOUCESTER. When shall I come to th' top of that same hill?

EDGAR. You do climb up it now. Look, how we labor.

GLOUCESTER. Methinks the ground is even.

EDGAR.   Horrible steep.
    Hark, do you hear the sea?

GLOUCESTER.   No, truly.

EDGAR. Why then your other senses grow imperfect
    By your eyes' anguish.°   5

GLOUCESTER.   So may it be indeed.
    Methinks thy voice is altered, and thou speak'st
    In better phrase and matter than thou didst.

EDGAR. Y'are much deceived: in nothing am I changed
    But in my garments.

GLOUCESTER.   Methinks y'are better spoken.   10

EDGAR. Come on, sir; here's the place: stand still. How fearful
    And dizzy 'tis to cast one's eyes so low!
    The crows and choughs° that wing the midway air°
    Show scarce so gross° as beetles. Half way down
    Hangs one that gathers sampire,° dreadful trade!   15
    Methinks he seems no bigger than his head.
    The fishermen that walk upon the beach
    Appear like mice; and yond tall anchoring° bark
    Diminished to her cock;° her cock, a buoy
    Almost too small for sight. The murmuring surge   20
    That on th' unnumb'red idle pebble° chafes
    Cannot be heard so high. I'll look no more,
    Lest my brain turn and the deficient sight
    Topple° down headlong.

GLOUCESTER.   Set me where you stand.

EDGAR. Give me your hand: you are now within a foot   25
    Of th' extreme verge: for all beneath the moon
    Would I not leap upright.°

IV.vi.   ⁶ *anguish* pain   ¹³ *choughs* a kind of crow   ¹³ *midway air* i.e., halfway down the cliff   ¹⁴ *gross* large   ¹⁵ *sampire* samphire, an aromatic herb associated with Dover Cliffs   ¹⁸ *anchoring* anchored   ¹⁹ *cock* cockboat, a small boat usually towed behind the ship   ²¹ *unnumb'red idle pebble* innumerable pebbles, moved to and fro by the waves to no purpose   ²³⁻²⁴ *the deficient sight/Topple* my failing sight topple me   ²⁷ *upright* i.e., even up in the air, to say nothing of forward, over the cliff

GLOUCESTER.   Let go my hand.
    Here, friend, 's another purse; in it a jewel
    Well worth a poor man's taking. Fairies° and gods   30
    Prosper it with thee! Go thou further off;
    Bid me farewell, and let me hear thee going.

EDGAR. Now fare ye well, good sir.

GLOUCESTER.   With all my heart.

EDGAR. [*Aside*] Why I do trifle thus with his despair
    Is done to cure it.°

GLOUCESTER.   O you mighty gods!

                                                   He kneels.

    This world I do renounce, and in your sights   35
    Shake patiently my great affliction off:
    If I could bear it longer and not fall
    To quarrel° with your great opposeless° wills,
    My snuff° and loathèd part of nature should
    Burn itself out. If Edgar live, O bless him!   40
    Now, fellow, fare thee well.

                                                   He falls.

EDGAR.   Gone, sir, farewell.
    And yet I know not how° conceit° may rob
    The treasury of life, when life itself
    Yields to° the theft. Had he been where he thought,
    By this had thought been past. Alive or dead?   45
    Ho, you sir! friend! Hear you, sir! speak!
    Thus might he pass° indeed: yet he revives.
    What are you, sir?

GLOUCESTER.   Away, and let me die.

EDGAR. Hadst thou been aught but gossamer, feathers, air,
    So many fathom down precipitating,°   50
    Thou'dst shivered like an egg: but thou dost breathe;
    Hast heavy substance; bleed'st not; speak'st; art sound.
    Ten masts at each° make not the altitude
    Which thou hast perpendicularly fell:
    Thy life's° a miracle. Speak yet again.   55

GLOUCESTER. But have I fall'n, or no?

EDGAR. From the dread summit of this chalky bourn.°

---

30 *Fairies* (who are supposed to guard and multiply hidden treasure)   34–35 *Why . . . it* I play
    on his despair in order to cure it   37–38 *fall/To quarrel with* rebel against   38 *opposeless*
    not to be, and not capable of being, opposed   39 *snuff* the guttering (and stinking) wick
    of a burnt-out candle   42 *how* but what   42 *conceit* imagination   44 *Yields to* allows
    47 *pass* die   50 *precipitating* falling   53 *at each* one on top of the other   55 *life's*
    survival   57 *bourn* boundary

Look up a-height;° the shrill-gorged° lark so far
Cannot be seen or heard: do but look up.

GLOUCESTER. Alack, I have no eyes.   60
Is wretchedness deprived that benefit,
To end itself by death? 'Twas yet some comfort,
When misery could beguile° the tyrant's rage
And frustrate his proud will.

EDGAR.   Give me your arm.
Up, so. How is 't? Feel you° your legs? You stand.   65

GLOUCESTER. Too well, too well.

EDGAR.   This is above all strangeness.
Upon the crown o' th' cliff, what thing was that
Which parted from you?

GLOUCESTER.   A poor unfortunate beggar.

EDGAR. As I stood here below, methought his eyes
Were two full moons; he had a thousand noses,   70
Horns whelked° and waved like the enridgèd° sea:
It was some fiend; therefore, thou happy father,°
Think that the clearest° gods, who make them honors
Of men's impossibilities,° have preserved thee.

GLOUCESTER. I do remember now: henceforth I'll bear   75
Affliction till it do cry out itself
''Enough, enough,'' and die. That thing you speak of,
I took it for a man; often 'twould say
''The fiend, the fiend''—he led me to that place.

EDGAR. Bear free° and patient thoughts.

          Enter Lear [fantastically dressed with wild flowers].

                                          But who comes here?   80
The safer° sense will ne'er accommodate°
His master thus.

LEAR. No, they cannot touch me for coining;° I am the King himself.

EDGAR. O thou side-piercing sight!

LEAR. Nature's above art in that respect.° There's your press-money.°   85

---

⁵⁸ *a-height* on high   ⁵⁸ *gorged* throated, voiced   ⁶³ *beguile* chest (i.e., by suicide)   ⁶⁵ *Feel you* have you any feeling in   ⁷¹ *whelked* twisted   ⁷¹ *enridgèd* i.e., furrowed into waves   ⁷² *happy father* fortunate old man   ⁷³ *clearest* purest   ⁷³⁻⁷⁴ *who . . . impossibilities* who cause themselves to be honored and revered by performing miracles of which men are incapable   ⁸⁰ *free* i.e., emancipated from grief and despair, which fetter the soul   ⁸¹ *safer* sounder, saner   ⁸¹ *accommodate* dress, adorn   ⁸³ *touch me for coining* arrest me for minting coins (the king's prerogative)   ⁸⁵ *Nature's . . . respect* i.e., a born king is superior to legal (and hence artificial) inhibition. There is also a glance here at the popular Renaissance debate, concerning the relative importance of nature (inspiration) and art (training)   ⁸⁵ *press-money* (paid to conscripted soldiers)

That fellow handles his bow like a crow-keeper;° draw me a
clothier's yard.° Look, look, a mouse! Peace, peace; this piece
of toasted cheese will do 't. There's my gauntlet;° I'll prove it
on° a giant. Bring up the brown bills.° O, well flown,° bird! i' th'
clout, i' th' clout:° hewgh!° Give the word.°   90

EDGAR. Sweet marjoram.°

LEAR. Pass.

GLOUCESTER. I know that voice.

LEAR. Ha! Goneril, with a white beard! They flattered me like a dog,°
and told me I had white hairs in my beard ere the black ones   95
were there.° To say "ay" and "no" to everything that I said!
"Ay" and "no" too was no good divinity.° When the rain came
to wet me once and the wind to make me chatter; when the
thunder would not peace at my bidding; there I found 'em,
there I smelt 'em out. Go to, they are not men o' their words;   100
they told me I was everything; 'tis a lie, I am not ague-proof.°

GLOUCESTER. The trick° of that voice I do well remember:
Is't not the king?

LEAR.   Ay, every inch a king.
When I do stare, see how the subject quakes.
I pardon that man's life. What was thy cause?°   105
Adultery?
Thou shalt not die: die for adultery! No:
The wren goes to 't, and the small gilded fly
Does lecher° in my sight.
Let copulation thrive; for Gloucester's bastard son   110
Was kinder to his father than my daughters
Got° 'tween the lawful sheets.
To 't, luxury,° pell-mell! for I lack soldiers.°
Behold yond simp'ring dame,

---

⁸⁶ *crow-keeper* a farmer scaring away crows   ⁸⁷ *clothier's yard* (the standard English arrow
was a cloth-yard long. Here the injunction is to draw the arrow back, like a powerful
archer, a full yard to the ear)   ⁸⁸ *gauntlet* armored glove, thrown down as a challenge
⁸⁸⁻⁸⁹ *prove it on* maintain my challenge even against   ⁸⁹ *brown bills* halberds varnished
to prevent rust (here the reference is to the soldiers who carry them)
⁸⁹ *well flown* (falconer's cry; and perhaps a reference to the flight of the arrow)
⁹⁰ *clout* the target shot at   ⁹⁰ *hewgh* ? imitating the whizzing of the arrow   ⁹⁰ *word*
password   ¹⁰⁰ *Sweet marjoram* herb, used as a remedy for brain disease   ⁹⁴ *like a dog*
as a dog flatters   ⁹⁵⁻⁹⁶ *I . . . there* I was wise before I had even grown a beard   ⁹⁷ *no
good divinity* (bad theology, because contrary to the Biblical saying [II Corinthians
1:18], "Our word toward you was not yea and nay." See also James 5:12 "But let your
yea be yea, and your nay, nay; lest ye fall into condemnation"; and Matthew 5:36–37)
¹⁰¹ *ague-proof* secure against fever   ¹⁰² *trick* intonation   ¹⁰⁵ *cause* offense   ¹⁰⁹ *lecher*
copulate   ¹¹² *Got* begot   ¹¹³ *luxury* lechery   ¹¹³ *for . . . soldiers* i.e., ? (1) whom copulation will supply (2) and am therefore powerless

Whose face between her forks presages snow,°   115
That minces° virtue and does shake the head
To hear of pleasure's name.°
The fitchew,° nor the soilèd° horse, goes to 't
With a more riotous appetite.
Down from the waist they are Centaurs,°   120
Though women all above:
But to the girdle° do the gods inherit,°
Beneath is all the fiend's.
There's hell, there's darkness, there is the sulphurous pit,
Burning, scalding, stench, consumption; fie, fie, fie! pah! pah!   125
Give me an ounce of civet;° good apothecary, sweeten my
imagination: there's money for thee.

GLOUCESTER. O, let me kiss that hand!

LEAR. Let me wipe it first; it smells of mortality.°

GLOUCESTER. O ruined piece of nature! This great world   130
Shall so wear out to nought.° Dost thou know me?

LEAR. I remember thine eyes well enough. Dost thou squiny° at me?
No, do thy worst, blind Cupid;° I'll not love. Read thou this challenge;° mark but the penning of it.

GLOUCESTER. Were all thy letters suns, I could not see.   135

EDGAR. I would not take° this from report: it is,
And my heart breaks at it.

LEAR. Read.

GLOUCESTER. What, with the case° of eyes?

LEAR. O, ho, are you there with me?° No eyes in your head, nor no   140
money in your purse? Your eyes are in a heavy case,° your
purse in a light,° yet you see how this world goes.

GLOUCESTER. I see it feelingly.°

LEAR. What, art mad? A man may see how this world goes with no
eyes. Look with thine ears: see how yond justice rails upon   145
yond simple° thief. Hark, in thine ear: change places, and,

---

[115] *Whose . . . snow* whose cold demeanor seems to promise chaste behavior ("forks":
legs)   [116] *minces* squeamishly pretends to   [117] *pleasure's name* the very name of sexual pleasure   [118] *fitchew* polecat (and slang for "prostitute")   [118] *soilèd* put to pasture,
and hence wanton with feeding   [120] *Centaurs* lustful creatures, half man and half
horse   [122] *girdle* waist   [122] *inherit* possess   [126] *civet* perfume   [129] *mortality* (1) death
(2) existence   [130-31] *This . . . nought* i.e., the universe (macrocosm) will decay to nothing in the same way as the little world of man (microcosm)   [132] *squiny* squint, look
sideways, like a prostitute   [133] *blind Cupid* the sign hung before a brothel
[133-34] *challenge* a reminiscence of II. 89–90.   [136] *take* believe   [139] *case* empty sockets
[140] *are . . . me* is that what you tell me   [141] *heavy case* sad plight (pun on 1.146)
[142] *light* i.e., empty   [143] *feelingly* (1) by touch (2) by feeling pain (3) with emotion
[146] *simple* common, of low estate

handy-dandy,° which is the justice, which is the thief? Thou
hast seen a farmer's dog bark at a beggar?

GLOUCESTER. Ay, sir.

LEAR. And the creature run from the cur? There thou mightst behold   150
the great image of authority;° a dog's obeyed in office.°
Thou rascal beadle,° hold thy bloody hand!
Why doest thou lash that whore? Strip thy own back;
Thou hotly lusts to use her in that kind°
For which thou whip'st her. The usurer hangs the cozener.°   155
Through tattered clothes small vices do appear;
Robes and furred gowns° hide all. Plate sin with gold,
And the strong lance of justice hurtless° breaks;
Arm it in rags, a pygmy's straw does pierce it.
None does offend, none, I say, none; I'll able° 'em: 160
Take that° of me, my friend, who have the power
To seal th' accuser's lips. Get thee glass eyes,°
And, like a scurvy politician,° seem
To see the things thou dost not. Now, now, now, now.
Pull off my boots: harder, harder: so.   165

EDGAR. O, matter and impertinency° mixed!
Reason in madness!

LEAR. If thou wilt weep my fortunes, take my eyes.
I know thee well enough; thy name is Gloucester:
Thou must be patient; we came crying hither: 170
Thou know'st, the first time that we smell the air
We wawl and cry. I will preach to thee: mark.

GLOUCESTER. Alack, alack the day!

LEAR. When we are born, we cry that we are come
To this great stage of fools. This'° a good block.°   175

---

[147] *handy-dandy* i.e., choose, guess (after the children's game—"Handy-dandy, prickly
prandy"—of choosing the right hand)   [151] *image of authority* symbol revealing the
true meaning of authority   [151] *a . . . office* i.e., whoever has power is obeyed
[152] *beadle* parish constable   [154] *kind* i.e., sexual act   [155] *The usurer . . . cozener* i.e., the
powerful moneylender, in his role as judge, puts to death the petty cheat   [157] *Robes
and furred gowns* (worn by a judge)   [158] *hurtless* i.e., without hurting the sinner
[160] *able* vouch for   [161] *that* (the immunity just conferred) (l. 170)   [162] *glass eyes*
spectacles   [163] *scurvy politician* vile politic man   [166] *matter and impertinency* sense
and nonsense   [175] *This'* this is   [175] *block* (various meanings have been suggested, for
example, the stump of a tree, on which Lear is supposed to climb; a mounting–block,
which suggests "horse" l.187; a hat (which Lear or another must be made to wear), from
the block on which a felt hat is molded, and which would suggest a "felt" l.187. The
proposal here is that "block" be taken to denote the quintain, whose function is to bear
blows, "a mere lifeless block" (*As You Like It*, l.ii.263), an object shaped like a man and
used for tilting practice. See also *Much Ado*, II.i.246–7, "she misused me past the endurance of a block!" and, in the same passage, the associated reference, "I stood like a
man at a mark (target)" (l.253))

It were a delicate° stratagem, to shoe
A troop of horse with felt: I'll put 't in proof;°
And when I have stol'n upon these son-in-laws,
Then, kill, kill, kill, kill, kill, kill!

Enter a Gentleman [with Attendants].

GENTLEMAN. O, here he is: lay hand upon him. Sir,   180
  Your most dear daughter—

LEAR. No rescue? What, a prisoner? I am even
  The natural fool° of fortune. Use me well;
  You shall have ransom. Let me have surgeons;
  I am cut° to th' brains.

GENTLEMAN.   You shall have anything.   185

LEAR. No seconds?° all myself?
  Why, this would make a man a man of salt,°
  To use his eyes for garden water-pots,
  Ay, and laying autumn's dust.

GENTLEMAN. Good sir—   190

LEAR. I will die bravely,° like a smug° bridegroom.° What!
  I will be jovial: come, come; I am a king;
  Masters, know you that?

GENTLEMAN. You are a royal one, and we obey you.

LEAR. Then there's life in 't.° Come, and you get it, you shall get
  it by running. Sa, sa, sa, sa.°   195

Exit [running; Attendants follow].

GENTLEMAN. A sight most pitiful in the meanest wretch,
  Past speaking of in a king! Thou hast one daughter
  Who redeems nature from the general curse
  Which twain have brought her to.°   200

EDGAR. Hail, gentle° sir.

GENTLEMAN.   Sir, speed° you: what's your will?

EDGAR. Do you hear aught, sir, of a battle toward?°

GENTLEMAN. Most sure and vulgar;° every one hears that,
  Which can distinguish sound.

---

[176] *delicate* subtle   [177] *put 't in proof* test it   [183] *natural fool* born sport (with pun on "natural": "imbecile")   [185] *cut* wounded   [186] *seconds* supporters   [187] *man of salt* i.e., all (salt) tears   [191] *bravely* (1) smartly attired (2) courageously   [191] *smug* spick and span   [191] *bridegroom* whose "brave" sexual feats are picked up in the pun on "die"   [195] *there's life in 't* there's still hope   [196] *Sa . . . sa* hunting and rallying cry; also an interjection of defiance   [199–200] *general . . . to* (1) universal condemnation which Goneril and Regan have made for (2) damnation incurred by the original sin of Adam and Eve   [201] *gentle* noble   [202] *speed* God speed   [203] *toward* impending   [204] *vulgar* common knowledge

EDGAR.   But, by your favor,   205
    How near's the other army?

GENTLEMAN. Near and on speedy foot; the main descry
    Stands on the hourly thought.°

EDGAR.   I thank you, sir: that's all.

GENTLEMAN. Though that the Queen on special cause is here,
    Her army is moved on.

EDGAR.   I thank you, sir.   210

                              Exit (Gentleman).

GLOUCESTER. You ever-gentle gods, take my breath from me;
    Let not my worser spirit° tempt me again
    To die before you please.

EDGAR.   Well pray you, father.

GLOUCESTER. Now, good sir, what are you?

EDGAR. A most poor man, made tame° to fortune's blows;   215
    Who, by the art of known and feeling sorrows,°
    Am pregnant° to good pity. Give me your hand,
    I'll lead you to some biding.°

GLOUCESTER.   Hearty thanks;
    The bounty and the benison° of heaven
    To boot, and boot.°
                    Enter Oswald.

OSWALD.   A proclaimed prize°! Most happy!°   220
    That eyeless head of thine was first framed° flesh
    To raise my fortunes. Thou old unhappy traitor,
    Briefly thyself remember:° the sword is out
    That must destroy thee.

GLOUCESTER.   Now let thy friendly° hand
    Put strength enough to 't.

                        (Edgar interposes.)

OSWALD.   Wherefore, bold peasant,   225
    Dar'st thou support a published° traitor? Hence!
    Lest that th' infection of his fortune take
    Like hold on thee. Let go his arm.

207–208 *the . . . thought* we expect to see the main body of the army any hour   212 *worser spirit* bad angel, evil side of my nature   215 *tame* submissive   216 *art . . . sorrows* instruction of sorrows painfully experienced   217 *pregnant* disposed   218 *biding* place of refuge   219 *benison* blessing   220 *To boot, and boot* also, and in the highest degree   220 *proclaimed prize* i.e., one with a price on his head   220 *happy* fortunate (for Oswald)   221 *framed* created   223 *thyself remember* i.e., pray, think of your sins   224 *friendly* i.e., because it offers the death Gloucester covets   226 *published* proclaimed

EDGAR. Chill° not let go, zir, without vurther 'casion.°

OSWALD. Let go, slave, or thou diest!   230

EDGAR. Good gentleman, go your gait,° and let poor volk° pass. And
chud ha' bin zwaggered° out of my life, 'twould not ha' bin zo
long as 'tis by a vortnight. Nay, come not near th' old man; keep
out, che vor' ye,° or I'se° try whether your costard° or my ballow°
be the harder: chill be plain with you.   235

OSWALD. Out, dunghill!

                                                        They fight.

EDGAR. Chill pick your teeth,° zir: come; no matter vor your foins.°

                                                        [*Oswald falls.*]

OSWALD. Slave, thou hast slain me. Villain, take my purse:
If ever thou wilt thrive, bury my body,
And give the letters which thou find'st about° me   240
To Edmund Earl of Gloucester; seek him out
Upon the English party.° O, untimely death!
Death!

                                                        He dies.

EDGAR. I know thee well. A serviceable° villain,
As duteous° to the vices of thy mistress   245
As badness would desire.

GLOUCESTER.   What, is he dead?

EDGAR. Sit you down, father; rest you.
Let's see these pockets: the letters that he speaks of
May be my friends. He's dead; I am only sorry
He had no other deathsman.° Let us see: 250
Leave,° gentle wax;° and, manners, blame us not:
To know our enemies' minds, we rip their hearts;
Their papers° is more lawful.

                              Reads the letter.

"Let our reciprocal vows be remembered. You have many
opportunities to cut him off: if your will want not,° time and   255
place will befruitfully offered. There is nothing done, if he return
the conqueror; then am I the prisoner, and his bed my jail; from

---

[229] *Chill . . .* (Edgar speaks in rustic dialect)   [229] *Chill* I will   [229] *vurther 'casion* further
occasion   [231] *gait* way   [231] *volk* folk   [231–232] *And chud ha' bin zwaggered* if I could
have been swaggered   [234] *Che vor' ye* I warrant you   [234] *I'se* I shall   [234] *costard* head
(literally, "apple")   [234] *ballow* cudgel   [237] *Chill pick your teeth* I will knock your teeth
out   [237] *foins* thrusts   [240] *about* upon   [242] *party* side   [244] *serviceable* ready to be
used   [245] *duteous* obedient   [250] *deathsman* executioner   [251] *Leave* by your leave
[251] *wax* (with which the letter is sealed)   [253] *Their papers* i.e., to rip their papers   [255] *if
. . . not* if your desire (and lust) be not lacking

the loathed warmth whereof deliver me, and supply the place
for your labor.
   ``Your—wife, so I would° say—affectionate servant, and
for you her own for venture,°   260
             `Goneril.' ''

O indistinguished space of woman's will!°
A plot upon her virtuous husband's life;
And the exchange° my brother! Here in the sands
Thee I'll rake up,° the post unsanctified°   265
Of murderous lechers; and in the mature° time,
With this ungracious paper° strike° the sight
Of the death-practiced° Duke: for him 'tis well
That of thy death and business I can tell.

GLOUCESTER. The King is mad: how stiff° is my vile sense,° 270
  That I stand up, and have ingenious° feeling
  Of my huge sorrows! Better I were distract:°
  So should my thoughts be severed from my griefs,
  And woes by wrong imaginations° lose
  The knowledge of themselves.
               Drum afar off.

EDGAR.   Give me your hand: 275
  Far off, methinks, I hear the beaten drum.
  Come, father, I'll bestow° you with a friend.
               Exeunt.

Scene VII. [*A tent in the French camp.*]

Enter Cordelia, Kent, Doctor, and Gentleman.

CORDELIA. O thou good Kent, how shall I live and work,
  To match thy goodness? My life will be too short,
  And every measure fail me.

KENT. To be acknowledged, madam, is o'erpaid.
  All my reports go° with the modest truth,   5
  Nor more nor clipped,° but so.

---

259 *would* would like to 260–61 *and . . . venture* i.e., and one who holds you her own for venturing (Edmund had earlier been promised union by Goneril, ``If you dare venture in your own behalf,'' IV.ii 22). 262 *indistinguished . . . will* unlimited range of woman's lust 264 *exchange* substitute 265 *rake up* cover up, bury 265 *post unsanctified* unholy messenger 266 *mature* ripe 267 *ungracious paper* wicked letter 267 *strike* blast 268 *death-practiced* whose death is plotted 270 *stiff* unbending 270 *vile sense* hateful capacity for feeling 270 *ingenious* conscious 271 *distract* distracted, mad 276 *wrong imaginations* delusions 303 *bestow* lodge
IV.vii. 5 *go* conform 6 *clipped* curtailed

CORDELIA.   Be better suited:°
  These weeds° are memories° of those worser hours:
  I prithee, put them off.

KENT.   Pardon, dear madam;
  Yet to be known shortens my made intent:°
  My boon I make it,° that you know me not   10
  Till time and I think meet.°

CORDELIA. Then be 't so, my good lord. (*To the Doctor.*) How does the
  King?

DOCTOR. Madam, sleeps still.

CORDELIA. O you kind gods!
  Cure this great breach in this abusèd° nature.   15
  Th' untuned and jarring senses, O, wind up°
  Of this child-changèd° father.

DOCTOR.   So please your Majesty
  That we may wake the King: he hath slept long.

CORDELIA. Be governed by your knowledge, and proceed
  I' th' sway of° your own will. Is he arrayed?   20

                Enter Lear in a chair carried by Servants.

GENTLEMAN. Ay, madam; in the heaviness of sleep
  We put fresh garments on him.

DOCTOR. Be by, good madam, when we do awake him;
  I doubt not of his temperance.°

CORDELIA.   Very well.

DOCTOR. Please you, draw near. Louder the music there!   25

CORDELIA. O my dear father, restoration hang
  Thy medicine on my lips, and let this kiss
  Repair those violent harms that my two sisters
  Have in thy reverence° made.

KENT.   Kind and dear Princess.

CORDELIA. Had you not been their father, these white flakes°   30
  Did challenge° pity of them. Was this a face
  To be opposed against the warring winds?
  To stand against the deep dread-bolted° thunder?
  In the most terrible and nimble stroke

---

⁶ *suited* attired   ⁷ *weeds* clothes   ⁷ *memories* reminders   ⁹ *Yet . . . intent* to reveal myself
just yet interferes with the plan I have made   ¹⁰ *My boon I make it* I ask this reward
¹¹ *meet* fitting   ¹⁵ *abusèd* disturbed   ¹⁶ *wind up* tune   ¹⁷ *child-changèd* changed,
deranged (and also, reduced to a child) by the cruelty of his children   ²⁰ *I' th' sway of*
according to   ²⁴ *temperance* sanity   ²⁹ *reverence* revered person   ³⁰ *flakes* hairs (in
long strands)   ³¹ *challenge* claim   ³³ *deep dread-bolted* deep-voiced and furnished
with the dreadful thunderbolt

Of quick, cross° lightning to watch—poor perdu!°—   35
With this thin helm?° Mine enemy's dog,
Though he had bit me, should have stood that night
Against my fire; and wast thou fain,° poor father,
To hovel thee with swine and rogues° forlorn,
In short° and musty straw? Alack, alack!   40
'Tis wonder that thy life and wits at once
Had not concluded all.° He wakes; speak to him.

DOCTOR. Madam, do you; 'tis fittest.

CORDELIA. How does my royal lord? How fares your Majesty?

LEAR. You do me wrong to take me out o' th' grave: 45
Thou art a soul in bliss; but I am bound
Upon a wheel of fire,° that mine own tears
Do scald like molten lead.

CORDELIA.   Sir, do you know me?

LEAR. You are a spirit, I know. Where did you die?

CORDELIA. Still, still, far wide.°   50

DOCTOR. He's scarce awake: let him alone awhile.

LEAR. Where have I been? Where am I? Fair daylight?
I am mightily abused.° I should ev'n die with pity,
To see another thus. I know not what to say.
I will not swear these are my hands: let's see;   55
I feel this pin prick. Would I were assured
Of my condition.

CORDELIA.   O, look upon me, sir,
And hold your hand in benediction o'er me.
You must not kneel.

LEAR.   Pray, do not mock me:
I am a very foolish fond° old man,   60
Fourscore and upward, not an hour more nor less;
And, to deal plainly,
I fear I am not in my perfect mind.
Methinks I should know you and know this man,
Yet I am doubtful; for I am mainly° ignorant   65

---

³⁵ *cross* zigzag   ³⁵ *perdu* (1) sentry in a forlorn position (2) lost one   ³⁶ *helm* helmet (his scanty hair)   ³⁸ *fain* pleased   ³⁹ *rogues* vagabonds   ⁴⁰ *short* (when straw is freshly cut, it is long, and suitable for bedding, given its flexibility and crispness. As it is used, it becomes musty, shreds into pieces, is "short." In contemporary Maine usage, "short manure" refers to dung mixed with straw that has been broken up; "long manure" refers to dung mixed with coarse new straw)   ⁴² *concluded all* come to a complete end   ⁴⁷ *wheel of fire* (torment associated by the Middle Ages with Hell, where Lear thinks he is)   ⁵⁰ *wide* i.e., of the mark (of sanity)   ⁵³ *abused* deluded   ⁶⁰ *fond* in dotage   ⁶⁵ *mainly* entirely

What place this is, and all the skill I have
Remembers not these garments, nor I know not
Where I did lodge last night. Do not laugh at me,
For, as I am a man, I think this lady
To be my child Cordelia.

CORDELIA.   And so I am, I am.   70

LEAR. Be your tears wet? Yes, faith. I pray, weep not.
   If you have poison for me, I will drink it.
   I know you do not love me; for your sisters
   Have, as I do remember, done me wrong.
   You have some cause, they have not.

CORDELIA.   No cause, no cause.   75

LEAR. Am I in France?

KENT.   In your own kingdom, sir.

LEAR. Do not abuse° me.

DOCTOR. Be comforted, good madam: the great rage,°
   You see, is killed in him: and yet it is danger   80
   To make him even o'er° the time he has lost,
   Desire him to go in; trouble him no more
   Till further settling.°

CORDELIA. Will 't please your Highness walk?°

LEAR. You must bear with me. Pray you now, forget and forgive. I am   85
   old and foolish.
                    Exeunt. Mane(n)t° Kent and Gentleman.

GENTLEMAN. Holds it true, sir, that the Duke of Cornwall was so slain?

KENT. Most certain, sir.

GENTLEMAN. Who is conductor of his people?

KENT. As 'tis said, the bastard son of Gloucester.   90

GENTLEMAN. They say Edgar, his banished son, is with the Earl of Kent
   in Germany.

KENT. Report is changeable.° 'Tis time to look about; the powers° of
   the kingdom approach apace.

GENTLEMAN. The arbitrement° is like to be bloody. Fare you well, sir.   95
                                                                  [*Exit.*]

KENT. My point and period will be throughly wrought,°
   Or well or ill, as this day's battle's fought.
                                                                  Exit.

---

[78] *abuse* deceive   [79] *rage* frenzy   [81] *even o'er* smooth over by filling in; and hence,
"recollect"   [83] *settling* calming   [84] *walk* (perhaps in the sense of "withdraw")   [87] s.d.
Mane(n)t remain   [93] *Report is changeable* rumors are unreliable   [93] *powers* armies
[95] *arbitrement* deciding encounter   [96] *My . . . wrought* the aim and end, the close of my
life will be completely worked out

ACT V

Scene I. [*The British camp near Dover.*]

Enter, with drum and colors, Edmund, Regan, Gentlemen, and Soldiers.

EDMUND. Know° of the Duke if his last purpose hold,°
    Or whether since he is advised° by aught
    To change the course: he's full of alteration
    And self-reproving: bring his constant pleasure.°
                            [*To a Gentleman, who goes out.*]

REGAN. Our sister's man is certainly miscarried.°   5

EDMUND. 'Tis to be doubted,° madam.

REGAN.   Now, sweet lord,
    You know the goodness I intend upon you:
    Tell me, but truly, but then speak the truth,
    Do you not love my sister?

EDMUND.   In honored° love.

REGAN. But have you never found my brother's way   10
    To the forfended° place?

EDMUND.   That thought abuses° you.

REGAN. I am doubtful that you have been conjunct
    And bosomed with her, as far as we call hers.°

EDMUND. No, by mine honor, madam.

REGAN. I shall never endure her: dear my lord,   15
    Be not familiar with her.

EDMUND.   Fear° me not.—
    She and the Duke her husband!

    Enter, with drum and colors, Albany, Goneril [and] Soldiers.

GONERIL. [*Aside*] I had rather lose the battle than that sister
    Should loosen° him and me.

ALBANY. Our very loving sister, well be-met.°   20
    Sir, this I heard, the King is come to his daughter,
    With others whom the rigor of our state°
    Forced to cry out. Where I could not be honest,°
    I never yet was valiant: for this business,

V.i.   ¹ *Know* learn   ¹ *last purpose hold* most recent intention (to fight) be maintained
    ² *advised* induced   ⁴ *constant pleasure* fixed (final) decision   ⁵ *miscarried* come to
    grief   ⁶ *doubted* feared   ⁹ *honored* honorable   ¹¹ *forfended* forbidden   ¹¹ *abuses* (1)
    deceives (2) demeans, is unworthy of   ¹²⁻¹³ *I . . . hers* I fear that you have united
    with her intimately, in the fullest possible way   ¹⁶ *Fear* distrust   ¹⁹ *loosen* separate
    ²⁰ *be-met* met   ²² *rigor . . . state* tyranny of our government   ²³ *honest* honorable

It touches us, as° France invades our land,   25
Not bolds the King, with others, whom, I fear,
Most just and heavy causes make oppose.°

EDMUND. Sir, you speak nobly.

REGAN.   Why is this reasoned?°

GONERIL. Combine together 'gainst the enemy;
For these domestic and particular broils°   30
Are not the question° here.

ALBANY.   Let's then determine
With th' ancient of war° on our proceeding.

EDMUND. I shall attend you presently at your tent.

REGAN. Sister, you'll go with us?°

GONERIL. No.   35

REGAN. 'Tis most convenient;° pray you, go with us.

GONERIL. (*Aside*) O, ho, I know the riddle.°—I will go.

          Exeunt both the Armies. Enter Edgar (disguised).

EDGAR. If e'er your Grace had speech with man so poor,
Hear me one word.

ALBANY. (*To those going out*) I'll overtake you. (*To Edgar*) Speak.   40

          Exeunt (all but Albany and Edgar).

EDGAR. Before you fight the battle, ope this letter.
If you have victory, let the trumpet sound
For° him that brought it: wretched though I seem,
I can produce a champion that will prove°
What is avouchèd° there. If you miscarry,   45
Your business of° the world hath so an end,
And machination° ceases. Fortune love you.

ALBANY. Stay till I have read the letter.

EDGAR.   I was forbid it.
When time shall serve, let but the herald cry,
And I'll appear again.   50

ALBANY. Why, fare thee well: I will o'erlook° thy paper.   *Exit (Edgar).*

          Enter Edmund.

---

²⁵ *touches us,* as concerns me, only in that   ²⁶⁻²⁷ *Not . . . oppose* and not in that France
emboldens the King and others, who have been led, by real and serious grievances, to
take up arms against us   ²⁸ *reasoned* argued   ³⁰ *particular broils* private quarrels
³¹ *question* issue   ³² *th' ancient of war* experienced commanders   ³⁴ *us* me (rather
than Edmund)   ³⁶ *convenient* fitting, desirable   ³⁷ *riddle* real reason (for Regan's curious request)   ⁴²⁻⁴³ *sound/For* summon   ⁴⁴ *prove* i.e., by trial of combat   ⁴⁵ *avouchèd*
maintained   ⁴⁶ *of* in   ⁴⁷ *machination* plotting   ⁵¹ *o'erlook* read over

EDMUND. The enemy's in view: draw up your powers.
    Here is the guess° of their true strength and forces
    By diligent discovery;° but your haste
    Is now urged on you.

ALBANY.   We will greet° the time.   *Exit.*   55

EDMUND. To both these sisters have I sworn my love;
    Each jealous° of the other, as the stung
    Are of the adder. Which of them shall I take?
    Both? One? Or neither? Neither can be enjoyed,
    If both remain alive: to take the widow   60
    Exasperates, makes mad her sister Goneril;
    And hardly° shall I carry out my side,°
    Her husband being alive. Now then, we'll use
    His countenance° for the battle; which being done,
    Let her who would be rid of him devise   65
    His speedy taking off. As for the mercy
    Which he intends to Lear and to Cordelia,
    The battle done, and they within our power,
    Shall never see his pardon; for my state
    Stands on me to defend, not to debate.°   *Exit.*   70

Scene II. [*A field between the two camps.*]

Alarum° within. Enter, with drum and colors, Lear, Cordelia, and Soldiers, over the stage; and exeunt.

Enter Edgar and Gloucester.

EDGAR. Here, father,° take the shadow of this tree
    For your good host; pray that the right may thrive.
    If ever I return to you again,
    I'll bring you comfort.

GLOUCESTER.   Grace go with you, sir.

                               Exit [Edgar].

Alarum and retreat° within. [Re-]enter Edgar.

EDGAR. Away, old man; give me thy hand; away!   5
    King Lear hath lost, he and his daughter ta'en:°
    Give me thy hand; come on.

---

[53] *guess* estimate   [54] *By diligent discovery* obtained by careful reconnoitering   [55] *greet* i.e., meet the demands of   [57] *jealous* suspicious   [62] *hardly* with difficulty   [62] *carry . . . side* (1) satisfy my ambition (2) fulfill my bargain (with Goneril)   [64] *countenance* authority   [69–70] *for . . . debate* my position requires me to act, not to reason about right and wrong   V.ii. s.d. *Alarum* a trumpet call to battle   [1] *father* i.e., venerable old man (Edgar has not yet revealed his identity)   [4] s.d. *retreat* (signaled by a trumpet)   [6] *ta'en* captured

GLOUCESTER. No further, sir; a man may rot even here.

EDGAR. What, in ill thoughts again? Men must endure
    Their going hence, even as their coming hither: 10
    Ripeness° is all. Come on.

GLOUCESTER.   And that's true too.

Exeunt.

Scene III. [*The British camp near Dover.*]

Enter, in conquest, with drum and colors, Edmund; Lear and Cordelia,
as prisoners; Soldiers, Captain.

EDMUND. Some officers take them away: good guard,°
    Until their greater pleasures° first be known
    That are to censure° them.

CORDELIA.   We are not the first
    Who with best meaning° have incurred the worst.
    For thee, oppressèd King, I am cast down;   5
    Myself could else out-frown false fortune's frown.
    Shall we not see these daughters and these sisters?

LEAR. No, no, no, no! Come, let's away to prison:
    We two alone will sing like birds i' th' cage:
    When thou dost ask me blessing, I'll kneel down   10
    And ask of thee forgiveness: so we'll live,
    And pray, and sing, and tell old tales, and laugh
    At gilded butterflies,° and hear poor rogues
    Talk of court news; and we'll talk with them too,
    Who loses and who wins, who's in, who's out;   15
    And take upon's the mystery of things,
    As if we were God's spies:° and we'll wear out,°
    In a walled prison, packs and sects of great ones
    That ebb and flow by th' moon.°

EDMUND.   Take them away.

LEAR. Upon such sacrifices, my Cordelia,   20
    The gods themselves throw incense.° Have I caught thee?
    He that parts us shall bring a brand from heaven,

---

¹¹ *Ripeness* maturity, as of fruit that is ready to fall   V.iii.   ¹ *good guard* let there be good
guard   ² *their greater pleasures* the will of those in command, the great ones
³ *censure* pass judgment on   ⁵ *meaning* intentions   ¹³ *gilded butterflies* i.e., gor-
geously attired courtiers, fluttering after nothing   ¹⁶⁻¹⁷ *take . . . spies* profess to read
the riddle of existence, as if endowed with divine omniscience   ¹⁷ *wear out* outlast
¹⁷⁻¹⁸ *packs . . . moon* intriguing and partisan cliques of those in high station, whose fortunes change every month   ²⁰⁻²¹ *Upon . . . incense* i.e., the gods approve our renun-
ciation of the world

And fire us hence like foxes.° Wipe thine eyes;
The good years° shall devour them,° flesh and fell,°
Ere they shall make us weep. We'll see 'em starved first. 　　25
Come. 　　　　　　　　*[Exeunt Lear and Cordelia, guarded.]*

EDMUND. Come hither, captain; hark.
　　Take thou this note: go follow them to prison:
　　One step I have advanced thee; if thou dost
　　As this instructs thee, thou dost make thy way 　　30
　　To noble fortunes: know thou this, that men
　　Are as the time is:° to be tender-minded
　　Does not become a sword:° thy great employment
　　Will not bear question;° either say thou'lt do 't,
　　Or thrive by other means.

CAPTAIN. 　　　　　　　　I'll do 't, my lord. 　　35

EDMUND. About it; and write happy° when th' hast done.
　　Mark; I say, instantly, and carry it so°
　　As I have set it down.

CAPTAIN. I cannot draw a cart, nor eat dried oats;
　　If it be man's work, I'll do 't. 　　　　*Exit Captain.* 　　40

Flourish. Enter Albany, Goneril, Regan [another Captain, and]
　Soldiers.

ALBANY. Sir, you have showed today your valiant strain,°
　　And fortune led you well: you have the captives
　　Who were the opposites of° this day's strife:
　　I do require them of you, so to use them
　　As we shall find their merits° and our safety 　　45
　　May equally determine.

EDMUND. 　　　　　　　　Sir, I thought it fit
　　To send the old and miserable King
　　To some retention and appointed guard;°
　　Whose° age had charms in it, whose title more,
　　To pluck the common bosom on his side,° 　　50
　　And turn our impressed lances in our eyes°

---

²²⁻²³ *He . . . foxes* no human agency can separate us, but only divine interposition, as of a
heavenly torch parting us like foxes who are driven from their place of refuge by fire and
smoke 　²⁴ *good years* plague and pestilence (``undefined malefic power or agency,''
N.E.D.) 　²⁴ *them* i.e., the enemies of Lear and Cordelia 　²⁴ *fell* skin 　³² *as the time is*
i.e., absolutely determined by the exigencies of the moment 　³³ *become a sword* befit
a soldier 　³⁴ *bear question* admit of discussion 　³⁶ *write happy* style yourself
fortunate 　³⁷ *carry it so* manage the affair in exactly that manner (as if Cordelia had
taken her own life) 　⁴¹ *strain* (1) stock (2) character 　⁴³ *opposites of* opponents in
⁴⁵ *merits* deserts 　⁴⁸ *retention . . . guard* confinement under duly appointed guard
⁴⁹ *Whose* i.e., Lear's 　⁵⁰ *pluck . . . side* win the sympathy of the people to himself
⁵¹ *turn . . . eyes* turn our conscripted lancers against us

Which do command them. With him I sent the Queen:
My reason all the same; and they are ready
Tomorrow, or at further space,° t' appear
Where you shall hold your session.° At this time   55
We sweat and bleed: the friend hath lost his friend;
And the best quarrels, in the heat, are cursed
By those that feel their sharpness.°
The question of Cordelia and her father
Requires a fitter place.

ALBANY.   Sir, by your patience,   60
I hold you but a subject of° this war,
Not as a brother.

REGAN.   That's as we list to grace° him.
Methinks our pleasure might have been demanded,
Ere you had spoke so far. He led our powers,
Bore the commission of my place and person;   65
The which immediacy may well stand up
And call itself your brother.°

GONERIL.   Not so hot:
In his own grace he doth exalt himself
More than in your addition.°

REGAN.   In my rights,
By me invested, he compeers° the best.   70

GONERIL. That were the most,° if he should husband you.°

REGAN. Jesters do oft prove prophets.

GONERIL.   Holla, holla!
That eye that told you so looked but a-squint.°

REGAN. Lady, I am not well; else I should answer
From a full·flowing stomach.° General,   75
Take thou my soldiers, prisoners, patrimony;°
Dispose of them, of me; the walls is thine:°
Witness the world, that I create thee here
My lord, and master.

---

⁵⁴ *further space* a later time   ⁵⁵ *session* trial   ⁵⁸ *the . . . sharpness* the worthiest causes
may be judged badly by those who have been affected painfully by them, and whose
passion has not yet cooled   ⁶¹ *subject of* subordinate in   ⁶² *list to grace* wish to
honor   ⁶⁵⁻⁶⁷ *Bore . . . brother* was authorized, as my deputy, to take command; his
present status, as my immediate representative, entitles him to be considered your
equal   ⁶⁹ *your addition* honors you have bestowed on him   ⁷⁰ *compeers* equals
⁷¹ *most* most complete investing in your rights   ⁷¹ *husband you* become your
husband   ⁷³ *a-squint* cross-eyed   ⁷⁵ *From . . . stomach* angrily   ⁷⁶ *patrimony*
inheritance   ⁷⁷ *walls is thine* i.e., Regan's person, which Edmund has stormed and won

GONERIL.   Mean you to enjoy him?

ALBANY. The let-alone° lies not in your good will.   80

EDMUND. Nor in thine, lord.

ALBANY.   Half-blooded° fellow, yes.

REGAN. [*To Edmund*] Let the drum strike, and prove my title thine.°

ALBANY. Stay yet; hear reason. Edmund, I arrest thee
   On capital treason; and in thy attaint°
   This gilded serpent [*pointing to Goneril*]. For your claim, fair
      sister,   85
   I bar it in the interest of my wife.
   'Tis she is subcontracted° to this lord,
   And I, her husband, contradict your banes.°
   If you will marry, make your loves° to me;
   My Lady is bespoke.°

GONERIL.   An interlude!°   90

ALBANY. Thou art armed, Gloucester: let the trumpet sound:
   If none appear to prove upon thy person
   Thy heinous, manifest, and many treasons,
   There is my pledge° [*throwing down a glove*]: I'll make° it on thy
      heart,
   Ere I taste bread, thou art in nothing less   95
   Than I have here proclaimed thee.

REGAN.   Sick, O, sick!

GONERIL. [*Aside*] If not, I'll ne'er trust medicine.°

EDMUND. [*Throwing down a glove*] There's my exchange:° what in the
      world he is
   That names me traitor, villain-like he lies:°
   Call by the trumpet:° he that dares approach,   100
   On him, on you—who not?—I will maintain
   My truth and honor firmly.

ALBANY. A herald, ho!

EDMUND.   A herald, ho, a herald!

ALBANY. Trust to thy single virtue;° for thy soldiers,

---

⁸⁰ *let-alone* power to prevent   ⁸¹ *Half-blooded* bastard, and so only half noble   ⁸² *prove . . .
thine* prove by combat your entitlement to my rights   ⁸⁴ *in thy attaint* as a sharer in the
treason for which you are impeached   ⁸⁷ *subcontracted* pledged by a contract which is
called into question by the existence of a previous contract (Goneril's marriage)
⁸⁸ *contradict your banes* forbid your announced intention to marry (by citing the
precontract)   ⁸⁹ *loves* love-suits   ⁹⁰ *bespoke* already pledged   ⁹⁰ *interlude* play
⁹³ *pledge* gage,   ⁹³ *make* prove   ⁹⁷ *medicine* poison   ⁹⁸ *exchange* (technical term,
denoting the glove Edmund throws down)   ⁹⁹ *villain-like he lies* (the lie direct, a challenge to mortal combat)   ¹⁰⁰ *trumpet* trumpeter   ¹⁰⁴ *single virtue* unaided valor

All levied in my name, have in my name   105
Took their discharge.

REGAN.   My sickness grows upon me.

ALBANY. She is not well; convey her to my tent.

                                   [*Exit Regan, led.*]

                      Enter a Herald.

Come hither, herald. Let the trumpet sound—
And read out this.

CAPTAIN. Sound, trumpet!   110

                   A trumpet sounds.

HERALD. *(Reads.)* "If any man of quality or degree° within the lists° of
the army will maintain upon Edmund, supposed Earl of
Gloucester, that he is a manifold traitor, let him appear by the
third sound of the trumpet: he is bold in his defense."

EDMUND. Sound!   115

                   First trumpet.

HERALD. Again!

                  Second trumpet.

HERALD. Again!

                   Third trumpet.

Trumpet answers within. Enter Edgar, at the third sound, armed, a
                 trumpet before him.°

ALBANY. Ask him his purposes, why he appears
Upon this call o' th' trumpet.

HERALD.   What are you?
Your name, your quality,° and why you answer   120
This present summons?

EDGAR.   Know, my name is lost;
By treason's tooth bare-gnawn and canker-bit:°
Yet am I noble as the adversary
I come to cope.°

ALBANY.   Which is that adversary?

EDGAR. What's he that speaks for Edmund, Earl of Gloucester?   125

EDMUND. Himself: what say'st thou to him?

EDGAR.   Draw thy sword,
That if my speech offend a noble heart,
Thy arm may do thee justice: here is mine.

Behold it is my privilege,
The privilege of mine honors,   130
My oath, and my profession.° I protest,
Maugre° thy strength, place, youth, and eminence,
Despite thy victor sword and fire-new° fortune,
Thy valor and thy heart,° thou art a traitor,
False to thy gods, thy brother, and thy father,   135
Conspirant° 'gainst this high illustrious prince,
And from th' extremest upward° of thy head
To the descent and dust below thy foot,°
A most toad-spotted traitor.° Say thou "No,"
This sword, this arm and my best spirits are bent°   140
To prove upon thy heart, whereto I speak,°
Thou liest.

EDMUND.   In wisdom° I should ask thy name,
But since thy outside looks so fair and warlike,
And that thy tongue some say° of breeding breathes,
What safe and nicely° I might well delay°   145
By rule of knighthood, I disdain and spurn:
Back do I toss these treasons° to thy head;
With the hell-hated° lie o'erwhelm thy heart;
Which for they yet glance by and scarcely bruise,
This sword of mine shall give them instant way,   150
Where they shall rest for ever.° Trumpets, speak!

         Alarums. [*They*] *fight.* [*Edmund falls.*]

ALBANY. Save° him, save him!

GONERIL.   This is practice,° Gloucester:
By th' law of war thou wast not bound to answer
An unknown opposite;° thou art not vanquished,
But cozened and beguiled.

ALBANY.   Shut your mouth, dame   155
Or with this paper shall I stop it. Hold, sir;°

[199–131] *it . . . profession* my knighthood entitles me to challenge you, and to have my challenge accepted   [132] *Maugre* despite   [133] *fire-new* fresh from the forge or mint   [134] *heart* courage   [136] *Conspirant* conspiring, a conspirator   [137] *extremest upward* the very top   [138] *the . . . foot* your lowest part (sole) and the dust beneath it   [139] *toad-spotted traitor* spotted with treason (and hence venomous, as the toad is allegedly marked with spots that exude venom)   [140] *bent* directed   [141] *whereto I speak* (Edgar speaks from the heart, and speaks to the heart of Edmund)   [142] *wisdom* prudence (since he is not obliged to fight with one of lesser rank)   [144] *say* assay (i.e., touch, sign)   [145] *safe and nicely* cautiously and punctiliously   [145] *delay* i.e., avoid   [147] *treasons* accusations of treason   [148] *hell-hated* hated like hell   [148–150] *Which . . . ever* which accusations of treason, since as yet they do no harm, even though I have hurled them back, I now thrust upon you still more forcibly, with my sword, so that they may remain with you permanently   [152] *Save* spare   [153] *practice* trickery   [155] *opposite* opponent   [156] *Hold, sir* (to Edmund: "Just a moment!")

Thou° worse than any name, read thine own evil.
No tearing, lady; I perceive you know it.

GONERIL. Say, if I do, the laws are mine, not thine:
Who can arraign me for 't?

ALBANY.   Most monstrous! O!   160
Know'st thou this paper?

GONERIL.   Ask me not what I know.

                                                                    Exit.

ALBANY. Go after her; she's desperate; govern° her.

EDMUND. What you have charged me with, that have I done;
And more, much more; the time will bring it out.
'Tis past, and so am I. But what art thou   165
That hast this fortune on° me? If thou 'rt noble,
I do forgive thee.

EDGAR.   Let's exchange charity.°
I am no less in blood° than thou art, Edmund;
If more,° the more th' hast wronged me.
My name is Edgar, and thy father's son.   170
The gods are just, and of our pleasant° vices
Make instruments to plague us:
The dark and vicious place° where thee he got°
Cost him his eyes.

EDMUND.   Th' hast spoken right, 'tis true;
The wheel is come full circle; I am here.°   175

ALBANY. Methought thy very gait did prophesy°
A royal nobleness: I must embrace thee:
Let sorrow split my heart, if ever I
Did hate thee or thy father!

EDGAR.   Worthy° Prince, I know 't.

ALBANY. Where have you hid yourself?   180
How have you known the miseries of your father?

EDGAR. By nursing them, my lord. List a brief tale;
And when 'tis told, O, that my heart would burst!
The bloody proclamation to escape°
That followed me so near—O, our lives' sweetness,   185
That we the pain of death would hourly die

---

[157] *Thou* (probably Goneril)   [162] *govern* control   [166] *fortune on* victory over   [167] *charity* forgiveness and love   [168] *blood* lineage   [169] *If more* if I am more noble (since legitimate)   [171] *of our pleasant* out of our pleasurable   [173] *place* i.e., the adulterous bed   [173] *got* begot   [175] *wheel . . . here* i.e., Fortune's wheel, on which Edmund ascended, has now, in its downward turning, deposited him at the bottom, whence he began   [176] *gait did prophesy* carriage did promise   [179] *Worthy* honorable   [184] *to escape* (my wish) to escape the sentence of death

Rather than die at once!°—taught me to shift
Into a madman's rags, t' assume a semblance
That very dogs disdained: and in this habit°
Met I my father with his bleeding rings,°   190
Their precious stones new lost; became his guide,
Led him, begged for him, saved him from despair;
Never—O fault!—revealed myself unto him,
Until some half-hour past, when I was armed,
Not sure, though hoping, of this good success,   195
I asked his blessing, and from first to last
Told him our pilgrimage.° But his flawed° heart—
Alack, too weak the conflict to support—
'Twixt two extremes of passion, joy and grief,
Burst smilingly.

EDMUND.   This speech of yours hath moved me,   200
And shall perchance do good: but speak you on;
You look as you had something more to say.

ALBANY. If there be more, more woeful, hold it in;
For I am almost ready to dissolve,°
Hearing of this.

EDGAR.   This would have seemed a period°   205
To such as love not sorrow; but another,
To amplify too much, would make much more,
And top extremity.°
Whilst I was big in clamor,° came there in a man,
Who, having seen me in my worst estate,°   210
Shunned my abhorred° society; but then, finding
Who 'twas that so endured, with his strong arms
He fastened on my neck, and bellowed out
As he'd burst heaven; threw him on my father;
Told the most piteous tale of Lear and him   215
That ever ear received: which in recounting
His grief grew puissant,° and the strings of life
Began to crack: twice then the trumpets sounded,
And there I left him tranced.°

ALBANY.   But who was this?

EDGAR. Kent, sir, the banished Kent; who in disguise   220
Followed his enemy° king, and did him service
Improper for a slave.

[185-187] *O . . . once* how sweet is life, that we choose to suffer death every hour rather than make an end at once   [189] *habit* attire   [190] *rings* sockets   [197] *our pilgrimage* of our (purgatorial) journey   [197] *flawed* cracked   [204] *dissolve* i.e., into tears   [205] *period* limit   [206-208] *but . . . extremity* just one woe more, described too fully, would go beyond the extreme limit   [209] *big in clamor* loud in lamentation   [210] *estate* condition   [211] *abhorred* abhorrent   [217] *puissant* overmastering   [219] *tranced* insensible   [221] *enemy* hostile

Enter a Gentleman, with a bloody knife.

GENTLEMAN. Help, help, O, help!

EDGAR.   What kind of help?

ALBANY.   Speak, man.   225

EDGAR. What means this bloody knife?

GENTLEMAN.   'Tis hot, it smokes;°
  It came even from the heart of—O, she's dead!

ALBANY. Who dead? Speak, man.

GENTLEMAN. Your lady, sir, your lady: and her sister
  By her is poisoned; she confesses it.   230

EDMUND. I was contracted° to them both: all three
  Now marry° in an instant.

EDGAR.   Here comes Kent.

ALBANY. Produce the bodies, be they alive or dead.

          (Exit Gentleman.)
  This judgment of the heavens, that makes us tremble,
  Touches us not with pity.

       Enter Kent.
       O, is this he?   235
  The time will not allow the compliment°
  Which very manners° urges.

KENT.   I am come
  To bid my king and master aye° good night:
  Is he not here?

ALBANY.   Great thing of° us forgot!
  Speak, Edmund, where's the King? and where's Cordelia?   240
  Seest thou this object,° Kent?

The bodies of Goneril and Regan are brought in.

KENT. Alack, why thus?

EDMUND.   Yet° Edmund was beloved:
  The one the other poisoned for my sake,
  And after slew herself.

ALBANY. Even so. Cover their faces.   245

EDMUND. I pant for life:° some good I mean to do,
  Despite of mine own nature. Quickly send,
  Be brief in it, to th' castle; for my writ°

---

²³⁶ *smokes* steams   ²³¹ *contracted* betrothed   ²³² *marry* i.e., unite in death
²³⁶ *compliment* ceremony   ²³⁷ *very manners* ordinary civility   ²³⁸ *aye* forever
²³⁹ *thing of* matter by   ²⁴¹ *object* sight (the bodies of Goneril and Regan)   ²⁴² *Yet* in
spite of all   ²⁴⁶ *pant for life* gasp for breath   ²⁴⁸ *writ* command (ordering the
execution)

    Is on the life of Lear and on Cordelia:
    Nay, send in time.

ALBANY.   Run, run, O, run!   250

EDGAR. To who, my lord? Who has the office?° Send
    Thy token of reprieve.°

EDMUND. Well thought on: take my sword,
    Give it the captain.

EDGAR.   Haste thee, for thy life.

                            (Exit Messenger.)

EDMUND. He hath commission from thy wife and me   255
    To hang Cordelia in the prison, and
    To lay the blame upon her own despair,
    That she fordid° herself.

ALBANY. The gods defend her! Bear him hence awhile.

                     (Edmund is borne off.)

    Enter Lear, with Cordelia in his arms (Gentleman and others
                      following).

LEAR. Howl, howl, howl, howl! O, you are men of stones: 260
    Had I your tongues and eyes, I'd use them so
    That heaven's vault should crack. She's gone for ever.
    I know when one is dead and when one lives;
    She's dead as earth. Lend me a looking-glass;
    If that her breath will mist or stain the stone,°   265
    Why, then she lives.

KENT.   Is this the promised end?°

EDGAR. Or image° of that horror?

ALBANY.   Fall and cease.°

LEAR. This feather stirs; she lives. If it be so,
    It is a chance which does redeem° all sorrows
    That ever I have felt.

KENT.   O my good master.   270

LEAR. Prithee, away.

EDGAR.   'Tis noble Kent, your friend.

LEAR. A plague upon you, murderers, traitors all!
    I might have saved her; now she's gone for ever.
    Cordelia, Cordelia, stay a little. Ha,
    What is 't thou say'st? Her voice was ever soft,   275

---

²⁵¹ *office* commission   ²⁵² *token of reprieve* sign that they are reprieved   ²⁵⁸ *fordid* destroyed   ²⁶⁵ *stone* i.e., the surface of the crystal looking glass   ²⁶⁶ *promised end* Doomsday   ²⁶⁷ *image* exact likeness   ²⁶⁸ *Fall and cease* i.e., let the heavens fall, and all things finish   ²⁶⁹ *redeem* make good

Gentle and low, an excellent thing in woman.
I killed the slave that was a-hanging thee.

GENTLEMAN. 'Tis true, my lords, he did.

LEAR.   Did I not, fellow?
I have seen the day, with my good biting falchion°
I would have made them skip: I am old now,   280
And these same crosses° spoil me.° Who are you?
Mine eyes are not o' th' best: I'll tell you straight.°

KENT. If Fortune brag of two° she loved and hated,
One of them we behold.

LEAR. This is a dull sight.° Are you not Kent?

KENT.   The same,   285
Your servant Kent. Where is your servant Caius?°

LEAR. He's a good fellow, I can tell you that;
He'll strike, and quickly too: he's dead and rotten.

KENT. No, my good lord; I am the very man.

LEAR. I'll see that straight.°   290

KENT. That from your first of difference and decay°
Have followed your sad steps.

LEAR.   You are welcome hither.

KENT. Nor no man else:° all's cheerless, dark and deadly.
Your eldest daughters have fordone° themselves,
And desperately° are dead.

LEAR.   Ay, so I think.   295

ALBANY. He knows not what he says, and vain is it
That we present us to him.

EDGAR.   Very bootless.°

Enter a Messenger.

MESSENGER. Edmund is dead, my lord.

ALBANY.   That's but a trifle here.
You lords and noble friends, know our intent.
What comfort to this great decay may come°   300

---

²⁷⁹ *falchion* small curved sword   ²⁸¹ *crosses* troubles   ²⁸¹ *spoil me* i.e., my prowess as a
swordsman   ²⁸² *tell you straight* recognize you straightway   ²⁸³ *two* i.e., Lear, and
some hypothetical second, who is also a prime example of Fortune's inconstancy
("loved and hated")   ²⁸⁵ *dull sight* (1) melancholy spectacle (2) faulty eyesight (Lear's
own, clouded by weeping)   ²⁸⁶ *Caius* (Kent's name, in disguise)   ²⁹⁰ *see that straight*
attend to that in a moment   ²⁹¹ *your . . . decay* beginning of your decline in fortune
²⁹³ *Nor no man else* no, I am not welcome, nor is anyone else   ²⁹⁴ *fordone* destroyed
²⁹⁵ *desperately* in despair   ³⁴⁶ *bootless* fruitless   ³⁰⁰ *What . . . come* whatever aid may
present itself to this great ruined man

Shall be applied. For us, we° will resign,
During the life of this old majesty,
To him our absolute power: [*To Edgar and Kent*] you, to your
 rights;
With boot,° and such addition° as your honors
Have more than merited. All friends shall taste   305
The wages of their virtue, and all foes
The cup of their deservings. O, see, see!

LEAR. And my poor fool° is hanged: no, no, no life?
 Why should a dog, a horse, a rat, have life,
 And thou no breath at all? Thou'lt come no more,   310
 Never, never, never, never, never.
 Pray you, undo this button.° Thank you, sir.
 Do you see this? Look on her. Look, her lips,
 Look there, look there.

He dies.

EDGAR.   He faints. My lord, my lord!

KENT. Break, heart; I prithee, break.

EDGAR.   Look up, my lord.   315

KENT. Vex not his ghost:° O, let him pass! He hates him
 That would upon the rack° of this tough world
 Stretch him out longer.°

EDGAR.   He is gone indeed.

KENT. The wonder is he hath endured so long:
 He but usurped° his life.   320

ALBANY. Bear them from hence. Our present business
 Is general woe. [*To Kent and Edgar*] Friends of my soul, you
 twain,
 Rule in this realm and the gored state sustain.

KENT. I have a journey, sir, shortly to go;
 My master calls me, I must not say no.   325

EDGAR. The weight of this sad time we must obey,°
 Speak what we feel, not what we ought to say.
 The oldest hath borne most: we that are young
 Shall never see so much, nor live so long.

Exeunt, with a dead march.

FINIS

[301] *us, we* (the royal "we")   [304] *boot* good measure   [304] *addition* additional titles and rights   [308] *fool* Cordelia ("fool" being a term of endearment. But it is perfectly possible to take the word as referring also to the Fool)   [312] *undo this button* i.e., to ease the suffocation Lear feels   [316] *Vex . . . ghost* do not trouble his departing spirit   [317] *rack* instrument of torture, stretching the victim's joints to dislocation   [318] *longer* (1) in time (2) in bodily length   [320] *usurped* possessed beyond the allotted term   [380] *obey* submit to

SUGGESTIONS FOR WRITING AND DISCUSSION

Act I

1. Why do you think Lear decides to give away his kingdom? Is there something wrong in his desire to abdicate or in his manner of going about it?
2. When Lear first asks Cordelia to tell him how much she loves him, she says "Nothing, my lord." It is only when Lear asks her for the third time that she tells him exactly how much she loves him. Discuss her initial reluctance and apparent coldness.
3. In Scene II Edmund pays homage to "nature." Later in the scene Gloucester comments on various unnatural events. In a two- to three-page essay discuss the different views of nature presented in this scene.
4. Using the descriptions of nature in the previous question, examine how Lear and other characters categorize events as "natural" or "unnatural" throughout the play. Look closely at the Fool's speeches.
5. Comment on Goneril's behavior to her father in Scene IV. Does she have any justification for her actions? Why is Lear upset when she tells him that he must dismiss some of his followers?

Act II

1. Looking at Act I and the beginning of Act II, do you think Gloucester is too easily persuaded that Edgar is wicked? Comment on the parallels between his behavior and King Lear's.
2. Discuss the irony in the speeches of Regan, Gloucester, Edmund, and Cornwall.
3. Does Kent's behavior toward Oswald change your impression of him?
4. What is the meaning of the Fool's speech in II.iv.45? Do the events of the play fulfill his prophecies?
5. Examine the images that Lear uses when talking to his daughters. What do these images convey? How are they pertinent to the theme of the play?
6. Can you distinguish any differences in attitude between Goneril and Regan? Discuss these differences in a one-page essay.
7. Look closely at Lear's speech in II.iv.257. Compare it to Cordelia's answer to her father in Act I. Discuss the characters' attitudes toward *need* and *duty*.

Act III

1. At the beginning of Act II and Act III we hear numerous rumors of political unrest. What do these rumors contribute to our perception of what is happening to Lear?
2. Compare Lear's incantation to nature with the speeches by Edmund and Gloucester in I.ii.
3. Discuss Lear's relationship with the Fool. How has this relationship deepened and developed since Act I?
4. With what is Lear preoccupied during the storm? What do these preoccu-

pations reveal about a change in his character? Why does he try to tear off his clothes?

5. Discuss the differences between the Fool's speeches and those of Edgar disguised as Poor Tom.

6. Examine Gloucester's relationship with the King. Does his behavior toward Lear make his behavior toward Edgar more surprising?

7. Look closely at III.vi. What sense is conveyed in the madness? What preoccupations recur?

8. Lear asks, "Is there any cause in nature that make these hard hearts?" (III.vi.71–72). Does the play provide any answers to this question?

9. Discuss the attitudes of the various servants. Are they more loyal than their masters?

Act IV

1. Edgar says, "The worst is not so long as we can say 'this is the worst.'" Discuss how this remark is true for one or more characters.

2. In IV.ii we learn that Albany no longer sides with his wife and sister-in-law. Is this change a surprise?

3. In IV.ii we learn that the invasion of which we have heard rumors has taken place. What effect does this have on the various characters?

4. While commenting on the difference between Cordelia and her sisters, Kent says, "The stars above us govern our conditions;/Else one self mate and make could not beget/such different issues." What do the extreme differences between the siblings in this play suggest?

5. Compare the description of Cordelia in IV.iii and her behavior in IV.iv with what we learned about her in Act I.

6. Discuss the reversals of traditional sex roles in Goneril's and Regan's marriages. How do these fit with the discussion of nature in the play?

7. What lies behind Edgar's dealings with his father in IV.vi? What is he trying to teach him? Are you surprised by the "cure" he brings about in Gloucester?

8. In IV.vi.94 Lear, by mentioning his beard, suggests the comparison between himself and Gloucester. Explore this comparison in a four- to five-page essay.

9. Explicate Lear's speech in IV.vi.150.

10. Why does Edgar drop the pretense of madness with Gloucester only after killing Oswald?

11. Look at the reconciliation between Lear and Cordelia. What changes do we see in each of them? Comment on Cordelia's speech about the storm. What does it recall?

Act V

1. Although both Goneril and Regan are almost entirely motivated by their lust for power, Edmund seems to pierce their defenses. What does this contribute to the theme of the play?

2. Examine Edmund's speech at the end of V.i. How do his sentiments at this point distinguish him from Goneril and Regan?

3. How does Lear react to his and Cordelia's imprisonment? Does he seem "mad"?

4. In IV.i.37 Gloucester says, "As flies to wanton boys, are we to th' gods,/They kill us for their sport." In V.iii.72 Edgar says, "The gods are just, and of our pleasant vices/Make instruments to plague us:" Compare these two views in a four- to five-page essay. How is each view borne out in the course of the play?

5. Is Edgar justified in blaming himself for his father's death?

6. In V.iii.305–307 Albany says, "All friends shall taste/The wages of their virtue, and all foes/The cup of their deservings." Is this ironic?

7. After Cordelia's death, does Lear ever truly believe she is alive? Why does he vacillate?

8. In a seven- to eight-page paper discuss the connection between the main plot and the various subplots that are brought together in the final act.

Generation to Generation: Thematic Questions

1. Some of the characters in the works in this section fit the traditional roles of mother or father; others do not. Which characters come closest to what you believe a mother or father should be?

2. King Lear says that it is "sharper than a serpent's tooth . . . to have a thankless child." "Mother's Day," "No Pictures," and "Daddy" show children who have strong negative feelings about their parents. Do you think that such feelings can be justified? Or do all children owe their parents affection and gratitude regardless of the circumstances?

3. Some parents, like Amanda in *The Glass Menagerie,* seem to want to keep their adult children from becoming independent. How much influence can or should parents have over their grown children?

4. In William Carlos Williams' poem "The Horse Show" the speaker claims at the age of sixty-four to be having the most intimate conversation he has ever had with his mother. Is a certain distance between parent and child necessary or desirable?

5. In *King Lear* we see two extreme kinds of competition: between parent and child and among siblings. Do you think that some degree of competition is present in all families? Is family competition always destructive, or can it be beneficial?

6. In Weldon Kees's sonnet "For My Daughter" the speaker announces that he does not wish to have a daughter. Given the present state of the world, is there a good argument for not having children? Is there a better reason for having them?

7. Discuss the role of money in family life in some of the works in this section and in real life.

Struggles

It seems clear to me that God designed us to live in society—just as He has given the bees honey; and as our social system could not subsist without the sense of justice and injustice, He has given us the power to acquire that sense.

VOLTAIRE

Essays

Jonathan Swift (British, 1667–1745)

A Modest Proposal

Swift was born in Dublin. He was educated at Trinity College, Dublin, and ordained as an Anglican priest. He was active in the Tory party, and spent several years in England. In 1713 he became Dean of St. Patrick's Cathedral, Dublin. As a writer he is best known for Gulliver's Travels, *a satire on human nature. Swift also attacked the Anglican church. "A Modest Proposal" was written in 1729, when there had been a famine in Ireland for several years.*

For Preventing the Children of Poor People in Ireland from Being a Burden to Their Parents or Country, and for Making Them Beneficial to the Public.

It is a melancholy object to those who walk through this great town or travel in the country, when they see the streets, the roads, and cabin doors, crowded with beggars of the female sex, followed by three, four, or six children, all in rags and importuning every passenger for an alms. These mothers, instead of being able to work for their honest livelihood, are forced to employ all their time in strolling to beg sustenance for their helpless infants: who as they grow up either turn thieves for want of work, or leave their dear native country to fight for the pretender in Spain, or sell themselves to the Barbadoes.

I think it is agreed by all parties that this prodigious number of children in the arms, or on the backs, or at the heels of their mothers, and frequently of their fathers, is in the present deplorable state of the kingdom a very great additional grievance; and therefore, whoever could find out a fair, cheap, and easy method of making these children sound, useful members of the commonwealth, would deserve so well of the public as to have his statue set up for a preserver of the nation.

But my intention is very far from being confined to provide only for the children of professed beggars; it is of a much greater extent, and shall take in the whole number of infants at a certain age who are born of parents in effect as little able to support them as those who demand our charity in the streets.

As to my own part, having turned my thoughts for many years upon this important subject, and maturely weighed the several schemes of our projectors, I have always found them grossly mistaken in their computation. It is true, a child just dropped from its dam may be supported by her milk for a solar year, with little other nourishment; at most not above the value of 2s. which the mother may certainly get, or the value in scraps, by her lawful occupation of begging; and it is exactly at one year old that I propose to provide for them in such a manner as instead of being a charge upon their parents or the parish, or wanting food and raiment for the rest of their lives, they shall on the contrary contribute to the feeding, and partly to the clothing, of many thousands.

There is likewise another great advantage in my scheme, that it will prevent those voluntary abortions, and that horrid practice of women murdering their bastard children, alas! too frequent among us! sacrificing the poor innocent babes I doubt more to avoid the expense than the shame, which would move tears and pity in the most savage and inhuman breast.

The number of souls in this kingdom being usually reckoned one million and a half, of these I calculate there may be about 200,000 couple whose wives are breeders; from which number I subtract 30,000 couple who are able to maintain their own children (although I apprehend there cannot be so many, under the present distress of the kingdom); but this being granted, there will remain 170,000 breeders. I again subtract 50,000 for those women who miscarry, or whose children die by accident or disease within the year. There only remain 120,000 children of poor parents annually born. The question therefore is, how this number shall be reared and provided for? which, as I have already said, under the present situation of affairs, is utterly impossible by all the methods hitherto proposed. For we can neither employ them in handicraft or agriculture; we neither build houses (I mean in the country) nor cultivate land; they can very seldom pick up a livelihood by stealing, till they arrive at six years old, except where they are of towardly parts; although I confess they learn the rudiments much earlier; during which time they can, however, be properly looked upon only as probationers; as I have been informed by a principal gentleman in the county of Cavan, who protested to me that he never knew above one or two instances under the age of six, even in a part of the kingdom so renowned for the quickest proficiency in that art.

I am assured by our merchants, that a boy or a girl before twelve years old is no saleable commodity; and even when they come to this age they will not yield above 3*l.* or 3*l.* 2*s.* 6*d.* at most on the exchange; which cannot turn to account either to the parents or kingdom, the charge of nutriment and rags having been at least four times that value.

I shall now therefore humbly propose my own thoughts, which I hope will not be liable to the least objection.

I have been assured by a very knowing American of my acquaintance in London, that a young healthy child well nursed is at a year old a most delicious, nourishing, and wholesome food, whether stewed, roasted, baked, or broiled; and I make no doubt that it will equally serve in a fricassee or a ragout.

I do therefore humbly offer it to public consideration that of the 120,000 children already computed, 20,000 may be reserved for breed, whereof only one-fourth part to be males; which is more than we allow to sheep, black cattle, or swine; and my reason is, that these children are seldom the fruits of marriage, a circumstance not much regarded by our savages; therefore one male will be sufficient to serve four females. That the remaining 100,000 may, at a year old, be offered in sale to the persons of quality and fortune through the kingdom; always advising the mother to let them suck plentifully in the last month, so as to render them plump and fat for a good table. A child will make two dishes at an entertainment for friends; and when the family dines alone, the fore or hind quarter will make a reasonable dish, and seasoned with a little pepper or salt will be very good boiled on the fourth day, especially in winter.

I have reckoned upon a medium that a child just born will weigh 12 pounds, and in a solar year, if tolerably nursed, will increase to 28 pounds.

I grant this food will be somewhat dear, and therefore very proper for landlords, who, as they have already devoured most of the parents, seem to have the best title to the children.

Infant's flesh will be in season throughout the year, but more plentiful in March, and a little before and after: for we are told by a grave author, an eminent French physician, that fish being a prolific diet, there are more children born in Roman Catholic countries about nine months after Lent than at any other season; therefore, reckoning a year after Lent, the markets will be more glutted than usual, because the number of popish infants is at least three to one in this kingdom: and therefore it will have one other collateral advantage, by lessening the number of papists among us.

I have already computed the charge of nursing a beggar's child (in which list I reckon all cottagers, laborers, and four-fifths of the farmers) to be about 2s. per annum, rags included; and I believe no gentleman would repine to give 10s. for the carcass of a good fat child, which, as I have said, will make four dishes of excellent nutritive meat, when he has only some particular friend or his own family to dine with him. Thus the squire will learn to be a good landlord, and grow popular among the tenants; the mother will have 8s. net profit, and be fit for work till she produces another child.

Those who are more thrifty (as I must confess the times require) may flay the carcass; the skin of which artificially dressed will make admirable gloves for ladies, and summer boots for fine gentlemen.

As to our city of Dublin, shambles may be appointed for this purpose in the most convenient parts of it, and butchers we may be assured will not be wanting: although I rather recommend buying the children alive, and dressing them hot from the knife as we do roasting pigs.

A very worthy person, a true lover of his country, and whose virtues I highly esteem, was lately pleased in discoursing on this matter to offer a refinement upon my scheme. He said that many gentlemen of this kingdom, having of late destroyed their deer, he conceived that the want of venison might be well supplied by the bodies of young lads and maidens, not exceeding fourteen years of age nor under twelve; so great a number of both sexes in every country being now ready to starve for want of work and service; and these to be disposed of by their parents, if alive, or otherwise by their nearest relations. But with due deference to so excellent a friend and so deserving a patriot, I cannot be altogether in his sentiments; for as to the males, my American acquaintance assured me from frequent experience that their flesh was generally tough and lean, like that of our schoolboys by continual exercise, and their taste disagreeable; and to fatten them would not answer the charge. Then as to the females, it would, I think, with humble submission be a loss to the public, because they soon would become breeders themselves: and besides, it is not improbable that some scrupulous people might be apt to censure such a practice (although indeed very unjustly), as a little bordering upon cruelty; which, I confess, has always been with me the strongest objection against any project, how well soever intended.

But in order to justify my friend, he confessed that this expedient was put into his head by the famous Psalmanazar, a native of the island Formosa, who came from thence to London about twenty years ago: and in conversation told my friend, that in his country when any young person happened to be put to death, the executioner sold the carcass of persons of quality as a prime dainty; and that in his time the body of a plump girl of fifteen, who was crucified for an attempt to poison the emperor, was sold to his imperial majesty's prime minister of state, and other great mandarins of the court, in joints from the gibbet, at 400 crowns. Neither indeed can I deny, that if the same use were made of several plump young girls in this town, who without one single groat to their fortunes cannot stir abroad without a chair, and appear at the playhouse and assemblies in foreign fineries which they never will pay for, the kingdom would not be the worse.

Some persons of a desponding spirit are in great concern about the vast number of poor people, who are aged, diseased, or maimed, and I have been desired to employ my thoughts what course may be taken to ease the nation of so grievous an encumbrance. But I am not in the least pain upon that matter, because it is well known that they are every day dying and rotting by cold and famine, and filth and vermin, as fast as can be reasonably expected. And as to the young laborers, they are now in as hopeful a condition: they cannot get work, and consequently pine away for want of nourishment, to a degree that if at any time they are accidentally hired to common labor, they have not strength to perform it; and thus the country and themselves are happily delivered from the evils to come.

I have too long digressed, and therefore shall return to my subject. I think the advantages by the proposal which I have made are obvious and many, as well as of the highest importance.

For first, as I have already observed, it would greatly lessen the number of papists, with whom we are yearly overrun, being the principal breeders of the nation as well as our most dangerous enemies; and who stay at home on purpose to deliver the kingdom to the Pretender, hoping to take their advantage by the absence of so many good Protestants, who have chosen rather to leave their country than stay at home and pay tithes against their conscience to an Episcopal curate.

Secondly, The poor tenants will have something valuable of their own, which by law may be made liable to distress and help to pay their landlord's rent, their corn and cattle being already seized, and money a thing unknown.

Thirdly, Whereas the maintenance of 100,000 children from two years old and upward, cannot be computed at less than 10s. a-piece per annum, the nation's stock will be thereby increased £50,000 per annum, beside the profit of a new dish introduced to the tables of all gentlemen of fortune in the kingdom who have any refinement in taste. And the money will circulate among ourselves, the goods being entirely of our own growth and manufacture.

Fourthly, The constant breeders, beside the gain of 8s. sterling per annum by the sale of their children, will be rid of the charge of maintaining them after the first year.

Fifthly, This food would likewise bring great custom to taverns, where the vintners will certainly be so prudent as to procure the best receipts for dressing it to perfection, and consequently have their houses frequented by all the fine gentlemen, who justly value themselves upon their knowledge in good eating; and a skilful cook, who understands how to oblige his guests, will contrive to make it as expensive as they please.

Sixthly, This would be a great inducement to marriage, which all wise nations have either encouraged by rewards or enforced by laws and penalties. It would increase the care and tenderness of mothers toward their children, when they were sure of a settlement for life to the poor babes, provided in some sort by the public, to their annual profit instead of expense. We should see an honest emulation among the married women, which of them would bring the fattest child to the market. Men would become as fond of their wives during the time of their pregnancy as they are now of their mares in foal, their cows in calf, their sows when they are ready to farrow; nor offer to beat or kick them (as is too frequent a practice) for fear of a miscarriage.

Many other advantages might be enumerated. For instance, the addition of some thousand carcasses in our exportation of barreled beef, the propagation of swine's flesh, and improvement in the art of making good bacon, so much wanted among us by the great destruction of pigs, too frequent at our table; which are no way comparable in taste or magnificence to a well-grown, fat, yearling child, which roasted whole will make a considerable figure at a lord mayor's feast or any other public entertainment. But this and many others I omit, being studious of brevity.

Supposing that 1,000 families in this city would be constant customers for infant's flesh, besides others who might have it at merrymeetings, particularly at weddings and christenings, I compute that Dublin would take off annually about 20,000 carcasses: and the rest of the kingdom (where probably they will be sold somewhat cheaper) the remaining 80,000.

I can think of no one objection that will possibly be raised against this proposal, unless it should be urged that the number of people will be thereby much lessened in the kingdom. This I freely own, and it was indeed one principal design in offering it to the world. I desire the reader will observe, that I calculate my remedy for this one individual kingdom of Ireland and for no other that ever was, or I think ever can be upon earth. Therefore let no man talk to me of other expedients: of taxing our absentees at 5s. a pound: of using neither clothes nor household furniture except what is of our own growth and manufacture: of utterly rejecting the materials and instruments that promote foreign luxury: of curing the expensiveness of pride, vanity, idleness, and gaming in our women: of introducing a vein of parsimony, prudence, and temperance: of learning to love our country, in the want of which we differ even from Laplanders and the inhabitants of Topinamboo: of quitting our animosities and factions, nor acting any longer like the Jews, who were murdering one another at the very moment their city was taken: of being a little cautious not to sell our country and conscience for nothing: of teaching landlords to have at least one degree of mercy toward their tenants: lastly, of putting a spirit of honesty, industry, and skill into our shopkeepers; who, if a resolution could now be taken to buy only our native goods, would immediately unite to cheat and exact upon us in the price, the measure, and the goodness, nor could ever yet be brought to make one fair proposal of just dealing, though often and earnestly invited to it.

Therefore I repeat, let no man talk to me of these and the like expedients, till he has at least some glimpse of hope that there will be ever some hearty and sincere attempt to put them in practice.

But as to myself, having been wearied out for many years with offering vain, idle, visionary thoughts, and at length utterly despairing of success, I fortunately fell upon this proposal; which, as it is wholly new, so it has something solid and real, of no expense and little trouble, full in our own power, and whereby we can incur no danger in disobliging England. For this kind of commodity will not bear exportation, the flesh being of too tender a consistence to admit a long continuance in salt, although perhaps I could name a country which would be glad to eat up our whole nation without it.

After all, I am not so violently bent upon my own opinion as to reject any offer proposed by wise men, which shall be found equally innocent, cheap, easy, and effectual. But before something of that kind shall be advanced in contradiction to my scheme, and offering a better, I desire the authors will be pleased maturely to consider two points. First, as things now stand, how they will be able to find food and raiment for 100,000 useless mouths and backs. And secondly, there being a round million of creatures in human figure throughout this kingdom, whose subsistence put into a common stock would leave them in debt

2,000,000*l.* sterling, adding those who are beggars by profession to the bulk of farmers, cottagers, and laborers, with the wives and children who are beggars in effect; I desire those politicians who dislike my overture, and may perhaps be so bold as to attempt an answer, that they will first ask the parents of these mortals, whether they would not at this day think it a great happiness to have been sold for food at a year old in the manner I prescribe, and thereby have avoided such a perpetual scene of misfortunes as they have since gone through by the oppression of landlords, the impossibility of paying rent without money or trade, the want of common sustenance, with neither house nor clothes to cover them from the inclemencies of the weather, and the most inevitable prospect of entailing the like or greater miseries upon their breed for ever.

I profess, in the sincerity of my heart, that I have not the least personal interest in endeavoring to promote this necessary work, having no other motive than the public good of my country, by advancing our trade, providing for infants, relieving the poor, and giving some pleasure to the rich. I have no children by which I can propose to get a single penny; the youngest being nine years old, and my wife past child-bearing.

SUGGESTIONS FOR WRITING AND DISCUSSION

1. When does it first become clear that Swift is being ironic? What is the purpose of his irony? Are there any points in the essay when you feel that Swift forgets to use this device?
2. Swift consistently compares poor people to animals. Choose some examples of this and discuss the effect.
3. What are the various stages in this argument? Is it a sound one? Write an outline of the argument.
4. The speaker of this essay is not Swift, but rather an invented persona. Why do you think Swift chose to present the proposal in this way?
5. ''A Modest Proposal'' was written in response to the apathy of the English toward the Irish during Ireland's great famine. This satirical piece is over 200 years old and it addresses a very specific problem at a specific point in history. Why is it still so widely read and discussed?
6. Look at the definition of satire in Chapter 9. Write a two- to three-page satirical essay about an issue that concerns you.

Thomas Jefferson (American, 1743–1826)

The Declaration of Independence

In Congress, July 4, 1776.

The Unanimous Declaration
of the Thirteen United States of America.

When in the Course of human events, it becomes necessary for one people to dissolve the political bands which have connected them with another, and to assume among the powers of the earth, the separate and equal station to which the Laws of Nature and of Nature's God entitle them, a decent respect to the opinions of mankind requires that they should declare the causes which impel them to the separation.

We hold these truths to be self-evident, that all men are created equal, that they are endowed by their Creator with certain unalienable Rights, that among these are Life, Liberty and the pursuit of Happiness.

That to secure these rights, Governments are instituted among Men, deriving their just powers from the consent of the governed.

That whenever any Form of Government becomes destructive of these ends, it is the Right of the People to alter or to abolish it, and to institute new Government, laying its foundation on such principles and organizing its powers in such form, as to them shall seem most likely to effect their Safety and Happiness. Prudence, indeed, will dictate that Governments long established should not be changed for light and transient causes; and accordingly all experience hath shewn, that mankind are more disposed to suffer, while evils are sufferable, than to right themselves by abolishing the forms to which they are accustomed. But when a long train of abuses and usurpations, pursuing invariably the same Object evinces a design to reduce them under absolute Despotism, it is their right, it is their duty, to throw off such Government, and to provide new Guards for their future security.

Such has been the patient sufferance of these Colonies; and such is now the necessity which constrains them to alter their former Systems of Government. The history of the present King of Great Britain is a history of repeated injuries and usurpations, all having in direct object the establishment of an absolute Tyranny over these States. To prove this, let Facts be submitted to a candid world.

He has refused his Assent to Laws, the most wholesome and necessary for the public good.

He has forbidden his Governors to pass Laws of immediate and pressing importance, unless suspended in their operation till his Assent should be obtained; and when so suspended, he has utterly neglected to attend to them.

He has refused to pass other Laws for the accommodation of large districts of people, unless those people would relinquish the right of Representation in the Legislature, a right inestimable to them and formidable to tyrants only.

He has called together legislative bodies at places unusual, uncomfortable, and distant from the depository of their public Records, for the sole purpose of fatiguing them into compliance with his measures.

He has dissolved Representative Houses repeatedly, for opposing with manly firmness his invasions on the rights of people.

He has refused for a long time, after such dissolutions, to cause others to be elected; whereby the Legislative powers, incapable of Annihilation, have returned to the People at large for their exercise; the State remaining in the mean time exposed to all the dangers of invasion from without, and convulsions within.

He has endeavoured to prevent the population of these States; for that purpose obstructing the Laws for Naturalization of Foreigners; refusing to pass others to encourage their migrations hither, and raising the conditions of new Appropriations of Lands.

He has obstructed the Administration of Justice, by refusing his Assent to Laws for establishing Judiciary powers.

He has made Judges dependent on his Will alone, for the tenure of their offices, and the amount and payment of their salaries.

He has erected a multitude of New Offices, and sent hither swarms of Officers to harass our people, and eat out their substance.

He has kept among us, in times of peace, Standing Armies without the Consent of our legislatures.

He has affected to render the Military independent of and superior to the Civil power.

He has combined with others to subject us to a jurisdiction foreign to our constitution, and unacknowledged by our laws; giving his Assent to their Acts of pretended Legislation:

For Quartering large bodies of armed troops among us:

For protecting them, by a mock Trial, from punishment for any Murders which they should commit on the Inhabitants of these States:

For cutting off our Trade with all parts of the world:

For imposing Taxes on us without our Consent:

For depriving us in many cases, of the benefits of Trial by Jury:

For transporting us beyond Seas to be tried for pretended offenses:

For abolishing the free System of English Laws in a neighbouring Province, establishing therein an Arbitrary government, and enlarging its Boundaries so as to render it at once an example and fit instrument for introducing the same absolute rule into these Colonies:

For taking away our Charters, abolishing our most valuable Laws, and altering fundamentally the Forms of our Governments:

For suspending our own Legislatures, and declaring themselves invested with power to legislate for us in all cases whatsoever.

He has abdicated Government here, by declaring us out of his Protection and waging War against us:

He has plundered our seas, ravaged our Coasts, burnt our towns, and destroyed the lives of our people.

He is at this time transporting large Armies of foreign Mercenaries to compleat the works of death, desolation and tyranny, already begun with circumstances of Cruelty & perfidy scarcely paralleled in the most barbarous ages, and totally unworthy the Head of a civilized nation.

He has constrained our fellow Citizens taken Captive on the high Seas to bear Arms against their Country, to become the executioners of their friends and Brethren, or to fall themselves by their Hands.

He has excited domestic insurrections amongst us, and has endeavoured to bring on the inhabitants of our frontiers, the merciless Indian Savages, whose known rule of warfare, is an undistinguished destruction of all ages, sexes and conditions. In every stage of these Oppressions We have Petitioned for Redress in the most humble terms: Our repeated Petitions have been answered only by repeated injury. A Prince, whose character is thus marked by every act which may define a Tyrant, is unfit to be the ruler of a free people. Nor have We been wanting in attentions to our British brethren. We have warned them from time to time of attempts by their legislature to extend an unwarrantable jurisdiction over us. We have reminded them of the circumstances of our emigration and settlement here. We have appealed to their native justice and magnanimity, and we have conjured them by the ties of our common kindred to disavow these usurpations, which, would inevitably interrupt our connections and correspondence. They too have been deaf to the voice of justice and of consanguinity. We must, therefore, acquiesce in the necessity, which denounces our Separation, and hold them, as we hold the rest of mankind, Enemies in War, in Peace Friends.

WE, THEREFORE, the Representatives of the UNITED STATES OF AMERICA, in General Congress Assembled, appealing to the Supreme Judge of the world for the rectitude of our intentions, do, in the Name and by Authority of the good People of these Colonies, solemnly publish and declare, That these United Colonies are, and of Right ought to be FREE AND INDEPENDENT STATES; that they are Absolved from all Allegiance to the British Crown, and that all political connection between them and the State of Great Britain, is and ought to be totally dissolved; and that as Free and Independent States, they have full Power to levy War, conclude Peace, contract Alliances, establish Commerce, and to do all other Acts and Things which Independent States may of right do.

And for the support of this Declaration, with a firm reliance on the protection of divine Providence, we mutually pledge to each other our Lives, our Fortunes and our sacred Honor.

SUGGESTIONS FOR WRITING AND DISCUSSION

1. What does the phrase "the pursuit of happiness" mean?
2. What is the effect of the long first sentence? Compare it with the final paragraph.
3. This document is now over 200 years old. Looking back on the history of the United States since it was written, do you think it still reflects the ideals of this country? Do you feel it should be amended or changed?
4. Compare this document with Martin Luther King, Jr.'s "Letter from Birmingham Jail." What do they share in style and content? How do they differ?
5. Using The Declaration of Independence as your model, write your own declaration supporting a principle important to you.

Chief Seattle (American, 1786–1866)

Reply to U.S. Government

Chief Seattle (1786–1866) was chief of the Suquamish and Duwamish tribes. In 1854 Governor Isaac Stevens, then Commissioner of Indian Affairs for the Washington Territories, arranged a treaty with the Indians in which two million acres of Indian territory would be turned over to the U.S. government. The Indians were powerless against the federal government, and the land, considered sacred by the Indians, was taken from them. What follows is Chief Seattle's direct reply to Stevens, translated by Henry A. Smith. This speech was delivered in 1853 in a tiny village that was later to become Seattle, Washington.

Yonder sky that has wept tears of compassion upon my people for centuries untold, and which to us appears changeless and eternal, may change. Today is fair. Tomorrow may be overcast with clouds. My words are like the stars that never change. Whatever Seattle says the great chief at Washington can rely upon with as much certainty as he can upon the return of the sun or the seasons. The White Chief says that Big Chief at Washington sends us greetings of friendship and goodwill. That is kind of him for we know he has little need of our friendship in return. His people are many. They are like the grass that covers vast prairies. My people are few. They resemble the scattering trees of a storm-swept plain. The great, and—I presume—good, White Chief sends us word that he wishes to buy our lands but is willing to allow us enough to live comfortably. This indeed appears just, even generous, for the Red Man no longer has rights that he need respect, and the offer may be wise also, as we are no longer in need of an extensive country. . . . I will not dwell on, nor mourn over, our untimely decay, nor reproach our paleface brothers with hastening it, as we too may have been somewhat to blame.

Youth is impulsive. When our young men grow angry at some real or imaginary wrong, and disfigure their faces with black paint, it denotes that their hearts are black, and then they are often cruel and relentless, and our old men and old women are unable to restrain them. Thus it has ever been. Thus it was when the white men first began to push our forefathers further westward. But let us hope that the hostilities between us may never return. We would have everything to lose and nothing to gain. Revenge by young men is considered gain, even at the cost of their own lives, but old men who stay at home in times of war, and mothers who have sons to lose, know better.

Our good father at Washington—for I presume he is now our father as well as yours, since King George has moved his boundaries further north—our great good father, I say, sends us word that if we do as he desires he will protect us. His brave warriors will be to us a bristling wall of strength, and his wonderful ships of war will fill our harbors so that our ancient enemies far to the northward—the Hydas and Tsimpsians— will cease to frighten our women, children, and old men. Then in reality will he be our father and we his children. But can that ever be? Your God is not our God! Your God loves your people and hates mine. He folds his strong and protecting arms lovingly about the paleface and leads him by the hand as a father leads his infant son—but He has forsaken His red children—if they really are his. Our God, the Great Spirit, seems also to have forsaken us. Your God makes your people wax strong every day. Soon they will fill the land. Our people are ebbing away like a rapidly receding tide that will never return. The white man's God cannot love our people or He would protect them. They seem to be orphans who can look nowhere for help. How then can we be brothers? How can your God become our God and renew our prosperity and awaken in us dreams of returning greatness? If we have a common heavenly father He must be partial—for He came to his paleface children. We never saw Him. He gave you laws but He had no word for His red children whose teeming multitudes once filled this vast continent as stars fill the firmament. No; we are two distinct races with separate origins and separate destinies. There is little in common between us.

To us the ashes of our ancestors are sacred and their resting place is hallowed ground. You wander far from the graves of your ancestors and seemingly without regret. Your religion was written upon tables of stone by the iron finger of your God so that you could not forget. The Red Man could never comprehend nor remember it. Our religion is the traditions of our ancestors—the dreams of our old men, given them in solemn hours of night by the Great Spirit; and the visions of our sachems; and it is written in the hearts of our people.

Your dead cease to love you and the land of their nativity as soon as they pass the portals of the tomb and wander way beyond the stars. They are soon forgotten and never return. Our dead never forget the beautiful world that gave them being.

Day and night cannot dwell together. The Red Man has ever fled the approach of the White Man, as the morning mist flees before the morning sun. However, your proposition seems fair and I think that my people will accept it and will retire to the reservation you offer them. Then we will dwell apart in peace, for the words of the Great White Chief seem to be the words of nature speaking to my people out of dense darkness.

It matters little where we pass the remnant of our days. They will not be many. A few more moons; a few more winters—and not one of the descendants of the mighty hosts that once moved over this broad land or lived in happy homes, protected by the Great Spirit, will remain to mourn over the graves of a people once more powerful and hopeful than yours. But why should I mourn at the untimely fate of my people? Tribe follows tribe, and nation follows nation, like the waves of the sea. It is the order of nature, and regret is useless. Your time of decay may be distant, but it will surely come, for even the White Man whose God walked and talked with him as friend with friend, cannot be exempt from the common destiny. We may be brothers after all. We will see.

We will ponder your proposition, and when we decide we will let you know. But should we accept it, I here and now make this condition that we will not be denied the privilege without molestation of visiting at any time the tombs of our ancestors, friends and children. Every part of this soil is sacred in the estimation of my people. Every hillside, every valley, every plain and grove, has been hallowed by some sad or happy event in days long vanished. . . . The very dust upon which you now stand responds more lovingly to their footsteps than to yours, because it is rich with the blood of our ancestors and our bare feet are conscious of the sympathetic touch. . . . Even the little children who lived here and rejoiced here for a brief season will love these somber solitudes and at eventide they greet shadowy returning spirits. And when the last Red Man shall have perished, and the memory of my tribe shall have become a myth among the White Men, these shores will swarm with the invisible dead of my tribe, and when your children's children think themselves alone in the field, the store, the shop, upon the highway, or in the silence of the pathless woods, they will not be alone. . . . At night when the streets of your cities and villages are silent and you think them deserted, they will throng with the returning hosts that once filled and still love this beautiful land. The White Man will never be alone.

Let him be just and deal kindly with my people, for the dead are not powerless. Dead, did I say? There is no death, only a change of worlds.

SUGGESTIONS FOR WRITING AND DISCUSSION

1. At the beginning of his speech Chief Seattle says that his words are like "the stars that never change." Further on, however, he compares the "red children" to the stars and comments on how many of them have vanished. Do these two comparisons contradict each other?
2. Why does Chief Seattle believe that the white people have a different god than the native Americans?
3. What kind of audience is Chief Seattle addressing? How is this evident?
4. Chief Seattle describes the native Americans as being very different from white people. In a one- to two-page essay discuss some of the more important differences and comment on Chief Seattle's belief that the two can never be reconciled.
5. In a two- to three-page essay compare this speech to The Declaration of Independence. Compare the use of language, using quotations from each, and show how they differ in tone and style.

Henry David Thoreau (American, 1817–1862)

Civil Disobedience

I heartily accept the motto—"That government is best which governs least"; and I should like to see it acted up to more rapidly and systematically. Carried out, it finally amounts to this, which also I believe,— "That government is best which governs not at all"; and when men are prepared for it, that will be the kind of government which they will have. Government is at best but an expedient; but most governments are usually, and all governments are sometimes, inexpedient. The objections which have been brought against a standing army, and they are many and weighty, and deserve to prevail, may also at last be brought against a standing government. The standing army is only an arm of the standing government. The government itself, which is only the mode which the people have chosen to execute their will, is equally liable to be abused and perverted before the people can act through it. Witness the present Mexican war, the work of comparatively a few individuals using the standing government as their tool; for, in the outset, the people would not have consented to this measure.

This American government—what is it but a tradition, though a recent one, endeavoring to transmit itself unimpaired to posterity, but each instant losing some of its integrity? It has not the vitality and force of a single living man; for a single man can bend it to his will. It is a sort of wooden gun to the people themselves. But it is not the less necessary for this; for the people must have some complicated machinery or other, and hear its din, to satisfy that idea of government which they have. Governments show us how successfully men can be imposed on, even impose on themselves, for their own advantage. It is excellent, we must all allow. Yet this government never of itself furthered any enterprise, but by the alacrity with which it got out of its way. *It* does not keep the country free. *It* does not settle the West. *It* does not educate. The character inherent in the American people has done all that has been accomplished; and it would have done somewhat more, if the government had not sometimes got in its way. For government is an expedient by which men would fain succeed in letting one another alone; and, as has been said, when it is most expedient, the governed are most let alone by it. Trade and commerce, if they were not made of India-rubber, would never manage to bounce over the obstacles which legislators are continually putting in their way; and, if one were to judge these men wholly by the effects of their actions and not partly by their intentions, they would deserve to be classed and punished with those mischievous persons who put obstructions on the railroads.

But, to speak practically and as a citizen, unlike those who call themselves no-government men, I ask for, not at once no government, but *at once* a better government. Let every man make known what kind of government would command his respect, and that will be one step toward obtaining it.

After all, the practical reason why, when the power is once in the hands of the people, a majority are permitted, and for a long period continue, to rule is not because they are most likely to be in the right, nor because this seems fairest to the minority, but because they are physically the strongest. But a government in which the majority rule in all cases cannot be based on justice, even as far as men understand it. Can there not be a government in which majorities do not virtually decide right and wrong, but conscience—in which majorities decide only those questions to which the rule of expediency is applicable? Must the citizen ever for a moment or in the last degree, resign his conscience to the legislator? Why has every man a conscience, then? I think that we should be men first, and subjects afterward. It is not desirable to cultivate a respect for the law so much as for the right. The only obligation which I have a right to assume is to do at any time what I think right. It is truly enough said, that a corporation has no conscience; but a corporation of conscientious men is a corporation *with* a conscience. Law never made men a whit more just; and, by means of their respect for it, even the well-disposed are daily made the agents of injustice. A common and natural result of an undue respect for law is, that you may see a file of soldiers, colonel, captain, corporal, privates, powder-monkeys, and all, marching in admirable order over hill and dale to the war, against their will, ay, against their common sense and consciences, which makes it very steep marching indeed, and produces a palpitation of the heart. They have no doubt that it is a damnable business in which they are concerned; they are all peaceably inclined. Now, what are they? Men at all? or small movable forts and magazines, at the service of some unscrupulous man in power? Visit the Navy-Yard, and behold a marine, such a man as an American government can make, or such as it can make a man with its black arts—a mere shadow and reminiscence of humanity, a man laid out alive and standing, and already, as one may say, buried under arms with funeral accompaniments, though it may be,—

> Not a drum was heard, not a funeral note,
> As his corpse to the rampart we hurried;
> Not a soldier discharged his farewell shot
> O'er the grave where our hero we buried.

The mass of men serve the state thus, not as men mainly, but as machines, with their bodies. They are the standing army, and the militia, jailors, constables, posse comitatus, etc. In most cases there is no free exercise whatever of the judgment or of the moral sense; but they put themselves on a level with wood and earth and stones; and wooden men can perhaps be manufactured that will serve the purpose as well. Such command no more respect than men of straw or a lump of dirt. They have the same sort of worth only as horses and dogs. Yet such as these even are commonly esteemed good citizens. Others—as most legislators, politicians, lawyers, ministers, and officeholders—serve the state chiefly with their heads; and, as they rarely make any moral distinctions, they are as likely to serve the Devil, without *intending* it, as God. A very few, as heroes, patriots, martyrs, reformers in the great sense, and *men*, serve the state with their consciences also, and so necessarily resist it for the most part; and they are commonly treated as enemies by it. A wise man will only be useful as a man, and will not submit to be "clay," and "stop a hole to keep the wind away," but leave that office to his dust at least:—

> I am too high-born to be propertied,
> To be a secondary at control,
> Or useful serving-man and instrument
> To any sovereign state throughout the world.

He who gives himself entirely to his fellow-men appears to them useless and selfish; but he who gives himself partially to them is pronounced a benefactor and philanthropist.

How does it become a man to behave toward this American government to-day? I answer, that he cannot without disgrace be associated with it. I cannot for an instant recognize that political organization as my government which is the *slave's* government also.

All men recognize the right of revolution; that is, the right to refuse allegiance to, and to resist, the government, when its tyranny or its inefficiency are great and unendurable. But almost all say that such is not the case now. But such was the case, they think, in the Revolution of '75. If one were to tell me that this was a bad government because it taxed certain foreign commodities brought to its ports, it is most probable that I should not make an ado about it, for I can do without them. All machines have their friction; and possibly this does enough good to counterbalance the evil. At any rate, it is a great evil to make a stir about it. But when the friction comes to have its machine, and oppression and robbery are organized, I say, let us not have such a machine any longer. In other words, when a sixth of the population of a nation which has undertaken to be the refuge of liberty are slaves, and a whole country is unjustly overrun and conquered by a foreign army, and subjected to military law, I think that it is not too soon for honest men to rebel and revolutionize. What makes this duty the more urgent is the fact that the country so overrun is not our own, but ours is the invading army . . .

> A drab of state, a cloth-o'-silver slut,
> To have her train borne up, and her soul trail in the
>   dirt

Practically speaking, the opponents to a reform in Massachusetts are not a hundred thousand politicians at the South, but a hundred thousand merchants and farmers here, who are more interested in commerce and agriculture than they are in humanity, and are not prepared to do justice to the slave and to Mexico, *cost what it may*. I quarrel not with far-off foes, but with those who, near at home, cooperate with, and do the bidding of, those far away, and without whom the latter would be harmless. We are accustomed to say, that the mass of men are unprepared; but improvement is slow, because the few are not materially wiser or better than the many. It is not so important that many should be as good as you, as that there be some absolute goodness somewhere; for that will leaven the whole lump. There are thousands who are *in opinion* opposed to slavery and to the war, who yet in effect do nothing to put an end to them; who, esteeming themselves children of Washington and Franklin, sit down with their hands in their pockets, and say that they know not what to do, and do nothing; who even postpone the question of freedom to the question of free-trade, and quietly read the prices-current along with the latest advices from Mexico, after dinner, and, it may be, fall asleep over them both. What is the price-current of an honest man and patriot today? They hesitate, and they regret, and sometimes they petition; but they do nothing in earnest and with effect. They will wait, well disposed, for others to remedy the evil, that they may no longer have it to regret. At most, they give only a cheap vote, and a feeble countenance and God-speed, to the right, as it goes by them. There are nine hundred and ninety-nine patrons of virtue to one virtuous man. But it is easier to deal with the real possessor of a thing than with the temporary guardian of it.

All voting is a sort of gaming, like checkers or backgammon, with a slight moral tinge to it, a playing with right and wrong, with moral questions; and betting naturally accompanies it. The character of the voters is not staked. I cast my vote, perchance, as I think right; but I am not vitally concerned that that right should prevail. I am willing to leave it to the majority. Its obligation, therefore, never exceeds that of expediency. Even voting *for the right* is *doing* nothing for it. It is only expressing to men feebly your desire that it should prevail. A wise man will not leave the right to the mercy of chance, nor wish it to prevail through the power of the majority. There is but little virtue in the action of masses of men. When the majority shall at length vote for the abolition of slavery, it will be because they are indifferent to slavery, or because there is but little slavery left to be abolished by their vote. *They* will then be the only slaves. Only *his* vote can hasten the abolition of slavery who asserts his own freedom by his vote.

I hear of a convention to be held at Baltimore, or elsewhere, for the selection of a candidate for the Presidency, made up chiefly of editors, and men who are politicians by profession; but I think, what is it to any independent, intelligent, and respectable man what decision they may come to? Shall we not have the advantage of his wisdom and honesty, nevertheless? Can we not count upon some independent votes? Are there not many individuals in the country who do not attend conventions? But no: I find that the respectable man, so called, has immediately drifted from his position, and despairs of his country, when his country has more reason to despair of him. He forthwith adopts one of the candidates thus selected as the only *available* one, thus proving that he is himself *available* for any purposes of the demagogue. His vote is of no more worth than that of any unprincipled foreigner or hireling native, who may have been bought. O for a man who is a *man,* and, as my neighbor says, has a bone in his back which you cannot pass your hand through! Our statistics are at fault: the population has been returned too large. How many *men* are there to a square thousand miles in this country? Hardly one. Does not America offer any inducement for men to settle here? The American has dwindled into an Odd Fellow,—one who may be known by the development of his organ of gregariousness, and a manifest lack of intellect and cheerful self-reliance; whose first and chief concern, on coming into the world, is to see that the Almshouses are in good repair; and, before yet he has lawfully donned the virile garb, to collect a fund for the support of the widows and orphans that may be; who, in short, ventures to live only by the aid of the Mutual Insurance Company, which has promised to bury him decently.

It is not a man's duty, as a matter of course, to devote himself to the eradication of any, even the most enormous wrong; he may still properly have other concerns to engage him; but it is his duty, at least, to wash his hands of it, and, if he gives it no thought longer, not to give it practically his support. If I devote myself to other pursuits and contemplations, I must first see, at least, that I do not pursue them sitting upon another man's shoulders. I must get off him first, that he may pursue his contemplations too. See what gross inconsistency is tolerated. I have heard some of my townsmen say, ``I should like to have them order me out to help put down an insurrection of the slaves, or to march to Mexico;—see if I would go''; and yet these very men have each, directly by their allegiance, and so indirectly, at least, by their money, furnished a substitute. The soldier is applauded who refuses to serve in an unjust war by those who do not refuse to sustain the unjust government which makes the war; is applauded by those whose own act and authority he disregards and sets at naught; as if the state were penitent to that degree that it hired one to scourge it while it sinned, but not to that degree that it left off sinning for a moment. Thus, under the name of Order and Civil Government, we are all made at last to pay homage to and support our own meanness. After the first blush of sin comes its indifference; and from immoral it becomes, as it were, unmoral, and not quite unnecessary to that life which we have made.

The broadest and most prevalent error requires the most disinterested virtue to sustain it. The slight reproach to which the virtue of patriotism is commonly liable, the noble are most likely to incur. Those who, while they disapprove of the character and measures of a government, yield to it their allegiance and support are undoubtedly its most conscientious supporters, and so frequently the most serious obstacles to reform. Some are petitioning the state to dissolve the Union, to disregard the requisitions of the President. Why do they not dissolve it themselves—the union between themselves and the state,—and refuse to pay their quota into its treasury? Do not they stand in the same relation to the state that the state does to the Union? And have not the same reasons prevented the state from resisting the Union which have prevented them from resisting the state?

How can a man be satisfied to entertain an opinion merely, and enjoy *it?* Is there any enjoyment in it, if his opinion is that he is aggrieved? If you are cheated out of a single dollar by your neighbor, you do not rest satisfied with knowing that you are cheated, or with saying that you are cheated, or even with petitioning him to pay you your due; but you take effectual steps at once to obtain the full amount, and see that you are never cheated again. Action from principle, the perception and the performance of right, changes things and relations; it is essentially revolutionary, and does not consist wholly with anything which was. It not only divides states and churches, it divides families; ay, it divides the *individual,* separating the diabolical in him from the divine.

Unjust laws exist: shall we be content to obey them, or shall we endeavor to amend them, and obey them until we have succeeded, or shall we transgress them at once? Men generally, under such a government as this, think that they ought to wait until they have persuaded the majority to alter them. They think that, if they should resist, the remedy would be worse than the evil. But it is the fault of the government itself that the remedy is worse than the evil. *It* makes it worse. Why is it not more apt to anticipate and provide for reform? Why does it not cherish its wise minority? Why does it cry and resist before it is hurt? Why does it not encourage its citizens to be on the alert to point out its faults, and *do* better than it would have them? Why does it always crucify Christ, and excommunicate Copernicus and Luther, and pronounce Washington and Franklin rebels?

One would think, that a deliberate and practical denial of its authority was the only offense never contemplated by government; else, why has it not assigned its definite, its suitable and proportionate penalty? If a man who has no property refuses but once to earn nine shillings for the state, he is put in prison for a period unlimited by any law that I know, and determined only by the discretion of those who placed him there; but if he should steal ninety times nine shillings from the state, he is soon permitted to go at large again.

If the injustice is part of the necessary friction of the machine of government, let it go, let it go: perchance it will wear smooth,—certainly the machine will wear out. If the injustice has a spring, or a pulley, or a rope, or a crank, exclusively for itself, then perhaps you may consider whether the remedy will not be worse than the evil; but if it is of such a nature that it requires you to be the agent of injustice to another, then, I say, break the law. Let your life be a counter friction to stop the machine. What I have to do is to see, at any rate, that I do not lend myself to the wrong which I condemn.

As for adopting the ways which the state has provided for remedying the evil, I know not of such ways. They take too much time, and a man's life will be gone. I have other affairs to attend to. I came into this world, not chiefly to make this a good place to live in, but to live in it, be it good or bad. A man has not everything to do, but something; and because he cannot do *everything,* it is not necessary that he should do *something* wrong. It is not my business to be petitioning the Governor or the Legislature any more than it is theirs to petition me; and if they should not hear my petition, what should I do then? But in this case the state has provided no way; its very Constitution is the evil. This may seem to be harsh and stubborn and unconciliatory; but it is to treat with the utmost kindness and consideration the only spirit that can appreciate or deserves it. So is all change for the better, like birth and death, which convulse the body.

I do not hesitate to say, that those who call themselves Abolitionists should at once effectually withdraw their support, both in person and property, from the government of Massachusetts and not wait till they constitute a majority of one, before they suffer the right to prevail through them. I think that it is enough if they have God on their side, without waiting for that other one. Moreover, any man more right than his neighbors constitutes a majority of one already.

I meet this American government, or its representative, the state government, directly, and face to face, once a year—no more—in the person of its tax-gatherer; this is the only mode in which a man situated as I am necessarily meets it; and it then says distinctly, Recognize me; and the simplest, most effectual, and in the present posture of affairs, the indispensablest mode of treating with it on this head, of expressing your little satisfaction with and love for it, is to deny it then. My civil neighbor, the tax-gatherer, is the very man I have to deal with,—for it is, after all, with men and not with parchment that I quarrel,—and he has voluntarily chosen to be an agent of the government. How shall he ever know well what he is and does as an officer of the government, or as a man, until he is obliged to consider whether he shall treat me, his neighbor, for whom he has respect, as a neighbor and well-disposed man, or as a maniac and disturber of the peace, and see if he can get over this obstruction to his neighborliness without a ruder and more impetuous thought or speech corresponding with his action. I know this well, that if one thousand, if one hundred, if ten men whom I could name,—if ten *honest* men only,—ay, if *one* HONEST man, in this State of Massachusetts, *ceasing to hold slaves,* were actually to withdraw from this copartnership, and be locked up in the county jail therefor, it would be the abolition of slavery in America. For it matters not how small the beginning may seem to be: what is once well done is done forever. But we love better to talk about it: that we say in our mission. Reform keeps many scores of newspapers in its service, but not one man. If my esteemed neighbor, the State's ambassador, who will devote his days to the settlement of the question of human rights in the Council Chamber, instead of being threatened with the prisons of Carolina, were to sit down the prisoner of Massachusetts, that State which is so anxious to foist the sin of slavery upon her sister,— though at present she can discover only an act of inhospitality to be the ground of a quarrel with her,—the Legislature would not wholly waive the subject the following winter.

Under a government which imprisons any unjustly, the true place for a just man is also a prison. The proper place to-day, the only place which Massachusetts has provided for her freer and less desponding spirits, is in her prisons, to be put out and locked out of the State by her own act, as they have already put themselves out by their principles. It is there that the fugitive slave, and the Mexican prisoner on parole, and the Indian come to plead the wrongs of his race should find them; on that separate, but more free and honorable ground, where the State places those who are not *with* her, but *against* her,—the only house in a slave State in which a free man can abide with honor. If any think that their influence would be lost there, and their voices no longer afflict the ear of the State, that they would not be as an enemy within its walls, they do not know by how much truth is stronger than error, nor how much more eloquently and effectively he can combat injustice who has experienced a little in his own person. Cast your whole vote, not a strip of paper merely, but your whole influence. A minority is powerless while it conforms to the majority; it is not even a minority then; but it is irresistible when it clogs by its whole weight. If the alternative is to keep all just men in prison, or give up war and slavery, the State will not hesitate which to choose. If a thousand men were not to pay their tax-bills this year, that would not be a violent and bloody measure, as it would be to pay them, and enable the State to commit violence and shed innocent blood. This is, in fact, the definition of a peaceable revolution, if any such is possible. If the tax-gatherer, or any other public officer, asks me, as one has done, "But what shall I do?" my answer is, "If you really wish to do anything, resign your office." When the subject has refused allegiance, and the officer has resigned his office, then the revolution is accomplished. But even suppose blood should flow. Is there not a sort of blood shed when the conscience is wounded? Through this wound a man's real manhood and immortality flow out, and he bleeds to an everlasting death. I see this blood flowing now.

I have contemplated the imprisonment of the offender, rather than the seizure of his goods,—though both will serve the same purpose—because they who assert the purest right, and consequently are most dangerous to a corrupt State, commonly have not spent much time in accumulating property. To such the State renders comparatively small service, and a slight tax is wont to appear exorbitant, particularly if they are obliged to earn it by special labor with their hands. If there were one who lived wholly without the use of money, the State itself would hesitate to demand it of him. But the rich man—not to make any invidious comparison—is always sold to the institution which makes him rich. Absolutely speaking, the more money, the less virtue; for money comes between a man and his objects, and obtains them for him; and it was certainly no great virtue to obtain it. It puts to rest many questions which he would otherwise be taxed to answer; while the only new question which it puts is the hard but superfluous one, how to spend it. Thus his moral ground is taken from under his feet. The opportunities of living are diminished in proportion as what are called the "means" are increased.

The best thing a man can do for his culture when he is rich is to endeavor to carry out those schemes which he entertained when he was poor. Christ answered the Herodians according to their condition. "Show me the tribute-money," said he;—and one took a penny out of his pocket;—if you use money which has the image of Caesar on it and which he has made current and valuable, that is, *if you are men of the State,* and gladly enjoy the advantages of Caesar's government, then pay him back some of his own when he demands it. "Render therefore to Caesar that which is Caesar's, and to God those things which are God's"—leaving them no wiser than before as to which; for they did not wish to know. . . .

I have paid no poll-tax for six years. I was put into a jail once on this account, for one night; and, as I stood considering the walls of solid stone, two or three feet thick, the door of wood and iron, a foot thick, and the iron grating which strained the light, I could not help being struck with the foolishness of that institution which treated me as if I were mere flesh and blood and bones, to be locked up. I wondered that it should have concluded at length that this was the best use it could put me to, and had never thought to avail itself of my services in some way. I saw that, if there was a wall of stone between me and my townsmen, there was a still more difficult one to climb or break through before they could get to be as free as I was. I did not for a moment feel confined, and the walls seemed a great waste of stone and mortar. I felt as if I alone of all my townsmen had paid my tax. They plainly did not know how to treat me, but behaved like persons who are underbred. In every threat and in every compliment there was a blunder; for they thought that my chief desire was to stand the other side of that stone wall. I could not but smile to see how industriously they locked the door on my meditations, which followed them out again without let or hindrance, and *they* were really all that was dangerous. As they could not reach me, they had resolved to punish my body; just as boys, if they cannot come at some person against whom they have a spite, will abuse his dog. I saw that the State was half-witted, that it was timid as a lone woman with her silver spoons, and that it did not know its friends from its foes, and I lost all my remaining respect for it, and pitied it.

Thus the State never intentionally confronts a man's sense, intellectual or moral, but only his body, his senses. It is not armed with superior wit or honesty, but with superior physical strength. I was not born to be forced. I will breathe after my own fashion. Let us see who is the strongest. What force has a multitude? They only can force me who obey a higher law than I. They force me to become like themselves. I do not hear of *men* being *forced* to live this way or that by masses of men. What sort of life were that to live? When I meet a government which says to me, "Your money or your life," why should I be in haste to give it my money? It may be in a great strait, and not know what to do: I cannot help that. It must help itself; do as I do. It is not worth the while to snivel about it. I am not responsible for the successful working of the machinery of society. I am not the son of the engineer. I perceive that, when an acorn and a chestnut fall side by side, the one does not remain inert to make way for the other, but both obey their own laws, and spring and grow and flourish as best they can, till one, perchance, overshadows and destroys the other. If a plant cannot live according to its nature, it dies; and so a man. . . .

When I came out of prison,—for some one interfered, and paid that tax,—I did not perceive that great changes had taken place on the common, such as he observed who went in a youth and emerged a tottering and gray-headed man; and yet a change had to my eyes come over the scene,—the town, and State, and country,—greater than any that mere time could effect. I saw yet more distinctly the State in which I lived. I saw to what extent the people among whom I lived could be trusted as good neighbors and friends; that their friendship was for summer weather only; that they did not greatly propose to do right; that they were a distinct race from me by their prejudices and superstitions, as the Chinamen and Malays are; that in their sacrifices to humanity they ran no risks, not even to their property; that after all they were not so noble but they treated the thief as he had treated them, and hoped, by a certain outward observance and a few prayers, and by walking in a particular straight though useless path from time to time, to save their souls. This may be to judge my neighbors harshly; for I believe that many of them are not aware that they have such an institution as the jail in their village.

It was formerly the custom in our village, when a poor debtor came out of jail, for his acquaintances to salute him, looking through their fingers, which were crossed to represent the grating of a jail window. ``How do ye do?'' My neighbors did not thus salute me, but first looked at me, and then at one another, as if I had returned from a long journey. I was put into jail as I was going to the shoemaker's to get a shoe which was mended. When I was let out the next morning, I proceeded to finish my errand, and, having put on my mended shoe, joined a huckleberry party, who were impatient to put themselves under my conduct; and in half an hour,—for the horse was soon tackled,—was in the midst of a huckleberry field, on one of our highest hills, two miles off, and then the State was nowhere to be seen. . . .

I have never declined paying the highway tax, because I am as desirous of being a good neighbor as I am of being a bad subject; and as for supporting schools, I am doing my part to educate my fellow-countrymen now. It is for no particular item in the tax-bill that I refuse to pay it. I simply wish to refuse all allegiance to the State, to withdraw and stand aloof from it effectually. I do not care to trace the course of my dollar, if I could, till it buys a man or a musket to shoot with,—the dollar is innocent,—but I am concerned to trace the effects of my allegiance. In fact, I quietly declare war with the State, after my fashion, though I will still make what use and get what advantage of her I can, as is usual in such cases.

If others pay the tax which is demanded of me, from a sympathy with the State, they do but what they have already done in their own case, or rather they abet injustice to a greater extent than the State requires. If they pay the tax from a mistaken interest in the individual taxed, to save his property, or prevent his going to jail, it is because they have not considered wisely how far they let their private feelings interfere with the public good.

This, then, is my position at present. But one cannot be too much on his guard in such a case, lest his action be biased by obstinacy or an undue regard for the opinions of men. Let him see that he does only what belongs to himself and to the hour.

I think sometimes, Why, these people mean well, they are only ignorant; they would do better if they knew how: why give your neighbors this pain to treat you as they are inclined to? But I think again. This is no reason why I should do as they do, or permit others to suffer much greater pain of a different kind. Again, I sometimes say to myself, When many millions of men, without heat, without ill will, without personal feeling of any kind, demand of you a few shillings only, without the possibility, such is their constitution, of retracting or altering their present demand, and without the possibility, on your side, of appeal to any other millions, why expose yourself to this overwhelming brute force? You do not resist cold and hunger, the winds and the waves, thus obstinately; you quietly submit to a thousand similar necessities. You do not put your head into the fire. But just in proportion as I regard this as not wholly a brute force, but partly a human force, and consider that I have relations to those millions as to many millions of men, and not of mere brute or inanimate things, I see that appeal is possible, first and instantaneously, from them to the Maker of them and, secondly, from them to themselves. But if I put my head deliberately into the fire, there is no appeal to fire or to the Maker of fire, and I have only myself to blame. If I could convince myself that I have any right to be satisfied with men as they are, and to treat them accordingly, and not according, in some respects, to my requisitions and expectations of what they and I ought to be, then, like a good Mussulman and fatalist, I should endeavor to be satisfied with things as they are, and say it is the will of God. And, above all, there is this difference between resisting this and a purely brute or natural force, that I can resist this with some effect; but I cannot expect, like Orpheus, to change the nature of the rocks and trees and beasts.

I do not wish to quarrel with any man or nation. I do not wish to split hairs, to make fine distinctions, or set myself up as better than my neighbors. I seek rather, I may say, even an excuse for conforming to the laws of the land. I am but too ready to conform to them. Indeed, I have reason to suspect myself on this head; and each year, as the tax-gatherer comes round, I find myself disposed to review the acts and position of the general and State governments, and the spirit of the people, to discover a pretext for conformity.

We must affect our country as our parents,
And if at any time we alienate
Our love or industry from doing it honor,

We must respect effects and teach the soul
Matter of conscience and religion,
And not desire of rule or benefit.

I believe that the State will soon be able to take all my work of this sort out of my hands, and then I shall be no better a patriot than my fellow-countrymen. Seen from a lower point of view, the Constitution, with all its faults, is very good; the law and the courts are very respectable; even this State and this American government are, in many respects, very admirable, and rare things, to be thankful for, such as a great many have described them; but seen from a point of view a little higher, they are what I have described them; seen from a higher still, and the highest, who shall say what they are, or that they are worth looking at or thinking of at all?

However, the government does not concern me much, and I shall bestow the fewest possible thoughts on it. It is not many moments that I live under a government, even in this world. If a man is thought-free, fancy-free, imagination-free, that which *is not* never for a long time appearing *to be* to him, unwise rulers or reformers cannot fatally interrupt him.

I know that most men think differently from myself; but those whose lives are by profession devoted to the study of these or kindred subjects content me as little as any. Statesmen and legislators, standing so completely within the institution, never distinctly and nakedly behold it. They speak of moving society, but have no resting-place without it. They may be men of a certain experience and discrimination, and have no doubt invented ingenious and even useful systems, for which we sincerely thank them; but all their wit and usefulness lie within certain not very wide limits. They are wont to forget that the world is not governed by policy and expediency. Webster never goes behind government, and so cannot speak with authority about it. His words are wisdom to those legislators who contemplate no essential reform in the existing government; but for thinkers, and those who legislate for all time, he never once glances at the subject. I know of those whose serene and wise speculations on this theme would soon reveal the limits of his mind's range and hospitality. Yet, compared with the cheap professions of most reformers, and the still cheaper wisdom and eloquence of politicians in general, his are almost the only sensible and valuable words, and we thank Heaven for him. Comparatively, he is always strong, original, and, above all, practical. Still, his quality is not wisdom, but prudence. The lawyer's truth is not Truth, but consistency or a consistent expediency. Truth is always in harmony with herself, and is not concerned chiefly to reveal the justice that may consist with wrong-doing. He well deserves to be called, as he has been called, the Defender of the Constitution. There are really no blows to be given by him but defensive ones. He is not a leader, but a follower. His leaders are the men of '87. "I have never made an effort," he says, "and never propose to make an effort; I have never countenanced an effort, and never mean to countenance an effort, to disturb the arrangement as originally made, by which the various States came into the Union." Still thinking of the sanction which the Constitution gives to slavery, he says, "Because it was a part of the original compact,—let it stand." Notwithstanding his special acuteness and ability, he is unable to take a fact out of its merely political relations, and behold it as it lies absolutely to be disposed of by the intellect,—what, for instance, it behooves a man to do here in America to-day with regard to slavery,—but ventures, or is driven, to make some such desperate answer as the following while professing to speak absolutely, and as a private man,—from which what new and singular code of social duties might be inferred? "The manner," says he, "in which the governments of those States where slavery exists are to regulate it is for their own consideration, under their responsibility to their constituents, to the general laws of propriety, humanity, and justice, and to God. Associations formed elsewhere, springing from a feeling of humanity, or other cause, have nothing whatever to do with it. They have never received any encouragement from me, and they never will."

They who know of no purer sources of truth, who have traced up its stream no higher, stand, and wisely stand, by the Bible and the Constitution, and drink at it there with reverence and humility; but they who behold where it comes trickling into this lake or that pool, gird up their loins once more, and continue their pilgrimage towards its fountainhead.

No man with a genius for legislation has appeared in America. They are rare in the history of the world. There are orators, politicians, and eloquent men, by the thousand; but the speaker has not yet opened his mouth to speak who is capable of settling the much-vexed questions of the day. We love eloquence for its own sake, and not for any truth which it may utter, or any heroism it may inspire. Our legislators have not yet learned the comparative value of free-trade and of freedom, of union, and of rectitude, to a nation. They have no genius or talent for comparatively humble questions of taxation and finance, commerce and manufactures and agriculture. If we were left solely to the wordy wit of legislators in Congress for our guidance, uncorrected by the seasonable experience and the effectual complaints of the people, America would not long retain her rank among the nations. For eighteen hundred years, though perchance I have no right to say it, the New Testament has been written; yet where is the legislator who has wisdom and practical talent enough to avail himself of the light which it sheds on the science of legislation?

The authority of government, even such as I am willing to submit to,—for I will cheerfully obey those who know and can do better than I, and in many things even those who neither know nor can do so well,—is still an impure one: to be strictly just, it must have the sanction and consent of the governed. It can have no pure right over my person and property but what I concede to it. The progress from an absolute to a limited monarchy, from a limited monarchy to a democracy, is a progress toward a true respect for the individual. Even the Chinese philosopher was wise enough to regard the individual as the basis of the empire. Is a democracy, such as we know it, the last improvement possible in government? Is it not possible to take a step further towards recognizing and organizing the rights of man? There will never be a really free and enlightened State until the State comes to recognize the individual as a higher and independent power, from which all its own power and authority are derived, and treats him accordingly. I please myself with imagining a State at last which can afford to be just to all men, and to treat the individual with respect as a neighbor; which even would not think it inconsistent with its own repose if a few were to live aloof from it, not meddling with it, nor embraced by it, who fulfilled all the duties of neighbors and fellow-men. A State which bore this kind of fruit, and suffered it to drop off as fast as it ripened, would prepare the way for a still more perfect and glorious State, which also I have imagined, but not yet anywhere seen.

SUGGESTIONS FOR WRITING AND DISCUSSION

1. Thoreau says "that government is best which governs least." What does this mean? Do you agree?
2. How does Thoreau construct his argument? Is it logical?
3. Give some examples of how acting on the right to be free might hurt other members of society.
4. What rights, if any, do you feel should be beyond the rule of law?
5. Write a two- to three-page response to Thoreau's rhetorical question "Is a democracy, such as we know it, the last improvement possible in government? Is it not possible to take a step further towards recognizing and organizing the rights of man?"
6. Many works in this section, such as those by Mohandas Gandhi, Margaret Sanger and Martin Luther King, Jr., show attempts to change prevailing laws. Research the background of one of these essays and in a four- to six-page paper show how the law was or was not changed.

Mohandas K. Gandhi (Indian, 1869–1948)

Nonviolence and Civil Disobedience

Gandhi was born in India and was educated in England. In 1893 he went to South Africa to practice law and became a leader in the campaign to end discrimination against Indians. It was at this time that he started to apply the principles of passive resistance in order to achieve social change.

From 1905 Gandhi followed the Hindu ideals of celibacy and asceticism. By the time he returned to India in 1915, he was a well-known leader. He campaigned for agrarian and labor reforms and for India's independence from Britain. Independence was achieved shortly before Gandhi was assassinated on his way to a prayer and pacifist meeting.

There is no defence for my conduct weighed only in the scales of *abiṃsā,* I draw no distinction between those who wield the weapons of destruction and those who do Red Cross work. Both participate in war and advance its cause. Both are guilty of the crime of war. But even after introspection during all these years, I feel that in the circumstances in which I found myself I was bound to adopt the course I did both during the Boer War and the Great European War and for that matter the so-called Zulu 'Rebellion' of Natal in 1906.

Life is governed by a multitude of forces. It would be smooth sailing, if one could determine the course of one's actions only by one general principle whose application at a given moment was too obvious to need even a moment's reflection. But I cannot recall a single act which could be so easily determined.

Being a confirmed war resister I have never given myself training in the use of destructive weapons in spite of opportunities to take such training. It was perhaps thus that I escaped direct destruction of human life. But so long as I lived under a system of government based on force and voluntarily partook of the many facilities and privileges it created for me, I was bound to help that government to the extent of my ability when it was engaged in a war unless I non-co-operated with that government and renounced to the utmost of my capacity the privileges it offered me.

Let me take an illustration. I am a member of an institution which holds a few acres of land whose crops are in imminent peril from monkeys. I believe in the sacredness of all life and hence I regard it a breach of *abiṃsā* to inflict any injury on the monkeys. But I do not hesitate to instigate and direct an attack on the monkeys in order to save the crops. I would like to avoid this evil. I can avoid it by leaving or breaking up the institution. I do not do so because I do not expect to be able to find a society where there will be no agriculture and therefore no destruction of some life. In fear and trembling, in humility and penance, I therefore participate in the injury inflicted on the monkeys, hoping some day to find a way out.

Even so did I participate in the three acts of war. I could not, it would be madness for me to, sever my connexions with the society to which I belong. And on those three occasions I had no thought of non-co-operating with the British Government. My position regarding the government is totally different today and hence I should not voluntarily participate in its wars and I should risk imprisonment and even the gallows if I was forced to take up arms or otherwise take part in its military operations.

But that still does not solve the riddle. If there was a national government, whilst I should not take any direct part in any war I can conceive occasions when it would be my duty to vote for the military training of those who wish to take it. For I know that all its members do not believe in non-violence to the extent I do. It is not possible to make a person or a society non-violent by compulsion.

Non-violence works in a most mysterious manner. Often a man's actions defy analysis in terms of non-violence; equally often his actions may wear the appearance of violence when he is absolutely non-violent in the highest sense of the term and is subsequently found so to be. All I can then claim for my conduct is that it was in the instances cited actuated in the interests of non-violence. There was no thought of sordid national or other interest. I do not believe in the promotion of national or any other interest at the sacrifice of some other interest.

I may not carry my argument any further. Language at best is but a poor vehicle for expressing one's thoughts in full. For me non-violence is not a mere philosophical principle. It is the rule and the breath of my life. I know I fail often, sometimes consciously, more often unconsciously. It is a matter not of the intellect but of the heart. True guidance comes by constant waiting upon God, by utmost humility, self-abnegation, by being ever ready to sacrifice one's self. Its practice requires fearlessness and courage of the highest order. I am painfully aware of my failings.

But the Light within me is steady and clear. There is no escape for any of us save through truth and non-violence. I know that war is wrong, is an unmitigated evil. I know too that it has got to go. I firmly believe that freedom won through bloodshed or fraud is no freedom. Would that all the acts alleged against me were found to be wholly indefensible rather than that by any act of mine non-violence was held to be compromised or that I was ever thought to be in favour of violence or untruth in any shape or form! Not violence, not untruth but non-violence, Truth is the law of our being.

.   .   .   .   .

Complete civil disobedience is rebellion without the element of violence in it. An out-and-out civil resister simply ignores the authority of the State. He becomes an outlaw claiming to disregard every unmoral State law. Thus, for instance, he may refuse to pay taxes, he may refuse to recognize the authority in his daily intercourse. He may refuse to obey the law of trespass and claim to enter military barracks in order to speak to the soldiers, he may refuse to submit to limitations upon the manner of picketing and may picket within the proscribed area. In doing all this he never uses force and never resists force when it is used against him. In fact, he invites imprisonment and other uses of force against himself. This he does because and when he finds the bodily freedom he seemingly enjoys to be an intolerable burden. He argues to himself that a State allows personal freedom only in so far as the citizen submits to its regulations. Submission to the State law is the price a citizen pays for his personal liberty. Submission, therefore, to a State law wholly or largely unjust is an immoral barter for liberty. A citizen who thus realizes the evil nature of a State is not satisfied to live on its sufferance, and therefore appears to the others who do not share his belief to be a nuisance to society whilst he is endeavouring to compel the State, without committing a moral breach, to arrest him. Thus considered, civil resistance is a most powerful expression of a soul's anguish and an eloquent protest against the continuance of an evil State. Is not this the history of all reform? Have not reformers, much to the disgust of their fellows, discarded even innocent symbols associated with an evil practice?

When a body of men disown the State under which they have hitherto lived, they nearly establish their own government. I say nearly, for they do not go to the point of using force when they are resisted by the State. Their 'business', as of the individual, is to be locked up or shot by the State, unless it recognizes their separate existence, in other words bows to their will. Thus three thousand Indians in South Africa after due notice to the Government of the Transvaal crossed the Transvaal border in 1914 in defiance of the Transvaal Immigration Law and compelled the government to arrest them. When it failed to provoke them to violence or to coerce them into submission, it yielded to their demands. A body of civil resisters is, therefore, like an army subject to all the discipline of a soldier, only harder because of want of excitement of an ordinary soldier's life. And as a civil resistance army is or ought to be free from passion because free from the spirit of retaliation, it requires the fewest number of soldiers. Indeed one *perfect* civil resister is enough to win the battle of Right against Wrong.

SUGGESTIONS FOR WRITING AND DISCUSSION

1. Gandhi says that he does not worry about being misrepresented. What does he mean? Why might this be a struggle in itself?
2. Do the first three paragraphs offer a consistent argument? Explain.
3. What other non-combatants besides Red Cross workers contribute either directly or indirectly to war?
4. Describe Gandhi's personality as shown in this essay. Pay particular attention to the ways he claims to have changed.
5. In a two- to three-page essay discuss whether you feel society could ever fully accept Gandhi's non-violent principles.
6. Gandhi greatly admired Thoreau. Compare this speech with "Civil Disobedience" in a three- to five-page essay.
7. Research Gandhi's life. Write a five- to seven-page paper in which you discuss other writings and speeches by Gandhi within their historical context. How effective were his principles in bringing about change? What other prominent leaders were influenced by him?

Martin Luther King, Jr. (American, 1929–1968)

Letter from Birmingham Jail[1]

My Dear Fellow Clergymen:

While confined here in the Birmingham city jail, I came across your recent statement calling my present activities ``unwise and untimely.''

[1]This response to a published statement by eight fellow clergymen from Alabama (Bishop C. C. J. Carpenter, Bishop Joseph A. Durick, Rabbi Milton L. Grafman, Bishop Paul Hardin, Bishop Holan B. Harmon, the Reverend George M. Murray, the Reverend Edward V. Ramage, and the Reverend Earl Stallings) was composed under somewhat constricting circumstances. Begun on the margins of newspaper in which the statement appeared while I was in jail, the letter was continued on scraps of writing paper supplied by a friendly Negro trusty, and concluded on a pad my attorneys were eventually permitted to leave me. Although the text remains in substance unaltered, I have indulged in the author's prerogative of polishing it for publication (King's note).

Seldom do I pause to answer criticism of my work and ideas. If I sought to answer all the criticisms that cross my desk, my secretaries would have little time for anything other than such correspondence in the course of the day, and I would have no time for constructive work. But since I feel that you are men of genuine good will and that your criticisms are sincerely set forth, I want to try to answer your statement in what I hope will be patient and reasonable terms.

I think I should indicate why I am here in Birmingham, since you have been influenced by the view which argues against "outsiders coming in." I have the honor of serving as president of the Southern Christian Leadership Conference, an organization operating in every southern state, with headquarters in Atlanta, Georgia. We have some eighty-five affiliated organizations across the South, and one of them is the Alabama Christian Movement for Human Rights. Frequently we share staff, educational, and financial resources with our affiliates. Several months ago the affiliate here in Birmingham asked us to be on call to engage in a nonviolent direct-action program if such were deemed necessary. We readily consented and when the hour came we lived up to our promise. So I, along with several members of my staff, am here because I was invited here. I am here because I have organizational ties here.

But more basically, I am in Birmingham because injustice is here. Just as the prophets of the eighth century B.C. left their villages and carried their "thus saith the Lord" far beyond the boundaries of their home towns, and just as the Apostle Paul left his village of Tarsus and carried the gospel of Jesus Christ to the far corners of the Greco-Roman world, so am I compelled to carry the gospel of freedom beyond my own home town. Like Paul, I must constantly respond to the Macedonian call for aid.

Moreover, I am cognizant of the interrelatedness of all communities and states. I cannot sit idly by in Atlanta and not be concerned about what happens in Birmingham. Injustice anywhere is a threat to justice everywhere. We are caught in an inescapable network of mutuality, tied in a single garment of destiny. Whatever affects one directly, affects all indirectly. Never again can we afford to live with the narrow, provincial "outside agitator" idea. Anyone who lives inside the United States can never be considered an outsider anywhere within its bounds.

You deplore the demonstrations taking place in Birmingham. But your statement, I am sorry to say, fails to express a similar concern for the conditions that brought about the demonstrations. I am sure that none of you would want to rest content with the superficial kind of social analysis that deals merely with effects and does not grapple with underlying causes. It is unfortunate that demonstrations are taking place in Birmingham, but it is even more unfortunate that the city's white power structure left the Negro community with no alternative.

In any nonviolent campaign there are four basic steps: collection of the facts to determine whether injustices exist; negotiation; self-purification; and direct action. We have gone through all these steps in Birmingham. There can be no gainsaying the fact that racial injustice engulfs this community. Birmingham is probably the most thoroughly segregated city in the United States. Its ugly record of brutality is widely known. Negroes have experienced grossly unjust treatment in the courts. There have been more unsolved bombings of Negro homes and churches in Birmingham than in any other city in the nation. These are the hard, brutal facts of the case. On the basis of these conditions, Negro leaders sought to negotiate with the city fathers. But the latter consistently refused to engage in good-faith negotiation.

Then, last September, came the opportunity to talk with leaders of Birmingham's economic community. In the course of the negotiations, certain promises were made by the merchants—for example, to remove the stores' humiliating racial signs. On the basis of these promises, the Reverend Fred Shuttlesworth and the leaders of the Alabama Christian Movement for Human Rights agreed to a moratorium on all demonstrations. As the weeks and months went by, we realized that we were the victims of a broken promise. A few signs, briefly removed, returned; the others remained.

As in so many past experiences, our hopes had been blasted, and the shadow of deep disappointment settled upon us. We had no alternative except to prepare for direct action, whereby we would present our very bodies as a means of laying our case before the conscience of the local and the national community. Mindful of the difficulties involved, we decided to undertake a process of self-purification. We began a series of workshops on nonviolence, and we repeatedly asked ourselves: "Are you able to accept blows without retaliating?" "Are you able to endure the ordeal of jail?" We decided to schedule our direct-action program for the Easter season, realizing that except for Christmas, this is the main shopping period of the year. Knowing that a strong economic-withdrawal program would be the by-product of direct action, we felt that this would be the best time to bring pressure to bear on the merchants for the needed change.

Then it occurred to us that Birmingham's mayoral election was coming up in March, and we speedily decided to postpone action until after election day. When we discovered that the Commissioner of Public Safety, Eugene "Bull" Connor, had piled up enough votes to be in the run-off, we decided again to postpone action until the day after the run-off so that the demonstrations could not be used to cloud the issues. Like many others, we wanted to see Mr. Connor defeated, and to this end we endured postponement after postponement. Having aided in this community need, we felt that our direct-action program could be delayed no longer.

You may well ask, "Why direct action? Why sit-ins, marches, and so forth? Isn't negotiation a better path?" You are quite right in calling for negotiation. Indeed, this is the very purpose of direct action. Nonviolent direct action seeks to create such a crisis and foster such a tension that a community which has constantly refused to negotiate is forced to confront the issue. It seeks so to dramatize the issue that it can no longer be ignored. My citing the creation of tension as part of the work of the nonviolent-resister may sound rather shocking. But I must confess that I am not afraid of the word "tension." I have earnestly opposed violent tension, but there is a type of constructive, nonviolent tension which is necessary for growth. Just as Socrates felt that it was necessary to create a tension in the mind so that individuals could rise from the bondage of myths and half-truths so the unfettered realm of creative analysis and objective appraisal, so must we see the need for nonviolent gadflies to create the kind of tension in society that will help men rise from the dark depths of prejudice and racism to the majestic heights of understanding and brotherhood.

The purpose of our direct-action program is to create a situation so crisis-packed that it will inevitably open the door to negotiation. I therefore concur with you in your call for negotiation. Too long has our beloved Southland been bogged down in a tragic effort to live in monologue rather than dialogue.

One of the basic points in your statement is that the action that I and my associates have taken in Birmingham is untimely. Some have asked: "Why didn't you give the new city administration time to act?" The only answer that I can give to this query is that the new Birmingham administration must be prodded about as much as the outgoing one, before it will act. We are sadly mistaken if we feel that the election of Albert Boutwell as mayor will bring the millennium to Birmingham. While Mr. Boutwell is a much more gentle person than Mr. Connor, they are both segregationists, dedicated to maintenance of the status quo. I have hoped that Mr. Boutwell will be reasonable enough to see the futility of massive resistance to desegregation. But he will not see this without pressure from devotees of civil rights. My friends, I must say to you that we have not made a single gain in civil rights without determined legal and nonviolent pressure. Lamentably, it is an historical fact that privileged groups seldom give up their privileges voluntarily. Individuals may see the moral light and voluntarily give up their unjust posture; but, as Reinhold Niebuhr has reminded us, groups tend to be more immoral than individuals.

We know through painful experience that freedom is never voluntarily given by the oppressor; it must be demanded by the opressed. Frankly, I have yet to engage in a direct-action compaign that was "well timed" in the view of those who have not suffered unduly from the disease of segregation. For years now I have heard the word "Wait!" It rings in the ear of every Negro with piercing familiarity. This "Wait" has almost always meant "Never." We must come to see, with one of our distinguished jurists, that "justice too long delayed is justice denied."

We have waited for more than 340 years for our constitutional and

God-given rights. The nations of Asia and Africa are moving with jetlike speed toward gaining political independence, but we still creep at horse-and-buggy pace toward gaining a cup of coffee at a lunch counter. Perhaps it is easy for those who have never felt the stinging darts of segregation to say, "Wait." But when you have seen vicious mobs lynch your mothers and fathers at will and drown your sisters and brothers at whim; when you have seen hate-filled policemen curse, kick, and even kill your black brothers and sisters; when you see the vast majority of your twenty million Negro brothers smothering in an airtight cage of poverty in the midst of an affluent society; when you suddenly find your tongue twisted and your speech stammering as you seek to explain to your six-year-old daughter why she can't go to the public amusement park that has just been advertised on television, and see tears welling up in her eyes when she is told that Funtown is closed to colored children, and see onimous clouds of inferiority beginning to form in her little mental sky, and see her beginning to distort her personality by developing an unconscious bitterness toward white people; when you have to concoct an answer for a five-year-old son who is asking, "Daddy, why do white people treat colored people so mean?"; when you take a cross-country drive and find it necessary to sleep night after night in the uncomfortable corners of your automobile because no motel will accept you; when you are humiliated day in and day out by nagging signs reading "white" and "colored"; when your first name becomes "nigger," your middle name becomes "boy," (however old you are) and your last name becomes "John," and your wife and mother are never given the respected title "Mrs."; when you are harried by day and haunted by night by the fact that you are a Negro, living constantly at tiptoe stance, never quite knowing what to expect next, and are plagued with inner fears and outer resentments; when you are forever fighting a degenerating sense of "nobodiness"—then you will understand why we find it difficult to wait. There comes a time when the cup of endurance runs over, and men are no longer willing to be plunged into the abyss of despair. I hope, sirs, you can understand our legitimate and unavoidable impatience.

You express a great deal of anxiety over our willingness to break laws. This is certainly a legitimate concern. Since we so diligently urge people to obey the Supreme Court's decision of 1954 outlawing segregation in the public schools, at first glance it may seem rather paradoxical for us consciously to break laws. One may well ask: "How can you advocate breaking some laws and obeying others?" The answer lies in the fact that there are two types of laws: just and unjust. I would be the first to advocate obeying just laws. One has not only a legal but a moral responsibility to obey just laws. Conversely, one has a moral responsibility to disobey unjust laws. I would agree with St. Augustine that "an unjust law is no law at all."

Now, what is the difference between the two? How does one determine whether a law is just or unjust? A just law is a man-made code that squares with the moral law or the law of God. An unjust law is a code that is out of harmony with the moral law. To put it in the terms of St. Thomas Aquinas: An unjust law is a human law that is not rooted in eternal law and natural law. Any law that uplifts human personality is just. Any law that degrades human personality is unjust. All segregation statutes are unjust because segregation distorts the soul and damages the personality. It gives the segregator a false sense of superiority and the segregated a false sense of inferiority. Segregation, to use the terminology of the Jewish philosopher Martin Buber, substitutes an ``I-it'' relationship for an ``I-thou'' relationship and ends up relegating persons to the status of things. Hence segregation is not only politically, economically, and sociologically unsound, it is morally wrong and sinful. Paul Tillich has said that sin is separation. Is not segregation an existential expression of man's tragic separation, his awful estrangement, his terrible sinfulness? Thus it is that I can urge men to obey the 1954 decision of the Supreme Court, for it is morally right; and I can urge them to disobey segregation ordinances, for they are morally wrong.

Let us consider a more concrete example of just and unjust laws. An unjust law is a code that a numerical or power majority group compels a minority group to obey but does not make binding on itself. This is *difference* made legal. By the same token, a just law is a code that a majority compels a minority to follow and that it is willing to follow itself. This is *sameness* made legal.

Let me give another explanation. A law is unjust if it is inflicted on a minority that, as a result of being denied the right to vote, had no part in enacting or devising the law. Who can say that the legislature of Alabama which set up that state's segregation laws was democratically elected? Throughout Alabama all sorts of devious methods are used to prevent Negroes from becoming registered voters, and there are some counties in which, even though Negroes constitute a majority of the population, not a single Negro is registered. Can any law enacted under such circumstatces be considered democratically structured?

Sometimes a law is just on its face and unjust in its application. For instance, I have been arrested on a charge of parading without a permit. Now, there is nothing wrong in having an ordinance which requires a permit for a parade. But such an ordinance becomes unjust when it is used to maintain segregation and to deny citizens the First-Amendment privilege of peaceful assembly and protest.

I hope you are able to see the distinction I am trying to point out. In no sense do I advocate evading or defying the law, as would the rabid segregationist. That would lead to anarchy. One who breaks an unjust law must do so openly, lovingly, and with a willingness to accept the penalty. I submit that an individual who breaks a law that conscience tells him is unjust, and who willingly accepts the penalty of imprisonment in order to arouse the conscience of the community over its injustice, is in reality expressing the highest respect for law.

Of course, there is nothing new about this kind of civil disobedience. It was evidenced sublimely in the refusal of Shadrach, Meshach, and Abednego to obey the laws of Nebuchadnezzar, on the ground that a higher moral law was at stake. It was practiced superbly by the early Christians, who were willing to face hungry lions and the excruciating pain of chopping blocks rather than submit to certain unjust laws of the Roman Empire. To a degree, academic freedom is a reality today because Socrates practiced civil disobedience. In our own nation, the Boston Tea Party represented a massive act of civil disobedience.

We should never forget that everything Adolf Hitler did in Germany was "legal" and everything the Hungarian freedom fighters did in Hungary was "illegal." It was "illegal" to aid and comfort a Jew in Hitler's Germany. Even so, I am sure that, had I lived in Germany at the time, I would have aided and comforted my Jewish brothers. If today I lived in a Communist country where certain principles dear to the Christian faith are suppressed, I would openly advocate disobeying that country's anti-religious laws.

I must make two honest confessions to you, my Christian and Jewish brothers. First, I must confess that over the past few years I have been gravely disappointed with the white moderate. I have almost reached the regrettable conclusion that the Negro's great stumbling block in his stride toward freedom is not the White Citizen's Counciler or the Ku Klux Klanner, but the white moderate, who is more devoted to "order" than to justice; who prefers a negative peace which is the absence of tension to a positive peace which is the presence of justice; who constantly says, "I agree with you in the goal you seek, but I cannot agree with your methods of direct action"; who paternalistically believes he can set the timetable for another man's freedom; who lives by a mythical concept of time and who constantly advises the Negro to wait for a "more convenient season." Shallow understanding from people of good will is more frustrating than absolute misunderstanding from people of ill will. Lukewarm acceptance is much more bewildering than outright rejection.

I had hoped that the white moderate would understand that law and order exist for the purpose of establishing justice and that when they fail in this purpose they become the dangerously structured dams that block the flow of social progress. I had hoped that the white moderate would understand that the present tension in the South is a necessary phase of the transition from an obnoxious negative peace, in which the Negro passively accepted his unjust plight, to a substantive and positive peace, in which all men will respect the dignity and worth of human personality. Actually, we who engage in nonviolent direct action are not the creators of tension. We merely bring to the surface the hidden tension that is already alive. We bring it out in the open, where it can be seen and dealt with. Like a boil that can never be cured so long as it is covered up but must be opened with all its ugliness to the natural medicines of air and light, injustice must be exposed, with all the tension its exposure creates, to the light of human conscience and the air of national opinion, before it can be cured.

In your statement you assert that our actions, even though peaceful, must be condemned because they precipitate violence. But is this a logical assertion? Isn't this like condemning a robbed man because his possession of money precipitated the evil act of robbery? Isn't this like condemning Socrates because his unswerving commitment to truth and his philosophical inquiries precipitated the act by the misguided populace in which they made him drink hemlock? Isn't this like condemning Jesus because his unique God-consciousness and never-ceasing devotion to God's will precipitated the evil act of crucifixion? We must come to see that, as the federal courts have consistently affirmed, it is wrong to urge an individual to cease his efforts to gain his basic constitutional rights because the quest may precipitate violence. Society must protect the robbed and punish the robber.

I had also hoped that the white moderate would reject the myth concerning time in relation to the struggle for freedom. I have just received a letter from a white brother in Texas. He writes: "All Christians know that the colored people will receive equal rights eventually, but it is possible that you are in too great a religious hurry. It has taken Christianity almost two thousand years to accomplish what it has. The teachings of Christ take time to come to earth." Such an attitude stems from a tragic misconception of time, from the strangely irrational notion that there is something in the very flow of time that will inevitably cure all ills. Actually, time itself is neutral; it can be used either destructively or constructively. More and more I feel that the people of ill will have used time much more effectively than have the people of good will. We will have to repent in this generation not merely for the hateful words and actions of the bad people, but for the appalling silence of the good people. Human progress never rolls in on wheels of inevitability; it comes through the tireless efforts of men willing to be co-workers with God, and without this hard work, time itself becomes an ally of the forces of social stagnation. We must use time creatively, in the knowledge that the time is always ripe to do right. Now is the time to make real the promise of democracy and transform our pending national elegy into a creative psalm of brotherhood. Now is the time to lift our national policy from the quicksand of racial injustice to the solid rock of human dignity.

You speak of our activity in Birmingham as extreme. At first I was rather disappointed that fellow clergymen would see my nonviolent efforts as those of an extremist. I began thinking about the fact that I stand in the middle of two opposing forces in the Negro community. One is a force of complacency, made up in part of Negroes who, as a result of long years of oppression, are so drained of self-respect and a sense of "somebodiness" that they have adjusted to segregation; and in part of a few middle-class Negroes who, because of a degree of academic and economic security and because in some ways they profit by segregation, have become insensitive to the problems of the masses. The other force is one of bitterness and hatred, and it comes perilously close to advocating violence. It is expressed in the various black nationalist groups that are springing up across the nation, the largest and best-known being Elijah Muhammad's Muslim movement. Nourished by the Negro's frustration over the continued existence of racial discrimination, this movement is made up of people who have lost faith in America, who have absolutely repudiated Christianity, and who have concluded that the white man is an incorrigible "devil."

I have tried to stand between these two forces, saying that we need emulate neither the "do-nothingism" of the complacent nor the hatred and despair of the black nationalist. For there is the more excellent way of love and nonviolent protest. I am grateful to God that, through the influence of the Negro church, the way of nonviolence became an integral part of our struggle.

If this philosophy had not emerged, by now many streets of the South would, I am convinced, be flowing with blood. And I am further convinced that if our white brothers dismiss as "rabblerousers" and "outside agitators" those of us who employ nonviolent direct action, and if they refuse to support our non-violent efforts, millions of Negroes will, out of frustration and despair, seek solace and security in black-nationalist ideologies—a development that would inevitably lead to a frightening racial nightmare.

Oppressed people cannot remain oppressed forever. The yearning for freedom eventually manifests itself, and that is what has happened to the American Negro. Something within has reminded him of his birthright of freedom, and something without has reminded him that it can be gained. Consciously or unconsciously, he has been caught up by the *Zeitgeist* (the spirit of the times), and with his black brothers of Africa and his brown and yellow brothers of Asia, South America, and the Caribbean, the United States Negro is moving with a sense of great urgency toward the promised land of racial justice. If one recognizes this vital urge that has engulfed the Negro community, one should readily understand why public demonstrations are taking place. The Negro has many pent-up resentments and latent frustrations, and he must release them. So let him march; let him make prayer pilgrimages to the city hall; let him go on freedom rides—and try to understand why he must do so. If his repressed emotions are not released in nonviolent ways, they will seek expression through violence; this is not a threat but a fact of history. So I have not said to my people, "Get rid of your discontent." Rather, I have tried to say that this normal and healthy discontent can be channeled into the creative outlet of nonviolent direct action. And now this approach is being termed extremist.

But though I was initially disappointed at being categorized as an extremist, as I continued to think about the matter I gradually gained a measure of satisfaction from the label. Was not Jesus an extremist for love: "Love your enemies, bless them that curse you, do good to them that hate you, and pray for them which despitefully use you, and persecute you." Was not Amos an extremist for justice: "Let justice roll down like waters and righteousness like an ever-flowing stream." Was not Paul an extremist for the Christian gospel: "I bear in my body the marks of the Lord Jesus." Was not Martin Luther an extremist: "Here I stand; I cannot do otherwise, so help me God." And John Bunyan: "I will stay in jail to the end of my days before I make a butchery of my conscience." And Abraham Lincoln: "This nation cannot survive half slave and half free." And Thomas Jefferson: "We hold these truths to be self-evident, that all men are created equal. . . ." So the question is not whether we will be extremists, but what kind of extremists we will be. Will we be extremists for hate or for love? Will we be extremists for the preservation of injustice or for the extension of justice? In that dramatic scene on Calvary's hill three men were crucified. We must never forget that all three men were crucified for the same crime—the crime of extremism. Two were extremists for immorality, and thus fell below their environment. The other, Jesus Christ, was an extremist for love, truth, and goodness, and thereby rose above his environment. Perhaps the South, the nation, and the world are in dire need of creative extremists.

I had hoped that the white moderate would see this need. Perhaps I was too optimistic; perhaps I expected too much. I suppose I should have realized that few members of the oppressor race can understand the deep groans and passionate yearnings of the oppressed race, and still fewer have the vision to see that injustice must be rooted out by strong, persistent, and determined action. I am thankful, however, that some of our white brothers in the South have grasped the meaning of this social revolution and committed themselves to it. They are still all too few in quantity, but they are big in quality. Some—such as Ralph McGill, Lillian Smith, Harry Golden, James McBridge Dabbs, Ann Braden, and Sarah Patton Boyle—have written about our struggle in eloquent and prophetic terms. Others have marched with us down nameless streets of the South. They have languished in filthy, roach-infested jails, suffering the abuse and brutality of policemen who view them as "dirty nigger-lovers." Unlike so many of their moderate brothers and sisters, they have recognized the urgency of the moment and sensed the need for powerful "action" antidotes to combat the disease of segregation.

Let me take note of my other major disappointment. I have been so greatly disappointed with the white church and its leadership. Of course, there are some notable exceptions. I am not unmindful of the fact that each of you has taken some significant stands on this issue. I commend you, Reverend Stallings, for your Christian stand of this past Sunday, in welcoming Negroes to your worship service on a nonsegregated basis. I commend the Catholic leaders of this state for integrating Spring Hill College several years ago.

But despite these notable exceptions, I must honestly reiterate that I have been disappointed with the church. I do not say this as one of those negative critics who can always find something wrong with the church. I say this as a minister of the gospel, who loves the church; who was nurtured in its bosom; who has been sustained by its spiritual blessings; and who will remain true to it as long as the cord of life shall lengthen.

When I was suddenly catapulted into the leadership of the bus protest in Montgomery, Alabama, a few years ago, I felt we would be supported by the white church. I felt that the white ministers, priests, and rabbis of the South would be among our strongest allies. Instead, some have been outright opponents, refusing to understand the freedom movement and misrepresenting its leaders; all too many others have been more cautious than courageous and have remained silent behind the anesthetizing security of stained-glass windows.

In spite of my shattered dreams, I came to Birmingham with the hope that the white religious leadership of this community would see the justice of our cause and, with deep moral concern, would serve as the channel through which our just grievances could reach the power structure. I had hoped that each of you would understand. But again I have been disappointed.

I have heard numerous southern religious leaders admonish their worshipers to comply with a desegregation decision because it is the law, but I have longed to hear white ministers declare: "Follow this decree because integration is morally right and because the Negro is your brother." In the midst of blatant injustices inflicted upon the Negro, I have watched white churchmen stand on the sideline and mouth pious irrelevancies and sanctimonious trivialities. In the midst of a mighty struggle to rid our nation of racial and economic injustice, I have heard many ministers say: "Those are social issues, with which the gospel has no real concern." And I have watched many churches commit themselves to a completely otherworldly religion which makes a strange, un-Biblical distinction between body and soul, between the sacred and the secular.

I have traveled the length and breadth of Alabama, Mississippi, and all the other southern states. On sweltering summer days and crisp autumn mornings I have looked at the South's beautiful churches with their lofty spires pointing heavenward. I have beheld the impressive outlines of her massive religious-education buildings. Over and over I have found myself asking: "What kind of people worship here? Who is their God? Where were their voices when the lips of Governor Barnett dripped with words of interposition and nullification? Where were they when Governor Wallace gave a clarion call for defiance and hatred? Where were their voices of support when bruised and weary Negro men and women decided to rise from the dark dungeons of complacency to the bright hills of creative protest?"

Yes, these questions are still in my mind. In deep disappointment I have wept over the laxity of the church. But be assured that my tears have been tears of love. There can be no deep disappointment where there is not deep love. Yes, I love the church. how could I do otherwise? I am in the rather unique position of being the son, the grandson, and the great-grandson of preachers. Yes, I see the church as the body of Christ. But, oh! How we have blemished and scarred that body through social neglect and through fear of being nonconformists.

There was a time when the church was very powerful—in the time when the early Christians rejoiced at being deemed worthy to suffer for what they believed. In those days the church was not merely a thermometer that recorded the ideas and principles of popular opinion; it was a thermostat that transformed the mores of society. Whenever the early Christians entered a town, the people in power became disturbed and immediately sought to convict the Christians for being "disturbers of the peace" and "outside agitators." But the Christians pressed on, in the conviction that they were "a colony of heaven," called to obey God rather than man. Small in number, they were big in commitment. They were too God-intoxicated to be "astronomically intimidated." By their effort and example they brought an end to such ancient evils as infanticide and gladiatorial contests.

Things are different now. So often the contemporary church is a weak, ineffectual voice with an uncertain sound. So often it is an archdefender of the status quo. Far from being disturbed by the presence of the church, the power structure of the average community is consoled by the church's silent—and often even vocal—sanction of things as they are.

But the judgment of God is upon the church as never before. If today's church does not recapture the sacrificial spirit of the early church, it will lose its authenticity, forfeit the loyalty of millions, and be dismissed as an irrelevant social club with no meaning for the twentieth century. Every day I meet young people whose disappointment with the church has turned into outright disgust.

Perhaps I have once again been too optimistic. Is organized religion too inextricably bound to the status quo to save our nation and the world? Perhaps I must turn my faith to the inner spiritual church, the church within the church, as the true *ekklesia* (the Greek New Testament word for the early Christian Church), and the hope of the world. But again

I am thankful to God that some noble souls from the ranks of organized religion have broken loose from the paralyzing chains of conformity and joined us as active partners in the struggle for freedom. They have left their secure congregations and walked the streets of Albany, Georgia, with us. They have gone down the highways of the South on tortuous rides for freedom. Yes, they have gone to jail with us. Some have been dismissed from their churches, have lost the support of their bishops and fellow ministers. But they have acted in the faith that right defeated is stronger than evil triumphant. Their witness has been the spiritual salt that has preserved the true meaning of the gospel in these troubled times. They have carved a tunnel of hope through the dark mountain of disappointment.

I hope the church as a whole will meet the challenge of this decisive hour. But even if the church does not come to the aid of justice, I have no despair about the future. I have no fear about the outcome of our struggle in Birmingham, even if our motives are at present misunderstood. We will reach the goal of freedom in Birmingham and all over the nation, because the goal of America is freedom. Abused and scorned though we may be, our destiny is tied up with America's destiny. Before the pilgrims landed at Plymouth, we were here. Before the pen of Jefferson etched the majestic words of the Declaration of Independence across the pages of history, we were here. For more than two centuries our forebears labored in this country without wages; they made cotton king; they built the homes of their masters while suffering gross injustice and shameful humiliation—and yet out of a bottomless vitality they continued to thrive and develop. If the inexpressible cruelties of slavery could not stop us, the opposition we now face will surely fail. We will win our freedom embodied in our echoing demands.

Before closing I feel impelled to mention one other point in your statement that has troubled me profoundly. You warmly commended the Birmingham police force for keeping ''order'' and ''preventing violence.'' I doubt that you would have so warmly commended the police force if you had seen its dogs sinking their teeth into unarmed, nonviolent Negroes. I doubt that you would so quickly commend the policemen if you were to observe their ugly and inhumane treatment of Negroes here in the city jail; if you were to watch them push and curse old Negro women and young Negro girls; if you were to see them slap and kick old Negro men and young boys; if you were to observe them, as they did on two occasions, refuse to give us food because we wanted to sing our grace together. I cannot join you in your praise of the Birmingham police department.

It is true that the police have exercised a degree of discipline in handling the demonstrators. In this sense they have conducted themselves rather ''nonviolently'' in public. But for what purpose? To preserve the evil system of segregation. Over the past few years I have consistently preached that nonviolence demands that the means we use must be as pure as the ends we seek. I have tried to make clear that it is wrong to use immoral means to attain moral ends. But now I must affirm that it is just as wrong, or perhaps even more so, to use moral means to preserve immoral ends. Perhaps Mr. Connor and his policemen have been rather nonviolent in public, as was Chief Pritchett in Albany, Georgia, but they have used the moral means of nonviolence to maintain the immoral end of racial injustice. As T. S. Eliot has said, ``The last temptation is the greatest treason: To do the right deed for the wrong reason.''

I wish you had commended the Negro sit-inners and demonstrators of Birmingham for their sublime courage, their willingness to suffer, and their amazing discipline in the midst of great provocation. One day the South will recognize its real heroes. They will be the James Merediths, with the noble sense of purpose that enables them to face jeering and hostile mobs, and with the agonizing loneliness that characterizes the life of the pioneer. They will be old, oppressed, battered Negro women, symbolized in a seventy-two-year-old woman in Montgomery, Alabama, who rose up with a sense of dignity and with her people decided not to ride segregated buses, and who responded with ungrammatical profundity to one who inquired about her weariness: ``My feets is tired, but my soul is at rest.'' They will be the young high school and college students, the young ministers of the gospel and a host of their elders, courageously and nonviolently sitting in at lunch counters and willingly going to jail for conscience' sake. One day the South will know that when these disinherited children of God sat down at lunch counters, they were in reality standing up for what is best in the American dream and for the most sacred values in our Judaeo-Christian heritage, thereby bringing our nation back to those great wells of democracy which were dug deep by the founding fathers in their formulation of the Constitution and the Declaration of Independence.

Never before have I written so long a letter. I'm afraid it is much too long to take your precious time. I can assure you that it would have been much shorter if I had been writing from a comfortable desk, but what else can one do when he is alone in a narrow jail cell, other than write long letters, think long thoughts, and pray long prayers?

If I have said anything in this letter that overstates the truth and indicates an unreasonable impatience, I beg you to forgive me. If I have said anything that understates the truth and indicates my having a patience that allows me to settle for anything less than brotherhood, I beg God to forgive me.

I hope this letter finds you strong in the faith. I also hope that circumstances will soon make it possible for me to meet each of you, not as an integrationist or a civil-rights leader but as a fellow clergyman and

a Christian brother. Let us all hope that the dark clouds of racial prejudice will soon pass away and the deep fog of misunderstanding will be
lifted from our fear-drenched communities, and in some not too distant
tomorrow the radiant stars of love and brotherhood will shine over our
great nation with all their scintillating beauty.

> Yours for the cause of Peace and Brotherhood,
> MARTIN LUTHER KING, JR.

1963

SUGGESTIONS FOR WRITING AND DISCUSSION

1. How does King justify his actions in Birmingham? What is his definition of
   an unjust law?
2. Why does King quote or refer to writings and teachings from so many different sources?
3. Why does King address the letter to eight clergymen, rather than, say, the
   editor of a newspaper or a politician?
4. Read Maya Angelou's "Graduation" (pp. 53–62) and in a two- to three-page
   essay compare her experiences with those King describes.
5. The sentiments expressed in this letter are quite similar to those of Gandhi
   and Thoreau. Compare the use of language in these three pieces. Which
   phrases or sentences do you find particularly effective?
6. Read background material about conditions in Birmingham at the time of
   King's arrest. Which laws in particular were civil rights workers struggling
   to change? What were the conditions for minorities elsewhere in the United
   States? Write a four- to six-page paper discussing the historical context of
   King's letter.

Margaret Sanger (American, 1883–1966)

The Turbid Ebb and Flow of Misery

*Sanger was born in Corning, New York, the sixth of eleven children. She
became a nurse and worked in the slums of the Lower East Side of New York
City. In 1914 she published a magazine entitled* The Woman Rebel *which
advocated the use of birth control. As a result of this she was briefly imprisoned. In 1916 she opened the first U.S. birth control clinic in Brooklyn; this
too resulted in a jail sentence. She is the author of numerous books, including*
What Every Girl Should Know, Motherhood and Bondage, *and* My Fight for
Birth Control.

> "Every night and every morn
> Some to misery are born.
> Every morn and every night

Some are born to sweet delight.
Some are born to sweet delight,
Some are born to endless night.''

WILLIAM BLAKE

During these years in New York trained nurses were in great demand. Few people wanted to enter hospitals; they were afraid they might be ''practiced'' upon, and consented to go only in desperate emergencies. Sentiment was especially vehement in the matter of having babies. A woman's own bedroom, no matter how inconveniently arranged, was the usual place for her lying-in. I was not sufficiently free from domestic duties to be a general nurse, but I could ordinarily manage obstetrical cases because I was notified far enough ahead to plan my schedule. And after serving my two weeks I could get home again.

Sometimes I was summoned to small apartments occupied by young clerks, insurance salesmen, or lawyers, just starting out, most of them under thirty and whose wives were having their first or second baby. They were always eager to know the best and latest method in infant care and feeding. In particular, Jewish patients, whose lives centered around the family, welcomed advice and followed it implicitly.

But more and more my calls began to come from the Lower East Side, as though I were being magnetically drawn there by some force outside my control. I hated the wretchedness and hopelessness of the poor, and never experienced that satisfaction in working among them that so many noble women have found. My concern for my patients was now quite different from my earlier hospital attitude. I could see that much was wrong with them which did not appear in the physiological or medical diagnosis. A woman in childbirth was not merely a woman in childbirth. My expanded outlook included a view of her background, her potentialities as a human being, the kind of children she was bearing, and what was going to happen to them.

The wives of small shopkeepers were my most frequent cases, but I had carpenters, truck drivers, dishwashers, and pushcart vendors. I admired intensely the consideration most of these people had for their own. Money to pay doctor and nurse had been carefully saved months in advance—parents-in-law, grandfathers, grandmothers, all contributing.

As soon as the neighbors learned that a nurse was in the building they came in a friendly way to visit, often carrying fruit, jellies, or gefüllter fish made after a cherised recipe. It was infinitely pathetic to me that they, so poor themselves, should bring me food. Later they drifted in again with the excuse of getting the plate, and sat down for a nice talk; there was no hurry. Always back of the little gift was the question, ''I am pregnant (or my daughter, or my sister is). Tell me something to keep from having another baby. We cannot afford another yet.''

I tried to explain the only two methods I had ever heard of among the middle classes, both of which were invariably brushed aside as unacceptable. They were of no certain avail to the wife because they placed the burden of responsibility solely upon the husband—a burden which he seldom assumed. What she was seeking was self-protection she could herself use, and there was none.

Below this stratum of society was one in truly desperate circumstances. The men were sullen and unskilled, picking up odd jobs now and then, but more often unemployed, lounging in and out of the house at all hours of the day and night. The women seemed to slink on their way to market and were without neighborliness.

These submerged, untouched classes were beyond the scope of organized charity or religion. No labor-union, no church, not even the Salvation Army reached them. They were apprehensive of everyone and rejected help of any kind, ordering all intruders to keep out; both birth and death they considered their own business. Social agents, who were just beginning to appear, were profoundly mistrusted because they pried into homes and lives, asking questions about wages, how many were in the family, had any of them ever been in jail. Often two or three had been there or were now under suspicion of prostitution, shoplifting, purse snatching, petty thievery, and, in consequence, passed furtively by the big blue uniforms on the corner.

The utmost depression came over me as I approached this surreptitious region. Below Fourteenth Street I seemed to be breathing a different air, to be in another world and country where the people had habits and customs alien to anything I had ever heard about.

There were then approximately ten thousand apartments in New York into which no sun ray penetrated directly; such windows as they had opened only on a narrow court from which rose fetid odors. It was seldom cleaned, though garbage and refuse often went down into it. All these dwellings were pervaded by the foul breath of poverty, that moldy, indefinable, indescribable smell which cannot be fumigated out, sickening to me but apparently unnoticed by those who lived there. When I set to work with antiseptics, their pungent sting, at least temporarily, obscured the stench.

I remember one confinement case to which I was called by the doctor of an insurance company. I climbed up the five flights and entered the airless rooms, but the baby had come with too great speed. A boy of ten had been the only assistant. Five flights was a long way; he had wrapped the placenta in a piece of newspaper and dropped it out the window into the court.

Many families took in ''boarders,'' as they were termed, whose small contributions paid the rent. These derelicts, wanderers, alternately working and drinking, were crowded in with the children; a single room sometimes held as many as six sleepers. Little girls were accustomed to dressing and undressing in front of the men, and were often violated, occasionally by their own fathers or brothers, before they reached the age of puberty.

Pregnancy was a chronic condition among the women of this class.

Suggestions as to what to do for a girl who was "in trouble" or a married woman who was "caught" passed from mouth to mouth—herb teas, turpentine, steaming, rolling downstairs, inserting slippery elm, knitting needles, shoe-hooks. When they had word of a new remedy they hurried to the drugstore, and if the clerk were inclined to be friendly he might say, "Oh, that won't help you, but here's something that may." The younger druggists usually refused to give advice because, if it were to be known, they would come under the law; midwives were even more fearful. The doomed women implored me to reveal the "secret" rich people had, offering to pay me extra to tell them; many really believed I was holding back information for money. They asked everybody and tried anything, but nothing did them any good. On Saturday nights I have seen groups of from fifty to one hundred with their shawls over their heads waiting outside of the office of a five-dollar abortionist.

Each time I returned to this district, which was becoming a recurrent nightmare, I used to hear that Mrs. Cohen "had been carried to a hospital, but had never come back," or that Mrs. Kelly "had sent the children to a neighbor and had put her head into the gas oven." Day after day such tales were poured into my ears—a baby born dead, great relief—the death of an older child, sorrow but again relief of a sort—the story told a thousand times of death from abortion and children going into institutions. I shuddered with horror as I listened to the details and studied the reasons back of them—destitution linked with excessive childbearing. The waste of life seemed utterly senseless. One by one worried, sad, pensive, and aging faces marshaled themselves before me in my dreams, sometimes appealingly, sometimes accusingly.

These were not merely "unfortunate conditions among the poor" such as we read about. I knew the women personally. They were living, breathing, human beings, with hopes, fears, and aspirations like my own, yet their weary, misshapen bodies, "always ailing, never failing," were destined to be thrown on the scrap heap before they were thirty-five. I could not escape from the facts of their wretchedness; neither was I able to see any way out. My own cozy and comfortable family existence was becoming a reproach to me.

Then one stifling mid-July day of 1912 I was summoned to a Grand Street tenement. My patient was a small, slight Russian Jewess, about twenty-eight years old, of the special cast of feature to which suffering lends a madonna-like expression. The cramped three-room apartment was in a sorry state of turmoil. Jake Sachs, a truck driver scarcely older than his wife, had come home to find the three children crying and her unconscious from the effects of a self-induced abortion. He had called the nearest doctor, who in turn had sent for me. Jake's earnings were trifling, and most of them had gone to keep the none-too-strong children clean and properly fed. But his wife's ingenuity had helped them to save a little, and this he was glad to spend on a nurse rather than have her go to a hospital.

The doctor and I settled ourselves to the task of fighting the septicemia. Never had I worked so fast, never so concentratedly. The sultry days and nights were melted into a torpid inferno. It did not seem possible there could be such heat, and every bit of food, ice, and drugs had to be carried up three flights of stairs.

Jake was more kind and thoughtful than many of the husbands I had encountered. He loved his children, and had always helped his wife wash and dress them. He had brought water up and carried garbage down before he left in the morning, and did as much as he could for me while he anxiously watched her progress.

After a fortnight Mrs. Sachs' recovery was in sight. Neighbors, ordinarily fatalistic as to the results of abortion, were genuinely pleased that she had survived. She smiled wanly at all who came to see her and thanked them gently, but she could not respond to their hearty congratulations. She appeared to be more despondent and anxious than she should have been, and spent too much time in meditation.

At the end of three weeks, as I was preparing to leave the fragile patient to take up her difficult life once more, she finally voiced her fears, "Another baby will finish me, I suppose?"

"It's too early to talk about that," I temporized.

But when the doctor came to make his last call, I drew him aside. "Mrs. Sachs is terribly worried about having another baby."

"She well may be," replied the doctor, and then he stood before her and said, "Any more such capers, young woman, and there'll be no need to send for me."

"I know, doctor," she replied timidly, "but," and she hestitated as though it took all her courage to say it, "what can I do to prevent it?"

The doctor was a kindly man, and he had worked hard to save her, but such incidents had become so familiar to him that he had long since lost whatever delicacy he might once have had. He laughed good-naturedly. "You want to have your cake and eat it too, do you? Well, it can't be done."

Then picking up his hat and bag to depart he said, "Tell Jake to sleep on the roof."

I glanced quickly at Mrs. Sachs. Even through my sudden tears I could see stamped on her face an expression of absolute despair. We simply looked at each other, saying no word until the door had closed behind the doctor. Then she lifted her thin, blue-veined hands and clasped them beseechingly. "He can't understand. He's only a man. But you do, don't you? Please tell me the secret, and I'll never breathe it to a soul. *Please!*"

What was I to do? I could not speak the conventionally comforting phrases which would be of no comfort. Instead, I made her as physically easy as I could and promised to come back in a few days to talk with her again. A little later, when she slept, I tiptoed away.

Night after night the wistful image of Mrs. Sachs appeared before me. I made all sorts of excuses to myself for not going back. I was busy on other cases; I really did not know what to say to her or how to convince her of my own ignorance; I was helpless to avert such monstrous atrocities. Time rolled by and I did nothing.

The telephone rang one evening three months later, and Jake Sachs' agitated voice begged me to come at once; his wife was sick again and from the same cause. For a wild moment I thought of sending someone else, but actually, of course, I hurried into my uniform, caught up my bag, and started out. All the way I longed for a subway wreck, an explosion, anything to keep me from having to enter that home again. But nothing happened, even to delay me. I turned into the dingy doorway and climbed the familiar stairs once more. The children were there, young little things.

Mrs. Sachs was in a coma and died within ten minutes. I folded her still hands across her breast, remembering how they had pleaded with me, begging so humbly for the knowledge which was her right. I drew a sheet over her pallid face. Jake was sobbing, running his hands through his hair and pulling it out like an insane person. Over and over again he wailed, ``My God! My God! My God!''

I left him pacing desperately back and forth, and for hours I myself walked and walked and walked through the hushed streets. When I finally arrived home and let myself quietly in, all the household was sleeping. I looked out my window and down upon the dimly lighted city. Its pains and griefs crowded in upon me, a moving picture rolled before my eyes with photographic clearness: women writhing in travail to bring forth little babies; the babies themselves naked and hungry, wrapped in newspapers to keep them from the cold; six-year-old children with pinched, pale, wrinkled faces, old in concentrated wretchedness, pushed into gray and fetid cellars, crouching on stone floors, their small scrawny hands scuttling through rags, making lamp shades, artificial flowers; white coffins, black coffins, coffins, coffins interminably passing in never-ending succession. The scenes piled one upon another on another. I could bear it no longer.

As I stood there the darkness faded. The sun came up and threw its reflection over the house tops. It was the dawn of a new day in my life also. The doubt and questioning, the experimenting and trying, were now to be put behind me. I knew I could not go back merely to keeping people alive.

I went to bed, knowing that no matter what it might cost, I was finished with palliatives and superficial cures; I was resolved to seek out the root of evil, to do something to change the destiny of mothers whose miseries were vast as the sky.

SUGGESTIONS FOR WRITING AND DISCUSSION

1. What are some of the distinctions Sanger makes about the different classes of women she knew?

2. Do you think this is a persuasive essay? Why or why not?
3. What is Sanger's attitude toward her patients?
4. Reread the poem by William Blake at the beginning of this essay. Why do you feel she included it?
5. At the time when Sanger was working as a nurse in the Lower East Side of New York City, the distribution of birth control information, as well as devices, was illegal. Sanger was arrested and jailed several times for violating this law. Are there any rules or laws which you feel should be changed? Write a three- to five-page paper in which you use your personal observations or experiences to illustrate why you think a particular law is unjust.

Anne Frank (German, 1929–1945)

From *The Diary of a Young Girl*

German-born Jews, Anne Frank and her family were living in Holland when they went into hiding in 1942 in an attempt to escape the concentration camps. They were joined in their hiding place, which Anne called "The Secret Annex," by another family, the Van Damms, who had a teenage son, Peter. Anne's diary is an account of the nearly three years she spent in hiding, during which she changed from a child to a young woman. It is also an account of her growing affection for Peter and a never-ending search for peace with her own family. She wrote the entries in the diary in the form of letters to an imaginary friend, whom she called Kitty.

"The Secret Annex" was discovered by the Gestapo in 1944 and all of its occupants sent to concentration camps. Anne died at Bergen-Belsen just two months before liberation. Only her father, Otto Frank, survived the camps, and it was he who found Anne's diary.

Saturday, 15 July, 1944

Dear Kitty,

We have had a book from the library with the challenging title of: *What Do You Think of the Modern Young Girl?* I want to talk about this subject today.

The author of this book criticized "the youth of today" from top to toe, without, however, condemning the whole of the young brigade as "incapable of anything good." On the contrary, she is rather of the opinion that if young people wished, they have it in their hands to make a bigger, more beautiful and better world, but that they occupy themselves with superficial things, without giving a thought to real beauty.

In some passages the writer gave me very much the feeling she was directing her criticisms at me, and that's why I want to lay myself completely bare to you for once and defend myself against this attack.

I have one outstanding trait in my character, which must strike anyone who knows me for any length of time, and that is my knowledge of myself. I can watch myself and my actions, just like an outsider. The Anne of every day I can face entirely without prejudice, without making excuses for her, and watch what's good and what's bad about her. This ``self-consciousness'' haunts me, and every time I open my mouth I know as soon as I've spoken whether ``that ought to have been different'' or ``that was right as it was.'' There are so many things about myself that I condemn. I couldn't begin to name them all. I understand more and more how true Daddy's words were when he said: ``All children must look after their own upbringing.'' Parents can only give good advice or put them on the right paths, but the final forming of a person's character lies in their own hands.

In addition to this, I have lots of courage. I always feel so strong and as if I can bear a great deal, I feel so free and so young! I was glad when I first realized it, because I don't think I shall easily bow down before the blows that inevitably come to everyone.

But I've talked about these things so often before. Now I want to come to the chapter of ``Daddy and Mummy don't understand me.'' Daddy and Mummy have always thoroughly spoiled me, were sweet to me, defended me, and have done all that parents could do. And yet I've felt so terribly lonely for a long time, so left out, neglected, and misunderstood. Daddy tried all he could to check my rebellious spirit, but it was no use, I have cured myself, by seeing for myself what was wrong in my behavior and keeping it before my eyes.

How is it that Daddy was never any support to me in my struggle, why did he completely miss the mark when he wanted to offer me a helping hand? Daddy tried the wrong methods, he always talked to me as a child who was going through difficult phases. It sounds crazy, because Daddy's the only one who has always taken me into his confidence, and no one but Daddy has given me the feeling that I'm sensible. But there's one thing he's omitted: you see, he hasn't realized that for me the fight to get on top was more important than all else. I didn't want to hear about ``symptoms of your age,'' or ``other girls,'' or ``it wears off by itself''; I didn't want to be treated as a-girl-like-all-others, but as Anne-on-her-own-merits. Pim didn't understand that. For that matter, I can't confide in anyone, unless they tell me a lot about themselves, and as I know very little about Pim, I don't feel that I can tread upon more intimate ground with him. Pim always takes up the older, fatherly attitude, tells me that he too has had similar passing tendencies. But still he's not able to feel with me like a friend, however hard he tries. These things have made me never mention my views on life nor my well-considered theories to anyone but my diary and, occasionally, to Margot. I concealed from Daddy everything that perturbed me; I never shared my ideals with him. I was aware of the fact that I was pushing him away from me.

I couldn't do anything else. I have acted entirely according to my feelings, but I have acted in the way that was best for my peace of mind. Because I should completely lose my repose and self-confidence, which I have built up so shakily, if, at this stage, I were to accept criticisms of my half-completed task. And I can't do that even from Pim, although it sounds very hard, for not only have I not shared my secret thoughts with Pim but I have often pushed him even further from me, by my irritability.

This is a point that I think a lot about: why is it that Pim annoys me? So much so that I can hardly bear him teaching me, that his affectionate ways strike me as being put on, that I want to be left in peace and would really prefer it if he dropped me a bit, until I felt more certain in my attitude towards him? Because I still have a gnawing feeling of guilt over that horrible letter that I dared to write him when I was so wound up. Oh, how hard it is to be really strong and brave in every way!

Yet this was not my greatest disappointment; no, I ponder far more over Peter than Daddy. I know very well that I conquered him instead of he conquering me. I created an image of him in my mind, pictured him as a quiet, sensitive, lovable boy, who needed affection and friendship. I needed a living person to whom I could pour out my heart; I wanted a friend who'd help to put me on the right road. I achieved what I wanted, and, slowly but surely, I drew him towards me. Finally, when I had made him feel friendly, it automatically developed into an intimacy which, on second thought, I don't think I ought to have allowed.

We talked about the most private things, and yet up till now we have never touched on those things that filled, and still fill, my heart and soul. I still don't know quite what to make of Peter, is he superficial, or does he still feel shy, even of me? But dropping that, I committed one error in my desire to make a real friendship: I switched over and tried to get at him by developing it into a more intimate relation, whereas I should have explored all other possibilities. He longs to be loved and I can see that he's beginning to be more and more in love with me. He gets satisfaction out of our meetings, whereas they just have the effect of making me want to try it out with him again. And yet I don't seem able to touch on the subjects that I'm so longing to bring out into the daylight. I drew Peter towards me, far more than he realizes. Now he clings to me, and for the time being, I don't see any way of shaking him off and putting him on his own feet. When I realized that he could not be a friend for my understanding, I thought I would at least try to lift him up out of his narrow-mindedness and make him do something with his youth.

"For in its innermost depths youth is lonelier than old age." I read this saying in some book and I've always remembered it, and found it to be true. Is it true then that grownups have a more difficult time here than we do? No. I know it isn't. Older people have formed their opinions about everything, and don't waver before they act. It's twice as hard for us young ones to hold our ground, and maintain our opinions, in a time when all ideals are being shattered and destroyed, when people are showing their worst side, and do not know whether to believe in truth and right and God.

Anyone who claims that the older ones have a more difficult time here certainly doesn't realize to what extent our problems weigh down on us, problems for which we are probably much too young, but which thrust themselves upon us continually, until, after a long time, we think we've found a solution, but the solution doesn't seem able to resist the facts which reduce it to nothing again. That's the difficulty in these times: ideals, dreams, and cherished hopes rise witin us, only to meet the horrible truth and be shattered.

It's really a wonder that I haven't dropped all my ideals, because they seem so absurd and impossible to carry out. Yet I keep them, because in spite of everything I still believe that people are really good at heart. I simply can't build up my hopes on a foundation consisting of confusion, misery, and death. I see the world gradually being turned into a wilderness, I hear the ever approaching thunder, which will destroy us too, I can feel the sufferings of millions and yet, if I look up into the heavens, I think that it will all come right, that this cruelty too will end, and that peace and tranquillity will return again.

In the meantime, I must uphold my ideals, for perhaps the time will come when I shall be able to carry them out.

Yours, *Anne*

SUGGESTIONS FOR WRITING AND DISCUSSION

1. What are some of the struggles to which Frank refers?
2. Frank describes a number of contradictory feelings toward her father. What are they? Is there a certain logic to these contradictions?
3. Why does Frank describe herself as idealistic?
4. Shortly after this diary entry was written, the Franks and four others who were hiding with them were discovered in their hiding place and sent to concentration camps. Does this knowledge change the way we read this particular entry? If so, how?
5. In a three- to five-page paper, compare Frank's idealism with that of some other author or character in this section.

Fiction

Richard Wright (American, 1908–1960)

The Man Who Saw the Flood

When the flood waters recede,
the poor folk along the river
start from scratch.

At last the flood waters had receded. A black father, a black mother, and a black child tramped through muddy fields, leading a tired cow by a thin bit of rope. They stopped on a hilltop and shifted the bundles on their shoulders. As far as they could see the ground was covered with flood silt. The little girl lifted a skinny finger and pointed to a mud-caked cabin.

"Look, Pa! Ain tha our home?"

The man, round-shouldered, clad in blue, ragged overalls, looked with bewildered eyes. Without moving a muscle, scarcely moving his lips, he said: "Yeah."

For five minutes they did not speak or move. The flood waters had been more than eight feet high here. Every tree, blade of grass, and stray stick has its flood mark; caky, yellow mud. It clung to the ground, cracking thinly here and there in spider web fashion. Over the stark fields came a gusty spring wind. The sky was high, blue, full of white clouds and sunshine. Over all hung a first-day strangeness.

"The henhouse is gone," sighed the woman.

"N the pigpen," sighed the man.

They spoke without bitterness.

"Ah reckon them chickens is all done drowned."

"Yeah."

"Miz Flora's house is gone, too," said the little girl.

They looked at a clump of trees where their neighbor's house had stood.

"Lawd!"

"Yuh reckon anybody knows where they is?"

"Hard t tell."

The man walked down down the slope and stood uncertainly.

"There wuz a road erlong here somewheres," he said.

But there was no road now. Just a wide sweep of yellow, scalloped silt.

"Look, Tom!" called the woman. "Here's a piece of our gate!"

The gatepost was half buried in the ground. A rusty hinge stood stiff, like a lonely finger. Tom pried it loose and caught it firmly in his hand. There was nothing particular he wanted to do with it; he just stood holding it firmly. Finally he dropped it, looked up, and said:

"C mon. Les go down n see whut we kin do."

Because it sat in a slight depression, the ground about the cabin was soft and slimy.

"Gimme the bag o lime, May," he said.

With his shoes sucking in mud, he went slowly around the cabin, spreading the white lime with thick fingers. When he reached the front again he had a little left; he shook the bag out on the porch. The fine grains of floating lime flickered in the sunlight.

"Tha oughta hep some," he said.

"Now, yuh be careful, Sal!" said May. "Don yuh go n fall down in all this mud, yuh hear?"

"Yessum."

The steps were gone. Tom lifted May and Sally to the porch. They stood a moment looking at the half-opened door. He had shut it when he left, but somehow it seemed natural that he should find it open. The planks in the porch floor were swollen and warped. The cabin had two colors; near the bottom it was a solid yellow; at the top it was the familiar gray. It looked weird, as though its ghost were standing beside it.

The cow lowed.

"Tie Pat t the pos on the en of the porch, May."

May tied the rope slowly, listlessly. When they attempted to open the front door, it would not budge. It was not until Tom placed his shoulder against it and gave it a stout shove that it scraped back jerkily. The front room was dark and silent. The damp smell of flood silt came fresh and sharp to their nostrils. Only one-half of the upper window was clear, and through it fell a rectangle of dingy light. The floors swam in ooze. Like a mute warning, a wavering flood mark went high around the walls of the room. A dresser sat cater-cornered, its drawers and sides bulging like a bloated corpse. The bed, with the mattress still on it, was like a giant casket forged of mud. Two smashed chairs lay in a corner, as though huddled together for protection.

"Les see the kitchen," said Tom.

The stovepipe was gone. But the stove stood in the same place.

"The stove's still good. We kin clean it."

"Yeah."

"But where's the table?"

"Lawd knows."

"It must've washed erway wid the rest of the stuff, Ah reckon."

They opened the back door and looked out. They missed the barn, the henhouse, and the pigpen.

"Tom, yuh bettah try tha ol pump n see ef eny watah's there."

The pump was stiff. Tom threw his weight on the handle and carried it up and down. No water came. He pumped on. There was a dry, hollow cough. Then yellow water trickled. He caught his breath and kept pumping. The water flowed white.

"Thank Gawd! We's got some watah."

"Yuh bettah boil it fo yuh use it," he said.

"Yeah. Ah know."

"Look, Pa! Here's yo ax," called Sally.

Tom took the ax from her. "Yeah. Ah'll need this."

"N here's somethin else," called Sally, digging spoons out of the mud.

"Waal, Ahma git a bucket n start cleanin," said May. "Ain no use in waitin, cause we's gotta sleep on them floors tonight."

When she was filling the bucket from the pump, Tom called from around the cabin. "May, look! Ah done foun mah plow!" Proudly he dragged the silt-caked plow to the pump. "Ah'll wash it n it'll be awright."

"Ahm hongry," said Sally.

"Now. yuh jus wait! Yuh et this mawnin," said May. She turned to Tom. "Now, whutcha gonna do, Tom?"

He stood looking at the mud-filled fields.

"Yuh goin back t Burgess?"

"Ah reckon Ah have to."

"Whut else kin yuh do?"

"Nothin," he said. "Lawd, but Ah sho hate t start all over wid tha white man. Ah'd leave here ef Ah could. Ah owes im nigh eight hundred dollahs. N we needs a hoss, grub, seed, n a lot mo other things. Ef we keeps on like this tha white man'll own us body n soul."

"But, Tom, there ain nothin else t do," she said.

"Ef we try t run erway they'll put us in jail."

"It coulda been worse," she said.

Sally come running from the kitchen. "Pa!"

"Hunh?"

"There's a shelf in the kitchen the flood didn git!"

"Where?"

"Right up over the stove."

"But, chile, ain nothin up there," said May.

"But there's somethin on it," said Sally.

"C mon. Les see."

High and dry, untouched by the flood-water, was a box of matches. And beside it a half-full sack of Bull Durham tobacco. He took a match from the box and scratched it on his overalls. It burned to his fingers before he dropped it.

"May!"

"Hunh?"

"Look! Here's ma bacco n some matches!"

She stared unbelievingly. "Lawd!" she breathed.

Tom rolled a cigarette clumsily.

May washed the stove, gathered some sticks, and after some diffi-culty, made a fire. The kitchen stove smoked, and their eyes smarted. May put water on to heat and went into the front room. It was getting dark. From the bundles they took a kerosene lamp and lit it. Outside Pat lowed longingly into the thickening gloam and tinkled her cowbell.

"Tha old cow's hongry," said May.

"Ah reckon Ah'll have t be gittin erlong t Burgess."

They stood on the front porch.

"Yuh bettah git on, Tom, fo it gits too dark."

"Yeah."

The wind had stopped blowing. In the east a cluster of stars hung.

"Yuh goin, Tom?"

"Ah reckon Ah have t."

"Ma, Ah'm hongry," said Sally.

"Wait erwhile, honey. Ma knows yuh's hongry."

Tom threw his cigarette away and sighed.

"Look! Here comes somebody!"

"Thas Mistah Burgess now!"

A mud-caked buggy rolled up. The shaggy horse was splattered all over. Burgess leaned his white face out of the buggy and spat.

"Well, I see you're back."

"Yessuh."

"How things look?"

"They don look so good, Mistah."

"What seems to be the trouble?"

"Waal. Ah ain got no hoss, no grub, nothin. The only thing Ah got is tha ol cow there . . .''

"You owe eight hundred dollahs down at the store, Tom."

"Yessuh, Ah know. But, Mistah Burgess, can't yuh knock somethin off of tha, seein as how Ahm down n out now?"

"You ate that grub, and I got to pay for it, Tom."

"Yessuh, Ah know."

"It's going to be a little tough, Tom. But you got to go through with it. Two of the boys tried to run away this morning and dodge their debts, and I had to have the sheriff pick em up. I wasn't looking for no trouble out of you, Tom . . . . The rest of the families are going back."

Leaning out of the buggy, Burgess waited. In the surrounding stillness the cowbell tinkled again. Tom stood with his back against a post.

"Yuh got t go on, Tom. We ain't got nothin here," said May.

Tom looked at Burgess.

"Mistah Burgess, Ah don wanna make no trouble. But this is jus *too* hard. Ahm worse off now than befo. Ah got to start from scratch."

"Get in the buggy and come with me. I'll stake you with grub. We can talk over how you can pay it back." Tom said nothing. He rested his back against the post and looked at the mud-filled fields.

"Well," asked Burgess. "You coming?" Tom said nothing. He got slowly to the ground and pulled himself into the buggy. May watched them drive off.

"Hurry back, Tom!"

"Awright."

"Ma, tell Pa t bring me some 'lasses," begged Sally.

"Oh, Tom!"

Tom's head came out of the side of the buggy.

"Hunh?"

"Bring some 'lasses!"

``Hunh?''
``Bring some 'lasses for Sal!''
``Awright!''
She watched the buggy disappear over the crest of the muddy hill. Then she sighed, caught Sally's hand, and turned back into the cabin.

SUGGESTIONS FOR WRITING AND DISCUSSION

1. How does Wright convey Tom and May's despair? Why do you think Wright describes their house in such detail?
2. Do the characters change during the course of the story?
3. Argue that Mr. Burgess is not a totally unsympathetic character.
4. What is the theme of this story?
5. What purpose is served by having the story begin after the flood?
6. Are the characters in this story defeated or undefeated? Weak or strong? Argue in a two- to three-page essay.

Nadine Gordimer (South African, 1923–

Some Monday For Sure

My sister's husband, Josias, used to work on the railways but then he got this job where they make dynamite for the mines. He was the one who sits out on that little iron seat clamped to the back of the big red truck, with a red flag in his hand. The idea is that if you drive up too near the truck or look as if you're going to crash into it, he waves the flag to warn you off. You've seen those trucks often on the Main Reef Road between Johannesburg and the mining towns—they carry the stuff and have DAN-GER—EXPLOSIVES painted on them. The man sits there, with an iron chain looped across his little seat to keep him from being thrown into the road, and he clutches his flag like a kid with a balloon. That's how Josias was, too. Of course, if you didn't take any notice of the warning and went on and crashed into the truck, he would be the first to be blown to high heaven and hell, but he always just sits there, this chap, as if he has no idea when he was born or that he might not die in a bed an old man of eighty. As if the dust in his eyes and the racket of the truck are going to last for ever.

My sister knew she had a good man but she never said anything about being afraid of this job. She only grumbled in winter, when he was stuck out there in the cold and used to get a cough (she's a nurse), and in summer when it rained all day and she said he would land up with rheumatism, crippled, and then who would give him work? The dynamite people? I don't think it ever came into her head that any day, every day, he could be blown up instead of coming home in the evening. Anyway, you wouldn't have thought so by the way she took it when he told us what it was he was going to have to do.

I was working down at a garage in town, that time, at the petrol pumps, and I was eating before he came in because I was on the night shift. Emma had the water ready for him and he had a wash without saying much, as usual, but then he didn't speak when they sat down to eat, either, and when his fingers went into the mealie meal he seemed to forget what it was he was holding and not to be able to shape it into a mouthful. Emma must have thought he felt too dry to eat, because she got up and brought him a jam tin of the beer she had made for Saturday. He drank it and then sat back and looked from her to me, but she said 'Why don't you eat?' and he began to, slowly. She said, 'What's the matter with you?' He got up and yawned and yawned, showing those brown chipped teeth that remind me of the big ape at the Johannesburg zoo that I saw once when I went with the school. He went into the other room of the house, where he and Emma slept, and he came back with his pipe. He filled it carefully, the way a poor man does; I saw, as soon as I went to work at the filling station, how the white men fill their pipes, stuffing the tobacco in, picking out any bits they don't like the look of, shoving the tin half-shut back into the glove-box of the car. 'I'm going down to Sela's place,' said Emma. 'I can go with Willie on his way to work if you don't want to come.'

'No. Not tonight. You stay here.' Josias always speaks like this, the short words of a schoolmaster or a boss-boy, but if you hear the way he says them, you know he is not really ordering you around at all, he is only asking you.

'No, I told her I'm coming.' Emma said, in the voice of a woman having her own way in a little thing.

'Tomorrow.' Josias began to yawn again, looking at us with wet eyes. 'Go to bed,' Emma said. 'I won't be late.'

'No, no, I want to . . .' He blew a sigh. 'When he's gone, man—' He moved his pipe at me. 'I'll tell you later.'

Emma laughed. 'What can you tell me that Willie can't hear.' I've lived with them ever since they were married. Emma always was the one who looked after me, even before, when I was a little kid. It was true that whatever happened to us happened to us together. He looked at me; I suppose he saw that I was a man, now: I was in my blue overalls with *Shell* on the pocket and everything.

He said, 'They want me to do something . . . a job with the truck.'

Josias used to turn out regularly to political meetings and he took part in a few protests before everything went underground, but he had never been more than one of the crowd. We had Mandela and the rest of the leaders, cut out of the paper, hanging on the wall, but he had never known, personally, any of them. Of course there were his friends Ndhlovu and Seb Masinde who said they had gone underground and who occasionally came late at night for a meal or slept in my bed for a few hours.

'They want to stop the truck on the road—'

'Stop it?' Emma was like somebody stepping into cold dark water;

with every word that was said she went deeper. 'But how can you do it—when? Where will they do it?' She was wild, as if she must go out and prevent it all happening right then.

I felt that cold water of Emma's rising round the belly because Emma and I often had the same feelings, but I caught also, in Josias's not looking at me, a signal Emma couldn't know. Something in me jumped at it like catching a swinging rope. 'They want the stuff inside . . .?'

Nobody said anything.

I said, 'What a lot of big bangs you could make with that, man,' and then shut up before Josias needed to tell me to.

'So what're you going to do?' Emma's mouth stayed open after she had spoken, the lips pulled back.

'They'll tell me everything. I just have to give them the best place on the road—that'll be the Free State road, the others're too busy . . . and . . . the time when we pass . . .'

'You'll be dead.' Emma's head was shuddering and her whole body shook; I've never seen anybody give up like that. He was dead already, she saw it with her eyes and she was kicking and screaming without knowing how to show it to him. She looked like she wanted to kill Josias herself, for being dead. 'That'll be the finish, for sure. He's got a gun, the white man in front, hasn't he, you told me. And the one with him? They'll kill you. You'll go to prison. They'll take you to Pretoria jail and hang you by the rope . . . Yes, he's got the gun, you told me, didn't you—many times you told me—'

'The others've got guns too. How d'you think they can hold us up? They've got guns and they'll come all round him. It's all worked out—'

'The one in front will shoot you, I know it, don't tell me, I know what I say . . .' Emma went up and down and around till I thought she would push the walls down—they wouldn't have needed much pushing, in that house in Alexandra Township—and I was scared of her. I don't mean for what she would do to me if I got in her way, or to Josias, but for what might happen to her: something like taking a fit or screaming that none of us would be able to forget.

I don't think Josias was sure about doing the job before but he wanted to do it now. 'No shooting. Nobody will shoot me. Nobody will know that I know anything. Nobody will tell them anything. I'm held up just the same like the others! Same as the white man in front! Who can shoot me? They can shoot me for that?'

'Someone else can go, I don't want it, do you hear? You will stay at home, I will say you are sick . . . You will be killed, they will shoot you . . . Josias, I'm telling you, I don't want . . . I won't . . .'

I was waiting my chance to speak, all the time, and I felt Josias was waiting to talk to someone who had caught the signal. I said quickly, while she went on and on, 'But even on that road there are some cars?'

'Roadblocks,' he said, looking at the floor. 'They've got the signs, the ones you see when a road's being dug up, and there'll be some men with picks. After the truck goes through they'll block the road so that any other cars turn off onto the old road there by Kalmansdrif. The same thing on the other side, two miles on. There where the farm road goes down to Nek Halt.'

'Hell, man! Did you have to pick that part of the road?'

'I know it like this yard. Don't I?'

Emma stood there, between the two of us, while we discussed the whole business. We didn't have to worry about anyone hearing, not only because Emma kept the window wired up in that kitchen, but also because the yard the house was in was a real Alexandra Township one, full of babies yelling and people shouting, night and day, not to mention the transistors playing in the houses all round. Emma was looking at us all the time and out of the corner of my eye I could see her big front going up and down fast in the neck of her dress.

`. . . so they're going to tie you up as well as the others?'

He drew on his pipe to answer me.

We thought for a moment and then grinned at each other; it was the first time for Josias, that whole evening.

Emma began collecting the dishes under our noses. She dragged the tin bath of hot water from the stove and washed up. 'I said I'm taking my day off on Wednesday. I suppose this is going to be next week.' Suddenly, yet talking as if carrying on where she let up, she was quite different.

'I don't know.'

'Well, I have to know because I suppose I must be at home.'

'What must you be at home for?' said Josias.

'If the police come I don't want them talking to *him*,' she said, looking at us both without wanting to see us.

'The police—' said Josias, and jerked his head to send them running, while I laughed, to show her.

'And I want to know what I must say.'

'What must you say? Why? They can get my statement from me when they find us tied up. In the night I'll be back here myself.'

'Oh yes,' she said, scraping the mealie meal he hadn't eaten back into the pot. She did everything as usual; she wanted to show us nothing was going to wait because of this big thing, she must wash the dishes and put ash on the fire. 'You'll be back, oh yes.—Are you going to sit here all night, Willie?—Oh yes, you'll be back.'

And then, I think, for a moment Josias saw himself dead, too; he didn't answer when I took my cap and said, so long, from the door.

I knew it must be a Monday. I notice that women quite often don't remember ordinary things like this, I don't know what they think about—for instance, Emma didn't catch on that it must be Monday, next Monday or the one after, some Monday for sure, because Monday was the day that we knew Josias went with the truck to the Free State mines. It was Friday when he told us and all day Saturday I had a terrible feeling that it was going to be *that* Monday, and it would be all over before I could—what? I didn't know, man. I felt I must at least see where it was going to happen. Sunday I was off work and I took my bicycle and rode into town before there was even anybody in the streets and went to the big station and found that although there wasn't a train on Sundays that would take me all the way, I could get one that would take me about thirty miles. I had to pay to put the bike in the luggage van as well as for my ticket, but I'd got my wages on Friday. I got off at the nearest halt to Kalmansdrif and then I asked people along the road the best way. It was a long ride, more than two hours. I came out on the main road from the sand road just at the turn-off Josias had told me about. It was just like he said: a tin sign KALMANSDRIF pointing down the road I'd come from. And the nice blue tarred road, smooth, straight ahead: was I glad to get on to it! I hadn't taken much notice of the country so far, while I was sweating along, but from then on I woke up and saw everything. I've only got to think about it to see it again now. The veld is flat round about there, it was the end of winter, so the grass was dry. Quite far away and very far apart, there was a hill and then another, sticking up in the middle of nothing, pink colour, and with its point cut off like the neck of a bottle. Ride and ride, these hills never got any nearer and there were none beside the road. It all looked empty and the sky much bigger than the ground, but there were some people there. It's funny you don't notice them like you do in town. All our people, of course; there were barbed-wire fences, so it must have been white farmers' land, but they've got the water and their houses are far off the road and you can usually see them only by the big dark trees that hide them. Our people had mud houses and there would be three or four in the same place made bare by goats and people's feet. Often the huts were near a kind of crack in the ground, where the little kids played and where, I suppose, in summer, there was water. Even now the women were managing to do washing in some places. I saw children run to the road to jig about and stamp when cars passed, but the men and women took no interest in what was up there. It was funny to think that I was just like them, now, men and women who are always busy inside themselves with jobs, plans, thinking about how to get money or how to talk to some-one about something important, instead of like the children, as I used to be only a few years ago, taking in each small thing around them as it happens.

Still, there were people living pretty near the road. What would they do if they saw the dynamite truck held up and a fight going on? (I couldn't think of it, then, in any other way except like I'd seen hold-ups in West-erns, although I've seen plenty of fighting, all my life, among the Location gangs and drunks—I was ashamed not to be able to forget those kid-stuff Westerns at a time like this.) Would they go running away to the white farmer? Would somebody jump on a bike and go for the police? Or if there was no bike, what about a horse? I saw someone riding a horse.

I rode slowly to the next turn-off, the one where a farm road goes down to Nek Halt. There it was, just like Josias said. Here was where the other roadblock would be. But when he spoke about it there was nothing inbetween! No people, no houses, no flat veld with hills on it! It had been just one of those things grown-ups see worked out in their heads: while all the time, here it was, a real place where people had cooking fires, I could hear a herdboy yelling at a dirty bundle of sheep, a big bird I've never seen in town balanced on the barbed-wire fence right in front of me . . . I got off my bike and it flew away.

I sat a minute on the side of the road. I'd had a cold drink in an Indian shop in the dorp where I'd got off the train, but I was dry again inside my mouth, while plenty of water came out of my skin, I can tell you. I rode back down the road looking for the exact place I would choose if I was Josias. There was a stretch where there was only one kraal with two houses, and that quite a way back from the road. Also there was a dip where the road went over a donga. Old stumps of trees and nothing but cows' business down there; men could hide. I got off again and had a good look round.

But I wondered about the people, up top. I don't know why it was, I wanted to know about those people just as though I was going to have to go and live with them or something. I left the bike down in the donga and crossed the road behind a Cadillac going so fast the air smacked together after it, and I began to trek over the veld to the houses. I know most of our people live like this, in the veld, but I'd never been into houses like that before. I was born in some Location (I don't know which one, I must ask Emma one day) and Emma and I lived in Moroka with our grand-mother. Our mother worked in town and she used to come and see us sometimes, but we never saw our father and Emma thinks perhaps we didn't have the same father, because she remembers a man before I was born, and after I was born she didn't see him again. I don't really remem-ber anyone, from when I was a little kid, except Emma. Emma dragging me along so fast my arm almost came off my body, because we had nearly been caught by the Indian while stealing peaches from his lorry: we did that every day.

We lived in one room with our grandmother but it was a tin house with a number and later on there was a streetlight at the corner. These houses I was coming to had a pattern all over them marked into the mud they were built of. There was a mound of dried cows' business, as tall as I was, stacked up in a pattern, too. And then the usual junk our people have, just like in the Location: old tins, broken things collected from white people's rubbish heaps. The fowls ran sideways from my feet and two old men let their talking die away into ahas and ehês as I came up. I greeted them the right way to greet old men and they nodded and went on ehêing and ahaing to show that they had been greeted properly. One of them had very clean ragged trousers tied with string and he sat on the ground, but the other, sitting on a bucket-seat that must have been taken from some scrapyard car, was dressed in a way I've never seen—from the old days, I suppose. He wore a black suit with very wide trousers, laced boots, a stiff white collar and black tie, and on top of it all, a broken old hat. It was Sunday, of course, so I suppose he was all dressed up. I've heard that these people who work for farmers wear sacks most of the time. The old ones didn't ask me what I wanted there. They just peered at me with their eyes gone the colour of soapy water because they were so old. And I didn't know what to say because I hadn't thought what I was going to say, I'd just walked. Then a little kid slipped out of the dark doorway quick as a cockroach. I thought perhaps everyone else was out because it was Sunday but then a voice called from inside the other house, and when the child didn't answer, called again, and a woman came to the doorway.

I said my bicycle had a puncture and could I have some water.

She said something into the house and in a minute a girl, about fifteen she must've been, edged past her carrying a paraffin tin and went off to fetch water. Like all the girls that age, she never looked at you. Her body shook under an ugly old dress and she almost hobbled in her hurry to get away. Her head was tied up in a rag-doek right down to the eyes the way old-fashioned people do, otherwise she would have been quite pretty, like any other girl. When she had gone a little way the kid went pumping after her, panting, yelling, opening his skinny legs wide as scissors over stones and antheaps, and then he caught up with her and you could see that right away she was quite different, I knew how it was, she yelled at him, you heard her laughter as she chased him with the tin, whirled around from out of his clutching hands, struggled with him; they were together like Emma and I used to be when we got away from the old lady, and from the school, and everybody. And Emma was also one of our girls who have the big strong comfortable bodies of mothers even when they're still kids, maybe it comes from always lugging the smaller one round on their backs.

A man came out of the house behind the woman and was friendly. His hair had the dusty look of someone who's been sleeping off drink. In fact, he was still a bit heavy with it.

'You coming from Jo'burg?'

But I wasn't going to be caught out being careless at all, Josias could count on me for that.

'Vereeniging.'

He thought there was something funny there—nobody dresses like a Jo'burger, you could always spot us a mile off—but he was too full to follow it up.

He stood stretching his sticky eyelids open and then he fastened on me the way some people will do: 'Can't you get me work there where you are?'

'What kind of work?'

He waved a hand describing me. 'You got a good work.'

' 'Sall right.'

'Where you working now?'

'Garden boy.'

He tittered, 'Look like you work in town,' shook his head.

I was surprised to find the woman handing me a tin of beer, and I squatted on the ground to drink it. It's mad to say that a mud house can be pretty, but those patterns made in the mud looked nice. They must have been done with a sharp stone or stick when the mud was smooth and wet, the shapes of things like big leaves and moons filled in with lines that went all one way in this shape, another way in that, so that as you looked at the walls in the sun, some shapes were dark and some were light, and if you moved the light ones went dark and the dark ones got light instead. The girl came back with the heavy tin of water on her head making her neck thick. I washed out the jam tin I'd had the beer in and filled it with water. When I thanked them, the old men stirred and ahaed and ehêd again. The man made as if to walk a bit with me, but I was lucky he didn't go more than a few yards. 'No good,' he said. 'Every morning, five o'clock, and the pay—very small.'

How I would have hated to be him, a man already married and with big children, working all his life in the fields wearing sacks. When you think like this about someone he seems something you could never possibly be, as if it's his fault, and not just the chance of where he happened to be born. At the same time I had a crazy feeling I wanted to tell him something wonderful, something he'd never dreamed could happen, something he'd fall on his knees and thank me for. I wanted to say, 'Soon you'll be the farmer yourself and you'll have shoes like me and your girl will get water from your windmill. Because on Monday, or another Monday, the truck will stop down there and all the stuff will be taken away and they—Josias, me; even you, yes—we'll win forever.' But instead all I said was, 'Who did that on your house?' He didn't understand and I made a drawing in the air with my hand. 'The women,' he said, not interested.

Down in the donga I sat a while and then threw away the tin and rode off without looking up again to where the kraal was.

It wasn't that Monday. Emma and Josias go to bed very early and of course they were asleep by the time I got home late on Sunday night— Emma thought I'd been with the boys I used to go around with at weekends. But Josias got up at half past four every morning, then, because it was a long way from the Location to where the dynamite factory was, and although I didn't usually even hear him making the fire in the kitchen which was also where I was sleeping, that morning I was awake the moment he got out of bed next door. When he came into the kitchen I was sitting up in my blankets and I whispered loudly, 'I went there yesterday. I saw the turn-off and everything. Down there by the donga, ay? Is that the place?'

He looked at me, a bit dazed. He nodded. Then: 'Wha'd' you mean you went there?'

'I could see that's the only good place. I went up to the house, too, just to see . . . the people are all right. Not many. When it's not Sunday there may be nobody there but the old man—there were two, I think one was just a visitor. The man and the women will be over in the fields somewhere, and that must be quite far, because you can't see the mealies from the road . . .' I could feel myself being listened to carefully, getting in with him (and if with him, with *them*) while I was talking, and I knew exactly what I was saying, absolutely clearly, just as I would know exactly what I was doing. He began to question me; but like I was an older man or a clever one; he didn't know what to say. He drank his tea while I told him all about it. He was thinking. Just before he left he said, 'I shouldn't've told you.'

I ran after him, outside, into the yard. It was still dark. I blurted in the same whisper we'd been using. 'Not today, is it?' I couldn't see his face properly but I knew he didn't know whether to answer or not. 'Not today.' I was so happy I couldn't go to sleep again.

In the evening Josias managed to make some excuse to come out with me alone for a bit. He said, 'I told them you were a hundred-per-cent. It's just the same as if I know.' 'Of course, no difference. I just haven't had much of a chance to do anything . . .' I didn't carry on: ' . . . because I was too young'; we didn't want to bring Emma into it. And anyway, no one but a real kid is too young any more. Look at the boys who are up for sabotage. I said, 'Have they got them all?'

He hunched his shoulders.

'I mean, even the ones for the picks and spades . . .?'

He wouldn't say anything, but I knew I could ask. 'Oh, boetie, man, even just to keep a lookout, there on the road . . .'

I know he didn't want it but once they knew I knew, and that I'd been there and everything, they were keen to use me. At least that's what I think. I never went to any meetings or anything where it was planned, and beforehand I only met the two others who were with me at the turn-off in the end, and we were told exactly what we had to do by Seb Masinde. Of course, Josias and I never said a word to Emma. The Monday that we did it was three weeks later and I can tell you, although a lot's happened to me since then, I'll never forget the moment when we flagged the truck through with Josias sitting there on the back in his little seat. Josias! I wanted to laugh and shout there in the veld; I didn't feel scared—what was there to be scared of, he'd been sitting on a load of dynamite every day of his life for years now, so what's the odds. We had one of those tins of fire and a bucket of tar and the real ROAD CLOSED signs from the P.W.D. and everything went smooth at our end. It was at the Nek Halt end that the trouble started when one of these A.A. patrol bikes had to come along (Josias says it was something new, they'd never met a patrol on that road that time of day, before) and get suspicious about the block there. In the meantime the truck was stopped all right but someone was shot and

Josias tried to get the gun from the white man up in front of the truck and there was a hell of a fight and they had to make a getaway with the stuff in a car and van back through our block, instead of taking over the truck and driving it to a hiding place to offload. More than half the stuff had to be left behind in the truck. Still, they got clean away with what they did get and it was never found by the police. Whenever I read in the papers here that something's been blown up back at home, I wonder if it's still one of our bangs. Two of our people got picked up right away and some more later and the whole thing was all over the papers with speeches by the chief of Special Branch about a master plot and everything. But Josias got away okay. We three chaps at the road block just ran into the veld to where there were bikes hidden. We went to a place we'd been told in Rustenburg district for a week and then we were told to get over to Bechuanaland. It wasn't so bad; we had no money but around Rustenburg it was easy to pinch pawpaws and oranges off the farms . . . Oh, I sent a message to Emma that I was all right; and at that time it didn't seem true that I couldn't go home again.

But in Bechuanaland it was different. We had no money, and you don't find food on trees in that dry place. They said they would send us money; it didn't come. But Josias was there too, and we stuck together; people hid us and we kept going. Planes arrived and took away the big shots and the white refugees but although we were told we'd go too, it never came off. We had no money to pay for ourselves. There were plenty others like us in the beginning. At last we just walked, right up Bechuanaland and through Northern Rhodesia to Mbeya, that's over the border in Tanganyika, where we were headed for. A long walk; took Josias and me months. We met up with a chap who'd been given a bit of money and from there sometimes we went by bus. No one asks questions when you're nobody special and you walk, like all the other African people themselves, or take the buses, that the whites never use; it's only if you've got the money for cars or to arrive at the airports that all these things happen that you read about: getting sent back over the border, refused permits and so on. So we got here, to Tanganyika at last, down to this town of Dar es Salaam where we'd been told we'd be going.

There's a refugee camp here and they give you a shilling or two a day until you get work. But it's out of town, for one thing, and we soon left there and found a room down in the shanty town. There are some nice buildings, of course, in the real town—nothing like Johannesburg or Durban, though—and that used to be the white town, the whites who are left still live there, but the Africans with big jobs in the government and so on live there too. Some of our leaders who are refugees like us live in these houses and have big cars; everyone knows they're important men, here, not like at home where if you're black you're just rubbish for the Locations. The people down where we lived are very poor and it's hard to get work because they haven't got enough work for themselves, but I've got my Standard Seven and I managed to get a small job as a clerk. Josias never found steady work. But that didn't matter so much because the big thing was that Emma was able to come to join us after five months, and she and I earn the money. She's a nurse, you see, and Africanization started in the hospitals and the government was short of nurses. So Emma got the chance to come up with a party of them sent for specially from South Africa and Rhodesia. We were very lucky because it's impossible for people to get their families up here. She came in a plane paid for by the government, and she and the other girls had their photograph taken for the newspaper as they got off at the airport. That day she came we took her to the beach, where everyone can bathe, no restrictions, and for a cool drink in one of the hotels (she'd never been in a hotel before), and we walked up and down the road along the bay where everyone walks and where you can see the ships coming in and going out so near that the men out there wave to you. Whenever we bumped into anyone else from home they would stop and ask her about home, and how everything was. Josias and I couldn't stop grinning to hear us all, in the middle of Dar, talking away in our language about the things we know. That day it was like it had happened already: the time when we are home again and everything is our way.

Well, that's nearly three years ago, since Emma came. Josias has been sent away now and there's only Emma and me. That was always the idea, to send us away for training. Some go to Ethiopia and some go to Algeria and all over the show and by the time they come back there won't be anything Verwoerd's men know in the way of handling guns and so on that they won't know better. That's for a start. I'm supposed to go too, but some of us have been waiting a long time. In the meantime I go to work and I walk about this place in the evenings and I buy myself a glass of beer in a bar when I've got money. Emma and I have still got the flat we had before Josias left and two nurses from the hospital pay us for the other bedroom. Emma still works at the hospital but I don't know how much longer. Most days now since Josias's gone she wants me to walk up to fetch her from the hospital when she comes off duty, and when I get under the trees on the drive I see her staring out looking for me as if I'll never turn up ever again. Every day it's like that. When I come up she smiles and looks like she used to for a minute but by the time we're ten yards on the road she's shaking and shaking her head until the tears come, and saying over and over, 'A person can't stand it, a person can't stand it.' She said right from the beginning that the hospitals here are not like the hospitals at home, where the nurses have to know their job. She's got a whole ward in her charge and now she says they're worse and worse and she can't trust anyone to do anything for her. And the staff don't like having strangers working with them anyway. She tells me every day like she's telling me for the first time. Of course it's true that some of the people don't like us being here. you know how it is, people haven't got enough jobs to go round, themselves. But I don't take much notice;

I'll be sent off one of these days and until then I've got to eat and that's that.

The flat is nice with a real bathroom and we are paying off the table and six chairs she liked so much, but when we walk in, her face is terrible. She keeps saying the place will never be straight. At home there was only a táp in the yard for all the houses but she never said it there. She doesn't sit down for more than a minute without getting up at once again, but you can't get her to go out, even on these evenings when it's so hot you can't breathe. I go down to the market to buy the food now, she says she can't stand it. When I asked why — because at the beginning she used to like the market, where you can pick a live fowl for yourself, quite cheap—she said those little rotten tomatoes they grow here, and dirty people all shouting and she can't understand. She doesn't sleep, half the time, at night, either, and lately she wakes me up. It happened only last night. She was standing there in the dark and she said, 'I felt bad.' I said, 'I'll make you some tea,' though what good could tea do. 'There must be something the matter with me,' she says. 'I must go to the doctor tomorrow.'

'Is it pains again or what?'

She shakes her head slowly, over and over, and I know she's going to cry again. 'A place where there's no one. I get up and look out the window and it's just like I'm not awake. And every day, every day. I can't ever wake up and be out of it. I always see this town.'

Of course it's hard for her. I've picked up Swahili and I can get around all right; I mean I can always talk to anyone if I feel like it, but she hasn't learnt more than *ahsante*—she could've picked it up just as easily, but she *can't*, if you know what I mean. It's just a noise to her, like dogs barking or those black crows in the palm trees. When anyone does come here to see her — someone else from home, usually, or perhaps I bring the Rhodesian who works where I do—she only sits there and whatever anyone talks about she doesn't listen until she can sigh and say, 'Heavy, heavy. Yes, for a woman alone. No friends, nobody. For a woman alone, I can tell you.'

Last night I said to her, 'It would be worse if you were at home, you wouldn't have seen Josias or me for a long time.'

But she said, 'Yes, it would be bad. Sela and everybody. And the old crowd at the hospital—but just the same, it would be bad. D'you remember how we used to go right into Jo'burg on my Saturday off? The people—ay! Even when you were twelve you used to be scared you'd lose me.'

'I wasn't scared, you were the one was scared to get run over sometimes.' But in the Location when we stole fruit, and sweets from the shops, Emma could always grab me out of the way of trouble, Emma always saved me. The same Emma. And yet it's not the same. And what could I do for her?

I suppose she wants to be back there now. But still she wouldn't be the same. I don't often get the feeling she knows what I'm thinking about, any more, or that I know what she's thinking, but she said, 'You and he go off, you come back or perhaps you don't come back, you know what you must do. But for a woman? What shall I do there in my life? What shall I do here? What time is this for a woman?'

It's hard for her. Emma. She'll say all that often now, I know. She tells me everything so many times. Well, I don't mind it when I fetch her from the hospital and I don't mind going to the market. But straight after we've eaten, now, in the evenings, I let her go through it once and then I'm off. To walk in the streets when it gets a bit cooler in the dark. I don't know why it is, but I'm thinking so bloody hard about getting out there in the streets that I push down my food as fast as I can without her noticing. I'm so keen to get going I feel queer, kind of tight and excited. Just until I can get out and not hear. I wouldn't even mind skipping the meal. In the streets in the evening everyone is out. On the grass along the bay the fat Indians in their white suits with their wives in those fancy coloured clothes. Men and their girls holding hands. Old watchmen like beggars, sleeping in the doorways of the shut shops. Up and down people walk, walk, just sliding one foot after the other because now and then, like somebody lifting a blanket, there's air from the sea. She should come out for a bit of air in the evening, man. It's an old, old place this, they say. Not the buildings, I mean; but the place. They say ships were coming here before even a place like London was a town. She thought the bay was so nice, that first day. The lights from the ships run all over the water and the palms show up a long time even after it gets dark. There's a smell I've smelled ever since we've been here—three years! I don't mean the smells in the shanty town; a special warm night-smell. You can even smell it at three in the morning. I've smelled it when I was standing about with Emma, by the window; it's as hot in the middle of the night here as it is in the middle of the day, at home—funny, when you look at the stars and the dark. Well, I'll be going off soon. It can't be long now. Now that Josias is gone. You've just got to wait your time; they haven't forgotten about you. Dar es Salaam. Dar. Sometimes I walk with another chap from home, he says some things, makes you laugh! He says the old watchmen who sleep in the doorways get their wives to come there with them. Well, I haven't seen it. He says we're definitely going with the next lot. Dar es Salaam. Dar. One day I suppose I'll remember it and tell my wife I stayed three years there, once. I walk and walk, along the bay, past the shops and hotels and the German church and the big bank, and through the mud streets between old shacks and stalls. It's dark there and full of other walking shapes as I wander past light coming from the cracks in the walls, where the people are in their homes.

SUGGESTIONS FOR WRITING AND DISCUSSION

1. Look at the dictionary definitions of *naivete* and *innocence*. What is the difference? Which term best describes the narrator of this story? Why

2. In a two- to three-page essay discuss the ways in which Willy matures in the course of three years and also the ways in which he remains the same.
3. The relationship between Willy and Emma is at the center of the story. Discuss how this relationship evolves.
4. Do you think Gordimer is sympathetic to apartheid or opposes it? Give evidence to support your answer. Compare this story with Barrio's "The Campesinos." Which has the more overt political message? Which is the more effective?
5. Various kinds of homes are described in this story. Examine these descriptions and in a short essay discuss their relevance to the theme of the story.

Raymond Barrio (American, 1921–

The Campesinos

Dawn.

Outside, the coolest night.

Outside, the soft, plush, lingering sheen of nightlight.

Within his breezy air-conditioned shack Manuel lay half asleep in the middle of the biggest apricot orchard in the world, nothing but apricot trees all around, in one of a long double row of splintered boards nailed together and called a shack. A migrant's shack. He struggled to come awake. Everything seemed to be plugged up. A distant roar closed in steadily. He awoke in a cold sweat. He sat up abruptly in the cold darkness.

The roar grew louder and louder. He leaned forward, hunched in his worn, torn covers, and peered through the grimy window. A huge black monster was butting through the trees, moving and pitching about, its headlights piercing the armor of night, then swinging away again as the roaring lessened. Manuel smiled. The roar of a tractor. He rubbed the sleep from his eyes. He stretched his aching arms and shoulders. He thought of Lupe and the kids back in Drawbridge.

On the very brink of the full onslaught of summer's punishing heat, with the plums and pears and apricots fattening madly on every vine, branch, bush, and limb in every section of every county in the country, pickers were needed right now immediately on every farm and orchard everywhere and all at once. The frantic demand for pickers increased rapidly as the hot days mounted. That sure looked good out there. What a cool job that was. Driving a tractor at night. Maybe he could get Ramiro to teach him to drive one.

Manuel well knew what his physical energy was.

His physical energy was his total worldly wealth.

No matter how anxious he was to work, he did have his limit. He had to rest his body. The finger joint he'd injured still hurt. He missed Lupe's chatter. He'd signed up with that shrewd contractor, Roberto Morales, that shrewd, fat, energetic contratista, manipulator of migrating farm workers, that smiling middleman who promised to deliver so many hands to the moon at such and such a time at such and such an orchard at such and such a price, for such a small commission. A tiny percentage. Such a little slice. Silvery slavery—modernized.

Roberto Morales, an organization man, was a built-in toll gate. A parasite. A collector of drops of human sweat. An efficiency expert. Had he not been Mexican, he would have made a fantastic capitalist, like Turner. He was Turner upside down. Sucking blood from his own people. With the help and convenient connivance of Turner's insatiable greed.

The agricultural combine's imperative need to have its capital personally plucked when ripe so as to materialize its honest return on its critical investment in order to keep its executives relaxed in blue splendor in far-off desert pools, was coupled to the migrant workers' inexorable and uncompromising need to earn pennies to fend off stark starvation.

Good money.

Good dough.

Good hard work.

Pick fast.

Penny a bucket.

Check off.

Get the count right.

Cotsplumsprunespeachesbeanspeas.

Pods.

The seed of life.

And:—don't complain. . . .

Manuel lay back in the blackness. As the darkness receded and the light of day started creeping imperiously across its own land, he thought that these powerful orchard land owners were awfully generous to give him such a beautiful hostel to stop in overnight. The skylight hotel. There the land stood. A heaving, sleeping mother earth. A marvelous land. Ripening her fruit once again. Once more. Ripening it fatly and pregnantly for the thousandth time. It must be plucked said the wise man. For it cannot hang around on limbs a minute extra. At no man's convenience. As soon as the baby's ready. Lush and full of plump juices. Hugging its new seed around its own ripeness. The plum and the cot and the peach and the pear must plummet again to earth. Carrying the seed of its own delicate rebirth and redestruction back home to earth again. A clever mother earth who in her all-but-unbelievable generosity was capable of giving man fivefold, tenfold the quanity of fruit he could himself eat, five times fifty, and yet the pickers were never paid enough to satisfy their hunger beyond their actual working hours. And yet it was called a moral world. An ethical world. A good world. A happy world. A world full of golden opportunities. Manuel simply couldn't figure it out.

What was wrong with the figures?

Why was mother earth so generous? And men so greedy?

You got twenty-five cents a basket for tomatoes. A dollar a crate for some fruit. You had to work fast. That was the whole thing. A frantic lunatic to make your barely living wage. If you had no rent to pay, it was OK.

You were ahead, amigo. Pay rent, however, stay in one place, and you couldn't migrate after the other easy pickings. The joy of working was looking over your dreams locked to hunger.

Manuel studied the whorls in the woodwork whirling slowly, revealed in the faint crepuscular light penetrating his shack. His cot was a slab of half-inch plywood board twenty-two inches wide and eight feet long, the width of the shack, supported by two two-by-four beams butted up against the wall at both ends beneath the side window. The shack itself was eight by twelve by seven feet high. Its roof had a slight pitch. The rain stains in the ceiling planks revealed the ease with which the rain penetrated. Except for two small panes of glass exposed near the top. most of the window at the opposite end was boarded up. A single, old, paint-encrusted door was the only entry. No curtains. No interior paneling. Just a shack. A shack of misery. He found he was able to admire and appreciate the simplicity and the strength of the construction. He counted the upright studs, level, two feet apart, the double joists across the top supporting the roof. Cracks and knotholes aplenty, in the wall siding, let in bright chinks of light during the day and welcome wisps of clear fresh air at night. The rough planking of the siding was stained dark. The floor was only partly covered with odd sections of plywood. Some of the rough planking below was exposed, revealing cracks leading down to the cool black earth beneath. A small thick table was firmly studded to a portion of the wall opposite the door. A few small pieces of clear lumber stood bunched together, unsung, unused, unhurried, in the far corner. An overhead shelf, supported from the ceiling by a small extending perpendicular arm, containing some boxes of left-over chemicals and fertilizers, completed the furnishings in his temporary abode.

It was habitable.

He could raise his family in it.

If they were rabbits.

The first rays of a brute new day clinked in through the small rectangle of panes. The ray hovered, then peaked, then rested on the covers pushed up by his knees. He recalled his mountain trips with his uncle to the great forbidding barrancas near Durango in Central Mexico, and stopping to rest in the middle of the wild woods, and coming unexpectedly upon a crumbling, splintered hulk of a shack that was all falling apart. It barely gave them shelter from the sudden pelting storm they were trying to escape, he as a young frightened boy, but shelter it was—and how beautiful that experience was, then, for they were free, daring, adventurers, out there in that wilderness, alone and daring, with nothing between them and God's own overpowering nature, alone. They belonged to nothing. To no one. But themselves. They were dignity purified. No one forced them to go or stay there. They were delighted and grateful to the shack. For the protection it afforded them. Though it was hardly more than a ratty pile of splinters. Far worse than this one he was now occupying . . . but also somehow far more beautiful in his memory.

And now. Here he was. Shut up in this miserable shack. So sturdily built. Thinking how it sickened him inside because it was more a jail cell than a shelter. He didn't care how comfortable and convenient the growers made the shacks for him. They were huts of slavery. What he wanted was an outlet for his pride. A sudden fierce wave of anger made him want to cross the shack with his fists. There had to be some way to cross the ungulfable bridge. Why was necessity always the bride of hunger? To be free . . . ah, and also to be able to eat all one wanted. My heart, mi corazon, why did work always have to blend with such misery? The welcome warmth of the sun's early rays, penetrating more, warmed his frame. But it was a false, false hope. He knew it. The work that lay ahead of him that day would drain and stupify and fatigue him once again to the point of senseless torpor, ready to fall over long before the work day was done. And that fatigue wasn't merely so bad to bear as the deadly repetitious monotony of never changing, never resting, doing the same plucking over and over and over again. But he had to do it. He had no choice. It was all he could do. It had to be done if he wanted the money. And he had to have the money, if he wanted to feed his family. The brain in his arms was his only capital. Not very much, true, but it was the only sacrifice he could offer the money gods, the only heart he could offer on a pyramid of gold.

His life. La gran vida.

Wide awake now, fully refreshed, his whole body lithe and toned, Manuel was ashamed to find himself eager to start in work, knowing that he would do well, but ashamed because he could think of nothing he would rather do more. The final step.

The final the final the final the final the final the final step.

To want to work oneself to death. A la muerte. It wasn't the work itself that bothered him. It was the total immersion, the endless, ceaseless, total use of all his energies and spirit and mind and being that tore him apart within. He didn't know what else he was good for or could do with his life. But there had to be something else. He had to be something more than a miserable plucking animal. Pluck pluck pluck. Feed feed feed. Glug glug glug. Dressing quickly, rolling up his blanket roll and stuffing it into a corner to use again that night, Manuel stepped coolly out into the morning sweetness and breathed the honey-scented humidity rinsing air rising from the honied soil, and joined the thickening throng of his fellow pluckers milling about the large open barn serving as a cookout. Feeding all the pickers was another of the fat man's unholy prerogatives, for he cheated and overpriced on meals too. Roberto Morales, the fat man, the shrewd contratista, was a bully man, busily darting his blob about, exhorting his priceless pickers to hurry, answering questions, giving advice, in the cool half-light, impatiently, pushing, giving orders. Manuel, in order to avoid having to greet him, scowled at his toes when Roberto came trouncing by, saying, ``Apurense, compañeros, hurry, hurry, hurry, amigos.'' Sure. Amigos. Si. Si. Frens. They all gulped their food down hurriedly, standing. Just like home. Paper plates, plastic cups. Wooden spoons. And bits of garbage flying into large canisters. Then in the still cool nightlike morning air, like a flood of disturbed birds, they all picked up their pails and filed into the orchard.

The apricots were plump.

Smooth.

A golden syrupy orange.

Manuel popped two into his mouth, enjoying their cool natural sweetness after the bitter coffee. He knew he could not eat too many. His stomach muscles would cramp. Other pickers started pulling rapidly away from him. Let them. Calmly he calculated the struggle. Start the pressure, slow, and keep it going steady. Piecework. Fill the bucket, fill another, and still another. The competition was among a set of savages, as savage for money as himself, savages with machetes, hacking their way through the thickets of modern civilization back to the good old Aztec days, waiting to see who'd be first in line to wrench his heart out. Savage beasts, eager to fill as many buckets as possible in as short a time as possible, cleaning out an entire orchard, picking everything in sight clean, tons of fruit, delivering every bit of ripe fruit to the accountants in their cool air-conditioned orifices.

The competition was not between pickers and growers.

It was between pickers—Jorge and Guillermo.

Between the poor and the hungry, the desperate, and the hunted, the slave and the slave, slob against slob, the depraved and himself. You were your own terrible boss. That was the cleverest part of the whole thing. The picker his own bone picker, his own willing built-in slave driver. God, that was good! That was where they reached into your scrotum and screwed you royally and drained your brain and directed your sinews and nerves and muscles with invisible fingers. To fatten their coffers. And drive you to your coffin. That sure was smart. Meant to be smart. Bookkeepers aren't dumb. You worked hard because you wanted to do that hard work above everything else. Pickfast pickhard pickfurious pick pick pick. They didn't need straw bosses studying your neck to see if you kept bobbing up and down to keep your picking pace up. Like the barn-stupid chicken, you drove yourself to do it. you were your own money monkey foreman, monkey on top of your own back.

You over-charged yourself.

With your own frenzy.

Neat.

You pushed your gut and your tired aching arms and your twitching legs pumping adrenalin until your tongue tasted like coarse sandpaper.

You didn't even stop to take a drink, let alone a piss, for fear you'd get fined, fired, or bawled out.

And then, after all that effort, you got your miserable pay.

Would the bobbing boss's sons stoop to that?

His fingers were loose and dexterous now. The plump orange balls plopped pitter patter like heavy drops of golden rain into his swaying, sweaty canvas bucket. His earnings depended entirely on how quickly he worked and how well he kept the pressure up. The morning sun was high. The sweet shade was fragrant and refreshing and comfortable under the leafy branches. The soil too was still cool and humid. It was going to be another hot one.

There.

Another row ended.

He swung around the end of the row and for a moment he was all alone, all by himself. He looked out far across the neighboring alfalfa field, dark green and rich and ripe. Then he looked at the long low Diablo Range close by, rising up into the misty pale blue air kept cool by the unseen bay nearby. This was all his. For a flowing, deceptive minute, all this rich, enormous terrain was all his. All this warm balmy baby air. All this healthful sunny breeze. All those hills, this rich fertile valley, these orchards, these tiled huertas, these magnificent farms all, all his . . . for his eyes to feast upon. It was a moment he wished he could capture forever and etch permanently on his memory, making it a part of living life for his heart to feast joyously on, forever. Why couldn't he stop? Why? Why couldn't he just put the bucket down and open his arms and walk into the hills and merge himself with the hills and just wander invisibly in the blue?

What Manuel couldn't really know was that he was completing yet another arc in the unending circle that had been started by one of his Mexican forebears exactly two hundred years before—for even the memory of history was also robbed from him—when Gaspar de Portola, hugging the coastline, nearing present-day San Francisco, climbed what is now Sweeney Ridge, and looked down upon San Francisco's magnificent land-locked Bay, overlooking what is now the International Airport.

Both Don Gaspar and Don Manuel were landlords and landless at precisely the same instant of viewing all this heady beauty. And both were equally dispossessed. Both were also possessed of a keen sense of pride and natural absorption with the ritual and mystery of all life. The living that looked mighty good in a flash to Manuel lasted a good deal longer for Don Gaspar whose stumbling accident swept him into the honored and indelible pages of glorious history.

Manuel was now a mere straw among the enormous sludge of humanity flowing past, a creature of limb and his own driving appetites, a creature of heed and need. Swinging around another end run he placed his ladder on the next heavy limb of the next pregnant tree. He reached up. He plucked bunches of small golden fruit with both hands. He worked like a frenzied windmill in slow motion. He cleared away an arc as far as the circumference of his plucking fingers permitted. A living model for da Vinci's outstretched man. Adam heeding God's moving finger. He moved higher. He repeated another circle. Then down and around again to another side of the tree, until he cleared it, cleared it of all visible, viable, delectable, succulent fruit. It was sweet work. The biggest difference between him and the honey-gathering ant was that the ant had a home.

Several pickers were halfway down the next row, well in advance of him. He was satisfied he was pacing himself well. Most of the band was still behind him. The moving sun, vaulting the sky dome's crackling earth parting with its bronzing rays, pounded its fierce heat into every dead and living crevice. Perspiration poured down his sideburns, down his forehead, down his cheek, down his neck, into his ears, off his chin. He tasted its saltiness with the tip of his dry tongue. He wished he'd brought some salt tablets. Roberto Morales wasn't about to worry about the pickers, and Manuel wasn't worried either. Despite the heat, he felt some protection from the ocean and bay. It had been much, much worse in Texas, and much hotter in Delano in the San Joaquin valley and worst of all in Satan's own land, the Imperial Valley.

No matter which way he turned, he was trapped in an endless maze of apricot trees, as though forever, neat rows of them, neatly planted, row after row, just like the blackest bars on the jails of hell. There had to be an end. There had to be. There—trapped. There had to be a way out. Locked. There had to be a respite. Animal. The buckets and the crates kept piling up higher. Brute. He felt alone. Though surrounded by other pickers. Beast. Though he was perspiring heavily, his shirt was powder dry. Savage. The hot dry air. The hot dry air sucking every drop of living moisture from his brute body. Wreck. He stopped and walked to the farthest end of the first row for some water, raised the dented dipper from the brute tank, drank the holy water in great brute gulps so he wouldn't have to savor its tastelessness, letting it spill down his torn shirt to cool his exhausted body, to replenish his brute cells and animal pores and stinking follicles and pig gristle, a truly refined wreck of an animal, pleased to meetcha. Predator.

Lunch.

Almost too exhausted to eat, he munched his cheese with tortillas, smoked on ashes, then lay back on the cool ground for half an hour. That short rest in the hot shade replenished some of his humor and resolve. He felt his spirit swell out again like a thirsty sponge in water.Then up again. The trees. The branches again. The briarly branches. The scratching leaves. The twigs tearing at his shirt sleeves. The ladder. The rough bark. The endlessly unending piling up of bucket upon box upon crate upon stack upon rack upon mound upon mountain. He picked a mountain of cots automatically. An automaton. A beast. A ray of enemy sun penetrated the tree that was hiding him and split his forehead open. His mind whirred. He blacked out. Luckily he'd been leaning against a heavy branch. His feet hooked to the ladder's rung. His half-filled bucket slipped from his grasp and fell in slow motion, splattering the fruit he'd so laboriously picked. To the ground. Roberto happened by and shook his head. ``Whatsamatter, can't you see straight, pendejo.'' Manuel was too tired even to curse. He should have had some salt pills.

Midafternoon.

The summer's fierce zenith passed overhead. It passed. Then

dropped. It started to light the ocean behind him, back of the hills. Sandy dreams. Cool nights. Cold drinks. Soft guitar music with Lupe sitting beside him. All wafting through his feverish moments. Tiredness drained his spirit of will. Exhaustion drained his mind. His fingers burned. His arms flailed the innocent trees. He was slowing down. He could hardly fill his last bucket. Suddenly the whistle blew. The day's work was at last ended.

Ended!

The contratista Roberto Morales stood there.

His feet straddled. Mexican style. A real robber. A Mexican general. A gentlemanly, friendly, polite, grinning, vicious, thieving brute. The worst kind. To his own people. Despite his being a fellow Mexican, despite his torn, old clothing, everyone knew what kind of clever criminal he was. Despite his crude, ignorant manner, showing that he was one of them, that he'd started with them, that he grew up with them, that he'd suffered all the sordid deprivations with them, he was actually the shrewdest, smartest, richest cannibal in forty counties around. They sure couldn't blame the gueros for this miscarriage. He was a crew chief. How could anyone know what he did to his own people? And what did the gueros care? So the anglo growers and guero executives, smiling in their cool filtered offices, puffing their elegant thin cigars, washed their clean blond bloodless dirtless hands of the whole matter. All they did was hire Roberto Morales. Firm, fair, and square. For an agreed-upon price. Good. How he got his people down to the pickings was no concern of theirs. They were honest, those gueros. They could sleep at night. They fulfilled their end of the bargain, and cheated no one. Their only crime; their only soul crime indeed was that they just didn't give a shit how that migratory scum lived. It was no concern of theirs. Their religion said it was no concern of theirs. Their wives said it was no concern of theirs. Their aldermen said it was no concern of theirs. Their—

Whenever Roberto Morales spoke, Manuel had to force himself not to answer. He had to keep his temper from flaring.

"Now," announced Morales at last, in his friendliest tone. "Now. I must take two cents from every bucket. I am sorry. There was a miscalculation. Everybody understands. Everybody?" He slid his eyes around smiling, palms up.

The tired, exhausted pickers gasped as one.

Yes. Everyone understood. Freezing in place. After all that hard work.

"Any questions, men?"

Still grinning, knowing, everyone realizing that he had the upper hand, that that would mean a loss of two or three dollars out of each picker's pay that day, a huge windfall for Morales.

"You promised to take nothing!" Manuel heard himself saying. Everyone turned in astonishment to stare at Manuel.

"I said two cents, hombre. You got a problem or what?"

"You promised."

The two men, centered in a huge ring of red-ringed eyes, glared at each other. Reaching for each other's jugular. The other exhausted animals studied the tableau through widening eyes. It was so unequal. Morales remained calm, confident, studying Manuel. As though memorizing his features. He had the whole advantage. Then, with his last remaining energy, Manuel lifted his foot and clumsily tipped over his own last bucket of cots. They rolled away in all directions around everyone's feet.

Roberto Morales' eyes blazed. His fists clenched. "You pick them up, Gutierrez."

So. He knew his name. After all. For answer, Manuel kicked over another bucket, and again the fruit rolled away in all directions.

Then an astonishing thing happened.

All the other pickers moved toward their own buckets still standing beside them on the ground awaiting the truck gatherer, and took an ominous position over them, straddling their feet over them. Without looking around, without taking his eyes off Manuel, Roberto Morales said sharply, "All right. All right, men, I shall take nothing this time."

Manuel felt a thrill of power course through his nerves.

He had never won anything before. He would have to pay for this, for his defiance, somehow, again, later. But he had shown defiance. He had salvaged his money savagely and he had earned respect from his fellow slaves. The gringo hijos de la chingada would never know of this little incident, and would probably be surprised, and perhaps even a little mortified, for a few minutes. But they wouldn't give a damn. It was bread, pan y tortillas out of his children's mouths. But they still wouldn't give a single damn. Manuel had wrenched Morales' greedy fingers away and removed a fat slug of a purse from his sticky grasp. And in his slow way, in his stupid, accidental, dangerous way, Manuel had made an extravagant discovery, as Don Gaspar had also made two centuries before, in almost exactly the same spot. And that was—that a man counted for something. For men, Manuel dimly suspected, are built for something more important and less trifling than the mere gathering of prunes and apricots, hour upon hour, decade upon decade, insensibly, mechanically, antlike. Men are built to experience a certain sense of honor and pride.

Or else they are dead before they die.

SUGGESTIONS FOR WRITING AND DISCUSSION

1. The language in this story is particularly rich in imagery that appeals to all the senses. List the ways Barrio's descriptions appeal to one of the senses.
2. Why does Barrio use a mixture of fairly long and extremely short sentences?
3. How is the end of the story foreshadowed?
4. Compare this story with "The Man Who Saw the Flood." How do the two authors approach somewhat similar subjects?

5. The final two lines of this story are the thesis of many of the other works in Struggles. In a two- to three-page essay, use this as a thesis for an essay about another work in this section.

Bernard Malamud (American, 1914–

Black Is My Favorite Color

Charity Sweetness sits in the toilet eating her two hard-boiled eggs while I'm having my ham sandwich and coffee in the kitchen. That's how it goes only don't get the idea of ghettoes. If there's a ghetto I'm the one that's in it. She's my cleaning woman from Father Divine and comes in once a week to my small three-room apartment on my day off from the liquor store. "Peace," she says to me, "Father reached on down and took me right up in Heaven." She's a small person with a flat body, frizzy hair, and a quiet face that the light shines out of, and Mama had such eyes before she died. The first time Charity Sweetness came in to clean, a little more than a year and a half, I made the mistake to ask her to sit down at the kitchen table with me and eat her lunch. I was still feeling not so hot after Ornita left but I'm the kind of a man—Nat Lime, forty-four, a bachelor with a daily growing bald spot on the back of my head, and I could lose frankly fifteen pounds—who enjoys company so long as he has it. So she cooked up her two hard-boiled eggs and sat down and took a small bite out of one of them. But after a minute she stopped chewing and she got up and carried the eggs in a cup in the bathroom, and since then she eats there. I said to her more than once, "Okay, Charity Sweetness, so have it your way, eat the eggs in the kitchen by yourself and I'll eat when you're done," but she smiles absentminded and eats in the toilet. It's my fate with colored people.

Although black is still my favorite color you wouldn't know it from my luck except in short quantities even though I do all right in the liquor store business in Harlem, on Eighth Avenue between 110th and 111th. I speak with respect. A large part of my life I've had dealings with Negro people, most on a business basis but sometimes for friendly reasons with genuine feeling on both sides. I'm drawn to them. At this time of my life I should have one or two good colored friends but the fault isn't necessarily mine. If they knew what was in my heart towards them, but how can you tell that to anybody nowadays? I've tried more than once but the language of the heart either is a dead language or else nobody understands it the way you speak it. Very few. What I'm saying is, personally for me there's only one human color and that's the color of blood. I like a black person if not because he's black, then because I'm white. It comes to the same thing. If I wasn't white my first choice would be black. I'm satisfied to be white because I have no other choice. Anyway, I got an eye for color. I appreciate. Who wants everybody to be the same? Maybe it's like some kind of a talent. Nat Lime might be a liquor dealer in Harlem, but once in the jungle in New Guinea in the Second War, I got the idea when I shot at a running Jap and missed him, that I had some kind of a talent, though maybe it's the kind where you have a marvelous idea now and then but in the end what do they come to? After all, it's a strange world.

Where Charity Sweetness eats her eggs makes me think about Buster Wilson when we were both boys in the Williamsburg section of Brooklyn. There was this long block of run-down dirty frame houses in the middle of a not-so-hot white neighborhood full of pushcarts. The Negro houses looked to me like they had been born and died there, dead not long after the beginning of the world. I lived on the next street. My father was a cutter with arthritis in both hands, big red knuckles and swollen fingers so he didn't cut, and my mother was the one who went to work. She sold paper bags from a second-hand pushcart in Ellery Street. We didn't starve but nobody ate chicken unless we were sick or the chicken was. This was my first acquaintance with a lot of black people and I used to poke around on their poor block. I think I thought, brother, if there can be like this, what can't there be? I mean I caught an early idea what life was about. Anyway I met Buster Wilson there. He used to play marbles by himself. I sat on the curb across the street, watching him shoot one marble lefty and the other one righty. The hand that won picked up the marbles. It wasn't so much of a game but he didn't ask me to come over. My idea was to be friendly, only he never encouraged, he discouraged. Why did I pick him out for a friend? Maybe because I had no others then, we were new in the neighborhood, from Manhattan. Also I liked his type. Buster did everything alone. He was a skinny kid and his brothers' clothes hung on him like worn-out potato sacks. He was a beanpole boy, about twelve, and I was then ten. His arms and legs were burnt out matchsticks. He always wore a brown wool sweater, one arm half unraveled, the other went down to the wrist. His long and narrow head had a white part cut straight in the short woolly hair, maybe with a ruler there, by his father, a barber but too drunk to stay a barber. In those days though I had little myself I was old enough to know who was better off, and the whole block of colored houses made me feel bad in the daylight. But I went there as much as I could because the street was full of life. In the night it looked different, it's hard to tell a cripple in the dark. Sometimes I was afraid to walk by the houses when they were dark and quiet. I was afraid there were people looking at me that I couldn't see. I liked it better when they had parties at night and everybody had a good time. The musicians played their banjos and saxophones and the houses shook with the music and laughing. The young girls, with their pretty dresses and ribbons in their hair, caught me in my throat when I saw them through the windows.

But with the parties came drinking and fights. Sundays were bad days after the Saturday night parties. I remember once that Buster's father, also long and loose, always wearing a dirty gray Homburg hat, chased another black man in the street with a half-inch chisel. The other one, maybe five feet high, lost his shoe and when they wrestled on the ground he was already bleeding through his suit, a thick red blood smearing the sidewalk. I was frightened by the blood and wanted to pour it back in the man who was bleeding from the chisel. On another time Buster's father was playing in a crap game with two big bouncy red dice, in the back of an alley between two middle houses. Then about six men started fist-fighting there, and they ran out of the alley and hit each other in the street. The neighbors, including children, came out and watched, everybody afraid but nobody moving to do anything. I saw the same thing near my store in Harlem, years later, a big crowd watching two men in the street, their breaths hanging in the air on a winter night, murdering each other with switch knives, but nobody moved to call a cop. I didn't either. Anyway, I was just a young kid but I still remember how the cops drove up in a police paddy wagon and broke up the fight by hitting everybody they could hit with big nightsticks. This was in the days before LaGuardia. Most of the fighters were knocked out cold, only one or two got away. Buster's father started to run back in his house but a cop ran after him and cracked him on his Homburg hat with a club, right on the front porch. Then the Negro men were lifted up by the cops, one at the arms and the other at the feet, and they heaved them in the paddy wagon. Buster's father hit the back of the wagon and fell, with his nose spouting very red blood, on top of three other men. I personally couldn't stand it, I was scared of the human race so I ran home, but I remember Buster watching without any expression in his eyes. I stole an extra fifteen cents from my mother's pocketbook and I ran back and asked Buster if he wanted to go to the movies. I would pay. He said yes. This was the first time he talked to me.

So we went more than once to the movies. But we never got to be friends. Maybe because it was a one-way proposition—from me to him. Which includes my invitations to go with me, my (poor mother's) movie money, Hershey chocolate bars, watermelon slices, even my best Nick Carter and Merriwell books that I spent hours picking up in the junk shops, and that he never gave me back. Once he let me go in his house to get a match so we could smoke some butts we found, but it smelled so heavy, so impossible, I died till I got out of there. What I saw in the way of furniture I won't mention—the best was falling apart in pieces. Maybe we went to the movies all together five or six matinees that spring and in the summertime, but when the shows were over he usually walked home by himself.

"Why don't you wait for me, Buster?" I said, "We're both going in the same direction."

But he was walking ahead and didn't hear me. Anyway he didn't answer.

One day when I wasn't expecting it he hit me in the teeth. I felt like crying but not because of the pain. I spit blood and said, "What did you hit me for? What did I do to you?"

"Because you a Jew bastard. Take your Jew movies and your Jew candy and shove them up your Jew ass."

And he ran away.

I thought to myself how was I to know he didn't like the movies. When I was a man I thought, you can't force it.

Years later, in the prime of my life, I met Mrs. Ornita Harris. She was standing by herself under an open umbrella at the bus stop, crosstown 110th, and I picked up her green glove that she had dropped on the wet sidewalk. It was the end of November. Before I could ask her was it hers, she grabbed the glove out of my hand, closed her umbrella, and stepped in the bus. I got on right after her.

I was annoyed so I said, "If you'll pardon me, Miss, there's no law that you have to say thanks, but at least don't make a criminal out of me."

"Well, I'm sorry," she said, "but I don't like white men trying to do me favors."

I tipped my hat and that was that. In ten minutes I got off the bus but she was already gone.

Who expected to see her again but I did. She came into my store about a week later for a bottle of scotch.

"I would offer you a discount," I told her, "but I know you don't like a certain kind of a favor and I'm not looking for a slap in the face."

Then she recognized me and got a little embarrassed.

"I'm sorry I misunderstood you that day."

"So mistakes happen."

The result was she took the discount. I gave her a dollar off.

She used to come in about every two weeks for a fifth of Haig and Haig. Sometimes I waited on her, sometimes my helpers, Jimmy or Mason, also colored, but I said to give the discount. They both looked at me but I had nothing to be ashamed. In the spring when she came in we used to talk once in a while. She was a slim woman, dark but not the most dark, about thirty years I would say, also well built, with a combination nice legs and good-size bosom that I like. Her face was pretty, with big eyes and high cheek bones, but lips a little thick and a nose a little broad. Sometimes she didn't feel like talking, she paid for the bottle, less discount, and walked out. Her eyes were tired and she didn't look to me like a happy woman.

I found out her husband was once a window cleaner on the big buildings, but one day his safety belt broke and he fell fifteen stories. After the funeral she got a job as a manicurist in a Times Square barber shop. I told her I was a bachelor and lived with my mother in a small three-room apartment on West Eighty-third near Broadway. My mother had cancer, and Ornita said she was very sorry.

One night in July we went out together. How that happened I'm still not so sure. I guess I asked her and she didn't say no. Where do you go out with a Negro woman? We went to the Village. We had a good dinner and walked in Washington Square Park. It was a hot night. Nobody was surprised when they saw us, nobody looked at us like we were against the law. If they looked maybe they saw my new lightweight suit that I bought yesterday and my shiny bald spot when we walked under a lamp, also how pretty she was for a man of my type. We went in a movie on West Eighth Street. I didn't want to go in but she said she had heard about the picture. We went in like strangers and we came out like strangers. I wondered what was in her mind and I thought to myself, whatever is in there it's not a certain white man that I know. All night long we went together like we were chained. After the movie she wouldn't let me take her back to Harlem. When I put her in a taxi she asked me, "Why did we bother?"

For the steak, I wanted to say. Instead I said, "You're worth the bother."

"Thanks anyway."

Kiddo, I thought to myself after the taxi left, you just found out what's what, now the best thing is to forget her.

It's easy to say. In August we went out the second time. That was the night she wore a purple dress and I thought to myself, my God, what colors. Who paints that picture paints a masterpiece. Everybody looked at us but I had pleasure. That night when she took off her dress it was in a furnished room I had the sense to rent a few days before. With my sick mother, I couldn't ask her to come to my apartment, and she didn't want me to go home with her where she lived with her brother's family on West 115th near Lenox Avenue. Under her purple dress she wore a black slip, and when she took that off she had white underwear. When she took off the white underwear she was black again. But I know where the next white was, if you want to call it white. And that was the night I think I fell in love with her, the first time in my life though I have liked one or two nice girls I used to go with when I was a boy. It was a serious proposition. I'm the kind of a man when I think of love I'm thinking of marriage. I guess that's why I am a bachelor.

That same week I had a holdup in my place, two big men—both black—with revolvers. One got excited when I rang open the cash register so he could take the money and he hit me over the ear with his gun. I stayed in the hospital a couple of weeks. Otherwise I was insured. Ornita came to see me. She sat on a chair without talking much. Finally I saw she was uncomfortable so I suggested she ought to go home.

"I'm sorry it happened," she said.

"Don't talk like it's your fault."

When I got out of the hospital my mother was dead. She was a wonderful person. My father died when I was thirteen and all by herself she kept the family alive and together. I sat *shive* for a week and remembered how she sold paper bags on her pushcart. I remembered her life and what she tried to teach me. Nathan, she said, if you ever forget you are a Jew a goy will remind you. Mama, I said, rest in peace on this subject. But if I do something you don't like, remember, on earth it's harder than where you are. Then when my week of mourning was finished, one night I said, "Ornita, let's get married. We're both honest people and if you love me like I love you it won't be such a bad time. If you don't like New York I'll sell out here and we'll move someplace else. Maybe to San Francisco where nobody knows us. I was there for a week in the Second War and I saw white and colored living together."

"Nat," she answered me, "I like you but I'd be afraid. My husband woulda killed me."

"Your husband is dead."

"Not in my memory."

"In that case I'll wait."

"Do you know what it'd be like—I mean the life we could expect?"

"Ornita," I said, "I'm the kind of a man, if he picks his own way of life he's satisfied."

"What about children? Were you looking forward to half-Jewish polka dots?"

"I was looking forward to children."

"I can't," she said.

Can't is can't. I saw she was afraid and the best thing was not to push. Sometimes when we met she was so nervous that whatever we did she couldn't enjoy it. At the same time I still thought I had a chance. We were together more and more. I got rid of my furnished room and she came to my apartment—I gave away Mama's bed and bought a new one. She stayed with me all day on Sundays. When she wasn't so nervous she was affectionate, and if I know what love is, I had it. We went out a couple of times a week, the same way—usually I met her in Times Square and sent her home in a taxi, but I talked more about marriage and she talked less against it. One night she told me she was still trying to convince herself but she was almost convinced. I took an inventory of my liquor stock so I could put the store up for sale.

Ornita knew what I was doing. One day she quit her job, the next day she took it back. She also went away a week to visit her sister in Philadelphia for a little rest. She came back tired but said maybe. Maybe is maybe so I'll wait. The way she said it it was closer to yes. That was the winter two years ago. When she was in Philadelphia I called up a friend of mine from the Army, now a CPA, and told him I would appreciate an invitation for an evening. He knew why. His wife said yes right away. When Ornita came back we went there. The wife made a fine dinner. It wasn't a bad time and they told us to come again. Ornita had a few drinks. She looked relaxed, wonderful. Later, because of a twenty-four hour taxi strike I had to take her home on the subway. When we got to the 116th Street station she told me to stay on the train, and she would walk the couple of blocks to her house. I didn't like a woman walking alone on the streets at that time of night. She said she never had any trouble but I insisted nothing doing. I said I would walk to her stoop with her and when she went upstairs I would go back to the subway.

On the way there, on 115th in the middle of the block before Lenox, we were stopped by three men—maybe they were boys. One had a black hat with a half-inch brim, one a green cloth hat, and the third wore a black leather cap. The green hat was wearing a short coat and the other two had long ones. It was under a street light but the leather cap snapped a six-inch switchblade open in the light.

"What you doin' with this white son of a bitch?" he said to Orntia.

"I'm minding my own business," she answered him, "and I wish you would too."

"Boys," I said, "we're all brothers. I'm a reliable merchant in the neighborhood. This young lady is my dear friend. We don't want any trouble. Please let us pass."

"You talk like a Jew landlord," said the green hat. "Fifty a week for a single room."

"No charge fo' the rats," said the half-inch brim.

"Believe me, I'm no landlord. My store is 'Nathan's Liquors' between Hundred Tenth and Eleventh. I also have two colored clerks, Mason and Jimmy, and they will tell you I pay good wages as well as I give discounts to certain customers."

"Shut your mouth, Jewboy," said the leather cap, and he moved the knife back and forth in front of my coat button. "No more black pussy for you."

"Speak with respect about this lady, please."

I got slapped on my mouth.

"That ain't no lady," said the long face in the half-inch brim, "that's black pussy. She deserve to have evvy bit of her hair shave off. How you like to have evvy bit of your hair shave off, black pussy?"

"Please leave me and this gentleman alone or I'm gonna scream long and loud. That's my house three doors down."

They slapped her. I never heard such a scream. Like her husband was falling fifteen stories.

I hit the one that slapped her and the next I knew I was lying in the gutter with a pain in my head. I thought, goodbye, Nat, they'll stab me for sure, but all they did was take my wallet and run in three different directions.

Ornita walked back with me to the subway and she wouldn't let me go home with her again.

"Just get home safely."

She looked terrible. Her face was gray and I still remembered her scream. It was a terrible winter night, very cold February, and it took me an hour and ten minutes to get home. I felt bad for leaving her but what could I do?

We had a date downtown the next night but she didn't show up, the first time.

In the morning I called her in her place of business.

"For God's sake, Ornita, if we got married and moved away we wouldn't have that kind of trouble that we had. We wouldn't come in that neighborhood any more.''

"Yes, we would. I have family there and don't want to move anyplace else. The truth of it is I can't marry you, Nat. I got troubles enough of my own.''

''I coulda sworn you love me.''

''Maybe I do but I can't marry you.''

''For God's sake, why?''

''I got enough trouble of my own.''

I went that night in a cab to her brother's house to see her. He was a quiet man with a thin mustache. ''She gone,'' he said, ''left for a long visit to some close relatives in the South. She said to tell you she appreciate your intentions but didn't think it will work out.''

''Thank you kindly,'' I said.

Don't ask me how I got home.

Once on Eighth Avenue, a couple of blocks from my store, I saw a blind man with a white cane tapping on the sidewalk. I figured we were going in the same direction so I took his arm.

''I can tell you're white,'' he said.

A heavy colored woman with a full shopping bag rushed after us.

''Never mind,'' she said, ''I know where he live.''

She pushed me with her shoulder and I hurt my leg on the fire hydrant.

That's how it is. I give my heart and they kick me in my teeth.

''Charity Sweetness—you hear me?—come out of that goddamn toilet!''

SUGGESTIONS FOR WRITING AND DISCUSSION

1. A paradox is a statement that initially seems self-contradictory or absurd but somehow is not. Nat makes a number of paradoxical statements in this story. Discuss some of them.
2. What is ironic about Ornita's statement that she can't marry Nat because she's got troubles of her own?
3. Initially Nat may seem like a sympathetic character. Does he change in the course of this story? Does your opinion of him change?
4. What ''talent'' does Nat describe in the second paragraph? Does this talent fail him or serve him well?
5. People like Nat mean well, yet they repeat their mistakes time and again. Write a two- to three-page profile of someone you know well who fits this description. Start with a summary of the story.

Poetry

John Milton (British, 1608–1674)

On the Late Massacre in Piedmont

On Easter Day, 1655 about 1,700 members of the Protestant Waldensian sect who lived in Piedmont, a region in the northwest of Italy, were killed by the Duke of Savoy's soldiers. The sect had existed since the twelfth century, "when all our fathers worshipped stocks and stones," and was especially critical of the materialism of the Roman Catholic church. "The triple tyrant" of line 12 is the Pope, whose tiara has three crowns. The Italian poet Petrarch described the papal court as being like Babylon, a biblical city famous for vice; "the Babylonian woe" refers to Catholicism in general.

Avenge, O Lord, thy slaughtered saints, whose bones
  Lie scattered on the Alpine mountains cold,
  Even them who kept thy truth so pure of old
  When all our fathers worshiped stocks and stones,
Forget not: in thy book record their groans
  Who were thy sheep and in their ancient fold
  Slain by the bloody Piedmontese that rolled
  Mother with infant down the rocks. Their moans
The vales redoubled to the hills, and they
  To Heaven. Their martyred blood and ashes sow
  O'er all th' Italian fields where still doth sway
The triple tyrant: that from these may grow
  A hundredfold, who having learnt thy way
  Early may fly the Babylonian woe.

SUGGESTIONS FOR WRITING AND DISCUSSION

1. The sonnet describes a very specific event. What is the larger point the sonnet makes?
2. Work out the rhyme scheme. Is this a Shakespearian or an Italian sonnet? What vowel sound occurs most frequently in the rhyming words? What is its effect?
3. Is Milton advocating revenge? Support your argument in a one- to two-page essay.

Matthew Arnold (British, 1822–1888)

Dover Beach

The sea is calm tonight,
The tide is full, the moon lies fair

Upon the straits;—on the French coast the light
Gleams and is gone; the cliffs of England stand,
Glimmering and vast, out in the tranquil bay.
Come to the window, sweet is the night-air!
Only, from the long line of spray
Where the sea meets the moon-blanched land,
Listen! you hear the grating roar
Of pebbles which the waves draw back, and fling,
At their return, up the high strand,
Begin, and cease, and then again begin,
With tremulous cadence slow, and bring
The eternal note of sadness in.

Sophocles long ago
Heard it on the Aegean, and it brought
Into his mind the turbid ebb and flow
Of human misery; we
Find also in the sound a thought,
Hearing it by this distant northern sea.

The Sea of Faith
Was once, too, at the full, and round earth's shore
Lay like the folds of a bright girdle furled.
But now I only hear
Its melancholy, long, withdrawing roar,
Retreating, to the breath
Of the night-wind, down the vast edges drear
And naked shingles of the world.

Ah, love, let us be true
To one another! for the world, which seems
To lie before us like a land of dreams,
So various, so beautiful, so new,
Hath really neither joy, nor love, nor light,
Nor certitude, nor peace, nor help for pain;
And we are here as on a darkling plain
Swept with confused alarms of struggle and flight,
Where ignorant armies clash by night.

SUGGESTIONS FOR WRITING AND DISCUSSION

1. The poem opens with a romantic description of a moonlit night. When does the tone of the description change? Point to the words and phrases that support your answer.
2. In the second stanza the speaker compares the English Channel to the Aegean sea as described by the Greek dramatist Sophocles in his play *Anti-*

gone. Write a stanza-by-stanza paraphrase of the poem, paying particular attention to what the sea symbolizes in stanzas one, two, and three.

3. Write an explication of the first and fourth stanzas and compare the two. How could the first be seen as an example of what the speaker describes more generally in the fourth?

4. Read Anthony Hecht's poem "The Dover Bitch" in Chapter 9. Does it change your impressions of "Dover Beach"? Write your own reply to Arnold's poem in either verse or prose.

William Butler Yeats (Irish, 1865–1939)

Easter, 1916

On Easter Monday 1916 an Irish Nationalist uprising began in Dublin. According-ing to D. B. Quinn in Chamber's Encyclopedia: *"Fifteen hundred men seized key points and an Irish republic was proclaimed from the General Post Office. After the initial surprise prompt British military action was taken, and when over three hundred lives had been lost the insurgents were forced to surren-der on 29 April . . . . The seven signatories of the republican proclamation, including (Padraic) Pearse and (James) Connolly, and nine others were shot after court martial between 3 and 12 May; 75 were reprieved and over 2,000 held prisoners."*

I have met them at close of day
Coming with vivid faces
From counter or desk among grey
Eighteenth-century houses.
I have passed with a nod of the head
Or polite meaningless words,
Or have lingered awhile and said
Polite meaningless words,
And thought before I had done
Of a mocking tale or a gibe
To please a companion
Around the fire at the club,
Being certain that they and I
But lived where motley is worn:
All changed, changed utterly:
A terrible beauty is born.

That woman's days were spent
In ignorant good-will,
Her nights in argument
Until her voice grew shrill.
What voice more sweet than hers
When, young and beautiful,
She rode to harriers?
This man had kept a school

And rode our wingèd horse;
This other his helper and friend
Was coming into his force;
He might have won fame in the end,
So sensitive his nature seemed,
So daring and sweet his thought.
This other man I had dreamed
A drunken, vainglorious lout.
He had done most bitter wrong
To some who are near my heart,
Yet I number him in the song;
He, too, has resigned his part
In the casual comedy;
He, too, has been changed in his turn,
Transformed utterly:
A terrible beauty is born.

Hearts with one purpose alone
Through summer and winter seem
Enchanted to a stone
To trouble the living stream.
The horse that comes from the road,
The rider, the birds that range
From cloud to tumbling cloud,
Minute by minute they change;
A shadow of cloud on the stream
Changes minute by minute;
A horse-hoof slides on the brim,
And a horse plashes within it;
The long-legged moor-hens dive,
And hens to moor-cocks call;
Minute by minute they live:
The stone's in the midst of all.

Too long a sacrifice
Can make a stone of the heart.
O when may it suffice?
That is Heaven's part, our part
To murmur name upon name,
As a mother names her child
When sleep at last has come
On limbs that had run wild.
What is it but nightfall?
No, no, not night but death;
Was it needless death after all?
For England may keep faith

For all that is done and said.
We know their dream; enough
To know they dreamed and are dead;
And what if excess of love
Bewildered them till they died?
I write it out in a verse—
MacDonagh and MacBride
And Connolly and Pearse
Now and in time to be,
Whatever green is worn,
Are changed, changed utterly:
A terrible beauty is born.

                              September 25, 1916

SUGGESTIONS FOR WRITING AND DISCUSSION

1. In the second stanza four people are mentioned. "That woman" is Countess
    Constance Georgina Markiewicz. The man who "kept a school" is Padraic
    Pearse. Like Yeats he was a prolific writer; he "rode our winged horse."
    "The other" is Thomas MacDonough, also a schoolteacher. The "drunken
    vainglorious lout" is Major John MacBride who was briefly married to
    Maud Gonne, the woman with whom Yeats was in love for many years.
    Looking at the first and second stanzas, describe the speaker's attitude to
    these people before and after the uprising. Why does Yeats use the words
    motley (first stanza) and *comedy* (second stanza)?
2. The first two stanzas describe a change or transformation. The third stanza
    contrasts the constancy of the nationalists with the changing world of
    nature. Write a two- to three-page essay analyzing the different ideas about
    change in the poem.
3. At several points in the poem words or phrases are repeated. Examine these
    repetitions and discuss their purpose.
4. What is the speaker's attitude to Heaven and revenge in the fourth stanza?
    Compare his attitude with that expressed in John Milton's sonnet "On the
    Late Massacre in Piedmont."
5. Yeats's poem "A Prayer for My Daughter" (p. 201) was written in 1919. Can
    you find evidence for the attitudes expressed in "Easter 1916" in this later
    poem? What similarities are there between the two poems?

Walt Whitman (American, 1819–1892)

The Wound-Dresser

1. An old man bending I come among new faces,
    Years looking backward resuming in answer to children,
    Come tell us old man, as from young men and maidens that love me,

(Arous'd and angry, I'd thought to beat the alarum, and urge relentless
    war,
But soon my fingers fail'd me, my face droop'd and I resign'd myself,
To sit by the wounded and soothe them, or silently watch the dead;)
Years hence of these scenes, of these furious passions, these chances,
Of unsurpass'd heroes, (was one side so brave? the other was equally
    brave;)
Now be witness again, paint the mightiest armies of earth,
Of those armies so rapid so wondrous what saw you to tell us?
What stays with you latest and deepest? of curious panics,
Of hard-fought engagements or sieges tremendous what deepest
    remains?

2. O maidens and young men I love and that love me,
   What you ask of my days those the strangest and sudden your talking
      recalls,
   Soldier alert I arrive after a long march cover'd with sweat and dust,
   In the nick of time I come, plunge in the fight,
      loudly shout in the rush of successful charge,
   Enter the captur'd works—yet lo, like a swift-running river they fade,
   Pass and are gone they fade—I dwell not on soldiers' perils or soldiers'
     joys,
   (Both I remember well—many the hardships, few the joys,
     yet I was content.)

   But in silence, in dreams' projections,
   While the world of gain and appearance and mirth goes on,
   So soon what is over forgotten, and waves wash the imprints off the
     sand,
   With hinged knees returning I enter the doors, (while for you up there,
   Whoever you are, follow without noise and be of strong heart.)

   Bearing the bandages, water and sponge,
   Straight and swift to my wounded I go,
   Where they lie on the ground after the battle brought in,
   Where their priceless blood reddens the grass the ground,
   Or to the rows of the hospital tent, or under the roof'd hospital,
   To the long rows of cots up and down each side I return,
   To each and all one after another I draw near, not one do I miss,
   An attendant follows holding a tray, he carries a refuse pail,
   Soon to be fill'd with clotted rags and blood, emptied, and fill'd again.

   I onward go, I stop,
   With hinged knees and steady hand to dress wounds,
   I am firm with each, the pangs are sharp yet unavoidable,
   One turns to me his appealing eyes—poor boy! I never knew you,

Yet I think I could not refuse this moment to die for you,
   if that would save you.

3. On, on I go, (open doors of time! open hospital doors!)
   The crush'd head I dress, (poor crazed hand tear not the bandage
      away.)
   The neck of the cavalry-man with the bullet through and through I
      examine,
   Hard the breathing rattles, quite glazed already the eye, yet life
      struggles hard,
   (Come sweet death! be persuaded O beautiful death!
   In mercy come quickly.)
   From the stump of the arm, the amputated hand,
   I undo the clotted lint, remove the slough, wash off the matter and
      blood,
   Back on his pillow the soldier bends with curv'd neck and side-falling
      head,
   His eyes are closed, his face is pale, he dares not look on the bloody
      stump,
   And has not yet look'd on it.

   I dress a wound in the side, deep, deep,
   But a day or two more, for see the frame all wasted and sinking,
   And the yellow-blue countenance see.

   I dress the perforated shoulder, the foot with the bullet-wound,
   Cleanse the one with a gnawing and putrid gangrene, so sickening, so
      offensive,
   While the attendant stands behind aside me holding the tray and pail.

   I am faithful, I do not give out,
   The fractur'd thigh, the knee, the wound in the abdomen,
   These and more I dress with impassive hand,
      (yet deep in my breast a fire, a burning flame.)

4. Thus in silence in dreams' projections,
   Returning, resuming, I thread my way through the hospitals,
   The hurt and wounded I pacify with soothing hand,
   I sit by the restless all the dark night, some are so young,
   Some suffer so much, I recall the experience sweet and sad,
   (Many a soldier's loving arms about this neck have cross'd and rested,
   Many a soldier's kiss dwells on these bearded lips.)

SUGGESTIONS FOR WRITING AND DISCUSSION

1. This poem is based on Whitman's experiences as a nurse during the Civil
   War. In the first stanza the young men and maidens ask the wound-dresser

to tell them about the war. How does he answer them? What does he remember most clearly? What has already faded from his memory?

2. Does the wound-dresser take a side in the war?
3. Write a one-paragraph character description of the wound-dresser.
4. What is the wound-dresser's attitude to the wounds he dresses? To the suffering he sees? To death?
5. In a two- to three-page essay compare this poem to Wilfred Owen's "Dulce et Decorum Est."

Wilfred Owen (British, 1893–1918)

Dulce et Decorum Est

Bent double, like old beggars under sacks,
Knock-kneed, coughing like hags, we cursed through sludge,
Till on the haunting flares we turned our backs,
And towards our distant rest began to trudge.
Men marched asleep. Many had lost their boots,
But limped on, blood-shod. All went lame, all blind;
Drunk with fatigue; deaf even to the hoots
Of gas-shells dropping softly behind.

Gas! Gas! Quick, boys!—An ecstasy of fumbling,
Fitting the clumsy helmets just in time,
But someone still was yelling out and stumbling
And flound'ring like a man in fire or lime.
Dim through the misty panes and thick green light,
As under a green sea, I saw him drowning.

In all my dreams before my helpless sight
He plunges at me, guttering, choking, drowning.

If in some smothering dreams, you too could pace
Behind the wagon that we flung him in,
And watch the white eyes writhing in his face,
His hanging face, like a devil's sick of sin,
If you could hear, at every jolt, the blood
Come gargling from the froth-corrupted lungs
Bitter as the cud
Of vile, incurable sores on innocent tongues,—
My friend, you would not tell with such high zest
To children ardent for some desperate glory,
The old lie: *Dulce et decorum est*
Pro patria mori.

1920

SUGGESTIONS FOR WRITING AND DISCUSSION

1. *Dulce et decorum est pro patria mori* is a Latin quotation from the Roman poet Horace. It means, "It is sweet and honorable to die for one's country." The title of the poem means "It is sweet and honorable." How is this title being used, and why does Owen use only a portion of the quotation?
2. How does the speaker characterize himself and his fellow soldiers? What similes and metaphors does he use?
3. Why does the poem describe a soldier being wounded by gas rather than by gunfire? How does this fit with the theme of the poem?
4. In a two- to three-page essay compare this poem with E. E. Cummings' "next to of course god america i." What statement do the two poems make about political rhetoric?

Osip Mandelstam (Russian, 1892–1940?)

The Stalin Epigram

Our lives no longer feel ground under them.
At ten paces you can't hear our words.

But whenever there's a snatch of talk
it turns to the Kremlin mountaineer,

the ten thick worms his fingers,
his words like measures of weight,

the huge laughing cockroaches on his top lip,
the glitter of his boot-rims.

Ringed with a scum of chicken-necked bosses
he toys with the tributes of half-men.

One whistles, another meouws, a third snivels.
He pokes out his finger and he alone goes boom.

He forges decrees in a line like horseshoes,
One for the groin, one the forehead, temple, eye.

He rolls the executions on his tongue like berries.
He wishes he could hug them like big friends from home.

SUGGESTIONS FOR WRITING AND DISCUSSION

1. In 1934 when this poem about Stalin, "the Kremlin mountaineer," became known to the authorities, they arrested Mandelstam. In the first draft Stalin was called a "murderer and peasant-slayer." Although Mandelstam later cut

this extreme condemnation, the poem is still severely critical of Stalin. How
is this criticism conveyed? What picture do you get of Stalin?

2. In a two- to three-page essay compare Mandelstam's portrait of Stalin with
   Pablo Neruda's depiction of various South American dictators in "The
   United Fruit Company."

Pablo Neruda (Chilean, 1904–1973)

The United Fruit Co.*

When the trumpet sounded, it was
all prepared on the earth,
and Jehovah parceled out the earth
to Coca-Cola, Inc., Anaconda,
Ford Motors, and other entities:
The Fruit Company, Inc.
reserved for itself the most succulent,
the central coast of my own land,
the delicate waist of America.
It rechristened its territories
as the "Banana Republics"
and over the sleeping dead,
over the restless heroes
who brought about the greatness,
the liberty and the flags,
it established the comic opera:
abolished the independencies,
presented crowns of Caesar,
unsheathed envy, attracted
the dictatorship of the flies,
Trujillo flies, Tacho flies,
Carias flies, Martinez flies,
Ubico flies, damp flies
of modest blood and marmalade,
drunken flies who zoom
over the ordinary graves,
circus flies, wise flies
well trained in tyranny.
Among the bloodthirsty flies
the Fruit Company lands its ships,

*"The Betrayed Sand" (a long poem by Neruda) concentrates on the men who allowed
South American nations to fall back on colonialism of the United States, and on the
men who support United States' interests today. He mentions the pressure from U.S.
companies to keep wages low. He describes especially events in the year 1946, while
he was senator in Chile. We have chosen one of the poems in the center of the section,
on the United Fruit Company. *(Translator's note)*

taking off the coffee and the fruit;
the treasure of our submerged
territories flows as though
on plates into the ships.

Meanwhile Indians are falling
into the sugared chasms
of the harbors, wrapped
for burial in the mist of the dawn:
a body rolls, a thing
that has no name, a fallen cipher,
a cluster of dead fruit
thrown down on the dump.

                    Translated by Robert Bly

SUGGESTIONS FOR WRITING AND DISCUSSION

1. What is the tone of the first five lines?
2. The poet describes various South American dictators as flies. What kinds of dictators do the different kinds of flies suggest?
3. In the second stanza Indians are compared to fruit. What does this metaphor suggest in the context of the poem as a whole?
4. This poem uses figurative language to describe the dictators and the Indians. Using figurative language, write a two- to three-page essay about some conflict that is currently in the news.

Phillis Wheatley (American, 1753?–1784)

On Being Brought from Africa to America

'Twas mercy brought me from my *Pagan* land,
Taught my benighted soul to understand
That there's a God, that there's a *Saviour* too:
Once I redemption neither sought nor knew.
Some view our sable race with scornful eye,
"Their color is a diabolic die."
Remember, *Christians, Negroes,* black as *Cain,*
May be refin'd, and join th' angelic train.

SUGGESTIONS FOR WRITING AND DISCUSSION

1. Although the speaker seems to be giving sincere thanks for being brought from Africa, this poem may strike readers today as ironic. Using the biographical information about Wheatley given at the end of this book, explicate the poem and discuss in a two-page essay the nature of this irony.
2. Compare this poem with Langston Hughes's "I, too" and "Dream Deferred." Write a one- to two-page essay showing how the two authors differ in their attitude to their race.

Langston Hughes (American, 1902–1967)

I, Too

I, too, sing America.

I am the darker brother.
They send me to eat in the kitchen
When company comes,
But I laugh,
And eat well,
And grow strong.

Tomorrow,
I'll be at the table
When company comes.
Nobody'll dare
Say to me,
"Eat in the kitchen,"
Then.

Besides,
They'll see how beautiful I am
And be ashamed—

I, too, am America.

Dream Deferred

What happens to a dream deferred?

Does it dry up
like a raisin in the sun?
Or fester like a sore—
And then run?
Does it stink like rotten meat?
Or crust and sugar over—
like a syrupy sweet?

Maybe it just sags
like a heavy load.

Or does it explode?

SUGGESTIONS FOR WRITING AND DISCUSSION

1. In "I, Too" there is an undercurrent of violence. In a one- to two-page essay
   pick out the words and phrases that suggest the presence of this undercurrent, and explain how the violence is resolved.

2. "Dream Deferred" asks a series of questions. The order in which these questions are asked creates the tension of the poem. Discuss how the tension builds.
3. Some poems deal with personal conflicts, whereas others are about larger more general issues. Which is the case in each of these poems? Give evidence to support your answer.

E. E. Cummings (American, 1894–1962)

"next to of course god america i"

"next to of course god america i
love you land of the pilgrims' and so forth oh
say can you see by the dawn's early my
country 'tis of centuries come and go
and are no more what of it we should worry
in every language even deafanddumb
thy sons acclaim your glorious name by gorry
by jingo by gee by gosh by gum
why talk of beauty what could be more beautiful than these heroic happy dead
who rushed like lions to the roaring slaughter
they did not stop to think they died instead
then shall the voice of liberty be mute?"

He spoke. And drank rapidly a glass of water

SUGGESTIONS FOR WRITING AND DISCUSSION

1. The poem contains many quotations and allusions. Read it aloud and identify as many of these as you can. From what common source do many of them come? Why are the quotations so short and why do they run together? Choose two or three lines and in a one- to two-page essay discuss the juxtaposition.
2. What does the last line of the poem suggest about the speaker's attitude to his speech?
3. What is Cummings's attitude to the speaker of the poem?

Adrienne Rich (American, 1929–

Necessities of Life

Piece by piece I seem
to re-enter the world: I first began

a small, fixed dot, still see
that old myself, a dark-blue thumbtack

pushed into the scene,
a hard little head protruding

from the pointillist's buzz and bloom.
After a time the dot

begins to ooze. Certain heats
melt it.
           Now I was hurriedly

blurring into ranges
of burnt red, burning green,

whole biographies swam up and
swallowed me like Jonah.

Jonah! I was Wittgenstein,
Mary Wollstonecraft, the soul

of Louis Jouvet, dead
in a blown-up photograph.

Till, wolfed almost to shreds,
I learned to make myself

unappetizing. Scaly as a dry bulb
thrown into a cellar

I used myself, let nothing use me.
Like being on a private dole,

sometimes more like kneading bricks in Egypt.
What life was there, was mine,

now and again to lay
one hand on a warm brick

and touch the sun's ghost
with economical joy,

now and again to name
over the bare necessities.

So much for those days. Soon
practice may make me middling-perfect, I'll

dare inhabit the world
trenchant in motion as an eel, solid

as a cabbage-head. I have invitations:
a curl of mist steams upward

from a field, visible as my breath,
houses along a road stand waiting

like old women knitting, breathless
to tell their tales.

SUGGESTIONS FOR WRITING AND DISCUSSION

1. The speaker is describing the various stages of her life and how they lead to
   her reentry into the world as a fully independent adult. (The first entry is
   birth.) What extended metaphor is used in the first part of the poem? How
   does this metaphor contribute to the theme of the poem?
2. Wittgenstein was an Austrian philosopher; Mary Wollstonecraft was an
   eighteenth-century English feminist; Louis Jouvet was a French actor and
   theater director. What role did these three play in the speaker's life?
3. Why does the speaker withdraw from the world? What qualities does she
   predict she will need to reenter successfully?
4. Write a three- to four-page essay analyzing the various stages of the speaker's life and the connections between them. What does she consider to be
   the necessities of life?

Drama

Sophocles (Greek, 495? B.C.–406? B.C.)

It is widely believed that Greek drama evolved from religious ceremonies. In the earliest productions, the actors were priests. Religious festivals were marked by drama competitions, attendance at which was more in the nature of an obligation than a mere pleasure. The cost of a ticket was roughly equivalent to the price of a loaf of bread.

Plays were performed in large open-air theaters. The audience sat in a semicircle on seats built into the hillside, looking down onto the stage. In front of the main acting area, there was an orchestra, *where the chorus sang and danced. Behind the chorus and the actors stood a building called the* skene *(from which comes our word* scene). *This building served as an all-purpose set and also improved the acoustics.*

The actors, all men, wore masks, which helped to amplify their voices, and platform shoes, or buskins, which made them seem taller. Prior to Sophocles, only two actors appeared on the stage at the same time; Sophocles introduced a third actor and fixed the size of the chorus at fifteen. The chorus provided a commentary on the action and also talked to the main characters. The terms strophe *and* antistrophe, *which appear before speeches by the chorus, are stage directions: The chorus danced across the stage in one direction in the strophe and in the opposite direction in the antistrophe.*

Sophocles was a successful general, poet, and playwright. In 486 B.C. the defeated Aeschylus, the reigning tragedian, and took first prize in the drama competition. Subsequently he wrote well over one hundred plays, of which only seven have survived in their entirety. Aristotle, the Greek philosopher, who wrote extensively about drama, used Sophocles's Oedipus Rex (c.429 B.C.) as a model of tragedy.

Antigonê

An English Version by Dudley Fitts and Robert Fitzgerald

LIST OF CHARACTERS

ANTIGONÊ
ISMENÊ
EURYDICÊ
CREON
HAIMON
TEIRESIAS
A SENTRY
A MESSENGER
CHORUS

Scene. Before the palace of CREON, *king of Thebes. A central double door, and two lateral doors. A platform extends the length of the façade, and from this platform three steps lead down into the "orchestra," or chorus-ground.*

Time. Dawn of the day after the repulse of the Argive army from the assault on Thebes.

Prologue

ANTIGONÊ *and* ISMENÊ *enter from the central door of the palace.*

ANTIGONÊ. Ismenê, dear sister,
 You would think that we had already suffered enough
 For the curse on Oedipus.°
 I cannot imagine any grief
 That you and I have not gone through. And now—   5
 Have they told you of the new decree of our King Creon?

ISMENÊ. I have heard nothing: I know
 That two sisters lost two brothers, a double death
 In a single hour; and I know that the Argive army
 Fled in the night; but beyond this, nothing.   10

ANTIGONÊ. I thought so. And that is why I wanted you
 To come out here with me. There is something we must do.

ISMENÊ. Why do you speak so strangely?

ANTIGONÊ. Listen, Ismenê:
 Creon buried our brother Eteoclês   15
 With military honors, gave him a soldier's funeral,
 And it was right that he should; but Polyneicês,
 Who fought as bravely and died as miserably,—
 They say that Creon has sworn
 No one shall bury him, no one mourn for him,   20
 But his body must lie in the fields, a sweet treasure
 For carrion birds to find as they search for food.
 That is what they say, and our good Creon is coming here
 To announce it publicly; and the penalty—
 Stoning to death in the public square!   25

---

[3]According to Greek legend, Oedipus was told by the Delphic oracle that he would kill his father and marry his mother. Although he tried his utmost to avoid his fate, both parts of this prophecy came true. Unwittingly he killed his father Laius, King of Thebes, and married Laius's widow, Jocasta, thereby becoming King of Thebes. Oedipus and Jocasta had four children: Polyneicês, Eteoclês, Antigonê and Ismenê. When Oedipus learned what he had done, he blinded himself and left Thebes. Eteoclês and Polyneicês quarreled and killed each other in battle. Creon who became King of Thebes decreed Polyneicês a traitor and ordered that he should not be buried.

There it is,
And now you can prove what you are:
A true sister, or a traitor to your family.

ISMENÊ. Antigonê, you are mad! What could I possibly do?

ANTIGONÊ. You must decide whether you will help me or not.   30

ISMENÊ. I do not understand you. Help you in what?

ANTIGONÊ. Ismenê, I am going to bury him. Will you come?

ISMENÊ. Bury him! You have just said the new law forbids it.

ANTIGONÊ. He is my brother. And he is your brother, too.

ISMENÊ. But think of the danger! Think what Creon will do!

ANTIGONÊ. Creon is not strong enough to stand in my way.   35

ISMENÊ. Ah sister!
Oedipus died, everyone hating him
For what his own search brought to light, his eyes
Ripped out by his own hand; and Iocastê died,
His mother and wife at once: she twisted the cords   40
That strangled her life; and our two brothers died,
Each killed by the other's sword. And we are left:
But oh, Antigonê,
Think how much more terrible than these
Our own death would be if we should go against Creon   45
And do what he has forbidden! We are only women,
We cannot fight with men, Antigonê!
The law is strong, we must give in to the law
In this thing, and in worse. I beg the Dead
To forgive me, but I am helpless: I must yield   50
To those in authority. And I think it is dangerous business
To be always meddling.

ANTIGONÊ.   If that is what you think,
I should not want you, even if you asked to come.
You have made your choice, you can be what you want to be.   55
But I will bury him; and if I must die,
I say that this crime is holy: I shall lie down
With him in death, and I shall be as dear
To him as he to me.
                    It is the dead,
Not the living, who make the longest demands:
We die for ever . . .
                    You may do as you like,   60
Since apparently the laws of the gods mean nothing to you.

ISMENÊ. They mean a great deal to me; but I have no strength
To break laws that were made for the public good.

ANTIGONÊ. That must be your excuse, I suppose. But as for me,
   I will bury the brother I love.

ISMENÊ.   Antigonê,   65
   I am so afraid for you!

ANTIGONÊ.   You need not be:
   You have yourself to consider, after all.

ISMENÊ. But no one must hear of this, you must tell no one!
   I will keep it a secret, I promise!

ANTIGONÊ.   O tell it! Tell everyone!
   Think of how they'll hate you when it all comes out   70
   If they learn that you knew about it all the time!

ISMENÊ. So fiery! You should be cold with fear.

ANTIGONÊ. Perhaps. But I am doing only what I must.

ISMENÊ. But can you do it? I say that you cannot.

ANTIGONÊ. Very well: when my strength gives out,
   I shall do no more.   75

ISMENÊ. Impossible things should not be tried at all.

ANTIGONÊ. Go away, Ismenê:
   I shall be hating you soon, and the dead will too,
   For your words are hateful. Leave me my foolish plan:
   I am not afraid of the danger; if it means death,   80
   It will not be the worst of deaths—death without honor.

ISMENÊ. Go then, if you feel that you must.
   You are unwise,
   But a loyal friend indeed to those who love you.

   Exit into the palace. ANTIGONÊ *goes off, left. Enter the* CHORUS.

Párodos

CHORUS. Now the long blade of the sun, lying   *Strophe 1*
   Level east to west, touches with glory
   Thebes of the Seven Gates. Open, unlidded
   Eye of golden day! O marching light
   Across the eddy and rush of Dircê's stream,°   5
   Striking the white shields of the enemy
   Thrown headlong backward from the blaze of morning!

CHORAGOS.° Polyneicês their commander
   Roused them with windy phrases,
   He the wild eagle screaming   10
   Insults above our land,

---

⁵*Dircê's stream*   a stream west of Thebes
⁸*Choragos*   leader of the Chorus

His wings their shields of snow,
His crest their marshalled helms.

CHORUS. Against our seven gates in a yawning ring *Antistrophe 1*
    The famished spears came onward in the night; 15
    But before his jaws were sated with our blood,
    Or pine fire took the garland of our towers,
    He was thrown back; and as he turned, great Thebes—
    No tender victim for his noisy power—
    Rose like a dragon behind him, shouting war. 20

CHORAGOS. For God hates utterly
    The bray of bragging tongues;
    And when he beheld their smiling,
    Their swagger of golden helms,
    The frown of his thunder blasted 25
    Their first man from our walls.

CHORUS. We heard his shout of triumph high in the air *Strophe 2*
    Turn to a scream; far out in a flaming arc
    He fell with his windy torch, and the earth struck him.
    And others storming in fury no less than his 30
    Found shock of death in the dusty joy of battle.

CHORAGOS. Seven captains at seven gates
    Yielded their clanging arms to the god
    That bends the battle-line and breaks it.
    These two only, brothers in blood, 35
    Face to face in matchless rage,
    Mirroring each the other's death,
    Clashed in long combat.

CHORUS. But now in the beautiful morning of victory *Antistrophe 2*
    Let Thebes of the many chariots sing for joy! 40
    With hearts for dancing we'll take leave of war:
    Our temples shall be sweet with hymns of praise,
    And the long nights shall echo with our chorus.

Scene I

CHORAGOS. But now at last our new King is coming:
    Creon of Thebes, Menoikeus' son.
    In this auspicious dawn of his reign
    What are the new complexities
    That shifting Fate has woven for him? 5
    What is his counsel? Why has he summoned
    The old men to hear him?

    Enter CREON *from the palace, center. He addresses the* CHORUS
    from the top step.

CREON. Gentlemen: I have the honor to inform you that our Ship of
State, which recent storms have threatened to destroy, has
come safely to harbor at last, guided by the merciful wisdom of   10
Heaven. I have summoned you here this morning because I
know that I can depend upon you: your devotion to King Laios
was absolute; you never hesitated in your duty to our late ruler
Oedipus; and when Oediups died, your loyalty was transferred
to his children. Unfortunately, as you know, his two sons, the   15
princes Eteoclês and Polyneicês, have killed each other in battle; and I, as the next in blood, have succeeded to the full
power of the throne.

    I am aware, of course, that no Ruler can expect complete
loyalty from his subjects until he has been tested in office.   20
Nevertheless, I say to you at the very outset that I have nothing
but contempt for the kind of Governor who is afraid, for whatever reason, to follow the course that he knows is best for the
State; and as for the man who sets private friendship above the
public welfare,—I have no use for him, either. I call God to wit-   25
ness that if I saw my country headed for ruin, I should not be
afraid to speak out plainly; and I need hardly remind you that I
would never have any dealings with an enemy of the people.
No one values friendship more highly than I; but we must
remember that friends made at the risk of wrecking our Ship   30
are not real friends at all.

    These are my principles, at any rate, and that is why I have
made the following decision concerning the sons of Oedipus:
Eteoclês, who died as a man should die, fighting for his country, is to be buried with full military honors, with all the cere-   35
mony that is usual when the greatest heroes die; but his
brother Polyneicês, who broke his exile to come back with fire
and sword against his native city and the shrines of his fathers'
gods, whose one idea was to spill the blood of his blood and
sell his own people into slavery—Polyneicês, I say, is to have   40
no burial: no man is to touch him or say the least prayer for
him; he shall lie on the plain, unburied; and the birds and the
scavenging dogs can do with him whatever they like.

    This is my command, and you can see the wisdom behind
it. As long as I am King, no traitor is going to be honored with   45
the loyal man. But whoever shows by word and deed that he is
on the side of the State,—he shall have my respect while he is
living and my reverence when he is dead.

CHORAGOS. If that is your will, Creon son of Menoikeus,
    You have the right to enforce it: we are yours.   50

CREON. That is my will. Take care that you do your part.

CHORAGOS. We are old men: let the younger ones carry it out.

CREON. I do not mean that: the sentries have been appointed.

CHORAGOS. Then what is it that you would have us do?

CREON. You will give no support to whoever breaks this law. 55

CHORAGOS. Only a crazy man is in love with death!

CREON. And death it is; yet money talks, and the wisest
    Have sometimes been known to count a few coins too many.

    Enter SENTRY *from left.*

SENTRY. I'll not say that I'm out of breath from running, King, because
    every time I stopped to think about what I have to tell you, I felt 60
    like going back. And all the time a voice kept saying, "You fool,
    don't you know you're walking straight into trouble?"; and then
    another voice: "Yes, but if you let somebody else get the news
    to Creon first, it will be even worse than that for you!" But good
    sense won out, at least I hope it was good sense, and here I am 65
    with a story that makes no sense at all; but I'll tell it anyhow,
    because, as they say, what's going to happen's going to hap-
    pen and—

CREON. Come to the point. What have you to say?

SENTRY. I did not do it. I did not see who did it. You must not punish 70
    me for what someone else has done.

CREON. A comprehensive defense! More effective, perhaps,
    If I knew its purpose. Come: what is it?

SENTRY. A dreadful thing . . . I don't know how to put it—

CREON. Out with it! 75

SENTRY.   Well, then;
    The dead man—
                        Polyneicês—

Pause. The SENTRY *is overcome, fumbles for words.* CREON *waits
impassively.*

                        out there—
                              someone,—
    New dust on the slimy flesh!

Pause. No sign from CREON.

    Someone has given it burial that way, and 80
    Gone . . .

Long pause. CREON *finally speaks with deadly control.*

CREON. And the man who dared do this?

SENTRY.   I swear I
    Do not know! You must believe me!
                              Listen:
    The ground was dry, not a sign of digging, no, 85

Not a wheeltrack in the dust, no trace of anyone.
It was when they relieved us this morning: and one of them,
The corporal, pointed to it.

                                  There it was,
The strangest—
                        Look: 90
The body, just mounded over with light dust: you see?
Not buried really, but as if they'd covered it
Just enough for the ghost's peace. And no sign
Of dogs or any wild animal that had been there.
And then what a scene there was! Every man of us   95
Accusing the other: we all proved the other man did it,
We all had proof that we could not have done it.
We were ready to take hot iron in our hands,
Walk through fire, swear by all the gods,
It was not I!   100
I do not know who it was, but it was not I!

CREON's *rage has been mounting steadily, but the* SENTRY *is too intent
upon his story to notice it.*

And then, when this came to nothing, someone said
A thing that silenced us and made us stare
Down at the ground: you had to be told the news,
And one of us had to do it! We threw the dice,
And the bad luck fell to me. So here I am   105
No happier to be here than you are to have me:
Nobody likes the man who brings bad news.

CHORAGOS. I have been wondering, King: can it be that the gods have
     done this?

CREON (*furiously*). Stop!
     Must you doddering wrecks   110
     Go out of your heads entirely? "The gods"!
     Intolerable!
     The gods favor this corpse? Why? How had he served them?
     Tried to loot their temples, burn their images,
     Yes, and the whole State, and its laws with it!   115
     Is it your senile opinion that the gods love to honor bad men?
     A pious thought!—
                         No, from the very beginning
     There have been those who have whispered together,
     Stiff-necked anarchists, putting their heads together,
     Scheming against me in alleys. These are the men,   120
     And they have bribed my own guard to do this thing.
     (*Sententiously.*) Money!
     There's nothing in the world so demoralizing as money.
     Down go your cities,

Homes gone, men gone, honest hearts corrupted,   125
Crookedness of all kinds, and all for money!
(*To* SENTRY.)   But you—!
I swear by God and by the throne of God,
The man who has done this thing shall pay for it!
Find that man, bring him here to me, or your death   130
Will be the least of your problems: I'll string you up
Alive, and there will be certain ways to make you
Discover your employer before you die;
And the process may teach you a lesson you seem to have
    missed:
The dearest profit is sometimes all too dear: 135
That depends on the source. Do you understand me?
A fortune won is often misfortune.

SENTRY. King, may I speak?

CREON.   Your very voice distresses me.

SENTRY. Are you sure that it is my voice, and not your conscience?   140

CREON. By God, he wants to analyze me now!

SENTRY. It is not what I say, but what has been done, that hurts you.

CREON. You talk too much.

SENTRY.   Maybe; but I've done nothing.

CREON. Sold your soul for some silver: that's all you've done.

SENTRY. How dreadful it is when the right judge judges wrong!

CREON. Your figures of speech
    May entertain you now; but unless you bring me the man,
    You will get little profit from them in the end.
    Exit CREON *into the palace.*

SENTRY. ``Bring me the man''—!
    I'd like nothing better than bringing him the man!
    But bring him or not, you have seen the last of me here.
    At any rate, I am safe!   (*Exit* SENTRY.)

Ode I

CHORUS. Numberless are the world's wonders, but none   *Strophe 1*
    More wonderful than man; the stormgray sea
    Yields to his prows, the huge crests bear him high;
    Earth, holy and inexhaustible, is graven
    With shining furrows where his plows have gone   5
    Year after year, the timeless labor of stallions.

    The lightboned birds and beasts that cling to cover,   *Antistrophe 1*
    The lithe fish lighting their reaches of dim water,
    All are taken, tamed in the net of his mind;

The lion on the hill, the wild horse windy-maned,   10
Resign to him; and his blunt yoke has broken
The sultry shoulders of the mountain bull.

Words also, and thought as rapid as air,   *Strophe 2*
He fashions to his good use; statecraft is his,
And his the skill that deflects the arrows of snow,   15
The spears of winter rain: from every wind
He has made himself secure—from all but one:
In the late wind of death he cannot stand.

O clear intelligence, force beyond all measure!   *Antistrophe 2*
O fate of man, working both good and evil!   20
When the laws are kept, how proudly his city stands!
When the laws are broken, what of his city then?
Never may the anarchic man find rest at my hearth,
Never be it said that my thoughts are his thoughts.

Scene II

Reenter SENTRY *leading* ANTIGONÊ.

CHORAGOS. What does this mean? Surely this captive woman
     Is the Princess, Antigonê. Why should she be taken?

SENTRY. Here is the one who did it! We caught her
     In the very act of burying him.—Where is Creon?

CHORAGOS. Just coming from the house.

     Enter CREON, *center.*

CREON.   What has happened?   5
     Why have you come back so soon? O King,

SENTRY *(expansively).*
     A man should never be too sure of anything:
     I would have sworn
     That you'd not see me here again: your anger
     Frightened me so, and the things you threatened me with;   10
     But how could I tell then
     That I'd be able to solve the case so soon?
     No dice-throwing this time: I was only too glad to come!
     Here is this woman. She is the guilty one:
     We found her trying to bury him.   15
     Take her, then; question her; judge her as you will.
     I am through with the whole thing now, and glad of it.

CREON. But this is Antigonê! Why have you brought her here?

SENTRY. She was buring him, I tell you!

CREON *(severely).*   Is this the truth?

SENTRY. I saw her with my own eyes. Can I say more?   20

CREON. The details: come, tell me quickly!

SENTRY.   It was like this:
    After those terrible threats of yours, King,
    We went back and brushed the dust away from the body.
    The flesh was soft by now, and stinking,
    So we sat on a hill to windward and kept guard.   25
    No napping this time! We kept each other awake.
    But nothing happened until the white round sun
    Whirled in the center of the round sky over us:
    Then, suddenly,
    A storm of dust roared up from the earth, and the sky   30
    Went out, the plain vanished with all its trees
    In the stinging dark. We closed our eyes and endured it.
    The whirlwind lasted a long time, but it passed;
    And then we looked, and there was Antigonê!
    I have seen   35
    A mother bird come back to a stripped nest, heard
    Her crying bitterly a broken note or two
    For the young ones stolen. Just so, when this girl
    Found the bare corpse, and all her love's work wasted,
    She wept, and cried on heaven to damn the hands   40
    That had done this thing.
                            And then she brought more dust
    And sprinkled wine three times for her brother's ghost.
    We ran and took her at once. She was not afraid,
    Not even when we charged her with what she had done.
    She denied nothing.
                            And this was a comfort to me,   45
    And some uneasiness: for it is a good thing
    To escape from death, but it is no great pleasure
    To bring death to a friend.
                            Yet I always say
    There is nothing so comfortable as your own safe skin!

CREON (*slowly, dangerously*). And you, Antigonê,   50
    You with your head hanging,—do you confess this thing?

ANTIGONÊ. I do. I deny nothing.

CREON (*to* SENTRY).   You may go.   (*Exit* SENTRY.)
    (*To* ANTIGONÊ.) Tell me, tell me briefly:
    Had you heard my proclamation touching this matter?

ANTIGONÊ. It was public. Could I help hearing it?   55

CREON. And yet you dared defy the law.

ANTIGONÊ.
    It was not God's proclamation. That final Justice
    That rules the world below makes no such laws.

Your edict, King, was strong,
But all your strength is weakness itself against   60
The immortal unrecorded laws of God.
They are not merely now: they were, and shall be,
Operative for ever, beyond man utterly.
I knew I must die, even without your decree:
I am only mortal. And if I must die   65
Now, before it is my time to die,
Surely this is no hardship: can anyone
Living, as I live, with evil all about me,
Think Death less than a friend? This death of mine
Is of no importance; but if I had left my brother   70
Lying in death unburied, I should have suffered.
Now I do not.
      You smile at me. Ah Creon,
Think me a fool, if you like; but it may well be
That a fool convicts me of folly.

CHORAGOS. Like father, like daughter: both headstrong, deaf to
  reason!   75
She has never learned to yield:

CREON.   She has much to learn.
The inflexible heart breaks first, the toughest iron
Cracks first, and the wildest horses bend their necks
At the pull of the smallest curb.
          Pride? In a slave?
This girl is guilty of a double insolence,   80
Breaking the given laws and boasting of it.
Who is the man here,
She or I, if this crime goes unpunished?
Sister's child, or more than sister's child,
Or closer yet in blood—she and her sister   85
Win bitter death for this!
(*To* SERVANTS.)   Go, some of you,
Arrest Ismenê. I accuse her equally.
Bring her: you will find her sniffling in the house there.
Her mind's a traitor: crimes kept in the dark
Cry for light, and the guardian brain shudders;   90
But how much worse than this
Is brazen boasting of barefaced anarchy!

ANTIGONÊ. Creon, what more do you want than my death?

CREON.   Nothing.
That gives me everything.

ANTIGONÊ.   Then I beg you: kill me.
This talking is a great weariness: your words   95
Are distasteful to me, and I am sure that mine

Seem so to you. And yet they should not seem so:
I should have praise and honor for what I have done.
All these men here would praise me
Were their lips not frozen shut with fear of you.   100
(Bitterly.) Ah the good fortune of kings,
Licensed to say and do whatever they please!

CREON. You are alone here in that opinion.

ANTIGONÊ. No, they are with me. But they keep their tongues in leash.

CREON. Maybe. But you are guilty, and they are not.   105

ANTIGONÊ. There is no guilt in reverence for the dead.

CREON. But Eteoclês—was he not your brother too?

ANTIGONÊ. My brother too.

CREON.   And you insult his memory?

ANTIGONÊ. *(softly)*. The dead man would not say that I insult it.

CREON. He would: for you honor a traitor as much as him.   110

ANTIGONÊ. His own brother, traitor or not, and equal in blood.

CREON. He made war on his country. Eteoclês defended it.

ANTIGONÊ. Nevertheless, there are honors due all the dead.

CREON. But not the same for the wicked as for the just.

ANTIGONÊ. Ah Creon, Creon,   115
Which of us can say what the gods hold wicked?

CREON. An enemy is an enemy, even dead.

ANTIGONÊ. It is my nature to join in love, not hate.

CREON *(finally losing patience)*. Go join them then; if you must have
your love,
Find it in hell!   120

CHORAGOS. But see, Ismenê comes:

Enter ISMENÊ, *guarded.*

Those tears are sisterly, the cloud
That shadows her eyes rains down gentle sorrow.

CREON. You too, Ismenê,
Snake in my ordered house, sucking my blood   125
Stealthily—and all the time I never knew
That these two sisters were aiming at my throne!
                                                 Ismenê,
Do you confess your share in this crime, or deny it?
Answer me.

ISMENÊ. Yes, if she will let me say so. I am guilty.   130

ANTIGONÊ *(coldly)*. No, Ismenê. You have no right to say so.
You would not help me, and I will not have you help me.

ISMENÊ. But now I know what you meant; and I am here
    To join you, to take my share of punishment.

ANTIGONÊ. The dead man and the gods who rule the dead   135
    Know whose act this was. Words are not friends.

ISMENÊ. Do you refuse me, Antigonê? I want to die with you:
    I too have a duty that I must discharge to the dead.

ANTIGONÊ. You shall not lessen my death by sharing it.

ISMENÊ. What do I care for life when you are dead?   140

ANTIGONÊ. Ask Creon. You're always hanging on his opinions.

ISMENÊ. You are laughing at me. Why, Antigonê?

ANTIGONÊ. It's a joyless laughter, Ismenê.

ISMENÊ.   But can I do nothing?

ANTIGONÊ. Yes. Save yourself. I shall not envy you.
    There are those who will praise you; I shall have honor, too.   145

ISMENÊ. But we are equally guilty!

ANTIGONÊ.   No more, Ismenê.
    You are alive, but I belong to Death.

CREON (*to the* CHORUS). Gentlemen, I beg you to observe these girls:
    One has just now lost her mind; the other,
    It seems, has never had a mind at all.   150

ISMENÊ. Grief teaches the steadiest minds to waver, King.

CREON. Yours certainly did, when you assumed guilt with the guilty!

ISMENÊ. But how could I go on living without her?

CREON.   You are.
    She is already dead.

ISMENÊ.   But your own son's bride!

CREON. There are places enough for him to push his plow.   155
    I want no wicked women for my sons!

ISMENÊ. O dearest Haimon, how your father wrongs you!

CREON. I've had enough of your childish talk of marriage!

CHORAGOS. Do you really intend to steal this girl from your son?

CREON. No; Death will do that for me.

CHORAGOS.   Then she must die?   160

CREON (*ironically.*) You dazzle me.
                  —But enough of this talk!
    (*To* GUARDS.) You, there, take them away and guard them well:
    For they are but women, and even brave men run
    When they see Death coming.

                        Exeunt ISMENÊ, ANTIGONÊ, *and* GUARDS.

Ode II

CHORUS. Fortunate is the man who has never tasted God's *Strophe 1*
    vengeance!
    Where once the anger of heaven has struck, that house is
      shaken
    For ever: damnation rises behind each child
    Like a wave cresting out of the black northeast,
    When the long darkness under sea roars up   5
    And bursts drumming death upon the windwhipped sand.

    I have seen this gathering sorrow from time long past *Antistrophe 1*
    Loom upon Oedipus' children: generation from generation
    Takes the compulsive rage of the enemy god.
    So lately this last flower of Oedipus' line   10
    Drank the sunlight! but now a passionate word
    And a handful of dust have closed up all its beauty.

        What mortal arrogance *Strophe 2*
        Transcends the wrath of Zeus?
    Sleep cannot lull him nor the effortless long months   15
    Of the timeless gods: but he is young for ever,
    And his house is the shining day of high Olympos.
        All that is and shall be,
        And all the past, is his.
    No pride on earth is free of the curse of heaven.   20

    The straying dreams of men *Antistrophe 2*
        May bring them ghosts of joy:
    But as they drowse, the waking embers burn them;
    Or they walk with fixed eyes, as blind men walk.
    But the ancient wisdom speaks for our own time: 25
        Fate works most for woe
        With Folly's fairest show.
    Man's little pleasure is the spring of sorrow.

Scene III

CHORAGOS. But here is Haimon, King, the last of all your sons.
    Is it grief for Antigonê that brings him here,
    And bitterness at being robbed of his bride?

    Enter HAIMON.

CREON. We shall soon see, and no need of diviners.
                           —Son,
    You have heard my final judgment on that girl: 5

Have you come here hating me, or have you come
With deference and with love, whatever I do?

HAIMON. I am your son, father. You are my guide.
You make things clear for me, and I obey you.
No marriage means more to me than your continuing wisdom. 10

CREON. Good. That is the way to behave: subordinate
Everything else, my son, to your father's will.
This is what a man prays for, that he may get
Sons attentive and dutiful in his house,
Each one hating his father's enemies, 15
Honoring his father's friends. But if his sons
Fail him, if they turn out unprofitably,
What has he fathered but trouble for himself
And amusement for the malicious?

　　　　　　　　　　　　　So you are right
Not to lose your head over this woman. 20
Your pleasure with her would soon grow cold, Haimon,
And then you'd have a hellcat in bed and elsewhere.
Let her find her husband in Hell!
Of all the people in this city, only she
Has had contempt for my law and broken it. 25

Do you want me to show myself weak before the people?
Or to break my sworn word? No, and I will not.
The woman dies.
I suppose she'll plead "family ties." Well, let her.
If I permit my own family to rebel, 30
How shall I earn the world's obedience?
Show me the man who keeps his house in hand,
He's fit for public authority.
　　　　　　　　　　　I'll have no dealings
With lawbreakers, critics of the government:
Whoever is chosen to govern should be obeyed— 35
Must be obeyed, in all things, great and small,
Just and unjust! O Haimon,
The man who knows how to obey, and that man only,
Knows how to give commands when the time comes.
You can depend on him, no matter how fast 40

The spears come: he's a good soldier, he'll stick it out.
Anarchy, anarchy! Show me a greater evil!
This is why cities tumble and the great houses rain down,
This is what scatters armies!
No, no: good lives are made so by discipline. 45
We keep the laws then, and the lawmakers,
And no woman shall seduce us. If we must lose,
Let's lose to a man, at least! Is a woman stronger than we?

CHORAGOS. Unless time has rusted my wits,
    What you say, King, is said with point and dignity.   50

HAIMON *(boyishly earnest)*. Father:
    Reason is God's crowning gift to man, and you are right
    To warn me against losing mine. I cannot say—
    I hope that I shall never want to say!—that you
    Have reasoned badly. Yet there are other men   55
    Who can reason, too; and their opinions might be helpful.
    You are not in a position to know everything
    That people say or do, or what they feel:
    Your temper terrifies—everyone
    Will tell you only what you like to hear.   60
    But I, at any rate, can listen; and I have heard them
    Muttering and whispering in the dark about this girl.
    They say no woman has ever, so unreasonably,
    Died so shameful a death for a generous act:
    "She covered her brother's body. Is this indecent?   65
    She kept him from dogs and vultures. Is this a crime?
    Death?—She should have all the honor that we can give her!"

    This is the way they talk out there in the city.

    You must believe me:
    Nothing is closer to me than your happiness.   70
    What could be closer? Must not any son
    Value his father's fortune as his father does his?
    I beg you, do not be unchangeable:
    Do not believe that you alone can be right.
    The man who thinks that,   75
    The man who maintains that only he has the power
    To reason correctly, the gift to speak, the soul—
    A man like that, when you know him, turns out empty

    It is not reason never to yield to reason!

    In flood time you can see how some trees bend,   80
    And because they bend, even their twigs are safe,
    While stubborn trees are torn up, roots and all.
    And the same thing happens in sailing:
    Make your sheet fast, never slacken,—and over you go,
    Head over heels and under: and there's your voyage.   85
    Forget you are angry! Let yourself be moved!
    I know I am young; but please let me say this:
    The ideal condition
    Would be, I admit, that men should be right by instinct;
    But since we are all too likely to go astray,   90
    The reasonable thing is to learn from those who can teach.

CHORAGOS. You will do well to listen to him, King,
    If what he says is sensible. And you, Haimon,
    Must listen to your father.—Both speak well.

CREON. You consider it right for a man of my years and experience   95
    To go to school to a boy?

HAIMON.   It is not right
    If I am wrong. But if I am young, and right,
    What does my age matter?

CREON. You think it right to stand up for an anarchist?

HAIMON. Not at all. I pay no respect to criminals.   100

CREON. Then she is not a criminal?

HAIMON. The City would deny it, to a man.

CREON. And the City proposes to teach me how to rule?

HAIMON. Ah. Who is it that's talking like a boy now?

CREON. My voice is the one voice giving orders in this City!   105

HAIMON. It is no City if it takes orders from one voice.

CREON. The State is the King!

HAIMON.   Yes, if the State is a desert.
    Pause.

CREON. This boy, it seems, has sold out to a woman.

HAIMON. If you are a woman: my concern is only for you.

CREON. So? Your "concern"! In a public brawl with your father!   110

HAIMON. How about you, in a public brawl with justice?

CREON. With justice, when all that I do is within my rights?

HAIMON. You have no right to trample on God's right.

CREON. *(completely out of control).* Fool, adolescent fool! Taken in by
    a woman!

HAIMON. You'll never see me taken in by anything vile.   115

CREON. Every word you say is for her!

HAIMON *(quietly, darkly).*   And for you.
    And for me. And for the gods under the earth.

CREON. You'll never marry her while she lives.

HAIMON. Then she must die.—But her death will cause another.

CREON. Another?   120
    Have you lost your senses? Is this an open threat?

HAIMON. There is no threat in speaking to emptiness.

CREON. I swear you'll regret this superior tone of yours!
    You are the empty one!

HAIMON.   If you were not my father,
    I'd say you were perverse.   125

CREON. You girlstruck fool, don't play at words with me!

HAIMON. I am sorry. You prefer silence.

CREON.   Now, by God—!
    I swear, by all the gods in heaven above us,
    You'll watch it, I swear you shall!
    (*To the* SERVANTS)   Bring her out!
    Bring the woman out! Let her die before his eyes!   130
    Here, this instant, with her bridegroom beside her!

HAIMON. Not here, no; she will not die here, King.
    And you will never see my face again.
    Go on raving as long as you've a friend to endure you.
                                       (*Exit* HAIMON.)

CHORAGOS. Gone, gone.   135
    Creon, a young man in a rage is dangerous!

CREON. Let him do, or dream to do, more than a man can.
    He shall not save these girls from death.

CHORAGOS.   These girls?
    You have sentenced them both?

CREON.   No, you are right.
    I will not kill the one whose hands are clean.   140

CHORAGOS. But Antigonê?

CREON. (*somberly*).   I will carry her far away
    Out there in the wilderness, and lock her
    Living in a vault of stone. She shall have food,
    As the custom is, to absolve the State of her death.
    And there let her pray to the gods of hell: 145
    They are her only gods:
    Perhaps they will show her an escape from death,
    Or she may learn,
               though late,
    That piety shown the dead is pity in vain.   (*Exit* CREON.)

Ode III

CHORUS. Love, unconquerable   *Strophe*
    Waster of rich men, keeper
    Of warm lights and all-night vigil
    In the soft face of a girl:
    Sea-wanderer, forest-visitor!   5
    Even the pure Immortals cannot escape you,

And mortal man, in his one day's dusk,
Trembles before your glory.

Surely you swerve upon ruin   *Antistrophe*
The just man's consenting heart,   10
As here you have made bright anger
Strike between father and son—
And none has conquered but Love!
A girl's glance working the will of heaven:
Pleasure to her alone who mocks us,   15
Merciless Aphroditê.°

Scene IV

CHORAGOS (*as* ANTIGONÊ *enters guarded*). But I can no longer stand in
awe of this,
Nor, seeing what I see, keep back my tears.
Here is Antigonê, passing to that chamber
Where all find sleep at last.

ANTIGONÊ. Look upon me, friends, and pity me   *Strophe 1*
Turning back at the night's edge to say
Good-by to the sun that shines for me no longer;
Now sleepy Death
Summons me down to Acheron,° that cold shore:
There is no bridesong there, nor any music.   10

CHORUS. Yet not unpraised, not without a kind of honor,
You walk at last into the underworld;
Untouched by sickness, broken by no sword.
What woman has ever found your way to death?

ANTIGONÊ. How often I have heard the story of Niobê,°   *Antistrophe 1*
Tantalos' wretched daughter, how the stone
Clung fast about her, ivy-close: and they say
The rain falls endlessly
And sifting soft snow; her tears are never done.
I feel the loneliness of her death in mine.   20

CHORUS. But she was born of heaven, and you
Are woman, woman-born. If her death is yours,
A mortal woman's, is this not for you
Glory in our world and in the world beyond?

Ode III.   ¹⁶*Aphroditê*   goddess of love
Scene IV.   ⁹*Acheron*   a river of the underworld, which was ruled by Hades
¹⁵*Niobê*, the daughter of Tantalos, boasted about her dozen children thereby provoking
Artemis and Apollo to kill them all. Crying inconsolably, Niobê fled to Mount Sipylus
where Zeus turned her into a stone image that wept perpetually.

ANTIGONÊ. You laugh at me. Ah, friends, friends,   *Strophe 2*
    Can you not wait until I am dead? O Thebes,
    O men many-charioted, in love with Fortune,
    Dear springs of Dircê, sacred Theban grove,
    Be witnesses for me, denied all pity,
    Unjustly judged! and think a word of love   30
    For her whose path turns
    Under dark earth, where there are no more tears.

CHORUS. You have passed beyond human daring and come at last
    Into a place of stone where Justice sits.
    I cannot tell   35
    What shape of your father's guilt appears in this.

ANTIGONÊ. You have touched it at last: that bridal bed   *Antistrophe 2*
    Unspeakable, horror of son and mother mingling:
    Their crime, infection of all our family!
    O Oedipus, father and brother!   40
    Your marriage strikes from the grave to murder mine.
    I have been a stranger here in my own land:
    All my life
    The blasphemy of my birth has followed me.

CHORUS. Reverence is a virtue, but strength   45
    Lives in established law: that must prevail.
    You have made your choice,
    Your death is the doing of your conscious hand.

ANTIGONÊ. Then let me go, since all your words are bitter,   *Epode*
    And the very light of the sun is cold to me.   50
    Lead me to my vigil, where I must have
    Neither love nor lamentation; no song, but silence.
    CREON *interrupts impatiently.*

CREON. If dirges and planned lamentations could put off death,
    Men would be singing for ever.
    (*To the* SERVANTS.)   Take her, go!
    You know your orders: take her to the vault   55
    And leave her alone there. And if she lives or dies,
    That's her affair, not ours: our hands are clean.

ANTIGONÊ. O tomb, vaulted bride-bed in eternal rock,
    Soon I shall be with my own again
    Where Persephonê° welcomes the thin ghosts underground: 60
    And I shall see my father again, and you, mother,
    And dearest Polyneicês
             —dearest indeed
    To me, since it was my hand

---

60 *Persephonê*   queen of the underworld

That washed him clean and poured the ritual wine:
And my reward is death before my time! 65
And yet, as men's hearts know, I have done no wrong,
I have not sinned before God. Or if I have,
I shall know the truth in death. But if the guilt
Lies upon Creon who judged me, then, I pray,
May his punishment equal my own. 70

CHORAGOS. O passionate heart,
Unyielding, tormented still by the same winds!

CREON. Her guards shall have good cause to regret their delaying.

ANTIGONÊ. Ah! That voice is like the voice of death!

CREON. I can give you no reason to think you are mistaken. 75

ANTIGONÊ. Thebes, and you my fathers' gods,
And rulers of Thebes, you see me now, the last
Unhappy daughter of a line of kings,
Your kings, led away to death. You will remember
What things I suffer, and at what men's hands, 80
Because I would not transgress the laws of heaven.
(*To the* GUARDS, *simply.*) Come: let us wait no longer.

(*Exit* ANTIGONÊ, *left, guarded.*)

Ode IV

CHORUS. All Danaê's beauty was locked away   *Strophe 1*
In a brazen cell where the sunlight could not come:
A small room still as any grave, enclosed her.
Yet she was a princess too.
And Zeus in a rain of gold poured love upon her. 5
O child, child.
No power in wealth or war
Or tough sea-blackened ships
Can prevail against untiring Destiny!

And Dryas' son° also, that furious king,   *Antistrophe 1*
Bore the god's prisoning anger for his pride:
Sealed up by Dionysos in deaf stone,
His madness died among echoes.
So at the last he learned what dreadful power
His tongue had mocked: 15
For he had profaned the revels,
And fired the wrath of the nine
Implacable Sisters° that love the sound of the flute.

---

[10] *Dryas' son* Lycurgus, King of Thrace
[18] *Sisters* the Muses

And old men tell a half-remembered tale *Strophe 2*
Of horror where a dark ledge splits the sea 20
And a double surf beats on the gray shores:
How a king's new woman,° sick
With hatred for the queen he had imprisoned,
Ripped out his two sons' eyes with her bloody hands
While grinning Arês° watched the shuttle plunge 25
Four times: four blind wounds crying for revenge,

Crying, tears and blood mingled.—Piteously born, *Antistrophe 2*
Those sons whose mother was of heavenly birth!
Her father was the god of the North Wind
And she was cradled by gales, 30
She raced with young colts on the glittering hills
And walked untrammeled in the open light:
But in her marriage deathless Fate found means
To build a tomb like yours for all her joy.

Scene V

Enter blind TEIRESIAS, *led by a boy. The opening speeches of* TEIRESIAS
should be in singsong contrast to the realistic lines of CREON.

TEIRESIAS. This is the way the blind man comes, Princes, Princes,
   Lock-step, two heads lit by the eyes of one.

CREON. What new thing have you to tell us, old Teiresias?

TEIRESIAS. I have much to tell you: listen to the prophet, Creon.

CREON. I am not aware that I have ever failed to listen. 5

TEIRESIAS. Then you have done wisely, King, and ruled well.

CREON. I admit my debt to you. But what have you to say?

TEIRESIAS. This, Creon: you stand once more on the edge of fate.

CREON. What do you mean? Your words are a kind of dread.

TEIRESIAS. Listen, Creon: 10
   I was sitting in my chair of augury, at the place
   Where the birds gather about me. They were all a-chatter,
   As is their habit, when suddenly I heard
   A strange note in their jangling, a scream, a
   Whirring fury; I knew that they were fighting, 15
   Tearing each other, dying
   In a whirlwind of wings clashing. And I was afraid.

---

[22] *king's new woman* Eidothea, second wife of King Phineus, blinded her stepsons. Their
   mother, Cleopatra, had been imprisoned in a cave. Phineus was the son of a king, and
   Cleopatra, his first wife, was the daughter of Boreas, the North wind, but this illustrious
   ancestry could not protect his sons from violence and darkness.
[25] *Arês* god of war

I began the rites of burnt-offering at the altar,
But Hephaistos° failed me: instead of bright flame,
There was only the sputtering slime of the fat thigh-flesh   20
Melting: the entrails dissolved in gray smoke,
The bare bone burst from the welter. And no blaze!

This was a sign from heaven. My boy described it,
Seeing for me as I see for others.

I tell you, Creon, you yourself have brought   25
This new calamity upon us. Our hearths and altars
Are stained with the corruption of dogs and carrion birds
That glut themselves on the corpse of Oedipus' son.
The gods are deaf when we pray to them, their fire
Recoils from our offering, their birds of omen   30
Have no cry of comfort, for they are gorged
With the thick blood of the dead.
                                    O my son,
These are no trifles! Think: all men make mistakes,
But a good man yields when he knows his course is wrong,
And repairs the evil. The only crime is pride.   35
Give in to the dead man, then: do not fight with a corpse—
What glory is it to kill a man who is dead?
Think, I beg you:
It is for your own good that I speak as I do.
You should be able to yield for your own good.   40

CREON. It seems that prophets have made me their especial
        province.
   All my life long
   I have been a kind of butt for the dull arrows
   Of doddering fortune-tellers
                        No, Teiresias:
   If your birds—if the great eagles of God himself   45
   Should carry him stinking bit by bit to heaven,
   I would not yield. I am not afraid of pollution:
   No man can defile the gods.
                        Do what you will,
   Go into business, make money, speculate
   In India gold or that synthetic gold from Sardis,   50
   Get rich otherwise than by my consent to bury him.
   Teiresias, it is a sorry thing when a wise man
   Sells his wisdom, lets out his words for hire!

TEIRESIAS. Ah Creon! Is there no man left in the world—

CREON. To do what?—Come, let's have the aphorism!   55

---

[19] *Hephaistos*   god of fire

TEIRESIAS. No man who knows that wisdom outweighs any wealth?

CREON. As surely as bribes are baser than any baseness.

TEIRESIAS. You are sick, Creon! You are deathly sick!

CREON. As you say: it is not my place to challenge a prophet.

TEIRESIAS. Yet you have said my prophecy is for sale. 60

CREON. The generation of prophets has always loved gold.

TEIRESIAS. The generation of kings has always loved brass.

CREON. You forget yourself! You are speaking to your King.

TEIRESIAS. I know it. You are a king because of me.

CREON. You have a certain skill; but you have sold out. 65

TEIRESIAS. King, you will drive me to words that—

CREON.   Say them, say them!
    Only remember: I will not pay you for them.

TEIRESIAS. No, you will find them too costly.

CREON.   No doubt. Speak:
    Whatever you say, you will not change my will.

TEIRESIAS. Then take this, and take it to heart! 70
    The time is not far off when you shall pay back
    Corpse for corpse, flesh of your own flesh.
    You have thrust the child of this world into living night,
    You have kept from the gods below the child that is theirs:
    The one in a grave before her death, the other, 75
    Dead, denied the grave. This is your crime:
    And the Furies and the dark gods of Hell
    Are swift with terrible punishment for you.
    Do you want to buy me now, Creon?
                                    Not many days,
    And your house will be full of men and women weeping, 80
    And curses will be hurled at you from far
    Cities grieving for sons unburied, left to rot
    Before the walls of Thebes.

    These are my arrows, Creon: they are all for you.

    (*To* BOY.) But come, child: lead me home. 85
    Let him waste his fine anger upon younger men.
    Maybe he will learn at last
    To control a wiser tongue in a better head.   (*Exit* TEIRESIAS.)

CHORAGOS. The old man has gone, King, but his words
    Remain to plague us. I am old, too, 90
    But I cannot remember that he was ever false.

CREON. That is true. . . . It troubles me.
    Oh it is hard to give in! but it is worse
    To risk everything for stubborn pride.

CHORAGOS. Creon: take my advice.

CREON. What shall I do? 95

CHORAGOS. Go quickly: free Antigonê from her vault
And build a tomb for the body of Polyneicês.

CREON. You would have me do this!

CHORAGOS. Creon, yes!
And it must be done at once: God moves
Swiftly to cancel the folly of stubborn men. 100

CREON. It is hard to deny the heart! But I
Will do it: I will not fight with destiny.

CHORAGOS. You must go yourself, you cannot leave it to others.

CREON. I will go.—Bring axes, servants: Come with me to the tomb.
I buried her, I 105
Will set her free.
Oh quickly! My mind misgives—
The laws of the gods are mighty, and a man must serve them
To the last day of his life! (*Exit* CREON.)

Paean°

CHORAGOS. God of many names *Strophe 1*

CHORUS. O Iacchos

son
of Kadmeian Sémelê
O born of the thunder!
Guardian of the West
Regent
of Eleusis' plain
O Prince of maenad Thebes
and the Dragon Field by rippling Ismenós:° 5

CHORAGOS. God of many names *Antistrophe 1*

CHORUS. the flame of torches
flares on our hills
the nymphs of Iacchos
dance at the spring of Castalia:°
from the vine-close mountain
come ah come in ivy:
Evohé evohé! sings through the streets of Thebes 10

Paean a hymn of praise. This paean is dedicated to Iacchos, also known as Dionysos, the
son of Zeus and Sémelê, daughter of Kadmos. Iacchos's worshipers were the Maenads,
whose cry was ''*Evohé evohé.*
[5] *Ismenos* a river near Thebes. Kadmos sowed a crop of dragon's teeth near the Ismenos.
From these teeth sprang men who were ancestors of Theban nobility.

CHORAGOS. God of many names   *Strophe 2*

CHORUS.   Iacchos of Thebes
    heavenly child
        of Sémelê bride of the Thunderer!
    The shadow of plague is upon us:
           come
    with clement feet
        oh come from Parnasos
    down the long slopes
        across the lamenting water   15

CHORAGOS. Iô Fire! Chorister of the throbbing stars!   *Antistrophe 2*
    O purest among the voices of the night!
    Thou son of God, blaze for us!

CHORUS. Come with choric rapture of circling Maenads
    Who cry *Iô Iacche!*
        God of many names!   20

Exodos

Enter MESSENGER *from left.*

MESSENGER. Men of the line of Kadmos,° you who live
    Near Amphion's citadel,°
        I cannot say
    Of any condition of human life "This is fixed,
    This is clearly good, or bad." Fate raises up,
    And Fate casts down the happy and unhappy alike: 5
    No man can fortell his Fate.
        Take the case of Creon:
    Creon was happy once, as I count happiness:
    Victorious in battle, sole governor of the land,
    Fortunate father of children nobly born.
    And now it has all gone from him! Who can say   10
    That a man is still alive when his life's joy fails?
    He is a walking dead man. Grant him rich,
    Let him live like a king in his great house:
    If his pleasure is gone, I would not give
    So much as the shadow of smoke for all he owns.   15

CHORAGOS. Your words hint at sorrow: what is your news for us?

MESSENGER. They are dead. The living are guilty of their death.

CHORAGOS. Who is guilty? Who is dead? Speak!

---

¹ *Kadmos,* see notes on page 510. Kadmos founded Thebes.
³ *Amphion's citadel* Amphion, a son of Zeus, played such sweet music that stones moved
   of their own will to form a wall around Thebes.

MESSENGER.   Haimon.
    Haimon is dead; and the hand that killed him
    Is his own hand.

CHORAGOS. His father's? or his own?   20

MESSENGER. His own, driven mad by the murder his father had done.

CHORAGOS. Teiresias, Teiresias, how clearly you saw it all!

MESSENGER. This is my news: you must draw what conclusions you
    can from it.

CHORAGOS. But look: Eurydicê, our Queen:
    Has she overheard us?   25

    Enter EURYDICÊ *from the palace, center.*

EURYDICÊ. I have heard something, friends:
    As I was unlocking the gate of Pallas'° shrine,
    For I needed her help today, I heard a voice
    Telling of some new sorrow. And I fainted
    There at the temple with all my maidens about me.   30
    But speak again: whatever it is, I can bear it:
    Grief and I are no strangers.

MESSENGER.   Dearest Lady,
    I will tell you plainly all that I have seen.
    I shall not try to comfort you: what is the use,
    Since comfort could lie only in what is not true?   35
    The truth is always best.

                 I went with Creon
    To the outer plain where Polyneicês was lying,
    No friend to pity him, his body shredded by dogs.
    We made our prayers in that place to Hecatê
    And Pluto,° that they would be merciful. And we bathed   40
    The corpse with holy water, and we brought
    Fresh-broken branches to burn what was left of it,
    And upon the urn we heaped up a towering barrow
    Of the earth of his own land.

                 When we were done, we ran
    To the vault where Antigonê lay on her couch of stone.   45
    One of the servants had gone ahead,
    And while he was yet far off he heard a voice
    Grieving within the chamber, and he came back
    And told Creon. And as the King went closer,
    The air was full of wailing, the words lost,   50
    And he begged us to make all haste. ``Am I a prophet?''
    He said, weeping, ``And must I walk this road,

---

²⁷ *Pallas, Pallas Athene*   goddess of wisdom
³⁹⁻⁴⁰ *Hecatê/And Pluto*   Hecatê and Pluto (also known as Hades) were deities of the
    underworld.

The saddest of all that I have gone before?
My son's voice calls me on. Oh quickly, quickly!
Look through the crevice there, and tell me   55
If it is Haimon, or some deception of the gods!"

We obeyed: and in the cavern's farthest corner
We saw her lying:
She had made a noose of her fine linen veil
And hanged herself. Haimon lay beside her,   60
His arms about her waist, lamenting her,
His love lost under ground, crying out
That his father had stolen her away from him.

When Creon saw him the tears rushed to his eyes
And he called to him: "What have you done, child? Speak to me. 65
What are you thinking that makes your eyes so strange?
O my son, my son, I come to you on my knees!"
But Haimon spat in his face. He said not a word,
Staring—
               And suddenly drew his sword
And lunged. Creon shrank back, the blade missed; and the boy,   70
Desperate against himself, drove it half its length
Into his own side, and fell. And as he died
He gathered Antigonê close in his arms again,
Choking, his blood bright red on her white cheek.
And now he lies dead with the dead, and she is his   75
At last, his bride in the house of the dead.

Exit EURYDICÊ *into the palace.*

CHORAGOS. She has left us without a word. What can this mean?

MESSENGER. It troubles me, too: yet she knows what is best,
    Her grief is too great for public lamentation,
    And doubtless she has gone to her chamber to weep   80
    For her dead son, leading her maidens in his dirge.

    Pause.

CHORAGOS. It may be so: but I fear this deep silence.

MESSENGER. I will see what she is doing. I will go in.

Exit MESSENGER *into the palace.*

Enter CREON *with attendants, bearing* HAIMON's *body.*

CHORAGOS. But here is the king himself: oh look at him,
    Bearing his own damnation in his arms.   85

CREON. Nothing you say can touch me any more.
    My own blind heart has brought me
    From darkness to final darkness. Here you see
    The father murdering, the murdered son—

And all my civic wisdom!   90
Haimon my son, so young, so young to die,
I was the fool, not you; and you died for me.

CHORAGOS. That is the truth; but you were late in learning it.

CREON. This truth is hard to bear. Surely a god
Has crushed me beneath the hugest weight of heaven,   95
And driven me headlong a barbaric way
To trample out the thing I held most dear.

The pains that men will take to come to pain!

Enter MESSENGER *from the palace.*

MESSENGER. The burden you carry in your hands is heavy,
But it is not all: you will find more in your house.   100

CREON. What burden worse than this shall I find there?

MESSENGER. The Queen is dead.

CREON. O port of death, deaf world,
Is there no pity for me? And you, Angel of evil,
I was dead, and your words are death again.   105
Is it true, boy? Can it be true?
Is my wife dead? Has death bred death?

MESSENGER. You can see for yourself.

The doors are opened and the body of EURYDICÈ *is disclosed within.*

CREON. Oh pity!
All true, all true, and more than I can bear!   110
O my wife, my son!

MESSENGER. She stood before the altar, and her heart
Welcomed the knife her own hand guided,
And a great cry burst from her lips for Megareus° dead,
And for Haimon dead, her sons; and her last breath   115
Was a curse for their father, the murderer of her sons.
And she fell, and the dark flowed in through her closing eyes.

CREON. O God, I am sick with fear.
Are there no swords here? Has no one a blow for me?

MESSENGER. Her curse is upon you for the deaths of both.   120

CREON. It is right that it should be. I alone am guilty.
I know it, and I say it. Lead me in,
Quickly, friends.
I have neither life nor substance. Lead me in.

CHORAGOS. You are right, if there can be right in so much wrong.   125
The briefest way is best in a world of sorrow.

---

[114] *Megareus,* brother of Haimon, had died in the assault on Thebes.

CREON. Let it come,
    Let death come quickly, and be kind to me.
    I would not ever see the sun again.

CHORAGOS. All that will come when it will; but we, meanwhile,   130
    Have much to do. Leave the future to itself.

CREON. All my heart was in that prayer!

CHORAGOS. Then do not pray any more: the sky is deaf.

CREON. Lead me away. I have been rash and foolish.
    I have killed my son and my wife.   135
    I look for comfort; my comfort lies here dead.
    Whatever my hands have touched has come to nothing.
    Fate has brought all my pride to a thought of dust.

As CREON *is being led into the house, the* CHORAGOS *advances and speaks directly to the audience.*

CHORAGOS. There is no happiness where there is no wisdom;
    No wisdom but in submission to the gods.   140
    Big words are always punished,
    And proud men in old age learn to be wise.

SUGGESTIONS FOR WRITING AND DISCUSSION

1. The Prologue is the means of exposition (see Chapter 8). How does it help us to appreciate what takes place in the rest of the play?
2. When Antigonê first announces to Ismenê her intention of burying Polyneicês, her courage and resolution seem admirable. Does our opinion of her character change when we see how she behaves toward Ismenê later in the play?
3. Is Antigonê simply being reactionary in following the old laws? Is Creon merely being tyrannical in insisting on the new laws?
4. Examine the speeches made by the Chorus. What is their relationship to the rest of the play? How do they deepen our understanding and response?
5. Is Creon a tragic hero? Read the definition of *tragedy* in Chapter 8 and answer this question in a two- to three-page essay.
6. Is Haimon trying to manipulate his father in Scene III, or is his concern for Creon genuine? In answering this question keep in mind both Creon's comments on his son in Scene II and how Haimon meets his end.
7. Does Creon capitulate too easily? Look at Teiresias's speeches and explain their effect on him.
8. Given that Eurydicê makes only a brief appearance, why do you think that Sophocles introduced this character into the play?
9. Throughout the play Creon argues for the needs of the state, whereas Antigonê puts forward the rights of the individual. Do you think that the play makes a clear-cut case for one side or the other? Support your answer in a two- to three-page essay.

10. Look up the definition of *hubris* in Chapter 8. Is Creon guilty of hubris? Is Antigonê?
11. What is the meaning of the last speech in the play? Could it apply to any other character in the play besides Creon?
12. The sea is used as a metaphor both by the chorus and by Creon and Haimon. Analyze in a three- to four-page essay the use of this metaphor.
13. The Greek philosopher Aristotle said that drama should preserve the three unities: unity of time, unity of place, and unity of action. How does *Antigonê* fulfill these criteria?
14. When Sophocles' plays were first performed in ancient Greece, attendance was considered a citizen's duty. There was even a fund to pay for the tickets of those who couldn't otherwise afford to go. In a three- to four-page essay discuss what this play teaches us about the rights and responsibilites of a citizen.
15. Thoreau was a great admirer of *Antigonê.* Read his essay "Civil Disobedience" and examine the play in the light of his arguments.

Henrik Ibsen (Norwegian, 1828–1906)

An Enemy of the People

CAST OF CHARACTERS

DR. THOMAS STOCKMANN, *medical officer at the Baths*
MRS. STOCKMANN, *his wife*
PETRA, *their daughter, a schoolteacher*
EILIF ⎱ *their sons, aged 13 and 10*
MORTEN ⎰
PETER STOCKMANN, *the Doctor's elder brother, Mayor and Chief Constable, Chairman of the Baths Committee, etc.*
MORTEN KIIL, *master tanner, foster father to Mrs. Stockmann*
HOVSTAD, *editor of the* People's Tribune
BILLING, *an employee of the newspaper*
HORSTER, *a sea captain*
ASLAKSEN, *a printer*
PEOPLE *at a public meeting—men of all classes, a few women and a bunch of schoolboys*

ACT ONE

Evening in DR STOCKMANN'S *living-room. It is humbly but neatly furnished and decorated. In the wall to the right are two doors, of which the further leads out to the hall and the nearer to the* DOCTOR'S *study. In the opposite wall, facing the hall door, is a door that leads to the other rooms occupied by the family. In the middle of this wall stands a tiled stove; further downstage is a sofa with a mirror above it. In front of the sofa is an oval table with a cloth on it. Upon this table stands a lighted lamp with a shade. Upstage, an open door to the dining-room in which can be seen a table laid for the evening meal, with a lamp on it.*

At this table BILLING *is seated, a napkin tucked beneath his chin.* MRS STOCKMANN *is standing by the table, offering him a plate with a large joint of beef on it. The other places around the table are empty, and this table is in the disorder of a meal that has been finished.*

MRS STOCKMANN. There, Mr. Billing! But if you will come an hour late, you'll have to put up with cold.

BILLING *(eating.)* Oh, but this is capital. Absolutely capital!

MRS STOCKMANN. Well, you know how punctually my husband always likes to eat—

BILLING. It doesn't bother me. I enjoy eating alone, without having to talk to anyone.

MRS STOCKMANN. Oh. Well, as long as you're *enjoying* it, that's—*(Listens towards the hall.)* Ah, this must be Mr Hovstad.

BILLING. Very likely.

MAYOR PETER STOCKMANN *enters wearing an overcoat and his official hat, and carrying a stick.*

MAYOR. Good evening to you, my dear sister-in-law.

MRS STOCKMANN *(goes into the living-room).* Why, good evening! Fancy seeing you here! How nice of you to come and call on us!

MAYOR. I just happened to be passing, so—*(Glances towards the dining-room.)* But I hear you have company.

MRS STOCKMANN *(a little embarrassed).* Oh, no, no, that's no one. *(Quickly.)* Won't you have something, too?

MAYOR: I? No, thank you! Good heavens, a cooked meal at night! My digestion would never stand that!

MRS STOCKMANN. Oh, but surely just for once—

MAYOR. No, no! It's very kind of you, but I'll stick to my tea and sandwiches. It's healthier in the long run; and a little less expensive.

MRS STOCKMANN *(smiles).* You speak as though Thomas and I were spendthrifts!

MAYOR. Not you, my dear sister-in-law. Such a thought was far from my mind. *(Points towards the* DOCTOR's *study.)* Isn't he at home?

MRS STOCKMANN. No, he's gone for a little walk with the boys.

MAYOR. I wonder if that's wise so soon after a meal? *(Listens.)* Ah, this must be he.

MRS STOCKMANN. No, I don't think it can be, yet. *(A knock on the door.)* Come in!

HOVSTAD, *the editor of the local newspaper, enters from the hall.*

MRS STOCKMANN. Oh— Mr Hovstad—?

HOVSTAD. Yes. Please excuse me, I was detained down at the printer's. Good evening, Your Worship.

MAYOR *(greets him somewhat stiffly).* Good evening. I suppose you are here on business?

HOVSTAD. Partly. About an article for my newspaper—

MAYOR. I guessed as much. I hear my brother is a regular contributor to the *People's Tribune.*

HOVSTAD. Yes, he usually drops us a line when he thinks the truth needs to be told about something.

MRS STOCKMANN *(to* HOVSTAD, *pointing towards the dining-room).* But—won't you—?

MAYOR. Great heavens, you mustn't think I blame him for writing for the kind of public he's most likely to find sympathetic to his ideas. Besides, I have no reason to bear your newspaper any ill will, Mr Hovstad—

HOVSTAD. I should hope not.

MAYOR. On the whole I think I may say that an admirable spirit of tolerance reigns in our town. A fine communal spirit! And the reason for this is that we have this great common interest that binds us together— an interest which is the close concern of every right-minded citi- zen—

HOVSTAD. You mean the Baths?

MAYOR. Exactly! Our magnificent new Baths. Mark my words, sir! These Baths will prove the very heart and essence of our life! There can be no doubt about it.

MRS STOCKMANN. Yes, that's just what Thomas says.

MAYOR. It's really astounding the strides this place has made during the past two or three years! The town is becoming prosperous. People are waking up and beginning to live. Buildings and ground rents are increasing in value every day.

HOVSTAD. And unemployment is going down.

MAYOR. Yes, there's that too. The burden upon the propertied classes of poor relief has been most gratifyingly reduced—and will be still more if only we have a really good summer this year, with plenty of visitors. What we want most is invalids. They'll give the Baths a good name.

HOVSTAD. And I hear the indications are promising.

MAYOR. They are indeed. Enquiries about accommodation are pouring in every day.

HOVSTAD. Well then, the Doctor's article will be most opportune.

MAYOR. Oh, has he written something new?

HOVSTAD. No, it's something he wrote last winter; a eulogy of the Baths and the excellent health facilities of the town. But I decided to hold it over.

MAYOR. Ah, there was a snag somewhere?

HOVSTAD. No, it wasn't that. I just thought it would be better to wait till the spring. Now people are thinking about where to spend their summer holidays—

MAYOR. Quite right! Quite right, Mr Hovstad!

MRS STOCKMANN. Thomas never stops thinking about those Baths.

MAYOR. Well, he *is* employed there.

HOVSTAD. Yes, and he was the one who really created it all, wasn't he?

MAYOR. Was he? Really? Yes, I have heard that certain people do hold that opinion. I must say I was labouring under the delusion that I had had some modest share in promoting the enterprise.

MRS STOCKMANN. That's what Thomas is always telling people.

HOVSTAD. No one denies that, Your Worship. You got it going and saw to all the practical details—we all know that. I only meant that the idea originated with the Doctor.

MAYOR. Yes, my brother's always been full of ideas—unfortunately. But when things have to be done, another kind of man is needed, Mr Hovstad. And I should have thought that least of all in this house would—

MRS STOCKMANN. But my dear brother-in-law—!

HOVSTAD. Surely Your Worship doesn't—?

MRS STOCKMANN. Do go inside and get yourself something to eat, Mr Hovstad. My husband will be here any moment.

HOVSTAD. Thank you—just a bite, perhaps. *(Goes into the dining-room.)*

MAYOR *(lowers his voice slightly)*. It's extraordinary about people of peasant stock. They never learn the meaning of tact.

MRS STOCKMANN. But is it really anything to bother about? Can't you and Thomas share the honour as brothers?

MAYOR. Well, I should have thought so. But it seems not everyone is content to share.

MRS STOCKMANN. Oh, nonsense! You and Thomas always get on so well together. Ah, this sounds like him.

Goes over and opens the door leading to the hall.

DR STOCKMANN *(laughing and boisterous)*. Hullo, Catherine! I've another guest for you here! The more the merrier, what? Come in, Captain

Horster! Hang your overcoat up there on the hook. No, of course, you don't wear an overcoat, do you? Fancy, Catherine, I bumped into him in the street! Had the devil of a job persuading him to come back with me!

CAPTAIN HORSTER *enters and shakes hands with* MRS STOCKMANN.

DR STOCKMANN *(in the doorway)*. Run along in now, lads. (*To* MRS STOCK-MANN.) They're hungry again already! This way, Captain Horster, you're going to have the finest roast beef you ever—!

Drives HORSTER *into the dining-room*. EILIF *and* MORTEN *go in too.*

MRS STOCKMANN. Thomas! Don't you see who's—?

DR STOCKMANN *(turns in the doorway)*. Oh, hullo, Peter! *(Goes over and shakes his hand.)* Well, it's good to see you!

MAYOR. I'm afraid I can only spare a few minutes—

DR STOCKMANN. Rubbish! We'll be having some hot toddy soon. You haven't forgotten the toddy, Catherine?

MRS STOCKMANN. No, of course not. I've got the kettle on— *(Goes into the dining-room.)*

MAYOR. Hot toddy too—!

DR STOCKMANN. Yes. Now sit down, and we'll have a good time.

MAYOR. Thank you. I never partake in drinking parties.

DR STOCKMANN. But this isn't a party.

MAYOR. Well, but—! *(Glance towards the dining-room.)* It's really extraordinary the amount they eat!

DR STOCKMANN *(rubs his hands)*. Yes, there's nothing better than to see young people tuck in, is there? Always hungry! That's the way it should be! They've got to have food! Gives them strength! They're the ones who've got to ginger up the future, Peter.

MAYOR. May one ask what it is that needs to be 'gingered up', as you put it?

DR STOCKMANN. You must ask the young ones that—when the time comes. We can't see it, of course. Obviously—a couple of old fogeys like you and me—

MAYOR. Well, really! That's a most extraordinary way to describe us—

DR STOCKMANN. Oh, you mustn't take me too seriously, Peter. I feel so happy and exhilarated, you see! It's so wonderful to be alive at a time like this, with everything germinating and bursting out all around us! Oh, it's a glorious age we live in! It's as though a whole new world were coming to birth before our eyes!

MAYOR. Do you really feel that?

DR. STOCKMANN. Yes. Of course, you can't see it as clearly as I do. You've spent your life in this background, so it doesn't make the same impression on you as it does on me. But I've had to spend all these years sitting up there in that damned northern backwater, hardly ever seeing a new face that had a stimulating word to say to me. To me it's as though I had moved into the heart of some pulsing metropolis—

MAYOR. Hm; metropolis—!

DR STOCKMANN. Oh, I know it must seem small in comparison with lots of other cities. But there's life here—promise—so many things to work and fight for! And that's what matters. *(Shouts.)* Catherine, hasn't the post come yet?

MRS STOCKMANN *(from the dining-room)*. No, not yet.

DR STOCKMANN. And to be making a decent living, Peter! That's something one learns to appreciate when one's been living on the edge of starvation, as we have—

MAYOR. Oh, surely—!

DR STOCKMANN. Oh yes, I can tell you we were often pretty hard pressed up there. But now, we can live like lords! Today, for instance, we had roast beef for dinner! *And* there was enough left over for supper! Won't you have a bit? Let me show it to you anyway. Come on, have a look—

MAYOR. No, really—

DR STOCKMANN. Well, look at this, then! Do you see? We've got a tablecloth!

MAYOR. Yes, I've noticed it.

DR STOCKMANN. And a lampshade too! See? All from what Catherine's managed to save! It makes the room so cosy, don't you think? Come and stand here—no, no, no, not there! There, now! Look! See how the light sort of concentrates downwards? I really think it looks very elegant, don't you?

MAYOR. Well, if one can indulge in that kind of luxury—

DR STOCKMANN. Oh, I think I can permit myself that now. Catherine says I earn almost as much as we spend.

MAYOR. Almost!

DR STOCKMANN. Well, a man of science ought to live in a little style. I'm sure any magistrate spends far more in a year than I do.

MAYOR. Yes, I should think so! After all, a magistrate is an important public official—

DR STOCKMANN. Well, a wholesale merchant, then. A man like that spends much more—

MAYOR. His circumstances are different.

DR STOCKMANN. Oh, it isn't that I'm wasteful, Peter. I just can't deny myself the pleasure of having people around me! I need that, you know. I've been living outside the world for so long, and for me it's a necessity to be with people who are young, bold and cheerful, and have lively, liberal minds—and that's what they are, all the men who are sitting in there enjoying a good meal! I wish you knew Hovstad a little better—

MAYOR. That reminds me, Hovstad told me he's going to print another article by you.

DR STOCKMANN. An article by me?

MAYOR. Yes, about the Baths. Something you wrote last winter.

DR STOCKMANN. Oh, that. No, I don't want them to print that now.

MAYOR. No? But I should have thought now would be the most suitable time.

DR STOCKMANN. I dare say it would under ordinary circumstances. *(Walks across the room.)*

MAYOR *(watches him).* and what is extraordinary about the circumstances now?

DR STOCKMANN *(stops).* I'm sorry, Peter, I can't tell you that yet. Not this evening, anyway. There may be a great deal that's extraordinary; or there may be nothing at all. It may be my imagination—

MAYOR. I must say you're making it all sound very mysterious. Is there something the matter? Something I musn't be told about? I should have thought that I, as Chairman of the Baths Committee—

DR STOCKMANN. And I should have thought that I, as—well, let's not start flying off the handle.

MAYOR. Heaven forbid. I'm not in the habit of flying off the handle, as you phrase it. But I must absolutely insist that all arrangements be made and executed through the proper channels (and through the authorities legally appointed for that purpose).[1] I cannot permit any underhanded or backdoor methods.

DR STOCKMANN. Have I ever used underhand or backdoor methods?

MAYOR. You will always insist on going your own way. And that's almost equally inadmissible in a well-ordered community. The individual must learn to fall in line with the general will—or, to be more accurate, with that of the authorities whose business it is to watch over the common good.

DR STOCKMANN. I dare say. But what the hell has that to do with me?

MAYOR. Because that, my dear Thomas, is what you seem never to be willing to learn. But take care. You'll pay for it some time. Well, I've warned you. Good-bye.

DR STOCKMANN. Are you raving mad? You're barking completely up the wrong tree—

MAYOR. I'm not in the habit of doing that. Well, if you'll excuse me—*(Bows towards the dining-room.)* Good-bye, sister-in-law. Good day, gentlemen. *(Goes.)*

---

[1]Square brackets in the text indicate suggested cuts for performance.

MRS STOCKMANN *(comes back into the living-room).* Has he gone?

DR STOCKMANN. Yes, Catherine, and in a damned bad temper.

MRS STOCKMANN. Oh, Thomas, what have you done to him now?

DR STOCKMANN. Absolutely nothing. He can't expect me to account to him until the time comes.

MRS STOCKMANN. Account to him? For what?

DR STOCKMANN. Hm; never mind, Catherine. Why the devil doesn't the post come?

HOVSTAD, BILLING *and* HORSTER *have got up from the dining table and come into the living-room.* EILIF *and* MORTEN *follow a few moments later.*

BILLING *(stretches his arms).* Ah, a meal like that makes one feel like a new man! By Jingo, yes!

HOVSTAD. His Worship wasn't in a very cheerful mood tonight.

DR STOCKMANN. Oh, that's his stomach. He's got a bad digestion.

HOVSTAD. I expect we radical journalists stuck in his gullet.

MRS STOCKMANN. I thought you were getting on rather well with him.

HOVSTAD. Oh, it's only an armistice.

BILLING. That's it! The word epitomizes the situation in a nutshell!

DR STOCKMANN. Peter's a lonely man, poor fellow. We must remember that. He has no home where he can relax; only business, business. And all that damned tea he pours into himself! Well, lads, pull up your chairs! Catherine, where's that toddy?

MRS STOCKMANN *(goes into the dining-room).* It's just coming.

DR STOCKMANN. You sit down here on the sofa with me, Captain Horster. You're too rare a guest in this house! Sit, sit, gentlemen!

THE GENTLEMEN *sit at the table.* MRS STOCKMANN *brings a tray with a kettle, decanters, glasses, etc.*

MRS STOCKMANN. Here you are. This is arrack, and this is rum; and there's the brandy. Now everyone must help himself.

DR STOCKMANN *(takes a glass).* Don't you worry about that! *(As the toddy is mixed.)* But where are the cigars? Eilif, you know where the box is. Morten, you can bring me my pipe. *(The* BOYS *go into the room on the right.)* I've a suspicion Eilif pinches a cigar once in a while, but I pretend I don't know! *(Shouts.)* And my smoking cap, Morten! Catherine, can't you tell him where I've put it? Oh, good, he's found it. *(The* BOYS *return with the things he asked for.)* Help yourselves, my friends! I stick to my pipe, you know; this old friend's been my companion on many a stormy round up there in the north. *(Clinks his glass with theirs.)* Skoal! Ah, I must say it's better to be sitting here, warm and relaxed.

MRS STOCKMANN *(who is sitting, knitting).* Will you be sailing soon, Captain Horster?

HORSTER. I expect to be off next week.

MRS STOCKMANN. It's America this time, isn't it?

HORSTER. That's the idea.

BILLING. But then you won't be able to vote in the next council elections!

(HORSTER. Is there going to be a new election?

BILLING. Didn't you know?

HORSTER. No, such things don't interest me.

BILLING. But you must care about public affairs?)

HORSTER. No, I don't understand these matters.

BILLING. All the same, one ought at least to vote.

HORSTER. Even if one doesn't understand what it's about?

BILLING. Understand? What's that got to do with it? Society's like a ship. Everyone's got to lend a hand at the rudder.

HORSTER. Not in my ship!

(HOVSTAD. It's curious how little sailors bother about what goes on in their own country.

BILLING. Most abnormal.)

DR STOCKMANN. Sailors are like birds of passage; wherever they happen to be, they regard that as home. Which means the rest of us must be all the more active, Mr Hovstad. Have you anything salutary to offer us in the *People's Tribune* tomorrow?

HOVSTAD. Nothing of local interest. But the day after, I thought of printing your article—

DR STOCKMANN. Oh God, yes, that article! No, look, you'll have to sit on that.

HOVSTAD. Oh? We've plenty of space just now; and I thought this would be the most suitable time—

DR STOCKMANN. Yes, yes, I dare say you're right, but you'll have to wait all the same. I'll explain later—

PETRA, *in hat and cloak, with a pile of exercise books under her arm, enters from the hall.*

PETRA. Good evening.

DR STOCKMANN. Hullo, Petra, is that you?

The others greet her, and she them. She puts down her cloak, hat and books on a chair by the door.

PETRA. And you're all sitting here having a party while I've been out working!

DR STOCKMANN. Well, come and have a party too.

BILLING. May I mix you a tiny glass?

PETRA *(comes over to the table)*. Thanks, I'll do it myself; you always make it too strong. Oh, by the way, father, I've a letter for you.

Goes over to the chair on which her things are lying.

DR STOCKMANN. A letter? Who from?

PETRA *(looks in her coat pocket)*. The postman gave it to me just as I was going out—

DR STOCKMANN *(gets up and goes over to her)*. Why on earth didn't you let me have it before?

PETRA. I really didn't have time to run up again. Here it is.

DR STOCKMANN *(seizes the letter)*. Let me see it, child, let me see it! *(Looks at the envelope.)* Yes, this is it!

MRS STOCKMANN. Is this what you've been waiting for so anxiously, Thomas?

DR STOCKMANN. It is indeed. I must go and read it at once. Where can I find a light, Catherine? Is there no lamp in my room again?

MRS STOCKMANN. Yes, there's one burning on your desk.

DR STOCKMANN. Good, good. Excuse me a moment—

Goes into the room on the right.

PETRA. What on earth can that be, Mother?

MRS STOCKMANN. I don't know. These last few days he's done nothing but ask about the post.

BILLING. Probably some patient out of town—

PETRA. Poor father! He'll soon find he's bitten off more than he can chew. *(Mixes herself a glass.)* Ah, that tastes good!

HOVSTAD. Have you been at evening classes tonight, too?

PETRA *(sips her drink)*. Two hours.

BILLING. And four hours this morning at the technical college—

PETRA *(sits at the table)*. Five hours.

MRS STOCKMANN. And you've got exercises to correct tonight, I see.

PETRA. Yes, lots.

HORSTER. You seem to have bitten off more than you can chew too, by the sound of it.

PETRA. Yes, but I like it. It makes you feel so wonderfully tired.

BILLING. Wonderfully?

PETRA. Yes. One sleeps so soundly afterwards.

MORTEN. You must be very wicked, Petra.

PETRA. Wicked?

MORTEN. Yes, if you work so much. Dr Roerlund says work is a punishment for our sins.

EILIF *(sniffs)*. Silly! Fancy believing stuff like that!

MRS STOCKMANN. Now, now, Eilif!

BILLING *(laughs).* Ha! Very good!

HOVSTAD. Don't you want to work hard too, Morten?

MORTEN. No! Not me!

HOVSTAD. But surely you want to become something?

MORTEN. I want to be a Viking!

EILIF. But then you'll have to be a heathen.

MORTEN. All right, I'll be a heathen!

BILLING. I'm with you there, Morten! That's just the way I feel!

MRS STOCKMANN *(makes a sign).* I'm sure you don't really, Mr Billing.

BILLING. By Jingo, I do! I *am* a heathen and I'm proud of it! Before long we'll all be heathens. Just you wait and see.

MORTEN. Shall we be able to do anything we like then?

BILLING. Yes, Morten! You see—

MRS STOCKMANN. Hurry off now, boys. I'm sure you've some homework to do.

EILIF. I can stay a few minutes longer—

MRS STOCKMANN. No, you can't. Be off, the pair of you!

The BOYS *say good night and go into the room on the left.*

HOVSTAD. Do you really think it can do the boys any harm to hear this kind of thing?

MRS STOCKMANN. Well, I don't know. I just don't like it.

PETRA. Oh, really, mother! I think you're being very stupid.

MRS STOCKMANN. Perhaps I am; but I don't like it. Not here in the home.

PETRA. Oh, there's so much fear of the truth everywhere! At home and at school. Here we've got to keep our mouths shut, and at school we have to stand up and tell lies to the children.

HORSTER. Lie to them?

PETRA. Yes, surely you realize we have to teach them all kinds of things we don't believe in ourselves.

BILLING. I fear that is all too true!

PETRA. If only I had the money, I'd start a school of my own. And there things would be different.

BILLING. Ah! Money!

HORSTER. If you mean that seriously, Miss Stockmann, I could gladly let you have a room at my place. My father's old house is almost empty; there's a great big dining-room downstairs—

PETRA *(laughs).* Thank you! But I don't suppose it'll ever come to anything.

HOVSTAD. No, I think Miss Petra will probably turn to journalism. By the way, have you found time to look at that English novel you promised to translate for us?

PETRA. Not yet. But I'll see you get it in time.

DR STOCKMANN *enters from his room with the letter open in his hand.*

DR STOCKMANN *(waves the letter).* Here's news that's going to set this town by the ears, believe you me!

BILLING. News?

MRS STOCKMANN. Why, what's happened?

DR STOCKMANN. A great discovery has been made, Catherine!

HOVSTAD. Really?

MRS STOCKMANN. By you?

DR STOCKMANN. Precisely! By me! *(Walks up and down.)* Now let them come as usual and say it's all madman's talk and I'm imagining things! But they'll have to watch their step this time! *(Laughs.)* Yes, I fancy they'll have to watch their step!

PETRA. Father, for Heaven's sake tell us what it is!

DR STOCKMANN. Yes, yes, just give me time and you'll hear everything. Oh, if only I had Peter here now! Well, it only goes to show how blindly we mortals can form our judgments—

HOVSTAD. What do you mean by that, Doctor?

DR STOCKMANN *(stops by the table).* Is it not popularly supposed that our town is a healthy place?

HOVSTAD. Yes, of course.

DR STOCKMANN. A quite unusually healthy place? A place which deserves to be recommended in the warmest possible terms both for the sick and for their more fortunate brethren?

MRS STOCKMANN. Yes, but my dear Thomas—!

DR STOCKMANN. And we ourselves have praised and recommended it, have we not? I have written thousands of words of eulogy both in the *People's Tribune,* and in pamphlets—

HOVSTAD. Yes, well, what of it?

DR STOCKMANN. These Baths, which have been called the artery of the town, and its central nerve and—and God knows what else—

BILLING. 'The pulsing heart of our city' is a phrase I once, in a festive moment, ventured to—

DR STOCKMANN. No doubt. But do you know what they really are, these beloved Baths of ours which have been so puffed up and which have cost so much money? Do you know what they are?

HOVSTAD. No, what are they?

Dr Stockmann. Nothing but a damned cesspit!

Petra. The Baths, father?

Mrs Stockmann *(simultaneously)*. Our Baths!

Hovstad *(simultaneously)*. But, Doctor—!

Billing. Absolutely incredible!

Dr Stockmann. These Baths are a whited sepulchre—and a poisoned one at that. Dangerous to health in the highest degree! All that filth up at Moelledal—you know, that stinking refuse from the tanneries— has infected the water in the pipes that feed the Pump Room. And that's not all. This damnable muck has even seeped out on to the beach—

Horster. Where the sea baths are?

Dr Stockmann. Exactly!

Hovstad. But how can you be so sure about all this, Doctor?

Dr Stockmann. I've investigated the whole thing most thoroughly. Oh, I've long suspected something of the kind. Last year there were a lot of curious complaints among visitors who'd come for the bathing— typhoid, and gastric troubles—

Mrs Stockmann. Yes, so there were.

Dr Stockmann. At the time we thought these people had brought the disease with them. But later, during the winter, I began to have other thoughts. So I set to work to analyse the water as closely as I was able.

Mrs Stockmann. So that's what you've been toiling so hard at!

Dr Stockmann. Yes, you may well say I have toiled, Catherine. But of course I lacked the proper scientific facilities. So I sent specimens of both the drinking water and the sea water to the University to have them analysed by a chemist.

Hovstad. And now you have that analysis?

Dr Stockmann *(shows the letter)*. Here it is! It establishes conclusively that the water here contains putrid organic matter—millions of bacteria! It is definitely noxious to the health even for external use.

Mrs Stockmann. What a miracle you found this out in time!

Dr Stockmann. You may well say that, Catherine.

Hovstad. And what do you intend to do now, Doctor?

Dr Stockmann. Put the matter right, of course.

Hovstad. Can that be done?

Dr Stockmann. It must be done! Otherwise the Baths are unusable—and all our work has been wasted. But don't worry. I'm pretty sure I know what needs to be done.

Mrs Stockmann. But, my dear Thomas, why have you kept all this so secret?

Dr Stockmann. Did you expect me to go round the town talking about it before I was certain? No, thank you, I'm not that mad.

Petra. You might have told us—

Dr Stockmann. I wasn't going to tell anyone. But tomorrow you can run along to the Badger and—

Mrs Stockmann. Thomas, really!

Dr Stockmann. Sorry, I mean your grandfather. It'll shock the old boy out of his skin. He thinks I'm a bit gone in the head anyway—oh, and there are plenty of others who think the same! I know! But now these good people shall see! Now they shall see! *(Walks around and rubs his hands.)* There's going to be such a to-do in this town, Catherine! You've no idea! The whole water system will have to be relaid.

Hovstad *(gets up)*. The whole of the water system—?

Dr Stockmann. Of course. The intake is too low. It'll have to be raised much higher up.

Petra. Then you were right after all!

Dr Stockmann. Yes, Petra, do you remember? I wrote protesting against the plans when they were about to start laying it. But no one would listen to me then. Well, now I'll give them a real broadside. Of course, I've written a full report to the Baths Committee; it's been ready for a whole week, I've only been waiting to receive this. *(Shows the letter.)* But now I shall send it to them at once! *(Goes into his room and returns with a sheaf of papers.)* Look at this! Ten foolscap pages—closely written! I'm sending the analysis with it. A newspaper, Catherine! Get me something to wrap these up in. Good! There, now! Give it to—to—! *(Stamps his foot.)* What the devil's her name? You know, the maid! Tell her to take it straight down to the Mayor.

MRS STOCKMANN *goes out through the dining-room with the parcel.*

Petra. What do you think Uncle Peter will say, father?

Dr Stockmann. What can he say? He must be grateful that so important a fact has been brought to light.

Hovstad. May I have your permission to print a short piece about your discovery in the *People's Tribune?*

Dr stockmann. I'd be very grateful if you would.

Hovstad. I think it's desirable that the community should be informed as quickly as possible.

Dr Stockmann. Yes, yes, of course.

Mrs Stockmann *(comes back)*. She's gone with it now.

BILLING. You'll be the first citizen in the town, Doctor, by Jingo, you will!

DR STOCKMANN *(walks round contendedly)*. Oh, nonsense, I've really done nothing except my duty. I dug for treasure and struck lucky, that's all. All the same—!

BILLING. Hovstad, don't you think the town ought to organize a torchlight procession in honour of Dr Stockmann?

HOVSTAD. I'll suggest it, certainly.

BILLING. And I'll have a word with Aslaksen.

DR STOCKMANN. No, my dear friends, please don't bother with that nonsense. I don't want any fuss made. And if the Baths Committee should decide to raise my salary, I won't accept it! It's no good, Catherine, I won't accept it!

MRS STOCKMANN. Quite right, Thomas.

PETRA *(raises her glass)*. Skoal, father!

HOVSTAD ⎫
           ⎬ Skoal, skoal, Doctor!
BILLING ⎭

HORSTER *(clinks his glass with the* DOCTOR's*)*. Here's hoping your discovery will bring you nothing but joy!

DR STOCKMANN. Thank you, my dear friends, thank you! I'm so deeply happy! Oh, it's good to know that one has the respect of one's fellow-citizens! Hurrah, Catherine!

Seizes her round the neck with both hands and whirls round with her. MRS STOCKMANN *screams and struggles. Laughter, applause, and cheers for the* DOCTOR. *The* BOYS *stick their heads in through the door.*

ACT TWO

The DOCTOR's *living-room. The door to the dining-room is shut. Morning.*

MRS STOCKMANN *(enters from the dining-room with a sealed letter in her hand, goes over to the door downstage right and peeps in)*. Are you at home, Thomas?

DR STOCKMANN *(offstage)*. Yes, I've just come in. *(Enters.)* What is it?

MRS STOCKMANN. A letter from your brother. *(Hands it to him.)*

DR STOCKMANN. Aha, let's see what he says. *(Opens the envelope and reads):* 'I return herewith the manuscript you sent me—' *(Reads on, mumbling.)* Hm—!

MRS STOCKMANN Well, what does he say?

DR STOCKMANN *(puts the papers in his pocket)*. No, he just writes that he'll be coming up here to see me towards noon.

MRS STOCKMANN. You must remember to stay at home, then.

DR STOCKMANN. Oh, that'll be all right. I've finished my round for today.

MRS STOCKMANN. I'm very curious to know how he's taken it.

DR STOCKMANN. You'll see. He won't like the fact that I made this discovery and not he.

MRS STOCKMANN. Doesn't it worry you? It does me.

DR STOCKMANN. Well, he'll be happy at heart, of course. The trouble is, Peter gets so damned angry at the idea of anyone but himself doing anything for the good of the town.

MRS STOCKMANN. You know, Thomas, I really think you ought to share the honour with him. Couldn't you say it was he who started you thinking along these lines—?

DR STOCKMANN. Gladly, as far as I'm concerned. As long as I get the matter put right, I—

OLD MORTEN KIIL (*puts his head in through the door leading from the hall, looks around inquiringly, chuckles to himself and asks slyly*). Is it— is it true?

MRS STOCKMANN. Why, father!

DR STOCKMANN. Hullo, father-in-law! Good morning, good morning!

MRS STOCKMANN. Well, aren't you going to come in?

MORTEN KIIL. I will if it's true. If not, I'll be off—

DR STOCKMANN. If what's true?

MORTEN KIIL. This nonsense about the water system. Is it true, eh?

DR STOCKMANN. Of course it's true. But how did you hear about it?

MORTEN KIIL (*comes in*). Petra looked in on her way to school—

DR STOCKMANN. Oh, did she?

MORTEN KIIL. Mm. And she told me. I thought she was just pulling my leg. But that's not like Petra.

DR STOCKMANN. How could you think she'd do a thing like that?

MORTEN KIIL. Never trust anyone. That's my motto. You get made a fool of before you know where you are. So it is true, then?

DR STOCKMANN. Absolutely true. Sit down now, father. (*Coaxes him down on to the sofa.*) Isn't it a stroke of luck for the town?

MORTEN KIIL (*stifles a laugh*). Stroke of luck for the town?

DR STOCKMANN. That I made this discovery in time—

MORTEN KILL (*as before*). Oh, yes, yes, yes! But I never thought you'd start playing monkey tricks with your own flesh and blood?

DR STOCKMANN. Monkey tricks?

MRS STOCKMANN. Father dear—?

MORTEN KIIL (*rests his hands and chin on the handle of his stick and winks slyly at the* DOCTOR). What was it, now? Didn't you say some animals had got into the water pipes?

DR STOCKMANN. Yes, bacteria.

MORTEN KIIL. Quite a number of them, so Petra told me. Regular army?

DR STOCKMANN. Millions, probably.

MORTEN KIIL. But no one can see them. Isn't that right?

DR STOCKMANN. Of course one can't *see* them.

MORTEN KIIL *(chuckles silently).* Devil take me if this isn't the best I've heard from you yet!

DR STOCKMANN. What do you mean?

MORTEN KIIL. But you'll never get the Mayor to believe a tale like that.

DR STOCKMANN. We'll see.

MORTEN KIIL. Do you think he's that daft?

DR STOCKMANN. I hope the whole town will be that daft.

MORTEN KIIL. The whole town? That's perfectly possible! Serve them right, it'll teach them a lesson! They hounded me out of the Council—yes, that's what I call it, for they drove me out like a dog, they did! But now they're going to pay for it! You make fools of them, Stockmann!

DR STOCKMANN. But, father—

MORTEN KIIL. You make fools of them, my boy! *(Gets up.)* If you can put the Mayor and his friends out of countenance, I'll give a hundred crowns to the poor immediately!

DR STOCKMANN. That's very generous of you.

MORTEN KIIL. I'm not a rich man, mind! But if you do that, I'll remember the poor to the tune of fifty crowns; at Christmas.

HOVSTAD *enters from the hall.*

HOVSTAD. Good morning! *(Stops.)* Oh, am I intruding?

DR STOCKMANN. No, come in, come in!

MORTEN KIIL *(chuckles again).* Him! Is he in with you on this?

HOVSTAD. What do you mean?

DR STOCKMANN. Indeed he is.

MORTEN KIIL. I might have guessed it! So it's to be in the papers! Yes, you're a card all right, Stockmann! Well, you two put your heads together. I'm off.

DR STOCKMANN. Oh, father, stay a little longer.

MORTEN KIIL. No, I'm off. Pull out all the tricks you know! By God, I'll see you don't lose by it! *(Goes.* MRS STOCKMANN *accompanies him out.)*

DR STOCKMANN *(laughs).* Imagine, Hovstad, the old man doesn't believe a word I say about the water system!

HOVSTAD. Oh, so *that* was—?

DR STOCKMANN. Yes, that's what we were talking about. I suppose that's why you've come too?

HOVSTAD. Yes. Can you spare me a moment or two, Doctor?

DR STOCKMANN. As long as you want, my dear fellow.

HOVSTAD. Have you heard anything from the Mayor?

DR STOCKMANN. Not yet. He'll be along shortly.

HOVSTAD. I've been thinking a lot about this since last night.

DR STOCKMANN. Yes?

HOVSTAD. You're a doctor and a man of science, and to you this business of the water is something to be considered in isolation. I think you don't perhaps realize how it's tied up with a lot of other things.

DR STOCKMANN. I don't quite understand you. (Let's sit down my dear chap. No, over there on the sofa.)

HOVSTAD *sits on the sofa,* DR STOCKMANN *in an armchair on the other side of the table.*

DR STOCKMANN. Well?

HOVSTAD. You said yesterday that the pollution of the water was the result of impurities in the soil.

DR STOCKMANN. Yes, we're pretty certain that filthy swamp up at Moelledal is the cause of the evil.

HOVSTAD. Forgive me, Doctor, but I believe the real cause of all the evil is to be found in quite a different swamp.

DR STOCKMANN. Which one?

HOVSTAD. The swamp in which our whole communal life is slowly rotting.

DR STOCKMANN. Damn it, Mr Hovstad, what kind of talk is this?

HOVSTAD. Little by little all the affairs of this town have fallen into the hands of a small clique of bureaucrats.

DR STOCKMANN. Oh, come, you can't group them all under that description.

HOVSTAD. No, but the ones who don't belong to it are the friends and hangers-on of the ones who do. It's the rich men, the ones with names— they're the people who rule our life.

DR STOCKMANN. They're shrewd and intelligent men.

HOVSTAD. Did they show shrewdness or intelligence when they laid the water pipes where they are now?

DR STOCKMANN. No, that was very stupid, of course. But it's going to be put right now.

HOVSTAD. You think they'll enjoy doing that?

DR STOCKMANN. Enjoy it or not, they'll be forced to do it.

HOVSTAD. If the press is allowed to use its influence.

DR STOCKMANN. That won't be necessary, my dear fellow. I'm sure my brother will—

HOVSTAD. I'm sorry, Doctor, but I intend to take this matter up myself.

DR STOCKMANN. In the newspaper?

HOVSTAD. When I took over the *People's Tribune* I did so with the fixed purpose of breaking up this ring of obstinate bigots who hold all the power in their hands.

DR STOCKMANN. But you told me yourself what happened as a result. The paper almost had to close down.

HOVSTAD. We had to play it easy then, that's true. There was a risk that if these men fell, the Baths might not be built. But now we have them, and these fine gentlemen have become dispensable.

DR STOCKMANN. Dispensable, perhaps. But we owe them a debt all the same.

HOVSTAD. Oh, that'll be handsomely acknowledged. But a radical writer like me can't let an opportunity like this pass unused. We must destroy the myth of these men's infallibility. It must be rooted out like any other kind of superstition.

DR STOCKMANN. Ah, I'm with you there! If it is a superstition, then away with it!

HOVSTAD. I'd prefer not to attack the Mayor, since he's your brother. But I know you feel as strongly as I do that truth must precede all other considerations.

DR STOCKMANN. Of course. *(Bursts out.)* But—! But—!

HOVSTAD. You mustn't think ill of me. I'm not more ambitious or self-seeking than most men.

DR STOCKMANN. But my dear fellow, who suggests you are?

HOVSTAD. I'm the son of poor people, as you know, and I've had the chance to see what's needed most in the lower strata of society. It's to have a share in the control of public affairs. That's what develops ability, and knowledge, and human dignity.

DR STOCKMANN. I appreciate that.

HOVSTAD. And then I think a journalist has a lot to answer for if he neglects an opportunity to achieve emancipation for the masses—[—the small and the oppressed]. Oh, I know—the big boys will call me a demagogue and all that—but I don't care. As long as my conscience is clear, I—

DR STOCKMAN. That's the point, yes! That's exactly it, Mr. Hovstad! All the same—damn it—*(A knock at the door.)* Come in!

ASLAKSEN, *the printer, appears in the doorway leading from the hall. He is humbly but decently dressed in black, with a white and somewhat crumpled cravat, gloves, and a silk hat in his hand.*

ASLAKSEN *(bows).* I trust you'll forgive me for being so bold, Doctor—

Dr Stockmann *(gets up)*. Why, hullo! Aren't you Aslaksen the printer?

Aslaksen. I am indeed, Doctor.

Hovstad *(gets up)*. Are you looking for me, Aslaksen?

Aslaksen. No, I'd no idea I'd see you here. It was the Doctor himself I—

Dr Stockmann. Well, what can I do for you?

Aslaksen. Is it true what Mr Billing tells me, that you're thinking of getting us a better water system?

Dr Stockmann. Yes, for the Baths.

Aslaksen. Ah, yes, I see. Well, I just came to say that I'm right behind you!

Hovstad *(to* dr stockmann*)*. You see!

Dr Stockmann. I'm most grateful; but—

Aslaksen. You might find it useful to have us tradespeople behind you. We form a pretty solid majority in this town—when we choose to, mind! And it's always good to have the majority behind you, Doctor.

Dr Stockmann. True enough. But I don't see that any special effort is necessary here. Surely it's a perfectly straightforward matter—

Aslaksen. Yes, but you might be glad of us all the same. I know these local authorities. The boys in power don't like accepting suggestions from outside. So I thought it might not be out of place if we organized a little demonstration.

Hovstad. That's just what I feel.

Dr Stockmann. Demonstration? In what way will you demonstrate?

Aslaksen. Oh, with restraint, Doctor. I always insist on restraint. Restraint is the primary virtue of every citizen. That's my opinion, anyway.

Dr Stockmann. Yes, yes, Mr. Aslaksen. Your views are well known—

Aslaksen. Yes, I fancy they are. Now this business of the water system is very important to us tradespeople. It looks as though the Baths are going to prove as you might say a little goldmine for the town. We'll all be depending on the Baths for our livelihood, especially us property owners. That's why we want to give the project every support we can. And seeing as I'm Chairman of the Property Owners' Association—

Dr Stockmann. Yes?

Aslaksen. And seeing as I'm also on the Council of the Temperance Society—you do know I'm a temperance worker—?

Dr Stockmann. Yes, yes.

Aslaksen. Well, so it stands to reason I come into contact with a lot of people. And seeing as I'm known to be a level-headed and law-abiding citizen, as you said yourself, it means I have a certain influence in the town—I wield a little power—though I say it myself.

Dr Stockmann. I'm well aware of that, Mr Aslaksen.

ASLAKSEN. Yes, well—so it'd be an easy matter for me to arrange an address, if the occasion should arise.

DR STOCKMANN. An address?

ASLAKSEN. Yes, a kind of vote of thanks from the citizens of this town to you for having carried this important matter to a successful conclusion. Of course, it stands to reason the wording's got to be restrained, so it won't offend the authorities and the other people as has the power. And so long as we're careful about that, I don't think anyone can take offence, can they?

HOVSTAD. Well, even if they don't particularly like it, they—

ASLAKSEN. No, no, no! We mustn't offend authority, Mr. Hovstad! We can't afford to defy the people on whom our lives depend. I've seen plenty of that in my time, and no good ever came out of it. But the sober expression of liberal sentiments can cause no affront.

DR STOCKMANN (shakes his hand). My dear Aslaksen, I can't tell you how deeply happy I am to find all this support among my fellow citizens. I am most moved, most moved. Well, now! What about a small glass of sherry?

ASLAKSEN. No, thank you! I never touch spirits.

DR STOCKMANN. A glass of beer, then? What do you say to that?

ASLAKSEN. No, thank you, not that either, Doctor. I never touch anything so early in the day. And now I must be getting back to town to talk to some of the other property owners and prepare the atmosphere.

DR STOCKMANN. It's really most kind of you, Mr Aslaksen. But I simply cannot get it into my head that all this fuss is really necessary. I should have thought the matter would solve itself.

ASLAKSEN. The authorities move somewhat ponderously, Doctor. Heaven knows I don't intend any reflection on them—!

HOVSTAD. We'll give them a drubbing in print tomorrow, Mr Aslaksen.

ASLAKSEN. But no violence, Mr Hovstad! Proceed with restraint! Otherwise you'll get nowhere with them. You can rely on my judgment, for I have culled my knowledge in the school of life. Yes, well, I must say good-bye. You know now that we tradespeople stand behind you like a wall, Doctor. You have the solid majority on your side, whatever else may happen.

DR STOCKMANN. Thank you, my dear Mr Aslaksen. (Shakes his hand.) Good-bye, good-bye!

ASLAKSEN. Are you coming down to the press too, Mr Hovstad?

HOVSTAD. I'll follow later. I've a few things to arrange first.

ASLAKSEN. Yes, yes.

Bows and goes out. DR STOCKMANN *accompanies him out into the hall.*

HOVSTAD *(as the* DOCTOR *returns).* Well, what do you say to that, Doctor? Don't you think it's time this town was shaken out of its torpidity and its weak-kneed half-heartedness?

DR STOCKMANN. You mean Aslaksen?

HOVSTAD. Yes, I do. Oh, he's honest enough in some respects, but he's stuck in the swamp. And most of the others are the same. They swing this way and that, and spend so much time looking at every side of the question that they never make a move in any direction.

DR STOCKMANN. But Aslaksen seemed very well-meaning, I thought.

HOVSTAD. There's something I regard as more important than that. To know your own mind and have the courage of your convictions.

DR STOCKMANN. Yes, you're right there.

HOVSTAD. That's why I'm so keen to seize this opportunity and see if I can't get these well-meaning idiots to act like men for once. All this grovelling to authority has got to be stopped. This blunder they've made about the water system is quite indefensible, and that fact's got to be drummed into the ears of every citizen who's got the right to vote.

DR STOCKMANN. Very well. If you think it's for the communal good, go ahead. But not till I've talked with my brother.

HOVSTAD. I'll get my editorial written anyway. And if the Mayor refuses to take action, then—

DR STOCKMANN. Oh, but that's unthinkable.

HOVSTAD. It's a possibility. And if it should happen—?

DR STOCKMANN. If it does, I promise you that—yes, you can print my report. Print the whole damned thing!

HOVSTAD. Is that a promise?

DR STOCKMANN *(hands him the manuscript).* Here it is. Take it with you. It won't do any harm for you to read through it; and you can give it back to me afterwards.

HOVSTAD. Right, I'll do that. Well, good-bye, Doctor.

DR STOCKMANN. Good-bye, good-bye! Don't you worry, Mr Hovstad—everything's going to go quite smoothly. Quite smoothly!

HOVSTAD. Hm. We shall see.

Nods and goes out through the hall.

DR STOCKMANN *(goes over to the dining-room and looks in).* Catherine—! Oh, hullo, Petra, are you here?

PETRA *(enters).* Hasn't he come yet?

DR STOCKMANN. Peter? No. But I've been having a long talk with Hovstad. He's quite excited about this discovery of mine. It seems it has a much wider significance than I'd supposed. So he's placed his newspaper at my disposal, if I should need it.

MRS STOCKMANN. But do you think you will?

DR STOCKMANN. Oh no, I'm sure I won't. But it's good to know that one has the free press on one's side—the mouthpiece of liberal opinion. And what do you think? I've had a visit from the Chariman of the Property Owners' Association?

MRS STOCKMANN. Oh? And what did he want?

DR STOCKMANN. He's going to support me too. They're all going to support me, if there's any trouble. Catherine, do you know what I have behind me?

MRS STOCKMANN. Behind you? No, what have you behind you?

DR STOCKMANN. The solid majority.

MRS STOCKMANN. I see. And that's a good thing, is it?

DR STOCKMANN. Of course it's a good thing! *(Rubs his hands, and walks up and down.)* How splendid to feel that one stands shoulder to shoulder with one's fellow citizens in brotherly concord!

PETRA. And that one's doing so much that's good and useful, father.

DR STOCKMANN. Yes, and for one's home town too!

MRS STOCKMANN. There's the doorbell.

DR STOCKMANN. Ah, this must be him! *(A knock on the inner door.)* Come in!

MAYOR *(enters from the hall).* Good morning.

DR STOCKMANN *(warmly).* Hullo, Peter!

MRS STOCKMANN. Good morning, brother-in-law. How are you?

MAYOR. Oh, thank you; so-so. *(To the DOCTOR.)* Last night, after office hours, I received a thesis from you regarding the state of the water at the Baths.

DR STOCKMANN. Yes. Have you read it?

MAYOR. I have.

DR STOCKMANN. Well! What do you think?

MAYOR *(glances at the others).* Hm—

MRS STOCKMANN. Come, Petra.

She and PETRA go into the room on the left.

MAYOR *(after a pause).* Was it necessary to conduct all these investigations behind my back?

DR STOCKMANN. Well, until I was absolutely certain, I—

MAYOR. And now you are?

DR STOCKMANN. Yes. Surely you must be convinced—?

Mayor. Is it your intention to place this document before the Baths Committee as an official statement?

Dr Stockmann. Of course? Something must be done. And quickly.

Mayor. I find your phraseology in this document, as usual, somewhat extravagant. Amongst other things, you say that all we have to offer our visitors at present is a permanent state of ill-health.

Dr Stockmann. Peter, how else can you describe it? Just think! That water's poisonous even if you bathe in it, let alone drink it! And we're offering this to unfortunate people who are ill and who have turned to us in good faith, and are paying us good money, in order to get their health back!

Mayor. And your conclusion is that we must build a sewer to drain away these aforesaid impurities from the swamp at Moelledal, and that the whole water system must be relaid.

Dr Stockmann. Can you think of any other solution? I can't.

Mayor. This morning I called upon the town engineer. In the course of our discussion I half jokingly mentioned these proposals as a thing we might possibly undertake some time in the future.

Dr Stockmann. Some time in the future?

Mayor. He smiled at what he obviously regarded as my extravagance— as I knew he would. Have you ever troubled to consider what these alterations you suggest would cost? According to the information I received, the expense would probably run into several hundred thousand crowns.

Dr Stockmann. Would it be that much?

Mayor. Yes. But that's not the worst. The work would take at least two years.

Dr Stockmann. Two years, did you say? Two whole years?

Mayor. At least. And what do we do with the Baths in the meantime? Close them? Yes, we'd be forced to. You don't imagine anyone would come here once the rumour got around that the water was impure?

Dr Stockmann. But, Peter, it is!

Mayor. (And for this to happen just now, when the whole enterprise is coming to fruition!) There are other towns around with qualifications to be regarded as health resorts. Do you think they won't start trying to attract the market? Of course they will. And there we shall be! We'll probably have to abandon the whole expensive scheme, and you will have ruined the town (that gave you birth).

Dr Stockmann. I—ruined—!

Mayor. It's only as a health resort—a Spa—that this town has any future worth speaking of. Surely you realize that as well as I do.

Dr Stockmann. But what do you propose we do?

Mayor. Your report has not completely convinced me that the situation is as dangerous as you imply.

Dr Stockmann. Oh, Peter, if anything it's worse! Or at least it will be in the summer, once the hot weather starts.

Mayor. As I said, I believe that you are exaggerating the danger. [A capable medical officer must be able to take measures. He must know how to forestall such unpleasantnesses, and how to remedy them if they should become obvious.

Dr Stockmann. Go on.]

Mayor. The existing water system at the Baths is a fact, and must be accepted as such. However, in due course I dare say the Committee might not be inflexibly opposed to considering whether, without unreasonable pecuniary sacrifice, it might not be possible to introduce certain improvements.

Dr Stockmann. And you think I'd lend me name to such chicanery?

Mayor. Chicanery!

Dr Stockmann. That's what it would be! A fraud, a lie, a crime against the community, against the whole of society!

Mayor. As I have already pointed out, I have not succeeded in convincing myself that any immediate or critical danger exists.

Dr Stockmann. Oh, yes you have! [You must have! My arguments are irrefutable—I know they are! And you know that as well as I do, Peter!] But you won't admit it, because it was you who forced through the proposal that the Baths and the water pipes should be sited where they are, and you refuse to admit that you made a gross blunder. Don't be such a fool, do you think I don't see through you?

Mayor. And suppose you were right? If I do guard my reputation with a certain anxiety, it is because I have the welfare of our town at heart. Without moral authority I cannot guide and direct affairs as I deem most fit for the general good. For this, and diverse other reasons, it is vital to me that your report should not be placed before the Baths Committee. It must be suppressed for the general good. At a later date I shall bring the matter up for discussion, and we shall discreetly do the best we can. But nothing, not a single word, about this unfortunate matter must come to the public ear.

Dr Stockmann. Well, it can't be stopped now, my dear Peter.

Mayor. It must and shall be stopped.

Dr Stockmann. It can't, I tell you. Too many people know.

Mayor. Know? Who knows? You don't mean those fellows from the *People's Tribune*—?

DR STOCKMANN. (Oh, yes, they too.) The free press of our country will see to it that you do your duty.

MAYOR *(after a short pause)*. You're an exceedingly foolish man, Thomas. Haven't you considered what the consequences of this action may be for you?

DR STOCKMANN. Consequences? Consequences for me?

MAYOR. Yes. For you and for your family.

DR STOCKMANN. What the devil do you mean by that?

MAYOR. I think I have always shown myself a good brother to you, whenever you've needed help.

DR STOCKMANN. You have, and I thank you for it.

MAYOR. I'm not asking for thanks. To a certain extent I've been forced to do it—for my own sake. (I always hoped I might be able to curb you a little if I could help to improve your economic position.

DR STOCKMANN. What! So it was only for your own sake that you—

MAYOR. Partly, I said.) It's painful for a public servant to see his next-of-kin spend his entire time compromising himself.

DR STOCKMANN. And you think I do that?

MAYOR. Unfortunately you do, without knowing it. You have a restless, combative, rebellious nature. And then you've this unfortunate passion for rushing into print upon every possible—and impossible—subject. The moment you get an idea you have to sit down and write a newspaper article or a whole pamphlet about it.

DR STOCKMANN. Surely if a man gets hold of a new idea it's his duty as a citizen to tell it to the public?

MAYOR. People don't want new ideas. They're best served by the good old accepted ideas they have already.

DR STOCKMANN. And you can say that to my face!

(MAYOR. Yes, Thomas. I'm going to speak bluntly to you for once. Up to now I've tried to avoid it, because I know how hasty you are; but now I've got to tell you the truth. You've no idea how much harm you do yourself by this impulsiveness of yours. You abuse the authorities, and even the government—you throw mud at them, you claim you've been cold-shouldered and persecuted. But what else can you expect, when you're such a difficult person?

DR STOCKMANN. Oh, so I'm difficult too, am I?)

MAYOR. Oh, Thomas, you're impossible to work with. (I've discovered that for myself.) You never consider anyone else's feelings. You even seem to forget it's me you have to thank for getting you your job at the Baths—

DR STOCKMANN. It was mine by right! I was the first person to see that this town could become a flourishing watering place! (And I was the only person who did see it at that time!) For many years I fought alone for this idea! I wrote, and wrote—

MAYOR. No one denies that. But the time wasn't ripe then. (Of course you weren't to know that, tucked away in your northern backwater.) But as soon as the right moment arrived, I—and others—took the matter up—

DR STOCKMANN. Yes, and made a mess of my wonderful plan! Oh yes, it's becoming very clear now what brilliant fellows you were!

MAYOR. As far as I can see, all you're looking for now is just another excuse for a fight. You've always got to pick a quarrel with your superiors—it's your old failing. You can't bear to have anyone in authority over you. (You look askance at anyone who occupies a position higher than yours. You regard him as a personal enemy— and then, as far as you're concerned, one weapon of attack is as good as another.) But now I've shown you what's at stake, for the whole town, and for myself too. And I'm not prepared to compromise.

DR STOCKMANN. What do you mean?

MAYOR. Since you have been so indiscreet as to discuss this delicate matter, which you ought to have kept a professional secret, the affair obviously cannot be hushed up. All kinds of rumours will spread around, and the malicious elements among us will feed these rumours with details of their own invention. It is therefore necessary that you publicly deny these rumours.

DR STOCKMANN. I don't understand you.

MAYOR. I feel sure that on further investigation you will convince yourself that the situation is not nearly as critical as you had at first supposed.

DR STOCKMANN. Aha; you feel sure, do you?

MAYOR. I also feel sure you will publicly express your confidence that the Committee will (painstakingly and conscientiously take all necessary measures to) remedy any possible defects which may exist.

DR STOCKMANN. But you can't remedy the defect by just patching things up! I'm telling you, Peter, unless you start again from scratch, it's my absolute conviction that—

MAYOR. As an employee you have no right to any independent conviction.

DR STOCKMANN *(starts).* No right!

MAYOR. As an employee. As a private person—well, heaven knows that's another matter. But as a subordinate official at the Baths, you have no right to express any opinion which conflicts with that of your superiors.

DR STOCKMANN. This is going too far! I, a doctor, a man of science, have no right—!

MAYOR. The question is not merely one of science. (The problem is complex.) The issues involved are both technical and economical.

DR STOCKMANN. I don't care how you define the bloody thing! I must be free to say what I think about anything!

MAYOR. Go ahead. As long as it isn't anything connected with the Baths. That we forbid you.

DR STOCKMANN (shouts). You forbid—! You—! Why, you're just a—

MAYOR. *I* forbid you—I, your chief! And when I forbid you to do something, you must obey!

DR STOCKMANN (controls himself). Peter—if you weren't my brother—!

PETRA (throws open the door). Father, don't put up with this!

MRS STOCKMANN (follows her). Petra, Petra!

MAYOR. Ha! Eavesdroppers!

MRS STOCKMANN. You were talking so loud—we couldn't help hearing—

PETRA. I was listening.

MAYOR. Well, I'm not altogether sorry—

DR STOCKMANN (goes closer to him). You spoke to me of forbidding and obeying?

MAYOR. You forced me to use that tone.

DR STOCKMANN. And you expect me to publicly swallow my own words?

MAYOR. We regard it as an unavoidable necessity that you issue a statement on the lines I have indicated.

DR STOCKMANN. And if I don't—obey?

MAYOR. Then we shall be forced to issue an explanation, to calm the public.

DR STOCKMANN. All right! But I shall write and refute you. I stick to my views. I shall prove that I am right and you are wrong. And what will you do then?

MAYOR. Then I shall be unable to prevent your dismissal.

DR STOCKMANN. What—!

PETRA. Father! Dismissal!

MRS STOCKMANN. Dismissal!

MAYOR. Dismissal from your post as public medical officer. I shall feel compelled to apply for immediate notice to be served on you, barring you from any further connection with the Baths.

DR STOCKMANN. You'd have the impudence to do that?

MAYOR. You're the one who's being impudent.

PETRA. Uncle, this is a disgraceful way to treat a man like father!

MRS STOCKMANN. Be quiet, Petra.

MAYOR (*looks at* PETRA). So we've opinions of our own already, have we? But of course! (*To* MRS STOCKMANN.) Sister-in-law, you seem to be the most sensible person in this house. Use what influence you have over your husband. Make him realize the consequences this will have both for his family and—

DR STOCKMANN. My family concerns no one but myself.

MAYOR. —both for his family, and for the town he lives in.

DR STOCKMANN. I'm the one who has the town's real interests at heart! I want to expose the evils that sooner or later must come to light. I'm going to prove to people that I love this town where I was born.

MAYOR. Oh, you're blind! All you're trying to do is to stop up the source of the town's prosperity.

DR STOCKMANN. That source is poisoned, man! Are you mad? We live by hawking filth and disease! And all this communal life you boast so much about is based upon a lie!

MAYOR. That's pure imagination—if nothing worse. The man who casts such foul aspersions against the town he lives in is an enemy of society.

DR STOCKMANN (*goes towards him*). You dare to—!

MRS STOCKMANN (*throws herself between them*). Thomas!

PETRA (*grasps her father by the arm*). Keep calm, father!

MAYOR. I shall not expose myself to violence. You've been warned. Consider what is your duty to yourself and your family. Good-bye. (*Goes.*)

DR STOCKMANN (*walks up and down*). And in my own house too, Catherine!

MRS STOCKMANN. Yes, Thomas. It's a shame and a scandal—

PETRA. I'd like to get my hands on him—!

DR STOCKMANN. It's my own fault. I ought to have exposed them long ago! I should have bared my teeth; and used them! Calling me an enemy of society! By God, I'm not going to take that lying down!

MRS STOCKMANN. But, Thomas dear, might is right—

DR STOCKMANN. I'm the one who's right!

MRS STOCKMANN. What's the good of being right if you don't have the might?

PETRA. Mother, how can you speak like that?

[DR STOCKMANN. So it's no use in a free society to have right on one's side? Don't be absurd, Catherine. Besides—don't I have the free press in front of me—and the solid majority behind me? That's might enough, I should have thought?

MRS STOCKMANN. For heaven's sake, Thomas, surely you're not thinking of setting yourself up against your brother?

DR STOCKMANN. What the devil else do you expect me to do? Don't you want me to stand up for what I believe to be right?

PETRA. Yes, father, you must!

MRS STOCKMANN. It'll do you no good. If they won't, they won't.]

DR STOCKMANN (laughs). Oh, Catherine, just give me time. You'll see! I'm going to fight this war to the end.

MRS STOCKMANN. Yes, and the end will be that you'll lose your job. [You'll see.

DR STOCKMANN. At least I shall have done my duty to the community; my duty to society. And they call me an enemy of society—!]

MRS STOCKMANN. What about your family, Thomas? [And your home? Do you think you'll be doing your duty to the ones who depend on you?]

PETRA. Oh, mother, don't always think only of us.

MRS STOCKMANN. It's easy for you to talk. You can stand on your own feet, if need be. But think of the boys, Thomas! [And think of yourself too—and me—]

DR STOCKMANN. You must be mad, Catherine! If I give in like a coward to Peter and his wretched gang, do you think I'd ever have another moment of happiness in my life?

MRS STOCKMANN. I don't know about that. But God preserve us from the happiness we're likely to enjoy if you go on digging your heels in. You'll have no means of livelihood, no regular income. Didn't we have enough of that in the old days? Remember that, Thomas. Think what it'll mean.

DR STOCKMANN (writhes, fighting with himself, and clenches his fists). And these office lackeys can do this to a free and honourable man! Isn't it monstrous, Catherine?

MRS STOCKMANN. Yes, they've behaved very wickedly to you, that's true. But heaven knows, there's so much injustice one has to put up with in this world. There are the boys, Thomas.] Look at them! What's to become of them? [No, no, you can't have the heart.]

EILIF and MORTEN have meanwhile entered, carrying their schoolbooks.

DR STOCKMANN. My sons! (Suddenly stands erect, his mind made up.) Even if my whole world crashes about me, I shall never bow my head. (Goes towards his room.)

MRS STOCKMANN. Thomas, what are you going to do?

DR STOCKMANN (in the doorway). I want to have the right to look my sons in the eyes when they grow up into free men! (Goes into his room.)

MRS STOCKMANN (bursts into tears). Oh, God help us!

(PETRA. Father's right, mother! He'll never give in.)

The boys ask in bewilderment what is the matter. PETRA *signs to them to go.*

ACT THREE

The editorial office of the People's Tribune. *On the left in the background is the entrance door; to the right in the same wall is another door with glass panes through which the composing room is visible. Another door is in the wall on the right. In the middle of the room is a big table covered with papers, newspapers and books. Downstage left is a window; by it is a writing desk with a high stool. Two armchairs stand by the table, and there are other chairs along the walls. The room is gloomy and uncomfortable; the furniture is old, the armchair, dirty and torn. In the composing room one or two* COMPOSITORS *are at work. Beyond them, a hand-press is being operated.*

HOVSTAD *sits writing at the desk. After a few moments,* BILLING *enters right, with the* DOCTOR *'s manuscript in his hand.*

BILLING. I say, I say, I say!

HOVSTAD *(writing).* Have you read it?

BILLING *(puts the manuscript on the desk).* I should say I have!

HOVSTAD. Pretty forceful, isn't it?

BILLING. Forceful? He'll butcher them, by Jingo! Every paragraph's a knock-out!

HOVSTAD. Those fellows won't give in at the first blow, though.

BILLING. That's true. But we'll go on bashing them, punch after punch, till their whole damned oligarchy falls to the ground! As I sat in there reading this, it was as though I saw the revolution dawning from afar!

HOVSTAD *(turns).* Hush, don't let Aslaksen hear.

BILLING *(lowers his voice).* Aslaksen's a coward, a jellyfish! He hasn't the guts of a man! But you'll have your way? You will publish the Doctor's article?

HOVSTAD. Yes, unless the Mayor backs down—

BILLING. That'd be a damned nuisance!

HOVSTAD. Whichever way it turns out we can exploit the situation. If the Mayor doesn't agree to the Doctor's proposal, he'll have all the tradespeople down on him—the Property Owners' association, and the rest. And if he does agree to it he'll antagonize all the big shareholders in the Baths who up to now have been his chief supporters—

BILLING. Of course! They'll have to fork out a pile of money—

HOVSTAD. You bet they will. And then the clique will be broken, and day after day we'll drum it into the public that the Mayor's incompetent in more respects than one, and that (all the responsible offices in the town,) the whole municipal authority, ought to be handed over to people of liberal opinions.

BILLING. By Jingo, that's the truth! I see it! I see it! We stand on the threshold of a revolution!

A knock on the door.

HOVSTAD. Quiet! *(Shouts.)* Come in.

DR STOCKMANN *enters through the door upstage left.*

HOVSTAD *(goes to greet him).* Ah, here is the Doctor! Well?

DR STOCKMANN. Print away, Mr Hovstad!

HOVSTAD. So it's come to that?

BILLING. Hurrah!

DR STOCKMANN. Print away, I say! Yes, it's come to that all right. Well, now they shall have it the way they want it. It's war now, Mr Billing!

BILLING. War to the death, I hope! Give it to them, Doctor!

DR STOCKMANN. This report is only the beginning. My head's already teeming with ideas for four or five other articles. Where's Aslaksen?

BILLING *(calls into the composing-room).* Aslaksen, come here a moment!

HOVSTAD. Four or five other articles, did you say? On the same theme?

DR STOCKMANN. No—oh, good heavens no, my dear fellow! No, they'll be about quite different things. But it all stems from this business of the water system and the sewer. One thing leads to another, you know. It's like when you start to pull down an old building. Exactly like that.

BILLING. By Jingo, that's true! You suddenly realize you'll never be finished till you've pulled down the whole rotten structure!

ASLAKSEN *(from the composing-room).* Pulled down! You're surely not thinking of pulling the Baths down, Doctor?

HOVSTAD. No, no, don't get frightened.

DR STOCKMAN. No, we were talking about something else. Well, Mr Hovstad, what do you think of my report?

HOVSTAD. I think it's an absolute masterpiece—

DR STOCKMANN. Do you think so? That makes me very happy—very happy.

HOVSTAD. It's so clear and to the point; you don't have to be a specialist to follow the argument. I'm sure you'll have every enlightened person on your side.

ASLAKSEN. Every discriminating one too, I trust?

BILLING. Discriminating or not—you'll have the whole town behind you.

ASLAKSEN. Well then, I don't think we need be afraid to print it.

DR STOCKMANN. I should damn well hope not.

HOVSTAD. It'll be in tomorrow morning.

DR STOCKMANN. Good God, yes, we can't afford to waste a single day. Oh, Mr Aslaksen, there was one thing I wanted to ask you. You must take charge of this manuscript yourself.

ASLAKSEN. If you wish.

DR STOCKMANN. Treat it as though it was gold. No misprints! Every word is important. I'll drop back later; perhaps you'd let me look at a proof. I can't tell you how eager I am to see this thing in print— launched—!

BILLING. Launched, yes! Like a thunderbolt!

DR STOCKMANN. —and submitted to the judgment of every intelligent citizen. Oh, you'd never guess what I've had to put up with today! I've been threatened with God knows what. They want to rob me of my elementary rights as a human being—

BILLING. Your rights as a human being!

DR STOCKMANN. (They want to degrade me, reduce me to the level of a beggar.) They demand that I put my private interests above my most sacred and innermost convictions—

BILLING. By Jingo, that's going too far!

HOVSTAD. You can expect anything from that lot.

DR STOCKMANN. (But they won't get far with me!) I'll give it to them in black and white! I'll grapple with them every day in the *People's Tribune!* I'll sweep them with one broadside after another—!

ASLAKSEN. Yes, but remember—

BILLING. Hurrah! It's war, it's war!

DR STOCKMANN. I'll beat them to the ground, (I'll crush them,) I'll flatten their defenses for every honest man to see! (By God I will!)

ASLAKSEN. But do it soberly, Doctor. Act with restraint—

BILLING. No, no! Don't spare your powder!

DR STOCKMANN (*continues imperturbably*). You see, it isn't just a question of the water system and the sewer. This whole community's got to be cleansed and decontaminated—

BILLING. That's the very word!

DR STOCKMANN. All these skimpers and compromisers have got to be thrown out! There's got to be a clean sweep! (Oh, such endless vistas have been opened up before my eyes today! I don't see my way quite clearly yet. But I will!) We need fresh standard-bearers, my friends! Young men! Our advance posts must be manned by new captains!

BILLING. Hear, hear!

DR STOCKMANN. As long as we stick together, (it'll all happen so easily!—) the whole revolution will glide into existence like a ship from the stocks! Don't you agree?

HOVSTAD. I think we've every prospect now for getting the helm into the right hands.

ASLAKSEN. As long as we proceed with restraint, I don't think there can be any danger.

DR STOCKMANN. Who the hell cares about danger? I'm doing this in the name of truth and of my conscience!

HOVSTAD. You're a man who deserves support, Doctor.

ASLAKSEN. Yes, the Doctor's a true friend of the town, that's certain. I'll go further; he's a friend of society!

BILLING. By Jingo, Mr Aslaksen, Dr Stockmann is a friend of the people!

(ASLAKSEN. I think the Property Owners' Association might be able to use that phrase.)

DR STOCKMANN (moved, presses their hands). Thank you, my dear, good friends—thank you! It's so refreshing for me to hear this. My brother described me in vastly different terms. By God, I'll give it back to him with interest! Now I must go and see a poor devil of a patient. But I'll be back! Take good care of that manuscript, Mr Aslaksen. And for heaven's sake don't cut out any of the exclamation marks! If anything, put in a few more! Good, good! Well, good-bye! Good-bye, good-bye!

He shakes hands with them as they accompany him to the door and he goes out.

HOVSTAD. He's going to be bloody useful to us.

ASLAKSEN. As long as he sticks to the Baths. But if he tries to go further, we'd be unwise to stay with him.

HOVSTAD. Hm; that all depends—

BILLING. You're such a damned coward, Aslaksen!

ASLAKSEN. Coward? Yes, when it's a question of fighting local authorities, I am a coward, Mr Billing. That's a lesson I have learned in the school of life. But elevate me into the field of high politics, confront me with the Government, and then see if I am a coward!

BILLING. No, no, I'm sure you're not. But that's just where you're so inconsistent.

ASLAKSEN. Because I know my responsibilities as a citizen! Throwing stones at the government can't harm society. It doesn't bother those fellows—they stay put. But local authorities can be overthrown, and then you may get inexperience at the helm. (With disastrous results for property owners and the like.)

HOVSTAD. But what about the education of people through self-government?

ASLAKSEN. When a man has interests to protect he can't think of everything, Mr Hovstad.

HOVSTAD. Then I hope to God I never have any interests to protect.

BILLING. Hear, hear!

HOVSTAD. I'm not a trimmer, and I never will be.

ASLAKSEN. A politician should never commit himself, Mr Hovstad. And you, Mr Billing, you ought to put a reef or two in your sails if you want that job of clerk to the council.

BILLING. I—!

HOVSTAD. *You*, Billing?

BILLING. Of course I only applied for it to put their backs up, you understand.

ASLAKSEN. Well, it's no business of mine. But since I'm being accused of cowardice and inconsistency, I'd like to make this clear. My political record is open for anyone to investigate. I've never changed my standpoint—apart from having learned more restraint. My heart still belongs with the people; but I don't deny that my head keeps one ear cocked towards the authorities. The local ones, anyway. *(Goes into the composing-room.)*

BILLING. Couldn't you change to some other printer, Hovstad?

HOVSTAD. Do you know anyone else who'd give us credit (for printing and paper)?

BILLING. It's a damned nuisance not having any capital!

HOVSTAD *(sits at the desk)*. Yes, if we only had that—

BILLING. Ever thought of trying Dr. Stockmann?

HOVSTAD *(glancing through his papers)*. What'd be the use of that? He hasn't a bean.

BILLING. No; but he's got a good man behind him. Old Morten Kiil—the fellow they call the Badger–

HOVSTAD *(writing)*. Do you really think he's got much?

BILLING. By Jingo, of course he has! And part of it must go to the Stockmanns. He's bound to provide for—well, the children anyway.

HOVSTAD *(half turns)*. Are you banking on that?

BILLING. Banking? I never bank on anything.

HOVSTAD. You'd better not. And don't bank on becoming clerk to the council either, because I can promise you you won't.

BILLING. Do you think I don't know? *Not* to get it is just what I want! A snub like that puts you on your mettle. It gives you a fresh supply of gall, and you need that in a backwater like this, where hardly anything really infuriating ever happens.

HOVSTAD *(writing)*. Yes, Yes.

BILLING. Well, they'll soon hear from me! I'll go and write that appeal for funds to the Property Owners' Association. *(Going into the room on the right.)*

HOVSTAD *(sitting at the desk, chews his pen and says slowly)*. Hm! So that's the way the wind blows! *(There is a knock on the door.)* Come In!

PETRA *enters through the door upstage left.*

HOVSTAD *(gets up)*. Why, hullo! Fancy seeing you here!

PETRA. Please forgive me—

HOVSTAD *(pushes forward an armchair)*. Won't you sit down?

PETRA. No, thank you. I'm only staying a moment.

HOVSTAD. Is it something from your father—?

PETRA. No, something from me. *(Takes a book from her coat pocket.)* Here's that English novel.

HOVSTAD. Why are you giving it back to me?

PETRA. I don't want to translate it.

HOVSTAD. But you promised—

PETRA. I hadn't read it then. You can't have, either!

HOVSTAD. No—you know I don't understand English. But—

PETRA. Exactly. That's why I wanted to tell you—you'll have to find something else to serialize. *(Puts the book on the table.)* You can't possibly print this in the *People's Tribune.*

HOVSTAD. Why not?

PETRA. Because it's diametrically opposed to what you believe.

HOVSTAD. Oh, that's the reason?

PETRA. I don't think you understand. Its theme is that there's a supernatural power which takes care of all the so-called good people in this world, and works things so that in the end everything turns out well for them and all the so-called bad people get punished.

HOVSTAD. Yes, well, that's all right. That's just what people want to read.

PETRA. But do you want to be the one who provides it for them? You don't believe a word of that! You know quite well it doesn't happen like that in real life.

HOVSTAD. Of course not. But an editor can't always do as he wishes. One often has to bow to people's feelings in minor matters. After all, politics are the most important things in life—for a newspaper, anyway. And if I want to win people over to my views about freedom and progress, I mustn't frighten them away. If they find a moral story like this in the back pages of the newspaper they're more likely to go along with what we print on the front page. It reassures them.

PETRA. Oh, really! You're not as crafty as that. I don't see you as a spider spinning webs to catch your readers!

HOVSTAD *(smiles)*. Thank you for holding such a high opinion of me. No, actually this was Billing's idea, not mine.

PETRA. Billing's!

HOVSTAD. Yes. He was talking on those lines here the other day. He's the one who's so keen that we should publish this novel. I'd never heard of the book.

PETRA. But Billing holds such progressive views—

HOVSTAD. Oh, there's more in Billing than meets the eye. I've just heard he's applied for the post of clerk to the council.

PETRA. I don't believe that, Mr. Hovstad. How could he reconcile himself to doing a thing like that?

HOVSTAD. You'd better ask him.

PETRA. I'd never have thought that of Billing.

HOVSTAD *(looks more closely at her.)* Wouldn't you? Does it so surprise you?

PETRA. Yes. Perhaps not, though. I don't really know—

HOVSTAD. We journalists aren't worth much, Miss Stockmann.

PETRA. How can you say that?

HOVSTAD. I sometimes think it.

PETRA. In the ordinary run of events, perhaps not—that I can understand. But now, when you've taken up such an important cause—

[HOVSTAD. This business with your father, you mean?

PETRA. Yes, that.] Now surely you must feel you're worth more than most men.

HOVSTAD. Yes, today I do feel a bit like that.

PETRA. It's true, isn't it? You do! Oh, it's a wonderful vocation you've chosen! To be able to pioneer neglected truths and brave new doctrines—the mere fact of standing fearlessly forth to defend a man who's been wronged—

HOVSTAD. Especially when this man who's been wronged is—hm—how shall I say—?

PETRA. When he is a man of such honour and integrity?

HOVSTAD *(more quietly)*. I was about to say: especially when he is your father.

PETRA *(astounded)*. Mr. Hovstad!

HOVSTAD. Yes, Petra—Miss Petra—

PETRA. Is that what seems important to you? Not the issue itself. Not the truth—or the fact that this means everything to Father—

HOVSTAD. Yes—yes, of course—those things too—

PETRA. No, thank you. You let the cat out of the bag there, Mr. Hovstad. Now I shall never believe you again. About anything.

HOVSTAD. Does it make you so angry that I've done this for your sake?

PETRA. I'm angry because you haven't been honest with Father. You've been talking to him as though truth and the good of the people were what mattered most to you. You've been fooling both of us. You're not the man you've been pretending you are. And that I'll never forgive you—never!

HOVSTAD. You shouldn't speak so sharply to me, Miss Petra. Least of all just now.

PETRA. Why not now?

HOVSTAD. Because your father needs my help.

PETRA. So that's the sort of man you are!

HOVSTAD. No, no, I didn't mean that. Please believe me—!

PETRA. I know what to believe. Good-bye.

ASLAKSEN *(hurries in furiously from the composing-room)*. For God's sake, Mr. Hovstad—! *(Sees* PETRA.*)* Oh, dear, that's unlucky—!

PETRA. There's the book. You can give it so someone else. *(Goes towards the door.)*

HOVSTAD *(goes after her)*. But, Miss Petra—!

PETRA. Good-bye. *(Goes)*.

ASLAKSEN. Mr. Hovstad, listen, please!

HOVSTAD. Yes, yes, what is it?

ASLAKSEN. The Mayor's standing outside there in the composing-room!

HOVSTAD. The Mayor?

ASLAKSEN. Yes. He wants to talk to you. He came in the back way—didn't want to be seen, I suppose.

HOVSTAD. What can he want? No, wait, I'd better—*(Goes to the door of the composing-room, opens it, bows and invites the* MAYOR *to enter.)*

HOVSTAD. Keep a look out, Aslaksen, and make sure no one—

ASLAKSEN. Of course. *(Goes into the composing-room.)*

MAYOR. You weren't expecting to see me here.

HOVSTAD. No, frankly, I wasn't.

MAYOR *(looks round).* You've done this up quite nicely. Very pleasant.

HOVSTAD. Oh—

MAYOR. And here I am, coming along and making demands on your time.

HOVSTAD. Not at all, sir. What can I do for you? Please allow me—*(Takes the* MAYOR*'s hat and stick and puts them on a chair.)* Won't you sit down?

MAYOR *(sits at the table).* Thank you.

HOVSTAD *also sits at the table.*

MAYOR. Something—something extremely irritating has happened to me today, Mr. Hovstad.

HOVSTAD. Really? Of course, Your Worship has so many responsibilities—

MAYOR. This particular matter concerns the medical officer at the Baths.

HOVSTAD. Oh—the Doctor—?

MAYOR. He's written a sort of—report to the Baths Committee regarding some supposed defects in the baths.

HOVSTAD. You amaze me.

MAYOR. Hasn't he told you? I thought he said—

HOVSTAD. Oh yes, that's true, he did say something—

ASLAKSEN *(from the composing-room).* I'd better have that manuscript—

HOVSTAD *(irritated).* Hm—it's there on the desk—

ASLAKSEN *(finds it).* Good.

MAYOR. Why, surely that's it!

ASLAKSEN. Yes, this is the Doctor's article, Your Worship.

HOVSTAD. Oh, is this what you were talking about?

MAYOR. The very thing. What do you think of it?

HOVSTAD. Of course I'm not a specialist, and I've only glanced through it—

MAYOR. But you're going to print it?

HOVSTAD. I can't very well refuse a signed contribution—

ASLAKSEN. I have no say in the contents of the paper, Your Worship—

MAYOR. Of course not.

ASLAKSEN. I only print what's put into my hands.

MAYOR. Absolutely.

ASLAKSEN. So if you'll excuse me—*(Goes towards the composing-room.)*

MAYOR. No, wait a moment, Mr Aslaksen. With your permission, Mr. Hovstad—

HOVSTAD. Of course, Your Worship.

MAYOR. You're an intelligent and discriminating man, Mr Aslaksen.

ASLAKSEN. I'm glad Your Worship thinks so.

MAYOR. And a man of wide influence in more circles than one.

ASLAKSEN. Oh—mostly among humble people—

MAYOR. The small taxpayers are the most numerous, here as elsewhere.

ASLAKSEN. Yes, that's true.

MAYOR. And I've no doubt you know how most of them feel. Don't you?

ASLAKSEN. Yes, I think I may say I do, Your Worship.

MAYOR. Well then, since the less affluent of the citizens of this town are so laudably disposed to make this sacrifice, I—

ASLAKSEN. What!

HOVSTAD. Sacrifice—?

MAYOR. It's a fine token of public spirit. A remarkably fine token. I was about to confess I hadn't expected it. But you know the mood of the people better than I do.

ASLAKSEN. But, Your Worship—

MAYOR. And it will probably be no mean sacrifice that the ratepayers will be called upon to make.

HOVSTAD. The ratepayers?

ASLAKSEN. But I don't understand—surely the shareholders—?

MAYOR. According to a provisional estimate, the alterations that the medical officer at the Baths regards as desirable will cost some two to three hundred thousand crowns.

ASLAKSEN. That's a lot of money; but—

MAYOR. We shall of course be forced to raise a municipal loan.

HOVSTAD (gets up). You surely don't mean that the ordinary citizens—?

ASLAKSEN. You mean you'd charge it on the rates! Empty the pockets of the tradespeople—?

MAYOR. Well, my dear Mr Aslaksen, where else is the money to come from?

ASLAKSEN. That's the business of gentlemen who own the Baths.

MAYOR. The Committee cannot see their way towards authorizing any further expenditure.

ASLAKSEN. Is that quite definite, Your Worship?

MAYOR. I have gone into the matter very thoroughly. If the people want all these comprehensive alterations, then the people themselves will have to pay for them.

ASLAKSEN. But, good God Almighty—oh, I beg Your Worship's pardon!—but this puts a completely different face on the situation, Mr Hovstad.

HOVSTAD. It certainly does.

MAYOR. The worst of the matter is that we shall be compelled to close the Baths for two to three years.

HOVSTAD. Close them? You mean—close them completely?

ASLAKSEN. For two years?

MAYOR. That's how long the work will take, at the lowest calculation.

ASLAKSEN. But, good heavens, we'll never be able to stand that, Your Worship! How are we property owners to live in the meantime?

MAYOR. I'm afraid that's a very difficult question to answer, Mr Aslaksen. But what do you expect us to do? Do you imagine we shall get a single visitor here if we start spreading the idea that the water is contaminated, that we are living over a cesspit, that the whole town—?

ASLAKSEN. And all this is just pure speculation?

MAYOR. With the best will in the world I have been unable to convince myself that it is anything else.

ASLAKSEN. But if that's the case it's monstrous of Dr Stockmann to have— I beg Your Worship's pardon, but—

MAYOR. I deplore your observation, Mr Aslaksen, But I'm afraid it represents the truth. My brother has unfortunately always been an impulsive man.

ASLAKSEN. And you still want to support him in this action. Mr. Hovstad?

HOVSTAD. But who could have possibly guessed that—?

MAYOR. I have written a brief *résumé* of the situation as it appears to an impartial observer; and in it I have suggested how any possible flaws in the existing arrangements could safely be remedied by measures within the financial resources at present possessed by the Baths.

HOVSTAD. Have you that document with you, Your Worship?

MAYOR *(feels in his pocket)*. Yes, I brought it with me just in case you—

ASLAKSEN *(quickly)*. Oh, my goodness, there he is!

MAYOR. Who? My brother?

HOVSTAD. Where—Where?

ASLAKSEN. He's just coming through the composing-room.

MAYOR. Most unfortunate! I don't want to meet him here, and I've something else I wanted to speak to you about.

HOVSTAD *(points towards the door, right)*. Go in there till he's gone.

MAYOR. But—?

HOVSTAD. There's only Billing there.

ASLAKSEN. Quick, quick, Your Worship! He's coming now!

MAYOR. Very well. But get rid of him as soon as you can.
Goes out through the door on the right, which ASLAKSEN *opens and closes for him.*

HOVSTAD. Find something to do, Aslaksen.

He sits down and writes. ASLAKSEN *starts looking through a pile of news-papers on a chair to the right.*

DR STOCKMANN *(enters from the composing-room).* Well, here I am again! *(Puts down his hat and stick.)*

HOVSTAD *(writing).* Already, Doctor? Aslaksen, hurry up with that thing we were talking about. We're badly behindhand today.

DR STOCKMANN *(to* ASLAKSEN). *No proofs yet, by the sound of it?*

ASLAKSEN *(without turning).* No, surely you didn't think they'd be ready yet.

DR STOCKMANN. That's all right. I'm just impatient, as I know you'll appreciate. I can't rest till I've seen that thing in print.

HOVSTAD. Hm—it'll be a good time yet. Won't it, Aslaksen?

ASLAKSEN. I'm afraid so.

DR STOCKMANN. Very well, my dear friends. I'll be back later. I don't mind making the journey twice if need be! (In such a vital matter, with the welfare of the whole town at stake, one mustn't grudge a little extra effort!) *(Is about to go, but stops and comes back.)* Oh, by the way, there's one more thing I must speak to you about.

HOVSTAD. I'm sorry, but couldn't it wait till another time—?

DR STOCKMANN. I can tell you in two words. It's just this—(when people read my article in the paper tomorrow and discover I've been racking my brains all winter working silently for the welfare of the town—

HOVSTAD. But, Doctor—

DR STOCKMANN. I know what you're going to say! You think it was no more than my damned duty—my job as a citizen. Yes, of course—I know that as well as you do. But) my fellow citizens, you see—oh dear, those good people, they're so fond of me—

ASLAKSEN. Yes, the people of this town have been very fond of you, Doctor, up to today.

(DR STOCKMANN. Yes, and that's exactly why I'm frightened that—what I mean is—when they read this—especially the poorer people—as a clarion call bidding them take the government of their town into their own hands—

HOVSTAD *(gets up).* Look, Doctor, I don't want to hide anything from you—

Dr Stockmann. Ah, something's already afoot! I might have guessed! But I don't want it! If anything like that's being organized, I—

Hovstad. Like what?)

Dr Stockmann. Well, if anything like a torchlight procession or a banquet or—a subscription for some little token of thanks is being organized, you must promise me solemnly you'll squash the idea. And you too, Mr Aslaksen! You hear?

Hovstad. I'm sorry, Doctor, but we might as well tell you the truth now as later—

MRS STOCKMANN, *in hat and cloak, enters through the door upstage, left.*

Mrs Stockmann *(sees the* DOCTOR*).* I knew it!

Hovstad *(goes towards her).* You here too, Mrs Stockmann?

Dr Stockmann. What the devil do you want here, Catherine?

Mrs Stockmann. Surely you can guess.

Hovstad. Won't you sit down? (Or perhaps—?)

Mrs Stockmann. Thank you, you needn't bother. And you mustn't take offence at my coming here to fetch my husband, for I'm the mother of three children, I'd have you realize.

Dr Stockmann. Oh really, Catherine, we know all this.

Mrs Stockmann. Well, it doesn't seem you've much thought for your wife and children today, or you wouldn't have come here to cause all of us misery.

Dr Stockmann. Are you quite mad, Catherine? Simply because a man has a wife and children, is he to be forbidden to proclaim the truth—to be a useful and active citizen—to serve the town he lives in?

Mrs Stockmann. Oh, Thomas, if only you'd use some restraint.

Aslaksen. That's exactly what I say. Restraint in all things.

Mrs Stockmann. And as for you, Mr Hovstad, it's not right for you to persuade my husband to leave his house and home and trick him into involving himself in all this—

Hovstad. I haven't tricked anyone—

Dr Stockmann. Tricked! You think *I* allow myself to be tricked?

Mrs Stockmann. Yes, you do. Oh, I know you're the cleverest man in the town, but you're so dreadfully easy to fool, Thomas. (*To* HOVSTAD.) And don't forget he'll lose his job at the Baths if you print that thing he's written—

Aslaksen. What!

Hovstad. But Doctor—I—

Dr Stockmann *(laughs).* Just let them try! Oh no, Catherine—they'll watch their step! You see, I have the majority behind me!

MRS STOCKMANN. Yes, that's just the trouble. They're an ugly thing to have behind you.

DR STOCKMANN. Rubbish, Catherine! You go home now and take care of the house, and let me take care of society. How can you be frightened when I feel so calm and happy? *(Rubs his hands and walks up and down.)* Truth and the people will win this battle, never you fear! Oh, I can see every liberal-minded citizen in this town marching forward in an unconquerable army—! *(Stops by a chair.)* What—the devil is this?

ASLAKSEN *(looks at it).* Oh dear!

DR STOCKMANN. The crown of authority! *(Takes the* MAYOR's *hat carefully in his fingers and holds it in the air.)*

MRS STOCKMANN. The Mayor's hat!

DR STOCKMANN. And his marshal's baton too. How in the name of hell—?

HOVSTAD. Well—

DR STOCKMANN. Ah, I see! He's been here to talk you over! *(Laughs.)* He came to the wrong men! And then he saw me in the composing-room—*(Roars with laughter.)* Did he run away, Mr Aslaksen?

ASLAKSEN *(quickly).* Oh yes, Doctor, he ran away.

DR STOCKMANN. Ran away leaving his stick and—? Rubbish! Peter never left anything behind in his life! But where the devil have you put him? Ah, yes, of course—in there! Now, Catherine, you watch!

MRS STOCKMANN. Thomas, I beg you—!

ASLAKSEN. Don't do anything rash, Doctor!

DR STOCKMANN *has put the* MAYOR's *hat on his head and taken his stick. Then he goes across, throws the door open and brings his hand up to the hat to salute. The* MAYOR *enters, red with anger.* BILLING *follows him.*

MAYOR. What is the meaning of this disorderly scene?

DR STOCKMANN. A little more respect if you please, my dear Peter. I am the supreme authority in this town now. *(He walks up and down.)*

MRS STOCKMANN *(almost in tears).* Thomas, please!

MAYOR *(follows him).* Give me my hat and stick!

DR STOCKMANN *(as before).* You may be Chief of Police, but I'm the Mayor! I'm master of this whole town, I am!

MAYOR. Take off that hat, I tell you! Remember that that hat is an official emblem—

DR STOCKMANN. Rubbish! Do you think the awakening lion of public opinion is going to let itself be frightened by a hat? We're starting a revolution tomorrow, I'd have you know! You threatened to sack me, but now I'm going to sack you—sack you from all your positions of responsibility! You think I can't? You're wrong, Peter! I have as my allies the conquering forces of social revolution! Hovstad and Billing will thunder in the *People's Tribune,* and Mr Aslaksen will march forth at the head of the entire Property Owner's Association—

ASLAKSEN. No, Doctor, I won't.

DR STOCKMANN. Indeed you will!.

MAYOR. Aha! But perhaps Mr Hovstad will support this up-rising!

HOVSTAD. No, Your Worship.

ASLAKSEN. Mr Hovstad isn't so mad as to ruin himself and his newspaper for the sake of an hallucination.

DR STOCKMANN *(looks around).* What the devil—?

HOVSTAD. You have presented your case in a false light, Doctor; and therefore I cannot support you.

BILLING. No, after what His Worship has had the grace to tell me in there, I shouldn't—

DR STOCKMANN. Lies! I'll answer for the truth of my report! You just print it. I shan't be frightened to defend it.

HOVSTAD. I'm not printing it. I can't and I won't and I dare not print it.

DR STOCKMANN. Dare not? What nonsense is this? You're the editor, and it's the editors who rule the press.

ASLAKSEN. No, Doctor. It's the subscribers.

MAYOR. Fortunately.

ASLAKSEN. It's public opinion, the educated reader, the property owners and so forth—they're the ones who rule the press.

DR STOCKMANN *(calmly).* And all these forces are ranged against me?

ASLAKSEN. They are. If your report got printed, it would mean ruin for the entire community.

DR STOCKMANN. I see.

MAYOR. My hat and stick!

DR STOCKMANN *takes off the hat and puts it on the table together with the stick.*

MAYOR *(takes them both).* Your little reign didn't last long.

DR STOCKMANN. It isn't over yet. (*To* HOVSTAD.) You refuse absolutely, then, to print my report in the *People's Tribune?*

HOVSTAD. Absolutely. Out of consideration for your family, if for no other reason.

MRS STOCKMANN. Never you mind his family, Mr Hovstad.

MAYOR *(takes a paper from his pocket).* This will give the public full possession of the facts. It's an official statement. Mr Hovstad—

HOVSTAD *(takes the paper).* Right. I'll see it's set up at once.

DR STOCKMANN. But not mine! You think you can gag me and stifle the truth! But it won't be as easy as you think. Mr Aslaksen, take this manuscript of mine and print it immediately as a pamplet—at my own expense! I'll publish it myself! I want four hundred copies—five— no, make it six hundred copies!

ASLAKSEN. I wouldn't give you the use of my press if you offered me gold, Doctor. I daren't. Public opinion wouldn't allow me. You won't find a printer to take it anywhere in this town.

DR STOCKMANN. Give it back to me than.

HOVSTAD *hands him the manuscript.*

DR STOCKMANN *(takes his hat and stick).* I'll see the contents are made known all the same. I'll summon a public meeting and read it! All my fellow citizens shall know the truth!

MAYOR. You won't find anyone in this town who'll lease you a hall for such a purpose.

ASLAKSEN. Not one. I'm sure of that.

BILLING. By Jingo, you won't.

MRS STOCKMANN. This is too disgraceful! Why are they all against you?

DR STOCKMANN *(hotly).* I'll tell you why! It's because in this town all the men are old women! Like you, they just think of their families and not of the community.

MRS STOCKMANN *(grasps his arm).* Then I'll show them that an—an old woman can be a man—for once. I'm sticking with you, Thomas.

DR STOCKMANN. Well said, Catherine! The truth shall be told—by God it will! If I can't lease a hall, I'll hire a drummer to march through the town with me, and I'll read it out at every street corner!

MAYOR. You can't be so crazy as to do that!.

DR STOCKMANN. I am!

ASLAKSEN. You won't find a single man in the whole town who'll go with you.

BILLING. No, by Jingo!

MRS STOCKMANN. Don't you give in, Thomas! I'll ask the boys to go with you.

DR STOCKMANN. That's a splendid idea!

MRS STOCKMANN. Morten will love to do it, And so will Eilif, I'm sure.

DR STOCKMANN. Yes, and Petra, too! And you, Catherine!

MRS STOCKMANN. No, no, not me. But I'll stand at the window and watch you. I'll do that.

DR STOCKMANN *(throws his arms around her and kisses her).* Thank you! Well, my fine gentlemen, let the trumpets sound! Let's see whether meanness and mediocrity have the power to gag a man who wants to clean up society!

DR *and* MRS STOCKMANN *go out through the door upstage left.*

MAYOR *(shakes his head thoughtfully).* Now he's driven her mad, too!

ACT FOUR

A big, old-fashioned room in CAPTAIN HORSTER's *house. In the background an open double-leaved door leads to a lobby. In the left-hand wall are three windows. Against the middle of the opposite wall has been placed a dais, on which stands a small table with two candles, a water carafe, a glass and a bell. The room is further illuminated by bracket lamps between the windows. Downstage left stands a table with a candle on it, and a chair. Downstage right is a door, with a few chairs by it.*

A large gathering of CITIZENS, *of all classes. Here and there,* WOMEN *can be seen among the crowd, and there are a few* SCHOOLBOYS. *More and more people gradually stream in from the back, filling the room.*

A CITIZEN *(to another, as he bumps against him).* Hullo, Lamstad! You here too this evening?

SECOND CITIZEN. I never miss a public meeting.

THIRD CITIZEN *(standing near them).* Brought your whistle, I hope?

SECOND CITIZEN. Course I have. Haven't you?

THIRD CITIZEN. You bet! And Skipper Evensen said he'd bring a bloody great horn!

SECOND CITIZEN. He's a card, old Evensen!

Laughter among the CROWD.

FOURTH CITIZEN *(joins them).* I say, what's this meeting about?

SECOND CITIZEN. Dr. Stockmann's going to deliver a lecture attacking the Mayor.

FOURTH CITIZEN. But the Mayor's his brother.

FIRST CITIZEN. That don't matter. Dr Stockmann ain't afraid of no one.

THIRD CITIZEN. But he's in the wrong. It said so in the *People's Tribune.*

SECOND CITIZEN. Yes, he must be in the wrong this time. The Property Owners wouldn't let him use their hall, nor the People's Club neither.

FIRST CITIZEN. He couldn't even get the hall at the Baths.

SECOND CITIZEN. Well, what do you expect?

FIRST CITIZEN. Which one do you think we ought to support?

FOURTH CITIZEN. Just keep your eye on old Aslaksen, and do as he does.

BILLING *(with a portfolio under his arm, pushes his way through the* CROWD*).* Excuse me, please, gentlemen! Can I get through, please? I'm reporting the meeting for the *People's Tribune.* Thank you! *(Sits down at the table, left.)*

[A Worker. Who was that?

Another Worker. Don't you know? It's that chap Billing, who works on Aslaksen's paper.]

captain horster escorts mrs stockmann and petra in through the door down-stage right. eilif and morten are with them.

Captain Horster. I thought you might sit here. You can slip out easily if anything should happen.

Mrs Stockmann. Do you think there'll be trouble?

Captain Horster. One never knows, with a crowd like this. But sit down, and don't worry.

Mrs Stockmann *(sits)*. It was very kind of you to offer my husband this room.

Captain Horster. Well, no one else would, so I—

Petra *(who has sat down too)*. It was brave of you, too, Captain Horster.

Captain Horster. Oh, that didn't call for much courage.

hovstad and aslaksen come through the crowd, at the same time but separately.

Aslaksen *(goes over to captain horster)*. Hasn't the Doctor come yet?

Captain Horster. He's waiting in there.

There is a stir among the crowd near the door backstage.

Hovstad *(to billing)*. There's the Mayor! See?

Billing. Yes, by Jingo! So he's come after all!

The mayor gently pushes his way through the crowd, greeting people politely, and stations himself against the wall on the left. A few moments later dr stockmann enters through the door downstage right. He is dressed in black, with a frock-coat and white cravat. A few people clap uncertainly, but are countered by subdued hissing. Silence falls.

Dr Stockmann *(in a low voice)*. How do you feel, Catherine?

Mrs Stockmann. I'm all right. *(More quietly.)* Now don't lose your temper, Thomas!

Dr Stockmann. Oh, I'll control myself, don't you worry. *(Looks at his watch, steps up on to the dais and bows.)* It's a quarter past, so I'll begin— *(Takes out his manuscript.)*

Aslaksen. Surely a Chairman ought to be elected first?

Dr Stockmann. No, no, there's no need for that.

Several Men *(shout)*. Yes, yes!

Mayor. I really think we should have someone in the chair.

Dr Stockmann. But, Peter, I've called this meeting to deliver a lecture!

MAYOR. The Doctor's lecture may possibly give rise to divergent expressions of opinion.

SEVERAL VOICES FROM THE CROWD. A Chairman! A Chairman!

HOVSTAD. Public opinion seem to demand a Chairman.

DR STOCKMANN (*controlling himself*). Very well. Let public opinion have its way.

ASLAKSEN. Would His Worship the Mayor be willing to undertake the function?

THREE MEN (*clap*). Bravo! Hear, hear!

MAYOR. For reasons which I'm sure you will appreciate, I must decline that honour. But fortunately we have among us a man whom I think we can all accept. I refer to the Chairman of the Property Owners' Association, Mr Aslaksen.

MANY VOICES. Yes, yes! Good old Aslaksen! Hurrah for Aslaksen.

DR STOCKMANN *picks up his manuscript and descends from the dais.*

ASLAKSEN. If my fellow citizens want to express their trust in me, I won't refuse their call.

Applause and cheers. ASLAKSEN *steps up on to the dais.*

BILLING (*writes*). 'Mr Aslaksen was chosen amid acclamation . . .

ASLAKSEN. Now that I stand here, may I crave permission to say a few brief words? I'm a mild and peace-loving man who believes in sensible discretion, and in—and in discreet good sense. Everyone who knows me knows that.

MANY VOICES. Yes! That's right, Aslaksen!

ASLAKSEN. Experience in the school of life has taught me that the most valuable virtue for any citizen is restraint—

MAYOR. Hear, hear!

ASLAKSEN. (And that discretion and restraint are the best servants of society.) I would therefore suggest to our respected fellow-citizen who has summoned this meeting that he endeavour to keep himself within the bounds of temperance.

DRUNKEN MAN (*by the entrance door*). Three cheers for the Temperance Society! Jolly good health!

A VOICE. Shut your bloody trap.

MANY VOICES. Hush, hush!

ASLAKSEN. No interruptions, gentlemen, please! Does anyone wish to say anything before I—?

MAYOR. Mr Chairman!

ASLAKSEN. Your Worship!

MAYOR. As everyone here is doubtless aware, I have close ties of relationship with the present medical officer at the Baths, and would consequently have preferred not to speak this evening. But my official position on the Committee of that organization, and my anxiety for the best interests of the town, force me to table a resolution. I hope I may assume that no citizen here present would regard it as desirable that dubious and exaggerated allegations concerning the sanitary conditions at the Baths should circulate outside this town.

MANY VOICES. No, no, no! Certainly not! We protest!

MAYOR. I therefore move that this meeting refuse the aforesaid medical officer permission to read or dilate upon his theories concerning the matter in question.

DR STOCKMANN *(explosively)*. Refuse permission? What the devil—?

MRS STOCKMANN *coughs.*

DR STOCKMANN *(composes himself)*. Very well. You refuse permission.

MAYOR. In my statement to the *People's Tribune* I have acquainted the public with the essential facts so that every intelligent citizen can form his own judgment. Amongst other things I pointed out that the medical officer's proposals—quite apart from the fact that they amount to a vote of no confidence in the leading citizens of this town—will burden the ratepayers with the unnecessary expenditure of at least a hundred thousand crowns.

Groans and a few whistles.

ASLAKSEN *(rings his bell)*. Order please, gentlemen! I beg leave to second His Worship's motion. I would add that in my view the Doctor has had an ulterior motive, no doubt unconscious, in stirring up this agitation; (he talks about the Baths, but) what he's really aiming at is a revolution. He wants to transfer authority into other hands. No one doubts the honesty of the Doctor's intentions. (Heaven knows, there can be no two opinions about that!) I too believe in popular self-government, so long as it doesn't impose too heavy an expense upon the taxpayer. But that's just what would happen here; so I'm blowed, if you'll excuse the expression, if I can support Dr Stockmann in this matter. One can pay too high a price for gold; that's my opinion.

(Lively expressions of assent from all sides.)

HOVSTAD. I too feel impelled to explain my position. Dr Stockmann's agitation won considerable sympathy at first, and I myself supported it as impartially as I was able. But then we found we had allowed ourselves to be misled by a false picture of the facts—

DR STOCKMANN. That's a lie!

Hovstad. A not completely reliable picture, then. His Worship's statement has proved that. I hope no one here doubts the liberality of my views. The *People's Tribune*'s attitude on major political questions is well known to you all. But I have learned from men of discretion and experience that in local matters it is the duty of a newspaper to observe a certain caution.

Aslaksen. Exactly my feelings.

Hovstad. Now in the matter under discussion it's quite clear that Dr Stockmann has popular opinion against him. Well, I ask you, gentlemen, what is the primary duty of an editor? Is it not to reflect the opinions of his readers? Has he not been entrusted with what might be described as an unspoken mandate to advance the cause of those who hold the same views as himself, with all the eloquence of which he is capable? Or am I mistaken?

Many Voices. No, no, no! Mr Hovstad is right!

Hovstad. It has caused me much heartsearching to break with a man under whose roof I have lately been a not infrequent guest—a man who has until this day rejoiced in the undivided affection of his fellow citizens—a man whose only, or anyway principal fault is that he follows his heart rather than his head.

Scattered Voices. That's true. Hurrah for Dr Stockmann!

Hovstad. But my duty towards society left me no alternative. And there's one further consideration which forces me to oppose him, in the hope of halting him on the inauspicious road he has now begun to tread—consideration for his family—

Dr Stockmann. Stick to the water system and the sewer!

Hovstad. —consideration for his wife and the children he has abandoned.

Morten. Does he mean us, Mother?

Mrs Stockmann. Hush!

Aslaksen. I shall now put His Worship's resolution to the vote.

Dr Stockmann. Don't bother! I won't say a word about those damned Baths. No. I've something else to tell you tonight.

Mayor *(in a low voice)*. What the devil's this?

Drunken Man *(near the entrance door)*. I pay my taxes! So I'm entitled to express my opinion! And it's my absolute 'n unintelligible opinion that—

Several Voices. Keep quiet there!

Others. He's drunk! Throw him out!

The drunk man *is removed.*

Dr Stockmann. Have I the floor?

Aslaksen *(rings his bell)*. Dr Stockmann has the floor.

DR STOCKMANN. A few days ago, if anyone had tried to gag me like this I'd have fought like a lion for my sacred human rights! But now that doesn't matter. Now I have more important things to talk about.

THE CROWD *moves closer around him.* MORTEN KIIL *can be seen among them.*

DR STOCKMANN *(continues).* I've been thinking a great deal these past few days. I've brooded so deeply that in the end my head began to spin—

MAYOR *(coughs).* Hm—!

DR STOCKMANN. But then everything began to fall into place. (I saw the whole picture of things quite clearly. And that's why I'm standing here this evening.) I'm going to make a mighty revelation to you, my friends! I'm going to tell you about a discovery that is infinitely more important than the middling little fact that our water system is poisoned and our health baths sited above a cesspit!

MANY VOICES *(shout).* Leave the Baths alone! Don't talk about them! We won't listen!

DR STOCKMANN. This great discovery that I have made during these last few days is that all our spiritual sources are poisoned, and that the whole of our vaunted social system is founded upon a cesspit of lies!

ASTONISHED VOICES *(mutter in low tones).* What's that! What did he say?

MAYOR. These are ridiculous insinuations—

ASLAKSEN *(his hand on the bell).* I must request the speaker to moderate his language.

DR STOCKMANN. (I have loved this birthplace of mine as dearly as any man can love the place where he spent his youth.) I was young when I left home, and distance, hunger and memory threw, as it were, a brighter lustre over this place and the people who dwelt here.

Some applause and cheers are heard.

DR STOCKMANN. For years I lived in a dreadful backwater far up in the north. (As I wandered among those people who lived scattered over the mountains, I often thought it would have been better for those poor degraded creatures if they'd had a vet instead of a man like me!

Murmurs.

BILLING *(puts down his pen).* By Jingo, I've never heard the like of that—!

HOVSTAD. That's a filthy slander against a worthy community!

DR STOCKMANN. Wait a moment! I don't think anyone could say that I forgot my birthplace up there. I sat there brooding like a duck on an egg; and the chick I hatched was—the plan for these Baths.

Clapping, and murmurs of disapproval.

DR STOCKMANN.) Then at long last fate smiled upon me and allowed me to return. [And then, my fellow-citizens, then I thought I had nothing left to wish for in this world. No—] I had one ambition left—a burning desire to work with all my heart and soul for the welfare of my home and my community.

MAYOR *(gazing into space)*. You've a strange way of showing it!

DR STOCKMANN. I went around here revelling blindly in my new-found happiness. But yesterday morning—no, it was the previous night, actually—my eyes were opened, and the first thing that greeted them was the stupendous imbecility of the authorities—

Noise, shouting and laughter. MRS STOCKMANN *coughs loudly.*

MAYOR. Mr Chairman!

ASLAKSEN *(rings his bell)*. As Chairman of this meeting, I—

DR STOCKMANN. Oh, let's not start quibbling about words, Mr Aslaksen. I only mean that I suddenly realized how really revoltingly our politicians had behaved down there at the Baths. I can't stand politicians! I've had all I can take of them. They're like goats in a plantation of young trees! They destroy everything! They block the way for a free man, however much he may twist and turn—and I'd like to see them rooted out and exterminated, like other vermin—

Commotion in the hall.

MAYOR. Mr Chairman, are such calumnies to be permitted?

ASLAKSEN *(his hand on the bell)*. Dr Stockmann—!

DR STOCKMANN. I can't understand why I'd never had a proper look at these gentlemen before. I'd had a prime example right in front of my eyes all the time—my brother Peter—procrastinating and purblind—!

Laughter, confusion and whistling. MRS STOCKMANN *sits and coughs.* ASLAKSEN *rings his bell loudly.*

THE DRUNK MAN *(who has come back)*. Are you referring to me? My name's Petersen, but don't you bloody well—

ANGRY VOICES. Throw that drunk out! Get rid of him!

The DRUNK MAN *is thrown out again.*

MAYOR. Who was that person?

A BYSTANDER. I don't know, Your Worship.

ASLAKSEN. The man was obviously intoxicated with German beer. Continue, Doctor; but please try to use restraint!

DR STOCKMANN. Well, my fellow-citizens, I won't say anything more about our politicians. If anyone imagines from what I've just said that I've come here this evening to crucify these gentlemen, he's wrong—

quite wrong. (For I cherish the comforting belief that these laggards, these survivors from a dying world, are studiously cutting their own throats. They need no doctor's help to hasten their demise. And anyway, it isn't they who are the chief danger to society!) They aren't the ones who are most active in poisoning the sources of our spiritual life (and contaminating the ground on which we tread)! It isn't they who are the most dangerous enemies of truth and freedom in our society!

SHOUTS FROM ALL SIDES. Who, then? Who is? Name them!

DR STOCKMANN. Don't worry, I'll name them! Because this is the great discovery I've made today! *(Raises his voice.)* The most dangerous enemies of truth and freedom are the majority! Yes, the solid, liberal, bloody majority—they're the ones we have to fear! Now you know!

Complete uproar. Nearly everyone is shouting, stamping and whistling. Some of the older men exchange covert glaces and seem to be enjoying the situation. MRS STOCKMANN *gets up anxiously.* EILIF *and* MORTEN *go threateningly over to the schoolboys, who are making a commotion.* ASLAKSEN *rings his bell and calls for silence.* HOVSTAD *and* BILLING *are both talking, but neither can be heard. At last silence is restored.*

ASLAKSEN. As Chairman I call upon the speaker to withdraw those mischievous observations.

DR STOCKMANN. Never, Mr Aslaksen! It's the majority in this community that is depriving me of my freedom and trying to forbid me to proclaim the truth.

HOVSTAD. The majority is always right.

BILLING. And speaks the truth, by Jingo!

DR STOCKMANN. The majority is never right! Never, I tell you! That's one of those community lies that free, thinking men have got to rebel against! Who form the majority—in any country? The wise, or the fools? I think we'd all have to agree that the fools are in a terrifying, overwhelming majority all over the world! But in the name of God it can't be right that the fools should rule the wise! *(Uproar and shouting.)* Yes, yes, you can shout me down! But you can't say I'm wrong! The majority has the power—unforunately—but the majority is not right! The ones who are right are a few isolated individuals like me! The minority is always right! *(Uproar again.)*

HOVSTAD. So Dr Stockmann's turned aristocrat since the day before yesterday!

DR STOCKMANN. I've already said I don't want to waste words on the little flock of short-winded sheep puffing along in the rear! Life has nothing exciting left to offer them. But I'm thinking of the few, the individuals amongst us, who have adopted the new, fresh, burgeoning truths as their watchword! These men stand at the outposts, so far forward that the compact majority hasn't yet arrived—and there they are fighting for those truths which are still too new to man's conscious mind to have any majority behind them.

HOVSTAD. I see, so you've become a revolutionary!

DR STOCKMANN. Yes, Mr. Hovstad, By God I have! I intend to start a revolution against the lie that truth is a monopoly of the majority! What are these truths to which the majority clings? They're the truths which are so old that they're on the way to becoming decrepit! But when a truth's as old as that, gentlemen, it's also well on the way to becoming a lie!

Laughter and jeers.

DR STOCKMANN. Yes, yes, you can believe me or not, as you wish; but truths aren't such long-lived Methuselahs as people imagine. A normal truth lives for—what shall I say?—seventeen to eighteen years on an average—twenty years at the most—seldom longer. But truths as old as that are always dreadfully thin. (All the same, it isn't until then that the majority cottons on to them, and commands them to society as sound spiritual fodder. But) there's no great nourishment in that sort of food, I can promise you (that; and as a doctor, I know about these things). All these majority truths are like last year's salt pork; they're hams that have gone sour and green and tainted. And they're the cause of all the moral scurvy that's rotting our society!

ASLAKSEN. It seems to me that the honourable speaker has strayed somewhat from his text.

MAYOR. I warmly endorse the Chairman's observation.

DR STOCKMANN. Oh, really, Peter, I think you must be quite mad! I'm sticking as close to my text as any man could! My whole point is precisely this, that it's the masses, the mob, this damned majority—they're the thing that's poisoning the sources of our spiritual life and contaminating the ground we walk on!

HOVSTAD. And the great progressive majority does this simply by being sensible enough to believe in those truths which are indisputable and generally acknowledged?

DR STOCKMANN. Oh, my good Mr Hovstad, don't talk to me about indisputable truths. The truths that the masses and the mob acknowledge are the ones that were held by advanced thinkers in our grandparents' time. We outrunners of today don't acknowledge them any longer. I really believe there's only one indisputable truth. It is that no society can live a healthy life if it feeds on truths that are old and marrowless.

HOVSTAD. Instead of all this generalizing why don't you give us a few examples of these old and marrowless truths on which we're living?

Murmurs of agreement from several quarters.

DR STOCKMANN. Oh, I could reel you off a whole list of the beastly things; but to start with I'll limit myself to one 'acknowledged' truth which is really a damned lie, but which Mr Hovstad and the *People's Tribune* and all the hangers-on of the *People's Tribune* feed on all the same.

HOVSTAD. And that is—?

DR STOCKMANN. That is the doctrine which you have inherited from your forefathers and which you continue thoughtlessly to proclaim far and wide—the doctrine that the plebs, the masses, the mob, are the living heart of the people—that they *are* the people—and that the common man, all those ignorant and incompetent millions, have the same right to sanction and condemn, to advise and to govern, as the few individuals who are intellectually aristocrats.

BILLING. Now, really, by Jingo—!

HOVSTAD *(simultaneously, shouts).* Mark that, fellow citizens!

FURIOUS VOICES. Oh-ho, so we're not the people, aren't we? So it's only the aristocrats who have the right to rule?

A WORKER. Throw him out if he talks like that!

OTHERS. Chuck him through the door!

A CITIZEN *(shouts).* Blow that horn, Evensen!

Loud blasts are heard. Whistles and furious uproar in the hall.

DR STOCKMANN *(when the noise has abated somewhat).* Can't you be reasonable? Can't you bear to hear the truth just for once? I'm not asking you all to agree with me immediately! But I did expect Mr Hovstad would admit I was right once he'd given the matter a little thought. After all, Mr Hovstad claims to be a freethinker—

SURPRISED VOICES *(murmur).* Freethinker, did he say? What? Is Mr Hovstad a freethinker?

HOVSTAD *(shouts).* Prove that, Dr Stockmann! When have I said so in print?

DR STOCKMANN *(thinks).* No, by Jove, you're right! You've never had the guts to admit it publicly. Well, I won't corner you, Mr Hovstad. Let me be the freethinker, then. From my knowledge of natural science I shall now reveal to you all that the *People's Tribune* is deceiving you most shamefully when it tells you that you, the common millions, the masses, the mob, are the true heart and core of the people! That's just a newspaper lie! The masses are nothing but raw material which may, some day, be refined into individuals!

Growls, laughter and disturbances in the hall.

DR STOCKMANN. Well, isn't that the way life works with the rest of creation? [Look at the enormous difference there is between a breed of animal that's cultivated and one that is uncultivated! Just look at the common farmyard hen. What is such a stunted piece of rubbish worth as flesh? Not much! And what kind of eggs does it lay? Any common rook or crow can lay eggs just as good. But take a cultivated Spanish or Japanese hen, or take a fine pheasant or turkey, and see the difference! Consider dogs, with which we human beings have so much in common! Think first of a simple mongrel—one of those filthy, ragged, common curs that lope along the streets and defile the wall of our houses. And then put that mongrel next to a greyhound with a distinguished pedigree whose ancestors have been fed delicate meals for generations and have had the opportunity to listen to harmonious voices and music. Don't you think the brain of that greyhound is differently developed from that of the mongrel? You bet your life it is! It's the pups of these cultivated animals that trainers teach to perform the most amazing tricks. A common mongrel couldn't learn to do such things if you stood it on its head!

Noise and laughter.

A CITIZEN *(shouts).* So we're dogs too now, are we?

ANOTHER. We're not animals, Doctor!

DR STOCKMANN. Yes, my friend, we are animals! But there aren't many aristocratic animals among us. And there's a terrifying difference between men who are greyhounds and men who are mongrels. And that's what's so absurd, that Mr Hovstad is quite at one with me as long we we're talking about four-legged animals—

HOVSTAD. Well, they're only beasts.

DR STOCKMANN. All right! But as soon as I start to apply the law to the ones who are two-legged, Mr Hovstad balks at the consequences; he turns his whole philosophy upside down, and proclaims in the *People's Tribune* that the street mongrel is the champion of the menagerie. But that's how it always is, as long as a man remains possessed by this blind worship of the mob and hasn't worked his way out of spiritual bondage into aristocracy.

HOVSTAD. I don't want any kind of aristocracy. I come of simple peasant stock; and I'm proud that I have my roots deep down in the mob, whom you deride.

MANY WORKERS. Hurrah for Hovstad! Hurrah, Hurrah!

DR STOCKMANN. The kind of mob I'm talking about isn't only to be found at the bottom of the barrel. It swarms and mills all around us, even among the high peaks of society. Just look at your own smug, sleek Mayor! My brother Peter's as good a mobster as ever walked in two shoes?

Laughter and hisses.

MAYOR. I protest against these personal insinuations.

(DR STOCKMANN *(unperturbed).* And that isn't because he stems like me from a villianous old pirate from Pomerania or somewhere down there—for we do—!

MAYOR. It's absurd, it's a myth! I deny it!)

DR STOCKMANN. Because he thinks what his superiors think, and his opinions are the opinions he's heard them express. The men who do that are spiritually of the mob; and that's why my noble brother Peter is so frighteningly unaristocratic in all essentials—and consequently so terrified of all things liberal.

MAYOR. Mr Chairman—!

HOVSTAD. So it's the aristocrats who are the liberals in this country? That really is a new discovery!

Laughter among the CROWD.

DR STOCKMANN. Yes, that's part of my discovery too. (And the reason is that liberality is almost exactly the same as morality.) And I say it's quite indefensible of the *Tribune* day after day to proclaim the false gospel that the masses, (the mob, the solid majority,) have a monopoly on liberality and morality, and that vice and corruption and every kind of spiritual filth are a kind of pus that oozes out of culture, just as all that beastly stuff in the Baths oozes down from the tanneries at Moelledal!

Confusion and interruptions.

DR STOCKMANN *(unperturbed, laughs in his excitment).* (And yet this same *People's Tribune* can preach that the masses and the mob must be elevated to a higher standard of living! Good God Almighty, if what the *People's Tribune* teaches were true, then to elevate the masses would simply be to start them on the road to ruin!) But luckily the idea that culture demoralizes is an old inherited fairy tale. No, it's stupidity, poverty and foul living conditions that do the Devil's work! In a house where the rooms aren't aired and the floors swept every day—my wife Catherine says they ought to be scrubbed too, but there can be two opinions on that—in such a house, I say, within two or three years people lose the capacity for moral thought and moral action. Lack of oxygen debilitates the conscience. And there's a shortage of oxygen in many, many houses in this town, from the sound of things, if the whole of this damned majority can be so devoid of conscience as to want to build the prosperity of their town on a quagmire of deceit and lies.

ASLAKSEN. You can't cast an accusation like that against a whole community!

A MAN. I appeal to the Chairman to order the speaker to stand down.

EXCITED VOICES. Yes, yes! That's right. Make him stand down!

DR STOCKMANN *(explodes).* Then I'll shout the truth at every street corner! I'll write in the newspapers of other towns! The whole country shall be told what is happening here!

HOVSTAD. It sounds almost as though the Doctor wishes to destroy this town.

DR STOCKMANN. Yes, I love this town where I was born so dearly that I would rather destroy it than see it flourish because of a lie!

ASLAKSEN. Those are strong words.

Shouts and whistling. MRS STOCKMANN *coughs in vain; the* DOCTOR *no longer hears her.*

HOVSTAD *(shouts through the uproar).* The man who can want to destroy a whole community must be a public enemy!

DR STOCKMANN *(with increasing excitement).* A community that lives on lies deserves to be destroyed! I say that the town that houses such a community should be levelled to the ground! All those who live by lies ought to be exterminated like vermin! You will end by contaminating the entire country! You will bring it to the pass where the whole land will deserve to be laid waste! And if things go that far, then I say with all my heart: 'Let the whole land be laid waste! Let the whole people be exterminated!'

A MAN. That's talking like an enemy of the people!

BILLING. There speaks the voice of the people, by Jingo!

THE WHOLE CROWD *(screams).* Yes, yes, yes! He's an enemy of the people! He hates his country! He hates the people!

ASLAKSEN. Both as a citizen and as a human being I am deeply shocked by what I have had to hear. Dr Stockmann has shown himself in his true colours—(in a manner of which I should never have dreamed him capable. I fear I must support the view expressed a moment ago by respected citizens; and) I move that (we embody this opinion in a resolution. I suggest the following:) 'This meeting declares (that it regard) the medical officer at the Baths, Dr Thomas Stockmann, an enemy of the people.'

Deafening cheers and applause. Many of the CROWD *form a circle around* DR STOCKMANN *and whistle at him.* MRS STOCKMANN *and* PETRA *have got to their feet.* MORTEN *and* EILIF *are fighting with the other* SCHOOLBOYS, *who have been whistling too. Some* ADULTS *part them.*

DR STOCKMANN *(to the people who have been whistling).* You fools! I tell you—!

ASLAKSEN (*rings his bell*). The Doctor no longer has the floor. A formal ballot will take place; (but to protect personal feelings the voting should be done in writing and anonymously.) Have you any clean paper, Mr Billing?

BILLING. I've both blue and white here—

ASLAKSEN (*descends from the dais*). Good, that'll save time. Tear it into squares; like that, yes. (*To the* CROWD.) Blue means no, white means yes. I'll collect the votes myself.

The MAYOR *leaves the hall.* ASLAKSEN *and a couple of other* CITIZENS *go around the* CROWD *with the pieces of paper in hats.*

FIRST CITIZEN (*to* HOVSTAD). What's come over the Doctor? What's one to think?

HOVSTAD. You know how impulsive he is.

SECOND CITIZEN (*to* BILLING). I say, you're a regular visitor in that house. Have you ever noticed—does the fellow drink?

BILLING. I don't know what to reply, by Jingo! There's always toddy on the table when anyone comes.

THIRD CITIZEN. I think he just goes off his head now and then.

FIRST MAN. Yes, don't they say there's madness in the family?

BILLING. Could be.

A FOURTH MAN. No, it's pure spite. Wants revenge for something or other.

BILLING. He did say something the other day about a rise in salary. But he didn't get it.

ALL THE MEN (*with one voice*). Ah, that explains it!

THE DRUNK MAN (*in the thick of the* CROWD). I want a blue one! And I want a white one too!

SHOUTS. There's the drunk man again! Throw him out!

MORTEN KIIL (*comes up to* DR STOCKMANN). Well, Stockmann, you see now what happens once you start playing monkey tricks?

DR STOCKMANN. I have done my duty.

MORTEN KIIL. What was that you were saying about the tanneries at Moelledal?

DR STOCKMANN. You heard. I said that that's where all the filth comes from.

MORTEN KIIL. From my tannery too?

DR STOCKMANN. I'm afraid your tannery is the worst of all.

MORTEN KIIL. Are you going to print that in the papers?

DR STOCKMANN. I shall hide nothing.

MORTEN KIIL. That'll cost you dear, Stockmann. (*Goes.*)

A FAT MAN (*goes across to* CAPTAIN HORSTER, *without greeting the* LADIES). Well, Captain, so you lend your house to enemies of the people?

CAPTAIN HORSTER. I reckon I can do what I like with my own property.

FAT MAN. Then you won't object if I do the same with mine?

CAPTAIN HORSTER. What do you mean?

FAT MAN. You'll hear from me tomorrow. *(Turns and goes.)*

PETRA. Isn't that the man who owns your ship, Captain Horster?

CAPTAIN HORSTER. Yes.

ASLAKSEN *(with the voting papers in his hand, steps up on to the dais and rings his bell).* Gentlemen, allow me to inform you of the result. With only a single dissentient vote—

A YOUNG MAN. That's the drunk man!

ASLAKSEN. With only one dissentient vote, and that of a man not sober, this gathering of citizens unanimously declares the medical officer of the Baths, Dr Thomas Stockmann, an enemy of the people! *(Shouts and gestures of approval.)* Long live our ancient and noble community! *(More cheers.)* Long live our worthy and active Mayor, who has so loyally ignored the ties of blood! *(Cheers.)* The meeting is closed. *(He steps down.)*

BILLING. Three cheers for the Chairman!

WHOLE CROWD. Hurrah for Mr Aslaksen! Hurrah! Hurrah!

DR STOCKMANN. My hat and coat, Petra. Captain, have you room in your ship for passengers to the new world?

CAPTAIN HORSTER. For you and yours, Doctor, I'll make room.

DR STOCKMANN *(as* PETRA *helps him on with his coat).* Good! Come, Catherine! Come, boys! *(He takes his wife by the arm.)*

MRS STOCKMANN *(quietly).* Thomas dear, let's go out the back way.

DR STOCKMANN. No back way for me, Catherine! *(Raises his voice.)* You'll hear from your enemy of the people before he shakes the dust of this town from his feet! I'm not so forgiving as a certain person. I don't say: 'I forgive ye, for ye know not what ye do!'

ASLAKSEN *(shouts).* That comparison's a blasphemy, Dr Stockmann!

BILLING. I'll say it is, by God—! What a dreadful thing for respectable people to hear!

A COARSE VOICE. He's threatening us now!

EXCITED SHOUTS. Let's break his windows! Throw him in the fjord!

A MAN *(in the* CROWD*).* Blow your horn, Evensen! *(He imitates the sound of the horn twice.)*

Blasts on the horn, whistles and wild cries. The DOCTOR *goes with his family towards the door.* CAPTAIN HORSTER *clears a way for them.*

THE WHOLE CROWD *(howls after them as they go).* Enemy of the people! Enemy of the people! Enemy of the people!

BILLING *(as he puts his notes in order).* I'm damned if I'll drink toddy with them tonight, by Jingo!

The CROWD *swarms towards the door. The shouting spreads outside. From the street can be heard the cry: 'Enemy of the people! Enemy of the People! Enemy of the people!'*

ACT FIVE

DR STOCKMANN*'s study. Bookshelves and cupboards containing medicine bottles, along the walls. In the background is the exit to the hall; down-stage left is the door to the living-room. In the wall on the right are two windows, all the panes of which are smashed. In the middle of the room stands the* DOCTOR*'s desk, covered with books and papers. The room is in disorder. It is morning.*

DR STOCKMANN, *in dressing-gown and slippers and with his smoking-cap on his head, is crouched down raking under one of the cupboards with an umbrella. At length he pulls out a stone.*

DR STOCKMANN *(speaks through the open door into the living-room).* Catherine, I've found another!

MRS STOCKMANN *(from the living-room).* Oh, you'll find a lot more yet.

DR STOCKMANN *(puts the stone among a heap of others on the table).* I shall keep these stones as sacred relics. Eilif and Morten shall see them every day, and when they're grown up they shall inherit them from me. *(Rakes under a bookshelf.)* Hasn't—what the devil's her name?—you know, the maid—hasn't she gone for the glazier yet?

MRS STOCKMANN *(enters).* He said he didn't know if he'd be able to come today.

[DR STOCKMANN. The truth is, he doesn't dare.

MRS STOCKMAN. Yes.] Randine says he daren't because of the neighbours. *(Speaks into the living-room.)* What is it, Randine? Very well. *(Goes inside and returns immediately.)* Here's a letter for you, Thomas.

DR STOCKMANN. Give it to me. *(Opens it and reads.)* I see.

MRS STOCKMANN. Who's it from?

DR STOCKMANN. The landlord. He's giving us notice to quit.

MRS STOCKMANN. Is he really? He seems such a decent man—

DR STOCKMANN *(looks at the letter).* [He daren't do otherwise, he says.] He's very sorry, but [he daren't do otherwise]—his fellow-citizens—respect for public opinion—certain obligations—dare not offend certain persons of influence—

MRS STOCKMANN. There, Thomas, you see?

DR STOCKMANN. Yes, yes, I see. They're all cowards in this town. None of them dares do anything for fear of the others. *(Throws the letter on the table.)* But we don't have to worry, Catherine. We're off to the new world now—

MRS STOCKMANN. Thomas, do you really think it's a good idea, this going away?

DR STOCKMANN. Am I to stay here when they've pilloried me as an enemy of the people, branded me, broken my windows? And just look at this, Catherine! They've torn my trousers, too!

MRS STOCKMANN. Oh no! And they're your best!

DR STOCKMANN. One should never wear one's best trousers when one goes out to fight for freedom and truth. [Oh, I don't mind so much about the trousers—you can always patch them up for me. It's the fact that these riff-raff dare to threaten me as though they were my equals— that's the thing I can't damned well stomach!

MRS STOCKMAN. Yes, Thomas, they've behaved shockingly to you in this town. But does that mean we have to leave the country?

DR STOCKMANN. Do you think the rabble aren't just as insolent in other towns? Oh, yes, Catherine. There isn't twopence to choose between them. To hell with the curs, let them yelp. That's not the worst. The worst is that throughout this country all the people are just party slaves. Mind you, they're probably not much better in America. The majority's rampant there too, and liberal public opinion and all the rest of the rubbish. But the context is larger there, you see. They may kill you, but they won't torture you slowly; they don't pin a free man in a vice like they do here. And if you want to, you can stay independent outside it all.] *(Walks across the room.)* If only I knew of some primeval forest or a little South Sea island that was going cheap—

[MRS STOCKMANN. But what about the boys, Thomas?

DR STOCKMANN *(stops).* How extraordinary you are, Catherine! Would you rather they grew up in a society like this? You saw for yourself last night that half the people are raving lunatics; and if the other half haven't lost their wits it's only because they're beasts that don't have any wits to lose.

MRS STOCKMANN. But, Thomas dear, you're so careless about what you say.

DR STOCKMANN. What! Don't I tell them the truth? Don't they turn every idea upside down? Don't they merge right and wrong so that they can't tell the difference? Don't they call everything a lie which I know to be true? But the maddest thing of all is that you get grown men of liberal inclinations getting together in groups and convincing themselves and other people that they're progressive thinkers! Did you ever hear the like, Catherine?

MRS STOCKMANN. Yes, yes, it's all very stupid, but—)

PETRA *enters from the living-room.*

MRS STOCKMANN. Are you back from school already?

PETRA. I've got the sack.

MRS STOCKMANN. The sack?

DR STOCKMANN. You too!

PETRA. Mrs Busk gave me notice. So I thought I'd better leave at once.

DR STOCKMANN. Quite right, by heaven!

MRS STOCKMANN. Who'd have thought Mrs Busk was such a nasty woman?

PETRA. Oh, mother, she's not nasty. It was quite obvious she didn't like doing it. But she said she dared not do otherwise. So I got the sack.

DR STOCKMANN *(laughs and rubs his hands).* (Dared not do otherwise!) She too! Oh, that's splendid!

MRS STOCKMANN. Well, after those dreadful scenes last night, you can't—

PETRA. It wasn't only that. Listen to this, father.

DR STOCKMANN. Yes?

PETRA. Mrs Busk showed me no less than three letters she'd received this morning—

DR STOCKMANN. Anonymous, of course?

PETRA. Yes.

DR STOCKMANN. They daren't even sign their names, Catherine.

PETRA. Two of them stated that a gentleman who frequents this house announced in the Club last night that I held excessively free views on various subjects—

DR STOCKMANN. I hope you didn't deny that.

PETRA. Not on your life! (Mrs Busk expresses pretty free views herself when we're alone together; but now that this has come out about me, she didn't dare to keep me.)

MRS STOCKMAN. (Fancy—'a gentleman who frequents this house'!) You see what thanks you get for your hospitality, Thomas!

DR STOCKMANN. We won't go on living in this jungle any longer. Pack the bags as quickly as you can, Catherine. The sooner we get away from here, the better.

MRS STOCKMANN. Hush! I think there's someone in the hall. Go and look, Petra.

PETRA *(opens the door).* Oh, is it you, Captain Horster? Please come in.

CAPTAIN HORSTER *(from the hall).* Good morning. I felt I had to come along and see how everything was.

DR STOCKMANN *(shakes his hand).* Thank you. It's extremely good of you.

MRS STOCKMANN. And thank you for seeing us safely back last night, Captain Horster.

PETRA. How did you manage to get home again?

CAPTAIN HORSTER. Oh, I managed; [I'm pretty strong, and] those fellows bark worse than they bite.

DR STOCKMANN. Yes, isn't it amazing what wretched cowards they are! [Come here, I'll show you something.] Look, here are all the stones they threw through our windows. Just look at them! Upon my soul, there aren't more than two decent rocks in the whole lot; the others are just pebbles—mere gravel! And yet they stood out there howling, and swearing they'd beat the life out of me—but action—action—no, you won't see much of that in this town.

CAPTAIN HORSTER. Just as well for you on this occasion, Doctor.

[DR STOCKMANN. Of course! But it annoys me all the same; for if it ever comes to a serious fight, in defence of our country, you'll see, Captain Horster—public opinion'll be for safety first, and this sacred majority'll run for their lives like a flock of sheep. That's what's so sad—it really hurts me to think of it—no, damn it, I'm just being stupid! They've said I'm an enemy of the people, so let me be an enemy of the people!

MRS STOCKMANN. You'll never be that, Thomas.

DR STOCKMANN. Don't be so sure, Catherine. An ugly word can be like the scratch of a needle on the lung. And that damned phrase—I can't forget it—it's got stuck down here in the pit of my stomach, and it's lying there chafing and corroding me like an acid. And there's no magnesia that will neutralize that.

PETRA. You must just laugh at them, father.

CAPTAIN HORSTER. People will think differently of you in time, Doctor.

MRS STOCKMANN. Yes, Thomas, that's as sure as you're standing here.]

DR STOCKMANN. [Perhaps, when it's too late.] Well, it's their funeral! [Let them live like beasts; they'll be sorry they drove a patriot into exile.] When do you sail, Captain Horster?

CAPTAIN HORSTER. Hm—that was what I came to talk to you about, as a matter of fact—

DR STOCKMANN. Why, has something happened to the ship?

CAPTAIN HORSTER. No. It's just that I shan't be going with her.

PETRA. They surely haven't given you the sack?

CAPTAIN HORSTER (smiles). Indeed they have!

PETRA. You, too!

MRS STOCKMANN. There, Thomas, you see!

DR STOCKMANN. And just because I spoke the truth! Oh, if I'd ever dreamed that such a thing could happen—

CAPTAIN HORSTER. Don't worry about me. I'll find a job with a company somewhere else.

DR STOCKMANN. But that boss of yours is a rich man, he's completely independent! Oh, damn, damn!

CAPTAIN HORSTER. He's fair enough in the ordinary way. He said himself, he'd have like to have kept me, if only he'd dared—

DR STOCKMAN *(laughs).* [But he didn't dare! No, of course not!]

CAPTAIN HORSTER. It isn't so easy, he said, when you belong to a party—

DR STOCKMANN. That's the truest word he ever uttered! A party is like a mincing machine. It grinds everyone's brains into a pulp, and all you're left with is human sausages, all identical!

MRS STOCKMANN. Thomas, really!

PETRA *(to* CAPTAIN HORSTER*).* If only you hadn't seen us home, this might never have happened.

CAPTAIN HORSTER. I don't regret it.

PETRA *(holds out her hand).* Thank you!

CAPTAIN HORSTER *(to* DR STOCKMANN*).* What I wanted to say was, if you still want to go, I have thought of another way—

DR STOCKMANN. Fine! As long as we can get away quickly—

MRS STOCKMANN. Hush—wasn't that a knock at the door?

PETRA. I think it's Uncle.

DR STOCKMANN. Aha! *(Shouts).* Come in!

MRS STOCKMANN. Now, Thomas dear, do promise me—

The MAYOR *enters from the hall.*

MAYOR *(in the doorway).* Oh, you're engaged. I'll come back later—

DR STOCKMANN. No, No. Please come in.

MAYOR. I wanted to speak to you privately.

MRS STOCKMANN. We'll go into the living-room.

CAPTAIN HORSTER. And I'll come back later.

DR STOCKMANN. No, you go in too. I want to know more about that—

CAPTAIN HORSTER. Right, I'll wait, then.

He goes with MRS STOCKMANN *and* PETRA *into the living-room. The* MAYOR *says nothing but glances at the windows.*

DR STOCKMANN. Do you find it draughty here today? Put your hat on.

MAYOR. Thank you, if I may. *(Does so.)* I think I caught a cold last night. [I stood there shivering—]

DR. STOCKMAN. Really? I found it warm enough.

MAYOR. I regret that it didn't lie within my power to prevent those nocturnal extravagancies.

Dr Stockmann. Did you come out here to tell me that?

Mayor *(takes out a large letter)*. I have this document for you, from the Directors of the Baths.

Dr Stockmann. Am I dismissed?

Mayor. From the date of writing. *(Puts the letter on the table.)* It distresses us; but, frankly, we had no choice. Public opinion being what it is, we didn't dare—

Dr Stockmann *(smiles)*. [Didn't dare?] I've heard that word before today.

Mayor. I beg you to realize your position. From now on you can't reckon on having any practice whatever in this town.

Dr Stockmann. To hell with the practice! But what makes you so sure?

Mayor. The Property Owners' Association has drawn up a round robin which it is sending from house to house. All respectable citizens are being urged not to employ you; and I'll guarantee that not a single householder will dare refuse to sign it. They just won't dare.

Dr Stockmann. Yes, yes, I don't doubt that. But what then?

Mayor. My advice would be that you should leave town for a while—

Dr Stockmann. Yes, I'm thinking of doing that.

Mayor. Good. Then, when you've had six months to think the matter over, you might, after mature consideration, possibly reconcile yourself to issuing a short statement admitting your error and expressing your regret—

Dr Stockmann. And then, you mean, I might get my job back?

Mayor. It's not unthinkable.

Dr Stockmann. But what about public opinion? You daren't offend that.

Mayor. Public opinion is very fickle. And, quite frankly, it's important to us that you should publish some such admission.

Dr Stockmann. Yes, that'd make you smack your lips, wouldn't it? But, damn it, haven't I told you already what I think of that kind of chicanery?

Mayor. Your position was somewhat stronger then. You had reason to suppose that the whole town was behind you—

Dr Stockmann. And now they're rubbing my face in the dirt! *(Flares up.)* [I don't care if I've got the Devil himself and his great-grandmother on my back!] Never, I tell you, never!

Mayor. A man with a family has no right to act as you're doing. You have no right, Thomas!

Dr Stockmann. No right! There's only one thing in the world that a free man has no right to do! Do you know what that is?

Mayor. No.

Dr Stockmann. No, of course you don't. But I'll tell you. A free man has no right to befoul himself like a beast. He has no right to get himself into the position where he feels the need to spit in his own face!

MAYOR. That all sounds very plausible—if only there didn't happen to exist another explanation for your stubbornness. (But there does.)

DR STOCKMANN. What do you mean by that?

MAYOR. You know perfectly well. But as your brother, and as a man of the world, I would advise you not to put too much trust in expectations that might so easily not be fulfilled.

DR STOCKMANN. What on earth are you talking about?

MAYOR. Do you seriously expect me to believe that you don't know of the arrangements that Morten Kiil has made in his will?

DR STOCKMANN. I know that what little he has is to go to a home for retired artisans. But what's that got to do with me?

MAYOR. To begin with, it's not so little. Morten Kiil is a pretty wealthy man.

DR STOCKMANN. I had no idea—!

MAYOR. Hm—hadn't you really? Then I suppose you also have no idea that a considerable proportion of his money is earmarked for your children, and that you and your wife will be able to enjoy the interest for the rest of your lives. Hasn't he told you?

DR STOCKMANN. Indeed he has not! On the contrary, he's done nothing but complain about how disgracefully overtaxed he is. But are you quite sure of this, Peter?

MAYOR. I have it from an impeccable source.

DR STOCKMANN. But, good heavens—that means Catherine's future is secured—and the children's, too! I say, I must tell her! (Shouts.) Catherine, Catherine!

MAYOR (holds him back). Hush, don't say anything yet.

MRS STOCKMANN (opens the door). What is it?

DR STOCKMANN. Nothing, my dear. Go back in again.

MRS STOCKMANN closes the door.

DR STOCKMANN (paces up and down the room). Their future secured! (I can't believe it! All of them—and for life! Oh, it's a wonderful feeling to know that one's future is secured.) For ever!

MAYOR. But that's just what it isn't. Morten Kiil can revoke that will any day or hour that he chooses.

DR STOCKMANN. But he won't, my dear Peter. The Badger's much too delighted at the embarrassment I've caused to you and your worthy friends.

MAYOR (starts and looks searchingly at him). Aha! So that's the explanation!

DR STOCKMANN. What do you mean?

MAYOR. This whole thing's been a conspiracy. These violent and unprincipled accusations which you've levelled against the authorities in the name of truth were simply your price for being remembered in that vindictive old idiot's will.

DR STOCKMANN *(almost speechless)*. Peter—you are the lowest bastard I have ever met in all my life!

MAYOR. Things are finished between us now. Your dismissal is final. Now we have a weapon against you. *(He goes.)*

DR STOCKMANN. The filthy—damn, damn! *(Shouts.)* Catherine! Scrub the floors behind him! Tell her to bring in a bucket—that girl—what the devil's her name?—the one who's always got a dirty nose—!

MRS STOCKMANN *(in the doorway to the living-room)*. Hush, hush, Thomas, please!

PETRA *(also in the doorway)*. Father, Grandfather's here and says, can he speak to you privately?

DR STOCKMANN. Yes, of course. *(At the door.)* Come in, father.

MORTEN KIIL *comes in.* DR STOCKMANN *closes the door behind him.*

DR STOCKMANN. Well, what is it? Sit down.

MORTEN KIIL. No, I won't sit. *(Looks around.)* Nice and cosy it looks here today, Stockmann.

DR STOCKMANN. Yes, doesn't it?

MORTEN KIIL. Very nice. And fresh air too! You've got enough of that oxygen you were talking about last night! Your conscience feels pretty good today, I suppose?

DR STOCKMANN. Yes, it does.

MORTEN KIIL. I thought it would. *(Thumps himself on the breast.)* But do you know what I've got here?

DR STOCKMANN. A good conscience too, I hope.

MORTEN KIIL *(snorts)*. No, something better than that.

Takes out a thick pocket-book, opens it and shows a wad of papers.

DR STOCKMANN *(looks at him in amazement)*. Shares in the Baths?

MORTEN KIIL. They weren't hard to come by today.

DR STOCKMANN. You mean you've been out and bought—?

MORTEN KIIL. As many as I could afford.

DR STOCKMANN. But, my dear Mr Kiil—the state those Baths are in now, you—!

MORTEN KIIL. If you act like a sensible man, you'll soon have them on their feet again.

DR STOCKMANN. You see for yourself I'm doing all I can, but—I [The people of this town are quite mad!]

MORTEN KIIL. You said last night that the worst of the filth comes from my tannery. But if that were true, then my grandfather and my father before me, and I myself, have been polluting this town for generations like three angels of death. Do you think I'm going to let an imputation like that hang over my head?

DR STOCKMANN. I'm afraid it looks as though you'll have to.

MORTEN KIIL. No, thank you! I value my name and reputation. People call me the 'the Badger,' I'm told. A badger's a dirty beast, isn't it? Well, I'll prove them wrong. I intend to live and die clean.

DR STOCKMANN. And how are you going to go about that?

MORTEN KIIL. You're going to make me clean, Stockmann.

DR STOCKMANN. I—!

MORTEN KIIL. Do you know what money I've used to buy these shares with? No, you can't; but I'll tell you. It's the money Catherine and Petra and the boys are going to inherit when I'm gone. I've managed to put a little aside, you see.

DR STOCKMANN *(flares up)*. You mean you've spent Catherine's money on this?

MORTEN KIIL. Yes, now it's all invested in the Baths. So now we'll see if you're really as daft as you pretend, Stockmann. Every time you say there's vermin coming out of my tannery, it'll be as though you were cutting a pound of flesh from your wife's body, and Petra's and the children's. But no self-respecting husband and father would do such a thing—unless he really was mad.

DR STOCKMANN *(walks up and down)*. Yes, but I *am* mad! I *am* mad!

MORTEN KIIL. You can't be that mad when your wife and children are at stake.

DR STOCKMANN *(stops in front of him)*. Why couldn't you have come and spoken to me before you went and bought all this waste paper?

MORTEN KIIL. Actions speak louder than words.

DR STOCKMANN *(wanders around restlessly)*. If only I weren't so sure—! But I *know* I'm right!

MORTEN KIIL *(weighs the pocketbook in his hand)*. If you persist in this lunacy, these shares won't be worth much, you know.

He puts the pocketbook back in his pocket.

DR STOCKMANN. But, damn it, science must be able to find some way. A preventative; or a purifier or something—

MORTEN KIIL. You mean something to kill these vermin?

DR STOCKMANN. Yes, or render them harmless.

MORTEN KIIL. Couldn't you try rat poison?

DR STOCKMANN. Oh, no, no! But everyone keeps saying it's just a fancy of mine. All right, then, let them have it that way. Those ignorant, narrow-minded curs denounced me as an enemy of the people, didn't they? And all but tore the clothes off my back!

MORTEN KIIL. And smashed your windows.

DR STOCKMANN. Yes. And then this question of my duty towards my family. I must talk to Catherine. She knows about these things.

MORTEN KIIL. That's a good idea. She's a sensible woman. Follow her advice.

DR STOCKMANN (turns on him). Why did you have to (do such a stupid thing? Hazard Catherine's money, and) put me in this frightful predicament? When I look at you, I feel as though I was looking at the Devil himself—

MORTEN KIIL. Then I'd best be off. But I want your answer by two o'clock. If it's no, I'm giving these shares to the Old Folks' Home—and I'll do it today.

DR STOCKMAN. And what will Catherine get then?

MORTEN KIIL. Not a farthing!

The door to the hall is opened. HOVSTAD *and* ASLAKSEN *are seen there.*

MORTEN KIIL. Well! Look whom we have here!

DR STOCKMANN (stares at them). What the devil—? Do you two still dare to visit me?

HOVSTAD. Indeed we do.

ASLAKSEN. We've something we want to talk to you about.

MORTEN KIIL (whispers). Yes or no—by two o'clock!

ASLAKSEN (glances at HOVSTAD). Aha!

MORTEN KIIL *goes.*

DR STOCKMANN. Well, what do you want? Make it short.

HOVSTAD. I dare say you don't feel too kindly towards us in view of the stand we took at last night's meeting—

DR STOCKMANN. Stand, you call it! A fine stand indeed! You just lay down like a couple of old women! Damn the pair of you!

HOVSTAD. Call it what you like; we *couldn't* do otherwise.

DR STOCKMANN. You *dared* not do otherwise! Isn't that what you mean?

HOVSTAD. If you wish.

ASLAKSEN. But why didn't you tip us off? You only needed to drop a hint to Mr Hovstad or me.

DR STOCKMANN. Hint? About what?

ASLAKSEN. Why you were doing it.

DR STOCKMANN. I don't understand.

ASLAKSEN *(nods conspiratorially)*. Oh, yes you do, Dr Stockmann.

HOVSTAD. There's no need to keep it secret any longer.

DR STOCKMANN *(looks from one to the other)*. What the devil—?

ASLAKSEN. Forgive the question, but isn't your father-in-law going round the town buying up all the shares in the Baths?

DR STOCKMANN. He has bought some today. But—

ASLAKSEN. You'd have done wiser to employ someone else. Someone not quite so close to you.

HOVSTAD. And you shouldn't have done all this under your own name. Nobody need have known that the attack on the Baths came from you. You ought to have taken me into your confidence, Dr Stockmann.

DR STOCKMANN *(stares straight in front of him. A light seems to dawn on him, and he says as though thunderstruck)*. Is it conceivable? Could such a thing really be *done?*

ASLAKSEN *(smiles)*. Apparently. But it ought to be done with a certain subtlety, you know.

HOVSTAD. And there ought to be more than one person in on it. A man doesn't have so much responsibility to bear if he's in partnership.

DR STOCKMANN *(composedly)*. In brief, gentlemen, what do you want?

ASLAKSEN. Mr Hovstad can explain better than—

HOVSTAD. No, you tell him, Aslaksen.

ASLAKSEN. Well, it's just this really, that now we know how the land lies, we think we might venture to put the *People's Tribune* at your disposal.

DR STOCKMANN. You think you dare risk it? But what about public opinion? Aren't you afraid we might cause a storm?

HOVSTAD. We shall have to ride that storm.

ASLASKEN. But you'll have to be quick on the trigger, Doctor. As soon as your campaign has done its job—

DR STOCKMANN. As soon as my father-in-law and I have got all the shares cheaply, you mean—?

HOVSTAD. It is of course principally in the cause of science that you are seeking to gain control of the Baths.

DR STOCKMANN. Of course. It was in the cause of science that I got the old Badger to come in with me on this. And then we'll tinker a bit with the water system and do a little digging on the beach and it won't cost the ratepayers half-a-crown. I think we'll get away with it, don't you? Eh?

HOVSTAD. I think so—if you have the *People's Tribune* behind you.

ASLAKSEN. In a free society the press is a power to be feared, Doctor.

DR STOCKMANN. Quite. And public opinion, too. Mr Aslaksen, you'll answer for the Property Owners' Association?

ASLAKSEN. The Property Owners' Association and the Temperance Society. Have no fear.

DR STOCKMANN. But gentlemen—I blush to mention the matter, but—what consideration—er—

HOVSTAD. Well, of course we'd like to help you absolutely gratis. But the *People's Tribune* is going through an awkward period; we're having a uphill struggle, and I'm very reluctant to wind things up just now, when there are such splendid causes that need our support.

DR STOCKMANN. Of course. That'd be a bitter pill for a friend of the people like you to have to swallow. *(Flares up.)* But I—I am an enemy of the people! *(Strides around the room.)* Where's that stick of mine? Where the devil did I put my stick?

HOVSTAD. What do you mean?

ASLAKSEN. You surely aren't thinking of—?

DR STOCKMANN *(stops).* And suppose I don't give you a penny of my shares? We rich men are pretty close with our money, you must remember.

HOVSTAD. And *you* must remember that this little business of the shares would bear more than one interpretation.

DR STOCKMANN. Yes, that'd be right up your street, wouldn't it? If I don't come to the aid of the *People's Tribune,* you'll misrepresent my motives—you'll start a witch-hunt, drive me to ground, and throttle the life out of me as a hound throttles a hare!

HOVSTAD. That's the law of nature. Every animal has to fight for survival, you know.

ASLAKSEN. Bread doesn't grow on trees. You must take it where you can find it.

DR STOCKMANN. Then see if you can find any in the gutter! *(Strides around the room.)* Now, by heaven, we'll see which is the strongest animal of us three! *(Finds his umbrella.)* Aha! *(Swings it.)* Now—!

HOVSTAD. You wouldn't dare to assault us!

ASLAKSEN. Be careful with that umbrella!

DR STOCKMANN. Out of the window with you, Mr Hovstad!

HOVSTAD *(at the doorway to the hall).* Are you out of your mind?

DR STOCKMANN. Get through that window, Mr Aslaksen! Jump, I tell you! Don't dally!

ASLAKSEN *(runs round the desk).* Doctor, Doctor, restrain yourself! I'm a weak man—I can't stand excitement—! *(Screams.)* Help, Help!

MRS STOCKMANN, PETRA *and* CAPTAIN HORSTER *enter from the living-room.*

MRS STOCKMANN. In heaven's name, Thomas, what's going on here?

DR STOCKMANN *(brandishes the umbrella).* Jump out, I tell you! Down into the gutter!

HOVSTAD. An unprovoked assault! I call you to witness, Captain Horster—! *(Runs out through the hall.)*

MRS STOCKMANN *(holds the* DOCTOR*).* Thomas, for mercy's sake control yourself!

ASLAKSEN *(desperate).* Restraint, Doctor! Restr—oh, dear! *(Scampers out through the living-room.)*

DR STOCKMANN *(throws away the umbrella).* Damn it, they got away after all!

MRS STOCKMANN. But what did they want?

DR STOCKMANN. I'll tell you later. I've other things to think about just now. *(Goes to the table and writes on a visiting card.)* Look at this, Catherine. What do you see here?

MRS STOCKMANN. 'No, no, no'—what does that mean?

DR STOCKMANN. I'll explain that later, too. *(Holds out the card.)* Here, Petra, tell that smutty-nosed girl to run up to the Badger with this as quickly as she can. Hurry!

PETRA *goes out with the card through the hall.*

DR STOCKMANN. If I haven't had all the devil's messengers after me today, I really don't know who's left! But now I'll sharpen my pen against them until it's like a dagger! I'll dip it in gall and venom! I'll fling my inkstand against their stupid skulls!

MRS STOCKMANN. But Thomas, we're leaving!

PETRA *returns.*

DR STOCKMANN. Well?

PETRA. She's taken it.

DR STOCKMANN. Good! Leaving, did you say? No, by God, we're not! We're staying here, Catherine!

PETRA. Staying?

MRS STOCKMANN. In this town?

DR STOCKMANN. Yes! This is the chosen battlefield, and it's here that the battle must be fought! And it's here that I shall win! As soon as you've sewn up those trousers of mine, I'll go into town and look for a house. We've got to have a roof over our heads (when winter comes).

CAPTAIN HORSTER. I can let you have my house.

DR STOCKMANN. Would you?

CAPTAIN HORSTER. Of course. I've plenty of rooms, and I'm hardly ever there.

MRS STOCKMANN. Oh, Captain Horster, how kind of you!

PETRA. Thank you!

DR STOCKMANN *(presses his hand).* Thank you, thank you! (Well, that prob-

lem's behind us! I'll start my campaign this very day!) Oh,
(Catherine,) there's so much to be done! But luckily I'll be able to
devote my whole time to it. Look at this. I've been sacked from the
Baths—

Mrs Stockmann *(sighs)*. Ah, well, I was expecting that.

Dr Stockmann. And they want to take away my practice too! All right, let
them! At least I'll keep my poor patients—they're the ones who
can't pay—well, heaven knows they're the ones who need me most.
But, by God, they'll have to listen to me! I'll preach to them morning,
noon and night.

Mrs Stockmann. Oh, Thomas, Thomas! Surely you've seen what good
preaching does!

Dr Stockmann. You really are absurd, Catherine! Am I to allow myself to
be chased from the field by public opinion, and the majority, and
such fiddle-faddle? No, thank you! (What I want is so simple and
straightforward and easy! I only want to knock it into the heads of
these curs that the Liberals are the most insidious enemies of freedom—that party programmes strangle every new truth that
deserves to live—and that expediency and self-interest turn morality
and justice upside down, so that in the end life here becomes intolerable. Well, Captain Horster, don't you think I ought to be able to
get people to grasp that?

Captain Horster. I dare say, I don't really understand these things.

Dr Stockmann. Well, you see, the real point is this! It's the party bosses—
they're the ones who've got to be rooted out! A party boss is like a
hungry wolf—he needs a certain number of baby lambs to devour
every year if he is to survive. Look at Hovstad and Aslaksen! How
many innocent and vital young idealists have they knocked on the
head! Or else they mangle and maul them till they're fit for nothing
but to be property owners or subscribers to the *People's Tribune!*
(Half-sits on the table.) Come here, Catherine! Look how beautifully
the sun's shining in through the windows today! And smell this glorious, fresh spring air which is being wafted in to us.

Mrs Stockmann. Oh, my dear Thomas, if only we could live on sunshine
and spring air!

Dr Stockmann. Well, you may have to pinch and scrape a little, but we'll
manage. That's the least of my worries. No, the worst is that I don't
know of anyone sufficiently free and—*unplebeian* to carry on my
work after me.

Petra. Oh, never mind that, father. You'll find someone in time. Look,
here are the boys!

EILIF *and* MORTEN *enter from the living-room.*

Mrs Stockmann. Have you been given a holiday today?

MORTEN. No. But we had a fight with the other boys in the break, so—

EILIF. That's not true! It was the other boys who fought with us!

MORTEN. Yes. So I said to Dr Roerlund I thought it would be better if we stayed at home for a few days.

DR STOCKMANN *(snaps his fingers and jumps from the table).* I've got it! By heaven, I've got it! Neither of you shall ever set foot in that school again!

THE BOYS. Not go to school?

MRS STOCKMANN. But, Thomas—!

DR STOCKMANN. Never, I say! I'll teach you myself! You won't learn a damned thing—

MORTEN. Hurray!

DR STOCKMANN. But I'll make you free men! Aristocrats! Petra, you'll have to help me.

PETRA. Yes, father, of course.

DR STOCKMANN. And we'll hold the school in the room where they branded me as an enemy of the people. But we need more pupils. I must have at least twelve to begin with.

MRS STOCKMANN. You won't find them in this town.

DR STOCKMANN. We shall see. *(To the* BOYS.*)* Do you know any street urchins—real guttersnipes—?

EILIF. Oh yes, father, I know lots!

DR STOCKMANN. That's fine! Get hold of a few for me. I'm going to experiment with mongrels for once. They have good heads on them sometimes.

EILIF. But what shall we do when we've become (free men and) aristocrats?

DR STOCKMANN. Then, my boys, you'll chase all these damned politicians into the Atlantic Ocean!

EILIF *looks somewhat doubtful.* MORTEN *jumps and cheers.*

MRS STOCKMANN. Let's hope it won't be the politicians who'll chase you out, Thomas.

DR STOCKMANN. Are you quite mad, Catherine? Chase me out? Now, when I am the strongest man in town?

MRS STOCKMANN. The strongest—now?

DR STOCKMANN. Yes! I'll go further! I am now one of the strongest men in the whole world.

MORTEN. Hurrah!

DR STOCKMANN *(lowers his voice).* Hush! You mustn't talk about it yet! But I've made a great discovery!

MRS STOCKMANN. Not again!

DR STOCKMANN. Yes—yes! *(Gathers them round him and whispers to them.)* The fact is, you see, that the strongest man in the world is he who stands most alone.

MRS STOCKMANN *(smiles and shakes her head)*. Oh, Thomas—!

PETRA *(warmly, clasps his hands)*. Father!

SUGGESTIONS FOR WRITING AND DISCUSSION

1. To some extent Dr. Stockmann is a comic character; Ibsen himself described him as "muddle-headed." Why do you think Ibsen chose to make him this way?

2. Throughout the play Dr. Stockmann is forced to choose among conflicting duties: loyalty to his town, his duty as a doctor, his duty to his family. Do you think he gives sufficient thought to the difficult choices he has to make?

3. Various characters tell Dr. Stockmann that he should put the welfare of his family above his concern for the community. In a three- to four-page essay argue that Dr. Stockmann either should or should not follow this advice.

4. Compare Dr. Stockmann and his brother. What do they have in common and how do they differ?

5. What is Peter Stockmann's main motivation in opposing his brother?

6. If Dr. Stockmann's advice had been followed many people in the town would have suffered severe hardships. Examine the arguments against Stockmann and in a two- to three-page essay make the strongest case you can against him.

7. In Act Three Mrs. Stockmann tries to prevent her husband from doing anything that will endanger the security of the family, but later she offers him her full support. Comment on this change. How does her behavior influence our perception of Dr. Stockmann?

8. Write a one- to two-page description of Petra showing how she acts as a foil to her mother and father.

9. Morten Kiil, Aslaksen, and Hovstad each try to change Dr. Stockmann's mind. Which character has the purest motives? Which the most corrupt? Which has the most influence on Dr. Stockmann?

10. In Act Four Dr. Stockmann says, "I'm going to tell you about a discovery that is infinitely more important than the fiddling little fact that our water system is poisoned and our baths sited above a cesspit!" What is his great discovery? Is it more or less acceptable to the people of the town than his original discovery?

11. Is the conflict of Act One the same as the conflict of Act Five?

12. Ibsen wrote this play after his play *Ghosts* was severely criticized by the press. In a two- to three-page essay analyze the comments various characters make about the function of the press.

13. At the end of the play Dr. Stockmann claims that the strongest man in the world is the man who stands most alone. Discuss in a four- to five-page paper the argument Ibsen offers about the relationship between society and the individual.

14. Discuss Ibsen's use of irony.
15. Read the formal description of plot in Chapter 8. How well does *An Enemy of the People* fit this description?
16. Ibsen is known for his realism (see Chapter 8). Read the descriptions of the settings in this play and discuss their significance.
17. Both Dr. Stockmann and Antigonê in Sophocle's play *Antigonê* are described by other characters as "enemies of the people." Compare them in a three- to four-page essay.
18. Compare Antigonê's sister Ismenê with Peter Stockmann. What does it add to each play that the protagonist has to struggle not only with society but also with a sibling?
19. Do you agree with Dr. Stockmann's statement in Act Five that a political party is a "mincing machine. It grinds everyone's brains into pulp, and all you're left with is human sausages, all identical"? Look at the essays in this section. Do any of them support this statement? Which would seem to contradict it most strongly? Write a two- to three-page paper interpreting Dr. Stockmann's statement in the light of one of the essays.
20. What contemporary social issue might turn you into a Dr. Stockmann? Write a three- to five-page essay in which you discuss what kinds of conflicts it would cause in your life if you were to imitate his behavior.

Struggles: Thematic Questions

1. A number of the authors in this section, such as Henry Thoreau, believed strongly in pacifism. Others, like Thomas Jefferson, considered war to be necessary. Which position is closest to your own?
2. Many of the authors in this section took unpopular minority positions, as Martin Luther King, Jr., did in opposing unjust and racist laws. Is there some cause you would be prepared to defend in the face of strong opposition?
3. Pablo Neruda shows how Indians in South America are mistreated by the United Fruit Company. Nadine Gordimer writes about apartheid in South Africa. Chief Seattle describes how his Indian tribe is being absorbed and destroyed by the whites. How does racism affect our society? How do the media help either to promote or to eliminate racism?
4. Do you believe in equality between the sexes? How would you define it? Do you think it is possible? Have you yourself ever been a victim of sexism?
5. *Antigonê* and *An Enemy of the People* portray struggles between the needs of the individual and the needs of society. Should the needs of the individual ever come before the needs of society? Give an example of this kind of conflict and explain how you think it should be resolved.

Places

Or Time and Space,
Or shape of Earth divine and wondrous,
Or some fair shape I viewing, worship,
Or lustrous orb of sun or star by night,
Be ye my Gods.

WALT WHITMAN

Essays

N. Scott Momaday (American, 1934–

A Kiowa Grandmother

A single knoll rises out of the plain in Oklahoma, north and west of the Wichita Range. For my people, the Kiowas, it is an old landmark, and they gave it the name Rainy Mountain. The hardest weather in the world is there. Winter brings blizzards, hot tornadic winds arise in the spring, and in summer the prairie is an anvil's edge. The grass turns brittle and brown, and it cracks beneath your feet. There are green belts along the rivers and creeks, linear groves of hickory and pecan, willow and witch hazel. At a distance in July or August the steaming foliage seems almost to writhe in fire. Great green and yellow grasshoppers are everywhere in the tall grass, popping up like corn to sting the flesh, and tortoises crawl about on the red earth, going nowhere in the plenty of time. Loneliness is an aspect of the land. All things in the plain are isolate; there is no confusion of objects in the eye, but *one* hill or *one* tree or *one* man. To look upon that landscape in the early morning, with the sun at your back, is to lose the sense of proportion. Your imagination comes to life, and this, you think, is where Creation was begun.

I returned to Rainy Mountain in July. My grandmother had died in the spring, and I wanted to be at her grave. She had lived to be very old and at last infirm. Her only living daughter was with her when she died, and I was told that in death her face was that of a child.

I like to think of her as a child. When she was born, the Kiowas were living the last great moment of their history. For more than a hundred years they had controlled the open range from the Smoky Hill River to the Red, from the headwaters of the Canadian to the fork of the Arkansas and Cimarron. In alliance with the Comanches, they had ruled the whole of the southern Plains. War was their sacred business, and they were among the finest horsemen the world has ever known. But warfare for the Kiowas was preeminently a matter of disposition rather than of survival, and they never understood the grim, unrelenting advance of the U.S. Cavalry. When at last, divided and ill-provisioned, they were driven onto the Staked Plains in the cold rains of autumn, they fell into panic. In Palo Duro Canyon they abandoned their crucial stores to pillage and had nothing then but their lives. In order to save themselves, they surrendered to the soldiers at Fort Sill and were imprisoned in the old stone corral that now stands as a military museum. My grandmother was spared the humiliation of those high gray walls by eight or ten years, but she must have known from birth the affliction of defeat, the dark brooding of old warriors.

Her name was Aho, and she belonged to the last culture to evolve in North America. Her forebears came down from the high country in western Montana nearly three centuries ago. They were a mountain people, a mysterious tribe of hunters whose language has never been positively classified in any major group. In the late seventeenth century they began a long migration to the south and east. It was a journey toward the dawn, and it led to a golden age. Along the way the Kiowas were befriended by the Crows, who gave them the culture and religion of the Plains. They acquired horses, and their ancient nomadic spirit was suddenly free of the ground. They acquired Tai-me, the sacred Sun Dance doll, from that moment the object and symbol of their worship, and so shared in the divinity of the sun. Not least, they acquired the sense of destiny, therefore courage and pride. When they entered upon the southern Plains they had been transformed. No longer were they slaves to the simple necessity of survival; they were a lordly and dangerous society of fighters and thieves, hunters and priests of the sun. According to their origin myth, they entered the world through a hollow log. From one point of view, their migration was the fruit of an old prophecy, for indeed they emerged from a sunless world.

Although my grandmother lived out her long life in the shadow of Rainy Mountain, the immense landscape of the continental interior lay like memory in her blood. She could tell of the Crows, whom she had never seen, and of the Black Hills, where she had never been. I wanted to see in reality what she had seen more perfectly in the mind's eye, and traveled fifteen hundred miles to begin my pilgrimage.

Yellowstone, it seemed to me, was the top of the world, a region of deep lakes and dark timber, canyons and waterfalls. But, beautiful as it is, one might have the sense of confinement there. The skyline in all directions is close at hand, the high wall of the woods and deep cleavages of shade. There is a perfect freedom in the mountains, but it belongs to the eagle and the elk, the badger and the bear. The Kiowas reckoned their stature by the distance they could see, and they were bent and blind in the wilderness.

Descending eastward, the highland meadows are a stairway to the plain. In July the inland slope of the Rockies is luxuriant with flax and buckwheat, stonecrop and larkspur. The earth unfolds and the limit of the land recedes. Clusters of trees, and animals grazing far in the distance, cause the vision to reach away and wonder to build upon the mind. The sun follows a longer course in the day, and the sky is immense beyond all comparison. The great billowing clouds that sail upon it are shadows that move upon the grain like water, dividing light. Farther down, in the land of the Crows and Blackfeet, the plain is yellow. Sweet clover takes hold of the hills and bends upon itself to cover and seal the soil. There the Kiowas paused on their way; they had come to the place where they must change their lives. The sun is at home on the plains. When the Kiowas came to the land of the Crows, they could see the dark lees of the hills at dawn across the Bighorn River, the profusion of light on the grain shelves, the oldest deity ranging after the solstices. Not yet would they veer southward to the caldron of the land that lay below; they must wean their blood from the northern winter and hold the mountains a while longer in their view. They bore Tai-me in procession to the east.

A dark mist lay over the Black Hills, and the land was like iron. At the top of a ridge I caught sight of Devil's Tower upthrust against the gray sky as if in the birth of time the core of the earth had broken through its crust and the motion of the world was begun. There are things in nature that engender an awful quiet in the heart of man; Devil's Tower is one of them. Two centuries ago, because they could not do otherwise, the Kiowas made a legend at the base of the rock. My grandmother said:

> Eight children were there at play, seven sisters and their brother. Suddenly the boy was struck dumb; he trembled and began to run upon his hands and feet. His fingers became claws, and his body was covered with fur. Directly there was a bear where the boy had been. The sisters were terrified; they ran, and the bear after them. They came to the stump of a great tree, and the tree spoke to them. It bade them climb upon it, and as they did so it began to rise into the air. The bear came to kill them, but they were just beyond its reach. It reared against the tree and scored the bark all around with its claws. The seven sisters were borne into the sky, and they became the stars of the Big Dipper.

From that moment, and so long as the legend lives, the Kiowas have kinsmen in the night sky. Whatever they were in the mountains, they could be no more. However tenuous their well-being, however much they had suffered and would suffer again, they had found a way out of the wilderness.

My grandmother had a reverence for the sun, a holy regard that now is all but gone out of mankind. There was a wariness in her, and an ancient awe. She was a Christian in her later years, but she had come a long way about, and she never forgot her birthright. As a child she had been to the Sun Dances; she had taken part in those annual rites, and by then she had learned the restoration of her people in the presence of Tai-me. She was about seven when the last Kiowa Sun Dance was held in 1887 on the Washita River above Rainy Mountain Creek. The buffalo were gone. In order to consummate the ancient sacrifice—to impale the head of a buffalo bull upon the medicine tree—a delegation of old men journeyed into Texas, there to beg and barter for an animal from the Goodnight herd. She was ten when the Kiowas came together for the last time as a living Sun Dance culture. They could find no buffalo; they had to hang an old hide from the sacred tree. Before the dance could begin, a company of soldiers rode out from Fort Sill under orders to disperse the tribe. Forbidden without cause the essential act of their faith, having seen the wild herds slaughtered and left to rot upon the ground, the Kiowas backed away forever from the medicine tree. That was July 20, 1890, at the great bend of the Washita. My grandmother was there. Without bitterness, and for as long as she lived, she bore a vision of deicide.

Now that I can have her only in memory, I see my grandmother in the several postures that were peculiar to her: standing at the wood stove on a winter morning and turning meat in a great iron skillet; sitting at the south window, bent above her beadwork, and afterwards, when her vision failed, looking down for a long time into the fold of her hands; going out upon a cane, very slowly as she did when the weight of age came upon her, praying. I remember her most often at prayer. She made long, rambling prayers out of suffering and hope, having seen many things. I was never sure that I had the right to hear, so exclusive were they of all mere custom and company. The last time I saw her she prayed standing by the side of her bed at night, naked to the waist, the light of a kerosene lamp moving upon her dark skin. Her long, black hair, always drawn and braided in the day, lay upon her shoulders and against her breasts like a shawl. I do not speak Kiowa, and I never understood her prayers, but there was something inherently sad in the sound, some merest hesitation upon the syllables of sorrow. She began in a high and descending pitch, exhausting her breath to silence; then again and again—and always the same intensity of effort, of something that is, and is not, like urgency in the human voice. Transported so in the dancing light among the shadows of her room, she seemed beyond the reach of time. But that was illusion; I think I knew then that I should not see her again.

Houses are like sentinels in the plain, old keepers of the weather watch. There, in a very little while, wood takes on the appearance of great age. All colors wear soon away in the wind and rain, and then the wood is burned gray and the grain appears and the nails turn red with rust. The windowpanes are black and opaque; you imagine there is nothing within, and indeed there are many ghosts, bones given up to the land. They stand here and there against the sky, and you approach them for a longer time than you expect. They belong in the distance; it is their domain.

Once there was a lot of sound in my grandmother's house, a lot of coming and going, feasting and talk. The summers there were full of excitement and reunion. The Kiowas are a summer people; they abide the cold and keep to themselves, but when the season turns and the land becomes warm and vital they cannot hold still; an old love of going returns upon them. The aged visitors who came to my grandmother's house when I was a child were made of lean and leather, and they bore themselves upright. They wore great black hats and bright ample shirts that shook in the wind. They rubbed fat upon their hair and wound their braids with strips of colored cloth. Some of them painted their faces and carried the scars of old and cherished enmities. They were an old council of warlords, come to remind and be reminded of who they were. Their wives and daughters served them well. The women might indulge themselves; gossip was at once the mark and compensation of their servitude. They made loud and elaborate talk among themselves, full of jest and gesture, fright and false alarm. They went abroad in fringed and flowered shawls, bright beadwork and German silver. They were at home in the kitchen, and they prepared meals that were banquets.

There were frequent prayer meetings, and great nocturnal feasts. When I was a child I played with my cousins outside, where the lamplight fell upon the ground and the singing of the old people rose up around us and carried away into the darkness. There were a lot of good things to eat, a lot of laughter and surprise. And afterwards, when the quiet returned, I lay down with my grandmother and could hear the frogs away by the river and feel the motion of the air.

Now there is a funeral of silence in the rooms, the endless wake of some final word. The walls have closed in upon my grandmother's house. When I returned to it in mourning, I saw for the first time in my life how small it was. It was late at night, and there was a white moon, nearly full. I sat for a long time on the stone steps by the kitchen door. From there I could see out across the land; I could see the long row of trees by the creek, the low light upon the rolling plains, and the stars of the Big Dipper. Once I looked at the moon and caught sight of a strange thing. A cricket had perched upon the handrail, only a few inches away from me. My line of vision was such that the creature filled the moon like a fossil. It had gone there, I thought, to live and die, for there, of all places, was its small definition made whole and eternal. A warm wind rose up and purled like the longing within me.

The next morning I awoke at dawn and went out on the dirt road to Rainy Mountain. It was already hot, and the grasshoppers began to fill the air. Still, it was early in the morning, and the birds sang out of the shadows. The long yellow grass on the mountain shone in the bright light, and a scissortail hied above the land. There, where it ought to be, at the end of a long and legendary way, was my grandmother's grave. Here and there on the dark stones were ancestral names. Looking back once, I saw the mountain and came away.

SUGGESTIONS FOR WRITING AND DISCUSSION

1. In what ways does Momaday connect himself to his grandmother? In what ways does he seem estranged from her?
2. How does Momaday's relationship to the Kiowa tribe influence this essay?
3. What audience is Momaday writing for? How can you tell?
4. Both Chief Seattle and Momaday talk about the significance of the land. Compare the two pieces in a two- to three-page essay.

E. B. White (American, 1899–1985)

Once More to the Lake

One summer, along about 1904, my father rented a camp on a lake in Maine and took us all there for the month of August. We all got ringworm from some kittens and had to rub Pond's Extract on our arms and legs night and morning, and my father rolled over in a canoe with all his clothes on; but outside of that the vacation was a success and from then on none of us ever thought there was any place in the world like that lake in Maine. We returned summer after summer—always on August 1 for one month. I have since become a salt-water man, but sometimes in summer there are days when the restlessness of the tides and the fearful cold of the sea water and the incessant wind that blows across the afternoon and into the evening make me wish for the placidity of a lake in the woods. A few weeks ago this feeling got so strong I bought myself a couple of bass hooks and a spinner and returned to the lake where we used to go, for a week's fishing and to revisit old haunts.

I took along my son, who had never had any fresh water up his nose and who had seen lily pads only from train windows. On the journey over to the lake I began to wonder what it would be like. I wondered how time would have marred this unique, this holy spot—the coves and streams, the hills that the sun set behind, the camps and the paths behind the camps. I was sure that the tarred road would have found it out, and I wondered in what other ways it would be desolated. It is strange how much you can remember about places like that once you allow your mind to return into the grooves that lead back. You remember one thing, and that suddenly reminds you of another thing. I guess I remembered clearest of all the early mornings, when the lake was cool and motionless, remembered how the bedroom smelled of the lumber it was made of and of the wet woods whose scent entered through the screen. The partitions in the camp were thin and did not extend clear to the top of the rooms, and as I was always the first up I would dress softly so as not to wake the others, and sneak out into the sweet outdoors and start out in the canoe, keeping close along the shore in the long shadows of the pines. I remembered being very careful never to rub my paddle against the gunwale for fear of disturbing the stillness of the cathedral.

The lake had never been what you would call a wild lake. There were cottages sprinkled around the shores, and it was a farming country although the shores of the lake were quite heavily wooded. Some of the cottages were owned by nearby farmers, and you would live at the shore and eat your meals at the farmhouse. That's what our family did. But although it wasn't wild, it was a fairly large and undisturbed lake and there were places in it that, to a child at least, seemed infinitely remote and primeval.

I was right about the tar: it led to within half a mile of the shore. But when I got back there, with my boy, and we settled into a camp near a farmhouse and into the kind of summertime I had known, I could tell that it was going to be pretty much the same as it had been before—I knew it, lying in bed the first morning, smelling the bedroom and hearing the boy sneak quietly out and go off along the shore in a boat. I began to sustain the illusion that he was I, and therefore, by simple transposition, that I was my father. This sensation persisted, kept cropping up all the time we were there. It was not an entirely new feeling, but in this setting it grew much stronger. I seemed to be living a dual existence. I would be in the middle of some simple act, I would be picking up a bait box or laying down a table fork, or I would be saying something, and suddenly it would be not I but my father who was saying the words or making the gesture. It gave me a creepy sensation.

We went fishing the first morning. I felt the same damp moss covering the worms in the bait can, and saw the dragonfly alight on the tip of my rod as it hovered a few inches from the surface of the water. It was the arrival of this fly that convinced me beyond any doubt that everything was as it always had been, that the years were a mirage and that there had been no years. The small waves were the same, chucking the rowboat under the chine as we fished at anchor, and the boat was the same boat, the same color green and the ribs broken in the same places, and under the floorboards the same fresh-water leavings and debris—the dead helgramite, the wisps of moss, the rusty discarded fishhook, the dried blood from yesterday's catch. We stared silently at the tips of our rods, at the dragonflies that came and went. I lowered the tip of mine into the water, tentatively, pensively dislodging the fly, which darted two feet away, poised, darted two feet back, and came to rest again a little farther up the rod. There had been no years between the ducking of this dragonfly and the other one—the one that was part of memory. I looked at the boy, who was silently watching his fly, and it was my hands that held his rod, my eyes watching. I felt dizzy and didn't know which rod I was at the end of.

We caught two bass, hauling them in briskly as though they were mackerel, pulling them over the side of the boat in a businesslike manner without any landing net, and stunning them with a blow on the back of the head. When we got back for a swim before lunch, the lake was exactly where we had left it, the same number of inches from the dock, and there was only the merest suggestion of a breeze. This seemed an utterly enchanted sea, this lake you could leave to its own devices for a few hours and come back to, and find that it had not stirred, this constant and trustworthy body of water. In the shallows, the dark, water-soaked sticks and twigs, smooth and old, were undulating in clusters on the bottom against the clean ribbed sand, and the track of the mussel was plain. A school of minnows swam by, each minnow with its small individual shadow, doubling the attendance, so clear and sharp in the sunlight. Some of the other campers were in swimming, along the shore, one of them with a cake of soap, and the water felt thin and clear and unsubstantial. Over the years there had been this person with the cake of soap, this cultist, and here he was. There had been no years.

Up to the farmhouse to dinner through the teeming, dusty field, the road under our sneakers was only a two-track road. The middle track was missing, the one with the marks of the hooves and the splotches of dried, flaky manure. There had always been three tracks to choose from in choosing which track to walk in; now the choice was narrowed down to two. For a moment I missed terribly the middle alternative. But the way led past the tennis court, and something about the way it lay there in the sun reassured me; the tape had loosened along the backline, the alleys were green with plantains and other weeds, and the net (installed in June and removed in September) sagged in the dry noon, and the whole place steamed with midday heat and hunger and emptiness. There was a choice of pie for dessert, and one was blueberry and one was apple, and the waitresses were the same country girls, there having been no passage of time, only the illusion of it as in a dropped curtain—the waitresses were still fifteen; their hair had been washed, that was the only difference—they had been to the movies and seen the pretty girls with the clean hair.

Summertime, oh, summertime, pattern of life indelible, the fade-proof lake, the woods unshatterable, the pasture with the sweetfern and the juniper forever and ever, summer without end; this was the background, and the life along the shore was the design, the cottagers with their innocent and tranquil design, their tiny docks with the flagpole and the American flag floating against the white clouds in the blue sky, the little paths over the roots of the trees leading from camp to camp and the paths leading back to the outhouses and the can of lime for sprinkling, and at the souvenir counters at the store the miniature birch-bark canoes and the postcards that showed things looking a little better than they looked. This was the American family at play, escaping the city heat, wondering whether the newcomers in the camp at the head of the cove were ``common'' or ``nice,'' wondering whether it was true that the people who drove up for Sunday dinner at the farmhouse were turned away because there wasn't enough chicken.

It seemed to me, as I kept remembering all this, that those times and those summers had been infinitely precious and worth saving. There had been jollity and peace and goodness. The arriving (at the beginning of August) had been so big a business in itself, at the railway station the farm wagon drawn up, the first smell of the pine-laden air, the first glimpse of the smiling farmer, and the great importance of the trunks and your father's enormous authority in such matters, and the feel of the wagon under you for the long ten-mile haul, and at the top of the last long hill catching the first view of the lake after eleven months of not seeing this cherished body of water. The shouts and cries of the other campers when they saw you, and the trunks to be unpacked, to give up their rich burden. (Arriving was less exciting nowadays, when you sneaked up in your car and parked it under a tree near the camp and took out the bags and in five minutes it was all over, no fuss, no loud wonderful fuss about trunks.)

Peace and goodness and jollity. The only thing that was wrong now, really, was the sound of the palce, an unfamiliar nervous sound of the outboard motors. This was the note that jarred, the one thing that would sometimes break the illusion and set the years moving. In those other summertimes all motors were inboard; and when they were at a little distance, the noise they made was a sedative, an ingredient of summer sleep. They were one-cylinder and two-cylinder engines, and some were make-and-break and some were jump-spark, but they all made a sleepy sound across the lake. The one-lungers throbbed and fluttered, and the twin-cylinder ones purred and purred, and that was a quiet sound, too. But now the campers all had outboards. In the daytime, in the hot mornings, these motors made a petulant, irritable sound; at night, in the still evening when the afterglow lit the water, they whined about one's ears like mosquitoes. My boy loved our rented outboard, and his great desire was to achieve single-handed mastery over it, and authority, and he soon learned the trick of choking it a little (but not too much), and the adjustment of the needle valve. Watching him I would remember the things you could do with the old one-cylinder engine with the heavy flywheel, how you could have it eating out of your hand if you got really close to it spiritually. Motorboats in those days didn't have clutches, and you would make a landing by shutting off the motor at the proper time and coasting in with a dead rudder. But there was a way of reversing them, if you learned the trick, by cutting the switch and putting it on again exactly on the final dying revolution of the flywheel, so that it would kick back against compression and begin reversing. Approaching a dock in a strong following breeze, it was difficult to slow up sufficiently by the ordinary coasting method, and if a boy felt he had complete mastery over his motor, he was tempted to keep it running beyond its time and then reverse it a few feet from the dock. It took a cool nerve, because if you threw the switch a twentieth of a second too soon you would catch the flywheel when it still had speed enough to go up past center, and the boat would leap ahead, charging bull-fashion at the dock.

We had a good week at the camp. The bass were biting well and the sun shone endlessly, day after day. We would be tired at night and lie down in the accumulated heat of the little bedrooms after the long hot day and the breeze would stir almost imperceptibly outside and the smell of the swamp drift in through the rusty screens. Sleep would come easily and in the morning the red squirrel would be on the roof, tapping out his gay routine. I kept remembering everything, lying in bed in the mornings—the small steamboat that had a long rounded stern like the lip of a Ubangi, and how quietly she ran on the moonlight sails, when the older boys played their mandolins and the girls sang and we ate doughnuts dipped in sugar, and how sweet the music was on the water in the shining night, and what it had felt like to think about girls then. After breakfast we would go up to the store and the things were in the same place—the minnows in a bottle, the plugs and spinners disarranged and pawed over by the youngsters from the boys' camp, the Fig Newtons and the Beeman's gum. Outside, the road was tarred and cars stood in front of the store. Inside, all was just as it had always been, except there was more Coca-Cola and not so much Moxie and root beer and birch beer and sarsaparilla. We would walk out with a bottle of pop apiece and sometimes the pop would backfire up our noses and hurt. We explored the streams, quietly, where the turtles slid off the sunny logs and dug their way into the soft bottom; and we lay on the town wharf and fed worms to the tame bass. Everywhere we went I had trouble making out which was I, the one walking at my side, the one walking in my pants.

One afternoon while we were there at that lake a thunderstorm came up. It was like the revival of an old melodrama that I had seen long ago with childish awe. The second-act climax of the drama of the electrical disturbance over a lake in America had not changed in any important respect. This was the big scene, still the big scene. The whole thing was so familiar, the first feeling of oppression and heat and a general air around camp of not wanting to go very far away. In mid-afternoon (it was all the same) a curious darkening of the sky, and a lull in everything that had made life tick; and then the way the boats suddenly swung the other way at their moorings with the coming of a breeze out of the new quarter, and the premonitory rumble. Then the kettle drum, then the snare, then the bass drum and cymbals, then crackling light against the dark, and the gods grinning and licking their chops in the hills. Afterward the calm, the rain steadily rustling in the calm lake, the return of light and hope and spirits, and the campers running out in joy and relief to go swimming in the rain, their bright cries perpetuating the deathless joke about how they were getting simply drenched, and the children screaming with delight at the new sensation of bathing in the rain, and the joke about getting drenched linking the generations in a strong indestructible chain. And the comedian who waded in carrying an umbrella.

When the others went swimming, my son said he was going in, too. He pulled his dripping trunks from the line where they had hung all through the shower and wrung them out. Languidly, and with no thought of going in, I watched him, his hard little body, skinny and bare, saw him wince slightly as he pulled up around his vitals the small, soggy, icy garment. As he buckled the swollen belt, suddenly my groin felt the chill of death.

SUGGESTIONS FOR WRITING AND DISCUSSION

1. How would you describe the tone at the beginning of this essay? At what point does the tone shift? Why does this happen?
2. What do you feel are the son's perceptions of his father during this trip?

3. How has the passage of time influenced the way White reacts to seeing the lake again?
4. What is implied by the last sentence of the essay? What effect does it have on your understanding of the rest of the essay?
5. Have you ever been in a position similar to that of White or his son? What was the experience like? Discuss it in a two- to three-page essay.

Shana Alexander (American, 1925–   )

America the Ugly

The other day a fragment of an old cockney song ran through my head. "Ain't it a bleedin' shame. They're shifting daddy's bones to build a sewer. Ain't it a bleedin' shame." I was standing on a New York street in the sunshine, watching a steel ball batter a fine old brown wall, and doing it great hurt. We were once again demolishing ourselves.

Now, I'm not against change. A great part of the American genius has been to sell its old timbers to pay for new hardware. We are, after all, the greatest consumer society the world has ever known. And the metabolism of a consumer society requires it continually to eat and excrete, every day throwing itself away in plastic bags.

But what I do object to is the violence done to the quality of life by all the wrapping and unwrapping. We allow some things to last, but very little to mature. That fine hundred-year-old wall in New York will be replaced by—what? Probably another parking pyramid. A ziggurat of stacked-up automobiles. Ain't it a bleedin' shame.

Tied to the question of waste is the question of taste. Contemporary culture seems to worship a freakish goddess. We have made waste and taste into Siamese twins, joined at the pocketbook. When something ugly comes down, something uglier nearly always rises in its place, and the explanation is always money.

Must we be forever re-creating ourselves as ugly America, battering down the cities and ploughing up the countryside to sow ever-more-freakish crops of gas stations and Laundromats? We have zoning laws, fire laws, earthquake laws. But we have no eyesight laws. An eyesight law might not have preserved my fine old wall . . . perhaps it had to come down. But it would preserve us from things like plastic pizza parlors. The public should also be protected from really overpriced tastelessness, such as the marble arrogance of the new Kennedy Performing Arts Center, in Washington.

What we may need is a Ralph Nader of America the Beautiful, someone to regularly question this cash-registering but consumer-consuming society of ours, that tears down to put up to tear down. Someone to ask, bravely and openly: why should *we* reshape *our* lives to fit *your* new hardware?

CBS "Spectrum"—October 18, 1971

SUGGESTIONS FOR WRITING AND DISCUSSION

1. Alexander's main argument against demolition is that it is often done only to make way for ugly, new buildings. What additional argument does she offer?
2. Write a two-page description of the ugliest building in your neighborhood.

Henry James (American, 1843–1916)

Venice

The danger is that you will not linger enough—a danger of which the author of these lines had known something. It is possible to dislike Venice, and to entertain the sentiment in a responsible and intelligent manner. There are travellers who think the place odious, and those who are not of this opinion often find themselves wishing that the others were only more numerous. The sentimental tourist's sole quarrel with his Venice is that he has too many competitors there. He likes to be alone; to be original; to have (to himself, at least) the air of making discoveries. The Venice of to-day is a vast museum where the little wicket that admits you is perpetually turning and creaking, and you march through the institution with a herd of fellow-gazers. There is nothing left to discover or describe, and originality of attitude is completely impossible. This is often very annoying: you can only turn your back on your impertinent playfellow and curse his want of delicacy. But this is not the fault of Venice; it is the fault of the rest of the world. The fault of Venice is that, though she is easy to admire, she is not so easy to live with as you count living in other places. After you have stayed a week and the bloom of novelty has rubbed off you wonder if you can accommodate yourself to the peculiar conditions. Your old habits become impracticable and you find yourself obliged to form new ones of an undesirable and unprofitable character. You are tired of your gondola (or you think you are) and you have seen all the principal pictures and heard the names of the palaces announced a dozen times by your gondolier, who brings them out almost as impressively as if he were an English butler bawling titles into a drawing-room. You have walked several hundred times round the Piazza and bought several bushels of photographs. You have visitied the antiquity mongers whose horrible signboards dishonour some of the grandest vistas in the Grand Canal; you have tried the opera and found it very bad; you have bathed at the Lido and found the water flat. You have begun to have a shipboard-feeling—to regard the Piazza as an enormous saloon and the Riva degli Schiavoni as a promenade-deck. You are obstucted and encaged; your desire for space is unsatisfied; you miss your usual exercise. You try to take a walk and you fail, and meantime, as I say, you have come to regard your gondola as a sort of magnified baby's cradle. You have no desire to be rocked to sleep, though you are sufficiently kept awake by the irritation produced, as you gaze across the shallow lagoon, by the attitude of the perpetual gondolier, with his turned-out toes, his protruded chin, his absurdly unscientific stroke. The canals have a horrible smell, and the everlasting Piazza, where you have looked repeatedly at every article in every shop-window and found them all rubbish, where the young Venetians who sell bead bracelets and ''panoramas'' are perpetually thrusting their wares at you, where the same tightly-buttoned officers are for ever sucking the same black weeds, at the same empty tables, in front of the same cafés—the Piazza, as I say, has resolved itself into a magnificent tread-mill. This is the state of mind of those shallow inquirers who find Venice all very well for a week; and if in such a state of mind you take your departure you act with fatal rashness. The loss is your own, moreover; it is not—with all deference to your personal attractions—that of your companions who remain behind; for though there are some disagreeable things in Venice there is nothing so disagreeable as the visitors. The conditions are peculiar, but your intolerance of them evaporates before it has had time to become a prejudice. When you have called for the bill to go, pay it and remain, and you will find on the morrow that you are deeply attached to Venice. It is by living there from day to day that you feel the fulness of her charm; that you invite her exquisite influence to sink into your spirit. The creature varies like a nervous woman, whom you know only when you know all the aspects of her beauty. She has high spirits or low, she is pale or red, grey or pink, cold or warm, fresh or wan, according to the weather or the hour. She is always interesting and almost always sad; but she has a thousand occasional graces and is always liable to happy accidents. You become extraordinarily fond of these things; you count upon them; they make part of your life. Tenderly fond you become; there is something indefinable in those depths of personal acquaintance that gradually establish themselves. The place seems to personify itself, to become human and sentient and conscious of your affection. You desire to embrace it, to caress it, to possess it; and finally a soft sense of possession grows up and your visit becomes a perpetual love-affair. It is very true that if you go, as the author of these lines on a certain occasion went, about the middle of March, a certain amount of disappointment is possible. He had paid no visit for several years, and in the interval the beautiful and helpless city had suffered an increase of inquiry. The barbarians are in full possession and you tremble for what they may do. You are reminded from the moment of your arrival that Venice scarcely exists any more as a city at all; that she exists only as a battered peep-show and bazaar. There was a horde of savage Germans encamped in the Piazza, and they filled the Ducal Palace and the Academy with their uproar. The English and Americans came a little later. They came in good time, with a great many French, who were discreet enough to make very long repasts at the Caffé Quadri, during which they were out of the way. The months of April and May of the year 1881 were not, as a general thing, a favourable season for visiting the Ducal Palace and the Academy. The *valet-de-place* had marked them for his own and held triumphant possession of them. He celebrates his triumphs in a terrible brassy voice, which resounds all over the place, and has, whatever language he be speaking, the accent of some other idiom. During all the spring months in Venice these gentry abound in the great resorts, and they lead their helpless captives through churches and galleries in dense irresponsible groups. They infest the Piazza; they pursue you along the Riva; they hang about the bridges and the doors of the cafés. In saying just now that I was disappointed at first, I had chiefly in mind the impression that assails me to-day in the whole precinct of St. Mark's. The condition of this ancient sanctuary is surely a great scandal. The pedlars and commissioners ply their trade—often a very unclean one—at the very door of the temple; they follow you across the threshold, into the sacred dusk, and pull your sleeve, and hiss into your ear, scuffling with each other for customers. There is a great deal of dishonour about St. Mark's altogether, and if Venice, as I say, has become a great bazaar, this exquisite edifice is now the biggest booth.

SUGGESTIONS FOR WRITING AND DISCUSSION

1. Why does James refer to Venice as "she"? What part does this personification play in his descriptions?
2. Does James's argument proceed logically? Do his feelings about his own last visit seem to contradict his arguments?
3. Consider a place you know well. Using the brainstorming technique described in Chapter 2, make a list of your thoughts and feelings about that place. Decide which information really helps to capture the essence of the place you are writing about and which can be discarded as too general. When you have done this, write a three- to five-page essay with the intent of either persuading your readers to visit the place or dissuading them from visiting it.

Andrea Lee (American, 1953–   )

Leningrad

When we got to Leningrad, two weeks ago, the branches of the trees around the Winter Palace were still white with the famous hoarfrost of this damp region; above the frozen Neva, in the stunningly clear light of a minus thirty-degree morning, the blue-green palace looked like the final step in a theorem proving that cold weather would be the eternal state of the world. As our taxi crossed the bridge to Vasilevsky Island, I saw people strolling on the ice of the river, all of them as bundled up as I was in fur coats and hats and tightly wrapped scarves. (I've found that by far the best way to deal with temperatures below twenty degrees Fahrenheit is to wrap my face like a mummy until only my eyes show, and then to breathe

the warmed air coming in through the cloth.) Far behind them, the gold spires of the Peter and Paul Fortress shone under the blinding sky like a signal to even colder countries, farther north.

Even then, the length of the days betrayed the approach of spring. Every day the twilight comes a bit later and hangs longer over the city, and in the afternoons, everyone, starved for light through the darkness of December and January, is out strolling along the streets and canals. After our arrival the weather swiftly grew warmer, the temperatures rising daily, until now the snow has turned to puddles of slush and it is possible to go outside in what Russians call a "*demi-saison*" (many of their fashion terms are French), a wool coat, instead of a fur or sheepskin. I paid careful attention to the Neva, so as not to miss the breakup of the ice. I imagined that I would be awakened one dawn by the fabled cracking sounds like gunfire that would mean that the river had wrestled itself free from winter. Instead, as I paused one sunny afternoon on the Dvortsovyi Bridge, I heard a light tinkling, like crystals in a chandelier, and looked down to see an open channel about two feet wide in the thick gray ice; inside was a swift eddy of brownish water where dozens of tiny pieces of ice were caught and ringing against one another. This delicate chiming seemed to be an apt voice for the ravishing artificial city of pastels, balanced on its marshes at the top of the world. The combination of Mediterranean colors and architectural shapes with the high white skies of the North gives Leningrad, to me, the disturbing glamor one finds in exotic hybrid fruits and flowers—wherever the hand of man has tampered outrageously with nature.

There is the Leningrad of Rastrelli and the Bronze Horseman, of Nevsky Prospekt and the Winter Palace, and then there is our corner of the city: a working-class neighborhood on Vasilevsky Island, which was filled with barricades during the revolutions of 1905 and 1917. We are staying in a small dormitory for Russian and foreign students that is set inconspicuously among brick apartment buildings and snowy open spaces that are becoming seas of mud as the snow melts. Our window looks out on what seems to be a boys' *gymnasium:* we often see the boys outside in their school uniforms, goose-stepping through some quasi-military drill. They also like to gather upstairs in the lavatory to laugh and smoke cigarettes and try to push one another out of the windows. Once there was a *skandal* when some of the pupils threw snowballs at one of the school cleaning women: she charged into the yard, her white kerchief flapping, yelling and flailing at them with a mop.

Shopping in the stores in this neighborhood makes it clear that we're no longer in a relatively privileged community, as we were in Moscow. There are fewer leather boots and blue jeans on the clientele, and more *valenki* (felt boots) and black quilted workmen's jackets. The stores are filled with crowds, strong smells, and puddles of soupy mud near the doors. Entering the *gastronom* on Malyi Prospekt, where I shop almost daily, one is assailed with the stink of stale meat and turning milk, of crowds who eat too much sausage and wash infrequently. Behind the counters, big slatternly women—who usually have crudely bleached hair above exhausted faces shining with grease and perspiration, faces whose fine-textured skin is a startling reminder that these women are quite young, perhaps thirty or thirty-five—slice kilos of cheese, weigh butter, and bring out the greenish bottles of *kefir* and acidophilus milk. The people in the endless jostling lines are constantly shouting orders and thrusting out their cashier slips, but these women in their bedraggled white coats do everything with an insolent slowness. Foul-tempered beyond any American's nightmare of a rude employee, they pounce, with shouts of abuse, on any customer whose demeanor offends them. In the line itself, there is always some nimble old woman who tries, without any subtlety, to dart to the front; a proper reaction might be to say "*Grazhdanka, vui byez orchered!*"—Citizeness, you're out of place in line!—or one can simply shove. (I prefer the latter response.) In the middle of the crowd, mothers in lacy knitted headshawls try to keep tabs on toddlers bundled in immense wooly coats, with scarves tied around their middles. Workmen with black-jowled faces and missing teeth line up for salted fish. Behind the welter of bodies, glass sale cases display huge yellowish pigs' heads.

In this uncertain transitional weather between winter and spring, this end of Vasilevsky Island, with its streets full of dirty snow and its dingy apartment buildings streaked with moisture, can seem intensely depressing, a bit like an American slum, though one devoid of any flamboyant signs of vice or suffering. Here, there is just a sense of incessant struggle, of the constant burden of a harsh life that squashes men into mean shapes. Yet something of the magic of Leningrad penetrates even to this lowly corner. The early evenings can be lovely. I get off the metro in the middle of a crowd and push my way outside through the masses of damp wool coats at the station door. At this hour dozens of people are waiting for the trolley on Sredny Prospekt. Some of the girls and young women have their heads uncovered for the first time since October, and their necks and faces look vulnerable and delicately colored after a winter of protection. The sky over Sredny is blue-white with a roseate tinge to it; the air is moist and cold, scented with whiffs of cabbage-flavored steam from a nearby cafeteria. By the bus stop stands a small open-air flower market, run mostly by Moldavian women; they sell hyacinths and red tulips, which the crowds carry away like torches. Across the street, there is often a line waiting to get into a candy store that has a mild blue neon sign depicting a squirrel. There are few cars in Leningrad, compared to Moscow, and so one can look far up the street, where slushy puddles gleam in the sunset, and watch the trolleys as they rattle from block to block, striking showers of sparks between the dark buildings.

SUGGESTIONS FOR WRITING AND DISCUSSION

1. What does Lee mean when she says that Leningrad has "disturbing glamor"?

2. Compare Lee's approach to Leningrad with James's approach to Venice.
3. What are some of the contradictions Lee discusses in this essay?
4. "Leningrad" is a chapter from *A Russian Journal,* an account of a year Lee spent in the Soviet Union while her husband was a graduate student there. Most of her journal describes time spent in Moscow, and this chapter is a digression, which creates a comparison between the two cities. In a three- to five-page essay compare two places in which you have lived or where you have visited.
5. Choose a place near where you now live that you have never visited (an ethnic restaurant, a museum, a shop) and visit it. Describe your impressions in a three- to five-page paper.

Lillian Hellman (American, 1905–1984)

The Fig Tree

There was a heavy fig tree on the lawn where the house turned the corner into the side street, and to the front and sides of the fig tree were three live oaks that hid the fig from my aunts' boardinghouse. I suppose I was eight or nine before I discovered the pleasures of the fig tree, and although I have lived in many houses since then, including a few I made for myself, I still think of it as my first and most beloved home.

I learned early, in our strange life of living half in New York and half in New Orleans, that I made my New Orleans teachers uncomfortable because I was too far ahead of my schoolmates, and my New York teachers irritable because I was too far behind. But in New Orleans, I found a solution: I skipped school at least once a week and often twice, knowing that nobody cared or would report my absence. On those days I would set out for school done up in polished strapped shoes and a prim hat against what was known as "the climate," carrying my books and a little basket filled with delicious stuff my Aunt Jenny and Carrie, the cook, had made for my school lunch. I would round the corner of the side street, move on toward St. Charles Avenue, and sit on a bench as if I were waiting for a streetcar until the boarders and the neighbors had gone to work or settled down for the post-breakfast rest that all Southern ladies thought necessary. Then I would run back to the fig tree, dodging in and out of bushes to make sure the house had no dangers for me. The fig tree was heavy, solid, comfortable, and I had, through time, convinced myself that it wanted me, missed me when I was absent, and approved all the rigging I had done for the happy days I spent in its arms: I had made a sling to hold the school books, a pulley rope for my lunch basket, a hole for the bottle of afternoon cream-soda pop, a fishing pole and a smelly little bag of elderly bait, a pillow embroidered with a picture of Henry Clay on a horse that I had stolen from Mrs. Stillman, one of my aunts' boarders, and a proper nail to hold my dress and shoes to keep them neat for the return to the house.

It was in that tree that I learned to read, filled with the passions that can only come to the bookish, grasping, very young, bewildered by almost all of what I read, sweating in the attempt to understand a world of adults I fled from in real life but desperately wanted to join in books. (I did not connect the grown men and women in literature with the grown men and women I saw around me. They were, to me, another species.)

It was in the fig tree that I learned that anything alive in water was of enormous excitement to me. True, the water was gutter water and the fishing could hardly be called that: sometimes the things that swam in New Orleans gutters were not pretty, but I didn't know what was pretty and I liked them all. After lunch—the men boarders returned for a large lunch and a siesta—the street would be safe again, with only the noise from Carrie and her helpers in the kitchen, and they could be counted on never to move past the back porch, or the chicken coop. Then I would come down from my tree to sit on the side street gutter with my pole and bait. Often I would catch a crab that had wandered in from the Gulf, more often I would catch my favorite, the crayfish, and sometimes I would, in that safe hour, have at least six of them for my basket. Then about 2:30, when house and street would stir again, I would go back to my tree for another few hours of reading and dozing or having what I called the ill hour. It is too long ago for me to know why I thought the hour ''ill,'' but certainly I did not mean sick. I think I meant an intimation of sadness, a first recognition that there was so much to understand that one might never find one's way and the first signs, perhaps, that for a nature like mine, the way would not be easy. I cannot be sure that I felt all that then, although I can be sure that it was in the fig tree, a few years later, that I was first puzzled by the conflict which would haunt me, harm me, and benefit me the rest of my life: simply, the stubborn, relentless, driving desire to be alone as it came into conflict with the desire not to be alone when I wanted not to be. I already guessed that other people wouldn't allow that, although, as an only child, I pretended for the rest of my life that they would and must allow it to me.

SUGGESTIONS FOR WRITING AND DISCUSSION

1. Why does Hellman characterize the fig tree as her most beloved home?
2. Hellman is not sure why she called a certain time of the day the ''ill hour.'' What are some possible meanings?
3. Hellman seems alone but not lonely. What specific details of the essay demonstrate this?
4. This essay discusses in part what a place can teach us about ourselves. What does Hellman say she learned about herself while sitting in her fig tree?
5. In a two- to three-page essay compare ''The Fig Tree'' with E. B. White's ''Once More to the Lake.''

Fiction

Ernest Hemingway (American, 1899–1961)

In Another Country

In the fall the war was always there, but we did not go to it any more. It was cold in the fall in Milan and the dark came very early. Then the electric lights came on, and it was pleasant along the streets looking in the windows. There was much game hanging outside the shops, and the snow powdered in the fur of the foxes and the wind blew their tails. The deer hung stiff and heavy and empty, and small birds blew in the wind and the wind turned their feathers. It was a cold fall and the wind came down from the mountains.

We were all at the hospital every afternoon, and there were different ways of walking across the town through the dusk to the hospital. Two of the ways were alongside canals, but they were long. Always, though, you crossed a bridge across a canal to enter the hospital. There was a choice of three bridges. On one of them a woman sold roasted chestnuts. It was warm, standing in front of her charcoal fire, and the chestnuts were warm afterward in your pocket. The hospital was very old and very beautiful, and you entered through a gate and walked across a courtyard and out a gate on the other side. There were usually funerals starting from the courtyard. Beyond the old hospital were the new brick pavilions, and there we met every afternoon and were all very polite and interested in what was the matter, and sat in the machines that were to make so much difference.

The doctor came up to the machine where I was sitting and said: "What did you like best to do before the war? Did you practise a sport?"

I said: "Yes, football."

"Good," he said. "You will be able to play football again better than ever."

My knee did not bend and the leg dropped straight from the knee to the ankle without a calf, and the machine was to bend the knee and make it move as in riding a tricycle. But it did not bend yet, and instead the machine lurched when it came to the bending part. The doctor said: "That will all pass. You are a fortunate young man. You will play football again like a champion."

In the next machine was a major who had a little hand like a baby's. He winked at me when the doctor examined his hand, which was between two leather straps that bounced up and down and flapped the stiff fingers, and said: "And will I too play football, captain-doctor?" He had been a very great fencer, and before the war the greatest fencer in Italy.

The doctor went to his office in a back room and brought a photograph which showed a hand that had been withered almost as small as the major's, before it had taken a machine course, and after was a little larger. The major held the photograph with his good hand and looked at it very carefully. ''A wound?'' he asked.

''An industrial accident,'' the doctor said.

''Very interesting, very interesting,'' the major said, and handed it back to the doctor.

''You have confidence?''

''No,'' said the major.

There were three boys who came each day who were about the same age I was. They were all three from Milan, and one of them was to be a lawyer, and one was to be a painter, and one had intended to be a soldier, and after we were finished with the machines, sometimes we walked back together to the Café Cova, which was next door to the Scala. We walked the short way through the communist quarter because we were four together. The people hated us because we were officers, and from a wine-shop some one called out, ''A basso gli ufficiali!'' as we passed. Another boy who walked with us sometimes and made us five wore a black silk handkerchief across his face because he had no nose then and his face was to be rebuilt. He had gone out to the front from the military academy and been wounded within an hour after he had gone into the front line for the first time. They rebuilt his face, but he came from a very old family and they could never get the nose exactly right. He went to South America and worked in a bank. But this was a long time ago, and then we did not any of us know how it was going to be afterward. We only knew then that there was always the war, but that we were not going to it any more.

We all had the same medals, except the boy with the black silk band-age across his face, and he had not been at the front long enough to get any medals. The tall boy with a very pale face who was to be a lawyer had been a lieutenant of Arditi and had three medals of the sort we each had only one of. He had lived a very long time with death and was a little detached. We were all a little detached, and there was nothing that held us together except that we met every afternoon at the hospital. Although, as we walked to the Cova through the tough part of town, walking in the dark, with light and singing coming out of the wine-shops, and sometimes having to walk into the street when the men and women would crowd together on the sidewalk so that we would have had to jostle them to get by, we felt held together by there being something that had happened that they, the people who disliked us, did not understand.

We ourselves all understood the Cova, where it was rich and warm and not too brightly lighted, and noisy and smoky at certain hours, and there were always girls at the tables and the illustrated papers on a rack on the wall. The girls at the Cova were very patriotic, and I found that the most patriotic people in Italy were the café girls—and I believe they are still patriotic.

The boys at first were very polite about my medals and asked me what I had done to get them. I showed them the papers, which were written in very beautiful language and full of *fratellanza* and *abnegazione,* but which really said, with the adjectives removed, that I had been given the medals because I was an American. After that their manner changed a little toward me, although I was their friend against outsiders. I was a friend, but I was never really one of them after they had read the citations, because it had been different with them and they had done very different things to get their medals. I had been wounded, it was true; but we all knew that being wounded, after all, was really an accident. I was never ashamed of the ribbons, though, and sometimes, after the cocktail hour, I would imagine myself having done all the things they had done to get their medals; but walking home at night through the empty streets with the cold wind and all the shops closed, trying to keep near the street lights, I knew that I would never have done such things, and I was very much afraid to die, and often lay in bed at night by myself, afraid to die and wondering how I would be when I went back to the front again.

The three with the medals were like hunting-hawks; and I was not a hawk, although I might seem a hawk to those who had never hunted; they, the three, knew better and so we drifted apart. But I stayed good friends with the boy who had been wounded his first day at the front, because he would never know now how he would have turned out; so he could never be accepted either, and I liked him because I thought perhaps he would not have turned out to be a hawk either.

The major, who had been the great fencer, did not believe in bravery, and spent much time while we sat in the machines correcting my grammar. He had complimented me on how I spoke Italian, and we talked together very easily. One day I had said that Italian seemed such an easy language to me that I could not take a great interest in it; everything was so easy to say. "Ah, yes," the major said. "Why, then, do you not take up the use of grammar?" So we took up the use of grammar, and soon Italian was such a difficult language that I was afraid to talk to him until I had the grammar straight in my mind.

The major came very regularly to the hospital. I do not think he ever missed a day, although I am sure he did not believe in the machines. There was a time when none of us believed in the machines, and one day the major said it was all nonsense. The machines were new then and it was we who were to prove them. It was an idiotic idea, he said, "a theory, like another." I had not learned my grammar, and he said I was a stupid impossible disgrace, and he was a fool to have bothered with me. He was a small man and he sat straight up in his chair with his right hand thrust into the machine and looked straight ahead at the wall while the straps thumped up and down with his fingers in them.

"What will you do when the war is over if it is over?" he asked me. "Speak grammatically!"

"I will go to the States."

"Are you married?"

"No, but I hope to be."

``The more of a fool you are,'' he said. He seemed very angry. ``A man must not marry.''

``Why, Signor Maggiore?''

``Don't call me 'Signor Maggiore.'''

``Why must not a man marry?''

``He cannot marry. He cannot marry,'' he said angrily. ``If he is to lose everything, he should not place himself in a position to lose that. He should not place himslef in a position to lose. He should find things he cannot lose.''

He spoke very angrily and bitterly, and looked straight ahead while he talked.

``But why should he necessarily lose it?''

``He'll lose it,'' the major said. He was looking at the wall. Then he looked down at the machine and jerked his little hand out from between the straps and slapped it hard aginst his thigh. ``He'll lose it,'' he almost shouted. ``Don't argue with me!'' Then he called to the attendant who ran the machines. ``Come and turn this damned thing off.''

He went back into the other room for the light treatment and the massage. Then I heard him ask the doctor if he might use his telephone and he shut the door. When he came back into the room, I was sitting in another machine. He was wearing his cape and had his cap on, and he came directly toward my machine and put his arm on my shoulder.

``I am so sorry,'' he said, and patted me on the shoulder with his good hand. ``I would not be rude. My wife has just died. You must forgive me.''

``Oh—'' I said, feeling sick for him. ``I am *so* sorry.''

He stood there biting his lower lip. ``It is very difficult,'' he said. ``I cannot resign myself.''

He looked straight past me and out through the window. Then he began to cry. ``I am utterly unable to resign myself,'' he said and choked. And then crying, his head up looking at nothing, carrying himself straight and soldierly, with tears on both his cheeks and biting his lips, he walked past the machines and out the door.

The doctor told me the major's wife, who was very young and whom he had not married until he was definitely invalided out of the war, had died of pneumonia. She had been sick only a few days. No one expected her to die. The major did not come to the hospital for three days. Then he came at the usual hour, wearing a black band on the sleeve of his uniform. When he came back, there were large framed photographs around the wall, of all sorts of wounds before and after they had been cured by the machines. In front of the machine the major used were three photographs of hands like his that were completely restored. I do not know where the doctor got them. I always understood we were the first to use the machines. The photographs did not make much difference to the major because he only looked out of the window.

SUGGESTIONS FOR WRITING AND DISCUSSION

1. What effect is created by the sustained use of *we* in the first two paragraphs? Why does the narrator not use *we* throughout the story?
2. Examine the various beliefs about bravery in this story. Is the narrator brave? What does he mean when he says the major "did not believe in bravery"? Is this story about kinds of bravery other than physical courage? Is Hemingway condemning cowardice? Is he condemning war?
3. Why is it significant that the major is a fencing champion and that he did not marry until after he became an invalid?
4. Look at the various descriptions of Milan. What kind of atmosphere do they create? How do they contribute to the theme of the story?
5. What do the machines symbolize?
6. There are many circumstances that keep the narrator separate emotionally and physically from others in this story. Analyze his separateness in a three- to four-page paper.
7. Write a one-page character sketch of the narrator, using what he tells us explicitly and what we can infer from the way other characters treat him.

E. M. Forster (British, 1879–1970)

The Road from Colonus

I

For no very intelligible reason, Mr. Lucas had hurried ahead of his party. He was perhaps reaching the age at which independence becomes valuable, because it is so soon to be lost. Tired of attention and consideration, he liked breaking away from the younger members, to ride by himself, and to dismount unassisted. Perhaps he also relished that more subtle pleasure of being kept waiting for lunch, and of telling the others on their arrival that it was of no consequence.

So, with childish impatience, he battered the animal's sides with his heels, and made the muleteer bang it with a thick stick and prick it with a sharp one, and jolted down the hill sides through clumps of flowering shrubs and stretches of anemones and asphodel, till he heard the sound of running water, and came in sight of the group of plane trees where they were to have their meal.

Even in England those trees would have been remarkable, so huge were they, so interlaced, so magnificently clothed in quivering green. And here in Greece they were unique, the one cool spot in that hard brilliant landscape, already scorched by the heat of an April sun. In their midst was hidden a tiny Khan or country inn, a frail mud building with a broad wooden balcony in which sat an old woman spinning, while a small brown pig, eating orange peel, stood beside her. On the wet earth below squatted two children, playing some primaeval game with their fingers; and their mother, none too clean either, was messing with some rice inside. As Mrs. Forman would have said, it was all very Greek, and the fastidious Mr. Lucas felt thankful that they were bringing their own food with them, and should eat it in the open air.

Still, he was glad to be there—the muleteer had helped him off—and glad that Mrs. Forman was not there to forestall his opinions—glad even that he should not see Ethel for quite half an hour. Ethel was his youngest daughter, still unmarried. She was unselfish and affectionate, and it was generally understood that she was to devote her life to her father, and be the comfort of his old age. Mrs. Forman always referred to her as Antigone, and Mr. Lucas tried to settle down to the role of Oedipus, which seemed the only one that public opinion allowed him.

He had this in common with Oedipus, that he was growing old. Even to himself it had become obvious. He had lost interest in other people's affairs, and seldom attended when they spoke to him. He was fond of talking himself but often forgot what he was going to say, and even when he succeeded, it seldom seemed worth the effort. His phrases and gestures had become stiff and set, his anecdotes, once so successful, fell flat, his silence was as meaningless as his speech. Yet he had led a healthy, active life, had worked steadily, made money, educated his children. There was nothing and no one to blame: he was simply growing old.

At the present moment, here he was in Greece, and one of the dreams of his life was realized. Forty years ago he had caught the fever of Hellenism, and all his life he had felt that could he but visit that land, he would not have lived in vain. But Athens had been dusty, Delphi wet, Thermopylae flat, and he had listened with amazement and cynicism to the rapturous exclamations of his companions. Greece was like England: it was a man who was growing old, and it made no difference whether that man looked at the Thames or the Eurotas. It was his last hope of contradicting that logic of experience, and it was failing.

Yet Greece had done something for him, though he did not know it. It had made him discontented, and there are stirrings of life in discontent. He knew that he was not the victim of continual ill-luck. Something great was wrong, and he was pitted against no mediocre or accidental enemy. For the last month a strange desire had possessed him to die fighting.

"Greece is the land for young people," he said to himself as he stood under the plane trees, "but I will enter into it, I will possess it. Leaves shall be green again, water shall be sweet, the sky shall be blue. They were so forty years ago, and I will win them back. I do mind being old, and I will pretend no longer."

He took two steps forward, and immediately cold waters were gurgling over his ankle.

"Where does the water come from?" he asked himself. "I do not even know that." He remembered that all the hill sides were dry; yet here the road was suddenly covered with flowing streams.

He stopped still in amazement, saying: "Water out of a tree—out of a hollow tree? I never saw nor thought of that before."

For the enormous plane that leant towards the Khan was hollow—it had been burnt out for charcoal—and from its living trunk there gushed an impetuous spring, coating the bark with fern and moss, and flowing over the mule track to create fertile meadows beyond. The simple country folk had paid to beauty and mystery such tribute as they could, for in the rind of the tree a shrine was cut, holding a lamp and a little picture of the Virgin, inheritor of the Naiad's and Dryad's joint abode.

"I never saw anything so marvellous before," said Mr. Lucas. "I could even step inside the trunk and see where the water comes from."

For a moment he hesitated to violate the shrine. Then he remembered with a smile his own thought—"the place shall be mine; I will enter it and possess it"—and leapt almost aggressively on to a stone within.

The water pressed up steadily and noiselessly from the hollow roots and hidden crevices of the plane, forming a wonderful amber pool ere it spilt over the lip of bark on the earth outside. Mr. Lucas tasted it and it was sweet, and when he looked up the black funnel of the trunk he saw sky which was blue, and some leaves which were green; and he remembered, without smiling, another of his thoughts.

Others had been before him—indeed he had a curious sense of companionship. Little votive offerings to the presiding Power were fastened on to the bark—tiny arms and legs and eyes in tin, grotesque models of the brain or the heart—all tokens of some recovery of strength or wisdom or love. There was no such thing as the solitude of nature, for the sorrows and joys of humanity had pressed even into the bosom of a tree. He spread out his arms and steadied himself against the soft charred wood, and then slowly leant back, till his body was resting on the trunk behind. His eyes closed, and he had the strange feeling of one who is moving, yet at peace—the feeling of the swimmer, who, after long struggling with chopping seas, finds that after all the tide will sweep him to his goal.

So he lay motionless, conscious only of the stream below his feet, and that all things were a stream, in which he was moving.

He was aroused at last by a shock—the shock of an arrival perhaps, for when he opened his eyes, something unimagined, indefinable, had passed over all things, and made them intelligible and good.

There was meaning in the stoop of the old woman over her work, and in the quick motions of the little pig, and in her diminishing globe of wool. A young man came singing over the streams on a mule, and there was beauty in his pose and sincerity in his greeting. The sun made no accidental patterns upon the spreading roots of the trees, and there was intention in the nodding clumps of asphodel, and in the music of the water. To Mr. Lucas, who, in a brief space of time, had discovered not only Greece, but England and all the world and life, there seemed nothing ludicrous in the desire to hang within the tree another votive offering—a little model of an entire man.

"Why, here's papa, playing at being Merlin."

All unnoticed they had arrived—Ethel, Mrs. Forman, Mr. Graham, and the English-speaking dragoman. Mr. Lucas peered out at them suspiciously. They had suddenly become unfamiliar, and all that they did seemed strained and coarse.

"Allow me to give you a hand," said Mr. Graham, a young man who was always polite to his elders.

Mr. Lucas felt annoyed. "Thank you, I can manage perfectly well by myself," he replied. His foot slipped as he stepped out of the tree, and went into the spring.

"Oh papa, my papa!" said Ethel, "what are you doing? Thank goodness I have got a change for you on the mule."

She tended him carefully, giving him clean socks and dry boots, and then sat him down on the rug beside the lunch basket, while she went with the others to explore the grove.

They came back in ecstasies, in which Mr. Lucas tried to join. But he found them intolerable. Their enthusiasm was superficial, commonplace, and spasmodic. They had no perception of the coherent beauty that was flowering around them. He tried at least to explain his feelings, and what he said was:

"I am altogether pleased with the appearance of this place. It impresses me very favourably. The trees are fine, remarkably fine for Greece, and there is something very poetic in the spring of clear running water. The people too seem kindly and civil. It is decidedly an attractive place."

Mrs. Forman upbraided him for his tepid praise.

"Oh, it is a place in a thousand!" she cried. "I could live and die here! I really would stop if I had not to be back at Athens! It reminds me of the Colonus of Sophocles."

"Well, *I* must stop," said Ethel. "I positively must."

"Yes, *do*! You and your father! Antigone and Oedipus. Of course you must stop at Colonus!"

Mr. Lucas was almost breathless with excitement. When he stood within the tree, he had believed that his happiness would be independent of locality. But these few minutes' conversation had undeceived him. He no longer trusted himself to journey through the world, for old thoughts, old wearinesses might be waiting to rejoin him as soon as he left the shade of the planes, and the music of the virgin water. To sleep in the Khan with the gracious, kind-eyed country people, to watch the bats flit about within the globe of shade, and see the moon turn the golden patterns into silver—one such night would place him beyond relapse, and confirm him for ever in the kingdom he had regained. But all his lips could say was: "I should be willing to put in a night here."

"You mean a week, papa! It would be sacrilege to put in less."

"A week then, a week," said his lips, irritated at being corrected, while his heart was leaping with joy. All through lunch he spoke to them no more, but watched the place he should know so well, and the people who would so soon be his companions and friends. The inmates of the Khan only consisted of an old woman, a middle-aged woman, a young man and two children, and to none of them had he spoken, yet he loved them as he loved everything that moved or breathed or existed beneath the benedictory shade of the planes.

"*En route!*" said the shrill voice of Mrs. Forman. "Ethel! Mr. Graham! The best of things must end."

"Tonight," thought Mr. Lucas, "they will light the little lamp by the shrine. And when we all sit together on the balcony, perhaps they will tell me which offering they put up."

"I beg your pardon, Mr. Lucas," said Graham, "but they want to fold up the rug you are sitting on."

Mr. Lucas got up, saying to himself: "Ethel shall go to bed first, and then I will try to tell them about my offering too—for it is a thing I must do. I think they will understand if I am left with them alone."

Ethel touched him on the cheek. "Papa! I've called you three times. All the mules are here."

"Mules? What mules?"

"Our mules. We're all waiting. Oh, Mr. Graham, do help my father on."

"I don't know what you're talking about, Ethel."

"My dearest papa, we must start. You know we have to get to Olympia to-night."

Mr. Lucas in pompous, confident tones replied: "I always did wish, Ethel, that you had a better head for plans. You know perfectly well that we are putting in a week here. It is your own suggestion."

Ethel was startled into impoliteness. "What a perfectly ridiculous idea. You must have known I was joking. Of course I meant I wished we could."

"Ah! if we could only do what we wished!" sighed Mrs. Forman, already seated on her mule.

"Surely," Ethel continued in calmer tones, "you didn't think I meant it."

"Most certainly I did. I have made all my plans on the supposition that we are stopping here, and it will be extremely inconvenient, indeed, impossible for me to start."

He delivered this remark with an air of great conviction, and Mrs. Forman and Mr. Graham had to turn away to hide their smiles.

"I am sorry I spoke so carelessly; it was wrong of me. But, you know, we can't break up our party, and even one night here would make us miss the boat at Patras."

Mrs. Forman, in an aside, called Mr. Graham's attention to the excellent way in which Ethel managed her father.

"I don't mind about the Patras boat. You said that we should stop here, and we are stopping."

It seemed as if the inhabitants of the Khan had divined in some mysterious way that the altercation touched them. The old woman stopped her spinning, while the young man and the two children stood behind Mr. Lucas, as if supporting him.

Neither arguments nor entreaties moved him. He said little, but he was absolutely determined, because for the first time he saw his daily life aright. What need had he to return to England? Who would miss him? His friends were dead or cold. Ethel loved him in a way, but, as was right, she had other interests. His other children he seldom saw. He had only one other relative, his sister Julia, whom he both feared and hated. It was no effort to struggle. He would be a fool as well as a coward if he stirred from the place which brought him happiness and peace.

At last Ethel, to humour him, and not disinclined to air her modern Greek, went into the Khan with the astonished dragoman to look at the rooms. The woman inside received them with loud welcomes, and the young man, when no one was looking, began to lead Mr. Lucas' mule to the stable.

"Drop it, you brigand!" shouted Graham, who always declared that foreigners could understand English if they chose. He was right, for the man obeyed, and they all stood waiting for Ethel's return.

She emerged at last, with close-gathered skirts, followed by the dragoman bearing the little pig, which he had bought at a bargain.

"My dear papa, I will do all I can for you, but stop in the Khan—no."

"Are there—fleas?" asked Mrs. Forman.

Ethel intimated that "fleas" was not the word.

"Well, I am afraid that settles it," said Mrs. Forman, "I know how particular Mr. Lucas is."

"It does not settle it," said Mr. Lucas. "Ethel, you go on. I do not want you. I don't know why I ever consulted you. I shall stop here alone."

"That is absolute nonsense," said Ethel, losing her temper. "How can you be left alone at your age? How would you get your meals or your bath? All your letters are waiting for you at Patras. You'll miss the boat. That means missing the London operas, and upsetting all your engagements for the month. And as if you could travel by yourself!"

"They might knife you," was Mr. Graham's contribution.

The Greeks said nothing; but whenever Mr. Lucas looked their way, they beckoned him towards the Khan. The children would even have drawn him by the coat, and the old woman on the balcony stopped her almost completed spinning, and fixed him with mysterious appealing eyes. As he fought, the issue assumed gigantic proportions, and he believed that he was not merely stopping because he had regained youth or seen beauty or found happiness, but because in that place and with those people a supreme event was awaiting him which would transfigure the face of the world. The moment was so tremendous that he abandoned words and arguments as useless, and rested on the strength of his mighty unrevealed allies: silent men, murmuring water, and whispering trees. For the whole place called with one voice, articulate to him, and his garrulous opponents became every minute more meaningless and absurd. Soon they would be tired and go chattering away into the sun, leaving him to the cool grove and the moonlight and the destiny he foresaw.

Mrs. Forman and the dragoman had indeed already started, amid the piercing screams of the little pig, and the struggle might have gone on indefinitely if Ethel had not called in Mr. Graham.

"Can you help me?" she whispered. "He is absolutely unmanageable."

"I'm no good at arguing—but if I could help you in any other way—" and he looked down complacently at his well-made figure.

Ethel hesitated. Then she said: "Help me in any way you can. After all, it is for his good that we do it."

"Then have his mule led up behind him."

So when Mr. Lucas thought he had gained the day, he suddenly felt himself lifted off the ground, and sat sideways on the saddle, and at the same time the mule started off at a trot. He said nothing, for he had nothing to say, and even his face showed little emotion as he felt the shade pass and heard the sound of the water cease. Mr. Graham was running at his side, hat in hand, apologizing.

"I know I had no business to do it, and I beg your pardon awfully. But I do hope that some day you too will feel that I was—damn!"

A stone had caught him in the middle of the back. It was thrown by the little boy, who was pursuing them along the mule track. He was followed by his sister, also throwing stones.

Ethel screamed to the dragoman, who was some way ahead with Mrs. Forman, but before he could rejoin them, another adversary appeared. It was the young Greek, who had cut them off in front, and now dashed down at Mr. Lucas' bridle. Fortunately Graham was an expert boxer, and it did not take him a moment to beat down the youth's feeble defence, and to send him sprawling with a bleeding mouth into the asphodel. By this time the dragoman had arrived, the children, alarmed at the fate of their brother, had desisted, and the rescue party, if such it is to be considered, retired in disorder to the trees.

"Little devils!" said Graham, laughing with triumph. "That's the modern Greek all over. Your father meant money if he stopped, and they consider we were taking it out of their pocket."

"Oh, they are terrible—simple savages! I don't know how I shall ever thank you. You've saved my father."

"I only hope you didn't think me brutal."

"No," replied Ethel with a little sigh. "I admire strength."

Meanwhile the cavalcade reformed, and Mr. Lucas, who, as Mrs. Forman said, bore his disappointment wonderfully well, was put comfortably on to his mule. They hurried up the opposite hillside, fearful of another attack, and it was not until they had left the eventful place far behind that Ethel found an opportunity to speak to her father and ask his pardon for the way she had treated him.

"You seemed so different, dear father, and you quite frightened me. Now I feel that you are your old self again."

He did not answer, and she concluded that he was not unnaturally offended at her behaviour.

By one of those curious tricks of mountain scenery, the place they had left an hour before suddenly reappeared far below them. The Khan was hidden under the green dome, but in the open there still stood three figures, and through the pure air rose up a faint cry of defiance or farewell.

Mr. Lucas stopped irresolutely, and let the reins fall from his hand.

"Come, father dear," said Ethel gently.

He obeyed, and in another moment a spur of the hill hid the dangerous scene for ever.

II

It was breakfast time, but the gas was alight, owing to the fog. Mr. Lucas was in the middle of an account of a bad night he had spent. Ethel, who was to be married in a few weeks, had her arms on the table, listening.

"First the door bell rang, then you came back from the theatre. Then the dog started, and after the dog the cat. And at three in the morning a young hooligan passed by singing. Oh yes: then there was the water gurgling in the pipe above my head."

"I think that was only the bath water running away," said Ethel, looking rather worn.

"Well, there's nothing I dislike more than running water. It's perfectly impossible to sleep in the house. I shall give it up. I shall give notice next quarter. I shall tell the landlord plainly, 'The reason I am giving up the house is this: it is perfectly impossible to sleep in it.' If he says—says—well, what has he got to say?"

"Some more toast, father?"

"Thank you, my dear." He took it, and there was an interval of peace.

But he soon recommenced. "I'm not going to submit to the practising next door as tamely as they think. I wrote and told them so—didn't I?"

"Yes," said Ethel, who had taken care that the letter should not reach. "I have seen the governess, and she has promised to arrange it differently. And Aunt Julia hates noise. It will sure to be all right."

Her aunt, being the only unattached member of the family, was coming to keep house for her father when she left him. The reference was not a happy one, and Mr. Lucas commenced a series of half articulate sighs, which was only stopped by the arrival of the post.

"Oh, what a parcel!" cried Ethel. "For me! What can it be! Greek stamps. This is most exciting!"

It proved to be some asphodel bulbs, sent by Mrs. Forman from Athens for planting in the conservatory.

"Doesn't it bring it all back! You remember the asphodels, father. And all wrapped up in Greek newspaper. I wonder if I can read them still. I used to be able to, you know."

She rattled on, hoping to conceal the laughter of the children next door—a favourite source of querulousness at breakfast time.

"Listen to me! 'A rural disaster.' Oh, I've hit on something sad. But never mind. 'Last Tuesday at Plataniste, in the province of Messenia, a shocking tragedy occured. A large tree'—aren't I getting on well?—'blew down in the night and'—wait a minute—oh, dear!' crushed to death the five occupants of the little Khan there, who had apparently been sitting in the balcony. The bodies of Maria Rhomaides, the aged proprietress, and of her daughter, aged forty-six, were easily recognizable, whereas that of her grandson'—oh, the rest is really too horrid; I wish I had never tried it, and what's more I feel to have heard the name Plataniste before. We didn't stop there, did we, in the spring?"

"We had lunch," said Mr. Lucas, with a faint expression of trouble on his vacant face. "Perhaps it was where the dragonman bought the pig."

"Of course," said Ethel in a nervous voice. "Where the dragoman bought the little pig. How terrible!"

"Very terrible!" said her father, whose attention was wandering to the noisy children next door. Ethel suddenly started to her feet with genuine interest.

"Good gracious!" she exclaimed. "This is an old paper. It happened not lately but in April—the night of Tuesday the eighteenth—and we—we must have been there in the afternoon."

"So we were," said Mr. Lucas. She put her hand to her heart, scarcely able to speak.

"Father, dear father, I must say it: you wanted to stop there. All those people, those poor half-savage people, tried to keep you and they're dead. The whole place, it says, is in ruins, and even the stream had changed its course. Father, dear, if it had not been for me, and if Arthur had not helped me, you must have been killed."

Mr. Lucas waved his hand irritably. "It is not a bit of good speaking to the governess, I shall write to the landlord and say, 'The reason I am giving up the house is this: the dog barks, the children next door are intolerable, and I cannot stand the noise of running water.'"

Ethel did not check his babbling. She was aghast at the narrowness of the escape, and for a long time kept silence. At last she said: "Such a marvellous deliverance does make one believe in Providence."

Mr. Lucas, who was still composing his letter to the landlord, did not reply.

SUGGESTIONS FOR WRITING AND DISCUSSION

1. The setting is of paramount importance in this story. Discuss how Forster uses the shrine. Examine how the contrast between Greece and England is portrayed.
2. What transformations does the shrine bring about?
3. Reread this story. How does the second part change the way we read the first part?
4. When Ethel learns how narrowly her father has escaped death, she says, "Such a marvellous deliverance does make one believe in Providence." Write a two- to three-page paper arguing that Mr. Lucas has *not* had a "marvellous deliverance." Is "providence" at work in this story?
5. This story has numerous allusions to the story of Oedipus. According to Greek legend, the oracle prophesied that Oedipus would kill his father and marry his mother. In his efforts to escape the prophecy, Oedipus unwittingly fulfilled it. When he discovered what he had done, he blinded himself. In Sophocles' play *Oedipus at Colonus,* the blind Oedipus is guided by his loyal daughter, Antigonê. When he reaches Colonus, Oedipus sits down in a sacred grove and refuses to leave until he is carried off by the gods. What does "The Road from Colonus" suggest about sight and insight? What is the significance of the allusions to Oedipus? Write a four- to six-page essay.

Joseph Conrad (British, b. Poland, 1857–1924)

The Lagoon

The white man, leaning with both arms over the roof of the little house in the stern of the boat, said to the steersman—

"We will pass the night in Arsat's clearing. It is late."

The Malay only grunted, and went on looking fixedly at the river. The white man rested his chin on his crossed arms and gazed at the wake of the boat. At the end of the straight avenue of forests cut by the intense glitter of the river, the sun appeared unclouded and dazzling, poised low over the water that shone smoothly like a band of metal. The forests, sombre and dull, stood motionless and silent on each side of the broad stream. At the foot of big, towering trees trunkless nipa palms rose from the mud of the bank, in bunches of leaves enormous and heavy, that hung unstirring over the brown swirl of eddies. In the stillness of the air every tree, every leaf, every bough, every tendril of creeper and every petal of minute blossoms seemed to have been bewitched into an immobility perfect and final. Nothing moved on the river but the eight paddles that rose flashing regularly, dipped together with a single splash; while the steersman swept right and left with a periodic and sudden flourish of his blade describing a glinting semicircle above his head. The churned-up water frothed alongside with a confused murmur. And the white man's canoe, advancing upstream in the short-lived disturbance of its own making, seemed to enter the portals of a land from which the very memory of motion had forever departed.

The white man, turning his back upon the setting sun, looked along the empty and broad expanse of the sea-reach. For the last three miles of its course the wandering, hesitating river, as if enticed irresistably by the freedom of an open horizon, flows straight into the sea, flows straight to the east—to the east that harbours both light and darkness. Astern of the boat the repeated call of some bird, a cry discordant and feeble, skipped along over the smooth water and lost itself, before it could reach the other shore, in the breathless silence of the world.

The steersman dug his paddle into the stream, and held hard with stiffened arms, his body thrown forward. The water gurgled aloud; and suddenly the long straight reach seemed to pivot on its centre, the forests swung in a semicircle, and the slanting beams of sunset touched the broadside of the canoe with a fiery glow, throwing the slender and distorted shadows of its crew upon the streaked glitter of the river. The white man turned to look ahead. The course of the boat had been altered at right-angles to the stream, and the carved dragon-head of its prow was pointing now at a gap in the fringing bushes of the bank. It glided through, brushing the overhanging twigs, and disappeared from the river like some slim and amphibious creature leaving the water for its lair in the forests.

The narrow creek was like a ditch: tortuous, fabulously deep; filled with gloom under the thin strip of pure and shining blue of the heaven. Immense trees soared up, invisible behind the festooned draperies of creepers. Here and there, near the glistening blackness of the water, a twisted root of some tall tree showed amongst the tracery of small ferns, black and dull, writhing and motionless, like an arrested snake. The short words of the paddlers reverberated loudly between the thick and somber walls of vegetation. Darkness oozed out from between the trees, through the tangled maze of the creepers, from behind the great fantastic and unstirring leaves; the darkness, mysterious and invincible; the darkness scented and poisonous of impenetrable forests.

The men poled in the shoaling water. The creek broadened, opening out into a wide sweep of a stagnant lagoon. The forests receded from the marshy bank, leaving a level strip of bright green, reedy grass to frame the reflected blueness of the sky, A fleecy pink cloud drifted high above, trailing the delicate colouring of its image under the floating leaves and the silvery blossoms of the lotus. A little house, perched on high piles, appeared black in the distance. Near it, two tall nibong palms, that seemed to have come out of the forests in the background, leaned slightly over the ragged roof, with a suggestion of sad tenderness and care in the droop of their leafy and soaring heads.

The steersman, pointing with his paddle, said, ``Arsat is there. I see his canoe fast between the piles.''

The polers ran along the sides of the boat glancing over their shoulders at the end of the day's journey. They would have preferred to spend the night somewhere else than on this lagoon of weird aspect and ghostly reputation. Moreover, they disliked Arsat, first as a stranger, and also because he who repairs a ruined house, and dwells in it, proclaims that he is not afraid to live amongst the spirits that haunt the places abandoned by mankind. Such a man can disturb the course of fate by glances or words; while his familiar ghosts are not easy to propitiate by casual wayfarers upon whom they long to wreak the malice of their human master. White men care not for such things, being unbelievers and in league with the Father of Evil, who leads them unharmed through the invisible dangers of this world. To the warnings of the righteous they oppose an offensive pretence of disbelief. What is there to be done?

So they thought, throwing their weight on the end of their long poles. The big canoe glided on swiftly, noiselessly, and smoothly, towards Arsat's clearing, till, in a great rattling of poles thrown down, and the loud murmurs of "Allah be praised!" it came with a gentle knock against the crooked piles below the house.

The boatmen with uplifted faces shouted discordantly, "Arsat! O Arsat!" Nobody came. The white man began to climb the rude ladder giving access to the bamboo platform before the house. The juragan of the boat said sulkily, "We will cook in the sampan, and sleep on the water."

"Pass my blankets and the basket," said the white man, curtly.

He knelt on the edge of the platform to receive the bundle. Then the boat shoved off, and the white man, standing up, confronted Arsat, who had come out through the low door of his hut. He was a man young, powerful, with broad chest and muscular arms. He had nothing on but his sarong. His head was bare. His big, soft eyes stared eagerly at the white man, but his voice and demeanour were composed as he asked, without any words of greeting—

"Have you medicine, Tuan?"

"No," said the visitor in a startled tone. "No. Why? Is there sickness in the house?"

"Enter and see," replied Arsat, in the same calm manner, and turning short round, passed again through the small doorway. The white man, dropping his bundles, followed.

In the dim light of the dwelling he made out on a couch of bamboos a woman stretched on her back under a broad sheet of red cotton cloth. She lay still, as if dead; but her big eyes, wide open, glittered in the gloom, staring upwards at the slender rafters, motionless and unseeing. She was in a high fever, and evidently unconscious. Her cheeks were sunk slightly, her lips were partly open, and on the young face there was the ominous and fixed expression—the absorbed, contemplating expression of the unconscious who are going to die. The two men stood looking down at her in silence.

"Has she been long ill?" asked the traveller.

"I have not slept for five nights," answered the Malay, in a deliberate tone. "At first she heard voices calling her from the water and struggled against me who held her. But since the sun of to-day rose she hears nothing—she hears not me. She sees nothing. She sees not me—me!"

He remained silent for a minute, then asked softly—

"Tuan, will she die?"

"I fear so," said the white man, sorrowfully. He had known Arsat years ago, in a far country in times of trouble and danger, when no friendship is to be despised. And since his Malay friend had come unexpectedly to dwell in the hut on the lagoon with a strange woman, he had slept many times there, in his journeys up and down the river. He liked the man who knew how to keep faith in council and how to fight without fear by the side of his white friend. He liked him—not so much perhaps as a man likes his favourite dog—but still he liked him well enough to help and ask no questions, to think sometimes vaguely and hazily in the midst of his own pursuits, about the lonely man and the long-haired woman with audacious face and triumphant eyes, who lived together hidden by the forests—alone and feared.

The white man came out of the hut in time to see the enormous conflagration of sunset put out by the swift and stealthy shadows that, rising like a black and impalpable vapour above the tree-tops, spread over the heaven, extinguishing the crimson glow of floating clouds and the red brilliance of departing daylight. In a few moments all the stars came out above the intense blackness of the earth and the great lagoon gleaming suddenly with reflected lights resembled an oval patch of night sky flung down into the hopeless and abysmal night of the wilderness. The white man had some supper out of the basket, then collecting a few sticks that lay about the platform, made up a small fire, not for warmth, but for the sake of the smoke, which would keep off the mosquitos. He wrapped himself in the blankets and sat with his back against the reed wall of the house, smoking thoughtfully.

Arsat came through the doorway with noiseless steps and squatted down by the fire. The white man moved his outstretched legs a little.

"She breathes," said Arsat in a low voice, anticipating the expected question. "She breathes and burns as if with a great fire. She speaks not; she hears not—and burns!"

He paused for a moment, then asked in a quiet, incurious tone—

"Tuan . . . will she die?"

The white man moved his shoulders uneasily and muttered in a hesitating manner—

"If such is her fate."

"No, Tuan," said Arsat, calmly. "If such is my fate. I hear, I see, I wait. I remember . . . Tuan, do you remember the old days? Do you remember my brother?"

"Yes," said the white man. The Malay rose suddenly and went in. The other, sitting still outside, could hear the voice in the hut. Arsat said: "Hear me! Speak!" His words were succeeded by a complete silence. "O

Diamelen!'' he cried, suddenly. After that cry there was a deep sigh. Arsat came out and sank down again in his old place.

They sat in silence before the fire. There was no sound within the house, there was no sound near them; but far away on the lagoon they could hear the voices of the boatmen ringing fitful and distinct on the calm water. The fire in the bows of the sampan shone faintly in the distance with a hazy red glow. Then it died out. The voices ceased. The land and the water slept invisible, unstirring and mute. It was as though there had been nothing left in the world but the glitter of stars streaming, ceaseless and vain, through the black stillness of the night.

The white man gazed straight before him into the darkness with wide-open eyes. The fear and fascination, the inspiration and the wonder of death—of death near, unavoidable, and unseen, soothed the unrest of his race and stirred the most indistinct, the most intimate of his thoughts. The ever-ready suspicion of evil, the gnawing suspicion that lurks in our hearts, flowed out into the stillness round him—into the stillness profound and dumb, and made it appear untrustworthy and infamous, like the placid and impenetrable mask of an unjustifiable violence. In that fleeting and powerful disturbance of his being the earth enfolded in the starlight peace became a shadowy country of inhuman strife, a battle-field of phantoms terrible and charming, august or ignoble, struggling ardently for the possession of our helpless hearts. An unquiet and mysterious country of inextinguishable desires and fears.

A plaintive murmur rose in the night; a murmur saddening and startling, as if the great solitudes of surrounding woods had tried to whisper into his ear the wisdom of their immense and lofty indifference. Sounds hesitating and vague floated in the air round him, shaped themselves slowly into words; and at last flowed on gently in a murmuring stream of soft and monotonous sentences. He stirred like a man waking up and changed his position slightly. Arsat, motionless and shadowy, sitting with bowed head under the stars, was speaking in a low and dreamy tone—

`` . . . for where can we lay down the heaviness of our trouble but in a friend's heart? A man must speak of war and of love. You, Tuan, know what war is, and you have seen me in time of danger seek death as other men seek life! A writing may be lost; a lie may be written; but what the eye has seen is truth and remains in the mind!''

"I remember," said the white man, quietly. Arsat went on with mournful composure—

"Therefore I shall speak to you of love. Speak in the night. Speak before both night and love are gone—and the eye of day looks upon my sorrow and my shame; upon my blackened face; upon my burnt-up heart."

A sigh, short and faint, marked an almost imperceptible pause, and then his words flowed on, without a stir, without a gesture.

"After the time of trouble and war was over and you went away from my country in the pursuit of your desires, which we, men of the islands, cannot understand, I and my brother became again, as we had been before, the sword bearers of the Ruler. You know we were men of family, belonging to a ruling race, and more fit than any to carry on our right shoulder the emblem of power. And in the time of prosperity Si Dendring showed us favour, as we, in time of sorrow, had showed to him the faithfulness of our courage. It was a time of peace. A time of deer-hunts and cock-fights; of idle talks and foolish squabbles between men whose bellies are full and weapons are rusty. But the sower watched the young rice-shoots grow up without fear, and the traders came and went, departed lean and returned fat into the river of peace. They brought news, too. Brought lies and truth mixed together, so that no man knew when to rejoice and when to be sorry. We heard from them about you also. They had seen you here and had seen you there. And I was glad to hear, for I remembered the stirring times, and I always remembered you, Tuan, till the time came when my eyes could see nothing in the past, because they had looked upon the one who is dying there—in the house.''

He stopped to exclaim in an intense whisper, "O Mara bahia! O Calamity!" then went on speaking a little louder:

''There's no worse enemy and no better friend than a brother, Tuan, for one brother knows another, and in perfect knowledge is strength for good or evil. I loved my brother. I went to him and told him that I could see nothing but one face, hear nothing but one voice. He told me: 'Open your heart so that she can see what is in it—and wait. Patience is wisdom. Inchi Midah may die or our Ruler may throw off his fear of a woman!' . . . I waited! . . . You remember the lady with the veiled face, Tuan, and the fear of our Ruler before her cunning and temper. And if she wanted her servant, what could I do? But I fed the hunger of my heart on short glances and stealthy words. I loitered on the path to the bath-houses in the daytime, and when the sun had fallen behind the forest I crept along the jasmine hedges of the women's courtyard. Unseeing, we spoke to one another through the scent of flowers, through the veil of leaves, through the blades of long grass that stood still before our lips; so great was our prudence, so faint was the murmur of our great longing. The time passed swiftly . . . and there were whispers amongst women—and our enemies watched—my brother was gloomy, and I began to think of killing and of a fierce death. . . . We are of a people who take what they want—like you whites. There is a time when a man should forget loyalty and respect. Might and authority are given to rulers, but to all men is given love and strength and courage. My brother said, 'You shall take her from their midst. We are two who are like one.' And I answered, 'Let it be soon, for I find no warmth in sunlight that does not shine upon her.' Our time came when the Ruler and all the great people went to the mouth of the river to fish by torchlight. There were hundreds of boats, and on the white sand, between the water and the forests, swellings of leaves were built for the households of the Rajahs. The smoke of cooking-fires was like a blue mist of the evening, and many voices rang in it joyfully. While they were making the boats ready to beat up the fish, my brother came to me and said, 'To-night!' I looked to my weapons, and when the time came our canoe took its place in the circle of boats carrying the torches. The lights blazed on the water, but behind the boats there was darkness. When the shouting began and the excitement made them like mad we dropped out. The water swallowed our fire, and we floated back to the shore that was dark with only here and there the glimmer of embers. We could hear the talk of slave-girls amongst the sheds. Then we found a place deserted and silent. We waited there. She came. She came running along the shore, rapid and leaving no trace, like a leaf driven by the wind into the sea. My brother said gloomily, 'Go and take her; carry her into our boat.' I lifted her in my arms. She panted. Her heart was beating against my breast. I said, 'I take you from those people. You came to the cry of my heart, but my arms take you into my boat against the will of the great!' 'It is right,' said my brother. 'We are men who take what we want and can hold it against many. We should have taken her in daylight.' I said, 'Let us be off'; for since she was in my boat I began to think of our Ruler's many men. 'Yes. Let us be off,' said my brother. 'We are cast out and this boat is our country now—and the sea is our refuge.' He lingered with his foot on the shore, and I entreated him to hasten, for I remembered the strokes of her against my breast and thought that two men cannot withstand a hundred. We left, paddling downstream close to the bank; and as we passed by the creek where they were fishing, the great shouting had ceased, but the murmur of voices was loud like the humming of insects flying at noonday. The boats floated, clustered together, in the red light of torches, under a black roof of smoke; and men talked of their sport. Men that boasted, and praised, and jeered—men that would have been our friends in the morning, but on that night were already our enemies. We paddled swiftly past. We had no more friends in the country of our birth. She sat in the middle of the canoe with covered face; silent as she is now; unseeing as she is now—and I had no regret at what I was leaving because I could hear her breathing close to me—as I can hear her now.''

He paused, listened with his ear turned to the doorway, then shook his head and went on:

''My brother wanted to shout the cry of challenge—one cry only—to let the people know we were freeborn robbers who trusted our arms and the great sea. And again I begged him in the name of our love to be silent. Could I not hear her breathing close to me? I knew the pursuit would come quick enough. My brother loved me. He dipped his paddle without a splash. He only said, 'There is a half a man in you now—the other half is in that woman. I can wait. When you are a whole man again, you will come back with me here to shout defiance. We are sons of the same mother.' I made no answer. All my strength and all my spirit were in my hands that held the paddle—for I longed to be with her in a safe place beyond the reach of men's anger and of women's spite. My love was so great, that I thought it could guide me to a country where death was unknown, if I could only escape from Inchi Midah's fury and from our Ruler's sword. We paddled with haste, breathing through our teeth. The blades bit deep into the smooth water. We passed out of the river; we flew in clear channels amongst the shallows. We skirted the black coast; we skirted the sand beaches where the sea speaks in whispers to the land; and the gleam of white sand flashed back past our boat, so swiftly she ran upon the water. We spoke not. Only once I said, 'Sleep, Diamelen, for soon you may want all your strength.' I heard the sweetness of her voice, but I never turned my head. The sun rose and still we went on. Water fell from my face like rain from a cloud. We flew in the light and heat. I never looked back, but I knew that my brother's eyes, behind me, were looking steadily ahead, for the boat went as straight as a bushman's dart, when it leaves the end of the sumpitan. There was no better paddler, no better steersman than my brother. Many times, together, we had won races in that canoe. But we never had put out our strength as we did then—then, when for the last time we paddled together! There was no braver or stronger man in our country than my brother. I could not spare the strength to turn my head and look at him, but every moment I heard the hiss of his breath getting louder behind me. Still he did not speak. The sun was high. The heat clung to my back like a flame of fire. My ribs were ready to burst, but I could no longer get enough air into my chest. And then I felt I must cry out with my last breath, 'Let us rest!' . . . 'Good!' he answered; and his voice was firm. He was strong. He was brave. He knew not fear and no fatigue . . . My brother!''

A murmur powerful and gentle, a murmur vast and faint; the murmur of trembling leaves of stirring boughs, ran through the tangled depths of the forests, ran over the starry smoothness of the lagoon, and the water between the piles lapped the slimy timber once with a sudden splash. A breath of warm air touched the two men's faces and passed on with a mournful sound—a breath loud and short like an uneasy sigh of the dreaming earth.

Arsat went on in an even, low voice.

''We ran our canoe on the white beach of a little bay close to a long tongue of land that seemed to bar our road; a long wooded cape going far into the sea. My brother knew that place. Beyond the cape a river has its entrance, and through the jungle of that land there is a narrow path. We made a fire and cooked rice. Then we lay down to sleep on the soft sand in the shade of our canoe, while she watched. No sooner had I closed my eyes than I heard her cry of alarm. We leaped up. The sun was halfway down the sky already, and coming in sight in the opening of the bay we saw a prau manned by many paddlers. We knew it at once; it was one of our Rajah's praus. They were watching the shore, and saw us. They beat the gong, and turned the head of the prau into the bay. I felt my heart become weak within my breast. Diamelen sat on the sand and covered her face. There was no escape by sea. My brother laughed. He had the gun you had given him, Tuan, before you went away, but there was only a handful of powder. He spoke to me quickly: 'Run with her along the path. I shall keep them back, for they have no firearms, and landing in the face of a man with a gun is certain death for some. Run with her. On the other side of that wood there is a fisherman's house—and a canoe. When I have fired all the shots I will follow. I am a great runner, and before they can come up we shall be gone. I will hold out as long as I can, for she is but a woman—that can neither run nor fight, but she has your heart in her weak hands.' He dropped behind the canoe. The prau was coming. She and I ran, and as we rushed along the path I heard shots. My brother fired—once—twice—and the booming of the gong ceased. There was silence behind us. That neck of land is narrow. Before I heard my brother fire the third shot I saw the shelving shore, and I saw the water again; the mouth of a broad river. We crossed a grassy glade. We ran down to the water. I saw a low hut above the black mud, and a small canoe hauled up. I heard another shot behind me. I thought, 'That is his last charge.' We rushed down to the canoe; a man came running from the hut, but I leaped on him, and we rolled together in the mud. Then I got up, and he lay still at my feet. I don't know whether I had killed him or not. I and Diamelen pushed the canoe afloat. I heard yells behind me, and I saw my brother run across the glade. Many men were bounding after him, I took her in my arms and threw her into the boat, then leaped in myself. When I looked back I saw that my brother had fallen. He fell and was up again, but the men were closing round him. He shouted, 'I am coming!' The men were close to him. I looked. Many men. Then I looked at her. Tuan, I pushed the canoe! I pushed it into deep water. She was kneeling forward looking at me, and I said, 'Take your paddle,' while I struck the water with mine. Tuan, I heard him cry. I heard him cry my name twice; and I heard voices shouting, 'Kill! Strike!' I never turned back. I heard him calling my name again with a great shriek, as when life is going out together with the voice—and I never turned my head. My own name! . . . My brother! Three times he called—but I was not afraid of life. Was she not there in that canoe? And could I not with her find a country where death is forgotten—where death is unknown?''

The white man sat up. Arsat rose and stood, an indistinct and silent figure above the dying embers of the fire. Over the lagoon a mist drifting and low had crept, erasing slowly the glittering images of the stars. And now a great expanse of white vapour covered the land: it flowed cold and gray in the darkness, eddied in noiseless whirls round the tree-trunks and about the platform of the house, which seemed to float upon a restless and impalpable illusion of a sea. Only far away the tops of the trees stood outlined on the twinkle of heaven, like a sombre and forbidding shore— a coast deceptive, pitiless and black.

Arsat's voice vibrated loudly in the profound peace.

''I had her there! I had her! To get her I would have faced all mankind. But I had her—and———''

His words went out ringing into the empty distances. He paused, and seemed to listen to them dying away very far—beyond help and beyond recall. Then he said quietly—

"Tuan, I loved my brother."

A breath of wind made him shiver. High above his head, high above the silent sea of mist the drooping leaves of the palms rattled together with a mournful and expiring sound. The white man stretched his legs. His chin rested on his chest, and he murmured sadly without lifting his head—

"We all love our brothers."

Arsat burst out with an intense whispering violence—

"What did I care who died? I wanted peace in my own heart."

He seemed to hear a stir in the house—listened—then stepped in noiselessly. The white man stood up. A breeze was coming in fitful puffs. The stars shone paler as if they had retreated into the frozen depths of immense space. After a chill gust of wind there were a few seconds of perfect calm and absolute silence. Then from behind the black and wavy line of the forests a column of golden light shot up into the heavens and spread over the semicircle of the eastern horizon. The sun had risen. The mist lifted, broke into drifting patches, vanished into thin flying wreaths; and the unveiled lagoon lay, polished and black, in the heavy shadows at the foot of the wall of trees. A white eagle rose over it with a slanting and ponderous flight, reached the clear sunshine and appeared dazzlingly brilliant for a moment, then soaring higher, became a dark and motionless speck before it vanished into the blue as if it had left the earth forever. The white man, standing gazing upwards before the doorway, heard in the hut a confused and broken murmur of distracted words ending with a loud groan. Suddenly Arsat stumbled out with outstretched hands, shivered, and stood still for some time with fixed eyes. Then he said—

"She burns no more."

Before his face the sun showed its edge above the tree-tops rising steadily. The breeze freshened; a great brilliance burst upon the lagoon, sparkled on the rippling water. The forests came out of the clear shadows of the morning, became distinct, as if they had rushed nearer—to stop short in a great stir of leaves, of nodding boughs, of swaying branches. In the merciless sunshine the whisper of unconscious life grew louder, speaking in an incomprehensible voice round the dumb darkness of that human sorrow. Arsat's eyes wandered slowly, then stared at the rising sun.

"I can see nothing," he said half aloud to himself.

"There is nothing," said the white man, moving to the edge of the platform and waving his hand to his boat. A shout came faintly over the lagoon and the sampan began to glide towards the abode of the friend of ghosts.

"If you want to come with me, I will wait all the morning," said the white man, looking away upon the water.

"No, Tuan," said Arsat, softly. "I shall not eat or sleep in this house, but I must first see my road. Now I can see nothing—see nothing! There is no light and no peace in the world; but there is death—death for many. We are sons of the same mother—and I left him in the midst of enemies; but I am going back now."

He drew a long breath and went on in a dreamy tone:

"In a little while I shall see clear enough to strike—to strike. But she has died, and . . . now . . . darkness."

He flung his arms wide open, let them fall along his body, then stood still with unmoved face and stony eyes, staring at the sun. The white man got down into his canoe. The polers ran smartly along the sides of the boat, looking over their shoulders at the beginning of a weary journey. High in the stern, his head muffled up in white rags, the juragan sat moody, letting his paddle trail in the water. The white man, leaning with both arms over the grass roof of the little cabin, looked back at the shining ripple of the boat's wake. Before the sampan passed out of the lagoon into the creek he lifted his eyes. Arsat had not moved. He stood lonely in the searching sunshine; and he looked beyond the great light of a cloudless day into the darkness of a world of illusions.

SUGGESTIONS FOR WRITING AND DISCUSSION

1. At the beginning of the story the white man is described as liking Arsat "not so much perhaps as a man likes his favourite dog" but well enough. Do his feelings change after the night he spends with Arsat?
2. What do Arsat and his brother have in common? How do they differ?
3. In what sense could the story be described as "romantic"?
4. Why does Arsat say, "There's no worse enemy and no better friend than a brother"? Has Arsat betrayed his brother? Argue in a three- to four-page essay.
5. In a two- to three-page essay, explicate one or several of the many paragraphs that describe the setting and discuss how these descriptions create a mood or govern the action or foreshadow events.

Ursula K. Le Guin (American, 1929–   )

Sur

A Summary Report of the Yelcho Expedition to the Antarctic, 1909–10

Although I have no intention of publishing this report, I think it would be nice if a grandchild of mine, or somebody's grandchild, happened to find it some day; so I shall keep it in the leather trunk in the attic, along with Rosita's christening dress and Juanito's silver rattle and my wedding shoes and finneskos.

The first requisite for mounting an expedition—money—is normally

The Ross Sea

King Edward VII Land

South Victoria Land

Mts. Erebus *Terror

Ross Island
McMurdo Sound

Orca Bay

South South America

Quixote

Garcilaso

The Great Ice Barrier

Miranda / Ercilla

Concolorcorvo

THE GATEWAY

Mt. Bolívar's Big Nose

Nightin-gale glacier

Mt. Whose Toe?

The Pampas

N W E S

90°

The Map in the Attic

the hardest to come by. I grieve that even in a report destined for a trunk in the attic of a house in a very quiet suburb of Lima I dare not write the name of the generous benefactor, the great soul without whose unstint-ing liberality the Yelcho Expedition would never have been more than the idlest excursion into daydream. That our equipment was the best and most modern—that our provisions were plentiful and fine—that a ship of the Chilean government, with her brave officers and gallant crew, was twice sent halfway round the world for our convenience: all this is due to that benefactor whose name, alas!, I must not say, but whose happiest debtor I shall be till death.

When I was little more than a child, my imagination was caught by a newspaper account of the voyage of the *Belgica,* which, sailing south from Tierra del Fuego, was beset by ice in the Billingshausen Sea and drifted a whole year with the floe, the men aboard her suffering a great deal from want of food and from the terror of the unending winter darkness, I read and reread that account, and later followed with excitement the reports of the rescue of Dr. Nordenskjöld from the South Shetland Islands by the dashing Captain Irizar of the *Uruguay,* and the adventures of the *Scotia* in the Weddell Sea. But all these expolits were to me but forerunners of the British National Antarctic Expedition of 1901–04, in the *Discovery,* and the wonderful account of that expedition by Captain Scott. This book, which I ordered from London and reread a thousand times, filled me with longing to see with my own eyes that strange continent, last Thule of the South, which lies on our maps and globes like a white cloud, a void, fringed here and there with scraps of coastline, dubious capes, supposititious islands, headlands that may or may not be there: Antarctica. And the desire was as pure as the polar snows: to go, to see—no more, no less. I deeply respect the scientific accomplishments of Captain Scott's expedition, and have read with passionate interest the findings of physicists, meterologists, biologists, etc.; but having had no training in any science, nor any opportunity for such training, my ignorance obliged me to forgo any thought of adding to the body of scientific knowledge concerning Antarctica, and the same is true for all the members of my expedition. It seems a pity; but there was nothing we could do about it. Our goal was limited to observation and exploration. We hoped to go a little farther, perhaps, and see a little more; if not, simply to go and to see. A simple ambition. I think, and essentially a modest one.

Yet it would have remained less than an ambition, no more than a longing, but for the support and encouragement of my dear cousin and friend Juana————. (I use no surnames, lest this report fall into strangers' hands at last, and embarrassment or unpleasant notoriety thus be brought upon unsuspecting husbands, sons, etc.) I had lent Juana my copy of *The Voyage of the ''Discovery,''* and it was she who, as we strolled beneath our parasols across the Plaza de Armas after Mass one Sunday in 1908, said, ''Well, if Captain Scott can do it, why can't we?''

It was Juana who proposed that we write Carlota————in Valparaíso. Through Carlota we met our benefactor, and so obtained our money, our ship, and even the plausible pretext of going on retreat in a Bolivian convent, which some of us were forced to employ (while the rest of us said we were going to Paris for the winter season). And it was my Juana who in the darkest moments remained resolute, unshaken in her determination to achieve our goal.

And there were dark moments, especially in the spring of 1909— times when I did not see how the Expedition would ever become more than a quarter ton of pemmican gone to waste and a lifelong regret. It was so very hard to gather our expeditionary force together! So few of those we asked even knew what we were talking about—so many thought we were mad, or wicked, or both! And of those few who shared our folly, still fewer were able, when it came to the point, to leave their daily duties and commit themselves to a voyage of at least six months, attended with not inconsiderable uncertainty and danger. An ailing parent; an anxious husband beset by business cares; a child at home with only ignorant or incompetent servants to look after it: these are not responsibilities lightly to be set aside. And those who wished to evade such claims were not the companions we wanted in hard work, risk, and privation.

But since success crowned our efforts, why dwell on the setbacks and delays, or the wretched contrivances and downright lies that we all had to employ? I look back with regret only to those friends who wished to come with us but could not, by any contrivance, get free—those we had to leave behind to a life without danger, without uncertainity, without hope.

On the seventeenth of August, 1909, in Punta Arenas, Chile, all the members of the Expedition met for the first time: Juana and I, the two Peruvians; from Argentina, Zoe, Berta, and Teresa; and our Chileans, Carlota and her friends Eva, Pepita, and Dolores. At the last moment I had received word that María's husband, in Quito, was ill and she must stay to nurse him, so we were nine, not ten. Indeed, we had resigned ourselves to being but eight when, just as night fell, the indomitable Zoe arrived in a tiny pirogue manned by Indians, her yacht having sprung a leak just as it entered the Straits of Magellan.

That night before we sailed we began to get to know one another, and we agreed, as we enjoyed our abominable supper in the abominable seaport inn of Punta Arenas, that if a situation arose of such urgent danger that one voice must be obeyed without present question, the unenviable honor of speaking with that voice should fall first upon myself; if I were incapacitated, upon Carlota: if she, then upon Berta. We three were then toasted as ``Supreme Inca,'' ``La Araucana.'' and ``The Third Mate,'' amid a lot of laughter and cheering. As it came out, to my very great pleasure and relief, my qualities as a ``leader'' were never tested: the nine of us worked things out amongst us from beginning to end without any orders being given by anybody, and only two or three times with recourse to a vote by voice or show of hands. To be sure, we argued a good deal. But then, we had time to argue. And one way or another the arguments always ended up in a decision, upon which action could be taken. Usually at least one person grumbled about the decision, sometimes bitterly. But what is life without grumbling and the occasional opportunity to say ``I told you so''? How could one bear housework, or looking after babies, let alone the rigors of sledge-hauling in Antarctica, without grumbling? Officers—as we came to understand aboard the *Yelcho*—are forbidden to grumble: but we nine were, and are, by birth and upbringing, unequivocally and irrevocably, all crew.

Though our shortest course to the southern continent, and that originally urged upon us by the captain of our good ship, was of the South Shetlands and the Bellingshausen Sea. or else by the South Orkneys into the

Weddell Sea, we planned to sail west to the Ross Sea, which Captain Scott had explored and described, and from which the brave Ernest Shackleton had returned only the previous autumn. More was known about this region than any other portion of the coast of Antarctica, and though that more was not much, yet it served as some insurance of the safety of the ship, which we felt we had no right to imperil. Captain Pardo had fully agreed with us after studying the charts and our planned itinerary; and so it was westward that we took our course out of the Straits next morning.

Our journey half round the globe was attended by fortune. The little *Yelcho* steamed cheerily along through gale and gleam, climbing up and down those seas of the Southern Ocean that run unbroken round the world. Juana, who had fought bulls and the far more dangerous cows on her family's *estancia,* called the ship *la vaca valiente,* because she always returned to the charge. Once we got over being seasick, we all enjoyed the sea voyage, though oppressed at times by the kindly but officious protectiveness of the captain and his officers, who felt that we were only ''safe'' when huddled up in the three tiny cabins that they had chivalrously vacated for our use.

We saw our first iceberg much farther south than we had looked for it, and saluted it with Veuve Clicquot at dinner. The next day we entered the ice pack, the belt of floes and bergs broken loose from the land ice and winter-frozen seas of Antarctica which drifts northward in the spring. Fortune still smiled on us: our little steamer, incapable, with her unreinforced metal hull, of forcing a way into the ice, picked her way from lane to lane without hesitation, and on the third day we were through the pack, in which ships have sometimes struggled for weeks and been obliged to turn back at last. Ahead of us now lay the dark-gray waters of the Ross Sea, and beyond that, on the horizon, the remote glimmer, the cloud-reflected whiteness of the Great Ice Barrier.

Entering the Ross Sea a little east of Longitude West 160°, we came in sight of the Barrier at the place where Captain Scott's party, finding a bight in the vast wall of ice, had gone ashore and sent up their hydrogen-gas balloon for reconnaissance and photography. The towering face of the Barrier, its sheer cliffs and azure and violet waterworn caves, all were as described, but the location had changed: instead of a narrow bight, there was a considerable bay, full of the beautiful and terrific orca whales playing and spouting in the sunshine of that brilliant southern spring.

Evidently masses of ice many acres in extent had broken away from the Barrier (which—at least for most of its vast extent—does not rest on land but floats on water) since the *Discovery's* passage in 1902. This put our plan to set up camp on the Barrier itself in a new light; and while we were discussing alternatives, we asked Captain Pardo to take the ship west along the Barrier face toward Ross Island and McMurdo Sound. As the sea was clear of ice and quite calm, he was happy to do so and, when we sighted the smoke plume of Mt. Erebus, to share in our celebration— another half case of Veuve Clicquot.

The *Yelcho* anchored in Arrival Bay, and we went ashore in the ship's boat. I cannot describe my emotions when I set foot on the earth, on that earth, the barren, cold gravel at the foot of the the long volcanic slope. I felt elation, impatience, gratitude, awe, familiarity. I felt that I was home at last. Eight Adélie penguins immediately came to greet us with many exclamations of interest not unmixed with disapproval. "Where on earth have you been? What took you so long? The Hut is around this way. Please come this way. Mind the rocks." They insisted on our going to visit Hut Point, where the large structure built by Captain Scott's party stood, looking just as in the photographs and drawings that illustrate his book. The area about it, however, was disgusting—a kind of graveyard of seal skins, seal bones, penguin bones, and rubbish, presided over by the mad, screaming skua gulls. Our escorts waddled past the slaughterhouse in all tranquillity, and one showed me personally to the door, though it would not go in.

The interior of the hut was less offensive but very dreary. Boxes of supplies had been stacked up into a kind of room within the room: it did not look as I had imagined it when the *Discovery* party put on their melodramas and ministrel shows in the long winter night. (Much later, we learned that Sir Ernest had rearranged it a good deal when he was there just a year before us.) It was dirty, and had about it a mean disorder. A pound tin of tea was standing open. Empty meat tins lay about; biscuits were spilled on the floor; a lot of dog turds were underfoot—frozen, of course, but not a great deal improved by that. No doubt the last occupants had had to leave in a hurry, perhaps even in a blizzard. All the same, they could have closed the tea tin. But housekeeping, the art of the infinite, is no game for amateurs.

Teresa proposed that we use the hut as our camp. Zoe counterproposed that we set fire to it. We finally shut the door and left it as we had found it. The penguins appeared to approve, and cheered us all the way to the boat.

McMurdo Sound was free of ice, and Captain Pardo now proposed to take us off Ross Island and across to Victoria Land, where we might camp at the foot of the Western Mountains, on dry and solid earth. But those mountains, with their storm-darkened peaks and hanging cirques and glaciers, looked as awful as Captain Scott had found them on his western journey, and none of us felt much inclined to seek shelter among them.

Aboard the ship that night we decided to go back and set up our base as we had originally planned, on the Barrier itself. For all available reports indicated that the clear way south was across the level Barrier surface until one could ascend one of the confluent glaciers to the high plateau that appears to form the whole interior of the continent. Captain Pardo argued strongly against this plan, asking what would become of us if the Barrier "calved"—if our particular acre of ice broke away and started to drift northward. "Well," said Zoe, "then you won't have to come so far to meet us." But he was so persuasive on this theme that he persuaded himself into leaving one of the *Yelcho's* boats with us when we camped, as a means of escape. We found it useful for fishing, later on.

My first steps on Antarctic soil, my only visit to Ross Island, had not been pleasure unalloyed. I thought of the words of the English poet.

> Though every prospect pleases.
> And only Man is vile.

But then, the backside of heroism is often rather sad; women and servants know that. They know also that the heroism may be no less real for that. But achievement is smaller than men think. What is large is the sky, the earth, the sea, the soul. I looked back as the ship sailed east again that evening. We were well into September now, with eight hours or more of daylight. The spring sunset lingered on the twelve-thousand-foot peak of Erebus and shone rosy-gold on her long plume of steam. The steam from our own small funnel faded blue on the twilit water as we crept along under the towering pale wall of ice.

On our return to "Orca Bay"—Sir Ernest, we learned years later, had named it the Bay of Whales—we found a sheltered nook where the Barrier edge was low enough to provide fairly easy access from the ship. The *Yelcho* put out her ice anchor, and the next long, hard days were spent in unloading our supplies and setting up our camp on the ice, a half kilometre in from the edge: a task in which the *Yelcho's* crew lent us invaluable aid and interminable advice. We took all the aid gratefully, and most of the advice with salt.

The weather so far had been extraordinarily mild for spring in this latitude; the temperature had not yet gone below −20°F, and there was only one blizzard while we were setting up camp. But Captain Scott had spoken feelingly of the bitter south winds on the Barrier, and we had planned accordingly. Exposed as our camp was to every wind, we built no rigid structures above-ground. We set up tents to shelter in while we dug out a series of cubicles in the ice itself, lined them with hay insulation and pine boarding, and roofed them with canvas over bamboo poles, covered with snow for weight and insulation. The big central room was instantly named Buenos Aires by our Argentineans, to whom the center, wherever one is, is always Buenos Aires. The heating and cooking stove was in Buenos Aires. The storage tunnels and the privy (called Punta Arenas) got some back heat from the stove. The sleeping cubicles opened off Buenos Aires, and were very small, mere tubes into which one crawled feet first; they were lined deeply with hay and soon warmed by one's body warmth. The sailors called them coffins and wormholes, and looked with horror on our burrows in the ice. But our little warren or prairie-dog village served us well, permitting us as much warmth and privacy as one could reasonably expect under the circumstances. If the *Yelcho* was unable to get through the ice in February and we had to spend the winter in Antarctica, we certainly could do so, though on very limited rations.

For this coming summer, our base—Sudamérica del Sur, South South America, but we generally called it the Base — was intended merely as a place to sleep, to store our provisions, and to give shelter from blizzards.

To Berta and Eva, however, it was more than that. They were its chief architect-designers, its most ingenious builder-excavators, and its most diligent and contented occupants, forever inventing an improvement in ventilation, or learning how to make skylights, or revealing to us a new addition to our suite of rooms, dug in the living ice. It was thanks to them that our stores were stowed so handily, that our stove drew and heated so efficiently, and that Buenos Aires, where nine people cooked, ate, worked, conversed, argued, grumbled, painted, played the guitar and banjo, and kept the Expedition's library of books and maps, was a marvel of comfort and convenience. We lived there in real amity; and if you simply had to be alone for a while, you crawled into your sleeping hole head first.

Berta went a little farther. When she had done all she could to make South South America livable, she dug out one more cell just under the ice surface, leaving a nearly transparent sheet of ice like a greenhouse roof; and there, alone, she worked at sculptures. They were beautiful forms, some like a blending of the reclining human figure with the subtle curves and volumes of the Weddell seal, others like the fantastic shapes of ice cornices and ice caves. Perhaps they are there still, under the snow, in the bubble in the Great Barrier. There where she made them, they might last as long as stone. But she could not bring them north. That is the penalty for carving in water.

Captain Pardo was reluctant to leave us, but his orders did not permit him to hang about the Ross Sea indefinitely, and so at last, with many earnest injunctions to us to stay put—make no journeys—take no risks—beware of frostbite—don't use edge tools—look out for cracks in the ice—and a heartfelt promise to return to Orca Bay on February 20th, or as near that date as wind and ice would permit, the good man bade us farewell, and his crew shouted us a great goodbye cheer as they weighed anchor. That evening, in the long orange twilight of October, we saw the topmast of the *Yelcho* go down the north horizon, over the edge of the world, leaving us to ice, and silence, and the Pole.

That night we began to plan the Southern Journey.

The ensuing month passed in short practice trips and depot-laying. The life we had led at home, though in its own way strenuous, had not fitted any of us for the kind of strain met with in sledge-hauling at ten or twenty degrees below freezing. We all needed as much working out as possible before we dared undertake a long haul.

My longest exploratory trip, made with Dolores and Carlota, was southwest toward Mt. Markham, and it was a nightmare—blizzards and pressure ice all the way out, crevasses and no view of the mountains when we got there, and white weather and sastrugi all the way back. The trip was useful, however, in that we could begin to estimate our capacities; and also in that we had started out with a very heavy load of provisions, which we depoted at a hundred and a hundred and thirty miles south-southwest of Base. Thereafter other parties pushed on farther, till we had a line of snow cairns and depots right down to Latitude 83° 43', where Juana and Zoe, on an exploring trip, had found a kind of stone gateway opening on a great glacier leading south. We established these depots to avoid, if possible, the hunger that had bedevilled Captain Scott's Southern Party, and the consequent misery and weakness. And we also established to our own satisfaction—intense satisfaction—that we were sledge-haulers at least as good as Captain Scott's husky dogs. Of course we could not have expected to pull as much or as fast as his men. That we did so was because we were favored by much better weather than Captain Scott's party ever met on the Barrier; and also the quantity and quality of our food made a very considerable difference. I am sure that the fifteen percent of dried fruits in our pemmican helped prevent scurvy; and the potatoes, frozen and dried according to an ancient Andean Indian method, were very nourishing yet very light and compact—perfect sledding rations. In any case, it was with considerable confidence in our capacities that we made ready at last for the Southern Journey.

The Southern Party consisted of two sledge teams: Juana, Dolores, and myself; Carlota, Pepita, and Zoe. The support team of Berta, Eva, and Teresa set out before us with a heavy load of supplies, going right up onto the glacier to prospect routes and leave depots of supplies for our return journey. We followed five days behind them, and met them returning between Depot Ercilla and Depot Miranda. That "night"—of course, there was no real darkness—we were all nine together in the heart of the level plain of ice. It was November 15th, Dolores's birthday. We celebrated by putting eight ounces of pisco in the hot chocolate, and became very merry. We sang. It is strange now to remember how thin our voices sounded in that great silence. It was overcast, white weather, without shadows and without visible horizon or any feature to break the level; there was nothing to see at all. We had come to that white place on the map, that void, and there we flew and sang like sparrows.

After sleep and a good breakfast the Base Party continued north and the Southern Party sledged on. The sky cleared presently. High up, thin clouds passed over very rapidly from southwest to northeast, but down on the Barrier it was calm and just cold enough, five or ten degrees below freezing, to give a firm surface for hauling.

On the level ice we never pulled less than eleven miles (seventeen kilometres) a day, and generally fifteen or sixteen miles (twenty-five kilometres). (Our instruments, being British-made, were calibrated in feet, miles, degrees Fahrenheit, etc., but we often converted miles to kilometres, because the larger numbers sounded more encouraging.) At the time we left South America, we knew only that Mr. Ernest Shackleton had mounted another expedition to the Antarctic in 1907, had tried to attain the Pole but failed and had returned to England in June of the current year, 1909. No coherent report of his explorations had yet reached South America when we left; we did not know what route he had gone, or how far he had got. But we were not altogether taken by surprise when, far across the featureless white plain, tiny beneath the mountain peaks and the strange silent flight of the rainbow-fringed cloud wisps, we saw a fluttering dot of black. We turned west from our course to visit it: a snow heap nearly buried by the winter's storms—a flag on a bamboo pole, a mere shred of threadbare cloth, an empty oilcan—and a few footprints standing some inches above the ice. In some conditions of weather the snow compressed under one's weight remains when the surrounding soft snow melts or is scoured away by the wind; and so these reversed footprints had been left standing all these months, like rows of cobbler's lasts—a queer sight.

We met no other such traces on our way. In general I believe our course was somewhat east of Mr. Shackleton's. Juana, our surveyor, had trained herself well and was faithful and methodical in her sightings and readings, but our equipment was minimal—a theodolite on tripod legs, a sextant with artifical horizon, two compasses, and chronometres. We had only the wheel meter on the sledge to give distance actually travelled.

In any case, it was the day after passing Mr. Shackleton's waymark that I first saw clearly the great glacier among the mountains to the southwest, which was to give us a pathway from the sea level of the Barrier up to the altiplano, ten thousand feet above. The approach was magnificent: a gateway formed by immense vertical domes and pillars of rock. Zoe and Juana had called the vast ice river that flowed through that gateway the Florence Nightingale Glacier, wishing to honor the British, who had been the inspiration and guide of our Expedition: that very brave and very peculiar lady seemed to represent so much that is best, and strangest, in the island race. On maps, of course, this glacier bears the name Mr. Shackleton gave it: the Beardmore.

The ascent of the Nightingale was not easy. The way was open at first, and well marked by our support party, but after some days we came among terrible crevasses, a maze of hidden cracks, from a foot to thirty feet wide and from thirty to a thousand feet deep. Step by step we went, and step by step, and the way always upward now. We were fifteen days on the glacier. At first the weather was hot—up to 20°F—and the hot nights without darkness were wretchedly uncomfortable in our small tents. And all of us suffered more or less from snow blindness just at the time when we wanted clear eyesight to pick our way among the ridges and crevasses of the tortured ice, and to see the wonders about and before us. For at every day's advance more great, nameless peaks came into view in the west and southwest, summit beyond summit, range beyond range, stark rock and snow in the unending noon.

We gave names to these peaks, not very seriously, since we did not expect our discoveries to come to the attention of geographers. Zoe had a gift for naming, and it is thanks to her that certain sketch maps in various suburban South American attics bear such curious features as "Bolivar's Big Nose," "I am General Rosas," "The Cloudmaker," "Whose Toe?," and "Throne of Our Lady of the Southern Cross." And when at last we got up onto the altiplano, the great interior plateau, it was Zoe who called it the pampa, and maintained that we walked there among vast herds of invisible cattle, transparent cattle pastured on the spindrift snow, their gauchos the restless, merciless winds. We were by then all a little crazy with exhaustion and the great altitude—twelve thousand feet—and the cold and the wind blowing and the luminous circles and crosses surrounding the suns, for often there were three or four suns in the sky, up there.

That is not a place where people have any business to be. We should have turned back; but since we had worked so hard to get there, it seemed that we should go on, at least for a while.

A blizzard came, with very low temperatures, so we had to stay in the tents, in our sleeping bags, for thirty hours—a rest we all needed, though it was warmth we needed most, and there was no warmth on that terrible plain anywhere at all but in our veins. We huddled close together all that time. The ice we lay on is two miles thick.

It cleared suddenly and became, for the plateau, good weather: twelve below zero and the wind not very strong. We three crawled out of our tent and met the others crawling out of theirs. Carlota told us then that her group wished to turn back. Pepita had been feeling very ill: even after the rest during the blizzard, her temperature would not rise above 94°. Carlota was having trouble breathing. Zoe was perfectly fit, but much preferred staying with her friends and lending them a hand in difficulties to pushing on toward the Pole. So we put the four ounces of pisco that we had been keeping for Christmas into the breakfast cocoa, and dug out our tents, and loaded our sledges, and parted there in the white daylight on the bitter plain.

Our sledge was fairly light by now. We pulled on to the south. Juana calculated our position daily. On the twenty-second of December, 1909, we reached the South Pole. The weather was, as always, very cruel. Nothing of any kind marked the dreary whiteness. We discussed leaving some kind of mark or monument, a snow cairn, a tent pole and flag; but there seemed no particular reason to do so. Anything we could do, anything we were, was insignificant, in that awful place. We put up the tent for shelter for an hour and made a cup of tea, and then struck "90° Camp."

Dolores, standing patient as ever in her sledging harness, looked at the snow; it was so hard frozen that it showed no trace of our footprints coming, and she said, "Which way?"

"North," said Juana.

It was a joke, because at that particular place there is no other direction. But we did not laugh. Our lips were cracked with frostbite and hurt too much to let us laugh. So we started back, and the wind at our backs pushed us along, and dulled the knife edges of the waves of frozen snow.

All that week the blizzard wind pursued us like a pack of mad dogs. I cannot describe it. I wished we had not gone to the Pole. I think I wish it even now. But I was glad even then that we had left no sign there, for some man longing to be first might come some day, and find it, and know then what a fool he had been, and break his heart.

We talked, when we could talk, of catching up to Carlota's party, since they might be going slower than we. In fact they used their tents as a sail to catch the following wind and had got far ahead of us. But in many places they had built snow cairns or left some sign for us; once, Zoe had written on the lee side of a ten-foot sastruga, just as children write on the sand of the beach at Miraflores, ``This Way Out!'' The wind blowing over the frozen ridge had left the words perfectly distinct.

In the very hour that we began to descend the glacier, the weather turned warmer, and the mad dogs were left to howl forever tethered to the Pole. The distance that had taken us fifteen days going up we covered in only eight days going down. But the good weather that had aided us descending the Nightingale became a curse down on the Barrier ice, where we had looked forward to a kind of royal progress from depot to depot, eating our fill and taking our time for the last three hundred-odd miles. In a tight place on the glacier I lost my goggles—I was swinging from my harness at the time in a crevasse—and then Juana broke hers when we had to do some rock-climbing coming down to the Gateway. After two days in bright sunlight with only one pair of snow goggles to pass amongst us, we were all suffering badly from snow blindness. It became acutely painful to keep lookout for landmarks or depot flags, to take sightings, even to study the compass, which had to be laid down on the snow to steady the needle. At Concolorcorvo Depot, where there was a particularly good supply of food and fuel, we gave up, crawled into our sleeping bags with bandaged eyes, and slowly boiled alive like lobsters in the tent exposed to the relentless sun. The voices of Berta and Zoe were the sweetest sound I ever heard. A little concerned about us, they had skied south to meet us. They led us home to Base.

We recovered quite swiftly, but the altiplano left its mark. When she was very little Rosita asked if a dog ``had bitted Mama's toes.'' I told her yes— a great, white, mad dog named Blizzard! My Rosita and my Juanito heard many stories when they were little, about that fearful dog and how it howled, and the transparent cattle of the invisible gauchos, and a river of ice eight thousand feet high called Nightingale, and how Cousin Juana drank a cup of tea standing on the bottom of the world under seven suns, and other fairy tales.

We were in for one severe shock when we reached Base at last. Teresa was pregnant. I must admit that my first response to the poor girl's big belly and sheepish look was anger—rage—fury. That one of us should have concealed anything, and such a thing, from the others! But Teresa had done nothing of the sort. Only those who had concealed from her what she most needed to know were to blame. Brought up by servants, with four years schooling in a convent, and married at sixteen, the poor girl was still so ignorant at twenty years of age that she had thought it was "the cold weather" that made her miss her periods. Even this was not entirely stupid, for all of us on the Southern Journey had seen our periods change or stop altogether as we experienced increasing cold, hunger, and fatigue. Teresa's appetite had begun to draw general attention; and then she had begun, as she said pathetically, "to get fat." The others were worried at the thought of all the sledge-hauling she had done, but she flourished, and the only problem was her positively insatiable appetite. As well as could be determined from her shy references to her last night on the hacienda with her husband, the baby was due at just about the same time as the *Yelcho,* February 20th. But we had not been back from the Southern Journey two weeks when, on February 14th, she went into labor.

Several of us had borne children and had helped with deliveries, and anyhow most of what needs to be done is fairly self-evident; but a first labor can be long and trying, and we were all anxious, while Teresa was frightened out of her wits. She kept calling for her José till she was as hoarse as a skua. Zoe lost all patience at last and said, "By God, Teresa, if you say 'José!' once more, I hope you have a penguin!" But what she had, after twenty long hours, was a pretty little red-faced girl.

Many were the suggestions for that child's name from her eight proud midwife aunts: Polita, Penguina, McMurdo, Victoria . . . But Teresa announced, after she had had a good sleep and a large serving of pemmican, "I shall name her Rosa—Rosa del Sur," Rose of the South. That night we drank the last two bottles of Veuve Clicquot (having finished the pisco at 88° 60' South) in toasts to our little Rose.

On the nineteenth of February, a day early, my Juana came down into Buenos Aires in a hurry. "The ship," she said, "the ship has come." and she burst into tears — she who had never wept in all our weeks of pain and weariness on the long haul.

Of the return voyage there is nothing to tell. We came back safe.

In 1912 all the world learned that the brave Norwegian Amundsen had reached the South Pole; and then, much later, we heard the accounts of how Captain Scott and his men had come there after him but did not come home again.

Just this year, Juana and I wrote to the captain of the *Yelcho,* for the newspapers have been full of the story of his gallant dash to rescue Sir Ernest Shackleton's men from Elephant Island, and we wished to congratulate him, and once more to thank him. Never one word has he breathed of our secret. He is a man of honor, Luis Pardo.

I add this last note in 1929. Over the years we have lost touch with one another. It is very difficult for women to meet, when they live as far apart as we do. Since Juana died, I have seen none of my old sledgemates, though sometimes we write. Our little Rosa del Sur died of the scarlet fever when she was five years old. Teresa had many other children. Carlota took the veil in Santiago ten years ago. We are old women now, with old husbands, and grown children, and granchildren who might some day like to read about the Expedition. Even if they are rather ashamed of having such a crazy grandmother, they may enjoy sharing in the secret. But they must not let Mr. Amundsen know! He would be terribly embarrassed and disappointed. There is no need for him or anyone else outside the family to know. We left no footprints, even.

SUGGESTIONS FOR WRITING AND DISCUSSION

1. Le Guin has said that imagination is necessary to the complete human being, that it must constantly be provoked. How does this belief in imagination manifest itself in "Sur"?
2. How did the women convince the captain to take them on the expedition?
3. How would you define what the word *freedom* means in this story?
4. Do you think this story is essentially feminist or antifeminist? Is there an argument to be made that it is both? Argue in a two- to three-page paper.
5. There is frequent mention of the lack of footprints. Why?
6. In a four- to six-page paper describe what you think each of the women did when she got home.

Poetry

John Keats (British, 1795–1821)

On First Looking into Chapman's Homer

Much have I traveled in the realms of gold,
  And many goodly states and kingdoms seen;
  Round many western islands have I been
Which bards in fealty to Apollo hold.
Oft of one wide expanse had I been told
  That deep-browed Homer ruled as his demesne.
  Yet did I never breathe its pure serene
Till I heard Chapman speak out loud and bold.
Then felt I like some watcher of the skies
  When a new planet swims into his ken;
Or like stout Cortez when with eagle eyes
  He stared at the Pacific—and all his men
Looked at each other with a wild surmise—
  Silent, upon a peak in Darien.

SUGGESTIONS FOR WRITING AND DISCUSSION

1. One evening in October 1816, Keats, who could not read Greek, was introduced to George Chapman's translations of Homer. The following morning he wrote this sonnet. Chapman was an Elizabethan poet; is there any evidence in the poem that this fact influenced Keats's choice of language?
2. What is the main metaphor of the poem? What other metaphors can you find?
3. Does the speaker suggest that the experience described in the last four lines of the sonnet is superior to that described in the first four lines? What supports your answer?
4. Using your answers to the first three questions, write a two-page explication of the poem.

Wallace Stevens (American, 1879–1955)

The House Was Quiet and the World Was Calm

The house was quiet and the world was calm.
The reader became the book; and summer night

Was like the conscious being of the book.
The house was quiet and the world was calm.

The words were spoken as if there was no book,
Except that the reader leaned above the page,

Wanted to lean, wanted much most to be
The scholar to whom his book is true, to whom

The summer night is like a perfection of thought.
The house was quiet because it had to be.

The quiet was part of the meaning, part of the mind:
The access of perfection to the page.

And the world was calm. The truth in a calm world,
In which there is no other meaning, itself

Is calm, itself is summer and night, itself
Is the reader leaning late and reading there.

SUGGESTIONS FOR WRITING AND DISCUSSION

1. Describe the reader. What is his or her attitude to the book? Does it change
   in the course of the poem?
2. How do the elements of the poem, the reader-scholar, the book, the truth,
   the house, the world, the night, transform into one another and comment
   on each other by that transformation?
3. Stevens repeats a number of phrases. Look at these repetitions and discuss
   what effect they have.
4. Both this poem and Keats's "On First Looking into Chapman's Homer" give
   an account of reading. In a two- to three-page essay compare the two poems.

Allen Ginsberg (American, 1926–   )

A Supermarket in California

What thoughts I have of you tonight, Walt Whitman, for I walked down the
sidestreets under the trees with a headache self-conscious looking at the
full moon.

In my hungry fatigue, and shopping for images, I went into the neon
fruit supermarket, dreaming of your enumerations!

What peaches and what penumbras! Whole families shopping at
night! Aisles full of husbands! Wives in the avocados, babies in the tomatoes!—and you, Garcia Lorca, what were you doing down by the
watermelons?

I saw you, Walt Whitman, childless, lonely old grubber, poking
among the meats in the refrigerator and eyeing the grocery boys.

I heard you asking questions of each: Who killed the pork chops? What price bananas? Are you my Angel?

I wandered in and out of the brilliant stacks of cans following you, and followed in my imagination by the store detective.

We strode down the open corridors together in our solitary fancy tasting artichokes, possessing every frozen delicacy, and never passing the cashier.

Where are we going, Walt Whitman? The doors close in an hour. Which way does your beard point tonight?

(I touch your book and dream of our odyssey in the supermarket and feel absurd.)

Will we walk all night through solitary streets? The trees add shade to shade, lights out in the houses, we'll both be lonely.

Will we stroll dreaming of the lost America of love past blue automobiles in driveways, home to our silent cottage?

Ah, dear father, graybeard, lonely old courage-teacher, what America did you have when Charon quit poling his ferry and you got out on a smoking bank and stood watching the boat disappear on the black waters of Lethe?

SUGGESTIONS FOR WRITING AND DISCUSSION

1. What is the speaker's attitude to the other people in the supermarket? To the supermarket itself? Compare the use of a supermarket with that in John Updike's story "A & P."
2. How is the supermarket emblematic of the speaker's attitude toward America?
3. In a two-page essay describe the relationship between the speaker and Walt Whitman. What does Whitman mean to the speaker?

W. H. Auden (British, 1907–1973)

Paysage Moralisé

Hearing of harvests rotting in the valleys,
Seeing at end of street the barren mountains,
Round corners coming suddenly on water,
Knowing them shipwrecked who were launched for islands,
We honour founders of these starving cities
Whose honour is the image of our sorrow,

Which cannot see its likeness in their sorrow
That brought them desperate to the brink of valleys;
Dreaming of evening walks through learned cities

They reined their violent horses on the mountains,
Those fields like ships to castaways on islands,
Visions of green to them who craved for water.

They built by rivers and at night the water
Running past windows comforted their sorrow;
Each in his little bed conceived of islands
Where every day was dancing in the valleys
And all the green trees blossomed on the mountains,
Where love was innocent, being far from cities.

But dawn came back and they were still in cities;
No marvellous creature rose up from the water;
There was still gold and silver in the mountains
But hunger was a more immediate sorrow,
Although to moping villages in valleys
Some waving pilgrims were describing islands . . .

'The gods,' they promised, 'visit us from islands,
Are stalking, head-up, lovely, through our cities;
Now is the time to leave your wretched valleys
And sail with them across the lime-green water,
Sitting at their white sides, forget your sorrow,
The shadow cast across your lives by mountains.'

So many, doubtful, perished in the mountains,
Climbing up crags to get a view of islands,
So many, fearful, took with them their sorrow
Which stayed them when they reached unhappy cities,
So many, careless, dived and drowned in water,
So many, wretched, would not leave their valleys.

It is our sorrow. Shall it melt? Then water
Would gush, flush, green these mountains and these valleys,
And we rebuild our cities, not dream of islands.

SUGGESTIONS FOR WRITING AND DISCUSSION

1. *Paysage Moralisé* means "moralized landscape." How does Auden "moralize"
   the landscape in the course of the poem?
2. The people who live in the valleys and mountains seem desperate to escape
   to the cities, but those who live in the cities are not satisfied either; they
   dream of islands. What do the islands represent or suggest?
3. This poem is a sestina. Write a paragraph about each of the six key words,
   discussing the different meanings each gains in the course of the poem.
4. In a two- to three-page essay discuss how this poem charts the spiritual fluc-
   tuations of a culture. What kind of culture? What kinds of changes occur?

Robert Frost (American, 1874–1963)

The Gift Outright

The land was ours before we were the land's.
She was our land more than a hundred years
Before we were her people. She was ours
In Massachusetts, in Virginia,
But we were England's, still colonials,
Possessing what we still were unpossessed by,
Possessed by what we now no more possessed.
Something we were withholding made us weak
Until we found it was ourselves
We were withholding from our land of living,
And forthwith found salvation in surrender.
Such as we were we gave ourselves outright
(The deed of gift was many deeds of war)
To the land vaguely realizing westward,
But still unstoried, artless, unenhanced,
Such as she was, such as she would become.

SUGGESTIONS FOR WRITING AND DISCUSSION

1. How is the land characterized? What kind of relationship exists between the land and the people? What stages does this relationship pass through?
2. Write a two- to three-page essay explicating the poem.
3. In "The Silken Tent" Frost compares a woman to a tent, and in "The Gift Outright" he calls the land "she." What feminine attributes do the two metaphors suggest?

May Swenson (American, 1919–   )

Bison Crossing Near Mt. Rushmore

There is our herd of cars stopped,
staring respectfully at the line of bison crossing.
One big-fronted bull nudges his cow into a run.
She and her calf are first to cross.
In swift dignity the dark-coated caravan sweeps through
the gap our cars leave in the two-way stall
on the road to The Presidents:
the polygamous bulls guarding their families from the
    rear,
the honey-brown calves trotting head-to-hip

by their mothers—who, lean and muscled as bulls,
have chin tassels and curved horns—
all leap the road like a river, and run,
the strong and somber remnant of western freedom
disappearing into the rough grass of the draw
around the point of the mountain.
The bison, orderly, disciplined by the prophet-faced,
heavy-headed fathers, threading the pass
of our awestruck stationwagons, airstreams and trailers,
if in dread of us give no sign,
go where their leaders twine them, over the prairie.
And we keep to our line,
staring, stirring, revving idling motors, moving
each behind the other, herdlike, where the highway
   leads.

SUGGESTIONS FOR WRITING AND DISCUSSION

1. What is the significance of the fact that this incident occurs on the way to Mt. Rushmore?
2. How does Swensen characterize the bison? Which words and phrases make her attitude to them especially clear?
3. In a two- to three-page essay discuss how Swensen compares and contrasts the motorists and the bison.

William Wordsworth (British, 1770–1850)

Composed upon Westminster Bridge, September 3, 1802

Earth has not anything to show more fair:
Dull would he be of soul who could pass by
A sight so touching in its majesty;
This City now doth, like a garment, wear
The beauty of the morning; silent, bare,
Ships, towers, domes, theaters, and temples lie
Open unto the fields, and to the sky;
All bright and glittering in the smokeless air.
Never did sun more beautifully steep
In his first splendor, valley, rock, or hill;
Ne'er saw I, never felt, a calm so deep!
The river glideth at his own sweet will:
Dear God! the very houses seem asleep;
And all that mighty heart is lying still.

SUGGESTIONS FOR WRITING AND DISCUSSION

1. This sonnet contains many examples of personification. List them. What effect does this personification have? Why do you think Wordsworth chose this technique?
2. The speaker says that the view is "touching in its majesty." In a two- to three-page essay show how the details of the poem bear out this description.
3. What does the last line mean?

William Butler Yeats (Irish, 1865–1939)

The Lake Isle of Innisfree

I will arise and go now, and go to Innisfree,
And a small cabin build there, of clay and wattles made:
Nine bean-rows will I have there, a hive for the honey-bee,
And live alone in the bee-loud glade.

And I shall have some peace there, for peace comes dropping slow,
Dropping from the veils of the morning to where the cricket sings;
There midnight's all a glimmer, and noon a purple glow,
And evening full of the linnet's wings.

I will arise and go now, for always night and day
I hear lake water lapping with low sounds by the shore;
While I stand on the roadway, or on the pavements gray,
I hear it in the deep heart's core.

SUGGESTIONS FOR WRITING AND DISCUSSION

1. Work out the rhyme scheme and then look for examples of alliteration, assonance, and consonance. How do these sounds reinforce the meaning of the poem?
2. Why does the poem end with hearing instead of seeing?
3. What is the mood of the speaker? Is he really about to depart for the lake? Support your answer in a one- to two-page essay.

Hart Crane (American, 1899–1932)

Repose of Rivers

The willows carried a slow sound,
A sarabande the wind mowed on the mead.
I could never remember
That seething, steady leveling of the marshes
Till age had brought me to the sea.

Flags, weeds. And remembrance of steep alcoves
Where cypresses shared the noon's
Tyranny; they drew me into hades almost.
And mammoth turtles climbing sulphur dreams
Yielded, while sun-silt rippled them
Asunder . . .

How much I would have bartered! the black gorge
And all the singular nestings in the hills
Where beavers learn stitch and tooth.
The pond I entered once and quickly fled—
I remember now its singing willow rim.

And finally, in that memory all things nurse;
After the city that I finally passed
With scalding unguents spread and smoking darts
The monsoon cut across the delta
At gulf gates . . . There, beyond the dykes

I heard wind flaking sapphire, like this summer,
And willows could not hold more steady sound.

SUGGESTIONS FOR WRITING AND DISCUSSION

1. There are three different landscapes in this poem: the landscape of the willows, the tropical dreamscape, the cityscape. What is the speaker's attitude toward each of these? What states of mind do each of these represent to the speaker? Discuss in a one- to two-page essay.
2. This poem is about a fall from a state of innocence and about remembering that innocence. Although the speaker is never explicit about his attitude to this fall, what do you think it is? What words and phrases support your answer?

Charlotte Mew (British, 1869–1928)

Moorland Night

My face is against the grass—the moorland grass is wet—
　　My eyes are shut against the grass, against my lips there are the little
　　　　　　　　blades,
　　　　Over my head the curlews call,
　　And now there is the night wind in my hair;
My heart is against the grass and the sweet earth,—it has gone still, at
　　　　　　　　last.
　　　　　It does not want to beat any more,
　　　　　　And why should it beat?

This is the end of the journey;
The Thing is found.

This is the end of all the roads—
Over the grass there is the night-dew
And the wind that drives up from the sea along the moorland road;
I hear a curlew start out from the heath.
And fly off, calling through the dusk,
The wild, long, rippling call.
The Thing is found and I am quiet with the earth.
Perhaps the earth will hold it, or the wind, or that bird's cry,
But it is not for long in any life I know. This cannot stay,
Not now, not yet, not in a dying world, with me, for very long.
I leave it here:
And one day the wet grass may give it back—

One day the quiet earth may give it back—
The calling birds may give it back as they go by—
To someone walking on the moor who starves for love and will not know
Who gave it to all these to give away;
Or, if I come and ask for it again,
Oh! then, to me.

SUGGESTIONS FOR WRITING AND DISCUSSION

1. How would you describe the speaker's mood in the first stanza? Does it change in the course of the second stanza?
2. Write a short description of the moor. What makes this place so important to the narrator?
3. The speaker never tells us what the Thing is. What do you think it is? Why can it not stay for very long? Why must she "leave it here"? In a one- to two-page essay analyze the effect of not naming the Thing. Why do you think Mew chooses to do this?

Dylan Thomas (Welsh, 1914–1953)

Fern Hill

Now as I was young and easy under the apple boughs
About the lilting house and happy as the grass was green,
The night above the dingle starry,
Time let me hail and climb
Golden in the heydays of his eyes,
And honored among wagons I was prince of the apple towns
And once below a time I lordly had the trees and leaves
Trail with daisies and barley
Down the rivers of the windfall light.

And as I was green and carefree, famous among the barns
About the happy yard and singing as the farm was home,
    In the sun that is young once only,
        Time let me play and be
    Golden in the mercy of his means,
And green and golden I was huntsman and herdsman, the calves
Sang to my horn, the foxes on the hills barked clear and cold,
        And the sabbath rang slowly
    In the pebbles of the holy streams.

All the sun long it was running, it was lovely, the hay
Fields high as the house, the tunes from the chimneys, it was air
    And playing, lovely and watery
        And fire green as grass.
    And nightly under the simple stars
As I rode to sleep the owls were bearing the farm away,
All the moon long I heard, blessed among stables, the night-jars
    Flying with the ricks, and the horses
        Flashing into the dark.

And then to awake, and the farm, like a wanderer white
With the dew, come back, the cock on his shoulder: it was all
    Shining, it was Adam and maiden,
        The sky gathered again
    And the sun grew round that very day.
So it must have been after the birth of the simple light
In the first, spinning place, the spellbound horses walking warm
    Out of the whinnying green stable
        On to the fields of praise.

And honored among foxes and pheasants by the gay house
Under the new made clouds and happy as the heart was long,
    In the sun born over and over,
        I ran my heedless ways,
    My wishes raced through the house high hay
And nothing I cared, at my sky blue trades, that time allows
In all his tuneful turning so few and such morning songs
    Before the children green and golden
        Follow him out of grace,

Nothing I cared, in the lamb white days, that time would take me
Up to the swallow thronged loft by the shadow of my hand,
    In the moon that is always rising,
        Nor that riding to sleep
    I should hear him fly with the high fields
And wake to the farm forever fled from the childless land.
Oh as I was young and easy in the mercy of his means,

> Time held me green and dying
> Though I sang in my chains like the sea.

SUGGESTIONS FOR WRITING AND DISCUSSION

1. This is an idealized remembrance of childhood. Write a two- to three-page essay in which, using details from the poem, you give an account of how the speaker spent a day.
2. How is time characterized? What is the speaker's attitude toward time? Does it change in the course of the poem?
3. What does the word *green* suggest in the first five stanzas of the poem? How does its meaning change in the sixth?
4. The speaker describes himself as "prince of the apple towns." What other words and phrases indicate that he felt in control of his world?
5. Write a two- to three-page essay comparing this poem with Philip Levine's "One for the Rose." What attitudes do the two speakers have toward the way in which they have spent their youth?

Philip Levine (American, 1929–   )

One for the Rose

Three weeks ago I went back
to the same street corner where
27 years before I took a bus for Akron,
Ohio, but now there was only a blank space
with a few concrete building blocks
scattered among the beer cans
and broken bottles and a view of
the blank backside of an abandoned hotel.
I wondered if Akron was still down there
hidden hundreds of miles south among
the small, shoddy trees of Ohio,
a town so ripe with the smell
of defeat that its citizens lied
about their age, their height, sex,
income, and previous condition
of anything. I spent all of a Saturday
there, disguised in a cashmere suit
stolen from a man twenty pounds
heavier than I, and I never unbuttoned
the jacket. I remember someone
married someone, but only the bride's
father and mother went out
on the linoleum dance floor and leaned

into each other like whipped school kids.
I drank whatever I could find and made
my solitary way back to the terminal
and dozed among the drunks and widows
toward dawn and the first thing north.
What was I doing in Akron, Ohio
waiting for a bus that groaned slowly
between the sickened farms of 1951
and finally entered the smeared air
of hell on US 24 where the Rouge plant
destroys the horizon? I could have been
in Paris at the foot of Gertrude Stein,
I could have been drifting among
the reeds of a clear stream
like the little Moses, to be found
by a princess and named after a conglomerate
or a Jewish hero. Instead I was born
in the wrong year and in the wrong place,
and I made my way so slowly and badly
that I remember every single turn,
and each one smells like an overblown rose,
yellow, American, beautiful, and true.

SUGGESTIONS FOR WRITING AND DISCUSSION

1. The speaker says that Akron is a town "ripe with the smell of defeat." What details in his description support this statement? Which of these details could the speaker have known and which are things that he must have imagined? Write your answer in a one- to two-page essay.
2. In a paragraph describe what the speaker's journey to Akron symbolizes to him about his life.
3. Describe the speaker of the poem.
4. Explicate the last sentence of the poem. How is it linked with the description of Akron?

Drama

Eugene O'Neill (American, 1888–1953)

Ile

CHARACTERS

BEN, *the cabin boy*
THE STEWARD
CAPTAIN KEENEY
SLOCUM, *second mate*
MRS. KEENEY
JOE, *a harpooner*
Members of the crew of the steam whaler Atlantic Queen

Scene. CAPTAIN KEENEY'S *cabin on board the steam whaling ship* Atlantic Queen—*a small, square compartment about eight feet high with a sky-light in the center looking out on the poop deck. On the left (the stern of the ship) a long bench with rough cushions is built in against the wall. In front of the bench, a table. Over the bench, several curtained portholes.*

In the rear, left, a door leading to the CAPTAIN'S *sleeping quarters. To the right of the door a small organ, looking as if it were brand-new, is placed against the wall.*

On the right, to the rear, a marble-topped sideboard. On the side-board, a woman's sewing basket. Farther forward, a doorway leading to the companionway, and past the officers' quarters to the main deck.

In the center of the room, a stove. From the middle of the ceiling a hanging lamp is suspended. The walls of the cabin are painted white.

There is no rolling of the ship, and the light which comes through the skylight is sickly and faint, indicating one of those gray days of calm when ocean and sky are alike dead. The silence is unbroken except for the mea-sured tread of someone walking up and down on the poop deck overhead.

It is nearing two bells—one o'clock—in the afternoon of a day in the year 1895.

At the rise of the curtain there is a moment of intense silence. Then THE STEWARD *enters and commences to clear the table of the few dishes which still remain on it after the* CAPTAIN'S *dinner. He is an old, grizzled man dressed in dungaree pants, a sweater, and a woolen cap with earflaps. His manner is sullen and angry. He stops stacking up the plates and casts a quick glance upward at the skylight; then tiptoes over to the closed door in rear and listens with his ear pressed to the crack. What he hears makes his face darken and he mutters a furious curse. There is a noise from the doorway on the right and he darts back to the table.*

BEN *enters. He is an overgrown, gawky boy with a long, pinched face. He is dressed in sweater, fur cap, etc. His teeth are chattering with the cold and he hurries to the stove, where he stands for a moment shivering, blowing on his hands, slapping them against his sides, on the verge of crying.*

THE STEWARD *(in relieved tones—seeing who it is).* Oh, 'tis you, is it? What're ye shiverin' 'bout? Stay by the stove where ye belong and ye'll find no need of chatterin'.

BEN. It's c-c-cold. *(Trying to control his chattering teeth—derisively)* Who d'ye think it were—the Old Man?

THE STEWARD *(makes a threatening move—*BEN *shrinks away).* None o' your lip, young un, or I'll learn ye. *(More kindly)* Where was it ye've been all o' the time—the fo'c's'tle?

BEN. Yes

THE STEWARD. Let the Old Man see ye up for'ard monkeyshinin' with the hands and ye'll get a hidin' ye'll not forget in a hurry.

BEN. Aw, he don't see nothin'. *(A trace of awe in his tones—he glances upward)* He just walks up and down like he didn't notice nobody—and stares at the ice to the no'th'ard.

THE STEWARD *(the same tone of awe creeping into his voice).* He's always starin' at the ice. *(In a sudden rage, shaking his fist at the skylight)* Ice, ice, ice! Damn him and damn the ice! Holdin' us in for nigh on a year—nothin' to see but ice—stuck in it like a fly in molasses!

BEN. *(apprehensively).* Ssshh! He'll hear ye.

THE STEWARD *(raging).* Aye, damn him, and damn the Arctic seas, and damn this stinkin' whalin' ship of his, and damn me for a fool to ever ship on it! *(Subsiding as if realizing the uselessness of this outburst—shaking his head—slowly, with deep conviction)* He's a hard man—as hard a man as ever sailed the seas.

BEN *(solemnly).* Aye.

THE STEWARD. The two years we all signed up for are done this day. Blessed Christ! Two years 'o this dog's life, and no luck in the fishin', and the hands half starved with the food runnin' low, rotten as it is, and not a sign of him turnin' back for home! *(Bitterly)* Home! I begin to doubt if ever I'll set foot on land again. *(Excitedly)* What is it he thinks he's goin' to do? Keep us all up here after our time is worked out till the last man of us is starved to death or frozen? We've grub enough hardly to last out the voyage back if we started now. What are the men goin' to do 'bout it? Did ye hear any talk in the fo'c's'tle?

BEN *(going over to him—in a half-whisper).* They said if he don't put back south for home today they're goin' to mutiny.

THE STEWARD *(with grim satisfaction).* Mutiny? Aye, 'tis the only thing they can do; and serve him right after the manner he's treated them—'s if they weren't no better nor dogs.

BEN. The ice is all broke up to s'uth'ard. They's clear water 's far 's you can see. He ain't got no excuse for not turnin' back for home, the men says.

THE STEWARD *(bitterly).* He won't look nowheres but no'th'ard where they's only the ice to see. He don't want to see no clear water. All he thinks on is gittin' the ile—'s if it was our fault he ain't had good luck with the whales. *(Shaking his head)* I think the man's mighty nigh losin' his senses.

BEN *(awed).* D'you really think he's crazy?

THE STEWARD. Aye, it's the punishment o' God on him. Did ye ever hear of a man who wasn't crazy do the things he does? *(Pointing to the door in rear)* Who but a man that's mad would take his woman—and as sweet a woman as ever was—on a stinkin' whalin' ship to the Arctic seas to be locked in by the rotten ice for nigh on a year, and maybe lose her senses forever—for it's sure she'll never be the same again.

BEN *(sadly).* She useter be awful nice to me before—*(His eyes grow wide and frightened.)* she got—like she is.

THE STEWARD. Aye, she was good to all of us. 'Twould have been hell on board without her; for he's a hard man—a hard, hard man—a driver if there ever were one. *(With a grim laugh)* I hope he's satisfied now—drivin' her on till she's near lost her mind. And who could blame her? 'Tis a God's wonder we're not a ship full of crazed people—with the damned ice all the time, and the quiet so thick you're afraid to hear your own voice.

BEN *(with a frightened glance toward the door on right).* She don't never speak to me no more—jest looks at me 's if she didn't know me.

THE STEWARD. She don't know no one—but him. She talks to him—when she does talk—right enough.

BEN. She does nothin' all day long now but sit and sew—and then she cries to herself without makin' no noise. I've seen her.

THE STEWARD. Aye, I could hear her through the door a while back.

BEN *(tiptoes over to the door and listens).* She's cryin' now.

THE STEWARD *(furiously—shaking his fist).* God send his soul to hell for the devil he is! *(There is the noise of someone coming slowly down the companionway stairs.* THE STEWARD *hurries to his stacked-up dishes. He is so nervous from fright that he knocks off the top one, which falls and breaks on the floor. He stands aghast, trembling with dread.* BEN *is violently rubbing off the organ with a piece of cloth which he has snatched from his pocket.* CAPTAIN KEENEY *appears in the doorway on right and comes into the cabin, removing his fur cap as he does so. He is a man of about forty, around five-ten in height but looking much shorter on account of the enormous proportions of his shoulders and chest. His face is massive and deeply lined, with gray-blue eyes of a bleak hardness, and a tightly clenched, thin-lipped mouth. His thick hair is long and gray. He is dressed in a heavy blue jacket and blue pants stuffed into his sea-boots.*

He is followed into the cabin by the SECOND MATE, *a rangy six-footer with a lean weather-beaten face. The* MATE *is dressed about the same as the* CAPTAIN. *He is a man of thirty or so.)*

KEENEY *(comes toward* THE STEWARD—*with a stern look on his face.* THE STEW-ARD *is visibly frightened and the stack of dishes rattle in his trembling hands.* KEENEY *draws back his fist and* THE STEWARD *shrinks away. The fist is gradually lowered and* KEENEY *speaks slowly).* 'Twould be like hitting a worm. It is nigh on two bells, Mr. Steward, and this truck not cleared yet.

THE STEWARD *(stammering).* Y-y-yes, sir.

KEENEY. Instead of doin' your rightful work ye've been below here gossipin' old woman's talk with that boy. *(To* BEN *fiercely)* get out o' this, you! Clean up the chart room. *(*BEN *darts past the* MATE *to the open doorway)* Pick up that dish, Mr. Steward!

THE STEWARD *(doing so with difficulty).* Yes, sir.

KEENEY. The next dish you break, Mr. Steward, you take a bath in the Bering Sea at the end of a rope.

THE STEWARD *(trembling).* Yes, sir. *(He hurries out. The* SECOND MATE *walks slowly over to the* CAPTAIN.*)*

MATE. I warn't 'specially anxious the man at the wheel should catch what I wanted to say to you, sir. That's why I asked you to come below.

KEENEY *(impatiently).* Speak your say, Mr. Slocum.

MATE *(unconsciously lowering his voice).* I'm afeard there'll be trouble with the hands by the look o' things. They'll likely turn ugly, every blessed one o' them, if you don't put back. The two years they signed up for is up today.

KEENEY. And d'you think you're tellin' me somethin' new, Mr. Slocum? I've felt it in the air this long time past. D'you think I've not seen their ugly looks and the grudgin' way they worked? *(The door in rear is opened and* MRS. KEENEY *stands in the doorway. She is a slight, sweet-faced little woman primly dressed in black. Her eyes are red from weeping and her face drawn and pale. She takes in the cabin with a frightened glance and stands as if fixed to the spot by some nameless dread, clasping and unclasping her hands nervously. The two men turn and look at her.)*

KEENEY *(with rough tenderness).* Well, Annie?

MRS. KEENEY *(as if awakening from a dream).* David, I—*(She is silent. The* MATE *starts for the doorway.)*

KEENEY *(turning to him—sharply)*. Wait!

MATE. Yes, sir.

KEENEY. D'you want anything, Annie?

MRS. KEENEY *(after a pause, during which she seems to be endeavoring to collect her thoughts)*. I thought maybe—I'd go up on deck, David, to get a breath of fresh air. *(She stands humbly awaiting his permission. He and the* MATE *exchange a significant glance.)*

KEENEY. It's too cold, Annie. You'd best stay below today. There's nothing to look at on deck—but ice.

MRS. KEENEY *(monotonously)*. I know—ice, ice, ice! But there's nothing to see down here but these walls. *(She makes a gesture of loathing.)*

KEENEY. You can play the organ, Annie.

MRS. KEENEY *(dully)*. I hate the organ. It puts me in mind of home.

KEENEY *(a touch of resentment in his voice)*. I got it jest for you.

MRS. KEENEY *(dully)*. I know. *(She turns away from them and walks slowly to the bench on left. She lifts up one of the curtains and looks through a porthole; then utters an exclamation of joy.)* Ah, water! Clear water! As far as I can see! How good it looks after all these months of ice! *(She turns around to them, her face transfigured with joy.)* Ah, now I must go up on the deck and look at it, David.

KEENEY *(frowning)*. Best not today, Annie. Best wait for a day when the sun shines.

MRS. KEENEY *(desperately)*. But the sun never shines in this terrible place.

KEENEY *(a tone of command in his voice)*. Best not today, Annie.

MRS. KEENEY *(crumbling before this command—abjectly)*. Very well, David. *(She stands there staring straight before her as if in a daze. The two men look at her uneasily.)*

KEENEY *(sharply)*. Annie!

MRS. KEENEY *(dully)*. Yes, David.

KEENEY. Me and Mr. Slocum has business to talk about—ship's business.

MRS. KEENEY. Very well, David. *(She goes slowly out, rear, and leaves the door three-quarters shut behind her.)*

KEENEY. Best not have her on deck if they's goin' to be any trouble.

MATE. Yes, sir.

KEENEY. And trouble they's goin' to be. I feel it in my bones. *(Takes a revolver from the pocket of his coat and examines it)* Got your'n?

MATE. Yes, sir.

KEENEY. Not that we'll have to use 'em—not if I know their breed of dog— just to frighten 'em up a bit. *(Grimly)* I ain't never been forced to use one yit; and trouble I've had by land and by sea 's long as I kin remember, and will have till my dyin' day, I reckon.

MATE *(hesitatingly)*. Then you ain't goin'—to turn back?

KEENEY. Turn back! Mr. Slocum, did you ever hear o' me pointin' s'uth for home with only a measly four hundred barrel of ile in the hold?

MATE *(hastily)*. No sir—but the grub's gittin' low.

KEENEY. They's enough to last a long time yit, if they're careful with it; and they's plenty o' water.

MATE. They say it's not fit to eat—what's left; and the two years they signed on fur is up today. They might make trouble for you in the courts when we git home.

KEENEY. To hell with 'em! Let them make what law trouble they kin. I don't give a damn 'bout the money. I've got to git the ile! *(Glancing sharply at the* MATE*)* You ain't turnin' no damned sea-lawyer, be you, Mr. Slocum?

MATE *(flushing)*. Not by a hell of a sight, sir.

KEENEY. What do the fools want to go home fur now? Their share o' the four hundred barrel wouldn't keep 'em in chewin' terbacco.

MATE *(slowly)*. They wants to git back to their folks an' things, I s'pose.

KEENEY *(looking at him searchingly)*. 'N you want to turn back, too. *(The* MATE *looks down confusedly before his sharp gaze.)* Don't lie, Mr. Slocum. It's writ down plain in your eyes. *(With grim sarcasm)* I hope, Mr. Slocum, you ain't agoin' to jine the men agin me.

MATE *(indignantly)*. That ain't fair, sir, to say sich things.

KEENEY *(with satisfaction)*. I warn't much afeard o' that, Tom. You been with me nigh on ten year and I've learned ye whalin'. No man kin say I ain't a good master, if I be a hard one.

MATE. I warn't thinkin' of myself, sir—'bout turnin' home, I mean. *(Desperately)* But Mrs. Keeney, sir—seems like she ain't jest satisfied up here, ailin' like—what with the cold an' bad luck an' the ice an' all.

KEENEY *(his face clouding—rebukingly but not severely)*. That my business, Mr. Slocum. I'll thank you to steer a clear course o' that. *(A pause)* The ice'll break up soon to no'th'ard. I could see it startin' today. And when it goes and we git some sun Annie'll perk up. *(Another pause—then he bursts forth.)* It ain't the damned money what's keepin' me up in the Northern seas, Tom. But I can't go back to Homeport with a measly four hundred barrel if ile. I'd die fust. I ain't never come back home in all my days without a full ship. Ain't that truth?

MATE. Yes, sir; but this voyage you been ice-bound, an'—

KEENEY *(scornfully)*. And d'you s'pose any of 'em would believe that—any o' them skippers I've beaten voyage after voyage? Can't you hear 'em laughin' and sneerin'—Tibbots 'n' Harris 'n' Simms and the rest—and all o' Homeport makin' fun o' me? ''Dave Keeney what boasts he's the best whalin' skipper out o' Homeport comin' back with a measly four hundred barrel of ile?'' *(The thought of this drives him into a frenzy, and he smashes his fist down on the marble top of the sideboard.)* Hell! I got to git the ile, I tell you. How could I figger on this ice? It's never been so bad before in the thirty year I been acomin' here. And now it's breakin' up. In a couple o' days it'll be all gone. And they's whale here, plenty of 'em. I know they is and I ain't never gone wrong yit. I got to git the ile! I got to git it in spite of all hell, and by God, I ain't agoin' home till I do git it! *(There is the sound of subdued sobbing from the door in rear. The two men stand silent for a moment, listening. Then* KEENEY *goes over to the door and looks in. He hesitates for a moment as if he were going to enter— then closes the door softly.* JOE, *the harpooner, an enormous six-footer with a battered, ugly face, enters from right and stands waiting for the* CAPTAIN *to notice him.)*

KEENEY *(turning and seeing him).* Don't be standin' there like a gawk, Harpooner. Speak up!

JOE *(confusedly).* We want—the men, sir—they wants to send a depitation aft to have a word with you.

KEENEY *(furiously).* Tell 'em to go to—*(Checks himself and continues grimly.)* Tell 'em to come, I'll see 'em.

JOE. Aye, aye, sir. *(He goes out.)*

KEENEY *(with a grim smile).* Here it comes, the trouble you spoke of, Mr. Slocum, and we'll make short shrift of it. It's better to crush such things at the start than let them make headway.

MATE *(worriedly).* Shall I wake up the First and Fourth, sir? We might need their help.

KEENEY. No, let them sleep. I'm well able to handle this alone, Mr. Slocum. *(There is the shuffling of footsteps from outside and five of the crew crowd into the cabin, led by* JOE. *All are dressed alike—sweaters, sea-boots, etc. They glance uneasily at the* CAPTAIN, *twirling their fur caps in their hands.)*

KEENEY *(after a pause).* Well? Who's to speak for ye?

JOE *(stepping forward with an air of bravado).* I be.

KEENEY *(eyeing him up and down coldly).* So you be. Then speak your say and be quick about it.

JOE *(trying not to wilt before the* CAPTAIN'S *glance and avoiding his eyes).* The time we signed up for is done today.

KEENEY *(icily).* You're telling me nothin' I don't know.

JOE. You ain't pintin' fur home yit, far 's we kin see.

KEENEY. No, and I ain't agoin' to till this ship is full of ile.

JOE. You can't go no further no'th with the ice afore ye.

KEENEY. The ice is breaking up.

JOE *(after a slight pause during which the others mumble angrily to one another).* The grub we're gittin' now is rotten.

KEENEY. It's good enough fur ye. Better men than ye are have eaten worse. *(There is a chorus of angry exclamations from the crowd.)*

JOE *(encouraged by this support).* We ain't agoin' to work no more less you puts back for home.

KEENEY *(fiercely).* You ain't, ain't you?

JOE. No; and the law courts'll say we was right.

KEENEY. To hell with your law courts! We're at sea now and I'm the law on this ship *(Edging up toward the* HARPOONER*)* And every mother's son of you what don't obey orders goes in irons. *(There are more angry exclamations from the crew.* MRS. KEENEY *appears in the doorway in the rear and looks on with startled eyes. None of the men notice her.)*

JOE *(with bravado).* Then we're agoin' to mutiny and take the old hooker home ourselves. Ain't we, boys? *(As he turns his head to look at the others,* KEENEY*'s fist shoots out to the side of his jaw.* JOE *goes down in a heap and lies there.* MRS. KEENEY *gives a shriek and hides her face in her hands. The men pull out their sheath knives and start a rush, but stop when they find themselves confronted by the revolvers of* KEENEY *and the* MATE.*)*

KEENEY *(his eyes and voice snapping).* Hold still! *(The men stand huddled together in a sullen silence.* KEENEY*'s voice is full of mockery.)* You've found out it ain't safe to mutiny on this ship, ain't you? And now git for'ard where ye belong, and—(He gives* JOE*'s body a contemptuous kick.)* drag him with you. And remember the first man of ye I see shirkin' I'll shoot dead as sure as there's a sea under us, and you can tell the rest the same. Git for'ard now! Quick! *(The men leave in cowed silence, carrying* JOE *with them.* KEENEY *turns to the* MATE *with a short laugh and puts his revolver back in his pocket.)* Best get up on deck, Mr. Slocum, and see to it they don't try none of their skulkin' tricks. We'll have to keep an eye peeled from now on. I know 'em.

MATE. Yes, sir. *(He goes out, right.* KEENEY *hears his wife's hysterical weeping and turns around in surprise—then walks slowly to her side.)*

KEENEY *(putting an arm around her shoulder—with gruff tenderness).* There, there. Annie. Don't be afeard. It's all past and gone.

MRS. KEENEY *(shrinking away from him).* Oh, I can't bear it! I can't bear it any longer!

KEENEY *(gently).* Can't bear what, Annie?

MRS. KEENEY *(hysterically).* All this horrible brutality, and these brutes of men, and this terrible ship, and this prison cell of a room and the ice all around, and the silence. *(After this outburst she calms down and wipes her eyes with her handkerchief.)*

KEENEY *(after a pause during which he looks down at her with a puzzled frown).* Remember, I warn't hankerin' to have you come on this voyage, Annie.

MRS. KEENEY. I wanted to be with you, David, don't you see? I didn't want to wait back there in the house all alone as I've been doing these last six years since we were married—waiting, and watching, and fearing—with nothing to keep my mind occupied—not able to go back teaching school on account of being Dave Keeney's wife. I used to dream of sailing on the great, wide, glorious ocean. I wanted to be by your side in the danger and vigorous life of it all. I wanted to see you the hero they make you out to be in Homeport. And instead—*(Her voice gows tremulous.)* all I find is ice and cold—and brutality! *(Her voice breaks.)*

KEENEY. I warned you what it'd be, Annie. ``Whalin' ain't no ladies' tea-party,'' I says to you, and ``you better stay to home where you've got all your woman's comforts.'' *(Shaking his head)* But you was so set on it.

MRS. KEENEY *(wearily).* Oh, I know it isn't your fault, David. You see, I didn't believe you. I guess I was dreaming about the old Vikings in the story books and I thought you were one of them.

KEENEY *(protestingly).* I done my best to make it as cozy and as comfortable as could be. *(MRS. KEENEY looks around her in wild scorn.)* I even sent to the city for that organ for ye, thinkin' it might be soothin' to ye to be playin' it times when they was calms and things was dull like.

MRS. KEENEY *(wearily).* Yes, you were very kind, David. I know that. *(She goes to left and lifts the curtains from the porthole and looks out— then suddenly bursts forth:)* I won't stand it—I can't stand it—pent up by these walls like a prisoner. *(She runs over to him and throws her arms around him, weeping. He puts his arm protectingly over her shoulders.)* Take me away from here, David! If I don't get away from here, out of this terrible ship, I'll go mad! Take me home, David! I can't think any more. I feel as if the cold and the silence were crushing down on my brain. I'm afraid. Take me home!

KEENEY *(holds her at arm's length and looks at her face anxiously).* Best go to bed, Annie. You ain't yourself. You got fever. Your eyes look so strange like. I ain't never seen you look this way before.

MRS. KEENEY *(laughing hysterically).* It's the ice and the cold and silence— they'd make any one look strange.

KEENEY *(soothingly).* In a month or two, with good luck, three at the most, I'll have her filled with ile and then we'll give her everything she'll stand and pint for home.

Mrs. Keeney. But we can't wait for that—I can't wait. I want to get home. And the men won't wait. They want to get home. It's cruel, it's brutal for you to keep them. You must sail back. You've got no excuse. There's clear water to the south now. If you've a heart at all you've got to turn back.

Keeney *(harshly)*. I can't, Annie.

Mrs. Keeney. Why can't you?

Keeney. A woman couldn't rightly understand my reason.

Mrs. Keeney *(wildly)*. Because it's a stupid, stubborn reason. Oh, I heard you talking with the Second Mate. You're afraid the other captains will sneer at you because you didn't come back with a full ship. You want to live up to your silly reputation even if you do have to beat and starve men and drive me mad to do it.

Keeney *(his jaw set stubbornly)*. It ain't that, Annie. Them skippers would never dare sneer to my face. It ain't so much what any one'd say— but—*(He hesitates, struggling to express his meaning.)* you see— I've always done it—since my first voyage as skipper. I always come back—with a full ship—and—it don't seem right not to—somehow. I been always first whalin' skipper out o' Homeport, and—Don't you see my meanin', Annie? *(He glances at her. She is not looking at him but staring dully in front of her, not hearing a word he is saying.)* Annie! *(She comes to herself with a start.)* Best turn in, Annie, there's a good woman. You ain't well.

Mrs. Keeney *(resisting his attempts to guide her to the door in rear)*. David! Won't you please turn back?

Keeney *(gently)*. I can't, Annie—not yet awhile. You don't see my meanin'. I got to git the ile.

Mrs. Keeney. It'd be different if you needed the money, but you don't. You've got more than plenty.

Keeney *(impatiently)*. It ain't the money I'm thinkin' of. D'you think I'm as mean as that?

Mrs. Keeney *(dully)*. No—I don't know—I can't understand—*(Intensely)* Oh, I want to be home in the old house once more and see my own kitchen again, and hear a woman's voice talking to me and be able to talk to her. Two years! It seems so long ago—as if I'd been dead and could never go back.

Keeney *(worried by her strange tone and the far-away look in her eyes)*. Best to go to bed, Annie. You ain't well.

Mrs. Keeney *(not appearing to hear him)*. I used to be lonely when you were away. I used to think Homeport was a stupid, monotonous place. Then I used to go down on the beach, especially when it was windy and the breakers were rolling in, and I'd dream of the fine free life you must be leading. *(She gives a laugh which is half a sob.)* I used to love the sea then. *(She pauses; then continues with slow intensity:)* But now—I don't ever want to see the sea again.

KEENEY *(thinking to humor her).* 'Tis no fit place for a woman, that's sure. I was a fool to bring ye.

MRS. KEENEY *(after a pause—passing her hand over her eyes with a gesture of pathetic weariness).* How long would it take us to reach home—if we started now?

KEENEY *(frowning).* 'Bout two months, I reckon, Annie, with fair luck.

MRS. KEENEY *(counts on her fingers—then murmurs wtih a rapt smile).* That would be August, the latter part of August, wouldn't it? It was on the twenty-fifth of August we were married, David, wasn't it?

KEENEY *(trying to conceal the fact that her memories have moved him—gruffly).* Don't *you* remember?

MRS. KEENEY *(vaguely—again passes her hand over her eyes).* My memory is leaving me—up here in the ice. It was so long ago. *(A pause—then she smiles dreamily.)* It's June now. The lilacs will be all in bloom in the front yard—and the climbing roses on the trellis to the side of house—they're budding. *(She suddenly covers her face wtih her hands and commences to sob.)*

KEENEY *(disturbed).* Go in and rest, Annie. You're all wore out cryin' over what can't be helped.

MRS. KEENEY *(suddenly throwing her arms around his neck and clinging to him).* You love me, don't you, David?

KEENEY *(in amazed embarrassment at this outburst).* Love you? Why d'you ask me such a question, Annie?

MRS. KEENEY *(shaking him—fiercely).* But you do, don't you, David? Tell me!

KEENEY. I'm your husband, Annie, and you're my wife. Could there be aught but love between us after all these years?

MRS. KEENEY *(shaking him again—still more fiercely).* Then you do love me. Say it!

KEENEY *(simply).* I do, Annie.

MRS. KEENEY *(shaking him again—her hands drop to her sides.* KEENEY *regards her anxiously. She passes her hand across her eyes and murmurs half to herself:)* I sometimes think if we could only have had a child. *(*KEENEY *turns away from her, deeply moved. She grabs his arm and turns him around to face her—intensely.)* And I've always been a good wife to you, haven't I, David?

KEENEY *(his voice betraying his emotion).* No man has ever had a better, Annie.

MRS. KEENEY. And I've never asked for much from you, have I, David? Have I?

KEENEY. You know you could have all I got the power to give ye, Annie.

MRS. KEENEY *(wildly)*. Then do this this once for my sake, for God's sake—take me home! It's killing me, this life—the brutality and cold and horror of it. I'm going mad. I can feel the threat in the air. I can hear the silence threatening me—day after gray day and every day the same. I can't bear it. *(Sobbing)* I'll go mad, I know I will. Take me home, David, if you love me as you say. I'm afraid. For the love of God, take me home! *(She throws her arms around him, weeping against his shoulder. His face betrays the trememdous struggle going on within him. He holds her out at arm's length, his expression softening. For a moment his shoulders sag, he becomes old, his iron spirit weakens as he looks at her tear-stained face.)*

KEENEY *(dragging out the words with an effort)*. I'll do it, Annie—for your sake—if you say it's needful for ye.

MRS. KEENEY *(wild with joy—kissing him)*. God bless you for that, David! *(He turns away from her silently and walks toward the companionway. Just at that moment there is a clatter of footsteps on the stairs and the* SECOND MATE *enters the cabin.)*

MATE *(excitedly)*. The ice is breakin' up to no'th'ard, sir. There's a clear passage through the floe, and clear water beyond, the lookout says. *(*KEENEY *straightens himself like a man coming out of a trance.* MRS. KEENEY *looks at the* MATE *with terrified eyes.)*

KEENEY *(dazedly—trying to collect his thoughts)*. A clear passage? To no'th'ard?

MATE. Yes, sir.

KEENEY *(his voice suddenly grim with determination)*. Then get her ready and we'll drive her through.

MATE. Aye, aye, sir.

MRS. KEENEY *(appealingly)*. David!

KEENEY *(not heeding her)*. Will the men turn to willin' or must we drag 'em out?

MATE. They'll turn to willin' enough. You put the fear o' God into 'em, sir. They're meek as lambs.

KEENEY. Then drive 'em—both watches. *(With grim determination)* They's whale t'other side o' this floe and we're going to git 'em.

MATE. Aye, aye, sir. *(He goes out hurriedly. A moment later there is the sound of scuffling feet from the deck outside and the* MATES' *voice shouting orders.)*

KEENEY *(speaking aloud to himself—derisively)*. And I was agoin' home like a yaller dog!

MRS. KEENEY *(imploringly)*. David!

KEENEY *(sternly)*. Woman, you ain't adoin' right when you meddle in men's business and weaken 'em. You can't know my feelin's. I got to prove a man to be a good husband for ye to take pride in. I got to get the ile, I tell ye.

MRS. KEENEY *(supplicatingly)*. David! Aren't you going home?

KEENEY *(ignoring this question—commandingly)*. You ain't well. Go and lay down a mite. *(He starts for the door.)* I got to git on deck. *(He goes out. She cries after him in anguish:)* David! *(A pause. She passes her hand across her eyes—then commences to laugh hysterically and goes to the organ. She sits down and starts to play wildly an old hymn.* KEENEY *reenters from the doorway to the deck and stands looking at her angrily. He comes over and grabs her roughly by the shoulder.)*

KEENEY. Woman, what foolish mockin' is this? *(She laughs wildly and he starts back from her in alarm.)* Annie! What is it? *(She doesn't answer him.* KEENEY*'s voice trembles.)* Don't you know me, Annie? *(He puts both hands on her shoulders and turns her around so that he can look into her eyes. She stares up at him with a stupid expression, a vague smile on her lips. He stumbles away from her, and she commences softly to play the organ again.)*

KEENEY *(swallowing hard—in a hoarse whisper, as if he had difficulty in speaking)*. You said—you was agoin' mad—God! *(A long wail is heard from the deck above)* Ah bl-o-o-o-ow! *(A moment later the* MATE*'s face appears through the skylight. He cannot see* MRS. KEENEY.*)*

MATE *(in great excitement)*. Whales, sir—a whole school of 'em—off the star'b'd quarter 'bout five miles away—big ones!

KEENEY *(galvanized into action)*. Are you lowerin' the boats?

MATE. Yes, sir.

KEENEY *(with grim decision)*. I'm acomin' with ye.

MATE. Aye, aye, sir. *(Jubilantly)* You'll git the ile now right enough, sir. *(His head is withdrawn and he can be heard shouting orders.)*

KEENEY *(turning to his wife)*. Annie? Did you hear him? I'll get the ile. *(She doesn't answer or seem to know he is there. He gives a hard laugh, which is almost a groan.)* I know you're foolin' me, Annie. You ain't out of your mind—(*Anxiously)* be you? I'll git the ile now right enough—jest a little while longer, Annie—then we'll turn hom'ard. I can't turn back now, you see that, don't ye? I've got to git the ile. *(in sudden terror)* Answer me? You ain't mad, be you? *(She keeps on playing the organ, but makes no reply. The* MATE*'s face appears again through the skylight.)*

MATE. All ready, sir. *(*KEENEY *turns his back on his wife and strides to the doorway, where he stands for a moment and looks back at her in anguish, fighting to control his feelings.)*

MATE. Comin', sir?

KEENEY *(his face suddenly grown hard with determination)*. Aye. *(He turns *abruptly and goes out.* MRS. KEENEY *does not appear to notice his departure. Her whole attention seems centered in the organ. She sits with half-closed eyes, her body swaying a little from side to side to the rhythm of the hymn. Her fingers move faster and faster and she is playing wildly and discordantly as*

The Curtain Falls.)

SUGGESTIONS FOR WRITING AND DISCUSSION

1. What do the sailors' attitudes towards Mrs. Keeney suggest about her? In what ways does she identify with them and they with her?
2. Why did Mrs. Keeney want to accompany her husband on the voyage? How have her feelings changed in the course of the trip?
3. The whaling ship has been icebound for a year. How does the claustrophobia affect each of the characters?
4. Why is Captain Keeney so determined to find whales? Why does he at one point give in to his wife and agree to go home? How does the thought of going home with an empty ship make him feel?
5. In a two- to three-page essay argue that Captain Keeney does or does not love his wife.
6. *Ile* is a one act play. Does this brevity make the events described seem less credible? Does the play have a traditional structure? Discuss in a three- to five-page essay the length and structure of *Ile*.

Places: Thematic Questions

1. To what extent are you defined by where you live or where you grew up— for example, as a suburbanite, a New Englander, or a Californian? How does this affect the way other people regard you? How does it affect the way you see yourself?
2. In John Keats's sonnet "On First Looking into Chapman's Homer" the speaker describes how, through reading, he visualizes places he has never visited. Is there any place of which you have a vivid picture through books or other people's accounts rather than through first-hand experience? What do you know about this place?
3. Where would you live if you could live anywhere in the world? What would be your ideal environment?
4. In "Once More to the Lake" E. B. White describes returning to a place after a long absence. Have you ever done this? Were you surprised, either by real changes or by the discovery that you remembered things differently from the way they really were?
5. In "The Gift Outright" Robert Frost describes the relationship between America and Americans in the following way: "The land was ours before we were the land's./She was our land more than a hundred years/Before we were her people." Do you think there is a two-way relationship between a people and their country? Are we "owned" by America, in the same way as we own it? And does this ownership carry certain rights and obligations?

Varieties of Love

I never asked thy leave to let me love thee—I have a right. I love thee not as something private and personal, which is your own, but as something universal and worthy of love, which I have found. Oh, how I think of you! You are purely good—you are infinitely good. I can trust you forever. I did not think that humanity was so rich. Give me an opportunity to live.

HENRY DAVID THOREAU
"ON FRIENDSHIP"

Essays

Plato (Greek, 427? B.C.*–347?* B.C.*)*

Symposium

Well then, Eryximachus, Aristophanes began, I propose, as you suggested, to take quite a different line from you and Pausanias. I am convinced that mankind has never had any conception of the power of Love, for if we had known him as he really is, surely we should have raised the mightiest temples and altars, and offered the most splendid sacrifices, in his honor, and not—as in fact we do—have utterly neglected him. Yet he of all the gods has the best title to our service, for he, more than all the rest, is the friend of man; he is our great ally, and it is he that cures us of those ills whose relief opens the way to man's highest happiness. And so, gentlemen, I will do my best to acquaint you with the power of Love, and you in turn shall pass the lesson on.

First of all I must explain the real nature of man, and the change which it has undergone—for in the beginning we were nothing like we are now. For one thing, the race was divided into three; that is to say, besides the two sexes, male and female, which we have at present, there was a third which partook of the nature of both, and for which we still have a name, though the creature itself is forgotten, for though 'hermaphrodite' is only used nowadays as a term of contempt, there really was a man-woman in those days, a being which was half male and half female.

And secondly, gentlemen, each of these beings was globular in shape, with rounded back and sides, four arms and four legs, and two faces, both the same, on a cylindrical neck, and one head, with one face one side and one the other, and four ears, and two lots of privates, and all the other parts to match. They walked erect, as we do ourselves, backward or forward, whichever they pleased, but when they broke into a run they simply stuck their legs straight out and went whirling round and round like a clown turning cartwheels. And since they had eight legs, if you count their arms as well, you can imagine that they went bowling along at a pretty good speed.

The three sexes, I may say, arose as follows. The males were descended from the Sun, the females from the Earth, and the hermaphrodites from the Moon, which partakes of either sex, and they were round and they *went* round, because they took after their parents. And such, gentlemen, were their strength and energy, and such their arrogance, that they actually tried—like Ephialtes and Otus in Homer—to scale the heights of heaven and set upon the gods.

At this Zeus took counsel with the other gods as to what was to be done. They found themselves in rather an awkward position; they didn't want to blast them out of existence with thunderbolts as they did the giants, because that would be saying good-by to all their offerings and devotions, but at the same time they couldn't let them get altogether out of hand. At last, however, after racking his brains, Zeus offered a solution.

I think I can see my way, he said, to put an end to this disturbance by weakening these people without destroying them. What I propose to do is to cut them all in half, thus killing two birds with one stone, for each one will be only half as strong, and there'll be twice as many of them which will suit us very nicely. They can walk about, upright, on their two legs, and if, said Zeus, I have any more trouble with them, I shall split them up again, and they'll have to hop about on one.

So saying, he cut them all in half just as you or I might chop up sorb apples for pickling, or slice an egg with a hair. And as each half was ready he told Apollo to turn its face, with the half-neck that was left, toward the side that was cut away—thinking that the sight of such a gash might frighten it into keeping quiet—and then to heal the whole thing up. So Apollo turned their faces back to front, and, pulling in the skin all the way round, he stretched it over what we now call the belly—like those bags you pull together with a string—and tied up the one remaining opening so as to form what we call the navel. As for the creases that were left, he smoothed most of them away, finishing off the chest with the sort of tool a cobbler uses to smooth down the leather on the last, but he left a few puckers round about the belly and the navel, to remind us of what we suffered long ago.

Now, when the work of bisection was complete it left each half with a desperate yearning for the other, and they ran together and flung their arms around each other's necks, and asked for nothing better than to be rolled into one. So much so, that they began to die of hunger and general inertia, for neither would do anything without the other. And whenever one half was left alone by the death of its mate, it wandered about questing and clasping in the hope of finding a spare half-woman—or a whole woman, as we should call her nowadays—or half a man. And so the race was dying out.

Fortunately, however, Zeus felt so sorry for them that he devised another scheme. He moved their privates round to the front, for of course they had originally been on the outside—which was now the back—and they had begotten and conceived not upon each other, but, like the grasshoppers, upon the earth. So now, as I say, he moved their members round to the front and made them propagate among themselves, the male begetting upon the female—the idea being that if, in all these clippings and claspings, a man should chance upon a woman, conception would take place and the race would be continued, while if man should conjugate with man, he might at least obtain such satisfaction as would allow him to turn his attention and his energies to the everyday affairs of life. So you see, gentlemen, how far back we can trace our innate love for one another, and how this love is always trying to reintegrate our former nature, to make two into one, and to bridge the gulf between one human being and another.

And so, gentlemen, we are all like pieces of the coins that children break in half for keepsakes—making two out of one, like the flatfish—and each of us is forever seeking the half that will tally with himself. The man who is a slice of the hermaphrodite sex, as it was called, will naturally be attracted by women—the adulterer, for instance—and women who run after men are of similar descent—as, for instance, the unfaithful wife. But the woman who is a slice of the original female is attracted by women rather than by men—in fact she is a Lesbian—while men who are slices of the male are followers of the male, and show their masculinity throughout their boyhood by the way they make friends with men, and the delight they take in lying beside them and being taken in their arms. And these are the most hopeful of the nation's youth, for theirs is the most virile constitution.

I know there are some people who call them shameless, but they are wrong. It is not immodesty that leads them to such pleasures, but daring, fortitude, and masculinity—the very virtues that they recognize and welcome in their lovers—which is proved by the fact that in after years they are the only men who show any real manliness in public life. And so, when they themselves have come to manhood, their love in turn is lavished upon boys. They have no natural inclination to marry and beget children. Indeed, they only do so in deference to the usage of society, for they would just as soon renounce marriage altogether and spend their lives with one another.

Such a man, then, gentlemen, is of an amorous disposition, and gives his love to boys, always clinging to his like. And so, when this boy lover—or any lover, for that matter—is fortunate enough to meet his other half, they are both so intoxicated with affection, with friendship, and with love, that they cannot bear to let each other out of sight for a single instant. It is such reunions as these that impel men to spend their lives together, although they may be hard put to it to say what they really want with one another, and indeed, the purely sexual pleasures of their friendship could hardly account for the huge delight they take in one another's company. The fact is that both their souls are longing for a something else—a something to which they can neither of them put a name, and which they can only give an inkling of in cryptic sayings and prophetic riddles.

Now, supposing Hephaestus were to come and stand over them with his tool bag as they lay there side by side, and suppose he were to ask, Tell me, my dear creatures, what do you really want with one another?

And suppose they didn't know what to say, and he went on. How would you like to be rolled into one, so that you could always be together, day and night, and never be parted again? Because if that's what you want, I can easily weld you together, and then you can live your two lives in one, and, when the time comes, you can die a common death and still be two-in-one in the lower world. Now, what do you say? Is that what you'd like me to do? And would you be happy if I did?

We may be sure, gentlemen, that no lover on earth would dream of refusing such an offer, for not one of them could imagine a happier fate. Indeed, they would be convinced that this was just what they'd been waiting for—to be merged, that is, into an utter oneness with the beloved.

And so all this to-do is a relic of that original state of ours, when we were whole, and now, when we are longing for and following after that primeval wholeness, we say we are in love. For there was a time, I repeat, when we were one, but now, for our sins, God has scattered us abroad, as the Spartans scattered the Arcadians. Moreover, gentlemen, there is every reason to fear that, if we neglect the worship of the gods, they will split us up again, and then we shall have to go about with our noses sawed asunder, part and counterpart, like the basso-relievos on the tombstones. And therefore it is our duty one and all to inspire our friends with reverence and piety, for so we may ensure our safety and attain that blessed union by enlisting in the army of Love and marching beneath his banners.

For Love must never be withstood—as we do, if we incur the displeasure of the gods. But if we cling to him in friendship and reconciliation, we shall be among the happy few to whom it is given in these latter days to meet their other halves. Now, I don't want any coarse remarks from Eryximachus. I don't mean Pausanias and Agathon, though for all I know they may be among the lucky ones, and both be sections of the male. But what I am trying to say is this—that the happiness of the whole human race, women no less than men, is to be found in the consummation of our love, and in the healing of our dissevered nature by finding each his proper mate. And if this be a counsel of perfection, then we must do what, in our present circumstances, is next best, and bestow our love upon the natures most congenial to our own.

And so I say that Love, the god who brings all this to pass, is worthy of our hymns, for his is the inestimable and present service of conducting us to our true affinities, and it is he that offers this great hope for the future—that, if we do not fail in reverence to the gods, he will one day heal us and restore us to our old estate, and establish us in joy and blessedness.

Such, Eryximachus, is my discourse on Love—as different as could be from yours. And now I must ask you again. Will you please refrain from making fun of it, and let us hear what all the others have to say—or rather, the other two, for I see there's no one left but Agathon and Socrates.

SUGGESTIONS FOR WRITING AND DISCUSSION

1. What is Aristophanes' account of the origin of love? What reasons does he give to support his account? How does a mythical account differ from a historical or scientific one? In what ways can a myth be true?
2. Do you think that Aristophanes deals fairly with women in his argument?
3. Aristophanes gives us an account of human behavior. Choose some social custom and make up your own mythical account of how it came into being.

Benjamin Franklin (American, 1706–1790)

Early Marriages Are Happy Ones

To John Alleyne

Craven Street, August 9, 1768

Dear Sir,

You made an apology to me for not acquainting me sooner with your marriage. I ought now to make an apology to you for delaying so long the answer to your letter. It was mislaid or hid among my papers and much business put it out of my mind, or prevented my looking for it and writing when I thought of it. So this account between us if you please may stand balanced. I assure you it gave me great pleasure to hear you were married, and into a family of reputation. This I learned from the public papers. The character you give me of your bride (as it included every qualification that in the married state conduces to mutual happiness) is an addition to that pleasure. Had you consulted me, as a friend, on the occasion, youth on both sides I should not have thought any objection. Indeed, from the matches that have fallen under my observation, I am rather inclined to think that early ones stand the best chance for happiness. The tempers and habits of young people are not yet become so stiff and uncomplying as when more advanced in life; they form more easily to each other, and hence many occasions of disgust are removed. And if youth has less of that prudence that is necessary to conduct a family, yet the parents and elder friends of young married persons are generally at hand to afford their advice, which amply supplies that defect; and, by early marriage, youth is sooner formed to regular and useful life; and possibly some of those accidents, habits or connections, that might have injured either the constitution, or the reputation, or both, are thereby happily prevented.

Particular circumstances of particular persons may possibly sometimes make it prudent to delay entering into that state; but in general, when nature has rendered our bodies fit for it, the presumption is in nature's favor, that she has not judged amiss in making us desire it. Late marriages are often attended, too, with this further inconvenience, that there is not the same chance the parents shall live to see their offspring educated. "Late children," says the Spanish proverb, "are early orphans." A melancholy reflection to those, whose case it may be! With us in America, marriages are generally in the morning of life; our children are therefore educated and settled in the world by noon; and thus, our business being done, we have an afternoon and evening of cheerful leisure to ourselves; such as your friend at present enjoys. By these early marriages we are blest with more children; and from the mode among us, founded in nature, of every Mother suckling and nursing her own child, more of them are raised. Thence the swift progress of population among us, unparalleled in Europe.

In fine, I am glad you are married, and congratulate you most cordially upon it. You are now in the way of becoming a useful citizen; and you have escaped the unnatural state of celibacy for life, the fate of many here, who never intended it, but who, having too long postponed the change of their condition, find at length that it is too late to think of it, and so live all their lives in a situation that greatly lessens a man's value. An odd volume of a set of books you know is not worth its proportion of the set, and what think you of the usefulness of an odd half of a pair of scissors? It cannot well cut anything. It may possibly serve to scrape a trencher.

Pray make my compliments and best wishes acceptable to your spouse. I am old and heavy and grow a little indolent, or I should ere this have presented them in person. I shall make but small use of the old man's privilege, that of giving advice to younger friends. Treat your wife always with respect; it will procure respect to you, not from her only but from all that observe it. Never use a slighting expression to her, even in jest, for slights in jest, after frequent bandyings, are apt to end in angry earnest. Be studious in your profession, and you will be learned. Be industrious and frugal, and you will be rich. Be sober and temperate, and you will be healthy. Be in general virtuous, and you will be happy. At least, you will, by such conduct, stand the best chance for such consequences. I pray God to bless you both; being ever your affectionate friend.

B. Franklin

SUGGESTIONS FOR WRITING AND DISCUSSION

1. What are Franklin's arguments in favor of early marriages? Are all these arguments practical?
2. Why does Franklin believe that early marriages are happier than late marriages?
3. This letter strongly suggests that a person is incomplete without a permanent relationship with another. Do you agree or disagree? Write your answer in a two- to three-page essay.
4. The final paragraph of this letter contains some of Franklin's most frequently quoted remarks. Use one of them as the thesis of a two- to three-page essay, either agreeing or disagreeing with its sentiment.

Emma Goldman (American, 1869–1940)

Marriage and Love

The popular notion about marriage and love is that they are synonymous, that they spring from the same motives, and cover the same human needs. Like most popular notions this also rests not on actual facts, but on superstition.

Marriage and love have nothing in common; they are as far apart as the poles; are, in fact, antagonistic to each other. No doubt some marriages have been the result of love. Not, however, because love could assert itself only in marriage; much rather is it because few people can completely outgrow a convention. There are today large numbers of men and women to whom marriage is naught but a farce, but who submit to it for the sake of public opinion. At any rate, while it is true that some marriages are based on love, and while it is equally true that in some cases love continues in married life, I maintain that it does so regardless of marriage, and not because of it.

On the other hand, it is utterly false that love results from marriage. On rare occasions one does hear of a miraculous case of a married couple falling in love after marriage, but on close examination it will be found that it is a mere adjustment to the inevitable. Certainly the growing-used to each other is far away from the spontaneity, the intensity, and beauty of love, without which the intimacy of marriage must prove degrading to both the woman and the man.

Marriage is primarily an economic arrangement, an insurance pact. It differs from the ordinary life insurance agreement only in that it is more binding, more exacting. Its returns are insignificantly small compared with the investments. In taking out an insurance policy one pays for it in dollars and cents, always at liberty to discontinue payments. If, however, woman's premium is a husband, she pays for it with her name, her privacy, her self-respect, her very life, ``until death doth part.'' Moreover, the marriage insurance condemns her to life-long dependency, to parasitism, to complete uselessness, individual as well as social. Man, too, pays his toll, but as his sphere is wider, marriage does not limit him as much as woman. He feels his chains more in an economic sense. . . .

Perchance the poor quality of the material whence woman comes is responsible for her inferiority. At any rate, woman has no soul—what is there to know about her? Besides, the less soul a woman has the greater her asset as a wife, the more readily will she absorb herself in her husband. It is this slavish acquiescence to man's superiority that has kept the marriage institution seemingly intact for so long a period. Now that woman is coming into her own, now that she is actually growing aware of herself as a being outside of the master's grace, the sacred institution of marriage is gradually being undermined, and no amount of sentimental lamentation can stay it.

From infancy, almost, the average girl is told that marriage is her ultimate goal; therefore her training and education must be directed towards that end. Like the mute beast fattened for slaughter, she is prepared for that. Yet, strange to say, she is allowed to know much less about her function as wife and mother than the ordinary artisan of his trade. It is indecent and filthy for a respectable girl to know anything of the marital relation. Oh, for the inconsistency of respectability, that needs the marriage vow to turn something which is filthy into the purest and most sacred arrangement that none dare question or criticize. Yet that is exactly the attitude of the average upholder of marriage. The prospective wife and mother is kept in complete ignorance of her only asset in the competitive field—sex. Thus she enters into life-long relations with a man only to find herself shocked, repelled, outraged beyond measure by the most natural and healthy instinct, sex. It is safe to say that a large percentage of the unhappiness, misery, distress, and physical suffering of matrimony is due to the criminal ignorance in sex matters that is being extolled as a great virtue. Nor is it at all an exaggeration when I say that more than one home has been broken up because of this deplorable fact.

If, however, woman is free and big enough to learn the mystery of sex without the sanction of State of Church, she will stand condemned as utterly unfit to become the wife of a "good" man, his goodness consisting of an empty brain and plenty of money. Can there be anything more outrageous than the idea that a healthy, grown woman, full of life and passion, must deny nature's demand, must subdue her most intense craving, undermine her health and break her spirit, must stunt her vision, abstain from the depth and glory of sex experience until a "good" man comes along to take her unto himself as a wife? That is precisely what marriage means. How can such an arrangement end except in failure? This is one, though not the least important, factor of marriage, which differentiates it from love.

Ours is a practical age. The time when Romeo and Juliet risked the wrath of their fathers for love, when Gretchen exposed herself to the gossip of her neighbors for love, is no more. If, on rare occasions, young people allow themselves the luxury of romance, they are taken in care by the elders, drilled and pounded until they become "sensible."

The moral lesson instilled in the girl is not whether the man has aroused her love, but rather is it, "How much?" The important and only God of practical American life: Can the man make a living? can he support a wife? That is the only thing that justifies marriage. Gradually this saturates every thought of the girl; her dreams are not of moonlight and kisses, of laughter and tears; she dreams of shopping tours and bargain counters. This soul poverty and sordidness are the elements inherent in the marriage institution. The State and the Church approve of no other ideal, simply because it is the one that necessitates the State and Church control of men and women.

Doubtless there are people who continue to consider love above dollars and cents. Particularly is this true of that class whom economic necessity has forced to become self-supporting. The tremendous change in woman's position, wrought by that mighty factor, is indeed phenomenal when we reflect that it is but a short time since she has entered the industrial arena. Six million women wage workers; six million women, who have the equal right with men to be exploited, to be robbed, to go on strike; aye, to starve even. Anything more, my lord? Yes, six million wage workers in every walk of life, from the highest brain work to the mines and railroad tracks; yes, even detectives and policemen. Surely the emancipation is complete.

Yet with all that, but a very small number of the vast army of women wage workers look upon work as a permanent issue, in the same light as does man. No matter how decrepit the latter, he has been taught to be independent, self-supporting. Oh, I know that no one is really independent in our economic treadmill; still, the poorest specimen of a man hates to be a parasite; to be known as such, at any rate.

The woman considers her position as worker transitory, to be thrown aside for the first bidder. That is why it is infinitely harder to organize women than men. "Why should I join a union? I am going to get married, to have a home." Has she not been taught from infancy to look upon that as her ultimate calling? She learns soon enough that the home, though not so large a prison as the factory, has more solid doors and bars. It has a keeper so faithful that naught can escape him. The most tragic part, however, is that the home no longer frees her from wage slavery; it only increases her task.

According to the latest statistics submitted before a Committee "on labor and wages, and congestion of population," ten per cent of the wage workers in New York City alone are married, yet they must continue to work at the most poorly paid labor in the world. Add to this horrible aspect the drudgery of housework, and what remains of the protection and glory of the home? As a matter of fact, even the middle-class girl in marriage can not speak of her home, since it is the man who creates her sphere. It is not important whether the husband is a brute or a darling. What I wish to prove is that marriage guarantees woman a home only by the grace of her husband. There she moves about in *his* home, year after year, until her aspect of life and human affairs becomes as flat, narrow, and drab as her surroundings. Small wonder if she becomes a nag, petty, quarrelsome, gossipy, unbearable, thus driving the man from the house. She could not go, if she wanted to; there is no place to go. Besides, a short period of married life, of complete surrender of all faculties, absolutely incapacitates the average woman for the outside world. She becomes reckless in appearance, clumsy in her movements, dependent in her decisions, cowardly in her judgment, a weight and a bore, which most men grow to hate and despise. Wonderfully inspiring atmosphere for the bearing of life, is it not?

But the child, how is it to be protected, if not for marriage? After all, is not that the most important consideration? The sham, the hypocrisy of it! Marriage protecting the child, yet thousands of children destitute and homeless. Marriage protecting the child, yet orphan asylums and reformatories overcrowded, the Society for the Prevention of Cruelty to Children keeping busy in rescuing the little victims from "loving" parents, to place them under more loving care, the Gerry Society. Oh, the mockery of it!

Marriage may have the power to bring the horse to water, but has it ever made him drink? The law will place the father under arrest, and put him in convict's clothes; but has that ever stilled the hunger of the child? If the parent has no work, or if he hides his identity, what does marriage do then? It invokes the law to bring the man to "justice," to put him safely behind closed doors; his labor, however, goes not to the child, but to the State. The child receives but a blighted memory of its father's stripes.

As to the protection of the woman—therein lies the curse of marriage. Not that it really protects her, but the very idea is so revolting, such an outrage and insult on life, so degrading to human dignity, as to forever condemn this parasitic institution.

It is like that other paternal arrangement—capitalism. It robs man of his birthright, stunts his growth, poisons his body, keeps him in ignorance, in poverty, and dependence, and then institutes charities that thrive on the last vestige of a man's self-respect.

The institution of marriage makes a parasite of woman, an absolute dependent. It incapacitates her for life's struggle, annihilates her social consciousness, paralyzes her imagination, and then imposes its gracious protection, which is in reality a snare, a travesty on human character.

If motherhood is the highest fulfillment of woman's nature, what other protection does it need, save love and freedom? Marriage but defiles, outrages, and corrupts her fulfillment. Does it not say to woman, Only when you follow me shall you bring forth life? Does it not condemn her to the block, does it not degrade and shame her if she refuses to buy her right to motherhood by selling herself? Does not marriage only sanction motherhood, even though conceived in hatred, in compulsion? Yet, if motherhood be of free choice, of love, of ecstasy, of defiant passion, does it not place a crown of thorns upon an innocent head and carve in letters of blood the hideous epithet, Bastard? Were marriage to contain all the virtues claimed for it, its crimes against motherhood would exclude it forever from the realm of love.

Love, the strongest and deepest element in all life, the harbinger of hope, of joy, of ecstasy; love, the defier of all laws, of all conventions; love, the freest, the most powerful moulder of human destiny; how can such an all-compelling force be synonymous with that poor little State and Church-begotten weed, marriage?

Free love? As if love is anything but free! Man has bought brains, but all the millions in the world have failed to buy love. Man has subdued bodies, but all the power on earth has been unable to subdue love. Man has conquered whole nations, but all his armies could not conquer love. Man has chained and fettered the spirit, but he has been utterly helpless before love. High on a throne, with all the splendor and pomp his gold can command, man is yet poor and desolate, if love passes him by. And if it stays, the poorest hovel is radiant with warmth, with life and color. Thus love has the magic power to make of a beggar a king. Yes, love is free; it can dwell in no other atmosphere. In freedom it gives itself unreservedly, abundantly, completely. All the laws on the statutes, all the courts in the universe, cannot tear it from the soil, once love has taken root. If, however, the soil is sterile, how can marriage make it bear fruit? It is like the last desperate struggle of fleeting life against death. . . .

SUGGESTIONS FOR WRITING AND DISCUSSION

1. Why does Goldman believe that love and marriage are incompatible?
2. Do you think that Goldman is fair in her description of women? Of men?
3. Does Goldman's argument progress logically? Are there flaws in the argument?
4. How would you defend the institution of marriage against the charges Goldman brings? Write your response in a two- to three-page essay.

Margaret Mead (American, 1901–1978)

From Popping the Question to Popping the Pill

There have been major changes in attitudes toward courtship and marriage among those middle-class, educated Americans who are celebrated in the media and who are style setters for American life. Courtship was once a regular part of American life; it was a long period, sometimes lasting for many years, and also a tentative one, during which a future husband or wife could still turn back but during which their relationship became more and more exclusive and socially recognized. Courtship both preceded the announcement of an engagement and followed the announcement, although a broken engagement was so serious that it could be expected to throw the girl into a depression from which she might never recover.

There were definite rules governing the courtship period, from the "bundling" permitted in early New England days, when young couples slept side by side with all their clothes on, to strict etiquette that prescribed what sort of gifts a man might give his fiancée in circles where expensive presents were customary. Gifts had to be either immediately consumable, like candy or flowers, or indestructible, like diamonds— which could be given back, their value unimpaired, if there was a rift in the relationship. Objects that could be damaged by use, like gloves and furs, were forbidden. A gentlemen might call for a lady in a cab or in his own equipage, but it was regarded as inappropriate for him to pay for her train fare if they went on a journey.

How much chaperoning was necessary, and how much privacy the courting couple was allowed, was a matter of varying local custom. Long walks home through country lanes after church and sitting up in the parlor after their elders had retired for the night may have been permitted, but the bride was expected to be a virgin at marriage. The procedure for breaking off an engagement, which included the return of letters and photographs, was a symbolic way of stating that an unconsummated relationship could still be erased from social memory.

The wedding day was the highest point in a girl's life—a day to which she looked forward all her unmarried days and to which she looked back for the rest of her life. The splendor of her wedding, the elegance of dress and veil, the cutting of the cake, the departure amid a shower of rice and confetti, gave her an accolade of which no subsequent event could completely rob her. Today people over 50 years of age still treat their daughter's wedding this way, prominently displaying the photographs of the occasion. Until very recently, all brides' books prescribed exactly the same ritual they had prescribed 50 years before. The etiquette governing wedding presents—gifts that were or were not appropriate, the bride's maiden initials on her linen—was also specified. For the bridegroom the wedding represented the end of his free, bachelor days, and the bachelor dinner the night before the wedding symbolized this loss of freedom. A woman who did not marry—even if she had the alibi of a fiancé who had been killed in war or had abilities and charm and money of her own—was always at a social disadvantage, while an eligible bachelor was sought after by hostess after hostess.

Courtship ended at the altar, as the bride waited anxiously for the bridegroom who might not appear or might have forgotten the ring. Suppliant gallantry was replaced overnight by a reversal of roles, the wife now becoming the one who read her husband's every frown with anxiety lest she displease him.

This set of rituals established a rhythm between the future husband and wife and between the two sets of parents who would later become co-grandparents. It was an opportunity for mistakes to be corrected; and if the parents could not be won over, there was, as a last resort, elopement, in which the young couple proclaimed their desperate attraction to each other by flouting parental blessing. Each part of the system could be tested out for marriage that was expected to last for life. We have very different ways today.

Since World War I, changes in relationships between the sexes have been occurring with bewildering speed. The automobile presented a challenge to chaperonage that American adults met by default. From then on, except in ceremonial and symbolic ways, chaperonage disappeared, and a style of premarital relationship was set up in which the onus was put on the girl to refuse inappropriate requests, while each young man declared his suitability by asking for favors that he did not expect to receive. The disappearance of chaperonage was facilitated by the greater freedom of middle-aged women, who began to envy their daughters' freedom, which they had never had. Social forms went through a whole series of rapid changes: The dance with formal partners and programs gave way to occasions in which mothers, or daughters, invited many more young men than girls, and the popular girl hardly circled the dance floor twice in the same man's arms. Dating replaced courtship—not as a prelude to anything but rather as a way of demonstrating popularity. Long engagements became increasingly unfashionable, and a series of more tentative commitments became more popular. As college education became the norm for millions of young people, "pinning" became a common stage before engagement. The ring was likely to appear just before the wedding day. And during the 1950's more and more brides got married while pregnant—but they still wore the long white veil, which was a symbol of virginity.

In this conservative, security-minded decade love became less important than marriage, and lovers almost disappeared from parks and riverbanks as young people threatened each other: "Either you marry me now, or I'll marry someone else." Courtship and dating were embraced by young people in lower grades in school, until children totally unready for sex were enmeshed by the rituals of pairing off. Marriage became a necessity for everyone, for boys as well as for girls: Mothers worried if their sons preferred electronic equipment or chess to girls and pushed their daughters relentlessly into marriage. Divorce became more and more prevalent, and people who felt their marriages were failing began to worry about whether they ought to get a divorce, divorce becoming a duty to an unfulfilled husband or to children exposed to an unhappy marriage. Remarriage was expected, until finally, with men dying earlier than women, there were no men left to marry. The United States became the most married country in the world. Children, your own or adopted, were just as essential, and the suburban life-style—each nuclear family isolated in its own home, with several children, a station wagon and a country-club membership—became the admired life-style, displayed in magazines for the whole world to see.

By the early sixties there were signs of change. We discovered we were running out of educated labor, and under the heading of self-fulfillment educated married women were being tempted back into the labor market. Young people began to advocate frankness and honesty, rebelling against the extreme hypocrisy of the 1950s, when religious and educational institutions alike connived to produce pregnancies that would lead to marriage. Love as an absorbing feeling for another person was rediscovered, as marriage as a goal for every girl and boy receded into the background.

A series of worldwide political and ecological events facilitated these changes. Freedom for women accompanied agitation for freedom for blacks, for other minorities, for the Third World, for youth, for gay people. Zero-population growth became a goal, and it was no longer unfashionable to admit one did not plan to have children, or perhaps even to marry. The marriage age rose a little, the number of children fell a little. The enjoyment of pornography and use of obscenity became the self-imposed obligation of the emancipated women. Affirmative action catapulted many unprepared women into executive positions. Men, weary of the large families of the '50s, began to desert them; young mothers, frightened by the prospect of being deserted, pulled up stakes and left their suburban split-levels to try to make it in the cities. "Arrangements," or public cohabitation of young people with approval and support from their families, college deans and employers, became common.

By the early 1970s the doomsters were proclaiming that the family was dead. There were over 9,000,000 single-parent households, most of them headed by poorly paid women. There were endless discussions of "open marriages," "group marriages," communes in which the children were children of the group, and open discussion of previously taboo subjects, including an emphasis on female sexuality. Yet most Americans continued to live as they always had, with girls still hoping for a permanent marriage and viewing "arrangements" as stepping-stones to marriage. The much-publicized behavior of small but conspicuous groups filtered through the layers of society, so that the freedoms claimed by college youth were being claimed five years later by blue-collar youth; "swinging" (mate swapping) as a pastime of a bored upper-middle-class filtered down.

Perhaps the most striking change of all is that courtship is no longer a prelude to consummation. In many levels of contemporary society, sex relations require no prelude at all; the courtship that exists today tends to occur between a casual sex encounter and a later attempt by either the man or the woman to turn it into a permanent relationship. Courtship is also seen as an act in which either sex can take the lead. Women are felt to have an alternative to marriage, as once they had in the Middle Ages, when convent life was the choice of a large part of the population. Weddings are less conventional, although new conventions, like reading from Kahlil Gibran's *The Prophet,* spread very quickly. There is also a growing rebellion against the kind of town planning and housing that isolate young couples from the help of older people and friends that they need.

But the family is not dead. It is going through stormy times, and millions of children are paying the penalty of current disorganization, experimentation and discontent. In the process, the adults who should never marry are sorting themselves out. Marriage and parenthood are being viewed as a vocation rather than as the duty of every human being. As we seek more human forms of existence, the next question may well be how to protect our young people from a premature, pervasive insistence upon precocious sexuality, sexuality that contains neither love nor delight.

The birthrate is going up a little; women are having just as many babies as before, but having them later. The rights of fathers are being discovered and placed beside the rights of mothers. Exploitive and commercialized abortion mills are being questioned, and the Pill is proving less a panacea than was hoped. In a world troubled by economic and political instability, unemployment, highjacking, kidnapping and bombs, the preoccupation with private decisions is shifting to concern about the whole of humankind.

Active concern for the world permits either celibacy *or* marriage, but continuous preoccupation with sex leaves no time for anything else. As we used to say in the '20s, promiscuity, like free verse, is lacking in structure.

SUGGESTIONS FOR WRITING AND DISCUSSION

1. What are the distinctions Mead makes between dating and courtship?
2. What argument does Mead make in favor of marriage?
3. Compare this essay with Emma Goldman's "Marriage and Love." Whose argument comes closer to your own point of view?
4. What comment does this essay make about the changing roles of women in American society?
5. This essay does not take into account failed marriages. Do you think this is deliberate on the author's part?
6. In a three- to five-page essay discuss what marriage means to you. Does it mean the end of romance? Is its primary function to preserve the family unit? Can our society function without marriage? Do people usually get married for the wrong reasons? Are most marriages based on realistic expectations?

Fiction

Mark Twain (American, 1835–1910)

The Diary of Adam and Eve

Part I—Extracts from Adam's Diary

Monday This new creature with the long hair is a good deal in the way. It is always hanging around and following me about. I don't like this; I am not used to company. I wish it would stay with the other animals. . . . Cloudy today, wind in the east; think we shall have rain. . . . *We?* Where did I get that word?—I remember now—the new creature uses it.

Tuesday Been examining the great waterfall. It is the finest thing on the estate, I think. The new creature calls it Niagara Falls—why, I am sure I do not know. Says it *looks* like Niagara Falls. That is not a reason, it is mere waywardness and imbecility. I get no chance to name anything myself. The new creature names everything that comes along, before I can get in a protest. And always that same pretext is offered—it *looks* like the thing. There is the dodo, for instance. Says the moment one looks at it one sees at a glance that it "looks like a dodo." It will have to keep that name, no doubt. It wearies me to fret about it, and it does no good, anyway. Dodo! It looks no more like a dodo than I do.

Wednesday Built me a shelter against the rain, but could not have it to myself in peace. The new creature intruded. When I tried to put it out it shed water out of the holes it looks with, and wiped it away with the back of its paws, and made a noise such as some of the other animals make when they are in distress. I wish it would not talk; it is always talking. That sounds like a cheap fling at the poor creature, a slur; but I do not mean it so. I have never heard the human voice before, and any new and strange sound intruding itself here upon the solemn hush of these dreaming solitudes offends my ear and seems a false note. And this new sound is so close to me; it is right at my shoulder, right at my ear, first on one side and then on the other, and I am used only to sounds that are more or less distant from me.

Friday The naming goes recklessly on, in spite of anything I can do. I had a very good name for the estate, and it was musical and pretty— GARDEN OF EDEN. Privately, I continue to call it that, but not any longer publicly. The new creature says it is all woods and rocks and scenery, and therefore has no resemblance to a garden. Says it *looks* like a park, and does not look like anything *but* a park. Consequently, without consulting me, it has been new-named—NIAGARA FALLS PARK. This is sufficiently high-handed, it seems to me. And already there is a sign up:

KEEP OFF

THE GRASS

My life is not as happy as it was.

Saturday The new creature eats too much fruit. We are going to run short, most likely. "We" again—that is *its* word; mine, too, now, from hearing it so much. Good deal of fog this morning. I do not go out in the fog myself. The new creature does. It goes out in all weathers, and stumps right in with its muddy feet. And talks. It used to be so pleasant and quiet here.

Sunday Pulled through. This day is getting to be more and more trying. It was selected and set apart last November as a day of rest. I had already six of them per week before. This morning found the new creature trying to clod apples out of that forbidden tree.

Monday The new creature says its name is Eve. That is all right, I have no objections. Says it is to call it by, when I want it to come. I said it was superfluous, then. The word evidently raised me in its respect; and indeed it is a large, good word and will bear repetition. It says it is not an It, it is a She. This is probably doubtful; yet it is all one to me; what she is were nothing to me if she would but go by herself and not talk.

Tuesday She has littered the whole estate with execrable names and offensive signs:

THIS WAY TO THE WHIRLPOOL

THIS WAY TO GOAT ISLAND

CAVE OF THE WINDS THIS WAY

She says this park would make a tidy summer resort if there was any custom for it. Summer resort—another invention of hers—just words, without any meaning. What is a summer resort? But it is best not to ask her, she has such a rage for explaining.

Friday She has taken to beseeching me to stop going over the Falls. What harm does it do? Says it makes her shudder. I wonder why; I have always done it—always like the plunge, and coolness. I supposed it was what the Falls were for. They have no other use that I can see, and they must have been made for something. She says they were only made for scenery—like the rhinoceros and the mastodon.

I went over the Falls in a barrel—not satisfactory to her. Went over in a tub—still not satisfactory. Swam the Whirlpool and the Rapids in a fig-leaf suit. It got much damaged. Hence, tedious complaints about my extravagance. I am too much hampered here. What I need is change of scene.

Saturday I escaped last Tuesday night, and traveled two days, and built me another shelter in a secluded place, and obliterated my tracks as well as I could, but she hunted me out by means of a beast which she has tamed and calls a wolf, and came making that pitiful noise again, and shedding that water out of the places she looks with. I was obliged to return with her, but will presently emigrate again when occasion offers. She engages herself in many foolish things; among others, to study out why the animals called lions and tigers live on grass and flowers, when, as she says, the sort of teeth they wear would indicate that they were intended to eat each other. This is foolish, because to do that would be to kill each other, and that would introduce what, as I understand it, is called ``death''; and death, as I have been told, has not yet entered the Park. Which is a pity, on some accounts.

Sunday Pulled through.

Monday I believe I see what the week is for: it is to give time to rest up from the weariness of Sunday. It seems a good idea. . . . She has been climbing that tree again. Clodded her out of it. She said nobody was looking. Seems to consider that a justification for chancing any dangerous thing. Told her that. The word justification moved her admiration—and envy, too, I thought. It is a good word.

Tuesday She told me she was made out of a rib taken from my body. This is at least doubtful, if not more than that. I have not missed any rib. . . . She is in much trouble about the buzzard; says grass does not agree with it; is afraid she can't raise it; thinks it was intended to live on decayed flesh. The buzzard must get along the best it can with what it is provided. We cannot overturn the whole scheme to accommodate the buzzard.

Saturday She fell in the pond yesterday when she was looking at herself in it, which she is always doing. She nearly strangled, and said it was most uncomfortable. This made her sorry for the creatures which live in there, which she calls fish, for she continues to fasten names on to things that don't need them and don't come when they are called by them, which is a matter of no consequence to her, she is such a numskull, anyway; so she got a lot of them out and brought them in last night and put them in my bed to keep warm, but I have noticed them now and then all day and I don't see that they are any happier there than they were before, only quieter. When night comes I shall throw them outdoors. I will not sleep with them again, for I find them clammy and unpleasant to lie among when a person hasn't anything on.

Sunday Pulled through.

Tuesday She has taken up with a snake now. The other animals are glad, for she was always experimenting with them and bothering them; and I am glad because the snake talks, and this enables me to get a rest.

Friday She says the snake advised her to try the fruit of that tree, and says the result will be a great and fine and noble education. I told her there would be another result, too—it would introduce death into the world. That was a mistake—it had been better to keep the remark to myself; it only gave her an idea—she could save the sick buzzard, and furnish fresh meat to the despondent lions and tigers. I advised her to keep away from the tree. She said she wouldn't. I foresee trouble. Will emigrate.

Wednesday I have had a variegated time. I escaped last night, and rode a horse all night as fast as he could go, hoping to get clear out of the Park and hide in some other country before the trouble should begin; but it was not to be. About an hour after sun-up, as I was riding through a flowery plain where thousands of animals were grazing, slumbering, or playing with each other, according to their wont, all of a sudden they broke into a tempest of frightful noises, and in one moment the plain was a frantic commotion and every beast was destroying its neighbor. I knew what it meant—Eve had eaten that fruit, and death was come into the world. . . . The tigers ate my horse, paying no attention when I ordered them to desist, and they would have eaten me if I had stayed—which I didn't, but went away in much haste. . . . I found this place, outside the Park, and was fairly comfortable for a few days, but she has found me out. Found me out, and has named the place Tonawanda—says it *looks* like that. In fact I was not sorry she came, for there are but meager pickings here, and she brought some of those apples. I was obliged to eat them, I was so hungry. It was against my principles, but I find that principles have no real force except when one is well fed. . . . She came curtained in boughs and bunches of leaves, and when I asked her what she meant by such nonsense, and snatched them away and threw them down, she tittered and blushed. I had never seen a person titter and blush before, and to me it seemed unbecoming and idiotic. She said I would soon know how it was myself. This was correct. Hungry as I was, I laid down the apple half-eaten—certainly the best one I ever saw, considering the lateness of the season—and arrayed myself in the discarded boughs and branches, and then spoke to her with some severity and ordered her to go and get some more and not make such a spectacle of herself. She did it, and after this we crept down to where the wild-beast battle had been, and collected some skins, and I made her patch together a couple of suits proper for public occasions. They are uncomfortable, it is true, but stylish, and that is the main point about clothes. . . . I find she is a good deal of a companion. I see I should be lonesome and depressed without her, now that I have lost my property. Another thing, she says it is ordered that we work for our living hereafter. She will be useful. I will superintend.

Ten Days Later   She accuses *me* of being the cause of our disaster! She says, with apparent sincerity and truth, that the Serpent assured her that the forbidden fruit was not apples, it was chestnuts. I said I was innocent, then, for I had not eaten any chestnuts. She said the Serpent informed her that "chestnut" was a figurative term meaning an aged and moldy joke. I turned pale at that, for I have made many jokes to pass the weary time, and some of them could have been of that sort, though I had honestly supposed that they were new when I made them. She asked me if I had made one just at the time of the catastrophe. I was obliged to admit that I had made one to myself, though not aloud. It was this. I was thinking about the Falls, and I said to myself, "How wonderful it is to see that vast body of water tumble down there!" Then in an instant a bright thought flashed into my head, and I let it fly, saying, "It would be a deal more wonderful to see it tumble *up* there!"—and I was just about to kill myself with laughing at it when all nature broke loose in war and death and I had to flee for my life. "There," she said, with triumph, "that is just it; the Serpent mentioned that very jest, and called it the First Chestnut, and said it was coeval with the creation." Alas, I am indeed to blame. Would that I were not witty; oh, that I had never had that radiant thought!

Next Year   We have named it Cain. She caught it while I was up country trapping on the North Shore of the Erie; caught it in the timber a couple of miles from our dug-out—or it might have been four, she isn't certain which. It resembles us in some ways, and may be a relation. That is what she thinks, but this is an error, in my judgment. The difference in size warrants the conclusion that it is a different and new kind of animal— a fish, perhaps, though when I put it in the water to see, it sank, and she plunged in and snatched it out before there was opportunity for the experiment to determine the matter. I still think it is a fish, but she is indifferent about what it is, and will not let me have it to try. I do not understand this. The coming of the creature seems to have changed her whole nature and made her unreasonable about experiments. She thinks more of it than she does of any of the other animals, but is not able to explain why. Her mind is disordered—everything shows it. Sometimes she carries the fish in her arms half the night when it complains and wants to get to the water. At such times the water comes out of the places in her face that she looks out of, and she pats the fish on the back and makes soft sounds with her mouth to soothe it, and betrays sorrow and solicitude in a hundred ways. I have never seen her do like this with any other fish, and it troubles me greatly. She used to carry the young tigers around so, and play with them, before we lost our property, but it was only play; she never took on about them like this when their dinner disagreed with them.

Sunday   She doesn't work, Sundays, but lies around all tired out, and likes to have the fish wallow over her; and she makes fool noises to amuse it, and pretends to chew its paws, and that makes it laugh. I have not seen a fish before that could laugh. This makes me doubt. . . . I have come to like Sunday myself. Superintending all the week tires a body so. There ought to be more Sundays. In the old days they were tough, but now they come in handy.

Wednesday   It isn't a fish. I cannot quite make out what it is. It makes curious devilish noises when not satisfied, and says ``goo-goo'' when it is. It is not one of us, for it doesn't walk; it is not a bird, for it doesn't fly; it is not a frog, for it doesn't hop; it is not a snake, for it doesn't crawl. I feel sure it is not a fish, though I cannot get a chance to find out whether it can swim or not. It merely lies around, and mostly on its back, with its feet up. I have not seen any other animal do that before. I said I believed it was an enigma; but she only admired the word without understanding it. In my judgment it is either an enigma or some kind of a bug. If it dies, I will take it apart and see what its arrangements are. I never had a thing perplex me so.

Three Months Later   The perplexity augments instead of diminishing. I sleep but little. It has ceased from lying around, and goes about on its four legs now. Yet it differs from the other four-legged animals, in that its front legs are unusually short, consequently this causes the main part of its person to stick up uncomfortably high in the air, and this is not attractive. It is built much as we are, but its method of traveling shows that it is not of our breed. The short front legs and long hind ones indicate that it is of the kangaroo family, but it is a marked variation of the species, since the true kangaroo hops, whereas this one never does. Still it is a curious and interesting variety, and has not been catalogued before. As I discovered it, I have felt justified in securing the credit of the discovery by attaching my name to it, and hence have called it *Kangaroorum Adamiensis.* . . . It must have been a young one when it came, for it has grown exceedingly since. It must be five times as big, now, as it was then, and when discontented it is able to make from twenty-two to thirty-eight times the noise it made at first. Coercion does not modify this, but has the contrary effect. For this reason I discontinued the system. She reconciles it by persuasion, and by giving it things which she had previously told me she wouldn't give it. As already observed, I was not at home when it first came, and she told me she found it in the woods. It seems odd that it should be the only one, yet it must be so, for I have worn myself out these many weeks trying to find another one to add to my collection, and for this one to play with; for surely then it would be quieter and we could tame it more easily. But I find none, nor any vestige of any; and strangest of all, no tracks. It has to live on the ground, it cannot help itself; therefore, how does it get about without leaving a track? I have set a dozen traps, but they do no good. I catch all small animals except that one; animals that merely go into the trap out of curiosity, I think, to see what the milk is there for. They never drink it.

Three Months Later   The Kangaroo still continues to grow, which is very strange and perplexing. I never knew one to be so long getting its growth. It has fur on its head now; not like kangaroo fur, but exactly like our hair except that it is much finer and softer, and instead of being black is red. I am like to lose my mind over the capricious and harassing developments of this unclassifiable zoological freak. If I could catch another one—but that is hopeless; it is a new variety, and the only sample; this is plain. But I caught a true kangaroo and brought it in, thinking that this one, being lonesome, would rather have that for company than have no kin at all, or any animal it could feel a nearness to or get sympathy from in its forlorn condition here among strangers who do not know its ways or habits, or what to do to make it feel that it is among friends; but it was a mistake—it went into such fits at the sight of the kangaroo that I was convinced it had never seen one before. I pity the poor noisy little animal, but there is nothing I can do to make it happy. If I could tame it—but that is out of the question; the more I try the worse I seem to make it. It grieves me to the heart to see it in its little storms of sorrow and passion. I wanted to let it go, but she wouldn't hear of it. That seemed cruel and not like her; and yet she may be right. It might be lonelier than ever; for since I cannot find another one, how could *it?*

Five Months Later It is not a kangaroo. No, for it supports itself by holding to her finger, and thus goes a few steps on its hind legs, and then falls down. It is probably some kind of a bear; and yet it has no tail—as yet—and no fur, except on its head. It still keeps on growing—that is a curious circumstance, for bears get their growth earlier than this. Bears are dangerous—since our catastrophe—and I shall not be satisfied to have this one prowling about the place much longer without a muzzle on. I have offered to get her a kangaroo if she would let this one go, but it did no good—she is determined to run us into all sorts of foolish risks, I think. She was not like this before she lost her mind.

A Fortnight Later I examined its mouth. There is no danger yet: it has only one tooth. It has no tail yet. It makes more noise now than it ever did before—and mainly at night. I have moved out. But I shall go over, mornings, to breakfast, and see if it has more teeth. If it gets a mouthful of teeth it will be time for it to go, tail or no tail, for a bear does not need a tail in order to be dangerous.

Four Months Later I have been off hunting and fishing a month, up in the region that she calls Buffalo; I don't know why, unless it is because there are not any buffaloes there. Meantime the bear has learned to paddle around all by itself on its hind legs, and says ``poppa'' and ``momma.'' It is certainly a new species. This resemblance to words may be purely accidental, of course, and may have no purpose or meaning; but even in that case it is still extraordinary, and is a thing which no other bear can do. This imitation of speech, taken together with general absence of fur and entire absence of tail, sufficiently indicates that this is a new kind of bear. The further study of it will be exceedingly interesting. Meantime I will go off on a far expedition among the forests of the north and make an exhaustive search. There must certainly be another one somewhere, and this one will be less dangerous when it has company of its own species. I will go straightway; but I will muzzle this one first.

Three Months Later It has been a weary, weary hunt, yet I have had no success. In the mean time, without stirring from the home estate, she has caught another one! I never saw such luck. I might have hunted these woods a hundred years, I never would have run across that thing.

Next Day I have been comparing the new one with the old one, and it is perfectly plain that they are the same breed. I was going to stuff one of them for my collection, but she is prejudiced against it for some reason or other; so I have relinquished the idea, though I think it is a mistake. It would be an irreparable loss to science if they should get away. The old one is tamer than it was and can laugh and talk like the parrot, having learned this, no doubt, from being with the parrot so much, and having the imitative faculty in a highly developed degree. I shall be astonished if it turns out to be a new kind of parrot; and yet I ought not to be astonished for it has already been everything else it could think of since those first days when it was a fish. The new one is as ugly now as the old one was at first; has the same sulphur-and-raw-meat complexion and the same singular head without any fur on it. She calls it Abel.

Ten Years Later They are *boys;* we found it out long ago. It was their coming in that small, immature shape that puzzled us; we were not used to it. There are some girls now. Abel is a good boy, but if Cain had stayed a bear it would have improved him. After all these years, I see that I was mistaken about Eve in the beginning; it is better to live outside the Garden with her than inside it without her. At first I thought she talked too much; but now I should be sorry to have that voice fall silent and pass out of my life. Blessed be the chestnut that brought us near together and taught me to know the goodness of her heart and the sweetness of her spirit!

Part II—Eve's Diary

(Translated from the original)

Saturday I am almost a whole day old, now. I arrived yesterday. That is as it seems to me. And it must be so, for if there was a day-before-yesterday I was not there when it happened, or I should remember it. It could be, of course, that it did happen, and that I was not noticing. Very well; I will be very watchful now, and if any day-before-yesterdays happen I will make a note of it. It will be best to start right and not let the record get confused, for some instinct tells me that these details are going to be important to the historian some day. For I feel like an experiment, I feel exactly like an experiment; it would be impossible for a person to feel more like an experiment than I do, and so I am coming to feel convinced that that is what I *am*—an experiment; just an experiment, and nothing more.

Then if I am an experiment, am I the whole of it? No, I think not; I think the rest of it is part of it. I am the main part of it, but I think the rest of it has its share in the matter. Is my position assured, or do I have to watch it and take care of it? The latter, perhaps. Some instinct tells me that eternal vigilance is the price of supremacy. (That is a good phrase, I think, for one so young.)

Everything looks better to-day than it did yesterday. In the rush of finishing up yesterday, the mountains were left in a ragged condition, and some of the plains were so cluttered with rubbish and remnants that the aspects were quite distressing. Noble and beautiful works of art should not be subjected to haste; and this majestic new world is indeed a most noble and beautiful work. And certainly marvelously near to being perfect, notwithstanding the shortness of the time. There are too many stars in some places and not enough in others, but that can be remedied presently, no doubt. The moon got loose last night, and slid down and fell out of the scheme—a very great loss; it breaks my heart to think of it. There isn't another thing among the ornaments and decorations that is comparable to it for beauty and finish. It should have been fastened better. If we can only get it back again—

But of course there is no telling where it went to. And besides, whoever gets it will hide it; I know it because I would do it myself. I believe I can be honest in all other matters, but I already begin to realize that the core and center of my nature is love of the beautiful, a passion for the beautiful, and that it would not be safe to trust me with a moon that belonged to another person and that person didn't know I had it. I could give up a moon that I found in the daytime, because I should be afraid some one was looking; but if I found it in the dark, I am sure I should find some kind of an excuse for not saying anything about it. For I do love moons, they are so pretty and so romantic. I wish we had five or six; I would never go to bed; I should never get tired lying on the moss-bank and looking up at them.

Stars are good, too. I wish I could get some to put in my hair. But I suppose I never can. You would be surprised to find how far off they are, for they do not look it. When they first showed, last night, I tried to knock some down with a pole, but it didn't reach, which astonished me; then I tried clods till I was all tired out, but I never got one. It was because I am left-handed and cannot throw good. Even when I aimed at the one I wasn't after I couldn't hit the other one, though I did make some close shots, for I saw the black blot of the clod sail right into the midst of the golden clusters forty or fifty times, just barely missing them, and if I could have held out a little longer maybe I could have got one.

So I cried a little, which was natural, I suppose, for one of my age, and after I was rested I got a basket and started for a place on the extreme rim of the circle, where the stars were close to the ground and I could get them with my hands, which would be better, anyway, because I could gather them tenderly then, and not break them. But it was farther than I thought, and at last I had to give it up; I was so tired I couldn't drag my feet another step; and besides, they were sore and hurt me very much.

I couldn't get back home; it was too far and turning cold; but I found some tigers and nestled in among them and was most adorably comfortable, and their breath was sweet and pleasant, because they live on strawberries. I had never seen a tiger before, but I knew them in a minute by the stripes. If I could have one of those skins, it would make a lovely gown.

To-day I am getting better ideas about distances. I was so eager to get hold of every pretty thing that I giddily grabbed for it, sometimes when it was too far off, and sometimes when it was but six inches away but seemed a foot—alas, with thorns between! I learned a lesson; also I made an axiom, all out of my own head—my very first one: *The scratched Experiment shuns the thorn.* I think it is a very good one for one so young.

I followed the other Experiment around, yesterday afternoon, at a distance, to see what it might be for, if I could. But I was not able to make it out. I think it is a man. I had never seen a man, but it looked like one, and I feel sure that that is what it is. I realize that I feel more curiosity about it than about any of the other reptiles. If it is a reptile, and I suppose it is; for it has frowsy hair and blue eyes, and looks like a reptile. It has no hips; it tapers like a carrot; when it stands, it spreads itself apart like a derrick; so I think it is a reptile, though it may be architecture.

I was afraid of it at first, and started to run every time it turned around, for I thought it was going to chase me; but by and by I found it was only trying to get away, so after that I was not timid any more, but tracked it along, several hours, about twenty yards behind, which made it nervous and unhappy. At last it was a good deal worried, and climbed a tree. I waited a good while, then gave it up and went home.

To-day the same thing over. I've got it up the tree again.

Sunday   It is up there yet. Resting, apparently. But that is a subterfuge: Sunday isn't the day of rest; Saturday is appointed for that. It looks to me like a creature that is more interested in resting than in anything else. It would tire me to rest so much. It tires me just to sit around and watch the tree. I do wonder what it is for; I never see it do anything.

They returned the moon last night, and I was *so* happy! I think it is very honest of them. It slid down and fell off again, but I was not distressed; there is no need to worry when one has that kind of neighbors; they will fetch it back. I wish I could do something to show my appreciation. I would like to send them some stars, for we have more than we can use. I mean I, not we, for I can see that the reptile cares nothing for such things.

It has low tastes, and is not kind. When I went there yesterday evening in the gloaming it had crept down and was trying to catch the little speckled fishes that play in the pool, and I had to clod it to make it go up the tree again and let them alone. I wonder if *that* is what it is for? Hasn't it any heart? Hasn't it any compassion for those little creatures? Can it be that it was designed and manufactured for such ungentle work? It has the look of it. One of the clods took it back of the ear, and it used language. It gave me a thrill, for it was the first time I had ever heard speech, except my own. I did not understand the words, but they seemed expressive.

When I found it could talk I felt a new interest in it, for I love to talk; I talk, all day, and in my sleep, too, and I am very interesting, but if I had another to talk to I could be twice as interesting, and would never stop, if desired.

If this reptile is a man, it isn't an *it*, is it? That wouldn't be grammatical, would it? I think it would be a *he*. I think so. In that case one would parse it thus: nominative, *he;* dative, *him;* possessive, *his'n.* Well, I will consider it a man and call it he until it turns out to be something else. This will be handier than having so many uncertainties.

Next week Sunday   All the week I tagged around after him and tried to get acquainted. I had to do the talking, because he was shy, but I didn't mind it. He seemed pleased to have me around, and I used the sociable "we" a good deal, because it seemed to flatter him to be included.

Wednesday   We are getting along very well indeed, now, and getting better and better acquainted. He does not try to avoid me any more, which is a good sign, and shows that he likes to have me with him. That pleases me, and I study to be useful to him in every way I can, so as to increase his regard. During the last day or two I have taken all the work of naming things off his hands, and this has been a great relief to him, for he has no gift in that line, and is evidently very grateful. He can't think of a rational name to save him, but I do not let him see that I am aware of his defect. Whenever a new creature comes along I name it before he has time to expose himself by an awkward silence. In this way I have saved him many embarrassments. I have no defect like his. The minute I set eyes on an animal I know what it is. I don't have to reflect a moment; the right name comes out instantly, just as if it were an inspiration, as no doubt it is, for I am sure it wasn't in me half a minute before. I seem to know just by the shape of the creature and the way it acts what animal it is.

When the dodo came along he thought it was a wildcat—I saw it in his eye. But I saved him. And I was careful not to do it in a way that could hurt his pride. I just spoke up in a quite natural way of pleased surprise, and not as if I was dreaming of conveying information, and said, ``Well, I do declare, if there isn't the dodo!'' I explained—without seeming to be explaining—how I knew it for a dodo, and although I thought maybe he was a little piqued that I knew the creature when he didn't, it was quite evident that he admired me. That was very agreeable, and I thought of it more than once with gratification before I slept. How little a thing can make us happy when we feel that we have earned it!

Thursday   My first sorrow. Yesterday he avoided me and seemed to wish I would not talk to him. I could not believe it, and thought there was some mistake, for I loved to be with him, and loved to hear him talk, and so how could it be that he could feel unkind toward me when I had not done anything? But at last it seemed true, so I went away and sat lonely in the place where I first saw him the morning that we were made and I did not know what he was and was indifferent about him; but now it was a mournful place, and every little thing spoke of him, and my heart was very sore. I did not know why very clearly, for it was a new feeling; I had not experienced it before, and it was all a mystery, and I could not make it out.

But when night came I could not bear the lonesomeness, and went to the new shelter which he has built, to ask him what I had done that was wrong and how I could mend it and get back his kindness again; but he put me out in the rain, and it was my first sorrow.

Sunday   It is pleasant again, now, and I am happy; but those were heavy days; I do not think of them when I can help it.

I tried to get him some of those apples, but I cannot learn to throw straight. I failed, but I think the good intention pleased him. They are forbidden, and he says I shall come to harm; but so I come to harm through pleasing him, why shall I care for that harm?

Monday   This morning I told him my name, hoping it would interest him. But he did not care for it. It is strange. If he should tell me his name,

I would care. I think it would be pleasanter in my ears than any other sound.

He talks very little. Perhaps it is because he is not bright, and is sensitive about it and wishes to conceal it. It is such a pity that he should feel so, for brightness is nothing; it is in the heart that values lie. I wish I could make him understand that a loving good heart is riches, and riches enough, and that without it intellect is poverty.

Although he talks so little, he has quite a considerable vocabulary. This morning he used a surprisingly good word. He evidently recognized, himself, that it was a good one, for he worked it in twice afterward, casually. It was not good casual art, still it showed that he possesses a certain quality of perception. Without a doubt that seed can be made to grow, if cultivated.

Where did he get that word? I do not think I have ever used it.

No, he took no interest in my name. I tried to hide my disappointment, but I suppose I did not succeed. I went away and sat on the mossbank with my feet in the water. It is where I go when I hunger for companionship, some one to look at, some one to talk to. It is not enough—that lovely white body painted there in the pool—but it is something, and something is better than utter loneliness. It talks when I talk; it is sad when I am sad; it comforts me with its sympathy; it says, ``Do not be downhearted, you poor friendless girl; I will be your friend.'' It *is* a good friend to me, and my only one; it is my sister.

That first time that she forsook me! Ah, I shall never forget that—never, never. My heart was lead in my body! I said, ``She was all I had, and now she is gone!'' In my despair I said, ``Break, my heart; I cannot bear my life any more!'' and hid my face in my hands, and there was no solace for me. And when I took them away, after a little, there she was again, white and shining and beautiful, and I sprang into her arms!

That was perfect happiness; I had known happiness before, but it was not like this, which was ecstasy. I never doubted her afterward. Sometimes she stayed away—maybe an hour, maybe almost the whole day, but I waited and did not doubt; I said, ``She is busy, or she is gone a journey, but she will come.'' And it was so: she always did. At night she would not come if it was dark, for she was a timid little thing; but if there was a moon she would come. I am not afraid of the dark, but she is younger than I am; she was born after I was. Many and many are the visits I have paid her; she is my comfort and my refuge when my life is hard—and it is mainly that.

Tuesday All the morning I was at work improving the estate; and I purposely kept away from him in the hope that he would get lonely and come. But he did not.

At noon I stopped for the day and took my recreation by flitting all about with the bees and the butterflies and reveling in the flowers, those beautiful creatures that catch the smile of God out of the sky and preserve it! I gathered them, and made them into wreaths and garlands and clothed myself in them while I ate my luncheon—apples, of course; then I sat in the shade and wished and waited. But he did not come.

But no matter. Nothing would have come of it, for he does not care for flowers. He calls them rubbish, and cannot tell one from another, and thinks it is superior to feel like that. He does not care for me, he does not care for flowers, he does not care for the painted sky at eventide—is there anything he does care for, except building shacks to coop himself up in from the good clean rain, and thumping the melons, and sampling the grapes, and fingering the fruit on the trees, to see how those properties are coming along?

I laid a dry stick on the ground and tried to bore a hole in it with another one, in order to carry out a scheme that I had, and soon I got an awful fright. A thin, transparent bluish film rose out of the hole, and I dropped everything and ran! I thought it was a spirit, and I *was* so frightened! But I looked back, and it was not coming; so I leaned against a rock and rested and panted, and let my limbs go on trembling until they got steady again; then I crept warily back, alert, watching, and ready to fly if there was occasion; and when I was come near, I parted the branches of a rose-bush and peeped through—wishing the man was about, I was looking so cunning and pretty—but the sprite was gone. I went there, and there was a pinch of delicate pink dust in the hole. I put my finger in, to feel it, and said *ouch!* and took it out again. It was a cruel pain. I put my finger in my mouth; and by standing first on one foot and then the other, and grunting, I presently eased my misery; then I was full of interest, and began to examine.

I was curious to know what the pink dust was. Suddenly the name of it occurred to me, though I had never heard of it before. It was *fire!* I was as certain of it as a person could be of anything in the world. So without hesitation I named it that—fire.

I had created something that didn't exist before; I had added a new thing to the world's uncountable properties; I realized this, and was proud of my achievement, and was going to run and find him and tell him about it, thinking to raise myself in his esteem—but I reflected, and did not do it. No—he would not care for it. He would ask what it was good for, and what could I answer? for if it were not *good* for something, but only beautiful, merely beautiful—

So I sighed, and did not go. For it wasn't good for anything; it could not build a shack, it could not improve melons, it could not hurry a fruit crop; it was useless, it was a foolishness and a vanity; he would despise it and say cutting words. But to me it was not despicable; I said, "Oh, you fire, I love you, you dainty pink creature, for you are *beautiful*—and that is enough!" and was going to gather it to my breast. But refrained. Then I made another maxim out of my own head, though it was so nearly like the first one that I was afraid it was only a plagiarism: "*The burnt Experiment shuns the fire.*"

I wrought again; and when I had made a good deal of fire-dust I emptied it into a handful of dry brown grass, intending to carry it home and keep it always and play with it; but the wind struck it and it sprayed up and spat out at me fiercely, and I dropped it and ran. When I looked back the blue spirit was towering up and stretching and rolling away like a cloud, and instantly I thought of the name of it—*smoke!*—though, upon my word, I had never heard of smoke before.

Soon, brilliant yellow and red flares shot up through the smoke, and I named them in an instant—*flames*—and I was right, too, though these were the very first flames that had ever been in the world. They climbed the trees, they flashed splendidly in and out of the vast and increasing volume of tumbling smoke, and I had to clap my hands and laugh and dance in my rapture, it was so new and strange and so wonderful and so beautiful!

He came running, and stopped and gazed, and said not a word for many minutes. Then he asked what it was. Ah, it was too bad that he should ask such a direct question. I had to answer it, of course, and I did. I said it was fire. If it annoyed him that I should know and he must ask, that was not my fault; I had no desire to annoy him. After a pause he asked:

"How did it come?"

Another direct question, and it also had to have a direct answer.

"I made it."

The fire was traveling farther and farther off. He went to the edge of the burned place and stood looking down, and said:

"What are these?"

"Fire-coals."

He picked up one to examine it, but changed his mind and put it down again. Then he went away. *Nothing* interests him.

But I was interested. There were ashes, gray and soft and delicate and pretty—I knew what they were at once. And the embers; I knew the embers, too. I found my apples, and raked them out, and was glad; for I am very young and my appetite is active. But I was disappointed; they were all burst open and spoiled. Spoiled apparently; but it was not so; they were better than raw ones. Fire is beautiful; some day it will useful, I think.

Friday   I saw him again, for a moment, last Monday at nightfall, but only for a moment. I was hoping he would praise me for trying to improve the estate, for I had meant well and had worked hard. But he was not pleased, and turned away and left me. He was also displeased on another account: I tried once more to persuade him to stop going over the Falls. That was because the fire had revealed to me a new passion—quite new, and distinctly different from love, grief, and those others which I had already discovered—*fear*. And it is horrible!—I wish I had never discovered it; it gives me dark moments, it spoils my happiness, it makes me shiver and tremble and shudder. But I could not persuade him, for he has not discovered fear yet, and so he could not understand me.

Extract from Adam's Diary

Perhaps I ought to remember that she is very young, a mere girl, and make allowances. She is all interest, eagerness, vivacity, the world is to her a charm, a wonder, a mystery, a joy; she can't speak for delight when she finds a new flower, she must pet it and caress it and smell it and talk to it, and pour out endearing names upon it. And she is color-mad: brown rocks, yellow sand, gray moss, green foliage, blue sky; the pearl of the dawn, the purple shadows on the mountains, the golden islands floating in crimson seas at sunset, the pallid moon sailing through the shredded cloud-rack, the star-jewels glittering in the wastes of space—none of them is of any practical value, so far as I can see, but because they have color and majesty, that is enough for her, and she loses her mind over them. If she could quiet down and keep still a couple of minutes at a time, it would be a reposeful spectacle. In that case I think I could enjoy looking at her; indeed I am sure I could, for I am coming to realize that she is a quite remarkably comely creature—lithe, slender, trim, rounded, shapely, nimble, graceful; and once when she was standing marble-white and sun-drenched on a boulder, with her young head tilted back and her hand shading her eyes, watching the flight of a bird in the sky, I recognized that she was beautiful.

Monday noon   If there is anything on the planet that she is not interested in it is not in my list. There are animals that I am indifferent to, but it is not so with her. She has no discrimination, she takes to all of them, she thinks they are all treasures, every new one is welcome.

When the mighty brontosaurus came striding into camp, she regarded it as an acquisition, I considered it a calamity; that is a good sample of the lack of harmony that prevails in our views of things. She wanted to domesticate it, I wanted to make it a present of the homestead and move out. She believed it could be tamed by kind treatment and would be a good pet; I said a pet twenty-one feet high and eighty-four feet long would be no proper thing to have about the place, because, even with the best intentions and without meaning any harm, it could sit down on the house and mash it, for any one could see by the look of its eye that it was absent-minded.

Still, her heart was set upon having that monster, and she couldn't give it up. She thought we could start a dairy with it, and wanted me to help her milk it; but I wouldn't; it was too risky. The sex wasn't right, and we hadn't any ladder anyway. Then she wanted to ride it, and look at the scenery. Thirty or forty feet of its tail was lying on the ground, like a fallen tree, and she thought she could climb it, but she was mistaken; when she got to the steep place it was too slick and down she came, and would have hurt herself but for me.

Was she satisfied now? No. Nothing ever satisfies her but demonstration; untested theories are not in her line, and she won't have them. It is the right spirit, I concede it; it attracts me; I feel the influence of it; if I were with her more I think I should take it up myself. Well, she had one theory remaining about this colossus: she thought that if we could tame him and make him friendly we could stand him in the river and use him for a bridge. It turned out that he was already plenty tame enough—at least as far as she was concerned—so she tried her theory, but it failed: every time she got him properly placed in the river and went ashore to cross over on him, he came out and followed her around like a pet mountain. Like the other animals. They all do that.

Friday Tuesday—Wednesday—Thursday—and to-day: all without seeing him. It is a long time to be alone; still, it is better to be alone than unwelcome.

I *had* to have company—I was made for it, I think—so I made friends with the animals. They are just charming, and they have the kindest disposition and politest ways; they never look sour, they never let you feel that you are intruding, they smile at you and wag their tail, if they've got one, and they are always ready for a romp or an excursion or anything you want to propose. I think they are perfect gentlemen. All these days we have had such good times, and it hasn't been lonesome for me, ever. Lonesome! No, I should say not. Why, there's always a swarm of them around—sometimes as much as four or five acres—you can't count them; and when you stand on a rock in the midst and look out over the furry expanse it is so mottled and splashed and gay with color and frisking sheen and sun-flash, and so rippled with stripes, that you might think it was a lake, only you know it isn't; and there's storms of sociable birds, and hurricanes of whirring wings; and when the sun strikes all that feathery commotion, you have a blazing up of all the colors you can think of, enough to put your eyes out.

We have made long excursions, and I have seen a great deal of the world; almost all of it, I think; and so I am the first traveler, and the only one. When we are on the march, it is an imposing sight—there's nothing like it anywhere. For comfort I ride a tiger or a leopard, because it is soft and has a round back that fits me, and because they are such pretty animals; but for long distance or for scenery I ride the elephant. He hoists me up with his trunk, but I can get off myself; when we are ready to camp, he sits and I slide down the back way.

The birds and animals are all friendly to each other, and there are no disputes about anything. They all talk, and they all talk to me, but it must be a foreign language, for I cannot make out a word they say; yet they often understand me when I talk back, particularly the dog and the elephant. It makes me ashamed. It shows that they are brighter than I am, and are therefore my superiors. It annoys me, for I want to be the principal Experiment myself—and I intend to be, too.

I have learned a number of things, and am educated, now, but I wasn't at first. I was ignorant at first. At first it used to vex me because, with all my watching, I was never smart enough to be around when the water was running uphill; but now I do not mind it. I have experimented and experimented until now I know it never does run uphill, except in the dark. I know it does in the dark, because the pool never goes dry, which it would, of course, if the water didn't come back in the night. It is best to prove things by actual experiment; then you *know;* whereas if you depend on guessing and supposing and conjecturing, you will never get educated.

Some things you *can't* find out; but you will never know you can't by guessing and supposing: no, you have to be patient and go on experimenting until you find out that you can't find out. And it is delightful to have it that way, it makes the world so interesting. If there wasn't anything to find out, it would be dull. Even trying to find out and not finding out is just as interesting as trying to find out and finding out, and I don't know but more so. The secret of the water was a treasure until I *got* it; then the excitement all went away, and I recognized a sense of loss.

By experiment I know that wood swims, and dry leaves, and feathers, and plenty of other things; therefore by all that cumulative evidence you know that a rock will swim; but you have to put up with simply knowing it, for there isn't any way to prove it—up to now. But I shall find a way—then *that* excitement will go. Such things make me sad; because by and by when I have found out everything there won't be any more excitements, and I do love excitements so! The other night I couldn't sleep for thinking about it.

At first I couldn't make out what I was made for, but now I think it was to search out the secrets of this wonderful world and be happy and thank the Giver of it all for devising it. I think there are many things to learn yet—I hope so; and by economizing and not hurrying too fast I think they will last weeks and weeks. I hope so. When you cast up a feather it sails away on the air and goes out of sight; then you throw up a clod and it doesn't. It comes down, every time. I have tried it and tried it, and it is always so. I wonder why it is? Of course it *doesn't* come down, but why should it *seem* to? I suppose it is an optical illusion. I mean, one of them is. I don't know which one. It may be the feather, it may be the clod; I can't prove which it is, I can only demonstrate that one or the other is a fake, and let a person take his choice.

By watching, I know that the stars are not going to last. I have seen some of the best ones melt and run down the sky. Since one can melt, they can all melt; since they can all melt, they can all melt the same night. That sorrow will come—I know it. I mean to sit up every night and look at them as long as I can keep awake; and I will impress those sparkling fields on my memory, so that by and by when they are taken away I can by my fancy restore those lovely myriads to the black sky and make them sparkle again, and double them by the blur of my tears.

After the Fall

When I look back, the Garden is a dream to me. It was beautiful, surpassingly beautiful, enchantingly beautiful; and now it is lost, and I shall not see it any more.

The Garden is lost, but I have found *him,* and am content. He loves me as well as he can; I love him with all the strength of my passionate nature, and this, I think, is proper to my youth and sex. If I ask myself why I love him, I find I do not know, and do not really much care to know; so I suppose that this kind of love is not a product of reasoning and statistics, like one's love for other reptiles and animals. I think that this must be so. I love certain birds because of their song; but I do not love Adam on account of his singing—no, it is not that; the more he sings the more I do not get reconciled to it. Yet I ask him to sing, because I wish to learn to like everything he is interested in. I am sure I can learn, because at first I could not stand it, but now I can. It sours the milk, but it doesn't matter; I can get used to that kind of milk.

It is not on account of his brightness that I love him—no, it is not that. He is not to blame for his brightness, such as it is, for he did not make it himself; he is as God made him, and that is sufficient. There was a wise purpose in it, *that* I know. In time it will develop, though I think it will not be sudden; and besides, there is no hurry; he is well enough just as he is.

It is not on account of his gracious and considerate ways and his delicacy that I love him. No, he has lacks in these regards, but he is well enough just so, and is improving.

It is not on account of his industry that I love him—no, it is not that. I think he has it in him, and I do not know why he conceals it from me. It is my only pain. Otherwise he is frank and open with me, now. I am sure he keeps nothing from me but this. It grieves me that he should have a secret from me, and sometimes it spoils my sleep, thinking of it, but I will put it out of my mind; it shall not trouble my happiness, which is otherwise full to overflowing.

It is not on account of his education that I love him—no, it is not that. He is self-educated, and does really know a multitude of things, but they are not so.

It is not on account of his chivalry that I love him—no, it is not that. He told on me, but I do not blame him; it is a peculiarity of sex, I think, and he did not make his sex. Of course I would not have told on him, I would have perished first; but that is a peculiarity of sex, too, and I do not take credit for it, for I did not make my sex.

Then why is it that I love him? *Merely because he is masculine,* I think.

At bottom he is good, and I love him for that, but I could love him without it. If he should beat me and abuse me, I should go on loving him. I know it. It is a matter of sex, I think.

He is strong and handsome, and I love him for that, and I admire him and am proud of him, but I could love him without those qualities. If he were plain, I should love him; if he were a wreck, I should love him; and I would work for him, and slave over him, and pray for him, and watch by his bedside until I died.

Yes, I think I love him merely because he is *mine* and is *masculine.*

There is no other reason, I suppose. And so I think it is as I first said: that this kind of love is not a product of reasonings and statistics. it just *comes*—none knows whence—and cannot explain itself. And doesn't need to.

It is what I think. But I am only a girl, and the first that has examined this matter, and it may turn out that in my ignorance and inexperience I have not got it right.

Forty Years Later

It is my prayer, it is my longing, that we may pass from this life together—a longing which shall never perish from the earth, but shall have place in the heart of every wife that loves, until the end of time; and it shall be called by my name.

But if one of us must go first, it is my prayer that it shall be I; for he is strong. I am weak, I am not so necessary to him as he is to me—life without him would not be life; how could I endure it? This prayer is also immortal, and will not cease from being offered up while my race continues. I am the first wife; and in the last wife I shall be repeated.

At Eve's Grave

Adam: Wheresoever she was, *there* was Eden.

SUGGESTIONS FOR WRITING AND DISCUSSION

1. Why do you think Twain attributes the discovery of fire to Eve rather than to Adam?
2. How are objects given names in this account of Adam and Eve? Does Twain attempt to find a logic to the way names are given?
3. This is a satire (see Chapter 9). What is being satirized? How?
4. How do Adam's and Eve's impressions of each other change throughout the story? Do they ever really fall in love?
5. How does this story use sexual stereotypes? What point is Twain trying to make by the use of these stereotypes? Do you feel Twain is a male chauvinist? Discuss in a three- to five-page essay.
6. What statement does this story make about the need for companionship?
7. Write a series of diary or journal entries for a biblical, fictional, or historical character, showing events from his or her point of view.

Anton Chekhov (Russian, 1860–1904)

A Lady with a Dog

I

There was said to be a new arrival on the Esplanade: a lady with a dog.

After spending a fortnight at Yalta, Dmitry Gurov had quite settled in and was now beginning to take an interest in new faces. As he sat outside

Vernet's café he saw a fair-haired young woman, not tall, walking on the promenade—wearing a beret, with a white Pomeranian dog trotting after her.

Then he encountered her several times a day in the municipal park and square. She walked alone, always with that beret, always with the white Pomeranian. Who she was no one knew, everyone just called her 'the dog lady'.

'If she has no husband or friends here she might be worth picking up,' calculated Gurov.

He was still in his thirties, but had a twelve-year-old daughter and two schoolboy sons. His marriage had been arranged early—during his second college year—and now his wife seemed half as old again as he. She was a tall, dark-browed woman: outspoken, earnest, stolid, and—she maintained—an 'intellectual'. She was a great reader, she favoured spelling reform, she called her husband 'Demetrius' instead of plain 'Dmitry', while he privately thought her narrow-minded, inelegant and slow on the uptake. He was afraid of her, and disliked being at home. He had begun deceiving her long ago, and his infidelities were frequent—which is probably why he nearly always spoke so disparagingly of women, calling them an 'inferior species' when the subject cropped up.

He was, he felt, sufficiently schooled by bitter experience to call them any name he liked, yet he still couldn't live two days on end without his 'inferior species'. Men's company bored him, making him ill at ease, tongue-tied and apathetic, whereas with women he felt free. He knew what to talk about, how to behave—he even found it easy to be with them without talking at all. In his appearance and character, in his whole nature, there was an alluring, elusive element which charmed and fascinated women. He knew it, and he was himself strongly attracted in return.

As experience multiple and—in the full sense of the word—bitter had long since taught him, every intimacy which so pleasantly diversifies one's life, which seems so easy, so delightfully adventurous at the outset . . . such an intimacy does, when reasonable people are involved (not least Muscovites—so hesitant and slow off the mark), develop willy-nilly into some vast, extraordinarily complex problem until the whole business finally becomes quite an ordeal. Somehow, though, on every new encounter with an attractive woman all this experience went for nothing—he wanted a bit of excitement and it all seemed so easy and amusing.

Well, he was eating in an open-air restaurant late one afternoon when the lady in the beret sauntered along and took the next table. Her expression, walk, clothes, hair-style . . . all told him that she was socially presentable, married, in Yalta for the first time, alone—and bored.

Much nonsense is talked about the looseness of morals in these parts, and he despised such stories, knowing that they were largely fabricated by people who would have been glad to misbehave themselves, given the aptitude! But when the young woman sat down at the next table, three paces away, he recalled those tales of trips into the mountains and easy conquests. The seductive thought of a swift, fleeting *affaire*—the romance with the stranger whose very name you don't know—suddenly possessed him. He made a friendly gesture to the dog. It came up. He wagged his finger. The dog growled and Gurov shook his finger again.

The lady glanced at him, lowered her eyes at once.

'He doesn't bite.' She blushed.

'May I give him a bone?'

She nodded.

'Have you been in Yalta long, madam?' he asked courteously.

'Five days.'

'Oh, I've nearly survived my first fortnight.'

There was a short pause.

'Time goes quickly, but it *is* so boring,' she said, not looking at him.

'That's what they all say, what a bore this place is. Your average tripper from Belyov, Zhizdra or somewhere . . . he doesn't know what boredom means till he comes here. Then it's ''Oh, what a bore! Oh, what dust!'' You might think he'd just blown in from sunny Spain!'

She laughed. Then both continued their meal in silence, as strangers. After dinner, though, they left together and embarked on the bantering chat of people who feel free and easy, who don't mind where they go or what they talk about. As they strolled they discussed the strange light on the sea: the water was of a soft, warm, mauve hue, crossed by a stripe of golden moonlight. How sultry it was after the day's heat, they said. Gurov described himself as a Muscovite who had studied literature but worked in a bank. He had once trained as an opera singer but had given that up and owned two houses in Moscow.

From her he learnt that she had grown up in St. Petersburg, but had married in the provincial town where she had now been living for two years, that she was staying in Yalta for another month, that her husband (who also wanted a holiday) might come and fetch her. She was quite unable to explain her husband's job—was it with the County Council or the Rural District?—and even she saw the funny side of this. Gurov also learnt that she was called Anne.

In his hotel room afterwards he thought about her. He was very likely to meet her tomorrow, bound to. As he went to bed he remembered that she had not long left boarding-school, that she had been a schoolgirl like his own daughter—remembered, too, how much shyness and stiffness she still showed when laughing and talking to a stranger. This must be her first time ever alone in such a place, with men following her around, watching her, talking to her: all with a certain privy aim which she could not fail to divine. He remembered her slender, frail neck, her lovely grey eyes.

'You can't help feeling sorry for her, though,' he thought. And dozed off.

II

A week had passed since their first meeting. It was a Sunday or some other holiday. Indoors was stifling, and outside flurries of dust swept the streets, whipping off hats. It was a thirsty day, and Gurov kept calling in at the café to fetch Anne a soft drink or an ice-cream. There was no escaping the heat.

In the evening things were a little easier, and they went on the pier to watch a steamer come in. There were a lot of people hanging around on the landing-stage: they were here to meet someone, and held bunches of flowers. Two features of the Yalta smart set were now thrown into sharp relief. The older women dressed like young ones. There were lots of generals.

As the sea was rough the steamer arrived late, after sunset, and manœuvred for some time before putting in at the jetty. Anne watched boat and passengers through her lorgnette as if seeking someone she knew. Whenever she turned to Gurov her eyes shone. She spoke a lot, asking quick-fire questions and immediately forgetting what they were. Then she lost her lorgnette: dropped it in the crowd.

The gaily-dressed gathering dispersed, no more faces could be seen, and the wind dropped completely while Gurov and Anne stood as if waiting for someone else to disembark. Anne had stopped talking, and sniffed her flowers without looking at Gurov.

'The weather's better now that it's evening,' said he. 'So where shall we go? How about driving somewhere?'

She did not answer.

Then he stared at her hard, embraced her suddenly and kissed her lips. The scent of her flowers, their dampness, enveloped him, and he immediately glanced around fearfully: had they been observed?

'Let's go to your room,' he said softly.

They set off quickly together.

Her room was stuffy and smelt of the scent which she had bought in the Japanese shop.

'What encounters one does have in life,' thought Gurov as he looked at her now.

He still retained memories of the easy-going, light-hearted women in his past: women happy in their love and grateful to him for that happiness, however brief. He also recalled those who, like his wife, made love insincerely, with idle chatter, affectations and hysteria, their expressions conveying that this was neither love nor passion but something more significant. He thought of two or three very beautiful frigid women whose faces would suddenly flash a rapacious, stubborn look of lust to seize, to snatch more from life than it can give . . . women no longer young, these: fractious, unreasonable, overbearing and obtuse. When Gurov had cooled towards them their beauty had aroused his hatred, and the lace on their underclothes had looked like a lizard's scales.

In this case, though, all was hesitancy, the awkwardness of inexperienced youth. There was the impression of her being taken aback, too, as by a sudden knock on the door. Anne, this 'lady with a dog', had her own special view—a very serious one—of what had happened. She thought of it as her 'downfall', it seemed, which was all very strange and inappropriate. Her features had sunk and faded, her long hair drooped sadly down each side of her face. She had struck a pensive, despondent pose, like the Woman Taken in Adultery in an old-fashioned picture.

'This is all wrong,' she said. 'Now you'll completely despise me.'

There was a water-melon on the table. Gurov cut a slice and slowly ate. Half an hour, at least, passed in silence.

He found Anne touching. She had that air of naïve innocence of a thoroughly nice unworldly woman. A solitary candle, burning on the table, barely lit her face, but it was obvious that she was ill at ease.

'Why should I lose respect for you?' asked Gurov. 'You don't know what you're saying.'

'God forgive me,' she said, her eyes brimming with tears. 'This is terrible.'

'You seem very much on the defensive, Anne.'

'How *can* I defend what I've done? I'm a bad, wicked woman, I despise myself and I'm not trying to make excuses. It's not my husband, it is *myself* I've deceived. I don't just mean what happened here, I've been deceiving myself for a long time. My husband may be a good, honourable man, but he *is* such a worm. What he does at that job of his I don't know—all I know is, he's a worm. I was twenty when I married him—I longed to know more of life. Then I wanted something better. There must *be* a different life, mustn't there? Or so I told myself. I wanted a little—well, rather *more* than a little—excitement. I was avid for experience. You won't understand me, I'm sure, but I could control myself no longer, I swear, something had happened to me, there was no holding me. So I told my husband I was ill and I came here. And I've been going round here in a daze as if I was off my head. But now I'm just another vulgar, worthless woman whom everyone is free to despise.'

Gurov was bored with all this. He was irritated by the naïve air, the unexpected, uncalled-for remorse. But for the tears in her eyes he might have thought her to be joking or play-acting.

'I don't understand,' said he softly. 'What is it you want?'

She hid her face on his breast and clung to him.

'Please, please believe me,' she implored. 'I long for a decent, moral life. Sin disgusts me, I don't know what I'm doing myself. The common people say the "Evil One" tempted them, and now I can say the same: I was tempted by the Evil One.'

'There there, that's enough,' he muttered.

He looked into her staring, frightened eyes, kissed her, spoke softly and gently. She gradually relaxed and cheered up again. Both laughed.

Then they went out. The promenade was deserted, the town with its cypresses looked quite dead, but the sea still roared, breaking on the beach. A single launch with a sleepily glinting lamp tossed on the waves.

They found a cab and drove to Oreanda.

'I've only just discovered your surname, downstairs in your hotel,' Gurov told her. '"Von Diederitz", it says on the board. Is your husband German?'

'No, his grandfather was, I think, but he's Russian.'

They sat on a bench near the church at Oreanda, gazing silently down at the sea. Yalta was barely visible through the dawn mist, white clouds hung motionless on the mountain peaks. Not a leaf stirred on the trees, cicadas chirped. Borne up from below, the sea's monotonous, muffled boom spoke of peace, of the everlasting sleep awaiting us. Before Yalta or Oreanda yet existed that surf had been thundering down there, it was roaring away now, and it will continue its dull booming with the same unconcern when we are no more. This persistence, this utter aloofness from all our lives and deaths . . . do they perhaps hold the secret pledge of our eternal salvation, of life's perpetual motion on earth, of its uninterrupted progress? As he sat there, lulled and entranced by the magic panorama—sea, mountains, clouds, broad sky—beside a young woman who looked so beautiful in the dawn, Gurov reflected that everything on earth is beautiful, really, when you consider it—everything except what we think and do ourselves when we forget the lofty goals of being and our human dignity.

Someone—a watchman, no doubt—came up, looked at them, went away. Even this incident seemed mysterious—beautiful, too. In the dawn they saw a steamer arrive from Feodosiya, its lights already extinguished.

'There's dew on the grass,' Anne said, after a pause.

'Yes, time to go home.'

They went back to town.

After this they met on the promenade each noon, lunched, dined, strolled, enthused about the sea together. She complained of sleeping badly, of palpitations. Disturbed by jealousy, and by the fear that he did not respect her enough, she kept repeating the same old questions. And often in the Square or Gardens, when there was nobody near them, he would suddenly draw her to him and kiss her ardently. This utter idleness, these kisses in broad daylight, these glances over the shoulder, this fear of being seen, the heat, the sea's smell, the repeated glimpses of idle, elegant, sleek persons . . . it all seemed to revitalize him. He told Anne how pretty she was, how provocative. He was impetuous, he was passionate, he never left her side, while she was for ever brooding and begging him to admit that he did not respect her, that he loved her not at all, that he could see in her no more than a very ordinary woman. Late almost every evening they would drive out of town: to Oreanda or the waterfall. These trips were invariably a great success, leaving an impression of majesty and beauty.

They had been expecting the husband to arrive, but he sent a letter to say that he had eye trouble, and begged his wife to come home soon. Anne bestirred herself.

'It's just as well I *am* leaving,' she told Gurov. 'This is fate.'

She left by carriage and he drove with her. This part of her journey took all day. When she took her seat in the express train, which was due to leave in five minutes, she asked to look at him once more.

'One last look—that's right.'

She did not cry, but was so sad that she seemed ill. Her face quivered.

'I'll think of you, I'll remember you,' she said. 'God bless and keep you. Don't think ill of me. We're parting for ever. We must, because we should never have met at all. God bless you.'

The train departed swiftly, its lights soon vanishing and its noise dying away within a minute, as though everything had conspired to make a quick end of that sweet trance, that madness. Alone on the platform, gazing into the dark distance, Gurov heard the chirp of grasshoppers and the hum of telegraph wires, feeling as if he had just awoken. Well, there went another adventure or episode in his life, he reflected. It too had ended, now only the memory was left.

He was troubled, sad, somewhat penitent. This young woman whom he would never see again . . . she hadn't been happy with him, now, had she? He had treated her kindly and affectionately. And yet his attitude to her, his tone, his caresses had betrayed a faint irony: the rather crude condescension of your conquering male—of a man nearly twice her age into the bargain. She had kept calling him kind, exceptional, noble—so she hadn't seen him as he really was, obviously, and he must have been deceiving her without meaning to.

Here at the station there was already a whiff of autumn in the air, and the evening was cool.

'It's time I went north too,' thought Gurov, leaving the platform. 'High time.'

III

Back home in Moscow it was already like winter. The stoves were alight. It was dark when his children breakfasted and got ready for school in the mornings, so their nanny lit the light for a short time. The frosts had begun. It is always such a joy to see the white ground and white roofs when the snow first falls, on that first day of sleigh-riding. The air is so fresh and good to breathe, and you remember the years of your youth. White with frost, the old limes and birches have a kindly look, they are dearer to your heart than any cypresses or palm-trees, and near them you no longer hanker after mountains and sea.

A Moscow man himself, Gurov had come home on a fine frosty day. He put on his fur coat and warm gloves and strolled down the Petrovka, he heard church bells pealing on Saturday evening . . . and his recent trip, all the places he had visited, lost all charm for him. He gradually plunged into Moscow life. He was zealously reading his three newspapers a day, now—while claiming to read no Moscow newspapers on principle! He felt the lure of restaurants, clubs, dinner parties, anniversary celebrations; he was flattered to be visited by famous lawyers and actors, flattered to play cards with a professor at the Doctors' Club. He could tackle a large helping of 'Moscow hotpot' straight from the pan.

In a month or two's time the memory of Anne would become blurred, thought he—he would just dream of her, of her adorable smile, occasionally as he used to dream of those other ones. But more than a month passed, real winter set in, and yet everything was still as clear in his mind as if they had parted only yesterday. His memories flared up ever more brightly. When, in the quiet of evening, his children's voices reached his study as they did their homework, when he heard a sentimental song or a barrel organ in a restaurant, when a blizzard howled in his chimney . . . it would all suddenly come back to him: that business on the pier, the early morning with the mist on the mountains, the Feodosiya steamer, the kisses. He would pace the room for hours, remembering and smiling until these recollections merged into fantasies: until, in his imagination, past fused with future. Though he did not dream of Anne, she pursued him everywhere like his shadow, watching him. If he closed his eyes he could see her vividly—younger, gentler, more beautiful than she really was. He even saw himself as a better man than he had been back in Yalta. She gazed at him from the book-case in the evenings, from the hearth, from a corner of the room. He heard her breathing, heard the delightful rustle of her dress. In the street he followed women with his eyes, seeking one like her.

He was plagued, now, by the urge to share his memories. But he could not talk about his love at home, and outside his home there was no one to tell—he couldn't very well discuss it with his tenants or at the bank! What was there to say, anyway? Had he really been in love? Had there really been anything beautiful or idyllic, anything edifying—anything merely interesting, even—in his relations with Anne? He was reduced to vague remarks about love and women, and no one guessed what he had in mind. His wife just twitched those dark eyebrows and told him that 'the role of lady-killer doesn't suit you at all, Demetrius'.

As he was leaving the Doctors' Club one night with his partner, a civil servant, he could not help saying that he had 'met such an enchanting woman in Yalta—did you but know!'

The civil servant climbed into his sledge and drove off, but suddenly turned round and shouted Gurov's name.

'What is it?'

'You were quite right just now, the sturgeon *was* a bit off.'

For some reason these words, humdrum though they were, suddenly infuriated Gurov, striking him as indelicate and gross. What barbarous manners, what faces, what meaningless nights, what dull, featureless days! Frantic card-playing, guzzling, drunkenness, endless chatter always on one and the same topic. Futile activities, repetitious talk, talk, talk . . . they engross most of your time, your best efforts, and you end up with a sort of botched, pedestrian life: a form of imbecility from which there's no way out, no escape. You might as well be in jail or in a madhouse!

Gurov lay awake all night, fuming—then had a headache all next day. He slept badly on the following nights, too, sitting up in bed thinking, or pacing the room. He was fed up with his children, fed up with his bank, there was nowhere he wanted to go, nothing he wanted to talk about.

Towards Christmas he prepared for a journey. He told his wife that he was going to St. Petersburg on a certain young man's business—but he actually went to the town where Anne lived. Why? He didn't really know himself. He wanted to see her, speak to her—make an assignation if he could.

He reached the town one morning and put up at a hotel, in the 'best' room with wall-to-wall carpeting in coarse field-grey material. On the table stood an inkstand, grey with dust and shaped as a horseman holding his hat up in one hand and minus a head. The porter told him what he needed to know: von Diederitz lived in Old Pottery Street in his own house near the hotel. He did things in style, kept his own horses, was known to everyone in town. The porter pronounced the name as 'Drearydits'. Gurov sauntered off to Old Pottery Street, found the house. Immediately facing it was a long, grey fence crowned with nails: 'a fence to run away from', thought Gurov, looking from windows to fence and back.

Local government offices were closed today, so the husband was probably at home, Gurov reckoned. In any case it would be tactless to go into the house and create a disturbance. If he sent a note, though, it might fall into the husband's hands and ruin everything. Better trust to chance. He paced the street near the fence, awaiting this chance. He saw a beggar go through the gate, saw him set upon by dogs. An hour later he heard the faint, muffled sound of a piano—that must be Anne playing. Suddenly the front door opened, and out came an old woman with the familiar white Pomeranian running after her. Gurov wanted to call the dog, but his heart suddenly raced and he was too excited to remember its name.

He paced about, loathing that grey fence more and more. In his irritation, he fancied that Anne had forgotten him and might be amusing herself with another man—what else could be expected of a young woman compelled to contemplate this confounded fence morning, noon and night? He went back to his room, sat on the sofa for hours not knowing what to do, then lunched and dozed for hours.

'It's all so stupid and distressing,' he thought, waking up and seeing the dark windows—it was already evening. 'Now I've had a good sleep for some reason, but what shall I do tonight?'

He sat on the bed—it was covered with a cheap, grey hospital blanket.

'So much for your ladies with dogs!' said he in petulant self-mockery. 'So much for your holiday romances—now you're stuck in this dump.'

In the station that morning his eye had been caught by a poster in bold lettering advertising the opening of *The Geisha*. Recalling this, he drove to the theatre, reflecting that she very probably attended first nights.

The theatre was full. As usual in provincial theatres a mist hung above the chandelier, while the gallery was restive and rowdy. In the first row before the performance began stood the local gallants, hands clasped behind their backs. In the Governor's box, in front, sat that worthy's daughter complete with feather boa, while the Governor himself lurked modestly behind a *portière*, only his hands showing. The curtain shook, the orchestra tuned up protractedly. As the audience came in and took its seats, Gurov peered frantically around.

In came Anne. She sat down in the third row, and when Gurov glimpsed her his heart seemed to miss a beat. He saw clearly, now, that she was nearer, dearer, more important to him than anyone in the whole world. Lost in the provincial crowd, this very ordinary little woman carrying her vulgar lorgnette now absorbed his whole being. She was his grief, his joy—the only happiness he wanted, now. To the strains of that abominable orchestra with its atrocious, tasteless fiddling he thought how lovely she was . . . thought and brooded.

A young man with short dundrearies, very tall, round-shouldered, had come in with Anne and sat down beside her. He kept bobbing his head as if making obeisance with every step he took. It must be the husband whom, in that bitter outburst back in Yalta, she had dubbed a 'worm'. His lanky figure, his side-whiskers, his small bald patch . . . there actually *was* something menial and flunkey-like about them. He gave an ingratiating smile, the emblem of some learned society glinting in his buttonhole like a hotel servant's number.

The husband went for a smoke in the first interval, while she remained seated. Gurov—his seat was also in the stalls—approached her. His voice trembling, forcing a smile, he wished her good evening.

She glanced at him, she blenched. Then she looked again—aghast, not believing her eyes, crushing fan and lorgnette together in her hands in an obvious effort to prevent herself from fainting. Neither spoke. She sat, he remained standing—alarmed by her discomfiture, not venturing to sit down beside her. Fiddles and flute started tuning up, and he suddenly panicked: from all the boxes eyes seemed to be staring at them. Then she stood up and quickly made for the exit, while he followed, both walking at random along corridors, up and down stairways, glimpsing men in the uniforms of the courts, the schools and the administration of crown lands, all wearing their decorations. There were glimpses of ladies and fur coats on pegs. A draught enveloped them with the smell of cigarette ends.

'Oh God—why all these people, this orchestra?' wondered Gurov, his heart pounding.

Suddenly he recalled the evening when he had seen Anne off at the station, when he had told himself that it was all over and that they would never meet again. How far they were now, though, from any ending!

On a narrow, gloomy staircase labelled ENTRANCE TO CIRCLE she stopped.

'How you did scare me,' she panted, still pale and dazed. 'I nearly died, you scared me so. Why, why, why are you here?'

'Try and understand, Anne,' he said in a rapid undertone. 'Understand, I implore you————'

She looked at him—fearfully, pleadingly, lovingly. She stared, trying to fix his features in her memory.

'I'm so miserable,' she went on, not hearing him. 'I've thought only of you all this time, my thoughts of you have kept me alive. Oh, I did so want to forget you—why, why, why are you here?'

On a landing higher up two schoolboys were smoking and looking down, but Gurov did not care. He pulled Anne to him, kissed her face, cheek, hands.

'Whatever are you doing?' she asked—horrified, pushing him from her. 'We must be out of our minds. You must go away today—leave this very instant, I implore you, I beg you in the name of all that is holy. Someone's coming.'

Someone indeed was coming upstairs.

'You *must* leave,' Anne went on in a whisper. 'Do you hear me, Gurov? I'll visit you in Moscow. I've never been happy, I'm unhappy now, and I shall never, never, never be happy. So don't add to my sufferings. I'll come to Moscow, I swear it, but we must part now. We must say goodbye, my good, kind darling.'

She pressed his hand and went quickly downstairs, looking back at him, and he could see from her eyes that she really was unhappy. Gurov waited a little, cocked an ear and, when all was quiet, found the peg with his coat and left the theatre.

IV

Anne took to visiting him in Moscow. Once every two or three months she would leave her home town, telling her husband that she was going to consult a professor about a female complaint. The husband neither believed nor disbelieved her. In Moscow she would put up at the Slav Fair Hotel, and at once send a red-capped messenger to Gurov. Gurov would visit her hotel, and no one in Moscow knew anything about it.

It thus chanced that he was on his way to see her one winter morning—her messenger had called on the previous evening, but had not found him at home. He was walking with his daughter, wanting to take her to school, which was on his way. There was a heavy downpour of sleet.

'It's three degrees above zero, yet look at the sleet,' said Gurov to his daughter. 'But it's only the ground which is warm, you see—the temperature in the upper strata of the atmosphere is quite different.'

'Why doesn't it thunder in winter, Daddy?'

He explained this too, reflecting as he spoke that he was on his way to an assignation. Not a soul knew about it—or ever would know, probably. He was living two lives. One of them was open to view by—and known to—the people concerned. It was full of stereotyped truths and stereotyped untruths, it was identical with the life of his friends and acquaintances. The other life proceeded in secret. Through some strange and possibly arbitrary chain of coincidences everything vital, interesting and crucial to him, everything which called his sincerity and integrity into play, everything which made up the core of his life . . . all that took place in complete secrecy, whereas everything false about him, the facade behind which he hid to conceal the truth—his work at the bank, say, his arguments at the club, that 'inferior species' stuff, attending anniversary celebrations with his wife—all that was in the open. He judged others by himself, disbelieving the evidence of his eyes, and attributing to everyone a real, fascinating life lived under the cloak of secrecy as in the darkness of the night. Each individual existence is based on mystery, which is perhaps why civilized man makes such a neurotic fuss about having his privacy respected.

After taking his daughter to school, Gurov made for the Slav Fair. He removed his coat downstairs, went up, tapped on the door. Anne was wearing his favourite grey dress, she was tired by the journey—and by the wait, after expecting him since the previous evening. She was pale, she looked at him without smiling, and no sooner was he in the room than she flung herself against his chest. Their kiss was as protracted and lingering as if they had not met for two years.

'Well, how are things with you?' he asked. 'What's the news?'

'Wait, I'll tell you in a moment—I can't now.'

Unable to speak for crying, she turned away and pressed a handkerchief to her eyes.

'Let her cry, I'll sit down for a bit,' thought he, and sat in the armchair.

Then he rang and ordered tea. Then he drank it while she still stood with her back to him, facing the window.

She wept as one distressed and woefully aware of the melancholy turn which their lives had taken. They met only in secret, they hid from other people like thieves. Their lives were in ruins, were they not?

'Now, do stop it,' he said.

He could see that this was no fleeting affair—there was no telling when it would end. Anne was growing more and more attached to him. She adored him, and there was no question of telling her that all this must finish one day. Besides, she would never believe him.

He went up to her, laid his hands on her shoulders, meaning to soothe her with a little banter—and then caught sight of himself in the mirror.

His hair was turning grey. He wondered why he had aged so much in the last few years and lost his looks. The shoulders on which his hands rested were warm and trembling. He pitied this life—still so warm and beautiful, but probably just about to fade and wither like his own. Why did she love him so? Women had never seen him as he really was. What they loved in him was not his real self but a figment of their own imaginations—someone whom they had dreamed of meeting all their lives. Then, when they realized their mistake, they had loved him all the same. Yet none of them had been happy with him. Time had passed, he had met new ones, been intimate with them, parted from them. Not once had he been in love, though. He had known everything conceivable—except love, that is.

Only now that his head was grey had he well and truly fallen in love: for the first time in his life.

Anne and he loved each other very, very dearly, like man and wife or bosom friends. They felt themselves predestined for each other. That he should have a wife, and she a husband . . . it seemed to make no sense. They were like two migratory birds, a male and a female, caught and put in separate cages. They had forgiven each other the shameful episodes of their past, they forgave each other for the present too, and they felt that their love had transformed them both.

Once, in moments of depression, he had tried to console himself with any argument which came into his head—but now he had no use for arguments. His deepest sympathies were stirred, he only wanted to be sincere and tender.

'Stop, darling,' he said. 'You've had your cry—that's enough. Now let's talk, let's think of something.'

Then they consulted at length about avoiding the need for concealment and deception, for living in different towns, for meeting only at rare intervals. How could they break these intolerable bonds? How, how, how?

He clutched his head and asked the question again and again.

Soon, it seemed, the solution would be found and a wonderful new life would begin. But both could see that they still had a long, long way to travel—and that the most complicated and difficult part was only just beginning.

SUGGESTIONS FOR WRITING AND DISCUSSION

1. At the beginning of this story Gurov refers to women as "the inferior species." What evidence does he give to substantiate this opinion? Does he regard Anne in this way?
2. Why does the remark of the civil servant have such an effect on Gurov?
3. How does Gurov's conversation with his daughter about sleet reflect what is happening to him?

4. The color grey is mentioned frequently in the descriptions of the town where Anne lives. What does this suggest? Does the significance of this color change in the last part of the story?
5. How does Chekhov's use of setting convey and emphasize the characters' thoughts and feelings?
6. Are Anne's and Gurov's spouses similar? Discuss this in a two- to three-page essay.
7. At the beginning and at the end of the story Anne and Gurov are alone in a room together. Compare these two occasions in a three- to four-page essay.
8. Write a two- to three-page description of Anne. How does she change during the course of this story?

Nathaniel Hawthorne (American, 1804–1864)

Wakefield

In some old magazine or newspaper I recollect a story, told as truth, of a man—let us call him Wakefield—who absented himself for a long time from his wife. The fact, thus abstractedly stated, is not very uncommon, nor—without a proper distinction of circumstances—to be condemned either as naughty or nonsensical. Howbeit, this, though far from the most aggravated, is perhaps the strangest, instance on record, of marital delinquency; and, moreover, as remarkable a freak as may be found in the whole list of human oddities. The wedded couple lived in London. The man, under pretence of going a journey, took lodgings in the next street to his own house, and there, unheard of by his wife or friends, and without the shadow of a reason for such self-banishment, dwelt upwards of twenty years. During that period, he beheld his home every day, and frequently the forlorn Mrs. Wakefield. And after so great a gap in his matrimonial felicity—when his death was reckoned certain, his estate settled, his name dismissed from memory, and his wife, long, long ago, resigned to her autumnal widowhood—he entered the door one evening, quietly, as from a day's absence, and became a loving spouse till death.

This outline is all that I remember. But the incident, though of the purest originality, unexampled, and probably never to be repeated, is one, I think, which appeals to the generous sympathies of mankind. We know, each for himself, that none of us would perpetrate such a folly, yet feel as if some other might. To my own contemplations, at least, it has often recurred, always exciting wonder, but with a sense that the story must be true, and a conception of its hero's character. Whenever any subject so forcibly affects the mind, time is well spent in thinking of it. If the reader choose, let him do his own meditation; or if he prefer to ramble with me through the twenty years of Wakefield's vagary, I bid him welcome; trusting that there will be a pervading spirit and a moral, even should we fail to find them, done up neatly, and condensed into the final sentence. Thought has always its efficacy, and every striking incident its moral.

What sort of a man was Wakefield? We are free to shape out our own idea, and call it by his name. He was now in the meridian of life; his matrimonial affections, never violent, were sobered into a calm, habitual sentiment; of all husbands, he was likely to be the most constant, because a certain sluggishness would keep his heart at rest, wherever it might be placed. He was intellectual, but not actively so; his mind occupied itself in long and lazy musings, that ended to no purpose, or had not vigor to attain it; his thoughts were seldom so energetic as to seize hold of words. Imagination, in the proper meaning of the term, made no part of Wakefield's gifts. With a cold but not depraved nor wandering heart, and a mind never feverish with riotous thoughts, nor perplexed with originality, who could have anticipated that our friend would entitle himself to a foremost place among the doers of eccentric deeds? Had his acquaintances been asked, who was the man in London the surest to perform nothing to-day which should be remembered on the morrow, they would have thought of Wakefield. Only the wife of his bosom might have hesitated. She, without having analyzed his character, was partly aware of a quiet selfishness that had rusted into his inactive mind; of a peculiar sort of vanity, the most uneasy attribute about him; sort of a disposition to craft, which had seldom produced more positive effects than the keeping of petty secrets, hardly worth revealing; and, lastly, of what she called a little strangeness, sometimes, in the good man. This latter quality is indefinable, and perhaps non-existent.

Let us now imagine Wakefield bidding adieu to his wife. It is the dusk of an October evening. His equipment is a drab great-coat, a hat covered with an oilcloth, top-boots, an umbrella in one hand and a small portmanteau in the other. He has informed Mrs. Wakefield that he is to take the night coach into the country. She would fain inquire the length of his journey, its object, and the probable time of his return; but, indulgent to his harmless love of mystery, interrogates him only by a look. He tells her not to expect him positively by the return coach, nor to be alarmed should he tarry three or four days; but, at all events, to look for him at supper on Friday evening. Wakefield himself, be it considered, has no suspicion of what is before him. He holds out his hand, she gives her own, and meets his parting kiss in the matter-of-course way of a ten years' matrimony; and forth goes the middle-aged Mr. Wakefield, almost resolved to perplex his good lady by a whole week's absence. After the door has closed behind him, she perceives it thrust partly open, and a vision of her husband's face, through the aperture, smiling on her, and gone in a moment. For the time, this little incident is dismissed without a thought. But, long afterwards, when she has been more years a widow than a wife, that smile recurs, and flickers across all her reminiscences of Wakefield's visage. In her many musings, she surrounds the original smile with a multitude of fantasies, which make it strange and awful: as, for instance, if she imagines him in a coffin, that parting look is frozen on his pale features; or, if she dreams of him in heaven, still his blessed spirit wears a quiet and crafty smile. Yet, for its sake, when all others have given him up for dead, she sometimes doubts whether she is a widow.

But our business is with the husband. We must hurry after him along the street, ere he lose his individuality, and melt into the great mass of London life. It would be vain searching for him there. Let us follow close at his heels, therefore, until, after several superfluous turns and doublings, we find him comfortably established by the fireside of a small apartment, previously bespoken. He is in the next street to his own, and at his journey's end. He can scarcely trust his good fortune, in having got thither unperceived—recollecting that, at one time, he was delayed by the throng, in the very focus of a lighted lantern; and, again, there were footsteps that seemed to tread behind his own, distinct from the multitudinous tramp around him; and, anon, he heard a voice shouting afar, and fancied that it called his name. Doubtless, a dozen busybodies had been watching him, and told his wife the whole affair. Poor Wakefield! Little knowest thou thine own insignificance in this great world! No mortal eye but mine has traced thee. Go quietly to thy bed, foolish man; and, on the morrow, if thou wilt be wise, get thee home to good Mrs. Wakefield, and tell her the truth. Remove not thyself, even for a little week, from thy place in her chaste bosom. Were she, for a single moment, to deem thee dead, or lost, or lastingly divided from her, thou wouldst be wofully conscious of a change in thy true wife forever after. It is perilous to make a chasm in human affections; not that they gape so long and wide—but so quickly close again!

Almost repenting of his frolic, or whatever it may be termed, Wakefield lies down betimes, and starting from his first nap, spreads forth his arms into the wide and solitary waste of the unaccustomed bed. "No,"—thinks he, gathering the bedclothes about him,—"I will not sleep alone another night."

In the morning he rises earlier than usual, and sets himself to consider what he really means to do. Such are his loose and rambling modes of thought that he has taken this very singular step with the consciousness of a purpose, indeed, but without being able to define it sufficiently for his own contemplation. The vagueness of the project, and the convulsive effort with which he plunges into the execution of it, are equally characteristic of a feeble-minded man. Wakefield sifts his ideas, however, as minutely as he may, and finds himself curious to know the progress of matters at home—how his exemplary wife will endure her widowhood of a week; and, briefly, how the little sphere of creatures and circumstances, in which he was a central object, will be affected by his removal. A morbid vanity, therefore, lies nearest the bottom of the affair. But, how is he to attain his ends? Not, certainly, by keeping close in this comfortable lodging, where, though he slept and awoke in the next street to his home, he is as effectually abroad as if the stage-coach had been whirling him away all night. Yet, should he reappear, the whole project is knocked in the head. His poor brains being hopelessly puzzled with this dilemma, he at length ventures out, partly resolving to cross the head of the street, and send one hasty glance towards his forsaken domicile. Habit—for he is a man of habits—takes him by the hand, and guides him, wholly unaware, to his own door, where, just at the critical moment, he is aroused by the scraping of his foot upon the step. Wakefield! whither are you going?

At that instant his fate was turning on the pivot. Little dreaming of the doom to which his first backward step devotes him, he hurries away, breathless with agitation hitherto unfelt, and hardly dares turn his head at the distant corner. Can it be that nobody caught sight of him? Will not the whole household—the decent Mrs. Wakefield, the smart maidservant, and the dirty little footboy—raise a hue and cry, through London streets, in pursuit of their fugitive lord and master? Wonderful escape! He gathers courage to pause and look homeward, but is perplexed with a sense of change about the familiar edifice, such as affects us all, when, after a separation of months or years, we again see some hill or lake, or work of art, with which we were friends of old. In ordinary cases, this indescribable impression is caused by the comparison and contrast between our imperfect reminiscences and the reality. In Wakefield, the magic of a single night has wrought a similar transformation, because, in that brief period, a great moral change has been effected. But this is a secret from himself. Before leaving the spot, he catches a far and momentary glimpse of his wife, passing athwart the front window, with her face turned towards the head of the street. The crafty nincompoop takes to his heels, scared with the idea that, among a thousand such atoms of mortality, her eye must have detected him. Right glad is his heart, though his brain be somewhat dizzy, when he finds himself by the coal fire of his lodgings.

So much for the commencement of this long whim-wham. After the initial conception, and the stirring up of the man's sluggish temperament to put it in practice, the whole matter evolves itself in a natural train. We may suppose him, as the result of deep deliberation, buying a new wig, of reddish hair, and selecting sundry garments, in a fashion unlike his customary suit of brown, from a Jew's old-clothes bag. It is accomplished. Wakefield is another man. The new system being now established, a retrograde movement to the old would be almost as difficult as the step that placed him in his unparalleled position. Furthermore, he is rendered obstinate by a sulkiness occasionally incident to his temper, and brought on at present by the inadequate sensation which he conceives to have been produced in the bosom of Mrs. Wakefield. He will not go back until she be frightened half to death. Well; twice or thrice has she passed before his sight, each time with a heavier step, a paler cheek, and more anxious brow; and in the third week of his non-appearance he detects a portent of evil entering the house, in the guise of an apothecary. Next day the knocker is muffled. Towards nightfall comes the chariot of a physician, and deposits its big-wigged and solemn burden at Wakefield's door, whence, after a quarter of an hour's visit, he emerges, perchance the herald of a funeral. Dear woman! Will she die? By this time, Wakefield is excited to something like energy of feeling, but still lingers away from his wife's bedside, pleading with his conscience that she must not be disturbed at such a juncture. If aught else restrains him, he does not know it. In the course of a few weeks she gradually recovers; the crisis is over; her heart is sad, perhaps, but quiet; and, let him return soon or late, it will never be feverish for him again. Such ideas glimmer through the mist of Wakefield's mind, and render him indistinctly conscious that an almost impassable gulf divides his hired apartment from his former home. ``It is but in the next street!'' he sometimes says. Fool! it is in another world. Hitherto, he has put off his return from one particular day to another; henceforward, he leaves the precise time undetermined. Not to-morrow—probably next week—pretty soon. Poor man! The dead have nearly as much chance of revisiting their earthly homes as the self-banished Wakefield.

Would that I had a folio to write, instead of an article of a dozen pages! Then might I exemplify how an influence beyond our control lays its strong hand on every deed which we do, and weaves its consequences into an iron tissue of necessity. Wakefield is spell-bound. We must leave him, for ten years or so, to haunt around his house, without once crossing the threshold, and to be faithful to his wife, with all the affection of which his heart is capable, while he is slowly fading out of hers. Long since, it must be remarked, he had lost the perception of singularity in his conduct.

Now for a scene! Amid the throng of a London street we distinguish a man, now waxing elderly, with few characteristics to attract careless observers, yet bearing, in his whole aspect, the handwriting of no common fate, for such as have the skill to read it. He is meagre; his low and narrow forehead is deeply wrinkled; his eyes, small and lustreless, sometimes wander apprehensively about him, but oftener seem to look inward. He bends his head, and moves with an indescribable obliquity of gait, as if unwilling to display his full front to the world. Watch him long enough to see what we have described, and you will allow that circumstances—which often produce remarkable men from nature's ordinary handiwork—have produced one such here. Next, leaving him to sidle along the footwalk, cast your eyes in the opposite direction, where a portly female, considerably in the wane of life, with a prayer-book in her hand, is proceeding to yonder church. She has the placid mien of settled widowhood. Her regrets have either died away, or have become so essential to her heart, that they would be poorly exchanged for joy. Just as the lean man and well-conditioned woman are passing, a slight obstruction occurs, and brings these two figures directly in contact. Their hands touch; the pressure of the crowd forces her bosom against his shoulder; they stand, face to face, staring into each other's eyes. After a ten years' separation, thus Wakefield meets his wife!

The throng eddies away, and carries them asunder. The sober widow, resuming her former pace, proceeds to church, but pauses in the portal, and throws a perplexed glance along the street. She passes in, however, opening her prayer-book as she goes. And the man! with so wild a face that busy and selfish London stands to gaze after him, he hurries to his lodgings, bolts the door, and throws himself upon the bed. The latent feelings of years break out; his feeble mind acquires a brief energy from their strength; all the miserable strangeness of his life is revealed to him at a glance: and he cries out, passionately, ``Wakefield! Wakefield! You are mad!''

Perhaps he was so. The singularity of his situation must have so moulded him to himself, that, considered in regard to his fellow-creatures and the business of life, he could not be said to possess his right mind. He had contrived, or rather he had happened, to dissever himself from the world—to vanish—to give up his place and privileges with living men, without being admitted among the dead. The life of a hermit is nowise parallel to his. He was in the bustle of the city, as of old; but the crowd swept by and saw him not; he was, we may figuratively say, always beside his wife and at his hearth, yet must never feel the warmth of the one nor the affection of the other. It was Wakefield's unprecedented fate to retain his original share of human sympathies, and to be still involved in human interests, while he had lost his reciprocal influence on them. It would be a most curious speculation to trace out the effect of such circumstances on his heart and intellect, separately, and in unison. Yet, changed as he was, he would seldom be conscious of it, but deem himself the same man as ever; glimpses of the truth, indeed, would come, but only for the moment; and still he would keep saying, ``I shall soon go back!''—nor reflect that he had been saying so for twenty years.

I conceive, also, that these twenty years would appear, in the retrospect, scarcely longer than the week to which Wakefield had at first limited his absence. He would look on the affair as no more than an interlude in the main business of his life. When, after a little while more, he should deem it time to reënter his parlor, his wife would clap her hands for joy, on beholding the middle-aged Mr. Wakefield. Alas, what a mistake! Would Time but await the close of our favorite follies, we should be young men, all of us, and till Doomsday.

One evening, in the twentieth year since he vanished, Wakefield is taking his customary walk towards the dwelling which he still calls his own. It is a gusty night of autumn, with frequent showers that patter down upon the pavement, and are gone before a man can put up his umbrella. Pausing near the house, Wakefield discerns, through the parlor windows of the second floor, the red glow and the glimmer and fitful flash of a comfortable fire. On the ceiling appears a grotesque shadow of good Mrs. Wakefield. The cap, the nose and chin, and the broad waist, form an admirable caricature, which dances, moreover, with the up-flickering and down-sinking blaze, almost too merrily for the shade of an elderly widow. At this instant a shower chances to fall, and is driven, by the unmannerly gust, full into Wakefield's face and bosom. He is quite penetrated with its autumnal chill. Shall he stand, wet and shivering here, when his own hearth has a good fire to warm him, and his own wife will run to fetch the gray coat and small-clothes, which, doubtless, she has kept carefully in the closet of their bed chamber? No! Wakefield is no such fool. He ascends the steps—heavily!—for twenty years have stiffened his legs since he came down—but he knows it not. Stay, Wakefield! Would you go to the sole home that is left you? Then step into your grave! The door opens. As he passes in, we have a parting glimpse of his visage, and recognize the crafty smile, which was the precursor of the little joke that he has ever since been playing off at his wife's expense. How unmercifully has he quizzed the poor woman! Well, a good night's rest to Wakefield!

This happy event—supposing it to be such—could only have occurred at an unpremeditated moment. We will not follow our friend across the threshold. He has left us much food for thought, a portion of which shall lend its wisdom to a moral, and be shaped into a figure. Amid the seeming confusion of our mysterious world, individuals are so nicely adjusted to a system, and systems to one another and to a whole, that, by stepping aside for a moment, a man exposes himself to a fearful risk of losing his place forever. Like Wakefield, he may become, as it were, the Outcast of the Universe.

SUGGESTIONS FOR WRITING AND DISCUSSION

1. What type of narrator is used? What is unique about the way this story is narrated?
2. What is the significance of the word *vanity*, which Hawthorne uses a number of times in describing Wakefield?
3. What does the narrator's comment that Wakefield's wife was aware of his "quiet selfishness" suggest? What does this term mean? Do you feel that Wakefield was essentially selfish?
4. Why does the narrator say that the twenty years Wakefield was away from his wife "would appear, in the retrospect, scarcely longer than the week to which Wakefield had at first limited his absence"?
5. What was his wife's life like while Wakefield was away? What was it like when he returned? Write a two- to three-page response to either of these questions.

Grace Paley (American, 1922–   )

Wants

I saw my ex-husband in the street. I was sitting on the steps of the new library.

Hello, my life, I said. We had once been married for twenty-seven years, so I felt justified.

He said, What? What life? No life of mine.

I said, O.K. I don't argue when there's real disagreement. I got up and went into the library to see how much I owed them.

The librarian said $32 even and you've owed it for eighteen years. I didn't deny anything. Because I don't understand how time passes. I have had those books. I have often thought of them. The library is only two blocks away.

My ex-husband followed me to the Books Returned desk. He interrupted the librarian, who had more to tell. In many ways, he said, as I look back, I attribute the dissolution of our marriage to the fact that you never invited the Bertrams to dinner.

That's possible, I said. But really, if you remember: first, my father was sick that Friday, then the children were born, then I had those Tuesday-night meetings, then the war began. Then we didn't seem to know them any more. But you're right. I should have had them to dinner.

I gave the librarian a check for $32. Immediately she trusted me, put my past behind her, wiped the record clean, which is just what most other municipal and/or state bureaucracies will *not* do.

I checked out the two Edith Wharton books I had just returned because I'd read them so long ago and they are more apropos now than ever. They were *The House of Mirth* and *The Children*, which is about how life in the United States in New York changed in twenty-seven years fifty years ago.

A nice thing I do remember is breakfast, my ex-husband said. I was surprised. All we ever had was coffee. Then I remembered there was a hole in the back of the kitchen closet which opened into the apartment next door. There, they always ate sugar-cured smoked bacon. It gave us a very grand feeling about breakfast, but we never got stuffed and sluggish.

That was when we were poor, I said.

When were we ever rich? he asked.

Oh, as time went on, as our responsibilities increased, we didn't go in need. You took adequate financial care, I reminded him. The children went to camp four weeks a year and in decent ponchos with sleeping bags and boots, just like everyone else. They looked very nice. Our place was warm in winter, and we had nice red pillows and things.

I wanted a sailboat, he said. But you didn't want anything.

Don't be bitter, I said. It's never too late.

No, he said with a great deal of bitterness. I may get a sailboat. As a matter of fact I have money down on an eighteen-foot two-rigger. I'm doing well this year and can look forward to better. But as for you, it's too late. You'll always want nothing.

He had had a habit throughout the twenty-seven years of making a narrow remark which, like a plumber's snake, could work its way through the ear down the throat, halfway to my heart. He would then disappear, leaving me choking with equipment. What I mean is, I sat down on the library steps and he went away.

I looked through *The House of Mirth,* but lost interest. I felt extremely accused. Now, it's true, I'm short of requests and absolute requirements. But I do want *something.*

I want, for instance, to be a different person. I want to be the woman who brings these two books back in two weeks. I want to be the effective citizen who changes the school system and addresses the Board of Estimate on the troubles of this dear urban center.

I *had* promised my children to end the war before they grew up.

I wanted to have been married forever to one person, my ex-husband or my present one. Either has enough character for a whole life, which as it turns out is really not such a long time. You couldn't exhaust either man's qualities or get under the rock of his reasons in one short life.

Just this morning I looked out the window to watch the street for a while and saw that the little sycamores the city had dreamily planted a couple of years before the kids were born had come that day to the prime of their lives.

Well! I decided to bring those two books back to the library. Which proves that when a person or an event comes along to jolt or appraise me I *can* take some appropriate action, although I am better known for my hospitable remarks.

SUGGESTIONS FOR WRITING AND DISCUSSION

1. How would you characterize the narrator of this story? How does she seem to regard her husband at their meeting at the library?
2. Does the narrator seem to miss being married to her former husband?
3. What part did finances play in their marriage?
4. To what extent do you think the narrator was responsible for the breakup of her first marriage?
5. All of us have important relationships in our lives that end for one reason or another. Write a three- to five-page essay about such a relationship in your life and what you would say to the person involved at a chance meeting.

Poetry

Catullus (Roman, 84? B.C.*–54* B.C.*)*

Vivamus, mea Lesbia, atque amemus

Lesbia, let's live and love
without one thought for gossip of
the boys grown old and stern.
Suns go down and can return,
but, once put out our own brief light,
we sleep through one eternal night.
Give me a thousand, a hundred kisses,
another thousand, a second hundred,
a thousand complete, a hundred repeat;
and when we've many thousand more,
we'll scramble them, forget the score
so Malice cannot know how high
the count, and cast its evil eye.

SUGGESTIONS FOR WRITING AND DISCUSSION

1. What does the speaker's mention of gossip suggest about his and Lesbia's position in society?
2. In a two-page essay compare this poem with Andrew Marvell's "To His Coy Mistress." Are the attitudes of the two speakers similar? From reading these two poems what can we learn about the women to whom they were addressed?

Lady Mary Wortley Montagu (British, 1689–1762)

The Lover: A Ballad

At length, by so much importunity pressed,
Take, C—, at once, the inside of my breast;
This stupid indifference so often you blame
Is not owing to nature, to fear, or to shame;
I am not as cold as a Virgin in lead,
Nor is Sunday's sermon so strong in my head;
I know but too well how time flies along,
That we live but few years and yet fewer are young.

But I hate to be cheated, and never will buy
Long years of repentance for moments of joy.
Oh was there a man (but where shall I find

Good sense and good nature so equally joined?)
Would value his pleasure, contribute to mine,
Not meanly would boast, nor would lewdly design,
Not over severe, yet not stupidly vain,
For I would have the power though not give the pain;

No pedant yet learned, not rakehelly gay
Or laughing becaues he has nothing to say,
To all my whole sex obliging and free,
Yet never be fond of any but me;
In public preserve the decorum that's just,
And show in his eyes he is true to his trust,
Then rarely approach, and respectfully-bow,
Yet not fulsomely pert, nor yet foppishly low.

But when the long hours of public are past
And we meet with champagne and a chicken at last,
May every fond pleasure that hour endear,
Be banished afar both discretion and fear,
Forgetting or scorning the airs of the crowd
He may cease to be formal, and I to be proud,
Till lost in the joy we confess that we live,
And he may be rude, and yet I may forgive.

And that my delight may be solidly fixed,
Let the friend and the lover be handsomely mixed,
In whose tender bosom my soul might confide,
Whose kindness can sooth me, whose counsel could guide.
From such a dear lover as here I describe
No danger should fright me, no millions should bribe;
But till this astonishing creature I know,
As I long have lived chaste, I will keep myself so.

I never will share with the wanton coquette,
Or be caught by a vain affectation of wit.
The toasters and songsters may try all their art
But never shall enter the pass of my heart.
I loathe the lewd rake, the dressed fopling despise;
Before such pursuers the nice virgin flies;
And as Ovid has sweetly in parables told
We harden like trees, and like rivers are cold.

SUGGESTIONS FOR WRITING AND DISCUSSION

1. The speaker says that her indifference to her suitors "is not owing to nature,
   to fear, or to shame." What are her reasons?

2. Write a one-page character description of the woman who is speaking in this poem.
3. What qualities does the speaker admire in a man?
4. Imagine that this poem is a reply to Andrew Marvell's "To His Coy Mistress." In a two- to three-page essay discuss whose argument you find more persuasive.

Christopher Marlowe (British, 1564–1616)

The Passionate Shepherd to His Love

Come live with me, and be my love,
And we will all the pleasures prove
That hills and valleys, dales and fields,
And all the craggy mountains yields.

And we will sit upon the rocks,
Seeing the shepherds feed their flocks,
By shallow rivers, to whose falls
Melodious birds sing madrigals.

And I will make thee beds of roses
And a thousand fragrant posies,
A cap of flowers, and a kirtle
Embroidered all with leaves of myrtle;

A gown made of the finest wool,
Which from our pretty lambs we pull,
Fair linèd slippers, for the cold,
With buckles of the purest gold;

A belt of straw and ivy-buds
With coral clasps and amber studs.
And if these pleasures may thee move,
Come live with me, and be my love.

The shepherds' swains shall dance and sing
For thy delight each May morning.
If these delights thy mind may move,
Then live with me, and be my love.

SUGGESTIONS FOR WRITING AND DISCUSSION

1. What is the mood of this poem?
2. Why does the shepherd describe in so much detail the clothes he would make for his love?

3. This poem is an idyll of rustic life. Would the life of the shepherd and his love really be as he describes? Is his argument persuasive?
4. Read Sir Walter Raleigh's "The Nymph's Reply to the Shepherd." Write a two- to three-page essay comparing the two poems.

Sir Walter Raleigh (British, 1552–1618)

The Nymph's Reply to the Shepherd

If all the world and love were young,
And truth in every shepherd's tongue,
These pretty pleasures might me move
To live with thee and be thy love.

Time drives the flocks from field to fold
When rivers rage and rocks grow cold,
And Philomel becometh dumb;
The rest complains of cares to come.

The flowers do fade, and wanton fields
To wayward winter reckoning yields;
A honey tongue, a heart of gall,
Is fancy's spring, but sorrow's fall.

Thy gowns, thy shoes, thy beds of roses,
Thy cap, thy kirtle, and thy posies
Soon break, soon wither, soon forgotten—
In folly ripe, in reason rotten.

Thy belt of straw and ivy buds,
Thy coral clasps and amber studs,
All these in me no means can move
To come to thee and be thy love.

But could youth last and love still breed,
Had joys no date nor age no need,
Then these delights my mind might move
To live with thee and be thy love.

SUGGESTIONS FOR WRITING AND DISCUSSION

1. What does the nymph tell us in the last stanza? How does this comment reflect on the rest of the poem?
2. Like the speaker in Andrew Marvell's "To His Coy Mistress," the nymph begins with the premise that time passes swiftly, but she reaches a very different conclusion. Compare these two arguments.

3. In a three- to five-page essay compare Raleigh's, Marlowe's, and Marvell's treatment of time and passion.

Andrew Marvell (British, 1621–1678)

To His Coy Mistress

Had we but world enough, and time,
This coyness, lady, were no crime,
We would sit down and think which way
To walk, and pass our long love's day.
Thou by the Indian Ganges' side
Should'st rubies find; I by the tide
Of Humber would complain. I would
Love you ten years before the Flood.
And you should, if you please, refuse
Till the conversion of the Jews.
My vegetable love should grow
Vaster than empires, and more slow.
An hundred years should go to praise
Thine eyes, and on thy forehead gaze,
Two hundred to adore each breast,
But thirty thousand to the rest.
An age at least to every part,
And the last age should show your heart.
For, lady, you deserve this state,
Nor would I love at lower rate.
    But at my back I always hear
Time's wingèd chariot hurrying near;
And yonder all before us lie
Deserts of vast eternity.
Thy beauty shall no more be found,
Nor in thy marble vault shall sound
My echoing song; then worms shall try
That long preserved virginity.
And your quaint honor turn to dust,
And into ashes all my lust.
The grave's a fine and private place,
But none, I think, do there embrace.
    Now therefore, while the youthful hue
Sits on thy skin like morning glew
And while thy willing soul transpires
At every pore with instant fires,
Now let us sport us while we may;
And now, like am'rous birds of prey,
Rather at once our time devour,

Than languish in his slow-chapped power.
Let us roll all our strength, and all
Our sweetness, up into one ball;
And tear our pleasures with rough strife
Thorough the iron gates of life.
Thus, though we cannot make our sun
Stand still, yet we will make him run.

SUGGESTIONS FOR WRITING AND DISCUSSION

1. What is the speaker trying to persuade his mistress to do? What can you deduce about her from the poem? Is the poem complimentary? Has the speaker previously made advances to her? Does she like the speaker? Is she likely to capitulate?
2. Identify as many figures of speech in the poem as you can.
3. Each of the three stanzas presents a step in the speaker's argument. Write a short paraphrase of this argument.
3. In a one- to two-page essay analyze the ways in which the speaker reinforces each step in his argument.
4. Lines 1 through 20 describe one kind of courtship, lines 33 through 42 another. Write a two- to three-page essay contrasting the tone and images in these two sections. How do lines 21 through 32 provide a contrast to both?
5. This is an example of a *carpe diem* poem, or a poem which urges us to seize the day. How does the speaker describe time? What is the connection between time and lovemaking?

John Crowe Ransom (American, 1888–1974)

Blue Girls

Twirling your blue skirts, traveling the sward
Under the towers of your seminary,
Go listen to your teachers old and contrary
Without believing a word.

Tie the white fillets then about your lustrous hair
And think no more of what will come to pass
Than bluebirds that go walking on the grass
And chattering on the air.

Practice your beauty, blue girls, before it fail;
And I will cry with my loud lips and publish
Beauty which all our power shall never establish,
It is so frail.

For I could tell you a story which is true:
I know a lady with a terrible tongue,
Blear eyes fallen from blue,
All her perfections tarnished—and yet it is not long
Since she was lovelier than any of you.

SUGGESTIONS FOR WRITING AND DISCUSSION

1. What is the connection between the girls in the first stanza and the woman in the final stanza?
2. How does the word *blue* change in meaning from stanza to stanza?
3. What do we learn about the speaker of the poem? Compare his attitude with that of the speaker in Weldon Kees's poem "For My Daughter" (p. 203).
4. Compare this poem with one or two others in this section that deal with the inevitable loss of youth and beauty. Discuss this theme in a three- to four-page essay.

Theodore Roethke (American, 1908–1963)

I Knew a Woman

I knew a woman, lovely in her bones,
When small birds sighed, she would sigh back at them;
Ah, when she moved, she moved more ways than one:
The shapes a bright container can contain!
Of her choice virtues only gods should speak,
Or English poets who grew up on Greek
(I'd have them sing in chorus, cheek to cheek).

How well her wishes went! She stroked my chin,
She taught me Turn, and Counter-turn, and Stand;
She taught me Touch, that undulant white skin;
I nibbled meekly from her proffered hand;
She was the sickle; I, poor I, the rake.
Coming behind her for her pretty sake
(But what prodigious mowing we did make).

Love likes a gander, and adores a goose:
Her full lips pursed, the errant note to seize;
She played it quick, she played it light and loose;
My eyes, they dazzled at her flowing knees;
Her several parts could keep a pure repose,
Or one hip quiver with a mobile nose
(She moved in circles, and those circles moved).

Let seed be grass, and grass turn into hay:
I'm martyr to a motion not my own;
What's freedom for? To know enternity.
I swear she cast a shadow white as stone.
But who would count eternity in days?
These old bones live to learn her wanton ways:
(I measure time by how a body sways).

SUGGESTIONS FOR WRITING AND DISCUSSION

1. This witty poem has numerous puns and figures of speech. Identify as many
   as you can.
2. The speaker pokes fun at both himself and the woman. How does he do this?
   In a one- to two-page essay discuss what this shows about the relationship
   between them.
3. How does the tone as conveyed by the diction compare with Roethke's poem
   ''My Papa's Waltz'' (p. 205)?

Walt Whitman (American, 1819–1892)

The Dalliance of the Eagles

Skirting the river road (my forenoon walk, my rest,)
Skyward in air a sudden muffled sound, the dalliance of the eagles,
The rushing amorous contact high in space together,
The clinching interlocking claws, a living, fierce, gyrating wheel,
Four beating wings, two beaks, a swirling mass tight grappling,
In tumbling turning clustering loops, straight downward falling,
Till o'er the river pois'd, the twain yet one, a moment's lull,
A motionless still balance in the air, then parting, talons loosing,
Upward again on slow-firm pinions slanting, their separate diverse flight,
She hers, he his, pursuing.

SUGGESTIONS FOR WRITING AND DISCUSSION

1. In a one-page essay discuss the word *dalliance.* Why is it particularly appropriate to describe the eagles? Is its meaning carried throughout the poem?
2. This poem is written in free verse. Does it contain end rhymes or internal
   rhymes?
3. Whitman uses many adjectives, especially participles, that is, adjectives
   formed from verbs. What is their effect? How do these participles give the
   poem a sense of continuing movement?
4. What is the point of view of the speaker? Is he solely an observer, or does
   he somehow participate in the dalliance?

Seamus Heaney (Irish, 1939–   )

Act of Union

I

To-night, a fast movement, a pulse,
As if the rain in bogland gathered head
To slip and flood: a bog-burst,
A gash breaking open the ferny bed.
Your back is a firm line of eastern coast
And arms and legs are thrown
Beyond your gradual hills. I caress
The heaving province where our past has grown.
I am the tall kingdom over your shoulder
That you would neither cajole nor ignore.
Conquest is a lie. I grow older
Conceding your half-independent shore
Within whose borders now my legacy
Culminates inexorably.

II

And I am still imperially
Male, leaving you with the pain,
The rending process in the colony,
The battering ram, the boom burst from within.
The act sprouted an obstinate fifth column
Whose stance is growing unilateral.
His heart beneath your heart is a wardrum
Mustering force. His parasitical
And ignorant little fists already
Beat at your borders and I know they're cocked
At me across the water. No treaty
I foresee will salve completely your tracked
And stretchmarked body, the big pain
That leaves you raw, like opened ground, again.

SUGGESTIONS FOR WRITING AND DISCUSSION

1. This poem describes not only the relationship between a man and a woman
   but also the political tension between Northern Ireland and the British government. In a brief essay show how the personal and political elements are
   woven together.
2. What does this poem say about the way in which a child may replace the
   father in the mother's affections?
3. How is the landscape used as a metaphor?

John Donne (British, 1572–1631)

A Valediction: Forbidding Mourning

1633

As virtuous men pass mildly away,
   And whisper to their souls to go,
Whilst some of their sad friends do say
   The breath goes now, and some say no:

So let us melt, and make no noise,
   No tear-floods, nor sigh-tempests move;
'Twere profanation of our joys
   To tell the laity our love.

Moving of th' earth brings harms and fears;
   Men reckon what it did and meant;
But trepidation of the spheres,
   Though greater far, is innocent.

Dull sublunary lovers' love
   (Whose soul is sense) cannot admit
Absence, because it doth remove
   Those things which elemented it.

But we, by a love so much refined
   That ourselves know not what it is,
Inter-assurèd of the mind,
   Care less, eyes, lips, and hands to miss.

Our two souls, therefore, which are one,
   Though I must go, endure not yet
A breach, but an expansion,
   Like gold to airy thinness beat.

If they be two, they are two so
   As stiff twin compasses are two:
Thy soul, the fixed foot, makes no show
   To move, but doth, if th' other do.

And though it in the center sit,
   Yet when the other far doth roam,
It leans and harkens after it,
   And grows erect as that comes home.

Such wilt thou be to me, who must,
  Like th' other foot, obliquely run;
Thy firmness makes my circle just,
  And makes me end where I begun.

SUGGESTIONS FOR WRITING AND DISCUSSION

1. This poem contains three similes which describe the parting of lovers. Find them and write a paragraph about each. Which is the most fanciful? Which is the most eloquent?
2. The speaker describes and contrasts two kinds of lovers. How does the speaker characterize them? What are the main differences between them? How does each behave on parting?
3. What figure of speech is used in the third stanza? Explicate it.

William Shakespeare (British, 1564–1616)

Sonnet 116

Let me not to the marriage of true minds
Admit impediments. Love is not love
Which alters when it alteration finds,
Or bends with the remover to remove.
O no! it is an ever-fixèd mark
That looks on tempests and is never shaken;
It is the star to every wand'ring bark,
Whose worth's unknown, although his height be taken.
Love's not Time's fool, though rosy lips and cheeks
Within his bending sickle's compass come.
Love alters not with his brief hours and weeks,
But bears it out even to the edge of doom.
    If this be error, and upon me proved,
    I never writ, nor no man ever loved.

SUGGESTIONS FOR WRITING AND DISCUSSION

1. What does "the marriage of true minds" mean? What does the speaker claim to be the main quality of love? How is "the marriage of true minds" contrasted with the physical changes that time brings?
2. In a one- to two-page essay compare this sonnet with Sonnet 18. How is time described in each? What do the final couplets in both sonnets show about the speakers' attitudes toward the art of poetry?
3. Compare the idea of love in this poem with that in John Donne's "Valediction: Forbidding Mourning."

Kuan Tao-Sheng (Japanese, 1282–1319)

Married Love

You and I
Have so much love,
That it
Burns like a fire,
In which we bake a lump of clay
Molded into a figure of you
And a figure of me.
Then we take both of them,
And break them into pieces,
And mix the pieces with water,
And mold again a figure of you,
And a figure of me.
I am in your clay.
You are in my clay.
In life we share a single quilt.
In death we will share one coffin.

SUGGESTIONS FOR WRITING AND DISCUSSION

1. The poem contains an extended metaphor. List the different stages of the metaphor. How do they parallel the different stages in the speaker's marriage?
2. Compare "Married Love" to Catullus's "Lesbia." What attitudes, if any, do the two speakers share? In what sense are these both love poems? How do the two speakers define love?
3. Write a one- or two-page essay explicating this poem.

Ezra Pound (American, 1885–1972)

The River-Merchant's Wife: A Letter

While my hair was still cut straight across my forehead
I played about the front gate, pulling flowers.
You came by on bamboo stilts, playing horse,
You walked about my seat, playing with blue plums.
And we went on living in the village of Chokan:
Two small people, without dislike or suspicion.

At fourteen I married My Lord you.
I never laughed, being bashful.
Lowering my head, I looked at the wall.
Called to, a thousand times, I never looked back.

At fifteen I stopped scowling,
I desired my dust to be mingled with yours
Forever and forever and forever.
Why should I climb the look out?

At sixteen you departed,
You went into far Ku-to-yen, by the river of swirling eddies,
And you have been gone five months.
The monkeys make sorrowful noise overhead.

You dragged your feet when you went out.
By the gate now, the moss is grown, the different mosses,
Too deep to clear them away!
The leaves fall early this autumn, in wind.
The paired butterflies are already yellow with August
Over the grass in the West garden;
They hurt me. I grow older.
If you are coming down through the narrows of the river Kiang,
Please let me known beforehand,
And I will come out to meet you
       As far as Cho-fu-Sa.

SUGGESTIONS FOR WRITING AND DISCUSSION

1. This poem is a free translation of one by the eighth-century Chinese poet Li Po. It is written in the form of a letter and tells the story of the river-merchant's relationship with his wife. Write a one- to two-page account of their relationship and show how the descriptive details are used to indicate the passage of time.
2. The wife does not blame her husband for being away but she misses him deeply. What details show her sadness?

Anne Bradstreet (American, 1612?–1672)

To My Dear and Loving Husband

If ever two were one, then surely we.
If every man were lov'd by wife, then thee;
If ever wife was happy in a man,
Compare with me ye women if you can.
I prize thy love more than whole Mines of gold,
Or all the riches that the East doth hold.
My love is such that Rivers cannot quench,
Nor ought but love from thee, give recompense.
Thy love is such I can no way repay,
The heavens reward thee manifold I pray.

Then while we live, in love lets so persever,
That when we live no more, we may live ever.

SUGGESTIONS FOR WRITING AND DISCUSSION

1. In the first eight lines the speaker discusses earthly love; in the last four she discusses a more spiritual kind of love. How is this progression mapped in the images?
2. In a one- to two-page essay compare this poem with Kuan Tao-Sheng's "Married Love."

Elizabeth Barrett Browning (British, 1809–1861)

Sonnet 43

How do I love thee? Let me count the ways.
I love thee to the depth and breadth and height
My soul can reach, when feeling out of sight
For the ends of Being and ideal Grace.
I love thee to the level of everyday's
Most quiet need, by sun and candle-light.
I love thee freely, as men strive for Right;
I love thee purely, as they turn from Praise.
I love thee with the passion put to use
In my old griefs, and with my childhood's faith.
I love thee with a love I seemed to lose
With my lost saints,—I love thee with the breath,
Smiles, tears, of all my life!—and, if God choose,
I shall but love thee better after death.

SUGGESTIONS FOR WRITING AND DISCUSSION

1. What does the speaker's choice of comparisons show about her attitude toward love?
2. Is this sonnet simply a love poem to the speaker's husband or is it also an explication of the different kinds of love that exist? Support your answer in a two-page essay.

Robert Browning (British, 1812–1889)

My Last Duchess

Ferrara, 1842

That's my last Duchess painted on the wall,
Looking as if she were alive. I call

That piece a wonder, now; Frà Pandolf's hands
Worked busily a day, and there she stands.
Will 't please you sit and look at her? I said
"Frà Pandolf" by design, for never read
Strangers like you that pictured countenance,
The depth and passion of its earnest glance,
But to myself they turned (since none puts by
The curtain I have drawn for you, but I)
And seemed as they would ask me, if they durst,
How such a glance came there; so, not the first
Are you to turn and ask thus. Sir, 'twas not
Her husband's presence only, called the spot
Of joy into the Duchess' cheek; perhaps
Frà Pandolf chanced to say, "Her mantle laps
Over my lady's wrist too much," or "Paint
Must never hope to reproduce the faint
Half-flush that dies along her throat." Such stuff
Was courtesy, she thought, and cause enough
For calling up that spot of joy. She had
A heart—how shall I say?—too soon made glad,
Too easily impressed; she liked whate'er
She looked on, and her looks went everywhere.
Sir, 'twas all one! My favor at her breast,
The dropping of the daylight in the West,
The bough of cherries some officious fool
Broke in the orchard for her, the white mule
She rode with round the terrace—all and each
Would draw from her alike the approving speech,
Or blush, at least. She thanked men,—good! but thanked
Somehow—I know not how—as if she ranked
My gift of a nine-hundred-years' old name
With anybody's gift. Who'd stoop to blame
This sort of trifling? Even had you skill
In speech—which I have not—to make your will
Quite clear to such an one, and say "Just this
Or that in you disgusts me; here you miss,
Or there exceed the mark"—and if she let
Herself be lessoned so, nor plainly set
Her wits to yours, forsooth, and made excuse—
E'en then would be some stooping; and I choose
Never to stoop. Oh, sir, she smiled, no doubt,
Whene'er I passed her; but who passed without
Much the same smile? This grew; I gave commands;
Then all smiles stopped together. There she stands
As if alive. Will 't please you rise? We'll meet
The company below, then. I repeat,

The Count your master's known munificence
Is ample warrant that no just pretense
Of mine for dowry will be disallowed;
Though his fair daughter's self, as I avowed
At starting, is my object. Nay, we'll go
Together down, sir. Notice Neptune, though,
Taming a sea-horse, thought a rarity,
Which Claus of Innsbruck cast in bronze for me!

SUGGESTIONS FOR WRITING AND DISCUSSION

1. Browning lets his readers know almost immediately that it is the Duke who is speaking this poem, but it is not until the last few lines that we learn to whom he is speaking and on what occasion. Why do you think Browning does this? How does the new information change the way we read the earlier part of the poem? What do the Duke's reminiscences of his last wife have to do with the present situation?
2. Both implicitly and explicitly the Duke tells us not only about his last Duchess but also about himself. Write a one- to two-page character description of the Duke.
3. For what does the Duke condemn the Duchess? Does she seem more or less likeable than her husband? How does Browning permit us to see her separately from her husband?
4. The Duke does not say exactly what happens to the Duchess. Does this weaken the poem? What do you think happened to her?

Thomas Wyatt (British, 1503–1542)

They Flee from Me

They flee from me that sometime did me seek
  With naked foot stalking in my chamber.
I have seen them gentle tame and meek
  That now are wild and do not remember
  That sometime they put themself in danger
To take bread at my hand; and now they range
Busily seeking with a continual change.

Thanked be Fortune it hath been otherwise
  Twenty times better; but once in special,
In thin array after a pleasant guise,
  When her loose gown from her shoulders did fall,
  And she me caught in her arms long and small;
And therewith all sweetly did me kiss,
And softly said, ``Dear heart, how like you this?''

It was no dream: I lay broad waking.
   But all is turned through my gentleness
Into a strange fashion of forsaking;
   And I have leave to go of her goodness,
   And she also to use newfangleness.
But since that I so kindely am served,
I fain would know what she hath deserved.

SUGGESTIONS FOR WRITING AND DISCUSSION

1. Who are "they" in the first stanza? To what are "they" being compared?
2. In the second stanza the speaker describes his relationship with a woman. What happens to their relationship? How does her behavior compare with that of other women the speaker has known?
3. Write a two-page essay comparing this poem with Theodore Roethke's "I Knew a Woman."

H. D. (Hilda Doolittle) (American, 1886–1961)

Never More Will the Wind

Never more will the wind
cherish you again,
never more will the rain.

Never more
shall we find you bright
in the snow and wind.

The snow is melted,
the snow is gone,
and you are flown:

Like a bird out of our hand,
like a light out of our heart,
you are gone.

SUGGESTIONS FOR WRITING AND DISCUSSION

1. Write a paraphrase of this short lyric poem.
2. Why does the speaker use *we* and *our?* What is the effect?

Edgar Allan Poe (American, 1809–1849)

Annabel Lee

It was many and many a year ago,
       In a kingdom by the sea,

That a maiden there lived whom you may know
                    By the name of Annabel Lee;—
And this maiden she lived with no other thought
                    Than to love and be loved by me.

She was a child and *I* was a child,
                    In this kingdom by the sea,
But we loved with a love that was more than love—
                    I and my Annabel Lee—
With a love that the winged seraphs of Heaven
                    Coveted her and me.

And this was the reason that, long ago,
                    In this kingdom by the sea,
A wind blew out of a cloud by night
                    Chilling my Annabel Lee;
So that her highborn kinsmen came
                    And bore her away from me,
To shut her up in a sepulchre
                    In this kingdom by the sea.

The angels, not half so happy in Heaven,
                    Went envying her and me—
Yes!—that was the reason (as all men know,
                    In this kingdom by the sea)
That the wind came out of the cloud chilling
                    And killing my Annabel Lee.

But our love it was stronger by far than the love
    Of those who were older than we—
    Of many far wiser than we—
And neither the angels in Heaven above,
    Nor the demons down under the sea,
Can ever dissever my soul from the soul
    Of the beautiful Annabel Lee:—

For the moon never beams without bringing me dreams
    Of the beautiful Annabel Lee;
And the stars never rise but I see the bright eyes
    Of the beautiful Annabel Lee;
And so, all the night-tide, I lie down by the side
Of my darling, my darling, my life and my bride,
    In her sepulchre there by the sea—
    In her tomb by the side of the sea.

SUGGESTION FOR WRITING AND DISCUSSION

1. Why is Annabel Lee taken away from the speaker?
2. The speaker seems to be in opposition both to the angels in heaven and to the demons under the sea. What does this say about the quality of his love?
3. What do you think Poe means by "we loved with a love that was more than love"? In a one- to two-page essay discuss why the speaker and Annabel Lee are punished for their love.

Emily Dickinson (American, 1830–1886)

I Cannot Live with You

I cannot live with You—
It would be Life—
And Life is over there—
Behind the Shelf

The Sexton keeps the Key to—
Putting up
Our Life—His Porcelain—
Like a Cup—

Discarded of the Housewife—
Quaint—or Broke—
A newer Sevres pleases—
Old Ones crack—

I could not die—with You—
For One must wait
To shut the Other's Gaze down—
You—could not—

And I—could I stand by
And see You—freeze—
Without my Right of Frost—
Death's privilege?

Nor could I rise—with You—
Because Your Face
Would put out Jesus'—
That New Grace

Glow plain—and foreign
On my homesick Eye—
Except that You than He
Shone closer by—

They'd judge Us—How—
For You—served Heaven—You know,
Or sought to—
I could not—

Because You saturated Sight—
And I had no more Eyes
For sordid excellence
As Paradise

And were You lost, I would be—
Though My Name
Rang loudest
On the Heavenly fame—

And were You—saved—
And I—condemned to be
Where You were not—
That self—were Hell to Me—

So We must meet apart—
You there—I—Here—
With just the Door ajar
That Oceans are—and Prayer—
And that White Sustenance—
Despair—

SUGGESTIONS FOR WRITING AND DISCUSSION

1. In a two-page essay discuss the various reasons why the speaker and the
   beloved cannot meet.
2. Characterize the beloved.
3. In the last stanza why is despair described as sustenance? What in the rest
   of the poem leads up to this description and makes it comprehensible?

Louise Bogan (American, 1897–1970)

Song for the Last Act

Now that I have your face by heart, I look
Less at its features than its darkening frame
Where quince and melon, yellow as young flame,
Lie with quilled dahlias and the shepherd's crook.
Beyond, a garden. There, in insolent ease
The lead and marble figures watch the show
Of yet another summer loath to go
Although the scythes hang in the apple trees.

Now that I have your face by heart, I look.

Now that I have your voice by heart, I read
In the black chords upon a dulling page
Music that is not meant for music's cage,
Whose emblems mix with words that shake and bleed.
The staves are shuttled over with a stark
Unprinted silence. In a double dream
I must spell out the storm, the running stream.
The beat's too swift. The notes shift in the dark.

Now that I have your voice by heart, I read.

Now that I have your heart by heart, I see
The wharves with their great ships and architraves;
The rigging and the cargo and the slaves
On a strange beach under a broken sky.
O not departure, but a voyage done!
The bales stand on the stone; the anchor weeps
Its red rust downward, and the long vine creeps
Beside the salt herb, in the lengthening sun.

Now that I have your heart by heart, I see.

SUGGESTIONS FOR WRITING AND DISCUSSION

1. The controlling metaphor of the first stanza is a garden; the controlling metaphor of the second stanza is music; the controlling metaphor of the third stanza is a voyage. Write a paragraph about each of these metaphors, discussing what they represent.
2. How do these metaphors act as the vehicles of the spiritual journey that the speaker is making?
3. The title, "Song for the Last Act," implies that this poem is about the end of a love affair. What details help to convey a sense of loss?
4. In a two- to three-page essay compare this poem to Elizabeth Bishop's "One Art." In what ways do the speakers of the two poems seem similar in their situations and reactions?

Elizabeth Bishop (American, 1911–1980)

One Art

The art of losing isn't hard to master;
so many things seem filled with the intent
to be lost that their loss is no disaster.

Lose something every day. Accept the fluster
of lost door keys, the hour badly spent.
The art of losing isn't hard to master.

Then practice losing farther, losing faster:
places, and names, and where it was you meant
to travel. None of these will bring disaster.

I lost my mother's watch. And look! my last, or
next-to-last, of three loved houses went.
The art of losing isn't hard to master.

I lost two cities, lovely ones. And, vaster,
some realms I owned, two rivers, a continent.
I miss them, but it wasn't a disaster.

—Even losing you (the joking voice, a gesture
I love) I shan't have lied. It's evident
the art of losing's not too hard to master
though it may look like (*Write* it!) like disaster.

SUGGESTIONS FOR WRITING AND DISCUSSION

1. This poem is written in a form devised by the French poets of the Middle
   Ages, the villanelle. Look up the definition of a villanelle and show why this
   poem is one. Because of their rigid form and repetition, villanelles are sometimes no more than exercises in ingenuity. How do you think "One Art"
   manages to avoid this?
2. What do we learn about the speaker of the poem and about the person to
   whom she is speaking?
3. The first and third lines of the first stanza are used as refrains throughout
   the poem. How does the meaning or emphasis of these lines change? In a
   two- to three-page essay analyze the changes in the speaker's thoughts and
   feelings.

William Shakespeare (British, 1564–1616)

Sonnet 18

Shall I compare thee to a summer's day?
Thou art more lovely and more temperate:
Rough winds do shake the darling buds of May,
And summer's lease hath all too short a date:
Sometime too hot the eye of heaven shines,
And often is his gold complexion dimmed;
And every fair from fair sometime declines,

By chance or nature's changing course untrimmed:
But thy eternal summer shall not fade
Nor lose possession of that fair thou ow'st,
Nor shall Death brag thou wand'rest in his shade,
When in eternal lines to time thou grow'st.
   So long as men can breathe or eyes can see,
   So long lives this, and this gives life to thee.

SUGGESTIONS FOR WRITING AND DISCUSSION

1. In this sonnet the speaker compares his beloved to a summer's day. How does he describe the day? In what respects does he claim the beloved to be superior (lines 9 through 11)? What new meaning is this claim given in the final three lines of the poem?
2. Is the speaker really praising his beloved? If not, who or what is being praised?
3. In line 11 death is personified as a braggart. Why is this personification apt? What does it show about the speaker?
4. In a one- or two-page essay analyze the use of figurative language in this sonnet.

Richard Wilbur (American, 1921–   )

Love Calls Us to the Things of This World

   The eyes open to a cry of pulleys,
And spirited from sleep, the astounded soul
Hangs for a moment bodiless and simple
As false dawn.
              Outside the open window
The morning air is all awash with angels.

   Some are in bed-sheets, some are in blouses,
Some are in smocks: but truly there they are.
Now they are rising together in calm swells
Of halcyon feeling, filling whatever they wear
With the deep joy of their impersonal breathing;

   Now they are flying in place, conveying
The terrible speed of their omnipresence, moving
And staying like white water; and now of a sudden
They swoon down into so rapt a quiet
That nobody seems to be there.
               The soul shrinks

From all that it is about to remember,
From the punctual rape of every blessed day,
And cries,
            ``Oh, let there be nothing on earth but laundry,
Nothing but rosy hands in the rising steam
And clear dances done in the sight of heaven.''

    Yet, as the sun acknowledges
With a warm look the world's hunks and colors,
The soul descends once more in bitter love
To accept the waking body, saying now
In a changed voice as the man yawns and rises,

    ``Bring them down from their ruddy gallows;
Let there be clean linen for the backs of thieves;
Let lovers go fresh and sweet to be undone,
And the heaviest nuns walk in a pure floating
Of dark habits,
                keeping their difficult balance.''

SUGGESTIONS FOR WRITING AND DISCUSSION

1. This poem is about someone waking up in the morning and hearing and seeing laundry being hung out to dry. How does Wilbur transform something as mundane as laundry into a metaphor expressing how ``love calls us to the things of this world''?
2. Why is the soul reluctant to enter the body on waking? In a one- or two-page essay discuss how the soul's attitude toward the body, and by extension the world, changes.
3. What do you think the poet means by the phrase *bitter love?*

Drama

Anton Chekhov (Russian, 1860–1904)

The Marriage Proposal   •

CHARACTERS

STEPHEN CHUBUKOV, *a landowner*
NATASHA, *his daughter, aged 25*
IVAN LOMOV, *a landowning neighbour of Chubukov's, hefty and well-nourished, but a hypochondriac*

The action takes place in the drawing-room of Chubukov's country-house

Scene I

[CHUBUKOV *and* LOMOV; *the latter comes in wearing evening dress and white gloves.*]

CHUBUKOV [*going to meet him*]. Why, it's Ivan Lomov—or do my eyes deceive me, old boy? Delighted. [*Shakes hands.*] I say, old bean, this is a surprise! How *are* you?

LOMOV. All right, thanks. And how might you be?

CHUBUKOV. Not so bad, dear boy. Good of you to ask and so on. Now, you simply must sit down. Never neglect the neighbours, old bean— what? But why so formal, old boy—the tails, the gloves and so on? Not going anywhere, are you, dear man?

LOMOV. Only coming here, my dear Chubukov.

CHUBUKOV. Then why the tails, my dear fellow? Why make such a great thing of it?

LOMOV. Well, look, the point is—. [*Takes his arm.*] I came to ask a favour, my dear Chubukov, if it's not too much bother. I have had the priv- ilege of enlisting your help more than once, and you've always, as it were—but I'm so nervous, sorry. I'll drink some water, my dear Chu- bukov. [*Drinks water.*]

CHUBUKOV [*aside*]. He's come to borrow money. Well, there's nothing doing! [*To him.*] What's the matter, my dear fellow?

LOMOV. Well, you see, my dear Dubukov—my dear Chubukov, I mean, sorry—that's to say, I'm terribly jumpy, as you see. In fact only you can help me, though I don't deserve it, of course and, er, have no claims on you either.

CHUBUKOV. Now don't muck about with it, old bean. Let's have it. Well?

LOMOV. Certainly, this instant. The fact is, I'm here to ask for the hand of your daughter Natasha.

CHUBUKOV (*delightedly*). My dear Lomov! Say that again, old horse, I didn't quite catch it.

LOMOV. I have the honour to ask—

CHUBUKOV (*interrupting him*). My dear old boy! I'm delighted and so on, er, and so forth—what? (*Embraces and kisses him.*) I've long wanted it, it's always been my wish. (*Sheds a tear.*) I've always loved you as a son, dear boy. May you both live happily ever after and so on. As for me, I've always wanted—. But why do I stand around like a blithering idiot? I'm tickled pink, I really am! Oh, I most cordially—. I'll go and call Natasha and so forth.

LOMOV (*very touched*). My dear Chubukov, what do you think—can I count on a favourable response?

CHUBUKOV. What—her turn down a good-looking young fellow like you! Not likely! I bet she's crazy about you and so on. One moment. (*Goes out.*)

Scene II

(LOMOV, *alone.*)

LOMOV. I feel cold, I'm shaking like a leaf. Make up your mind, that's the great thing. If you keep chewing things over, dithering on the brink, arguing the toss and waiting for your ideal woman or true love to come along, you'll never get hitched up. Brrr! I'm cold. Natasha's a good housewife. She's not bad-looking and she's an educated girl— what more can you ask? But I'm so jumpy, my ears have started buzzing. (*Drinks water.*) And get married I must. In the first place, I'm thirty-five years old—a critical age, so to speak. Secondly, I should lead a proper, regular life. I've heart trouble and constant palpitations, I'm irritable and nervous as a kitten. See how my lips are trembling now? See my right eyelid twitch? But my nights are the worst thing. No sooner do I get in bed and start dozing off than I have a sort of shooting pain in my left side. It goes right through my shoulder and head. Out I leap like a lunatic, walk about a bit, then lie down again—but the moment I start dropping off I get this pain in my side again. And it happens twenty times over.

Scene III

(NATASHA *and* LOMOV.)

NATASHA (*comes in*). Oh, it's you. That's funny, Father said it was a dealer collecting some goods or something. Good morning, Mr. Lomov.

LOMOV. And good morning to you, my dear Miss Chubukov.

NATASHA. Excuse my apron, I'm not dressed for visitors. We've been shelling peas—we're going to dry them. Why haven't you been over for so long? Do sit down. (*They sit.*) Will you have lunch?

LOMOV. Thanks, I've already had some.

NATASHA. Or a smoke? Here are some matches. It's lovely weather, but it rained so hard yesterday—the men were idle all day. How much hay have you cut? I've been rather greedy, you know—I mowed all mine, and now I'm none too happy in case it rots. I should have hung on. But what's this I see? Evening dress, it seems. That *is* a surprise! Going dancing or something? You're looking well, by the way—but why on earth go round in that get-up?

LOMOV (*agitated*). Well, you see, my dear Miss Chubukov. The fact is, I've decided to ask you to—er, lend me your ears. You're bound to be surprised—angry, even. But I— (*Aside.*) I feel terribly cold.

NATASHA. What's up then? (*Pause.*) Well?

LOMOV. I'll try to cut it short. Miss Chubukov, you are aware that I have long been privileged to know your family—since I was a boy, in fact. My dear departed aunt and her husband—from whom, as you are cognizant, I inherited the estate—always entertained the deepest respect for your father and dear departed mother. We Lomovs and Chubukovs have always been on the friendliest terms—you might say we've been pretty thick. And what's more, as you are also aware, we own closely adjoining properties. You may recall that my land at Oxpen Field is right next to your birch copse.

NATASHA. Sorry to butt in, but you refer to Oxpen Field as 'yours'? Surely you're not serious!

LOMOV. I am, madam.

NATASHA. Well, I like that! Oxpen Field is ours, it isn't yours.

LOMOV. You're wrong, my dear Miss Chubukov, that's my land.

NATASHA. This is news to me. How can it be yours?

LOMOV. How? What do you mean? I'm talking about Oxpen Field, that wedge of land between your birch copse and Burnt Swamp.

NATASHA. That's right. It's our land.

LOMOV. No, you're mistaken, my dear Miss Chubukov. It's mine.

NATASHA. Oh, come off it, Mr. Lomov. How long has it been yours?

LOMOV. How long? As long as I can remember—it's always been ours.

NATASHA. I say, this really is a bit steep!

LOMOV. But you have only to look at the deeds, my dear Miss Chubukov. Oxpen Field once *was* in dispute, I grant you, but it's mine now—that's common knowledge, and no argument about it. If I may explain, my aunt's grandmother made over that field rent free to your father's grandfather's labourers for their indefinite use in return for firing her bricks. Now, your great-grandfather's people used the place rent free for forty years or so, and came to look on it as their own. Then when the government land settlement was brought out—

NATASHA. No, that's all wrong. My grandfather and great-grandfather both claimed the land up to Burnt Swamp as theirs. So Oxpen Field was ours. Why argue? That's what I can't see. This is really rather aggravating.

LOMOV. I'll show you the deeds, Miss Chubukov.

NATASHA. Oh, you must be joking or having me on. This *is* a nice surprise! You own land for nearly three hundred years, then someone ups and tells you it's not yours! Mr. Lomov, I'm sorry, but I simply can't believe my ears. I don't mind about the field—it's only the odd twelve acres, worth the odd three hundred roubles. But it's so unfair—that's what infuriates me. I can't stand unfairness, I don't care what you say.

LOMOV. Do hear me out, please! With due respect, your great-grandfather's people baked bricks for my aunt's grandmother, as I've already told you. Now, my aunt's grandmother wanted to do them a favour—

NATASHA. Grandfather, grandmother, aunt—it makes no sense to me. The field's ours, and that's that.

LOMOV. It's mine.

NATASHA. It's ours! Argue till the cows come home, put on tailcoats by the dozen for all I care—it'll still be ours, ours, ours! I'm not after your property, but I don't propose losing mine either, and I don't care what you think!

LOMOV. My dear Miss Chubukov, it's not that I need that field—it's the principle of the thing. If you want it, have it. Take it as a gift.

NATASHA. But it's mine to give *you* if I want—it's my property. This is odd, to put it mildly. We always thought you such a good neighbour and friend, Mr. Lomov. We lent you our threshing-machine last year, and couldn't get our own threshing done till November in consequence. We might be gipsies, the way you treat us. Making me a present of my own property! I'm sorry, but that's not exactly neighbourly of you. In fact, if you ask me, it's sheer howling cheek.

LOMOV. So I'm trying to pinch your land now, am I? It's not my habit, madam, to grab land that isn't mine, and I won't have anyone say it is! (*Quickly goes to the carafe and drinks some water.*) Oxpen Field belongs to me.

NATASHA. That's a lie, it's ours.

LOMOV. It's mine.

NATASHA. That's a lie and I'll nail it! I'll send my men to cut that field this very day.

Lomov. What do you say?

Natasha. My men will be out on that field today!

Lomov. Too right, they'll be out! Out on their ear!

Natasha. You'd never dare.

Lomov (*clutches his heart*). Oxpen Field belongs to me, do you hear? It's mine!

Natasha. Kindly stop shouting. By all means yell yourself blue in the face when you're in your own home, but I'll thank you to keep a civil tongue in your head in this house.

Lomov. Madam, if I hadn't got these awful, agonizing palpitations and this throbbing in my temples, I'd give you a piece of my mind! (*Shouts.*) Oxpen Field belongs to me.

Natasha. To us, you mean!

Lomov. It's mine!

Natasha. It's ours!

Lomov. Mine!

Scene IV

(*The above and* CHUBUKOV.)

Chubukov (*coming in*). What's going on, what are you shouting about?

Natasha. Father, who owns Oxpen Field? Would you mind telling this gentleman? Is it his or ours?

Chubukov (*to* Lomov). That field's ours, old cock!

Lomov. Now look here, Chubukov, how can it be? You at least might show some sense! My aunt's grandmother made over that field to your grandfather's farm-labourers rent free on a temporary basis. Those villagers had the use of the land for forty years and came to think of it as theirs, but when the settlement happened—

Chubukov. Now hang on, dear man, you forget one thing. That field was in dispute and so forth even in those days—and that's why the villagers paid your grandmother no rent and so on. But now it belongs to us, every dog in the district knows that, what? You can't have seen the plans.

Lomov. It's mine and I'll prove it.

Chubukov. Oh no you won't, my dear good boy.

Lomov. Oh yes, I will.

Chubukov. No need to shout, old bean. Shouting won't prove anything, what? I'm not after your property, but I don't propose losing mine, either. Why on earth should I? If it comes to that, old sausage, if you're set on disputing the field and so on, I'd rather give it to the villagers than you. So there.

LOMOV. This makes no sense to me. What right have you to give other people's property away?

CHUBUKOV. Permit me to be the best judge of that. Now, look here, young feller-me-lad—I'm not used to being spoken to like this, what? I'm twice your age, boy, and I'll thank you to talk to me without getting hot under the collar and so forth.

LOMOV. Oh, really, you must take me for a fool. You're pulling my leg. You say my land's yours, then you expect me to keep my temper and talk things over amicably. I call this downright unneighbourly, Chubukov. You're not a neighbour, you're a thorough-going shark!

CHUBUKOV. I *beg* your pardon! What did you say?

NATASHA. Father, send the men out to mow that field this very instant!

CHUBUKOV (*to* LOMOV). What was it you said, sir?

NATASHA. Oxpen Field's ours and I won't let it go, I won't, I won't!

LOMOV. We'll see about that! I'll have the law on you!

CHUBUKOV. You will, will you? Then go right ahead, sir, and so forth, go ahead and sue, sir! Oh, I know your sort! Just what you're angling for and so on, isn't it—a court case, what? Quite the legal eagle, aren't you? Your whole family's always been litigation-mad, every last one of 'em!

LOMOV. I'll thank you not to insult my family. We Lomovs have always been honest, we've none of us been had up for embezzlement like your precious uncle.

CHUBUKOV. The Lomovs have always been mad as hatters!

NATASHA. Yes! All of you! Mad!

CHUBUKOV. Your grandfather drank like a fish, and your younger Aunt What's-her-name—Nastasya—ran off with an architect and so on.

LOMOV. And your mother was a cripple. (*Clutches his heart.*) There's that shooting pain in my side, and a sort of blow on the head. Heavens alive! Water!

CHUBUKOV. Your father gambled and ate like a pig!

NATASHA. Your aunt was a most frightful busybody!

LOMOV. My left leg's gone to sleep. And you're a very slippery customer. Oh my heart! And it's common knowledge that at election time you bri—. I'm seeing stars. Where's my hat?

NATASHA. What a rotten, beastly, filthy thing to say.

CHUBUKOV. You're a thoroughly nasty, cantankerous, hypocritical piece of work, what? Yes, sir!

Lomov. Ah, there's my hat. My heart—. Which way do I go? Where's the door? Oh, I think I'm dying. I can hardly drag one foot after another. [*Moves to the door.*]

Chubukov [*after him*]. You need never set either of those feet in my house again, sir.

Natasha. Go ahead and sue, we'll see what happens.

[Lomov *goes out staggering.*]

Scene V

[Chubukov *and* Natasha.]

Chubukov. Oh, blast it! [*Walks up and down in agitation.*]

Natasha. The rotten cad! So much for trusting the dear neighbours!

Chubukov. Scruffy swine!

Natasha. He's an out-and-out monster! Pinches your land and then has the cheek to swear at you!

Chubukov. And this monstrosity, this blundering oaf, has the immortal rind to come here with his proposal and so on, what? A proposal! I ask you!

Natasha. A proposal, did you say?

Chubukov. Not half I did! He came here to propose to you!

Natasha. Propose? To me? Then why didn't you say so before?

Chubukov. That's why he dolled himself up in tails. Damn popinjay! Twerp!

Natasha. Me? Propose to me? Oh! [*Falls in an armchair and groans.*] Bring him back! Bring him back! Bring him back, I tell you!

Chubukov. Bring who back?

Natasha. Hurry up, be quick, I feel faint. Bring him back. [*Has hysterics.*]

Chubukov. What's this? What do you want? [*Clutches his head.*] Oh, misery! I might as well go and boil my head! I'm fed up with them!

Natasha. I'm dying. Bring him back!

Chubukov. Phew! All right then. No need to howl. [*Runs out.*]

Natasha [*alone, groans*]. What have we done! Bring him, bring him back!

Chubukov [*runs in*]. He'll be here in a moment and so on, damn him! Phew! You talk to him—I don't feel like it, what?

Natasha [*groans*]. Bring him back!

Chubukov [*shouts*]. He's coming, I tell you

> 'My fate, ye gods, is just too bad—
> To be a grown-up daughter's dad!'

I'll cut my throat, I'll make a point of it. We've sworn at the man, insulted him and kicked him out of the house. And it was all your doing.

NATASHA. It was *not,* it was yours!

CHUBUKOV. So now it's my fault, what?

[LOMOV *appears in the doorway.*]

CHUBUKOV. All right, now you talk to him. (*Goes out.*)

Scene VI

[NATASHA *and* LOMOV.]

LOMOV (*comes in, exhausted*). My heart's fairly thumping away, my leg's gone to sleep and there's this pain in my side—

NATASHA. I'm sorry we got a bit excited, Mr. Lomov. I've just remembered—Oxpen Field really belongs to you.

LOMOV. My heart's fairly thumping away. That field's mine. I've a nervous tic in both eyes.

NATASHA. The field *is* yours, certainly. Do sit down. (*They sit.*) We were mistaken.

LOMOV. This is a question of principle. It's not the land I mind about, it's the principle of the thing.

NATASHA. Just so, the principle. Now let's change the subject.

LOMOV. Especially as I can prove it. My aunt's grandmother gave your father's grandfather's villagers—

NATASHA. All right, that'll do. (*Aside.*) I don't know how to start. (*To him.*) Thinking of going shooting soon?

LOMOV. Yes, I'm thinking of starting on the woodcock after the harvest, my dear Miss Chubukov. I say, have you heard? What awful bad luck! You know my dog Tracker? He's gone lame.

NATASHA. Oh, I am sorry. How did it happen?

LOMOV. I don't know. Either it must be a sprain, or the other dogs bit him. (*Sighs.*) My best dog, to say nothing of what he set me back! Do you know, I gave Mironov a hundred and twenty-five roubles for him?

NATASHA. Then you were had, Mr. Lomov.

LOMOV. He came very cheap if you ask me—he's a splendid dog.

NATASHA. Father only gave eighty-five roubles for Rover. And Rover's a jolly sight better dog than Tracker, you'll agree.

LOMOV. Rover better than Tracker! Oh come off it! (*Laughs.*) Rover a better dog than Tracker!

NATASHA. Of course he is. Rover's young, it's true, and not yet in his prime. But you could search the best kennels in the county without finding a nippier animal, or one with better points.

LOMOV. I am sorry, Miss Chubukov, but you forget he has a short lower jaw, and a dog like that can't grip.

NATASHA. Oh, can't he! That's news to me!

LOMOV. He has a weak chin, you can take that from me.

NATASHA. Why, have you measured it?

LOMOV. Yes, I have. Naturally he'll do for coursing, but when it comes to retrieving, that's another story.

NATASHA. In the first place, Rover has a good honest coat on him, and a pedigree as long as your arm. As for that mud-coloured, piebald animal of yours, his antecedents are anyone's guess, quite apart from him being ugly as a broken-down old cart-horse.

LOMOV. Old he may be, but I wouldn't swap him for half a dozen Rovers—not on your life! Tracker's a real dog, and Rover—why, it's absurd to argue. The kennels are lousy with Rovers, he'd be dear at twenty-five roubles.

NATASHA. You *are* in an awkward mood today, Mr. Lomov. First you decide our field is yours, now you say Tracker's better than Rover. I dislike people who won't speak their mind. Now, you know perfectly well that Rover's umpteen times better than that—yes, that stupid Tracker. So why say the opposite?

LOMOV. I see you don't credit me with eyes or brains, Miss Chubukov. Well, get it in your head that Rover has a weak chin.

NATASHA. That's not true.

LOMOV. Oh yes it is!

NATASHA [*shouts*]. Oh no it isn't!

LOMOV. Don't you raise your voice at me, madam.

NATASHA. Then don't you talk such utter balderdash! Oh, this is infuriating! It's time that measly Tracker was put out of his misery—and you compare him with Rover!

LOMOV. I can't go on arguing, sorry—it's my heart.

NATASHA. Men who argue most about sport, I've noticed, are always the worst sportsmen.

LOMOV. Will you kindly hold your trap, madam—my heart's breaking in two. [*Shouts.*] You shut up!

NATASHA. I'll do nothing of the sort till you admit Rover's a hundred times better than Tracker.

LOMOV. A hundred times worse, more like! I hope Rover drops dead! Oh, my head, my eye, my shoulder—

NATASHA. That half-wit Tracker doesn't need to drop dead—he's pretty well a walking corpse already.

LOMOV (*weeps*). Shut up! I'm having a heart attack!

NATASHA. I will *not* shut up!

Scene VII

[*The above and* CHUBUKOV.]

CHUBUKOV (*comes in*). What is it this time?

NATASHA. Father, I want an honest answer: which is the better dog, Rover or Tracker?

LOMOV. Will you kindly tell us just one thing, Chubukov: has Rover got a weak chin or hasn't he? Yes or no?

CHUBUKOV. What if he has? As if that mattered! Seeing he's only the best dog in the county and so on.

LOMOV. Tracker's better and you know it! Be honest!

CHUBUKOV. Keep your shirt on, dear man. Now look here. Tracker has got some good qualities, what? He's a pedigree dog, has firm paws, steep haunches and so forth. But that dog has two serious faults if you want to know, old bean: he's old and he's pug-nosed.

LOMOV. I'm sorry—it's my heart! Let's just look at the facts. You may recall that Tracker was neck and neck with the Count's Swinger on Maruskino Green when Rover was a good half-mile behind.

CHUBUKOV. He dropped back because the Count's huntsman fetched him a crack with his whip.

LOMOV. Serve him right. Hounds are all chasing the fox and Rover has to start worrying a sheep!

CHUBUKOV. That's not true, sir. I've got a bad temper, old boy, and the fact is—let's please stop arguing, what? He hit him because everyone hates the sight of another man's dog. Oh yes they do. Loathe 'em, they do. And you're no one to talk either, sir! The moment you spot a better dog than the wretched Tracker, you always try to start something and, er, so forth—what? I don't forget, you see.

LOMOV. Nor do I, sir.

CHUBUKOV (*mimics him*). 'Nor do I, sir.' What is it you don't forget then?

LOMOV. My heart! My leg's gone to sleep. I can't go on.

NATASHA (*mimics him*). 'My heart' Call yourself a sportsman! You should be lying on the kitchen stove squashing black-beetles, not fox-hunting. His heart!

CHUBUKOV. Some sportsman, I must say! With that heart you should stay at home, not bob around in the saddle, what? I wouldn't mind if you hunted properly, but you only turn out to pick quarrels and annoy the hounds and so on. I have a bad temper, so let's change the subject. You're no sportsman, sir—what?

Lomov. What about you then? You only turn out so you can get in the Count's good books and intrigue against people. Oh, my heart! You're a slippery customer, sir!

Chubukov. What's that, sir? Oh, I am, am I? [*Shouts.*] Hold your tongue!

Lomov. You artful old dodger!

Chubukov. Why, you young puppy!

Lomov. Nasty old fogy! Canting hypocrite!

Chubukov. Shut up, or I'll pot you like a ruddy partridge. And I'll use a dirty gun too, you idle gasbag!

Lomov. And it's common knowledge that—oh, my heart—your wife used to beat you. Oh, my leg! My head! I can see stars! I can't stand up!

Chubukov. And your housekeeper has you eating out of her hand!

Lomov. Oh, oh! My heart's bursting. My shoulder seems to have come off—where is the thing? I'm dying. [*Falls into an armchair.*] Fetch a doctor. [*Faints.*]

Chubukov. Why, you young booby! Hot air merchant! I think I'm going to faint. [*Drinks water.*] I feel unwell.

Natasha. Calls himself a sportsman and can't even sit on a horse! [*To her father.*] Father, what's the matter with him? Father, have a look. [*Falls into an armchair.*] Fetch a doctor, a doctor! [*Has hysterics.*]

Chubukov. I feel faint. I can't breathe! Give me air!

Natasha. He's dead. [*Tugs* Lomov*'s sleeve.*] Mr. Lomov, Mr. Lomov! What have we done? He's dead. [*Falls into an armchair.*] Fetch a doctor, a doctor! [*Has hysterics.*]

Chubukov. Oh! What's happened? What's the matter?

Natasha [*groans*]. He's dead! Dead!

Chubukov. Who's dead? [*Glancing at* Lomov.] My God, you're right! Water! A doctor! [*Holds a glass to* Lomov*'s mouth.*] Drink! No, he's not drinking. He must be dead, and so forth. O misery, misery! Why don't I put a bullet in my brain? Why did I never get round to cutting my throat? What am I waiting for? Give me a knife! A pistol! [Lomov *makes a movement.*] I think he's coming round. Drink some water! That's right.

Lomov. I can see stars! There's a sort of mist. Where am I?

Chubukov. Hurry up and get married an—oh, to hell with you! She says yes. [*Joins their hands.*] She says yes, and so forth. You have my blessing, and so on. Just leave me in peace, that's all.

LOMOV. Eh? What? (*Raising himself.*) Who?

CHUBUKOV. She says yes. Well, what about it? Kiss each other and—oh, go to hell!

NATASHA (*groans*). He's alive. Yes, yes, yes! I agree.

CHUBUKOV. Come on, kiss.

LOMOV. Eh? Who? (*Kisses* NATASHA.) Very nice too. I say, what's all this about? Oh, I see—. My heart! I'm seeing stars! Miss Chubukov, I'm so happy. (*Kisses her hand.*) My leg's gone to sleep.

NATASHA. I, er, I'm happy too.

CHUBUKOV. Oh, what a weight off my mind! Phew!

NATASHA. Still, you must admit now that Tracker's not a patch on Rover.

LOMOV. Oh yes he is!

NATASHA. Oh no he isn't!

CHUBUKOV. You can see those two are going to live happily ever after! Champagne!

LOMOV. He's better.

NATASHA. He's worse, worse, worse.

CHUBUKOV (*trying to shout them down*). Champagne, champagne, champagne!

SUGGESTIONS FOR WRITING AND DISCUSSION

1. What do we learn about Chubukov from the way he treats Lomov in Scene I?
2. Why does Lomov wish to marry Natasha? Why does she wish to marry him? Does either of them have good reasons?
3. Describe the relationship between Natasha and her father. Are there any family traits they seem to share?
4. What do we learn about Natasha in Scene III? What impression does she make on Lomov?
5. Do traditional terms apply to this play? Is there a protagonist? an antagonist? a foil? Does the play have a climax?
6. In Scene VII Chubukov suddenly announces that he is not feeling well. What does this suggest about the relative strengths and weaknesses of men and women in this play?
7. In a three- to five-page essay compare this play with Eugene Ionesco's "The Gap." In what respects are they both farcical or absurd? How are the characters exaggerated? What, if any, serious statements do they make?
8. Write your own short (three- to four-page) play in which one character tries to propose to another but the two keep arguing.

Varieties of Love: Thematic Questions

1. The rising divorce rate in America seems to support Emma Goldman's claim that love and marriage are incompatible. Nevertheless, every year more marriages occur. What do you think contributes to this enduring optimism? Can marriage work?

2. In Plato's "Symposium" Aristophanes tells the story that humans used to be both male and female until they were divided in two, and that ever since they have been preoccupied with searching for their missing halves. Do you think it makes sense to describe the search for love as a search for one's "other half"? Is it possible to have a successful life without a loving partnership? What else is important in life?

3. Is love defined differently in different cultures? Compare love in contemporary America to love in another society or period.

4. In a number of the poems in this section the speaker describes to his beloved the speed with which time is passing and the necessity of making the most of it. Do you think the kind of passion described in these poems can survive in a long relationship?

Work and Reward

That which a man has not fairly earned, and, further, that which he cannot fully enjoy, does not belong to him, but is a part of mankind's treasure which he holds as a steward on parole. To mankind, then, it must be made profitable; and how this should be done is . . . a problem which each man must solve for himself, and about which none has a right to judge him.

ROBERT LOUIS STEVENSON

Essays

Henry David Thoreau (American, 1817–1862)

The Bean-Field

Meanwhile my beans, the length of whose rows, added together, was seven miles already planted, were impatient to be hoed, for the earliest had grown considerably before the latest were in the ground; indeed they were not easily to be put off. What was the meaning of this so steady and self-respecting, this small Herculean labor, I knew not. I came to love my rows, my beans, though so many more than I wanted. They attached me to the earth, and so I got strength like Antaeus. But why should I raise them? Only Heaven knows. This was my curious labor all summer,—to make this portion of the earth's surface, which had yielded only cinque-foil, blackberries, johnswort, and the like, before, sweet wild fruits and pleasant flowers, produce instead this pulse. What shall I learn of beans or beans of me? I cherish them, I hoe them, early and late I have an eye to them; and this is my day's work. It is a fine broad leaf to look on. My auxiliaries are the dew and rains which water this dry soil, and what fertility is in the soil itself, which for the most part is lean and effete. My enemies are worms, cool days, and most of all woodchucks. The last have nibbled for me a quarter of an acre clean. But what right had I to oust johnswort and the rest, and break up their ancient herb garden? Soon, however, the remaining beans will be too tough for them, and go forward to meet new foes.

When I was four years old, as I well remember, I was brought from Boston to this my native town, through these very woods and this field, to the pond. It is one of the oldest scenes stamped on my memory. And now to-night my flute has waked the echoes over that very water. The pines still stand here older than I; or, if some have fallen, I have cooked my supper with their stumps, and a new growth is rising all around, preparing another aspect for new infant eyes. Almost the same johnswort springs from the same perennial root in this pasture, and even I have at length helped to clothe that fabulous landscape of my infant dreams, and one of the results of my presence and influence is seen in these bean leaves, corn blades, and potato vines.

I planted about two acres and a half of upland; and as it was only about fifteen years since the land was cleared, and I myself had got out two or three cords of stumps, I did not give it any manure; but in the course of the summer it appeared by the arrowheads which I turned up in hoeing, that an extinct nation had anciently dwelt here and planted corn and beans ere white men came to clear the land, and so, to some extent, had exhausted the soil for this very crop.

Before yet any woodchuck or squirrel had run across the road, or the sun had got above the shrub-oaks, while all the dew was on, though the farmers warned me against it,—I would advise you to do all your work if possible while the dew is on,—I began to level the ranks of haughty weeds in my bean-field and throw dust upon their heads. Early in the morning I worked barefooted, dabbling like a plastic artist in the dewy and crumbling sand, but later in the day the sun blistered my feet. There the sun lighted me to hoe beans, pacing slowly backward and forward over that yellow gravelly upland, between the long green rows, fifteen rods, the one end terminating in a shrub oak copse where I could rest in the shade, the other in a blackberry field where the green berries deepened their tints by the time I had made another bout. Removing the weeds, putting fresh soil about the bean stems, and encouraging this week which I had sown, making the yellow soil express its summer thought in bean leaves and blossoms rather than in wormwood and piper and millet grass, making the earth say beans instead of grass,—this was my daily work. As I had little aid from horses or cattle, or hired men or boys, or improved implements of husbandry, I was much slower, and became much more intimate with my beans than usual. But labor of the hands, even when pursued to the verge of drudgery, is perhaps never the worst form of idleness. It has a constant and imperishable moral, and to the scholar it yields a classic result. A very *agricola laboriosus* was I to travellers bound westward through Lincoln and Wayland to nobody knows where; they sitting at their ease in gigs, with elbows on knees, and reins loosely hanging in festoons; I the home-staying, laborious native of the soil. But soon my homestead was out of their sight and thought. It was the only open and cultivated field for a great distance on either side of the road; so they made the most of it; and sometimes the man in the field heard more of travellers' gossip and comment than was meant for his ear: "Beans so late! peas so late!"—for I continued to plant when others had begun to hoe,—the ministerial husbandman had not suspected it. "Corn, my boy, for fodder; corn for fodder." "Does he *live* there?" asks the black bonnet of the gray coat; and the hard-featured farmer reins up his grateful dobbin to inquire what you are doing where he sees no manure in the furrow, and recommends a little chip dirt, or any little waste stuff, or it may be ashes or plaster. But here were two acres and a half of furrows, and only a hoe for cart and two hands to draw it,—there being an aversion to other carts and horses,—and chip dirt far away. Fellow-travellers as they rattled by compared it aloud with the fields which they had passed, so that I came to know how I stood in the agricultural world. This was one field not in Mr. Colman's report. And, by the way, who estimates the value of the crop which Nature yields in the still wilder fields unimproved by man? The crop of *English* hay is carefully weighed, the moisture calculated, the silicates and the potash; but in all dells and pond holes in the woods and pastures and swamps grows a rich and various crop only unreaped by man. Mine was, as it were, the connecting link between wild and cultivated fields; as some states are civilized, and others half-civilized, and others savage or barbarous, so my field was, though not in a bad sense, a half-cultivated field. They were beans cheerfully returning to their wild and primitive state that I cultivated, and my hoe played the *Ranz des Vaches* for them.

Near at hand, upon the topmost spray of a birch, sings the brown-thrasher—or red mavis, as some love to call him—all the morning, glad of your society, that would find out another farmer's field if yours were not here. While you are planting the seed, he cries,—``Drop it, drop it,—cover it up, cover it up,—pull it up, pull it up, pull it up.'' But this was not corn, and so it was safe from such enemies as he. You may wonder what his rigmarole, his amateur Paganini performances on one string or on twenty, have to do with your planting, and yet prefer it to leached ashes or plaster. It was a cheap sort of top dressing in which I had entire faith.

As I drew a still fresher soil about the rows with my hoe, I disturbed the ashes of unchronicled nations who in primeval years lived under these heavens, and their small implements of war and hunting were brought to the light of this modern day. They lay mingled with other natural stones, some of which bore the marks of having been burned by Indian fires, and some by the sun, and also bits of pottery and glass brought hither by the recent cultivators of the soil. When my hoe tinkled against the stones, that music echoed to the woods and sky, and was an accompaniment to my labor which yielded an instant and immeasurable crop. It was no longer beans that I hoed, nor I that hoed beans; and I remembered with as much pity as pride, if I remembered at all, my acquaintances who had gone to the city to attend the oratorios. The night-hawk circled overhead in the sunny afternoons—for I sometimes made a day of it—like a mote in the eye, or in heaven's eye, falling from time to time with a swoop and a sound as if the heavens were rent, torn at last to very rags and tatters, and yet a seamless cope remained; small imps that fill the air and lay their eggs on the ground on bare sand or rocks on the tops of hills, where few have found them; graceful and slender like ripples caught up from the pond, as leaves are raised by the wind to float in the heavens; such kindredship is in Nature. The hawk is aerial brother of the wave which he sails over and surveys, those his perfect air-inflated wings answering to the elemental unfledged pinions of the sea. Or sometimes I watched a pair of hen-hawks circling high in the sky, alternately soaring and descending, approaching and leaving one another, as if they were the imbodiment of my own thoughts. Or I was attracted by the passage of wild pigeons from this wood to that, with a slight quivering winnowing sound and carrier haste; or from under a rotten stump my hoe turned up a sluggish portentous and outlandish spotted salamander, a trace of Egypt and the Nile, yet our contemporary. When I paused to lean on my hoe, these sounds and sights I heard and saw any where in the row, a part of the inexhaustible entertainment which the country offers.

On gala days the town fires its great guns, which echo like popguns to these woods, and some waifs of martial music occasionally penetrate thus far. To me, away there in my bean-field at the other end of the town, the big guns sounded as if a puff ball had burst; and when there was a military turnout of which I was ignorant, I have sometimes had a vague sense all the day of some sort of itching and disease in the horizon, as if some eruption would break out there soon, either scarlatina or canker-rash, until at length some more favorable puff of wind, making haste over the fields and up the Wayland road, brought me information of the ''train-ers.'' It seemed by the distant hum as if somebody's bees had swarmed, and that the neighbors, according to Virgil's advice, by a faint *tintinnab-ulum* upon the most sonorous of their domestic utensils, were endeav-oring to call them down into the hive again. And when the sound died quite away, and the hum had ceased, and the most favorable breezes told no tale, I knew that they had got the last drone of them all safely into the Middlesex hive, and that now their minds were bent on the honey with which it was smeared.

I felt proud to know that the liberties of Massachusetts and of our fatherland were in such safe keeping; and as I turned to my hoeing again I was filled with an inexpressible confidence, and pursued my labor cheer-fully with a calm trust in the future.

When there were several bands of musicians, it sounded as if all the village was a vast bellows, and all the buildings expanded and collapsed alternately with a din. But sometimes it was a really noble and inspiring strain that reached these woods, and the trumpet that sings of fame, and I felt as if I could spit a Mexican with a good relish,—for why should we always stand for trifles?—and looked round for a woodchuck or a skunk to exercise my chivalry upon. These martial strains seemed as far away as Palestine, and reminded me of a march of crusaders in the horizon, with a slight tantivy and tremulous motion of the elm-tree tops which overhang the village. This was one of the *great* days; though the sky had from my clearing only the same everlastingly great look that it wears daily, and I saw no difference in it.

It was a singular experience that long acquaintance which I culti-vated with beans, what with planting, and hoeing, and harvesting, and threshing, and picking over, and selling them,—the last was the hardest of all,—I might add eating, for I did taste. I was determined to know beans. When they were growing, I used to hoe from five o'clock in the morning till noon, and commonly spent the rest of the day about other affairs. Consider the intimate and curious acquaintance one makes with various kinds of weeds,—it will bear some iteration in the account, for there was no little iteration in the labor,—disturbing their delicate orga-nizations so ruthlessly, and making such invidious distinctions with his hoe, levelling whole ranks of one species, and sedulously cultivating another. That's Roman wormwood,—that's pigweed,—that's sorrel,—that's piper-grass,—have at him, chop him up, turn his roots upward to the sun, don't let him have a fibre in the shade, if you do he'll turn himself t'other side up and be as green as a leek in two days. A long war, not with cranes, but with weeds, those Trojans who had sun and rain and dews on their side. Daily the beans saw me come to their rescue armed with a hoe, and thin the ranks of their enemies, filling up the trenches with weedy dead. Many a lusty crest-waving Hector, that towered a whole foot above his crowding comrades, fell before my weapon and rolled in the dust.

Those summer days which some of my contemporaries devoted to the fine arts in Boston or Rome, and others to contemplation in India, and others to trade in London or New York, I thus, with the other farmers of New England, devoted to husbandry. Not that I wanted beans to eat, for I am by nature a Pythagorean, so far as beans are concerned, whether they mean porridge or voting, and exchanged them for rice; but, perchance, as some must work in fields if only for the sake of tropes and expression, to serve a parable-maker one day. It was on the whole a rare amusement, which, continued too long, might have become a dissipation. Though I gave them no manure, and did not hoe them all once, I hoed them unusually well as far as I went, and was paid for it in the end, "there being in truth," as Evelyn says, "no compost or laetation whatsoever comparable to this continual motion, repastination, and turning of the mould with the spade." "The earth," he adds elsewhere, "especially if fresh, has a certain magnetism in it, by which it attracts the salt, power, or virtue (call it either) which gives it life, and is the logic of all the labor and stir we keep about it, to sustain us; all dungings and other sordid temperings being but the vicars succedaneous to this improvement." Moreover, this being one of those "worn-out and exhausted lay fields which enjoy their sabbath," had perchance, as Sir Kenelm Digby thinks likely, attracted "vital spirits" from the air. I harvested twelve bushels of beans.

But to be more particular; for it is complained that Mr. Colman has reported chiefly the expensive experiments of gentlemen farmers; my outgoes were,—

For a hoe,	$0 54
Ploughing, harrowing, and furrowing,	7 50, Too much.
Beans for seed,	3 12½
Potatoes "	1 33
Peas "	0 40
Turnip seed,	0 06
White line for crow fence,	0 02
Horse cultivator and boy three hours,	1 00
Horse and cart to get crop,	0 75
In all,	$14 72½

My income was, (patrem familias vendacem, non emacem esse oportet,) from

Nine bushels and twelve quarts of beans sold,	$16 94
Five " large potatoes,	2 50
Nine " small . . . "	2 25
Grass,	1 00
Stalks,	0 75
In all,	$23 44

Leaving a pecuniary profit, as I have elsewhere said, of $8 71½.

This is the result of my experience in raising beans. Plant the common small white bush bean about the first of June, in rows three feet by eighteen inches apart, being careful to select fresh round and unmixed seed. First look out for worms, and supply vacancies by planting anew. Then look out for woodchucks, if it is an exposed place, for they will nibble off the earliest tender leaves almost clean as they go; and again, when the young tendrils make their appearance, they have notice of it, and will shear them off with both buds and young pods, sitting erect like a squirrel. But above all harvest as early as possible, if you would escape frosts and have a fair and saleable crop; you may save much loss by this means.

This further experience also I gained. I said to myself, I will not plant beans and corn with so much industry another summer, but such seeds, if the seed is not lost, as sincerity, truth, simplicity, faith, innocence, and the like, and see if they will not grow in this soil, even with less toil and manurance, and sustain me, for surely it has not been exhausted for these crops. Alas! I said this to myself; but now another summer is gone, and another, and another, and I am obliged to say to you, Reader, that the seeds which I planted, if indeed they *were* the seeds of those virtues, were wormeaten or had lost their vitality, and so did not come up. Commonly men will only be brave as their fathers were brave, or timid. This generation is very sure to plant corn and beans each new year precisely as the Indians did centuries ago and taught the first settlers to do, as if there were a fate in it. I saw an old man the other day, to my astonishment, making the holes with a hoe for the seventieth time at least, and not for himself to lie down in! But why should not the New Englander try new adventures, and not lay so much stress on his grain, his potato and grass crop, and his orchards?—raise other crops than these? Why concern ourselves so much about our beans for seed, and not be concerned at all about a new generation of men? We should really be fed and cheered if when we met a man we were sure to see that some of the qualities which I have named, which we all prize more than those other productions, but which are for the most part broadcast and floating in the air, had taken root and grown in him. Here comes such a subtle and ineffable quality, for instance, as truth or justice, though the slightest amount or new variety of it, along the road. Our ambassadors should be instructed to send home such seeds as these, and Congress help to distribute them over all the land. We should never stand upon ceremony with sincerity. We should never cheat and insult and banish one another by our meanness, if there were present the kernel of worth and friendliness. We should not meet thus in haste. Most men I do not meet at all, for they seem not to have time; they are busy about their beans. We would not deal with a man thus plodding ever, leaning on a hoe or a spade as a staff between his work, not as a mushroom, but partially risen out of the earth, something more than erect, like swallows alighted and walking on the ground.—

"And as he spake, his wings would now and then
Spread, as he meant to fly, then close again,"

so that we should suspect that we might be conversing with an angel. Bread may not always nourish us; but it always does us good, it even takes stiffness out of our joints, and makes us supple and buoyant, when we knew not what ailed us, to recognize any generosity in man or Nature, to share any unmixed and heroic joy.

Ancient poetry and mythology suggest, at least, that husbandry was once a sacred art; but it is pursued with irreverent haste and heedlessness by us, our object being to have large farms and large crops merely. We have no festival, nor procession, nor ceremony, not excepting our Cattle-shows and so called Thanksgivings, by which the farmer expresses a sense of the sacredness of his calling, or is reminded of its sacred origin. It is the premium and the feast which tempt him. He sacrifices not to Ceres and the Terrestrial Jove, but to the infernal Plutus rather. By avarice and selfishness, and a grovelling habit, from which none of us is free, of regarding the soil as property, or the means of acquiring property chiefly, the landscape is deformed, husbandry is degraded with us, and the farmer leads the meanest of lives. He knows Nature but as a robber. Cato says that the profits of agriculture are particularly pious or just, (*maximeque pius quæstus,*) and according to Varro the old Romans "called the same earth Mother and Ceres, and thought that they who cultivated it led a pious and useful life, and that they alone were left of the race of King Saturn."

We are wont to forget that the sun looks on our cultivated fields and on the prairies and forests without distinction. They all reflect and absorb his rays alike, and the former make but a small part of the glorious picture which he beholds in his daily course. In his view the earth is all equally cultivated like a garden. Therefore we should receive the benefit of his light and heat with a corresponding trust and magnanimity. What though I value the seed of these beans, and harvest that in the fall of the year? This broad field which I have looked at so long looks not to me as the principal cultivator, but away from me to influences more genial to it, which water and make it green. These beans have results which are not harvested by me. Do they not grow for woodchucks partly? The ear of wheat, (in Latin *spica*, obsoletely *speca*, from *spe*, hope,) should not be the only hope of the husbandman; its kernel or grain (*granum*, from *gerendo*, bearing,) is not all that it bears. How, then, can our harvest fail? Shall I not rejoice also at the abundance of the weeds whose seeds are the granary of the birds? It matters little comparatively whether the fields fill the farmer's barns. The true husbandman will cease from anxiety, as the squirrels manifest no concern whether the woods will bear chestnuts this year or not, and finish his labor with every day, relinquishing all claim to the produce of his fields, and sacrificing in his mind not only his first but his last fruits also.

SUGGESTIONS FOR WRITING AND DISCUSSION

1. Why does Thoreau feel qualified to criticize the farmers?
2. Thoreau says, "I was determined to know beans." What does he mean by this statement? How does this set him apart from other farmers?
3. Compare this with Thoreau's "Civil Disobedience" (pp. 395–409). What in style and content shows that the same author wrote both?
4. In a three- to five-page essay argue for or against the idea that this is an essay about the rewards of work.
5. Should you be more concerned about the financial rewards of work or the spiritual rewards? Argue in a three- to five-page essay.

Studs Terkel (American, 1912–   )

Waitress: Dolores Dante

She has been a waitress in the same restaurant for twenty-three years. Many of its patrons are credit card carriers on an expense account—conventioneers, politicians, labor leaders, agency people. Her hours are from 5:00 P.M. to 2:00 A.M. six days a week. She arrives earlier "to get things ready, the silverware, the butter. When people come in and ask for you, you would like to be in a position to handle them all, because that means more money for you.

"I became a waitress because I needed money fast and you don't get it in an office. My husband and I broke up and he left me with debts and three children. My baby was six months. The fast buck, your tips. The first ten-dollar bill that I got as a tip, a Viking guy gave to me. He was a very robust, terrific atheist. Made very good conversation for us, 'cause I am too.

"Everyone says all waitresses have broken homes. What they don't realize is when people have broken homes they need to make money fast, and do this work. They don't have broken homes because they're waitresses."

I have to be a waitress. How else can I learn about people? How else does the world come to me? I can't go to everyone. So they have to come to me. Everyone wants to eat, everyone has hunger. And I serve them. If they've had a bad day, I nurse them, cajole them. Maybe with coffee I give them a little philosophy. They have cocktails, I give them political science.

I'll say things that bug me. If they manufacture soap, I say what I think about pollution. If it's automobiles, I say what I think about them. If I pour water I'll say, "Would you like your quota of mercury today?" If I serve cream, I say, "Here is your substitute. I think you're drinking plastic." I just can't keep quiet. I have an opinion on every single subject there is. In the beginning it was theology, and my bosses didn't like it.

Now I am a political and my bosses don't like it. I speak *sotto voce.* But if I get heated, then I don't give a damn. I speak like an Italian speaks. I can't be servile. I give service. There is a difference.

I'm called by my first name. I like my name. I hate to be called Miss. Even when I serve a lady, a strange woman, I will not say madam. I hate ma'am. I always say milady. In the American language there is no word to address a woman, to indicate whether she's married or unmarried. So I say milady. And sometimes I playfully say to the man milord.

It would be very tiring if I had to say, "Would you like a cocktail?" and say that over and over. So I come out different for my own enjoyment. I would say, "What's exciting at the bar that I can offer?" I can't say, "Do you want coffee?" Maybe I'll say, "Are you in the mood for coffee?" Or, "The coffee sounds exciting." Just rephrase it enough to make it interesting for me. That would make them take an interest. It becomes theatrical and I feel like Mata Hari and it intoxicates me.

People imagine a waitress couldn't possibly think or have any kind of aspiration other than to serve food. When somebody says to me, "You're great, how come you're *just* a waitress?" *Just* a waitress. I'd say, "Why, don't you think you deserve to be served by me?" It's implying that he's not worthy, not that I'm not worthy. It makes me irate. I don't feel lowly at all. I myself feel sure. I don't want to change the job. I love it.

Tips? I feel like Carmen. It's like a gypsy holding out a tambourine and they throw the coin. (Laughs.) If you like people, you're not thinking of the tips. I never count my money at night. I always wait till morning. If I thought about my tips I'd be uptight. I never look at a tip. You pick it up fast. I would do my bookkeeping in the morning. It would be very dull for me to know I was making so much and no more. I do like challenge. And it isn't demeaning, not for me.

There might be occasions when the customers might intend to make it demeaning—the man about town, the conventioneer. When the time comes to pay the check, he would do little things, "How much should I give you?" He might make an issue about it. I did say to one, "Don't play God with me. Do what you want." Then it really didn't matter whether I got a tip or not. I would spit it out, my resentment—that he dares make me feel I'm operating only for a tip.

He'd ask for his check. Maybe he's going to sign it. He'd take a very long time and he'd make me stand there, "Let's see now, what do you think I ought to give you?" He would not let go of that moment. And you knew it. You know he meant to demean you. He's holding the change in his hand, or if he'd sign, he'd flourish the pen and wait. These are the times I really get angry. I'm not reticent. Something would come out. Then I really didn't care. "Goddamn, keep your money!"

There are conventioneers, who leave their lovely wives or their bad wives. They approach you and say, "Are there any hot spots?" "Where can I find girls?" It is, of course, first directed at you. I don't mean that as a compliment, 'cause all they're looking for is females. They're not looking for companionship or conversation. I am quite adept at understanding this. I think I'm interesting enough that someone may just want to talk to me. But I would philosophize that way. After all, what is left after you talk? The hours have gone by and I could be home resting or reading or studying guitar, which I do on occasion. I would say, "What are you going to offer me? Drinks?" And I'd point to the bar, "I have it all here." He'd look blank and then I'd say, "A man? If I need a man, wouldn't you think I'd have one of my own? Must I wait for you?"

Life doesn't frighten me any more. There are only two things that relegate us—the bathroom and the grave. Either I'm gonna have to go to the bathroom now or I'm gonna die now. I go to the bathroom.

And I don't have a high opinion of bosses. The more popular you are, the more the boss holds it over your head. You're bringing them business, but he knows you're getting good tips and you won't leave. You have to worry not to overplay it, because the boss becomes resentful and he uses this as a club over your head.

If you become too good a waitress, there's jealousy. They don't come in and say, "Where's the boss?" They'll ask for Dolores. It doesn't make a hit. That makes it rough. Sometimes you say, Aw hell, why am I trying so hard? I did get an ulcer. Maybe the things I kept to myself were twisting me.

It's not the customers, never the customers. It's injustice. My dad came from Italy and I think of his broken English—*injoost.* He hated injustice. If you hate injustice for the world, you hate more than anything injustice toward you. Loyalty is never appreciated, particularly if you're the type who doesn't like small talk and are not the type who makes reports on your fellow worker. The boss wants to find out what is going on surreptitiously. In our society today you have informers everywhere. They've informed on cooks, on coworkers. "Oh, someone wasted this." They would say I'm talking to all the customers. "I saw her carry such-and-such out. See if she wrote that on her check." "The salad looked like it was a double salad." I don't give anything away. I just give myself. Informers will manufacture things in order to make their job worthwhile. They're not sure of themselves as workers. There's always someone who wants your station, who would be pretender to the crown. In life there is always someone who wants somebody's job.

I'd get intoxicated with giving service. People would ask for me and I didn't have enough tables. Some of the girls are standing and don't have customers. There is resentment. I feel self-conscious. I feel a sense of guilt. It cramps my style. I would like to say to the customer, "Go to so-and-so." But you can't do that, because you feel a sense of loyalty. So you would rush, get to your customers quickly. Some don't care to drink and still they wait for you. That's a compliment.

There is plenty of tension. If the cook isn't good, you fight to see that the customers get what you know they like. You have to use diplomacy with cooks, who are always dangerous. (Laughs.) They're madmen.

(Laughs.) You have to be their friend. They better like you. And your bartender better like you too, because he may do something to the drink. If your bartender doesn't like you, your cook doesn't like you, your boss doesn't like you, the other girls don't like you, you're in trouble.

And there will be customers who are hypochondriacs, who feel they can't eat, and I coax them. Then I hope I can get it just the right way from the cook. I may mix the salad myself, just the way they want it.

Maybe there's a party of ten. Big shots, and they'd say, "Dolores, I have special clients, do your best tonight." You just hope you have the right cook behind the broiler. You really want to pleasure your guests. He's selling something, he wants things right, too. You're giving your all. How does the steak look? If you cut his steak, you look at it surreptitiously. How's it going?

Carrying dishes is a problem. We do have accidents. I spilled a tray once with steaks for seven on it. It was a big, gigantic T-bone, all sliced, and the bosses are watching. If you get the wrong shoes and you get the wrong stitch in that shoe, that does bother you. Your feet hurt, your body aches. If you come out in anger at things that were done to you, it would only make you feel cheapened. Really I've been keeping it to myself. But of late, I'm beginning to spew it out. It's almost as thought I sensed my body and soul had had quite enough.

It builds and builds and builds in your guts. Near crying. I can think about it . . . (She cries softly.) 'Cause you're tired. When the night is done, you're tired. You've had so much, there's so much going . . . You had to get it done. The dread that something wouldn't be right, because you want to please. You hope everyone is satisfied. The night's done, you've done your act. The curtains close.

The next morning is pleasant again. I take out my budget book, write down how much I made, what my bills are. I'm managing. I won't give up this job as long as I'm able to do it. I feel out of contact if I just sit at home. At work they all consider me a kook. (Laughs.) That's okay. No matter where I'd be, I would make a rough road for me. It's just me, and I can't keep still. It hurts, and what hurts has to come out.

POSTSCRIPT: *"After sixteen years—that was seven years ago—I took a trip to Hawaii and the Caribbean for two weeks. Went with a lover. The kids saw it—they're all married now. (Laughs.) One of my daughters said, "Act your age." I said, "Honey, if I were acting my age, I wouldn't be walking. My bones would ache. You don't want to hear about my arthritis. Aren't you glad I'm happy?"*

SUGGESTIONS FOR WRITING AND DISCUSSION

1. Explain Dante's distinction between giving service and being servile.
2. It seems surprising that Dante cries at the end of the interview. Why does her mood change?

3. Do you think that anyone, in any job, could find dignity in work?

4. Why does Dante try to use new phrases when waiting on her customers? What effect does this have on the customers?

5. In a three- to five-page paper discuss a job you have had. What problems did you have?

Pauline Newman (American, 1893–   )

Union Organizer

The calamitous Triangle Shirtwaist Factory fire of 1911, in which 146 women and girls lost their lives, was a landmark in American labor history. It galvanized public opinion behind the movement to improve conditions, hours, and wages in the sweatships. Pauline Newman went to work in the Triangle Shirtwaist Factory at the age of eight, shortly after coming to the Lower East Side of New York City. Many of her friends lost their lives in the fire. She went on to become an organizer and later an executive of the newly formed International Ladies Garment Workers' Union. At the age of eighty-six, she was the education director of the union's health center.

The village I came from was very small. One department store, one synagogue, and one church. There was a little square where the peasants would bring their produce, you know, for sale. And there was one teahouse where you could have a glass of tea for a penny and sit all day long and play checkers if you wanted.

In the winter we would skate down the hilltop toward the lake, and in the summer we'd walk to the woods and get mushrooms, raspberries. The peasants lived on one side of the lake, and the Jewish people on the other, in little square, thatched-roofed houses. In order to go to school you had to own land and we didn't own land, of course. Very few Jews did. But we were allowed to go to Sunday School and I never missed going to Sunday School. They would sing Russian folk songs and recite poetry. I liked it very much. It was a narrow life, but you didn't miss anything because you didn't know what you were missing.

That was the time, you see, when America was known to foreigners as the land where you'd get rich. There's gold on the sidewalk—all you have to do is pick it up. So people left that little village and went to America. My brother first and then he sent for one sister, and after that, a few years after that, my father died and they sent for my mother and my other two sisters and me. I was seven or eight at the time. I'm not sure exactly how old, because the village I came from had no registration of birth, and we lost the family Bible on the ship and that was where the records were.

Of course we came steerage. That's the bottom of the ship and three layers of bunks. One, two, three, one above the other. If you were lucky, you got the first bunk. Of course you can understand that it wasn't all that pleasant when the people on the second bunk or the third bunk were ill. You had to suffer and endure not only your own misery, but the misery from the people above you.

My mother baked rolls and things like that for us to take along, because all you got on the boat was water, boiled water. If you had tea, you could make tea, but otherwise you just had the hot water. Sometimes they gave you a watery soup, more like a mud puddle than soup. It was stormy, cold, uncomfortable. I wasn't sick, but the other members of my family were.

When we landed at Ellis Island our luggage was lost. We inquired for it and they said, "Come another time. Come another time. You'll find it. We haven't got time now." So we left and we never saw our luggage again. We had bedding, linen, beautiful copper utensils, that sort of thing.

From Ellis Island we went by wagon to my brother's apartment on Hester Street. Hester Street and Essex on the Lower East Side. We were all bewildered to see so many people. Remember we were from a little village. And here you had people coming and going and shouting. Peddlers, people on the streets. Everything was new, you know.

At first we stayed in a tiny apartment with my brother and then, finally, we got one of our own. Two rooms. The bedroom had no windows. The toilets were in the yard. Just a coal stove for heat. The rent was ten dollars a month.

A cousin of mine worked for the Triangle Shirtwaist Company and she got me on there in October of 1901. It was probably the largest shirtwaist factory in the city of New York then. They had more than two hundred operators, cutters, examiners, finishers. Altogether more than four hundred people on two floors. The fire took place on one floor, the floor where we worked. You've probably heard about that. But that was years later.

We started work at seven-thirty in the morning, and during the busy season we worked until nine in the evening. They didn't pay you any overtime and they didn't give you anything for supper money. Sometimes they'd give you a little apple pie if you had to work very late. That was all. Very generous.

What I had to do was not really very difficult. It was just monotonous. When the shirtwaists were finished at the machine there were some threads that were left, and all the youngsters—we had a corner on the floor that resembled a kindergarten—we were given little scissors to cut the threads off. It wasn't heavy work, but it was monotonous, because you did the same thing from seven-thirty in the morning till nine at night.

What about the child labor laws?

Well, of course, there were laws on the books, but no one bothered to enforce them. The employers were always tipped off if there was going to be an inspection. "Quick," they'd say, "into the boxes!" And we children would climb into the big boxes the finished shirts were stored in. Then some shirts were piled on top of us, and when the inspector came— no children. The factory always got an okay from the inspector, and I suppose someone at City Hall got a little something, too.

The employers didn't recognize anyone working for them as a human being. You were not allowed to sing. Operators would have liked to have sung, because they, too, had the same thing to do and weren't allowed to sing. We weren't allowed to talk to each other. Oh, no, they would sneak up behind if you were found talking to your next colleague. You were admonished: "If you keep on you'll be fired." If you went to the toilet and you were there longer than the floor lady thought you should be, you would be laid off for half a day and sent home. And, of course, that meant no pay. You were not allowed to have your lunch on the fire escape in the summertime. The door was locked to keep us in. That's why so many people were trapped when the fire broke out.

My pay was $1.50 a week no matter how many hours I worked. My sisters made $6.00 a week; and the cutters, they were the skilled workers, they might get as much as $12.00. The employers had a sign in the elevator that said: "If you don't come in on Sunday, don't come in on Monday." You were expected to work every day if they needed you and the pay was the same whether you worked extra or not. You had to be there at seven-thirty, so you got up at five-thirty, took the horse car, then the electric trolley to Greene Street, to be there on time.

At first I tried to get somebody who could teach me English in the evening, but that didn't work out because I don't think he was a very good teacher, and, anyhow, the overtime interfered with private lessons. But I mingled with people. I joined the Socialist Literary Society. Young as I was and not very able to express myself, I decided that it wouldn't hurt if I listened. There was a Dr. Newman, no relation of mine, who was teaching in City College. He would come down to the Literary Society twice a week and teach us literature, English literature. He was very helpful. He gave me a list of books to read, and, as I said, if there is a will you can learn. We read Dickens, George Eliot, the poets. I remember when we first heard Thomas Hood's "Song of the Shirt." I figured that it was written for us. You know, because it told the long hours of "stitch, stitch, stitch." I remember one of the girls said, "He didn't know us, did he?" And I said, "No, he didn't." But it had an impact on us. Later on, of course, we got to know Shelley. Shelley's known for his lyrics, but very few people know his poem dealing with slavery, called "The Masque of Anarchy." It appealed to us, too, because it was a time when we were ready to rise and that helped us a great deal. (*Recites:* "Rise like Lions after slumber.")

I regretted that I couldn't go even to evening school, let alone going to day school; but it didn't prevent me from trying to learn and it doesn't have to prevent anybody who wants to. I was then and still am an avid reader. Even if I didn't go to school I think I can hold my own with anyone, as far as literature is concerned.

Conditions were dreadful in those days. We didn't have anything. If the season was over, we were told, "You're laid off. Shift for yourself." How did you live? After all, you didn't earn enough to save any money. Well, the butcher trusted you. He knew you'd pay him when you started work again. Your landlord, he couldn't do anything but wait, you know. Sometimes relatives helped out. There was no welfare, no pension, no unemployment insurance. There was nothing. We were much worse off than the poor are today because we had nothing to lean on; nothing to hope for except to hope that the shop would open again and that we'd have work.

But despite that, we had good times. In the summer we'd go to Central Park and stay out and watch the moon arise; go to the Palisades and spend the day. We went to meetings, too, of course. We had friends and we enjoyed what we were doing. We had picnics. And, remember, in that time you could go and hear Caruso for twenty-five cents. We heard all the giants of the artistic world—Kreisler, Pavlova. We only had to pay twenty-five cents. Of course, we went upstairs, but we heard the greatest soloists, all for a quarter, and we enjoyed it immensely. We loved it. We'd go Saturday night and stand in line no matter whan the weather. In the winter we'd bring blankets along. Just imagine, the greatest artists in the world, from here and abroad, available to you for twenty-five cents. The first English play I went to was *Peer Gynt*. The actor's name was Mansfield. I remember it very well. So, in spite of everything, we had fun and we enjoyed what we learned and what we saw and what we heard.

I stopped working at the Triangle Factory during the strike in 1909 and I didn't go back. The union sent me out to raise money for the strikers. I apparently was able to articulate my feelings and opinions about the criminal conditions, and they didn't have anyone else who could do better, so they assigned me. And I was successful getting money. After my first speech before the Central Trade and Labor Council I got front-page publicity, including my picture. I was only about fifteen then. Everybody saw it. Wealthy women were curious and they asked me if I would speak to them in their homes. I said I would if they would contribute to the strike, and they agreed. So I spent my time from November to the end of March upstate in New York, speaking to the ladies of the Four Hundred (the elite of New York's society) and sending money back.

Those ladies were very kind and generous. I had never seen or dreamed of such wealth. One Sunday, after I had spoken, one of the women asked me to come to dinner. And we were sitting in the living room in front of a fireplace; remember it was winter. A beautiful library and comfort that I'd never seen before and I'm sure the likes of me had never seen anything like it either. And the butler announced that dinner was ready and we went into the dining room and for the first time I saw the silver and the crystal and the china and the beautiful tablecloth and vases—beautiful vases, you know. At that moment I didn't know what the hell I was doing there. The butler had probably never seen anything like me before. After the day was over, a beautiful limousine took me back to the YWCA where I stayed.

In Buffalo, in Rochester, it was the same thing. The wealthy ladies all asked me to speak, and they would invite me into their homes and contribute money to the strike. I told them what the conditions were that made us get up: the living conditions, the wages, the shop conditions. They'd probably never heard anything like this. I didn't exaggerate. I didn't have to. I remember one time in Syracuse a young woman sitting in front of me wept.

We didn't gain very much at the end of the strike. I think the hours were reduced to fifty-six a week or something like that. We got a 10 percent increase in wages. I think that the best thing that the strike did was to lay a foundation on which to build a union. There was so much feeling against unions then. The judge, when one of our girls came before him, said to her: "You're not striking against your employer, you know, young lady. You're striking against God," and sentenced her to two weeks on Blackwell's Island, which is now Welfare Island. And a lot of them got a taste of the club.

I can look back and find that there were some members of the union who might very well be compared to the unknown soldier. I'll never forget one member in the Philadelphia union. She was an immigrant, a beautiful young woman from Russia, and she was very devoted to the local union. And one Friday we were going to distribute leaflets to a shop that was not organized. They had refused to sign any agreement and we tried to work it that way to get the girls to join. But that particular day—God, I'll never forget the weather. Hail, snow, rain, cold. It was no weather for any human being to be out in, but she came into my office. I'd decided not to go home because of the weather and I'd stayed in the office. She came in and I said, "You're not going out tonight. I wouldn't send a dog out in weather like this." And I went to the window and I said, "Look." And while my back was turned, she grabbed a batch of leaflets and left the office. And she went out. And the next thing I heard was that she had pneumonia and she went to the hospital and in four days she was gone. I can't ever forget her. Of course, perhaps it was a bit unrealistic on her part, but on the other hand, I can't do anything but think of her with admiration. She had the faith and the will to help build the organization and, as I often tell other people, she was really one of the unknown soldiers.

After the 1909 strike I worked with the union, organizing in Philadelphia and Cleveland and other places, so I wasn't at the Triangle Shirtwaist Factory when the fire broke out, but a lot of my friends were. I was in Philadelphia for the union and, of course, someone from here called me immediately and I came back. It's very difficult to describe the feeling because I knew the place and I knew so many of the girls. The thing that bothered me was the employers got a lawyer. How anyone could have *defended* them!—because I'm quite sure that the fire was planned for insurance purposes. And no one is going to convince me otherwise. And when they testified that the door to the fire escape was open, it was a lie! It was never open. Locked all the time. One hundred and forty-six people were sacrificed, and the judge fined Blank and Harris seventy-five dollars!

Conditions were dreadful in those days. But there was something that is lacking today and I think it was the devotion and the belief. We *believed* in what we were doing. We fought and we bled and we died. Today they don't have to.

You sit down at the table, you negotiate with the employers, you ask for 20 percent, they say 15, but the girls are working. People are working. They're not disturbed, and when the negotiations are over they get the increases. They don't really have to fight. Of course, they'll belong to the union and they'll go on strike if you tell them to, but it's the inner faith that people had in those days that I don't see today. It was a terrible time, but it was interesting. I'm glad I lived then.

Even when things were terrible, I always had that faith. . . . Only now, I'm a little discouraged sometimes when I see the workers spending their free hours watching television—trash. We fought so hard for those hours and they waste them. We used to read Tolstoy, Dickens, Shelley, by candlelight, and they watch the ''Hollywood Squares.'' Well, they're free to do what they want. That's what we fought for.

SUGGESTIONS FOR WRITING AND DISCUSSION

1. How did Newman's childhood shape her strong feelings about the need for unions?
2. Is Newman optimistic or idealistic? Discuss the difference between the two terms and justify your answer by reference to the text.
3. How would you describe Newman's attitude to what workers do with their leisure time? Does she feel they have betrayed her efforts?
4. Interview someone who has held a particular job for a long period of time. Write up the interview and include your own observations about the person you interview.

Virginia Woolf (British, 1882–1941)

Professions for Women[1]

When your secretary invited me to come here, she told me that your Society is concerned with the employment of women and she suggested that I might tell you something about my own professional experiences. It is true I am a woman; it is true I am employed; but what professional experiences have I had? It is difficult to say. My profession is literature; and in that profession there are fewer experiences for women than in any other, with the exception of the stage—fewer, I mean, that are peculiar to For the road was cut many years ago—by Fanny Burney, by Aphra Behn, by Harriet Martineau, by Jane Austen, by George Eliot—many famous women, and many more unknown and forgotten, have been before me, making the path smooth, and regulating my steps. Thus, when I came to

[1]A paper read to the Women's Service League.

write, there were very few material obstacles in my way. Writing was a reputable and harmless occupation. The family peace was not broken by the scratching of a pen. No demand was made upon the family purse. For ten and sixpence one can buy paper enough to write all the plays of Shakespeare—if one has a mind that way. Pianos and models, Paris, Vienna and Berlin, masters and mistresses, are not needed by a writer. The cheapness of writing paper is, of course, the reason why women have succeeded as writers before they have succeeded in the other professions.

But to tell you my story—it is a simple one. You have only got to figure to yourselves a girl in a bedroom with a pen in her hand. She had only to move that pen from left to right—from ten o'clock to one. Then it occurred to her to do what is simple and cheap enough after all—to slip a few of those pages into an envelope, fix a penny stamp in the corner, and drop the envelope into the red box at the corner. It was thus that I became a journalist; and my effort was rewarded on the first day of the following month—a very glorious day it was for me—by a letter from an editor containing a cheque for one pound ten shillings and sixpence. But to show you how little I deserve to be called a professional woman, how little I know of the struggles and difficulties of such lives, I have to admit that instead of spending that sum upon bread and butter, rent, shoes and stockings, or butcher's bills, I went out and bought a cat—a beautiful cat, a Persian cat, which very soon involved me in bitter disputes with my neighbours.

What could be easier than to write articles and to buy Persian cats with the profits? But wait a moment. Articles have to be about something. Mine, I seem to remember, was about a novel by a famous man. And while I was writing this review, I discovered that if I were going to review books I should need to do battle with a certain phantom. And the phantom was a woman, and when I came to know her better I called her after the heroine of a famous poem, The Angel in the House. It was she who used to come between me and my paper when I was writing reviews. It was she who bothered me and wasted my time and so tormented me that at last I killed her. You who come of a younger and happier generation may not have heard of her—you may not know what I mean by the Angel in the House. I will describe her as shortly as I can. She was intensely sympathetic. She was immensely charming. She was utterly unselfish. She excelled in the difficult arts of family life. She sacrificed herself daily. If there was chicken, she took the leg; if there was a draught she sat in it—in short she was so constituted that she never had a mind or a wish of her own, but preferred to sympathize always with the minds and wishes of others. Above all—I need not say it—she was pure. Her purity was supposed to be her chief beauty—her blushes, her great grace. In those days—the last of Queen Victoria—every house had its Angel. And when I came to write I encountered her with the very first words. The shadow of her wings fell on my page; I heard the rustling of her skirts in the room. Directly, that is to say, I took my pen in hand to review that novel by a famous man, she slipped behind me and whispered: ``My dear, you are a young woman. You are writing about a book that has been written by a man. Be sympathetic; be tender; flatter; deceive; use all the arts and wiles of our sex. Never let anybody guess that you have a mind of your own. Above all, be pure.'' And she made as if to guide my pen. I now record the one act for which I take some credit to myself, though the credit rightly belongs to some excellent ancestors of mine who left me a certain sum of money—shall we say five hundred pounds a year?—so that it was not necessary for me to depend solely on charm for my living. I turned upon her and caught her by the throat. I did my best to kill her. My excuse, if I were to be had up in a court of law, would be that I acted in self-defence. Had I not killed her she would have killed me. She would have plucked the heart out of my writing. For, as I found, directly I put pen to paper, you cannot review even a novel without having a mind of your own, without expressing what you think to be the truth about human relations, morality, sex. And all these questions, according to the Angel in the House, cannot be dealt with freely and openly by women; they must charm, they must conciliate, they must—to put it bluntly—tell lies if they are to succeed. Thus, whenever I felt the shadow of her wing or the radiance of her halo upon my page, I took up the inkpot and flung it at her. She died hard. Her fictitious nature was of great assistance to her. It is far harder to kill a phantom than a reality. She was always creeping back when I thought I had despatched her. Though I flatter myself that I killed her in the end, the struggle was severe; it took much time that had better have been spent upon learning Greek grammar; or in roaming the world in search of adventures. But it was a real experience; it was an experience that was bound to befall all women writers at that time. Killing the Angel in the House was part of the occupation of a woman writer.

But to continue my story. The Angel was dead; what then remained? You may say that what remained was a simple and common object—a young woman in a bedroom with an inkpot. In other words, now that she had rid herself of falsehood, that young woman had only to be herself. Ah, but what is ``herself''? I mean, what is a woman? I assure you, I do not know. I do not believe that you know. I do not believe that anybody can know until she has expressed herself in all the arts and professions open to human skill. That indeed is one of the reasons why I have come here—out of respect for you, who are in process of showing us by your experiments what a woman is, who are in process of providing us, by your failures and successes, with that extremely important piece of information.

But to continue the story of my professional experiences. I made one pound ten and six by my first review; and I bought a Persian cat with the proceeds. Then I grew ambitious. A Persian cat is all very well, I said; but a Persian cat is not enough. I must have a motor car. And it was thus that I became a novelist—for it is a very strange thing that people will give you a motor car if you will tell them a story. It is a still stranger thing that there is nothing so delightful in the world as telling stories. It is far pleasanter than writing reviews of famous novels. And yet, if I am to obey your secretary and tell you my professional experiences as a novelist, I must tell you about a very strange experience that befell me as a novelist. And to understand it you must try to imagine a novelist's state of mind. I hope I am not giving away professional secrets if I say that a novelist's chief desire is to be as unconscious as possible. He has to induce in himself a state of perpetual lethargy. He wants life to proceed with the utmost quiet and regularity. He wants to see the same faces, to read the same books, to do the same things day after day, month after month, while he is writing, so that nothing may break the illusion in which he is living—so that nothing may disturb or disquiet the mysterious nosings about, feelings round, darts, dashes and sudden discoveries of that very shy and illusive spirit, the imagination. I suspect that this state is the same both for men and women. Be that as it may, I want you to imagine me writing a novel in a state of trance. I want you to figure to yourselves a girl sitting with a pen in her hand, which for minutes, and indeed for hours, she never dips into the inkpot. The image that comes to my mind when I think of this girl is the image of a fisherman lying sunk in dreams on the verge of a deep lake with a rod held out over the water. She was letting her imagination sweep unchecked round every rock and cranny of the world that lies submerged in the depths of our unconscious being. Now came the experience, the experience that I believe to be far commoner with women writers than with men. The line raced through the girl's fingers. Her imagination had rushed away. It had sought the pools, the depths, the dark places where the largest fish slumber. And then there was a smash. There was an explosion. There was foam and confusion. The imagination had dashed itself against something hard. The girl was roused from her dream. She was indeed in a state of the most acute and difficult distress. To speak without figure she had thought of something, something about the body, about the passions which it was unfitting for her as a woman to say. Men, her reason told her, would be shocked. The consciousness of what men will say of a woman who speaks the truth about her passions had roused her from her artist's state of unconsciousness. She could write no more. The trance was over. Her imagination could work no longer. This I believe to be a very common experience with women writers—they are impeded by the extreme conventionality of the other sex. For though men sensibly allow themselves great freedom in these respects, I doubt that they realize or can control the extreme severity with which they condemn such freedom in women.

These then were two very genuine experiences of my own. These were two of the adventures of my professional life. The first—killing the Angel in the House—I think I solved. She died. But the second, telling the truth about my own experiences as a body, I do not think I solved. I doubt that any woman has solved it yet. The obstacles against her are still immensely powerful—and yet they are very difficult to define. Outwardly, what is simpler than to write books? Outwardly, what obstacles are there for a woman rather than for a man? Inwardly, I think, the case is very different; she has still many ghosts to fight, many prejudices to overcome. Indeed it will be a long time still, I think, before a woman can sit down to write a book without finding a phantom to be slain, a rock to be dashed against. And if this is so in literature, the freest of all professions for women, how is it in the new professions which you are now for the first time entering?

Those are the questions that I should like, had I time, to ask you. And indeed, if I have laid stress upon these professional experiences of mine, it is because I believe that they are, though in different forms, yours also. Even when the path is nominally open—when there is nothing to prevent a woman from being a doctor, a lawyer, a civil servant—there are many phantoms and obstacles, as I believe, looming in her way. To discuss and define them is I think of great value and importance; for thus only can the labour be shared, the difficulties be solved. But besides this, it is necessary also to discuss the ends and the aims for which we are fighting, for which we are doing battle with these formidable obstacles. Those aims cannot be taken for granted; they must be perpetually questioned and examined. The whole position, as I see it—here in this hall surrounded by women practising for the first time in history I know not how many different professions—is one of extraordinary interest and importance. You have won rooms of your own in the house hitherto exclusively owned by men. You are able, though not without great labour and effort, to pay the rent. You are earning your five hundred pounds a year. But this freedom is only a beginning; the room is your own, but it is still bare. It has to be furnished; it has to be decorated; it has to be shared. How are you going to furnish it, how are you going to decorate it? With whom are you going to share it, and upon what terms? These, I think are questions of the utmost importance and interest. For the first time in history you are able to ask them; for the first time you are able to decide for yourselves what the answers should be. Willingly would I stay and discuss those questions and answers—but not tonight. My time is up; and I must cease.

SUGGESTIONS FOR WRITING AND DISCUSSION

1. In the first paragraph Woolf says, "My profession is literature; and in that profession there are fewer experiences for women than in any other, with the exception of the stage—fewer, I mean, that are peculiar to women." What does she mean by this statement? Do you think it is true? Justify your answers by referring to Woolf's account of her experiences as a writer.
2. Discuss Woolf's description of "the Angel in the House." Is her tone ironic? What part does this description play in her argument?
3. Who is Woolf's audience? How does it shape her speech?
4. Are Woolf's views old-fashioned? Are they consistent with contemporary feminism? In a three- to four-page essay discuss how Woolf's views either do or do not apply to women in general.

Fiction

Luke (first century A.D.*)*

The Parable of the Prodigal Son

Luke 15: 11–32, King James Version of the Bible

And he said, "A certain man had two sons: and the younger of them said to his father. 'Father, give me the portion of goods that falleth to me.' And he divided unto them his living. And not many days after, the younger son gathered all together, and took his journey into a far country, and there wasted his substance with riotous living. And when he had spent all, there arose a mighty famine in that land, and he began to be in want. And he went and joined himself to a citizen of that country, and he sent him into his fields to feed swine. And he would fain have filled his belly with the husks that the swine did eat: and no man gave unto him. And when he came to himself, he said, 'How many hired servants of my father's have bread enough and to spare, and I perish with hunger? I will arise and go to my father, and will say unto him, "Father, I have sinned against heaven, and before thee, and am no more worthy to be called thy son: make me as one of thy hired servants."' And he arose, and came to his father. But when he was yet a great way off, his father saw him, and had compassion, and ran, and fell on his neck, and kissed him. And the son said unto him, 'Father, I have sinned against heaven, and in thy sight, and am no more worthy to be called thy son.' But the father said to his servants, 'Bring forth the best robe, and put it on him, and put a ring on his hand, and shoes on his feet. And bring hither the fatted calf, and kill it, and let us eat, and be merry. For this my son was dead, and is alive again; he was lost, and is found.' And they began to be merry. Now his elder son was in the field, and as he came and drew nigh to the house, he heard music and dancing. And he called one of the servants, and asked what these things meant. And he said unto him, 'Thy brother is come, and thy father hath killed the fatted calf, because he hath received him safe and sound.' And he was angry, and would not go in: therefore came his father out, and entreated him. And he answering said to his father, 'Lo, these many years do I serve thee, neither transgressed I at any time thy commandment, and yet thou never gavest me a kid, that I might make merry with my friends: but as soon as this thy son was come, which hath devoured thy living with harlots, thou hast killed for him the fatted calf.' And he said unto him, 'Son, thou art ever with me, and all that I have is thine. It was meet that we should make merry, and be glad: for this thy brother was dead, and is alive again: and was lost, and is found.'"

SUGGESTIONS FOR WRITING AND DISCUSSION

1. Compare the two brothers.
2. What comment does this parable make about our attitude toward material goods?
3. What values does this parable promote? Do you agree with them?

Nikolai Gogol (Russian, 1809–1852)

The Overcoat

In the department of . . . but I had better not mention in what department. There is nothing in the world more readily moved to wrath than a department, a regiment, a government office, and in fact any sort of official body. Nowadays every private individual considers all society insulted in his person. I have been told that very lately a petition was handed in from a police-captain of what town I don't recollect, and that in this petition he set forth clearly that the institutions of the State were in danger and that its sacred name was being taken in vain; and, in proof thereof, he appended to his petition an enormously long volume of some work of romance in which a police-captain appeared on every tenth page, occasionally, indeed, in an intoxicated condition. And so, to avoid any unpleasantness, we had better call the department of which we are speaking a certain department.

And so, in a certain department there was a government clerk; a clerk of whom it cannot be said that he was very remarkable; he was short, somewhat pock-marked, with rather reddish hair and rather dim, bleary eyes, with a small bald patch on the top of his head, with wrinkles on both sides of his cheeks and the sort of complexion which is usually associated with hæmorrhoids . . . no help for that, it is the Petersburg climate. As for his grade in the service (for among us the grade is what must be put first), he was what is called a perpetual titular councillor, a class at which, as we all know, various writers who indulge in the praiseworthy habit of attacking those who cannot defend themselves jeer and jibe to their hearts' content. This clerk's surname was Bashmatchkin. From the very name it is clear that it must have been derived from a shoe *(bashmak);* but when and under what circumstances it was derived from a shoe, it is impossible to say. Both his father and his grandfather and even his brother-in-law, and all the Bashmatchkins without exception wore boots, which they simply re-soled two or three times a year. His name was Akaky Akakyevitch. Perhaps it may strike the reader as a rather strange and far-fetched name, but I can assure him that it was not far-fetched at all, that the circumstances were such that it was quite out of the question to give him any other name. Akaky Akakyevitch was born towards nightfall, if my memory does not deceive me, on the twenty-third of March. His mother, the wife of a government clerk, a very good woman, made arrangements in due course to christen the child. She was still lying in bed, facing the door, while on her right hand stood the godfather, an excellent man called Ivan Ivanovitch Yeroshkin, one of the head clerks of the Senate, and the godmother, the wife of a police official, and a woman of rare qualities. Arina Semyonovna Byelobryushkov. Three names were offered to the happy mother for selection—Moky, Sossy, or the name of the martyr Hozdazat. "No," thought the poor lady, "they are all such names!" To satisfy her, they opened the calendar at another place, and the names which turned up were: Trifily, Dula, Varahasy. "What an infliction!" said the mother. "What names they all are! I really never heard such names. Varadat or Varuh would be bad enough, but Trifily and Varahasy!" They turned over another page and the names were: Pavsikahy and Vahtisy. "Well, I see," said the mother, "it is clear that it is his fate. Since that is how it is, he had better be called after his father, his father is Akaky, let the son be Akaky, too." This was how he came to be Akaky Akakyevitch. The baby was christened and cried and made wry faces during the ceremony, as though he foresaw that he would be a titular councillor. So that was how it all came to pass. We have recalled it here so that the reader may see for himself that it happened quite inevitably and that to give him any other name was out of the question. No one has been able to remember when and how long ago he entered the department, nor who gave him the job. However many directors and higher officials of all sorts came and went, he was always seen in the same place, in the same position, at the very same duty, precisely the same copying clerk, so that they used to declare that he must have been born a copying clerk in uniform all complete and with a bald patch on his head. No respect at all was shown him in the department. The porters, far from getting up from their seats when he came in, took no more notice of him than if a simple fly had flown across the vestibule. His superiors treated him with a sort of domineering chilliness. The head clerk's assistant used to throw papers under his nose without even saying: "Copy this" or "Here is an interesting, nice little case" or some agreeable remark of the sort, as is usually done in well-behaved offices. And he would take it, gazing only at the paper without looking to see who had put it there and whether he had the right to do so; he would take it and at once set to work to copy it.

The young clerks jeered and made jokes at him to the best of their clerkly wit, and told before his face all sorts of stories of their own invention about him; they would say of his landlady, an old woman of seventy, that she beat him, would enquire when the wedding was to take place, and would scatter bits of paper on his head, calling them snow. Akaky Akakyevitch never answered a word, however, but behaved as though there were no one there. It had no influence on his work even; in the midst of all this teasing, he never made a single mistake in his copying. Only when the jokes were too unbearable, when they jolted his arm and prevented him from going on with his work, he would bring out: "Leave me alone! Why do you insult me?" and there was something strange in the words and in the voice in which they were uttered. There was a note in it of something that aroused compassion, so that one young man, new to the office, who, following the example of the rest, had allowed himself to mock at him, suddenly stopped as though cut to the heart, and from that time forth, everything was, as it were, changed and appeared in a different light to him. Some unnatural force seemed to thrust him away from the companions with whom he had become acquainted, accepting them as well-bred, polished people. And long afterwards, at moments of the greatest gaiety, the figure of the humble little clerk with a bald patch on his head rose before him with his heart-rending words: ``Leave me alone! Why do you insult me?'' and in those heart-rending words he heard others: ``I am your brother.'' And the poor young man hid his face in his hands, and many times afterwards in his life he shuddered, seeing how much inhumanity there is in man, how much savage brutality lies hidden under refined, cultured politeness, and, my God! even in a man whom the world accepts as a gentleman and a man of honor. . . .

It would be hard to find a man who lived in his work as did Akaky Akakyevitch. To say that he was zealous in his work is not enough; no, he loved his work. In it, in that copying, he found a varied and agreeable world of his own. There was a look of enjoyment on his face; certain letters were favorites with him, and when he came to them he was delighted; he chuckled to himself and winked and moved his lips, so that it seemed as though every letter his pen was forming could be read in his face. If rewards had been given according to the measure of zeal in the service, he might to his amazement have even found himself a civil councillor; but all he gained in the service, as the wits, his fellow-clerks, expressed it, was a buckle in his button-hole and a pain in his back. It cannot be said, however, that no notice had ever been taken of him. One director, being a good-natured man and anxious to reward him for his long service, sent him something a little more important than his ordinary copying; he was instructed from a finished document to make some sort of report for another office; the work consisted only of altering the headings and in places changing the first person into the third. This cost him such an effort that it threw him into a regular perspiration: he mopped his brow and said at last, ``No, better let me copy something.''

From that time forth they left him to go on copying forever. It seemed as though nothing in the world existed for him outside his copying. He gave no thought at all to his clothes; his uniform was—well, not green but some sort of rusty, muddy color. His collar was very short and narrow, so that, although his neck was not particularly long, yet, standing out of the collar, it looked as immensely long as those of the plaster kittens that wag their heads and are carried about on trays on the heads of dozens of foreigners living in Russia. And there were always things sticking to his uniform, either bits of hay or threads; moreover, he had a special art of passing under a window at the very moment when various rubbish was being flung out into the street, and so was continually carrying off bits of melon rind and similar litter on his hat. He had never once in his life noticed what was being done and going on in the street, all those things at which, as we all know, his colleagues, the young clerks, always stare, carrying their sharp sight so far even as to notice any one on the other side of the pavement with a trouser strap hanging loose—a detail which always calls forth a sly grin. Whatever Akaky Akakyevitch looked at, he saw nothing anywhere but his clear, evenly written lines, and only perhaps when a horse's head suddenly appeared from nowhere just on his shoulder, and its nostrils blew a perfect gale upon his cheek, did he notice that he was not in the middle of his writing, but rather in the middle of the street.

On reaching home, he would sit down at once to the table, hurriedly sip his soup and eat a piece of beef with an onion; he did not notice the taste at all, but ate it all up together with the flies and anything else that Providence chanced to send him. When he felt that his stomach was beginning to be full, he would rise up from the table, get out a bottle of ink and set to copying the papers he had brought home with him. When he had none to do, he would make a copy expressly for his own pleasure, particularly if the document were remarkable not for the beauty of its style but for the fact of its being addressed to some new or important personage.

Even at those hours when the gray Petersburg sky is completely overcast and the whole population of clerks have dined and eaten their fill, each as best he can, according to the salary he receives and his personal tastes; when they are all resting after the scratching of pens and bustle of the office, their own necessary work and other people's, and all the tasks that an over-zealous man voluntarily sets himself even beyond what is necessary; when the clerks are hastening to devote what is left of their time to pleasure; some more enterprising are flying to the theatre, others to the street to spend their leisure, staring at women's hats, some to spend the evening paying compliments to some attractive girl, the star of a little official circle, while some—and this is the most frequent of all— go simply to a fellow-clerk's flat on the third or fourth story, two little rooms with an entry or a kitchen, with some pretentions to style, with a lamp or some such article that has cost many sacrifices of dinners and excursions—at the time when all the clerks are scattered about the little flats of their friends, playing a tempestuous game of whist, sipping tea out of glasses to the accompaniment of farthing rusks, sucking in smoke from long pipes, telling, as the cards are dealt, some scandal that has floated down from higher circles, a pleasure which the Russian can never by any possibility deny himself, or, when there is nothing better to talk about, repeating the everlasting anecdote of the commanding officer who was told that the tail had been cut off the horse on the Falconet monument— in short, even when every one was eagerly seeking entertainment, Akaky Akakyevitch did not give himself up to any amusement. No one could say that they had ever seen him at an evening party. After working to his heart's content, he would go to bed, smiling at the thought of the next day and wondering what God would send him to copy. So flowed on the peaceful life of a man who knew how to be content with his fate on a salary of four hundred roubles, and so perhaps it would have flowed on to extreme old age, had it not been for the various calamities that bestrew the path through life, not only of titular, but even of privy, actual court and all other councillors, even those who neither give council to others nor accept it themselves.

There is in Petersburg a mighty foe of all who receive a salary of four hundred roubles or about that sum. That foe is none other than our northern frost, although it is said to be very good for the health. Between eight and nine in the morning, precisely at the hour when the streets are full of clerks going to their departments, the frost begins giving such sharp and stinging flips at all their noses indiscriminately that the poor fellows don't know what to do with them. At that time, when even those in the higher grade have a pain in their brows and tears in their eyes from the frost, the poor titular councillors are sometimes almost defenceless. Their only protection lies in running as fast as they can through five or six streets in a wretched, thin little overcoat and then warming their feet thoroughly in the porter's room, till all their faculties and qualifications for their various duties thaw again after being frozen on the way. Akaky Akakyevitch had for some time been feeling that his back and shoulders were particularly nipped by the cold, although he did try to run the regular distance as fast as he could. He wondered at last whether there were any defects in his overcoat. After examining it thoroughly in the privacy of his home, he discovered that in two or three places, to wit on the back and the shoulders, it had become a regular sieve; the cloth was so worn that you could see through it and the lining was coming out. I must observe that Akaky Akakyevitch's overcoat had also served as a butt for the jibes of the clerks. It had even been deprived of the honorable name of overcoat and had been referred to as the "dressing jacket." It was indeed of rather a strange make. Its collar had been growing smaller year by year as it served to patch the other parts. The patches were not good specimens of the tailor's art, and they certainly looked clumsy and ugly. On seeing what was wrong, Akaky Akakyevitch decided that he would have to take the overcoat to Petrovitch, a tailor who lived on a fourth story up a back staircase, and, in spite of having only one eye and being pock-marked all over his face, was rather successful in repairing the trousers and coats of clerks and others—that is, when he was sober, be it understood, and had no other enterprise in his mind.

Of this tailor I ought not, of course, to say much, but since it is now the rule that the character of every person in a novel must be completely drawn, well, there is no help for it, here is Petrovitch too. At first he was called simply Grigory, and was a serf belonging to some gentleman or other. He began to be called Petrovitch from the time that he got his freedom and began to drink rather heavily on every holiday, at first only on the chief holidays, but afterwards on all church holidays indiscriminately, wherever there is a cross in the calendar. On that side he was true to the customs of his forefathers, and when he quarrelled with his wife used to call her ''a worldly woman and a German.'' Since we have now mentioned the wife, it will be necessary to say a few words about her too, but unfortunately not much is known about her, except indeed that Petrovitch had a wife and that she wore a cap and not a kerchief, but apparently she could not boast of beauty; anyway, none but soldiers of the Guards peeped under her cap when they met her, and they twitched their moustaches and gave vent to a rather peculiar sound.

As he climbed the stairs, leading to Petrovitch's—which, to do them justice, were all soaked with water and slops and saturated through and through with that smell of spirits which makes the eyes smart, and is, as we all know, inseparable from the backstairs of Petersburg houses— Akaky Akakyevitch was already wondering how much Petrovitch would ask for the job, and inwardly resolving not to give more than two roubles. The door was open, for Petrovitch's wife was frying some fish and had so filled the kitchen with smoke that you could not even see the black-beetles. Akaky Akakyevitch crossed the kitchen unnoticed by the good woman, and walked at last into a room where he saw Petrovitch sitting on a big, wooden, unpainted table with his legs tucked under him like a Turkish Pasha. The feet, as is usual with tailors when they sit at work, were bare; and the first object that caught Akaky Akakyevitch's eye was the big toe, with which he was already familiar, with a misshapen nail as thick and strong as the shell of a tortoise. Round Petrovitch's neck hung a skein of silk and another of thread and on his knees was a rag of some sort. He had for the last three minutes been trying to thread his needle, but could not get the thread into the eye and so was very angry with the darkness and indeed with the thread itself, muttering in an undertone: ''It won't go in, the savage! You wear me out, you rascal.'' Akaky Akakyevitch was vexed that he had come just at the minute when Petrovitch was in a bad humor; he liked to give him an order when he was a little ''elevated,'' or, as his wife expressed it, ''had fortified himself with fizz, the one-eyed devil.'' In such circumstances Petrovitch was as a rule very ready to give way and agree, and invariably bowed and thanked him, indeed. Afterwards, it is true, his wife would come wailing that her husband had been drunk and so had asked too little, but adding a single ten-kopeck piece would settle that. But on this occasion Petrovitch was apparently sober and consequently curt, unwilling to bargain, and the devil knows what price he would be ready to lay on. Akaky Akakyevitch perceived this, and was, as the saying is, beating a retreat, but things had gone too far, for Petrovitch was screwing up his solitary eye very attentively at him and Akaky Akakyevitch involuntarily brough out: ''Good day, Petrovitch!'' ''I wish you a good day, sir,'' said Petrovitch, and squinted at Akaky Akakyevitch's hands, trying to discover what sort of goods he had brought.

"Here I have come to you, Petrovitch, do you see . . . !"

It must be noticed that Akaky Akakyevitch for the most part explained himself by apologies, vague phrases, and particles which have absolutely no significance whatever. If the subject were a very difficult one, it was his habit indeed to leave his sentences quite unfinished, so that very often after a sentence had begun with the words, "It really is, don't you know . . . " nothing at all would follow and he himself would be quite oblivious, supposing he had said all that was necessary.

"What is it?" said Petrovitch, and at the same time with his solitary eye he scrutinized his whole uniform from the collar to the sleeves, the back, the skirts, the button holes—with all of which he was very familiar, they were all his own work. Such scrutiny is habitual with tailors, it is the first thing they do on meeting one.

"It's like this, Petrovitch . . . the overcoat, the cloth . . . you see everywhere else it is quite strong; it's a little dusty and looks as though it were old, but it is new and it is only in one place just a little . . . on the back, and just a little worn on one shoulder and on this shoulder, too, a little . . . do you see? that's all, and it's not much work. . . . "

Petrovitch took the "dressing jacket," first spread it out over the table, examined it for a long time, shook his head and put his hand out to the window for a round snuff-box with a portrait on the lid of some general—which precisely I can't say, for a finger had been thrust through the spot where a face should have been, and the hole had been pasted up with a square bit of paper. After taking a pinch of snuff, Petrovitch held the "dressing jacket" up in his hands and looked at it against the light, and again he shook his head; then he turned it with the lining upwards and once more shook his head; again he took off the lid with the general pasted up with paper and stuffed a pinch into his nose, shut the box, put it away and at last said: "No, it can't be repaired; a wretched garment!" Akaky Akakyevitch's heart sank at those words.

"Why can't it, Petrovitch?" he said, almost in the imploring voice of a child. "Why, the only thing is it is a bit worn on the shoulders; why, you have got some little pieces. . . . "

"Yes, the pieces will be found all right," said Petrovitch, "but it can't be patched, the stuff is quite rotten; if you put a needle in it, it would give way."

"Let it give way, but you just put a patch on it."

"There is nothing to put a patch on. There is nothing for it to hold on to; there is a great strain on it, it is not worth calling cloth, it would fly away at a breath of wind."

"Well, then, strengthen it with something—upon my word really, this is . . . !"

"No," said Petrovitch resolutely, "there is nothing to be done, the thing is no good at all. You had far better, when the cold winter weather comes, make yourself leg wrappings out of it, for there is no warmth in stockings, the Germans invented them just to make money." (Petrovitch was fond of a dig at the Germans occasionally.) "And as for the overcoat, it is clear that you will have to have a new one."

At the word "new" there was a mist before Akaky Akakyevitch's eyes, and everything in the room seemed blurred. He could see nothing clearly but the general with the piece of paper over his face on the lid of Petrovitch's snuff-box.

"A new one?" he said, still feeling as though he were in a dream; "why, I haven't the money for it."

"Yes, a new one," Petrovitch repeated with barbarous composure.

"Well, and if I did have a new one, how much would it . . . ?"

"You mean what will it cost?"

"Yes."

"Well, three fifty-rouble notes or more," said Petrovitch, and he compressed his lips significantly. He was very fond of making an effect, he was fond of suddenly disconcerting a man completely and then squinting sideways to see what sort of a face he made.

"A hundred and fifty roubles for an overcoat," screamed poor Akaky Akakyevitch—it was perhaps the first time he had screamed in his life, for he was always distinguished by the softness of his voice.

"Yes," said Petrovitch, "and even then it's according to the coat. If I were to put marten on the collar, and add a hood with silk linings, it would come to two hundred."

"Petrovitch, please," said Akaky Akakyevitch in an imploring voice, not hearing and not trying to hear what Petrovitch said, and missing all his effects, "do repair it somehow, so that it will serve a little longer."

"No, that would be wasting work and spending money for nothing," said Petrovitch, and after that Akaky Akakyevitch went away completely crushed, and when he had gone Petrovitch remained standing for a long time with his lips pursed up significantly before he took up his work again, feeling pleased that he had not demeaned himself nor lowered the dignity of the tailor's art.

When he got into the street, Akaky Akakyevitch was as though in a dream. "So that is how it is," he said to himself. "I really did not think it would be so . . ." and then after a pause he added, "So there it is! so that's how it is at last! and I really could never have supposed it would have been so. And there . . ." There followed another long silence, after which he brought out: "So there it is! well, it really is so utterly unexpected . . . who would have thought . . . what a circumstance . . ." Saying this, instead of going home he walked off in quite the opposite direction without suspecting what he was doing. On the way a clumsy sweep brushed the whole of his sooty side against him and blackened all his shoulder; a regular hatful of plaster scattered upon him from the top of a house that was being built. He noticed nothing of this, and only after he had jostled against a sentry who had set his halberd down beside him and was shaking some snuff out of his horn into his rough fist, he came to himself a little and then only because the sentry said: "Why are you poking yourself right in one's face, haven't you the pavement to yourself?" This made him look round and turn homeward; only there he began to collect his thoughts, to see his position in a clear and true light and began talking to himself no longer incoherently but reasonably and openly as with a sensible friend with whom one can discuss the most intimate and vital matters. "No, indeed," said Akaky Akakyevitch, "it is no use talking to Petrovitch now; just now he really is . . . his wife must have been giving it to him. I had better go to him on Sunday morning; after the Saturday evening he will be squinting and sleepy, so he'll want a little drink to carry it off and his wife won't give him a penny. I'll slip ten kopecks into his hand and then he will be more accommodating and maybe take the overcoat. . . ."

So reasoning with himself, Akaky Akakyevitch cheered up and waited until the next Sunday; then, seeing from a distance Petrovitch's wife leaving the house, he went straight in. Petrovitch certainly was very tipsy after the Saturday. He could hardly hold his head up and was very drowsy: but, for all that, as soon as he heard what he was speaking about, it seemed as though the devil had nudged him. "I can't," he said, "you must kindly order a new one." Akaky Akakyevitch at once slipped a ten-kopeck piece into his hand. "I thank you, sir, I will have just a drop to your health, but don't trouble yourself about the overcoat; it is not a bit of good for anything. I'll make you a fine new coat, you can trust me for that."

Akaky Akakyevitch would have said more about repairs, but Petrovitch, without listening, said: "A new one now I'll make you without fail; you can rely upon that, I'll do my best. It could even be like the fashion that has come in with the collar to button with silver claws under appliqué."

Then Akaky Akakyevitch saw that there was no escape from a new overcoat and he was utterly depressed. How indeed, for what, with what money could he get it? Of course he could to some extent rely on the bonus for the coming holiday, but that money had long ago been appropriated and its use determined beforehand. It was needed for new trousers and to pay the cobbler an old debt for putting some new tops to some old boot-legs, and he had to order three shirts from a seamstress as well as two specimens of an undergarment which it is improper to mention in print; in short, all that money absolutely must be spent, and even if the director were to be so gracious as to assign him a gratuity of forty-five or even fifty, instead of forty roubles, there would be still left a mere trifle, which would be but as a drop in the ocean beside the fortune needed for an overcoat. Though, of course, he knew that Petrovitch had a strange craze for suddenly putting on the devil knows what enormous price, so that at times his own wife could not help crying out: "Why, you are out of your wits, you idiot! Another time he'll undertake a job for nothing, and here the devil has bewitched him to ask more than he is worth himself." Though, of course, he knew that Petrovitch would undertake to make it for eighty roubles, still where would he get those eighty roubles? He might manage half of that sum; half of it could be found, perhaps even a little more; but where could he get the other half? . . . But, first of all, the reader ought to know where that first half was to be found. Akaky Akakyevitch had the habit every time he spent a rouble of putting aside two kopecks in a little locked-up box with a slit in the lid for slipping the money in. At the end of every half-year he would inspect the pile of coppers there and change them for small silver. He had done this for a long time, and in the course of many years the sum had mounted up to forty roubles and so he had half the money in his hands, but where was he to get the other half, where was he to get another forty roubles? Akaky Akakyevitch pondered and pondered and decided at last that he would have to diminish his ordinary expenses, at least for a year; give up burning candles in the evening, and if he had to do anything he must go into the landlady's room and work by her candle; that as he walked along the streets he must walk as lightly and carefully as possible, almost on tiptoe, on the cobbles and flagstones, so that his soles might last a little longer than usual; that he must send his linen to the wash less frequently, and that, to preserve it from being worn, he must take it off every day when he came home and sit in a thin cotton-shoddy dressing-gown, a very ancient garment which Time itself had spared. To tell the truth, he found it at first rather hard to get used to these privations, but after a while it became a habit and went smoothly enough—he even became quite accustomed to being hungry in the evening; on the other hand, he had spiritual nourishment, for he carried ever in his thoughts the idea of his future overcoat. His whole existence had in a sense become fuller, as though he had married, as though some other person were present with him, as though he were no longer alone, but an agreeable companion had consented to walk the path of life hand in hand with him, and that companion was no other than the new overcoat with its thick wadding and its strong, durable lining. He became, as it were, more alive, even more strong-willed, like a man who has set before himself a definite aim. Uncertainty, indecision, in fact all the hesitating and vague characteristics vanished from his face and his manners.

At times there was a gleam in his eyes, indeed, the most bold and audacious ideas flashed through his mind. Why not really have marten on the collar? Meditation on the subject always made him absent-minded. On one occasion when he was copying a document, he very nearly made a mistake, so that he almost cried out "ough" aloud and crossed himself. At least once every month he went to Petrovitch to talk about the overcoat, where it would be best to buy the cloth, and what color it should be, and what price, and, though he returned home a little anxious, he was always pleased at the thought that at last the time was at hand when everything would be bought and the overcoat would be made. Things moved even faster than he had anticipated. Contrary to all expectations, the director bestowed on Akaky Akakyevitch a gratuity of no less than sixty roubles. Whether it was that he had an inkling that Akaky Akakyevitch needed a greatcoat, or whether it happened so by chance, owing to this he found he had twenty roubles extra.

This circumstance hastened the course of affairs. Another two or three months of partial fasting and Akaky Akakyevitch had actually saved up nearly eighty roubles. His heart, as a rule very tranquil, began to throb. The very first day he set off in company with Petrovitch to the shops. They bought some very good cloth, and no wonder, since they had been thinking of it for more than six months before, and scarcely a month had passed without their going to the shop to compare prices; now Petrovitch himself declared that there was no better cloth to be had. For the lining they chose calico, but of a stout quality, which in Petrovitch's words was even better than silk, and actually as strong and handsome to look at. Marten they did not buy, because it certainly was dear, but instead they chose cat fur, the best to be found in the shop—cat which in the distance might almost be taken for marten. Petrovitch was busy over the coat for a whole fortnight, because there were a great many button holes, otherwise it would have been ready sooner. Petrovitch asked twelve roubles for the work; less than that it hardly could have been, everything was sewn with silk, with fine double seams, and Petrovitch went over every seam afterwards with his own teeth, imprinting various figures with them. It was . . . it is hard to say precisely on what day, but probably on the most triumphant day of the life of Akaky Akakyevitch that Petrovitch at last brought the overcoat. He brought it in the morning, just before it was time to set off for the department. The overcoat could not have arrived more in the nick of time, for rather sharp frosts were just beginning and seemed threatening to be even more severe. Petrovitch brought the greatcoat himself as a good tailor should. There was an expression of importance on his face, such as Akaky Akakyevitch had never seen there before. He seemed fully conscious of having completed a work of no little moment and of having shown in his own person the gulf that separates tailors who only put in linings and do repairs from those who make up new materials. He took the greatcoat out of the pocket-handerkerchief in which he had brought it (the pocket-handerkerchief had just come home from the wash), he then folded it up and put it in his pocket for future use. After taking out the overcoat, he looked at it with much pride and, holding it in both hands, threw it very deftly over Akaky Akakyevitch's shoulders, then pulled it down and smoothed it out behind with his hands; then draped it about Akaky Akakyevitch with somewhat jaunty carelessness. The latter, as a man advanced in years, wished to try it with his arms in the sleeves. Petrovitch helped him to put it on, and it appeared that it looked splendid too with his arms in the sleeves. In fact it turned out that the overcoat was completely and entirely successful. Petrovitch did not let slip the occasion for observing that it was only because he lived in a small street and had no signboard, and because he had known Akaky

Akakyevitch so long, that he had done it so cheaply, but on the Nevsky Prospect they would have asked him seventy-five roubles for the work alone. Akaky Akakyevitch had no inclination to discuss this with Petrovitch, besides he was frightened of the big sums that Petrovitch was fond of flinging airily about in conversation. He paid him, thanked him, and went off on the spot, with his new overcoat on, to the department. Petrovitch followed him out and stopped in the street, staring for a good time at the coat from a distance and then purposely turned off and, taking a short cut by a side street, came back into the street and got another view of the coat from the other side, that is, from the front.

Meanwhile Akaky Akakyevitch walked along with every emotion in its most holiday mood. He felt every second that he had a new overcoat on his shoulders, and several times he actually laughed from inward satisfaction. Indeed, it had two advantages, one that it was warm and the other that it was good. He did not notice the way at all and found himself all at once at the department; in the porter's room he took off the overcoat, looked it over and put it in the porter's special care. I cannot tell how it happened, but all at once every one in the department learned that Akaky Akakyevitch had a new overcoat and that the "dressing jacket" no longer existed. They all ran out at once into the porter's room to look at Akaky Akakyevitch's new overcoat, they began welcoming him and congratulating him so that at first he could do nothing but smile and afterwards felt positively abashed. When, coming up to him, they all began saying that he must "sprinkle" the new overcoat and that he ought at least to stand them all a supper, Akaky Akakyevitch lost his head completely and did not know what to do, how to get out of it, nor what to answer. A few minutes later, flushing crimson, he even began assuring them with great simplicity that it was not a new overcoat at all, that it was just nothing, that it was an old overcoat. At last one of the clerks, indeed the assistant of the head clerk of the room, probably in order to show that he was not proud and was able to get on with those beneath him, said: "So be it, I'll give a party instead of Akaky Akakyevitch and invite you all to tea with me this evening; as luck would have it, it is my name-day."

The clerks naturally congratulated the assistant head clerk and eagerly accepted the invitation. Akaky Akakyevitch was beginning to make excuses, but they all declared that it was uncivil of him, that it was simply a shame and a disgrace and that he could not possibly refuse. However, he felt pleased about it afterwards when he remembered that through this he would have the opportunity of going out in the evening, too, in his new overcoat. That whole day was for Akaky Akakyevitch the most triumphant and festive day in his life. He returned home in the happiest frame of mind, took off the overcoat and hung it carefully on the wall, admiring the cloth and lining once more, and then pulled out his old "dressing jacket," now completely coming to pieces, on purpose to compare them. He glanced at it and positively laughed, the difference was

In the distance, goodness knows where, there was a gleam of light from some sentry-box which seemed to be standing at the end of the world. Akaky Akakyevitch's light-heartedness grew somehow sensibly less at this place. He stepped into the square, not without an involuntary uneasiness, as though his heart had a foreboding of evil. He looked behind him and to both sides—it was as though the sea were all round him. "No, better not look," he thought, and walked on, shutting his eyes, and when he opened them to see whether the end of the square were near, he suddenly saw standing before him, almost under his very nose, some men with mustaches; just what they were like he could not even distinguish. There was a mist before his eyes and a throbbing in his chest. "I say the overcoat is mine!" said one of them in a voice like a clap of thunder, seizing him by the collar. Akaky Akakyevitch was on the point of shouting "Help!" when another put a fist the size of a clerk's head against his very lips, saying: "You just shout now." Akaky Akakyevitch felt only that they took the overcoat off, and gave him a kick with their knees, and he fell on his face in the snow and was conscious of nothing more. A few minutes later he came to himself and got on to his feet, but there was no one there. He felt that it was cold on the ground and that he had no overcoat, and began screaming, but it seemed as though his voice could not carry to the end of the square. Overwhelmed with despair and continuing to scream, he ran across the square straight to the sentry-box, beside which stood a sentry leaning on his halberd and, so it seemed, looking with curiosity to see who the devil the man was who was screaming and running towards him from the distance.

As Akaky Akakyevitch reached him he began breathlessly shouting that he was asleep and not looking after his duty not to see that a man was being robbed. The sentry answered that he had seen nothing, that he had only seen him stopped in the middle of the square by two men, and supposed that they were his friends, and that, instead of abusing him for nothing, he had better go the next day to the superintendent and that he would find out who had taken the overcoat. Akaky Akakyevitch ran home in a terrible state: his hair, which was still comparatively abundant on his temples and the back of his head, was completely dishevelled; his sides and chest and his trousers were all covered with snow. When his old landlady heard a fearful knock at the door she jumped hurriedly out of bed and, with only one slipper on, ran to open it, modestly holding her shift across her bosom; but when she opened it she stepped back, seeing what a state Akaky Akakyevitch was in. When he told her what had happened, she clasped her hands in horror and said that he must go straight to the superintendent, that the police constable of the quarter would deceive him, make promises and lead him a dance; that it would be best of all to go to the superintendent, and that she knew him indeed, because Anna the Finnish girl who was once her cook was now in service as a nurse at the superintendent's; and that she often saw him himself when he passed by their house, and that he used to be every Sunday at church too, saying his prayers and at the same time looking good-humoredly at every one, and that therefore by every token he must be a kind-hearted man. After listening to this advice, Akaky Akakyevitch made his way very gloomily to his room, and how he spent that night I leave to the imagination of those who are in the least able to picture the position of others. Early in the morning he set off to the police superintendent's, but was told that he was asleep. He came at ten o'clock, he was told again that he was asleep; he came at eleven and was told that the superintendent was not at home; he came at dinner-time, but the clerks in the anteroom would not let him in, and insisted on knowing what was the matter and what business had brought him and exactly what had happened; so that at last Akaky Akakyevitch for the first time in his life tried to show the strength of his character and said curtly that he must see the superintendent himself, that they dare not refuse to admit him, that he had come from the department on government business, and that if he made complaint of them they would see. The clerks dared say nothing to this, and one of them went to summon the superintendent.

The latter received his story of being robbed of his overcoat in an extremely strange way. Instead of attending to the main point, he began asking Akaky Akakyevitch questions, why had he been coming home so late? Wasn't he going, or hadn't he been, to some house of ill-fame? so that Akaky Akakyevitch was overwhelmed with confusion, and went away without knowing whether or not the proper measures would be taken in regard to his overcoat. He was absent from the office all that day (the only time that it had happened in his life). Next day he appeared with a pale face, wearing his old ``dressing jacket'' which had become a still more pitiful sight. The tidings of the theft of the overcoat—though there were clerks who did not let even this chance slip of jeering at Akaky Akakyevitch—touched many of them. They decided on the spot to get up a subscription for him, but collected only a very trifling sum, because the clerks had already spent a good deal on subscribing to the director's portrait and on the purchase of a book, at the suggestion of the head of their department, who was a friend of the author, and so the total realized was very insignificant. One of the clerks, moved by compassion, ventured at any rate to assist Akaky Akakyevitch with good advice, telling him not to go to the district police inspector, because, though it might happen that the latter might be sufficiently zealous of gaining the approval of his superiors to succeed in finding the overcoat, it would remain in the possession of the police unless he presented legal proofs that it belonged to him; he urged that far the best thing would be to appeal to a Person of Consequence; that the Person of Consequence, by writing and getting into communication with the proper authorities, could push the matter through more successfully. There was nothing else for it. Akaky Akakyevitch made up his mind to go to the Person of Consequence. What precisely was the nature of the functions of the Person of Consequence has remained a matter of uncertainty. It must be noted that this Person of Consequence had only lately become a Person of Consequence, and until recently had been a Person of No Consequence. Though, indeed, his position even now was not reckoned of consequence in comparison with others of still greater consequence. But there is always to be found a circle of persons to whom a Person of Little Consequence in the eyes of others is a Person of Consequence. It is true that he did his utmost to increase the consequence of his position in various ways, for instance by insisting that his subordinates should come out onto the stairs to meet him when he arrived at his office; that no one should venture to approach him directly but all proceedings should be by the strictest order of precedence, that a collegiate registration clerk should report the matter to the provincial secretary, and the provincial secretary to the titular councillor or whomsoever it might be, and that business should only reach him by this channel. Every one in Holy Russia has a craze for imitation, every one apes and mimics his superiors. I have actually been told that a titular councillor who was put in charge of a small separate office, immediately partitioned off a special room for himself, calling it the head office, and set special porters at the door with red collars and gold lace, who took hold of the handle of the door and opened it for every one who went in, though the ''head office'' was so tiny that it was with difficulty that an ordinary writing table could be put into it.

The manners and habits of the Person of Consequence were dignified and majestic but not complex. The chief foundation of his system was strictness, ''strictness, strictness, and—strictness!'' he used to say, and at the last word he would look very significantly at the person he was addressing, though, indeed, he had no reason to do so, for the dozen clerks who made up the whole administrative mechanism of his office stood in befitting awe of him; any clerk who saw him in the distance would leave his work and remain standing at attention till his superior had left the room. His conversation with his subordinates was usually marked by severity and almost confined to three phrases: ''How dare you? Do you know to whom you are speaking? Do you understand who I am?'' He was, however, at heart a good-natured man, pleasant and obliging with his colleagues; but the grade of general had completely turned his head. When he received it, he was perplexed, thrown off his balance, and quite at a loss how to behave. If he chanced to be with his equals, he was still quite a decent man, a very gentlemanly man, in fact, and in many ways even an intelligent man, but as soon as he was in company with men who were even one grade below him, there was simply no doing anything with him: he sat silent and his position excited compassion, the more so as he himself felt that he might have been spending his time to incomparably more advantage. At times there could be seen in his eyes an intense desire to join in some interesting conversation, but he was restrained by the doubt whether it would not be too much on his part, whether it would not be too great a familiarity and lowering of his dignity, and in consequence of these reflections he remained everlastingly in the same mute condition, only uttering from time to time monosyllabic sounds, and in this way he gained the reputation of being a very tiresome man.

So this was the Person of Consequence to whom our friend Akaky Akakyevitch appealed, and he appealed to him at a most unpropitious moment, very unfortunate for himself, though fortunate, indeed, for the Person of Consequence. The latter happened to be in his study, talking in the very best of spirits with an old friend of his childhood who had only just arrived and whom he had not seen for several years. It was at this moment that he was informed that a man called Bashmatchkin was asking to see him. He asked abruptly, ''What sort of man is he?'' and received the answer, ''A government clerk.'' ''Ah! he can wait, I haven't time now,'' said the Person of Consequence. Here I must observe that this was a complete lie on the part of the Person of Consequence: he had time; his friend and he had long ago said all they had to say to each other and their conversation had begun to be broken by very long pauses during which they merely slapped each other on the knee, saying, ''So that's how things are, Ivan Abramovitch!''—''There it is, Stepan Varlamovitch!'' but, for all that, he told the clerk to wait in order to show his friend, who had left the service years before and was living at home in the country, how long clerks had to wait in his anteroom.

At last after they had talked, or rather been silent to their heart's content and had smoked a cigar in very comfortable armchairs with sloping backs, he seemed suddenly to recollect, and said to the secretary, who was standing at the door with papers for his signature: ''Oh, by the way, there is a clerk waiting, isn't there? Tell him he can come in.'' When he saw Akaky Akakyevitch's meek appearance and old uniform, he turned to him at once and said: ''What do you want?'' in a firm and abrupt voice, which he had purposely practised in his own room in solitude before the looking-glass for a week before receiving his present post and the grade of a general. Akaky Akakyevitch, who was overwhelmed with befitting awe beforehand, was somewhat confused and, as far as his tongue would allow him, explained to the best of his powers, with even more frequent ''ers'' than usual, that he had had a perfectly new overcoat and now he had been robbed of it in the most inhuman way, and that now he had come to beg him by his intervention either to correspond with his honor the head policemaster or anybody else, and find the overcoat. This mode of proceeding struck the general for some reason as taking a great liberty. ''What next, sir,'' he went on as abruptly, ''don't you know the way to proceed? To whom are you addressing yourself? Don't you know how things are done? You ought first to have handed in a petition to the office; it would have gone to the head clerk of the room, and to the head clerk of the section, then it would have been handed to the secretary and the secretary would have brought it to me. . . .''

''But, your Excellency,'' said Akaky Akakyevitch, trying to collect all the small allowance of presence of mind he possessed and feeling at the same time that he was getting into a terrible perspiration, ''I ventured, your Excellency, to trouble you because secretaries . . . er . . . are people you can't depend on.''

"What? what? what?" said the Person of Consequence, "where did you get hold of that spirit? Where did you pick up such ideas? What insubordination is spreading among young men against their superiors and betters?" The Person of Consequence did not apparently observe that Akaky Akakyevitch was well over fifty, and therefore if he could have been called a young man it would only have been in comparison with a man of seventy. "Do you know to whom you are speaking? Do you understand who I am? Do you understand that, I ask you?" At this point he stamped, and raised his voice to such a powerful note that Akaky Akakyevitch was not the only one to be terrified. Akaky Akakyevitch was positively petrified; he staggered, trembling all over, and could not stand; if the porters had not run up to support him, he would have flopped upon the floor; he was led out almost unconscious. The Person of Consequence, pleased that the effect had surpassed his expectations and enchanted at the idea that his words could even deprive a man of consciousness, stole a sideway glance at his friend to see how he was taking it, and perceived not without satisfaction that his friend was feeling very uncertain and even beginning to be a little terrified himself.

How he got downstairs, how he went out into the street—of all that Akaky Akakyevitch remembered nothing, he had no feeling in his arms or his legs. In all his life he had never been so severely reprimanded by a general, and this was by one of another department, too. He went out into the snowstorm, that was whistling through the streets, with his mouth open, and as he went he stumbled off the pavement; the wind, as its way is in Petersburg, blew upon him from all points of the compass and from every side street. In an instant it had blown a quinsy into his throat, and when he got home he was not able to utter a word; with a swollen face and throat he went to bed. So violent is sometimes the effect of a suitable reprimand!

Next day he was in a high fever. Thanks to the gracious assistance of the Petersburg climate, the disease made more rapid progress than could have been expected, and when the doctor came, after feeling his pulse he could find nothing to do but prescribe a fomentation, and that simply that the patient might not be left without the benefit of medical assistance; however, two days later he informed him that his end was at hand, after which he turned to his landlady and said: "And you had better lose no time, my good woman, but order him now a deal coffin, for an oak one will be too dear for him." Whether Akaky Akakyevitch heard these fateful words or not, whether they produced a shattering effect upon him, and whether he regretted his pitiful life, no one can tell, for he was all the time in delirium and fever. Apparitions, each stranger than the one before, were continually haunting him: first, he saw Petrovitch and was ordering him to make a greatcoat trimmed with some sort of traps for robbers, who were, he fancied, continually under the bed, and he was calling his landlady every minute to pull out a thief who had even got under the quilt; then he kept asking why his old "dressing jacket" was hanging before him when he had a new overcoat, then he fancied he was standing before the general listening to the appropriate reprimand and saying "I am sorry, your Excellency," then finally he became abusive, uttering the most awful language, so that his old landlady positively crossed herself, having never heard anything of the kind from him before, and the more horrified because these dreadful words followed immediately upon the phrase "your Excellency." Later on, his talk was a mere medley of nonsense, so that it was quite unintelligible; all that could be seen was that his incoherent words and thoughts were concerned with nothing but the overcoat. At last poor Akaky Akakyevitch gave up the ghost. No seal was put upon his room nor upon his things, because in the first place, he had no heirs and, in the second, the property left was very small, to wit, a bundle of goose-feathers, a quire of white government paper, three pairs of socks, two or three buttons that had come off his trousers, and the "dressing jacket" with which the reader is already familiar. Who came into all this wealth God only knows, even I who tell the tale must own that I have not troubled to enquire. And Petersburg remained without Akaky Akakyevitch, as though, indeed, he had never been in the city. A creature had vanished and departed whose cause no one had championed, who was dear to no one, of interest to no one, who never even attracted the attention of the student of natural history, though the latter does not disdain to fix a common fly upon a pin and look at him under the microscope—a creature who bore patiently the jeers of the office and for no particular reason went to his grave, though even he at the very end of his life was visited by a gleam of brightness in the form of an overcoat that for one instant brought color into his poor life—a creature on whom calamity broke as insufferably as it breaks upon the heads of the mighty ones of this world . . . !

Several days after his death, the porter from the department was sent to his lodgings with instructions that he should go at once to the office, for his chief was asking for him; but the porter was obliged to return without him, explaining that he could not come, and to the inquiry "Why?" he added, "Well, you see: the fact is he is dead, he was buried three days ago." This was how they learned at the office of the death of Akaky Akakyevitch, and the next day there was sitting in his seat a new clerk who was very much taller and who wrote not in the same upright hand but made his letters more slanting and crooked.

But who could have imagined that this was not all there was to tell about Akaky Akakyevitch, that he was destined for a few days to make a noise in the world after his death, as though to make up for his life having been unnoticed by any one? But so it happened, and our poor story unexpectedly finishes with a fantastic ending. Rumors were suddenly floating about Petersburg that in the neighborhood of the Kalinkin Bridge and for a little distance beyond, a corpse had taken to appearing at night in the form of a clerk looking for a stolen overcoat, and stripping from the shoulders of all passers-by, regardless of grade and calling, overcoats of all descriptions—trimmed with cat fur, or beaver or wadded, lined with raccoon, fox and bear—made, in fact, of all sorts of skin which men have adapted for the covering of their own. One of the clerks of the department saw the corpse with his own eyes and at once recognized it as Akaky Akakyevitch; but it excited in him such terror, however, that he ran away as fast as his legs could carry him and so could not get a very clear view of him, and only saw him hold up his finger threateningly in the distance.

From all sides complaints were continually coming that backs and shoulders, not of mere titular councillors, but even of upper court councillors, had been exposed to taking chills, owing to being stripped of their greatcoats. Orders were given to the police to catch the corpse regardless of trouble or expense, alive or dead, and to punish him in the cruellest way, as an example to others, and, indeed, they very nearly succeeded in doing so. The sentry of one district police station in Kiryushkin Place snatched a corpse by the collar on the spot of the crime in the very act of attempting to snatch a frieze overcoat from a retired musician, who used in his day to play the flute. Having caught him by the collar, he shouted until he had brought two other comrades, whom he charged to hold him while he felt just a minute in his boot to get out a snuff-box in order to revive his nose which had six times in his life been frost bitten, but the snuff was probably so strong that not even a dead man could stand it. The sentry had hardly had time to put his finger over his right nostril and draw up some snuff in the left when the corpse sneezed violently right into the eyes of all three. While they were putting their fists up to wipe them, the corpse completely vanished, so that they were not even sure whether he had actually been in their hands. From that time forward the sentries conceived such a horror of the dead that they were even afraid to seize the living and confined themselves to shouting from the distance: "Hi, you there, be off!" and the dead clerk began to appear even on the other side of the Kalinkin Bridge, rousing no little terror in all timid people.

We have, however, quite deserted the Person of Consequence, who may in reality almost be said to be the cause of the fantastic ending of this perfectly true story. To begin with, my duty requires me to do justice to the Person of Consequence by recording that soon after poor Akaky Akakyevitch had gone away crushed to powder, he felt something not unlike regret. Sympathy was a feeling not unknown to him; his heart was open to many kindly impulses, although his exalted grade very often prevented them from being shown. As soon as his friend had gone out of his study, he even began brooding over poor Akaky Akakyevitch, and from that time forward he was almost every day haunted by the image of the poor clerk who had succumbed so completely to the befitting reprimand. The thought of the man so worried him that a week later he actually decided to send a clerk to find out how he was and whether he really could help him in any way. And when they brought him word that Akaky Akakyevitch had died suddenly in delirium and fever, it made a great impression on him, his conscience reproached him and he was depressed all day. Anxious to distract his mind and to forget the unpleasant impression, he went to spend the evening with one of his friends, where he found a genteel company and, what was best of all, almost every one was of the same grade so that he was able to be quite free from restraint. This had a wonderful effect on his spirits, he expanded, became affable and genial; in short, spent a very agreeable evening. At supper he drank a couple of glasses of champagne—a proceeding which we all know has a happy effect in inducing good-humor. The champagne made him inclined to do something unusual, and he decided not to go home yet but to visit a lady of his acquaintance, one Karolina Ivanovna—a lady apparently of German extraction, for whom he entertained extremely friendly feelings. It must be noted that the Person of Consequence was a man no longer young, an excellent husband, and the respectable father of a family. He had two sons, one already serving in his office, and a nice-looking daughter of sixteen with a rather turned-up, pretty little nose, who used to come every morning to kiss his hand, saying: *"Bon jour, Papa."* His wife, who was still blooming and decidedly good-looking, indeed, used first to give him her hand to kiss and then would kiss his hand, turning it the other side upwards. But though the Person of Consequence was perfectly satisfied with the kind amenities of his domestic life, he thought it proper to have a lady friend in another quarter of the town. This lady friend was not a bit better looking nor younger than his wife, but these mysterious facts exist in the world and it is not our business to criticize them.

And so the Person of Consequence went downstairs, got into his sledge, and said to his coachman, "To Karolina Ivanovna," while luxuriously wrapped in his warm fur coat he remained in that agreeable frame of mind sweeter to a Russian than anything that could be invented, that is, when one thinks of nothing while thoughts come into the mind of themselves, one pleasanter than the other, without the labor of following them or looking for them. Full of satisfaction, he recalled all the amusing moments of the evening he had spent, all the phrases that had set the little circle laughing; many of them he repeated in an undertone and found them as amusing as before, and so, very naturally, laughed very heartily at them again. From time to time, however, he was disturbed by a gust of wind which, blowing suddenly, God knows whence and wherefore, cut him in the face, pelting him with flakes of snow, puffing out his coat-collar like a sack or suddenly flinging it with unnatural force over his head and giving him endless trouble to extricate himself from it. All at once, the Person of Consequence felt that some one had clutched him very tightly by the collar. Turning round he saw a short man in a shabby old uniform, and not without horror recognized him as Akaky Akakyevitch. The clerk's face was white as snow and looked like that of a corpse, but the horror of the Person of Consequence was beyond all bounds when he saw the mouth of the corpse distorted into speech and, breathing upon him the chill of the grave, it uttered the following words: "Ah, so here you are at last! At last I've . . . er . . . caught you by the collar. It's your overcoat I want, you refused to help me and abused me into the bargain! So now give me yours!'' The poor Person of Consequence very nearly died. Resolute and determined as he was in his office and before subordinates in general, and though any one looking at his manly air and figure would have said: ``Oh, what a man of character!'' yet in this plight he felt, like very many persons of athletic appearance, such terror that not without reason he began to be afraid he would have some sort of fit. He actually flung his overcoat off his shoulders as fast as he could and shouted to his coachman in a voice unlike his own: ``Drive home and make haste!'' The coachman, hearing the tone which he had only heard in critical moments and then accompanied by something even more rousing, hunched his shoulders up to his ears in case of worse following, swung his whip and flew on like an arrow. In a little over six minutes the Person of Consequence was at the entrance of his own house. Pale, panic-stricken, and without his overcoat, he arrived home instead of at Karolina Ivanovna's, dragged himself to his own room and spent the night in great perturbation, so that next morning his daughter said to him at breakfast, ``You look quite pale today, Papa'': but her papa remained mute and said not a word to any one of what had happened to him, where he had been, and where he had been going. The incident made a great impression upon him. Indeed, it happened far more rarely that he said to his subordinates, ``How dare you? Do you understand who I am?'' and he never uttered those words at all until he had first heard all the rights of the case.

What was even more remarkable is that from that time the apparition of the dead clerk ceased entirely: apparently the general's overcoat had fitted him perfectly, anyway nothing more was heard of overcoats being snatched from any one. Many restless and anxious people refused, however, to be pacified, and still maintained that in remote parts of the town the ghost of the dead clerk went on appearing. One sentry in Kolomna, for instance, saw with his own eyes a ghost appear from behind a house; but, being by natural constitution somewhat feeble—so much so that on one occasion an ordinary, well-grown pig, making a sudden dash out of some building, knocked him off his feet to the vast entertainment of the cabmen standing round, from whom he exacted two kopecks each for snuff for such rudeness—he did not dare to stop it, and so followed it in the dark until the ghost suddenly looked round and, stopping, asked him: ``What do you want?'' displaying a fist such as you never see among the living. The sentry said: ``Nothing,'' and turned back on the spot. This ghost, however, was considerably taller and adorned with immense mustaches, and, directing its steps apparently towards Obuhov Bridge, vanished into the darkness of the night.

SUGGESTIONS FOR WRITING AND DISCUSSION

1. What does the term ``Person of Consequence'' mean? To whom does it refer? Can it be applied to something other than an individual?
2. How would you describe the tone of this story?

3. How does the overcoat change Akakyevitch? How does its value change during the course of the story?
4. Why does the ghost appear at the end of the story? What is its significance?
5. In a two- to three-page essay discuss an object that has been unusually important to you. How did it gain greater significance than its monetary worth?

Guy de Maupassant (French, 1850–1893)

The Necklace

She was one of those pretty and charming girls who are sometimes, as if by a mistake of destiny, born in a family of clerks. She had no dowry, no expectations, no means of being known, understood, loved, wedded by any rich and distinguished man; and she let herself be married to a little clerk at the Ministry of Public Instruction.

She dressed plainly because she could not dress well, but she was as unhappy as though she had really fallen from her proper station, since with women there is neither caste nor rank: and beauty, grace, and charm act instead of family and birth. Natural fineness, instinct for what is elegant, suppleness of wit, are the sole hierarchy, and make from women of the people the equals of the very greatest ladies.

She suffered ceaselessly, feeling herself born for all the delicacies and all the luxuries. She suffered from the poverty of her dwelling, from the wretched look of the walls, from the worn-out chairs, from the ugliness of the curtains. All those things, of which another woman of her rank would never even have been conscious, tortured her and made her angry. The sight of the little Breton peasant who did her humble housework aroused in her regrets which were despairing, and distracted dreams. She thought of the silent antechambers hung with Oriental tapestry, lit by tall bronze candelabra, and of the two great footmen in knee breeches who sleep in the big armchairs, made drowsy by the heavy warmth of the hot-air stove. She thought of the long *salons* fitted up with ancient silk, of the delicate furniture carrying priceless curiosities, and of the coquettish perfumed boudoirs made for talks at five o'clock with intimate friends, with men famous and sought after, whom all women envy and whose attention they all desire.

When she sat down to dinner, before the round table covered with a tablecloth three days old, opposite her husband, who uncovered the soup tureen and declared with an enchanted air, ''Ah, the good *pot-au-feu!* I don't known anything better than that,'' she thought of dainty dinners, of shining silverware, of tapestry which peopled the walls with ancient personages and with strange birds flying in the midst of a fairy forest; and she thought of delicious dishes served on marvelous plates, and of the whispered gallantries which you listen to with a sphinxlike smile, while you are eating the pink flesh of a trout or the wings of a quail.

She had no dresses, no jewels, nothing. And she loved nothing but that; she felt made for that. She would so have liked to please, to be envied, to be charming, to be sought after.

She had a friend, a former schoolmate at the convent, who was rich, and whom she did not like to go and see any more, because she suffered so much when she came back.

But one evening, her husband returned home with a triumphant air, and holding a large envelope in his hand.

"There," said he. "Here is something for you."

She tore the paper sharply, and drew out a printed card which bore these words:

"The Minister of Public Instruction and Mme. Georges Ramponneau request the honor of M. and Mme. Loisel's company at the palace of the Ministry on Monday evening, January eighteenth."

Instead of being delighted, as her husband hoped, she threw the invitation on the table with disdain, murmuring:

"What do you want me to do with that?"

"But, my dear, I thought you would be glad. You never go out, and this is such a fine opportunity. I had awful trouble to get it. Everyone wants to go; it is very select, and they are not giving many invitations to clerks. The whole official world will be there."

She looked at him with an irritated eye, and she said, impatiently:

"And what do you want me to put on my back?"

He had not thought of that; he stammered:

"Why, the dress you go to the theater in. It looks very well, to me."

He stopped, distracted, seeing that his wife was crying. Two great tears descended slowly from the corners of her eyes toward the corners of her mouth. He stuttered:

"What's the matter? What's the matter?"

But, by violent effort, she had conquered her grief, and she replied, with a calm voice, while she wiped her wet cheeks:

"Nothing. Only I have no dress and therefore I can't go to this ball. Give your card to some colleague whose wife is better equipped than I."

He was in despair. He resumed:

"Come, let us see, Mathilde. How much would it cost, a suitable dress, which you could use on other occasions, something very simple?"

She reflected several seconds, making her calculations and wondering also what sum she could ask without drawing on herself an immediate refusal and a frightened exclamation from the economical clerk.

Finally, she replied, hesitatingly:

"I don't know exactly, but I think I could manage it with four hundred francs."

He had grown a little pale, because he was laying aside just that amount to buy a gun and treat himself to a little shooting next summer on the plain of Nanterre, with several friends who went to shoot larks down there, of a Sunday.

But he said:

"All right. I will give you four hundred francs. And try to have a pretty dress."

The day of the ball drew near, and Mme. Loisel seemed sad, uneasy, anxious. Her dress was ready, however. Her husband said to her one evening:

"What is the matter? Come, you've been so queer these last three days."

And she answered:

"It annoys me not to have a single jewel, not a single stone, nothing to put on. I shall look like distress. I should almost rather not go at all."

He resumed:

"You might wear natural flowers. It's very stylish at this time of the year. For ten francs you can get two or three magnificent roses."

She was not convinced.

"No; there's nothing more humiliating than to look poor among other women who are rich."

But her husband cried:

"How stupid you are! Go look up your friend Mme. Forestier, and ask her to lend you some jewels. You're quite thick enough with her to do that."

She uttered a cry of joy:

"It's true. I never thought of it."

The next day she went to her friend and told of her distress.

Mme. Forestier went to a wardrobe with a glass door, took out a large jewel-box, brought it back, opened it, and said to Mme. Loisel:

"Choose, my dear."

She saw first of all some bracelets, then a pearl necklace, then a Venetian cross, gold and precious stones of admirable workmanship. She tried on the ornaments before the glass, hesitated, could not make up her mind to part with them, to give them back. She kept asking:

"Haven't you any more?"

"Why, yes. Look. I don't know what you like."

All of a sudden she discovered, in a black satin box, a superb necklace of diamonds, and her heart began to beat with an immoderate desire. Her hands trembled as she took it. She fastened it around her throat, outside her high-necked dress, and remained lost in ecstasy at the sight of herself.

Then she asked, hesitating, filled with anguish:

"Can you lend me that, only that?"

"Why, yes, certainly."

She sprang upon the neck of her friend, kissed her passionately, then fled with her treasure.

The day of the ball arrived. Mme. Loisel made a great success. She was prettier than them all, elegant, gracious, smiling, and crazy with joy. All the men looked at her, asked her name, endeavored to be introduced. All the attachés of the Cabinet wanted to waltz with her. She was remarked by the minister himself.

She danced with intoxication, with passion, made drunk by pleasure, forgetting all, in the triumph of her beauty, in the glory of her success, in a sort of cloud of happiness composed of all this homage, of all this admiration, of all these awakened desires, and of that sense of complete victory which is so sweet to a woman's heart.

She went away about four o'clock in the morning. Her husband had been sleeping since midnight, in a little deserted anteroom, with three other gentlemen whose wives were having a very good time. He threw over her shoulders the wraps which he had brought, modest wraps of common life, whose poverty contrasted with the elegance of the ball dress. She felt this, and wanted to escape so as not to be remarked by the other women, who were enveloping themselves in costly furs.

Loisel held her back.

"Wait a bit. You will catch cold outside. I will go and call a cab."

But she did not listen to him, and rapidly descended the stairs. When they were in the street they did not find a carriage; and they began to look for one, shouting after the cabmen whom they saw passing by at a distance.

They went down toward the Seine, in despair, shivering with cold. At last they found on the quay one of those ancient noctambulant coupés which, exactly as if they were ashamed to show their misery during the day, are never seen round Paris until after nightfall.

It took them to their door in the Rue des Martyrs, and once more, sadly, they climbed up homeward. All was ended, for her. And as to him, he reflected that he must be at the Ministry at ten o'clock.

She removed the wraps, which covered her shoulders, before the glass, so as once more to see herself in all her glory. But suddenly she uttered a cry. She had no longer the necklace around her neck!

Her husband, already half undressed, demanded:

"What is the matter with you?"

She turned madly towards him:

"I have—I have—I've lost Mme. Forestier's necklace."

He stood up, distracted.

"What!—how?—impossible!"

And they looked in the folds of her dress, in the folds of her cloak, in her pockets, everywhere. They did not find it.

He asked:

"You're sure you had it on when you left the ball?"

"Yes, I felt it in the vestibule of the palace."

"But if you had lost it in the street we should have heard it fall. It must be in the cab."

"Yes. Probably. Did you take his number?"

"No. And you, didn't you notice it?"

"No."

They looked, thunderstruck, at one another. At last Loisel put on his clothes.

"I shall go back on foot," said he, "over the whole route which we have taken to see if I can find it."

And he went out. She sat waiting on a chair in her ball dress, without strength to go to bed, overwhelmed, without fire, without a thought.

Her husband came back about seven o'clock. He had found nothing.

He went to Police Headquarters, to the newspaper offices, to offer a reward; he went to the cab companies—everywhere, in fact, whither he was urged by the least suspicion of hope.

She waited all day, in the same condition of mad fear before this terrible calamity.

Loisel returned at night with a hollow, pale face; he had discovered nothing.

"You must write to your friend," said he, "that you have broken the clasp of her necklace and that you are having it mended. That will give us time to turn round."

She wrote at his dictation.

At the end of a week they had lost all hope.

And Loisel, who had aged five years, declared:

"We must consider how to replace that ornament."

The next day they took the box which had contained it, and they went to the jeweler whose name was found within. He consulted his books.

"It was not I, madame, who sold that necklace; I must simply have furnished the case."

Then they went from jeweler to jeweler, searching for a necklace like the other, consulting their memories, sick both of them with chagrin and anguish.

They found, in a shop at the Palais Royal, a string of diamonds which seemed to them exactly like the one they looked for. It was worth forty thousand francs. They could have it for thirty-six.

So they begged the jeweler not to sell it for three days yet. And they made a bargain that he should buy it back for thirty-four thousand francs, in case they found the other one before the end of February.

Loisel possessed eighteen thousand francs which his father had left him. He would borrow the rest.

He did borrow, asking a thousand francs of one, five hundred of another, five louis here, three louis there. He gave notes, took up ruinous obligations, dealt with usurers and all the race of lenders. He compromised all the rest of his life, risked his signature without even knowing if he could meet it, and, frightened by the pains yet to come, by the black misery which was about to fall upon him, by the prospect of all the physical privations and of all the moral tortures which he was to suffer, he went to get the new necklace, putting down upon the merchant's counter thirty-six thousand francs.

When Mme. Loisel took back the necklace, Mme. Forestier said to her, with a chilly manner:

"You should have returned it sooner; I might have needed it."

She did not open the case, as her friend had so much feared. If she had detected the substitution, what would she have thought, what would she had said? Would she not have taken Mme. Loisel for a thief?

Mme. Loisel now knew the horrible existence of the needy. She took her part, moreover, all of a sudden, with heroism. That dreadful debt must be paid. She would pay it. They dismissed their servant; they changed their lodgings; they rented a garret under the roof.

She came to know what heavy housework meant and the odious cares of the kitchen. She washed the dishes, using her rosy nails on the greasy pots and pans. She washed the dirty linen, the shirts, and the dishcloths, which she dried upon a line; she carried the slops down to the street every morning, and carried up the water, stopping for breath at every landing. And, dressed like a woman of the people, she went to the fruiterer, the grocer, the butcher, her basket on her arm, bargaining, insulted, defending her miserable money sou by sou.

Each month they had to meet some notes, renew others, obtain more time.

Her husband worked in the evening making a fair copy of some tradesman's accounts, and late at night he often copied manuscript for five sous a page.

And this life lasted for ten years.

At the end of ten years, they had paid everything, everything, with the rates of usury, and the accumulations of the compound interest.

Mme. Loisel looked old now. She had become the woman of impoverished households—strong and hard and rough. With frowsy hair, skirts askew, and red hands, she talked loud while washing the floor with great swishes of water. But sometimes, when her husband was at the office, she sat down near the window, and she thought of that gay evening of long ago, of that ball where she had been so beautiful and so fêted.

What would have happened if she had not lost that necklace? Who knows? Who knows? How life is strange and changeful! How little a thing is needed for us to be lost or to be saved!

But, one Sunday, having gone to take a walk in the Champs Elysées to refresh herself from the labor of the week, she suddenly perceived a woman who was leading a child. It was Mme. Forestier, still young, still beautiful, still charming.

Mme. Loisel felt moved. Was she going to speak to her? Yes, certainly. And now that she had paid, she was going to tell her all about it. Why not?

She went up.

"Good-day, Jeanne."

The other, astonished to be familiarly addressed by this plain good-wife, did not recognize her at all, and stammered:

"But—madam!—I do not know—You must be mistaken."

"No. I am Mathilde Loisel."

Her friend uttered a cry.

"Oh, my poor Mathilde! How you are changed!"

"Yes, I have had days hard enough, since I have seen you, days wretched enough—and that because of you!"

"Of me! How so?"

"Do you remember that diamond necklace which you lent me to wear at the ministerial ball?"

"Yes. Well?"

"Well, I lost it."

"What do you mean? You brought it back."

"I brought you back another just like it. And for this we have been ten years paying. You can understand that it was not easy for us, us who had nothing. At last it is ended, and I am very glad."

Mme. Forestier had stopped.

"You say that you bought a necklace of diamonds to replace mine?"

"Yes. You never noticed it, then! They were very like."

And she smiled with a joy which was proud and naïve at once.

Mme. Forestier, strongly moved, took her two hands.

"Oh, my poor Mathilde! Why, my necklace was paste. It was worth at most five hundred francs!"

SUGGESTIONS FOR WRITING AND DISCUSSION

1. This brief story covers more than ten years. Examine and discuss de Maupassant's use of summary and details.
2. What comment does this story make about the value of work?
3. This story has a surprise ending. How does the ending change your perception of the rest of the story? Do you think the ending is ironic?
4. Describe the husband. What part does he play in the story?
5. In a two- to three-page essay write a character sketch of Mathilde. How would you describe her at the beginning of the story? How does she change in the course of the story? At what point in the story does she seem happiest?
6. Write a short (five- to seven-page) story in which an object plays a major role.

Sarah Orne Jewett (American, 1849–1909)

Tom's Husband

I shall not dwell long upon the circumstances that led to the marriage of my hero and heroine; though their courtship was, to them, the only one that has ever noticeably approached the ideal, it had many aspects in which it was entirely commonplace in other people's eyes. While the world in general smiles at lovers with kindly approval and sympathy, it refuses to be aware of the unprecedented delight which is amazing to the lovers themselves.

But, as has been true in many other cases, when they were at last married, the most ideal of situations was found to have been changed to the most practical. Instead of having shared their original duties, and, as school-boys would say, going halves, they discovered that the cares of life had been doubled. This led to some distressing moments for both our friends; they understood suddenly that instead of dwelling in heaven they were still upon earth, and had made themselves slaves to new laws and limitations. Instead of being freer and happier than ever before, they had assumed new responsibilities; they had established a new household, and must fulfill in some way or another the obligations of it. They looked back with affection to their engagement; they had been longing to have each other to themselves, apart from the world, but it seemed that they never felt so keenly that they were still units in modern society. Since Adam and Eve were in Paradise, before the devil joined them, nobody has had a chance to imitate that unlucky couple. In some respects they told the truth when, twenty times a day, they said that life had never been so pleasant before; but there were mental reservations on either side which might have subjected them to the accusation of lying. Somehow, there was a little feeling of disappointment, and they caught themselves wondering—though they would have died sooner than confess it—whether they were quite so happy as they had expected. The truth was, they were much happier than people usually are, for they had an uncommon capacity for enjoyment. For a little while they were like a sail-boat that is beating and has to drift a few minutes before it can catch the wind and start off on the other tack. And they had the same feeling, too, that any one is likely to have who has been long pursuing some object of his ambition or desire. Whether it is a coin, or a picture, or a stray volume of some old edition of Shakespeare, or whether it is an office under government or a lover, when fairly in one's grasp there is a loss of the eagerness that was felt in pursuit. Satisfaction, even after one has dined well, is not so interesting and eager a feeling as hunger.

My hero and heroine were reasonably well established to begin with: they each had some money, though Mr. Wilson had most. His father had at one time been a rich man, but with the decline, a few years before, of manufacturing interests, he had become, mostly through the fault of others, somewhat involved; and at the time of his death his affairs were in such a condition that it was still a question whether a very large sum or a moderately large one would represent his estate. Mrs. Wilson, Tom's step-mother, was somewhat of an invalid; she suffered severely at times with asthma, but she was almost entirely relieved by living in another part of the country. While her husband lived, she had accepted her illness as inevitable, and rarely left home; but during the last few years she had lived in Philadelphia with her own people, making short and wheezing visits only from time to time, and had not undergone a voluntary period of suffering since the occasion of Tom's marriage, which she had entirely approved. She had a sufficient property of her own, and she and Tom were independent of each other in that way. Her only other step-child was a daughter, who had married a navy officer, and had at this time gone out to spend three years (or less) with her husband, who had been ordered to Japan.

It is not unfrequently noticed that in many marriages one of the persons who choose each other as partners for life is said to have thrown himself or herself away, and the relatives and friends look on with dismal forebodings and ill-concealed submission. In this case it was the wife who might have done so much better, according to public opinion. She did not think so herself, luckily, either before marriage or afterward, and I do not think it occurred to her to picture to herself the sort of career which would have been her alternative. She had been an only child, and had usually taken her own way. Some one once said that it was a great pity that she had not been obliged to work for her living, for she had inherited a most uncommon business talent, and, without being disreputably keen at a bargain, her insight into the practical working of affairs was very clear and far-reaching. Her father, who had also been a manufacturer, like Tom's, had often said it had been a mistake that she was a girl instead of a boy. Such executive ability as hers is often wasted in the more contracted sphere of women, and is apt to be more a disadvantage than a help. She was too independent and self-reliant for a wife; it would seem at first thought that she needed a wife herself more than she did a husband. Most men like best the women whose natures cling and appeal to theirs for protection. But Tom Wilson, while he did not wish to be protected himself, liked these very qualities in his wife which would have displeased some other men; to tell the truth, he was very much in love with his wife just as she was. He was a successful collector of almost everything but money, and during a great part of his life he had been an invalid, and he had grown, as he laughingly confessed, very old-womanish. He had been badly lamed, when a boy, by being caught in some machinery in his father's mill, near which he was idling one afternoon, and though he had almost entirely outgrown the effect of his injury, it had not been until after many years. He had been in college, but his eyes had given out there, and he had been obliged to leave in the middle of his junior year, though he had kept up a pleasant intercourse with the members of his class, with whom he had been a great favorite. He was a good deal of an idler in the world. I do not think his ambition, except in the case of securing Mary Dunn for his wife, had ever been distinct; he seemed to make the most he could of each day as it came, without making all his days' works tend toward some grand result, and go toward the upbuilding of some grand plan and purpose. He consequently gave no promise of being either distinguished or great. When his eyes would allow, he was an indefatigable reader; and although he would have said that he read only for amusement, yet he amused himself with books that were well worth the time he spent over them.

The house where he lived nominally belonged to his step-mother, but she had taken for granted that Tom would bring his wife home to it, and assured him that it should be to all intents and purposes his. Tom was deeply attached to the old place, which was altogether the pleasantest in town. He had kept bachelor's hall there most of the time since his father's death, and he had taken great pleasure, before his marriage, in refitting it to some extent, though it was already comfortable and furnished in remarkably good taste. People said of him that if it had not been for his illnesses, and if he had been a poor boy, he probably would have made something of himself. As it was, he was not very well known by the townspeople, being somewhat reserved, and not taking much interest in their every-day subjects of conversation. Nobody liked him so well as they liked his wife, yet there was no reason why he should be disliked enough to have much said about him.

After our friends had been married for some time, and had outlived the first strangeness of the new order of things, and had done their duty to their neighbors with so much apparent willingness and generosity that even Tom himself was liked a great deal better than he ever had been before, they were sitting together one stormy evening in the library, before the fire. Mrs. Wilson had been reading Tom the letters which had come to him by the night's mail. There was a long one from his sister in Nagasaki, which had been written with a good deal of ill-disguised reproach. She complained of the smallness of the income of her share in her father's estate, and said that she had been assured by American friends that the smaller mills were starting up everywhere, and beginning to do well again. Since so much of their money was invested in the factory, she had been surprised and sorry to find by Tom's last letters that he had seemed to have no idea of putting in a proper person as superintendent, and going to work again. Four per cent on her other property, which she had been told she must soon expect instead of eight, would make a great difference to her. A navy captain in a foreign port was obliged to entertain a great deal, and Tom must know that it cost them much more to live than it did him, and ought to think of their interests. She hoped he would talk over what was best to be done with their mother (who had been made executor, with Tom, of his father's will).

Tom laughed a little, but looked disturbed. His wife had said something to the same effect, and his mother had spoken once or twice in her letters of the prospect of starting the mill again. He was not a bit of a business man, and he did not feel certain, with the theories which he had arrived at of the state of the country, that it was safe yet to spend the money which would have to be spent in putting the mill in order. "They think that the minute it is going again we shall be making money hand over hand, just as father did when we were children," he said. "It is going to cost us no end of money before we can make anything. Before father died he meant to put in a good deal of new machinery, I remember. I don't know anything about the business myself, and I would have sold out long ago if I had had an offer that came anywhere near the value. The larger mills are the only ones that are good for anything now, and we should have to bring a crowd of French Canadians here; the day is past for the people who live in this part of the country to go into the factory again. Even the Irish all go West when they come into the country, and don't come to places like this any more."

"But there are a good many of the old work-people down in the village," said Mrs. Wilson. "Jack Towne asked me the other day if you weren't going to start up in the spring."

Tom moved uneasily in his chair. "I'll put you in for superintendent, if you like," he said, half angrily, whereupon Mary threw the newspaper at him; but by the time he had thrown it back he was in good humor again.

"Do you know, Tom," she said, with amazing seriousness, "that I believe I should like nothing in the world so much as to be the head of a large business? I hate keeping house,—I always did; and I never did so much of it in all my life put together as I have since I have been married. I suppose it isn't womanly to say so, but if I could escape from the whole thing I believe I should be perfectly happy. If you get rich when the mill is going again, I shall beg for a housekeeper, and shirk everything. I give you fair warning. I don't believe I keep this house half so well as you did before I came here."

Tom's eyes twinkled. "I am going to have that glory,—I don't think you do, Polly; but you can't say that I have not been forbearing. I certainly have not told you more than twice how we used to have things cooked. I'm not going to be your kitchen-colonel."

"Of course it seemed the proper thing to do," said his wife, meditatively; "but I think we should have been even happier than we have if I had been spared it. I have had some days of wretchedness that I shudder to think of. I never know what to have for breakfast; and I ought not to say it, but I don't mind the sight of dust. I look upon housekeeping as my life's great discipline"; and at this pathetic confession they both laughed heartily.

"I've a great mind to take it off your hands," said Tom. "I always rather liked it, to tell the truth, and I ought to be a better housekeeper,—I have been at it for five years; though housekeeping for one is different from what it is for two, and one of them a woman. You see you have brought a different element into my family. Luckily, the servants are pretty well drilled. I do think you upset them a good deal at first!"

Mary Wilson smiled as if she only half heard what he was saying. She drummed with her foot on the floor and looked intently at the fire, and presently gave it a vigorous poking. "Well?" said Tom, after he had waited patiently as long as he could.

"Tom! I'm going to propose something to you. I wish you would really do as you said, and take all the home affairs under your care, and let me start the mill. I am certain I could manage it. Of course I should get people who understood the thing to teach me. I believe I was made for it; I should like it above all things. And this is what I will do: I will bear the cost of starting it, myself,—I think I have money enough, or can get it; and if I have not put affairs in the right trim at the end of a year I will stop, and you may make some other arrangement. If I have, you and your mother and sister can pay me back."

"So I am going to be the wife, and you the husband," said Tom, a little indignantly; "at least, that is what people will say. It's a regular Darby and Joan affair, and you think you can do more work in a day than I can do in three. Do you know that you must go to town to buy cotton? And do you know there are a thousand things about it that you don't know?"

"And never will?" said Mary, with perfect good humor. "Why, Tom, I can learn as well as you, and a good deal better, for I like business, and you don't. You forget that I was always father's right-hand man after I was a dozen years old, and that you have let me invest my money and some of your own, and I haven't made a blunder yet."

Tom thought that his wife had never looked so handsome or so happy. "I don't care, I should rather like the fun of knowing what people will say. It is a new departure, at any rate. Women think they can do everything better than men in these days, but I'm the first man, apparently, who has wished he were a woman."

"Of course people will laugh," said Mary, "but they will say that it's just like me, and think I am fortunate to have married a man who will let me do as I choose. I don't see why it isn't sensible: you will be living exactly as you were before you married, as to home affairs; and since it was a good thing for you to know something about housekeeping then, I can't imagine why you shouldn't go on with it now, since it makes me miserable, and I am wasting a fine business talent while I do it. What do we care for people's talking about it?"

"It seems to me that it is something like women's smoking: it isn't wicked, but it isn't the custom of the country. And I don't like the idea of your going among business men. Of course I should be above going with you, and having people think I must be an idiot; they would say that you married a manufacturing interest, and I was thrown in. I can foresee that my pride is going to be humbled to the dust in every way," Tom declared in mournful tones, and began to shake with laughter. "It is one of your lovely castles in the air, dear Polly, but an old brick mill needs a better foundation than the clouds. No, I'll look around, and get an honest, experienced man for agent. I suppose it's the best thing we can do, for the machinery ought not to lie still any longer; but I mean to sell the factory as soon as I can. I devoutly wish it would take fire, for the insurance would be the best price we are likely to get. That is a famous letter from Alice! I am afraid the captain has been growling over his pay, or they have been giving too many little dinners on board ship. If we were rid of the mill, you and I might go out there this winter. It would be capital fun."

Mary smiled again in an absent-minded way. Tom had an uneasy feeling that he had not heard the end of it yet, but nothing more was said for a day or two. When Mrs. Tom Wilson announced, with no apparent thought of being contradicted, that she had entirely made up her mind, and she meant to see those men who had been overseers of the different departments, who still lived in the village, and have the mill put in order at once, Tom looked disturbed, but made no opposition; and soon after breakfast his wife formally presented him with a handful of keys, and told him there was some lamb in the house for dinner; and presently he heard the wheels of her little phaeton rattling off down the road. I should be untruthful if I tried to persuade any one that he was not provoked; he thought she would at least have waited for his formal permission, and at first he meant to take another horse, and chase her, and bring her back in disgrace, and put a stop to the whole thing. But something assured him that she knew what she was about, and he determined to let her have her own way. If she failed, it might do no harm, and this was the only ungallant thought he gave her. He was sure that she would do nothing unladylike, or be unmindful of his dignity; and he believed it would be looked upon as one of her odd, independent freaks, which always had won respect in the end, however much they had been laughed at in the beginning. "Susan," said he, as that estimable person went by the door with the dust-pan, "you may tell Catherine to come to me for orders about the house, and you may do so yourself. I am going to take charge again, as I did before I was married. It is no trouble to me, and Mrs. Wilson dislikes it. Besides, she is going into business, and will have a great deal else to think of."

"Yes, sir; very well, sir," said Susan, who was suddenly moved to ask so many questions that she was utterly silent. But her master looked very happy; there was evidently no disapproval of his wife; and she went on up the stairs, and began to sweep them down, knocking the dust-brush about excitedly, as if she were trying to kill a descending colony of insects.

Tom went out to the stable and mounted his horse, which had been waiting for him to take his customary after-breakfast ride to the post-office, and he galloped down the road in quest of the phaeton. He saw Mary talking with Jack Towne, who had been an overseer and a valued workman of his father's. He was looking much surprised and pleased.

"I wasn't caring so much about getting work, myself," he explained; "I've got what will carry me and my wife through; but it'll be better for the young folks about here to work near home. My nephews are wanting something to do; they were going to Lynn next week. I don't say but I should like to be to work in the old place again. I've sort of missed it, since we shut down."

"I'm sorry I was so long in overtaking you," said Tom, politely, to his wife. "Well, Jack, did Mrs. Wilson tell you she's going to start the mill? You must give her all the help you can."

"'Deed I will," said Mr. Towne, gallantly, without a bit of astonishment.

"I don't know much about the business yet," said Mrs. Wilson, who had been a little overcome at Jack Towne's lingo of the different rooms and machinery, and who felt an overpowering sense of having a great deal before her in the next few weeks. "By the time the mill is ready, I will be ready, too," she said, taking heart a little; and Tom, who was quick to understand her moods, could not help laughing, as he rode alongside. "We want a new barrel of flour, Tom, dear," she said, by way of punishment for his untimely mirth.

If she lost courage in the long delay, or was disheartened at the steady call for funds, she made no sign; and after a while the mill started up, and her cares were lightened, so that she told Tom that before next pay day she would like to go to Boston for a few days, and go to the theatre, and have a frolic and a rest. She really looked pale and thin, and she said she never worked so hard in all her life; but nobody knew how happy she was, and she was so glad she had married Tom, for some men would have laughed at it.

"I laughed at it," said Tom, meekly. "All is, if I don't cry by and by, because I am a beggar, I shall be lucky." But Mary looked fearlessly serene, and said that there was no danger at present.

It would have been ridiculous to expect a dividend the first year, though the Nagasaki people were pacified with difficulty. All the business letters came to Tom's address, and everybody who was not directly concerned thought that he was the motive power of the reawakened enterprise. Sometimes business people came to the mill, and were amazed at having to confer with Mrs. Wilson, but they soon had to respect her talents and her success. She was helped by the old clerk, who had been promptly recalled and reinstated, and she certainly did capitally well. She was laughed at, as she had expected to be, and people said they should think Tom would be ashamed of himself; but it soon appeared that he was not to blame, and what reproach was offered was on the score of his wife's oddity. There was nothing about the mill that she did not understand before very long, and at the end of the second year she declared a small dividend with great pride and triumph. And she was congratulated on her success, and every one thought of her project in a different way from the way they had thought of it in the beginning. She had singularly good fortune: at the end of the third year she was making money for herself and her friends faster than most people were, and approving letters began to come from Nagasaki. The Ashtons had been ordered to stay in that region, and it was evident that they were continually being obliged to entertain more instead of less. Their children were growing fast, too, and constantly becoming more expensive. The captain and his wife had already begun to congratulate themselves secretly that their two sons would in all probability come into possession, one day, of their uncle Tom's handsome property.

For a good while Tom enjoyed life, and went on his quiet way serenely. He was anxious at first, for he thought that Mary was going to make ducks and drakes of his money and her own. And then he did not exactly like the looks of the thing, either; he feared that his wife was growing successful as a business person at the risk of losing her womanliness. But as time went on, and he found there was no fear of that, he accepted the situation philosophically. He gave up his collection of engravings, having become more interested in one of coins and medals, which took up most of his leisure time. He often went to the city in pursuit of such treasures, and gained much renown in certain quarters as a numismatologist of great skill and experience. But at last his house (which had almost kept itself, and had given him little to do beside ordering the dinners, while faithful old Catherine and her niece Susan were his aids) suddenly became a great care to him. Catherine, who had been the mainstay of the family for many years, died after a short illness, and Susan must needs choose that time, of all others, for being married to one of the second hands in the mill. There followed a long and dismal season of experimenting, and for a time there was a procession of incapable creatures going in at one kitchen door and out of the other. His wife would not have liked to say so, but it seemed to her that Tom was growing fussy about the house affairs, and took more notice of those minor details than he used. She wished more than once, when she was tired, that he would not talk so much about the housekeeping; he seemed sometimes to have no other thought.

In the early days of Mrs. Wilson's business life, she had made it a rule to consult her husband on every subject of importance; but it had speedily proved to be a formality. Tom tried manfully to show a deep interest which he did not feel, and his wife gave up, little by little, telling him much about her affairs. She said that she liked to drop business when she came home in the evening; and at last she fell into the habit of taking a nap on the library sofa, while Tom, who could not use his eyes much by lamp-light, sat smoking or in utter idleness before the fire. When they were first married his wife had made it a rule that she should always read him the evening papers, and afterward they had always gone on with some book of history or philosophy, in which they were both interested. These evenings of their early married life had been charming to both of them, and from time to time one would say to the other that they ought to take up again the habit of reading together. Mary was so unaffectedly tired in the evening that Tom never liked to propose a walk; for, though he was not a man of peculiarly social nature, he had always been accustomed to pay an occasional evening visit to his neighbors in the village. And though he had little interest in the business world, and still less knowledge of it, after a while he wished that his wife would have more to say about what she was planning and doing, or how things were getting on. He thought that her chief aid, old Mr. Jackson, was far more in her thoughts than he. She was forever quoting Jackson's opinions. He did not like to find that she took it for granted that he was not interested in the welfare of his own property; it made him feel like a sort of pensioner and dependent, though, when they had guests at the house, which was by no means seldom, there was nothing in her manner that would imply that she thought herself in any way the head of the family. It was hard work to find fault with his wife in any way, though, to give him his due, he rarely tried.

But, this being a wholly unnatural state of things, the reader must expect to hear of its change at last, and the first blow from the enemy was dealt by an old woman, who lived near by, and who called to Tom one morning, as he was driving down to the village in a great hurry (to post a letter, which ordered his agent to secure a long-wished-for ancient copper coin, at any price), to ask him if they had made yeast that week, and if she could borrow a cupful, as her own had met with some misfortune. Tom was instantly in a rage, and he mentally condemned her to some undeserved fate, but told her aloud to go and see the cook. This slight delay, besides being killing to his dignity, caused him to lose the mail, and in the end his much-desired copper coin. It was a hard day for him, altogether; it was Wednesday, and the first days of the week having been stormy the washing was very late. And Mary came home to dinner provokingly good-natured. She had met an old school-mate and her husband driving home from the mountains, and had first taken them over her factory, to their great amusement and delight, and then had brought them home to dinner. Tom greeted them cordially, and manifested his usual graceful hospitality; but the minute he saw his wife alone he said in a plaintive tone of rebuke, ``I should think you might have remembered that the servants are unusually busy to-day. I do wish you would take a little interest in things at home. The women have been washing, and I'm sure I don't know what sort of a dinner we can give your friends. I wish you had thought to bring home some steak. I have been busy myself, and couldn't go down to the village. I thought we would only have a lunch.''

Mary was hungry, but she said nothing, except that it would be all right,—she didn't mind; and perhaps they could have some canned soup.

She often went to town to buy or look at cotton, or to see some improvement in machinery, and she brought home beautiful bits of furniture and new pictures for the house, and showed a touching thoughtfulness in remembering Tom's fancies; but somehow he had an uneasy suspicion that she could get along pretty well without him when it came to the deeper wishes and hopes of her life, and that her most important concerns were all matters in which he had no share. He seemed to himself to have merged his life in his wife's; he lost his interest in things outside the house and grounds; he felt himself fast growing rusty and behind the times, and to have somehow missed a good deal in life; he had a suspicion that he was a failure. One day the thought rushed over him that his had been almost exactly the experience of most women, and he wondered if it really was any more disappointing and ignominious to him than it was to women themselves. "Some of them may be contented with it," he said to himself, soberly. "People think women are designed for such careers by nature, but I don't know why I ever made such a fool of myself."

Having once seen his situation in life from such a standpoint, he felt it day by day to be more degrading, and he wondered what he should do about it; and once, drawn by a new, strange sympathy, he went to the little family burying-ground. It was one of the mild, dim days that come sometimes in early November, when the pale sunlight is like the pathetic smile of a sad face, and he sat for a long time on the limp, frost-bitten grass beside his mother's grave.

But when he went home in the twilight his step-mother, who just then was making them a little visit, mentioned that she had been looking through some boxes of hers that had been packed long before and stowed away in the garret. "Everything looks very nice up there," she said, in her wheezing voice (which, worse than usual that day, always made him nervous); and added, without any intentional slight to his feelings, "I do think you have always been a most excellent housekeeper."

"I'm tired of such nonsense!" he exclaimed, with surprising indignation. "Mary, I wish you to arrange your affairs so that you can leave them for six months at least. I am going to spend this winter in Europe."

"Why, Tom, dear!" said his wife, appealingly. "I couldn't leave my business any way in the"—

But she caught sight of a look on his usually placid countenance that was something more than decision, and refrained from saying anything more.

And three weeks from that day they sailed.

SUGGESTIONS FOR WRITING AND DISCUSSION

1. Jewett tells us that Tom was not as well liked as Mary. Discuss the reasons for this.

2. In a two- to three-page essay discuss the ways in which Tom becomes Mary's wife.

3. At the end of the story Tom insists that they go to Europe. Does this seem consistent with his role as the wife? What does it suggest about the future of Tom and Mary's relationship?

4. Mary obviously gets considerable satisfaction from her work. Is this also true for Tom? Does the story suggest that running a factory is more valuable than running a house? What comment does the story make on the effect of housework?
5. Are there jobs which can only be done by one sex? If so, why? Make an argument for allowing either men or women to enter some profession which has not been traditionally open to them.
6. This story makes a strong case for the right to satisfying work. Jewett does not, however, seem to take account of the fact that many people work not for satisfaction but out of need. In a three- to four-page essay analyze the importance of money in this story. Is it possible to imagine Jewett setting this story against a less affluent background?

John Updike (American, 1932–   )

A & P

In walks these three girls in nothing but bathing suits I'm in the third checkout slot, with my back to the door, so I don't see them until they're over by the bread. The one that caught my eye first was the one in the plaid green two-piece. She was a chunky kid, with a good tan and a sweet broad soft-looking can with those two crescents of white just under it, where the sun never seems to hit, at the top of the backs of her legs. I stood there with my hand on a box of HiHo crackers trying to remember if I rang it up or not. I ring it up again and the customer starts giving me hell. She's one of these cash-register-watchers, a witch about fifty with rouge on her cheekbones and no eyebrows, and I know it made her day to trip me up. She's been watching cash registers for fifty years and probably never seen a mistake before.

By the time I got her feathers smoothed and her goodies into a bag—she gives me a little snort in passing, if she'd been born at the right time they would have burned her over in Salem—by the time I get her on her way the girls had circled around the bread and were coming back, without a pushcart, back my way along the counters, in the aisle between the checkouts and the Special bins. They didn't even have shoes on. There was this chunky one, with the two-piece—it was bright green and the seams on the bra were still sharp and her belly was still pretty pale so I guessed she just got it (the suit)—there was this one, with one of those chubby berry-faces, the lips all bunched together under her nose, this one, and a tall one, with black hair that hadn't quite frizzed right, and one of these sunburns right across under the eyes, and a chin that was too long—you know, the kind of girl other girls think is very ``striking'' and ``attractive'' but never quite makes it, as they very well know, which is why they like her so much—and then the third one, that wasn't quite so tall. She was the queen. She kind of led them, the other two peeking around and making their shoulders round. She didn't look around, not this queen, she just walked straight on slowly, on these long white pri-madonna legs. She came down a little hard on her heels, as if she didn't walk in bare feet that much, putting down her heels and then letting the weight move along to her toes as if she was testing the floor with every step, putting a little deliberate extra action into it. You never know for sure how girls' minds work (do you really think it's a mind in there or just a little buzz like a bee in a glass jar?) but you got the idea she had talked the other two into coming in here with her, and now she was showing them how to do it, walk slow and hold yourself straight.

She had on a kind of dirty-pink—beige maybe, I don't know—bath-ing suit with a little nubble all over it and, what got me, the straps were down. They were off her shoulders looped loose around the cool tops of her arms, and I guess as a result the suit had slipped a little on her, so all around the top of the cloth there was this shining rim. If it hadn't been there you wouldn't have known there could have been anything whiter than those shoulders. With the straps pushed off, there was nothing between the top of the suit and the top of her head except just *her,* this clean bare plane of the top of her chest down from the shoulder bones like a dented sheet of metal tilted in the light. I mean, it was more than pretty.

She had a sort of oaky hair that the sun and salt had bleached, done up in a bun that was unravelling, and a kind of prim face. Walking into the A & P with your straps down, I suppose it's the only kind of face you *can* have. She held her head so high her neck, coming up out of those white shoulders, looked kind of stretched, but I didn't mind. The longer her neck was, the more of her there was.

She must have felt in the corner of her eye me and over my shoulder Stokesie in the second slot watching, but she didn't tip. Not this queen. She kept her eyes moving across the racks, and stopped, and turned so slow it made my stomach rub the inside of my apron, and buzzed to the other two, who kind of huddled against her for relief, and then they all three of them went up the cat-and-dog-food-breakfast-cereal-macaroni-rice-raisins-seasonings-spreads-spaghetti-soft-drinks-crackers-and-cook-ies aisle. From the third slot I look straight up this aisle to the meat counter, and I watched them all the way. The fat one with the tan sort of fumbled with the cookies, but on second thought she put the package back. The sheep pushing their carts down the aisle—the girls were walk-ing against the usual traffic (not that we have one-way signs or any-thing)—were pretty hilarious. You could see them, when Queenie's white shoulders dawned on them, kind of jerk, or hop, or hiccup, but their eyes snapped back to their own baskets and on they pushed. I bet you could set off dynamite in an A & P and the people would by and large keep reaching and checking oatmeal off their lists and muttering ``Let me see, there was a third thing, began with A, asparagus, no, ah, yes, apple-sauce!'' or whatever it is they do mutter. But there was no doubt, this jiggled them. A few house-slaves in pin curlers even looked around after pushing their carts past to make sure what they had seen was correct.

You know, it's one thing to have a girl in a bathing suit down on the beach, where what with the glare nobody can look at each other much anyway, and another thing in the cool of the A & P, under the fluorescent lights, against all those stacked packages, with her feet paddling along naked over our checker-board green-and-cream rubber-tile floor.

"Oh Daddy," Stokesie said beside me. "I feel so faint."

"Darling," I said. "Hold me tight." Stokesie's married, with two babies chalked up on his fuselage already, but as far as I can tell that's the only difference. He's twenty-two, and I was nineteen this April.

"Is it done?" he asks, the responsible married man finding his voice. I forgot to say he thinks he's going to be manager some sunny day, maybe in 1990 when it's called the Great Alexandrov and Petrooshki Tea Company or something.

What he meant was, our town is five miles from a beach, with a big summer colony out on the Point, but we're right in the middle of town, and the women generally put on a shirt or shorts or something before they get out of the car into the street. And anyway these are usually women with six children and varicose veins mapping their legs and nobody, including them, could care less. As I say, we're right in the middle of town, and if you stand at our front doors you can see two banks and the Congregational church and the newspaper store and three real-estate offices and about twenty-seven old freeloaders tearing up Central Street because the sewer broke again. It's not as if we're on the Cape; we're north of Boston and there's people in this town haven't seen the ocean for twenty years.

The girls had reached the meat counter and were asking McMahon something. He pointed, they pointed, and they shuffled out of sight behind a pyramid of Diet Delight peaches. All that was left for us to see was old McMahon patting his mouth and looking after them sizing up their joints. Poor kids, I began to feel sorry for them, they couldn't help it.

Now here comes the sad part of the story, at least my family says it's sad, but I don't think it's so sad myself. The store's pretty empty, it being Thursday afternoon, so there was nothing much to do except lean on the register and wait for the girls to show up again. The whole store was like a pinball machine and I didn't know which tunnel they'd come out of. After a while they come around out of the far aisle, around the light bulbs, records at discount of the Caribbean Six or Tony Martin Sings or some such gunk you wonder they waste the wax on, six-packs of candy bars, and plastic toys done up in cellophane that fall apart when a kid looks at them anyway. Around they come, Queenie still leading the way, and holding a little gray jar in her hand. Slots Three through Seven are unmanned and I could see her wondering between Stokes and me, but Stokesie with his usual luck draws an old party in baggy gray pants who stumbles up with four giant cans of pineapple juice (what do these bums *do* with all that pineapple juice? I've often asked myself) so the girls come to me.

Queenie puts down the jar and I take it into my fingers icy cold. Kingfish Fancy Herring Snacks in Pure Sour Cream: 49¢. Now her hands are empty, not a ring or a bracelet, bare as God made them, and I wonder where the money's coming from. Still with that prim look she lifts a folded dollar bill out of the hollow at the center of her nubbled pink top. The jar went heavy in my hand. Really, I thought that was so cute.

Then everybody's luck begins to run out. Lengel comes in from haggling with a truck full of cabbages on the lot and is about to scuttle into that door marked MANAGER behind which he hides all day when the girls touch his eye. Lengel's pretty dreary, teaches Sunday school and the rest, but he doesn't miss that much. He comes over and says, "Girls, this isn't the beach."

Queenie blushes, though maybe it's just a brush of sunburn I was noticing for the first time, now that she was so close. "My mother asked me to pick up a jar of herring snacks." Her voice kind of startled me, the way voices do when you see the people first, coming out so flat and dumb yet kind of tony, too, the way it ticked over "pick up" and "snacks." All of a sudden I slid right down her voice into her living room. Her father and the other men were standing around in ice-cream coats and bow ties and the women were in sandals picking up herring snacks on toothpicks off a big glass plate and they were all holding drinks the color of water with olives and sprigs of mint in them. When my parents have somebody over they get lemonade and if it's a real racy affair Schlitz in tall glasses with "They'll Do It Every Time" cartoons stencilled on.

"That's all right," Lengel said. "But this isn't the beach." His repeating this struck me as funny, as if it had just occurred to him, and he had been thinking all these years the A & P was a great big dune and he was the head lifeguard. He didn't like my smiling—as I say he doesn't miss much—but he concentrates on giving the girls that sad Sunday-school-superintendent stare.

Queenie's blush is no sunburn now, and the plump one in plaid, that I liked better from the back—a really sweet can—pipes up. "We weren't doing any shopping. We just came in for the one thing."

"That makes no difference," Lengel tells her, and I could see from the way his eyes went that he hadn't noticed she was wearing a two-piece before. "We want you decently dressed when you come in here."

"We *are* decent," Queenie says suddenly, her lower lip pushing, getting sore now that she remembers her place, a place from which the crowd that runs the A & P must look pretty crummy. Fancy Herring Snacks flashed in her very blue eyes.

"Girls, I don't want to argue with you. After this come in here with your shoulders covered. It's our policy." He turns his back. That's policy for you. Policy is what the kingpins want. What the others want is juvenile delinquency.

All this while, the customers had been showing up with their carts but, you know, sheep, seeing a scene, they had all bunched up on

Stokesie, who shook open a paper bag as gently as peeling a peach, not wanting to miss a word. I could feel in the silence everybody getting nervous, most of all Lengel, who asks me, "Sammy, have you rung up their purchase?"

I thought and said "No" but it wasn't about that I was thinking. I go through the punches, 4, 9, GROC, TOT—it's more complicated than you think, and after you do it often enough, it begins to make a little song, that you hear words to, in my case "Hello *(bing)* there, you *(gung)* hap-py pee-pul *(splat)*!"—the *splat* being the drawer flying out, I uncrease the bill, tenderly as you may imagine, it just having come from between the two smoothest scoops of vanilla I had ever known there were, and pass a half and a penny into her narrow pink palm, and nestle the herrings in a bag and twist its neck and hand it over, all the time thinking.

The girls, and who'd blame them, are in a hurry to get out, so I say "I quit" to Lengel quick enough for them to hear, hoping they'll stop and watch me, their unsuspected hero. They keep right on going, into the electric eye; the door flies open and they flicker across the lot to their car, Queenie and Plaid and Big Tall Goony-Goony (not that as raw material she was so bad), leaving me with Lengel and a kink in his eyebrow.

"Did you say something, Sammy?"

"I said I quit."

"I thought you did."

"You didn't have to embarrass them."

"It was they who were embarrassing us."

I started to say something that came out "Fiddle-de-do." It's a saying of my grandmother's, and I know she would have been pleased.

"I don't think you know what you're saying," Lengel said.

"I know you don't," I said. "But I do." I pull the bow at the back of my apron and start shrugging it off my shoulders. A couple of customers that had been heading for my slot begin to knock against each other, like scared pigs in a chute.

Lengel sighs and begins to look very patient and old and gray. He's been a friend of my parents for years. "Sammy, you don't want to do this to your Mom and Dad," he tells me. It's true, I don't. But it seems to me that once you begin a gesture it's fatal not to go through with it. I fold the apron, "Sammy" stitched in red on the pocket, and put it on the counter, and drop the bow tie on top of it. The bow tie is theirs, if you've ever wondered. "You'll feel this for the rest of your life," Lengel says, and I know that's true, too, but remembering how he made that pretty girl blush makes me so scrunchy inside I punch the No Sale tab and the machine whirs "pee-pul" and the drawer splats out. One advantage to this scene taking place in summer, I can follow this up with a clean exit, there's no fumbling around getting your coat and galoshes, I just saunter into the electric eye in my white shirt that my mother ironed the night before, and the door heaves itself open, and outside the sunshine is skating around on the asphalt.

I look around for my girls, but they're gone, of course. There wasn't anybody but some young married screaming with her children about some candy they didn't get by the door of a powder-blue Falcon station wagon. Looking back in the big windows, over the bags of peat moss and aluminum lawn furniture stacked on the pavement, I could see Lengel in my place in the slot, checking the sheep through. His face was dark gray and his back stiff, as if he'd just had an injection of iron, and my stomach kind of fell as I felt how hard the world was going to be to me hereafter.

SUGGESTIONS FOR WRITING AND DISCUSSION

1. At what point in his life is the narrator telling the story? Do you think he has already found a new job?
2. Examine Sammy's descriptions of the three girls. What makes Queenie so different from the other two and from the other customers in the store?
3. What do we learn about Sammy's family in the course of the story? How does his background affect his response to Queenie?
4. Why does Sammy quit his job? What in the story prepares us for this gesture? Is it admirable or foolish?
5. What kind of man do you think Lengel is? Is he completely a villain? Are you sympathetic to him at any point?
6. Reread the final sentence of the story. Write a two- to three-page essay about a time in your life that marked the end of your innocence about economic or social realities.

Poetry

Thomas Gray (British, 1716–1771)

Elegy Written in a Country Churchyard

The curfew tolls the knell of parting day;
The lowing herd wind slowly o'er the lea;
The plowman homeward plods his weary way,
And leaves the world to darkness and to me.

Now fades the glimmering landscape on the sight,
And all the air a solemn stillness holds,
Save where the beetle wheels his droning flight,
And drowsy tinklings lull the distant folds;

Save that from yonder ivy-mantled tow'r,
The moping owl does to the moon complain
Of such as, wand'ring near her secret bow'r,
Molest her ancient solitary reign.

Beneath those rugged elms, that yew tree's shade,
Where heaves the turf in many a mold'ring heap,
Each in his narrow cell for ever laid,
The rude forefathers of the hamlet sleep.

The breezy call of incense-breathing Morn,
The swallow twitt'ring from the straw-built shed,
The cock's shrill clarion, or the echoing horn,
No more shall rouse them from their lowly bed.

For them no more the blazing hearth shall burn,
Or busy housewife ply her evening care;
No children run to lisp their sire's return,
Or climb his knees the envied kiss to share.

Oft did the harvest to their sickle yield;
Their furrow oft the stubborn glebe has broke;
How jocund did they drive their team afield!
How bowed the woods beneath their sturdy stroke!

Let not Ambition mock their useful toil,
Their homely joys, and destiny obscure;
Nor Grandeur hear with a disdainful smile,
The short and simple annals of the poor.

The boast of heraldry, the pomp of pow'r,
And all that beauty, all that wealth, e'er gave
Awaits alike th' inevitable hour.
The paths of glory lead but to the grave.

Nor you, ye proud, impute to these the fault
If Mem'ry o'er their tomb no trophies raise,
Where, through the long-drawn aisle and fretted vault,
The pealing anthem swells the note of praise.

Can storied urn or animated bust
Back to its mansion call the fleeting breath?
Can Honor's voice provoke the silent dust,
Or Flattery soothe the dull cold ear of Death?

Perhaps in this neglected spot is laid
Some heart once pregnant with celestial fire;
Hands that the rod of empire might have swayed,
Or waked to ecstasy the living lyre.

But Knowledge to their eyes her ample page,
Rich with the spoils of time, did ne'er unroll;
Chill Penury repressed their noble rage,
And froze the genial current of the soul.

Full many a gem of purest ray serene
The dark unfathomed caves of ocean bear;
Full many a flower is born to blush unseen,
And waste its sweetness on the desert air.

Some village Hampden,* that with dauntless breast
The little tyrant of his fields withstood;
Some mute inglorious Milton here may rest,
Some Cromwell guiltless of his country's blood.

Th' applause of list'ning senates to command,
The threats of pain and ruin to despise,
To scatter plenty o'er a smiling land,
And read their hist'ry in a nation's eyes,

Their lot forbade: nor circumscribed alone
Their growing virtues, but their crimes confined;
Forbade to wade through slaughter to a throne
And shut the gates of mercy on mankind,

*John Hampden, a cousin of Oliver Cromwell, was a vigorous opponent of Charles I.

The struggling pangs of conscious truth to hide,
To quench the blushes of ingenuous shame,
Or heap the shrine of Luxury and Pride
With incense kindled at the Muse's flame.

Far from the madding crowd's ignoble strife,
Their sober wishes never learned to stray;
Along the cool sequestered vale of life
They kept the noiseless tenor of their way.

Yet ev'n these bones from insult to protect,
Some frail memorial still erected nigh,
With uncouth rimes and shapeless sculpture decked,
Implores the passing tribute of a sigh.

Their name, their years, spelt by th' unlettered Muse,
The place of fame and elegy supply;
And many a holy text around she strews,
That teach the rustic moralist to die.

For who, to dumb Forgetfulness a prey,
This pleasing anxious being e'er resigned,
Left the warm precincts of the cheerful day,
Nor cast one longing ling'ring look behind?

On some fond breast the parting soul relies,
Some pious drops the closing eye requires;
Ev'n from the tomb the voice of Nature cries,
Ev'n in our ashes live their wanted fires.

For thee who, mindful of th' unhonored dead,
Dost in these lines their artless tale relate,
If chance, by lonely contemplation led,
Some kindred spirit shall inquire thy fate,

Haply some hoary-headed swain may say,
"Oft have we seen him at the peep of dawn
Brushing with hasty steps the dews away
To meet the sun upon the upland lawn.

"There at the foot of yonder nodding beech
That wreathes its old fantastic roots so high,
His listless length at noontide would he stretch,
And pore upon the brook that babbles by.

"Hard by yon wood, now smiling as in scorn,
Mutt'ring his wayward fancies he would rove,
Now drooping, woeful wan, like one forlorn,
Or crazed with care, or crossed in hopeless love.

"One morn I missed him on the customed hill,
Along the heath and near his fav'rite tree;
Another came; nor yet beside the rill,
Nor up the lawn, nor at the wood was he;

"The next, with dirges due in sad array
Slow through the church-way path we saw him borne.
Approach and read (for thou canst read) the lay,
Graved on the stone beneath yon aged thorn."

The Epitaph

Here rests his head upon the lap of Earth
A youth to fortune and to fame unknown.
Fair Science frowned not on his humble birth,
And Melancholy marked him for her own.

Large was his bounty, and his soul sincere,
Heav'n did a recompense as largely send:
He gave to Misery all he had, a tear;
He gained from heav'n ('twas all he wished) a friend.

No farther seek his merits to disclose,
Or draw his frailties from their dread abode
(There they alike in trembling hope repose),
The bosom of his Father and his God.

SUGGESTIONS FOR WRITING AND DISCUSSION

1. The speaker compares the graves in the village churchyard with the graves of the rich. How does he describe the two kinds of graves? Which does he think is superior? Why? In a two- to three-page essay analyze this comparison.
2. Write a one-page description of rural life based on the details of this poem.
3. What comment does the speaker make about fame? Is fame the reward of hard work?
4. In the twenty-fourty quatrain the speaker says, "For thee who, mindful of th' unhonored dead." Who is "thee"? For whom is the epitaph at the end of the poem?

William Blake (British, 1757–1827)

The Chimney Sweeper

When my mother died I was very young,
And my father sold me while yet my tongue
Could scarcely cry "'weep! 'weep! 'weep!"
So your chimneys I sweep, & in soot I sleep.

There's little Tom Dacre, who cried when his head,
That curl'd like a lamb's back, was shav'd: so I said
"Hush, Tom! never mind it, for when your head's bare
You know that the soot cannot spoil your white hair."

And so he was quiet, & that very night,
As Tom was a-sleeping, he had such a sight!
That thousands of sweepers, Dick, Joe, Ned, & Jack,
Were all of them lock'd up in coffins of black.

And by came an Angel who had a bright key,
And he open'd the coffins & set them all free;
Then down a green plain leaping, laughing, they run,
And wash in a river, and shine in the Sun.

Then naked & white, all their bags left behind,
They rise upon clouds and sport in the wind;
And the Angel told Tom, if he'd be a good boy,
He'd have God for his father, & never want joy.

And so Tom awoke; and we rose in the dark,
And got with our bags & our brushes to work.
Tho' the morning was cold, Tom was happy & warm;
So if all do their duty they need not fear harm.

SUGGESTIONS FOR WRITING AND DISCUSSION

1. In eighteenth-century England, chimney sweeps used small boys to climb up and down inside the chimneys gathering soot. Such boys were often sold by their parents to the chimney sweep, as was the speaker of this poem. The speaker is quite matter-of-fact about his situation. Is this also Blake's attitude? In what lines do you think Blake's attitude shows through? In a one- or two-page essay discuss Blake's use of irony in this poem.
2. What symbolic meanings does Tom Dacre's dream have?

William Wordsworth (British, 1770–1850)

The World Is Too Much with Us

The world is too much with us; late and soon,
Getting and spending, we lay waste our powers;
Little we see in Nature that is ours;
We have given our hearts away, a sordid boon!
This Sea that bares her bosom to the moon;
The winds that will be howling at all hours,
And are up-gathered now like sleeping flowers;
For this, for everything, we are out of tune;
It moves us not. Great God! I'd rather be
A Pagan suckled in a creed outworn;
So might I, standing on this pleasant lea,
Have glimpses that would make me less forlorn;
Have sight of Proteus rising from the sea;
Or hear old Triton blow his wreathèd horn.

SUGGESTIONS FOR WRITING AND DISCUSSION

1. What comment is the speaker making about the value of work? Is there
   something on which he places a higher value?
2. Compare this sonnet with "Composed upon Westminster Bridge" (pp. 657–
   658). In a two- to three-page essay compare the attitudes of the two speakers
   to beauty and the importance of taking time to appreciate it.

Samuel Taylor Coleridge (British, 1772–1834)

Work Without Hope

Lines Composed 21st February 1825

All Nature seems at work. Slugs leave their lair—
The bees are stirring—birds are on the wing—
And Winter slumbering in the open air
Wears on his smiling face a dream of Spring!
And I the while, the sole unbusy thing,
Nor honey make, nor pair, nor build, nor sing.

Yet well I ken the banks where amaranths blow,
Have traced the fount whence streams of nectar flow.
Bloom, O ye amaranths! bloom for whom ye may,
For me ye bloom not! Glide, rich streams, away!
With lips unbrightened, wreathless brow, I stroll:
And would you learn the spells that drowse my soul?
Work without Hope draws nectar in a sieve,
And Hope without an object cannot live.

SUGGESTIONS FOR WRITING AND DISCUSSION

1. What comment does the speaker make in the first stanza regarding his condition? How would you describe his mood?
2. After 1802 Coleridge wrote very little poetry. The speaker in the second stanza describes being in a similar position. Once he "traced the fount whence streams of nectar flow" but now the amaranths "bloom not." Write a short paraphrase of the second stanza.
3. What does this sonnet suggest about the value and importance of work?
4. Using your answers to the first two questions, write a two-page explication of the poem.

Theodore Roethke (American, 1908–1963)

Dolor

I have known the inexorable sadness of pencils,
Neat in their boxes, dolor of pad and paper-weight,
All the misery of manilla folders and mucilage,
Desolation in immaculate public places,
Lonely reception room, lavatory, switchboard,
The unalterable pathos of basin and pitcher,
Ritual of multigraph, paper-clip, comma,
Endless duplication of lives and objects.
And I have seen dust from the walls of institutions,
Finer than flour, alive, more dangerous than silica,
Sift, almost invisible, through long afternoons of tedium,
Dropping a fine film on nails and delicate eyebrows,
Glazing the pale hair, the duplicate gray standard faces.

SUGGESTIONS FOR WRITING AND DISCUSSION

1. What does the speaker suggest about the power of work to shape our lives?
2. How is this poem an example of synecdoche?
3. In a one- or two-page essay show how the listing of objects piles up to make a statement about the nature of work.

Philip Larkin (British, 1922–   )

Toads

Why should I let the toad *work*
    Squat on my life?
Can't I use my wit as a pitchfork
    And drive the brute off?

Six days of the week it soils
    With its sickening poison—

Just for paying a few bills!
   That's out of proportion.

Lots of folk live on their wits:
   Lecturers, lispers,
Losels, loblolly-men, louts—
   They don't end as paupers;

Lots of folk live up lanes
   With fires in a bucket,
Eat windfalls and tinned sardines—
   They seem to like it.

Their nippers have got bare feet,
   Their unspeakable wives
Are skinny as whippets—and yet
   No one actually *starves*.

Ah, were I courageous enough
   To shout *Stuff your pension!*
But I know, all too well, that's the stuff
   That dreams are made on;

For something sufficiently toad-like
   Squats in me, too;
Its hunkers are heavy as hard luck,
   And cold as snow,

And will never allow me to blarney
   My way to getting
The fame and the girl and the money
   All at one sitting.

I don't say, one bodies the other
   One's spiritual truth;
But I do say it's hard to lose either,
   When you have both.

SUGGESTIONS FOR WRITING AND DISCUSSION

1. In stanzas three, four, and five the speaker describes two groups of people whose way of getting on in the world is different from his. From these descriptions, and from what he tells us in the rest of the poem, what kind of job do you think the speaker has?
2. In the first two stanzas the speaker describes the oppression of work as being like a toad squatting on his life. In the last three stanzas he describes a second toad. What is the second toad?

3. The speaker cannot shout "stuff your pension" in spite of the arguments for doing so. In a two- or three-page essay discuss why not.
4. Compare "Toads" with Theodore Roethke's "Dolor." Are Larkin and Roethke talking about the same kind of work as Robert Frost in "Two Tramps in Mud Time"?

Philip Larkin (British, 1922–   )

Toads Revisited

Walking around in the park
Should feel better than work:
The lake, the sunshine,
The grass to lie on,

Blurred playground noises
Beyond black-stockinged nurses—
Not a bad place to be.
Yet it doesn't suit me,

Being one of the men
You meet of an afternoon:
Palsied old step-takers,
Hare-eyed clerks with the jitters,

Waxed-fleshed out-patients
Still vague from accidents,
And characters in long coats
Deep in the litter-baskets—

All dodging the toad work
By being stupid or weak.
Think of being them!
Hearing the hours chime,

Watching the bread delivered,
The sun by clouds covered,
The children going home;
Think of being them,

Turning over their failures
By some bed of lobelias,
Nowhere to go but indoors,
No friends but empty chairs—

No, give me my in-tray,
My loaf-haired secretary,
My shall-I-keep-the-call-in-Sir:
What else can I answer,

When the lights come on at four
At the end of another year?
Give me your arm, old toad;
Help me down Cemetery Road.

SUGGESTIONS FOR WRITING AND DISCUSSION

1. How does the speaker feel about the people in the park? Why do they make him grateful for his in-tray and secretary?
2. In a three- or four-page essay compare "Toads" to "Toads Revisited." Compare the descriptions of the people who do not work in the two poems. What do these descriptions convey? Does the speaker's attitude to work change from the first poem to the second? How does the second poem comment on the conclusion of the first?

Margaret Walker (American, 1915–   )

Lineage

My grandmothers were strong.
They followed plows and bent to toil.
They moved through fields sowing seed.
They touched earth and grain grew.
They were full of sturdiness and singing.
My grandmothers were strong.

My grandmothers are full of memories
Smelling of soap and onions and wet clay
With veins rolling roughly over quick hands
They have many clean words to say.
My grandmothers were strong.
Why am I not as they?

SUGGESTIONS FOR WRITING AND DISCUSSION

1. The grandmothers described in this poem work hard and yet are "full of sturdiness and singing." How does the speaker feel about them and the work they did? In a one- to two-page essay discuss to what extent the speaker seems to romanticize her ancestors.
2. What does the last line suggest about the kind of work the speaker does?

Robert Frost (American, 1874–1963)

Two Tramps in Mud Time

Out of the mud two strangers came
And caught me splitting wood in the yard.
And one of them put me off my aim
By hailing cheerily "Hit them hard!"
I knew pretty well why he dropped behind
And let the other go on a way.
I knew pretty well what he had in mind:
He wanted to take my job for pay.

Good blocks of beech it was I split,
As large around as the chopping block;
And every piece I squarely hit
Fell splinterless as a cloven rock.
The blows that a life of self-control
Spares to strike for the common good
That day, giving a loose to my soul,
I spent on the unimportant wood.

The sun was warm but the wind was chill.
You know how it is with an April day
When the sun is out and the wind is still,
You're one month on in the middle of May.
But if you so much as dare to speak,
A cloud comes over the sunlit arch,
A wind comes off a frozen peak,
And you're two months back in the middle of March.

A bluebird comes tenderly up to alight
And fronts the wind to unruffle a plume,
His song so pitched as not to excite
A single flower as yet to bloom.
It is snowing a flake: and he half knew
Winter was only playing possum.
Except in color he isn't blue,
But he wouldn't advise a thing to blossom.

The water for which we may have to look
In summertime with a witching-wand,
In every wheelrut's now a brook,
In every print of a hoof a pond.
Be glad of water, but don't forget
The lurking frost in the earth beneath

That will steal forth after the sun is set
And show on the water its crystal teeth.

The time when most I loved my task
These two must make me love it more
By coming with what they came to ask.
You'd think I never had felt before
The weight of an ax-head poised aloft,
The grip on earth of outspread feet,
The life of muscles rocking soft
And smooth and moist in vernal heat.

Out of the woods two hulking tramps
(From sleeping God knows where last night,
But not long since in the lumber camps).
They thought all chopping was theirs of right.
Men of the woods and lumberjacks,
They judged me by their appropriate tool.
Except as a fellow handled an ax,
They had no way of knowing a fool.

Nothing on either side was said.
They knew they had but to stay their stay
And all their logic would fill my head:
As that I had no right to play
With what was another man's work for gain.
My right might be love but theirs was need.
And where the two exist in twain
Theirs was the better right—agreed.

But yield who will to their separation,
My object in living is to unite
My avocation and my vocation
As my two eyes make one in sight.
Only where love and need are one,
And the work is play for mortal stakes,
Is the deed ever really done
For Heaven and the future's sakes.

SUGGESTIONS FOR WRITING AND DISCUSSION

1. Write a one-paragraph description of the two tramps. How does the speaker's attitude toward splitting wood differ from their attitude? Does he think that they are presumptuous in wanting to chop his wood for money?
2. In stanzas three, four, and five the speaker describes the April day. What

does the description convey about the day? Why are so many stanzas devoted to this? How does the description relate to the theme of the poem?
3. In a two- or three-page essay analyze the speaker's attitude toward work. What should work be? How should we feel about it? Should work have a reward or be its own reward?

Seamus Heaney (Irish, 1939–   )

Digging

Between my finger and my thumb
The squat pen rests; snug as a gun.

Under my window, a clean rasping sound
When the spade sinks into gravelly ground:
My father, digging. I look down

Till his straining rump among the flowerbeds
Bends low, comes up twenty years away
Stooping in rhythm through potato drills
Where he was digging.

The coarse boot nestled on the lug, the shaft
Against the inside knee was levered firmly.
He rooted out tall tops, buried the bright edge deep
To scatter new potatoes that we picked
Loving their cool hardness in our hands.

By God, the old man could handle a spade.
Just like his old man.

My grandfather cut more turf in a day
Than any other man on Toner's bog.
Once I carried him milk in a bottle
Corked sloppily with paper. He straightened up
To drink it, then fell to right away

Nicking and slicing neatly, heaving sods
Over his shoulder, going down and down
For the good turf. Digging.

The cold smell of potato mould, the squelch and slap
Of soggy peat, the curt cuts of an edge
Through living roots awaken in my head.
But I've no spade to follow men like them.

Between my finger and my thumb
The squat pen rests.
I'll dig with it.

SUGGESTIONS FOR WRITING AND DISCUSSION

1. What do the speaker's father and grandfather have in common?
2. We sometimes think of manual work as being of little value. Do the descriptions in this poem of digging and cutting turf suggest this attitude?
3. In a one-page essay explain how the speaker carries on the work of his family.

Marianne Moore (American, 1887–1982)

The Grasshopper and the Ant

Until fall, a grasshopper
Chose to chirr;
With starvation as foe
When northeasters would blow,
And not even a gnat's residue
Or caterpillar's to chew,
She chirred a recurrent chant
Of want beside an ant,
Begging it to rescue her
With some seeds it could spare
Till the following year's fell.

"By August you shall have them all,
Interest and principal."
Share one's seeds? Now what is worse
For any ant to do?
Ours asked, "When fair, what brought you through?"
—"I sang for those who might pass by chance—
Night and day. Please do not be repelled."
—"Sang? A delight when someone has excelled.
A singer! Excellent. Now dance."

SUGGESTIONS FOR WRITING AND DISCUSSION

1. In two paragraphs characterize the grasshopper and the ant.
2. The ant's reply suggests that singing is of less value than working. Do you agree? Why should the ant who has worked hard all summer share with the grasshopper? Write a two-page essay arguing either for or against the ant's position.

Drama

Eugene Ionesco (Rumanian, 1912–   )

The Gap

Translated by Rosette Lamont

CHARACTERS

THE FRIEND
THE ACADEMICIAN
THE ACADEMICIAN'S WIFE
THE MAID

SET. *A rich bourgeois living room with artistic pretensions. One or two sofas, a number of armchairs, among which, a green, Régence style one, right in the middle of the room. The walls are covered with framed diplomas. One can make out, written in heavy script at the top of a particularly large one, "Doctor Honoris causa." This is followed by an almost illegible Latin inscription. Another equally impressive diploma states: "Doctorat honoris causa," again followed by a long, illegible text. There is an abundance of smaller diplomas, each of which bears a clearly written "doctorate."*
     A door to the right of the audience.
     As the curtain rises, one can see THE ACADEMICIAN'S WIFE *dressed in a rather crumpled robe. She has obviously just gotten out of bed, and has not had time to dress.* THE FRIEND *faces her. He is well dressed: hat, umbrella in hand, stiff collar, black jacket and striped trousers, shiny black shoes.*

THE WIFE. Dear friend, tell me all.

THE FRIEND. I don't know what to say.

THE WIFE. I know.

THE FRIEND. I heard the news last night. I did not want to call you. At the same time I couldn't wait any longer. Please forgive me for coming so early with such terrible news.

THE WIFE. He didn't make it! How terrible! We were still hoping. . . .

THE FRIEND. It's hard, I know. He still had a chance. Not much of one. We had to expect it.

THE WIFE. I didn't expect it. He was always so successful. He could always manage somehow, at the last moment.

THE FRIEND. In that state of exhaustion. You shouldn't have let him!

THE WIFE. What can we do, what can we do! . . . How awful!

THE FRIEND. Come on, dear friend, be brave. That's life.

THE WIFE. I feel faint: I'm going to faint. *(She falls in one of the armchairs.)*

THE FRIEND *(holding her, gently slapping her cheeks and hands).* I shouldn't have blurted it out like that. I'm sorry.

THE WIFE. No, you were right to do so. I had to find out somehow or other.

THE FRIEND. I should have prepared you, carefully.

THE WIFE. I've got to be strong. I can't help thinking of him, the wretched man. I hope they won't put it in the papers. Can we count on the journalists' discretion?

THE FRIEND. Close your door. Don't answer the telephone. It will still get around. You could go to the country. In a couple of months, when you are better, you'll come back, you'll go on with your life. People forget such things.

THE WIFE. People won't forget so fast. That's all they were waiting for. Some friends will feel sorry, but the others, the others. . . . (THE ACA-DEMICIAN *comes in, fully dressed: uniform, chest covered with decorations, his sword on his side.)*

THE ACADEMICIAN. Up so early, my dear? *(To* THE FRIEND.*)* You've come early too. What's happening? Do you have the final results?

THE WIFE. What a disgrace!

THE FRIEND. You mustn't crush him like this, dear friend. *(To* THE ACADEMI-CIAN.*)* You have failed.

THE ACADEMICIAN. Are you quite sure?

THE FRIEND. You should never have tried to pass the baccalaureate examination.

THE ACADEMICIAN. They failed me. The rats! How dare they do this to me!

THE FRIEND. The marks were posted late in the evening.

THE ACADEMICIAN. Perhaps it was difficult to make them out in the dark. How could you read them?

THE FRIEND. They had set up spotlights.

THE ACADEMICIAN. They're doing everything to ruin me.

THE FRIEND. I passed by in the morning; the marks were still up.

THE ACADEMICIAN. You could have bribed the concierge into pulling them down.

THE FRIEND. That's exactly what I did. Unfortunately the police were there. Your name heads the list of those who failed. Everyone's standing in line to get a look. There's an awful crush.

THE ACADEMICIAN. Who's there? The parents of the candidates?

THE FRIEND. Not only they.

THE WIFE. All your rivals, all your colleagues must be there. All those you attacked in the press for ignorance: your undergraduates, your graduate students, all those you failed when you were chairman of the board of examiners.

THE ACADEMICIAN. I am discredited! But I won't let them. There must be some mistake.

THE FRIEND. I saw the examiners. I spoke with them. They gave me your marks. Zero in mathematics.

THE ACADEMICIAN. I had no scientific training.

THE FRIEND. Zero in Greek, zero in Latin.

THE WIFE (*to her husband*). You, a humanist, the spokesman for humanism, the author of that famous treatise ``The Defense of Poesy and Humanism.''

THE ACADEMICIAN. I beg your pardon, but my book concerns itself with twentieth century humanism. (*To* THE FRIEND.) What about composition? What grade did I get in composition?

THE FRIEND. Nine hundred. You have nine hundred points.

THE ACADEMICIAN. That's perfect. My average must be all the way up.

THE FRIEND. Unfortunately not. They're marking on the basis of two thousand. The passing grade is one thousand.

THE ACADEMICIAN. They must have changed the regulations.

THE WIFE. They didn't change them just for you. You have a frightful persecution complex.

THE ACADEMICIAN. I tell you they changed them.

THE FRIEND. They went back to the old ones, back to the time of Napoleon.

THE ACADEMICIAN. Utterly outmoded. Besides, when did they make those changes? It isn't legal. I'm chairman of the Baccalaureate Commission of the Ministry of Public Education. They didn't consult me, and they cannot make any changes without my approval. I'm going to expose them. I'm going to bring government charges against them.

THE WIFE. Darling, you don't know what you're doing. You're in your dotage. Don't you recall handing in your resignation just before taking the examination so that no one could doubt the complete objectivity of the board of examiners?

THE ACADEMICIAN. I'll take it back.

THE WIFE. You should never have taken that test. I warned you. After all, it's not as if you needed it. But you have to collect all the honors, don't you? You're never satisfied. What did you need this diploma for? Now all is lost. You have your Doctorate, your Master's, your high school diploma, your elementary school certificate, and even the first part of the baccalaureate.

THE ACADEMICIAN. There was a gap.

THE WIFE. No one suspected it.

THE ACADEMICIAN. But *I* knew it. Others might have found out. I went to the office of the Registrar and asked for a transcript of my record. They said to me: "Certainly Professor, Mr. President, Your Excellency. . . ." Then they looked up my file, and the Chief Registrar came back looking embarrassed, most embarrassed indeed. He said: "There's something peculiar, very peculiar, You have your Master's, certainly, but it's no longer valid." I asked him why, of course. He answered: "There's a gap behind your Master's. I don't know how it happened. You must have registered and been accepted at the University without having passed the second part of the baccalaureate examination."

THE FRIEND. And then?

THE WIFE. Your Master's degree is no longer valid?

THE ACADEMICIAN. No, not quite. It's suspended. "The duplicate you are asking for will be delivered to you upon completion of the baccalaureate. Of course you will pass the examination with no trouble." That's what I was told, so you see now that I had to take it.

THE FRIEND. Your husband, dear friend, wanted to fill the gap. He's a conscientious person.

THE WIFE. It's clear you don't know him as I do. That's not it at all. He wants fame, honors. He never had enough. What does one diploma more or less matter? No one notices them anyway, but he sneaks in at night, on tiptoe, into the living room, just to look at them, and count them.

THE ACADEMICIAN. What else can I do when I have insomnia?

THE FRIEND. The questions asked at the baccalaureate are usually known in advance. You were admirably situated to get this particular information. You could also have sent in a replacement to take the test for you. One of your students, perhaps. Or if you wanted to take the test without people realizing that you already knew the questions, you could have sent your maid to the black market, where one can buy them.

THE ACADEMICIAN. I don't understand how I could have failed in my composition. I filled three sheets of paper, I treated the subject fully, taking into account the historical background. I interpreted the situation accurately . . . at least plausibly. I didn't deserve a bad grade.

THE FRIEND. Do you recall the subject?

THE ACADEMICIAN. Hum . . . let's see. . . .

THE FRIEND. He doesn't even remember what he discussed.

THE ACADEMICIAN. I do . . . wait . . . hum.

THE FRIEND. The subject to be treated was the following: "Discuss the influence of Renaissance painters on novelists of the Third Republic." I have here a photostatic copy of your examination paper. Here is what you wrote.

THE ACADEMICIAN *(grabbing the photostat and reading).* "The trial of Benjamin: After Benjamin was tried and acquitted, the assessors holding a different opinion from that of the President murdered him, and condemned Benjamin to the suspension of his civic rights, imposing on him a fine of nine hundred francs. . . ."

THE FRIEND. That's where the nine hundred points come from.

THE ACADEMICIAN. "Benjamin appealed his case . . . Benjamin appealed his case. . . ." I can't make out the rest. I've always had bad handwriting. I ought to have taken a typewriter along with me.

THE WIFE. Horrible handwriting, scribbling and crossing out; ink spots didn't help you much.

THE ACADEMICIAN *(goes on with his reading after having retrieved the text his wife had pulled out of his hand).* "Benjamin appealed his case. Flanked by policemen dressed in zouave uniforms . . . in zouave uniforms. . . ." It's getting dark. I can't see the rest. . . . I don't have my glasses.

THE WIFE. What you've written has nothing to do with the subject.

THE FRIEND. You wife's quite right, friend. It has nothing to do with the subject.

THE ACADEMICIAN. Yes, it has. Indirectly.

THE FRIEND. Not even indirectly.

THE ACADEMICIAN. Perhaps I chose the second question.

THE FRIEND. There was only one.

THE ACADEMICIAN. Even if there was only that one, I treated another quite adequately. I went to the end of the story. I stressed the important points, explaining the motivations of the characters, highlighting their behavior. I explained the mystery, making it plain and clear. There was even a conclusion at the end. I can't make out the rest. *(To* THE FRIEND.*)* Can you read it?

THE FRIEND. It's illegible. I don't have my glasses either.

THE WIFE *(taking the text).* It's illegible and I have excellent eyes. You pretended to write. Mere scribbling.

THE ACADEMICIAN. That's not true. I've even provided a conclusion. It's clearly marked here in heavy print: "Conclusion or sanction . . . Conclusion or sanction. . . ." They can't get away with it. I'll have this examination rendered null and void.

THE WIFE. Since you treated the wrong subject, and treated it badly, setting down only titles, and writing nothing in between, the mark you received is justified. You'd lose your case.

THE FRIEND. You'd most certainly lose. Drop it. Take a vacation.

THE ACADEMICIAN. You're always on the side of the Others.

THE WIFE. After all, these professors know what they're doing. They haven't been granted their rank for nothing. They passed examinations, received serious training. They know the rules of composition.

THE ACADEMICIAN. Who was on the board of examiners?

THE FRIEND. For Mathematics, a movie star. For Greek, one of the Beatles. For Latin, the champion of the automobile race, and many others.

THE ACADEMICIAN. But these people aren't any more qualified than I am. And for composition?

THE FRIEND. A woman, a secretary in the editorial division of the review *Yesterday, the Day Before Yesterday, and Today.*

THE ACADEMICIAN. Now I know. This wretch gave me a poor grade out of spite because I never joined her political party. It's an act of vengeance. But I have ways and means of rendering the examination null and void. I'm going to call the President.

THE WIFE. Don't. You'll make yourself look even more ridiculous. *(To THE FRIEND.)* Please try to restrain him. He listens to you more than to me. *(THE FRIEND shrugs his shoulders, unable to cope with the situation. THE WIFE turns to her husband, who has just lifted the receiver off the hook.)* Don't call!

THE ACADEMICIAN *(on the telephone).* Hello, John? It is I . . . What? . . . What did you say? . . . But, listen, my dear friend . . . but, listen to me . . . Hello! Hello! *(Puts down the receiver.)*

THE FRIEND. What did he say?

THE ACADEMICIAN. He said . . . He said. . . . ''I don't want to talk to you. My mummy won't let me make friends with boys at the bottom of the class.'' Then he hung up on me.

THE WIFE. You should have expected it. All is lost. How could you do this to me? How could you do this to me?

THE ACADEMICIAN. Think of it! I lectured at the Sorbonne, at Oxford, at American universities. Ten thousand theses have been written on my work; hundreds of critics have analyzed it. I hold an *honoris causa* doctorate from Amsterdam as well as a secret university Chair with the Duchy of Luxembourg. I received the Nobel Prize three times. The King of Sweden himself was amazed by my erudition. A doctorate *honoris causa, honoris causa* . . . and I failed the baccalaureate examination!

THE WIFE. Everyone will laugh at us!

THE ACADEMICIAN *takes off his sword and breaks it on his knee.*

THE FRIEND *(picking up the two pieces).* I wish to preserve these in memory of our ancient glory.

THE ACADEMICIAN *meanwhile in a fit of rage is tearing down his decorations, throwing them on the floor, and stepping on them.*

THE WIFE *(trying to salvage the remains).* Don't do this! Don't! That's all we've got left.

Curtain

SUGGESTIONS FOR WRITING AND DISCUSSION

1. Why does Ionesco give his characters titles instead of names?
2. The Academician decides to take the Baccalaureate because there is a gap in his record. Do you think there is anything laudable in his motives? Or is he simply after more fame and honors, as his wife says?
3. What attitudes do the three main characters have toward academic work? Do their attitudes change during the course of the play?
4. This play begins with a fairly plausible situation and moves gradually to an absurd conclusion. At what point does the play start to become fantastical? In a two- or three-page essay describe this progression.
5. How does the Academician react to the news that he has failed? How is his reaction to failure like and unlike that of Willy Loman in *Death of a Salesman*? Compare the two in a three- or four-page essay.
6. In this play Ionesco satirizes universities. How fairly do you think he treats universities and academics? To what extent is he exaggerating? What is the overall tone of this satire?

Arthur Miller (American, 1915–   )

Death of a Salesman

Certain Conversations in Two Acts and a Requiem

CHARACTERS

WILLY LOMAN
LINDA
BIFF
HAPPY
BERNARD
THE WOMAN
CHARLEY
UNCLE BEN
HOWARD WAGNER
JENNY
STANLEY
MISS FORSYTHE
LETTA

The action takes place in WILLY LOMAN'S *house and yard and in various places he visits in the New York and Boston of today.*

   Throughout the play, in the stage directions, left and right mean stage left and stage right.

ACT ONE

An Overture

A melody is heard, played upon a flute. It is small and fine, telling of grass and trees and the horizon. The curtain rises.

Before us is the Salesman's house. We are aware of towering, angular shapes behind it, surrounding it on all sides. Only the blue light of the sky falls upon the house and forestage; the surrounding area shows an angry glow of orange. As more light appears, we see a solid vault of apartment houses around the small, fragile-seeming home. An air of the dream clings to the place, a dream rising out of reality. The kitchen at center seems actual enough, for there is a kitchen table with three chairs, and a refrigerator. But no other fixtures are seen. At the back of the kitchen there is a draped entrance, which leads to the living room. To the right of the kitchen, on a level raised two feet, is a bedroom furnished only with a brass bedstead and a straight chair. On a shelf over the bed a silver athletic trophy stands. A window opens onto the apartment house at the side.

Behind the kitchen, on a level raised six and a half feet, is the boys' bedroom, at present barely visible. Two beds are dimly seen, and at the back of the room a dormer window. (This bedroom is above the unseen living room.) At the left a stairway curves up to it from the kitchen.

The entire setting is wholly or, in some places, partially transparent. The roof-line of the house is one-dimensional; under and over it we see the apartment buildings. Before the house lies an apron, curving beyond the forestage into the orchestra. This forward area serves as the back yard as well as the locale of all WILLY's *imaginings and of his city scenes. Whenever the action is in the present the actors observe the imaginary wall-lines, entering the house only through its door at the left. But in the scenes of the past these boundaries are broken, and characters enter or leave a room by stepping "through" a wall onto the forestage.*

From the right, WILLY LOMAN, *the Salesman, enters, carrying two large sample cases. The flute plays on. He hears but is not aware of it. He is past sixty years of age, dressed quietly. Even as he crosses the stage to the doorway of the house, his exhaustion is apparent. He unlocks the door, comes into the kitchen, and thankfully lets his burden down, feeling the soreness of his palms. A word-sigh escapes his lips—it might be "Oh, boy, oh, boy." He closes the door, then carries his cases out into the living room, through the draped kitchen doorway.*

LINDA, his wife, has stirred in her bed at the right. She gets out and puts on a robe, listening. Most often jovial, she has developed an iron repression of her exceptions to WILLY's *behavior—she more than loves him, she admires him, as though his mercurial nature, his temper, his massive dreams and little cruelties, served her only as sharp reminders of the turbulent longings within him, longings which she shares but lacks the temperament to utter and follow to their end.*

LINDA *(hearing* WILLY *outside the bedroom, calls with some trepidation).* Willy!

WILLY. It's all right. I came back.

LINDA. Why? What happened? *(Slight pause)* Did something happen, Willy?

WILLY. No, nothing happened.

LINDA. You didn't smash the car, did you?

WILLY *(with casual irritation).* I said nothing happened. Didn't you hear me?

LINDA. Don't you feel well?

WILLY. I'm tired to the death. *(The flute has faded away. He sits on the bed beside her, a little numb)* I couldn't make it. I just couldn't make it, Linda.

LINDA *(very carefully, delicately).* Where were you all day? You look terrible.

WILLY. I got as far as a little above Yonkers. I stopped for a cup of coffee. Maybe it was the coffee.

LINDA. What?

WILLY *(after a pause).* I suddenly couldn't drive any more. The car kept going off onto the shoulder, y'know?

LINDA *(helpfully).* Oh. Maybe it was the steering again. I don't think Angelo knows the Studebaker.

WILLY. No, it's me, it's me. Suddenly I realize I'm goin' sixty miles an hour and I don't remember the last five minutes. I'm—I can't seem to—keep my mind to it.

LINDA. Maybe it's your glasses. You never went for your new glasses.

WILLY. No, I see everything. I came back ten miles an hour. It took me nearly four hours from Yonkers.

LINDA *(resigned).* Well, you'll just have to take a rest, Willy, you can't continue this way.

WILLY. I just got back from Florida.

LINDA. But you didn't rest your mind. Your mind is overactive, and the mind is what counts, dear.

WILLY. I'll start out in the morning. Maybe I'll feel better in the morning. *(She is taking off his shoes)* These goddam arch supports are killing me.

LINDA. Take an aspirin. Should I get you an aspirin? It'll soothe you.

WILLY *(with wonder).* I was driving along, you understand? And I was fine. I was even observing the scenery. You can imagine, me looking at scenery, on the road every week of my life. But it's so beautiful up there, Linda, the trees are so thick, and the sun is warm. I opened the windshield and just let the warm air bathe over me. And then all of a sudden I'm goin' off the road! I'm tellin' ya, I absolutely forgot I was driving. If I'd've gone the other way over the white line I might've killed somebody. So I went on again—and five minutes later I'm dreamin' again, and I nearly—*(He presses two fingers against his eyes)* I have such thoughts, I have such strange thoughts.

LINDA. Willy, dear. Talk to them again. There's no reason why you can't work in New York.

WILLY. They don't need me in New York. I'm the New England man. I'm vital in New England.

LINDA. But you're sixty years old. They can't expect you to keep traveling every week.

WILLY. I'll have to send a wire to Portland. I'm supposed to see Brown and Morrison tomorrow morning at ten o'clock to show the line. Goddammit, I could sell them! *(He starts putting on his jacket)*

LINDA *(taking the jacket from him)*. Why don't you go down to the place tomorrow and tell Howard you've simply got to work in New York? You're too accommodating, dear.

WILLY. If old man Wagner was alive I'd a been in charge of New York now! That man was a prince, he was a masterful man. But that boy of his, that Howard, he don't appreciate. When I went north the first time, the Wagner Company didn't know where New England was!

LINDA. Why don't you tell those things to Howard, dear?

WILLY *(encouraged)*. I will, I definitely will. Is there any cheese?

LINDA. I'll make you a sandwich.

WILLY. No, go to sleep. I'll take some milk. I'll be up right away. The boys in?

LINDA. They're sleeping. Happy took Biff on a date tonight.

WILLY *(interested)*. That so?

LINDA. It was so nice to see them shaving together, one behind the other, in the bathroom. And going out together. You notice? The whole house smells of shaving lotion.

WILLY. Figure it out. Work a lifetime to pay off a house. You finally own it, and there's nobody to live in it.

LINDA. Well, dear, life is a casting off. It's always that way.

WILLY. No, no, some people—some people accomplish something. Did Biff say anything after I went this morning?

LINDA. You shouldn't have criticized him, Willy, especially after he just got off the train. You mustn't lose your temper with him.

WILLY. When the hell did I lose my temper? I simply asked him if he was making any money. Is that a criticism?

LINDA. But, dear, how could he make any money?

WILLY *(worried and angered).* There's such an undercurrent in him. He became a moody man. Did he apologize when I left this morning?

LINDA. He was crestfallen, Willy. You know how he admires you. I think if he finds himself, then you'll both be happier and not fight any more.

WILLY. How can he find himself on a farm? Is that a life? A farmhand? In the beginning, when he was young, I thought, well, a young man, it's good for him to tramp around, take a lot of different jobs. But it's more than ten years now and he has yet to make thirty-five dollars a week!

LINDA. He's finding himself, Willy.

WILLY. Not finding yourself at the age of thirty-four is a disgrace!

LINDA. Shh!

WILLY. The trouble is he's lazy, goddammit!

LINDA. Willy, please!

WILLY. Biff is a lazy bum!

LINDA. They're sleeping. Get something to eat. Go on down.

WILLY. Why did he come home? I would like to know what brought him home.

LINDA. I don't know. I think he's still lost, Willy. I think he's very lost.

WILLY. Biff Loman is lost. In the greatest country in the world a young man with such—personal attractiveness, gets lost. And such a hard worker. There's one thing about Biff—he's not lazy.

LINDA. Never.

WILLY *(with pity and resolve).* I'll see him in the morning; I'll have a nice talk with him. I'll get him a job selling. He could be big in no time. My God! Remember how they used to follow him around in high school? When he smiled at one of them their faces lit up. When he walked down the street . . . *(He loses himself in reminiscences)*

LINDA *(trying to bring him out of it).* Willy, dear, I got a new kind of American-type cheese today. It's whipped.

WILLY. Why do you get American when I like Swiss?

LINDA. I just thought you'd like a change—

WILLY. I don't want a change! I want Swiss cheese. Why am I always being contradicted?

LINDA *(with a covering laugh).* I thought it would be a surprise.

WILLY. Why don't you open a window in here, for God's sake?

LINDA *(with infinite patience).* They're all open, dear.

WILLY. The way they boxed us in here. Bricks and windows, windows and bricks.

LINDA. We should've bought the land next door.

WILLY. The street is lined with cars. There's not a breath of fresh air in the neighborhood. The grass don't grow any more, you can't raise a carrot in the back yard. They should've had a law against apartment houses. Remember those two beautiful elm trees out there? When I and Biff hung the swing between them?

LINDA. Yeah, like being a million miles from the city.

WILLY. They should've arrested the builder for cutting those down. They massacred the neighborhood. *(Lost)* More and more I think of those days, Linda. This time of year it was lilac and wisteria. And then the peonies would come out, and the daffodils. What fragrance in this room!

LINDA. Well, after all, people had to move somewhere.

WILLY. No, there's more people now.

LINDA. I don't think there's more people. I think—

WILLY. There's more people! That's what's ruining this country! Population is getting out of control. The competition is maddening! Smell the stink from that apartment house! And another one on the other side . . . How can they whip cheese?

On WILLY's *last line,* BIFF *and* HAPPY *raise themselves up in their beds, listening.*

LINDA. Go down, try it. And be quiet.

WILLY *(turning to* LINDA, *guiltily).* You're not worried about me, are you, sweetheart?

BIFF. What's the matter?

HAPPY. Listen!

LINDA. You've got too much on the ball to worry about.

WILLY. You're my foundation and my support, Linda.

LINDA. Just try to relax, dear. You make mountains out of molehills.

WILLY. I won't fight with him any more. If he wants to go back to Texas, let him go.

LINDA. He'll find his way.

WILLY. Sure. Certain men just don't get started till later in life. Like Thomas Edison, I think. Or B. F. Goodrich. One of them was deaf. *(He starts for the bedroom doorway)* I'll put my money on Biff.

LINDA. And Willy—if it's warm Sunday we'll drive in the country. And we'll open the windshield, and take lunch.

WILLY. No, the windshields don't open on the new cars.

LINDA. But you opened it today.

WILLY. Me? I didn't. *(He stops)* Now isn't that peculiar! Isn't that a remark-able—*(He breaks off in amazement and fright as the flute is heard distantly)*

LINDA. What, darling?

WILLY. That is the most remarkable thing.

LINDA. What, dear?

WILLY. I was thinking of the Chevvy. *(slight pause)* Nineteen twenty-eight . . . when I had that red Chevvy—*(Breaks off)* That funny? I coulda sworn I was driving that Chevvy today.

LINDA. Well, that's nothing. Something must've reminded you.

WILLY. Remarkable. Ts. Remember those days? The way Biff used to simonize that car? The dealer refused to believe there was eighty thousand miles on it. *(He shakes his head)* Heh! *(To* LINDA*)* Close your eyes, I'll be right up. *(He walks out of the bedroom)*

HAPPY *(to* BIFF*)*. Jesus, maybe he smashed up the car again!

LINDA *(calling after* WILLY*)*. Be careful on the stairs, dear! The cheese is on the middle shelf! *(She turns, goes over to the bed, takes his jacket, and goes out of the bedroom)*

Light has risen on the boys' room. Unseen, WILLY'S *is heard talking to him-self, "Eighty thousand miles," and a little laugh.* BIFF *gets out of bed, comes downstage a bit, and stands attentively.* BIFF *is two years older than his brother* HAPPY*, well built, but in these days bears a worn air and seems less self-assured. He has succeeded less, and his dreams are stronger and less acceptable than* HAPPY'S. HAPPY *is tall, powerfully made. Sexuality is like a visible color on him, or a scent that many women have discovered. He, like his brother, is lost, but in a different way, for he has never allowed himself to turn his face toward defeat and is thus more confused and hard-skinned, although seemingly more content.*

HAPPY *(getting out of bed)*. He's going to get his license taken away if he keeps that up. I'm getting nervous about him, y'know, Biff?

BIFF. His eyes are going.

HAPPY. No, I've driven with him. He sees all right. He just doesn't keep his mind on it. I drove into the city with him last week. He stops at a green light and then it turns red and he goes. *(He laughs)*

BIFF. Maybe he's color-blind.

HAPPY. Pop? Why he's got the finest eye for color in the business. You know that.

BIFF *(sitting down on his bed)*. I'm going to sleep.

HAPPY. You're not still sour on Dad, are you, Biff?

BIFF. He's all right, I guess.

WILLY *(underneath them, in the living-room).* Yes, sir, eighty thousand miles—eighty-two thousand!

BIFF. You smoking?

HAPPY *(holding out a pack of cigarettes).* Want one?

BIFF *(taking a cigarette).* I can never sleep when I smell it.

WILLY. What a simonizing job, heh!

HAPPY *(with deep sentiment).* Funny, Biff, y'know? Us sleeping in here again? The old beds. *(He pats his bed affectionately)* All the talk that went across those two beds, huh? Our whole lives.

BIFF. Yeah. Lotta dreams and plans.

HAPPY *(with a deep and masculine laugh).* About five hundred women would like to know what was said in this room.

They share a soft laugh.

BIFF. Remember that big Betsy something—what the hell was her name—over on Bushwick Avenue?

HAPPY *(combing his hair).* With the collie dog!

BIFF. That's the one. I got you in there, remember?

HAPPY. Yeah, that was my first time—I think. Boy, there was a pig! *(They laugh, almost crudely)* You taught me everything I know about women. Don't forget that.

BIFF. I bet you forgot how bashful you used to be. Especially with girls.

HAPPY. Oh, I still am, Biff.

BIFF. Oh, go on.

HAPPY. I just control it, that's all. I think I got less bashful and you got more so. What happened, Biff? Where's the old humor, the old confidence? *(He shakes BIFF's knee. BIFF gets up and moves restlessly about the room)* What's the matter?

BIFF. Why does Dad mock me all the time?

HAPPY. He's not mocking you, he—

BIFF. Everything I say there's a twist of mockery on his face. I can't get near him.

HAPPY. He just wants you to make good, that's all. I wanted to talk to you about Dad for a long time, Biff. Something's—happening to him. He—talks to himself.

BIFF. I noticed that this morning. But he always mumbled.

HAPPY. But not so noticeable. It got so embarrassing I sent him to Florida. And you know something? Most of the time he's talking to you.

BIFF. What's he say about me?

HAPPY. I can't make it out.

BIFF. What's he say about me?

HAPPY. I think the fact that you're not settled, that you're still kind of up in the air . . .

BIFF. There's one or two other things depressing him, Happy.

HAPPY. What do you mean?

BIFF. Never mind. Just don't lay it all to me.

HAPPY. But I think if you just got started—I mean—is there any future for you out there?

BIFF. I tell ya, Hap, I don't know what the future is. I don't know—what I'm supposed to want.

HAPPY. What do you mean?

BIFF. Well, I spent six or seven years after high school trying to work myself up. Shipping clerk, salesman, business of one kind or another. And it's a measly manner of existence. To get on that subway on the hot mornings in summer. To devote your whole life to keeping stock, or making phone calls, or selling or buying. To suffer fifty weeks of the year for the sake of a two-week vacation, when all you really desire is to be outdoors, with your shirt off. And always to have to get ahead of the next fella. And still—that's how you build a future.

HAPPY. Well, you really enjoy in on a farm? Are you content out there?

BIFF (*with rising agitation*). Hap, I've had twenty or thirty different kinds of jobs since I left home before the war, and it always turns out the same. I just realized it lately. In Nebraska when I herded cattle, and the Dakotas, and Arizona, and now in Texas. It's why I came home now, I guess, because I realized it. This farm I work on, it's spring there now, see? And they've got about fifteen new colts. There's nothing more inspiring or—beautiful than the sight of a mare and a new colt. And it's cool there now, see? Texas is cool now, and it's spring. And whenever spring comes to where I am, I suddenly get the feeling, my God, I'm not gettin' anywhere! What the hell am I doing, playing around with horses, twenty-eight dollars a week! I'm thirty-four years old, I oughta be makin' my future. That's when I come running home. And now, I get here, and I don't know what to do with myself. (*After a pause*) I've always made a point of not wasting my life, and everytime I come back here I know that all I've done is to waste my life.

HAPPY. You're a poet, you know that, Biff? You're a—you're an idealist!

BIFF. No, I'm mixed up very bad. Maybe I oughta get married. Maybe I oughta get stuck into something. Maybe that's my trouble. I'm like a boy. I'm not married, I'm not in business, I just—I'm like a boy. Are you content, Hap? You're a success, aren't you? Are you content?

HAPPY. Hell, no!

BIFF. Why? You're making money, aren't you?

HAPPY *(moving about with energy, expressiveness).* All I can do now is wait for the merchandise manager to die. And suppose I get to be merchandise manager? He's a good friend of mine, and he just built a terrific estate on Long Island. And he lived there about two months and sold it, and now he's building another one. He can't enjoy it once it's finished. And I know that's just what I would do. I don't know what the hell I'm workin' for. Sometimes I sit in my apartment—all alone. And I think of the rent I'm paying. And it's crazy. But then, it's what I always wanted. My own apartment, a car, and plenty of women. And still, goddammit, I'm lonely.

BIFF *(with enthusiasm).* Listen, why don't you come out West with me?

HAPPY. You and I, heh?

BIFF. Sure, maybe we could buy a ranch. Raise cattle, use our muscles. Men built like we are should be working out in the open.

HAPPY *(avidly).* The Loman Brothers, heh?

BIFF *(with vast affection)* Sure, we'd be known all over the counties!

HAPPY *(enthralled).* That's what I dream about, Biff. Sometimes I want to just rip my clothes off in the middle of the store and outbox that goddam merchandise manager. I mean I can outbox, outrun, and outlift anybody in that store, and I have to take orders from those common, petty sons-of-bitches till I can't stand it any more.

BIFF. I'm tellin' you, kid, if you were with me I'd be happy out there.

HAPPY *(enthused).* See, Biff, everybody around me is so false that I'm constantly lowering my ideals . . .

BIFF. Baby, together we'd stand up for one another, we'd have someone to trust.

HAPPY. If I were around you—

BIFF. Hap, the trouble is we weren't brought up to grub for money. I don't know how to do it.

HAPPY. Neither can I!

BIFF. Then let's go!

HAPPY. The only thing is—what can you make out there?

BIFF. But look at your friend. Builds an estate and then hasn't the peace of mind to live in it.

HAPPY. Yeah, but when he walks into the store the waves part in front of him. That's fifty-two thousand dollars a year coming through the revolving door, and I got more in my pinky finger than he's got in his head.

BIFF. Yeah, but you just said—

HAPPY. I gotta show some of those pompous, self-important executives over there that Hap Loman can make the grade. I want to walk into the store the way he walks in. Then I'll go with you, Biff. We'll be together yet, I swear. But take those two we had tonight. Now weren't they gorgeous creatures?

BIFF. Yeah, yeah, most gorgeous I've had in years.

HAPPY. I get that any time I want, Biff. Whenever I feel disgusted. The only trouble is, it gets like bowling or something. I just keep knockin' them over and it doesn't mean anything. You still run around a lot?

BIFF. Naa. I'd like to find a girl—steady, somebody with substance.

HAPPY. That's what I long for.

BIFF. Go on! You'd never come home.

HAPPY. I would! Somebody with character, with resistance! Like Mom, y'know? You're gonna call me a bastard when I tell you this. That girl Charlotte I was with tonight is engaged to be married in five weeks. *(He tries on his new hat)*

BIFF. No kiddin'!

HAPPY. Sure, the guy's in line for the vice-presidency of the store. I don't know what gets into me, maybe I just have an overdeveloped sense of competition or something, but I went and ruined her, and furthermore I can't get rid of her. And he's the third executive I've done that to. Isn't that a crummy characteristic? And to top it all, I go to their weddings! *(Indignantly, but laughing)* Like I'm not supposed to take bribes. Manufacturers offer me a hundred-dollar bill now and then to throw an order their way. You know how honest I am, but it's like this girl, see. I hate myself for it. Because I don't want the girl, and, still, I take it and—I love it!

BIFF. Let's go to sleep.

HAPPY. I guess we didn't settle anything, heh?

BIFF. I just got one idea that I think I'm going to try.

HAPPY. What's that?

BIFF. Remember Bill Oliver?

HAPPY. Sure, Oliver is very big now. You want to work for him again?

BIFF. No, but when I quit he said something to me. He put his arm on my shoulder, and he said, "Biff, if you ever need anything, come to me."

HAPPY. I remember that. That sounds good.

BIFF. I think I'll go to see him. If I could get ten thousand or even seven or eight thousand dollars I could buy a beautiful ranch.

HAPPY. I bet he'd back you. 'Cause he thought highly of you, Biff. I mean, they all do. You're well liked, Biff. That's why I say to come back here, and we both have the apartment. And I'm tellin' you, Biff, any babe you want . . .

BIFF. No, with a ranch I could do the work I like and still be something. I just wonder though. I wonder if Oliver still thinks I stole that carton of basketballs.

HAPPY. Oh, he probably forgot that long ago. It's almost ten years. You're too sensitive. Anyway, he didn't really fire you.

BIFF. Well, I think he was going to. I think that's why I quit. I was never sure whether he knew or not. I know he thought the world of me, though. I was the only one he'd let lock up the place.

WILLY (below). You gonna wash the engine, Biff?

HAPPY. Shh!

BIFF *looks at* HAPPY, *who is gazing down, listening.* WILLY *is mumbling in the parlor.*

HAPPY. You hear that?

They listen. WILLY *laughs warmly.*

BIFF (growing angry). Doesn't he know Mom can hear that?

WILLY. Don't get your sweater dirty, Biff!

A look of pain crosses BIFF'S *face.*

HAPPY. Isn't that terrible? Don't leave again, will you? You'll find a job here. You gotta stick around. I don't know what to do about him, it's getting embarrassing.

WILLY. What a simonizing job!

BIFF. Mom's hearing that!

WILLY. No kiddin', Biff, you got a date? Wonderful!

HAPPY. Go on to sleep. But talk to him in the morning, will you?

BIFF (reluctantly getting into bed). With her in the house. Brother!

HAPPY (getting into bed). I wish you'd have a good talk with him.

The light on their room begins to fade.

BIFF (to himself in bed). That selfish, stupid . . .

HAPPY. Sh . . . Sleep, Biff.

Their light is out. Well before they have finished speaking, WILLY'S *form is dimly seen below in the darkened kitchen. He opens the refrigerator, searches in there, and takes out a bottle of milk. The apartment houses are fading out, and the entire house and surroundings become covered with leaves. Music insinuates itself as the leaves appear.*

WILLY. Just wanna be careful with those girls, Biff, that's all. Don't make any promises. No promises of any kind. Because a girl, y'know, they always believe what you tell 'em, and you're very young, Biff, you're too young to be talking seriously to girls.

Light rises on the kitchen, WILLY, talking, shuts the refrigerator door and comes downstage to the kitchen table. He pours milk into a glass. He is totally immersed in himself, smiling faintly.

WILLY. Too young entirely, Biff. You want to watch your schooling first. Then when you're all set, there'll be plenty of girls for a boy like you. *(He smiles broadly at a kitchen chair)* That so? The girls pay for you? *(He laughs)* Boy, you must really be makin' a hit.

WILLY is gradually addressing—physically—a point offstage, speaking through the wall of the kitchen, and his voice has been rising in volume to that of a normal conversation.

WILLY. I been wondering why you polish the car so careful. Ha! Don't leave the hubcaps, boys. Get the chamois to the hubcaps. Happy, use newspaper on the windows, it's the easiest thing. Show him how to do it, Biff! You see, Happy? Pad it up, use it like a pad. That's it, that's it, good work. You're doin' all right, Hap. *(He pauses, then nods in approbation for a few seconds, then looks upward)* Biff, first thing we gotta do when we get time is clip that big branch over the house. Afraid it's gonna fall in a storm and hit the roof. Tell you what. We get a rope and sling her around, and then we climb up there with a couple of saws and take her down. Soon as you finish the car, boys, I wanna see ya. I got a surprise for you, boys.

BIFF *(offstage).* Whatta ya got, Dad?

WILLY. No, you finish first. Never leave a job till you're finished—remember that. *(Looking toward the "big trees")* Biff, up in Albany I saw a beautiful hammock. I think I'll buy it next trip, and we'll hang it right between those two elms. Wouldn't that be something? Just swingin' there under those branches. Boy, that would be . . .

Young BIFF and Young HAPPY appear from the direction WILLY was addressing. HAPPY carries rags and a pail of water. BIFF, wearing a sweater with a block "S," carries a football.

BIFF *(pointing in the direction of the car offstage).* How's that, Pop, professional?

WILLY. Terrific. Terrific job, boys. Good work, Biff.

HAPPY. Where's the surprise, Pop?

WILLY. In the back seat of the car.

HAPPY. Boy! *(He runs off)*

BIFF. What is it, Dad? Tell me, what'd you buy?

WILLY *(laughing, cuffs him).* Never mind, something I want you to have.

BIFF *(turns and starts off).* What is it, Hap?

HAPPY *(offstage).* It's a punching bag!

BIFF. Oh, Pop!

WILLY. It's got Gene Tunney's signature on in!

HAPPY *runs onstage with a punching bag.*

BIFF. Gee, how'd you know we wanted a punching bag?

WILLY. Well, it's the finest thing for the timing.

HAPPY *(lies down on his back and pedals with his feet).* I'm losing weight, you notice, Pop?

WILLY *(to HAPPY).* Jumping rope is good too.

BIFF. Did you see the new football I got?

WILLY *(examining the ball).* Where'd you get a new ball?

BIFF. The coach told me to practice my passing.

WILLY. That so? And he gave you the ball, heh?

BIFF. Well, I borrowed it from the locker room. *(He laughs confidentially)*

WILLY *(laughing with him at the theft).* I want you to return that.

HAPPY. I told you he wouldn't like it!

BIFF *(angrily).* Well, I'm bringing it back!

WILLY *(stopping the incipient argument, to HAPPY).* Sure, he's gotta practice with a regulation ball, doesn't he? *(To BIFF)* Coach'll probably congratulate you on your initiative!

BIFF. Oh, he keeps congratulating my initiative all the time, Pop.

WILLY. That's because he likes you. If somebody else took that ball there'd be an uproar. So what's the report, boys, what's the report?

BIFF. Where'd you go this time, Dad? Gee we were lonesome for you.

WILLY *(pleased, puts an arm around each boy and they come down to the apron).* Lonesome, heh?

BIFF. Missed you every minute.

WILLY. Don't say? Tell you a secret, boys. Don't breathe it to a soul. Someday I'll have my own business, and I'll never have to leave home any more.

HAPPY. Like Uncle Charley, heh?

WILLY. Bigger than Uncle Charley! Because Charley is not—liked. He's liked, but he's not—well liked.

BIFF. Where'd you go this time, Dad?

WILLY. Well, I got on the road, and I went north to Providence. Met the Mayor.

BIFF. The Mayor of Providence!

WILLY. He was sitting in the hotel lobby.

BIFF. What'd he say?

WILLY. He said, ``Morning!'' And I said, ``You got a fine city here, Mayor.'' And then he had coffee with me. And then I went to Waterbury.

Waterbury is a fine city. Big clock city, the famous Waterbury clock. Sold a nice bill there. And then Boston—Boston is the cradle of the Revolution. A fine city. And a couple of other towns in Mass., and on to Portland and Bangor and straight home!

Biff. Gee, I'd love to go with you sometime, Dad.

Willy. Soon as summer comes.

Happy. Promise?

Willy. You and Hap and I, and I'll show you all the towns. America is full of beautiful towns and fine, upstanding people. And they know me, boys, they know me up and down New England. The finest people. And when I bring you fellas up, there'll be open sesame for all of us, 'cause one thing, boys: I have friends. I can park my car in any street in New England, and the cops protect it like their own. This summer, heh?

Biff and Happy *(together)*. Yeah! You bet!

Willy. We'll take our bathing suits.

Happy. We'll carry your bags, Pop!

Willy. Oh, won't that be something! Me comin' into the Boston stores with you boys carryin' my bags. What a sensation!

Biff *is prancing around, practicing passing the ball.*

Willy. You nervous, Biff, about the game?

Biff. Not if you're gonna be there.

Willy. What do they say about you in school, now that they made you captain?

Happy. There's a crowd of girls behind him everytime the classes change.

Biff *(taking* Willy's *hand)*. This Saturday, Pop, this Saturday—just for you, I'm going to break through for a touchdown.

Happy. You're supposed to pass.

Biff. I'm taking one play for Pop. You watch me, Pop, and when I take off my helmet, that means I'm breakin' out. Then you watch me crash through that line!

Willy *(kisses* Biff*)*. Oh, wait'll I tell this in Boston!

Bernard *enters in knickers. He is younger than* Biff, *earnest and loyal, a worried boy.*

Bernard. Biff, where are you? You're supposed to study with me today.

Willy. Hey, looka Bernard. What're you lookin' so anemic about, Bernard?

Bernard. He's gotta study, Uncle Willy. He's got Regents next week.

Happy *(tauntingly, spinning* Bernard *around)*. Let's box, Bernard!

Bernard. Biff! *(He gets away from* Happy*)* Listen, Biff, I heard Mr. Burnbaum say that if you don't start studyin' math he's gonna flunk you, and you won't graduate. I heard him!

WILLY. You better study with him, Biff. Go ahead now.

BERNARD. I heard him!

BIFF. Oh, Pop, you didn't see my sneakers! *(He holds up a foot for* WILLY *to look at)*

WILLY. Hey, that's a beautiful job of printing!

BERNARD *(wiping his glasses)*. Just because he printed University of Virginia on his sneakers doesn't mean they've got to graduate him, Uncle Willy!

WILLY *(angrily)*. What're you talking about? With scholarships to three universities they're gonna flunk him?

BERNARD. But I heard Mr. Birnbaum say—

WILLY. Don't be a pest, Bernard! *(To his boys)* What an anemic!

BERNARD. Okay, I'm waiting for you in my house, Biff.

BERNARD *goes off. The* LOMANS *laugh.*

WILLY. Bernard is not well liked, is he?

BIFF. He's liked, but he's not well liked.

HAPPY. That's right, Pop.

WILLY. That's just what I mean. Bernard can get the best marks in school, y'understand, but when he gets out in the business world, y'understand, you are going to be five times ahead of him. That's why I thank Almighty God you're both built like Adonises. Because the man who makes an appearance in the business world, the man who creates personal interest, is the man who gets ahead. Be liked and you will never want. You take me, for instance. I never have to wait in line to see a buyer. "Willy Loman is here!" That's all they have to know, and I go right through.

BIFF. Did you knock them dead, Pop?

WILLY. Knocked 'em cold in Providence, slaughtered 'em in Boston.

HAPPY *(on his back, pedaling again)*. I'm losing weight, you notice, Pop?

LINDA *enters, as of old, a ribbon in her hair, carrying a basket of washing.*

LINDA *(with youthful energy)*. Hello, dear!

WILLY. Sweetheart!

LINDA. How'd the Chevvy run?

WILLY. Chevrolet, Linda, is the greatest car ever built. *(To the boys)* Since when do you let your mother carry wash up the stairs?

BIFF. Grab hold there, boy!

HAPPY. Where to, Mom?

LINDA. Hang them up on the line. And you better go down to your friends, Biff. The cellar is full of boys. They don't know what to do with themselves.

BIFF. Ah, when Pop comes home they can wait!

WILLY *(laughs appreciatively)*. You better go down and tell them what to do, Biff.

BIFF. I think I'll have them sweep the furnace room.

WILLY. Good work, Biff.

BIFF *(goes through wall-line of kitchen to doorway at back and calls down)*. Fellas! Everybody sweep out the furnace room! I'll be right down!

VOICES. All right! Okay, Biff.

BIFF. George and Sam and Frank, come out back! We're hangin' up the wash! Come on, Hap, on the double! *(He and* HAPPY *carry out the basket)*

LINDA. The way they obey him!

WILLY. Well, that's training, the training. I'm tellin' you, I was sellin' thousands and thousands, but I had to come home.

LINDA. Oh, the whole block'll be at that game. Did you sell anything?

WILLY. I did five hundred gross in Providence and seven hundred gross in Boston.

LINDA. No! Wait a minute, I've got a pencil. *(She pulls pencil and paper out of her apron pocket)* That makes your commission . . . Two hundred—my God! Two hundred and twelve dollars!

WILLY. Well, I didn't figure it yet, but . . .

LINDA. How much did you do?

WILLY. Well, I—I did—about a hundred and eighty gross in Providence. Well, no—it came to—roughly two hundred gross on the whole trip.

LINDA *(without hesitation)*. Two hundred gross. That's . . . *(She figures)*

WILLY. The trouble was that three of the stores were half closed for inventory in Boston. Otherwise I woulda broke records.

LINDA. Well, it makes seventy dollars and some pennies. That's very good.

WILLY. What do we owe?

LINDA. Well, on the first there's sixteen dollars on the refrigerator—

WILLY. Why sixteen?

LINDA. Well, the fan belt broke, so it was a dollar eighty.

WILLY. But it's brand new.

LINDA. Well, the man said that's the way it is. Till they work themselves in, y'know.

They move through the wall-line into the kitchen.

WILLY. I hope we didn't get stuck on that machine.

LINDA. They got the biggest ads of any of them!

WILLY. I know, it's a fine machine. What else?

LINDA. Well, there's nine-sixty for the washing machine, And for the vacuum cleaner there's three and a half due on the fifteenth. Then the roof, you got twenty-one dollars remaining.

WILLY. It don't leak, does it?

LINDA. No, they did a wonderful job. Then you owe Frank for the carburetor.

WILLY. I'm not going to pay that man! That goddam Chevrolet, they ought to prohibit the manufacture of that car!

LINDA. Well, you owe him three and a half. And odds and ends, comes to around a hundred and twenty dollars by the fifteenth.

WILLY. A hundred and twenty dollars! My God, if business don't pick up I don't know what I'm gonna do!

LINDA. Well, next week you'll do better.

WILLY. Oh, I'll knock 'em dead next week. I'll go to Hartford. I'm very well liked in Hartford. You know, the trouble is, Linda, people don't seem to take to me.

They move onto the forestage.

LINDA. Oh, don't be foolish.

WILLY. I know it when I walk in. They seem to laugh at me.

LINDA. Why? Why would they laugh at you? Don't talk that way, Willy.

WILLY *moves to the edge of the stage.* **LINDA** *goes into the kitchen and starts to darn stockings.*

WILLY. I don't know the reason for it, but they just pass me by. I'm not noticed.

LINDA. But you're doing wonderful, dear. You're making seventy to a hundred dollars a week.

WILLY. But I gotta be at it ten, twelve hours a day. Other men—I don't know—they do it easier. I don't know why—I can't stop myself—I talk too much. A man oughta come in with a few words. One thing about Charley. He's a man of few words, and they respect him.

LINDA. You don't talk too much, you're just lively.

WILLY *(smiling).* Well, I figure, what the hell, life is short, a couple of jokes. *(To himself)* I joke too much! *(The smile goes)*

LINDA. Why? You're—

WILLY. I'm fat. I'm very—foolish to look at, Linda. I didn't tell you, but Christmas time I happened to be calling on F. H. Stewarts, and a salesman I know, as I was going in to see the buyer I heard him say something about—walrus. And I—I cracked him right across the face. I won't take that. I simply will not take that. But they do laugh at me. I know that.

LINDA. Darling . . .

WILLY. I gotta overcome it. I know I gotta overcome it. I'm not dressing to advantage, maybe.

LINDA. Willy, darling, you're the handsomest man in the world—

WILLY. Oh, no, Linda.

LINDA. To me you are. *(Slight pause)* The handsomest.

From the darkness is heard the laughter of a woman. WILLY doesn't turn to it, but it continues through LINDA's lines.

LINDA. And the boys, Willy. Few men are idolized by their children the way you are.

Music is heard as behind a scrim, to the left of the house. THE WOMAN, dimly seen, is dressing.

WILLY *(with great feeling).* You're the best there is, Linda, you're a pal, you know that? On the road—on the road I want to grab you sometimes and just kiss the life outa you.

The laughter is loud now, and he moves into a brightening area at the left, where THE WOMAN has come from behind the scrim and is standing, putting on her hat, looking into a ''mirror'' and laughing.

WILLY. 'Cause I get so lonely—especially when business is bad and there's nobody to talk to. I get the feeling that I'll never sell anything again, that I won't make a living for you, or a business, a business for the boys. *(He talks through THE WOMAN's subsiding laughter; THE WOMAN primps at the ''mirror.'')* There's so much I want to make for—

THE WOMAN. Me? You didn't make me, Willy. I picked you.

WILLY *(pleased).* You picked me?

THE WOMAN *(who is quite proper-looking, WILLY's age).* I did. I've been sitting at that desk watching all the salesmen go by, day in, day out. But you've got such a sense of humor, and we do have such a good time together, don't we?

WILLY. Sure, sure. *(He takes her in his arms)* Why do you have to go now?

THE WOMAN. It's two o'clock . . .

WILLY. No, come on in! *(He pulls her)*

THE WOMAN. . . . . my sister'll be scandalized. When'll you be back?

WILLY. Oh, two weeks about. Will you come up again?

THE WOMAN. Sure thing. You do make me laugh. It's good for me. *(She squeezes his arm, kisses him)* And I think you're a wonderful man.

WILLY. You picked me, heh?

THE WOMAN. Sure. Because you're so sweet. And such a kidder.

WILLY. Well, I'll see you next time I'm in Boston.

THE WOMAN. I'll put you right through to the buyers.

WILLY *(slapping her bottom)*. Right. Well, bottoms up!

THE WOMAN *(slaps him gently and laughs)*. You just kill me, Willy. *(He suddenly grabs her and kisses her roughly)* You kill me. And thanks for the stockings. I love a lot of stockings. Well, good night.

WILLY. Good night. And keep your pores open!

THE WOMAN. Oh, Willy!

THE WOMAN *bursts out laughing, and* LINDA*'s laughter blends in.* THE WOMAN *disappears into the dark. Now the area at the kitchen table brightens.* LINDA *is sitting where she was at the kitchen table, but now is mending a pair of her silk stockings.*

LINDA. You are, Willy. The handsomest man. You've got no reason to feel that—

WILLY *(coming out of* THE WOMAN*'s dimming area and going over to* LINDA*)*. I'll make it all up to you, Linda, I'll—

LINDA. There's nothing to make up, dear. You're doing fine, better than—

WILLY *(noticing her mending)*. What's that?

LINDA. Just mending my stockings. They're so expensive—

WILLY *(angrily, taking them from her)*. I won't have you mending stockings in this house! Now throw them out!

LINDA *puts the stockings in her pocket.*

BERNARD *(entering on the run)*. Where is he? If he doesn't study!

WILLY *(moving to the forestage, with great agitation)*. You'll give him the answers!

BERNARD. I do, but I can't on a Regents! That's a state exam! They're liable to arrest me!

WILLY. Where is he? I'll whip him, I'll whip him!

LINDA. And he'd better give back that football, Willy, it's not nice.

WILLY. Biff! Where is he? Why is he taking everything?

LINDA. He's too rough with the girls, Willy. All the mothers are afraid of him!

WILLY. I'll whip him!

BERNARD. He's driving the car without a license!

THE WOMAN*'s laugh is heard.*

WILLY. Shut up!

LINDA. All the mothers—

WILLY. Shut up!

BERNARD (*backing quietly away and out*). Mr. Birnbaum says he's stuck up.

WILLY. Get outa here!

BERNARD. If he doesn't buckle down he'll flunk math! (*He goes off*)

LINDA. He's right, Willy, you've gotta—

WILLY (*exploding at her*). There's nothing the matter with him! You want him to be a worm like Bernard? He's got spirit, personality . . .

As he speaks, LINDA, *almost in tears, exits into the living room.* WILLY *is alone in the kitchen, wilting and staring. The leaves are gone. It is night again, and the apartment houses look down from behind.*

WILLY. Loaded with it. Loaded! What is he stealing? He's giving it back, isn't he? Why is he stealing? What did I tell him? I never in my life told him anything but decent things.

HAPPY *in pajamas has come down the stairs;* WILLY *suddenly becomes aware of* HAPPY's *presence.*

HAPPY. Let's go now, come on.

WILLY (*sitting down at the kitchen table*). Huh! Why did she have to wax the floors herself? Everytime she waxes the floors she keels over. She knows that!

HAPPY. Shh! Take it easy. What brought you back tonight?

WILLY. I got an awful scare. Nearly hit a kid in Yonkers. God! Why didn't I go to Alaska with my brother Ben that time! Ben! That man was a genius, that man was success incarnate! What a mistake! He begged me to go.

HAPPY. Well, there's no use in—

WILLY. You guys! There was a man started with the clothes on his back and ended up with diamond mines!

HAPPY. Boy, someday I'd like to know how he did it.

WILLY. What's the mystery? The man knew what he wanted and went out and got it! Walked into a jungle, and comes out, the age of twenty-one, and he's rich! The world is an oyster, but you don't crack it open on a mattress!

HAPPY. Pop, I told you I'm gonna retire you for life.

WILLY. You'll retire me for life on seventy goddam dollars a week? And your women and your car and your apartment, and you'll retire me for life! Christ's sake, I couldn't get past Yonkers today! Where are you guys, where are you? The woods are burning! I can't drive a car!

CHARLEY *has appeared in the doorway. He is a large man, slow of speech, laconic, immovable. In all he says, despite what he says, there is pity, and, now, trepidation. He has a robe over pajamas, slippers on his feet. He enters the kitchen.*

CHARLEY. Everything all right?

HAPPY. Yeah, Charley, everything's . . .

WILLY. What's the matter?

CHARLEY. I heard some noise. I thought something happened. Can't we do something about the walls? You sneeze in here, and in my house hats blow off.

HAPPY. Let's go to bed, Dad. Come on.

CHARLEY *signals to* HAPPY *to go.*

WILLY. You go ahead, I'm not tired at the moment.

HAPPY *(to* WILLY*).* Take it easy, huh? *(He exits)*

WILLY. What're you doin' up?

CHARLEY *(sitting down at the kitchen table opposite* WILLY*).* Couldn't sleep good. I had a heartburn.

WILLY. Well, you don't know how to eat.

CHARLEY. I eat with my mouth.

WILLY. No, you're ignorant. You gotta know about vitamins and things like that.

CHARLEY. Come on, let's shoot. Tire you out a little.

WILLY *(hesitantly).* All right. You got cards?

CHARLEY *(taking a deck from his pocket).* Yeah, I got them. Someplace. What is it with those vitamins?

WILLY *(dealing).* They build up your bones. Chemistry.

CHARLEY. Yeah, but there's no bones in a heartburn.

WILLY. What are you talkin' about? Do you know the first thing about it?

CHARLEY. Don't get insulted.

WILLY. Don't talk about something you don't know anything about.

They are playing. Pause.

CHARLEY. What're you doin' home?

WILLY. A little trouble with the car.

CHARLEY. Oh. *(Pause)* I'd like to take a trip to California.

WILLY. Don't say.

CHARLEY. You want a job?

WILLY. I got a job, I told you that. *(After a slight pause)* What the hell are you offering me a job for?

CHARLEY. Don't get insulted.

WILLY. Don't insult me.

CHARLEY. I don't see no sense in it. You don't have to go on this way.

WILLY. I got a good job. *(Slight pause)* What do you keep comin' in here for?

CHARLEY. You want me to go?

WILLY *(after a pause, withering).* I can't understand it. He's going back to Texas again. What the hell is that?

CHARLEY. Let him go.

WILLY. I got nothin' to give him, Charley. I'm clean, I'm clean.

CHARLEY. He won't starve. None a them starve. Forget about him.

WILLY. Then what have I got to remember?

CHARLEY. You take it too hard. To hell with it. When a deposit bottle is broken you don't get your nickel back.

WILLY. That's easy enough for you to say.

CHARLEY. That ain't easy for me to say.

WILLY. Did you see the ceiling I put up in the living-room?

CHARLEY. Yeah, that's a piece of work. To put up a ceiling is a mystery to me. How do you do it?

WILLY. What's the difference?

CHARLEY. Well, talk about it.

WILLY. You gonna put up a ceiling?

CHARLEY. How could I put up a ceiling?

WILLY. Then what the hell are you bothering me for?

CHARLEY. You're insulted again.

WILLY. A man who can't handle tools is not a man. You're disgusting.

CHARLEY. Don't call me disgusting, Willy.

UNCLE BEN, *carrying a valise and an umbrella, enters the forestage from around the right corner of the house. He is a stolid man, in his sixties, with a mustache and an authoritative air. He is utterly certain of his destiny, and there is an aura of far places about him. He enters exactly as* WILLY *speaks.*

WILLY. I'm getting awfully tired, Ben.

BEN's *music is heard.* BEN *looks around at everything.*

CHARLEY. Good, keep playing; you'll sleep better. Did you call me Ben?

BEN *looks at his watch.*

WILLY. That's funny. For a second there you reminded me of my brother Ben.

BEN. I only have a few minutes. *(He strolls, inspecting the place.* WILLY *and* CHARLEY *continue playing)*

CHARLEY. You never heard from him again, heh? Since that time?

WILLY. Didn't Linda tell you? Couple of weeks ago we got a letter from his wife in Africa. He died.

CHARLEY. That so.

BEN *(chuckling).* So this is Brooklyn, eh?

CHARLEY. Maybe you're in for some of his money.

WILLY. Naa, he had seven sons. There's just one opportunity I had with that man . . .

BEN. I must make a train, William. There are several properties I'm looking at in Alaska.

WILLY. Sure, sure! If I'd gone with him to Alaska that time, everything would've been totally different.

CHARLEY. Go on, you'd froze to death up there.

WILLY. What're you talking about?

BEN. Opportunity is tremendous in Alaska, William. Surprised you're not up there.

WILLY. Sure, tremendous.

CHARLEY. Heh?

WILLY. There was the only man I ever met who knew the answers.

CHARLEY. Who?

BEN. How are you all?

WILLY *(taking a pot, smiling).* Fine, fine.

CHARLEY. Pretty sharp tonight.

BEN. Is Mother living with you?

WILLY. No, she died a long time ago.

CHARLEY. Who?

BEN. That's too bad. Fine specimen of a lady, Mother.

WILLY *(to* CHARLEY*).* Heh?

BEN. I'd hoped to see the old girl.

CHARLEY. Who died?

BEN. Heard anything from Father, have you?

WILLY *(unnerved).* What do you mean, who died?

CHARLEY *(taking a pot).* What're you talkin' about?

BEN *(looking at his watch).* William, it's half-past eight!

WILLY *(as though to dispel his confusion he angrily stops* CHARLEY*'s hand).* That's my build!

CHARLEY. I put the ace—

WILLY. If you don't know how to play the game I'm not gonna throw my money away on you!

CHARLEY *(rising).* It was my ace, for God's sake!

WILLY. I'm through, I'm through!

BEN. When did Mother die?

WILLY. Long ago. Since the beginning you never knew how to play cards.

CHARLEY *(picks up the cards and goes to the door).* All right! Next time I'll bring a deck with five aces.

WILLY. I don't play that kind of game!

CHARLEY *(turning to him).* You ought to be ashamed of yourself!

WILLY. Yeah?

CHARLEY. Yeah! *(He goes out)*

WILLY *(slamming the door after him).* Ignoramus!

BEN *(as* WILLY *comes toward him through the wall-line of the kitchen).* So you're William.

WILLY *(shaking* BEN*'s hand).* Ben! I've been waiting for you so long! What's the answer? How did you do it?

BEN. Oh, there's a story in that.

LINDA *enters the forestage, as of old, carrying the wash basket.*

LINDA. Is this Ben?

BEN *(gallantly).* How do you do, my dear.

LINDA. Where've you been all these years? Willy's always wondered why you—

WILLY *(pulling* BEN *away from her impatiently).* Where is Dad? Didn't you follow him? How did you get started?

BEN. Well, I don't know how much you remember.

WILLY. Well, I was just a baby, of course, only three or four years old—

BEN. Three years and eleven months.

WILLY. What a memory, Ben!

BEN. I have many enterprises, William, and I have never kept books.

WILLY. I remember I was sitting under the wagon in—was it Nebraska?

BEN. It was South Dakota, and I gave you a bunch of wild flowers.

WILLY. I remember you walking away down some open road.

BEN *(laughing).* I was going to find Father in Alaska.

WILLY. Where is he?

BEN. At that age I had a very faulty view of geography, William. I discovered after a few days that I was heading due south, so instead of Alaska, I ended up in Africa.

LINDA. Africa!

WILLY. The Gold Coast!

BEN. Principally diamond mines.

LINDA. Diamond mines!

BEN. Yes, my dear. But I've only a few minutes—

WILLY. No! Boys! Boys! *(Young* BIFF *and* HAPPY *appear)* Listen to this. This is your Uncle Ben, a great man! Tell my boys, Ben!

BEN. Why, boys, when I was seventeen I walked into the jungle, and when I was twenty-one I walked out. *(He laughs)* And by God I was rich.

WILLY *(to the boys).* You see what I been talking about? The greatest things can happen!

BEN *(glancing at his watch).* I have an appointment in Ketchikan Tuesday week.

WILLY. No, Ben! Please tell about Dad. I want my boys to hear. I want them to know the kind of stock they spring from. All I remember is a man with a big beard, and I was in Mamma's lap, sitting around a fire, and some kind of high music.

BEN. His flute. He played the flute.

WILLY. Sure, the flute, that's right!

New music is heard, a high, rollicking tune.

BEN. Father was a very great and a very wild-hearted man. We would start in Boston, and he'd toss the whole family into the wagon, and then he'd drive the team right across the country; through Ohio, and Indiana, Michigan, Illinois, and all the Western states. And we'd stop in the towns and sell the flutes that he'd made on the way. Great inventor, Father. With one gadget he made more in a week than a man like you could make in a lifetime.

WILLY. That's just the way I'm bringing them up, Ben—rugged, well liked, all-around.

BEN. Yeah? *(To* BIFF*)* Hit that, boy—hard as you can. *(He pounds his stomach)*

BIFF. Oh, no, sir!

BEN *(taking boxing stance).* Come on, get to me! *(He laughs)*

WILLY. Go to it, Biff! Go ahead, show him!

BIFF. Okay! *(He cocks his fists and starts in)*

LINDA *(to* WILLY*).* Why must he fight, dear?

BEN *(sparring with* BIFF*).* Good boy! Good boy!

WILLY. How's that, Ben, heh?

HAPPY. Give him the left, Biff!

LINDA. Why are you fighting?

BEN. Good boy! *(Suddenly comes in, trips* BIFF, *and stands over him, the point of his umbrella poised over* BIFF'*s eye)*

LINDA. Look out, Biff!

BIFF. Gee!

BEN *(patting* BIFF'*s knee).* Never fight fair with a stranger, boy. You'll never get out of the jungle that way. *(Taking* LINDA'*s hand and bowing)* It was an honor and a pleasure to meet you, Linda.

LINDA *(withdrawing her hand coldly, frightened).* Have a nice—trip.

BEN *(to* WILLY*).* And good luck with your—what do you do?

WILLY. Selling.

BEN. Yes. Well . . . *(He raises his hand in farewell to all)*

WILLY. No, Ben, I don't want you to think . . . *(He takes* BEN'*s arm to show him)* It's Brooklyn, I know, but we hunt too.

BEN. Really, now.

WILLY. Oh, sure, there's snakes and rabbits and—that's why I moved out here. Why, Biff can fell any one of these trees in no time! Boys! Go right over to where they're building the apartment house and get some sand. We're gonna rebuild the entire front stoop right now! Watch this, Ben!

BIFF. Yes, sir! On the double, Hap!

HAPPY *(as he and* BIFF *run off).* I lost weight, Pop, you notice?

CHARLEY *enters in knickers, even before the boys are gone.*

CHARLEY. Listen, if they steal any more from that building the watchman'll put the cops on them!

LINDA *(to* WILLY*).* Don't let Biff . . .

BEN *laughs lustily.*

WILLY. You shoulda seen the lumber they brought home last week. At least a dozen six-by-tens worth all kinds a money.

CHARLEY. Listen, if that watchman—

WILLY. I gave them hell, understand. But I got a couple of fearless characters there.

CHARLEY. Willy, the jails are full of fearless characters.

BEN *(clapping* WILLY *on the back, with a laugh at* CHARLEY*).* And the stock exchange, friend!

WILLY *(joining in* BEN'*s laughter).* Where are the rest of your pants?

CHARLEY. My wife bought them.

WILLY. Now all you need is a golf club and you can go upstairs and go to sleep. *(To* Ben*)* Great athlete! Between him and his son Bernard they can't hammer a nail!

BERNARD *(rushing in).* The watchman's chasing Biff!

WILLY *(angrily).* Shut up! He's not stealing anything!

LINDA *(alarmed, hurrying off left).* Where is he? Biff, dear! *(She exits)*

WILLY *(moving toward the left, away from* Ben*).* There's nothing wrong. What's the matter with you?

BEN. Nervy boy. Good!

WILLY *(laughing).* Oh, nerves of iron, that Biff!

CHARLEY. Don't know what it is. My New England man comes back and he's bleedin', they murdered him up there.

WILLY. It's contacts, Charley, I got important contacts!

CHARLEY *(sarcastically).* Glad to hear it, Willy. Come in later, we'll shoot a little casino. I'll take some of your Portland money. *(He laughs at* WILLY *and exits)*

WILLY *(turning to* Ben*).* Business is bad, it's murderous. But not for me, of course.

BEN. I'll stop by on my way back to Africa.

WILLY *(longingly).* Can't you stay a few days? You're just what I need, Ben, because I—I have a fine position here, but I—well, Dad left when I was such a baby and I never had a chance to talk to him and I still feel—kind of temporary about myself.

BEN. I'll be late for my train.

They are at opposite ends of the stage.

WILLY. Ben, my boys—can't we talk? They'd go into the jaws of hell for me, see, but I—

BEN. William, you're being first-rate with your boys. Outstanding, manly chaps!

WILLY *(hanging on to his words).* Oh, Ben, that's good to hear! Because sometimes I'm afraid that I'm not teaching them the right kind of—Ben, how should I teach them?

BEN *(giving great weight to each word, and with a certain vicious audacity).* William, when I walked into the jungle, I was seventeen. When I walked out I was twenty-one. And, by God, I was rich! *(He goes off into darkness around the right corner of the house)*

WILLY. . . . was rich! That's just the spirit I want to imbue them with! To walk into a jungle! I was right! I was right! I was right!

BEN *is gone, but* WILLY *is still speaking to him as* LINDA, *in nightgown and robe, enters the kitchen, glances around for* WILLY, *then goes to the door* *of the house, looks out and sees him. Comes down to his left. He looks at her.*

LINDA. Willy, dear? Willy?

WILLY. I was right!

LINDA. Did you have some cheese? *(He can't answer)* It's very late, darling. Come to bed, heh?

WILLY *(looking straight up)*. Gotta break your neck to see a star in this yard.

LINDA. You coming in?

WILLY. Whatever happened to that diamond watch fob? Remember? When Ben came from Africa that time? Didn't he give me a watch fob with a diamond in it?

LINDA. You pawned it, dear. Twelve, thirteen years ago. For Biff's radio correspondence course.

WILLY. Gee, that was a beautiful thing. I'll take a walk.

LINDA. But you're in your slippers.

WILLY *(starting to go around the house at the left)*. I was right! I was! *(Half to* LINDA, *as he goes, shaking his head)* What a man! There was a man worth talking to. I was right!

LINDA *(calling after* WILLY). But in your slippers, Willy!

WILLY *is almost gone when* BIFF, *in his pajamas, comes down the stairs and enters the kitchen.*

BIFF. What is he doing out there?

LINDA. Sh!

BIFF. God Almighty, Mom, how long has he been doing this?

LINDA. Don't, he'll hear you.

BIFF. What the hell is the matter with him?

LINDA. It'll pass by morning.

BIFF. Shouldn't we do anything?

LINDA. Oh, my dear, you should do a lot of things, but there's nothing to do, so go to sleep.

HAPPY *comes down the stairs and sits on the steps.*

HAPPY. I never heard him so loud, Mom.

LINDA. Well, come around more often; you'll hear him. *(She sits down at the table and mends the lining of* WILLY*'s jacket.)*

BIFF. Why didn't you ever write me about this, Mom?

LINDA. How would I write to you? For over three months you had no address.

BIFF. I was on the move. But you know I thought of you all the time. You know that, don't you, pal?

LINDA. I know, dear, I know. But he likes to have a letter. Just to know that there's still a possibility for better things.

BIFF. He's not like this all the time, is he?

LINDA. It's when you come home he's always the worst.

BIFF. When I come home?

LINDA. When you write you're coming, he's all smiles, and talks about the future, and—he's just wonderful. And then the closer you seem to come, the more shaky he gets, and then, by the time you get here, he arguing, and he seems angry at you. I think it's just that maybe he can't bring himself to—to open up to you. Why are you so hateful to each other? Why is that?

BIFF *(evasively).* I'm not hateful, Mom.

LINDA. But you no sooner come in the door than you're fighting!

BIFF. I don't know why. I mean to change. I'm tryin', Mom, you understand?

LINDA. Are you home to stay now?

BIFF. I don't know. I want to look around, see what's doin'.

LINDA. Biff, you can't look around all your life, can you?

BIFF. I just can't take hold, Mom. I can't take hold of some kind of a life.

LINDA. Biff, a man is not a bird, to come and go with the springtime.

BIFF. Your hair . . . *(he touches her hair)* Your hair got so gray.

LINDA. Oh, it's been gray since you were in high school. I just stopped dyeing it, that's all.

BIFF. Dye it again, will ya? I don't want my pal looking old. *(He smiles)*

LINDA. You're such a boy! You think you can go away for a year and . . . You've got to get it into your head now that one day you'll knock on this door and there'll be strange people here—

BIFF. What are you talking about? You're not even sixty, Mom.

LINDA. But what about your father?

BIFF *(lamely).* Well, I meant him too.

HAPPY. He admires Pop.

LINDA. Biff, dear, if you don't have any feeling for him, then you can't have any feeling for me.

BIFF. Sure I can, Mom.

LINDA. No. You can't just come to see me, because I love him. *(With a threat, but only a threat, of tears)* He's the dearest man in the world to me, and I won't have anyone making him feel unwanted and low and blue. You've got to make up your mind now, darling, there's no leeway any more. Either he's your father and you pay him that respect, or else you're not to come here. I know he's not easy to get along with—nobody knows that better than me—but . . .

WILLY *(from the left, with a laugh)*. Hey, hey, Biffo!

BIFF *(starting to go out after* WILLY*)*. What the hell is the matter with him? *(*HAPPY *stops him)*

LINDA. Don't—don't go near him!

BIFF. Stop making excuses for him! He always, always wiped the floor with you. Never had an ounce of respect for you.

HAPPY. He's always had respect for—

BIFF. What the hell do you know about it?

HAPPY *(surlily)*. Just don't call him crazy!

BIFF. He's got no character—Charley wouldn't do this. Not in his own house—spewing out that vomit from his mind.

HAPPY. Charley never had to cope with what he's got to.

BIFF. People are worse off than Willy Loman. Believe me, I've seen them!

LINDA. Then make Charley your father, Biff. You can't do that, can you? I don't say he's a great man. Willy Loman never made a lot of money. His name was never in the paper. He's not the finest character that ever lived. But he's a human being, and a terrible thing is happening to him. So attention must be paid. He's not to be allowed to fall into his grave like an old dog. Attention, attention must be finally paid to such a person. You called him crazy—

BIFF. I didn't mean—

LINDA. No, a lot of people think he's lost his—balance. But you don't have to be very smart to know what his trouble is. The man is exhausted.

HAPPY. Sure!

LINDA. A small man can be just as exhausted as a great man. He works for a company thirty-six years this March, opens up unheard-of territories to their trademark, and now in his old age they take his salary away.

HAPPY *(indignantly)*. I didn't know that, Mom.

LINDA. You never asked, my dear! Now that you get your spending money someplace else you don't trouble your mind with him.

HAPPY. But I gave you money last—

LINDA. Christmas time, fifty dollars! To fix the hot water it cost ninety-seven fifty! For five weeks he's been on straight commission, like a beginner, an unknown!

BIFF. Those ungrateful bastards!

LINDA. Are they any worse than his sons? When he brought them business, when he was young, they were glad to see him. But now his old friends, the old buyers that loved him so and always found some order to hand him in a pinch—they're all dead, retired. He used to be able to make six, seven calls a day in Boston. Now he takes his valises out of the car and puts them back and takes them out again and he's exhausted. Instead of walking he talks now. He drives seven hundred miles, and when he gets there no one knows him any more, no one welcomes him. And what goes through a man's mind, driving seven hundred miles home without having earned a cent? Why shouldn't he talk to himself? Why? When he has to go to Charley and borrow fifty dollars a week and pretend to me that it's his pay? How long can that go on? How long? You see what I'm sitting here and waiting for? And you tell me he has no character? The man who never worked a day but for your benefit? When does he get the medal for that? Is this his reward—to turn around at the age of sixty-three and find his sons, who he loved better than his life, one a philandering bum—

HAPPY. Mom!

LINDA. That's all you are, my baby! *(To Biff)* And you! What happened to the love you had for him? You were such pals! How you used to talk to him on the phone every night! How lonely he was till he could come home to you!

BIFF. All right, Mom. I'll live here in my room, and I'll get a job. I'll keep away from him, that's all.

LINDA. No, Biff. You can't stay here and fight all the time.

BIFF. He threw me out of this house, remember that.

LINDA. Why did he do that? I never knew why.

BIFF. Because I know he's a fake and he doesn't like anybody around who knows!

LINDA. Why a fake? In what way? What do you mean?

BIFF. Just don't lay it all at my feet. It's between me and him—that's all I have to say. I'll chip in from now on. He'll settle for half my pay check. He'll be all right. I'm going to bed. *(He starts for the stairs)*

LINDA. He won't be all right.

BIFF *(turning on the stairs, furiously)*. I hate this city and I'll stay here. Now what do you want?

LINDA. He's dying, Biff.

HAPPY *turns quickly to her, shocked.*

BIFF *(after a pause)*. Why is he dying?

LINDA. He's been trying to kill himself.

BIFF *(with great horror)*. How?

LINDA. I live from day to day.

Biff. What're you talking about?

Linda. Remember I wrote you that he smashed up the car again? In February?

Biff. Well?

Linda. The insurance inspector came. He said that they have evidence. That all these accidents in the last year—weren't—weren't— accidents.

Happy. How can they tell that? That's a lie.

Linda. It seems there's a woman . . . *(She takes a breath as . . .)*

⎡ **Biff** *(sharply but contained)*   What woman?

⎣ **Linda** *(simultaneously)*   . . . and this woman . . .

Linda. What?

Biff. Nothing. Go ahead.

Linda. What did you say?

Biff. Nothing. I just said what woman?

Happy. What about her?

Linda. Well, it seems she was walking down the road and saw his car. She says that he wasn't driving fast at all, and that he didn't skid. She says he came to that little bridge, and then deliberately smashed into the railing, and it was only the shallowness of the water that saved him.

Biff. Oh, no, he probably just fell asleep again.

Linda. I don't think he fell asleep.

Biff. Why not?

Linda. Last month . . . *(With great difficulty)* Oh, boys, it's so hard to say a thing like this! He's just a big stupid man to you, but I tell you there's more good in him than in many other people. *(She chokes, wipes her eyes)* I was looking for a fuse. The lights blew out, and I went down the cellar. And behind the fuse box—it happened to fall out— was a length of rubber pipe—just short.

Happy. No kidding?

Linda. There's a little attachment on the end of it. I knew right away. And sure enough, on the bottom of the water heater there's a new little nipple on the gas pipe.

Happy *(angrily)*. That—jerk.

Biff. Did you have it taken off?

Linda. I'm—I'm ashamed to. How can I mention it to him? Every day I go down and take away that little rubber pipe. But, when he comes home, I put it back where it was. How can I insult him that way? I don't know what to do. I live from day to day, boys. I tell you, I know every thought in his mind. It sounds so old-fashioned and silly, but

I tell you he put his whole life into you and you've turned your backs on him. *(She is bent over in the chair, weeping, her face in her hands)* Biff, I swear to God! Biff, his life is in your hands!

HAPPY *(to BIFF)*. How do you like that damned fool!

BIFF *(kissing her)*. All right, pal, all right. It's all settled now. I've been remiss. I know that, Mom. But now I'll stay, and I swear to you, I'll apply myself. *(Kneeling in front of her, in a fever of self-reproach)* It's just—you see, Mom, I don't fit in business. Not that I won't try. I'll try, and I'll make good.

HAPPY. Sure you will. The trouble with you in business was you never tried to please people.

BIFF. I know, I—

HAPPY. Like when you worked for Harrison's. Bob Harrison said you were tops, and then you go and do some damn fool thing like whistling whole songs in the elevator like a comedian.

BIFF *(against HAPPY)*. So what? I like to whistle sometimes.

HAPPY. You don't raise a guy to a responsible job who whistles in the elevator!

LINDA. Well, don't argue about it now.

HAPPY. Like when you'd go off and swim in the middle of the day instead of taking the line around.

BIFF *(his resentment rising)*. Well, don't you run off? You take off sometimes, don't you? On a nice summer day?

HAPPY. Yeah, but I cover myself!

LINDA. Boys!

HAPPY. If I'm going to take a fade the boss can call any number where I'm supposed to be and they'll swear to him that I just left. I'll tell you something that I hate to say, Biff, but in the business world some of them think you're crazy.

BIFF *(angered)*. Screw the business world!

HAPPY. All right, screw it! Great, but cover yourself!

LINDA. Hap, Hap!

BIFF. I don't care what they think! They've laughed at Dad for years, and you know why? Because we don't belong in this nuthouse of a city! We should be mixing cement on some open plain, or—or carpenters. A carpenter is allowed to whistle!

WILLY *walks in from the entrance of the house, at left.*

WILLY. Even your grandfather was better than a carpenter. *(Pause. They watch him)* You never grew up. Bernard does not whistle in the elevator, I assure you.

BIFF *(as though to laugh* WILLY *out of it).* Yeah, but you do, Pop.

WILLY. I never in my life whistled in an elevator! And who in the business world thinks I'm crazy?

BIFF. I didn't mean it like that, Pop. Now don't make a whole thing out of it, will ya?

WILLY. Go back to the West! Be a carpenter, a cowboy, enjoy yourself!

LINDA. Willy, he was just saying—

WILLY. I heard what he said!

HAPPY *(trying to quiet* WILLY*).* Hey, Pop, come on now . . .

WILLY *(continuing over* HAPPY*'s line).* They laugh at me, heh? Go to Filene's, go the the Hub, go to Slattery's, Boston. Call out the name Willy Loman and see what happens! Big shot!

BIFF. All right, Pop.

WILLY. Big!

BIFF. All right!

WILLY. Why do you always insult me?

BIFF. I didn't say a word. *(To* LINDA*)* Did I say a word?

LINDA. He didn't say anything, Willy.

WILLY *(going to the doorway of the living-room).* All right, good night, good night.

LINDA. Willy dear, he just decided . . .

WILLY *(to* BIFF*).* If you get tired hanging around tomorrow, paint the ceiling I put up in the living-room.

BIFF. I'm leaving early tomorrow.

HAPPY. He's going to see Bill Oliver, Pop.

WILLY *(interestedly).* Oliver? For what?

BIFF *(with reserve, but trying, trying).* He always said he'd stake me. I'd like to go into business, so maybe I can take him up on it.

LINDA. Isn't that wonderful?

WILLY. Don't interrupt. What's wonderful about it? There's fifty men in the City of New York who'd stake him. *(To* BIFF*)* Sporting goods?

BIFF. I guess so. I know something about it and—

WILLY. He knows something about it! You know sporting goods better than Spalding, for God's sake! How much is he giving you?

BIFF. I don't know, I didn't even see him yet, but—

WILLY. Then what're you talkin' about?

BIFF *(getting angry).* Well, all I said was I'm gonna see him, that's all!

WILLY *(turning away).* Ah, you're counting your chickens again.

BIFF *(starting left for the stairs).* Oh, Jesus, I'm going to sleep!

Willy *(calling after him)*. Don't curse in this house!

Biff *(turning)*. Since when did you get so clean?

Happy *(trying to stop them)*. Wait a . . .

Willy. Don't use that language to me! I won't have it!

Happy *(grabbing* Biff, *shouts)*. Wait a minute! I got an idea. I got a feasible idea. Come here, Biff, let's talk this over now. Let's talk some sense here. When I was down in Florida last time, I thought of a great idea to sell sporting goods. It just came back to me. You and I, Biff—we have a line, the Loman Line. We train a couple of weeks, and put on a couple of exhibitions, see?

Willy. That's an idea!

Happy. Wait! We form two basketball teams, see? Two water-polo teams. We play each other. It's a million dollars' worth of publicity. Two brothers, see? The Loman Brothers. Displays in the Royal Palms— all the hotels. And banners over the ring and the basketball court: ''Loman Brothers.'' Baby, we could sell sporting goods!

Willy. That is a one-million-dollar idea!

Linda. Marvelous!

Biff. I'm in great shape as far as that's concerned.

Happy. And the beauty of it is, Biff, it wouldn't be like a business. We'd be out playin' ball again . . .

Biff *(enthused)*. Yeah, that's . . .

Willy. Million-dollar . . .

Happy. And you wouldn't get fed up with it, Biff. It'd be the family again. There'd be the old honor, and comradeship, and if you wanted to go off for a swim or somethin'—well, you'd do it! Without some smart cooky gettin' up ahead of you!

Willy. Lick the world! You guys together could absolutely lick the civilized world.

Biff. I'll see Oliver tomorrow. Hap, if we could work that out . . .

Linda. Maybe things are beginning to—

Willy *(wildly enthused, to* Linda*)*. Stop interrupting! *(To* Biff*)* But don't wear sport jacket and slacks when you see Oliver.

Biff. No, I'll—

Willy. A business suit, and talk as little as possible, and don't crack any jokes.

Biff. He did like me. Always liked me.

Linda. He loved you!

Willy *(to* Linda*)*. Will you stop! *(To* Biff*)* Walk in very serious. You are not applying for a boy's job. Money is to pass. Be quiet, fine, and serious. Everybody likes a kidder, but nobody lends him money.

HAPPY. I'll try to get some myself, Biff. I'm sure I can.

WILLY. I see great things for you kids, I think your troubles are over. But remember, start big and you'll end big. Ask for fifteen. How much you gonna ask for?

BIFF. Gee, I don't know—

WILLY. And don't say "Gee." "Gee" is a boy's word. A man walking in for fifteen thousand dollars does not say "Gee!"

BIFF. Ten, I think, would be top though.

WILLY. Don't be so modest. You always started too low. Walk in with a big laugh. Don't look worried. Start off with a couple of your good stories to lighten things up. It's not what you say, it's how you say it— because personality always wins the day.

LINDA. Oliver always thought the highest of him—

WILLY. Will you let me talk?

BIFF. Don't yell at her, Pop, will ya?

WILLY *(angrily)*. I was talking, wasn't I?

BIFF. I don't like you yelling at her all the time, and I'm tellin' you, that's all.

WILLY. What're you, takin' over this house?

LINDA. Willy—

WILLY *(turning on her)*. Don't take his side all the time, goddammit!

BIFF *(furiously)*. Stop yelling at her!

WILLY *(suddenly pulling on his cheek, beaten down, guilt ridden)*. Give my best to Bill Oliver—he may remember me. *(He exits through the living-room doorway)*

LINDA *(her voice subdued)*. What'd you have to start that for? (BIFF *turns away)* You see how sweet he was as soon as you talked hopefully? *(She goes over to* BIFF*)* Come up and say good night to him. Don't let him go to bed that way.

HAPPY. Come on, Biff, let's buck him up.

LINDA. Please, dear. Just say good night. It takes so little to make him happy. Come. *(She goes through the living-room doorway, calling upstairs from within the living-room)* Your pajamas are hanging in the bathroom, Willy!

HAPPY *(looking toward where* LINDA *went out)*. What a woman! They broke the mold when they made her. You know that, Biff?

BIFF. He's off salary. My God, working on commission!

HAPPY. Well, let's face it: he's no hot-shot selling man. Except that sometimes, you have to admit, he's a sweet personality

BIFF *(deciding)*. Lend me ten bucks, will ya? I want to buy some new ties.

HAPPY. I'll take you to a place I know. Beautiful stuff. Wear one of my striped shirts tomorrow.

BIFF. She got gray. Mom got awful old. Gee, I'm gonna go in to Oliver tomorrow and knock him for a—

HAPPY. Come on up. Tell that to Dad. Let's give him a whirl. Come on.

BIFF *(steamed up)*. You know, with ten thousand bucks, boy!

HAPPY *(as they go into the living-room)*. That's the talk, Biff, that's the first time I've heard the old confidence out of you! *(From within the living-room, fading off)* You're gonna live with me, kid, and any babe you want just say the word . . .

The last lines are hardly heard. They are mounting the stairs to their parents' bedroom.

LINDA *(entering her bedroom and addressing* WILLY, *who is in the bathroom. She is straightening the bed for him)*. Can you do anything about the shower? It drips.

WILLY *(from the bathroom)*. All of a sudden everything falls to pieces! Goddam plumbing, oughta be sued, those people. I hardly finished putting it in and the thing . . . *(His words rumble off)*

LINDA. I'm just wondering if Oliver will remember him. You think he might?

WILLY *(coming out of the bathroom in his pajamas)*. Remember him? What's the matter with you, you crazy? If he'd've stayed with Oliver he'd be on top by now! Wait'll Oliver gets a look at him. You don't know the average caliber any more. The average young man today—*(he is getting into bed)*—is got a caliber of zero. Greatest thing in the world for him was to bum around.

BIFF *and* HAPPY *enter the bedroom. Slight pause.*

WILLY *(stops short, looking at* BIFF*)*. Glad to hear it, boy.

HAPPY. He wanted to say good night to you, sport.

WILLY *(to* BIFF*)*. Yeah. Knock him dead, boy. What'd you want to tell me?

BIFF. Just take it easy, Pop. Good night. *(He turns to go)*

WILLY *(unable to resist)*. And if anything falls off the desk while you're talking to him—like a package or something—don't you pick it up. They have office boys for that.

LINDA. I'll make a big breakfast—

WILLY. Will you let me finish? *(To* BIFF*)* Tell him you were in the business in the West. Not farm work.

BIFF. All right, Dad.

LINDA. I think everything—

WILLY *(going right through her speech)*. And don't undersell yourself. No less than fifteen thousand dollars.

Biff *(unable to bear him)*. Okay. Good night, Mom. *(He starts moving)*

Willy. Because you got a greatness in you, Biff, remember that. You got all kinds a greatness . . . *(He lies back, exhausted.* Biff *walks out)*

Linda *(calling after* Biff*)*. Sleep well, darling!

Happy. I'm gonna get married, Mom. I wanted to tell you.

Linda. Go to sleep, dear.

Happy *(going)*. I just wanted to tell you.

Willy. Keep up the good work. *(*Happy *exits)* God . . . remember that Ebbets Field game? The championship of the city?

Linda. Just rest. Should I sing to you?

Willy. Yeah. Sing to me. *(*Linda *hums a soft lullaby)* When that team came out—he was the tallest, remember?

Linda. Oh yes. And in gold.

Biff *enters the darkened kitchen, takes a cigarette, and leaves the house. He comes downstage into a golden pool of light. He smokes, staring at the night.*

Willy. Like a young god. Hercules—something like that. And the sun, the sun all around him. Remember how he waved to me? Right up from the field, with the representatives of three colleges standing by? And the buyers I brought, and the cheers when he came out—Loman, Loman, Loman! God almighty, he'll be great yet. A star like that, magnificent, can never really fade away!

The light on Willy *is fading. The gas heater begins to glow through the kitchen wall, near the stairs, a blue flame beneath red coils.*

Linda *(timidly)*. Willy dear, what has he got against you?

Willy. I'm so tired. Don't talk any more.

Biff *slowly returns to the kitchen. He stops, stares toward the heater.*

Linda. Will you ask Howard to let you work in New York?

Willy. First thing in the morning. Everything'll be all right.

Biff *reaches behind the heater and draws out a length of rubber tubing. He is horrified and turns his head toward* Willy's *room, still dimly lit, from which the strains of* Linda's *desperate but monotonous humming rise.*

Willy *(staring through the window into the moonlight)*. Gee, look at the moon moving between the buildings!

Biff *wraps the tubing around his hand and quickly goes up the stairs.*

Curtain

ACT TWO

Music is heard, gay and bright. The curtain rises as the music fades away. WILLY, *in shirt sleeves, is sitting at the kitchen table, sipping coffee, his hat in his lap.* LINDA *is filling his cup when she can.*

WILLY. Wonderful coffee. Meal in itself.

LINDA. Can I make you some eggs?

WILLY. No. Take a breath.

LINDA. You look so rested, dear.

WILLY. I slept like a dead one. First time in months. Imagine, sleeping till ten on a Tuesday morning. Boys left nice and early, heh?

LINDA. They were out of here by eight o'clock.

WILLY. Good work!

LINDA. It was so thrilling to see them leaving together. I can't get over the shaving lotion in this house!

WILLY *(smiling).* Mmm—

LINDA. Biff was very changed this morning. His whole attitude seemed to be hopeful. He couldn't wait to get downtown to see Oliver.

WILLY. He's heading for a change. There's no question, there simply are certain men that take longer to get—solidified. How did he dress?

LINDA. His blue suit. He's so handsome in that suit. He could be a—anything in that suit!

WILLY *gets up from the table.* LINDA *holds his jacket for him.*

WILLY. There's no question, no question at all. Gee, on the way home tonight I'd like to buy some seeds.

LINDA *(laughing).* That'd be wonderful. But not enough sun gets back there. Nothing'll grow any more.

WILLY. You wait, kid, before it's all over we're gonna get a little place out in the country, and I'll raise some vegetables, a couple of chickens . . .

LINDA. You'll do it yet, dear.

WILLY *walks out of his jacket.* LINDA *follows him.*

WILLY. And they'll get married, and come for a weekend. I'd build a little guest house. 'Cause I got so many fine tools, all I'd need would be a little lumber and some peace of mind.

LINDA *(joyfully).* I sewed the lining . . .

WILLY. I could build two guest houses, so they'd both come. Did he decide how much he's going to ask Oliver for?

LINDA *(getting him into the jacket).* He didn't mention it, but I imagine ten or fifteen thousand. You going to talk to Howard today?

WILLY. Yeah. I'll put it to him straight and simple. He'll just have to take me off the road.

LINDA. And Willy, don't forget to ask for a little advance, because we've got the insurance premium. It's the grace period now.

WILLY. That's a hundred . . . ?

LINDA. A hundred and eight, sixty-eight. Because we're a little short again.

WILLY. Why are we short?

LINDA. Well, you had the motor job on the car . . .

WILLY. That goddam Studebaker!

LINDA. And you got one more payment on the refrigerator . . .

WILLY. But it just broke again!

LINDA. Well, it's old, dear.

WILLY. I told you we should've bought a well-advertised machine. Charley bought a General Electric and it's twenty years old and it's still good, that son-of-a-bitch.

LINDA. But, Willy—

WILLY. Whoever heard of a Hastings refrigerator? Once in my life I would like to own something outright before it's broken! I'm always in a race with the junkyard! I just finished paying for the car and it's on its last legs. The refrigerator consumes belts like a goddam maniac. They time those things. They time them so when you finally paid for them, they're used up.

LINDA *(buttoning up his jacket as he unbuttons it)*. All told, about two hundred dollars would carry us, dear. But that includes the last payment on the mortgage. After this payment, Willy, the house belongs to us.

WILLY. It's twenty-five years!

LINDA. Biff was nine years old when we bought it.

WILLY. Well, that's a great thing. To weather a twenty-five-year mortgage is—

LINDA. It's an accomplishment.

WILLY. All the cement, the lumber, the reconstruction I put in this house! There ain't a crack to be found in it any more.

LINDA. Well, it served its purpose.

WILLY. What purpose? Some stranger'll come along, move in, and that's that. If only Biff would take this house, and raise a family . . . *(He starts to go)* Good-by, I'm late.

LINDA *(suddenly remembering)*. Oh, I forgot! You're supposed to meet them for dinner.

WILLY. Me?

LINDA. At Frank's Chop House on Forty-eighth near Sixth Avenue.

WILLY. Is that so! How about you?

LINDA. No, just the three of you. They're gonna blow you to a big meal!

WILLY. Don't say! Who thought of that?

LINDA. Biff came to me this morning, Willy, and he said, "Tell Dad, we want to blow him to a big meal." Be there six o'clock. You and your two boys are going to have dinner.

WILLY. Gee whiz! That's really somethin'. I'm gonna knock Howard for a loop, kid. I'll get an advance, and I'll come home with a New York job. Goddammit, now I'm gonna do it!

LINDA. Oh, that's the spirit, Willy!

WILLY. I will never get behind a wheel the rest of my life!

LINDA. It's changing, Willy, I can feel it changing!

WILLY. Beyond a question. G'by, I'm late. *(He starts to go again)*

LINDA *(calling after him as she runs to the kitchen table for a hand-kerchief)*. You got your glasses?

WILLY *(feels for them, then comes back in)*. Yeah, yeah, got my glasses.

LINDA *(giving him the handkerchief)*. And a handkerchief.

WILLY. Yeah, handkerchief.

LINDA. And your saccharin?

WILLY. Yeah, my saccharin.

LINDA. Be careful on the subway stairs.

She kisses him, and a silk stocking is seen hanging from her hand. WILLY *notices it.*

WILLY. Will you stop mending stockings? At least while I'm in the house. It gets me nervous. I can't tell you. Please.

LINDA *hides the stocking in her hand as she follows* WILLY *across the fore-stage in front of the house.*

LINDA. Remember, Frank's Chop House.

WILLY *(passing the apron)*. Maybe beets would grow out there.

LINDA *(laughing)*. But you tried so many times.

WILLY. Yeah. Well, don't work hard today. *(He disappears around the right corner of the house)*

LINDA. Be careful!

As WILLY *vanishes,* LINDA *waves to him. Suddenly the phone rings. She runs across the stage and into the kitchen and lifts it.*

LINDA. Hello? Oh, Biff! I'm so glad you called, I just . . . Yes, sure, I just told him. Yes, he'll be there for dinner at six o'clock, I didn't forget. Listen, I was just dying to tell you. You know that little rubber pipe I told you about? That he connected to the gas heater? I finally decided to go down the cellar this morning and take it away and destroy it. But it's gone! Imagine? He took it away himself, it isn't there! *(She listens)* When? Oh, then you took it. Oh—nothing, it's just that I'd hoped he'd taken it away himself. Oh, I'm not worried, darling, because this morning he left in such high spirits, it was like the old days! I'm not afraid any more. Did Mr. Oliver see you? . . . Well, you wait there then. And make a nice impression on him, darling. Just don't perspire too much before you see him. And have a nice time with Dad. He may have big news too! . . . That's right, a New York job. And be sweet to him tonight, dear. Be loving to him. Because he's only a little boat looking for a harbor. *(She is trembling with sorrow and joy)* Oh, that's wonderful, Biff, you'll save his life. Thanks, darling. Just put your arm around him when he comes into the restaurant. Give him a smile. That's the boy . . . Good-by, dear. . . . You got your comb? . . . That's fine. Good-by, Biff dear.

In the middle of her speech, HOWARD WAGNER, *thirty-six, wheels on a small typewriter table on which is a wire-recording machine and proceeds to plug it in. This is on the left forestage. Light slowly fades on* LINDA *as it rises on* HOWARD. HOWARD *is intent on threading the machine and only glances over his shoulder as* WILLY *appears.*

WILLY. Pst! Pst!

HOWARD. Hello, Willy, come in.

WILLY. Like to have a little talk with you, Howard.

HOWARD. Sorry to keep you waiting. I'll be with you in a minute.

WILLY. What's that, Howard?

HOWARD. Didn't you ever see one of these? Wire recorder.

WILLY. Oh. Can we talk a minute?

HOWARD. Records things. Just got delivery yesterday. Been driving me crazy, the most terrific machine I ever saw in my life. I was up all night with it.

WILLY. What do you do with it?

HOWARD. I bought it for dictation, but you can do anything with it. Listen to this. I had it home last night. Listen to what I picked up. The first one is my daughter. Get this. *(He flicks the switch and ``Roll out the Barrel'' is heard being whistled)* Listen to that kid whistle.

WILLY. That is lifelike, isn't it?

HOWARD. Seven years old. Get that tone.

WILLY. Ts, ts. Like to ask a little favor if you . . .

The whistling breaks off, and the voice of HOWARD's *daughter is heard.*

HIS DAUGHTER. ``Now you, Daddy.''

HOWARD. She's crazy for me! *(Again the same song is whistled)* That's me! Ha! *(He winks)*

WILLY. You're very good!

The whistling breaks off again. The machine runs silent for a moment.

HOWARD. Sh! Get this now, this is my son.

HIS SON. "The capital of Alabama is Montgomery; the capital of Arizona is Phoenix; the capital of Arkansas is Little Rock; the capital of California is Sacramento . . ." *(and on, and on)*

HOWARD *(holding up five fingers)*. Five years old, Willy!

WILLY. He'll make an announcer some day!

HIS SON *(continuing)*. "The capital . . . "

HOWARD. Get that—alphabetical order! *(The machine breaks off suddenly)* Wait a minute. The maid kicked the plug out.

WILLY. It certainly is a—

HOWARD. Sh, for God's sake!

HIS SON. "It's nine o'clock, Bulova watch time. So I have to go to sleep."

WILLY. That really is—

HOWARD. Wait a minute! The next is my wife.

They wait.

HOWARD'S VOICE. "Go on, say something." *(Pause)* "Well, you gonna talk?"

HIS WIFE. "I can't think of anything."

HOWARD'S VOICE. "Well, talk—it's turning."

HIS WIFE *(shyly, beaten)*. "Hello." *(Silence)* "Oh, Howard, I can't talk into this . . . "

HOWARD *(snapping the machine off)*. That was my wife.

WILLY. That is a wonderful machine. Can we—

HOWARD. I tell you, Willy, I'm gonna take my camera, and my bandsaw, and all my hobbies, and out they go. This is the most fascinating relaxation I ever found.

WILLY. I think I'll get one myself.

HOWARD. Sure, they're only a hundred and a half. You can't do without it. Supposing you wanna hear Jack Benny, see? But you can't be at home at that hour. So you tell the maid to turn the radio on when Jack Benny comes on, and this automatically goes on with the radio . . .

WILLY. And when you come home you . . .

HOWARD.. You can come home twelve o'clock, one o'clock, any time you like, and you get yourself a Coke and sit yourself down, throw the switch, and there's Jack Benny's program in the middle of the night!

WILLY. I'm definitely going to get one. Because lots of times I'm on the road, and I think to myself, what I must be missing on the radio!

HOWARD. Don't you have a radio in the car?

WILLY. Well, yeah, but who ever thinks of turning it on?

HOWARD. Say, aren't you supposed to be in Boston?

WILLY. That's what I want to talk to you about, Howard. You got a minute? *(He draws a chair in from the wing)*

HOWARD. What happened? What're you doing here?

WILLY. Well . . .

HOWARD. You didn't crack up again, did you?

WILLY. Oh, no. No . . .

HOWARD. Geez, you had me worried there for a minute. What's the trouble?

WILLY. Well, tell you the truth, Howard. I've come to the decision that I'd rather not travel any more.

HOWARD. Not travel! Well, what'll you do?

WILLY. Remember, Christmas time, when you had the party here? You said you'd try to think of some spot for me here in town.

HOWARD. With us?

WILLY. Well, sure.

HOWARD. Oh, yeah, yeah. I remember. Well, I couldn't think of anything for you, Willy.

WILLY. I tell ya, Howard. The kids are all grown up, y'know. I don't need much any more. If I could take home—well, sixty-five dollars a week, I could swing it.

HOWARD. Yeah, but Willy, see I—

WILLY. I tell ya why, Howard. Speaking frankly and between the two of us, y'know—I'm just a little tired.

HOWARD. Oh, I could understand that, Willy. But you're a road man, Willy, and we do a road business. We've only got a half-dozen salesmen on the floor here.

WILLY. God knows, Howard, I never asked a favor of any man. But I was with the firm when your father used to carry you in here in his arms.

HOWARD. I know that, Willy, but—

WILLY. Your father came to me the day you were born and asked me what I thought of the name of Howard, may he rest in peace.

HOWARD. I appreciate that, Willy, but there just is no spot here for you. If I had a spot I'd slam you right in, but I just don't have a single solitary spot.

He looks for his lighter. WILLY *has picked it up and gives it to him. Pause.*

WILLY *(with increasing anger)*. Howard, all I need to set my table is fifty dollars a week.

HOWARD. But where am I going to put you, kid?

WILLY. Look, it isn't a question of whether I can sell merchandise, is it?

HOWARD. No, but it's a business, kid, and everybody's gotta pull his own weight.

WILLY *(desperately)*. Just let me tell you a story, Howard—

HOWARD. 'Cause you gotta admit, business is business.

WILLY *(angrily)*. Business is definitely business, but just listen for a minute. You don't understand this. When I was a boy—eighteen, nineteen—I was already on the road. And there was a question in my mind as to whether selling had a future for me. Because in those days I had a yearning to go to Alaska. See, there were three gold strikes in one month in Alaska, and I felt like going out. Just for the ride, you might say.

HOWARD *(barely interested)*. Don't say.

WILLY. Oh, yeah, my father lived many years in Alaska. He was an adventurous man. We've got quite a little streak of self-reliance in our family. I thought I'd go out with my older brother and try to locate him, and maybe settle in the North with the old man. And I was almost decided to go, when I met a salesman in the Parker House. His name was Dave Singleman. And he was eighty-four years old, and he'd drummed merchandise in thirty-one states. And old Dave, he'd go up to his room, y'understand, put on his green velvet slippers—I'll never forget—and pick up his phone and call the buyers, and without ever leaving his room, at the age of eighty-four, he made his living. And when I saw that, I realized that selling was the greatest career a man could want. 'Cause what could be more satisfying than to be able to go, at the age of eighty-four, into twenty or thirty different cities, and pick up a phone, and be remembered and loved and helped by so many different people? Do you know? when he died—and by the way he died the death of a salesman, in his green velvet slippers in the smoker of the New York, New Haven and Hartford, going into Boston—when he died, hundreds of salesmen and buyers were at his funeral. Things were sad on a lotta trains for months after that. *(He stands up.* HOWARD *has not looked at him)* In those days there was personality in it, Howard. There was respect, and comradeship, and gratitude in it. Today, it's all cut and dried, and there's no chance for bringing friendship to bear—or personality. You see what I mean? They don't know me any more.

HOWARD *(moving away, to the right)*. That's just the thing, Willy.

WILLY. If I had forty dollars a week—that's all I'd need. Forty dollars, Howard.

HOWARD. Kid, I can't take blood from a stone, I—

WILLY *(desperation is on him now).* Howard, the year Al Smith was nominated, your father came to me and—

HOWARD *(starting to go off).* I've got to see some people, kid.

WILLY *(stopping him).* I'm talking about your father! There were promises made across this desk! You mustn't tell me you've got people to see—I put thirty-four years into this firm, Howard, and now I can't pay my insurance! You can't eat the orange and throw the peel away—a man is not a piece of fruit! *(After a pause)* Now pay attention. Your father—in 1928 I had a big year. I averaged a hundred and seventy dollars a week in commissions.

HOWARD *(impatiently).* Now, Willy, you never averaged—

WILLY *(banging his hand on the desk).* I averaged a hundred and seventy dollars a week in the year of 1928! And your father came to me—or rather, I was in the office here—it was right over this desk—and he put his hand on my shoulder—

HOWARD *(getting up).* You'll have to excuse me, Willy, I gotta see some people. Pull yourself together. *(Going out)* I'll be back in a little while.

On HOWARD'*s exit, the light on his chair grows very bright and strange.*

WILLY. Pull myself together! What the hell did I say to him? My God, I was yelling at him! How could I! *(*WILLY *breaks off, staring at the light, which occupies the chair, animating it. He approaches this chair, standing across the desk from it)* Frank, Frank, don't you remember what you told me that time? How you put your hand on my shoulder, and Frank . . .

He leans on the desk and as he speaks the dead man's name he accidentally switches on the recorder, and instantly

HOWARD'S SON. `` . . . of New York is Albany. The capital of Ohio is Cincinnati, the capital of Rhode Island is . . .'' *(The recitation continues)*

WILLY *(leaping away with fright, shouting).* Ha! Howard! Howard! Howard!

HOWARD *(rushing in).* What happened?

WILLY *(pointing at the machine, which continues nasally, childishly, with the capital cities).* Shut it off! Shut it off!

HOWARD *(pulling the plug out).* Look, Willy . . .

WILLY *(pressing his hands to his eyes).* I gotta get myself some coffee. I'll get some coffee . . .

Willy starts to walk out. HOWARD *stops him.*

HOWARD *(rolling up the cord).* Willy, look . . .

WILLY. I'll go to Boston.

HOWARD. Willy, you can't go to Boston for us.

WILLY. Why can't I go?

HOWARD. I don't want you to represent us. I've been meaning to tell you for a long time now.

WILLY. Howard, are you firing me?

HOWARD. I think you need a good long rest, Willy.

WILLY. Howard—

HOWARD. And when you feel better, come back, and we'll see if we can work something out.

WILLY. But I gotta earn money, Howard. I'm in no position to—

HOWARD. Where are your sons? Why don't your sons give you a hand?

WILLY. They're working on a very big deal.

HOWARD. This is no time for false pride, Willy. You go to your sons and you tell them that you're tired. You've got two great boys, haven't you?

WILLY. Oh, no question, no question, but in the meantime . . .

HOWARD. Then that's that, heh?

WILLY. All right, I'll go to Boston tomorrow.

HOWARD. No, no.

WILLY. I can't throw myself on my sons. I'm not a cripple!

HOWARD. Look kid, I'm busy this morning.

WILLY (*grasping* HOWARD*'s arm*). Howard, you've got to let me go to Boston!

HOWARD (*hard, keeping himself under control*). I've got a line of people to see this morning. Sit down, take five minutes, and pull yourself together, and then go home, will ya? I need the office, Willy. (*He starts to go, turns, remembering the recorder, starts to push off the table holding the recorder*) Oh, yeah. Whenever you can this week, stop by and drop off the samples. You'll feel better, Willy, and then come back and we'll talk. Pull yourself together, kid, there's people outside.

HOWARD *exits, pushing the table off left.* WILLY *stares into space, exhausted. Now the music is heard*—BEN*'s music*—*first distantly, then closer, closer. As* WILLY *speaks,* BEN *enters from the right. He carries valise and umbrella.*

WILLY. Oh, Ben, how did you do it? What is the answer? Did you wind up the Alaska deal already?

BEN. Doesn't take much time if you know what you're doing. Just a short business trip. Boarding ship in an hour. Wanted to say good-by.

WILLY. Ben, I've got to talk to you.

BEN (*glancing at his watch*). Haven't the time, William.

WILLY (*crossing the apron to* BEN). Ben, nothing's working out. I don't know what to do.

Ben. Now, look here, William. I've bought timberland in Alaska and I need a man to look after things for me.

Willy. God, timberland! Me and my boys in those grand outdoors!

Ben. You've a new continent at your doorstep, William. Get out of these cities, they're full of talk and time payments and courts of law. Screw on your fists and you can fight for a fortune up there.

Willy. Yes, yes! Linda, Linda!

Linda *enters as of old, with the wash.*

Linda. Oh, you're back?

Ben. I haven't much time.

Willy. No, wait! Linda, he's got a proposition for me in Alaska.

Linda. But you've got— *(To Ben)* He's got a beautiful job here.

Willy. But in Alaska, kid, I could—

Linda. You're doing well enough, Willy!

Ben *(to Linda).* Enough for what, my dear?

Linda *(frightened of Ben and angry at him).* Don't say those things to him! Enough to be happy right here, right now. *(To Willy, while Ben laughs)* Why must everybody conquer the world? You're well liked, and the boys love you, and someday— *(to Ben)*—why, old man Wagner told him just the other day that if he keeps it up he'll be a member of the firm, didn't he, Willy?

Willy. Sure, sure. I am building something with this firm, Ben, and if a man is building something he must be on the right track, mustn't he?

Ben. What are you building? Lay your hand on it. Where is it?

Willy *(hesitantly).* That's true, Linda, there's nothing.

Linda. Why? *(To Ben)* There's a man eighty-four years old—

Willy. That's right, Ben, that's right. When I look at that man I say, what is there to worry about?

Ben. Bah!

Willy. It's true, Ben. All he has to do is go into any city, pick up the phone, and he's making his living and you know why?

Ben *(picking up his valise).* I've got to go.

Willy *(holding Ben back).* Look at this boy!

Biff, *in his high school sweater, enters carrying suitcase.* Happy *carries* Biff's *shoulder guards, gold helmet, and football pants.*

Willy. Without a penny to his name, three great universities are begging for him, and from there the sky's the limit, because it's not what you do, Ben. It's who you know and the smile on your face! It's contacts,

Ben, contacts! The whole wealth of Alaska passes over the lunch table at the Commodore Hotel, and that's the wonder, the wonder of this country, that a man can end with diamonds here on the basis of being liked! *(He turns to* BIFF*)* And that's why when you get out on that field today it's important. Because thousands of people will be rooting for you and loving you. *(To* BEN, *who has again begun to leave)* And Ben! when he walks into a business office his name will sound out like a bell and all the doors will open to him! I've seen it, Ben, I've seen it a thousand times! You can't feel it with your hand like timber, but it's there!

BEN. Good-by, William.

WILLY. Ben, am I right? Don't you think I'm right? I value your advice.

BEN. There's a new continent at your doorstep, William. You could walk out rich. Rich! *(He is gone)*

WILLY. We'll do it here, Ben! You hear me? We're gonna do it here!

Young BERNARD *rushes in. The gay music of the Boys is heard.*

BERNARD. Oh, gee, I was afraid you left already!

WILLY. Why? What time is it?

BERNARD. It's half-past one!

WILLY. Well, come on, everybody! Ebbets Field next stop! Where's the pennants? *(He rushes through the wall-line of the kitchen and out into the living-room)*

LINDA *(to* BIFF*)*. Did you pack fresh underwear?

BIFF *(who has been limbering up)*. I want to go!

BERNARD. Biff, I'm carrying your helmet, ain't I?

HAPPY. No, I'm carrying the helmet.

BERNARD. Oh, Biff, you promised me.

HAPPY. I'm carrying the helmet.

BERNARD. How am I going to get in the locker room?

LINDA. Let him carry the shoulder guards. *(She puts her coat and hat on in the kitchen)*

BERNARD. Can I, Biff? 'Cause I told everybody I'm going to be in the locker room.

HAPPY. In Ebbets Field it's the clubhouse.

BERNARD. I meant the clubhouse. Biff!

HAPPY. Biff!

BIFF *(grandly, after a slight pause)*. Let him carry the shoulder guards.

HAPPY *(as he gives* BERNARD *the shoulder guards)*. Stay close to us now.

WILLY *rushes in with the pennants.*

WILLY *(handing them out).* Everybody wave when Biff comes out on the field. *(*HAPPY *and* BERNARD *run off)* You set now, boy?

The music has died away.

BIFF. Ready to go, Pop. Every muscle is ready.

WILLY *(at the edge of the apron).* You realize what this means?

BIFF. That's right, Pop.

WILLY *(feeling* BIFF'S *muscles).* You're comin' home this afternoon captain of the All-Scholastic Championship Team of the City of New York.

BIFF. I got it, Pop. And remember, pal, when I take off my helmet, that touchdown is for you.

WILLY. Let's go! *(He is starting out, with his arm around* BIFF, *when* CHARLEY *enters, as of old, in knickers)* I got no room for you, Charley.

CHARLEY. Room? For what?

WILLY. In the car.

CHARLEY. You goin' for a ride? I wanted to shoot some casino.

WILLY *(furiously).* Casino! *(Incredulously)* Don't you realize what today is?

LINDA. Oh, he knows, Willy. He's just kidding you.

WILLY. That's nothing to kid about!

CHARLEY. No, Linda, what's goin' on?

LINDA. He's playing in Ebbets Field.

CHARLEY. Baseball in this weather?

WILLY. Don't talk to him. Come on, come on! *(He is pushing them out)*

CHARLEY. Wait a minute, didn't you hear the news?

WILLY. What?

CHARLEY. Don't you listen to the radio? Ebbets Field just blew up.

WILLY. You go to hell! *(*CHARLEY *laughs) (Pushing them out)* Come on, come on! We're late.

CHARLEY *(as they go).* Knock a homer, Biff, knock a homer!

WILLY *(the last to leave, turning to* CHARLEY*).* I don't think that was funny, Charley. This is the greatest day of his life.

CHARLEY. Willy, when are you going to grow up?

WILLY. Yeah, heh? When this game is over, Charley, you'll be laughing out of the other side of your face. They'll be calling him another Red Grange. Twenty-five thousand a year.

CHARLEY *(kidding).* Is that so?

WILLY. Yeah, that's so.

CHARLEY. Well, then, I'm sorry, Willy. But tell me something.

WILLY. What?

CHARLEY. Who is Red Grange?

WILLY. Put up your hands. Goddam you, put up your hands!

CHARLEY, *chuckling, shakes his head and walks away, around the left corner of the stage.* WILLY *follows him. The music rises to a mocking frenzy.*

WILLY. Who the hell do you think you are, better than everybody else? You don't know everything, you big, ignorant, stupid . . . Put up your hands!

Light rises, on the right side of the forestage, on a small table in the reception room of CHARLEY's *office. Traffic sounds are heard.* BERNARD, *now mature, sits whistling to himself. A pair of tennis rackets and an overnight bag are on the floor beside him.*

WILLY *(offstage).* What are you walking away for? Don't walk away! If you're going to say something say it to my face! I know you laugh at me behind my back. You'll laugh out of the other side of your goddam face after this game. Touchdown! Touchdown! Eighty thousand people! Touchdown! Right between the goal posts.

BERNARD *is a quiet, earnest, but self-assured young man.* WILLY's *voice is coming from right upstage now.* BERNARD *lowers his feet off the table and listens.* JENNY, *his father's secretary, enters.*

JENNY *(distressed).* Say, Bernard, will you go out in the hall?

BERNARD. What is that noise? Who is it?

JENNY. Mr. Loman. He just got off the elevator.

BERNARD *(getting up).* Who's he arguing with?

JENNY. Nobody. There's nobody with him. I can't deal with him any more, and your father gets all upset everytime he comes. I've got a lot of typing to do, and your father's waiting to sign it. Will you see him?

WILLY *(entering).* Touchdown! Touch—*(He sees* JENNY*)* Jenny, Jenny, good to see you. How're ya? Workin'? Or still honest?

JENNY. Fine. How've you been feeling?

WILLY. Not much any more, Jenny. Ha, Ha! *(He is surprised to see the rackets)*

BERNARD. Hello, Uncle Willy.

WILLY *(almost shocked).* Bernard! Well, look who's here! *(He comes quickly, guiltily, to* BERNARD *and warmly shakes his hand)*

BERNARD. How are you? Good to see you.

WILLY. What are you doing here?

BERNARD. Oh, just stopped by to see Pop. Get off my feet till my train leaves. I'm going to Washington in a few minutes.

WILLY. Is he in?

BERNARD. Yes, he's in his office with the accountant. Sit down.

WILLY *(sitting down)*. What're you going to do in Washington?

BERNARD. Oh, just a case I've got there, Willy.

WILLY. That so? *(Indicating the rackets)* You going to play tennis there?

BERNARD. I'm staying with a friend who's got a court.

WILLY. Don't say. His own tennis court. Must be fine people, I bet.

BERNARD. They are, very nice. Dad tells me Biff's in town.

WILLY *(with a big smile)*. Yeah, Biff's in. Working on a very big deal, Bernard.

BERNARD. What's Biff doing?

WILLY. Well, he's been doing very big things in the West. But he decided to establish himself here. Very big. We've having dinner. Did I hear your wife had a boy?

BERNARD. That's right. Our second.

WILLY. Two boys! What do you know!

BERNARD. What kind of a deal has Biff got?

WILLY. Well, Bill Oliver—very big sporting-goods man—he wants Biff very badly. Called him in from the West. Long distance, carte blanche, special deliveries. Your friends have their own private tennis court?

BERNARD. You still with the old firm, Willy?

WILLY *(after a pause)*. I'm—I'm overjoyed to see how you made the grade, Bernard, overjoyed. It's an encouraging thing to see a young man really—really—Looks very good for Biff—very—*(He breaks off, then)* Bernard—*(He is so full of emotion, he breaks off again)*

BERNARD. What is it, Willy?

WILLY *(small and alone)*. What—what's the secret?

BERNARD. What secret?

WILLY. How—how did you? Why didn't he ever catch on?

BERNARD. I wouldn't know that, Willy.

WILLY *(confidentially, desperately)*. You were his friend, his boyhood friend. There's something I don't understand about it. His life ended after that Ebbets Field game. From the age of seventeen nothing good ever happened to him.

BERNARD. He never trained himself for anything.

WILLY. But he did, he did. After high school he took so many correspondence courses. Radio mechanics; television; God knows what, and never made the slightest mark.

BERNARD *(taking off his glasses)*. Willy, do you want to talk candidly?

WILLY *(rising, faces BERNARD)*. I regard you as a very brilliant man, Bernard. I value your advice.

BERNARD. Oh, the hell with the advice, Willy. I couldn't advise you. There's just one thing I've always wanted to ask you. When he was supposed to graduate, and the math teacher flunked him—

WILLY. Oh, that son-of-a-bitch ruined his life.

BERNARD. Yeah, but, Willy, all he had to do was go to summer school and make up that subject.

WILLY. That's right, that's right.

BERNARD. Did you tell him not to go to summer school?

WILLY. Me? I begged him to go. I ordered him to go!

BERNARD. Then why wouldn't he go?

WILLY. Why? Why! Bernard, that question has been trailing me like a ghost for the last fifteen years. He flunked the subject, and laid down and died like a hammer hit him!

BERNARD. Take it easy, kid.

WILLY. Let me talk to you—I got nobody to talk to. Bernard, Bernard, was it my fault? Y'see? It keeps going around in my mind, maybe I did something to him. I got nothing to give him.

BERNARD. Don't take it so hard.

WILLY. Why did he lay down? What is the story there? You were his friend!

BERNARD. Willy, I remember, it was June, and our grades came out. And he'd flunked math.

WILLY. That son-of-a-bitch!

BERNARD. No, it wasn't right then. Biff just got very angry, I remember, and he was ready to enroll in summer school.

WILLY *(surprised)*. He was?

BERNARD. He wasn't beaten by it at all. But then, Willy, he disappeared from the block for almost a month. And I got the idea that he'd gone up to New England to see you. Did he have a talk with you then?

WILLY *stares in silence.*

BERNARD. Willy?

WILLY *(with a strong edge of resentment in his voice)*. Yeah, he came to Boston. What about it?

BERNARD. Well, just that when he came back—I'll never forget this, it always mystifies me. Because I'd thought so well of Biff, even though he'd always taken advantage of me. I loved him, Willy, y'know? And he came back after that month and took his sneakers—remember those sneakers with "University of Virginia" printed on them? He was so proud of those, wore them every day. And he took them down in the cellar, and burned them up in the furnace. We had a fist fight. It lasted at least half an hour. Just the two of us, punching each other down the cellar, and crying right through it. I've often thought of how strange it was that I knew he'd given up his life. What happened in Boston, Willy?

WILLY *looks at him as at an intruder.*

BERNARD. I just bring it up because you asked me.

WILLY *(angrily)*. Nothing. What do you mean, "What happened?" What's that got to do with anything?

BERNARD. Well, don't get sore.

WILLY. What are you trying to do, blame it on me? If a boy lays down is that my fault?

BERNARD. Now, Willy, don't get—

WILLY. Well, don't—don't talk to me that way! What does that mean, "What happened?"

CHARLEY *enters. He is in his vest, and he carries a bottle of bourbon.*

CHARLEY. Hey, you're going to miss that train. *(He waves the bottle)*

BERNARD. Yeah, I'm going. *(He takes the bottle)* Thanks, Pop. *(He picks up his rackets and bag)* Good-by, Willy, and don't worry about it. You know, "If at first you don't succeed . . ."

WILLY. Yes, I believe in that.

BERNARD. But sometimes, Willy, it's better for a man just to walk away.

WILLY. Walk away?

BERNARD. That's right.

WILLY. But if you can't walk away?

WILLY *(after a slight pause)*. I guess that's when it's tough. *(Extending his hand)* Good-by, Willy.

WILLY *(shaking* BERNARD*'s hand)*. Good-by, boy.

CHARLEY *(an arm on* BERNARD*'s shoulder)*. How do you like this kid? Gonna argue a case in front of the Supreme Court.

BERNARD *(protesting)*. Pop!

WILLY *(genuinely shocked, pained, and happy)*. No! The Supreme Court!

BERNARD. I gotta run. 'By, Dad!

CHARLEY. Knock 'em dead, Bernard!

BERNARD *goes off.*

WILLY *(as* CHARLEY *takes out his wallet)*. The Supreme Court! And he didn't even mention it!

CHARLEY *(counting out money on the desk)*. He don't have to—he's gonna do it.

WILLY. And you never told him what to do, did you? You never took any interest in him.

CHARLEY. My salvation is that I never took any interest in anything. There's some money—fifty dollars. I got an accountant inside.

WILLY. Charley, look . . . *(With difficulty)* I got my insurance to pay. If you can manage it—I need a hundred and ten dollars.

CHARLEY *doesn't reply for a moment; merely stops moving.*

WILLY. I'd draw it from my bank but Linda would know, and I . . .

CHARLEY. Sit down, Willy.

WILLY *(moving toward the chair)*. I'm keeping an account of everything, remember. I'll pay every penny back. *(He sits)*

CHARLEY. Now listen to me, Willy.

WILLY. I want you to know I appreciate . . .

CHARLEY *(sitting down on the table)*. Willy, what're you doin'? What the hell is goin' on in your head?

WILLY. Why? I'm simply . . .

CHARLEY. I offered you a job. You can make fifty dollars a week. And I won't send you on the road.

WILLY. I've got a job.

CHARLEY. Without pay? What kind of a job is a job without pay? *(He rises)* Now, look, kid, enough is enough. I'm no genius but I know when I'm being insulted.

WILLY. Insulted!

CHARLEY. Why don't you want to work for me?

WILLY. What's the matter with you? I've got a job.

CHARLEY. Then what're you walkin' in here every week for?

WILLY *(getting up)*. Well, if you don't want me to walk in here—

CHARLEY. I am offering you a job.

WILLY. I don't want your goddam job!

CHARLEY. When the hell are you going to grow up?

WILLY *(furiously)*. You big ignoramus, if you say that to me again I'll rap you one! I don't care how big you are! *(He's ready to fight)*

Pause.

CHARLEY *(kindly, going to him)*. How much do you need, Willy?

WILLY. Charley, I'm strapped. I'm strapped. I don't know what to do. I was just fired.

CHARLEY. Howard fired you?

WILLY. That snotnose. Imagine that? I named him. I named him Howard.

CHARLEY. Willy, when're you gonna realize that them things don't mean anything? You named him Howard, but you can't sell that. The only thing you got in this world is what you can sell. And the funny thing is that you're a salesman, and you don't know that.

WILLY. I've always tried to think otherwise, I guess. I always felt that if a man was impressive, and well liked, that nothing—

CHARLEY. Why must everybody like you? Who liked J. P. Morgan? Was he impressive? In a Turkish bath he'd look like a butcher. But with his pockets on he was very well liked. Now listen, Willy, I know you don't like me, and nobody can say I'm in love with you, but I'll give you a job because—just for the hell of it, put it that way. Now what do you say?

WILLY. I—I just can't work for you, Charley.

CHARLEY. What're you, jealous of me?

WILLY. I can't work for you, that's all, don't ask me why.

CHARLEY (angered, takes out more bills). You been jealous of me all your life, you damned fool! Here, pay your insurance. (He puts the money in WILLY's hand)

WILLY. I'm keeping strict accounts.

CHARLEY. I've got some work to do. Take care of yourself. And pay your insurance.

WILLY (moving to the right). Funny, y'know? After all the highways, and the trains, and the appointments, and the years, you end up worth more dead than alive.

CHARLEY. Willy, nobody's worth nothin' dead. (After a slight pause) Did you hear what I said?

WILLY stands still, dreaming.

CHARLEY. Willy!

WILLY. Apologize to Bernard for me when you see him. I didn't mean to argue with him. He's a fine boy. They're all fine boys, and they'll end up big—all of them. Someday they'll all play tennis together. Wish me luck, Charley. He saw Bill Oliver today.

CHARLEY. Good luck.

WILLY (on the verge of tears). Charley, you're the only friend I got. Isn't that a remarkable thing? (He goes out)

CHARLEY. Jesus!

CHARLEY stares after him a moment and follows. All light blacks out. Suddenly raucous music is heard, and a red glow rises behind the screen at right. STANLEY, a young waiter, appears, carrying a table, followed by HAPPY, who is carrying two chairs.

STANLEY (putting the table down). That's all right, Mr. Loman, I can handle it myself. (He turns and takes the chairs from HAPPY and places them at the table)

HAPPY (*glancing around*). Oh, this is better.

STANLEY. Sure, in the front there you're in the middle of all kinds a noise. Whenever you got a party, Mr. Loman, you just tell me and I'll put you back here. Y'know, there's a lotta people they don't like it private, because when they go out they like to see a lotta action around them because they're sick and tired to stay in the house by theirself. But I know you, you ain't from Hackensack. You know what I mean?

HAPPY (*sitting down*). So how's it coming, Stanley?

STANLEY. Ah, it's a dog's life. I only wish during the war they'd a took me in the Army. I coulda been dead by now.

HAPPY. My brother's back, Stanley.

STANLEY. Oh, he come back, heh? From the Far West.

HAPPY. Yeah, big cattle man, my brother, so treat him right. And my father's coming too.

STANLEY. Oh, your father too!

HAPPY. You got a couple of nice lobsters?

STANLEY. Hundred per cent, big.

HAPPY. I want them with the claws.

STANLEY. Don't worry, I don't give you no mice. (HAPPY *laughs*) How about some wine? It'll put a head on the meal.

HAPPY. No. You remember, Stanley, that recipe I brought you from overseas? With the champagne in it?

STANLEY. Oh, yeah, sure. I still got it tacked up yet in the kitchen. But that'll have to cost a buck apiece anyways.

HAPPY. That's all right.

STANLEY. What'd you, hit a number or somethin'?

HAPPY. No, it's a little celebration. My brother is—I think he pulled off a big deal today. I think we're going into business together.

STANLEY. Great! That's the best for you. Because a family business, you know what I mean?—that's the best.

HAPPY. That's what I think.

STANLEY. 'Cause what's the difference? Somebody steals? It's in the family. Know what I mean? (*Sotto voce*) Like this bartender here. The boss is goin' crazy what kinda leak he's got in the cash register. You put it in but it don't come out.

HAPPY (*raising his head*). Sh!

STANLEY. What?

HAPPY. You notice I wasn't lookin' right or left, was I?

STANLEY. No.

HAPPY. And my eyes are closed.

STANLEY. So what's the—?

HAPPY. Strudel's comin'.

STANLEY *(catching on, looks around).* Ah, no, there's no—

He breaks off as a furred, lavishly dressed girl enters and sits at the next table. Both follow her with their eyes.

STANLEY. Geez, how'd ya know?

HAPPY. I got radar or something. *(Staring directly at her profile)* Oooooooo . . . Stanley.

STANLEY. I think that's for you, Mr. Loman.

HAPPY. Look at that mouth. Oh, God. And the binoculars.

STANLEY. Geez, you got a life, Mr. Loman.

HAPPY. Wait on her.

STANLEY *(going to the* GIRL*'s table).* Would you like a menu, ma'am?

GIRL. I'm expecting someone, but I'd like a—

HAPPY. Why don't you bring her—excuse me, miss, do you mind? I sell champagne, and I'd like you to try my brand. Bring her a champagne, Stanley.

GIRL. That's awfully nice of you.

HAPPY. Don't mention it. It's all company money. *(He laughs)*

GIRL. That's a charming product to be selling, isn't it?

HAPPY. Oh, gets to be like everything else. Selling is selling, y'know.

GIRL. I suppose.

HAPPY. You don't happen to sell, do you?

GIRL. No, I don't sell.

HAPPY. Would you object to a compliment from a stranger? You ought to be on a magazine cover.

GIRL *(looking at him a little archly).* I have been.

STANLEY *comes in with a glass of champagne.*

HAPPY. What'd I say before, Stanley? You see? She's a cover girl.

STANLEY. Oh, I could see, I could see.

HAPPY *(to the* GIRL*).* What magazine?

GIRL. Oh, a lot of them. *(She takes the drink)* Thank you.

HAPPY. You know what they say in France, don't you? "Champagne is the drink of the complexion"—Hya, Biff!

BIFF *has entered and sits with* HAPPY.

BIFF. Hello, kid. Sorry I'm late.

HAPPY. I just got here. Uh, Miss—?

GIRL. Forsythe.

HAPPY. Miss Forsythe, this is my brother.

BIFF. Is Dad here?

HAPPY. His name is Biff. You might've heard of him. Great football player.

GIRL. Really? What team?

HAPPY. Are you familiar with football?

GIRL. No, I'm afraid I'm not.

HAPPY. Biff is quarterback with the New York Giants.

GIRL. Well, that is nice, isn't it? *(She drinks)*

HAPPY. Good health.

GIRL. I'm happy to meet you.

HAPPY. That's my name. Hap. It's really Harold, but at West Point they called me Happy.

GIRL *(now really impressed)*. Oh, I see. How do you do? *(She turns her profile)*

BIFF. Isn't Dad coming?

HAPPY. You want her?

BIFF. Oh, I could never make that.

HAPPY. I remember the time that idea would never come into your head. Where's the old confidence, Biff?

BIFF. I just saw Oliver—

HAPPY. Wait a minute. I've got to see that old confidence again. Do you want her? She's on call.

BIFF. Oh, no. *(He turns to look at the* GIRL*)*

HAPPY. I'm telling you. Watch this. *(Turning to the* GIRL*)* Honey? *(She turns to him)* Are you busy?

GIRL. Well, I am . . . but I could make a phone call.

HAPPY. Do that, will you, honey? And see if you can get a friend. We'll be here for a while. Biff is one of the greatest football players in the country.

GIRL *(standing up)*. Well, I'm certainly happy to meet you.

HAPPY. Come back soon.

GIRL. I'll try.

HAPPY. Don't try, honey, try hard.

The GIRL *exits.* STANLEY *follows, shaking his head in bewildered admiration.*

HAPPY. Isn't that a shame now? A beautiful girl like that? That's why I can't get married. There's not a good woman in a thousand. New York is loaded with them, kid!

Biff. Hap, look—

Happy. I told you she was on call!

Biff *(strangely unnerved)*. Cut it out, will ya? I want to say something to you.

Happy. Did you see Oliver?

Biff. I saw him all right. Now look, I want to tell Dad a couple of things and I want you to help me.

Happy. What? Is he going to back you?

Biff. Are you crazy? You're out of your goddam head, you know that?

Happy. Why? What happened?

Biff *(breathlessly)*. I did a terrible thing today, Hap. It's been the strangest day I ever went through. I'm all numb, I swear.

Happy. You mean he wouldn't see you?

Biff. Well, I waited six hours for him, see? All day. Kept sending my name in. Even tried to date his secretary so she'd get me to him, but no soap.

Happy. Because you're not showin' the old confidence, Biff. He remembered you, didn't he?

Biff *(stopping Happy with a gesture)*. Finally, about five o'clock, he comes out. Didn't remember who I was or anything. I felt like such an idiot, Hap.

Happy. Did you tell him my Florida idea?

Biff. He walked away. I saw him for one minute. I got so mad I could've torn the walls down! How the hell did I ever get the idea I was a salesman there? I even believed myself that I'd been a salesman for him! And then he gave me one look and—I realized what a ridiculous lie my whole life has been! We've been talking in a dream of fifteen years. I was a shipping clerk.

Happy. What'd you do?

Biff *(with great tension and wonder)*. Well, he left, see. And the secretary went out. I was all alone in the waiting-room. I don't know what came over me, Hap. The next thing I know I'm in his office—paneled walls, everything. I can't explain it. I—Hap, I took his fountain pen.

Happy. Geez, did he catch you?

Biff. I ran out. I ran down all eleven flights. I ran and ran and ran.

Happy. That was an awful dumb—what'd you do that for?

Biff *(agonized)* . I don't know, I just—wanted to take something, I don't know. You gotta help me, Hap. I'm gonna tell Pop.

Happy. You crazy? What for?

BIFF. Hap, he's got to understand that I'm not the man somebody lends that kind of money to. He thinks I've been spiting him all these years and it's eating him up.

HAPPY. That's just it. You tell him something nice.

BIFF. I can't.

HAPPY. Say you got a lunch date with Oliver tomorrow.

BIFF. So what do I do tomorrow?

HAPPY. You leave the house tomorrow and come back at night and say Oliver is thinking it over. And he thinks it over for a couple of weeks, and gradually it fades away and nobody's the worse.

BIFF. But it'll go on forever!

HAPPY. Dad is never so happy as when he's looking forward to something!

WILLY *enters.*

HAPPY. Hello, scout!

WILLY. Gee, I haven't been here in years!

STANLEY *has followed* WILLY *in and sets a chair for him.* STANLEY *starts off but* HAPPY *stops him.*

HAPPY. Stanley!

STANLEY *stands by, waiting for an order.*

BIFF *(going to* WILLY *with guilt, as to an invalid).* Sit down, Pop. You want a drink?

WILLY. Sure, I don't mind.

BIFF. Let's get a load on.

WILLY. You look worried.

BIFF. N-no. *(To* STANLEY*)* Scotch all around. Make it doubles.

STANLEY. Doubles, right. *(He goes)*

WILLY. You had a couple already, didn't you?

BIFF. Just a couple, yeah.

WILLY. Well, what happened, boy? *(Nodding affirmatively, with a smile)* Everything go all right?

BIFF *(takes a breath, then reaches out and grasps* WILLY's *hand).* Pal . . . *(He is smiling bravely, and* WILLY *is smiling too)* I had an experience today.

HAPPY. Terrific, Pop.

WILLY. That so? What happened?

BIFF *(high, slightly alcoholic, above the earth).* I'm going to tell you every-thing from first to last. It's been a strange day. *(Silence. He looks around, composes himself as best he can, but his breath keeps break-ing the rhythm of his voice)* I had to wait quite a while for him, and—

WILLY. Oliver?

BIFF. Yeah, Oliver. All day, as a matter of cold fact. And a lot of—instances—facts, Pop, facts about my life came back to me. Who was it, Pop? Who ever said I was a salesman with Oliver?

WILLY. Well, you were.

BIFF. No, Dad, I was a shipping clerk.

WILLY. But you were practically—

BIFF (with determination). Dad, I don't know who said it first, but I was never a salesman for Bill Oliver.

WILLY. What're you talking about?

BIFF. Let's hold on to the facts tonight, Pop. We're not going to get anywhere bullin' around. I was a shipping clerk.

WILLY (angrily). All right, now listen to me—

BIFF. Why don't you let me finish?

WILLY. I'm not interested in stories about the past or any crap of that kind because the woods are burning, boys, you understand? There's a big blaze going on all around. I was fired today.

BIFF (shocked). How could you be?

WILLY. I was fired, and I'm looking for a little good news to tell your mother, because the woman has waited and the woman has suffered. The gist of it is that I haven't got a story left in my head, Biff. So don't give me a lecture about facts and aspects. I am not interested. Now what've you got to say to me?

STANLEY *enters with three drinks. They wait until he leaves.*

WILLY. Did you see Oliver?

BIFF. Jesus, Dad!

WILLY. You mean you didn't go up there?

HAPPY. Sure he went up there.

BIFF. I did. I—saw him. How could they fire you?

WILLY (on the edge of his chair). What kind of a welcome did he give you?

BIFF. He won't even let you work on commission?

WILLY. I'm out! (Driving) So tell me, he gave you a warm welcome?

HAPPY. Sure, Pop, sure!

BIFF (driven). Well, it was kind of—

WILLY. I was wondering if he'd remember you. (To HAPPY) Imagine, man doesn't see him for ten, twelve years and gives him that kind of a welcome!

HAPPY. Damn right!

BIFF (trying to return to the offensive). Pop, look—

WILLY. You know why he remembered you, don't you? Because you impressed him in those days.

BIFF. Let's talk quietly and get this down to the facts, huh?

WILLY *(as though* BIFF *had been interrupting)*. Well, what happened? It's great news, Biff. Did he take you into his office or'd you talk in the waiting-room?

BIFF. Well, he came in, see, and—

WILLY *(with a big smile)*. What'd he say? Betcha he threw his arm around you.

BIFF. Well, he kinda—

WILLY. He's a fine man. *(To* HAPPY*)* Very hard man to see, y'know.

HAPPY *(agreeing)*. Oh, I know.

WILLY *(to* BIFF*)*. Is that where you had the drinks?

BIFF. Yeah, he gave me a couple of—no, no!

HAPPY *(cutting in)*. He told him my Florida idea.

WILLY. Don't interrupt. *(To* BIFF*)* How'd he react to the Florida idea?

BIFF. Dad, will you give me a minute to explain?

WILLY. I've been waiting for you to explain since I sat down here! What happened? He took you into his office and what?

BIFF. Well—I talked. And—and he listened, see.

WILLY. Famous for the way he listens, y'know. What was his answer?

BIFF. His answer was—*(He breaks off, suddenly angry)* Dad, you're not letting me tell you what I want to tell you!

WILLY *(accusing, angered)*. You didn't see him, did you?

BIFF. I did see him!

WILLY. What'd you insult him or something? You insulted him, didn't you?

BIFF. Listen, will you let me out of it, will you just let me out of it!

HAPPY. What the hell!

WILLY. Tell me what happened!

BIFF *(to* HAPPY*)*. I can't talk to him!

A single trumpet note jars the ear. The light of green leaves stains the house, which holds the air of night and a dream. Young BERNARD *enters and knocks on the door of the house.*

YOUNG BERNARD *(frantically)*. Mrs. Loman, Mrs. Loman!

HAPPY. Tell him what happened!

BIFF *(to* HAPPY*)*. Shut up and leave me alone!

WILLY. No, no! You had to go and flunk math!

BIFF. What math? What're you talking about?

YOUNG BERNARD. Mrs. Loman, Mrs. Loman!

LINDA *appears in the house, as of old.*

WILLY *(wildly).* Math, math, math!

BIFF. Take it easy, Pop!

YOUNG BERNARD. Mrs. Loman!

WILLY *(furiously).* If you hadn't flunked you'd've been set by now!

BIFF. Now, look, I'm gonna tell you what happened, and you're going to listen to me.

YOUNG BERNARD. Mrs. Loman!

BIFF. I waited six hours—

HAPPY. What the hell are you saying?

BIFF. I kept sending in my name but he wouldn't see me. So finally he . . . *(He continues unheard as light fades low on the restaurant)*

YOUNG BERNARD. Biff flunked math!

LINDA. No!

YOUNG BERNARD. Birnbaum flunked him! They won't graduate him!

LINDA. But they have to. He's gotta go to the university. Where is he? Biff! Biff!

YOUNG BERNARD. No, he left. He went to Grand Central.

LINDA. Grand—You mean he went to Boston!

YOUNG BERNARD. Is Uncle Willy in Boston?

LINDA. Oh, maybe Willy can talk to the teacher. Oh, the poor, poor boy!

Light on house area snaps out.

BIFF *(at the table, now audible, holding up a gold fountain pen)* . . . . so I'm washed up with Oliver, you understand? Are you listening to me?

WILLY *(at a loss).* Yeah, sure. If you hadn't flunked—

BIFF. Flunked what? What're you talking about?

WILLY. Don't blame everything on me! I didn't flunk math—you did! What pen?

HAPPY. That was awful dumb, Biff, a pen like that is worth—

WILLY *(seeing the pen for the first time).* You took Oliver's pen?

BIFF *(weakening).* Dad, I just explained it to you.

WILLY. You stole Bill Oliver's fountain pen!

BIFF. I didn't exactly steal it! That's just what I've been explaining to you!

HAPPY. He had it in his hand and just then Oliver walked in, so he got nervous and stuck it in his pocket!

WILLY. My God, Biff!

BIFF. I never intended to do it, Dad!

OPERATOR'S VOICE. Standish Arms, good evening!

WILLY *(shouting)*. I'm not in my room!

BIFF *(frightened)*. Dad, what's the matter? *(He and* HAPPY *stand up)*

OPERATOR. Ringing Mr. Loman for you!

WILLY. I'm not there, stop it!

BIFF *(horrified, gets down on one knee before* WILLY*)*. Dad, I'll make good, I'll make good. *(*WILLY *tries to get to his feet.* BIFF *holds him down)* Sit down now.

WILLY. No, you're no good, you're no good for anything.

BIFF. I am, Dad, I'll find something else, you understand? Now don't worry about anything. *(He holds up* WILLY*'s face)* Talk to me, Dad.

OPERATOR. Mr. Loman does not answer. Shall I page him?

WILLY *(attempting to stand, as though to rush and silence the Operator)*. No, no, no!

HAPPY. He'll strike something, Pop.

WILLY. No, no . . .

BIFF *(desperately, standing over* WILLY*)*. Pop, listen! Listen to me! I'm telling you something good. Oliver talked to his partner about the Florida idea. You listening? He—he talked to his partner, and he came to me . . . I'm going to be all right, you hear? Dad, listen to me, he said it was just a question of the amount!

WILLY. Then you . . . got it?

HAPPY. He's gonna be terrific, Pop!

WILLY *(trying to stand)*. Then you got it, haven't you? You got it! You got it!

BIFF *(agonized, holds* WILLY *down)*. No, no. Look, Pop. I'm supposed to have lunch with them tomorrow. I'm just telling you this so you'll know that I can still make an impression, Pop. And I'll make good somewhere, but I can't go tomorrow, see?

WILLY. Why not? You simply—

BIFF. But the pen, Pop!

WILLY. You give it to him and tell him it was an oversight!

HAPPY. Sure, have lunch tomorrow!

BIFF. I can't say that—

WILLY. You were doing a crossword puzzle and accidentally used his pen!

BIFF. Listen, kid, I took those balls years ago, now I walk in with his fountain pen? That clinches it, don't you see? I can't face him like that! I'll try elsewhere.

PAGE'S VOICE. Paging Mr. Loman!

WILLY. Don't you want to be anything?

BIFF. Pop, how can I go back?

WILLY. You don't want to be anything, is that what's behind it?

BIFF *(now angry at* WILLY *for not crediting his sympathy).* Don't take it that way! You think it was easy walking into that office after what I'd done to him? A team of horses couldn't have dragged me back to Bill Oliver!

WILLY. Then why'd you go?

BIFF. Why did I go? Why did I go! Look at you! Look at what's become of you!

Off left, THE WOMAN *laughs.*

WILLY. Biff, you're going to go to that lunch tomorrow, or—

BIFF. I can't go. I've got no appointment!

HAPPY. Biff, for . . . !

WILLY. Are you spiting me?

BIFF. Don't take it that way! Goddammit!

WILLY *(strikes* BIFF *and falters away from the table).* You rotten little louse! Are you spiting me?

THE WOMAN. Someone's at the door, Willy!

BIFF. I'm no good, can't you see what I am?

HAPPY *(separating them).* Hey, you're in a restaurant! Now cut it out, both of you! *(The girls enter)* Hello, girls, sit down.

THE WOMAN *laughs, off left.*

MISS FORSYTHE. I guess we might as well. This is Letta.

THE WOMAN. Willy, are you going to wake up?

BIFF *(ignoring* WILLY*).* How're ya, miss, sit down. What do you drink?

MISS FORSYTHE. Letta might not be able to stay long.

LETTA. I gotta get up very early tomorrow. I got jury duty. I'm so excited! Were you fellows ever on a jury?

BIFF. No, but I been in front of them! *(The girls laugh)* This is my father.

LETTA. Isn't he cute? Sit down with us, Pop.

HAPPY. Sit him down, Biff!

BIFF *(going to him).* Come on, slugger, drink us under the table. To hell with it! Come on, sit down, pal.

On BIFF's *last insistence,* WILLY *is about to sit.*

THE WOMAN *(now urgently).* Willy, are you going to answer the door!

THE WOMAN's *call pulls* WILLY *back. He starts right, befuddled.*

BIFF. Hey, where are you going?

WILLY. Open the door.

BIFF. The door?

WILLY. The washroom . . . the door . . . where's the door?

BIFF *(leading* WILLY *to the left).* Just go straight down.

WILLY *moves left.*

THE WOMAN. Willy, Willy, are you going to get up, get up, get up, get up?

WILLY *exits left.*

LETTA. I think it's sweet you bring your daddy along.

MISS FORSYTHE. Oh, he isn't really your father!

BIFF *(at left, turning to her resentfully).* Miss Forsythe, you've just seen a prince walk by. A fine, troubled prince. A hard-working, unappreciated prince. A pal, you understand? A good companion. Always for his boys.

LETTA. That's so sweet.

HAPPY. Well, girls, what's the program? We're wasting time. Come on, Biff. Gather round. Where would you like to go?

BIFF. Why don't you do something for him?

HAPPY. Me!

BIFF. Don't you give a damn for him, Hap?

HAPPY. What're you talking about? I'm the one who—

BIFF. I sense it, you don't give a good goddam about him. *(He takes the rolled-up hose from his pocket and puts it on the table in front of* HAPPY*)* Look what I found in the cellar, for Christ's sake. How can you bear to let it go on?

HAPPY. Me? Who goes away? Who runs off and—

BIFF. Yeah, but he doesn't mean anything to you. You could help him—I can't! Don't you understand what I'm talking about? He's going to kill himself, don't you know that?

HAPPY. Don't I know it! Me!

BIFF. Hap, help him! Jesus . . . help him . . . Help me, help me, I can't bear to look at his face! *(Ready to weep, he hurries out, up right)*

HAPPY *(starting after him).* Where are you going?

MISS FORSYTHE. What's he so mad about?

HAPPY. Come on, girls, we'll catch up with him.

MISS FORSYTHE *(as* HAPPY *pushes her out).* Say, I don't like that temper of his!

HAPPY. He's just a little overstrung, he'll be all right!

WILLY *(off left, as* THE WOMAN *laughs).* Don't answer! Don't answer!

LETTA. Don't you want to tell your father—

HAPPY. No, that's not my father. He's just a guy. Come on, we'll catch Biff, and honey, we're going to paint this town! Stanley, where's the check! Hey, Stanley!

They exit. STANLEY *looks toward left.*

STANLEY *(calling to* HAPPY *indignantly).* Mr. Loman! Mr. Loman!

STANLEY *picks up a chair and follows them off. Knocking is heard off left.* The WOMAN *enters, laughing.* WILLY *follows her. She is in a black slip; he is buttoning his shirt. Raw, sensuous music accompanies their speech.*

WILLY. Will you stop laughing? Will you stop?

THE WOMAN. Aren't you going to answer the door? He'll wake the whole hotel.

WILLY. I'm not expecting anybody.

THE WOMAN. Whyn't you have another drink, honey, and stop being so damn self-centered?

WILLY. I'm so lonely.

THE WOMAN. You know you ruined me, Willy? From now on, whenever you come to the office, I'll see that you go right through to the buyers. No waiting at my desk any more, Willy. You ruined me.

WILLY. That's nice of you to say that.

THE WOMAN. Gee, you are self-centered! Why so sad? You are the saddest, self-centeredest soul I ever did see-saw. *(She laughs. He kisses her)* Come on inside, drummer boy. It's silly to be dressing in the middle of the night. *(As knocking is heard)* Aren't you going to answer the door?

WILLY. They're knocking on the wrong door.

THE WOMAN. But I felt the knocking. And he heard us talking in here. Maybe the hotel's on fire!

WILLY *(his terror rising).* It's a mistake.

THE WOMAN. Then tell him to go away!

WILLY. There's nobody there.

THE WOMAN. It's getting on my nerves, Willy. There's somebody standing out there and it's getting on my nerves!

WILLY *(pushing her away from him).* All right, stay in the bathroom here, and don't come out. I think there's a law in Massachusetts about it, so don't come out. It may be that new room clerk. He looked very mean. So don't come out. It's a mistake, there's no fire.

The knocking is heard again. He takes a few steps away from her, and she vanishes into the wing. The light follows him, and now he is facing YOUNG BIFF, *who carries a suitcase.* BIFF *steps toward him. The music is gone.*

BIFF. Why didn't you answer?

WILLY. Biff! What are you doing in Boston?

BIFF. Why didn't you answer? I've been knocking for five minutes, I called you on the phone—

WILLY. I just heard you. I was in the bathroom and had the door shut. Did anything happen home?

BIFF. Dad—I let you down.

WILLY. What do you mean?

BIFF. Dad . . .

WILLY. Biffo, what's this about? *(putting his arm around* BIFF*)* Come on, let's go downstairs and get you a malted.

BIFF. Dad, I flunked math.

WILLY. Not for the term?

BIFF. The term. I haven't got enough credits to graduate.

WILLY. You mean to say Bernard wouldn't give you the answers?

BIFF. He did, he tried, but I only got a sixty-one.

WILLY. And they wouldn't give you four points?

BIFF. Birnbaum refused absolutely. I begged him, Pop, but he won't give me those points. You gotta talk to him before they close the school. Because if he saw the kind of man you are, and you just talked to him in your way, I'm sure he'd come through for me. The class came right before practice, see, and I didn't go enough. Would you talk to him? He'd like you, Pop. You know the way you could talk.

WILLY. You're on. We'll drive right back.

BIFF. Oh, Dad, good work! I'm sure he'll change it for you!

WILLY. Go downstairs and tell the clerk I'm checkin' out. Go right down.

BIFF. Yes, sir! See, the reason he hates me, Pop—one day he was late for class so I got up at the blackboard and imitated him. I crossed my eyes and talked with a lithp.

WILLY *(laughing).* You did? The kids like it?

BIFF. They nearly died laughing!

WILLY. Yeah? What'd you do?

BIFF. The thquare root of thixthy twee is . . . *(*WILLY *bursts out laughing;* BIFF *joins him)* And in the middle of it he walked in!

WILLY *laughs and* THE WOMAN *joins in offstage.*

WILLY *(without hesitation).* Hurry downstairs and—

BIFF. Somebody in there?

WILLY. No, that was next door.

THE WOMAN *laughs offstage.*

BIFF. Somebody got in your bathroom!

WILLY. No, it's the next room, there's a party—

THE WOMAN *(enters, laughing. She lisps this).* Can I come in? There's some-thing in the bathtub, Willy, and it's moving!

WILLY *looks at* BIFF, *who is staring open-mouthed and horrified at* THE WOMAN.

WILLY. Ah—you better go back to your room. They must be finished paint-ing by now. They're painting her room so I let her take a shower here. Go back, go back . . . *(He pushes her)*

THE WOMAN *(resisting).* But I've got to get dressed, Willy, I can't—

WILLY. Get out of here! Go back, go back . . . *(Suddenly striving for the ordi-nary)* This is Miss Francis, Biff, she's a buyer. They're painting her room. Go back, Miss Francis, go back . . .

BIFF *slowly sits down on his suitcase as the argument continues offstage.*

THE WOMAN. Where's my stockings? You promised me stockings, Willy!

WILLY. I have no stockings here!

THE WOMAN. You had two boxes of size nine sheers for me, and I want them!

WILLY. Here, for God's sake, will you get outa here!

THE WOMAN *(enters holding a box of stockings).* I just hope there's nobody in the hall. That's all I hope. *(To* BIFF*)* Are you football or baseball?

BIFF. Football.

THE WOMAN *(angry, humiliated).* That's me too. G'night. *(She snatches her clothes from* WILLY, *and walks out)*

WILLY *(after a pause).* Well, better get going. I want to get to the school first thing in the morning. Get my suits out of the closet. I'll get my valise. *(BIFF doesn't move)* What's the matter? *(BIFF remains motionless, tears falling)* She's a buyer. Buys for J. H. Simmons. She lives down the hall—they're painting. You don't imagine—*(He breaks off. After a pause)* Now listen, pal, she's just a buyer. She sees merchandise in her room and they have to keep it looking just so . . . *(Pause. Assuming command)* All right, get my suits. *(BIFF doesn't move)* Now stop crying and do as I say. I gave you an order. Biff, I gave you an order! Is that what you do when I give you an order? How dare you cry! *(Putting his arm around* BIFF*)* Now look, Biff, when you grow up you'll understand about these things. You mustn't—you mustn't overemphasize a thing like this. I'll see Birnbaum first thing in the morning.

BIFF. Never mind.

WILLY *(getting down beside* BIFF*).* Never mind! He's going to give you those points. I'll see to it.

BIFF. He wouldn't listen to you.

WILLY. He certainly will listen to me. You need those points for the U. of Virginia.

BIFF. I'm not going there.

WILLY. Heh? If I can't get him to change that mark you'll make it up in summer school. You've got all summer to—

BIFF *(his weeping breaking from him).* Dad . . .

WILLY *(infected by it).* Oh, my boy . . .

BIFF. Dad . . .

WILLY. She's nothing to me, Biff. I was lonely, I was terribly lonely.

BIFF. You—you gave her Mama's stockings! *(His tears break through and he rises to go)*

WILLY *(grabbing for* BIFF*).* I gave you an order!

BIFF. Don't touch me, you—liar!

WILLY. Apologize for that!

BIFF. You fake! You phony little fake! You fake! *(Overcome, he turns quickly and weeping fully goes out with his suitcase.* WILLY *is left on the floor on his knees)*

WILLY. I gave you an order! Biff, come back here or I'll beat you! Come back here! I'll whip you!

STANLEY *comes quickly in from the right and stands in front of* WILLY.

WILLY *(shouts at* STANLEY*).* I gave you an order . . .

STANLEY. Hey, let's pick it up, pick it up, Mr. Loman. *(He helps* WILLY *to his feet)* Your boys left with the chippies. They said they'll see you home.

A second WAITER *watches some distance away.*

WILLY. But we were supposed to have dinner together.

Music is heard, WILLY*'s theme.*

STANLEY. Can you make it?

WILLY. I'll—sure, I can make it. *(Suddenly concerned about his clothes)* Do I—I look all right?

STANLEY. Sure, you look all right. *(He flicks a speck off* WILLY*'s lapel)*

WILLY. Here—here's a dollar.

STANLEY. Oh, your son paid me. It's all right.

WILLY *(putting it in* STANLEY*'s hand).* No, take it. You're a good boy.

STANLEY. Oh, no, you don't have to . . .

WILLY. Here—here's some more, I don't need it any more. *(After a slight pause)* Tell me—is there a seed store in the neighborhood?

STANLEY. Seeds? You mean like to plant?

As WILLY *turns,* STANLEY *slips the money back into his jacket pocket.*

WILLY. Yes. Carrots, peas . . .

STANLEY. Well, there's hardware stores on Sixth Avenue, but it may be too late now.

WILLY *(anxiously)*. Oh, I'd better hurry. I've got to get some seeds. *(He starts off to the right)* I've got to get some seeds, right away. Nothing's planted. I don't have a thing in the ground.

WILLY *hurries out as the light goes down.* STANLEY *moves over to the right after him, watches him off. The other* WAITER *has been staring at* WILLY.

STANLEY *(to the* WAITER*)*. Well, whatta you looking at?

The WAITER *picks up the chairs and moves off right.* STANLEY *takes the table and follows him. The light fades on this area. There is a long pause, the sound of the flute coming over. The light gradually rises on the kitchen, which is empty.* HAPPY *appears at the door of the house, followed by* BIFF. HAPPY *is carrying a large bunch of long-stemmed roses. He enters the kitchen, looks around for* LINDA. *Not seeing her, he turns to* BIFF, *who is just outside the house door, and makes a gesture with his hands, indicating "Not here, I guess." He looks into the living-room and freezes. Inside,* LINDA, *unseen, is seated,* WILLY'S *coat on her lap. She rises ominously and quietly and moves toward* HAPPY, *who backs up into the kitchen, afraid.*

HAPPY. Hey, what're you doing up? *(*LINDA *says nothing but moves toward him implacably)* Where's Pop? *(He keeps backing to the right, and now* LINDA *is in full view in the doorway to the living-room)* Is he sleeping?

LINDA. Where were you?

HAPPY *(trying to laugh it off)*. We met two girls, Mom, very fine types. Here, we brought you some flowers. *(Offering them to her)* Put them in your room, Ma.

She knocks them to the floor at BIFF'S *feet. He has now come inside and closed the door behind him. She stares at* BIFF, *silent.*

HAPPY. Now what'd you do that for? Mom, I want you to have some flowers—

LINDA *(cutting* HAPPY *off, violently to* BIFF*)*. Don't you care whether he lives or dies?

HAPPY *(going to the stairs)*. Come upstairs, Biff.

BIFF *(with a flare of disgust, to* HAPPY*)*. Go away from me! *(To* LINDA*)* What do you mean, lives or dies? Nobody's dying around here, pal.

LINDA. Get out of my sight! Get out of here!

BIFF. I wanna see the boss.

LINDA. You're not going near him!

BIFF. Where is he? *(He moves into the living-room and* LINDA *follows)*

LINDA *(shouting after* BIFF*).* You invite him for dinner. He looks forward to it all day—*(*BIFF *appears in his parents' bedroom, looks around, and exits)*—and then you desert him there. There's no stranger you'd do that to!

HAPPY. Why? He had a swell time with us. Listen, when I—*(*LINDA *comes back into the kitchen)*—desert him I hope I don't outlive the day!

LINDA. Get out of here!

HAPPY. Now look, Mom . . .

LINDA. Did you have to go to women tonight? You and your lousy rotten whores!

BIFF *re-enters the kitchen.*

HAPPY. Mom, all we did was follow Biff around trying to cheer him up! *(To* BIFF*)* Boy, what a night you gave me!

LINDA. Get out of here, both of you, and don't come back! I don't want you tormenting him any more. Go on now, get your things together! *(To* BIFF*)* You can sleep in his apartment. *(She starts to pick up the flowers and stops herself)* Pick up this stuff, I'm not your maid any more. Pick it up, you bum, you!

HAPPY *turns his back to her in refusal.* BIFF *slowly moves over and gets down on his knees, picking up the flowers.*

LINDA. You're a pair of animals! Not one, not another living soul would have had the cruelty to walk out on that man in a restaurant!

BIFF *(not looking at her).* Is that what he said?

LINDA. He didn't have to say anything. He was so humiliated he nearly limped when he came in.

HAPPY. But, Mom, he had a great time with us—

BIFF *(cutting him off violently).* Shut up!

Without another word, HAPPY *goes upstairs.*

LINDA. You! You didn't even go in to see if he was all right!

BIFF *(still on the floor in front of* LINDA, *the flowers in his hand; with self-loathing).* No. Didn't. Didn't do a damned thing. How do you like that, heh? Left him babbling in a toilet.

LINDA. You louse. You . . .

BIFF. Now you hit it on the nose! *(He gets up, throws the flowers in the wastebasket)* The scum of the earth, and you're looking at him!

LINDA. Get out of here!

BIFF. I gotta talk to the boss, Mom. Where is he?

LINDA. You're not going near him. Get out of this house!

BIFF *(with absolute assurance, determination)*. No. We're gonna have an abrupt conversation, him and me.

LINDA. You're not talking to him!

Hammering is heard from outside the house, off right. BIFF turns toward the noise.

LINDA *(suddenly pleading)*. Will you please leave him alone?

BIFF. What's he doing out there?

LINDA. He's planting the garden!

BIFF *(quietly)*. Now? Oh, my God!

BIFF moves outside, LINDA following. The light dies down on them and comes up on the center of the apron as WILLY walks into it. He is carrying a flashlight, a hoe, and a handful of seed packets. He raps the top of the hoe sharply to fix it firmly, and then moves to the left, measuring off the distance with his foot. He holds the flashlight to look at the seed packets, reading off the instructions. He is in the blue of night.

WILLY. Carrots . . . quarter-inch apart. Rows . . . one-foot rows. *(He measures it off)* One foot. *(He puts down a package and measures off)* Beets. *(He puts down another package and measures again)* Lettuce. *(He reads the package, puts it down)* One foot—*(He breaks off as BEN appears at the right and moves slowly down to him)* What a proposition, ts, ts. Terrific, terrific. 'Cause she's suffered, Ben, the woman has suffered. You understand me? A man can't go out the way he came in, Ben, a man has got to add up to something. You can't, you can't—*(BEN moves toward him as though to interrupt)* You gotta consider, now. Don't answer so quick. Remember, it's a guaranteed twenty-thousand-dollar proposition. Now look, Ben, I want you to go through the ins and outs of this thing with me. I've got nobody to talk to, Ben, and the woman has suffered, you hear me?

BEN *(standing still, considering)*. What's the proposition?

WILLY. It's twenty thousand dollars on the barrelhead. Guaranteed, gilt-edged, you understand?

BEN. You don't want to make a fool of yourself. They might not honor the policy.

WILLY. How can they dare refuse? Didn't I work like a coolie to meet every premium on the nose? And now they don't pay off? Impossible!

BEN. It's called a cowardly thing, William.

WILLY. Why? Does it take more guts to stand here the rest of my life ringing up a zero?

BEN *(yielding)*. That's a point, William. *(He moves, thinking, turns)* And twenty thousand—that *is* something one can feel with the hand, it is there.

WILLY *(now assured, with rising power).* Oh, Ben, that's the whole beauty of it! I see it like a diamond, shining in the dark, hard and rough, that I can pick up and touch in my hand. Not like—like an appointment! This would not be another damned-fool appointment, Ben, and it changes all the aspects. Because he thinks I'm nothing, see, and so he spites me. But the funeral—*(Straightening up)* Ben, that funeral will be massive! They'll come from Maine, Massachusetts, Vermont, New Hampshire! All the old-timers with the strange license plates—that boy will be thunderstruck, Ben, because he never realized—I am known! Rhode Island, New York, New Jersey—I am known, Ben, and he'll see it with his eyes once and for all. He'll see what I am, Ben! He's in for a shock, that boy!

BEN *(coming down to the edge of the garden).* He'll call you a coward.

WILLY *(suddenly fearful).* No, that would be terrible.

BEN. Yes. And a damned fool.

WILLY. No, no, he mustn't, I won't have that! *(He is broken and desperate)*

BEN. He'll hate you, William.

The gay music of the Boys is heard.

WILLY. Oh, Ben, how do we get back to all the great times? Used to be so full of light, and comradeship, the sleigh-riding in winter, and the ruddiness on his cheeks. And always some kind of good news coming up, always something nice coming up ahead. And never even let me carry the valises in the house, and simonizing, simonizing that little red car! Why, why can't I give him something and not have him hate me?

BEN. Let me think about it. *(He glances at his watch)* I still have a little time. Remarkable proposition, but you've got to be sure you're not making a fool of yourself.

BEN *drifts off upstage and goes out of sight.* BIFF *comes down from the left.*

WILLY *(suddenly conscious of* BIFF, *turns and looks up at him, then begins picking up the packages of seeds in confusion).* Where the hell is that seed? *(Indignantly)* You can't see nothing out here! They boxed in the whole goddam neighborhood!

BIFF. There are people all around here. Don't you realize that?

WILLY. I'm busy. Don't bother me.

BIFF *(taking the hoe from* WILLY). I'm saying good-by to you, Pop. *(*WILLY *looks at him, silent, unable to move)* I'm not coming back any more.

WILLY. You're not going to see Oliver tomorrow?

BIFF. I've got no appointment, Dad.

WILLY. He put his arm around you, and you've got no appointment?

BIFF. Pop, get this now, will you? Everytime I've left it's been a fight that sent me out of here. Today I realized something about myself and I tried to explain it to you and I—I think I'm just not smart enough to make any sense out of it for you. To hell with whose fault it is or anything like that . *(He takes* WILLY's *arm)* Let's just wrap it up, heh? Come on in, we'll tell Mom. *(He gently tries to pull* WILLY *to left)*

WILLY *(frozen, immobile, with guilt in his voice).* No, I don't want to see her.

BIFF. Come on! *(He pulls again, and* WILLY *tries to pull away)*

WILLY *(highly nervous).* No, no, I don't want to see her.

BIFF *(tries to look into* WILLY's *face, as if to find the answer there).* Why don't you want to see her?

WILLY *(more harshly now).* Don't bother me, will you?

BIFF. What do you mean, you don't want to see her? You don't want them calling you yellow, do you? This isn't your fault; it's me, I'm a bum. Now come inside! *(*WILLY *strains to get away)* Did you hear what I said to you?

WILLY *pulls away and quickly goes by himself into the house.* BIFF *follows.*

LINDA *(to* WILLY*).* Did you plant, dear?

BIFF *(at the door, to* LINDA*).* All right, we had it out. I'm going and I'm not writing any more.

LINDA *(going to* WILLY *in the kitchen).* I think that's the best way, dear. 'Cause there's no use drawing it out, you'll just never get along.

WILLY *doesn't respond.*

BIFF. People ask where I am and what I'm doing, you don't know, and you don't care. That way it'll be off your mind and you can start brightening up again. All right? That clears it, doesn't it? *(*WILLY *is silent, and* BIFF *goes to him)* You gonna wish me luck, scout? *(He extends his hand)* What do you say?

LINDA. Shake his hand, Willy.

WILLY *(turning to her, seething with hurt).* There's no necessity to mention the pen at all, y'know.

BIFF *(gently).* I've got no appointment, Dad.

WILLY *(erupting fiercely).* He put his arm around . . . ?

BIFF. Dad, you're never going to see what I am, so what's the use of arguing? If I strike oil I'll send you a check. Meantime forget I'm alive.

WILLY *(to* LINDA*).* Spite, see?

BIFF. Shake hands, Dad.

WILLY. Not my hand.

BIFF. I was hoping not to go this way.

WILLY. Well, this is the way you're going. Good-by.

BIFF *looks at him a moment, then turns sharply and goes to the stairs.*

WILLY (*stops him with*). May you rot in hell if you leave this house!

BIFF (*turning*). Exactly what is it that you want from me?

WILLY. I want you to know, on the train, in the mountains, in the valleys, wherever you go, that you cut down your life for spite!

BIFF. No, no.

WILLY. Spite, spite, is the word of your undoing! And when you're down and out, remember what did it. When you're rotting somewhere beside the railroad tracks, remember, and don't you dare blame it on me!

BIFF. I'm not blaming it on you!

WILLY. I won't take the rap for this, you hear?

HAPPY *comes down the stairs and stands on the bottom step, watching.*

BIFF. That's just what I'm telling you!

WILLY (*sinking into a chair at the table, with full accusation*). You're trying to put a knife in me—don't think I don't know what you're doing!

BIFF. All right, phony! Then let's lay it on the line. (*He whips the rubber tube out of his pocket and puts in on the table*)

HAPPY. You crazy—

LINDA. Biff! (*She moves to grab the hose, but* BIFF *holds it down with his hand*)

BIFF. Leave it there! Don't move it!

WILLY (*not looking at it*). What is that?

BIFF. You know goddam well what that is.

WILLY (*caged, wanting to escape*). I never saw that.

BIFF. You saw it. The mice didn't bring it into the cellar! What is this supposed to do, make a hero out of you? This supposed to make me sorry for you?

WILLY. Never heard of it.

BIFF. There'll be no pity for you, you hear it? No pity!

WILLY (*to* LINDA). You hear the spite!

BIFF. No, you're going to hear the truth—what you are and what I am!

LINDA. Stop it!

WILLY. Spite!

HAPPY (*coming down toward* BIFF). You cut it now!

BIFF (*to* HAPPY). The man don't know who we are! The man is gonna know! (*To* WILLY) We never told the truth for ten minutes in this house!

HAPPY. We always told the truth!

BIFF (*turning on him*). You big blow, are you the assistant buyer? You're one of the two assistants to the assistant, aren't you?

Happy. Well, I'm practically—

Biff. You're practically full of it! We all are! And I'm through with it. *(To* Willy*)* Now hear this, Willy, this is me.

Willy. I know you!

Biff. You know why I had no address for three months? I stole a suit in Kansas City and I was in jail. *(To* Linda, *who is sobbing)* Stop crying. I'm through with it.

Linda *turns away from them, her hands covering her face.*

Willy. I suppose that's my fault!

Biff. I stole myself out of every good job since high school!

Willy. And whose fault is that?

Biff. And I never got anywhere because you blew me so full of hot air I could never stand taking orders from anybody! That's whose fault it is!

Willy. I hear that!

Linda. Don't, Biff!

Biff. It's goddam time you heard that! I had to be boss big shot in two weeks, and I'm through with it!

Willy. Then hang yourself! For spite, hang yourself!

Biff. No! Nobody's hanging himself, Willy! I ran down eleven flights with a pen in my hand today. And suddenly I stopped, you hear me? And in the middle of that office building, do you hear this? I stopped in the middle of that building and I saw—the sky. I saw the things that I love in this world. The work and the food and time to sit and smoke. And I looked at the pen and said to myself, what the hell am I grabbing this for? Why am I trying to become what I don't want to be? What am I doing in an office, making a contemptuous, begging fool of myself, when all I want is out there, waiting for me the minute I say I know who I am! Why can't I say that, Willy? *(He tries to make* Willy *face him, but* Willy *pulls away and moves to the left)*

Willy *(with hatred, threateningly).* The door of your life is wide open!

Biff. Pop! I'm a dime a dozen, and so are you!

Willy *(turning on him now in an uncontrolled outburst).* I am not a dime a dozen! I am Willy Loman, and you are Biff Loman!

Biff *starts for* Willy, *but is blocked by* Happy. *In his fury,* Biff *seems on the verge of attacking his father.*

Biff. I am not a leader of men, Willy, and neither are you. You were never anything but a hard-working drummer who landed in the ash can like all the rest of them! I'm one dollar an hour, Willy! I tried seven states and couldn't raise it. A buck an hour! Do you gather my meaning? I'm not bringing home any prizes any more, and you're going to stop waiting for me to bring them home!

WILLY *(directly to* BIFF*)*. You vengeful, spiteful mutt!

BIFF *breaks from* HAPPY. WILLY, *in fright, starts up the stairs.* BIFF *grabs him.*

BIFF *(at the peak of his fury)*. Pop, I'm nothing! I'm nothing, Pop. Can't you understand that? There's no spite in it any more. I'm just what I am, that's all.

BIFF's *fury has spent itself, and he breaks down, sobbing, holding on to* WILLY, *who dumbly fumbles for* BIFF's *face.*

WILLY *(astonished)*. What're you doing? What're you doing? *(To* LINDA*)* Why is he crying?

BIFF *(crying, broken)*. Will you let me go, for Christ's sake? Will you take that phony dream and burn it before something happens? *(Struggling to contain himself, he pulls away and moves to the stairs)* I'll go in the morning. Put him—put him to bed. *(Exhausted,* BIFF *moves up the stairs to his room)*

WILLY *(after a long pause, astonished, elevated)*. Isn't that—isn't that remarkable? Biff—he likes me!

LINDA. He loves you, Willy!

HAPPY *(deeply moved)*. Always did, Pop.

WILLY. Oh, Biff! *(Staring wildly)* He cried! Cried to me. *(He is choking with his love, and now cries out his promise)* That boy—that boy is going to be magnificent!

BEN *appears in the light just outside the kitchen.*

BEN. Yes, outstanding, with twenty thousand behind him.

LINDA *(sensing the racing of his mind, fearfully, carefully)*. Now come to bed, Willy. It's all settled now.

WILLY *(finding it difficult not to rush out of the house)*. Yes, we'll sleep. Come on. Go to sleep, Hap.

BEN. And it does take a great kind of a man to crack the jungle.

In accents of dread, BEN's *idyllic music starts up.*

HAPPY *(his arm around* LINDA*)*. I'm getting married, Pop, don't forget it. I'm changing everything. I'm gonna run that department before the year is up. You'll see, Mom. *(He kisses her)*

BEN. The jungle is dark but full of diamonds, Willy.

WILLY *turns, moves, listening to* BEN.

LINDA. Be good. You're both good boys, just act that way, that's all.

HAPPY. 'Night, Pop. *(He goes upstairs)*

LINDA *(to* WILLY*).* Come, dear.

BEN *(with greater force).* One must go in to fetch a diamond out.

WILLY *(to* LINDA, *as he moves slowly along the edge of the kitchen toward the door).* I just want to get settled down, Linda. Let me sit alone for a little.

LINDA *(almost uttering her fear).* I want you upstairs.

WILLY *(taking her in his arms).* In a few minutes, Linda. I couldn't sleep right now. Go on, you look awful tired. *(He kisses her)*

BEN. Not like an appointment at all. A diamond is rough and hard to the touch.

WILLY. Go on now. I'll be right up.

LINDA. I think this is the only way, Willy.

WILLY. Sure, it's the best thing.

BEN. Best thing!

WILLY. The only way. Everything is gonna be—go on, kid, get to bed. You look so tired.

LINDA. Come right up.

WILLY. Two minutes.

LINDA *goes into the living-room, then reappears in her bedroom.* WILLY *moves just outside the kitchen door.*

WILLY. Loves me. *(Wonderingly)* Always loved me. Isn't that a remarkable thing? Ben, he'll worship me for it!

BEN *(with promise).* It's dark there, but full of diamonds.

WILLY. Can you imagine that magnificence with twenty thousand dollars in his pocket?

LINDA *(calling from her room).* Willy! Come up!

WILLY *(calling into the kitchen).* Yes! Yes. Coming! It's very smart, you realize that, don't you, sweetheart? Even Ben sees it. I gotta go, baby. 'By! 'By! *(Going over to* BEN, *almost dancing)* Imagine? When the mail comes he'll be ahead of Bernard again!

BEN. A perfect proposition all around.

WILLY. Did you see how he cried to me? Oh, if I could kiss him, Ben!

BEN. Time, William, time!

WILLY. Oh, Ben, I always knew one way or another we were gonna make it, Biff and I!

BEN *(looking at his watch).* The boat. We'll be late. *(He moves slowly off into the darkness)*

WILLY *(elegiacally, turning to the house).* Now when you kick off, boy, I want a seventy-yard boot, and get right down the field under the ball, and when you hit, hit low and hit hard, because it's important, boy. *(He swings around and faces the audience)* There's all kinds of important people in the stands, and the first thing you know . . . *(Suddenly realizing he is alone)* Ben! Ben, where do I . . . ? *(He makes a sudden movement of search)* Ben, how do I . . . ?

LINDA *(calling)*. Willy, you coming up?

WILLY *(uttering a gasp of fear, whirling about as if to quiet her)*. Sh! *(He turns around as if to find his way; sounds, faces, voices, seem to be swarming in upon him and he flicks at them, crying)* Sh! Sh! *(Suddenly music, faint and high, stops him. It rises in intensity, almost to an unbearable scream. He goes up and down on his toes, and rushes off around the house)* Shhh!

LINDA. Willy?

There is no answer. LINDA *waits.* BIFF *gets up off his bed. He is still in his clothes.* HAPPY *stands listening.*

LINDA *(with real fear)*. Willy, answer me! Willy!

There is the sound of a car starting and moving away at full speed.

LINDA. No!

BIFF *(rushing down the stairs)*. Pop!

As the car speeds off, the music crashes down in a frenzy of sound, which becomes the soft pulsation of a single cello string. BIFF *slowly returns to his bedroom. He and* HAPPY *gravely don their jackets.* LINDA *slowly walks out of her room. The music has developed into a dead march. The leaves of day are appearing over everything.* CHARLEY *and* BERNARD, *somberly dressed, appear and knock on the kitchen door.* BIFF *and* HAPPY *slowly descend the stairs to the kitchen as* CHARLEY *and* BERNARD *enter. All stop a moment when* LINDA, *in clothes of mourning, bearing a little bunch of roses, comes through the draped doorway into the kitchen. She goes to* CHARLEY *and takes his arm. Now all move toward the audience, through the wall-line of the kitchen. At the limit of the apron,* LINDA *lays down the flowers, kneels, and sits back on her heels. All stare down at the grave.*

REQUIEM

CHARLEY. It's getting dark, Linda.

LINDA *doesn't react. She stares at the grave.*

BIFF. How about it, Mom? Better get some rest, heh? They'll be closing the gate soon.

LINDA *makes no move. Pause.*

HAPPY *(deeply angered)*. He had no right to do that. There was no necessity for it. We would've helped him.

CHARLEY *(grunting)*. Hmmm.

BIFF. Come along, Mom.

LINDA. Why didn't anybody come?

CHARLEY. It was a very nice funeral.

LINDA. But where are all the people he knew? Maybe they blame him.

CHARLEY. Naa. It's a rough world, Linda. They wouldn't blame him.

LINDA. I can't understand it. At this time especially. First time in thirty-five years we were just about free and clear. He only needed a little salary. He was even finished with the dentist.

CHARLEY. No man only needs a little salary.

LINDA. I can't understand it.

BIFF. There were a lot of nice days. When he'd come home from a trip; or on Sundays, making the stoop; finishing the cellar; putting on the new porch; when he built the extra bathroom; and put up the garage. You know something, Charley, there's more of him in that front stoop than in all the sales he ever made.

CHARLEY. Yeah. He was a happy man with a batch of cement.

LINDA. He was so wonderful with his hands.

BIFF. He had the wrong dreams. All, all, wrong.

HAPPY *(almost ready to fight BIFF)*. Don't say that!

BIFF. He never knew who he was.

CHARLEY *(stopping HAPPY's movement and reply. To BIFF)*. Nobody dast blame this man. You don't understand: Willy was a salesman. And for a salesman, there is no rock bottom to the life. He don't put a bolt to a nut, he don't tell you the law or give you medicine. He's a man way out there in the blue, riding on a smile and a shoeshine. And when they start not smiling back—that's an earthquake. And then you get yourself a couple of spots on your hat, and you're finished. Nobody dast blame this man. A salesman is got to dream, boy. It comes with the territory.

BIFF. Charley, the man didn't know who he was.

HAPPY *(infuriated)*. Don't say that!

BIFF. Why don't you come with me, Happy?

HAPPY. I'm not licked that easily. I'm staying right in this city, and I'm gonna beat this racket! *(He looks at BIFF, his chin set)* The Loman Brothers!

BIFF. I know who I am, kid.

HAPPY. All right, boy. I'm gonna show you and everybody else that Willy Loman did not die in vain. He had a good dream. It's the only dream you can have—to come out number-one man. He fought it out here, and this is where I'm gonna win it for him.

BIFF *(with a hopeless glance at* HAPPY, *bends toward his mother).* Let's go, Mom.

LINDA. I'll be with you in a minute. Go on, Charley. *(He hesitates)* I want to, just for a minute. I never had a chance to say good-by.

CHARLEY *moves away, followed by* HAPPY. BIFF *remains a slight distance up and left of* LINDA. *She sits there, summoning herself. The flute begins, not far away, playing behind her speech.*

LINDA. Forgive me, dear. I can't cry. I don't know what it is, but I can't cry. I don't understand it. Why did you ever do that? Help me, Willy, I can't cry. It seems to me that you're just on another trip. I keep expecting you. Willy, dear, I can't cry. Why did you do it? I search and search and I search, and I can't understand it, Willy. I made the last payment on the house today. Today, dear. And there'll be nobody home. *(A sob rises in her throat)* We're free and clear. *(Sobbing more fully, released)* We're free. *(BIFF comes slowly toward her)* We're free . . . We're free . . .

BIFF *lifts her to her feet and moves out up right with her in his arms.* LINDA *sobs quietly.* BERNARD *and* CHARLEY *come together and follow them, followed by* HAPPY. *Only the music of the flute is left on the darkening stage as over the house the hard towers of the apartment buildings rise into sharp focus, and*

The Curtain Falls

SUGGESTIONS FOR WRITING AND DISCUSSION

1. What is Willy's attitude to selling and being a salesman? Describe the way he sees his job. In a two- or three-page essay compare this with his attitude to sports and manual work.
2. Does Willy have a realistic view of what it takes to succeed in business? Discuss his theory about being liked and being well liked. To what extent does his theory fit the various characters in the play?
3. Do Willy and his sons share a common attitude toward women?
4. Is Willy a victim of circumstances or of his own self-delusions? Is it correct to regard him as a tragic hero? (See Chapter 8.) Discuss in a three- or four-page essay.
5. Is Willy's suicide an act of courage or cowardice? Will it really help his family?
6. Biff tells Linda that Willy "always, always wiped the floor with you. Never had an ounce of respect for you." Is this true? In a two- or three-page essay support your answer.
7. Look at the various places in the play where Linda describes her husband. Does she have a clear view of him?

8. Biff and Happy comment frequently on what a good wife Linda is. Do you agree with them? In answering consider the results of her behavior.

9. Both Happy and Biff compare their women friends to Linda. Are these comparisons favorable? Do you think either of them will ever marry, and if so, will it be to someone like Linda?

10. Linda calls Happy "a philandering bum." Is this an accurate description? Does Happy have any good qualities?

11. Happy and Willy are both younger brothers who grew up in the shadow of exalted older brothers. Has this common background given them characteristics in common? If so, what?

12. In a one- or two-page essay describe Biff's attitude toward work and explain why he has such a hard time keeping a job.

13. How would you describe Biff before he visits his father in Boston? How does he seem to have changed by the age of thirty-four?

14. What happens to Biff during the day he spends waiting to see Oliver? What makes this day so crucial?

15. Toward the end of the play Biff tries to force his family to see the truth about Willy and about themselves. Does he succeed?

16. What part does Ben play in Willy's life? Is he a foil to Willy? Is he largely a product of Willy's imagination? What does he symbolize to Willy?

17. In a three- or four-page essay compare the relationship between Ben and Willy with that between Biff and Happy.

18. How do Charley and Bernard act as foils to Willy and his family?

19. Why does Willy continue to refuse Charley's offer of a job?

20. Of all the characters in the play, whose view of Willy do you most nearly share? Explain in a two-page essay.

21. In Act Two Howard fires Willy. Describe his attitude to Willy and what we learn about Willy from him.

22. Although we never see the members of Howard's family, we hear them on his tape recorder. In a short essay show how they provide an ironic contrast to Willy's family.

23. On several occasions Linda compares Biff's and Happy's attitudes to their father with that of the company. How valid is this comparison?

24. In the Requiem at the end of the play Charley and Linda both make lyrical speeches about Willy and what his life has meant. Write a three- or four-page essay examining these speeches in the context of the rest of the play and discussing whether they are sincere or insincere, truthful or false. (You might want to look back at Linda's speech in Act One, "attention must be paid.")

25. What is the climax of the play, and what makes it so?

26. Go through Act One and make a list of all the scenes that are set in the past. As far as possible establish the chronology of these scenes. Examine the reasons why Willy remembers particular events.

27. Miller takes considerable pains to describe the setting of the play. In a three- or four-page essay analyze the importance of the setting, including lighting and music.

28. How would you describe the American dream of success. What comment does this play make about it?
29. Miller did a translation of Ibsen's play *An Enemy of the People.* Does reading *Death of a Salesman* give you ideas about why Ibsen's play was of special interest to Miller?

Work and Reward: Thematic Questions

1. In "Working" a waitress describes the dignity she finds in work. Besides earning a living, what can people gain from their work? Do you believe that work is its own reward?
2. In her account of working for the garment workers' union Pauline Newman describes the extremely long hours that people used to have to work. Many of us now regard leisure time as our birthright. What does the value we put on leisure suggest about the way we perceive work?
3. Do you believe in mandatory retirement at a certain age? If so, at what age, and why?
4. It is clear that Virginia Woolf, the author of "Professions for Women," did not have to work to support herself; nevertheless she did work. Would life be better if we did not have to work? If you didn't have to worry about earning a living, how would you spend your time?
5. To what extent are people defined by their jobs? What effect does this have on the unemployed or on those who choose not to work?
6. In "Two Tramps in Mud Time" Robert Frost claims that ideally work should be not only a duty or a need but also something that one loves. However, many unpleasant jobs are necessary to society. Should people be paid more to do these jobs than to do more enjoyable ones? Give examples.
7. What are the advantages and disadvantages of being one's own boss?
8. In *Death of a Salesman* Willy Loman is fired from his job after more than thirty years' service to the company. What sorts of responsibilities does a company have toward its employees?

Part III

Other Approaches to Writing

Other Ways of
Reading and Writing

The first eight chapters focused on the kind of writing you are most often asked to do in literature courses: critical essays about works of literature. The skill of writing a well-structured and persuasive essay is an important one. But there are other ways of writing about a work of literature. Sometimes your instructor may give you an assignment for which some other form would be appropriate; other times a work you read may inspire you to write something on your own. Some of the questions listed after the works in the anthology call for more imaginative forms of writing. For example, we ask you to imagine that you are the author of a work or that you are writing a letter to a character. Other forms you might experiment with include reviews, parodies, satires, journal entries, and imitations of a work of literature.

Reviews

Students are sometimes confused about the difference between a *critical essay* and a *review.* Briefly stated, in a critical essay the author assumes that the reader has some familiarity with the work and offers an interpretation of some aspect of the text. The writer of the review assumes that the reader is unfamiliar with the work and writes the review either to encourage or to discourage the reader from reading the book or seeing the play or film in question. Reviews are usually (although not always) shorter than critical essays, and they cannot usually explore a work in depth. (Some reviews get their point across with great succinctness. The *New York Times,* which gives one- or two-line reviews of the movies in its television listings, evaluated the film *Sex Kittens Go to College* as follows: "Magna Cum Lousy.")

A review almost always includes a brief summary; this is necessary to give the reader a sense of the work. Here is the beginning of a review of the film *The Godfather, Part II* by Pauline Kael, film critic of *The New Yorker*.

> At the close of *The Godfather*, Michael Corleone has consolidated his power by a series of murders and has earned the crown his dead father, Don Vito, handed him. In the last shot, Michael—his eyes clouded—assures his wife, Kay, that he is not responsible for the murder of his sister's husband. The door closes Kay out while he receives the homage of subordinates, and if she doesn't know that he lied, it can only be because she doesn't want to. *The Godfather, Part II* begins where the first film ended: before the titles there is a view behind that door. The new king stands in the dark, his face lusterless and dispassionate as his hand is being kissed. The familiar *Godfather* waltz is heard in an ambiguous, melancholy tone. Is it our imagination, or is Michael's face starting to rot? The dramatic charge of that moment is Shakespearean. The waltz is faintly, chillingly ominous.

This review immediately gives us a context. We know precisely the points on which Kael is about to build her review. She pulls us into the sinister feeling of the film, and she makes us believe she has given it careful consideration. This sense of careful thought on the reviewer's part is the basis for a successful review. Like any other essay, a review must convey a sense that the author is trustworthy. It is easy for a novice reviewer to abandon objectivity and to fall into the trap of relying on hyperbole. Imagine reading a review of the novel *Ordinary People* that contained paragraphs like this one:

> Conrad's mother shows just how rotten a person she is, but Conrad is too much of a wimp to stand up to her. The same is true of the father, who is a marshmallow. I don't know why the author thought anyone would be interested in people like this.

Would you trust the judgment of this critic? A reviewer is entitled to dislike the book, but reviewers who respond without justifying their reactions are not likely to persuade the reader to share them. We get no sense that this reviewer has considered the book on any level beyond an immediate emotional response. There is no information about the characters or the plot that would allow us to decide whether we agree or disagree with the judgments the reviewer makes.

What follows is a review of *Death of a Salesman* by Brooks Atkinson, a drama critic for the *New York Times*. The review appeared the morning after the play opened on Broadway in 1949. Notice that Atkinson does not hesitate to use superlatives in his review, but that at the same time, he is careful to give us enough information about the play so that we can judge whether the superlatives are merited.

> Arthur Miller has written a superb drama. From every point of view *Death of a Salesman*, which was acted at the Morosco last evening, is rich and memorable drama. It is so simple in style and so inevitable in theme that it scarcely seems like a thing that has been written and acted. For Mr. Miller has looked with compassion into the hearts of some ordinary Americans and quietly transferred their hope and anguish to the theatre. Under Elia Kazan's masterly direction, Lee J. Cobb

gives a heroic performance, and every member of the cast plays like a person inspired.

Two seasons ago Mr. Miller's *All My Sons* looked like the work of an honest and able playwright. In comparison with the new drama, that seems like a contrived play now. For *Death of a Salesman* has the flow and spontaneity of a suburban epic that may not be intended as poetry but becomes poetry in spite of itself because Mr. Miller has drawn it out of so many intangible sources.

It is the story of an aging salesman who has reached the end of his usefulness on the road. There has always been something unsubstantial about his work. But suddenly the unsubstantial aspects of it overwhelm him completely. When he was young, he looked dashing; he enjoyed the comradeship of other people—the humor, the kidding, the business.

In his early sixties he knows his business as well as he ever did. But the unsubstantial things have become decisive; the spring has gone from his step, the smile from his face and the heartiness from his personality. He is through. The phantom of his life has caught up with him. As literally as Mr. Miller can say it, dust returns to dust. Suddenly there is nothing.

This is only a little of what Mr. Miller is saying. For he conveys this elusive tragedy in terms of simple things—the loyalty and understanding of his wife, the careless selfishness of his two sons, the sympathetic devotion of a neighbor, the coldness of his former boss' son—the bills, the car, the tinkering around the house. And most of all: the illusions by which he has lived—opportunities missed, wrong formulas for success, fatal misconceptions about his place in the scheme of things.

Writing like a man who understands people, Mr. Miller has no moral precepts to offer and no solutions of the salesman's problems. He is full of pity, but he brings no piety to it. Chronicler of one frowsy corner of the American scene, he evokes a wraithlike tragedy out of it that spins through the many scenes of his play and gradually envelops the audience.

As theatre *Death of a Salesman* is no less original than it is as literature. Jo Mielziner, always equal to an occasion, has designed a skeletonized set that captures the mood of the play and serves the actors brilliantly. Although Mr. Miller's text may be diffuse in form, Mr. Kazan has pulled it together into a deeply moving performance.

Mr. Cobb's tragic portrait of the defeated salesman is acting of the first rank. Although it is familiar and folksy in the details, it has something of the grand manner in the big size and the deep tone. Mildred Dunnock gives the performance of her career as the wife and mother—plain of speech but indomitable in spirit. The parts of the thoughtless sons are extremely well played by Arthur Kennedy and Cameron Mitchell, who are all youth, brag and bewilderment.

Other parts are well played by Howard Smith, Thomas Chalmers, Don Keefer, Alan Hewitt and Tom Pedi. If there were time, this report would gratefully include all the actors and fabricators of illusion. For they all realize that for once in their lives they are participating in a rare event in the theatre. Mr. Miller's elegy in a Brooklyn sidestreet is superb.

The following steps will help you organize and write a review:

1. Pay careful attention to the subject and theme of the work you are reviewing. Naturally, if you are reviewing a written work you will read it more than once.

2. Organize your first paragraph in such a way that it opens up the work for further discussion. (Notice how the first paragraph of Pauline Kael's review does this.) It is better to postpone proclaiming your own emotional response until later in the review, after you have convinced your readers that you have considered the work carefully. You should give an overview of the content of the work near the beginning of your review, as Atkinson does in his third and fourth paragraphs.

3. Discuss the strengths of the work. Particularly if your review is going to be unfavorable, it is a good idea to discuss the positive aspects first. You will be a more credible critic if the reader can tell that you have given the work a fair chance and considered its good points as well as its failings.

4. Discuss the work's weaknesses, if you feel it has weaknesses. Your review will sound strained if the shortcomings you mention seem too minor to mention: "The problem with *Death of a Salesman* is that Happy and Biff are ridiculous names." Your reasons for liking or disliking a work should be substantial: "The writing in 'I Stand Here Ironing' has a self-conscious quality that makes it hard to lose sight of the fact that this is a story."

5. In your conclusion, restate the major point or points of the review. Be sure to make adequate transitions from what you saw or read to what you felt about it. All along, remember that the burden of proof falls on you as the reviewer.

Parody

Another way of responding to a work of literature is to write a *parody*. A parody is an imitation, usually a humorous one, of a particular work. An author may also parody a genre rather than a specific work, as Robert Benchley does in this parody of a Greek myth.

Endremia and Liason

Endremia was the daughter of Polyganimous, the God of Ensilage, and Reba, the Goddess of Licorice. She was the child of a most unhappy union, it later turned out, for when she was a tiny child her father struck her mother with an anvil and turned himself into a lily pad to avoid the vengeance of Jove. But Jove was too sly for Polyganimous and struck him with a bolt of lightning the size of the Merchant's Bank Building, which threw him completely off his balance so that he toppled over into a chasm and was dashed to death.

In the meantime, Little Endremia found herself alone in the world with nobody but Endrocine, the Goddess of Lettuce, and her son Bilax, the God of Gum Arabic, to look after her. But, as Polygaminous (her father: have you forgotten so soon, you dope?) had turned Endremia into a mushroom before he turned himself into a lily pad, neither of her guardians knew who she was, so their protection did her no good.

But Jove had not so soon forgotten the daughter of his favorite (Reba), and appeared to her one night in the shape of a mushroom gatherer. He asked her how she would like to get off that tree (she was one of those mushrooms that grow on trees) and get into his basket. Endremia, not knowing that it was Jove who was asking her, said not much. Whereupon Jove unloosened his mighty wrath and struck down the whole tree with the bolt of lightning which he had brought with him in case Endremia wouldn't listen to reason.

This is why it is never safe to eat the mushrooms which grow on trees, or to refuse to get into Jove's basket.*

Note that Benchley assumes some familiarity with Greek mythology on the reader's part, but not so much that only experts can enjoy the parody. Even if we have only a vague idea of what a Greek myth is like, we pick up Benchley's humorous exaggeration. But note, too, that the parody would lose much of its humor and its point if we did not know anything at all about Greek myths. A parody takes its meaning, its reason for existing, from the work it imitates. Benchley's parody works partly because he never seems to be trying to make any point other than the parody itself.

If you decide to write a parody, keep the following in mind:

1. Choose a work or a genre that lends itself well to imitation.
2. Stay close to the original, so that your readers will be sure to recognize the parody for what it is.
3. Find aspects of the original on which you can focus. Benchley parodies the names of the gods and goddesses, and he retains just enough of the serious, formal tone of an authentic Greek myth to create humor by the contrast between his tone and what he says.

Responding in a Literary Form

Another way to respond in writing to a work of literature is to put yourself in the position of the author, or of one of the characters or some third party, and to write from that point of view. You may want to use the original work as a model—for example, by writing a poem about a poem. Or you may adopt the persona of an author or character but use a different form: for example, writing a letter from one character in a play to another or keeping a journal for a character in a story. These kinds of writing allow you to respond to literature in a more personal way than you can do in critical essays.

In the following poem, the poet Anthony Hecht imagines how the woman addressed by the speaker in Matthew Arnold's "Dover Beach" must have felt.

The Dover Bitch, A Criticism of Life

For Andrews Wanning

So there stood Matthew Arnold and this girl
With the cliffs of England crumbling away behind them,
And he said to her, "Try to be true to me,

---

*From *The Benchley Roundup* by Robert Benchley (New York: Dell, 1962), p. 152.

And I'll do the same for you, for things are bad
All over, etc., etc.''
Well now, I knew this girl. It's true she had read
Sophocles in a fairly good translation
And caught that bitter allusion to the sea,
But all the time he was talking she had in mind
The notion of what his whiskers would feel like
On the back of her neck. She told me later on
That after a while she got to looking out
At the lights across the channel, and really felt sad,
Thinking of all the wine and enormous beds
And blandishments in French and the perfumes.
And then she got really angry. To have been brought
All the way down from London, and then be addressed
As a sort of mournful cosmic last resort
Is really tough on a girl, and she was pretty.
Anyway, she watched him pace the room
And finger his watch-chain and seem to sweat a bit,
And then she said one or two unprintable things.
But you mustn't judge her by that. What I mean to say is,
She's really all right. I still see her once in a while
And she always treats me right. We have a drink
And I give her a good time, and perhaps it's a year
Before I see her again, but there she is,
Running to fat, but dependable as they come.
And sometimes I bring her a bottle of *Nuit d'Amour.*

   This poem is not a parody: Hecht is not imitating or exaggerating the original work. Rather, he is imagining the circumstances of the original and writing
from the point of view of a friend of one of the characters. Although the poem
has a humorous tone, it has a serious purpose. Hecht is questioning and criticizing the values expressed in ''Dover Beach.''
   Some works of literature may inspire you to write about them in the form
of a *journal* or a *diary*. A student was asked to write about a section of *Walden,*
Thoreau's journal of his life at Walden Pond. Instead of analyzing the text or
comparing life at Walden in Thoreau's day and today, the student visited the
pond several times and wrote his own journal entries, keeping Thoreau's work
in mind. His observations and reflections made up a close response to *Walden.*
   Another student found she could not write a critical essay about Anne
Frank's *Diary of a Young Girl* because she could not be objective about it. She
decided to write a final entry in the diary, in Anne's voice, as Anne herself
might have written it had she lived. This project allowed the student to explore
the text, to use historical information, and also to express her emotional
response to the work.
   Writing a paper in the form of a letter is another way to respond to a work
of literature. The letter form requires you as the writer to develop a vivid sense
of character, place, and history. If one of the ''Blue Girls'' read John Crowe
Ransom's poem of that title, what might she write in a letter to the poet? If

Tom Wingfield of *The Glass Menagerie* eventually decided to write to his mother and sister, what would he say in his letter? Here is what one student imagined Tom might say if he wrote to Amanda long after leaving home.

Dear Mother,

I have no idea whether you will get this letter or not. The thought that you and Laura might have moved has crossed my mind more than once.

As you can see by the postmark, I am in New York. It's where I always thought a writer should be, but ironically I feel less like a writer than I did when I lived in St. Louis. Here every other person you meet says he or she is a writer and that somehow makes me feel less special, less like the "Shakespeare" the guys used to call me. I still do a lot of manual labor just like in St. Louis, so I guess you can say that I at least got some skills back there.

Even now I wish I could explain to you why I left. I knew that I had to write you a letter at least. I still feel the hurt from the two-line card that Dad sent. But if my experience tells me anything, he must still think about you, as I do. I think about you and Laura constantly. In my fantasies you are both well taken care of, happy, part of the world. In my fantasy Gentleman Callers call on you both. How I wish it is so.

I guess that mainly I want you to forgive me for leaving. You can never know what it took for me to leave. And you'll never know how often I think of you and wish you well.

Always,
Tom

This letter is carefully based on the original text: The guys in St. Louis did call Tom "Shakespeare"; his father did write only a two-line card after leaving home. At the same time, the student has been inventive and imagined what Tom might have felt about living in New York and about being out of touch with his family. This combination of fidelity to the original and inventiveness is essential to the creative kinds of writing about literature we have discussed in this section.

You can learn a good deal about a work by responding to it in a literary form. You might, for example, write an updated version of Chekhov's play *The Marriage Proposal*, using different types of characters—perhaps a more feminist woman. Or you might write a continuation of the story "My Oedipus Complex" in which you show the child narrator grown up, perhaps a father himself. Writing in these ways allows you to be subjective, to explore the original text, and to have fun with it.

Satire

Unlike the other types of writing that we have described in this chapter, *satire* is not a direct response to a text. The satirist uses irony and sarcasm to point out the vices or folly of individuals or of groups or institutions. Satire, unlike parody, often has a larger purpose beneath the humor. It is a joke with a purpose.

Jonathan Swift wrote "A Modest Proposal" as a response to what he saw as a terrible social injustice. English economic policy had impoverished Ireland, and in 1728 a famine compounded the disaster. Instead of writing a straightforward editorial condemning the policies of the English, Swift adopted a fictitious persona and offered an ironic—and satirical—solution to Ireland's problems. "A Modest Proposal" reads like an economist's report until it becomes clear that this economist's "solution" is that children can be sold and eaten.

> I have been assured by a very knowing American of my acquaintance in London, that a young healthy child well nursed is at a year old a most delicious, nourishing, and wholesome food, whether stewed, roasted, baked, or broiled; and I make no doubt that it will equally serve in a fricassee or a ragout.

Part of what Swift is doing is satirizing the English ruling class, implying that even if they stop short of eating babies, they exploit the Irish ruthlessly, figuratively if not literally devouring them. The civility of language and style in this "proposal" makes the solution proposed all the more chilling.

You might decide to use one of the satires in this book as a model for constructing your own, or you might get an idea for something that you wish to satirize from reading the works in this anthology.

10

Writing Literary Research Essays

Writing a research essay about literature is simply an extension of what you have been doing throughout this book: It requires the same steps of reading in depth, finding a topic, and developing a thesis. It also requires one further step: gathering information from other sources that will help you to define your topic or to support your thesis. This is research.

Perhaps the simplest form of research is to read several works by the same author. This will increase your understanding of the texts individually and as a group. If you enjoyed reading Flannery O'Connor's story "Everything that Rises Must Converge," you might read one of her collections of stories. This would enable you to write an essay comparing "Everything that Rises Must Converge" with one or several of her other stories. Or you might focus your essay on one story but bring in insights gained from your reading of the others.

Other areas you might explore through research include an author's life and the historical background to a literary work. Before writing about Virginia Woolf's essay "Professions for Women," for example, you might read parts of her diaries or a historical account of the kinds of jobs that were open to women in the early part of this century. Either of these approaches would enable you to write about Woolf's essay from a fresh perspective. You might discuss how feasible it was for women at that time to follow her advice. Or you might examine the extent to which she followed it in her own life.

A third kind of research is reading critical books and essays about the work itself and about other works by the same author with an eye toward making your own critical statement. When you write literary criticism your research is directed toward an evaluation of a work of literature from a particular perspective. Literary critics not only look at a text closely but also look at it in the light of a particular theory. For example, you might write an essay about Nathaniel Hawthorne's story "Wakefield," using current psychoanalytic theories about the nature of depression. Or you could discuss the treatment of women in Arthur Miller's play *Death of a Salesman* from a feminist perspective.

The writer of the sample essay at the end of this chapter read literary criticism to deepen her understanding of Herman Melville's novella *Billy Budd*. She used what other critics had written about *Billy Budd* to support her own evaluation of the novella. When writing this kind of paper you should be sure to read more than one critic to get an idea of the different ways a work of literature can be interpreted.

In talking about the material used for research, we make a distinction between primary and secondary sources. The work (or works) of literature that you are writing about is your primary source. For the student writing about *Billy Budd*, the novella itself is the primary source. Works that give background information or criticism are secondary sources. The writer of the sample essay consulted some critical essays; these are secondary sources.

Most often when doing research, you will have to rely on secondary sources, but sometimes you may find unexpected primary sources. If you were writing about the jobs that were open to women when Virginia Woolf gave her speech "Professions for Women," you would most likely be consulting secondary sources. It is possible, however, that you could find some elderly women to interview about what jobs were available when they were young. These interviews, along with the essay itself, would be your primary sources.

Choosing a Topic

When choosing a topic for a research essay, you should ask yourself the same kinds of questions you would for any other kind of essay:

1. Which authors, subjects, or literary periods interest you? If you are interested in a subject, you will enjoy finding out more about it.

2. Do you know enough to write about the topic? Of course, you are doing research to find out about your subject, but if your time is limited it is a good idea to choose a topic you already know something about.

3. How long is the assignment, and how much time do you have to do it? (See Chapter 2.)

4. Will you be able to find enough information on your topic? If you choose to write about a contemporary author, you may find very little secondary material by or about that author. Or you might want to write about the family life of the seventeenth-century poet Ben Jonson and again find yourself faced with an extreme shortage of sources of information. The availability of information is crucial in choosing a good research topic.

Finding Material

Once you have decided on a subject for your research essay, the next step is to find secondary sources. Although there are other forms of research, such as interviewing people or visiting a museum, in this chapter we focus on the kind of research that you do in your college library. Books in college libraries are usually classified under one of two systems: the Dewey Decimal system or the Library of Congress system. To find a book under either system, consult the card catalogue. Library catalogues list books by author, by title, and by subject. Suppose you are looking for a book about Robert Frost. If you know the author of the book, you can simply look up the author's name in the catalogue. You can find the book, however, even if you only know that it is about Robert Frost. If you look up Robert Frost in the card catalogue, you will find cards listing both books *by* Frost and books *about* him. You will also find cross-references to essays about him that appear in books on wider subjects.

Books that contain articles about Frost, or references to him, are also listed under wider subject headings, for example, "Twentieth-Century American Poetry." Besides the author's name, the title of the book, and other information, catalogue cards also list which subject headings the book is listed under. If you want to do some preliminary research about an author or topic, or if you simply want to see what is available in your library, looking under the subject heading is a good way to begin.

All catalogue cards show the call number of the book in the upper left-hand corner. This tells you where the book is shelved in the library. Copy the call number from the card, along with the author's name and the title of the book. Then compare the call number with the numbers displayed on the library shelves to find the shelf where your book is kept.

Scholarly or critical articles published in journals rather than in books are not listed individually in the card catalogue (although bound volumes of back issues of journals are listed). Various reference books that can help you locate these articles are kept in the reference section of the library.

The *MLA* (Modern Language Association) *International Bibliography*, published annually, lists all the articles on literary subjects published in a given year. These articles come from a vast number of different journals. The material is divided by nationality and grouped chronologically. To find material about Frost, you would look in the section on American literature and turn to the part that deals with the twentieth century.

Since 1969 the *MLA International Bibliography* has become so large that it is now divided into two volumes. Articles on texts written in English are listed in one volume; articles on European literature, in another. Therefore, for example, the listings for essays about Nadine Gordimer, a South African writer, appear in the same volume as those on Frost, and essays about Osip Mandelstam, a Russian writer, are listed in the other volume.

The *MLA International Bibliography* contains the most comprehensive list of journal articles. Other reference books can be useful precisely because they are more selective and less comprehensive. *The Year's Work in English Studies* lists only books and articles about English authors and includes brief reviews of some of these works, which can help you select useful material. A comparable book dealing with American authors is *American Literary Scholarship*. The *Essay and General Literature Guide*, published quarterly, is a comprehensive guide to essays by and about writers. The main reference book to consult for articles about classical literature is the *Humanities Index*.

Another source of information is *Dissertations Abstracts International.* Published monthly, it lists by subject all the dissertations that have been completed each month.

Specialized encyclopedias and dictionaries, such as the *Oxford Companion to American Literature* and the *Princeton Encyclopedia of Poetry and Poetics,* can be excellent sources of information. They are easy to use and they often suggest other books you might consult. *Twentieth Century Literary Criticism* and *Contemporary Literary Criticism* both give helpful summaries and excerpts from contemporary criticism.

These reference books list scholarly works, not popular ones. If you wanted to find a recent review of a play in *Newsweek* or an article about John Updike from *The New Yorker,* you would consult the *Reader's Guide to Periodical Literature,* which is published monthly and lists articles from a wide variety of popular American magazines. The *New York Times Index,* published annually, lists all the articles and features that have appeared in that newspaper.

In addition to these reference books, there are a number of others that can help you find recent works of literary criticism. Your librarian can show you where to find them.

Once you have made a list of the articles that sound helpful, the next step is to find them. Recent journals are usually kept on display; less recent ones are bound and kept in the stacks. Sometimes journals are kept on microfilm or microfiche. You will have to learn what your particular library does. Reference librarians are trained to answer your questions about how to find research material. With experience you will become more familiar with which material is readily available.

In addition to all these sources, many libraries now have computer facilities that you can use to find out what material there is about your chosen topic. Sometimes computers can provide not only a bibliography but also copies of the various essays and articles.

Finding lists of what has been written about your topic is not, or course, at all the same thing as actually finding the material itself. Research is full of frustrations, and it may happen that your library does not carry the journal you need or that someone else has checked out the book of essays you want to consult. If there is sufficient time, your library can usually arrange to borrow material through the interlibrary loan system or to recall a book from the previous borrower. If you need to get to work immediately, however, you should be prepared to tailor your research to the available material. It is always a good plan to have a list of more material than you could realistically consult, just in case you may not be able to find all of it.

Taking Notes

Once you have found books or articles on your subject, the next step is to find relevant material in them. You will probably want to skim the articles and look at the introduction or table of contents of each book in order to select what seems most useful. Once you have narrowed down your material, or at least arranged it according to a system of priorities, the next step is to read through it carefully, taking notes as you read.

Here are some suggestions on how to take notes.

1. Use file cards, rather than a notebook or odd pieces of paper. Notes on file cards are easy to keep track of, and you can easily shuffle, rearrange, and revise them. The cards also remind you to keep your notes concise. Copying out too much of a book or article is a waste of time.

2. Your file cards will be most useful if you make notes in the following way:

Vere: books

Vere's taste in books reflects
the kind of person he is.

Melville : _Billy Budd_, 36

Use each card for a single note on a single topic from a single source. Write the subject of the note in the top right-hand corner, so that you will be able to sort your cards at a glance. At the bottom of the card, identify the source of the note: List the author's last name and an abbreviation of the title. And always give the page number so that later if you want to reexamine the source it will be easy to trace.

3. Either quote or paraphrase. A common mistake is to do something in between these two—to make notes that are very close to the original but are not exact quotations. To reproduce these notes in an essay without acknowledging the source is plagiarism. (We will discuss plagiarism more fully in the section on citing sources.)

Taking notes is a way of getting to know your material. The most useful kind of note is one in which you summarize the main ideas or the important facts in your own words. If you think you may want to quote a passage, copy it out _exactly_ and record the source carefully, so that if you do decide to use it your note card will contain all the information you need. Remember that you should use a quotation only if it is necessary to make a particular point.

Writing Your Essay

When you have taken as many notes as you think you will need, it is time to begin writing your essay. First go over your file cards and study your notes carefully. Try to make a broad outline, beginning with your thesis and listing various subtopics. It will be easy to organize your file cards by topic because you have given each one a subject heading. Like any essay, a research essay must be coherent and focused. You may have to leave out material because it is not relevant.

One common problem in writing research essays is that after doing careful research you may end up writing an inconclusive paper that is simply a list of other people's opinions: Critic A says this; Critic B says that. A research paper should not be a mechanical regurgitation of your newfound knowledge. You are the author of your essay, and your reader wants to know your thoughts and opinions.

One way to avoid writing an inconclusive essay is to think of your thesis as a question rather than a statement, for example, "Was Captain Vere responsible for Billy Budd's untimely death?" rather than "Captain Vere was responsible for Billy Budd's untimely death." Having a question to answer, something to prove or establish, will help you to write a more conclusive essay.

A second, closely linked problem is that your finished essay may look as if it was organized from your note cards, with alternate paragraphs beginning "Critic A says" and "Critic B says." Having made thorough notes, don't be afraid to summarize or paraphrase your sources as necessary (but be sure to give credit to your sources). After you have written a rough draft of your essay, reread it and make revisions to be sure that it doesn't sound mechanical; check also to be sure you are using each paragraph to advance your thesis.

Citing Sources

In writing a research essay you must give the source of any quotation you use. You also must give the source whenever you are paraphrasing or borrowing someone else's idea or opinion. In his essay on Robert Frost in *Poetry and the Age,* Randall Jarrell argues that Frost is well known for all the wrong reasons. Suppose this idea catches your attention and you decide to use it in your essay. To do so without attributing it to Jarrell would be plagiarism. You have two alternatives. You can quote Jarrell's own words, giving him appropriate credit. Or you can paraphrase him, perhaps saying something like this: "As Randall Jarrell argues in *Poetry and the Age,* Robert Frost's reputation rests on his worst poems rather than on his best." The important thing is that whichever way you use Jarrell's idea, you have to attribute it to him, and you have to give your reader all the information to identify the correct source.

It is not necessary to give sources for facts everyone knows or for information anyone could find in several sources, such as the year *King Lear* was first performed or the dictionary definition of *allegory.*

To inform your reader of the source of a piece of information, you need to do two things. In the body of your essay, you must name the original author of the information and, where appropriate, give the page number. Then, at the end of your essay you must give a list of the works you have cited in your text. Another name for this list is a *bibliography*—but it may include not only the titles of books and articles but also interviews, films, recordings, and other sources you have used.

We will first discuss how to include information about sources within the actual essay and then show how to provide a list of works cited. There are a number of ways of doing these things, and you should check to see which style your instructor prefers. In this chapter we follow the rules in the *MLA Handbook for Writers of Research Papers,* 2d ed. (1984) because these rules are favored by many instructors in the humanities. For more detailed information, consult this useful handbook.

The crucial thing to remember when referring to a source in your text is that you must give enough information to direct your reader to the correct work in the list of works cited. Normally, if your list includes only one work by a given author, mentioning the author's last name in the text will be sufficient. To tell your reader exactly where in the author's work you found the quotation you are paraphrasing, you should also give a page number. (If you are referring to an entire work, be sure to mention the author's name in your text, and do not give page numbers.)

1. One way to give credit to an author is to mention his or her name in a sentence of your text and to put the page number in parentheses at the end of the sentence, before the period. The number alone is enough; no abbreviation for "page" is needed. In the following example, note that the source is named in the text but not quoted directly.

Thomas Scorza points out that as captain of the ship, Vere has certain

obligations (49).

2. If you do not name the author in your text, his or her last name should appear inside the parentheses with the page number.

Another critic points out that as captain of the ship, Vere has certain

obligations (Scorza 49).

3. If you are using a direct quotation from the author rather than paraphrasing, the same rules of citation apply. The author's name and the page number, or if the author is named in your text, the page number alone, appears in parentheses between the final quotation mark and the punctuation mark that ends the sentence.

Another critic points out that Vere, as captain of the ship, must "act

for the common good" (Scorza 49).

4. If you are quoting only part of an author's sentence but enough so that your reader might get the impression that the quotation is a complete sentence (or sentences), use ellipsis points to indicate that you have omitted something.

If you have omitted the end of a sentence, put the ellipsis points just before the final quotation mark. In either case, the source citation appears, as before, between the final quotation mark and the concluding punctuation.

> Scorza says of Billy Budd that "His was the virtue of bringing
>
> about . . . a thoughtless harmony accidentally in phase with the
>
> enlightened philosophers' rationalistic expectations" (51).

> Scorza says of Billy Budd that "His was the virtue of bringing
>
> about not an active loyalty, but a quiescent harmony . . ." (51).

5. When referring to an idea that occupies several pages or to one that an author deals with on several different occasions, give all necessary page numbers.

> Reich argues that Vere used his responsibility well, in the only way he
>
> could (57–60).

6. When giving a long, indented quotation, place the parenthetical information on the same line as the end of the quotation, after the final period. Note how this differs from the form used with shorter quotations, which are run in with your text rather than indented, and in which the information in parentheses comes before the final period.

> Scorza argues that Billy Budd
>
> > could not be the "spokesman" nor could he establish a
> >
> > position of leadership in society. His was the virtue of
> >
> > bringing about not an active loyalty, but a quiescent
> >
> > harmony, or a thoughtless harmony accidentally in phase
> >
> > with the enlightened philosophers' rationalistic
> >
> > expectations. (51)

7. If your list of works cited contains more than one volume of a multi-volume work, include the volume number as well as the page number in the parenthetical citation. Here the reference is to volume 4 of *The Letters of Virginia Woolf*, which were published in six volumes, all of which are listed in this student's list of works cited.

> Virginia Woolf complains that her novel Night and Day is interminable
>
> (4: 231).

8. In referring to classic literary works, of which there may be several editions, it is a good idea to include a chapter number, a part number, or a scene number where appropriate, to help the reader locate the reference even in a different edition. Use a semicolon between the page number and the additional information.

Although Melville compares Billy Budd to Hercules, he takes pains to

emphasize Billy's fair Anglo-Saxon complexion (15; ch. 2).

9. When referring in the same sentence to two or more works by different authors, follow the same procedure as for citing single works. Put citations for both authors in the same set of parentheses, separating them by a semicolon. Note that in this case, to avoid ambiguity, you should repeat the authors' names within the parentheses even if you mention them in your sentence.

Scorza and Reich both agree that Captain Vere is a man of moral

stamina (Scorza 49; Reich 57–60).

10. If your essay contains references to more than one work by a single author, additional information is needed to enable the reader to identify which of the author's works you are citing in a particular instance. In such a case, either include the title in the text or give a short form of it in parentheses before the page number. In the following example, both Yeats's *Autobiography* and *The Collected Poems of W. B. Yeats* appear in the list of cited works.

Yeats claims that he wanted to live on the island of Innisfree in

imitation of Thoreau (Autobiography 103).

11. In the following example, the reference is to the entry in *The New Columbia Encyclopedia* for Herman Melville. No page number is given because the encyclopedia is arranged alphabetically, and the reader will look up Melville by name rather than by page number. In the list of works cited the work is listed under its title, "Herman Melville." When referring to a work that is cited by title rather than by author, use the title (a shortened form is acceptable) to indicate the source.

After the critical and commercial failure of Moby Dick, Melville

"became absorbed in mysticism" ("Herman Melville").

Preparing a List of Works Cited

The list of works cited should appear after the end of your essay, as it does after the sample essay at the end of this chapter. Type the list of works cited on a separate page after the last page of your text.

Type the title "Works Cited" in the center of the top line. The entire list, like the rest of your essay, should be double-spaced. Begin each new entry at the left-hand margin. If an entry is longer than one line, indent the second and subsequent lines five spaces. List works alphabetically by author's last name, or if no author is specified, alphabetically by title.

The rules for listing sources will seem less complicated if you remember the aim of the list, namely, to identify your sources accurately.

Citing a Book

The general model for citing books is as follows:

Author (last name first). <u>Title</u>. Publication Information.

For example,

Scorza, Thomas J. <u>In the Time Before Steamships</u>. Dekalb: Northern

Illinois UP, 1979.

Note that the author's name, the title, and the publication information are followed by periods.

1. If there are two or more books by the same author, list the author only the first time. For each subsequent book, the name of the author is indicated by three hyphens followed by a period. The books are listed alphabetically by title.

Yeats, W. B. <u>The Autobiography of William Butler Yeats</u>. New York:

Macmillan, 1965.

---. <u>The Collected Poems of W. B. Yeats</u>. New York: Macmillan,

1956.

2. If a book has more than one author, list the subsequent authors exactly as they appear on the title page; do not put their last names first.

Blake, Kathryn A., and Mary Louise McBee. <u>Essays</u>. Encino: Glencoe,

1978.

3. If there are more than three authors, name only the first one and refer to the others by *et al.* (an abbreviation of the Latin *et alii,* "and others").

Knickerbocker, K. L., *et al.,* <u>Interpreting Literature</u>. 7th ed. New York:

Holt, 1985.

4. If a book has been issued in more than one edition, you must specify which edition you are using. This information appears after the title of the book (see the previous example).

Hillway, Tyrus. <u>Herman Melville</u>. Rev. ed. Boston: Twayne, 1979.

5. If a book has been reprinted, give the original date of publication as well as the date of the reprint. Otherwise your reader may think the book was first published at the later date. It is not necessary to do this in the case of a well-known book like *Moby Dick,* for which your reader would be unlikely to make this mistake.

Connell, Evan S. <u>Mrs. Bridge</u>. 1959. San Francisco: North Point Press,

1981.

6. The name of an editor or translator, if the book has one, usually appears after the book's title.

Melville, Herman. Billy Budd, Sailor. Ed. Milton R. Stearn. Indianapolis:

Bobbs-Merrill, 1975.

Chekhov, Anton. Lady with Lapdog and Other Stories. Trans. David

Magarshak. Bucks, Gt. Brit.: Penguin, 1964.

7. If, however, the reference is to the introduction or preface of a book, cite the author of that first, rather than the author of the main book.

Stearn, Milton R. Introduction. Billy Budd, Sailor. By Herman Melville.

Indianapolis: Bobbs-Merrill, 1975.

8. Similarly, the name of the translator appears first if the reference is to the translator's comments or notes.

Magarshak, David, trans. Lady with Lapdog and Other Stories. By

Anton Chekhov. Bucks, Gt. Brit.: Penguin, 1964.

9. When the reference is to a work in an anthology or a collection, the author and title of the individual work come first:

Hughes, Langston. "Conversation on the Corner." The Story and Its

Writer. Ed. Ann Charters. New York: St. Martin's, 1983.

Citing an Article in a Journal

To cite an article in a journal, give the following information, with punctuation as shown here:

Author. "Title of Article." Name of Periodical Series and/or volume

number (date of publication): page numbers.

For example:

Reich, Charles A. "The Tragedy of Justice in Billy Budd." Yale Review

56 (1967): 376–89.

It is not necessary to give the place of publication. It is, however, necessary to give the page numbers of the articles.

Whenever possible, you should cite material from its original source. In the case of journal articles, however, you may often find that you have to cite a collection in which the article has been reprinted. When you cite an article in a collection, give the information about the original publication as well as the information about the collection.

Reich, Charles A. "The Tragedy of Justice in Billy Budd." Yale

Review 56 (March 1967): 376–89. Rpt. in Twentieth Century

Interpretations of Billy Budd. Ed. Howard P. Vincent.

Englewood Cliffs: Prentice, 1971. 56–66.

Note that when a title that would normally be underlined appears within a title which should also be underlined, the internal title is not underlined.

Writing Endnotes and Footnotes

If it would be cumbersome to put in your text, either directly or in parentheses, all the information necessary to direct your reader to the correct entry in the list of works cited, then you will need to use a note. You may also need to use a note to explain or amend some particular point without interrupting the main flow of your argument. You should use this second kind of note sparingly. If a piece of information is not worth including in the body of your essay, it is probably not important enough to include in a note. Alternatively, if you believe it is something your reader really needs to know, you probably should include it in the body of the essay.

Notes can be either footnotes, which appear at the bottom of the text page to which they refer, or endnotes, which are typed together in one list at the end of your essay. Unless your instructor tells you otherwise, the *MLA Handbook* recommends typing your notes as endnotes rather than footnotes. It is easier to type a list of notes at the end than to fit notes at the bottom of pages of text. Notes are numbered consecutively throughout an essay. The numbers should be typed without a period or any other form of punctuation, slightly above the line, like this: [1]. Note numbers should ideally appear at the end of sentences or clauses, after the punctuation mark, in order to interrupt the reader as little as possible.

Type your endnotes on a separate page at the end of the essay. The title "Notes" should appear in the center of the top line. Indent five spaces for the first line of each new note; then type the number the same way as in the text, followed by the note. Second and subsequent lines begin at the left-hand margin. Type the notes double-spaced throughout.

In a note referring to a book, the same information is given as in the list of works cited, but the form and punctuation differ.

Works cited:

Scorza, Thomas J. In the Time Before Steamships. Dekalb: Northern

Illinois UP, 1979.

Notes:

[1]Thomas J. Scorza, In the Time Before Steamships (Dekalb:

Northern Illinois UP, 1979) 51.

If you are using footnotes rather than endnotes, when you type a page that includes one or more notes, be sure to leave enough space after the text to fit them in. Skip three lines after the last line of text and begin the footnote on the fourth line at the left-hand margin. Type each footnote single-spaced, but leave a double space between them. Except for being single-spaced the form for footnotes is the same as for endnotes. For more details consult the *MLA Handbook for Writers of Research Papers.*

SAMPLE STUDENT RESEARCH ESSAY

Assignment: Write a seven- to ten-page literary research paper analyzing the concept of responsibility in *Billy Budd.*

Jeanne Widen

English 191

Professor Warren

March 8, 1986

Reason and Responsibility in Billy Budd

After reading Herman Melville's Billy Budd, and witnessing, so to speak, the public hanging of a naive and morally innocent young man, I was plagued by the question that has plagued so many critics before me: Was this the only course of action Captain Vere could take? Or, in other words, how much is he to be held responsible for Billy's untimely death? In an effort to answer this question I will look at some of these earlier critics.

First, one must determine if Vere is dutifully carrying out the law or if he is influencing--if not designing--the process of law, that is, determine if he is responsible to or for the law.

Charles Reich argues that Vere is responsible to the law, albeit a law with "terrible shortcomings" (60). For Reich, the case of Billy Budd is "a case where compromise is impossible, and where Vere, and we, are forced to confront the imperatives of law"; a case where "Melville allows Vere no choice within the terms of the law itself . . ." (57–58). Thomas Scorza agrees and points out that Vere, as captain of the ship, must "act for the common good" (49). He must stick to the rule and not be swayed by exceptional circumstances. These critics both conclude that Vere used his responsibility well, <u>in the only way he could</u>. According to their arguments, Vere is, indeed, a heroic man whose outward rigidity is the shadow of an inner, courageous moral stamina.

However, I am not so easily convinced. Granted, Vere is responsible for the ship and therefore for every member of the crew, as well as the country for which it fights. Granted, <u>within</u> the terms of the law, Vere does not have a choice. But just how is Vere "forced" to follow this law? Melville does allow him alternatives; indeed, he gives him several opportunities to actively make a choice. Vere chooses to employ the Mutiny Act when it may not be "imperative" that he do so. The fact is, he has several options. Even Reich brings up the question of whether Vere could have mitigated the penalty and points out that he "did have the option of holding the case for the Admiral, instead of summoning his own drumhead court" (57). For the sake of argument, I'll agree with Reich that "if the law is obeyed, Billy must hang" (57). And, as for the drumhead court, it is easy to justify Vere's reasons for holding an early trial for Billy: namely, "the urgency of preventing any slumbering embers of the Nore Mutiny from igniting among the crew overruled for him every other consideration" (Reich 57).

But more important than why Vere constructs a trial is the way he conducts that trial. It is important to note that, first of all, Vere openly acknowledges that he has final responsibility for the court's decision: "reserving to himself, as the one on whom the ultimate accountability would rest" (Melville 99; ch. 20). Not only does he claim the responsibility for the court's conclusion, but he undoubtedly and forcefully dictates that outcome. He urges his fellow officers not to be guided by their natural feelings, by that which he calls the "feminine in man" (106; ch. 22), and directs them not to listen to their own "private consciences" (107; ch. 22). Perhaps Vere made a decision to suppress his personal feelings for sound reasons, but the fact that he persuades the other officers to do the same is evidence that he is steering the law in the direction of <u>his</u> choosing.

Less obvious, but perhaps more significant than the way Vere controls the officers' thought processes, is the way he controls the witness's defense. Vere must understand, as we surely do, Billy's pitiful lament: "'Could I have used my tongue I would not have struck him'" (102; ch. 22). Yet, when is it crucial that Billy does use his tongue, when Billy has the chance to save his life--if not that of Claggart--by speaking, Vere discourages him from doing so. Upon being asked for any last words, "the young sailor turned another quick glance towards Captain Vere; then, as taking a hint from that aspect . . . replied to the Lieutenant, 'I have said all, Sir'" (104; ch. 22). One may argue that Vere wants to prevent Billy from getting in even more trouble. But if this is so, then why doesn't Vere, a man who has the ability both to address and to manipulate the court--a man who we are supposed to believe has great sympathy, if not affection, for Billy--use this ability to help him, and speak on his behalf?

One may justify Vere's refusal to extend himself for Billy's sake by citing the need to protect what Scorza calls the "political community" of the ship (59). But just how much does Vere "act for the common good"? That is, how much does he include the ideas and feelings of the political community in his own? When we look closely at the story, we see that Vere decides Billy's fate before he gathers a court; that he decides it from the moment Billy strikes Claggart, when he exclaims "the angel must hang!" (95; ch. 20). The force and immediacy of that statement are evidence that Vere had come to a decision before he convened a court; that the court is, in effect, a public justification for his private judgment. Vere, we are told, is a man who "loved books," a man whose

> bias was towards those books to which every serious mind of superior order occupying any active post of authority in the world, naturally inclines: books, treating of actual men and events no matter of what era . . . writers, like Montaigne, who . . . philosophize upon realities.
>
> In this line of reading he found confirmation of his own

more reserved thoughts—confirmation which he had vainly sought in social converse. (36; ch. 7)

It's as if Vere has jumped at the chance to finally get social recognition for his ideas (and for his bias toward authority); it's as if he has waited for an opportunity such as this to take his private ideas and try them out on the public, to take a private drama and play it out in front of an audience, with himself in the role of director.

Just as Vere does not really act for the "common good," neither does he, "despite his desire to 'philosophize upon realities' . . . come to act upon 'indisputable' appearances," as Scorza maintains (125). On the contrary, it seems that Vere is, indeed, trying very hard to "philosophize upon realities." Richard Fogle writes that "Billy Budd makes a clear distinction between the sphere of the actual and the sphere of the ideal," that "Vere is equally clear on the distinction," and acted accordingly (45). However, Vere seems to abandon the "actual" in favor of the "ideal" instead of the other way around. The actual, the world of human impulses, limits, feelings, and messy mistakes, is distasteful to "Starry" Vere, who prefers loftier ideals of law and order. He removes himself from the human world and adopts a stance of distant observation and ultimate responsibility: the position of an executor of a Last Judgment. In "Melville's Quarrel with God" Lawrence Thompson explores Vere's Godlike role and argues that "By emblematic and allegorical extension, Claggart is an agent of Vere, an agent of God. . . . By extension, then, Claggart and Vere do indeed share the infamy and depravity, but only through the permissive will of the 'Maker of All that is Fair.'" When Thompson asks "Who is to blame? On whom does the ultimate responsibility rest?" he points a steady finger at Captain Vere (412–14).

Whether or not one sees Vere as an allegory for God, it is clear that the ultimate responsibility does indeed fall to him. He not only welcomes this responsibility, he monopolizes it. Whether or not Vere abuses his power by employing it to justify his own, personal biases, it is clear that he takes too much responsibility concerning Billy's fate, and for this he is to blame.

Works Cited

Fogle, Richard Harter. "Billy Budd—Acceptance or Irony." Tulane Studies
    in English 8 (1958): 107–13. Rpt. in Twentieth Century
    Interpretations of Billy Budd. Ed. Howard P. Vincent. Englewood
    Cliffs: Prentice, 1971. 41–47.

Melville, Herman. Billy Budd, Sailor. Ed. Milton R. Stearn. Indianapolis:
    Bobbs-Merrill, 1975.

Reich, Charles A. "The Tragedy of Justice in Billy Budd." Yale Review 56
    (March 1967): 376–89. Rpt. in Twentieth Century Interpretations of
    Billy Budd. Ed. Howard P. Vincent. Englewood Cliffs: Prentice, 1971.
    56–66.

Scorza, Thomas J. In the Time Before Steamships. Dekalb: Northern Illinois
    UP, 1979.

Thompson, Lawrence. Melville's Quarrel with God. Princeton: Princeton UP,
    Princeton Paperbacks, 1952.

Biographical Notes

Alexander, Shana (1925–   )
Alexander was born in New York City and educated at Vassar. She has written for numerous magazines and appeared on the television show "Sixty Minutes." Her books include *The Feminine Eye* (1970) and *Talking Woman* (1976).

Angelou, Maya (1928–   )
Maya Angelou was born in St. Louis and attended school in Arkansas and California. She has been a professional singer, dancer, and actress in touring companies and on Broadway. She has written several volumes of autobiography, *I Know Why the Caged Bird Sings*, including *Gather Together in My Name*, and *The Heart of a Woman*. She has also published fiction and poetry.

Arnold, Matthew (1822–1888)
Arnold was born in England and educated at Oxford. He wrote several volumes of poetry including *Poems* (1853) and *Merope: a Tragedy* (1858). As an influential literary critic, he attacked the narrow provincialism of the middle classes.

Auden, W. H. (1907–1973)
Auden was born in York, England, and educated at Oxford. He moved to America in 1939 and became a U.S. citizen in 1945. He published numerous volumes of poetry, several plays, and some travel books. *The Age of Anxiety,* a volume of poems, won him the Pulitzer Prize in 1947.

Barrett Browning, Elizabeth (1806–1861)
Born in Durham, England, Elizabeth Barrett Browning grew up as an invalid. In 1844 she published *Poems.* Robert Browning admired her work and the two corresponded secretly and married in 1846. Her work includes *Sonnets from the Portuguese* (1850).

Barrio, Raymond (1921–   )
Barrio was born in New Jersey and educated at the University of Southern California and Yale University. He lives and works in Santa Clara County, California. He has taught at several colleges in California and is the author of books about art, as well as fiction.

Bishop, Elizabeth (1911–1979)
Bishop was born in Worcester, Massachusetts, and was educated at Vassar. Her books include *North and South—A Gold Spring,* which won the 1955 Pulitzer Prize, as well as *Complete Poems* (1969) and travel books.

Blake, William (1757–1827)
Blake was born in London and spent almost his entire life there. Trained as an

engraver, he illustrated and published all his own books, with the exception of his first. Blake's poems include *Songs of Innocence* and *Songs of Experience* (1789, 1794).

Bogan, Louise (1897–1970)
Bogan was born in Livermore, Maine, and lived most of her life in New York, where she was poetry editor of *The New Yorker* for many years. Her best-known collection of poetry is *The Blue Estuaries: Poems, 1923–1968* (1968).

Bradstreet, Anne (1612–1672)
Bradstreet was born in England and came to Massachusetts in 1630 to join the Puritan colony. Her husband later became governor of Massachusetts. She published two books of poems.

Browning, Robert (1812–1889)
Browning was born in England. In 1846 he married Elizabeth Barrett, and they lived in Italy until her death. As a young man he wrote several verse plays. Later he abandoned this form, but it provided the basis for the dramatic monologues for which he is best known as a poet. Among these are "Fra Lippo Lippi" and "The Bishop Orders His Tomb."

Catullus (84 B.C.?–54 B.C.?)
Catullus was born in Verona, Italy. As a young man he fell in love with a woman whom he called Lesbia and to whom he wrote many poems.

Cheever, John (1912–1982)
Cheever was born in Quincy, Massachusetts. After his expulsion from prep school, his formal education ended. Throughout his life he wrote stories and novels and in 1978 *The Stories of John Cheever* won the Pulitzer Prize.

Chekhov, Anton (1860–1904)
Chekhov was born in Russia, the son of a grocer, and began writing to earn money while studying for his medical degree in Moscow. Chekhov practiced medicine and wrote stories and plays. Among the latter are *Uncle Vanya* (1899), *The Three Sisters* (1901), and *The Cherry Orchard* (1904).

Coleridge, Samuel Taylor (1772–1834)
Coleridge was born in Devon, England. After he left Cambridge he began writing, but it was not until he became friendly with William Wordsworth that he produced his best work. Together they began the Romantic movement in English poetry. After 1802 Coleridge wrote few poems, though he wrote critical works until his death.

Conrad, Joseph (1857–1924)
Conrad was born in Poland. He joined the French Merchant Navy in 1874, and his fiction draws heavily on that experience. In 1894 he left the navy to live in England. He wrote in English although it was his second language. Among his

best-known stories are "Heart of Darkness" and "The Secret Sharer." His novels include *Lord Jim* (1900), *Typhoon* (1903), and *Nostromo* (1904).

Crane, Hart (1899–1932)
Crane was born in Garrittsville, Ohio. In 1926 he published his first collection of poetry, *White Buildings*. This was followed by his only other book, *The Bridge*, in 1930. He committed suicide at the age of thirty-two.

Cummings, E. E. (1894–1962)
Cummings was born in Cambridge, Massachusetts, and educated at Harvard. He served with an ambulance unit during World War I and was imprisoned by the French authorities. He eventually settled in New York. He wrote poetry, drama, and criticism.

Dickinson, Emily (1830–1886)
Dickinson was born in Amherst, Massachusetts, the daughter of a lawyer. She attended Amherst Academy and Mount Holyoke Seminary. Although she continued to correspond with her friends, she gradually became a recluse. She published only seven poems during her life, but over a thousand were discovered after her death.

Donne, John (1572–1631)
Donne was born in England. He moved in court circles until he married and fell out of favor. In 1615 he became an Anglican clergyman and in 1621 Dean of St. Paul's. He is the best known of the metaphysical poets.

Dunne, John Gregory (1932–   )
Dunne was born in Connecticut and educated at Princeton. He has written several screenplays and novels. He is married to the essayist and novelist Joan Didion.

Forster, E. M. (1879–1970)
Forster was born in London and educated at Cambridge, England. He traveled widely in Italy and Greece and many of his best-known works are set abroad. He wrote short stories, novels, essays, and literary criticism. The last novel published in his lifetime was *Passage to India* (1924). His most important critical work is *Aspects of the Novel* (1927).

Frank, Anne (1929–1944)
Frank was born in Frankfurt-am-Main, Germany. Her family was Jewish, and fled to Holland when the Nazis rose to power. When the Nazis invaded they went into hiding in the attic of an Amsterdam warehouse. It was there that Anne wrote her diary. The police discovered the Franks' hiding place, and Anne and her family were sent to concentration camps. Anne's father, Otto, was the only surviving member of the family. He was instrumental in the diary's publication.

Franklin, Benjamin (1706–1790)

Born in Boston, Franklin was an inventor, printer, ambassador to France, signer of the Declaration of Independence, writer, publisher, and scientist. He is the author of *Poor Richard's Almanac.*

Freud, Sigmund (1856–1939)

Freud was born in Czechoslovakia and lived in Vienna for most of his life. He studied medicine, and in the course of treating patients with symptoms of hysteria, he gradually developed his theories of psychoanalysis. He is known as the father of psychoanalysis. His theories about infant sexuality, including the Oedipus complex, antagonized his contemporaries, but the concepts he developed remain the basis for modern psychiatry.

Frost, Robert (1874–1963)

Frost was born in San Francisco and grew up in Massachusetts. After studying briefly at Dartmouth, he worked as a bobbin boy in a cotton mill, a shoemaker, a schoolteacher, and a journalist. He also studied briefly at Harvard. In 1912 he went to England, where he was first acclaimed as a poet. He returned to America and settled on a farm in New Hampshire. He taught and lectured at several universities. He was awarded the Pulitzer Prize for Poetry in 1924, 1931, 1937, and 1943.

Gandhi, Mohandas K. (Mahatma) (1869–1948)

Gandhi was born in India and educated in England. In 1893 he went to South Africa to practice law and became a leader in the campaign to end discrimination against Indians. It was at this time that he started to apply the principles of passive resistance to achieve social change.

From 1905 Gandhi followed the Hindu ideals of celibacy and asceticism. By the time he returned to India in 1915, he was a well-known leader. He campaigned for agrarian and labor reforms and for India's independence from Britain. Independence was achieved shortly before Gandhi was assassinated in 1948.

Ginsberg, Allen (1926–   )

Ginsberg was born in Paterson, New Jersey, and is known as a member of the Beat Generation of poets. His most famous work is the long poem *Howl* (1956).

Gogol, Nikolai (1809–1852)

Gogol was born in the Ukraine. Local folktales influenced his early work; his later work also reflects his growing awareness of poverty and corruption. His best-known works are *The Inspector General* (1836) and *Dead Souls* (1842).

Goldman, Emma (1869–1940)

Goldman was born in Lithuania and came to America in 1886. She became an anarchist, feminist, and labor agitator and was deported to Russia in 1919. She left Russia in 1921 after a disagreement with the Bolshevik government. Among her works are *My Disillusionment in Russia* (1923) and *Living My Life* (1931).

Gordimer, Nadine (1923–   )
Gordimer was born in the Transvaal, South Africa. She attended a convent school and Witwatersrand University. She continues to live and write in South Africa although her work is often critical of apartheid. She has published several novels and collections of stories.

Gray, Thomas (1716–1761)
Gray was educated at Eton and Cambridge. He spent most of his life in Cambridge, living quietly and studying. He was asked to become Britain's poet laureate, but refused.

Hawthorne, Nathaniel (1804–1864)
Hawthorne was born in Salem, Massachusetts. His father was a ship's captain who died during a voyage, leaving his widow without adequate means to care for their three children. Hawthorne attended Bowdoin College in Maine and spent the next years writing and publishing such short fiction as "My Kinsman, Major Molineaux" and "Young Goodman Brown." He went to work for the Custom House in 1845 and was dismissed after three years. He subsequently wrote his novels *The Scarlet Letter* (1850) and *The House of Seven Gables* (1851).

Hayden, Robert (1913–1980)
Hayden was born in Detroit and educated at Wayne State University. He became a professor of English in 1946 at Fisk University. In 1966 his collection of poems, *Ballad of Remembrance,* won a prize at the World Festival of Negro Arts in Dakar, Senegal.

H. D. (Hilda Doolittle) (1886–1961)
H. D. was born in Bethlehem, Pennsylvania, and was educated at Bryn Mawr. She lived most of her adult life abroad. In England she became associated with Ezra Pound and other imagist poets. She published several volumes of poetry.

Heaney, Seamus (1939–   )
Heaney was born in County Derry, Ireland, and educated at Queen's University in Belfast. His first collection of poetry was *Death of a Naturalist* (1966). He has published several volumes including *Poems: 1965–1975* (1980).

Hellman, Lillian (1905–1984)
Hellman, a successful playwright, was born in New Orleans. Among her works are *The Children's Hour* (1934), *The Little Foxes* (1939), and *Watch on the Rhine* (1941). She is also the author of three volumes of memoirs.

Hemingway, Ernest (1899–1961)

Hemingway was born in Oak Park, Illinois. In 1917 he went to work as a journalist and then became an ambulance driver during World War I. While in Italy, he was seriously wounded. After the war he started to write fiction. Among his works are *The Sun Also Rises* (1926), *A Farewell to Arms* (1929), and *For Whom the Bell Tolls* (1940). He won the Nobel Prize for Literature in 1954. He committed suicide in 1961.

Hughes, Langston (1902–1967)

Hughes was born in Joplin, Missouri. He published his first volume of poetry, *The Weary Blues,* in 1926. A major figure in the Harlem Renaissance, he wrote novels, plays, poetry, and newspaper sketches.

Ibsen, Henrik (1828–1906)

Ibsen was born in Norway. In the mid-1830s his father went bankrupt and the family had to leave their home. Ibsen said that this move from familiar surroundings and the humiliation of his father's bankruptcy were the major influences on his work. The members of his family became the models for many of his characters. He lived abroad for twenty-seven years, returning to Norway in 1891. His major works include *Peer Gynt* (1867), *A Doll's House* (1879), *Ghosts* (1881), *The Wild Duck* (1886), *Hedda Gabler* (1890), and *The Master Builder* (1892).

Ionesco, Eugene (1912–   )

Ionesco was born in Rumania and settled in France in 1938. He is probably best known for his play *The Bald Soprano* (1950), a classic of the theater of the absurd. His other works include *Rhinoceros* (1959) and his memoir, *Present Past, Past Present* (1968).

James, Henry (1843–1916)

James was born in New York City and privately educated. He moved to Europe in 1875 and eventually settled in London. His novels include *Daisy Miller* (1879), *Portrait of a Lady* (1881), and *The Golden Bowl* (1904). He also wrote travel books, literary criticism, and memoirs.

Jefferson, Thomas (1743–1826)

Jefferson was born near Charlottesville, Virginia, and graduated from the College of William and Mary. Though primarily known as a statesman, he was also an architect and inventor. He was the third president of the United States.

Jewett, Sarah Orne (1849–1909)

Jewett was born in South Berwick, Maine, and lived there for most of her life. Her father was a doctor, and as a child Jewett often accompanied him on his rounds, thus becoming familiar with the local countryside, which later formed the background of much of her work. She wrote several volumes of stories, including *A White Heron* (1886) and *The Country of The Pointed Firs* (1896), and two novels.

Jonson, Ben (1572–1637)
Born in London, Jonson worked briefly as a bricklayer and did military service before beginning work as an actor and playwright. His plays include *Volpone* (1606) and *The Alchemist* (1610). He also wrote several volumes of poetry.

Joyce, James (1882–1941)
Joyce was born in Dublin, Ireland. He moved to the Continent in 1904 and never returned to Ireland. A collection of stories, *Dubliners,* was published in 1914. The novel *A Portrait of the Artist as a Young Man* followed in 1916. His two greatest works are *Ulysses* (1922) and *Finnegans Wake* (1939).

Justice, Donald (1925–   )
Justice was born in Miami, Florida, and attended the University of Iowa Writers' Workshop. He is the author of eight collections of poetry, including *The Summer Anniversaries* and *Departures.* He teaches at the University of Florida. His *Selected Poems* won the 1980 Pulitzer Prize.

Keats, John (1795–1821)
Keats was born in London, the son of a livery stable keeper. In 1811 he was apprenticed to a surgeon, but in 1816 he gave up surgery to write poetry. He published his first volume of poems in 1817. Some of his most famous poems are "Ode to a Nightingale," "Ode on a Grecian Urn," and "La Belle Dame Sans Merci." He died in Rome at the age of twenty-five.

Kees, Weldon (1914–1955?)
Kees was born in Beatrice, Nebraska. After graduating from the University of Nebraska, he worked as director of the Bibliographical Center of Research, made documentary films, painted, played jazz piano, and wrote poetry. On July 18, 1955, his abandoned car was found; Kees has not been seen since.

King, Martin Luther, Jr. (1929–1968)
King was born in Atlanta, the son and grandson of Baptist ministers. He attended Morehouse College and received a doctorate in theology from Boston University. He became a minister in Montgomery, Alabama, and president of the Southern Christian Leadership Conference. As a prominent leader of the civil rights movement, King urged nonviolent resistance. In 1964 he won the Nobel Peace Prize. He was assassinated in Memphis, Tennessee.

Kuan Tao-Shêng (1262–1319)
Kuan was a Chinese painter and calligrapher as well as a poet. Her husband was also a painter and calligrapher.

Larkin, Philip (1922–   )
Larkin was educated at Oxford and worked for many years as a university librarian. He has written volumes of poetry, novels, reviews, and essays.

Lawrence, D. H. (1885–1930)

Lawrence was born in Nottinghamshire, England, and studied to become an elementary school teacher. After his marriage to Freda von Richthofen, Lawrence lived mainly abroad. He wrote fiction, poetry, criticism, and translations. His most famous works are *Sons and Lovers* (1913), *Women in Love* (1921), and *Lady Chatterley's Lover* (1928).

Lear, Martha Weinman (1930–   )

Lear was born in Massachusetts and educated at Boston University. She is a journalist who writes frequently for the *New York Times*. Her book *Heartsounds* (1978) documents her husband's battle with heart disease.

Lee, Andrea (1953–   )

Lee was born in Philadelphia and educated at Harvard. *Russian Journal* is an account of the year she spent in Russia while her husband was studying there. Her first novel, *Sarah Phillips*, was published in 1984.

Le Guin, Ursula K. (1929–   )

Le Guin was born in Berkeley, California, and educated at Radcliffe and Columbia. She is a prolific writer of fiction and has won numerous awards. Among her novels are *The Earthsea Trilogy* (1968, 1971, 1972), *The Left Hand of Darkness* (1969), and *The Dispossessed* (1974).

Levine, Philip (1928–   )

Levine was born in Detroit and attended Wayne State University and the Iowa Writers' Workshop. He has published several collections of poetry including *Not This Pig, They Feed, the Lion,* and *One for the Rose*. His *Selected Poems* was published in 1984.

Lowell, Robert (1917–1977)

Lowell was born in Boston. He graduated from Harvard and studied poetry with John Crowe Ransom at Kenyon College. His collection *Life Studies* won the National Book Award in 1959. In the 1960s Lowell was active in the civil rights and antiwar movements.

Malamud, Bernard (1914–   )

Malamud was born in Brooklyn and educated at the City College of New York and Columbia. His novels include *The Natural* (1952), *The Assistant* (1957), and *The Fixer* (1966). He won the Pulitzer Prize for Fiction in 1966. He teaches at Bennington College in Vermont.

Mandelstam, Osip (1892–1938?)

Mandelstam was born in Warsaw and grew up in St. Petersburg. He was a political prisoner under Stalin and is believed to have died in a prison camp. It is only in the last twenty years that Mandelstam's work has become widely known in the West.

Marlowe, Christopher (1564–1593)
Marlowe was born in Canterbury, England. He wrote several verse plays including *Dr. Faustus* (1588).

Marvell, Andrew (1621–1678)
Marvell was born in England. In 1659 he was elected to Parliament. He wrote political poems and satires as well as lyric poems. He belongs to the group of metaphysical poets.

Maupassant, Guy de (1850–1893)
Maupassant grew up in France and apprenticed himself to the novelist Flaubert. In the course of his short life he wrote more than three hundred stories and several novels, plays, and travel books.

Mead, Margaret (1901–1978)
Mead grew up in Philadelphia and studied anthropology at Barnard College and Columbia University. She is the author of more than twenty-five books, including *Coming of Age in Samoa* (1928) and *Male and Female* (1949).

Mew, Charlotte (1869–1928)
Mew was born in London and attended a private girls' school. She wrote prose and poetry throughout her life and published a collection of poems, *The Farmer's Bride*, in 1916. She committed suicide.

Mezey, Robert (1935–   )
Mezey was born in Philadelphia. He won the Lamont Poetry Prize in 1960 and has published several collections of poetry, including *The Door Standing Open* (1970). He teaches at the University of Utah.

Miller, Arthur (1915–   )
Miller was born in New York City, the son of a wealthy clothing manufacturer. He started writing plays while a student at the University of Michigan. His plays include *All My Sons* (1947), *Death of a Salesman* (1949), *The Crucible* (1953), and *The Price* (1968). In 1956 Miller was indicted by the House Un-American Activities Committee, but he was later cleared.

Milton, John (1608–1674)
Milton was born in London and educated at Cambridge, where he began to write poetry. He wrote pamphlets advocating reforms in the Anglican church. Later he became the Latin secretary for Oliver Cromwell, and although he went blind, continued to carry out his duties with the help of secretaries, including the poet Andrew Marvell. After the Restoration in 1660 Milton gave up politics and devoted himself to writing poetry. He wrote two epic poems, *Paradise Lost* and *Paradise Regained.*

Momaday, N. Scott (1934–   )
Momaday was born in Oklahoma, educated at the University of New Mexico,

and received a doctorate from Stanford. He is a strong advocate of Native American rights and won a Pulitzer Prize in 1968 for *House Made of Dawn.*

Montagu , Lady Mary Wortley (1689–1762)
Montagu was the daughter of the first Duke of Kingston. She married Edward Wortley Montagu but later left him and went to live in Europe. She is best known for her letters and for her *Town Eclogues* (first published 1716).

Moore, Marianne (1887–1972)
Moore was born in St. Louis and attended Bryn Mawr. She worked as a librarian and editor and lived mostly in Brooklyn. Among her works are *Poems* (1921), *Observations* (1924), and *Collected Poems* (1951), which won a Pulitzer Prize.

Neruda, Pablo (1904–1973)
Neruda was born in Chile. He joined the foreign service as a diplomat. After becoming a senator in 1945 he was exiled for his radical political activities. He returned to Chile in 1953 and won the Nobel Prize for Literature in 1971.

Norman, Howard (1949–   )
Norman was born in Michigan and spent a good deal of his childhood in the Canadian wilderness, where he learned a number of Eskimo and Indian languages. His books include *Where the Chill Came From* (1982) and *The Wishing Bone Cycle* (1982).

O'Connor, Flannery (1925–1964)
Flannery O'Connor was born in Georgia. She attended the Iowa Writers' Workshop and spent two years in New York before serious illness forced her to return to her family farm in Milledgeville, Georgia. There she wrote and raised peacocks until her death in 1964. Her writing, which is both grotesque and comic, consistently reflects her devout Catholicism. Among her best-known works are *Wise Blood* (1952) and *A Good Man Is Hard to Find* (1955).

O'Connor, Frank (1903–1966)
O'Connor was born Michael O'Donovan in Cork, Ireland. He was for a short time a member of the Irish Republican Army and worked as a librarian and later as director of the Abbey Theatre. After he became known as a short story writer, he taught in America.

Olsen, Tillie (1913–   )
Olsen was born in Omaha, Nebraska. She has spent most of her life looking after her children and earning a living. Her collection of stories, *Tell Me a Riddle* (1961), attracted considerable attention.

O'Neill, Eugene (1888–1953)
O'Neill was born in New York City and expelled from Princeton in 1907. He worked as a sailor until he contracted tuberculosis in 1912, when he began

writing plays. His major works include *Desire Under the Elms* (1924), *Strange Interlude* (1928), and *Mourning Becomes Electra* (1931).

Owen, Wilfred (1893–1918)
Owen was born in Shropshire, England. During World War I he was a company commander in the Artist's Rifles. He was killed on November 4, 1918, one week before the Armistice.

Paley, Grace (1922–   )
Paley was born in New York City and attended Hunter College. Writer, teacher, and political activist, she has published three volumes of short stories, *The Little Disturbances of Man* (1959), *Enormous Changes at the Last Minute* (1974), and *Later the Same Day* (1985).

Plath, Sylvia (1932–1963)
Plath was born in Boston. Her father, a professor of German and biology, died while Plath was a child. She was educated at Smith College, married the English poet Ted Hughes, and had two children. Her best-known works are her collection of poems, *Ariel* (1968), and her novel, *The Bell Jar* (1971). She committed suicide at the age of thirty.

Plato (427 B.C.–347 B.C.)
Plato was a student and friend of Socrates. He founded the Academy in Athens, where he taught philosophy and mathematics. The dialogue *The Symposium* was probably written during his middle years.

Poe, Edgar Allan (1809–1849)
Poe was born in Boston. For most of his life he supported himself as a journalist and wrote poems and such stories as "The Tell-Tale Heart" and "The Fall of the House of Usher."

Pound, Ezra (1885–1972)
Pound was born in Hailey, Idaho, and was educated at the University of Pennsylvania. He lived in Europe for many years and was an important figure in the avant-garde literary movement. During World War II he did radio broadcasts on behalf of the Fascist Italian government. He was subsequently indicted for treason and from 1946 to 1958 was confined to a mental hospital in Washington, D.C. His work includes *Personae* (1909), *Hugh Selwyn Mauberly* (1920), and the *Cantos* (1925–1960).

Raleigh, Sir Walter (1554?–1618)
Raleigh was born in England and was a member of the court of Elizabeth I. He led expeditions to both North and South America and wrote prose and poetry.

Rich, Adrienne (1929–   )
Rich was born in Baltimore and educated at Radcliffe. A feminist poet, critic,

and essayist, she has won the Yale University Younger Poets Award and National Institute of Arts and Letters Award. Her books include *Diving Into the Wreck: Poems 1971–1972* (1973) and *Collected Poems* (1985).

Roethke, Theodore (1908–1963)
Roethke was born in Saginaw, Michigan, and educated at the University of Michigan and Harvard. He taught at a number of universities. He wrote several books of poetry, including *The Waking* (1953), for which he won the Pulitzer Prize, and a collection of poetry for children, *I Am! Says the Lamb* (1961).

Sanger, Margaret (1883–1966)
Sanger was born in Corning, New York, the sixth of eleven children. She became a nurse and worked in the slums of the Lower East Side of New York City. In 1914 she published a magazine entitled *The Woman Rebel,* which advocated the use of birth control. As a result she was briefly imprisoned. In 1916 she opened the first U.S. birth control clinic in Brooklyn; this too resulted in a jail sentence. She is the author of numerous books including *What Every Girl Should Know, Motherhood and Bondage,* and *My Fight for Birth Control.*

Seattle, Chief (1786–1866)
Chief Seattle was chief of the Suquamish and Duwamish tribes in the Washington territories. He converted to Catholicism as a young man. His orations, including "Reply to the U.S. Government," are mainly concerned with the rights of Native Americans to retain possession of their land.

Steffens, Lincoln (1866–1936)
Steffens was born in San Francisco and studied at the University of California. He wrote numerous articles about politics in which he exposed the corruption of local politicians. These were later collected as *The Shame of the Cities* (1904).

Stevens, Wallace (1879–1955)
Stevens was born in Reading, Pennsylvania, and graduated from New York University Law School in 1904. His books of poetry include *Ideas of Order* (1935), *The Man with the Blue Guitar* (1937), and *Parts of the World* (1942), and in 1954 he won a Pulitzer Prize. From 1916 until his death, Stevens worked at the Hartford Accident and Indemnity Co.

Swenson, May (1919–   )
Swenson was born in Utah and educated at Utah State University. From 1959 to 1966 she was an editor of New Directions Press. Her collections of poetry include *Another Animal* (1954), *Half Sun Half Asleep* (1967), and *More Poems to Solve* (1971).

Swift, Jonathan (1667–1745)
Swift was born in Dublin. He was educated at Trinity College, Dublin, and

ordained as an Anglican priest. He was active in the Tory party, and spent several years in England. In 1713 he became Dean of St. Patrick's Cathedral, Dublin. As a writer he is best known for *Gulliver's Travels,* a satire on human nature. Swift also attacked the Anglican church. *A Modest Proposal* was written in 1729, when there had been a famine in Ireland for several years.

Terkel, Studs (1912–   )
Terkel was born in New York City and educated in Chicago, where he studied law. The selection "Waitress" is from his book *Working* (1974), a collection of interviews in which people discuss their jobs.

Thomas, Dylan (1914–1953)
Thomas was born in Swansea, Wales, and left school at seventeen to become a journalist. His volumes of poetry include *Twenty-five Poems* (1936) and *Deaths and Entrances* (1946). He also wrote stories, autobiographical sketches, and the radio play *Under Milkwood* (1954).

Thomas, Lewis (1913–   )
Thomas was born in New York City. He studied medicine and has worked in a number of different hospitals. He is president of the Memorial Sloan-Kettering Cancer Center in New York City. His earliest essays were published in medical journals. His books include *The Lives of the Cell* (1972) and *The Medusa and the Snail* (1979).

Thoreau, Henry David (1817–1862)
Thoreau was born in Concord, Massachusetts, and graduated from Harvard in 1837. He worked in his father's pencil shop, taught in a grammar school, and helped Ralph Waldo Emerson edit the transcendentalist magazine *The Dial.* In 1845 Thoreau moved to a small cabin near Walden Pond and worked to be self-sufficient, growing his own vegetables and leading a simple life. His journals about life at Walden Pond are among his most famous writings.

In 1849 he spent a night in jail for refusing to pay a surtax to support the Mexican-American War. Shortly thereafter he wrote "Civil Disobedience."

Twain, Mark (Samuel Langhorn Clemens; 1835–1910)
Twain was born in Hannibal, Missouri, the setting of *The Adventures of Huckleberry Finn* (1814) and *The Adventures of Tom Sawyer* (1846). He also wrote numerous other novels, short stories, autobiographical works, and travel books.

Walker, Margaret (1915–   )
Walker was born in Birmingham, Alabama, and attended Northwestern University. She taught at Jackson State College and later became director of the Institute for the Study of History, Life and Culture of Black People. Her book *For My People* (1942) won the Yale University Younger Poets Award.

Wheatley, Phillis (1753?–1784)
Wheatley was born in Africa and was brought to America as a slave in 1761. She was owned by the Wheatley family, who educated her and encouraged her writing. She traveled to England, where her work was widely admired.

White, E. B. (1899–1985)
White was born in New York City and educated at Cornell. He joined the staff of *The New Yorker* magazine shortly after it was founded and continued to write for this publication. In addition to his essays, White wrote children's books, *Charlotte's Web* (1952) and *Stuart Little* (1945). He was coauthor of *Elements of Style* (1959), a well-known reference work for writers.

Whitman, Walt (1819–1892)
Born on Long Island, Whitman left school in 1830 to become a printer's apprentice. He later worked as a journalist. In 1855 he published his most famous volume of poems, *Leaves of Grass,* which he revised until his death. He was a spokesperson for individual liberty, and in 1871 he published the prose collection *Democratic Vistas.* His most famous poems include "Song of Myself," "I Sing the Body Electric," "O Captain! My Captain!" and "When Lilacs Last in the Dooryard Bloomed."

Wilbur, Richard (1921–   )
Wilbur was born in New York City and educated at Harvard and Amherst. He teaches at Wesleyan University. He has published several collections of poems and translations. His books include *Things of This World* (1956) and *Walking to Sleep: New Poems and Translations* (1969).

Williams, Tennessee (1911–1982)
Williams was born in Columbus, Mississippi. When he was twelve, his family moved to St. Louis. He worked his way through the University of Iowa and began writing plays. While working as a script writer in Hollywood, he wrote *The Glass Menagerie*, which was immediately successful. His other plays include *A Streetcar Named Desire* (1949), *Cat on a Hot Tin Roof* (1955), *Sweet Bird of Youth* (1959), and *Night of the Iguana* (1961).

Williams, William Carlos (1883–1963)
Williams was born in Rutherford, New Jersey. He received his M.D. from the University of Pennsylvania. In 1910 he returned to his hometown, where he spent the rest of his life practicing medicine and writing. His major work includes the long poem *Paterson* (1946–1958). He was posthumously awarded the Pulitzer Prize for Poetry.

Wolitzer, Hilma (1930–   )
Wolitzer was born in Brooklyn. She is the author of several novels including *Ending* (1974), *In the Flesh* (1977), and *Hearts* (1980). She has also written books for children.

Woolf, Virginia (1882–1941)
Woolf was born in London and educated at home. She married Leonard Woolf, a journalist and writer. She wrote novels, reviews, stories, and essays. Her works include *To the Lighthouse* (1927), *The Waves* (1931), and *The Death of the Moth and Other Essays*. With her husband she founded and ran the Hogarth Press. She drowned herself in 1941.

Wordsworth, William (1770–1850)
Wordsworth was born in Cumberland, England, and was educated at Cambridge. With the poet Samuel Coleridge he founded the Romantic movement of poetry, and together they published *Lyrical Ballads* in 1798.

Wright, Richard (1908–1960)
Wright was born in Mississippi. His father left home when he was five and his mother became disabled a few years later. Wright had no formal schooling. He gradually traveled north, working at various unskilled jobs. During the Depression, he worked for the Federal Writers' Project. After World War II he moved to Paris. He wrote several collections of stories and novels, including *Black Boy* (1945).

Wyatt, Thomas (1503–1542)
Wyatt was born in England and was a courtier of Henry VIII. His poetry was strongly influenced by the Italian poet Petrarch.

Yeats, William Butler (1865–1939)
Yeats was born in Dublin and as a boy became fascinated by Irish legends. He was a prolific writer of poetry, drama, and prose. His works include the plays *Cathleen Ni Houlihan* (1902) and *The Land of Heart's Desire* (1904) and the collections of poetry *In the Seven Woods* (1903), *The Wild Swans at Coole* (1917), and *The Tower* (1928). He was a member of the Irish Senate (1922–1928) and won the Nobel Prize for Literature in 1923.

Yosano, Akiko (1878–1942)
Akiko, the daughter of a Japanese merchant, studied with and married the poet Yosano Hiroshi. A feminist, pacifist, and socialist sympathizer, she wrote poetry, novels, essays, and children's stories. She had eleven children.

Glossary

act The major division of a play.

action The behavior of characters and the events that tell the story.

allegory A type of narrative in which there is a second deeper meaning below the surface.

alliteration Repetition of the first stressed syllable, usually a consonant, in two or more words (for example, "*live* and *let live*").

allusion Reference to another literary work or historical event, a work of art, and so forth.

analysis See Chapter 4.

anapest A metrical unit consisting of three syllables, the first two stressed and the last unstressed.

anecdote A short narrative relating a single event pertaining to the subject of an essay or story.

antagonist The character in fiction or drama who is the obstacle to the protagonist.

apostrophe Addressing a person who is either absent or dead, or a thing, as if they were present and could listen and reply.

archetype A universal theme or image.

argument The main idea of a literary work or the thesis a work presents.

assonance The repetition of vowel sounds in stressed syllables.

ballad A poem originally meant to be sung, passed down through an oral tradition. Poetry also regarded as folktales, such as "Frankie and Johnny."

blank verse Unrhymed iambic pentameter.

cacophony An unpleasant combination of sounds.

caesura The major pause in a line of verse, usually occurring in the middle.

carpe diem Latin phrase meaning "seize the day." Usually applies to love poems in which a lover is encouraged not to hesitate in expressing affection.

character A personality as created in a work of fiction or drama.

chorus In ancient Greek drama a group of actors who commented on the action.

chronicle An accounting of events in the order in which they occurred.

chronological order The order in which events actually occur, regardless of the order in which they are presented in a work of literature.

cliché Any overused phrase.

climax The highest point in an escalating series; the point at which events reach an emotional peak.

comedy A drama in which the events change from bad to good for the protagonist.

comparison and contrast A means of showing similarities (comparison) and differences (contrast).

conceit A figure of speech that is intended to surprise or amuse.

conflict In drama or fiction, the major disagreement between characters or within a character.

connotation The association a word carries with it. *Kids* and *chil-*

dren have approximately the same meaning, yet *kids* is more casual.

consonance The repetition of final consonants or consonant sounds in stressed syllables.

couplet Two successive rhymed or unrhymed lines.

dactyl A foot of poetry composed of one accented syllable followed by two unaccented syllables.

denotation The literal meaning of a word (see *connotation*).

denouement The unknotting of a plot; the point in a play or work of fiction when the fate of the characters becomes clear.

deus ex machina Latin for "the god from the machine." In ancient Greek drama an actor portraying a god literally appeared from a mechanized basket to rescue the protagonist. More recently, any unexpected or unlikely event that saves the protagonist.

dialogue The speech of characters in a story or essay; the speeches of characters in a play.

diction An author's choice of words: formal, casual, conversational, and so forth.

didactic Narratives that aim to teach; this term most often has negative connotations.

elegy A poem in lament or praise of the dead.

end rhyme A rhyme at the end of a line of poetry.

end-stopped line A line of poetry that ends at a clear pause, the end of a sentence or end of a unit of words.

enjambment A run-on line that carries its sense or meaning into the next stanza, without a pause at the end of the line.

epic A long narrative poem, usually passed down orally (such as Homer's *Odyssey*).

epilogue A speech that occurs at the end of a play.

epistle A letter or message; any work of prose or poetry written in the form of a letter.

epistolary poem A letter in verse form.

euphony Literally "good sounding"; a pleasant combination of sounds.

explication Explaining or making clear the meaning of a work.

exposition The part of a work of fiction or drama in which details essential to the plot are established.

fable A story with a moral. A fable often involves animals or nonhuman characters; for example, "The Fir Tree" or "Billy Goat's Gruff."

falling action In tragedy, the part of the play that shows the hero's or heroine's fall from power.

farce A broadly humorous play.

feminine rhyme A rhyme of two, or sometimes more, syllables. The stress falls on a syllable other than the last.

figurative language The nonliteral use of language, e.g., metaphors, similes, metonomy, and other figures of speech.

flat character A stereotype or character who is easily recognizable because of familiar characteristics (see *round character*).

foil A character whose characteristics or behavior are in contrast to those of another character.

foot A metrical unit in a line of poetry.

foreshadow The indication or suggestion of an event yet to happen.

free verse Poetry without a regular meter.

genre A term used to describe and categorize works of literature. The four major genres—fiction, nonfiction, poetry, and drama—can be further divided, for example, into letters, satire, comedy, romance novels, etc.

heptameter A metrical line composed of seven feet.

hero/heroine The main character or protagonist of a work of literature.

heroic couplet An end-stopped rhymed couplet in iambic pentameter.

hexameter A metrical line composed of eight feet.

hubris In Greek tragedy, overweening pride, usually manifested by a character who tries to defy the gods.

hyperbole An exaggerated statement, a statement disproportionate to the event it discusses. ("The math exam was the worst two hours of my life.")

iamb An iambic foot, consisting of an unaccented syllable followed by an accented syllable.

imagery Language that appeals to the senses: sight, touch, sound, taste, and smell.

internal rhyme Rhyme that occurs in the middle of a line.

irony The contrast between what *appears* to be true and what is true. In *verbal irony* the difference between what someone says and what is actually meant. In *dramatic irony* the difference between what the characters perceive and what the audience knows to be true.

Italian sonnet Also called a *Petrarchan sonnet*. A fourteen-line poem. The first eight lines rhyme *abba abba*. The second six lines rhyme *cdc cdc, cde cde,* or *cde dce.*

jargon Technical or specialized language, such as that used in business or the sciences.

logic Thinking based on established evidence or criteria and methods of reasoning.

lyric A poem that communicates personal emotions, usually by using a first-person speaker; considered to be the most emotionally intense type of poetry.

masculine rhyme The rhyme of one-syllable words, like *breath* and *death;* or in words of more than one syllable, the rhyme of the final stressed syllable.

melodrama A sensational—and usually improbable—drama, usually having a happy ending.

metaphor A figure of speech that equates one thing with another in a fresh way; a figure of speech in which two dissimilar things are equated and implicitly compared in one respect.

meter The pattern of stressed and unstressed syllables in a line of verse. In *regular meter* stresses occur at regular intervals.

metonymy A figure of speech that uses a single word to represent a complex situation or experience; for example, the *media* is used as a blanket term for print journalism, radio, and television.

monologue A long speech by one character in a play.

monometer A metrical line of one foot.

motif An idea or theme or element that recurs in a work of literature.

narrative The recounting of action or events in a work of prose or poetry.

narrator The voice or speaker of a work of prose or poetry. (See *point of view.*)

near rhyme Two words or syllables that have similar but not identical sounds, such as *licks* and *likes* (see *slant rhyme*).

novel The longest form of fiction, usually having more characters and more fully developed plot than in shorter fiction.

novella A work of fiction that is longer than a short story and shorter than a novel.

objective Presenting ideas in a detached, impersonal manner.

octave/octet The first eight lines of a sonnet, especially an Italian sonnet, or an eight-line stanza.

ode A serious formal poem, often addressed to someone or written to mark an occasion. Odes are usually of considerable length.

off rhyme See *slant rhyme.*

onomatopoeia The use of words whose sound imitates their meaning, for example, *cuckoo, hiss.*

oxymoron A figure of speech in which seemingly contradictory terms are juxtaposed; a compact paradox.

parable A short narrative that illustrates a moral or spiritual truth.

paradox A statement that at first seems contradictory because it contains apparently incompatible elements.

parody An imitation of another work. Parodies are usually humorous.

pathos The quality in events or situations that evokes pity or sadness.

pentameter A line of verse that contains five feet.

persona Literally means "mask"; the speaker of a poem or a ficti-tious mouthpiece devised by an author, as in "A Modest Proposal."

personification A figure of speech in which an animal, object, or concept is said to possess human qualities.

persuasion Seeks to convince a reader to share an idea or opinion. Logic, argument, wit, and rhetoric can all play a part in persuasive writing.

plot The events in a play or story and the ordering or structuring of those events.

point of view The angle or perspective from which an author chooses to tell a story or present material (see Chapter 6).

prologue The introduction to a poem or play. Greek tragedies usually began with a *prologos,* in which the necessary exposition was given.

protagonist The central character in a play or story.

pun Humorous play on words.

quatrain A four-line stanza in a poem or a group of four lines in a sonnet where the lines have an independent rhyme.

realistic drama Plays, like Ibsen's *An Enemy of the People,* that attempt to give a faithful depiction of everyday life. A reaction against romanticism.

refrain A word, phrase, or line that is repeated throughout a poem.

reversal A sudden change, or transformation, in the fortunes of the protagonist. In tragedy, the change is from good to bad.

rhetoric The art of persuasive speaking or writing; the art of making language serve one's purpose.

rhyme The repetition of stressed vowel sounds. (See also *slant rhyme.*)

rhyme scheme The pattern of rhymes throughout a stanza or poem.

rhythm The alternation of stressed and unstressed syllables in a line of verse. A regular alternation is called *meter.*

rising action The events in a play or story that lead up to the turning point; the part of the plot that precedes the climax.

round character A many-sided character in fiction or drama (see *flat character*).

run-on line A line of verse that does not end in a pause or punctuation and therefore flows into the next line without interruption.

sarcasm Bitter or wounding remark.

satire A work that ridicules the vices and follies of individuals, groups, or institutions.

scansion The process of dividing lines of verse into metrical feet and identifying the meter.

scene A subdivision of an act of a play; an episode in a play or story.

sentimentality Excessive emotion in literature that seems unjustified by the circumstances; an attempt to play on the feelings of the reader.

sestet A six-line stanza of poetry or the last six lines of a sonnet, most commonly of an Italian sonnet.

sestina A poem with six stanzas of six lines each and a concluding stanza of three lines. The last word of each line in stanza one is used as the last word of each line in the other five stanzas, but in a different order. In the final three-line stanza the six words are used at the middle and end of each line. Very occasionally sestinas are rhymed. For an example see Auden's "Paysage Moralisé."

setting The context for the events of a story or play. The time, the place, and the circumstances are all part of the setting.

Shakespearian sonnet A sonnet with the rhyme scheme *ab ab cd cd ef ef gg.* This was the form used by Shakespeare.

short story A short work of prose fiction.

simile A figure of speech in which one thing is compared to another by the use of *as* or *like*

slant rhyme Also called *near rhyme, approximate rhyme,* and *half rhyme.* The rhyming words or syllables do not have exactly the same sound, but they do have a marked resemblance.

soliloquy A speech in a play in which a character speaks his or her thoughts aloud. The character is usually alone on the stage.

sonnet A fourteen-line lyric poem written in iambic pentameter.

spondee A metrical foot consisting of two equally stressed syllables.

stanza A group of lines in a poem that form a unit. The metrical pattern of a stanza is usually repeated throughout the poem.

stock character A character in fiction or drama whom we recognize as a stereotype. Such characters usually have only a few qualities, all of which are exaggerated and familiar.

stress The emphasis on a word or syllable.

style An author's manner of expression characterized by his or her use of language and punctuation.

subjective Writing that emphasizes the author's intellectual and emotional attitudes toward a subject.

subplot A secondary plot in a play or work of fiction that relates to the main plot.

summary A synopsis or condensation of part or all of a work of literature.

symbol An object, person, action, or situation that stands for or suggests another thing.

synecdoche A special kind of metonymy; a figure of speech in which a part of something is named but the whole is understood.

syntax Sentence structure.

tale A short, simple narrative.

tetrameter Line of verse composed of four feet.

theme The deeper meaning or purpose of a work.

thesis The main idea or point that an author is making.

tone The manner of writing that conveys a certain attitude on the part of the writer.

tragedy A serious play in which the protagonist's fortunes change from good to bad.

tragicomedy A play having both tragic and comic elements.

transition The way an author connects one idea to the next.

trimeter A metrical line with three feet.

triplet A group of three lines, usually but not always rhymed.

trochee A foot containing two syllables, the first stressed, the second unstressed.

understatement A form of irony in which less is expressed than might be expected.

verse A line or lines of poetry.

villanelle A poem with five stanzas of three lines and a concluding stanza of four lines. The first and third lines of the first stanza rhyme and are repeated as the third line of alternate stanzas. They form the last two lines of the final quatrain. For an example, see Elizabeth Bishop's ''One Art.''

ACKNOWLEDGMENTS

YOSANO AKIKO, from *Women Poets of Japan* by Kenneth Rexroth. Copyright © 1977 by Kenneth Rexroth. Reprinted by permission of New Directions Publishing Corporation.

MAYA ANGELOU, from *I Know Why The Caged Bird Sings* by Maya Angelou: Copyright © 1969 by Maya Angelou. Reprinted by permission of Random House, Inc.

BROOKS ATKINSON, review of *Death of a Salesman,* February 11, 1949. Copyright 1949 by the New York Times Company. Reprinted by permission.

W. H. AUDEN, copyright 1937 and renewed 1965 by W. H. Auden. Reprinted from *W. H. Auden: Collected Poems,* edited by Edward Mendelson, by permission of Random House, Inc., and by permission of Faber and Faber, Ltd., London.

RAYMOND BARRIO, from *The Plum, Plum Pickers.* Published by Harper & Row, Publishers, Inc.

ROBERT C. BENCHLEY, from pp. 152–153 of "Happy Childhood Tales," from *The Benchley Roundup,* selected and edited by Nathaniel Benchley. Copyright 1932 by Robert C. Benchley, renewed © 1959 by Gertrude Benchley. Reprinted by permission of Harper & Row, Publishers, Inc.

ELIZABETH BISHOP, "One Art," from *The Complete Poems 1927–1979* by Elizabeth Bishop. Copyright © 1971, 1976 by Elizabeth Bishop. Copyright renewed © 1983 by Alice Helen Methfessel. Originally published in *The New Yorker.* Reprinted by permission of Farrar, Straus & Giroux, Inc.

LOUISE BOGAN, "Song for the Last Act" from *The Blue Estuaries* by Louise Bogan. Copyright 1949 by Louise Bogan. Copyright renewed © 1968 by Louise Bogan. Reprinted by permission of Farrar, Straus & Giroux, Inc.

JOHN CHEEVER, copyright © 1964 by John Cheever. Reprinted from *The Collected Stories of John Cheever* by permission of Alfred A. Knopf, Inc.

ANTON CHEKHOV, "A Lady with a Dog" from *Eleven Stories by Anton Chekhov,* translated by Ronald Hingley (1975). Copyright © 1975 by Ronald Hingley. Reprinted by permission of Oxford University Press. "The Marriage Proposal" reprinted from *The Oxford Chekhov:* vol. 1 *Short Plays;* translated and edited by Ronald Hingley (1968) by permission of Oxford University Press.

JOSEPH CONRAD, "The Lagoon" from *Tales of Unrest.* Reprinted by permission of Doubleday & Company, Inc.

HART CRANE, "Repose of Rivers" is reprinted from *The Complete Poems and Selected Letters and Prose of Hart Crane,* edited by Brom Weber, by permission of Liveright Publishing Corpora-

tion. Copyright 1933, © 1958, 1966 by Liveright Publishing Corporation.

E. E. CUMMINGS, "next to of course god america i" is reprinted from *IS 5 poems* by E. E. Cummings, by permission of Liveright Publishing Corporation. Copyright 1926 by Horace Liveright. Copyright renewed 1953 by E. E. Cummings.

EMILY DICKINSON, reprinted by permission of the publishers and the Trustees of Amherst College from *The Poems of Emily Dickinson,* edited by Thomas H. Johnson, Cambridge, Mass.: The Belknap Press of Harvard University Press, Copyright 1951, © 1955, 1979, 1983 by the President and Fellows of Harvard College.

HILDA DOOLITTLE (H.D.), from *H.D. Selected Poems.* Copyright 1957 by Norman Holmes Pearson. Reprinted by permission of New Directions Publishing Corporation.

JOHN GREGORY DUNNE, from *Quintana and Friends,* copyright © 1961, 1965, 1966, 1967, 1969, 1970, 1971, 1973, 1974, 1976, 1977, 1978 by John Gregory Dunne. Reprinted by permission of the publisher, E. P. Dutton, a division of New American Library.

ANNE FRANK, excerpt from "Saturday 1st, July 1944" from *Diary of a Young Girl.* Copyright 1952 by Otto H. Frank. Reprinted by permission of Doubleday & Company, Inc., and Valentine Mitchell Co., Ltd.

E. M. FORSTER, from *The Collected Tales of E. M. Forster.* Published 1947 by Alfred A. Knopf, Inc. Reprinted by permission of Alfred A. Knopf, Inc., King's College, Cambridge, and The Society of Authors as the literary representatives of the E. M. Forster Estate.

SIGMUND FREUD, reprinted by permission of Sigmund Freud Copyrights Ltd., the Institute of Psycho-Analysis, the Hogarth Press, and Basic Books from *The Standard Edition of the Complete Psychological Works of Sigmund Freud* translated and edited by James Strachey.

ROBERT FROST, from *The Poetry of Robert Frost,* edited by Edward Connery Lathem. Copyright © 1969 by Holt, Rinehart and Winston. Copyright 1936, 1942 by Robert Frost. Copyright © 1964, © 1970 by Lesley Frost Ballantine. Reprinted by permission.

ALLEN GINSBERG, "A Supermarket in California" from *Collected Poems, 1947–1980.* Copyright © 1955 by Allen Ginsberg. Reprinted by permission of Harper & Row, Publishers, Inc.

NIKOLAI GOGOL, from *Tales of Good and Evil,* copyright 1957 by Doubleday & Company, Inc., and reprinted by permission of the publisher.

NADINE GORDIMER, from *Selected Stories.* Copyright © 1965 by Nadine Gordimer. Reprinted by permission of Viking Penguin, Inc.

ROBERT HAYDEN, "Those Winter Sundays" is

reprinted from *Angle of Ascent, New and Selected Poems* by Robert Hayden, by permission of Liveright Publishing Corporation. Copyright © 1975, 1972, 1970, 1966 by Robert Hayden.

SEAMUS HEANEY, "Act of Union" and "Digging" from *Poems 1965–1975.* Copyright © 1966, 1969, 1972, 1975, 1980 by Seamus Heaney. Reprinted by permission of Farrar, Straus & Giroux, Inc. "Act of Union" reprinted from *North* by Seamus Heaney and "Digging" reprinted from *Death of a Naturalist* by Seamus Heaney by permission of Faber and Faber Ltd, London.

ANTHONY HECHT, © 1967 by Anthony E. Hecht. Reprinted by permission of Atheneum Publishers, Inc.

LILLIAN HELLMAN, from *Unfinished Woman.* Reprinted by permission of The Lantz Office.

ERNEST HEMINGWAY, "In Another Country" from *Men Without Women.* Copyright 1922 Charles Scribner's Sons; copyright renewed 1955 Ernest Hemingway. Reprinted with the permission of Charles Scribner's Sons.

A. E. HOUSMAN, from "A Shropshire Lad"—Authorised Edition—from *The Collected Poems of A. E. Housman.* Copyright 1939, 1940, © 1965 by Holt, Rinehart and Winston. Copyright © 1967, 1968 by Robert E. Symons. Reprinted by permission of Holt, Rinehart and Winston, Publishers and The Society of Authors as the literary representative of the estate of A. E. Housman, and Jonathan Cape Ltd., publishers of A. E. Housman's *Collected Poems.*

LANGSTON HUGHES, "Dream Deferred," copyright 1951 by Langston Hughes; "I, Too" copyright 1926 by Alfred A. Knopf, Inc. and renewed 1954 by Langston Hughes. Reprinted from *Selected Poems of Langston Hughes,* by permission of Alfred A. Knopf, Inc.

HENRIK IBSEN, from *Four Great Plays,* translated by R. Farquharson Sharp, 1959. Reprinted by permission of J. M. Dent and Sons Ltd, Publishers.

EUGENE IONESCO, reprinted from *The Massachusetts Review,* © 1969 The Massachusetts Review, Inc.

JAMES JOYCE, from *Dubliners.* Copyright 1916 by B. W. Huebsch. Definitive text edition. Copyright © 1967 by the Estate of James Joyce. Reprinted by permission of Viking Penguin, Inc.

DONALD JUSTICE, copyright © 1966 by Donald Justice. Reprinted from *Night Light* by permission of Wesleyan University Press.

WELDON KEES, reprinted from *The Collected Poems of Weldon Kees* by permission of the University of Nebraska Press. Copyright © 1975 by the University of Nebraska Press.

MARTIN LUTHER KING, JR. "Letter from Birmingham Jail"—April 16, 1963—in *Why We Can't Wait* by Martin Luther King, Jr. Copyright © 1963 by Martin Luther King, Jr. Reprinted by permission of Harper & Row, Publishers, Inc.

PHILLIP LARKIN, from *The Less Decided.* Reprinted by permission of The Marvell Press.

MARTHA WEINMAN LEAR, "Mother's Day" from *Heartsounds.* Copyright © 1980 by Martha Weinman Lear. Reprinted by permission of Simon & Schuster, Inc.

D. H. LAWRENCE, from *The Complete Short Stories, Vol. III.* Copyright 1933 by the Estate of D. H. Lawrence, renewed © 1961 by Angelo Ravagli and C. M. Weekley, Executors of the Estate of Frieda Lawrence Ravagli. All rights reserved. Reprinted by permission of Viking Penguin, Inc.

ANDREA LEE, "Leningrad" from *Russian Journal* by Andrea Lee. Copyright © 1979, 1980, 1981 by Andrea Lee. Reprinted by permission of Random House, Inc.

URSULA K. LE GUIN, copyright © 1982 by Ursula K. Le Guin: first appeared in *The New Yorker;* reprinted by permission of the author and the author's agent, Virginia Kidd.

PHILIP LEVINE, "One for the Rose" from *One for the Rose,* copyright © 1981 Philip Levine. Reprinted by permission of Atheneum Publishers, Inc.

ROBERT LOWELL, "Dunbarton" from *Life Studies* by Robert Lowell. Copyright © 1956, 1959 by Robert Lowell. Reprinted by permission of Farrar, Straus & Giroux, Inc.

BERNARD MALAMUD, "Black Is My Favorite Color" from *Idiots First* by Bernard Malamud. Copyright © 1963 by Bernard Malamud. Reprinted by permission of Farrar, Straus & Giroux, Inc.

DAVID MAMET, reprinted by permission of The Grove Press.

OSIP MANDELSTAM, CLARENCE BROWN and W. S. MERWIN, "The Stalin Epigram" from *Selected Poems.* Translation copyright © 1963 Clarence Brown and W. S. Merwin. Reprinted with permission of Atheneum Publishers, Inc.

GUY DE MAUPASSANT, reprinted by permission of The Bodley Head from *Boule de Suif and Other Short Stories* by Guy de Maupassant: translated by M. Laurie.

MARGARET MEAD, first appeared in *McCall's* magazine, April 1976. Reprinted by permission of Dr. Mary Catherine Bateson.

ROBERT MEZEY, "My Mother" reprinted by permission of the author.

ARTHUR MILLER, *Death of a Salesman.* Copyright 1949, renewed © 1977 by Arthur Miller. Reprinted by permission of Viking Penguin, Inc.

N. SCOTT MOMADAY, first published in *The Reporter,* 26 January 1967. Reprinted from *The*

Way to Rainy Mountain by permission of The University of New Mexico Press. Copyright © 1969 by The University of New Mexico Press.

MARIANNE MOORE, "The Grasshopper and the Ant" from *Fables of La Fontaine*, translated by Marianne Moore. Copyright © 1952, 1953, 1954, 1964 by Marianne Moore. Copyright renewed 1980, 1981, 1982 by Lawrence E. Brinn and Louise Crane. Reprinted by permission of Viking Penguin, Inc.

PABLO NERUDA, reprinted from *Neruda and Vallejo: Selected Poems*, Beacon Press, Boston 1971 by Robert Bly, James Wright, and John Knoepfle. Copyright © 1971 by Robert Bly. Reprinted by permission of Robert Bly.

PAULINE NEWMAN, from *American Mosaic: The Immigrant Experience in the Words of Those Who Lived it.* Copyright © 1980 by Joan Morrison and Charlotte Zabusky. Reprinted by permission of the publisher, E. P. Dutton, Inc.

FLANNERY O'CONNOR, "Everything That Rises Must Converge" from *Everything That Rises Must Converge.* Copyright © 1961, 1965 by Flannery O'Connor. Reprinted by permission of Farrar, Straus & Giroux, Inc.

FRANK O'CONNOR, copyright 1950 by Frank O'Connor. Reprinted from *Collected Stories* by Frank O'Connor, by permission of Alfred A. Knopf, Inc. and by permission of Joan Daves.

TILLIE OLSEN, "I Stand Here Ironing" excerpted from the book *Tell Me a Riddle* by Tillie Olsen. Copyright © 1956 by Tillie Olsen. Reprinted by permission of Delacorte Press/Seymour Lawrence.

EUGENE O'NEILL, copyright 1919 and renewed 1947 by Eugene O'Neill. Reprinted from *The Long Voyage Home: Seven Plays of the Sea*, by Eugene O'Neill, by permission of Random House, Inc.

WILFRED OWEN, from *The Collected Poems of Wilfred Owen.* Copyright © 1963 by Chatto and Windus. Reprinted by permission of New Directions Publishing Corporation.

GRACE PALEY, Reprinted by permission of Farrar, Straus & Giroux, Inc.

SYLVIA PLATH, "Daddy" from *The Collected Poems of Sylvia Plath*, edited by Ted Hughes. Copyright © 1963, 1981 by Ted Hughes. Reprinted by permission of Harper & Row, Publishers, Inc. Published by Faber and Faber, Ltd. London.

PLATO, "Symposium," translated by Michael Joyce; from *Collected Dialogues of Plato*, Hamilton and Cairns, Eds. (1961).

EZRA POUND, from *Personae.* Copyright 1926 by Ezra Pound. Reprinted by permission of New Directions Publishing Corporation.

JOHN CROWE RANSOM, reprinted from *Selected Poems, Third Edition Revised and Enlarged*, by John Crowe Ransom by permission of Alfred A. Knopf, Inc. Copyright 1927 by Alfred A. Knopf, Inc. and renewed 1955 by John Crowe Ransom.

ADRIENNE RICH, "Necessities of Life" is reprinted from *The Fact of a Doorframe, Poems Selected and New, 1950–1984*, by Adrienne Rich by permission of W. W. Norton & Company, Inc. Copyright © 1984 by Adrienne Rich. Copyright © 1975, 1978 by W. W. Norton & Company, Inc. Copyright © 1981 by Adrienne Rich.

THEODORE ROETHKE, "Dolor," copyright 1943 by Modern Poetry Association, Inc.; "I Knew a Woman," copyright 1954 by Theodore Roethke; "My Papa's Waltz," copyright 1942 by Hearst Magazine, Inc., all from the book *Collected Poems of Theodore Roethke* by Theodore Roethke. Reprinted by permission of Doubleday & Company, Inc.

MARGARET SANGER, from *An Autobiography.* Copyright 1938.

From *The Tragedy of King Lear* by William Shakespeare, edited by Russell Fraser. Copyright © 1963 by Russell Fraser. Copyright © 1963 by Sylvan Barnet. Reprinted by arrangement with New American Library, New York, New York.

The Antigone of Sophocles, an English version by Dudley Fitts and Robert Fitzgerald. Copyright 1939 by Harcourt Brace Jovanovich, Inc.: renewed 1967 by Dudley Fitts and Robert Fitzgerald: By permission of the publisher.

LINCOLN STEFFENS, from *The Autobiography of Lincoln Steffens*, copyright 1931 by Harcourt Brace Jovanovich, Inc.; renewed 1959 by Peter Steffens. Reprinted by permission of the publisher.

WALLACE STEVENS, copyright 1947 by Wallace Stevens. Reprinted from *The Collected Poems of Wallace Stevens* by permission of Alfred A. Knopf, Inc.

MAY SWENSON, from *Bison Crossing Near Mt. Rushmore* by May Swenson. Copyright © 1975 by May Swenson. Reprinted by permission of the author.

KUAN TAO-SHÊNG, from *Women Poets of China* by Kenneth Rexroth. Copyright © 1972 by Kenneth Rexroth and Ling Chung. Reprinted by permission of New Directions Publishing Corporation.

STUDS TERKEL, from *Working: People Talk About What They Do All Day and How They Feel About What They Do.* Copyright © 1972, 1974 by Studs Terkel. Reprinted by permission of Pantheon Books, a Division of Random House, Inc.

DYLAN THOMAS, from *The Poems of Dylan Thomas.* Copyright 1945 by the Trustees for the Copyrights of Dylan Thomas. Reprinted by permission of New Directions Publishing Corporation and of David Higham Associates Limited.

LEWIS THOMAS, from *Medusa and the Snail.* Copyright © 1979 by Lewis Thomas. Reprinted by permission of Viking Penguin, Inc.

JOHN UPDIKE, reprinted from *Pigeon Feathers and Other Stories* by permission of Alfred A. Knopf, Inc. Originally appeared in *The New Yorker.* Copyright © 1962 by John Updike.

MARGARET WALKER, from *For My People.* Published by Yale University 1942. Copyright 1942 by Margaret Walker Alexander. Reprinted by permission of the author.

PHILLIS WHEATLEY, from the *Poems of Phillis Wheatley,* edited by Julian D. Mason, Jr. Copyright © 1966 University of North Carolina Press. Reprinted by permission of the publisher.

E. B. WHITE, "Once More to the Lake" from *Essays of E. B. White.* Copyright 1941, © 1969 by E. B. White. Reprinted by permission of Harper & Row, Publishers, Inc.

RICHARD WILBUR, from *Things of This World* by Richard Wilbur. Copyright 1956 by Richard Wilbur. Reprinted by permission of Harcourt Brace Jovanovich, Inc.

TENNESSEE WILLIAMS, *The Glass Menagerie.* Copyright 1945 by Tennessee Williams and Edwina D. Williams and renewed 1973 by Tennessee Williams. Reprinted by permission of Random House, Inc.

WILLIAM CARLOS WILLIAMS, from *Collected Later Poems.* Copyright 1949 by William Carlos Williams. Reprinted by permission of New Directions Publishing Corporation.

HILMA WOLITZER, from *In the Flesh.* Originally published in *Esquire,* 1976, 1977. Reprinted by permission of William Morrow and Company.

VIRGINIA WOOLF, from *The Death of the Moth and Other Essays,* by Virginia Woolf. Copyright 1942 by Harcourt Brace Jovanovich, Inc.; renewed 1970 by Marjorie T. Parsons, Executrix, and Chatto and Windus: The Hogarth Press. Reprinted by permission of Harcourt Brace Jovanovich, Inc.

RICHARD WRIGHT, "The Man Who Saw the Flood." Reprinted by permission of United Feature Syndicate, Inc.

WILLIAM BUTLER YEATS, reprinted with permission of Macmillan Publishing Co., Inc. and Michael B. Yeats and Macmillan Ltd, London from *The Poems,* edited by Richard J. Finneran. Copyright 1924 by Macmillan Publishing Co., Inc., renewed 1952 by Bertha Georgie Yeats.

Subject Index

Index of Names, Titles, and First Lines of Poems